Contemporary
Black American
Playwrights
and Their Plays

D0209833

Contemporary Black American Playwrights and Their Plays

A Biographical Directory and Dramatic Index

BERNARD L. PETERSON, JR.

Foreword by JAMES V. HATCH

GREENWOOD PRESS

NEW YORK
WESTPORT, CONNECTICUT
LONDON

Ref
PS
153
.N5
P43
1988

Library of Congress Cataloging-in-Publication Data

Peterson, Bernard L.
  Contemporary black American playwrights and their plays.

  Bibliography: p.
  1. Afro-American dramatists—20th century—
Biography—Dictionaries.   2. American drama—Afro-
American authors—Bio-bibliography—Dictionaries.
3. American drama—20th century—Bio-bibliography—
Dictionaries.   4. Afro-American theater—Directories.
I. Title.
PS153.N5P43   1988   812′.54′09896   87–17814
ISBN 0–313–25190–8 (lib. bdg. : alk. paper)

British Library Cataloguing in Publication Data is available.

Library of Congress Catalog Card Number: 87–17814
ISBN: 0–313–25190–8

First published in 1988

Greenwood Press, Inc.
88 Post Road West, Westport, Connecticut 06881

Printed in the United States of America

The paper used in this book complies with the
Permanent Paper Standard issued by the National
Information Standards Organization (Z39.48–1984).

10 9 8 7 6 5 4 3 2 1

To HOBSON THOMPSON, JR., former Head Librarian of the G. R. Little Library, Elizabeth City State University, Elizabeth City, North Carolina, and currently Head Librarian of the Legler Branch of the Chicago Public Library—for suggesting that I write this book, and for his generosity in making available to me all the research facilities of both libraries for the completion of this project;

To DR. WALTER N. RIDLEY, former President of Elizabeth City State University—for his wise counsel, generosity, and encouragement, and for his enthusiastic support of the drama during his administration, including the building of a theatre in the G. R. Little Library of the University, which eventually led to the combining of drama and research and the writing of this book; *and*

To DR. ANNE M. HENDERSON, Chairperson of the Department of Language, Literature, and Communication—my "boss" and good friend for more than 20 years—for her unfailing support of all of my professional endeavors, for providing a climate of academic freedom within the department, and for her generosity in relieving me of many of my departmental responsibilities in order that I could bring this project to its conclusion.

CONTENTS

FOREWORD

James V. Hatch

Most play scripts are never published; even the majority of produced plays never see print. The reason is not entirely a publisher's prejudice that only Broadway and Off-Broadway scripts have merit; rather, the hundreds of community and university theatres that purchase the acting editions and pay the author royalties too often acquiesce to their audiences' wishes to see a "known" play.

This is not a happy situation for the "unknown" playwright, for then he or she, unaided, must make the plays "known" to directors across the continent, a formidable task. If one is a black playwright, such efforts must generate despair.

Each year, the Hatch-Billops Collection, an archives of black cultural history, receives a number of letters and phone calls requesting copies of plays and addresses of black playwrights; the collection can satisfy only a few of the requests, for playwrights are an itinerant group, and the library does not hold production rights to the plays. Hence the need for this Directory. At last, producing groups, teachers of drama, and theatre historians have a comprehensive list of contemporary black playwrights.

The past three decades, certainly the most prolific period in black theatre, have enabled a few playwrights to achieve international acclaim: Baraka, Bullins, Fuller, Childress, Shange. Their plays are listed here along with the hundreds of other scripts written by authors who depend upon word of mouth in order to find productions. For these, the majority of playwrights, this Directory will serve as a liaison between them and the producers.

The amassing of the names and the plays of black playwrights in a discrete volume reflects, on the one hand, that these men and women have not been fully welcomed into the mainstream theatre; their names and plays have been routinely neglected. On the other hand, this Directory encourages young talents by its recognition of them. In addition, it serves as a document to preserve the names of playwrights and productions that otherwise might disappear from theatre history.

In the early 1960s, American playwriting still suffered from the neglect engendered by World War II; only Tennessee Williams and Arthur Miller offered fresh visions, or so it seemed. Mainstream theatre expected the future to be like its past, in which only a half dozen blacks had been accorded professional productions. But help was on its way. Black American playwrights were about to create a quantity and a quality of plays previously undreamed of by the American theatre.

Among the early vanguard of this awakening, Louis Peterson, Alice Childress, James Baldwin, and Loften Mitchell deserve special notice: Peterson for *Take a Giant Step,* a drama of adolescence that opened on Broadway in October 1953 with 17-year-old Louis Gossett in his first professional role; Alice Childress for challenging white concepts of black stereotypes with her fighting black actress, Wiletta, who walked on stage with *Trouble in Mind* at the Greenwich Mews Theatre in 1955; James Baldwin, for his first play, *The Amen Corner,* which premiered at Howard University in 1955 under the direction of the "Dean of Black Theatre," Owen Dodson; and finally, Loften Mitchell for his dramatic documentary on school segregation, *Land Beyond the River,* 1957.

These playwrights were not alone: William Branch's *In Splendid Error* dramatized the conflict between Frederick Douglass and John Brown. A Katherine Dunham dancer, Charles Sebree, wrote *Mrs. Patterson,* a dream play starring Eartha Kitt. The decade climaxed with the New York Drama Critics Circle Award going to *A Raisin in the Sun.* The cast of this Lorraine Hansberry masterpiece of a family's dream of owning a new home in Chicago reads like a who's who in black theatre: Sidney Poitier, Ruby Dee, Glynn Turman, Diana Sands, Claudia McNeil, Ivan Dixon, Louis Gossett, and Lonne Elder III. Lloyd Richards directed, the first black man to do so on Broadway.

Many of these plays of the 1950s, by and large, were plays that emphasized family life, that reflected the integrationist dream of Martin Luther King when he led the Birmingham bus strike and the march to Selma, Alabama. In this optimistic era, Ossie Davis mocked racism with his comedy *Purlie Victorious,* as did Bernard Jackson and J. V. Hatch in the "sit-in" musical *Fly Blackbird.*

As the civil rights movement peaked with the March on Washington and the passage by Congress of the Civil Rights Act of 1964, the mood of the country changed: the black theatre began to reflect an increasing militancy. The young man who led the new wave, LeRoi Jones, soon cast aside his "slave name" for an African name, Amiri Baraka. Theatre critics and audiences were startled and amazed by Baraka's *Dutchman, The Slave,* and *The Toilet.* The fury with which the author attacked racism opened the floodgates for an army of playwrights who unleashed their militant vehicles upon the stages of America. And if the commercial theatre was slow to accept these plays, amateur groups across the nation sprang up like dragon's teeth. Six hundred community and university black theatre organizations burgeoned during the sixties and seventies to produce the scripts of Ben Caldwell, Sonia Sanchez, Martie Charles, Kalamu Ya Salaam, Barbara and Carlton Molette, Ted Shine, and dozens of others.

Among the university theatre teachers who led in the development of black playwrights were Owen Dodson at Howard, Tom Pawley at Lincoln University, Randolph Edmonds at Florida A & M; Ted Shine at Prairie View, George Bass at Brown, and William R. Reardon at Santa Barbara. Other writers found production at Karamu in Cleveland, Inner City in Los Angeles, the Frank Silvera Writers' Workshop, the Richard Allen Center, the AMAS Theatre and the New Federal Theatre in New York City.

In the sixties, black professional ensembles appeared. In Harlem, the New Lafayette Theatre, under the direction of Robert Macbeth, produced black theatre's most prolific writer, Ed Bullins, as well as future screenwriter Richard Wesley and actor-writer Sonny Jim Gaines. The Negro Ensemble produced playwrights Lonne Elder III, Douglas Turner Ward, Steve Carter, and Leslie Lee. Charles Gordone closed the decade of the sixties by being the first black playwright to capture a Pulitzer Prize.

Black women of the sixties created new images of women: *Funnyhouse of a Negro* by Adrienne Kennedy won an Obie Award as the best Off-Broadway play, as did Micki Grant for her musical *Don't Bother Me, I Can't Cope*. Alice Childress's *Wine in the Wilderness* appeared first as a television drama and then went on to become one of the most widely performed scripts of the decade. The greatest change of image for black women burst upon Broadway in 1977 with Ntozake Shange's *For Colored Girls Who Have Considered Suicide/When the Rainbow Is Enuf*.

By the mid-seventies, the momentum of community black theatre abated; however, in part, some of the energy surfaced on Broadway in black musicals: *Bubbling Brown Sugar, Eubie, The Wiz,* and *Your Arms Too Short to Box with God*. The black dramatists too invaded the Great White Way: Joseph Walker with *The River Niger;* Melvin Van Peebles's *Don't Play Us Cheap;* Phillip Hayes Dean with his controversial *Paul Robeson;* and Samm-Art Williams's *Home*. Two dramas opened with strong acting performances; nonetheless, the productions did not last: A. Marcus Hemphill's *Inacent Black,* starring Melba Moore, and Richard Wesley's *The Mighty Gents,* starring Morgan Freeman. Off-Broadway produced J. E. Franklin, Don Evans, Bill Gunn, Gus Edwards, and Ray Aranha.

Encouraged by this flurry of activity and by the rapid increase in numbers of black people in the audiences, black theatre artists decided that they would recognize their own talents: an organization known as AUDELCO (Audience Development Committee) founded in 1973 by Vivian Robinson, has had a continuous record of knighting the best in black playwrights, many included in this book.

The eighties, too, produced their share of new talents. To Charles Fuller, the decade brought a Pulitzer Prize for *A Soldier's Play* in 1982. George Wolfe, who arrived on Theatre Row in 1985 with his musical *Paradise,* took the critics by storm with his satirical revue, *The Colored Museum,* which opened at the Public Theatre in 1986. Vy Higginsen's *Mama, I Want to Sing* delighted family audiences for five years (at this writing). Finally, August Wilson, who in 1984 made his debut on Broadway with *Ma Rainey's Black Bottom,* returned in 1987 to win the Pulitzer for his play on family life, *Fences.*

If a reader reviews the playwrights and the plays of the last three decades indexed in this Directory, he or she will be cognizant of the "golden years" of black theatre.

ACKNOWLEDGMENTS

Appreciation is hereby expressed to all playwrights who furnished information concerning themselves and their plays, and to the following individuals and organizations for their assistance in completing this Directory:

To Dr. James V. Hatch, Curator of the Hatch-Billops Collection, New York City—for furnishing a list of scripts located in his archives; to Diana Lachathanere, Assistant Archivist, Rare Books, Manuscripts and Archives Section, Schomburg Center for Research in Black Culture, New York Public Library— for a list of scripts in the Archives of the Frank Silvera Writers' Workshop, located in the Schomburg Collection; and to Dorothy L. Swerdlove, Curator, The Billy Rose Theatre Collection, New York Public Library, Performing Arts Research Center—for providing information concerning pertinent materials in that collection.

To the following individuals who provided names and addresses and other pertinent information on playwrights: Tacquiena Boston, William Branch, Dr. Sandra Anderson Garcia, Townsend Brewster, P. J. Gibson, Theodore E. Gilliam, Maxwell Glanville, Rudy Gray, Gertrude Greenidge, Vera Katz, Maryat Lee, Mike Malone, Sharon Stockard Martin, Lionel Mitchell (deceased), Ric Richardson, Garland Lee Thompson, Donald Todd, Tad Truesdale, William Mayfield, and Lucy Walker.

To Dr. Claude Green, Administrative Librarian of the G. R. Little Library, Elizabeth City State University, Elizabeth City, North Carolina; to his predecessor, Hobson Thompson, Jr.; and to the past and present members of their respective staffs: Gwendolyn Midgette, Dr. Benjamin F. Speller, James B. Law, Donald Bradsher, Jutta D. Choudhury, Patricia C. Hines, Rebecca A. Ware, Berthel W. Penrose, Odessa A. Williams, Kathy McCuller Turner, Burnella White Griffin, Evelyn Garner Blount, Rosamond Panda, Cornelius Goodwin, Georgia Morgan, Brenda Sawyer, Freida Burke, James Blount, Handsel Ingram, Juanita Combs, Paul Mills, Valerie Villines, Mary Williams, Shirley Perry, and Christine Williams (deceased)—for location, acquisition, and loan of all books, periodicals, and reference materials needed by this researcher; for making available all the facilities and services of the G. R. Little Library, even during off-duty hours, and the facilities of other major libraries in North Carolina through Interlibrary Loan; and for their gracious cooperation and assistance in all phases of the research and writing of this book, from its inception to completion.

To Augustus Sutton, English teacher in the Public Schools of Washington, DC, for research assistance over more than a ten-year period. To Russell A. Gray of Richmond, Virginia, for secretarial services during the early stages of this work.

To Dr. Anne M. Henderson, Chairperson, Dr. Carol C. Jones, and Dr. Robert E. Thorne, Professors of English, Department of Language, Literature, and Communication; and to Dr. Dale E. Henderson, Professor, Department of Social Studies, Elizabeth City State University—for editorial assistance and proofing of the manuscript.

To Russell A. Gray, Robin L. Beamon, Valerie Lumsden, Evyonne Wilson, James A. Barnes, Clennie Razor, and Gladys Banks—for typing and photocopying; to Susan Henderson Mahaffey, Eric White, Carlotta Jordan, Brenda Newsome, James D. Collins, Thomas E. Brown, Harold D. Coppedge, Casper McDaniel, Joyce Sutton, and Willie Moore—for research and clerical services.

To my two sisters, Lena McPhatter of New York City, for keeping me informed of many dramatic events that came to her attention through the mails and the media, and for introducing me to a number of authors, playwrights, critics, and performers among her circle of friends; and Lorraine Cockrell of Reston, Virginia, for her warm encouragement and generous support of my creative efforts throughout the years.

To my buddies and gadflies, William T. Skinner, Lawrence E. Gatling, William D. Butts, Joseph Amanchukwu, and Benjamin Hardy—for a variety of services which helped to make my life easier while completing this book—and for providing the social companionship and camaraderie without which this book might have been completed one year sooner.

And to my editor, Marilyn Brownstein at Greenwood Press—for her insight, skill, understanding, patience, and—above all—tact, in guiding me through the long and arduous process of shaping this book into its present form.

PREFACE

Contemporary Black American Playwrights and Their Plays: A Biographical Directory and Dramatic Index is a comprehensive reference work, providing, in encyclopedia format, a convenient source of information on more than 700 contemporary black American and U.S. resident dramatists, screenwriters, radio and television scriptwriters, musical theatre collaborators, and other originators of theatrical and dramatic works, written, produced, and/or published between 1950 and the present. In this Preface, all these writers are called playwrights, and their works are called plays.

Information contained in *Contemporary Black American Playwrights* will be of obvious value to producers, directors, agents, performing groups, other playwrights, and all persons connected with the theatre. As a reference tool, it will be of inestimable value to graduate and undergraduate students, teachers, librarians, and individuals and institutions engaged in black studies, black literature, or black drama.

The Directory is not a "Who's Who Among Contemporary Black American Playwrights." It represents and includes a wide range of writers, from well-known dramatists (whose reputations in the American theatre and/or their respective media have been securely established and who have been awarded or nominated for one or more of the coveted annual dramatic prizes) to little-known playwrights whose plays have been produced primarily by regional, community, educational, or church-related theatre groups, or which remain largely unproduced.

The information contained in *Contemporary Black American Playwrights* has been based primarily on the continuing research and the collection of black theatre materials by the writer over a period of more than 20 years, as well as on questionnaires, telephone calls, and mailgrams to more than 2,000 playwrights, directors, agents, heads of theatrical and writers' organizations, and other resource persons in the fields of black American drama and theatre.

The playwrights included in the Directory were selected from a list of nearly

1,200 playwrights compiled by the writer since the mid-1960s from reliable published and unpublished sources, including bibliographies, anthologies, dissertations and theses, play manuscripts, periodicals, newspapers, programs, advertisements, announcements, and other types of printed matter located either in the writers' personal collection or in the major libraries and archives of North Carolina, Virginia, Washington, DC, New York City, Boston, and Chicago.

In an effort to make the Directory comprehensive, the writer has sought to include as many major, significant, prolific, and promising playwrights as possible, as well as nearly all published playwrights, and all who responded to questionnaires and requests for resumes and dramatic bibliographies.

Of the more than 700 playwrights included in this Directory, only about two-thirds were actually located by mail or by telephone, and of this number, only about one-half, or 200 playwrights, actually responded to requests for information. Thus, over 60 percent of the entries in the Directory were compiled from the existing published and unpublished sources listed above.

To achieve the degree of comprehensiveness desired for *Contemporary Black American Playwrights,* especially in view of the limited responses of many playwrights (including established authors) to requests for information, several goals or criteria originally established for inclusion in this Directory had to be abandoned. One of these goals was to include full biographical information and a completely annotated list of dramatic works for each playwright. Another was to include only those playwrights who had written at least two plays, of which at least one had been produced and/or published, and for which an adequate description had been located. A third goal was to be the inclusion of a mailing address for each playwright, in order that access to his/her unproduced and unpublished works could be achieved.

Thus, in the interest of including as many playwrights as possible, it was the decision of the writer and his editor to establish only four firm criteria for inclusion in the Directory:

1. All playwrights must be black, or partly black. (In some instances, where the racial identity of the playwright has not been definitely established, the entry will begin with these words: "Racial identity not verified.")

2. All must be American citizens or long-term residents of the United States (even if such residency is intermittent).

3. All must have been living in 1950, or born since that date, and all must have written, produced, and/or published at least one play between 1950 and 1985.

4. There must have been available to the writer enough information on either the playwright or his/her plays in order to construct a respectable entry. This criterion has been waived in the case of (a) published playwrights, (b) playwrights whose plays are available or accessible in major black theatre archives or repositories, and (c) playwrights for whom a mailing address has been located.

For playwrights whose work is both unproduced and unpublished, two additional criteria were established:

1. These playwrights must have written at least two plays.
2. There must be a mailing address for them in order that their unproduced/unpublished plays might be accessible to interested users of this Directory.

Every effort has been made to provide some biographical information for the majority of playwrights, ranging in length from one line or a few lines of identification to a brief or full biographical sketch of from one-half to two or even three pages. (Even with this effort, however, for some playwrights no biographical information has been located.)

Depending upon the availability of information, a playwright's entry in the Directory begins with a biographical sketch that seeks to include the following information, roughly in the order given:

1. The playwright's name or names, including pseudonyms, nicknames, ethnic names, married names, and/or titles, etc.
2. Date of birth (and death, if deceased).
3. Major fields of specialization, including theatrical, artistic, literary, and other occupations.
4. Place of birth, followed by other places in which the playwright was reared, educated, lived, worked, and/or currently resides.
5. Family background, if pertinent to the sketch, including relationships to other playwrights, theatrical personalities, and celebrities.
6. Education, including degrees, certificates, and private study.
7. Military or other service.
8. Marital status and children.
9. Highlights of career, with emphasis on literary, artistic, and theatrical activities and achievements.
10. Nondramatic writings and publications.
11. Memberships and offices held.
12. Honors and awards, including fellowships, grants, and honorary degrees.
13. Address of playwright, agent, and/or other representative.

Biographical sketches are immediately followed, where applicable, by one or more of the following types of collective works, analyzed for their individual plays or components, if possible:

1. The author's published collections and self-edited anthologies that include one or more of his/her plays. (Other anthologies, not edited by the playwright, are not included in this section, but may be located in the "Title List of Play Anthologies" in the back of the Directory.)
2. Groups of related plays, including programs of two or more one-act plays, which are produced under a different title than that of the individual plays, or cycles and series

of plays (including trilogies) which are of special significance. (When such programs consist of a series of sketches, skits, or very short pieces, these programs are listed as individual plays, and not under groups of related plays.)

The last section of a playwright's entry is devoted to an annotated list or index of the author's individual plays and dramatic works, which may be divided into two groups: "Representative Plays and Dramatic Works" and "Other Plays and Dramatic Works." Under the first group are listed only fully annotated plays, and under the second group those works for which only a limited amount of information is available. Whether the listing is in a single group or divided into two groups, the plays are always presented in chronological order within each group.

Full annotations of plays and dramatic works include the following information, if available:

1. Title of dramatic work. If the title is foreign, or in dialect, the standard English equivalent is given in quotation marks within parentheses. If the work has been produced under, or known by, another title than its present title, other titles are also given (and labeled as original title, alternate title, other titles, etc.).

2. Genre, length, and earliest date of completion, copyright, production, or publication—given within parentheses after the title(s).

3. Subtitle sometimes given under genre and length, when applicable—for example: **The Duplex** ("A Black Love Fable in Four Movements" [subtitle], 1970); but in most instances given separately, following 2 above.

4. Coauthor, or collaborators, including their specific contributions, if known (especially for musicals), and identification of those collaborators *known* to be black. If the collaborator is another playwright listed in the Directory, then his/her name is put in all capitals (e.g., LANGSTON HUGHES). An asterisk (*) is used to identify black collaborators not listed separately in the Directory. If the black collaborator is a significant early playwright, an obelisk or dagger (†) is used to identify such a playwright.

5. Title and author of original work on which each dramatic work is based, if adapted or dramatized (including date, if known). As described above, black authors are identified mainly by asterisks. (See also "Symbols," below.)

6. Circumstances which led to writing of work, if commissioned or written under special circumstances.

7. Synopsis of plot, or description, or theme.

8. Significance of work, if applicable, and/or awards received by the play or playwright or other contributors. (NOTE: The position of this information may vary considerably within a given entry, in order to place awards as close to related information as possible. Also, there is a certain amount of redundancy in listing awards that are also mentioned in the biographical section of the playwright's entry.)

9. Production history, including identification of black producers, all known directors,

and best-known actors featured in the cast. (Because of space limitations, important actors are named mainly in professional productions.)

10. Location of published or unpublished scripts (or films, or recordings, etc.), if available from sources other than the playwright or his/her agent. Prominent among these sources are the Hatch-Billops Collection and the Schomburg Collection (New York Public Library), which are frequently mentioned throughout.

As a supplement to the main directory of more than 700 playwrights, there are two appendixes: Appendix A lists more than 100 additional playwrights whose scripts are located in special repositories. Appendix B lists more than 75 other contemporary black American playwrights whose works are known to have been produced in the United States since 1950.

These two appendixes are followed by an extensive bibliography of information sources on black American playwrights and plays, which includes a list of libraries and repositories with strong collections in black theatre and drama; a title index of play anthologies that contain one or more plays by black American playwrights; an author list of reference books and critical studies pertinent to black theatre; a list of dissertations and theses, most available from University Microfilms International; and a list of periodicals, both active and no longer published, which regularly featured articles, reviews, and/or biographical materials on black plays and playwrights from 1950 to the present.

The Directory concludes with two indexes: a title index of all plays by black American playwrights listed or referred to throughout the book, and a general index of theatrical names, organizations, and awards. (NOTE: Names of playwrights included in the main directory are not indexed unless they are also referred to in other entries, or in other sections of the book.)

Since this directory was compiled from many different sources, the amount of information for each playwright varies substantially, and it is inevitable that there will be errors of omission, attribution, and even of fact. It is hoped that these will be minimal. The writer assumes sole responsibility for such errors, apologizes for them in advance, and will make every effort to correct them in any future editions.

In anticipation that a new edition may be forthcoming within the next several years, the writer wishes to be notified of any incorrect or incomplete information in this Directory and would welcome the receipt of information concerning new playwrights who should be included, of published or unpublished source materials, and of the activities of black theatre organizations and performing groups.

New playwrights are asked to submit their resumes and dramatic bibliographies, using the form outlined above for a full entry; and playwrights now included are asked to expand and update the information on themselves periodically and to keep the writer posted on any change of address (or to provide one, if one has not been located), in order that contact may be either maintained or established.

In any event, all criticisms, suggestions, or corrections that will help to improve the content and quality of any future edition of *Contemporary Black American Playwrights and Their Plays* will be greatly appreciated.

Bernard L. Peterson, Jr.
413 Massachusetts Ave., Suite 3
Elizabeth City, NC 27909

ABBREVIATIONS

A. & I.	Agricultural and Industrial
A. & M.	Agricultural and Mechanical
A. & T.	Agricultural and Technical
AAUP	American Association of University Professors
ABC	American Broadcasting Companies
ACLU	American Civil Liberties Union
ACT	American Community Theatre (New York City); American Conservatory Theatre (San Francisco)
ACTF	American College Theatre Festival
ACT/Pro/ Workshop	American Community Theatre Professional Workshop
AEA	Actors Equity Association
AFI	American Film Institute
AFL-CIO	American Federation of Labor and Congress of Industrial Organizations
AFTRA	American Federation of Television and Radio Artists
AGVA	American Guild of Variety Artists
ALA	American Library Association
A.M.A.	American Medical Association
A.M.E.	African Methodist Episcopal
ANT	American Negro Theatre
ANTA	American National Theatre and Academy
APT	American Place Theatre
ASCAP	American Society of Composers, Authors and Publishers
ATA	American Theatre Association
ATPAM	Association of Theatrical Press Agents and Managers
AUDELCO	Audience Development Committee
BA/W	Black Arts/West
BBC	British Broadcasting Corporation
B.D.	Bachelor of Divinity
B.F.A.	Bachelor of Fine Arts
B. Litt.	Bachelor of Literature

B.L.S.	Bachelor of Library Science
B.M.	Bachelor of Music
BMI	Broadcast Music Company
BTA	Black Theatre Alliance
Bway	Broadway
CAPS	Creative Artists Public Service (Program/Fellowship)
CBS	Columbia Broadcasting System
CCLA	City College of Los Angeles
CCNY	City College of New York
CET	Concept East Theatre
CLGA	Composers and Lyricists Guild of America
COFO	Council of Federated Organizations (Southern civil rights organizations)
Conf.	Conference
CORE	Congress of Racial Equality
CPB	Corporation for Public Broadcasting
CUNY	City University of New York
CWO	Council of Writers Organizations
D.B.A.	Doctor of Business Administration
D.D.	Doctor of Divinity
D.D.S.	Doctor of Dental Surgery/Science
DG	Dramatists Guild
DGA	Directors Guild of America
dir.	directed
D.L.S.	Doctor of Library Science
doc.	documentary
D.S.W.	Doctor of Social Work
D.V.M.	Doctor of Veterinary Medicine
Ed.D.	Doctor of Education
ELT	Equity Library Theatre
E.T.C.	Experimental Theatre Club (La Mama E.T.C.)
FDCAC	Frederick Douglass Creative Arts Center
FESTAC	[Black and African] Festival of Arts and Culture (Lagos, Nigeria)
fl.	flourished
FST	Free Southern Theater
FSWW	Frank Silvera Writers' Workshop
FTP	Federal Theatre Project
HARYOU-ACT	Harlem Youth Opportunities Unlimited, Inc., and Associated Community Teams
HEW	[Department of] Health, Education and Welfare
IATSE	International Alliance of Theatrical Stage Employees
ICCC	Inner City Cultural Center
ICM	International Creative Management
Inst.	Institute
instr.	instructor
J.D.	Doctor of Laws
LC	Library of Congress
L.H.D.	Doctor of Humane Letters
LCR	Lincoln Center Repertory

Lib.	Library
Litt.B.	Bachelor of Letters
LL.B.	Bachelor of Laws
LL.D.	Doctor of Laws
LSU	Louisiana State University
M.B.A.	Master of Business Administration
M.F.A.	Master of Fine Arts
M.L.S.	Master of Library Science
M.Mus.	Master of Music
M.S.W.	Master of Social Work
NAACP	National Association for the Advancement of Colored People
NAG	Negro Actors Guild
NADSA	National Association of Dramatic and Speech Arts
NARAS	National Academy of Recording Arts and Sciences
NATAS	National Academy of Television Arts and Sciences
NBC	National Broadcasting Company
NBT	National Black Theatre
NEA	National Endowment for the Arts
N.E.A.	National Education Association
NEC	Negro Ensemble Company
NEH	National Endowment for the Humanities
NET	National Educational Television
NFT	New Federal Theatre
NHT, NHRT	New Heritage Theatre, New Heritage Repertory Theatre
NLT	New Lafayette Theatre
NRT	National Repertory Theatre
NSF	National Science Foundation
NWC	National Writers Club
NYPL	New York Public Library
NYSF	New York Shakespeare Festival
NYTE	New York Theatre Ensemble
NYU	New York University
orig.	original
PASLA	Performing Arts Society of Los Angeles
PBS	Public Broadcasting Service
P.E.N.	Poets, Playwrights, Essayists, Editors and Novelists
prod.	produced
prodn.	production
pseud.	pseudonym
pub.	published
RAF	Royal Air Force
SADSA	Southern Association of Dramatic and Speech Arts
SAG	Screen Actors Guild
SCLC	Southern Christian Leadership Conference
SNCC	Student Non-Violent Coordinating Committee
SPJ	Society of Professional Journalists
SSDC	Society of Stage Directors and Choreographers

SUNY	State University of New York
TOBA	Theatre Owners Booking Association, Tough on Black Actors
UAC	Urban Arts Corps
UC	University of California
UCLA	University of California at Los Angeles
U.K.	United Kingdom
U.N.	United Nations
UNESCO	United Nations Educational, Scientific and Cultural Organization
unpub.	unpublished
USO	United Service Organizations
WGA	Writers Guild of America
WGA/E	Writers Guild of America, East
WGA/West	Writers Guild of America, West
WPA	Works Projects Administration
YMCA	Young Men's Christian Association
YWCA	Young Women's Christian Association
YUL	Yale University Library

SYMBOLS

1. Symbols used for playwrights and their collaborators:
   a. ALL CAPITALS used for a name within an entry indicates that the person is a contemporary black American playwright whose separate entry is also included in the Directory.
   b. An asterisk (*) before the name of a collaborator, when the name is in roman type, indicates that the collaborator is known to be black, but is not included as a separate entry in the directory. Asterisks are also used to identify black authors of original works (such as novels, poetry, and plays) which are adapted for the stage by other playwrights.
   c. An obelisk or single dagger (†) before the name of a collaborator, or any other individual within an entry, indicates that the person is a significant *early* black American playwright who is not included in the Directory.
   d. A name in quotation marks indicates a nickname.
   e. A name in parentheses indicates another name, an original name, or part of a name, by which the playwright is also known. (For a woman playwright, this may also include a married name or a single name.)
2. Symbols used in titles of plays and other dramatic works:
   a. **Boldface type** is used within an entry to indicate the titles of plays and dramatic works written by the playwright who is the subject of the entry.
   b. **"BOLDFACE CAPITALS"** within quotation marks are used to indicate overall production titles (also called blanket titles) covering a group of at least two plays by the subject playwright.
   c. *ITALICIZED CAPITALS* are used to indicate *published* collections of plays by the subject playwright.
   d. "ROMAN CAPITALS" within quotation marks are used to indicate *unpublished* collections of plays by the subject playwright, such as doctoral dissertations, master's theses, or mimeographed collections.

e. *Italic type* is used to indicate most titles of plays, films, and published works, other than titles of television series, songs, and very short segments or sketches within a single dramatic work.

f. "Titles in Quotation Marks" are used to indicate subtitles of plays, English translation of foreign titles or titles in dialect, and for titles of TV series, songs, and very short segments or sketches within a single play or dramatic work.

g. Double virgules (//) are usually used to separate current titles from original or earlier titles of the same work, or vice versa.

3. Symbols used in dating plays:

   a. Dashes (–) are ordinarily used to separate consecutive years of a single dramatic season, such as 1983–84.

   b. Single virgules (/) are ordinarily used to separate a span of more than two consecutive years, during which a play was either written or produced, such as 1983/86.

4. Other symbols are explained immediately prior to their use.

A BIOGRAPHICAL
DIRECTORY

A

ABAKARI, DEMANI (Demon Smith, also known as Damani Abubakari),
Playwright, director. Former director of the Afro-Centric Theatre Movement in
Detroit, where he was also associated with the Concept East Theatre (CET) and
the Mwongi Art Theatre.

PLAYS:
White Sale (short revolutionary skit, c. 1972). A black salesman is chastised by a
black customer for trying to sell him the "white things" that he has on special clearance
sale. Prod. by CET, prior to being pub. in *Guerrilla Theatre* (Weisman, 1973). **Inn
Crowd** (1 act, 1973). Prod. by Mwongi Art Theatre, 1973. **Pvt. Huckleberry** (1 act,
1973). Prod. by CET, 1973.

ABDULLAH, AHMED MAARIFA, Playwright. Formerly associated with
Oduduwa Production, Black Studies Dept., Univ. of Pittsburgh, PA.

PLAY:
A Malcom [*sic*] **Play** (children's play, 2 acts, 1970). About Malcolm X; written to
instill racial pride in children. Pub. in *Connection* (Porter, 1970).

ABIODUNJI, SYL, Playwright. Formerly associated with Oduduwa Production, Black Studies Dept., Univ. of Pittsburgh, PA.

PLAY:
For Malcolm X (1970). An arrangement of the words of Malcolm X, in which America
is put on trial and executed for crimes against black people. Pub. in *Connection* (Porter,
1970).

ABNEY, ROBERT, JR. (1949–   ), Author, playwright, library technician,
and human relations consultant. Born and resides in Washington, DC. Librarian
technician in the DC Public Lib. (now the Martin Luther King Memorial Lib.).

Author of plays, fiction, and poetry. Member of N.E.A., Operation PUSH, and the NAACP.

PLAYS:
Credited with two dozen plays, notably: **The Sofa** (morality, 1 act, 1973). A black man must choose between a black woman and a white "drag queen." **The Interview** (morality play, 1 act, 1974). Attacks the portrayal and use of women as sex objects. **Killing Me Softly** (pantomime, 1 act, 1974). Deals with the psychological problems of aging. **The Liquor Store** (6 movements, 1974). Four black drunks use street wisdom to help members of the black community deal with personal problems. **What Mama Don't See** (adolescent drama, 1 act, 1974). Delinquent teenagers discuss their lives. **What We Said We Was** (morality, 3 acts, 1974). Young black man tries to cope with his sister's death from a drug overdose. **Loving Conversation** (morality, 1 act, 1975). Bedroom conversation between lovers. **Maybe We Should Call Ourselves I Don't Know** (morality, 6 movements, 1975). Four black men use individual approaches to realize their dreams. **Who's Driving This Bus?** (children's play, 1 act, 1975). Concerns what happens when some black children misbehave on a school bus. **On the Verge of the Lying Truth** (morality, 1 act, 1970s). Explores the problem of sex roles in society.

ABRAMSON, DOLORES, Poet, short-story writer, playwright. An alumna of the Sonia Sanchez Writers Workshop in Harlem, 1970–71. Her poetry has been published in *A Rock Against the Wind* (Patterson, 1973) and the anthology cited below.

PLAY:
The Light (ritual, 1 act, 1971). Verbal dispute between God and the devil over the proper behavior of black women. Pub. in *Three Hundred and Sixty Degrees of Blackness Comin at You* (Sanchez, 1971).

ABUBAKARI, DAMANI. See ABAKARI, DEMANI.

ABUDU, MUNGU KIMYA (Carl F. Morrison, Jr.) (1948–   ), Poet-playwright and theatrical director. Former resident playwright and director of the Antioch Area Theatre, Yellow Springs, OH. Born in Lincoln, NB. Received the A.B. degree in theatre and black studies from California State Univ./San Jose, and the M.F.A. in playwriting and directing from the Univ. of Massachusetts/Amherst. Several of his poems have been published in *Drum* magazine, a literary publication of black experience originating at the Univ. of Massachusetts/Amherst.

PLAYS:
The Contract (morality play, full length [9 scenes], 1972). The problem of a man desperately trying to get out of debt to an underworld character. Prod. at California State Coll. (now Univ.)/San Jose, 1972; dir. by author.

And (morality drama, 1 act, 1974). A black man in search of his identity wishes to enter into a polygamous marriage with three black women, representative of the diverse types within the black race. Although each tries to win his undivided love, all finally agree to accept his joint marriage proposal. Prod. at the Fine Arts Center, Univ. of Massachusetts/Amherst, 1972; dir. by author.

The Black Egg ("A Spiritual in Three Movements" [subtitle], 1975). The problem faced by black students trying to get a culturally relevant education at predominantly white colleges. Prod. at the Fine Arts Center, Univ. of Massachusetts/Amherst, 1975; dir. by author.

ACAZ, MBA, Playwright. Brother Acaz was associated with the Writers Workshop of the New York Public Theatre.

PLAY:

The Ambassadors (drama, 1 act, c. 1970). Portrayal of teenage gang culture, in which the Ambassadors are engaged in a feud with the Jumbos, a rival gang. First prod. as a workshop production by the Public Theatre, at the Other Stage, during the 1970–71 season; dir. by DAMON KENYATTA. Again prod. in New York, July 1971; dir. by author.

ADDERLEY, JULIAN "CANNONBALL" (Julian Edwin Adderley) (1928–1975), and **NAT ADDERLEY (Nathaniel)** (1931–   ), Jazz musician brothers and composers. "Cannonball" Adderley was a noted alto saxophonist and band leader. Born in Gary, IN. Played with Lionel Hampton, Woody Herman, J. J. Johnson, Miles Davis, and George Shearing. Named *Down Beat* magazine's new Alto Star of the Year, 1959. Won *Playboy* magazine's Reader's Poll for First Alto Sax, 1962–71.

Nat Adderley is a well-known cornetist, composer, educator, and lecturer, and one of the pioneers of jazz. Born in Tampa, FL; currently resides in New York City. He has traveled throughout Europe and Japan, as well as in this country, playing the music that has made him a living legend. He also conducts musical clinics and seminars, and recently made his acting debut in *Mahalia,* an Off-Broadway showcase production based on the life of Mahalia Jackson.

DRAMATIC WORK:

Big Man (musical play, full length, 1974). Subtitled "The Legend of John Henry." Cowritten by Julian "Cannonball" and Nat Adderley. About the legendary railroad worker who outdistanced all other workers in the laying of railroad tracks with his famous hammer. World premiere in a concert version at Carnegie Hall, New York City, July 1976. Recording released in 1975 by Fantasy (F-79006), starring Joe Williams, Randy Crawford, and ROBERT GUILLAUME (of TV's "Benson" series).

ADDERLEY, NAT (Nathaniel). See ADDERLEY, JULIAN "CANNONBALL," and NAT ADDERLEY.

ADELL, ILUNGA (William Adell Stevenson III) (1948–   ), Actor, theatrical director, stage manager, television scriptwriter, editor, and playwright. Born in Memphis, TN, where he now resides. Educated at Memphis State Univ., Morehouse Coll., the Univ. of Massachusetts, and Wesleyan Univ. Directed the New York stage production of *Five on the Black Hand Side* (1969). Former scriptwriter and editor for the "Sanford and Son" TV series; currently story editor of "The Redd Foxx Show." Member of AEA, AFTRA, New Dramatists, and WGA. *Address:* 265 S. Main St., Memphis, TN 38103. *Agent:* Diana Hunt Management, 44 W. 44th St., New York, NY 10017.

PLAYS AND DRAMATIC WORKS:

One: The Two of Us (drama, 1 act, 1972). Black man tries to educate his mate as to what will be required of them in the black revolution. Prod. as a work-in-progress by the Public Theatre, New York, at the Other Stage, May 16, 1972, on a program of four one-act plays, under the prodn. title *Four for One*. Pub. in *Scripts* 7 (NYSF/Public Theatre), May 1972.

Superflyer (TV comedy, 1 act, 1972). Coauthor, with Charles T. Williams. From the "Sanford and Son" TV series. Fred Sanford inherits $15,000 upon the death of an uncle and flies to St. Louis to arrange for the funeral and to claim his inheritance. Telecast on NBC-TV, c. 1972–73. Pub. by Samuel French, New York, 1974.

Tooth or Consequences (TV comedy, 1 act, 1972). From the "Sanford and Son" TV series. Fred Sanford is frightened by the prospect of having his tooth pulled out but is coerced by his son, Lamont. Telecast on NBC-TV, c. 1972–73. Pub. by Samuel French, New York, 1974.

OTHER PLAYS AND DRAMATIC WORKS:

(All pre-1976.) **No Drums, No Bugles. Bulldogs. Love, Love. Stone and Steel** (TV script). Coauthor, with *John Forbes.

AHLERT, RICHARD, Composer-lyricist. Based in New York City.

DRAMATIC WORK:

Adam ("A . . . musical drama about Adam Clayton Powell, Jr." [subtitle] full length, 1983). Book by JUNE TANSEY (Mrs. Richard Ahlert). Music and lyrics by Ahlert. The fall from power of the flamboyant black congressman, the forces that contributed to it, and its effect on the black community. Prod. Off-Bway by WOODIE KING, JR., and the New Federal Theatre (NFT) at the Henry St. Playhouse, Jan. 20–Feb. 6, 1983; dir. by DON EVANS. With Reuben Green in the title role.

AHMAD, DOROTHY, Author and playwright; a product of the Black Arts movement on the West Coast during the late 1960s. Resides in San Francisco, CA. Married to an artist; the mother of three children. Her work has been published in *Black Dialogue* and *Soulbook*.

PLAY:

Papa's Daughter (drama, 1 act, 1957). Explores the unwholesome relationship that has developed between a father and daughter after the death of the mother, and the daughter's attempt to cope with this problem. First prod. by the Black Arts Alliance, in conjunction with the Black Communications Project. Prod. by the Dillard Univ. Players, New Orleans, 1969. Pub. in *Black Dialogue* (San Francisco), c. 1967, and in *The Drama Review,* Summer 1968, pp. 139–45.

AJAMU (Robert Crawford) (1952?–), Playwright. Resides in Philadelphia, PA. Studied playwriting at Howard Univ., Washington, DC, under the tutelage of JOHN O. KILLENS, mid-1970s, and in the M.F.A. Playwriting Program of UCLA, 1976. *Address:* 6638 Greene St., Philadelphia, PA 19119.

PLAY:

The Brass Medallion (drama, 1975). Deals with the illusions of black manhood within a prison, where a seasoned inmate has used intimidation to gain control of the drug use and homosexual activities of the other inmates. His macho reputation is destroyed when he is beaten up in a fight with a new prisoner whom he has brutally raped and eventually murders. Written in Killens's writing workshop at Howard Univ., where it was first prod. in 1975; dir. by St. Clair Christmas. Presented at the American Coll. Theatre Festival (ACTF), held at the Kennedy Center, Washington, DC, 1976.

AJANAKU, AMANA M. (1953–), Playwright, poet, and writer. Resides in Nashville and Memphis, TN. Began creative writing at age 11. Received the B.A. in general speech from Memphis State Univ., 1977. Presently working toward a master's degree in speech communication and theatre at Tennessee State Univ., Nashville. *Address:* Ajanaku African Research Institute, 891 Claybrook St., Memphis, TN 38107. Alternate: 876 37th St., Nashville, TN 37209.

PLAY:

D Dog Dreams (tragedy, 1 act, 1977). About a young woman in love with a married man, who becomes the source of her discontent. Their clandestine meeting place is a Tennessee beer joint and pool hall named Butterball's. When the wife dies, thus removing the last barrier to their happiness, the young woman receives the ultimate rejection and commits suicide in Butterball's. Prod. by LEVI FRAZIER, JR., as a cable public access TV production, in Nashville, 1977; dir. by H. Henderson, Jr.

AJAYI, AFOLABI, Nigerian actor, director, producer, and playwright, associated with the Negro Ensemble Co. (NEC) in New York City. Former director of the Mbari-Mbayo Players, a Nigerian performing group. Has performed in NEC's productions of *Kongi's Harvest* (1968), *Man Better Man* (1969), and *The Dream on Monkey Mountain* (1971). Coproduced the Off-Bway production of *The Strong Breed* and *The Trials of Brother Jero* (1979) by Nigerian playwright Wole Soyinka.

DRAMATIC WORK:

Akokawe ("Initiation"; theatrical collage, full length, 1970). Presentation of traditional African writings through drama, poetry, dance, and song, selected and directed by Ajayi. "The vignettes focused on the conflict between African and European civilization in Act I, and the malaise felt by African expatriates in Act II."—*Dictionary of the Black Theatre* (Woll, 1983), p. 6. Prod. Off-Bway jointly by NEC and the Mbari-Mbayo Players, at St. Marks Playhouse, New York, May 19–June 1970, for 44 perfs. With Esther Rolle, Frances Foster, Clarice Taylor, and Tanzanian actress Amandina Lihamba. Also presented at the Drama Workshop of the Harlem School of the Arts, at St. James Presbyterian Church, presumably during the same year. According to *Black World* (undated clipping): "Mbari-Mbayo means 'to delight the ears and enlighten the mind.' . . . A special feature of the players' appearance was the original African music played on traditional instruments, with lyrics in Swahili, Yoruba and English.''

AKINWOLE, OBATAIYI B., Playwright, postal service employee, teacher, musician, journalist, and recreational consultant. Has written over two dozen plays, 100 musical compositions, and 50 articles and book reviews for publication. Educated at North Carolina Central Univ. (B.A. in music, 1969; M.A. in musical theory and composition, 1976). Has also attended numerous institutes and workshops in educational broadcasting, business management, and music. Presently employed by the U.S. Postal Service. In Durham, NC, he has held the following positions: station manager, WAFR-FM Radio, 1971–73; vice pres. and cofounder, Community Radio Workshop, 1973–75; substitute teacher, Durham City Schools, at frequent intervals, 1976–present; cultural coordinator, Parks and Recreation Dept., 1977–78; and music teacher, Y.E. Smith and Morehead Schools, 1980. Member of Kappa Alpha Psi Fraternity. Recipient of Award for Outstanding Achievement in Programming for Local Audiences (Children's Radio Workshop), Corp. for Public Broadcasting (CPB), 1973; Notable Americans Award, American Biographical Inst., 1976–77; honorable mention, American Songwriters Festival Lyric Competition, 1983. Visiting Artists Program Candidate, North Carolina Arts Council, for playwriting and directing, 1977. *Address:* 3208–D Shire Lane, Raleigh, NC 27606.

PLAYS AND DRAMATIC WORKS:
(All pre-1986) **Project** (2 acts). Dramatization of tenement life in a large northern city. **Guitar Slim Moore** (1 act). About a record company's attempt to get an old blues singer to go to New York to record for them. **Something for Pee Wee** (1 act). A young black girl who is an overachiever is preoccupied with her own youthful thoughts until she begins to take pride in caring for her retarded older brother. **The Road to Freedom** (musical, 2 acts). About the capture, transportation, inculturation, and rise of the African American. Oba, a Yoruba chief, tells the story of how he and his family and his people were captured and brought to America. **Six Bridges I've Crossed** (1 act). **Does Anybody Really Know What Time It Is?** (1 act). Sandra spends a summer afternoon pestering everyone in the neighborhood. Unknown to them, she just wants some attention on her birthday. **The Bully** (1 act). Josephine, the neighborhood tomboy and pest, spends her day dodging the neighborhood bully whose personality is drastically altered by a head injury. **Flip Side** (comedy, 1 act; also a teleplay). Serious comedy that not only entertains but has something to say about the generation gap (the old and new values) in the black community. The story centers around the rejection of an older, less fortunate black man by the youth of the community. **She Never Said I Love You** (teleplay). Rousing story of a black woman who rose from the obscurity of drug addiction to found a national organization for the care of unwanted children.

ALAMAJI, JIWE. See WILKS, PETER YOUNG, III.

ALEXANDER, DONALD W., Playwright. Based in Berkeley and San Francisco, CA. An alumnus of the San Francisco Black Writers Workshop. Member of the Frank Silvera Writers' Workshop (FSWW), New York City. Also associated with the American Conservatory Theatre (ACT), San Francisco.

PLAYS:
(A script and tape recording of at least one of the author's unpublished plays is deposited in the FSWW Archives/Schomburg Collection.) **Ask Your Mama** (morality play, 1 act, 1975). Encounter between a white man and a black woman—or is she a woman? Pub. in *Time to Greez! Incantations from the Third World* (Clay et al., 1975). **Omens** (drama, 1 act, 1975). A black couple are entrapped in their home by unknown persons and must come to grips with their predicament. Prod. by ACT, May 1975. **Tricks** (musical comedy-drama, 2 acts, 1970s). Portrays the tricks that Uncle Sam plays on blacks. **Black Rats** (domestic drama, 1 act, 1970s). During the night, while her husband is asleep, a black woman tries to cope with her fears and frustrations. **We Don't Play That in the Projects** (drama, 1 act, 1970s). Conflict and violence break out within a teenage gang, with tragic results.

ALEXANDER, ROBERT, Playwright, novelist, and writer. Grew up in Washington, DC, the son of a prominent DC attorney. Educated at Oberlin Coll. (B.A. in English, 1975) and San Francisco State Univ. (completed studies for M.F.A. in playwriting, 1980s). Before graduating from Oberlin, he spent a year at Columbia Univ., developing his skills as a writer under the direction of JOHN O. KILLENS and DAMON KENYATTA. Married; one son. Currently resides in Oakland, CA. Author of "The Sandman and the Dreamer," an unpublished novel, and "San Pablo People," a novel in progress. Frequently contributed articles to *City Arts Monthly,* a publication of City Celebrations, Inc. A member of West Oakland Writers Workshop, the Playwrights Unit of the One Act Theatre Co. of San Francisco and DG. *Address:* 2638 78th Ave., Oakland, CA 94605.

PLAYS AND DRAMATIC WORKS:
A Place to Call Home (1978). Prod. at the Oakland Public Auditorium in an arts festival sponsored by the Rotary Club, Oct. 1978. Subsequently prod. by A Black Box, Inc., San Francisco, May 1980.

The Hourglass (drama, 2 acts, 1979). About a woman's obsession with the past and the unrequited love of her deceased husband. Deals with the tensions that mount when her expatriate son returns from Europe to find his mother trapped in a time zone, participating in a bizarre ritual of turning over "the hourglass." First prod. by First World Productions, at the Buriel Clay Theatre, San Francisco, Sept. 1979. Subsequently prod. at Soul People Repertory in Indianapolis, IN, Oct. 1981. A one-act version was prod. at the One Act Theatre of San Francisco, April 1972, playing to packed houses. Also received staged readings by the Los Angeles Cultural Center, the Karamu House in Cleveland, and the Frank Silvera Writers' Workshop (FSWW) in New York. Unpub. script and tape recording located in the FSWW Archives/Schomburg Collection. Pub. in *Center Stage* (Ostrow, 1981).

Home Free (drama, 1 act, 1981). Concerns a man paroled from prison who attempts to recapture lost time with his family, only to be disillusioned by the inevitable change in himself and his loved ones, including his dope-peddling son, whom he tries to save from a fate similar to his own. Showcased at the Black Rep Theatre in Berkeley, April 1981. Prod. in a full production by the Inner City Cultural Center (ICCC), Los Angeles, Oct.-Nov. 1981. Plans were under way in 1983 for productions by the Los Angeles Cultural Center, the Howard Univ. Drama Dept., and the San Jose Black Theatre Workshop. Staged readings given by the One Act Theatre Co. of San Francisco and the Karamu House in Cleveland. Pub. in *West Coast Plays* (California Theatre Council, Berkeley, 1982).

Factwino vs. Armageddon // Orig. title: **Fact Wino Meets Armageddon Man** (mime troupe play, 1 act, 1982). Written in collaboration with the San Francisco Mime Troupe. Toured the Bay Area parks, summer 1982, playing before an estimated 20,000 people; then on tour of the United States, where the author estimates that it was seen by more than 100,000 people.

Secrets of the Sand (mime troupe play, 1 act, 1982). Written in collaboration with the San Francisco Mime Troupe. A fictionalized account of the tragic aftermath of the John Wayne movie *The Conquerer*, a blood-and-sand epic filmed on location in Nevada near an atomic weapons test site. According to recent revelations, 90 members of the 220–member cast and crew contracted cancer later in life, and of this number 46 had died by 1980 (including John Wayne, costar Agnes Moorehead, and director Dick Powell). The play concerns the efforts of a black soul singer, the daughter of a celebrated black actor who had died from cancer after making a film similar to *The Conquerer*, to establish the true cause of her father's death as due to radioactive sands. Played to free admission in Bay Area parks. It was called by critics one of the best mime troupe plays in years. Was being translated into French in 1983, and sched. to tour Canada and Europe.

We Almost Made It to the Super Bowl (tragi-fantasy, 2 acts, 1982). A fantasy nightmare about the loss of the American dream, centered around a sports motif. Deals with a black running back, approaching the end of his playing career, unable to face his prospects after retirement. Also touches on several aspects of the game that confront black players in the 1980s: racism, drug abuse, etc. Received an unrehearsed cold reading in July 1982 at the Julian Theatre. Premiered at the Lorraine Hansberry Theatre in Jan. 1982, where it ran for 30 perfs. Was under option for prodn. by NEC in the 1983–84 season, with DOUGLAS TURNER WARD slated to direct.

Rock Fantasy (musical comedy, full length, pre-1983). Music and lyrics by *Alan Dones and *David Daniels, with additional lyrics by the author. About a middle-aged black certified public accountant who attempts to find refuge from his everyday problems by delving into rock-and-roll fantasies. In a fanciful dreamlike world, Albert Jackson gets discovered playing a tennis racket and becomes America's latest overnight sensation. The music is contemporary black new wave that incorporates sounds of Prince and Michael Jackson with the arty sounds of Talking Heads or Grace Jones. Was under option to premiere at the Lorraine Hansberry Theatre of San Francisco in 1983.

ALFORD, LAMAR, Actor, singer, composer, musician, and musical playwright. Associated with La Mama E.T.C. in New York during the 1970s. He has composed for and/or performed in several Off-Bway shows, including *Caution: A Love Story* (1969), *The Moondreamers* (1969), *Arden of Faversham* (1970), *Ubu* (1970), and *A Rat's Mass* (1972).

DRAMATIC WORK:

Thoughts (collection of musical sketches, full length, 1972). Book, music, and lyrics by Alford. With additional lyrics by Megan Terry and JOSE TAPIA. Based on the author's reminiscences of his growing up as black youth in the Deep South. According to Jeff Sweet, "Time and time again, the rhythms of gospel and soul roused the audience to hand-clapping, foot-stomping enthusiasm, a high point being Mary Alice's rendition of

'Sunshine.' ''—*The Best Plays of 1972–1973,* p. 45. First prod. Off-Bway at La Mama E.T.C., Dec. 6, 1972; dir. by Jan Mickens. Presented Off-Bway, at Theatre De Lys, March 19–April 6, 1973, for 24 perfs.; dir. by Michael Schultz. With Mary Alice, Jean Andelman, Martha Flowers, Robin LaMont, Baruk Levin, Bob Molock, Barbara Montgomery, Jeffery Mylett, Howard Porter, Sarallen, and E. H. Wright. Presented in the Off-Bway version by the New Theatre Club of Washington, DC, at the Washington Theatre Club, Jan. 23, 1974, for 23 perfs.

ALI, KENSHAKA, Playwright, director, and actor. Resides in New York City. Received the B.A. degree cum laude from CUNY, Special Baccalaureate Program, 1983, with a major in directing/playwriting. Associated with Theatre in Progress, NY. Listed in *Who's Who Among Students in American Universities and Colleges* (1983). Recipient of a Humanitarian Award from the Harlem Consumer Education Council for Outstanding Service to the Harlem Community, 1982. *Address:* 780 Grand Concourse #1M, Bronx, NY 10451.

PLAYS AND DRAMATIC WORKS:

No Crystal Stair (musical choreopoem, 1980). A collage of poems, songs, and anecdotes depicting the historical struggle of black youth in America. Prod. by AMAS Repertory Theatre, New York, 1980.

Bully (children's play, c. 1981). Young classmates accidentally discover the meaning of unity when they are forced to deal with a bully in their school. Prod. by the New Paltz Children's Theatre, around 1981.

The Calling (1 act, 1981). A couple discovers what happens when rigorous artistic training is not equally balanced by spiritual development. Prod. at Brooklyn Coll., New York, 1981.

Lil Miss Red Ridin Hood (one-character piece, 1 act, c. 1981). A vibrant warrior woman grows up in the ghetto discovering the power of the matriarch.

Lines to the Black Oak (for Paul Robeson) (ritual choreopoem, 1982). A celebration of and salute to Paul Robeson through poetry, dance, song, and scenes. Prod. at the AUDELCO (Audience Development Co.) First Black Theatre Festival, New York, 1982. Prod. by the New Heritage Theatre (NHT), New York, 1984.

Madahah's Song (children's choreopoem, 2 acts, 1983). A children's celebration of life. Prod. at the Lehman Coll. Performing Arts Center, New York, 1983.

A Try Is a Failure (social drama, 1 act, 1983). Addicts in a drug detoxification center try to kick not only heroin and methadone addiction, but the loneliness and despair inherent in ghetto lifestyles. Public reading by the Frank Silvera Writers' Workshop (FSWW), New York, 1983. Also prod. by Theatre in Progress, NY, 1983. Unpub. script in the FSWW Archives/Schomburg Collection.

A Teenage Love Play (musical, 2 acts, 1985). Two aspiring dancers must deal with drug abuse, child abuse, pregnancy, and a plethora of other crises threatening their ambitions. Sched. for prodn. by Mind Builders' Positive Youth Troupe, on New York City school tour, March 1985.

ALI, LATEEF, Playwright. Associated with Oduduwa Production, Black Studies Dept., Univ. of Pittsburgh, PA.

PLAY:

How Long How Long How Long (ritual, 1 act, 1970). White devil teaches black people how to be "niggers." Pub. in *Connection* (Porter, 1970).

ALLADYCE, DARRYL (Eric), Actor-playwright. Has appeared frequently in soap operas, situation comedies, and television commercials, and has performed in a number of plays in and around the New York City area and in the Southeast. His poetry has been performed in New York and elsewhere, and pub. in *New City Voices, Young Anthology of Poets, American Rag, Easy, Essence,* and *Long Journey.* Member of the Frank Silvera Writers' Workshop (FSWW) in New York. Recipient of the Theodore Goodman Playwriting Award at CCNY, 1977.

PLAYS:

Buddies (two-character piece, 1 act, 1977). Concerns the developing relationship between two friends who move toward intimacy. Staged reading by FSWW, at CCNY, March 1977. Prod. as a full production at the Urban Arts Corps (UAC), New York, 1978. Unpub. script and tape recording in the FSWW Archives/Schomburg Collection. **Peter and Karen** (two-character piece, 1 act, pre-1985). Concerns the parting of two friends in a subway station. Prod. by Actors Theatre of Louisville, KY, 1979. **Douglas and Juanita** (two-character piece, 1 act, pre-1985). Concerns the discoveries two cousins make about one another, their family, and the world. **Woodside** (drama, 2 acts, pre-1985). Concerns the tensions that erupt outside a New York City taxi garage when a driver's body is discovered.

ALLEN, PAUL R., Playwright. Former managing editor of the Black American Theatre of Washington, DC, later known as the American Theatre.

PLAYS:

Blues Life of Billie Holiday (1970s). About the well-known blues singer. Prod. by Black American Theatre, 1970s. **Raise Up** (1970s). About a floating numbers racket. Prod. by Black American Theatre, 1970s.

ALLEN, RICHARD, Playwright.

PLAY:

Take Me to Your Leader (children's comedy, 1 act, 1969). Some outer space visitors encounter an earth automobile, with predictable results. Pub. in *We Are Black* (Science Research Assocs., Chicago, 1969).

ALLEN, SENA. See ALLEN, THOMASENA DAVIS.

ALLEN, THOMASENA DAVIS (Sena Allen), Playwright and theatrical director. Based in Washington, DC, where she was associated with the Black American Theatre, later renamed the American Theatre. More recently, she was director of the New Theatre Center in Washington.

DRAMATIC WORK:

Songs My Father Taught Me (musical, full length, 1973). Focuses on the spiritual values and truths which American blacks have inherited from their ancestors. Prod. by Black American Theatre, Washington, DC, March 1974.

ALONZO, CECIL, Playwright, actor, poet, producer, director, composer, teacher, and administrator. Founder, administrator, director, producer, and principal playwright of the Alonzo Players, Brooklyn, NY, 1968–present. (The group was originally called Cecil Alonzo and the Players Eight.) Alonzo grew up in Williamsburg, VA, where he made his stage debut in a church pageant at age five. Received the B.A. in theatre arts and English education from Norfolk State Coll., VA, 1965. Studied acting and speech with the American Academy of Dramatic Arts, 1968; film and television production, and public relations, with Third World Cinema Productions, 1972. Has held a number of administrative positions in New York City, with the Dept. of Social Services, 1970–79. Artistic director, Brooklyn Masonic Temple (now the home of Alonzo Players), 1982–present. Since 1981 has taught communication skills and public speaking for Empire State Coll., the School Arts League, and the New York City Board of Education. His extensive acting career ranges from Off-Off-Bway to radio, television, stage, and movie appearances. Performed in the radio soap opera "Sounds of the City"; was asst. director to Gordon Parks, Jr., in the making of the film *Superfly;* and was production asst. on FRED WILLIAMSON's film *Black Caesar,* in which Alonzo also appeared as Williamson's bodyguard. Other stage appearances include *Day of Absence, Teahouse of the August Moon,* and *Murder in the Cathedral.* His choral works have been premiered by the Hampton Institute Choir and recorded by the Hartford Symphony Orchestra. His poetry and prose works have been performed by the Alonzo Players and published in various newsletters and anthologies. Memberships and associations include panelist, New York City Dept. of Cultural Affairs; panelist, Brooklyn Arts and Cultural Assn.; acting chairman and later vice pres., Black Theatre Alliance (BTA) of America; pres., Clairmont Area Housing Development Corp.; member, Pratt Area Community Council. Twice voted Outstanding Young Man of the Year by the Jaycees of America, 1980 and 1981; nominated for seven AUDELCO awards for theatre excellence, 1980–81; and recipient of the New York City Citizenship Award and the People in Profile Community Service Award. *Address:* Alonzo Players, 317 Clermont Ave., Brooklyn, NY 11205.

REPRESENTATIVE PLAYS AND DRAMATIC WORKS:

Black Voices // Orig. title: **Four Hundred Years Overdue** (poetic revue, 2 acts, 1969). Excerpts from black writers, laced with Alonzo's own material. A poetic retelling of the history of blacks in America from the slave era to the 1960s. First prod. under its original title by the Alonzo Players, Brooklyn, 1969; dir. by author. Prod. under its present title by the Alonzo Players, at the Courtyard Playhouse, New York, opening March 5, 1971; dir. by author. Aired on PBS, 1973, and telecast in the Tri-State Area (around New York City), c. 1973. Also presented at the Billie Holiday Theatre, Brooklyn, 1973.

Somewhere Between Us Two (poetic love story, 1 act, 1972). Coauthor, with ROB TAYLOR. Story of two pen pals who finally meet and are disappointed that the words on paper do not match all the images that they have conjured up during their correspondence. Concerns their attempt to bridge the gap that lies "somewhere between us two." Apparently written through correspondence with the collaborator, who was then an inmate at Riker's Island, NY. [See also **Strike One Blow,** immediately below.] Presented by the Alonzo Players, Brooklyn, at the Billie Holiday Theatre, 1973; dir. by author. Perfd. at the BTA annual festival, New York, 1974. Perfd. at the Seafood Playhouse, New York, June 1975.

Strike One Blow (drama, 1 act, 1973). Coauthor, with ROB TAYLOR. A true story of the feelings and thoughts of an inmate on Riker's Island, NY, whose personal beliefs run afoul of the law and keep him in hot water with the authorities. Focuses on the joys and sadness of his past and his determination not to give in to the physical and emotional pressures of prison life. Based on the experiences of the coauthor, and written through correspondence with Alonzo. [See also **Somewhere Between Us Two,** immediately above.]

Circus Maxi-Us ("A contemporary fairy tale with music" [sub-title], full length, 1974). The story of a group of trained circus animals who run away from the circus rather than perform for kids who are not as kind and respectful to people and animals as they ought to be. A kind ringmaster convinces the animals to go off strike and return to performing for the children, to give them a lesson in caring, sharing, and brotherhood. Prod. by the Alonzo Players, at the Brooklyn Academy of Music's Children's Christmas Festival, Dec. 1980, where it played to over 7,500 children in five days. Has been prod. by several children's theatre companies in New York City.

1999: (The Beginning of the End—The End of the Beginning) (musical, 3 acts, 1980). Book and lyrics by Alonzo. Music by Alonzo and JaSun. Apparently based on Alonzo's one act play, **1999** (1975) [see OTHER PLAYS AND DRAMATIC WORKS below]. A futuristic musical that blends Biblical fact and predictions with science fiction. The story of a family caught between the forces of good and evil in the last seven days of time. Nominated for seven AUDELCO awards during the 1980–81 season, including Best Musical, Best Production, and Best Female in a Musical. Prod. in repertory by the Alonzo Players, opening Feb. 1980; dir. by author.

Beulah Johnson (soap opera for the stage, more than 36 full length episodes, 1976/81). Subtitled "The World's First Live Continuing Saga in Soap." A series of staged episodes based on the format of the soaps. The continuing story of a colorful beautician who is discovered to have a rare singing voice and an assortment of crazed, serious, charming, and desperate people around her, providing classic lessons in living within New York's Melting Pot neighborhoods. The story line deals with Beulah's and her neighbors' turmoils, trails, tribulations, and triumphs. Each of the more than three dozen complete episodes ranges in length from 60 to 90 minutes. Written and prod. by Alonzo in bimonthly segments in Brooklyn, starring Carol Mitchell-Smith and John Furbert as the Johnsons, Beulah and Reuben. Aired on cable TV and local news shows. Has also been presented in Houston, Chicago, and Williamsburg, VA. Pub. in monthly installments in *Soap Opera Digest* from Dec. 1979 to June 1981, the only untelevised work to be afforded this treatment.

OTHER PLAYS AND DRAMATIC WORKS:

A Big Wheel a' Spinning and a' Spinning // Also known as **Big Wheel** (literary anthology, full length, 1968). Adaptn. of prose and poetry of black American writers combined with some of Alonzo's own works. Prod. by Cecil Alonzo and the Players Eight (orig. name of the Alonzo Players) and presented in the sanctuary of St. Luke's Lutheran Church, on Washington Ave. in Brooklyn, Jan. 1968. **Patchwork** (drama, 1 act, 1973). A black youth recalls, to an assortment of his peers in a classroom rollicking with fun, "The Summer When Black Kids Died in Atlanta." (One of the kids was his brother.) Prod. by the Alonzo Players, 1973; dir. by author. Also presented at the Billie Holiday Theatre, 1975. **Breakfast Is Served** (dramatic comedy, 1 act, 1974). Written in Georgetown, Guyana. About a domestic who wants her constantly unemployed actor-husband to get a job of any kind. A two-character study of high hopes and failed ambitions that leads to the death of one of the parties. Prod. by the Alonzo Players, 1974; dir. by author. **1999** // Also known as **Ghettoes 1999** (1 act, 1975). Based on a concept by *John Ajala Williams. Prod. by the Alonzo Players under the auspices of the Harlem Cultural Council; dir. by author. [See also **1999** (1980) above.] **AWOL** (sociopolitical satire, full length, 1987). "Pokes fun at the chaotic situation that results when Blacks stay home for one day and don't show up."—*New York Amsterdam News,* March 7, 1987. Prod. by the Alonzo Players, opening March 12, 1987.

AMIS, LOLA JONES. See JONES, LOLA E.

AMOS, JOHN (1939–   ), Actor, scriptwriter, producer, and former athlete. Best known for his television roles as Gordy the Weatherman on "The Mary Tyler Moore Show," James Evans on "Good Times," and the adult Kunta Kinte in *Roots.* Born in Newark, NJ; grew up in East Orange, NJ. Currently lives in Tarzana, CA. Educated at Long Beach City Coll. (CA.); transferred to Colorado State Univ. (B.A. in sociology); also attended Bronx Community Coll. Played football in college, and with semiprofessional teams for about three years. Worked briefly as a stand-up comic in nightclubs. Around 1965 began writing copy for an advertising agency, which eventually led to his TV and film career. Made his TV debut as a writer and performer on "The Lohman and Barkley Show." Other TV appearances include "The Tim Conway Show," "The Merv Griffin Show," "The Bill Cosby Show," and "Maude," where he made a few brief appearances as the husband of Maude's maid Florida, played by Esther Rolle. The chemistry between the two was so good that a spinoff from "Maude" developed into the "Good Times" show. Has also appeared in several films, including *Sweet Sweetback's Baadasssss Song* (1971), *The World's Greatest Athlete* (1973), and *Let's Do It Again* (1975).

DRAMATIC WORKS:
"**The Leslie Uggams Show**" (TV scripts, 1969). "**The Bill Cosby Show**" (TV scripts, 1969/71). **Norman Is That You?** (screenplay, full length, early 1970s). Based on the stage play of the same title in which Amos starred in the Los Angeles prodn. (It is not known whether or not this script was used for the 1976 film by the same title starring Redd Foxx and Pearl Bailey.) **Truth and Soul** (1972). Pub. in *Soul Illustrated,* Spring 1972, pp. 17, 64. **Shaka** (screenplay for a doc. film, full length, 1976). The life story of the nineteenth century black Zulu warrior-king, who rose from illegitimacy to become the most powerful military, cultural, and spiritual leader of the Zulu nation. Sched. for production and presumably prod. in Liberia around 1976 by John Amos Productions; dir. and starred in by author.

ANDERSON, ODIE (1943–   ), Broker, public speaker and playwright. Born and resides in Chicago, IL. Educated at DePaul Univ. (A.A., 1966; B.A., 1970; J.D., 1970). Married; the father of three children. Formerly associated with the brokerage firm of Williams & Williams, Chicago, 1967– c. 1978. Member of Urban League, Council of Foreign Relations, World Federalist Org., Pi Gamma Mu, and vice pres. of Phi Ro Pi. Winner of numerous public speaking and sales achievement awards.

PLAY:
The Trial of God (verse drama, 3 acts, 1970). God is accused, indicted, and tried for causing the evils and suffering of mankind. Pub. by Exposition Press, New York, 1970.

ANDERSON, T. DIANNE (1937–1983), Playwright, TV scriptwriter, author, theatrical technician, songwriter, and teacher. Born in Buffalo, NY, where she attended the public schools, received several awards for writing and oratory, and was class poet of her high school graduating class. Studied playwriting at Stanford Univ., 1956–58, where she was also electrician for a number of campus productions. Attended the Gene Frankel Theatre Workshop in New York, where she continued her study of playwriting with Ben Zavin and audited directing with Frankel. In 1958 she began experiencing the early symptoms of multiple sclerosis. For about ten years, 1958–67, she worked in Off-Bway theatre as a stagehand and electrician. During this period, she wrote poetry, songs, fiction, and her first plays, which were produced by the West Side YMCA Theatre and the West End Repertory Theatre. She spent three years in Washington, DC, 1968–71, working for HEW and the Center for Human Systems, while also serving as resident playwright and instructor at the Back Alley Theatre, which was then beginning its operations as a racially integrated community theatre. Wrote about 20 half-hour weekly TV scripts for "Our Street," a black series telecast by the Maryland Center for Public Broadcasting, 1970–71. Director, Black Free-Form Theatre, Grand Rapids, MI, 1971–72. Wrote a film treatment for John Secondari Productions, New York, and a feature film script for Cine/Orb, Inc., of Philadelphia, 1971–72. Visiting artist/lecturer, Univ. of South Florida at Tampa, 1972–73. By 1974 the severity of the multiple sclerosis made it impossible for her to continue working and writing. Admitted to Goldwater Memorial Hosp., Roosevelt Island, NY, where she remained active in literary groups at the hospital until her death in Oct. 1983. *Literary Executor* (and sister): Dr. Sandra Anderson Garcia, 807 Lorena Rd., Lutz, FL 33549; or Dept. of Psychology, College of Behavioral Sciences, University of South Florida at Tampa, FL 33620.

COLLECTION:
THE UNICORN DIED AT DAWN: Plays, Poems, Songs and Other Writings. Anderson Publishing (c/o Literary Executor above), Lutz, FL, 1981. Contains **Nightcap** (1964), **Just Friendly** (1964), **Come Yesterday** (1964), **Home to Roost** (1966), **The Unicorn Died at Dawn** (1967), **Closing Time** (1967), **Black Sparrow** (1972), **Cyro** (1976), **A Gift of Harmonia** (1981), and the following scripts dated 1970–71: **Keep Track, The**

Good Book Says, Let Me Count the Ways, Baby, Happy Birthday Brother, If I Were a Chameleon, Unpaid Dues, OFF & T Co., Inc., I'm Staying, and **Audition.**

REPRESENTATIVE PLAYS AND DRAMATIC WORKS:

Nightcap (comedy, 1 act, 1964). A man attempts to seduce a woman after forcing himself into her apartment for a nightcap. First prod. at the Lincoln Square Theatre, West Side YMCA, April 1974; dir. by Vernon Washington. Prod. by West End Repertory Theatre, July 1965. Pub. in the author's *THE UNICORN DIED AT DAWN.*

Just Friendly (semicomedy, 1 act, 1964). Concerns the seemingly friendly reunion of a lawyer and his client, a year after the client has been tried and acquitted, in which they hold their own private reenactment of the trial. Prod. by Lincoln Square Theatre, West Side YMCA, April 1964; dir. by Vernon Washington. Prod. by Back Alley Theatre, Washington, DC, Dec. 1968 and Jan. 1969. Pubic reading by Long Island Univ., Brooklyn; dir. by author. Pub. in the author's *THE UNICORN DIED AT DAWN.*

Come Yesterday (tragedy, 1 act, 1964). A young black man's search for faith ends in disillusionment. Prod. by the Lincoln Square Theatre, West Side YMCA, April 1964; dir. by Vernon Washington. Prod. by the West End Repertory Theatre, July 1964. Pub. in the author's *THE UNICORN DIED AT DAWN.*

Home to Roost (domestic comedy, 3 acts, 1966). A mother returns home unexpectedly, after an absence of several years, and brings turmoil into the lives of the men in the home, whose lifestyles have changed considerably during her absence. Prod. by the West End Repertory Theatre, 1966; dir. by Vernon Washington. Pub. in the author's *THE UNICORN DIED AT DAWN.*

The Unicorn Died at Dawn (drama, 2 acts, 1967). (Not to be confused with the author's collection by the same title.) Written for the National Urban League. "Centers around a musician . . . who is the son of a Baptist minister. Talented and successful, [he] comes home from the nightclub life in New York with the purpose of shaking up his middle-class family. During the weekend visit, the entire family copes with changes in their lives, racism, black awareness and communication. The title is derived from a mythical story of awakening and loss of innocence and Miss Anderson's admiration of the Unicorn tapestries at the Cloisters in New York."—*Evening Star* (Washington, DC), Jan. 27, 1971, p. B-8. Public reading (excerpts) by the Back Alley Theatre, at the Sheraton Park Hotel, Washington, July 1969; dir. by Kay Ford. Full prodn. by the Back Alley Theatre, Jan. 1971, running on weekends through Feb. 22, 1971; dir. by Robert Maddox. Prod. by The New Place, a black community center in Ybor City, FL.; dir. by Tito Shaw, June 1974. Pub. in the author's *THE UNICORN DIED AT DAWN.* Unpub. script also in the Hatch-Billops Collection.

Closing Time (comedy-skit, 1967). At closing time, a woman comes into a shoe store trying to buy one shoe (she has lost the other one). The tired salesman cannot cope, but the experienced manager makes the sale, charging the customer for both shoes but pretending to throw in the second one free of charge. Prod. at the New York City Rosicrucian Lodge, 1967; dir. by author. Pub. in the author's *THE UNICORN DIED AT DAWN.*

"Our Street" (TV series, 20 half-hr. scripts, 1970–71). The following scripts were written for and prod. by "Our Street," a 30-minute weekly TV series presented by the Maryland Center for Public Broadcasting, between Nov. 1970 and Aug. 1971. Although the author wrote over 20 scripts for the series, only the following were actually prod. on TV, and are pub. in the author's collection, *THE UNICORN DIED AT DAWN:* **Keep**

Track, The Good Book Says, Let Me Count the Ways, Baby, Happy Birthday, If I Were a Chameleon, Unpaid, OFF&T Co., Inc., I'm Staying, and **Audition** (co-authored with TED SHINE).

OTHER PLAYS:
A (one-act play with 6 songs, 1969). Prod. by Back Alley Theatre, Feb. 1970. **Black Sparrow** (drama, full length, 1972). Concerns the problems faced by a black veteran who returns from the war in Vietnam. Written while the author was in residence as a visiting artist/lecturer at the Univ. of South Florida at Tampa, Fall 1972, where it was prod. July 1973; dir. by Charles Briggs. Pub. in the author's *THE UNICORN DIED AT DAWN.* **Cyro** (biographical sketch, 1 act, 1976). Dramatization of the author's hospital experience before, during, and immediately following a surgical procedure called cyrothalamectomy. Pub. in the author's *THE UNICORN DIED AT DAWN.* **A Gift of Harmonia** (drama, 2 acts, 1981). In Greek mythology, Aphrodite gave her daughter Harmonia a necklace which was to bring disaster in a later generation. That is the theme of this play, which concerns a musician who sacrifices his principles in order to gain a much-desired commission. Pub. in the author's *THE UNICORN DIED AT DAWN.*

ANDERSON, THOMAS (1906–   ), Veteran stage and film actor-singer. Born in Pasadena, CA. Educated at Pasadena Jr. Coll. and the American Theatre Wing. His numerous stage appearances include the Federal Theatre production of *Macbeth* (1936), *Cabin in the Sky* (1940), *Native Son* (1941), *The Great White Hope* (1968), *Hello Dolly!* (1969), and *Don't Play Us Cheap* (1972). Film appearances include *The Learning Tree* (1969), *The Legend of Nigger Charley* (1972), and *Gordon's War* (1973).

PLAY:
Crispus Attucks (historical drama, full length, 1970). About the first black American hero to be killed in the American Revolution. Pub. by New Dimensions, New York, 1970.

ANDERSON, WALT, Playwright.
PLAY:
Bitter Bread! ("A Dramatic Reading" [subtitle], 1974). Pub. by Seabury Press, New York, 1974.

ANGELOU, MAYA (Marguerite Johnson, 1928–   ), Author, theatrical performer, playwright, scriptwriter, filmmaker, television personality, educator, and one of the world's most versatile and articulate women. Best known for her first autobiographical novel, *I Know Why the Caged Bird Sings* (1969), which was a Book-of-the-Month Club selection, nominated for a National Book Award, and made into a film for television. Born in St. Louis, MO. Raised from age three by her paternal grandmother in Stamps, AR, a racist community where she received her public school education and gained experiences that were to provide the material for her first book. Moved to California at age 13; graduated from George Washington H.S., San Francisco, 1945. Mother of one son. After taking a number of commonplace jobs, she decided on a theatrical career and began to take night courses in music, dance, and drama. Married a man of Greek origin (marriage dissolved around 1952) from which she took her professional surname, Angelou; the name Maya was adopted from her brother's familiar name for her. Became a nightclub performer in 1952, specializing in calypso songs and dances. Appeared in clubs in San Francisco, Chicago, and New York City. Joined the Harlem Writers' Guild and began serious study of writing, while continuing to pursue her theatrical career. Performed as a singer and premiere danseuse in the 22–nation European tour of *Porgy and Bess*, 1954–55, sponsored by the U.S. Dept. of State. Appeared Off-Broadway in *Calypso Heat Wave* (1958) and *The Blacks* (1960). Performed the title role in Brecht's *Mother Courage* (1964) at the Univ. of Ghana; the nurse in Frank Silvera's Los Angeles production of Anouilh's *Medea* (1966); and Mary Todd Lincoln's dressmaker and confidante on Broadway in *Look Away* (1973), for which she received a Tony nomination as best supporting actress in a dramatic role. Lived for several years in Africa, where she was editor of the *Arab Observer*, 1961–62; writer for the *Ghanaian Times* and contributor to the Ghanaian Broadcasting Corp., 1963–64; prof. of music and drama at the Univ. of Ghana, 1963–64; and feature editor of the *African Review*, 1966. Returned to Los Angeles, where she lectured at the Univ. of California, completed her first autobiography, and wrote a number of plays, poems, songs, and TV scripts, 1966–69. Wrote four more autobiographical volumes: *Gather Together in My Name* (1974), *Singin' and Swingin' and Gettin' Merry Like Christmas* (1976), and *The Heart of a Woman* (1982), and *All God's Children Need Traveling Shoes* (1986). Her volumes of poetry include *Just Give Me a Drink of Water 'Fore I Diiie* (1971), which was nominated for a Pulitzer Prize, *Oh, Pray My Wings Are Gonna Fit Me Well* (1975), *And Still I Rise* (1978), and *Shaker, Why Don't You Sing?* (1983). Her articles, stories, and poems have been published in numerous national periodicals. Since 1970 she has become increasingly involved in writing for television and films and has made numerous TV appearances as actress, host, narrator, interviewer, and celebrity guest. Her most notable TV appearances include narrator of "The Slave Coast," part 3 of the four-part "Black American Heritage" series, presented on WCBS-TV, Spring 1972; interview with Bill Moyers, Nov. 21, 1973; a cameo appearance as Kunta Kinte's African grandmother, Nyo Boto, in the original production of Alex Haley's *Roots* (1977); narrator of the PBS series "Humanities Through the Arts" (1982); and featured subject of the first episode of the Emmy Award-winning 17–part series, "Creativity with Bill Moyers." In 1976 she directed her first film, **All Day Long,** and is credited with being the first professional black woman film director. Married Paul DeFeu, a San Francisco builder, 1973 (marriage dissolved, late 1970s). In 1981 she was appointed Reynolds Prof. of American Studies at Wake Forest Univ., Winston-Salem, NC, where she now maintains her permanent home. Appointed member of the Board of Trustees of the American Film Inst. (AFI), 1975, and member of the American Revolution Bicentennial Council (by Pres. Gerald Ford), 1975–76. Named Woman of the Year in Communications by *Ladies' Home Journal*, 1976. Educational honors include a Chubb Fellowship at Yale Univ., 1970; writer-in-residence at the Univ. of Kansas (at Lawrence), Fall 1980; distinguished visiting professorships at Wake Forest Univ., Wichita State Univ., and California State Univ./Sacramento, 1970s; recipient of honorary doctor's degrees from Smith Coll., 1975; Mills Coll., 1975; Lawrence Univ., 1977; Howard Univ., 1985; and several other institutions. *Address*—Office: Wake Forest Univ., Winston-Salem, NC 27109. Home: 3240 Valley Rd., Winston-Salem, NC 27106. Alternate: c/o Random House, 201 E. 50th St., New York, NY 10022.

REPRESENTATIVE PLAYS AND DRAMATIC WORKS:

Cabaret for Freedom (nightclub revue, full length, 1960). Coauthored, costarred, and coproduced with the late actor-comedian GODFREY CAMBRIDGE. Topical revue in support of the civil rights movement and to raise funds for SCLC. Prod. Off-Bway at the Village Gate, Summer 1960, sponsored by the Emergency Committee for the Southern Freedom Struggle; with an integrated cast of unemployed actors, singers, dancers, and musicians; dir. by Hugh Herd.

Georgia, Georgia (feature film, full length: screenplay with musical score, 1972). Possibly the first orig. screenplay by a black woman to be prod. as a feature film (cf. MARY ELIZABETH VROMAN). Concerns a black singer on a tour of Sweden, who is strongly attracted to a group of white American ex-partriates and who becomes romantically involved with one of them, a photographer. Her racial attitude is in direct contrast with that of her traveling companion, an angry and bitter black woman. Independently prod. in Sweden by Quentin Kelly; dir. by Stig Bjorkman and distributed by Cinerama, 1972. Hugh A. Robertson, a black director, was consultant on this film, which featured Diana Sands as Georgia, the singer; MINNIE GENTRY as her companion; ROGER FURMAN as her homosexual black manager; and Dirk Benedict as her white lover. Available from Cinema Releasing, St. Louis, MO.

All Day Long (film: screenplay and musical score, 1974). Adapt. from her short story by the same title. Credited with being the first film professionally dir. by a black woman. Prod. by AFI, Los Angeles, 1974; dir. by author.

I Know Why the Caged Bird Sings (film for TV, full length: script and musical score, c. 1974). Script coauthored with Leonora Thuna. Adapt. from her best-selling autobiographical novel by the same title. About her childhood experiences in the racist town of Stamps, AR, where she was raised by her paternal grandmother; a year in St. Louis, where she was sexually assaulted by her mother's boyfriend; and her return to Stamps, where she was rehabilitated under the guidance of one of her teachers, who was to become a major influence in Maya's life. Script completed around 1974. Prod. as a two-hour special and first telecast on NBC-TV, April 27, 1979; dir. by Fielder Cook. Featured Constance Good as the young Maya and Esther Rolle as the grandmother who raised her; with Diahann Carroll, RUBY DEE, PAUL BENJAMIN, Roger E. Mosely, and Madge Sinclair. Pub. only as a novel by Random House, New York, 1969.

And Still I Rise (theatrical collage, full length, 1979). Afro-American poetry, music, and dance, apparently based on the author's book of poetry by the same title. Prod. by the Oakland Ensemble Theatre, CA, opening Oct. 18, 1979, for 14 perfs.; dir. by author. Pub. only as a volume of poetry by Random House, New York, 1978.

Sister, Sister (TV film, full length, 1979). Commissioned by NBC. "About three women whose conflicting values with the men in their lives strain family ties."—*Jet*, June 14, 1982. "The story line pits the three sisters against each other at a reunion at the family home in [a] small town in North Carolina.''—Ibid., June 21, 1982. Televised by NBC in Feb. 1969, but not released for three years because of network concern that it would not draw the necessary ratings. First aired on NBC-TV, June 7, 1982, and rebroadcast in June 1986. Featured Diahann Carroll, Carolyn Lovejoy, and Rosalind Cash as the three sisters; with Dick Anthony Williams, Paul Winfield, and Robert Hooks as the men in their lives.

On a Southern Journey (drama, full length, 1983). According to *Jet* (Dec. 19, 1983, p. 61). ''The plot of the play centers on three characters who are thrown together at a train station. Each is headed for the same small southern town to attend a trial which affects their lives individually and collectively.'' Premiered at the Spirit Square Theatre, Charlotte, NC, Winter 1983, with Berlinda Tolbert of CBS-TV's ''The Jeffersons'' in the starring role.

OTHER PLAYS, DRAMATIC WORKS, AND RELATED WRITINGS FOR TV AND FILMS:

The Least of These (drama, 1 act, 1966). Prod. in Los Angeles, 1966. **The Clawing Within** (drama, 3 acts, 1966). **Adjoa Amissah** (musical, 2 acts, 1967). Set in Ashanti, Ghana, in 1958. **Gettin' Up Stayed on My Mind** (1967). **Blacks! Blues! Blacks!** (series of ten 1–hr. TV programs, 1968). Written, prod., and hosted by Angelou. According to the author, the title means ''that in Africa we were Blacks, brought by slavery to the U.S. Our condition of misery could be called the Blues and now through our awareness of our African heritage, we were proudly becoming Blacks again. The series dealt with the Africanisms still current in the U.S., which I had known in my Southern days and nights.'' —*Ebony,* Feb. 1982, p. 133. **For Love of Ivy** (feature film, full length: songs only, 1968). Angelou wrote two songs for this film, which dealt with a floating gambling racketeer and his love for a housemaid. Prod. by Cinerama, 1968; dir. by Daniel Mann, with music by Quincy Jones. Starring Sidney Poitier and ABBEY LINCOLN. **Ajax** (adapt. from Sophocles's play, 2 acts, 1974). Written for and prod. by the Mark Taper Forum, Los Angeles, Feb. 5, 1974. **Assignment America** (six half-hr. TV programs, 1975). Interviews and profiles. Premiered Jan. 1975. **The Inheritors** (TV script, 1976). Afro-American TV special. Prod. 1976. **The Legacy** (TV script, 1976). Afro-American TV special.

ANTHONY, EARL (Leon), Black nationalist author, editor, playwright, theatrical director, and political leader. Educated at the Univ. of Southern California (A.B. in English, 1963). Author of *Picking Up the Gun* (1970), an inside report on the Black Panther Party, and *Time of the Furnaces* (1971), a case study of the black student revolt. Coeditor, with WOODIE KING, JR., of *Black Poets and Prophets* (1972), an anthology of writings on the Pan African Revolution. Member of the Black Panther Party of Southern California, rising to the position of Deputy Minister of Information before leaving because of ideological differences. Former director of the African People's Repertory Theatre in San Francisco, which in 1971 produced a collective theatrical work entitled *Babylon,* directed by Anthony.

REPRESENTATIVE PLAYS:

Charlie Still Can't Win No Wars on the Ground (1 act, 1971). A group of blacks of diverse socioeconomic and political backgrounds assemble to watch the first moon landing. Prod. Off-Off-Bway by the New Federal Theatre (NFT), at St. Augustine's Chapel, opening Jan. 8, 1971.

(Mis)Judgment (drama, 1 act, 1971). (Also cited as *The Misjudgment.*) After a black liberation group has "eliminated" a suspected informer, one of the group's most militant members is discovered to be the real informer. Prod. Off-Off-Bway by NFT, at St. Augustine's Chapel, opening Jan. 8, 1981.

The Black People's Party (drama, 2 acts, 1981). About the Black Panther Party, apparently based on the author's book *Picking Up the Gun* (1970). Prod. Off-Bway by NFT, opening Oct. 22, 1981, for 12 perfs.; dir. by Norman Riley. Prod. by the Theatre of Universal Images, Newark, NJ, Jan. 30–March 3, 1985; also dir. by Norman Riley.

OTHER PLAYS AND DRAMATIC WORKS:

A Long Way from Here (1 act, 1971). Prod. by the African People's Theatre, San Francisco, 1971; dir. by author. **Time** (drama, full length, 1970s). Concerns the experiences of violence and homosexuality encountered by a musician and his girlfriend while serving time in the same penitentiary for passing bad checks. **The Works of Franz Fanon** (adaptn., 1980s?). Unpub. script in the Hatch-Billops Collection.

ARANHA, RAY (1939–   ), Actor-playwright. Recipient of a Drama Desk Award for playwriting, 1974, for **My Sister, My Sister** (1973). Born in Miami, FL. Received the B.S. degree from Florida A. & M. Univ. Studied acting at the American Academy of Dramatic Arts. Has taught drama and conducted acting and writing workshops for numerous community and school groups. Theatrical appearances include *The Firebugs* (1970), produced by the McCarter Theatre, Princeton, NJ; *The Indians* (1970) and *The Tempest* (1970), both produced by the Missouri Repertory Theatre; *Ododo* (1970), produced by the Negro Ensemble Co. (NEC), New York; *Macbeth* (1977) and *Othello* (1978), both produced at the Champlain Shakespeare Festival, Univ. of Vermont; *The Shadow Box* (1978), produced by the Alliance Theatre in Atlanta; and *Benefit of a Doubt* (1979), produced by the Folger Theatre Group in Washington, DC. Recipient of a Rockefeller Playwright-in-Residence Grant, 1975. *Address:* GPO Box 1743, New York, NY 10001.

PLAYS AND DRAMATIC WORKS:

My Sister, My Sister (drama, full length, 1973). "About a young girl in the South of the 1950s, attempting to cope with her family, the world and her feelings."—*Black World,* April 1975. Earned for the author a Drama Desk Award, and for the leading actresses several acting awards cited below. First prod. by the Hartford Stage Co. (CT), opening Sept. 28, 1973, for 44 perfs. Prod. Off-Off-Bway in a tryout production at U.R.G.E.N.T. on 44th St., presumably in 1975. Prod. Off-Off-Bway by black producer Ashton Springer at the Little Theatre in Greenwich Village, New York City, April 30–Jan. 5, 1975, for 119 perfs.; dir. by Paul Weidner. With Seret Scott (who won a Drama Desk Award) as the young girl and Barbara Montgomery (who won both the AUDELCO and Obie awards) as the mother. Pub. by Samuel French, New York, 1973.

The Estate (historical drama, full length, 1976). Focuses on a confrontation between Benjamin Banneker, the black scientist who surveyed and designed Washington, DC, and Thomas Jefferson—also dealing with Jefferson's romantic involvement with his slave mistress. Prod. by the Hartford Stage Co., opening Jan. 23, 1976, for 44 perfs. Prod. Off-Bway by the Afro-American Total Theatre, Jan. 1978; dir. by Duane Jones.

Sons and Fathers of Sons (drama, full length [2 parts], 1983). Contrasts developments in the lives of three young men—a student, a sharecropper's son, and a college professor—during three successive decades, the 1940s, 50s, and 60s. The action centers "in the first two on the lynchings of similar youths in a small Mississippi town, and in the third on the effort of another youth to work out his relation to the past and future in the setting of a Black college in Tallahassee, Fla."—*New York Amsterdam News,* Feb. 12, 1983. Prod. by NEC at Theatre Four, New York, Jan. 28–Feb. 20, 1983, for 29 perfs.; dir. by Walter Dallas. With Olivia Virgil Harper, Sarallen, Ethel Ayler, Phylicia Ayers-Allen, Eugene Lee, Robert Gossett, Howard Baines, and Graham Brown.

OTHER PLAYS AND DRAMATIC WORKS:
The Clown's Corner Concert (play for children and adults, 1975). Prod. by the Hartford Stage Co. and by the Young People's Theatre of Center Stage, Baltimore, 1975–76. **I Am Black** (one-man show, 1975). Compiled, arranged, and performed by Aranha. Prod. by the Missouri Repertory Theatre, at the Univ. of Missouri, opening June 6, 1975, for 6 perfs. **Way Back When . . .** (bicentennial play for children, 1976). Stories and songs of Puritan New England. Prod. by the Hartford Stage Co. and the Young People's Theatre of Center Stage, 1976–77. **Akosu'a of the First and Final Day** (1977). Prod. by Stage West, Springfield, MA, opening March 13, 1977, for 2 perfs.; dir. by author. **New Year's** (1 act, 1979). One of a number of plays prod. under the title *Holidays* by the Actor's Theatre of Louisville (KY) at the Victor Jorey Theatre, opening Jan. 26, 1979. **Snow Pressings** (1979). Prod. by the National Playwrights Conf., at the Eugene O'Neill Theatre Center, Waterford, CT, July 21, 1979. **Remington** (1980). Prod. by the Actor's Theatre of Louisville, at the Victor Jorey Theatre, 1980, for 2 perfs.

ARKANSAW, TIM (Eddie Lewis Hudgons) (1925–   ), Songwriter, folk-singer, recording artist, ceramics artist, and playwright. Born in Anniston, AL, one of ten children. After the death of his parents, the family moved to live with an aunt in Atlanta's Summerhill Community, a ghetto rich in black folk history. Began writing songs at age five and helping the family survive the Depression by selling tiny birds (chickens, ducks, etc.) that he molded by hand out of mud and flour, or wax and tar, and painted with fingernail polish. Served a stint in the U.S. Navy after completing high school at night in Atlanta. Attended City Coll. of New York, receiving his A.B. in music, with a minor in business administration, 1951. Remained in New York City to become a professional songwriter and folksinger, playing in clubs around the city. Has performed throughout the United States, Canada, Europe, West Africa, and Australia, meeting with great success. Founder and pres., Atsumhill Enterprises, a music publishing, recording, public relations, and ceramics business, also known as Atsumhill-Birdworld Studios, located in Atlanta. Published and recorded two LP's of original songs on Atsumhill Record label, including his successful ballad "Hell Raisers of Summerhill," a true account of his experiences growing up in that community, which has sold 2 million copies. Now concentrates on his first love—making ceramic birds, which he sells through the better gift shops and galleries in the Atlanta area. Taught guitar and related music at the Atlanta Public

Schools, 1972. Currently works in public relations at Grady Memorial Hosp. Life member of NAACP; member of American Guild of Variety Artists (AGVA) and Atlanta Federation of Musicians; named Seaman of the Year, 1955, for composing two hit songs about sea life; also received a Silver Medal from the United Seaman's Service in New York; recently received an award for outstanding community service in Dekalb County, GA, by the DeKalb-Atlanta Voters Council. *Address*—Office: Atsumhill-Birdworld Studios, 1344 Hardee St., N.E., Atlanta, GA 30307.

DRAMATIC WORK:
The Successful Side of Summerhill (doc. play, 1972; also a doc. film, 1973). Written as a stage play while the author was teaching guitar and related music at E. P. Johnson Elementary School in 1972, under the Model Cities Extended Day Program. The school was located in Summerhill, where the author had grown up during the Depression. Having previously written a successful folksong called "Hell Raisers of Summerhill," which had shown the seamier side of Summerhill, he was encouraged to write something more positive about the community, showing its rich contributions to Atlanta, the South, and the nation. The resulting play sought to educate the area's disadvantaged youth about the many prominent persons, churches, and businesses that had flourished in Summerhill, to convince them that if earlier black citizens had succeeded there, they could do better in these days. Prod. at E. P. Johnson Elementary School, July 18, 1972, with the entire community working together with school personnel to get it staged, bringing about a form of unity that Summerhill had not known before. The Atlanta Board of Education officials were so impressed with the public response that another stage version was presented at the school board's prestigious Instructional Services Center "for all the big wheels to see." It was decided at this level to produce a film version for the mass media. The film premiered on April 23, 1973, on WPHA-TV, formerly WETV, Channel 30, Atlanta. It is still being shown on Southern Television Network Systems, especially during Black History Month.

ARRINGTON, JOHN, Playwright. Former lighting director for the DC Black Repertory Co., Washington, DC.

PLAY:
Strange Generation (drama, 3 acts, 1976). Depicts the aspirations of the young black generation of the 1950s who were determined to improve the racial climate of the South. Pub. by Vantage Press, New York, 1976.

ASHBY, DOROTHY. See ASHBY, JOHN (Tooley), and DOROTHY J. ASHBY.

ASHBY, JOHN (Tooley), and DOROTHY J. ASHBY (1932–   ), Playwriting couple. Former directors of the Ashby Players, Detroit, MI. JOHN ASHBY is a playwright, director, producer, arranger, actor, musician, and draftsman. Dorothy Ashby, his wife, is a singer, actress, composer-lyricist, and well-known jazz pianist, and harpist.

DRAMATIC WORKS:
The Choice and **The Duffers** (two musicals, full length, pre-1968). Books by John Ashby. Music and lyrics by Dorothy Ashby. The stories were mainly about ghetto life—hustlers, welfare agents, numbers racketeers, etc. They were presented at the Dexter Theatre, Detroit; dir. by John Ashby. **The Game** (musical satire, full length, 1968). The Ashbys' third musical. Book by John Ashby. Music and lyrics by Dorothy Ashby. "Revolves around a scheme by a Negro group to divert a City Hall fund that was to be used to avert future riots."—*Jet,* Oct. 3, 1968. (The title is based on the meaning implied by "con game.") Prod. by the Ashby Players, at the Dexter Theatre, Detroit, at the Detroit Lib., and in Toronto between March and Sept. 1968; dir. by John Ashby.

ASHLEY, RICHARD, Playwright. *Address:* 327 Central Park West, New York, NY 10025.

PLAY:
Nothing for Elizabeth (1967). A black man and his white wife are forced by a black playwright to come to grips with their racial identities.

AS-SALAAM, JAMAAL (1955?–   ), Poet, actor, photographer, playwright, and screenwriter. A native of Albany, NY. Now living in Denver, CO. Attended Empire State Coll. of the State Univ. of New York (SUNY), 1972–74, majoring in English literature, and SUNY/Purchase, NY, 1974–76, majoring in film history. Presently enrolled at the Univ. of Northern Colorado/Greeley, majoring in business administration. Has also attended numerous workshops and special classes, including Donald Todd's Voice and Diction Workshop, 1978–83. Married; the father of three children. Has performed as an actor in the Denver community, appearing in productions of the Bonfils Theatre, the Touchstone Theatre, the Children's Museum, Eden Theatrical Workshop, and the Donald Todd Theatre. Has given poetry readings throughout the Denver area. His collection of poetry, "Philopena: The Love Thing Shared" (1983), is as yet unpublished. Has freelanced as an editor, reporter, cable TV production asst., and photographer. Founder of Infinite Images Production Co., his own film and video firm. Employed by Burlington Northern Railroad. Also works as an intensive tutor in computer-aided instruction for the Denver school system. Member of AFTRA, the National Writers Club, the Society of Technical Writers, and the Win/Win Business Forum. *Address*—Home: 2837 Steele St., Denver, CO 80305. Office: Infinite Images Production Co., 2531 High St., Denver, CO 80205.

REPRESENTATIVE PLAYS AND DRAMATIC WORKS:
It's Real on the Corner, Also 30 Minutes Without a Commercial (ritual play, 1975). Conceived for a class at Empire State Coll., Albany, NY. First perfd. at the Milne School mini-theatre, Albany, June 12–13, 1975, with improvised music by Abdul Lateem, and orig. movement designed by Alex Thomas, Clive Thomas, Diahann Stevens, Angel Scott, and the author. Revised 1980.
Weapons of Survival (screenplay for a short video film [15 min.], 1977). A revolutionary black man converts a gang of youths using the tactics of street hustlers.

Some Kind of Night (screenplay for a short video film [20 min.], 1981). Based on a story pub. in *Black World* magazine. About a man on a blind date with a buddy who is involved with a hooker; the setting is a summer night in Los Angeles.

Harriet Tubman: Moses to Freedom (historical drama, 3 acts, 1982). About the Underground Railroad and the life of Harriet Tubman.

The Leak (short Betamax video film [30 min.], 1982). Script by As-Salaam in collaboration with Larry Copeland, who also wrote the story. About a group of hoods trying to discover who is snitching to the cops. Prod. and dir. by As-Salaam, and made in association with United Cable Television of Colorado, Inc., 1982.

OTHER PLAYS:
The Assassin (in progress, 1982). In collaboration with Larry Copeland. A man hires a professional assassin to kill his wife. **The Black Value System** (in progress, 1982). Adaptn. of AMIRI BARAKA's political proposition on black values. **The Final Act** (surrealistic tragic drama, 3 acts, in progress, 1983). About a dead man who relives his life. **Lightland Caravan** (adventure drama, 3 acts, in progress, 1983). Futuristic play about a mythical prince and princess who escape from evil sorcerers and search for the Flaming Rainbow.

ATKINS, RUSSELL (1926–   ), Poet, composer, editor, and playwright. Born in Cleveland, OH. Educated in the Cleveland public schools; at the Cleveland School (now Institute) of Art; on scholarship to the Cleveland Museum of Art, Karamu House, and the Cleveland Music School Settlement; and privately, under Milton Fox, Paul Travis, and J. Harold Brown. Founder and editor of *Free Lance,* a magazine of poetry and prose published semiannually in Cleveland from 1950 to 1980. Author of *A Psychovisual Perspective for Musical Composition* (published in two parts, 1956 and 1958), which describes a composing technique that he invented and introduced at the Darmstadt Festival of Avant-Garde Music held in Germany in 1956. Composer of works for violin, piano, cello, and orchestra, many of which have been performed by members of the Cleveland Symphony Orchestra and other musical groups. Has served as consultant for numerous writers' and poets' workshops and conferences in Ohio and elsewhere, and is in great demand as a lecturer and reader in schools and colleges. Former creative writing instructor at Karamu House, where his works have been performed by the Karamu Theatre; and former writer-in-residence for the One World Theatre Project, which was an annual fine arts festival in Cleveland during the 1970s. Received an honorary doctorate from Cleveland State Univ., 1976. Recipient of an Ohio Arts Council Individual Artists Fellowship of $5,000 in 1978 to support the writing of his three-act play **Children's Bones** (1979). *Address:* 6005 Grand Ave., Cleveland, OH 44104.

COLLECTIONS:
PHENOMENA. Wilberforce Univ. Press, Wilberforce, OH, 1961. Contains **The Drop of Blood** (1961) and **The Exoneration** (1961).

TWO BY ATKINS. Free Lance, Cleveland, 1963. Contains **The Corpse** (1954) and **The Abortionist** (1954).

HERETOFORE. Heritage Series 7. Paul Breman, London, 1968. Contains **The Seventh Circle** (1957).

PLAYS AND DRAMATIC WORKS:

The Corpse (poem in play form, to be set to music, 1 act, 1954). Utilizes a technique which the author calls the "music form idea," of which this work is the first example [see also **The Drop of Blood** (1961)]. A mentally unstable widow makes an annual visit to the tomb of her deceased husband to witness his corpse's progressive deterioration and loss of identity. Also developed into an opera, **The Widow** (1982). Pub. in *Western Review* (Univ. of Iowa), Winter 1954, and in the author's *TWO BY ATKINS*.

The Abortionist (poem in play form, to be set to music, 1 act, 1954). A physician gets revenge on one of his most despised colleagues when he performs a savage operation on his enemy's daughter. First pub. in *Free Lance*, 1954; republished, slightly revised, in the author's *TWO BY ATKINS*.

The Seventh Circle (poem in radio-play format, 1 act, 1957). Psychological play showing the dilemma of a man torn between involvement and noninvolvement. Written in 1957 for *Experiment Magazine*'s play issue, where it was first pub.; also pub. in the author's *HERETOFORE*.

The Nail (a play to be set to music, also called a libretto, 3 acts, 1957). Adapt. from a short story of the same title by Pedro Antonio de Alarcon, about a female fugitive who is hunted down by her lover. Written in 1957 at the suggestion of composer Hale Smith, but the planned opera was never composed. Pub. in *Free Lance, 1971.*

The Drop of Blood (poem in play form, 1 act, 1961). Further development of the "music form idea" as technique begun in **The Corpse**. Because of her mistrust of a young lover, an older woman drives herself into a mentally unstable condition. Pub. in the author's *PHENOMENA*.

The Exoneration (poetic drama, 1 act, 1961). A black suspect is falsely arrested and subjected to police brutality. Prod. at Karamu Theatre, 1971. Prod. at the Second One World Theatre Project, Cleveland, Summer 1973. Pub. in the author's *PHENOMENA*.

Brother Bad (screenplay, full length, 1974). Written while the author was with the Bertha Klausner Agency, New York, 1974. ("No sales, however, and I am no longer with the agency."—Author.)

Children's Bones (poetic drama, 3 acts, 1979). Uses the "music form idea" which the author began in **The Corpse** (1954) and developed in **The Drop of Blood** (1961). Written with the support of an Ohio Arts Council Individual Artists Fellowship of $5,000, awarded in 1978 for the use of the "music form idea" for a three-act play. A mentally unstable young man is visited by his cousin, a football star, whose confidence he destroys.

The Widow (opera, 1 act [of 3 acts], 1982). Words and piano score by Atkins. Based on the author's play **The Corpse** (1954), which concerns a mentally unstable widow who makes an annual pilgrimage to the tomb of her dead husband to witness the progressive deterioration and loss of identity of his corpse.

ATTAWAY, WILLIAM (1912–   ), Novelist, television scriptwriter, screenwriter, composer, former stage actor. Born in Greenville, MS, the son of a physician and the brother of Broadway actress Ruth Attaway. Grew up in Chicago, where he was educated in the public schools and at the Univ. of Illinois. Before completing his B.A., he left college for two years, pursuing the life of a vagabond and working as a seaman, salesman, and labor organizer. Influenced by his sister, he became interested in writing and the theatre, and wrote plays and short stories while in high school and at the university. During the 1930s he acted in the road company of *You Can't Take It with You,* in which his sister had appeared on Broadway in the original production. Author of two novels, both strongly influenced by John Steinbeck: *Let Me Breathe Thunder* (1939), a record of his vagabond days, and *Blood on the Forge* (1931), which deals with the adjustment problems of southern black sharecroppers to the conditions of factory life in the North during World War I. Arranger of songs for Harry Belafonte and a contributing editor of *The Calypso Song Book* (1957).

REPRESENTATIVE DRAMATIC WORK:
A Time for Laughter (TV script, full length, 1967). Based on a concept by *Harry Belafonte, who first prod. the show. Described by *Ebony* (May 1967) as "a show based on the humor of the Negro," which featured "most of the top Negro comedians of the century in sketches that encapsulated Negro comedy from minstrelsy to the ribald, often irreverent wit of the ghetto and to the rich humor that has grown out of the civil rights revolution." Telecast on ABC-TV, Spring 1967.

OTHER DRAMATIC WORKS:
Although only one of Attaway's dramatic works has been identified with certainty, according to *The Negro Vanguard* (Bardolph, 1959, p. 279), "Attaway, after earlier dependence upon menial jobs, earned . . . substantial fees by writing and consulting for the film industries." He is also credited in a number of sources, including *Cavalcade* (Davis & Redding, 1971, p. 378), with having written "the script for the screen version of Irving Wallace's *The Man,*" a novel about a black senator who becomes president of the United States after the incumbent president is killed in a freak accident. However, it is not known whether or not Attaway's script was actually used in connection with the 1972 Paramount film of the same title starring James Earl Jones, the screenplay of which is attributed to Rod Serling.

AURANSIA. See WILLIAMS, SANDA BETH.

AURELIUS, NEVILLE, International actor-playwright. Has lived in London, Dublin, Paris, and the United States. Educated at Clark Coll. (London). Served five years with the RAF, 1960–65. Received theatrical experience with the London Negro Theatre Workshop. Cofounded the Action Theatre in Paris, 1968. Has performed in London in *Boys in the Band, The Black Macbeth,* and *Benito Cereno,* and in Dublin in *Slow Dance on the Killing Ground.* Films abroad include *Pope Joan* and *The National Health.* In the United States, he has performed with the Actors Theatre of Louisville, KY; the Negro Ensemble Co. (NEC) and the Hudson Guild Theatre in New York City; and the American Shakespeare Theatre in Stratford, CT. In 1984–85 he was playing the recurring role of Hank Waters in the NBC daytime drama "Search for Tomorrow." Member of the Frank Silvera Writers' Workshop (FSWW) in New York City *Address:* 32 W. 82nd St., Apt. 2D, New York, NY 10024.

PLAYS:
Reflection of the Man // Orig. title: **Reflections, or the Indictment** (drama, 1974). Focuses on the relationship between a young black man and a middle-aged white man, both strangers, who seek refuge in a London laundromat on a winter night. Public reading by FSWW, Nov. 1974. Prod. by the National Art Theatre, New York, Nov. 1, 1974; dir. by Robert Stocking. Unpub. script and tape recording in FSWW Archives/Schomburg Collection.

A Long Night's Dying (political drama, c. 1974). Focuses on the aftermath of civil war in a mythical African country. Public reading by FSWW, around 1974. Unpub. script and tape recording in FSWW Archives/Schomburg Collection.

In Memoriam (drama, 1 act, c. 1976). Deals with the crisis in the life of a popular black English TV star whose interracial marriage is on the decline at the same time that his career is in danger of being destroyed by an old enemy. Public reading by FSWW, around 1976. Unpub. script and tape recording in FSWW Archives/Schomburg Collection.

Yesterday Once More (drama, c. 1976). Coauthor, with Alice Spivak. A young drifter becomes involved with two older women (one black, one white) in a small southern town and has a detrimental effect upon their lives. Public reading by FSWW, mid-1970s. Unpub. script and tape recording in FSWW Archives/Schomburg Collection.

It Always Rains on Sundays (1984). According to the author, it was being prepared for a public reading by FSWW in 1984.

AYERS, VIVIAN, Artist, poet and playwright. Born in Chester, SC. Mother of Debbie Allen and Phylicia Ayers–Allen Rashad. Author of two volumes of poetry, *Spice of Dawns* (1953) and *Hawk* (1957). Her work has been anthologized in *Negro Poets USA* (Huges, 1964).

PLAY:
Bow Boly (musical tragicomedy, 1970s).

B

BACON, CARLTON, Musician, composer, and actor. Former resident of Denver, CO. Currently resides in the Bronx, NY.

PLAY:

Barca! Men of Lightning (musical, full length, 1982). Book and lyrics by KEN GRIMES. Music by Bacon. Based on the story of Hannibal's historic attempt to conquer Rome. Hannibal was the black man who took the elephants over the Alps. For this production, the elephants were portrayed by dancers. Prod. by the Black Arts Co., at the Community House Theatre, Denver, July 29–Aug. 7, 1982; dir. by John McCallum.

BAHATI, AMIRH T., Poet, playwright. Born in Pittsburgh, PA. Currently resides in New York City. Educated at CCNY, where she majored in English and creative writing. An alumna of several writing workshops, including the Playwrights Workshop of the Negro Ensemble Co. (NEC), the Writers Unit of the Public Theatre, and the Frank Silvera Writers' Workshop (FSWW). She has given poetry readings at numerous locations in New York and on several radio stations.

PLAYS:

Castles in the Air (1 act, 1975). Staged reading by FSWW at the Teachers Inn, New York, Dec. 1975. Unpub. script and tape recording in the FSWW Archives/Schomburg Collection. **Attachments** (drama, full length, mid-1970s). Members of a black family, "out of sibling rivalry," fight constantly "to establish, maintain, or break attachments and connections to each other." —*The National Playwrights Directory* (Kaye, 1977), p. 11. Prod. by the Public Theatre, New York, as a workshop production, mid-1970s. **The Roomer** (1 act, mid-1970s). Prod. by the Public Theatre, as a workshop production, mid-1970s. **The Butterfly . . . The Bee** (1970s). **Victims** (1982). Subtitled "The Triangle." Described by Eddie O'Jay as "a real slice of life in New York City [in] 1982." —*New York Amsterdam News,* Dec. 11, 1982. Presented at the Vital Arts Theatre, New York, Dec. 1982; prod. and dir. by Nathan George.

BAILEY, HORACE (1925–   ), Ex-boxer, actor, playwright, director, singer, and postal employee. Founder-director of the Horace Bailey Players in the Bronx, NY. Born in La Grange, GA. Moved to New York, where he attended public school and high school. Learned to box at a Harlem church group, and won the Metro Boxing Championship. Served in the U.S. Army, where he won four boxing championships, learned to play the piano, and performed in USO shows. After being discharged, he turned to boxing professionally, fighting for eight years. Also played semiprofessional baseball in the Federation League of New York. Continued to develop his talents in music and theatre. Studied with the Joseph Da Narto School for Acting, the New York Playwriting School, and the Frank Silvera Writers' Workshop (FSWW). Has appeared in numerous commercials, soaps (such as "The Edge of Night"), and other television shows, including "The Doctors" and "N.Y.P.D." Has performed in more than 15 films, including *The Hostage, Cotton Comes to Harlem, Come Back Charleston Blue, The Godfather, Claudine, The French Connection, Raging Bull,* and *Nothing but a Man.* Has worked on and off for the U.S. Postal Service for 34 years, when he is not acting. *Address:* 2715 Third Ave., Bronx, NY 10451.

PLAYS AND DRAMATIC WORKS:

(All pre-1983, and apparently prod. by the Horace Bailey Players, Bronx, NY; dir. by author.) **Too Late** (drama and screenplay). Deals with a mother and her teenage son who live with her sister in the ghetto. The son and aunt are in conflict. **In and Out** (drama and screenplay). About a prize fighter turned singer. **Blood Count** (drama and screenplay). A black army veteran has a rare blood type and someone is in need of his blood. **Wade in the Water** (drama). A sister tries to keep her family together after the death of her mother and father.

BAILEY, SHERI, Author-playwright. Resides in Venice, CA. Educated at the Univ. of Pennsylvania (B.A. in English, with honors, 1979); currently pursuing M.F.A. studies in playwriting at the Univ. of California at Los Angeles (UCLA). Attended the Breadloaf Writers' Conf., 1980, and completed a five-week stay at the Dorland Mountain Colony artists retreat in 1984. Has worked with Aaron Spelling Productions, and as the executive story editor's assistant on *Hollywood Beat.* One of her plays was entered in the American College Theatre Festival (ACTF) by UCLA in 1982. Currently she runs a workshop at the Venice (CA) Community Theatre. She has been associated with Lee Strasberg Inst.'s Playwrights Wing, the American Black Book Writers Assn., and the Dramatists Guild (DG). In 1981 she received the Donald Davis Playwriting Award for **All Kinds of Blue** (1981). *Address:* 2128 Penmar Ave. #5, Venice, CA 90291.

PLAYS:

All Kinds of Blue (1981). Winner of the Donald Davis Award, 1981. Prod. as a special perf. for inmates of Terminal Island Prison, June 12, 1981. Prod. by ANTA West, at the Hearst Discovery Theatre, Los Angeles, March 1982. Presented as UCLA's official entry in the 1982–83 ACTF, Dec. 1982. **Southern Girls** (1982). Coauthor, with Dura Michl. Prod. at the Deja Vu Coffee House, Los Angeles, Fall 1981, where it enjoyed an extended run. **Dannie-n-Laurence** (1983). Prod. as a staged reading at the Company of Angels' first annual New Playwrights' Festival in Los Angeles, Nov. 1982. Prod. in an extended run by the Company of Angels, Los Angeles, June 1983. The author was completing a screen version in 1985. **Sad Song/Backdrop** (1984). Completed at the Dorland Mountain Colony artists' retreat, 1984.

BALDWIN, JAMES (Arthur) (1925–1987), Major American novelist and essayist; short-story writer and playwright. Born in New York City. Educated at P.S. 139 in Harlem and DeWitt Clinton H.S. in the Bronx. During the 1950s and 1960s, he was actively involved in the civil rights struggle as a literary spokesman and lecturer. Lived in Paris, 1948–56; and during the early 1970s lived for a while in Istanbul, where he was involved in writing, directing, and making films. Resided for many years in the South of France, where he died of cancer. Author of more than 15 books. Novels include *Go Tell It on the Mountain* (1953), *Giovanni's Room* (1956), *Another Country* (1962), *Tell Me How Long the Train's Been Gone* (1968), and *If Beale Street Could Talk* (1974). Other books include *Notes of a Native Son* (1955), *Nobody Knows My Name* (1961), *The Fire Next Time* (1963), *Nothing Personal* (with Richard Avedon, 1964), *Going to Meet the Man* (short stories, 1965), *A Rap on Race* (with Margaret Mead, 1971), *No Name in the Street* (1971), *A Dialogue: James Baldwin and Nikki Giovanni* (1973), *Little Man, Little Man* (children's book, 1975), and *The Devil Finds Work: An Essay* (1976). Member of Actors Studio, New York, the National Advisory Board of CORE (Congress of Racial Equality), the National Committee for a Sane Nuclear Policy, and the National Board of Arts and Letters. Recipient of Saxton Fellowship, 1956; Rosenwald Fellowship, 1956; Guggenheim Fellowship, 1954; National Inst. of Arts and Letters Grant, 1956; National Conf. of Christians and Jews Brotherhood Award, 1962; George Polk Award, 1963; Foreign Drama Critics Award, 1964; and D.Litt. from the Univ. of British Columbia at Vancouver, 1964. *Agent:* Edward J. Acton, Inc., 17 Grove St., New York, NY 10014.

REPRESENTATIVE PLAYS AND DRAMATIC WORKS:

The Amen Corner (drama, 3 acts, 1954). Partly autobiographical play, concerning the collapsing world of a strong woman preacher when the elders of the church begin to question her ability to lead them spiritually. First prod. at Howard Univ., Washington, DC, May 11–14, 1955; dir. by OWEN DODSON. Prod. and dir. by Frank Silvera at the Robertson Playhouse, Los Angeles, opening in March 1968, where it ran for about a year; then transferred to Bway (prod. by Mrs. Nat King Cole), opening at the Barrymore Theatre, April 15, 1964, for 84 perfs.; also dir. by Frank Silvera. Featuring BEAH RICHARDS, whose perf. won for her both the *Theatre World* Award and *Variety*'s annual New York Drama Critics' Poll. Prod. in a second professional version in 1965, starring Claudia McNeil, which toured many cities in Western Europe and the Near East, including Edinburgh, Tel Aviv, Vienna and London; dir. by Lloyd Richards. Also made into a musical, 1983 [see **Amen Corner** below]. Pub. by Dial Press, New York, 1965, and by Samuel French, New York; in *Black Theater* (Patterson, 1971); also in *Black Theater, U.S.A.* (Hatch & Shine, 1974).

Giovanni's Room (drama, 1957). Based on his novel by the same title. Concerns a young white American's discovery of his latent homosexuality while living in France. Staged by Actors Studio Workshop, New York, 1965. Pub. only as a novel by Dial Press, New York, 1965.

Blues for Mister Charlie (drama, 3 acts, 1964). Loosely based on the Emmett Till murder case in Mississippi, and dedicated "to the memory of the dead children of Birmingham." Concerns the reactions of both whites and blacks in a small southern community to the brutal slaying by a bigoted white storekeeper of a rebellious black youth on his return home from the North. Prod. on Bway by the Actors Studio, at the ANTA Theatre, April 23, 1964, for 148 perfs.; dir. by Burgess Meredith. Featuring AL FREEMAN, JR., Rip Torn, Percy Rodrigues, Wayne Grice, ROSETTA LeNOIRE, and Diana Sands. Also prod. in London, 1965. Pub. by Dial, New York, 1964; by Dell, New York, 1965; by Samuel French, New York, c. 1965; in *The Best American Plays, 6th Series, 1963–1967* (Gassner & Barnes, 1971); and in *Contemporary Black Drama* (Oliver & Sills, 1971).

Amen Corner (gospel musical, full length, 1983). Based on Baldwin's play **The Amen Corner** (1954). Book by Phil Rose and Peter Udell, who also wrote the lyrics and prod. the show. Music by Garry Sherman. About a woman preacher "whose life is turned upside down by the reappearance of her husband, a jazz musician." —*New York Amsterdam News,* Nov. 4, 1983, p. 23. Prod. on Bway at the Nederlander Theatre, Nov. 10–Dec. 4, 1983, for 29 perfs.; dir. by Philip Rose. Featuring Rhetta Hughes as the lady preacher and Ruth Brown as her mother.

OTHER PLAYS AND DRAMATIC WORKS:
One Day When I Was Lost (screenplay, full length, 1972). Subtitled "A Scenario Based on Alex Haley's *The Autobiography of Malcolm X.*" Pub. by Dial Press, New York, and Michael Joseph, London, 1972. **The Inheritors** (film: screenplay, 1971). Prod. 1973, presumably in Istanbul; dir. by author. **A Deed from the King of Spain** (1974). Prod. Off-Bway by the American Center for Stanislavski Theatre Art, opening Jan. 24, 1974; dir. by author.

BANKS, BOBBY, Composer-musician. Associated with the Afro-American Folkloric Troupe in New York City.

DRAMATIC WORK:
High John De Conquer (musical, full length, 1969). Script by MARC PRIMUS, who also directed. Music written and conducted by Banks. Based on the folk legend of High John the Conqueror. Perfd. by the Afro-American Folkloric Troupe, at City Center, New York, opening April 23, 1969.

BARAKA, AMIRI (LeRoi Jones; also known as Imamu Amiri Baraka) (1934–   ), Prolific poet, playwright, author, and educator. Cultural and spiritual leader of the revolutionary Black Arts and Black Theatre movements of the 1960s. Born in Newark, NJ. Educated at Rutgers Univ., 1951–52; Howard Univ. (B.A. in English, 1954); Columbia Univ. (M.A. in philosophy); the New School for Social Research (M.A. in German literature). Married to Amina Baraka, the former Sylvia Robinson; father of eight children, five by his present wife. Founder and director of the short-lived Black Arts Repertory Theatre and

School in Harlem, 1964–65, funded by New York's HARYOU-ACT. Founder and director of Spirit House, a Newark community arts center and the home of Baraka's Spirit House Movers, a repertory theatre group which later changed its name to the African Revolutionary Movers. Organizer of the Malcolm X Writers' Workshop, a Newark-based group. Has taught poetry at the New School, 1962–64 and Summer 1977–79; drama at Columbia, 1965, and a special series of lectures on American poetry, Spring 1980; literature at the Univ. of Buffalo, 1964; and was visiting prof. at San Francisco State Univ., 1977. Has also taught at Yale, 1977–78, and George Washington Univ., 1978–79. Most recently, asst. prof. of African Studies at SUNY/Stony Brook, and teacher of a special writing course at the Coll. of New Rochelle, South Bronx campus. Founder of Totem Press, 1958, which first published works by Allen Ginsberg, Frank O'Hara, and others. Editor of *Yugen* magazine, an early publisher of new American writing in the late 1950s. Coeditor of *The Floating Bear,* 1961–62, a literary newsletter. Former editor of *Cricket,* a magazine devoted to Afro-American music. Director of publications of Jihad Press (now People's War Publications) in Newark. Has written and edited more than two dozen books, not including plays. Volumes of poetry include *The Dead Lecturer* (1964), *Preface to a Twenty Volume Suicide Note* (1967), *Black Magic: Sabotage: Target Study: Black Art: Collected Poetry, 1961–67* (which includes four previously published books, 1969), *In Our Terribleness: Pictures of the Hip World* (with Billy Abernathy, 1970), *Spirit Reach* (1972), *African Revolution: A Poem* (1973), *Reggae or Not* (1981), and *In the Tradition* (1982). His two volumes of fiction are *The System of Dante's Hell* (a novel, 1965) and *Tales* (short stories, 1967). Nonfiction includes *Blues People: Negro Music in White America* (1967), *A Black Value System* (1970), *Raise Race Rays Raze: Essays Since 1965* (1971), *Selected Prose and Plays* (1979), and *Daggers & Javelins, Essays 1974–79* (1983). Editor of *Four Young Lady Poets* (1962), *The Moderns: An Anthology of New Writing in America* (1963), *Black Fire: An Anthology of Afro-American Writing* (with LARRY NEAL, 1968), *African Congress: A Documentary of the First Modern Pan-African Congress* (1972), *The Floating Bear: A Newsletter Numbers 1–37, 1961–69: A Completely Annotated Facsimile Edition* (with Diana di Prima, 1973), *Confirmation: An Anthology of African American Women* (with Amina Baraka, 1972). Organizational involvements include United Brothers, Newark, 1967–69; one of the founders and chairman, Congress of African People, 1970–75; chairman, Committee for United Newark, 1968–75; one of the chief organizers and co-governor, National Black Political Convention, held at Gary, IN, 1972. Currently active in the National Black United Front, the Black Writers' Union, the League of Revolutionary Struggle, and the Newark Writers Collective. Recipient of an Obie Award for **Dutchman** as the Best American Off-Broadway Play of 1964. Other honors and awards include Whitney Fellowship, 1964; Guggenheim Fellowship, 1965; Doctor of Humane Letters, Malcolm X Coll., Chicago, 1972; Rockefeller Foundation Award (drama), 1981; New Jersey State Council of Arts poetry grant, 1982; and a National Endowment for the Arts poetry grant, 1981.

Address: 708 S. 10th St., Newark, NJ 07101. *Agent:* Joan Brandt, Sterling Lord Agency, 660 Madison Ave., New York, NY 10021.

COLLECTIONS:

DUTCHMAN AND THE SLAVE. (As LeRoi Jones.) William Morrow/Apollo, New York, 1964; Faber & Faber, London, 1965. Contains **Dutchman** (1964) and **The Slave** (1964).

THE BAPTISM AND THE TOILET. (As LeRoi Jones.) Grove Press/Evergreen, New York, 1967. Contains **The Baptism** (1964) and **The Toilet** (1964).

BLACK FIRE: An Anthology of Afro-American Writings. Edited (as LeRoi Jones) with Larry Neal. William Morrow, New York, 1968. Contains **Madheart** (1967).

FOUR BLACK REVOLUTIONARY PLAYS. (As LeRoi Jones.) Bobbs-Merrill, Indianapolis, and Calder & Boyers, London, 1969. Contains **Experimental Death Unit #1** (1965), **A Black Mass** (1965), **Great Goodness of Life (A Coon Show)** (1967), and **Madheart** (1967).

A BLACK QUARTET: Four New Black Plays. Written (as Amiri Baraka) with BEN CALDWELL, RON MILNER, and ED BULLINS. Signet Books/New American Lib., New York, 1970. Contains **Great Goodness of Life (A Coon Show)** (1967).

THE MOTION OF HISTORY & OTHER PLAYS. (As Amiri Baraka.) William Morrow, New York, 1978. Contains **The Motion of History** (1975), **Slave Ship** (1967), and **S-1** (1976).

SELECTED PROSE AND PLAYS. (As Amiri Baraka/LeRoi Jones.) William Morrow, New York, 1979. Contents not analyzed.

REPRESENTATIVE PLAYS AND DRAMATIC WORKS:

The Eighth Ditch // Orig. title: **Dante** (symbolic drama, 1 act, 1961). Drama of black awareness, set in a boyscout camp during the late 1940s, in which a middle-class black youth is raped by an impoverished young black man from the "street." First prod. under its orig. title at the Off-Bowery Theatre, New York, opening Oct. 29, 1961, for 16 perfs. Prod. at the New Bowery Theatre, New York, early March 1964, but was closed by the authorities after a few days. First pub. in *The Floating Bear* (a newsletter edited by Baraka and Diana di Prima), June 1961, pp. 1–8. Pub. as a chapter in the author's novel, *The System of Dante's Hell* (1965).

Dutchman (absurdist drama, 1 act, 1964; also a full length film: screenplay, 1967). Modern allegory, with symbolic relationships to both the Garden of Eden myth and the legend of the Flying Dutchman. A young Ivy League black man is enticed, provoked to anger, and eventually murdered by a sexy white blonde aboard a subway "in the flying underbelly of the city." Winner of an Obie Award as the Best American Off-Broadway play of 1964. First prod. by Theatre 1964 Playwrights Unit, at the Village South Theatre, opening Jan. 12, 1964, for 2 perfs. Moved Off-Bway to the Cherry Lane Theatre, March 24, 1964–Feb. 6, 1965, for 232 perfs.; dir. by Edward Parone. With Robert Hooks and Jennifer West. Also presented in Berlin, Paris, and Spoleto, Italy. Prod. as a film by Gene Persson Enterprises, Ltd.; released by the Walter Reade Org., 1967. With AL FREEMAN, JR., and Shirley Knight. Pub. by Samuel French, New York; in the author's collection *DUTCHMAN AND THE SLAVE;* in *Drama* (Parone, 1965), with the text of the Off-Bway version; in *The American Theatre Today* (Downer, 1967); in *The New Writing in the USA* (Creeley, 1967); in *Icarus* (Bens & Baugh, 1970); in *Keys to Understanding* (Reinert, 1970); in *A Treasury of the Theatre,* vol. 2, 4th ed. (Gassner & Dukore, 1970); in *Contemporary Black Drama* (Oliver & Sills, 1971); in *Black Theatre* (Patterson, 1971); in *Types* *of Drama* (Barnet, Berman, & Burto, 1972); in *Introduction to Drama* (Dolan & Dolan, 1974); in *The Literature of America* (Dolan & Dolan, c. 1975).

The Baptism (comic fantasy, 1 act, 1964). Satire of religious and sexual hypocrisy, set in a Baptist church, in which a black preacher and a homosexual devil vie for the soul of a young black savior figure. First prod. at the Writers' Stage, New York, opening May 1, 1964, for 3 perfs., before being closed under duress. Presented in other Off-Bway theatres during the spring of 1964, on a once-a-week basis, while an unsuccessful attempt was made to raise funds for a regular prodn. Prod. by the Afro-American Studio for Acting and Speech, New York, 1971. Prod. in London, 1970–71, for 12 perfs. Prod. at the Writers' Workshop in New York's East Village, at a festival of black plays, Oct. 7, 1972. Pub. in the author's *THE BAPTISM AND THE TOILET*.

The Slave (revolutionary ritual drama, prologue and 2 short acts, 1964; also a film: screenplay, 1971). Subtitled "A Fable." During a black uprising, a black militant, formerly married to a white woman, attempts to exorcise all that is white in his past by murdering his ex-wife's present white husband, leaving her and their mulatto children to die in the wreckage of an explosion that destroys their home. First prod. Off-Bway at St. Marks Playhouse, Dec. 16, 1964–April 25, 1965, for 151 perfs.; dir. by Leo Garen. With Al Freeman, Jr., Nan Martin, and Jerome Raphel. Prod. at the International Festival of Negro Arts at Dakar, Senegal, 1966, where it won second prize. Prod. at Wellesley Coll. (MA), June 1968. Prod. Off-Bway by the Players Workshop, 1961; dir. by Clay Stevenson. Prod. by the American Center for Stanislavski Theatre Art, New York, 1972/73. Prod. as a film, under its subtitle **A Fable,** by MFR Productions, 1971. Pub. in the author's *DUTCHMAN AND THE SLAVE;* in *Three Plays* (Bigsby, 1964); in *Drama and Revolution* (Dukore, 1971); in *Ritual, Realism, and Revolt* (Taylor & Thompson, 1972); in *Black Theater, U.S.A.* (Hatch & Shine, 1974); in *Seventeen Plays* (Dukore, 1976).

The Toilet (revolutionary drama, 1 act, 1964). Violent allegory of black-white relations in America, in which a white homosexual is beaten by a gang of black youths in a school restroom because he sent a love letter to their leader. A Burns Mantle Theatre Yearbook "Best Play" of 1964–65. Prod. Off-Bway at St. Marks Playhouse, Dec. 16, 1964–April 25, 1965, for 151 perfs. Pub. in the author's *THE BAPTISM AND THE TOILET;* abridged in *The Best Plays of 1964–1965* (Guernsey, 1965); in *The Best American Plays, 6th Series, 1963–67* (Gassner & Barnes, 1971); in *Black Drama in America* (Turner, 1971); in *Masterpieces of the Drama* (Allison et, al., 1974); in *Grove Press Modern Drama* (Lahr, 1975).

A Recent Killing (drama, 3 acts, 1964). Concerns a poet-turned-militant, based on the author's experiences in the air force. Prod. by the New Federal Theatre (NFT), New York, opening Jan. 26, 1973. Unpub. script in the Hatch-Billops Collection.

J-E-L-L-O (absurdist comedy, 1 act, 1965). Satire of the old Jack Benny radio show (sponsored by Jello Gelatin) in which Ratfester (Rochester) is a black militant, only pretending to be an Uncle Tom, who robs his master Jack Penny. Prod. by the author's Black Arts Repertory Theatre in Harlem, 1965. Pub. by Jihad Press, Newark, and by Third World Press, Chicago, 1970.

A Black Mass (1 act, 1965). Dramatization of a Muslim allegory. A black magician creates a white beast (the white man) who spreads evil and destruction throughout the earth, also destroying the creator. First prod. by the author's Black Arts Repertory Theatre, at Proctor's Theatre, Newark, May 1966. Prod. at the East Wind in Harlem, opening Oct. 18, 1968. Prod. by Blackarts Midwest, Minneapolis, 1969. Prod. by the Berkeley

Black Cultural Center, at the Univ. of California/Berkeley, 1971, with electronic music composed by *Olly Wilson. Prod. in repertory by the Afro-American Studio in Harlem, 1972. Recording issued by Jihad Productions, Newark, with a "cast of seven plus a narrator and music by the Sun Ray Myth-Science Archestra [sic]. Mono only."—Catalog of the Drama Book Shop, New York. Pub. in *Liberator*, June 1966, pp. 14–17; also in the author's *FOUR BLACK REVOLUTIONARY PLAYS*.

The Death of Malcolm X (scenario, 1 act, 1965). Described by the editor of the pub. script as "The White conspiracy to murder Malcolm." Prod. by Spirit House, Newark, 1965. Pub. in *New Plays from the Black Theatre* (Bullins, 1969).

Experimental Death Unit #1 (revolutionary drama, 1 short act, 1965). Army unit of black militants murders two white homosexuals and a black prostitute who has befriended them. First prod. Off-Bway by the author's Black Arts Repertory Theatre, at St. Marks Playhouse, New York, opening March 1, 1965. Prod. by the Afro-American Studio in Harlem, opening Oct. 1, 1972, in repertory. Pub. in *East Side Review*, Jan.-Feb. 1966. Also in author's *FOUR BLACK REVOLUTIONARY PLAYS*.

Slave Ship ("Historical Pageant" [subtitle], full length [1 long act], 1967). Ritualistic drama, set in the hold of a slave ship, designed to make black audiences more sensitive to and aware of the horrible conditions under which their ancestors were transported to America. First prod. by the Spirit House Movers, Newark, March 1967; dir. by author. Prod. by the Chelsea Theatre Center, at the Brooklyn Academy of Music, Nov. 19, 1969–Jan. 3, 1970, for 53 perfs.; reopened at Theatre-in-the-Church at Washington Square (Washington Square Methodist Church), Jan. 13–20, 1970, for 4 perfs.; dir. by GILBERT MOSES, who also wrote the music with ARCHIE SHEPP. Prod. by the Free Southern Theatre, at The East in Brooklyn, opening March 29, 1974, in repertory, for 3 perfs. each weekend; dir. by JUSEF IMAN. Pub. in *Negro Digest*, April 1967; by Jihad Press, Newark, 1969; in *The Off-Broadway Book* (Poland & Mailman, 1972); in *The Great American Life Show* (Lahr and Price, 1974); in the author's *THE MOTION OF HISTORY AND OTHER PLAYS*.

Black Spring (doc. film, 1967). Made by Baraka and the Black Arts Alliance in San Francisco. "A documentary of the Black Arts Alliance travels on the West Coast, Spring 1967. Features: Stokely Carmichael, H. Rapp Brown, Hewey P. Newton, LeRoi Jones, Floyd McKissick."—*Negro Digest*, March 1970. Prod. Spring 1967. Was available on a rental-fee basis from Jihad Productions, Newark.

Home on the Range (absurdist comedy, 1 act, 1967). Designed by the author as "a play to be performed with the music of Albert Ayler improvised in the background." Symbolic of the black revolution, a black militant easily invades and takes over the home of an idiotic white family, while its members chatter in a nonsense language, eat popcorn and watch TV. Read publicly as part of the Black Communications Project, San Francisco, Spring 1967. First prod. at Spirit House, Spring 1968; then taken on tour to Boston and New York City, where it opened at the Fillmore East, May 20, 1968. Pub. in *The Drama Review*, Summer 1968, pp. 10–11.

Madheart ("Morality Drama" [subtitle], 1 act, 1967). Ritual drama, symbolizing the abasement and destruction of the "white devil," which causes black women to imitate the clothes, makeup, and hair styles of white women. First prod. by the Black Arts Alliance in San Francisco, 1967. Prod. by the Spirit House Movers, 1970. Prod. by the Afro-American Studio, opening June 11, 1971, in repertory. Pub. in the author's *BLACK FIRE* and in his *FOUR BLACK REVOLUTIONARY PLAYS;* also in *Nommo* (Robinson, 1972).

Great Goodness of Life (A Coon Show) (revolutionary play, 1 act, 1967). The trial and purgation of the soul of a middle-class black assimilationist, reminiscent of Kafka's *The Trial*. First Prod. at Spirit House, 1967. Prod. at the East Wind, opening Oct. 18, 1968. Prod. Off-Bway at Tambellini's Gate Theatre, July 30–Nov. 2, 1969, for 111 perfs., on a program of four one-act plays, under the prodn. title *A Black Quartet;* dir. by Irving Vincent. Pub. in *Best Short Plays of the World Theatre 1958–1967* (Richards, 1968); in the author's *FOUR BLACK REVOLUTIONARY PLAYS* and in his *A BLACK QUARTET;* in *Kuntu Drama* (Harrison, 1974); in *The Disinherited* (Ravitz, 1974).

Arm Yrself or Harm Yrself (revolutionary fable, 1 act, 1967). Subtitled ''A Message of Self-Defense to Black Men!'' Agitprop play which bears the message that unless black men arm themselves and defend themselves and their families against police brutality, they will be destroyed. Prod. at Spirit House, 1967. Pub. by Jihad Press, Newark, 1967.

Junkies Are Full of (Shhh . . .) (antidrug play, 1 act, 1968). (The obscenity represented by ''Shhh'' is used both scatalogically and as a street term for heroin.) White Newark, NJ, drug pushers are murdered and their black flunky given a drug overdose as a warning by black nationalists to the rest of the community. First prod. at Spirit House, 1968. Prod. by the Afro-American Studio, opening Oct. 1, 1972, in repertory. Pub. in *Black Drama Anthology* (King & Milner, 1972).

The Sidney Poet Heroical // Complete title: **The Sidney Poet Heroical or If in Danger of Suit, the Kid Poet Heroical** // Former title: **The Kid Poeta Tragical** (satirical comedy, 1 act, 1970/75). On the black ''success syndrome,'' with the well-known black film star as the apparent target of attack. Prod. Off-Off-Bway by NFT, at the Henry St. Playhouse, opening May 1975. Pub. by Ishmael Reed Books, New York, 1979, and by Nkiru International Book Enterprises, 1980.

The Motion of History (revolutionary play, 4 acts, 1975). Described by the author as a vehicle for the following message:

The only solution to our problems, i.e., the majority of us in this society, is revolution! And that revolution, socialist revolution, is inevitable. *The Motion of History* brings it back through the years, focusing principally on the conscious separation created between black and white workers who are being exploited by the same enemy. The play sets itself the task of exposing this treachery and sham, but also of telling of this nation's history through its recurrent rebellions. [Intro. to pub. script.]

Prod. by the New York Theatre Ensemble, May 27, 1977; dir. by author. Pub. in the author's *THE MOTION OF HISTORY & OTHER PLAYS*.

S-1 (''A Play with Music in 26 Scenes'' [subtitle], 1976). An argument against Senate Bill S-1, also known as the Criminal Justice Codification, Revision and Reform Act, which Baraka denounces as ''a bold attempt to legalize much of the repression that had to be done semi-cover before by FBI, CIA and local police.''—Pub. script. Prod. by the Congress of African People, April 1976, and presented at the Washington Square Methodist Church, New York, July 23, 1976, and at the Afro-American Studio, Aug. 1976; dir. by author. Pub. in the author's *THE MOTION OF HISTORY & OTHER PLAYS*.

OTHER PLAYS AND DRAMATIC WORKS:

A Good Girl Is Hard to Find (1958). His first play. Prod. at Sterlington House, Montclair, NJ, Aug. 28, 1958. **Revolt of the Moonflowers** (1 act, 1969). Lost in ms.

Black Power Chant (very short ritual, 1968). (Also cited as *B.P. Chant.*) Designed to create black awareness of the need for greater togetherness, militancy, and knowledge of self-defense, if the race is to avoid extermination by whites. Prod. at Spirit House, 1968. Pub. in *Black Theatre* #4, 1969, p. 35. **Chant** (short ritual, 1968). In praise of blackness and the building of a black nation. Prod. at Spirit House, 1968. **Insurrection** // Also called **Resurrection in Life** (pantomime, 1 act, 1968). Dramatizes how knowledge, art, and religion were taken from black people by the white man and used to overpower and enslave them, until a strong black liberator comes to free them. Prod. as **Insurrection** by Spirit House, 1968. **Board of Education** (children's play, 1968). Perfd. by children of the African Free School, at Spirit House, 1968. **The Coronation of the Black Queen** (scenario, 1970). Ceremony for the crowning of a black campus or beauty queen, modeled after African rituals. Pub. in *Black Scholar,* June 1970, pp. 46–48. **Bloodrites** (ritual drama, 1 act, 1971). According to playwright ERROL HILL, "Whites are fun-toting devils that masquerade as artists, musicians and hipsters to seduce Blacks struggling toward spiritual reconstruction."—*Contemporary Dramatists* (Vinson, 1973). Pub. in *Black Drama Anthology* (King & Milner, 1972). **Black Dada Nihilism** (1 act, 1971). Prod. Off-Bway by the Afro-American Studio, opening June 11, 1971. **Ba-Ra-Ka** (poetic ritual, 1 act, 1972). Concerns the origin of Baraka and the black race. Pub. in *Spontaneous Combustion* (Owens, 1972). **Columbia, Gem of the Ocean** (theatrical collage, 1972). Scenes from the black experience and slide projections to unite black people and liberate their minds from the evils of Western civilization. Prod. by the Spirit House Movers at Howard Univ., Washington, DC, 1972. **America More or Less** (musical, 1976). Written with Frank Chin and Leslie Siko. Conception, continuity, and lyrics by Arnold Weinstein. Music by Tony Greco. Prod. by the American Conservatory Theatre, at the Marine's Memorial Theatre, San Francisco, opening April 21, 1976, for 20 perfs. **Money** // Orig. title (and genre): **Jazz Opera** (libretto, 1979). Score by Swiss composer George Gruntz. Commissioned in 1979 by the Paris Opera. Prod. as a workshop production by La Mama E.T.C., Jan. 1982, and presented at the Kool Jazz Festival, New York, July 3–5, 1982. **What Was the Relationship of the Lone Ranger to the Means of Production** (1979). Prod. at Ladies Fort, New York, May 1979. Pub. by the Anti-Imperialist Cultural Union, 1978. **Boy and Tarzan Appear in a Clearing** (1980). Prod. by NFT, at the Henry St. Playhouse, New York, opening Oct. 9, 1981, for 12 perfs.; dir. by George Ferenez. **Dim/Crackr Party Convention** (1980). Prod. at Columbia Univ., New York, July 1980. **Song** (1 act, 1982). Subtitled "A One Act Play about the Relationship of Art to Real Life." Public reading at the Richard Allen Center, New York, 1982. Prod. in Jamaica, NY, Oct. 14–16, 1983, during Black Theatre Weekend, under the auspices of the New York State Council on the Arts.

BARBOUR, FLOYD, Playwright, author, teacher, and editor. Best known as the editor of two anthologies: *The Black Power Revolt* (1967) and *The Black Seventies* (1970). Born in Washington, DC, where he attended Dunbar H.S. Studied at Bowdoin Coll., Brunswick, ME; then traveled and studied further in Europe. Has taught English at Howard Univ. under a teaching fellowship, and Afro-American literature and culture at Boston Univ. and MIT. His plays have been performed in Washington, Boston, and New Haven.

PLAYS:
The Bird Cage (drama, 1 act, 1969). Concerns the dreams and frustrations of a young black man living in a small southern town, where he feels trapped and unfulfilled. Prod.

at Bowdoin Coll.; the Inst. for Advanced Studies in the Theatre Arts; and on an evening of one-act plays at Howard Univ., around 1969; dir. by OWEN DODSON. Excerpt (1 scene) pub. in *Black Scenes* (Childress, 1971). **Sweet Jesus** (drama, 1 act?, pre-1970). Apparently prod. during the late 1960s. Translated into Dutch by Rosey Pool. **Anthony and Cleopatra** (adaptn.?, 1971) and **Day Work** (drama, 1 act, 1971). Both prod. by the MIT Community Players, Cambridge, MA, opening Nov. 9, 1971, on double bill.

BARCLAY, PARRIS, Playwright. *Address:* 820 Tenth Ave., New York, NY 10019.

PLAY:
Almos' a Man (musical drama, full length, 1985). Based on a short story by *Richard Wright. A young black farmhand's dreams of becoming a man turn to tragedy. Prod. by the Soho Repertory Theatre, New York, April 12–May 5, 1985; dir. by Tazewell Thompson.

BARNES, AUBREY, Playwright. Based in New York City, where he was a participant in the New York Black Writers Conf. in 1971.

PLAY:
The Superheroes (comedy-drama, 2 acts, 1974). The superheroes try to resolve the weakening of their powers and find a way to defeat the forces of "honkeyism." Sched. for publication by Amuru Press, New York, 1974, but apparently never pub.

BARNETT, MARGO (Margaret) (1931–1982), Actress and compiler of one-woman shows. Formerly associated with the Back Alley Theatre, Washington, DC. Died of cancer.

DRAMATIC WORK:
Black Is a Beautiful Woman (one-woman show, full length, 1973). Compiled by Barnett and DOUGLAS JOHNSON. A perfd. reading of the works of Mari Evans, Nikki Giovanni, LANGSTON HUGHES, Margaret Walker, and other black writers. Perfd. by author at the Back Alley Theatre, opening Jan. 18, 1973. Also telecast on NET, 1973.

BARNWELL, NICK, Playwright. An alumnus of the Frank Silvera Writers' Workshop (FSWW) in New York City. *Address:* 355 W. 85th St., New York, NY 10024.

PLAY: Only in the Movies (pre-1985). Unpub. script in the FSWW Archives/ Schomburg Collection.

BARRETT, LINDSAY (Euseoghene Lindsay Barrett), Author, journalist, lecturer, playwright. Born in Jamaica, West Indies. His poetry, short stories, and nonfiction have been published in *Negro Digest/Black World, Black Lines, Black Fire,* and *Black Arts.* Winner of the Fifth Conrad Kent Rivers Memorial Award, 1971, sponsored by *Black World.*

DRAMATIC WORK:
Sighs of a Slave Dream (theatrical collage, 1970s). Depicts through dance, music, and drama the cruelty involved in the capture and enslavement of Africans, their trans-

portation to America, and their treatment on the plantations. Prod. in London and in the Keskidee Center of Islington during the early 1970s; dir. by Pat Amadu Maddy.

BARRETT, NATHAN N. (N. Noble Barrett) (1933–   ), Freelance writer. Born in New York City. Lived for ten years in Jamaica, West Indies. Educated in New York City, where he received the bachelor's degree from Brooklyn Coll. and his state certificate as an English teacher from Hunter Coll. Also attended the Frank Silvera Writers' Workshop (FSWW) in New York City. Author of *Floating World* (1972), a volume of poetry, and *Bars of Adamant* (1966), "a tropical novel." Recipient of a Huntington Hartford Foundation Award, 1961, and a John Hay Whitney Opportunity Fellowship in playwriting, 1965–66. *Address:* 35 E. First St., New York, NY 10003.

REPRESENTATIVE PLAYS:
The Aunts of Antioch City (comedy, 4 scenes, 1964). A black grandmother is determined that her mulatto granddaughter shall receive support from the girl's two affluent white aunts. Apparently first prod. by the Negro Ensemble Co. (NEC), New York, 1964. Prod. by the National Arts Theatre, New York, Feb. 1977; dir. by Cynthia Belgrave.

Baker-Maker (farce, 2 acts, 1971). About the life and involvement of a Harlem baker whose bread comes to life. Prod. by Playwrights' Horizons, New York, 1971.

Bird Food (protest play, 1 act, 1973). A black man is enslaved by a white cripple who attempts to control his mind. First prod. by the National Arts Theatre, Feb. 1977; dir. by Charles Pegues.

Why Lily Won't Spin (children's play, 1976). Music by Lucas Mason. Although Lily refuses to spin, she finds another way to get the prince to marry her. Prod. by the Greenwich Mews Theatre, New York, Oct. 1976.

OTHER PLAYS:
S-C-A-R-E-W-E-D (drama, 1 act, 1960). Prod. Off-Bway by NEC, 1960. **A Room of Roses** (melodrama, 3 scenes, 1964). A mother is honored by the town when her dead son is brought home, but is later run out of town because of her behavior. **Engagement in San Dominque** (historical melodrama, 3 acts, 1964). Love story set in the final days of the French occupation of Haiti. **Square Root of Mother** (domestic farce, 6 scenes, 1967). An interracial couple is visited on their first anniversary by both their mothers, and receive an additional surprise. **Cut-Ups & Cut-Outs** (comedy, 2 acts, 1973). The story of 16 forgotten World War II heroes who live out their lives in a secluded seashore home.

BASCOMBE, RONALD D., Poet-playwright. An alumnus of the Sonia Sanchez Writers Workshop in Harlem, New York City, 1970–71. His poetry has been published in *Black Creation, The Universal Black Writer,* and in the anthology cited below. *Address:* 128 Ft. Washington Ave. #16D, New York, NY 10032.

PLAY:
The Unifier (satire, 1 act, 1971). The "Unifier" is an Uncle Tom whose job is to keep blacks quiet and contented, while making no progress. Pub. in *Three Hundred and Sixty Degrees of Blackness Comin at You* (Sanchez, 1971).

BASHIRA, DAMALI, Playwright. A native of Greenville, SC. Member of the Frank Silvera Writers' Workshop (FSWW) in New York City.

PLAYS:
(At least one of the author's scripts is deposited in the FSWW Archives/Schomburg Collection.) **A New Day** (series of monologues, 3 acts, 1970). Concerned with black/white relationships, interests, and events of the 1960s and 1970s. **Just Like His Mama** (drama, 1 act, 1974). In the setting of a laundromat, a grassroots mother shares her street wisdom with a middle-class black female college student concerning male-female relationships and the raising of children.

BASS, GEORGE HOUSTON (1938–   ), Actor, playwright, screenwriter, director, producer, author, editor, and teacher. Born in Murfreesboro, TN. Educated at Fisk Univ. (A.B. with honors in mathematics, 1959), Columbia Univ. Graduate School of Business (1959–60), N.Y. Univ. (NYU) Film School (M.A. 1964), and Yale Univ. School of Drama. Secy. and literary asst. to LANGSTON HUGHES, New York, 1959–64; editorial asst. to Daisy Bates in the writing of her book, *Long Shadow over Little Rock,* 1962. Member of Voices, Inc., a group for which he wrote original scripts, 1960–63. Freelance writer, play doctor, and director, New York City, 1964–70. Artistic director, Jacob Riis Amphitheatre, New York, 1964–70; artistic director, *The Third Party,* produced by the Long Wharf Summer Theatre, New Haven, CT, Summer 1958. Assoc. producer and story editor, "On Being Black," a series of 13 original teleplays, WGBH-TV, Boston, 1968–69; assoc. to the director and resident playwright, Urban Arts Corps, New York City, 1969–70. Since 1969 has been on the faculty of Brown Univ., Providence, RI, where he is now Prof. of Theatre Arts and Afro-American Studies, and artistic director and founder of Rites and Reason (R&R), the university-based, community-oriented research theatre of the Afro-American Studies program. Since its founding, R&R has served as a laboratory for systematic and ongoing efforts by Bass, in collaboration with Prof. Rhett S. Jones, in the development of a research-to-performance method for original theatre productions. Since 1976 Bass has been working on the construction of an American myth of recreation through ritual drama and community celebrations. In addition to the writing and production of more than 20 original works, since coming to Brown, Bass has been involved in the creation, production, and/or direction of more than 30 original works by other playwrights, including ALICE CHILDRESS, J. FRANKLIN, PHILLIP HAYES DEAN, P. J. GIBSON, ADRIENNE KENNEDY, and RAY ARANHA, whose dramatic works have been presented by R&R. As a lecturer on black theatre, culture, history, and specific projects relating to his work with R&R, Bass has appeared on more than 40 talk shows for local TV programs and has presented papers at an equal number of scholarly conferences, conventions, forums, institutes, and convocations throughout the United States and abroad (including Japan and India). Cofounder of the Langston Hughes Soc., 1981; exec. editor of *The Langston Hughes Review,* 1981–present. His articles have been published in *Black Scholar, The Langston Hughes Review,* and *Black American Literature Forum;* his poetry has been included in *The Book of Negro Humor* (Hughes, 1966), *Poets for Today* (Lowenfels, 1970), *BOP: Blacks on Paper* (Vols. 1 and 2), *Fresh Fruit* (Spring 1973), and *22 Currents of an Ancient Stream Are Still Flowing* (1980). Memberships and affiliations include Arts Rhode Island and United Arts Rhode Island, Board of Directors, 1972–76, Long Range Planning Committee, 1974–76; Board of Directors, Afro-Arts Center, Providence, 1972–73; Expansion Arts Panel, NEA, 1973–75; Task Force Committee of Community Access to Public TV, Rhode Island Dept. of Education, Spring 1975; Task Force Committee on Arts and Education, Rhode Island Dept. of Education, Fall 1974; Rhode Island State Council on the Arts, 1976–83, vice chairman, 1980–83. Honors, grants, and awards include John Hay Whitney Fellowship, 1963–64; American Society of Cinematologists' Rosenthal Award, 1964; John Golden Playwriting Fellowship, Yale Univ. School of Drama, 1966–68; Harlem Cultural Council Award, 1969; Fulbright Research Scholarship (India), 1977; Howard Foundation Fellowship, 1977–78; Ford Foundation Travel and Study Grant, 1978; and Delta Sigma Theta Community Award of the Decade, 1980. Also recipient, jointly with Rhett S. Jones, of more than $600,000 in grants from various sources outside of Brown Univ. to support the works of Rites and Reason, 1971–84. *Address*—Home: 11 Poplar St., Providence, RI 02906. Office: Afro-American Studies, Box 1904, Brown University, Providence, RI 02912.

GROUPS OF RELATED PLAYS:

"A TRIO FOR THE LIVING" (3 one-act plays, 1968). Includes **Loop-De-Loo** (also known as **Games**) (1966), **Catch Us Alone** (1968), and **Mourners at the Bier** (1966). Prod. at Yale Univ. Chapel, April 1968, with incidental music (soloists, chorus, and organ) by *Noel Da Costa. A doc. film of the rehearsal process of **"TRIO . . . "** was prod. by WGBH-TV, Boston, under the title *In Rehearsal,* and telecast over all NET stations in Oct. 1969.

"FUNCTION AT THE JUNCTION" (2 plays for improvisation, 1972). Includes **Lonely Women** (1972) and **Buckwheat Revue** (1972). Prod. by New Junction, Providence, RI, May 1972.

REPRESENTATIVE PLAYS AND DRAMATIC WORKS:

Games // Orig. title: **Loop-De-Loo** (absurdist drama, 1 act, 1966; also prod. as a short film entitled **The Game:** screenplay, 1967). Utilizes a ghetto background, Puerto Rican and black characters, and the metaphor of children's games to dramatize the hostility, cruelty, and suffering experienced by minority and disavantaged children growing up in the United States. First performed as **Games** by the Cultural Arts Program of Mobilization for Youth, New York, the antipoverty, antidelinquency agency for New York's Lower East Side, Summer 1966; dir. by WOODIE KING, JR. Prod. as a film entitled **The Game** by the same group and director, and presented at the 1967 Venice Film Festival, where it won the Plaque of the Lion of St. Mark. Film version available from Grove Press, Film Distribution, New York Prod. as **Loop-De-Loop** at Yale Univ. on a program of three one-act plays, under the blanket title **"A TRIO FOR THE LIVING,"** April 1968 [see GROUPS OF RELATED PLAYS above]. Pub. as **Games** in *Readers and*

Writers Magazine, Spring 1967; *Introduction to Black Literature in America* (Patterson, 1968); and *Scott Foresman Reader* (1970).

Mama Etta's Chitlin Circuit ("Soul Revue" [subtitle], 3 scenes, 1973). Famous black entertainers (portrayed by actors) perform their own specialty numbers. Prod. at Brown Univ., April 1973. Pub. in *Rites and Reason* (Purdin, 1973).

The Providence Garden Blues (play with music, full length, 1975). Music by *Jonas Gwangwa. Concerns the problem of racism in Providence from the 1920s to the 1980s. Based on information gathered during an oral history research study. Prod. by R&R, March 1975; dir. by Bass. Scenes pub. in *BOP: Blacks on Paper*, vol. 3.

OTHER PLAYS AND DRAMATIC WORKS:

Roots (dramatic narrative, 1963). Commissioned for the Alvin Ailey Dance Co. and Voices, Inc., by NAACP of Stamford, CT, for its Centennial Celebration of the Emancipation Proclamation, May 1963. **One More Mile to Go** (teleplay, 1965). Prod. by WNJU-TV, Newark, NJ, June 1965, starring Louis Gossett, Jr. **Once I Heard Buddy Bolden Play** (musical, 1965). Book by Bass. Lyrics and music by Mildred Kayden. **The Booby** // Also known as **The Booby Prize, the Booby Hatch, the Booby Trap, the Booby** (ritual, 1 act, 1965). Prod. by the Yale School of Drama, New Haven, CT, 1966–67. **Due Day** (1 act, 1966). Prod. by Yale School of Drama, 1966–67. **Twelve Noon at the Lido** (1 act, 1966). Prod by Yale School of Drama, 1966–67. **Twelve Mortal Men** (1 act, 1966). Prod. by Yale School of Drama, 1966–67. **Kaleidoscope in Black** (multimedia environmental experience, 1966). Coproduced (with Onaway Millar) by Straight Gate Pentacostal Church, Mamaroneck, NY, Sept. 1966. **Mourners at the Bier** (1 act, 1966). Prod. by Yale Univ. three times between 1966 and 1968, the last time on a program of three one-act plays, April 1968, under the prodn. title **"A TRIO FOR THE LIVING"** [see GROUPS OF RELATED PLAYS above]. **Portraits of a People** (gospel song-play, 1967). Adapt. from the poetry of Langston Hughes. Performed by the Utterbach Ensemble, Carnegie Hall, New York, Oct. 1967. **Catch Us Alone** (1 act, 1968). Prod. at Yale Univ. Chapel, April 1968, with incidental music by Noel Da Costa. **Black Blues** (multimedia environmental experience, 1968). Scenario for improvisations of scenes from Black life. Prod. by the Black Arts Theatre, New Haven, June 1968. **The Funhouse** (full length, 1968). Prod. by the Long Wharf Summer Theatre, New Haven, Sept. 1968, with incidental music (soloists, chorus, and instrumental ensemble) by Noel Da Costa. **Soul Convention** (gospel song-play, 1968). Performed by the Utterbach Concert Ensemble, Carnegie Hall, Oct. 1968. **The How Long Suite** (ritual, 1 act, 1968). Prod. by the Black Arts Theatre (of New Haven) at the Onyx Conf. on the Arts, New York City, Nov. 1968. **Oh, Lord This World** (musical, full length, 1969). Subtitled "Get It Together." Book and lyrics by Bass. Music by Clinton Utterbach. Prod. by the Queen of Angels Players, Newark, NJ, Nov.-Dec. 1969; dir. by Bass. Perfs. also given by several high school and college groups. **Black Masque** (historical ritual, 1971). Prod. by R&R, April 1971; revised and revived, April 1981. **Buckwheat Revue** (1 act, 1972). Prod. at the New Junction, Providence, May 1972, on a program of two one-act plays for improvisation, under the prodn. title **"FUNCTION AT THE JUNCTION"** [see GROUPS OF RELATED PLAYS above]. **Lonely Women** (1 act, 1972). Prod. by the New Junction, May 1972, on same program as **Buckwheat Revue,** directly above. **African Vibrations** (ritual, 1973). Music by *Ndikho Xaba. Prod. July 1973. **Dreamdust** (6 Afro-American folk tales, 1974). Adapt. by Bass, *Dorothy Clark, and others. Music by *Kambon Obayani. Prod. as street theatre in numerous cities and towns throughout the state of

Rhode Island, 1974. **The Knee-High Man** (children's play, 1 act, 1974). Based on an Afro-American folk tale adapted by Bass. First prod. at the Manhattan Country School, New York City, 1974, with music by Noel Da Costa. **Babu's Juju** (children's play, 1 act, 1974). Libretto by Bass. Music by Noel Da Costa. First performed in the Flint, MI, school system, 1974. Also prod. at the Manhattan Country School, 1974. **One into the Other** (series of vaudeville spoofs, one-act length, 1974). Includes "Two Moves Plus Tag," "Remnants of a Dream" "Encore," and "A New Recipe." Prod. by the Wastepaper Theatre, Providence, Dec. 1974. **Mama Do Blew** (musical, full length, 1975). Music by Thomas Riggsbee and Kambon Obayani. Prod. by R&R at Brown Univ. and Lincoln Center, New York, July-Aug. 1975; dir. by Bass. **Malacoff Blue** (1976). Prod. by R&R, July 1976, April 1977, and Nov.-Dec. 1981; dir. by Bass. **The Articulate Sound of an Articulate Tale** (1977). Prod. by R&R, April 1977. **The Blacker the Berry** (a 40-day ritual drama, 1980). Prod. by R&R, 1980; dir. by Bass. **De Day of No Mo'** (1980). Prod. by R&R, March 1980. **Brer Rabbit Whole** (musical, full length, 1984). Book and lyrics by Bass. Music by Robert L. Holmes, Jr. Showcase prodn., Fisk Univ., Nashville, TN, Oct. 11–13, 1984. Premiere, R&R, March 8–24, 1985; dir. by Bass. **Peelings** (theatrical collage, full length, 1986). Coauthor and codirector, with Akin Babatunda. Prod. by R&R, March 7–23, 1986.

BATSON, SUSAN (1944–   ), Actress, poet, playwright. Born in Roxbury, MA. Has appeared in stage productions in Baltimore and Los Angeles and on television. Films include *WUSA* (1970) and *AC/DC* (1971), for which she received an Obie Award. Recently appeared in the TV film *Stone Pillow* (1985), which starred Lucille Ball as a bag woman.

PLAY:
Hoodoo Talkin (1 act, 1971). Discussion among four black women on various aspects of the black experience. Pub. in *Three Hundred and Sixty Degrees of Blackness Comin at You* (Sanchez, 1971), pp. 145–78.

BATTLE, SOL (Solomon Oden Battle) (1934–   ), Editor, author, filmmaker. Born in Talladega, AL. Educated at Temple Univ. (B.A., 1955), Brooklyn Coll., and the New School for Social Research. Has been a freelance photographer and TV scriptwriter. Editor and creative director of Panther House, Ltd., New York (now quiescent), which for many years published *Black List,* "the standard guide to Black publications and broadcasting media." Also edited *Ghetto '68* (1970), an anthology of young Harlem writers, and wrote a novel, *Melange in Black* (1970).

DRAMATIC WORKS
All doc. films, prod. and pub. by Panther House, Ltd., New York, 1970s, under the imprint of Contemporary Classics. **Harlem Etude. Julie Loves a Mugger. Only 'Til Spring. Underground Man. The Vow** (coauthored with *Wale Ogunyemi).

BEALE, TITA, Playwright.
PLAY:
A Just Piece (1970). Pub. in *Liberator,* June 1970, p. 16.

BEAN, MONROE (1947–), Playwright, actor, activist, director. Resides in New Orleans, LA, where he studied drama at Loyola Univ. and the Univ. of New Orleans. Has also studied under Nick Stewart of the Ebony Showcase Theater of Los Angeles. Cofounder and executive director of the Ethiopian Theatre in New Orleans, 1973–present. He describes the Ethiopian Theater as one of the oldest black, semiprofessional community theatres in the South. It continues to produce original plays by local and regional playwrights, such as TOM DENT, KALAMU YA SALAAM, N. R. DAVIDSON, JR., JUDY ANN MASON, and CHAKULA CHA JUA. As an actor, Bean has performed in over 50 plays, including *The Amen Corner, Sugar Mouth Sam . . . ,Sty of the Blind Pig, and Purlie Victorious*. He has taught creative writing to inmates at Orleans Parish Prison and conducted directing workshops in North Louisiana. He states that his dream is to keep theatre alive within the New Orleans community, and describes his work as an "activist/community leader, . . . doing what is necessary to stay on top of the political/economic situation."*Address:* Ethiopian Theatre, 2001 Laperouse St., New Orleans, LA 70116. *Agent:* Sabrina T. Bean, 1333 France St., New Orleans, LA 70117.

PLAYS AND DRAMATIC WORKS:

Yes, Dear (domestic comedy, full length, 1973). About a father who questions his children's sexuality. Premiered at Dashiki Theater of New Orleans, 1973. Also ran at Ethiopian Theatre, c. 1973.

Ain't Got Nothin' but the Blues (domestic drama, full length, 1977). Deals with an unemployed musician's attempt to portray himself to the family as successful. Prod. by Ethiopian Theatre, 1977.

Nobody Wins (social drama, full length, 1977). Deals with a black family's struggles to break the poverty cycle. Prod. by Ethiopian Theater, 1977.

Bad Times (social drama, 1 act, 1979). Depicts a black man's experience with employment discrimination. Prod. by Ethiopian Theatre, 1979.

Bucket of Blood (social drama, 1 act, 1979). Depicts a Vietnam vet's return home to fight poverty and black-on-black crime in his community. Prod. by Ethiopian Theatre, 1979.

Ghetto Christmas (Christmas play, full length, 1980). Deals with the real meaning of Christmas as experienced in a low-income black neighborhood. Prod. by Ethiopian Theater, 1980.

The Name of the Game (drama, full length, 1981). Illustrates black political life through a local mayoral race. Prod. by Ethiopian Theater, 1981.

Five Gold Rings (drama, full length, 1982). Tells the story of Billie Jean, a young black woman who seeks to avenge with all black men the hurt she has experienced with one. Prod. at the Masonic Temple, New Orleans, 1982.

The Soldier (social drama, full length, 1983). Depicts the struggles of a World War II veteran on the German warfront and at home on the American battleground as a civil rights soldier. Told in a series of flashbacks. Premiered to audiences at the Southern Black Cultural Alliance Conf. in Miami, FL, 1983. Has run locally at Ethiopian Theater, Copastetic Theater/Dinner Club, Hope House, and local churches.

Runnin' Out of Gas (drama, full length, 1984). About three old men who try to recapture their youth. Sched. for prodn. by Ethiopian Theater, early 1986.

BEAN, PATRICIA A. (Pat Bean) (1956–   ), Playwright, dancer, choreographer, black theatre founder-director, and teacher. Resides in Denver, CO. Educated at the Univ. of Colorado (B.A. in communications and theatre, 1978) and Metropolitan State Coll., Denver (theatre and black studies, 1974–76). Currently employed at the Colorado Civil Rights Div. Has been a member of the Ajoss African Dancers and is currently a member of the Irepo African Dance Group. Founder-director of the East Side Drama Group (ESDG), 1976–present, which she describes as a multitalented group of young people, mainly black, ranging in age from 17 to 26, who reside in northeast Denver. ESDG has presented a number of original plays, including her own works, and has developed *Black Experience* Programs, consisting of dance, skits, and singing, which have been presented in elementary schools throughout the Denver area, and taken on tour of a number of cities in Colorado, Mississippi, Tennessee, and Oklahoma. The group also toured with the program *Footsteps,* dramatizing the life of Mary McLeod Bethune, for the National Council of Negro Women, in 1982. It has also presented a program of monologues for the 1982 Martin Luther King celebration, which were performed at various locations in Denver. Bean is the recipient of an award from the Eden Theatrical Workshop for outstanding contribution to the arts, 1982. *Address:* 3049 Leyden, Denver, CO 80207.

PLAYS AND DRAMATIC WORKS:
Till Death Do Us Part (drama, 2 acts, 1978). Coauthor, with *Robert Kelley (deceased). About a black mother with a teenage daughter who remarries a younger man. The daughter is raped by her new stepfather; rather than spoil her mother's newfound happiness, she commits suicide. Prod. by ESDG, May 1978.

Getting It Together (comedy, 2 acts, 1978). About a little black girl who discovers the principles and concepts of Kwanza celebration through her favorite doll, which comes to life. Prod. by ESDG, Dec. 1978.

You Me and Us (abstract drama, 2 acts, 1979). Deals with the black male-female relationship. The beginning of the play focuses on what tears a relationship apart. The second half gives guidelines on how a couple can make their relationship work. Prod. by ESDG, Aug. 1983.

T.I.M.E. Is What Time Is It (drama, 2 acts, 1983). Documentary on the historical background of the black race, starting in the New Stone Age, and ending with what the author feels should be the 1980 revolution. Famous leaders highlighted include Marcus Garvey, Martin Luther King, Malcolm X, Eldridge Cleaver, Huey Newton, and Bobby Seales.

BECKHAM, BARRY (Earl) (1944–   ), Novelist, author, editor, playwright, and creative writing teacher. Asst. prof. of English at Brown Univ., Providence, RI. Born in Philadelphia, PA. Received the A.B. from Brown, 1966. Author of three novels: *My Main Mother* (1969), *Runner Mack* (1972), and *Double Dunk* (1980). His shorter writings have been published in *Esquire, New York Times Book Review, and Brown Alumni Monthly. Address:* Creative Writing Program, Box 1821, Brown University, Providence, RI 02912.

PLAY:
Garvey Lives! (ritual drama, 1972). Music by Richard Humes. About Marcus Garvey, advocate of the "Back-to-Africa" movement. Prod. by Rites and Reason, at Rhode Island Churchill House, Brown Univ., Nov. 1972; dir. by GEORGE HOUSTON BASS.

BEIM, NORMAN, Actor-playwright. Based in New York City.

PLAYS:
The Dark Corner of an Empty Room (pre-1972). A black youth, pressured into a life of crime, is finally killed by a white policeman. **Inside** (1981). Prod. by the Quaigh Theatre, New York, May 11, 1981; dir. by author.

BELL, DENISE, Short-story writer, poet, and playwright. Born in New York City; grew up in New Jersey. Educated at Seton Hall Univ. (B.S. in education, with a social studies major and an English minor) and Jersey City State Coll. (graduate work in education). Also studied with ADRIENNE KENNEDY and with the Frank Silvera Writers' Workshop (FSWW). Her mentors include Kennedy, Billie Allen, GARLAND LEE THOMPSON, FRED HUDSON, and DAN OWENS. The author of a number of short stories and poems, and five plays, of which only three are listed below. Her work concerns the conflict of black women in an upwardly mobile world. Her characters come to grips with their identity and their need for security. She has been a nominee for the AUDELCO theatre awards. *Address:* 650 Lenox Ave. #4H, New York, NY 10037.

PLAYS:
Dialogues of the Shadow Women (drama, 2 acts, 1977). Deals with a power struggle among women to gain control of a church. Prod. by the Director's Unit of FSWW, at the Urban Arts Corps, New York, opening Jan. 27, 1977; dir. by Sam Shepard. Unpub. script and tape recording in the FSWW Archives/Schomburg Collection. Script also in the Hatch-Billops Collection. **Lush Life** (1977). Public reading by FSWW at City Coll., New York, Jan. 1977. Unpub. script and tape recording in the FSWW Archives/Schomburg Collection. **Cliches, Soliloquies and Lies** (1970). Public reading by FSWW, Jan. 30, 1978. Unpub. script and tape recording in the FSWW Archives/Schomburg Collection. Script also in the Hatch-Billops Collection. **Mournings After** (1987). Public reading by FSWW, Feb. 16, 1987. Dir. by Pat White.

BEN HASSEN, UMAR. See HASSAN, UMAR BIN.

BENJAMIN, PAUL, Actor, poet-playwright, and director. Formerly associated with the New York Shakespeare Festival Public Theatre. Among his theatrical performances are *Hamlet* (1967), *Cities in Bezique (The Owl Answers)* (1969), *No Place to Be Somebody* (1969), *Camino Real* (1970), and *The Black Terror* (1971).

PLAYS:
Memoirs of a Junkie (morality drama, 2 acts, 1975). Deals with the lives of three drug addicts trying to rehabilitate themselves. Prod. by the Moravia Players, at CCNY, and at the Billie Holiday Theatre, Brooklyn, 1975. **A Twosome** (early 1970s). **The**

Carrier (drama, 1 act, 1985). About the tribal abuse of barren married women among some black tribes in South Africa. In Benjamin's play, a young wife's ''ability to bear children is crucial to her survival and well being and . . . [without] this ability, she [is subject to being] humiliated, ostracized, and [having] her dignity as a member of the human race totally stripped away.''—*New York Amsterdam News,* Aug. 17, 1985, p. 27 (Sinclair). Prod. at the Riverwest Theatre in the West Village, New York, Aug. 1985. **The Box** (avant-garde drama, 1 act, 1985). A companion piece to the above play, also set in South Africa. Described by Abiola Sinclair (*New York Amsterdam News,* Sept. 7, 1985, p. 23) as ''a rather surreal, almost existential, work [which examines] the question of living versus survival,'' as well as ''the value of concern.'' The topic of concern is, of course, apartheid. The setting is a ''shebeen,'' which is an illegal after-hours establishment in a private home, where friends drink, socialize, and hold political meetings. Prod. at the Riverwest Theatre in the West Village, New York, Aug. 1985, on double bill with **The Carrier.** Featuring Themba Ntinga, MINNIE GENTRY, Regina Taylor, and the author in the leading roles.

BERNIER, BHUNNIE. See MOLETTE, BHUNNIE BERNIER.

BERRY, KELLEY-MARIE, Actress-playwright. Formerly resided in New York City, where she was associated with the Black Repertory Theatre/School and the New Lafayette Theatre during the 1960s. Performed in *Dutchman* (1965) and *Clara's Ole Man* (1968). Now resides in Los Angeles.

PLAYS:
(All except the first are presumably children's plays.) **Black Happenin'** (drama, 1 act, 1967). Depicts the struggles of a black family ''to make it with the White man.'' **Baku, or How to Save the Whale's Tale** (1972). **The Boomp Song** (1973). **Alonzo Jason Jefferson Jones** (1970s).

BETTER, ANTHONY, Playwright. A resident of Washington, DC.

PLAY:
The Window of Our Dreams (1975). ''A fight for love and dignity in the Black ghetto.''—*Black World,* April 1976, p. 84. Prod. by Federal City Coll., Washington DC, 1975.

BIN HASSAN, UMAR. See HASSAN, UMAR BIN

BLACK, ISAAC J., Poet-playwright. A resident of New York City, where in 1975 he was involved in the rehabilitation of drug addicts. His poetry has appeared in *Obsidian, Callaloo, Hoodoo, First World, Black World, Black Creation, Black Dialogue,* the *Journal of Black Poetry,* and *New Black Voices.* Recipient of a Broadside Press Award for poetry in 1973. *Address:* 119–20 225th St., Cambria Heights, NY 11411.

PLAY:
Niggeramus (1971). Prod. by the Muse Theatre Workshop, Brooklyn, NY, 1971.

BLACK, WILLIAM ELECTRIC (Ian Ellis James), Playwright and director, specializing in jazz musicals, which he terms "jazzicals." Based in New York City. Educated at Brockport State Coll., Dept. of Drama; Southern Illinois Univ. Graduate School of Playwriting; the Frank Silvera Writers' Workshop (FSWW) and the Negro Ensemble Co. (NEC) Writers Workshop in New York City; and privately under Wesley Jensby (of La Mama E.T.C.), Andrei Serban, Elizabeth Swados, and Ching Yeh. Described by LIONEL MITCHELL, former drama critic of the *New York Amsterdam News,* as "the most exciting new playwright" of the 1982 season. Honors and awards include Best Play Award, Ajabu Children's Theatre, Chicago, 1977; Honorable Mention, American Song Festival, 1975; Long Play Honorable Mention Award, Southern Illinois Univ., 1978; Best Short Play Award, Southern Illinois Univ., 1978; Honorable Mention, American Song Festival, 1979; Faculty Grant, Riverdale Country Day School, for screenwriting, 1981; artist-in-residence, Tompkins Square Lib., New York City, 1981; and AUDELCO Award Honorable Mention, 1982. *Address:* 441 E. 12th St. #5A, New York, NY 10009.

REPRESENTATIVE PLAYS AND DRAMATIC WORKS:

Romeo & Juliet: New Wave // Formerly prod. as **Romeo & Juliet (A Rock Musical)** and **Romeo-Rock & Juliet Jazzical** (musical adaptn. of Shakespeare's tragedy, full length, 1981/84). Described by Robert Massa as a revamp of Shakespeare's tragedy into a lower East Side story. "Romeo wears blue hair and a 'no shit' button, while Juliet always seems about to burst into 'Girls Just Wanna Have Fu-un.' By remaining faithful to Shakespeare's words, the production doesn't give itself room to explore the close relationship of death and eros in punk . . . but the rock club ambience . . . makes the comic scenes delightfully vivid and gives the fight scenes more true street beat than any clash of Jets and Sharks I've seen."—*Village Voice,* March 13, 1984, p. 79. "Black's lively music, which ranges from rock to funk to reggae to rap, makes up in rhythm what it lacks in melody, and the expressionist staging gives the barebone production (performed with only worklights!) as much sheer surreal energy as any rock video I've seen"—Ibid. First prod. as **Romeo-Rock & Juliet-Jazzical** at Club 57, New York, June 20–July 6, 1981, for 3 perfs. Prod. as **Romeo & Juliet (A Rock Musical)** at the Bridgehampton Theatre, Long Island, Aug. 1983. Prod. as **Romeo & Juliet: New Wave** at Entermedia Marquee, New York, Feb. 21–March 11, 1984. All perfs. were dir. by author.

Whatever Happened Ta Amos 'N Andy? (comedy, 2 acts, 1982). Depicts an attempt at a comeback by the various members of the original "Amos 'n' Andy" TV show, after the show was cancelled during the mid-1950s. The play utilizes "a whole host of incredible slapstick routines," which "deal with both the before-camera situation and the desperate pitiful real life situations of top Black actors who could never get jobs after the series was taken off the air."—*New York Amsterdam News,* May 9, 1982, p. 25. Prod. by FSWW, April 29–May 16, 1982, for 12 perfs.; dir. by Pat White. The limited engagement was made possible only after extensive legal negotiations with CBS, which considered the play an infringement on their rights and had threatened to obtain an injunction to halt the show. Cast included William Williams as the Kingfish, Margaret Bynum as his wife Sapphire, Dorothy Fox as Mama, Rob Ashley Bowles as Calhoun, Gregory Holtz, Sr., as Lightin', Eldon Bullock as Amos, and Helmar Augustus Cooper as Andy. Unpub. script and tape recording in the FSWW Archives/Schomburg Collection.

The Sun Gets Blue (jazz musical, full length, 1982). Subtitled "A Jazzical." Book, lyrics, and choreography by Black; music by Paul Shapiro. Described by Lionel Mitchell (cited above) as "a staging of the Harlem riots in a way that doesn't allow us to forget the greater uprising of the people. The piece gets operative in time, very Aaron Copland (Billy the Kid ballet), ultra modern in sounds and movement."—Ibid. Prod. by FSWW, at the Theatre of the Open Eye, New York, April 14–May 2, 1982, for 15 perfs.; dir. by Amy Brockway. Unpub. script in the FSWW Archives/Schomburg Collection.

Frankenstein: New Wave (rock musical, full length, 1985). Book, music, and direction by Black. Described by the *New York Native*, Nov. 4–10, 1985, as "a kind of big-fun blend of *Cats* and *Rocky Horror* with tremendous reverence for its source, Mary Shelley's novel—and not without gay overtones (the monster reminded [the reviewer] of Truman Capote on acid, and there's a great deal made of the relationship between Dr. Frankenstein and Henry Clerval)." Prod. at the Kraine Gallery Theatre, New York, Sept.-Nov. 1985.

OTHER PLAYS AND DRAMATIC WORKS:

Jack (1976). Prod. at the Billie Holiday Theatre, Brooklyn, May 1976. **The Death of a Black Man** (1977). Prod. at LaMont Zeno Theatre, Chicago, Oct. 1977. **Alice Digs Soulland** (1978). Prod. by LaMont Zeno Theatre, Chicago, Jan. 1978, and by Triton Coll., Chicago, Feb. 79. **Ulysses (The Jazzical)** (full length, 1978). Written and dir. by Black. Prod. at Southern Illinois Univ., April 1978. Prod. by Entermedia Marquee Theatre, New York, Aug. 25–Sept. 12, 1982, with music by Hilary Schmidt. **Billy Stars & Kid Jupiter** (a sci-fi jazzical, full length, 1980). Written and dir. by Black. Music by Paul Schapiro. Prod. at the Theatre for the New City, New York, June 26–July 13, 1980. **L.A. Sunset** (rock jazzical, full length, 1981). **The Son** (1981). Written, dir., and choreographed by Black. Prod. at the Nat Horne Musical Theatre, New York, Oct. 15–Nov. 1, 1981. **Road to Timbuktu** (c. 1982). Unpub. script and tape recording of a reading by FSWW are located in the FSWW Archives/Schomburg Collection. **Hotel Toby** (c. 1982). Unpub. script and tape recording of a reading by FSWW are located in the FSWW Archives/Schomburg Collection.

BLACKWELL, CHARLES (Charlie) (1930–   ), Dancer, choreographer, stage manager, actor, producer, screenwriter, and playwright. Born in Philadelphia, PA. Resides in New York City. A former dancer with Pearl Primus, Blackwell has built a reputation as a stage manager of numerous hit Broadway shows for about 20 years and is considered one of the best in the business. Coproduced the New York production of *Ain't Supposed to Die a Natural Death* (1971). *Address:* c/o Fifi Oscard Associates, 19 W. 44th St., New York, NY 10036.

DRAMATIC WORKS:

A Piece of the Action (feature film, full length: screenplay, 1977). Music and lyrics by *Curtis Mayfield. Comic crime drama, set in Chicago, with Bill Cosby and Sidney Poitier as two successful crooks who are blackmailed by a police lieutenant played by James Earl Jones into volunteering their services at a community center (helping rehabilitate ghetto kids) or facing a prison sentence. Much of the dramatic action involves Cosby and Poitier's attempts to escape from some mobsters who are pursuing them. Prod.

1977; dir. by Poitier. The cast also included Denise Nicholas, HOPE CLARKE, and JA'NET DuBOIS.

The Tap Dance Kid (musical prologue and 2 acts, 1983). Book by Blackwell. Lyrics by Robert Lorick. Music by Henry Krieger. Based on the novel *Nobody's Family Is Going to Change* by Louise Fitzhugh, which had been produced as a TV drama (also entitled *The Tap Dance Kid)* by NBC, Oct. 24, 1978, with Blackwell in the role of the father. The story concerns a black youth's desire to become a successful dancer on the New York stage in spite of his father's objections. According to the New York *Amsterdam News* (Jan. 28, 1984, p. 26), the song and dance plot is built around "Blackwell's idea of a nuclear Black middle-class family. At all times he wanted to [show] . . . that they could be upwardly mobile and strive for better things without being preachy." Prod. on Bway, opening first at the Bradhurst Theatre, Dec. 21, 1983; then moved to the Minskoff Theatre in early 1974; choreographed by Danny Daniels, who won a Tony Award as best choreographer, with Hinton Battle (who also won a Tony as best featured actor in a musical) in the title role. The show closed March 11, 1985, after 705 perfs.

BLAINE, LAURENCE, Playwright. Associated with the Concept East Theatre (CET) of Detroit, MI, and the Detroit Repertory Theatre, during the late 1960s.

PLAYS:
Dark Night, Angry Faces (1968). Prod. by CET, Spring 1968. **Soul of Darkness** (1968). Prod. by the Detroit Repertory Theatre, 1968. **A Rose for Cousin Henry** (tragedy, 2 acts, 1971). Depicts the decline of a former husband, gardener, and self-respecting man, who ends up literally in the gutter.

BLAIR, CLIFTON, Playwright. Based in New York City.

PLAY:
Skillet (comedy, 3 acts, 1984). "The play, which has a setting . . . 'anywhere in the south,' . . . highlights activities and conversations in a boarding house between its various characters."—*New York Amsterdam News,* April 7, 1984. Prod. by Arts and Culture, Inc., New York, opening April 6, 1984; dir. by Andre Mtumi, and featuring Lex Monson.

BLAKELY, NORA, Poet and musical writer. Daughter of poet Gwendolyn Brooks. Blakely's poetry has been anthologized in a volume dedicated to her mother, *To Gwen with Love* (Brown, Lee, & Ward, 1971).

DRAMATIC WORK:
Future Spirits (musical, 1975).

BLANK, ROGER, Playwright. Based in New York City.

PLAY:
Blink Your Eyes (1975). Deals with those fleeting feelings that occur within the blink of an eye. Prod. by the Astral Players, New York, 1975.

BOHANON, MARY, Poet-playwright. Her poems and other writings have been published in *Earth Bosom and Collected Poems* (1960s), *Poems and Character Sketches* (1967), and in the anthology cited below.

PLAY:
Find the Girl (1970). Pub. in *A Galaxy of Black Writing* (Shuman, 1970).

BOLANDE, GENE (Eugene K. Bolande), Caribbean-born actor, playwright, TV scriptwriter, screenwriter, and producer. Has appeared several times on Broadway. Currently director of the Touring Readers Theatre Program of the Inner City Cultural Center (ICCC) in Los Angeles. Appeared in the New York stage productions of *The Cool World* and *The Great Indoors,* and in such productions of ICCC as *Sleep No More,* a successful adaptation of Shakespeare's *Macbeth,* in which he played the key role of the Porter. Television roles include "Dragnet," "Chips," and "The Young and the Restless." Motion picture appearances include *Airport I* and *II, Hotel, The Reincarnation of Peter Proud,* and *Pendulum.* Credited with being the first black staff writer of several major television shows, including "Peyton Place," "Julia," and "That Girl," and was an NBC casting director for "Sanford and Son." Has also written short stories, poetry, and a novelette entitled "Billie the Innocent," as yet unpublished. *Address:* c/o Inner City Cultural Center, 1308 S.New Hampshire, Los Angeles, CA 90006. *Agents:* Ivan Green Agency, 911 Pico Blvd., Los Angeles, CA 90035. Playwriting agent: William Talbot, Samuel French, Inc., 45 W. 25th St., New York, NY 10010.

REPRESENTATIVE PLAYS AND DRAMATIC WORKS:
Late for the Funeral (teleplay, also performed as a one-act drama, c. 1970). An incisive character study of what happens when a young black actress who is living in a common-law relationship with a well-to-do young white architect discovers that he is dying of cancer and, after his estranged family arrives in town, proceeds to shut her out of his life. Prod. by ICCC's Readers Theatre Repertory Co., Los Angeles; then on tour of the United States concert circuit, early 1970s.

The Unforgiving Minute (comedy-drama with music, 3 acts, 1971). Deals with a young son moving from adolescence into adulthood. Determined to seek his manhood, the son returns home after many years and triggers into sharp focus a searching, deep-seated drama which threatens to destroy his whole family, which is precariously held together by the slim thread of a guilty secret. The author's most successful and widely prod. play. Prod. first in London, 1971. Prod. in Charleston, SC, 1973, at the Charleston Municipal Auditorium. Prod. in 1975 by ICCC in Los Angeles and presented at numerous colleges and universities throughout the United States as well as on TV. Prod. in Haarlem, Holland, 1984.

OTHER PLAYS AND DRAMATIC WORKS:
Has cowritten TV scripts as a staff writer for the following shows: **"Peyton Place"** (1964/69). Prod. by 20th Century-Fox. **"Julia"** (1968/71). Prod. by 20th Century-Fox, starring Diahann Carroll. **"That Girl"** (1966/71). Prod. by Daisy Productions, starring Marlo Thomas. NOTE: The following plays are all pre-1985: **How the Black Experience Became Theatre** (TV doc.). Written with Angelo Presenti. An educational filmscript that traces the evolution of the black experience in America from an African village in centuries past to the legitimate stage and motion pictures of 1980. Prod. by Communications Group West. **In Italy Again** (story premise, applicable to TV or stage play). A neurotic, age-conscious, but beautiful woman meets a handsome, young Italian ex-priest

at a busstop. They become lovers and in the course of their relationship decide to travel through Europe together in a VW camper. The psychological events, both internal and external, that occur, coupled with her neurosis, eat away at their relationship, destroy their love, and finally send him back to the priesthood. **Is Jesus Still Minding the Store** (drama, 3 acts). Written with Welles Root. A dedicated, staunch, courtly, old world, white New England minister finds he is losing the young people of his parish. He appoints a black 30–year-old Vietnam veteran as asst. pastor and unleashes a fury of subliminal and overt racial prejudice which threatens to shatter his 50–year ministry and his childhood friendships and bring down his church. **Moving Backwards, Going Forward** (teleplay, full length). Written with Brenda Joyce. The death of his parents leaves a young black boy and his sister orphaned. To avoid becoming wards of the state and being placed in a foster home, he launches a genealogical search which turns up his only living relative— a proud, wise, and fascinating African widow—whose arrival in a small southern town triggers an emotional explosion of joy, self-knowledge, rape, and death that changes the lives of the townspeople forever. **Reap the Whirlwind** (TV soap opera/screenplay, full length). Blond, virile, southern-born, and bad, Garson Garvey wants to be a star, and becomes one. Tortured, misguided, possibly insane, he takes his wife, his best friend, and his lover down a dusty road to death—through the wind that he sowed and the whirlwind they all reaped. **The Slave Brothers** // Also known as **The Engineers** (screen-play/teleplay, full length). Written with ERIC MONTE. A panoramic adventure story of two brothers, one a house slave, the other a field slave, who escape bondage and follow the Underground Railroad to "freedom" in the North. Focuses on the love/hate rela-tionship of the brothers, and the triumph over the frailty of human nature when they discover that no man is free while his brother is in chains. This revelation leads them to return South to "engineer" a long line of escapes on their own Underground Railroad. **A Child Grows Up** (educational film). Prod. by Britannica Films (staff writer). **Miss Corey** (screenplay). Under option by Levy, Gardner & Laven to United Artists.

BOOKER, MARY, Director-playwright. Founder and director of the Black Experience Theatre of San Francisco, the name of which was later changed to the B & B Experimental Theatre.

> **PLAYS:**
> **Upon This Rock** (drama, 1972). Prod. by the Black Experience Theatre, at Black Expo, San Francisco, Aug. 1972. **A Black Woman Speaks** (theatrical collage, 1972). Collection of poems and scenes. Created and perfd. by the B & B Experimental Theatre during Black History Week, San Francisco, 1972. **Roll Dem Bones** (collective theatre work, 1973). Created and perfd. by the B & B Experimental Theatre, San Francisco, 1973; dir. by Booker.

BOOKER, STELLA. See MARRS, STELLA.

BOOKER, SUE (1946–   ), TV producer, director, writer; playwright. Born in Jersey City, NJ. Currently resides in Los Angeles, CA. Prodn. asst., "Sesame Street," Children's TV Workshop, New York, 1968. Producer, director, writer, KNBC-TV, Los Angeles, 1972–74. Assoc. prof., Dept. of Radio and TV, California State Univ. at Long Branch, 1973. Currently TV producer, Black News Bureau.

PLAY:

The Flags (drama, 1 act, 1971). An impoverished black woman loses her only means of income—selling Confederate flags—when she is persuaded to do so by a zealous young white civil rights worker. Pub. in *Cry at Birth* (Booker et al., 1971).

BOURNE, ST. CLAIR (Cecil) (1943–   ), Independent film producer, director, journalist, critic, and theoretician/teacher. Born in New York City. Educated at Georgetown Univ., Syracuse Univ. (B.A. 1967), and Columbia Univ. Served in the Peace Corps, 1964–66. Engineer, WBAI-FM, 1968. Taught film courses at Queens Coll., 1968; California State Coll., 1970; and Univ. of California at Los Angeles (UCLA) (guest lecturer), 1975. Designed and taught a film course at Cornell Univ. for several years. Was staff producer/director for *Black Journal* (NET series), 1968–70, during the year that the program won an Emmy Award. Film supervisor/consultant/coordinator for World Black and African Festival of the Arts and Culture (FESTAC), Lagos, Nigeria, 1976. Founder and pres., the Chamba Org., his film production and distribution operation. Productions of Chamba have included documentaries for ABC-TV and educational films in collaboration with such client institutions as the "Sesame Street" program, the American Inst. of Architecture, and the College Entrance Examination Board. Bourne has produced and/or directed such films as *Telephone* (1971) for "Sesame Street," *Ourselves* (1971), *Statues Hardly Ever Smile* (1971), *A Piece of the Block* (1972), *Pusher Man* (1972), *Zaire 1974* (production consultant, 1972), and *The Long Night* (1976), based on the JULIAN MAYFIELD novel. Publisher of *Chamba Notes* (a quarterly film newsletter), 1970–   ; film critic for *Black Scholar* and *New York Amsterdam News;* editor of *Bright Moments: A Media Guide and Reader*. Recipient of several fellowships from the National Endowment for the Arts (NEA); John Russworm Citation for excellence in broadcast journalism (New York Urban League), 1969; Bronze Award (New York International Film-TV Festival), 1974. *Address:* The Chamba Organization, 230 W. 105th St. #12A, New York, NY 10025.

REPRESENTATIVE FILM WORKS:
(All apparently prod. by the Chamba Org. and dir. by Bourne.)

Something to Build On (doc. film, 1973). Motivational tool to persuade black students to get a college education, prod. for the College Entrance Examination Board. Included animation by James Mannas of Jaymie Productions, the musical skills of Herbie Hancock, and narration by Ed Williams.

Let the Church Say Amen! (feature length doc., 1973). Commissioned by a group of black churchmen. According to Michael Mattox, writing in *Black Creation* (Summer 1973, p. 34), "In this film [Bourne] departs from the pure documentary form used in journalistic or educational films, and imposes a plot on the real life situations faced by a young Black graduate from a Seminary venturing out on his maiden voyage." The film was shot at the Interdenominational Theological Center in Atlanta; in Mound Bayou, MS, the oldest black community in the United States; and in Chicago. Featured music by B. B. King, Roberta Flack, and Donny Hathaway. All roles were played by nonprofessional actors. Presented by the Whitney Museum of American Art, New York, as part of its fifth season of New American Filmmakers series, 1974.

The Black and the Green (narrative film, 40 min., 1983). About what happens to a group of black American activists when they journey to Belfast, Northern Ireland, on a fact-finding mission. Explores parallels between American blacks and Northern Irish-Catholics in their fight for civil rights. Presented at the National Conf. on the Documentary Film, at the Kennedy Center, Washington, DC, 1983, sponsored by the American Film Inst. and the Corp. for Public Broadcasting.

In Motion: Amiri Baraka (TV doc., 1 hr., 1983). A portrait of the controversial poet/playwright/author/activist AMIRI BARAKA (LeRoi Jones). Telecast on PBS, June 1, 1983.

OTHER FILM WORKS:
Nothing But Common Sense (doc. film, 1973). **A Piece of the Block** (doc. film, c. 1973). For the Harlem Commonwealth Council. His first documentary to use actors to make a point. **Point of Entry** (feature film, in process, 1973). Sched. to be completed on a grant from the National Endowment for the Arts (NEA), and was to be his first feature film. No record of the actual prodn. **Shepperd's Blues** (TV drama, full length, in process, 1973). Commissioned by American Playhouse, to be coauthored by CLAYTON RILEY. No record of actual prodn. **A Nation of Common Sense** (doc. film, 1975). **Big City Blues** (doc film, c. 1980). A Chicago blues documentary for the premiere of the now defunct CBS Cable Network. Also wrote an extensive film treatment, with RICHARD WESLEY, on a black love story.

BOYKIN, ELIJAH, Playwright. Formerly associated with the Concept East Theatre (CET) in Detroit, MI. An alumnus of the Frank Silvera Writers' Workshop (FSWW) in New York City.

PLAYS:
Theme for a Black Cowboy (early 1970s). Prod. by CET, early 1970s. **Solomon Grant's Tales of the Ghetto** (1970s). Unpub. script and tape recording in FSWW Archives/Schomburg Collection.

BRADLEY, DAVID, Author and playwright. Prof. of English and dean at Temple Univ., Philadelphia, PA. Author of *The Cheneysville Incident* (1982), which won the P.E.N./Faulkner Award for fiction.

DRAMATIC WORK:
[An untitled screenplay on Malcolm X] (in progress, 1985). According to the *New York Amsterdam News* (June 13, 1985), "After his article, 'My Hero, Malcolm X,' appeared in the December 1983 *Esquire* magazine, [Bradley] was asked to write the screenplay for a Warner Bros. film about the fiery civil rights leader. It was a task Bradley eagerly accepted, even though he knew that at least four previous scripts by other writers had been rejected in the past for various reasons."

BRADSHAW, BOOKER T., JR., Actor, guitarist, folksinger, and TV scriptwriter. The son of a Richmond, VA, insurance executive. Appeared in a number of TV plays and films during the 1960s and 1970s, including an episode of

Tarzan and as the young law student in LUTHER JAMES'S *Liberty*. Starred as Brunswick in the film *Coffee* (1975).

DRAMATIC WORKS:

And People All Around (musical, full length, 1967). Music and lyrics by Bradshaw. Book by George Sklar. Prod. by the Bristol Old Vic Theatre, England, 1967. Prod. by the John Fernald Co., at the Meadow Brook Theatre, Rochester, MI, around 1970. **Night Train to L.A.** (TV script, full length [1 hr.], 1975). For the "Macmillan and Wife" series, with Rock Hudson, Susan St. James, and Paul Burke. Telecast on CBS-TV, 1975.

BRANCH, WILLIAM B. (Blackwell) (1928–   ), Playwright, screenwriter, scriptwriter, producer, director, journalist. and consultant. Born in New Haven, CT. Educated at Northwestern Univ. (B.S. in speech, 1949); Columbia Univ. (M.F.A. in dramatic arts, 1958; postgraduate study, 1958–59); and Yale Univ. School of Drama (screenwriting, 1965–66) on a Yale-ABC Fellowship. Divorced; one daughter. His first play, **A Medal for Willie,** was prod. in New York City on the day before he was drafted into the U.S. Army, 1951–52, where he served as an educational instructor in Germany. Performed as an actor in New York City during the mid-1950s. Since 1959 has written extensively for the stage, TV, radio, and films. Was staff writer-producer for New York's Channel 13, Educational Broadcasting Corp., 1962–64. Directed NBC's "The Alma John Show," 1963–69. Writer-producer, Special Unit, NBC News, 1972– 73. Executive producer, "Black Perspectives on the News," PBS, 1978–79. Writer-producer, multimedia project on the African Presence in the Art of the Americas, conducted by the African American Exchange Program, Inc., Chicago, completed 1981. Since 1973, founder and pres. of his own consulting firm, William Branch Assocs., based in New Rochelle, NY, where he writes, produces films and TV programs, and furnishes consultant services and expertise in these fields. Visiting playwright at Smith Coll., Northampton, MA, Spring 1970; North Carolina Central Univ., Durham, Spring-Summer 1971; St. Lawrence Univ., Canton, NY, Spring 1973. Visiting prof. at Univ. of Ghana, Summer 1963; visiting prof. of African American Studies, Univ. of Maryland/ Baltimore County, Sept. 1979–June 1981. Guest lecturer at numerous colleges and universities, including Harvard, Columbia, Syracuse, Temple, UCLA, UC/ Santa Barbara, Duke, San Jose State, Spellman, Univ. of Utah, Northwestern, Bluefield State, Livingstone, Southampton, Fisk, Fairleigh-Dickinson, Howard, UC/Berkeley, UC/San Diego, Univ. of Maryland/College Park, and SUNY/ Purchase. Consultancies include Ford Foundation, Office of Communications, 1976; Afro-American History Caravan, New York City Board of Education, 1975–77; and Black Citizens for a Fair Media, 1973–present. His articles have been published in *Black Scholar, New York Times, Spelman Messenger, Television Quarterly, New York Post, Ebony,* and *His Roots* (1960). Delegate to International Conf. on the Arts, Lagos, Nigeria, Dec. 1961. Board member, American Soc. of African Culture, 1963–70; National Citizens Committee for Broadcasting, 1969–71; and National Advisory Board, Center for the Book, Lib.

of Congress, 1979–present. Recipient of Guggenheim Fellowship for creative writing in the drama, 1959–60; Yale Univ.-ABC Fellowship, for creative writing in television drama, 1965–66; American Film Festival Blue Ribbon Award, 1969, and Emmy Award nomination, 1969, for **Still a Brother: Inside the Negro Middle Class** (1968); National Council of Christians and Jews Citation, 1958, for NBC television drama, **Light in the Southern Sky;** and Hannah B. Del Vecchio Award, from the Trustees of Columbia Univ., for achievement in playwriting, 1958. *Address*—Office: William Branch Associates, 53 Cortlandt Ave., New Rochelle, NY 10801. *Agent:* Bridget Ashenberg, International Creative Management (ICM), 40 W. 57th St., New York, NY 10019.

REPRESENTATIVE PLAYS AND DRAMATIC WORKS:

A Medal for Willie (drama, full length [prologue, 8 scenes, epilogue], 1951). A black mother in the Deep South expresses her disgust with southern white hypocrisy by refusing to accept an army medal awarded posthumously to her son for bravery in Korea. According to the author, "It dramatically underscored the ironies of a black soldier fighting and dying to secure freedoms for others abroad that he was unable to enjoy at home."— Resume, 1975. First prod. by the Committee for the Negro in the Arts, at Club Baron, a Harlem cabaret, Oct. 15, 1951–Jan. 1952; dir. by Elwood Smith. Cast included JULIAN MAYFIELD, Clarice Taylor, ROGER FURMAN, and Eli Rill. Since prod. by numerous groups in the United States and abroad (including Bermuda and the Phillippines). Pub. in *Black Drama Anthology* (King & Milner, 1972).

In Splendid Error // Orig. title: **Frederick Douglass** (historical drama, 3 acts [5 scenes], 1954). Deals with a disagreement between Frederick Douglass and John Brown concerning the best way to help the cause of abolition. First prod. Off-Bway at the Greenwich Mews Theatre, Oct. 17–Dec. 5, 1954, for nine weeks, starring film actor William Marshall as Douglass and Alfred Sandor as Brown. Reopened in Jan. 1955 for a short run. Prod. at Theatre XIV, Philadelphia, May 23–26, for 3 perfs. Since prod. by numerous theatre groups all over the United States. Prod. by the New Federal Theatre (NFT), New York, as part of its Retrospective Series, opening Dec. 14, 1978, for 12 perfs.; dir. by Charles Turner. Pub. in *Black Theater* (Patterson, 1971) and in *Black Theater, U.S.A.* (Hatch & Shine, 1974).

Light in the Southern Sky (TV drama, half hour, 1958; also a stage play, 1 act). About the life of the noted black educator and humanitarian Mary McLeod Bethune. Winner of a Robert E. Sherwood Television Award, 1958, and a Special Citation from the National Council of Christians and Jews, 1958. Prod. on NBC-TV, 1958. Cast included Elwood Smith, Hilda Haynes, and Clarice Taylor. Prod. as a stage work for the National Council of Negro Women, in New York and Washington, DC, 1958–59.

Fifty Steps Toward Freedom (stage doc., full length, 1959). Subtitled "A Dramatic Presentation in Observance of the Fiftieth Anniversary of the National Association for the Advancement of Colored People, 1909–1959." Prod. by the NAACP, at the 50th Anniversary celebration, in the New York Coliseum, 1959, starring OSSIE DAVIS. Cast also included GODFREY CAMBRIDGE. Pub. by the NAACP, New York, 1959; copies available from University Microfilms.

To Follow the Phoenix (historical drama, 2 acts, 1960). "Commissioned by the Delta Sigma Theta Sorority. In commemoration of the life work and inspiration of Mary Church Terrell (1863–1954)."—Pub. script. Prod. by the Civic Opera House, Chicago, 1960;

dir. by Osceola Archer. Cast included Ellen Holly (as Mary Church Terrell), Frederick O'Neal, Gail Fisher, Novella Nelson, and Robert Graham Brown. Excerpt (1 scene) pub. in *Black Scenes* (Childress, 1971); also in *Standing Room Only* (Dalgon & Bernier, 1977) and *Meeting Challenges* (Nelson, 1980).

A Wreath for Udomo (drama, 3 acts, 1960). Based on the novel by black South African writer *Peter Abramson (1956). About the rise and fall of an African dictator. First prod. at the Karamu Theatre, Cleveland, opening March 8, 1960. This prodn. included African dances and an orig. drum score. Prod. in London in its first professional production at the Lyric-Hammersmith Theatre, opening Nov. 2, 1961. Also prod. twice in Ghana. Unpub. script in the Schomburg Collection.

Still a Brother: Inside the Negro Middle Class (film doc., 90 min., 1968). Shows the black community from an inside point of view. "This film is organized in three main sections: the social and business life of the Negro middle-class; its reactions to an involvement in the civil-rights struggle of the lower-class brothers; and the newer mental revolution which may be signalling a separatist withdrawal from the mainstream of an American society."—*Guide to Films (16 mm.) About Negroes* (Sprecher), p. 56. Winner of the Blue Ribbon Award of the 1969 American Film Festival, and nominated for an Emmy Award—the first black prod. film to receive either honor. Prod. by the author on NET, 1968; repeat showing 1969. Exhibition in Independent Black American Cinema Retrospective, Paris, Summer 1981. Available from Contemporary Films, with offices in San Francisco, Evanston, IL, and New York City.

Together for Days (feature film, full length: screenplay, 1971). Concerns the problems of a black revolutionary who falls in love with a white girl. Based on a screen story by a white writer, previously acquired by the producers, who hired Branch to develop it into a screenplay. Prod. by Olas Corp. (independent film producers), New York, 1971. Filmed on location in Atlanta, GA, 1971; dir. by Robert Schultz, formerly associated with the Negro Ensemble Co. (NEC). Featured players include Clifton Davis, Liz Wright, Lois Chiles, and WOODIE KING, JR.

Afro-American Perspectives (TV doc., 30 programs, 1973/74). On black history and culture. Prod. by the Maryland Center for Public Broadcasting in cooperation with the Univ. of Maryland, 1973–74. In repeated broadcasts over Maryland PBS TV stations, 1974–80, as part of graduate education courses at Univ. of Maryland, College Park. On Howard Univ., Washington, DC, PBS Station Channel 32, Spring and Fall 1981. On WNYC-TV, New York, PBS Station Channel 31, Spring and Fall 1982. Also on other PBS stations across the United States.

Baccalaureate (domestic drama, 3 acts, 1975). A young black female student is torn between the prospect of an exciting but hazardous involvement with a young black activist—a college graduate involved in voter registration in the Deep South—and her more secure and comfortable middle-class aspirations. Prod. at City Hall Theatre, Hamilton, Bermuda, 1975. Unpub. script in the Schomburg Collection.

OTHER PLAYS, DRAMATIC WORKS AND RELATED WRITINGS:
"The Way" (TV drama, 1955). Script for the ABC-TV series by the same title. Prod. by ABC-TV, 1955. **What Is Conscience?** (TV doc., 1955). Script for the "Look Up and Live" series, prod. by CBS-TV, 1955. **Experiment in Black** (musical and dramatic revue, full length, 1955). Prod. at a Harlem cabaret (presumably Club Baron), starring Elwood Smith, Isabel Sanford, Johnny Barracuda, and Irene Senior. **Decision in Hongkong** (doc. film narration, 1956). Prod. by Dynamic Films, New York, 1956. **The Seed**

of Hope (TV drama, 1 hr., 1957). **The Man on Meeting Street** (doc. drama, 1 act, 1960). About Judge J. Waites Waring, for Alpha Kappa Alpha Sorority. Prod. at the New York City banquet, starring Ossie Davis and RUBY DEE. **Gypsy in My Soul** (TV doc., 1964). For "The City" series. Prod. by Educational Broadcasting Corp. (EBC), Channel 13, New York, 1964. **Legacy of a Prophet** (TV doc., 1964). Tribute to W.E.B. Du Bois. Prod. by EBC, Channel 13, New York, 1964. **"Let's Find Out"** (syndicated doc. TV series, 1956). For National Council of Churches. Prod. 1956. **The Rock Cried Out: No Hiding Place** (TV play, 1 hr., 1966). Written for Ossie Davis. **Judgment!** (motion picture outline, 1969). For Harry Belafonte. **Benefit Performance** (motion picture outline, for full length film, 1969). For Universal Studios. Prod. by NBC-TV, 1969. **As If a Mighty River: Paul Robeson** (filmstrip, half hr., 1970). On the famed singer-actor-athlete-activist. For Buckingham Learning Corp., New York, 1970. **Marcus Garvey: Black Messiah** (filmstrip, half hr., 1970). On the early U.S. black leader—father of the Back-to-Africa movement. Distributed by McGraw-Hill, 1970. In continuous use in school systems across the United States. **No Room to Run, No Place to Hide** (doc. TV report, 1972). **Red, White and Black** (motion picture outline, 1972). For Sidney Poitier. **The 20 Billion Dollar Rip-Off** (doc. TV report, 1972). **Adam Clayton Powell Jr.: Young Moses of Harlem** (filmstrip, half hr., 1975) and **Meet Harlem, USA** (filmstrip, half hr., 1976). Both written for and prod. by Afro-American Caravan, New York City Board of Education, in the years indicated.

BRANCHCOMB, SYLVIA WOINGUST (1933–   ), Author, editor, journalist, publisher, freelance photographer, artist, teacher, and lecturer. Born in Baltimore, MD, where she graduated from St. Frances Academy. Currently lives in Yonkers, NY. "A self-disciplined student" of the arts and sciences, she has also studied American legal procedure. Married; the mother of four children. Also foster parent of many other children for 22 years, for the Westchester Co. (NY) Dept. of Social Services, from which she received an appreciation award in 1980. Her artistic and cultural endeavors in Yonkers (too numerous to list in entirety) include art, drama, and creative writing workshop instructor at Runyon Heights Community Center, 1969–72; consultant in the arts and counselor for Getty Square Neighborhood Center, 1969–72; and program coordinator for several Bicentennial cultural arts programs and black history celebrations, 1976. Other activities include designer of greeting cards, artistic consultant, freelance photographer, grants writer, commissioned artist, writer, director, editor, building supervisor, and legal secretary. Author of two books: *Togetherness* (poetry, 1977) and *I Saw the Catalyst Forming* (1980), described as "an analysis of child care and adult behavior." Member of the American Soc. of Composers, Authors and Publishers (ASCAP); National Writers Club, Denver; National Soc. of Poets, Inc. Recipient of numerous awards for cultural and community activities, including plaques, trophies, the Margaret Pratt Boynton Award, and the Yonkers Chamber of Commerce Award. *Address:* The Catalyst Publishing Co., 18 Dearborne St., Yonkers, NY 10710.

PLAYS AND DRAMATIC WORKS:
If the Shoe Fits (drama, 1969). Dramatizes the peer pressure of youngsters and the covert racial disguises of bourgeois blacks. Prod. at Runyon Heights Community Center, Yonkers, NY, 1969/72.

It's Our Time to Speak (comedy, 2 acts, 1969). Subtitled "Rated X-ACTLY for Adults." Described by the author as "a dramatic presentation of the monotonies and antiquities of our educational system depicting our inability to communicate with other nations due to our being limited in linguistics." Prod. by the Getty Square Neighborhood Center, Yonkers, Nov. 1975. Unpub. script in the Hatch-Billops Collection.

Goin' Downtown to See Jesus ("disco-gospel musical" [author], 1978). According to the author, this musical was "written for the goddess of song, world renowned 'Queen Yahna,' " and "explains that Jesus is within 'Love.' " Premiered in Yonkers, Dec. 1978; then on extended tour of Africa, Greece, Egypt, and Germany, where it was twice presented in concert to standing room only crowds at the Berlin Philharmonie. Also presented in France, Italy, Switzerland, Austria, Japan, the Philippines, and Jamaica. Unpub. script on file with Capaquarius Management, Inc., c/o Cecil J. Morgan, Agent, 750 Kappock St., Suite 1015, New York, NY 10463.

BREWER, ROGER, Playwright. *Address:* Route 1, Box 123, Roopville, GA 20170.

PLAYS:

(All prod. in Hartford, CT.) **He Who's Ugly** (children's play in rhyme, 1973). Satirical treatment of prejudices in which the beautiful people of an imaginary town discriminate against the ugly people. **A Little Red Chicken** (protest drama, 2 acts, 1973). An attack upon the evils of commercialized educational systems. **No Grace for a God** (drama, 1 act, 1973). A newly released prisoner believes that he is God and plans to save the world. **What Is a Home Without a Mother?** (domestic drama, 2 acts, 1973). Explores the influence that mothers exert on the lives and destinies of their children.

BREWSTER, BESS E. CODLING (Bess Codling), Playwright. Based in New York City.

PLAYS:

Mama's Crazyhorse Rockin' Again (3 acts, 1974). Prod. Off-Bway by the Clark Center for the Performing Arts (Playwrights' Horizons), May 15, 1974; dir. by I. Allen Lee. Sched. for publication by Amuru Press, New York, 1974, but apparently never pub. **Elegy to X** (1970). Also sched. for publication by Amuru Press, New York, 1974, but apparently never pub. **The Assassin** (early 1970s).

BREWSTER, TOWNSEND (1924–   ), Linguist, poet, librettist, lyricist, playwright, teacher, and critic. Born in Glen Cove, NY. Now resides in Jamaica, NY. Educated at Queens Coll. (now of CCNY) (B.A. in classical languages, 1947) and Columbia Univ. (M.A. in French, 1962). Playwright-in-residence of CCNY, 1969–73, during which time he introduced a course in black theatre to the curriculum. Translated and adapted several operas for "NBC Television Opera," 1950–51, including **Carmen** (1950), **Hansel and Gretel** (1950), **Gianni Schicchi** (1951), and **Pagliacci** (1951). Contributed television, theatre, and book reviews to the trade paper *Show Business* and such periodicals as *Commonwealth, Denver Quarterly,* and *Players* magazine. Theatre critic for the *New York Amsterdam News* and the *Harlem Cultural Review,* of which he is currently editor. His poetry has appeared in *The Oracle, Dasein,* and *Common-*

wealth, and was anthologized in *Today's Negro Voices* (Murphy, 1970). An article on libretto writing was published in *Author and Publisher,* and his translation of the *Cid* Controversy Papers appeared in the anthology *Dramatic Theory and Criticism: The Greeks to Grotowsky* (1974). An alumnus of the New Dramatists Committee and a member of the Outer Critics Circle. His contributions to the theatre include original dramatic works as well as translations and adaptations of plays by foreign authors, many of them black. Board member of the Frank Silvera Writers' Workshop (FSWW) in New York City. Recipient of National Theatre Conf. Playwrights' Fellowship, 1949; Koussavitsky Foundation Librettists' Grant, 1959; *Story* magazine Citation of Honor, 1969; CCNY Research Grant for two programs on black theatre for Denmarks Radio in Copenhagen, 1972. Other honors and awards include William Morris Playwriting Scholarship at the American Theatre Wing, Louise Bogan Memorial Prize in Poetry, Jonathan Swift Award, and NEA Librettist Grant. *Address*— Home: 171–29 103rd Rd., Jamaica, NY 11433. Office: Harlem Cultural Review, 1 W. 125th St., New York, NY 10027. *Agent:* Ronalda Roberts, 1215 Ridge Blvd., Suite 3F, Brooklyn, NY 11209.

GROUPS OF RELATED PLAYS:

"PLEASE DON'T CRY AND SAY NO" (program of 3 one-act plays, 1972). Includes **The Brown Overcoat** (1972). **The Botany Lesson** (1972), and **Please Don't Cry and Say No** (1972). Prod. Off-Bway at the Circle-in-the-Square, New York, Dec. 6–17, 1972, for 15 perfs.

"MATTERS OF LIFE AND . . . " (bill of 3 one-act plays, 1973). Includes **The Ecologists** (1973), **Waiting for Godzilla** (1973), and a third play (title unknown).

"BLACK HIGH" (bill of 3 one-act plays, 1975–77). Includes **Though It's Been Said Many Times, Many Ways** (1975), **Black-Belt Bertram** (1974), and **The Girl Beneath the Tulip Tree** (1971).

"MEMORIALS" (bill of 4 one-act plays, 1975–80s). Includes **Idomeneus** (1976), **The Jade Funerary Suit** (1975), **Praise Song** (1980s), and **This Is the Gloaming of the Age of Aquarius** (1980s).

"VIGNETTES FROM WORLDS I AND III" (bill of 4 one-act plays, 1975–80). Includes **Ebur and Ebony** (1975), **The Fun People** (1980s), **Mood Indigo** (1976), and **There Was Something About Mr. Henderson** (1980s).

"THREE BY ONE" (bill of 3 one-act plays, 1977). Titles of individual plays unknown. Prod. at the Harlem Performance Center, New York, Dec. 8, 1977.

"UP AND DOWN" (bill of 2 one-act plays, 1980s). Includes **Party Down** (1980s) and **Meet Me up the Garden Path** (1980s).

REPRESENTATIVE PLAYS AND DRAMATIC WORKS:

Little Girl, Big Town (revue, 2 acts, 1953). Book and lyrics by Brewster. Music by Jacques Urbent, Mel Waldren, Jack Gottlieb, and Anthony Bruno. Depicts the adventures of a newcomer to Manhattan. Includes a one-act ballet-opera, **Slappy Hooper** (music by Jacques Urbent), which tells how sign painter Slappy paints a billboard of a stove that is so realistic that the poor of the city flock to it to warm themselves. Prod. at Queens College, New York, May 1, 1953.

Singapore Sling (comedy, 1 act, 1955). Girl from Dusty Gulch, TX, breaks into the International Set. Prod. by the Queens Community Theatre, New York, 1955.

The Tower (comic opera, 1 act [5 scenes], 1957). Musical score by Marvin David Levi. Without success, King Solomon attempts to prevent the realization of a prophecy that his daughter will marry the poorest man in the land. Prod. by the Santa Fe Opera, NM, during its initial season, Aug. 2, 1957. Pub. by Boosey & Hawkes, New York, 1958.

The Bougival Vampire (farce, 1 act, 1984). Translation of *Le Vampire de Bougival* by Georges Neveaux. Even now, this vampire may be among us. Prod. at the Univ. of Denver, CO, 1968. Public readings at the Ubu Repertory Theatre, 1984, and Fourth Friday Playwrights, 1985, both in New York.

Chief Rathebe ("Chief Rather-Be") (sketch, 1 act, 1968). Tarzan and Jane invite an African chief to dinner. Prod. at the Univ. of Denver, 1968.

How the West Was Fun (1 act, 1968). Ecological study of life in Surburban Gulch, a frontier town of the Old West. Western Robin Hood undoes a thieving banker. Prod. at the Univ. of Denver, 1968.

The Botany Lesson (comedy, 1 act, 1972). English translation of *Licão de Botânica,* a comedy by *Joaquim Maria Machado de Assis. A clever woman wins a marriage proposal, both for herself and her younger sister, by pretending to be interested in botany. First prod. (in this translation) Off-Bway at the Circle-in-the-Square, Dec. 6–17, 1972, for 15 perfs., on a bill of three one-act plays written or translated by Brewster, under the production title **"PLEASE DON'T CRY AND SAY NO."** [See GROUPS OF RELATED PLAYS above.]

The Brown Overcoat (comedy, 1 act, 1972). English translation of *Le Paletot Brun,* a comedy by the American-born French mulatto playwright *Victor Séjour. Nineteenth century comedy of manners in which a widowed countess, having fallen in love with a young pianist, wishes to drop her current suitor, the baron, without coming out and telling him so. First prod. (in this translation) Off-Bway at the Circle-in-the-Square, Dec. 6–17, 1972, for 15 perfs., on a bill of three one-act plays written or translated by Brewster, under the production title **"PLEASE DON'T CRY AND SAY NO."** [See GROUPS OF RELATED PLAYS above.] Prod. at Armstrong State Coll., 1979. Prod. by the Theatre of Riverside Church, New York, 1979.

Please Don't Cry and Say No (comedy with music, 1 act [5 scenes], 1972). A modern tale of a busy executive's wife having an affair with a teenage man. Includes four songs and orchestral number. Received a Citation of Honor from *Story* magazine in 1969. Prod. Off-Bway at the Circle-in-the-Square, Dec. 6–17, 1972, for 15 perfs., on a bill of three one-act plays written or translated by Brewster, under the production title **"PLEASE DON'T CRY AND SAY NO,"** of which this was the title play. [See GROUPS OF RELATED PLAYS above.]

The Cocktail Sip (comic opera, 1 act, 1973). Libretto by Brewster. Musical score by *Noel Da Costa. A parody of T. S. Eliot's *The Cocktail Party,* with the guests changed to pseudo-sophisticated blacks in Newark, NJ. Pub. by ATSOC Music.

Waiting for Godzilla (comedy, 1 act, c. 1973). One of a bill of three one-act comedies, entitled **"MATTERS OF LIFE AND...."** [See GROUPS OF RELATED PLAYS above.] The Frankenstein Monster, Dracula, Wolf Man, and company rescue a little black boy from some murderous white neighbors. Prod. by the Trent Gough Workshop, New York, 1973.

Amator, Amator (TV comedy, 3 acts, 1973). Modern adaptn. of the classical myth "The Judgment of Paris," set in a contemporary schoolroom, with a handsome Latin and Greek teacher as the counterpart of Paris. He attributes his effect on the ladies to awe of his erudition rather than as a response to his good looks. Prod. by the Trent Gough Workshop, New York, 1973. Finalist in the 1980 Writers Guild of America, East (WGA/ E) Foundation Fellowship for a screenplay or teleplay.

The Ecologists (radio play, 1 act, 1973). One of a bill of three 1 act comedies, entitled **"MATTERS OF LIFE AND. . . . "** [See GROUPS OF RELATED PLAYS above.] In the next century, the ecologists deal with the problem of people pollution. Winner of the Jonathan Swift Award for Satire, Virginia Commonwealth Univ., Richmond, 1979.

Black-Belt Bertram (farce, 1 act, 1974). One of a bill of three one-act plays entitled **"BLACK HIGH."** [See GROUPS OF RELATED PLAYS above.] Wealthy Bertram Butterworth tries to escape paying off on a bet by pretending to be a karate expert, until a real black belt both exposes him and wins his fiancee. Public reading by FSWW at the Martinique Theatre, New York, Oct. 14, 1974. Prod. by the Harlem Performance Center, 1977. Prod. in the Double Image Theatre's Short Play Festival, New York, 1979. Unpub. script in the FSWW Archieves/Schomburg Collection.

Arthur Ashe and I (comedy, 1 act, 1975). A young black college teacher, who is almost browbeaten by two colleagues into letting them take advantage of a black student, rises to the occasion when Arthur Ashe wins at Wimbledon. Prod. by the Theatre of the Riverside Church, New York, June 20, 1979. Unpub. script in the FSWW Archives/ Schomburg Collection.

Though It's Been Said Many Times, Many Ways (comedy, 1 act, 1975). One of a bill of three one act plays entitled **"BLACK HIGH."** [See GROUPS OF RELATED PLAYS above.] Zwarte Piet, Santa Claus's assistant, engineers a jail break using Santa's sleigh. Public reading by FSWW, at the Harlem Performance Center, New York, Dec. 22, 1976. Unpub. script may be in the FSWW Archives/Schomburg Collection.

The Cable (musical comedy, 5 acts, 1975). Musical adaptn. of the *Rudens* of Plautus, the only Roman comedy to take place in Africa. A long-lost daughter, who has fallen into the clutches of a pimp, finds her parents and weds her suitor. Pub. by Continental Play Service, New York, 1975.

The Jade Funerary Suit (comedy, 1 act, 1975). One of a bill of three one-act plays entitled **"MEMORIALS."** [See GROUPS OF RELATED PLAYS above.] An impoverished black family steals an ancient Chinese burial suit for their father's interment. Public reading by FSWW, New York. Unpub. script in the FSWW Archives/Schomburg Collection.

Mood Indigo (verse play, 1 act, 1976). One of a bill of four one-act plays entitled **VIGNETTES FROM WORLDS I AND III."** [See GROUPS OF RELATED PLAYS above.] A black bishop is doomed to disappointment in his hopes that his way of life will win him the acclaim accorded to the great Paul Robeson. Public reading by FSWW, New York. Unpub. script may be in the FSWW Archives/Schomburg Collection.

The Girl Beneath the Tulip Tree (comedy, 1 act, 1977). One of a bill of three one-act plays entitled *"BLACK HIGH."* [See GROUPS OF RELATED PLAYS above.] A beautiful woman inspires a young black lawyer to immigrate with her to Ghana. Prod. at the Harlem Performance Center, New York, Dec. 8, 1977.

The Complete Works of Kalkbrenner (comedy, 3 acts, 1970s). A young novelist decides that the surest way to succeed is by not really trying; however, he lacks the makings of a true "heel." Prod. at the Thirteenth St. Theatre, New York, 1970s.

The Liar (comedy, full length, 1984). Verse translation of Pierre Corneille's comedy *Le Menteur*. Dorante's superior imagination embroiders reality, gets him into trouble, but finally saves the day. First prod. (in this translation) by Apollo Drama Co., opening

March 29, 1984, at the Theatre of the Greek Orthodox Church, 91st St. and West End
Ave., New York.

Monsieur Thôgô-Gnini (comedy, 6 tableaux, 1986). Translation of the comedy by
Bernard Binlin Dadie. The cane-bearer of an African king becomes a dictator. Commis-
sioned by Ubu Repertory Theatre for 1986 prodn. Prod. at a Festival of Francophone
Plays by African and Caribbean Authors, New York City, Feb. 21, 1986; dir. by Billie
Allen.

OTHER PLAYS AND DRAMATIC WORKS:

The Choreography of Love (comic opera, 1 act, 1946). Libretto by Brewster. Musical
score by Mitzi Goldreyer. Two shy young persons in Central Park, who are unable to
bring themselves to speak, finally communicate through dance. Prod. at Queens Coll.,
New York, c. 1945. Broadcast over WYNC-Radio, New York, Feb. 16, 1946. **Egmont**
(adaptn., 1947). Condensation of Goethe's tragedy for orchestral performance of Bee-
thoven's music. Prod. at the Goethe Festival of the Berkshire Music Center, Tanglewood,
MA, July 29, 1947. **Letter and Lottery** (harlequinade, 1 act, 1948). Translation of *Les
Deux Billets* by Jean-Pierre Claris de Florian. Harlequin's sweetheart, Ricciolina, regains
the winning lottery ticket that Scapino has stolen from him. Presented by the Queens
Coll. Community Theatre, New York, Fall 1948. [See also **The Reversed Deception**
(1950) below.] **Andromeda** (musical, full length [1 long act], 1949). Book and lyrics
by Brewster. Lyric comedy dramatizing the myth of rescue of the Aethiopian princess
Andromeda by Perseus. The first of a trio of musicals which won for the author a National
Theatre Conf. Playwrights' Fellowship, 1949. **Look Eastward** (musical, 2 acts, 1949).
Lyric comedy about the fund-raising efforts of two men from one of the emerging nations.
The second of a trio of musicals which won for the author a National Theatre Conf.
Playwrights' Fellowship, 1949. **Rough and Ready** (lyric comedy, 2 acts, 1949). Book
and lyrics by Brewster. About a black student who writes for both of two inimical
publications on a college campus. The third of a trio of musicals which won for the
author a National Theatre Conf. Playwrights' Fellowship, 1949. **The Reversed Deception**
(comic opera, 1 act, 1950). Libretto by Brewster. Harlequin loses a winning lottery ticket
but gets it back through trickery. Apparently based on Brewster's **Letter and Lottery**
(1948), which was a translation of *Les Deux Billets* of Jean-Pierre Claris de Florian.
Carmen (translation of the Bizet opera, 1950). Broadcast by the NBC Television Opera,
1950. Repeated as the first opera telecast in compatible color, 1953, and as part of the
Highlights of Opera Historical Educational Television Series, 1957. **Hansel and Gretel**
(trans. of the Humperdinck opera, 1950). Broadcast by NBC Television Opera, 1950.
Gianni Schicchi (trans. of the Puccini opera, 1951). Broadcast by the NBC Television
Opera, 1951. Subsequently sung by the Metropolitan Opera Co. **Pagliacci** (trans. of the
Leoncavallo opera, 1951). Broadcast by the NBC Television Opera, 1951. **Medora and
the Rustics** (comic opera, 2 acts, 1954). Libretto by Brewster. "A fashionable lady loses
the man of her choice because, during her stay in Paris, he, along with the rest of her
set, has succumbed to the craze for folksey things."—Author, as quoted in *Black Playwrights, 1823–1977* (Hatch & Abdullah, 1977), p. 26. **Oh, What a Beautiful City!**
(verse comedy, 2 acts, 1954). By passing an examination, a committee chosen by the
mayor of New York City can win Heaven for all humanity. **Mowgli** (parody of Kipling's
Jungle Book, 1948). Prod. at the Univ. of Denver, CO., 1968. **What Are Friends For?**
(lyric comedy, 2 acts, 1968). Adapt. from Eugène Scribe's *La Camaraderie*. With the
help of friends, a second-choice candidate wins a federal arts grant, edging out a black

who is favored to win. **Harlequinades for Mourners** (4 acts, 1970). Play by *Shirley Guy. Lyrics by Brewster. Music by Basheer Qadar. Prod. Off-Bway at the New Theatre, 1970. **Pinter's Revue Sketches** (lyrics only, 1970). Play by Harold Pinter. Music by William Feingold. The song "Squaw Winter," of which Brewster wrote the lyrics, was sung between the Pinter sketches. Prod. by the Weathervane Theatre, Akron, OH, opening Aug. 8, 1970. **Lady Plum Blossom** (children's musical, 2 acts, 1972). Book by Madeline Davidson. Lyrics by Brewster. Musical score by Mark Ollinger. Prod. by Oregon State Univ., Corvallis, April 14, 1972. Pub. by Modern Theatre for Youth, Inc., Manhattan, KS, 1973. **The Main Chance Rag** (comedy, 1 act, 1972). Adapt. from *La Question d'argent* by French mulatto playwright *Alexandre Dumas fils. Despite opposition from some middle-class blacks, a young man from the streets marries the girl he loves. **The Adventurous Petticoat** (opera, 1 act, 1974). Libretto by Brewster. An adventurous woman helps to make Paul Revere's famous ride possible, thus demonstrating that at least one woman did take an active part in the American Revolution. **Johnny Renaissance** (lyric comedy, 1 act, 1974). Concept musical which extolls the achievements of a contemporary Renaissance man. **Ebur and Ebony** (comedy, 1 act, 1975). One of a bill of four one-act comedies entitled **"VIGNETTES FROM WORLDS I AND III."** [See GROUPS OF RELATED PLAYS above.] The patron saint of actors, with the help of some of the great actor-characters of dramatic literature, tries to write a play devoid of racial strife, but he is opposed in his efforts by Beelzebub. **The Finger Hole in the River** (musical, 1 act, 1975). Dramatizes the proverb that no one is indispensable. **Oh, My Pretty Quintroon** (jazz opera, 1975). Libretto by Brewster. Music by SAM RIVERS. Prod. by the Harlem Cultural Center, New York, 1975. **The Palm Leaf Boogie** (comedy, 1 act, 1975). Adapt. from *L'Invitation à la valse* by French mulatto playwright *Alexandre Dumas père. Having sent her young lover away while her husband was still alive, an attractive widow meets him again, after he has returned from fighting in Angola, and barely recognizes him. **To See the World in a Drop of Brine** (verse-comedy, 1 act, 1975). The two rulers of the Atlantic and Pacific oceans are involved in a dispute over their respective territories, and threaten to flood the Earth. **The Anonymous Lover** (opera, 2 acts, 1976). Translation of *Amant anonyme,* a comic opera by the eighteenth century black composer *Joseph Boulogne (Chevalier de Saint-Georges), under a grant from the Harlem Cultural Council. Prod. at Symphony Space, New York, 1976. **Idomeneus** (verse comedy, 1 act, 1976). One of a bill of four one-act plays entitled **"MEMORIALS."** (See GROUPS OF RELATED PLAYS above.) A black winner of the Nobel Prize for Literature regrets the toll that success has taken on his personal life. **Thirteen Ways of Looking at Merle** (1976). A beautiful black girl in the subway is unconsciously responsible for a variety of reactions from those who observe her. **Chocolat Volatil** (bill of 3 one-act lyric comedies, full length, 1977). Updated translations/for black actors of three French comedies of the eighteenth, nineteenth, and twentieth centuries. Includes **The Harlequin Twins,** from *Les Jumeaux de Bergame* by Jean-Pierre Claris de Florian; **Hot Love in Harlem,** from *Amour africaine* by Prosper Mérimée; and **No More Ego Tripping,** from *Modestie!* by Paul Hervieu. Written on a National Endowment for the Arts (NEA) Grant, 1977. **Arrangement in Rose and Silver** (comedy, 1 act, 1970s). An artist succeeds in convincing his new sweetheart that painting is not an impractical field. **I Was a Teeny Swodd** (sketch, 1 act, 1970s). Teenage Vampire, Werewolf, and Frankenstein form a rock group headed by the teenage Demon Barber of Fleet Street. **Mascara and Confetti** (revue, 2 acts, 1970s). On the theme of the modern woman. **A Threnody for the Newly Born** (opera libretto, 1 act, 1970s). A dialogue between Medea and Jason just after the birth of their first son. **The Washerwoman** (children's musical, 1 act, 1970s). Adapt. from one of the sketches in Lafcadio Hearn's *Two Years in the French West Indies*. Cinderella story of a poor girl who marries a successful young man with the help of some washerwomen on a Caribbean island. **Queen Olympia** (miniature opera libretto, 1 act, 1984). Looking back on the year 1984, a devotee of George Orwell finds that the Olympics prevented the author's predictions from coming true. **à** (1 act, 1980s). A companion piece to **On the Case,** cited below. Adaptn. of *La Dame aux jambes d'azur* by Marc Michel and Eugène Labiche. An actor-turned-playwright rehearses his drama about Thomas à Becket. **Ananias, Jr.** (lyric comedy for children, 2 acts, 1980s). Conflation of two children's plays by the Comtesse de Ségur. Adults scandalized by a little boy's fanciful fabrications must face up to their own dishonesty. **Bird Music** (verse comedy, 1 act, 1980s). Through the words of a ballad, parents learn that their dead son has not, as they had feared, gone down in history as a traitor. **Clytie Belle** (sketch, 1 act, 1980s). Clytemnestra, Penelope, Cassandra, Electra, Agamemnon, et al. in a *Gone with the Wind* setting. **Cute Root** (comic opera, 1 act, 1980s). A young man wins the woman he loves despite her preference for a visiting African. Commissioned by the Harlem Opera Society. **The Dianists** (comic opera libretto, 3 acts, 1980s). Conflation of the myths of Daphne and Endymion. **Experimental Life Unit** (sketch, 1 act, 1980s). Parody of AMIRI BARAKA's *Experimental Death Unit #1*. **The Fun People** (comedy, 1 act, 1980s). One of a bill of four one-act plays entitled **"VIGNETTES FROM WORLDS I AND III."** [See GROUPS OF RELATED PLAYS above.] A young man must conceal from the puritanical step-father of his fiancee an affair he has not yet had the heart to break off. **Hero and Leander** (monologue, 1 act, 1980s). Translation of the monologue by Jean-Pierre Claris de Florian. After waiting for Leander, Hero commits suicide when, at dawn, she sees his corpse in the waves. **Incomputability** (miniature opera, 1 act, 1980s). Score by Grenoldo. Satire of computerized dating. **Inklings** (revue, 2 acts, 1980s). **Mr. Macdougall** (TV comedy, 2 acts, 1980s). A patient tries to take advantage of the uniformity of hospital garb to pass himself off as a man of wealth and influence. **Meet Me up the Garden Path** (lyric comedy, 1 act, 1980s). One of a bill of two one-act plays entitled **"UP AND DOWN."** [See GROUPS OF RELATED PLAYS above.] Adaptn. of Jean Regnard's *Attendez-moi sous l'orme*. Resigned to settling for a wealthy match, a fortune hunter, to his astonishment, finds love as well. **The Midwife of Us All** (1 act, 1980s). Gertrude Stein parody/tribute subtitled "A Landscape in Memory of Isobel Wentworth." **Nefertiti** (TV fantasy, 1 act, 1980s). Adaptn. of "Omphale," a short story by Théophile Gautier. An actor learns about life and love from a painting of Nefertiti. **No Place for a Lady** (revue, 2 acts, 1980s). **Of Angels and Donkeys** (comic opera libretto, 1 act, 1980s). Dramatization of the Biblical story of Balaam. Commissioned by Israeli Music Publications. **On the Case** (comedy, 2 acts, 1980s). Translation of the comedy *Une Cause sans effet* by Léon Laleau and Georges N. Léger. A companion piece to **à,** cited above. A clientless lawyer cannot resist taking on the divorce case of his fiancee's sister. **The One-Man Greatest Show on Earth** (TV play, 3 acts, 1980s). The story of black cowboy Isom Dart. **Party Down** (lyric comedy, 1 act, 1980s). One of a bill of two one-act plays entitled **"UP AND DOWN."** [See GROUPS OF RELATED PLAYS above.] Adaptn. of Jean Regnard's *Le Bal*. Manipulative father meets his match in the superstar colleague of his daughters' suitors. **Polyxo** (opera libretto, 1 act, 1980s). Polyxo avenges her husband's death in the Trojan War by murdering Helen. **Praise Song** (verse comedy, 1 act, 1980s). One of a bill of four one-act plays entitled **"MEMORI-ALS."** [See GROUPS OF RELATED PLAYS above.] After being emancipated, a black mother becomes reunited with all her children though they had been sold off in various parts of the country. **Reprieves** (comic opera libretto, 2 acts, 1980s). Adapt. from Charles Lamb's farce, *The Pawnbroker's Daughter*. After being falsely arrested, a man feels himself to be too much degraded to marry his fiancee until she herself has also been falsely arrested. **Sexy Girl** (sketch, 1 act, 1980s). Mae West as Cinderella. **Sight Unseen** (children's opera libretto, 2 acts, 1980s). Adapt. from Hans Christian Andersen's "The Emperor's New Clothes." **Sometimes I Feel Like an Eagle in the Air** (comedy, 1 act, 1980s). A quiet, harmless husband views himself as a dangerous rake. **Spaced Out** (film short, 1980s). Alien enables little boy to play on his big brother's basketball team. **The Tip of the Ice Cube** (sketch, 1 act, 1980s). Ernest Hemingway parody. **La Tragedie de Rigoletto** (sketch, 1 act, 1980s). Parody of the Verdi opera. **There Was Something About Mr. Henderson** (comedy, 1 act, 1980s). One of a bill of four one-act plays entitled **"VIGNETTES FROM WORLDS I AND III."** [See GROUPS OF RELATED PLAYS above.] A black leader, faced with mutual attraction to a white woman, sets out to prove to her that other blacks are equally eligible. **This Is the Gloaming of the Age of Aquarius** (comedy, 1 act, 1980s). One of a bill of four one-act plays entitled **"MEMORIALS."** [See GROUPS OF RELATED PLAYS above.] Three blacks find their way back to their sixties ideals.

BROOKS, CHARLOTTE KENDRICK, Author, educator, scriptwriter. For many years supervisor of public schools, Washington, DC. During the 1960s, she was a teacher at Banneker Jr. H.S. and was a frequent contributor to the *Negro History Bulletin*. More recently, a member of the faculty of the American Univ. in Washington and a member of the advisory board of *Black American Literature Forum*.

PLAY:
Firm Foundations (radio skit for Negro History Week, 1954). Prod. as part of the "Americans All" program over Radio Station WOOK, Washington, DC, Feb. 7, 1954. Pub. in *Negro History Bulletin*, March 1954, pp. 128–31.

BROOME, BARBARA CUMMINGS, Playwright. Theatre director of the International Black Writers Conf. (IBWC), Chicago.

PLAY:
The Fat Sisters (comedy, 1 act, 1976). About weight watchers. Presented at the Fourth Annual IBWC, Chicago, 1976, where it won the June Clemmons Drama Award. **Millie Brown** (1977). Prod. in Chicago, June 1977, presumably at the Fifth Annual IBWC.

BROWN, AARION, Playwright. Based in New York City.

PLAY:
Onica Mitchell Is in Double Jeopardy: She's Black and Female . . . (AND SHE HATES EVERYBODY?). A black girl struggles to offset the double jeopardy stated in the title, while at the same time maintaining her individuality. Prod. at the Nat Horne Theatre, New York, 1977.

BROWN, BEVERLY S., Playwright.

PLAY:

The Snake Chief (drama, 1 act, [2 scenes], 1971). Adapt. from South African myths and legends. Pub. in *Negro History Bulletin,* March 1971, pp. 70–71.

BROWN, CECIL M., Playwright, author, and teacher. Born in Bolton, NC. Educated at Columbia Univ. (B.A., 1966) and the Univ. of Chicago (M.A., 1967). Taught English at the Univ. of Illinois, the Univ. of California/Berkeley, and Merritt Coll. in Oakland. His plays have been produced by the Grassroots Experimental Group in San Francisco. Author of two novels: *The Life and Loves of Mr. Jiveass Nigger* (1970) and *Days Without Weather* (1982). His criticism has appeared in *Evergreen Review, Partisan Review, Kenyon Review,* and *Black World.*

PLAYS AND DRAMATIC WORKS:

Gila Monster (1 act, 1969). Prod. by the Grassroots Experimental Group, at the Merritt Coll. Jazz Festival, Oakland, March 1969. Reportedly made into a film, 1972. **Real Nigger** (1 act, 1969). Subtitled "On the Minstrel Revolution." Prod. by the Grassroots Experimental Group, at the Merritt Coll. Jazz Festival, Oakland, March 1969. **The African Shades** (comedy, 1 act, 1972). A young black theatrical producer gets the best of a white producer of black exploitation films. Apparently presented at the International Film Festival at Cannes, 1968. Pub. in *Yardbird Reader* (Reed, 1972). **Our Sisters Are Pregnant** (1 act, 1973). Prod. by the Grassroots Experimental Group, at Julian Theatre, San Francisco, April 1972. Presented at the Petreto Hill Neighborhood House, San Francisco, 1973. **Which Way Is Up?** (feature film, full length: screenplay, 1977). Coauthor, with RICHARD PRYOR. Americanized version of the Italian film *The Seduction of Mimi* (1974). Prod. 1977; dir. by Michael Schultz, starring Richard Pryor.

BROWN, CLAUDETTE, Playwright. Based in New York City, where she is associated with the Frank Silvera Writers' Workshop (FSWW) and the West End Theatre. Received the B.A. in political science from Howard Univ., 1942, and also took graduate courses in history at Howard, 1973–74; received the M.A. in American history from the Univ. of Wisconsin at Madison, 1977. *Address:* 961 St. Nicholas Ave. #37, New York, NY 10032.

REPRESENTATIVE PLAYS AND DRAMATIC WORKS:

Conversations with a Friend (four-character play, 1983). Focuses on the relationships and the emotional turmoil which men and women accept in love relationships. Major focus surrounds two women friends—one's descent into hell, and the other's ascent toward maturity. Prod. Off-Off-Bway, at the West End Theatre, New York, 1983.

Ties That Bind (family drama, 2 acts [1 hr., 45 min.], 1984–85). // Also available in a second version entitled **Ties** (2 acts [2 hrs., 15 min.], 1984–85). About the preparations for a family reunion and cementing the familial bonds between parents and adult children. Prod. Off-Off-Bway at the West End Theatre, opening Nov. 24, 1984.

The Long Oppression (2 acts, 1986). Concerns the civil rights movement coming to a small southern town and the decisions everyone has to make about the price of freedom and dignity in their lives. Sched. to be read at NYU's Summer Writers' Conf., July 1986.

Something of Myself (one-woman show, full length, 1986). A commissioned play. Traces the growing consciousness of an older woman to the growing civil rights movement and the need for her continued political growth and involvement. Opens in 1954 and advances to the March on Washington in Aug. 1963. Sched. for prodn. in Sept. 1986.

OTHER PLAYS AND DRAMATIC WORKS:
(All pre-1986:) **All My Earthly Goods** (musical book). The story of young mothers who fight a baby-food corporate conglomerate which is manufacturing harmful products. **Don Giovanni** (musical adaptn. of Mozart's opera: book only, 2 acts). For six characters and a dance troupe. **Bearing Witness** (drama, 1 act). The interaction of two women in prison—one a political prisoner, the other a murder and robbery suspect. Deals with their concessions to the penal system while trying to retain their integrity. **Animal Murders** (one-character drama, 1 act). A mother's murder of her children, using an animal characterization to tell the story. The play portrays the mother as an animal gone wild who kills her own offspring.

BROWN, FRANK LONDON (1927–1962), Novelist, poet, essayist, short-story writer, and playwright. Born in Kansas City, MO. Grew up in Chicago, IL. Assoc. editor of *Ebony* magazine. Director of Union Research Center, Univ. of Chicago. Author of two novels: *Trumbull Park* (1959) and *The Myth Makers* (1969). Recipient of a John Hay Whitney Foundation Award for Creative Writing.

PLAY:
Short Ribs (late 1950s). Prod. by the Penthouse Players, Chicago, during the late 1950s.

BROWN, GERARD, Playwright. Born in Asbury Park, NJ. Now based in New York City. Graduated from Howard Univ., 1975, where he studied playwriting under JOHN O. KILLENS and majored in communications. Worked for a few months as a TV engineer at WNJU, Channel 47, NJ.

PLAYS:
[Two One Act Plays] (titles unknown, 1970s). Written while a student at Howard Univ. Prod. by the DC Black Repertory Co., Washington, DC, mid-1970s. **Jonin'** ("comedic drama," full length, 1982). Described by Joyce N. Caldwell in the *New York Amsterdam News* (June 3, 1984) as a "sensitive portrait of Black college frat life," dealing "with one of the traditional activities, pledging, which teaches the student how to 'play the game' by being responsible for his actions and taking charge of his life." The title "is a southern colloquialism for 'playing the dozens.' "—Ibid. First prod. by the Renaissance Drama Workshop at Tiffany's, 87–20 Parsons Ave., Long Island, NY, Sept.-Oct. 1982; dir. by Randy Frazier. Prod. as an Equity Showcase Production at the American Theatre of Actors, 314 W. 54th St., New York City, April 27–May 20, 1984; dir. by Noble Lee Lester. Prod. at the Paul Robeson Theatre, Brooklyn, New York, June 2–19, 1984. **Together for Life** (drama, c. 1982).

BROWN, JAMES NELSON, Playwright. Associated with Florida A. & M. Coll. (now Univ.) during the 1950s.

PLAYS:
The Barren Heritage (1 act, 1946). Presented by Florida A. & M. Coll., at the Tenth Annual Conf. of the Southern. Assn. of Dramatic and Speech Arts (SADSA), held at Tennessee A. & I. State Univ., Nashville, April 10, 1946. **Tomorrow Was Yesterday** (drama, 9 scenes, 1966). Pub. by Exposition Press, Hicksville, NY, 1966.

BROWN, LENNOX (John) (1934–   ), International prizewinning playwright, journalist, and poet. Born in Trinidad. Lived for many years in Toronto. In the late 1970s, he resided in the United States and taught at the Univ. of Hartford (CT) and CUNY. Educated at St. Mary's Coll. in Trinidad (Senior Cambridge Certificate), the Univ. of Western Ontario (B.A., 1961), and the Univ. of Toronto (M.A., 1969). Worked as a civil servant and freelance journalist in Trinidad; as a journalist and reporter for a number of Canadian newspapers and magazines, 1956–63; and as editor-producer for the Canadian Broadcasting Corp. (CBC) and the National Network Radio News, 1963–67. Has had numerous stage, radio, and TV productions of his plays in Canada, the United States, the Netherlands, and the Caribbean. His poetry has been published in numerous periodicals in Canada and London. Memberships include the Ebo Soc. for Black Art, Black Arts of Canada, National Black Coalition of Canada, Canadian Newspaper and Wireless Guild, Canadian Assn. of Radio and Television Actors' and Writers' Assn. Recipient of the Minnesota Mining and Manufacturing Undergraduate Fellowship, 1959; Canada Council Short Term Promising Artist Grant, 1969; Canada Council Short Term Artist Grant, 1970. Four-time winner in the Canadian National One-Act Playwriting Competition, Ottawa, 1965, 1966, 1967, and 1968—the first playwright in the history of the competition to win prizes in four consecutive years; first prize winner in the National Univ. Drama League Competition, 1969; runner-up for the Norma Epstein National Creative Award, Univ. of Toronto, 1969; runner-up for the Schubert Fellowship, Univ. of Michigan Theatre School, 1970; winner of the Canada Council Arts Bursary Contest, 1970; winner of the Eugene O'Neill Memorial Playwriting Competition, 1971. *Address:* 100 West 94th St. #16D, New York, NY 10025.

COLLECTION:
THE TWILIGHT DINNER AND OTHER PLAYS. Talonbooks, Canada, 1981. Contains **The Twilight Dinner** (1977), **Fog Drifts in the Spring** (1970), and **The Blood Promise of a Shopping Plaza** (1980).

GROUPS OF RELATED PLAYS:
"**THE CRYSTAL TREE**" (group of three plays, 1970/71). Includes **Fog Drifts in the Spring** (1979), **Summer Screen** (1971), and **Throne in the Autumn Room** (1970).

Brown states that he is writing "two cycles of plays, [more than] twenty of which have already been completed." One cycle, "**BEHIND THE BRIDGE**," deals with the black mythological Consciousness in the Caribbean." The other, "**WEST INDIAN WINTER**," deals "with the Consciousness in North America and Europe."—*Black American Writers* (Rush, Myers, & Arata, 1976), pp. 108–9. No attempt has been made in this entry to identify which of Brown's plays belong to each of these cycles.

REPRESENTATIVE PLAYS AND DRAMATIC WORKS:

The Captive // Orig. title and present subtitle: **Snow Dark Sunday** (1 act, 1965). A white southerner is held captive by a group of black American militants. Winner of the Birks Medal, Canadian National One-Act Play Competition, Ottawa, 1965. Prod. at the Museum Theatre, Toronto, 1965. Pub. in *Ottawa Little Theatre, Ranking Play Series 2, Catalog No. 43,* Sept. 1965.

The Meeting (1 act, 1965). Confrontation between a husband and his unfaithful wife. Winner of the Dorothy White Award, Canadian National One-Act Play Competition, Ottawa. Prod. by CBC Television, March 1969. Prod. at the Ontario Drama Festival and the Alberta Drama Festival. Prod. at the Dutch Centre for Amateur Theatre, the Netherlands, Feb. 1972. Prod. by Trinidad and Tobago Television. Pub. in *Ottawa Little Theatre, Ranking Play Series 2, Catalog No. 56,* Oct. 1966, and in *Performing Arts of Canada,* Winter 1970.

Night Sun (1 act, 1967). Winner of the Birks Medal, Canadian National One-Act Play Competition, Ottawa, 1967.

Jour Ouvert ("Daybreak") // Alternate title: **I Have to Call My Father** (1 act, 1968). Confrontation between a sensitive black man and a neurotic white woman on New Year's Eve. Winner of the Birks Medal in the Canadian National One-Act Play Competition, Ottawa, 1968. Under its alternate title, it won first prize in the Canadian National Univ. Drama League Competition, 1969. Pub. in *Ottawa Little Theatre, Ranking Play Series 2, Catalog No. 56,* Oct. 1966, and in *Drama and Theatre* (Fredonia State Univ., NY), Winter 1969–70, pp. 118–30.

The Night Class (2 acts, 1969). Morality drama in which Catholic priests and students are trapped by a storm in a night class, forcing them to come to grips with their views on death and suicide. Runner-up for the Norma Epstein National Creative Writing Award, Univ. of Toronto, 1969.

Fog Drifts in the Spring (1 act, 1970). One of a group of three related plays called **"THE CRYSTAL TREE"** [see GROUPS OF RELATED PLAYS above]. An encounter between a West Indian and an American in Paris. Prod. by the Caribbean-American Repertory Theatre, at the Billie Holiday Theatre, Brooklyn, Feb. 1976. Also prod. by the Trinidad Theatre Workshop; by the IRT Loft Theatre; and by the El Monte Theatre. Pub. in the author's *THE TWILIGHT DINNER AND OTHER PLAYS.*

Song of the Spear (radio drama, 2 acts, 1970). Concerns a friendship between a black Ghanaian and a black West Indian, which is finally destroyed by a white woman. Prod. on CBC Radio, Sept. 1970. Prod. on Radio 610, Trinidad, 1973.

Throne in the Autumn Room (3 acts, 1970). The second of a group of related plays called **"THE CRYSTAL TREE"** [see GROUPS OF RELATED PLAYS above]. About problems facing black West Indians in Toronto. Prod. by CBC Radio, Aug. 1971; by Radio 610, Trinidad, 1972; by the Trinidad Theatre Workshop, Jan. 1973; and by the Keskidee Theatre, London, 1979.

The Winti Train ("The Winter Train") (2 acts, 1970). About "six people aboard a train bound for Harlem and a Black World Festival, when it is learned that . . . two Festival members plan to blow up the train."—*New York Amsterdam News,* May 19, 1977. Winner of the Humanitarian Art Award, Hartford, CT, 1974. First prod. at the Billie Holiday Theatre, Brooklyn, opening March 12, 1977; dir. by GLENDA DICKERSON. Prod. by the Univ. of Hartford (CT). Sched. for pub. in *Black Drama* (a Simon & Schuster anthology), which was reportedly in progress during the mid-1970s.

Prodigal in Black Stone (2 acts, 1971). The return of a prodigal West Indian to his home after his father's death, and his confrontation with his embittered mother. Winner of the Eugene O'Neill Memorial Playwriting National Competition, 1971. Prod. as a staged reading by the Playwrights Conf. of the Eugene O'Neill Theatre Center, Waterford, CT, opening July 18, 1972, for 2 perfs.

A Ballet Behind the Bridge (drama, 2 acts, 1972). A revelation of the cultural, racial, and family factions which influence political and revolutionary activity in Trinidad. Prod. by CBC Television, Jan. 1971. Prod. by the Negro Ensemble Co. (NEC), at St. Marks Playhouse, New York, opening March 7, 1972, for 39 perfs.; dir. by DOUGLAS TURNER WARD. Cast included David Downing, Frances Foster, ADOLPH CAESAR, and Esther Rolle. Prod. by the Theatre Guild of Guyana.

The Trinity of Four (1 act, 1974). About a black slave rebellion in the West Indies in 1700. Prod. by the Caribbean American Repertory Theatre, at the Billie Holiday Theatre, Feb. 1976. Also prod. by the IRT Loft Theatre, New York, Dec. 1975. Pub. in *Caribbean Rhythms: The Emerging English Literature of the West Indies* (Livingstone, 1974).

Devil Mas' ("Devil Mass"). Ritualistic play which deals with the mystical and occult aspects of Caribbean life, set in a carnival in Trinidad. First broadcast on radio by Trinidad Theatre Workshop. Prod. by Karamu House, Cleveland, Oct. 1976, and by Western State Univ. (IL). Pub. in *Kuntu Drama* (Harrison, 1974).

The Twilight Dinner (drama, 1 act, 1977). Two former black militants, now middle-aged, reminisce about their college days and the events that have transpired since that time. Prod. at the IRT Loft Theatre, New York, Feb. 1977. Also prod. at the Harlem Performance Center, New York. Prod. by the Frank Silvera Writers' Workshop, as part of the Writers/Directors Project Series, at the Theatre of the Open Eye, New York, Nov. 2–6, 1977; dir. by Lincia Colombi. Prod. by NEC, at St. Marks Playhouse, April 14–May 14, 1978, for 27 perfs.; dir. by Douglas Turner Ward. Pub. in the author's *THE TWILIGHT DINNER AND OTHER PLAYS*.

The Blood Promise of a Shopping Plaza (drama, 1980). Concerns a ritualistic murder in a shopping plaza by a white teenager who thinks he is black. Pub. in the author's *THE TWILIGHT DINNER AND OTHER PLAYS*.

OTHER PLAYS AND DRAMATIC WORKS:
A Ballet in a Bear Pit (2 acts, 1966). Concerns a Caribbean immigrant couple living in North America (United States or Canada) who are determined, in spite of obstacles, to make a success of their lives according to white Protestant standards. **The Burning Sky** (1 act, 1966). **Fire for an Ice Age** (1 act, 1967). Prod. at the Univ. of Toronto, 1968. **Saturday's Druid** (radio play, 1 act, 1969). Prod. by CBC Radio, March 1969. **Moon in the Mirror** (1 act, 1969). **The Voyage Tonight** (1967). Runner-up for the Schubert Fellowship, Univ. of Michigan, 1970. **Wine in the Winter** (radio play, 1 act, 1971). Prod. by the Trinidad Theatre Workshop, on Radio 610, Trinidad, March 1972. **Summer Screen** (1971). The third of a group of related plays called **"THE CRYSTAL TREE"** [see GROUPS OF RELATED PLAYS above.] **A Communion at Dark Sun** (3 acts, 1973). **Ritual of the Shanti Golden Stool** (TV play, 1972). First prod. on Trinidad and Tobago Television, Aug. 1976. **The Conversion** (2 acts, 1975). **A Procession from La Basse** (2 acts, 1975). **Sisterhood of a Spring Night** (2 acts, 1974). A trio of black women, living in Canada, are disappointed in their search for satisfactory black male companionship. Prod. at Queens Coll. Theatre, New York, Oct. 1974. **Home Is a**

Long Way (radio/TV script, 1974). A West Indian immigrant tries to achieve success in the white society of Canada. [Cf. **A Ballet in a Bear Pit** (1966) above.] **A Last Dance in the Sun** (TV play, 2 acts, 1975). After an absence of several years, a group of West Indians returns to an island which has supposedly achieved its independence. Prod. on Trinidad and Tobago Television, Aug. 1975. **Three Colors of a Dream Quartet** (1 act, 1975). **A Clean Sweep** (TV play, 1976). Explores the problem of employment in the multiracial society of the West Indies. Prod. on Trinidad and Tobago Television, Aug. 1976. **The Gold Coast of Times Square** (1 act, 1976). **Becoming Persons** (2 acts, 1970s). **The Scent of Incense** (radio play, 1970s). (Also cited as **This Scent of Incense.**) Prod. by CBC Radio, early 1970s.

BROWN, OSCAR, JR. (1926–   ), Composer, singer, dancer, lyricist, producer, and playwright. Considered a multitalented show business phenomenon. Born in Chicago, IL. Graduated from Howard Univ. Began his theatrical career as a child actor, poet, and songwriter. Came to national attention in 1961 when his playwriting efforts gained the interest of Dave Garroway (the original "Today Show" TV host), playwright LORRAINE HANSBERRY, and her husband Robert Nemiroff. With their help, he secured the financial backing needed to produce his first musical, **Kicks & Company** (1961). Since 1961 he has written, produced, and directed more than eight additional musicals, in which he also costarred with his wife and on-stage partner, choreographer-singer Jean Pace, sister of actress Judy Pace. Brown's musical compositions include "Brown Baby" (sung by Mahalia Jackson), "Dat Der," "Muffled Drums," and "Work Song" (written with NAT ADDERLEY). His recordings include *Fresh, Brother Where Are You?, Moving On* (recorded by Atlantic), and *Between Heaven and Hell* (recorded by Columbia). He has appeared on a number of television shows, including "The Today Show" (1961), "One of a Kind" (a special, 1974), "Positively Black," and "Kup's Show" (1976), and has hosted two TV series: "Jazz Scene USA" (1962) and "From Jump Street: A Story of Black Music" (13 programs, 1980). Member of Authors League of America. *Address*—Office: WETA, P.O. Box 2626, Washington, DC 20012.

REPRESENTATIVE DRAMATIC WORKS:
Kicks & Company (musical, 2 acts, 1961). Book, music, and lyrics in collaboration with Robert Nemiroff. Described as "a musical about O. D. Kicks, a devil-figure, involved in, and working against, the Southern 'Sit-in' movement."—*Black Drama* (Mitchell, 1967). Brown's first playwriting effort was financed by Dave Garroway, playwright Lorraine Hansberry, and her husband, Robert Nemiroff. First auditioned on "The Dave Garroway Show" (the orig. "Today Show"), prior to being prod. at the Arie Crown Theatre, Chicago, where it ran for only 4 perfs., Oct. 11–14, 1961; staged by Hansberry following the resignation of VINNETTE CARROLL as director. Cast included Vi Velasco, Lonnie Sattin, and Burgess Meredith.

Worlds of Oscar Brown, Jr. (one-man show, full length, 1965). "Solo evening of songs, impressions and improvisations created and performed by Oscar Brown, Jr."—*The Best Plays of 1965–1966*, p. 355. Prod. Off-Bway at Gramercy Arts Theatre, Feb. 18–April 4, 1965, for 55 perfs.

Summer in the City (musical, full length, 1965). Cowritten with KENT FOREMAN, who also directed. "Although the motif in the production had an integrated background, the gut and beauty of it came entirely from Black life."—*Black World,* April 1973, pp. 28–29. Prod. at the Harper Theatre in Hyde Park, Chicago, 1965.

Joy (revue, full length, 1966). Written, directed, and starred in by Brown. "A collection of songs in the Brazilian style."—*Jet,* Feb. 12, 1970, p. 62. First prod. at the Happy Medium Theatre, Chicago, 1966. Prod. Off-Bway at the New Theatre, Jan. 27–July 26, 1970, for 208 perfs., with the author, Judy Pace, and Sivucca (an albino Brazilian performer) on the accordian.

Buck White (musical, full length, 1969). Based on the play *Big Time Buck White* (1966) by Joseph Dolan Tuotti. A black militant leader comes, along with his entourage, to address a meeting of the Beautiful Allelujah Days (BAD) organization, a black social group. First prod. at the Committee Theatre, San Francisco, opening Feb. 12, 1969, for a successful run; dir. by author, who also starred in the prodn. Prod. on Bway, at the George Abbott Theatre, Dec. 2–6, 1969, for 7 perfs.; also dir. by author, with Muhammad Ali in the title role. Act 1 of this prodn. was presented Off-Bway, at the Village Gate Theatre, Jan. 8–18, 1970, for 18 perfs. Cast album of the San Francisco prodn. released by Buddah records.

OTHER PLAYS AND DRAMATIC WORKS:
Opportunity, Please Knock (musical, full length, 1969). Prod. in Chicago and on national TV in 1969, with members of the Black P. Stone Rangers (a South Side Chicago youth gang), Oscar Brown, Jr., Jean Pace, B. B. King, Dick Gregory, and the SPENCER JACKSON family; dir. by author. Revived briefly in Jan. 1970, with many of the orig. cast members. **Slave Song** (musical, 1974). Sched. for prodn. by the Lamont Zeno Community Theatre, Chicago, March 1974. **Sunshine and Shadows** (poetic collage, 1974). Dramatized reading of †Paul Laurence Dunbar's poetry, with orig. music by *Phil Cochran. Prod. by the Black Heritage Theatrical Players, Chicago, 1974. **In De Beginning** (musical, full length, 1977). The Genesis story in music and verse. Reviewed as "A Story of Sin on a Stage Full of Kin." Prod. at the Body Politic Theatre, Chicago, Aug. 3, 1977.

BROWN, RHOZIER T. ("Roach" Brown) (1944–   ), Television and film writer-producer, who received a presidential pardon for his outstanding service to the community while serving a life sentence in Lorton Reformatory. Born and resides in Washington, DC. Educated at Federal City Coll., 1970–72. Founder and executive director of Inner Voices Multi-Media Service Center, 1968–present. Producer-writer, public television, 1970. Assoc. producer, WTTC-TV, 1970–72; producer of "Black News," 1972–74. Winner of numerous awards for his documentary films cited below. Member of ACLU National Prison Project, American Film Inst., Big Brothers of America, Lifers for Penal Reform, Communications Assn., and NAACP

PLAYS AND DRAMATIC WORKS:
Xmas in Time (drama, 1 act, 1969). Prod. by the Inner Voices, at Lorton Reformatory, Lorton, VA, Dec. 22, 1969. **Circle of Love** (doc. film, 1975). Winner, International Film Festival. **Holidays—Hollowdays** (doc. film, 1975). Prod. 1975; winner, Blue Rib-

bon Award, New York Film Festival. **Roach** (autobiographical doc. film, 1976). Prod. 1976; recipient of an Emmy nomination, and winner of a Broadcast Media Award.

BROWN, RICARDO, Playwright. An alumnus of the Frank Silvera Writers' Workshop (FSWW) in New York City. *Address:* 156 E. 35th St., Brooklyn, NY 11203.
  PLAYS:
  (Both unpub. scripts are in the FSWW Archives/Schomburg Collection.) **Comparsa** (pre-1985). **No Alterations** (pre-1985).

BROWN, WESLEY (1934–   ), Poet, writer, and playwright. Born and currently residing in New York City. Educated at Oswego State Univ. (B.A. in political science and history, 1968). Also studied writing in the John O. Killens Writers Workshop and the Sonia Sanchez Writers Workshop, New York. In 1973 he was imprisoned at Lewisburg, PA, as a conscientious objector to the Vietnam War. Author of a novel, *Tragic Magic* (1978). His poetry, fiction, and articles have been published in *Essence, Black Creation, Broadway Boogie, We Be Word Sorcerers* (Sanchez, 1973), and in the anthology cited below. Currently teaches creative writing at Rutgers Univ. in New Jersey. Member of Poets and Writers, Inc. Recipient of a P.E.N. Fellowship. *Address:* 103 W. 141st St., New York, NY 10030.
  PLAYS:
  And Now, Will the Real Bud Jones Stand Up (ritual, 1 act, 1971). Concerns a black man's attempt to cope with the philosophical question, "What is Truth?" Pub. in *Three Hundred and Sixty Degrees of Blackness Comin at You* (Sanchez, 1971).
  Boogie Woogie and Booker T (black history docudrama, full length, 1986). "The story centers around a meeting of the most influential leaders of Black America called by Booker T. Washington [Dr. W.E.B. Du Bois, Ida B. Wells, William Monroe Trotter, and Mary Church Terrell]. When this meeting was held in 1904, Washington was the most powerful Black man in America. . . . The drama lies in the tensions resulting from the conflicting views of the radicals and conservatives in the group."—*New York Amsterdam News,* Feb. 28, 1987, p. 34. Prod. by the New Federal Theatre, New York, Feb. 1987, with CHARLES DUMAS in the title role. Unpub. script in the Hatch-Billops Collection.

BROWNE, PATRICIA ANN WILKINS. See MANDULO, RHEA MAKEDA ZAWADIE.

BROWNE, ROSCOE LEE (1925–   ), Distinguished actor of stage, screen, and television, noted for his portrayal of articulate, educated, and arrogant black bourgeoisie characters. Born in Woodbury, NJ. Educated at Lincoln Univ. (PA), the Univ. of Florence (Italy), Middlebury Coll. (VT), and Columbia Univ. Formerly a track star—twice All-American, indoor 1,000 yard run; world champion, 800 meter run, Paris, 1951. Instr. of French and English, Lincoln Univ., 1946–47 and 1949–50, after which he gave up teaching to go into the theatre.

Among his stage acting credits are *Titus Andronicus* (1957), *The Cool World* (1960), *The Blacks* (1961), *General Seeger* (Bway, 1962), *The Ballad of the Sad Cafe* (1963), *Benito Cereno* (1967), and *The Dream on Monkey Mountain*. Films include *The Connection* (1960), *Black Like Me* (1964), *The Cool World* (1964), *Uptight* (1968), *The Comedians* (1969), and *The Liberation of L. B. Jones* (1970), in which he played the title role. His television acting credits include "Mannix," "The Invaders," "Outcasts," "Name of the Game," "Bonanza," "All in the Family," "The Flip Wilson Show," "Good Times," "Planet of the Apes," "Barney Miller," "The Streets of San Francisco," "Maude," and "The Bill Cosby Show."

DRAMATIC WORKS:

A Hand Is on the Gate // Orig. title: **An Evening of Negro Poetry and Folk Music** (theatrical collage, full length, 1966). Conceived, arranged, and directed by Browne. Described in *The Best Plays of 1966–1967* as "a collection of readings from the works of Negro authors and renditions of folk songs." According to Floyd Gaffney, writing in *Educational Theatre Journal* (May 1969), it "relates the story of the black man from his origin in Africa through captivity and enslavement to his present position in the United States." First prod. Off-Bway, under its orig. title, by the New York Shakespeare Festival (NYSF), at the Delacorte Theatre, Aug. 15, 1966, for 1 perf. Opened on Bway, under its present title (borrowed from a poem by †Arna Bontemps), at the Longacre Theatre, Sept. 21, 1966, for 21 perfs. Cast included Leon Bibb, Roscoe Lee Browne, Gloria Foster, Moses Gunn, Ellen Holly, James Earl Jones, Josephine Prenice, and Cicely Tyson. Prod. as an all-black showcase by the Ohio Univ. School of Theatre, Athens, OH, during the 1968–69 season. Prod. Off-Bway by the Afro-American Studio, opening Nov. 1974, continuing through 1975; dir. by ERNIE McCLINTOCK. Revived, under the title *A Hand Is on the Gate—'76*, March 5, 1976; also dir. by McClintock. Cast recording of the Bway prodn. released by Verve/Folkways in both monaural (9040–2-OC) and stereo (s-9040–2-OC).

Behind the Broken Words (theatre piece, 2 parts, 1981). According to *Theatre World*, 1981–82, p. 72, it "presents a poetic journey into some of America's outstanding literary works." Prod. by the American Place Theatre (APT), New York, Dec. 8–20, 1981, for 19 perfs.; cocreated by and costarring Roscoe Lee Browne and Anthony Zerbe.

BROWN-GUILLORY, ELIZABETH (1954–   ), Playwright, author, scholar, and critic. Born in Church Point, LA. Educated at the Univ. of Southwestern Louisiana (B.A. in English and psychology, 1975; M.A. in English, 1977) and Florida State Univ. (Ph.D. in British and American drama and American literature [with emphasis on black literature], 1980). Currently asst. prof. of English at Dillard Univ. in New Orleans. Has also taught at the Univ. of Southwestern Louisiana (grad. asst.), 1966–77; Florida State Univ. (grad. asst.), 1977–79; and the Univ. of South Carolina at Spartanburg (asst. prof. of English), 1980–82. Brown-Guillory has contributed scholarly articles to *The Dictionary of Literary Biography, Phylon, Sage, Helicon Nine: The Journal of Women's Arts and Letters, Xavier Review, and Salem Press*. Her play **Snapshots of Broken Dolls** was produced at Lincoln Center in New York City, Oct. 1986.

Memberships include National Council of Teachers of English, College Language Assn., South Carolina Modern Language Assn., Modern Language Assn., Southern Afro-American Studies Assn., Mississippi Philological Assn., Philological Assn. of Louisiana, National Writers Club, International Women's Writing Guild, American Black Book Writers Assn., International Black Women's Congress, Black Theatre Network, and NADSA. Recipient of a United Negro College Foundation grant, 1986–87, Brown-Guillory is at work on a book examining the development of black women playwriting in America. *Address:* 13075 Deauville Ct., New Orleans, LA 70129; alternate: 688 N. Wilson St., Church Point, LA 70525.

PLAYS:

Bayou Relics (comedy, 1 long act [1 hr., 15 min.], 1981). A play about senior citizens, set in a nursing home in southwest Louisiana. It makes the point that the elderly are spunky, funny, and sometimes pensive, and that they want what young people want: respect, love, and support. Contains twists in plot, suspense, screen scenes, asides, and repartee, and pokes fun at the shoddy treatment of elderly people in nursing homes. First prod. at the Spartanburg Arts Center, Spartanburg, SC, March 1981. Prod. at Dillard Univ., New Orleans March 1983, and at colleges and universities throughout the United States since 1983. Pub. by Contemporary Drama Service, Colorado Springs, CO, 1983; reprinted 1986.

Mam Phyllis (comedy, full length, 1981). Set in southwest Louisiana during the Depression, this play deals with the impact of Mam Phyllis—a midwife, nanny, friend, and grandmother—on her community. She is an example of a devoted, unselfish, Christian servant who is constantly tested by the diabolical, cynical, gossiping Sister Viola and the haughty, rich blacks of the community. At one point, Mam Phyllis says, "Some people think they roots in they teeth or they spring from a bottle of chablis." First prod. at Concourse Coll., Oct. 1981, as a project of the South Carolina Sesquicentennial Commission's Focus on Women's Drama Subcommittee. Revised and prod. at Dillard Univ., and various locations statewide, March 1985.

Marry Me Again (comedy, 1 act, 1984). About a newlywed couple learning to cope with each other's idiosyncrasies. Nita is driven by her need for attention, affection, and perfection. Manly, her husband, has a difficult time communicating. On another level, the play has talking pieces of furniture which give a running commentary on their owners as well as engage in their own conflicts—for example, "Bookshelf" is haughty, "Loveseat" is chauvinistic, "Armchair" is an instigative motor-mouth. Prod. at Dillard Univ., March 1984, then at various locations in Louisiana, winning a statewide first-place playwriting competition and garnering a commendation from the mayor of New Orleans, 1984.

Snapshots of Broken Dolls (comedy, 1 act, 1986). Set in a labor room of a hospital in Bayoutown, this play centers around three generations of women waiting for the birth of the fourth. On one hand, the nerdy, clumsy father-to-be bungles everything as he practices Lamaze with his laboring wife. Simultaneously, the gossiping grandmother levels verbal blows at her daughter, who pretends she's a prostitute only to pain the mother she once caught in bed with a relative. The four characters, all of whom are broken dolls, labor and give birth to their suppressed fears, secrets, and old wounds concurrently as the expectant mother progresses through labor and delivery. Prod. at

Dillard Univ. and at various locations in Louisiana in the fall of 1986. Prod. at New York's Lincoln Center, Oct. 1986. Pub. by Contemporary Drama Service, Colorado Springs, CO, 1987.

BROWNING, ALICE C. (Mrs. Charles P. Browning; Richard Bentley [pseudonym]) (1907–1985), Editor, author, playwright; former social worker, elementary school teacher. Born and currently living in Chicago. Educated at the Univ. of Chicago (B.A., 1935) and Columbia Univ. (M.A.). Editor of *Negro Story Magazine,* 1944–46; *Black Writers News;* and other periodicals. Founder-director of International Black Writers Conf. (IBWC), Chicago, which calls itself "the oldest ongoing annual conference of Black writers in the world." Recipient of an award from Modill School of Journalism, 1959. *Pertinent address:* International Black Writers' Conference, Inc., 4019 South Vincennes Ave., Chicago, IL 60653.

PLAYS AND DRAMATIC WORKS:
It's Fun to Be Black (children's musical, 1973). Prod. by the Actors of America, at Malcolm X Coll., Chicago, during the 1973–74 season. **How to Beat Old Age** (comedy, 1976). Described by the producer as a "hilarious . . . satire on the world today." Prod. at McCormick Inn, Chicago, opening Aug. 20, 1976; dir. by Glorissa Johnson. **How to Be Happy Though Married** (musical satire, 1977). Prod. for IBWC, June 1977. **How's Your Sex Life** (musical satire, 1977). Comedy on sex. Prod. for IBWC, June 1977; dir. by Jimmidee Smith, producer of Actors of America, Chicago. **Good Time Harry** (1980s). **A New Race** (science fiction, 1981). Prod. in Chicago, 1981, presumably for IBWC.

BRUMMIT, (Dr.) HOUSTON (1928–   ), Playwright, producer, lyricist, composer, educator, writer of fiction and nonfiction, psychoanalyst, and child psychiatrist. Born in Cincinnati, OH. Educated at the Univ. of Cincinnati (1944–46), Wilberforce Univ. (B.S., 1953), Ohio State Univ. Graduate School (1948–49), Meharry Medical Coll. (M.D., 1953), and American Inst. of Psychoanalysis (1960–63, 1972–73). Board certified in adult and child psychiatry. Served in the U.S. Air Force as captain, 1954–56. Director, Child Psychiatry, Brooklyn Cumberland Hosp., 1964–70. Consultant, New York City Board of Education, 1964–. Member of faculty, American Inst. for Psychoanalysis, 1977–78. Producer, *Raisin' Hell in the Son,* at the Providence Playhouse, New York City, 1962 (the first black-produced Equity Off-Broadway play, out of which came playwrights BARBARA ANN TEER and HAL DeWINDT and actors Janet MacLachlan and Arthur French). Author of half a dozen psychiatric articles; three unpublished novellas ("Gretchen," "Trick or Treat," and "Meshuggeneh") and a volume of nonfiction *(Counterculture),* which in 1983 was being edited for publication. Organizer and director of psychiatric clinics. Member of A.M.A., American Academy of Psychoanalysis, American Psychiatric Assn., NAACP, Urban League, United Negro College Fund, SCLC, and Dramatists Guild. *Address*—Office: 145 E. 49th St., New York, NY 10017.

DRAMATIC WORKS:

Too Late for Tears (musical drama, 2 acts, 1978). Music cocomposed with Roger Hamilton Spotts. The story of an upper-middle-class, idealistic white psychiatrist and his Pygmalion attempt to rehabilitate a young black female drug addict in a women's prison, only to have his Galatea crumble when she confronts the harsh realities of the street world. Showcased in New York, 1978.

Isabel Rising // Orig. title: **Evita Del Barrio** (musical, 2 acts, 1979). A fantasy-laden melodrama about life in the theatre and the power of the imagination. There are four principal roles that weave in and out of the legends of Eva and Isabel Peron, Catherine of Russia, and Tito Luciardo. Songs sung by the four leading characters include both original Latin-like pop songs and Bway operatic scores. Showcased under its original title (as a musical play, with only five songs) at El Porton Theatre, New York, July 1979. Revised under its present title as a full length musical.

Makin' It (musical comedy, 2 acts, 1981). About a young ingenue who comes to New York to get into show business. She becomes infatuated with a seasoned song and dance man and is almost seduced by a lecherous producer. Showcased at the Perry St. Theatre, New York, Dec. 1981.

BRUNO, JOANN, Author-playwright. Born in Opelousas, LA. Resides in Los Angeles, CA, where she gained theatrical experience with the Los Angeles Little Theatre and studied writing at the Watts Writers Workshop. One of her children's stories was used on TV's "Sesame Street."

PLAYS:

Sister Selena Got the Gift (comedy, 1 act, 1975). About a faith-healing woman with a questionable past. Prod. by the DC Repertory Theatre, Washington, DC, opening Jan. 8, 1975; dir. by Motojicho (VANTILE WHITFIELD). **Uncle Bud's No Stranger** (1970s).

BRUNSON, DORIS, Playwright. One of the cofounders of the New Heritage Theatre (NHT; now the New Heritage Repertory Theatre [NHRT]), New York, 1960s.

PLAY:

Three Shades of Harlem (comedy-drama, 3 acts, 1964). Coauthor, with ROGER FURMAN. Depicts the problems (shade 1), joys (shade 2), and hopes (shade 3) of the Harlem community. Prod. by NHT, in repertory, 1964–66, and presented at the Harlem YWCA, New York, opening June 18, 1965, where it played for a number of weekends; then moved to Walter Cooper's Sunset Ballroom in Harlem, where it continued to play throughout the summer of 1965; opened again at the Harlem YWCA, Feb. 18, 1966.

BRYANT, FREDERICK JAMES, JR. (1942–   ), Playwright, poet, social worker, and freelance photographer. Born in Philadelphia, PA. Worked as a casework supervisor with the Philadelphia Dept. of Public Welfare. His poetry has been published in several anthologies, including *Black Poets, Write On!, Extension, The New Black Poetry,* and *New Black Voices.*

PLAY:

Lord of the Mummy Wrappings (1967). Prod. at Lincoln Univ., Lincoln, PA, 1969.

BRYANT, HAZEL (1939–1983), Actress-singer, director, producer, theatrical administrator, teacher, and playwright. Founder and artistic director of the Afro-American Total Theatre, New York, 1968–73, which was superceded by the Richard Allen Center for Culture and Arts, of which she was also founder-director. One of the organizers and first president of the Black Theatre Alliance, 1969–73. Credited with having produced over 200 musicals and plays. Born in Zanesville, OH, the daughter of an A.M.E. bishop. Grew up in Baltimore, MD. Studied singing at the Peabody Preparatory School of Music in Baltimore, from which she graduated. Received the B.A. from Oberlin Conservatory of Music, 1962. Went to Europe to pursue a career in opera, studying at the Mozarteum School of Music in Salzburg, Austria. Sang operatic roles during the 1960s in most of the major opera houses in Italy, France, Austria, Germany, and the Soviet Union. Returned to the United States late 1960s to pursue a career in the theatre. Studied acting with Harold Clurman and Stella Adler. Performed in the Equity Library Theatre production of *Lost in the Stars* (1968) and the Milwaukee Repertory Theatre production of *That's the Game, Jack* (1969). During this period, she also studied theatre administration at Columbia Univ. Member of the Theatre Panel of the New York State Council on the Arts and the New York City Board of Cultural Affairs. Panelist and councilman to the National Endowment for the Arts (NEA) and the National Opera Inst. Recipient of the Harold Jackman Memorial Award for outstanding contribution to the arts in New York, 1976; a special citation from the governor of New York for having produced the 1970 Black Theatre Festival at Lincoln Center. In 1971 Bryant was the biographical subject of a 30–minute documentary film, produced by Gregory Peterson, entitled *Hazel Hazel Hazel Hazel Hazel* (also known as "Hazel 5X" ["Hazel five times"]). Died of heart disease in her home in New York City after having spoken earlier the same day at the United Nations.

REPRESENTATIVE PLAYS:

(All prod. by the Afro-American Total Theatre, New York City; dir. by author.) **Black Circles 'Round Angela** // Later prod. as **Black Circles** and as **Black Circles, Black Spirits** (musical, 1 act, 1970). Frequently prod. and revised musical which remained in the repertory of the Afro-American Total Theatre from 1970 to 1974. (Description follows prodn. history below.) First prod. as **Black Circles 'Round Angela** at the International House, New York, Feb. 19 and 22, 1970. Perfd. as **Black Circles** at the Halsey St. Block Assn., Brooklyn, Aug. 26, 1971. Perfd. as **Black Circles 'Round Angela** at the Afro-American Studio Theatre in Harlem, Feb. 1973. Perfd. as **Black Circles, Black Spirits,** at the Martinique Theatre, New York, March 1974. This latter prodn. was described as a confrontation in a beauty parlor setting between four women—Peaches, Aunt Sarah, Saffronia, and Sweetthing—representative of four distinct black lifestyles (depicted by Nina Simone in her recording of "Four Women," made several years ago). According to the *New York Amsterdam News* (March 9, 1974, p. D-14): "Vignettes and speeches of Angela Davis serve as the catalyst, while the women engage in a verbal brawl occasionally, defending their roles. Angela's role, however, is that of a spiritual entity interspersed throughout the performance, causing each woman to reflect as her words are spoken.'' Unpub. script of **Black Circles 'Round Angela** in the Schomburg Collection.

Makin' It (musical, full length, 1970). Book written in collaboration with GERTRUDE GREENIDGE and WALTER MILES. Music by JIMMY JUSTICE and HOLLY HAMILTON. The trials and tribulations of a young man from a small town as he tries to make it in show business. Written 1970. Prod. by the Afro-American Total Theatre, and perfd. at the following locations: International House, Jan. 14–16, 1972; Riverside Church, March 6–12, 1972; Finch Coll., March 1972; as a street theatre prodn. in the five boroughs of New York City, July 31–Aug. 14, 1972; Lincoln Center, Nov. 3, 1972. Remained in repertory until June 10, 1973.

Sheba (musical, 1 act, 1972). Music by Jimmy Justice. First prod. at the Riverside Church Theatre, Dec. 11–17, 1972. The premiere perf. was sponsored by Frederick Talbot, Guyana's ambassador to the United States, and his wife, and was attended by over 30 African, Asian, and Latin American ambassadors and some 150 black American artists and celebrities in every area of the arts. Presented at the Third Annual Black Theatre Festival, held at the Brooklyn Academy of Music, 1973. Remained in repertory until April 1974. Unpub. script in the Schomburg Collection.

OTHER PLAYS AND DRAMATIC WORKS:

(Also prod. by the Afro-American Total Theatre, New York; dir. by author.) **Mae's Amees** (musical, 1 act, 1979). Written with HOPE CLARKE and HANK JOHNSON. Prod. at the Riverside Church Theatre, Aug. 9–10, 1969. Apparently remained in repertory until Oct. 1969. **An Evening of Black Poetry** (''black music and letters event,'' 1969). Performance of 200 years of black poetry from Phillis Wheatley and Paul Laurence Dunbar to LeRoi Jones, MAYA ANGELOU, and members of the company. Prod. at the Riverside Church Theatre, July 25–27, 1969. **Origins** (musical, 1 act, 1969). Written with BEVERLY TODD and Hank Johnson. Prod. at the Riverside Church Theatre, Oct. 1969. **On Being Black in White America** (1970). Prod. at International House, Jan.-March 1970. **Soul Politiken** (1973). Music by Jimmy Justice. Prod. as a street theatre prodn., at Lincoln Center, July 27, 1973. **Carnival Song** (1973). Unpub. script in the Schomburg Collection. **Star** (1970s). Unpub. script in the Schomburg Collection.

BUDDE, JORDAN, Playwright. Based in New York City, where his work has been produced by the New Federal Theatre (NFT).

PLAY:

Fraternity (comedy, 1984). ''About five Southern Methodist University seniors facing graduation. They are planning to end their college days with a bang—but find they are forced to confront the conflicting issues of friendship, fraternity, and their futures.''— *New York Amsterdam News,* March 24, 1984. Prod. by WOODIE KING, JR., and NFT, at the Colonnades Theatre, New York, March 15–April 24, 1984, for 15 perfs.

BULLINS, ED (1936–   ), One of America's leading and most prolific black playwrights; editor, essayist, poet, novelist, filmmaker, and teacher. Recipient of an Obie Award for **The Fabulous Miss Marie** (1971) and a New York Drama Critics Circle Award for **The Taking of Miss Janie** (1975), as the Best American Play of 1974–75. Born in Philadelphia, PA, where he attended the public schools and William Penn Inst. Moved to California, where he lived for a number of years and wrote and produced his early plays. Attended Los Angeles City Coll. and San Francisco State Coll. Was one of the leaders of the Black Arts movement on the West Coast during the 1950s, and one of the founders of Black Arts/ West (BA/W), an experimental theatre group in the Fillmore District of San Francisco, patterned after AMIRI BARAKA's (LeRoi Jones's) Black Arts Repertory Theatre in Harlem. Moved back to the East Coast in 1967. Playwright-in-residence and assoc. director of the New Lafayette Theatre (NLT) in Harlem, 1968–72. Founder and editor of *Black Theatre* magazine, 1969–72. Founder of the Surviving Theatre, Bronx, NY, 1974–c. 1980. After the demise of NLT, he took a position on the staff of the New York Shakespeare Festival (NYSF), where he coordinated a playwrights' workshop and worked in the Publicity and Press Dept. During this period, he worked on a dramatization of Gorki's **The Lower Depths** for Joseph Papp and the book of a new musical, **Satchmo.** Has taught English and writing at a number of colleges, including Darmouth, Talladega, Clark (Atlanta), and the Univ. of California at Berkeley. Recently returned to California, where he lives and writes in the San Francisco Bay area and is on the drama faculty of City Coll. of San Francisco. In addition to his plays and writings on the theatre, Bullins is the author of *The Hungered One: Early Writings* (1971), *The Reluctant Rapist* (novel, 1973), and a number of articles and reviews which have been published in *Black World, Black Theatre, The Drama Review, Journal of Black Poetry, Liberator, New York Times, Performance,* and other periodicals. Member of DG, P.E.N. International, and WGA/East. In addition to the Obie and New York Drama Critics Circle awards, he is the recipient of three Rockefeller Foundation playwriting grants, a grant from the Guggenheim Foundation, and a CAPS Award for playwriting. Also awarded an honorary Doctor of Letters from Columbia Coll., Chicago. *Address:* 2124–B 5th St., Berkeley, CA 94710. *Agent:* Helen Merrill, 337 W. 22nd St., New York, NY 10011.

GROUP OF RELATED PLAYS:

"THE ELECTRONIC NIGGER AND OTHERS" (program of 3 one-act plays, 1968). Includes **The Electronic Nigger** (1968), **Clara's Ole Man** (1965), and **A Son, Come Home** (1968). Prod. Off-Bway, with members of NLT, at the American Place Theatre (APT), March 6–16, 1968; reopened Off-Bway at the Martinique Theatre (with title changed to "THREE PLAYS BY ED BULLINS"), March 28–May 26, 1968, where it continued to run for a total of 86 perfs., all dir. by ROBERT MACBETH.

NOTE: See also the following related plays in the author's projected Twentieth-Century Cycle: **In the Wine Time** (1968), **In New England Winter** (1968), **The Duplex** (1970), **The Fabulous Miss Marie** (1971), **Home Boy** (1972), and **DADDY!** (1974).

COLLECTIONS:

FIVE PLAYS BY ED BULLINS. Bobbs-Merrill, Indianapolis, 1969. Contains **Goin' a Buffalo** (1968), **In the Wine Time** (1968), **A Son, Come Home** (1968), **The Electronic Nigger** (1968), and **Clara's Ole Man** (1965). Same contents as *THE ELECTRONIC NIGGER AND OTHER PLAYS* below.

NEW PLAYS FROM THE BLACK THEATRE. Bantam Books, New York, 1969. Contains **In New England Winter** (1968) and **We Righteous Bombers** (1969).

THE ELECTRONIC NIGGER AND OTHER PLAYS. Faber & Faber, London, 1970. Contains same plays as *FIVE PLAYS BY ED BULLINS* above.

A BLACK QUARTET. Four plays by BEN CALDWELL, RON MILNER, Ed Bullins, and Amiri Baraka. With an introduction by CLAYTON RILEY. Signet Books, New American Lib., New York, 1970. Contains **The Gentleman Caller** (1969).

FOUR DYNAMITE PLAYS. Morrow, New York, 1972. Contains **It Bees Dat Way** (1970), **Death List** (1970), **The Pig Pen** (1969), and **Night of the Beast** (1972).

FOUR ONE ACT PLAYS. Morrow, New York, 1972. Contains **How Do You Do?** (1965), **A Minor Scene** (1966), **Dialect Determinism** (1965), and **It Has No Choice** (1966).

THE THEME IS BLACKNESS: The Corner and Other Plays. Morrow, New York, 1973. Contains **Dialect Determinism** (or *The Rally*) (1965), **It Has No Choice** (1966), **The Helper** (1966), **A Minor Scene** (1966), **The Theme Is Blackness** (1966), **The Man Who Dug Fish** (1967), **The Corner** (1968), **Black Commercial #2** (1967), **The American Flag Ritual** (1969), **State Office Building Curse** (1969), **One-Minute Commercial** (1969), **A Street Play** (1970), **Street Sounds** (1970), **A Short Play for a Small Theatre** (1971), and **The Play of the Play** (1970).

THE NEW LAFAYETTE THEATRE PRESENTS: Four Plays with Aesthetic Comment by Six Black Playwrights. Anchor Press/Doubleday, Garden City, NY, 1974. Contains **The Fabulous Miss Marie** (1971).

REPRESENTATIVE PLAYS AND DRAMATIC WORKS:

Clara's Ole Man (drama, 1 act, 1965). Subtitled "A Play of Lost Innocence." An Ivy League college student visits a young woman while her "ole man" is supposedly at work. There he meets an assortment of strange and unpleasant characters and gains some first-hand experience in the realities of ghetto life, finally learning that Clara's "ole man" is a lesbian. First prod. by the San Francisco Drama Circle, at the Firehouse Repertory Theatre, Aug. 5, 1965; dir. by Robert Hartman. With Blanche Richardson, Margo Norman, and James Robinson. Prod. Off-Bway, with members of NLT, at the APT, March 6–16 and March 28–May 6, 1986, for 86 perfs. [See **"THE ELECTRONIC NIGGER AND OTHERS"** under GROUP OF RELATED PLAYS above.] Cast included Kelly-Marie Berry, Caroline Y. Cardwell, and Roscoe Orman. Prod. by Afro-American Studio in Harlem during the 1969–70 season; dir. by ERNIE McCLINTOCK. Prod. as a workshop production by the D.C. Black Repertory Theatre, Washington, DC, 1973, on a program of three one-act plays, under the production title *Lifestyles*. Prod. by Theatre for New York City, Jan. 22, 1977. Prod. by The Family, Feb. 1977, as part of Festival '77; dir. by Marvin Felix Camillo. Pub. in *The Drama Review*, Summer 1968, pp. 159–71; in *FIVE PLAYS BY ED BULLINS*; in *The Best Short Plays, 1969* (Richards, 1969); in the author's *THE ELECTRONIC NIGGER AND OTHER PLAYS*; in *Cavalcade* (Davis & Redding, 1971); and in *The Off-Broadway Book* (Poland & Mailman, 1972).

The Electronic Nigger ("A Tragi-Comedy" [subtitle], 1 act, 1968). Described by Peter Bailey as "a cutting satire on the kind of 'Negro' who, with monotonous regularity and pompous pretensions, parrots the current white-establishment line on everything."— *Ebony*, Sept. 1968. Prod. Off-Bway, with members of NLT, at APT, March 6–16 and March 28–May 26, 1968, for 86 perfs. [See **"THE ELECTRONIC NIGGER AND OTHERS"** under GROUP OF RELATED PLAYS above.] Pub. in *New American Plays*, vol. 3 (Hoffman, 1968); in *FIVE PLAYS BY ED BULLINS*; and in *Nommo* (Robinson, 1972).

A Son, Come Home (drama, 1 act, 1968). A son who returns home after a ten-year absence finds that his relationship with his mother has deteriorated beyond repair. First prod. Off-Bway, with members of NLT, at APT, March 6–16 and March 28–May 26, 1968, for 86 perfs. [See **"THE ELECTRONIC NIGGER AND OTHERS"** under GROUP OF RELATED PLAYS above.] Pub. in *FIVE PLAYS BY ED BULLINS*; in Bullins's *THE ELECTRONIC NIGGER AND OTHER PLAYS;* in *Contemporary Drama: Thirteen Plays,* 2nd ed. (Clayes & Spencer, 1970); in *The Norton Introduction to Literature: Drama* (Bain, 1973); and in *Drama and Discussion,* 2nd ed. (Clayes, 1978). Excerpt (1 scene) in *Black Scenes* (Childress, 1971).

In the Wine Time (drama, 3 acts, 1968). The first play in the author's projected Twentieth-Century Cycle. Described by Darwin T. Turner as "the story of a black youth maturing in the ghetto with only the dreams of an unattainable woman."—*Black Drama in America* (Turner, 1971), p. 20. Prod. by NLT in Harlem, Dec. 10, 1968–Jan. 28, 1969; dir. by ROBERT MACBETH. With Sonny Jim (J. E. GAINES). Pub. in *FIVE PLAYS BY ED BULLINS*; in Bullins's *THE ELECTRONIC NIGGER AND OTHER PLAYS;* in *Black Theater* (Patterson, 1971); and in *The Great American Life Show* (Lahr & Price, 1974).

In New England Winter (drama, prologue and 7 scenes, 1968). The second play in the author's projected Twentieth-Century Cycle. A study of black lifestyle and survival, which continues the story of a group of black characters and a family begun in **In the Wine Time** (1968). First prod. Spring 1968 by NLT in Harlem. Prod. Off-Bway by NLT, at the Henry St. Playhouse, opening Jan. 26, 1971, for 8 perfs.; dir. by Dick Williams. Pub. in the author's *NEW PLAYS FROM THE BLACK THEATRE.*

Goin' a Buffalo ("Tragifantasy" [subtitle], 1968; also a film, 1971). Described by Darwin T. Turner as a drama "in which a Black hustler is betrayed by the man he has befriended and trusted."—*Black Drama in America* (Turner, 1971). First presented Off-Bway as a staged reading at APT, June 6–7, 1968, for 2 perfs.; dir. by Roscoe Orman. Prod. by NLT in Harlem, Oct. 25–Dec. 7, 1969. Made into a film by NLT, 1971. Pub. in *New Black Playwrights* (Couch, 1968); in *FIVE PLAYS BY ED BULLINS*; in Bullins's *THE ELECTRONIC NIGGER AND OTHER PLAYS*; and in Black Theater, U.S.A. (Hatch & Shine, 1974).

The Corner (drama, 1 act, 1968). "A typical Bullins character expresses his hope of escaping from the drinking, carousing, street corner way of life by which he has been trapped."—*The Best Plays of 1971–1972.* First prod. by the Theatre Co. of Boston, 1968; dir. by David Wheeler. With William Adell Stevenson III (ILUNGA ADELL). Prod. as a work-in-progress by NEC, at St. Marks Playhouse, for 2 perfs.; dir. by Kris Keiser. Prod. Off-Bway by NYSF, at the Other Stage, on a work-in-progress program of four one-act plays, May 16, 1972, under the prodn. title *Four for One.* Again prod. by the same group as the title play on a program of three one-act plays, June 22–July 30, 1972, for 46 perfs.; dir. by Sonny Jim Gaines (J. E. Gaines). Pub. in *Black Drama Anthology* (King & Milner, 1972) and in the author's *THE THEME IS BLACKNESS.*

The Gentleman Caller (satire, 1 act, 1969). Avant-garde play symbolizing the new black militance and nationalism of the 1960s. A black (typical "darky" stereotype) maid shakes off her Aunt Jemima image and murders both her white mistress and master, in the presence of a frightened young Ivy League black man whom her mistress was trying to seduce. Prod. Off-Bway by WOODIE KING, JR., at Tambellini's Gate Theatre, July 30–Nov. 2, 1969, for 111 perfs.; dir. by Allie Woods, on a program of four one-act plays, under the prodn. title *A Black Quartet.* With MINNIE GENTRY as the maid and

Dennis Tate as the gentleman. Pub. in the author's *A BLACK QUARTET; The Best Short Plays, 1970* (Richards, 1970); *Contemporary Black Drama* (Oliver & Sills, 1971); and *Illuminations* 5 (Mill Valley, CA.), 1971.

We Righteous Bombers (revolutionary play, 4 acts, 1969). Generally believed to be written by Bullins, although authorship was originally attributed by him to Kingsley B. Bass, Jr.—originally described as "a twenty-four-year-old Black man killed by Detroit police during the uprising in 1967."—*New Plays from the Black Theatre* (Bullins, 1969). Described by Peter Bailey as "an overly-long but righteous play dealing with the psychological and physical problems facing a group of Black revolutionaries."—*Negro Digest,* April 1970, p. 25. Considered in the late 1960s to be one of the most controversial plays of the contemporary Black Theatre movement, and denounced by black critics not only as a literary hoax and an unauthorized adaptation, but also as a negative portrayal of black revolutionaries. Prod. by NLT, April 18–June 3, 1969. Pub. in the author's *NEW PLAYS FROM THE BLACK THEATRE* and in *Black Drama in America* (Turner, 1971).

The Duplex ("A Black Fable in Four Movements" [subtitle], 1970). The third play in the author's projected Twentieth-Century Cycle. In this play, according to John M. Reilly, "the theme of the cycle is fully established: the difficulties of love, and by implication group solidarity, and the complicity of people in disabling themselves."—*Contemporary Dramatists* (Vinson, 1973). According to the editor of the published text, this play "deals with the search for love by a Black girl." It is also described as "a slice-of-life play about an all-night party in a Black California community (stylistically akin to the same author's *The Pig Pen* [see OTHER PLAYS below]. " —*The Best Plays of 1971–1972.* First prod. by NLT, May 22–July 5, 1970; dir. by Robert Macbeth. Prod. Off-Bway (in a controversial prodn. publicly denounced by the author) by the Repertory Theatre of Lincoln Center, at the Forum Theatre, March 9–April 1, 1972, for 34 perfs.; dir. by GILBERT MOSES. Pub. by Morrow, New York, 1970.

The Fabulous Miss Marie (play of black life, full length, 1971). The fourth play in the author's projected Twentieth-Century Cycle. According to John M. Reilly, this play "carries Bullins' cycle forward with a character who makes a brief appearance in *The Duplex* [see directly above]. Miss Marie, vital and vulgar, demonstrates the vigor that sustains humanity, even carries it to a level of achievement."—*Contemporary Dramatists* (Vinson, 1973). First prod. by NLT, March 5–May 2, 1971; dir. by Robert Macbeth, earning two Obie Awards—one for the playwright and the other for actor Sonny Jim (J. E. Gaines). Pub. in *Scripts* 4 (NYSF), 1972, and in the author's *THE NEW LAFAYETTE THEATRE PRESENTS.*

Home Boy (drama, full length, 1972). Music by Aaron Bell. The fifth play in the author's projected Twentieth-Century Cycle. "Two Southern black men plan to emigrate to the North. One does, but both are victims, survivors, and casualties of the America of the 1950s and 1960s."—*Black Playwrights, 1823–1977* (Hatch & Abdullah, 1977), p. 36. Prod. by the Perry St. Theatre, Sept. 23, 1976; dir. by Patricia Golden. With Thommi Blackwell, Rodney Hudson, Danna Manno, Pamela Poitier, and WINSTON LOVETT.

DADDY! (drama, full length, 1974). The sixth play in the author's projected Twentieth-Century Cycle. A truant father returns home and tries to make amends to the family that he has abandoned. Coproduced Off-Bway by Woodie King, Jr. and Joseph Papp, at NFT, opening June 9, 1977.

The Taking of Miss Janie (satirical drama, full length, 1975). "A parable of race relations in the 1960s in the encounter between a black would-be poet (Adeyemi Lythcott) and blond classmate and devoted friend (Hilary Jean Beane) whom he suddenly rapes after years of friendship."—*The Best Plays of 1974–1975*. A Burns Mantle Theatre Yearbook "Best Play" of 1974–75. Winner of the Drama Critics Circle Award as the Best American Play of 1974–75, and the second black play to win this award (the first being *A Raisin in the Sun* by LORRAINE HANSBERRY). Also won an Obie Award for distinguished direction. Prod. Off-Bway, jointly by NFT and NYSF/Lincoln Center, at the Mitzie E. Newhouse Theatre, May 4–June 15, 1975, for 42 perfs.; dir. by Gilbert Moses. With Adeyemi Lythcott and Hilary Jean Beane. Pub. in *Famous American Plays of the 1970s* (Hoffman, 1981). Abridged in *The Best Plays of 1974–1975*.

OTHER PLAYS:

Dialect Determinism (or *The Rally*) (absurdist drama, 1 act, 1965). Satire of the rhetoric of black militancy, in which a self-appointed Messiah is executed by the crowd when he convinces them that their cause needs a martyr. Prod. by the San Francisco Drama Circle, at the Firehouse Repertory Theatre, Aug. 5, 1965; dir. by Robert Hartman. Pub. in *Ante* (Los Angeles), 1966; in the author's *FOUR ONE ACT PLAYS*; in *Spontaneous Combustion* (Owens & Feingold, 1972); and in the author's *THE THEME IS BLACKNESS*. **How Do You Do?** (absurdist drama, 1 act, 1965). Subtitled "A Nonsense Drama." Satire on the black stereotypes that are found within the black community, the various postures assumed by two characters, one male and one female—the events taking place within the mind of a black writer. Prod. by the San Francisco Drama Circle, at the Firehouse Repertory Theatre, Aug. 5, 1965; dir. by Robert Hartman. Prod. by the Theatre Co. of Boston, 1969. Pub. in *Black Dialogue*, July-Aug., 1965, pp. 55–61; by Illuminations Press, Mill Valley, CA, 1968; and in the author's *FOUR ONE ACT PLAYS*. **It Has No Choice** (melodrama, 1 act, 1966). Title taken from a quotation by Kafka: "The world will freely offer itself to you to be unmasked, it has no choice. . . . " Concerns a white woman who tries unsuccessfully to break off her relationship with her black lover. Prod. at the BA/W Repertory Theatre, San Francisco, Spring 1966; dir. by Hillery L. Broadous. Pub. in the author's *FOUR ONE ACT PLAYS* and *THE THEME IS BLACK-NESS*. **A Minor Scene** (skit, 1 act, 1966). Sexual encounter between a foul-speaking black man and a shocked middle-class white woman at a bus stop, which ends in her seduction. Prod. at the BA/W Repertory Theatre, San Francisco, Spring 1966; dir. by Hillery L. Broadous. Pub. in the author's *FOUR ONE ACT PLAYS* and in his *THE THEME IS BLACKNESS*. **The Theme Is Blackness** ("A One-Act Play to Be Given Before Predominantly White Audiences" [subtitle], 1966). Consists of two short statements: one delivered before, and one after the lights have been turned out for 20 minutes, during which the audience is expected to contemplate "the theme of blackness." Prod. at various locations in the San Francisco Bay area, 1966–67. Later prod. at BA/W Repertory Theatre, with music and sound effects during the period of blackness. Performed at CCNY, 1973. Pub. in the author's *THE THEME IS BLACKNESS*. **The Helper** (satire, 1 act, 1966). A white family, moving into another apartment, engages the services of a black male helper, then proceeds to demonstrate all the clichés of racism through their conversation and actions, while trying to keep an outward posture of liberalism. Prod. at the New Dramatists Workshop, June 1, 1970; dir. by Allie Woods. Pub. in the author's *THE THEME IS BLACKNESS*. **Black Commercial #2** (short TV commercial, 1967). Two black men, who are trying to kill each other in a "pig feet emporium and whiskey, beer, and wine joint'' in the black community on a Saturday night, learn a lesson in black unity and brotherhood. Pub. in *The Drama Review,* Summer 1969, pp. 144–45, and in the author's *THE THEME IS BLACKNESS.* **The Man Who Dug Fish** (absurdist play, 1 act, 1967). A dignified man purchases a fish and a shovel, and deposits both in a safety deposit box at the bank, paying ten years' rent in advance. First prod. as a staged reading by the Theatre Co. of Boston, c. 1969. Prod. as a workshop production at the New Dramatists, New York, June 1, 1970. Pub. in *Nexus* (San Francisco), 1967, and in the author's *THE THEME IS BLACKNESS.* **The American Flag Ritual** ("A Short Play or Scenario" [subtitle], 1969). A man ceremoniously unfolds a large American flag on the ground, stands in the center, urinates on it while the National Anthem is played, then wipes his feet on the flag and exits. **State Office Building Curse** ("A Scenario to Ultimate Action" [subtitle], 1969). A New York state office building located in the Harlem community is blown up, following its public opening ceremonies. Performed by NLT, early 1970s. Pub. in *Negro Digest,* April 1970, pp. 54–55; in *The Drama Review,* Sept. 1970; and in the author's *THE THEME IS BLACKNESS.* **One Minute Commercial** (short TV commercial, 1969). Advertisement for NLT's prodn. of *A Ritual to Raise the Dead and Foretell the Future,* which was presented in Harlem in 1969. Written Dec. 26, 1969. Pub. in the author's *THE THEME IS BLACKNESS.* **You Gonna Let Me Take You Out Tonight, Baby?** (monologue, 1 act, 1969). Hip, smooth-talking young black man tries to get a date via telephone, apparently without much success. Prod. Off-Bway by NYSF, at the Other Stage, May 16, 1972, on a program of four one-act plays, under the prodn. title *Four for One.* Pub. in *Black Arts* (Alhamisi & Wangara, 1969). **The Pig Pen** (drama, full length, 1969). "An interracial party, loud and raucous, is twice interrupted by the comically bullying White policeman (Pig Pen) on the night that Malcolm X was killed."—*The Best Plays of 1969–1970.* Prod. Off-Bway by APT, at St. Clement's Church, April 29–June 6, 1970, for 46 perfs.; dir. by Dick Williams. Pub. in the author's *FOUR DYNAMITE PLAYS.* **A Street Play** (short scenario, 1970). Revolutionary script, in which two black "brothers" rap on a street corner about an approaching race war which to them seems inevitable. Written May 1970. Pub. in the author's *THE THEME IS BLACKNESS.* **Street Sounds** ("Dialogues with Black Existence" [subtitle], 1970). Thirty-eight brief monologues, depicting various character types familiar to the black community, including Pigs, Dope Seller, Soul Sister, Corner Brother, Harlem Mother, Non-Ideological Niggers, etc. First prod. Off-Off-Bway by the Players Workshop, at a festival of black plays, Oct. 7, 1972. Prod. by BA/W, Seattle, 1972. Pub. in the author's *THE THEME IS BLACKNESS.* **Death List** (revolutionary play, 1 act, 1970). "Dedicated to the Palestine National Liberation Movement." Blackman, the revolutionary, reads a list of so-called "enemies of the Black people," both black and white. Blackwoman, who represents a moderate point of view, attempts to save them from execution, to no avail. Prod. by Theatre Black, at the Univ. of the Streets [Auditorium], Lower East Side, New York, beginning Oct. 16, 1970. Pub. in *Black Theatre #5,* 1971, and in the author's *FOUR DYNAMITE PLAYS.* **The Devil Catchers** (short ritual, 1970). May have been written in collaboration with members of NLT. To strengthen black consciousness and nationalism. Prod. by NLT, Nov. 27, 1970–Jan. 10, 1971; also presented at the Cathedral of St. John the Divine, New York, Oct. 17, 1976—all prodns. dir. by Robert Macbeth. **The Box Office** ("A Scenario for a Short Film" [subtitle], 1970). "By Ed Bullins as Related by Robert Macbeth."—Pub. script. Apparently an advertisement for the reopening of NLT in Harlem. Pub. in *Black Theatre #3,* 1970, pp. 17–19. **Play of the Play** (scenario, apparently for a short "happening," 1970). The audience's own sounds and movements are picked up by hidden microphones and broadcast throughout the room. "Anything can be laid on the people that you wish through lights, images, sound, movement and color."—Pub. script. Written Dec. 1970. Pub. in the author's *THE THEME IS BLACKNESS*. **A Short Play for a Small Theatre** (short scenario, 1971). Set in a little theatre which holds no more than 90 people, of which at least two-thirds are black, this revolutionary script calls for a tall black man to apply bizarre makeup (war paint) to his face, don black gloves, and then shoot each white person in the audience. Pub. in *Black World,* April 1971, p. 39, and in the author's *THE THEME IS BLACKNESS*. **The Psychic Pretenders** ("A Black Magic Show" [subtitle], also called "A Pageant of the Black Passion in Three Motions," full length, 1971). May have been written in collaboration with members of NLT. A black pilgrim, pretending to be white, is led by a "spirit presence" on a "pilgrim's progress" back to his blackness. Prod. by NLT, Dec. 1971. **The Night of the Beast** (screenplay, 1972). A revolutionary Harlem group attempts to combat police brutality by patrolling its own community. Pub. in the author's *FOUR DYNAMITE PLAYS*. **Next Time** (drama, 1 act, 1975). Examines the shooting of black poet Henry Dumas by a white policeman. Pub. in *Spirit* (magazine of black culture), Spring 1975. **House Party** ("A Soulful Happening" [subtitle], full length, 1973). Described by the author as "a compilation of scenes and people you find in the Black existence. . . . It's a house party from the '20s to the present. It has militants, politicians, dope sellers, and Harlem mothers."—Advertisement. Prod. Off-Bway at APT, Oct. 16–Nov. 24, 1973, for 42 perfs.; dir. by Roscoe Orman, based on a prodn. concept by Robert Macbeth. **Malcolm. '71, or Publishing Blackness** (1 act, 1975). Subtitle: "Based on a Real Experience." A serious black revolutionary poet (Blackman) refuses to allow his work to be published in an anthology to be edited by a young white woman whose dog has been named after Malcolm X. Pub. in *Black Scholar,* June 1975, pp. 84–85. **The Mystery of Phillis Wheatley** (historical musical for children, 1976). Black and white forces contend for the soul of black American poet Phillis Wheatley as she begins to achieve international recognition. Prod. by NFT, Feb. 1976; dir. by Elizabeth Van Dyke. Unpub. script in Hatch-Billops Collection. **I Am Lucy Terry** (historical fantasy "for young Americans," 1976). About a young slave poet who was educated illegally by her mistress. She falls in love with and marries a free black man. Commissioned by the New York State Council of the Arts. Prod. by APT, Feb. 1976. **Jo Anne!** (satirical drama, 2 acts, 1976). Focuses on the famous Jo Anne Little case, in which she was acquitted of murdering a white North Carolina prison guard who had sexually assaulted her. Prod. at the Riverside Church Theatre, New York, Oct. 1976. **Sepia Star** (musical, 1977). Music and lyrics by Mildred Kayden. About the life of an early black blues singer. Prod. at Stage 73, New York City, Aug. 1977. **Storyville** (musical comedy, 1977). Music and lyrics by Mildred Kayden. "Set in New Orleans in 1917, a singer gets involved with a musician and they form their own band as they work their way up the river."—*Black American,* May 1977. Prod. at the Mandeville Theatre, Univ. of California/La Jolla, May 1977. **Michael** (1978). Prod. by the New Heritage Repertory Theatre, New York City, May 1978. **C'mon Back to Heavenly House** (1978). Prod. by Amherst Coll. Theatre, MA. 1978. **Do-Wah!** (musical, 1970s). The setting is the 1950s. **Leavings** (1980). Prod. by Syncopation, New York City, Aug. 1980. **Steve and Velma** (1980). Prod. by the New African Co., New York City, Aug. 1980. **High John Da Conqueror—The Musical** ("Musical folkloric fantasy," full length, 1985). Music by Lewis Tucker and Salaelo Maredi. "Set around a campfire in the 18th century, fieldhands have an evening of 'one-ups-menship' *[sic]* as they alternate singing and telling of hilarious stories about High

John's trickery. Washboards, handbone juice harps and makeshift drums are played to create a little fun in da 'bad old days'.''—Producer. Prod. by the African American Drama Co. (of San Francisco) at the Black Repertory Group's theatre, Berkeley, July 4–7, 1985; then moved to Potrero Hill Neighborhood House Theatre, San Francisco, playing through July 28, 1985. Sched. to tour the country, beginning in Jan. 1986.

BURGHARDT, ARTHUR N. (Arthur Burghardt-Banks) (1947–   ), Stage, film and television actor, noted for his portrayals of Frederick Douglass; also credited with two stage adaptations of Douglass's writings. Born in Georgia. While a federal pisoner in Sandstone, MN., Burghardt did extensive research on the life and works of the well-known nineteenth century former slave and abolitionist. Apparently through arrangement with prison authorities, he adapted and performed in a one-man show on Douglass in Town Hall and the Triangle Theatre in New York in 1971, and has since portrayed Douglass in several shows and films, including Gil Noble's *The Life and Times of Frederick Douglass* on "Close Up," in 1976, and *In Search of Frederick Douglass,* a 30–minute film which was shown in churches throughout Harlem during Black History Week in 1976. Other TV appearances by Burghardt include "Like It Is" and "Black Journal." His film appearances include *Cotton Comes to Harlem* (1969) and *Network* (1976). Also noted as a Shakespearean actor, he has performed Hamlet and Othello at a number of schools and churches in the New York area. Recipient of an Emmy Award, 1976.

PLAYS:
Frederick Douglass: An Evening in Memoriam, in Praise and in Glory of Our Black Nigger Father (one-man show, full length, 1971). Written and performed by Burghardt. Prod. Off-Bway, apparently at Town Hall and the Triangle Theatre, New York, 1971. **Frederick Douglass . . . Through His Own Words** (adapt., full length, 1972). Written in collaboration with Michael Egan. Based on the writings of Frederick Douglass. Prod. by the Negro Ensemble Co. (NEC), New York, May 9–June 4, 1972, for 12 perfs., with Burghardt in the title role.

BURGIE, IRVING (Louis) ("Lord Burgess") (1924–   ), Composer-singer. Born in Brooklyn, New York, of part West Indian heritage—his mother from Barbardos, his father from Virginia. Educated at the Juilliard School of Music (1946–48) and the Univ. of Southern California at Los Angeles (1949–50). Served in the U.S. Army, 1942–45. Best known as the author of more than three dozen songs for Harry Belafonte, including "Day-O," "Jamaica Farewell," "A Little Girl in Kingston Town," and "Island in the Sun" (which was the theme song for the film of the same title, in which Belafonte starred with Dorothy Dandridge). Also wrote *The West Indian Songbook* (1972). A new album of songs featuring his current group, The Crew, entitled "Lord Burgess Rides Again," was recently released in 1984, on the occasion of his election to the Songwriters Hall of Fame, in recognition of the sale of over 100 million recordings of his songs.

DRAMATIC WORKS:
Ballad for Bimshire (musical, 2 acts [prologue and 11 scenes], 1963) // Revised and retitled **Calalou** (1978). Book by Burgie and LOFTEN MITCHELL. Music and lyrics by Burgie. Love story with an island atmosphere, involving a native girl and a New York playboy, set in Barbados (nicknamed "Bimshire"). Prod. Off-Bway, at the Mayfair Theatre, Oct. 15–Dec. 15, 1963, for 74 perfs. Co-produced by OSSIE DAVIS, who also starred in the prodn.; dir. by Ed Cambridge. Orig. cast recording (selections) released by London in both monaural (48002) and stereo (78002); copy in the Schomburg Collection. Revised and prod. under the title **Calalou** in 1978. **Like Hogs** (1970s). Unpub. script and tape recording in the FSWW (Frank Silvera Writers' Workshop) Archives/Schomburg Collection.

BURR, ANN, Prize-winning Oswego, New York, playwright. (Racial identity not verified.) *Address:* 182 W. Seneca St., Oswego, New York 13126

PLAY:
Brothers (biographical drama, full length, 1962). About Martin Luther King, Jr. Winner of the third biennial international playwriting competition conducted by Southern Illinois Univ. at Carbondale, 1962. The contest was sponsored by the Dept. of Theatre and the Dept. of Black American Studies.

BURRELL, WALTER PRICE, JR. (1944–   ), Journalist, film publicist, critic, and playwright. Born in Portsmouth, Va. Resided in Beverly Hills, CA. Former critic and columnist for **Black Stars** magazine. Former unit publicist for both Universal Studios and 20th Century-Fox.

DRAMATIC WORKS:
(Both pre-1976.) **All for a Place. Free Black & 21.**

BURROWS, VINIE (1928–   ), Actress, director, and producer. Born in New York City. Received the B.A. from New York Univ. Has appeared in the stage productions of *The Wisteria Trees* (1950), *The Green Pastures* (1951), *Mrs. Patterson* (1954), *The Skin of Our Teeth* (1955), and *Nat Turner* (1960), *Mandingo* (1961), *The Worlds of Shakespeare* (1953), and *Black Medea* (1978), as well as in her one-woman shows cited below. Her television appearances have included "Christopher Closeup," "Camera Three," "The Merv Griffin Show," and "The Tonight Show." Affiliate member of the New York Black Theatre Alliance (BTA). *Address:* Ananse Productions, 63 Avenue A, New York, NY 10009.

REPRESENTATIVE DRAMATIC WORKS:
(All one-woman shows, adapted, arranged, and perfd. by Burrows.) **Shout Freedom** (program of dramatic readings, full length, 1963). Deals with themes of women's lib, nonconformity, and rebellion of children against parental authority. First perfd. at Antioch Coll., Yellow Springs, OH, 1963.
　　Walk Together Children (program of poetry, prose, and songs by black authors, 2 acts, 1968). Depicts "the Black journey from auction block to new nation time."—Program Notes. Her best-known show. First prod. Off-Bway by Robert Hooks at the

Greenwich Mews Theatre, Nov. 11–Dec. 1, 1968, for 24 perfs. Revived Off-Bway at the Mercer-Brecht Theatre, March 16–July 2, 1972, for 89 perfs.

Phillis Wheatley, Gentle Poet, Child of Africa (poetic collage, full length, 1973). A dramatic portrait of Phillis Wheatley's life, composed of selections from her poetry and letters, dramatic readings, dance, and music. Perfd. at the Phillis Wheatley Poetry Festival, held at Jackson State Coll., MS., Nov. 6, 1973, with the assistance of drummer Alphonse Climber and dancer Pearl Primus.

OTHER DRAMATIC WORKS:

(All one-woman shows.) **Dark Fire** (program of African legends, folktales, myths, and proverbs, full length, 1965). First perfd. at Pratt Univ., New York, 1965. **Sister! Sister!** (theatrical collage, full length, early 1970s). Commissioned by the A.M.E. Church, and first presented at the A.M.E. Conf., Los Angeles, early 1970s. Presented at Martha's Vineyard, MA., July 1975, subtitled "A Theatre Celebration of International Women's Year." Presented in a gala performance at Ford's Theatre, Washington, DC, subtitled "All Sorts and Conditions of Women." **Echoes of Africa** (poetic collage, full length, pre-1976). Program of dramatic readings in English and French, from contemporary African writers. **The Female of the Species** (poetic collage, full length, pre-1976). Incidental music composed by ULYSSES KAY. Portrait of seven women from literature and drama. Authors include Shakespeare, Oscar Wilde, Edgar Allan Poe, Lewis Carroll, and LANGSTON HUGHES. **From Swords to Plowshares** (program of readings, full length, pre-1976). Centered around the conflicts of war and peace.

BUTLER, GLEN ANTHONY (Glen Anthony Ravelomanantsoa) (1948–   ), Author, journalist, playwright, actor, and dancer. Born and residing in Omaha, NE, where he worked as a reporter for the *Omaha World-Herald,* was a co-pywriter for Mutual of Omaha, and acted with the Omaha Community Playhouse. Was also a member of the Afro-Academy of Dramatic Arts and the Beth Gaynes Dance Studio in Omaha.

PLAYS:

(All pre-1976.) **Obsolete Bird** (melodrama, 1 act, 1972). About the death of a black pimp. **Resurrection and Kingly Rites** (morality). About Martin Luther King, Jr. **19th Nervous Breakdown.**

BUTLER, RUFUS, Actor-playwright. Associated with the Inner City Cultural Center (ICCC), Los Angeles, CA.

DRAMATIC WORK:

Pushkin (one-man show, 1973). Adaptn. of a series of letters of Alexander Pushkin, the black Russian poet and dramatist of the nineteenth century. Prod. by ICCC, 1973; perfd. by author.

BUTLER, TOMMY, Playwright, composer, actor, singer, producer. Associated with the Inner City Cultural Center (ICCC), Los Angeles, CA.

DRAMATIC WORK:

Selma (dramatic musical, full length, 1975). Book, music, and lyrics by Butler. "Celebration of the life and works of Dr. Martin Luther King, Jr.," which "tells the story of the Civil Rights Struggle of the '50s and '60s.''—*ICCC Calendar,* May 26, 1975. Coproduced by the author and ICCC, opening March 16, 1975; dir. by Cliff Roquemore. Moved uptown to the Huntington-Hartford Theatre, Los Angeles, apparently in 1976, backed by Redd Foxx Productions. Closed, after a nationwide tour, in 1977. Prod. Off-Off-Bway by the New Federal Theatre (NFT), New York, opening Feb. 16, 1984. Unpub. script in the Hatch-Billops Collection.

C

CAESAR, ADOLPH (1934–1986), Veteran actor of stage, screen, and television, and originator of a one-man show. Best-known for his performance as Tech. Sgt. Vernon Waters in CHARLES FULLER's Pulitzer Prize-winning play, *A Soldier's Play* (1981), which was also made into a film, retitled *A Soldier's Story* (1984), in which Caesar repeated his stage role and was nominated for an Oscar as Best Supporting Actor. Gained theatrical experience during his 15-year association with the Negro Ensemble Co. (NEC), and through performances in Shakespearean plays and numerous television commercials. Other stage acting credits include *Day of Absence* (1965), *The Sty of the Blind Pig* (1971), *Nowhere to Run, Nowhere to Hide* (1974), *The Brownsville Raid* (1976), *The Truth About the Truth* (1978), and *Lagrima Del Diablo* (1980). As a memorial to Caesar, the NEC has established an annual Adolph Caesar Performing Arts Award Benefit, the first of which was held on April 26, 1987.

DRAMATIC WORK:
The Square Root of Soul (one-man show, full length, 1976). Conceived and performed by Caesar. A staged reading, with connecting narrative, of the works of 27 black poets, including †Paul Laurence Dunbar, †James Weldon Johnson, LANGSTON HUGHES, Gwendolyn Brooks, and Don Lee. Described as a show which "floats halfway between a recitation and a play."—*Encore,* Aug. 1, 1977. Prod. by NEC; dir. by Perry Schwartz; opening first at the American Theatre, Washington, DC, Feb. 4, 1976, for 15 perfs.; then on tour of cities and campuses outside New York for a year and a half. Opened Off-Bway at the Theatre De Lys, June 14, 1977, for 28 perfs.

CAIN, ORLANDO, Playwright. Formerly associated with the South Side Community Theatre in Chicago, IL.

PLAY:
Cry of the Still Blacks (1973). Deals with "a myriad of themes: interracial marriage, homosexuality, alcoholism and family disunity." —*Black World,* April 1974, p. 52 (Perkins). Prod. by the South Side Community Theatre, Nov. 1973.

CALDWELL, BEN (1937–   ), Playwright, essayist, and graphic artist. Born in Harlem, New York City, one of nine children. Attended the School of Industrial Arts in New York City, with the intent of becoming a commercial artist, but left school in 1954, after the death of his father, to support his family. The author of more than 20 short plays in the black revolutionary agitprop style of the late 1960s, written largely under the influence of AMIRI BARAKA (LeRoi Jones) and his repertory group formerly known as the Spirit House Movers. Caldwell's plays have been produced at Spirit House in Newark, NJ; by the Black Arts Alliance on the West Coast; and throughout the United States, including Off-Broadway. He is the author, with Askia Muhammad Toure, of *Juju (Magic Songs for the Black Nation* (1970). *Address:* c/o Third World Cultural Center, 400 E. 167th St., Bronx, NY 10456.

COLLECTION:

A BLACK QUARTET. Four plays by Ben Caldwell, RON MILNER, ED BULLINS, and Amiri Baraka (LeRoi Jones). Signet Books/New American Lib., New York, 1970. Contains **Prayer Meeting, or The First Militant Minister** (1967).

GROUP OF RELATED PLAYS:

"WHAT IS GOING ON" (5 one-act plays, 1973). Includes **All White Caste** (1971), **Family Portrait** (1969), **Rights and Reasons** (1973), **The Job** (1966), and **Top Secret** (1969). Prod. by the New Federal Theatre (NFT), New York, opening Nov. 23, 1973.

REPRESENTATIVE PLAYS:

Hypnotism (revolutionary play, 1 act, 1966). Ridicules the philosophy of nonviolence as another device used by whites to "hypnotize" blacks in order to keep them under control. Pub. in *Afro-Arts Anthology* (1968); also in *Black Culture* (Simmons & Hutchinson, 1972).

The Job (revolutionary skit, 1 act, 1966). A call for revolt against against black employment opportunity projects as devices used by whites to control blacks. Prod. Off-Bway by NFT, opening Nov. 23, 1973, on a program of five one-act plays, under the prodn. title **"WHAT IS GOING ON"** [see GROUP OF RELATED PLAYS above]. His most widely published play. Pub. in *The Drama Review,* Summer 1968, pp. 43–46; in *Black Identity* (Kearns, 1970); in *Points of Departure* (Kelly, 1972); in *Nommo* (Robinson, 1972); in *A Gathering of Ghetto Writers* (Millner, 1972).

Mission Accomplished (revolutionary skit, 1967). Ridicules the work of white missionaries in Africa. First performed in 1967. Pub. in *The Drama Review,* Summer 1968, pp. 50–52.

Prayer Meeting, or The First Militant Minister (comedy, 1 act, 1967). (Also cited frequently by subtitle alone, and as *The First Militant Preacher.*) An "Uncle Tom" preacher is converted into a black militant by a thief posing as the voice of God. Caldwell's most popular play. First prod. by the Spirit House Movers, 1967. Prod. Off-Bway by WOODIE KING Assocs. Inc., at Tambellini's Gate Theatre, July 30–Nov. 2, 1969, for 111 perfs., on a program of four one-act plays, under the prodn. title *A Black Quartet;* dir. by Irving Vincent. With Dennis Tate as the burglar and L. Errol Jaye as the minister. Pub. by Jihad Press, Newark, 1967; in *Black Fire* (Jones & Neal, 1968); and in the author's collection, *A BLACK QUARTET.*

The Wall (1 act, 1967). Concerns a grafitti wall and its different effects on blacks and whites. Pub. in *Scripts* #7 (NYSF/Public Theatre), May 1972, pp. 91–93.

Riot Sale, or Dollar Psyche Fake Out (revolutionary skit, 1 act, 1968). A white policeman breaks up a mob of black freedom rioters by shooting money into the crowd. Pub. in *The Drama Review,* Summer 1968, pp. 41–42. Also in *Black Culture* (Simmons & Hutchinson, 1972).

Top Secret, or A Few Million After B.C. (revolutionary skit, 1 act, 1969). Criticizes birth-control (B.C.) schemes as devices used by whites to eliminate the black population. Prod. by PASLA (the Performing Arts Soc. of Los Angeles), 1969. Prod. Off-Bway by NFT, opening Nov. 23, 1973, on a program of five one-act plays, under the prodn. title **"WHAT IS GOING ON"** [see GROUP OF RELATED PLAYS above]. Pub. in *The Drama Review,* Summer 1968, pp. 47–50.

Family Portrait, or My Son the Black Nationalist (revolutionary drama, 1 act, 1969). Concerns the generation gap between a black middle-class father and his militant son. Prod. Off-Bway by NFT, opening Nov. 23, 1973, on a program of five one-act plays, under the prodn. title **"WHAT IS GOING ON"** [see GROUP OF RELATED PLAYS above]. Pub. in *New Plays from the Black Theatre* (Bullins, 1969).

The King of Soul, or The Devil and Otis Redding ("A One Act Musical Tragedy" [subtitle], 1969). Modern version of the Faust legend, in which a black "soul" singer achieves fame and fortune by making a deal with the "White devil." Pub. in *Black Theatre* #3, 1969, pp. 28–33; in *New Plays from the Black Theatre* (Bullins, 1969); and in *The Disinherited* (Ravitz, 1974).

All White Caste (revolutionary drama, 1 act, 1971). Subtitled "After the Separation." Rejected by blacks and hated by whites, the white liberal becomes the "nigger" of the future, condemned to life imprisonment in a Harlem ghetto. Prod. Off-Bway by NFT, opening Nov. 23, 1973, on a program of five one-act plays, under the prodn. title **"WHAT IS GOING ON"** [see GROUP OF RELATED PLAYS above]. Pub. in *Black Drama Anthology* (King & Milner, 1972).

The World of Ben Caldwell (series of skits and monologues, making a full length prodn., 1982). Prod. Off-Bway by NFT, April 1, 1982, for 12 perfs.; dir. by Richard Gant. With Kirk Kirksey, REGINALD VEL JOHNSON, Morgan Freeman, GARRETT MORRIS, Steve Coats, B. Jerome Smith, Dianne Kirksey, and Terria Joseph.

OTHER PLAYS AND DRAMATIC WORKS:
The Fanatic (1 act, 1968). Subtitled "Testifyin.' " A white man is "moved by the Spirit" to testify in a black church concerning the wrongs that he has inflicted on black people during his life. Unpub. script in the Hatch-Billops Collection. **Recognition** (ritual, 1 act, 1968). God advises the black man as to the cause of his problems and how they can be solved. Unpub. script in the Hatch-Billops Collection. **Unpresidented** (drama, 1 act, 1968). Subtitled "What Needs to Be Done." Confrontation between a militant civil rights group and the President of the United States. **Runaround** (1 act, 1970). Prod. by the Third World House Black Magicians in Harlem, June 25, 1970. **An Obscene Play (for Adults Only)** (1971). Pub. in *Alafia,* Winter 1971, pp. 14–15. **Rights and Reason** (1 act, 1973). Prod. Off-Bway by NFT, opening Nov. 23, 1973, on a program of five one-act plays, under the prodn. title **"WHAT IS GOING ON"** [see GROUP OF RE-LATED PLAYS above). **Yesterday, Today and Tomorrow** (historical pageant, full length, 1974). Subtitled "The 7 Principles." By Ben Caldwell and YUSEF IMAN. A dramatization of the Seven Principles of the Black Value System, called the Nguso Saba. Prod. by the Weusi Kuumba Troupe, at the Black Theatre Alliance annual festival, New York, Summer 1974. **The Great New York City Crisis** (1987). Public reading by the

Frank Silvera Writers' Workshop (FSWW), Feb. 23, 1987, dir. by WOODIE KING, JR. Unpub. script in the FSWW Archives/Schomburg Collection. **Moms** (a comedy with music, 1987). [Second version of the script described on p. 108 under ALICE CHILDRESS.]

CALEB, J. RUFUS (1948–   ), Playwright, TV scriptwriter, author, editor, and teacher. Winner of an ABC television Award in conjunction with the Eugene O'Neill Playwrights Conf., 1981. His TV script **Benny's Place** (1980) was selected by Judith Christ of *TV Guide* as one of the 10 Best TV Movies of 1982, and was nominated for a Humanitas Prize, an NAACP Image Award, and a WGA TV/Radio Writing Award. Born in Dorchester Co., SC; grew up in Coatesville, PA. Educated at Dickenson Coll., Carlisle, PA (A.B. in political science/ English, 1971) and Johns Hopkins Univ., Baltimore (M.A. in creative writing, 1973). Instr. of English at Dickenson Coll., 1973–75; instr. of fiction and playwriting, the Pennsylvania Governor's School for the Arts, 1976–79; asst. prof. of English, Community Coll. of Pennsylvania, 1975; writer-in-residence, Phillips Andover Academy, Andover, MA, 1979–80; William Neal Reynolds Visiting Prof. and playwright-in-residence, Univ. of North Carolina/Chapel Hill, 1983. His short fiction and poetry have appeared in *Journal of Black Poetry, Obsidian, Poetry Now, Salome, Shenandoah, Trellis,* and *William and Mary Review*. Feature editor, *Black America Magazine,* 1976–79; editor, *Pennsylvania English,* 1975–78; and coeditor, *The New Heroin Addict* (project of the National Inst. of Drug Abuse, in progress, 1983). Organizational memberships include American Federation of Teachers, WGA/East, Coll. English Assn., Pennsylvania Coll. English Assn., ACLU, and NAACP. Other awards (not mentioned above) include Fellow, Eugene O'Neill Playwrights Conf., 1981; Playwriting Fellow, Pennsylvania Council on the Arts; Pennsylvania Council on the Humanities playwriting residencies at Wayne Middle School and Charlestown School, 1985–86. *Address:* 421 E. Woodlawn St., Philadelphia, PA 19144.

PLAYS AND DRAMATIC WORKS:
Fixed Points (1972). Prod. at Johns Hopkins Univ., Baltimore, 1972; dir. by author. Again prod. Baltimore, 1974; dir. by Phillip Arnoulh.
Benny's Place (drama/TV film, full length, 1980). Concerns the crisis of an aging black tool repairman who is employed to operate a repair shop ("Benny's Place") in a steel mill. Pressure is placed on him by his superiors to train a younger black man to do his job, in order that a token black might be qualified for a management position. Rather than give in to this pressure, Benny destroys his shop—a wire cage that he has built himself. (In the TV version, however, Benny is accidentally electrocuted, and his shop is inadvertently destroyed.) Recipient of numerous production awards, including ABC-TV/Eugene O'Neill Theatre Award, 1981, presented to the best play from the summer conference of the Eugene O'Neill Playwrights Conf.; Writers Guild of America (WGA) TV/Radio Writing Awards nomination for "Original Television Drama," 1982; finalist, Humanitas Prize, 1982; Image Award nomination, Los Angeles Chapter, NAACP, 1982, for "Best Television Movie"; and inclusion in "The 10 Best TV Movies of 1982," by Judith Christ, *TV Guide*. Prod. at North Carolina Central Univ., Durham, 1980; dir. by Linda Kerr Norflett. Prod. by the Eugene O'Neill Playwrights Conf., Waterford, CT.,

1981; dir. by Barnet Kellman. Featuring Bill Cobbs and Ethel Ayler. Telecast by ABC-TV as a Theatre Special, prod. by Titus Productions, Spring 1982; dir. by Michael Schultz. Featuring Louis Gossett, Jr., and Cicely Tyson.

City Lights: An Urban Sprawl (full length, 1983). Houston Baker has described this play as one which "expansively and surrealistically ranges over countless generations and generalities of Afro-American existence" to present "a collage of repeatedly deferred dreams." Baker considers the play a negative portrayal of black progress, in which "the march of the New Negro is but a futile duplication of the old Negro's treadmill stumblings in the dark night of an undemocratic America."—*Black American Literature Forum,* Spring 1983, p. 116. Staged readings by the Playmakers Repertory Co., Univ. of North Carolina/Chapel Hill, Spring 1983. Prod. by the People's Light and Theatre Co., Malvern, PA, June-Aug. 1984; dir. by Murphy Geyer. Featuring RAY ARANHA.

Men of Bronze (treatment for an 8-hr. TV mini-series, c. 1985). The story of the 369th (Colored) Infantry Regiment during World War I. The regiment, born of a political pay-off—officered by the sons of New York State's first families and soldiered by such notable blacks as jazz musicians James Reese Europe and Noble Sissle and artist Horace Pippin—fought both U.S. and southern racism, to go on to win distinction as part of the French army. Under contract to Ted Landreth, producer, and Danny Arnold, exec. producer.

Houston: The Day of, and the Night After (TV drama, full length, c. 1985). A day in the life of an Afro-American college student. The story takes place on the day Martin Luther King, Jr., was assassinated. Houston (the student) and an interracial group of friends who have invested themselves in racial understanding must come to terms with what King's death means for the bonds of friendship they have developed. And Houston himself, in the aftermath of the assassination, must struggle to resist the rising tide of black anger and rage that threatens to sweep away all he has learned from the words of Martin Luther King.

Jean Toomer's Cane (adaptn., full length, c. 1985). From the 1923 book, *Cane,* by Jean Toomer. The protagonist is an Afro-American whose skin is fair enough for him to "pass" as white. To reestablish contact with that part of his ancestral past, and his psyche, that is represented in the Afro-American folk culture of the rural South, the character journeys to Georgia. Amid the awesome beauty and the undercurrent of terror there, he undergoes a transformation and is able to accept not only the South, in all its contradictions, but himself as well.

CAMBRIDGE, GODFREY (1933–1976), Actor-comedian. Born in New York City. Educated at Hofstra Univ., and CCNY (1954). Stage acting credits include Gitloe in *Purlie Victorious* (1961); Diouf in *The Blacks* (1961), for which he won an Obie Award; and Pseudolus the slave in *A Funny Thing Happened on the Way to the Forum* (1967). His best-known films are *The Biggest Bundle of Them All* (1968), *Cotton Comes to Harlem* (1970), and *Watermelon Man* (1970), in which he played a white man who turns black overnight. Numerous nightclub and TV appearances.

DRAMATIC WORKS:

Cabaret for Freedom (nightclub revue, full length, 1960). Coauthored, costarred, and coproduced with MAYA ANGELOU. Topical revue in support of the civil rights movement and to raise funds for SCLC. Prod. Off-Bway at the Village Gate, Summer 1960, sponsored by the Emergency Committee for the Southern Freedom Struggle; with an integrated cast of unemployed actors, singers, dancers, and musicians; dir. by Hugh Herd. **Pusher Man** (antidrug doc. film, 1972). Written and prod. by Cambridge, 1972, and taken on road tour for two years.

CAMERON, NORMAN E., Playwright.

PLAY:

Jamaica Joe (drama, 3 acts, 1962). The story of a Jamaican laborer who comes to the United States during World War II, and his eventual return to his country to help improve the political and economic conditions there. Pub. by the author, Georgetown, Guyana, 1962.

CAMPBELL, DICK (Cornelius C. Campbell) (1903–   ), Veteran pro-

ducer-director, publicist, writer, actor, singer, and black theatre organizer—a pioneer in the fight against discrimination and segregation in the performing arts. Currently director of the Sickle Cell Anemia Foundation of Greater New York. Born in Beaumont, TX. Received the A.B. in sociology from Paul Quinn Coll. and the M.A. from Catholic Univ. During his early years as a singer-actor, was featured in such musicals as *Hot Chocolates* (1929), seven editions of Lew Leslie's *Blackbirds* (1928–   ), *Brain Sweat* (1934), and *Cabin in the Sky* (1941). Organized the Negro People's Theatre in Harlem, with actress Rose McClendon, 1935; and in 1938, after McClendon's death, organized the Rose McClendon Players, with the help of his singer-actress wife, the late Muriel Rahn. During World War II, organized more than 65 all-black USO touring camp shows. Directed *On Striver's Row,* 1945. Was field representative for ANTA and chairman of the Board of Directors of the Coordinating Council for Negro Performers, Inc., 1950s. Served as company manager for *Tambourines to Glory,* 1963, and during the same year produced and acted in *A Ballad for Bimshire.* Served as director of information for Operation Crossroads-Africa and chairman of the Committee for the Desegregation of the Arts, 1960s. Appeared in the film *Come Back Charleston Blue* (1972). Member of the Coordinating Council for Negro Performers and numerous other theatrical organizations. *Address*—Home: 321 W. 24th St., New York, NY 10011. Office: 209 W. 125th St., New York, NY 10027.

PLAYS:

The Watchword Is Forward (1 act, 1942). Written for and prod. at the Madison Square Garden mass meeting of the "March on Washington Movement," New York, June 16, 1942. Unpub. script in the Moorland-Spingarn Collection. **Jim Crow Must Go** (1 act, 1952). Prod. and pub. by the NAACP, New York, 1952. **Toll the Liberty Bell** (1 act, 1953). Prod. and pub. by the NAACP, New York, 1953.

CAMPBELL, HERBERT, Playwright. Formerly associated with the Bed-Stuy

Theatre in Brooklyn, NY.

PLAYS:

Middle-Class Black (drama, 3 acts, 1970). (Title originally punctuated *Middle Class! Black?*) Concerns the conflict between two branches of a black family, one middle-class, the other "grassroots." First prod. by the Black Vibrations, at the annual Black Theatre Alliance Festival, New York, 1974; dir. by Maxie Bailey. **Rape** (1971). Prod. by the Bed-Stuy Theatre, Brooklyn, Oct. 1971.

CAMPBELL, RALPH, Playwright.

PLAYS:
Nigger (1972). Pub. by Broadside Press, Detroit, 1972. **The Death of a Crow** (pre-1976).

CANNON, STEVE (1935–   ), Self-taught author, folklorist, artist, and playwright. Born in New Orleans, LA. Has been a radio-TV technician, teacher, and book publisher (in association with Reed, Cannon and Johnson Press, Berkeley, CA, now quiescent). Author of a novel, *Groove, Bang and Jive Around* (1968), an excerpt of which is published in *Nineteen Necromancers from Now* (Reed, 1970). Other writings have been published in *American Rag, Sunbury 9, Callaloo,* and *Pulp. Address:* 285 E. 3rd St., New York, NY 10009.

PLAY:
Snakeshiiiit (tragicomic pageant, 3 acts, 1975). Written with CORRINE JENNINGS and JOE OVERSTREET. Public reading by the New Federal Theatre, New York, 1975. Unpub. script in the Hatch-Billops Collection.

CAPEL, SHARON, Playwright. An alumna of the Frank Silvera Writers' Workshop (FSWW) in New York City. *Address—* Family home: 1507 Teller Ave., Bronx, NY.

PLAY:
Dreams Are for the Dead (1975). Public reading by FSWW, at the Martinique Theatre, New York, June 1975. Unpub. script and tape recording in the FSWW Archives/Schomburg Collection.

CARROLL, VINNETTE (1922–   ), Actress, black theatre organizer, director, playwright, and conceiver of original shows. Considered to be one of the outstanding black female directors in America. Recipient of numerous awards for acting, directing, playwriting, and other contributions to the theatre, cited below. Born in New York City's Harlem. Lived from age three to eight in Jamaica, West Indies. Educated at Long Island Univ. (B.A. in psychology, 1944), NYU (M.A. in psychology, 1946), and Columbia Univ. (Ph.D. studies—all but dissertation). Also studied with Erwin Piscator at the Dramatic Workshop; Lee Strassberg at the Actors Studio, 1948–50; and Stella Adler, 1954–65. Taught for several years at the H.S. for the Performing Arts in New York. Also headed the Ghetto Arts Program of the New York State Council on the Arts. Organizer and artistic director, since the early 1960s, of the Urban Arts Corps (UAC) in Greenwich Village, where most of her dramatic works were originally conceived and staged. Former member of the Directors Unit of the Actors Studio. Stage acting credits include *Outside the Door* (1949), *Caesar and Cleopatra* (1955),

The Crucible (1958), *Jolly's Progress* (1959), and *Moon on a Rainbow Shawl* (1961) for which she won an Obie Award. Films include *One Potato, Two Potato* (1964), *Up the Down Staircase* (1967), and *Alice's Restaurant* (1969). TV appearances include *Member of the Wedding* (London, 1960), "All in the Family" (1976), and a segment of the CBS-TV program, "We, the Women," in which she was highly praised for her performance as Sojourner Truth; she has also appeared frequently on "Sesame Street" as Lillian. In addition to her own dramatic works, she directed the original Off-Broadway productions of LANGSTON HUGHES's *Black Nativity* and *Prodigal Son;* and the Urban Arts Corps production of JOSEPH WHITE's *Old Judge Mose Is Dead* (1969) and PETER DeANDA's *Ladies in Waiting* (1970). For the Inner City Repertory Company in Los Angeles, she directed *Slow Dance on the Killing Ground* (1966) and *The Flies* (1967). In addition to the Obie Award in acting, 1961, mentioned above, she has received the following honors and awards: Ford Foundation grant for directors, 1960–61; Emmy Award for "conceiving, adapting and supervising *Beyond the Blues,*" presented on CBS-TV, 1964; Outer Critics' Circle Award for directing, 1971–72; NAACP Image Award (Los Angeles), 1972; Harold Jackman Memorial Award, 1973; three Tony nominations—two for directing, 1973 and 1977, and one for the best book for a musical, 1976; AUDELCO Board of Directors Award for contributions to the theatre, 1973; Frank Silvera Writers' Workshop Foundation Award, 1977; and the Dramatists Guild Committee for Women's first annual award, 1972, given to an outstanding woman dramatist for her contributions to the theatre (shared with playwright ALICE CHILDRESS). *Address:* Urban Arts Corps, 302 W. 12th St., New York, NY 10011.

REPRESENTATIVE PLAYS AND DRAMATIC WORKS:

Trumpets of the Lord (musical, full length, 1963). Adapt. by Carroll from †James Weldon Johnson's *God's Trombones* (1927). Described by *Jet* magazine (April 17, 1969, p. 59) as "a series of sermons and intermittent singing of gospel liturgical songs in a rustic country church." First prod. Off-Bway, at the Astor Place Playhouse, Dec. 21, 1963–May 17, 1964, for 161 perfs.; dir. by Donald McKayle. With AL FREEMAN, JR., Theresa Merritt, Lex Monson, and Cicely Tyson. Also prod. in Rome during the mid-1960s "by a small group of [black] artists who remained . . . after the filming of Cleopatra, forming an acting company under the direction of Jay J. Riley." —*Black Magic* (Hughes & Meltzer, 1967). Prod. Off-Bway at the Circle in the Square, April 29–May 3, 1969, for 7 perfs. Prod. at the Ford Theatre, Washington, DC, 1969, for a run of six weeks. Sched. to open at the Brooks Atkinson Theatre on Bway in 1969; no record of the actual prodn. [See also **The Great Gettin' Up Morning** under OTHER PLAYS AND DRAMATIC WORKS below.]

Beyond the Blues (TV show, 1964). Conceived, adapt., and dir. by Carroll. Televised by CBS-TV, 1964, and won for the author an Emmy Award. [This prodn. may have used material from the author's **Jubilation,** cited below under OTHER PLAYS AND DRAMATIC WORKS.]

But Never Jam Today // Also prod. as **Alice** (musical, full length, 1969). Conceived and dir. by Carroll. Music originally by Gershon Kinsley and others. [See below for other musical contributors.] "An Afro-American adaptation of Lewis Carroll's *Alice in Wonderland* and *Through the Looking Glass*."—Program notes. First prod. by UAC opening April 24, 1969, presumably as part of New York's Black Expo. Also presented (in this first prodn.) at the City Center, "for the Summer 1970 tour of New York City parks and streets."—Ibid. Cast included Marie Thomas as Alice and Sherman Hemsley (costar of "The Jeffersons" TV show) as the Mad Hatter and the Seven of Spades. Prod. in a pre-Bway tryout, entitled *Alice,* with book by Carroll, music and lyrics by MICKI GRANT; presented at the Forrest Theatre in Philadelphia, May 31–June 11, 1978, with Debbie Allen (of TV's "Fame") as Alice, and featuring Clevant Derricks, Clinton Derricks-Carroll, Alice Ghostley, and Paula Kelly. This prodn. closed prior to reaching Bway. Prod. on Bway in a third version, under its orig. title, with book by Carroll and Bob Larimer, who also coauthored the music (with Bert Keys) and wrote the lyrics alone. This prodn. was presented at the Longacre Theatre, July 31–Aug. 5, 1979, for 8 perfs. With Marilyn Winbush as Alice, and Clevant Derricks from the previous cast; playwright REGINALD VEL JOHNSON also appeared in this prodn.

Don't Bother Me, I Can't Cope (musical entertainment, 2 acts, 1970). Conceived by Carroll, who dir. all professional prodns. Book, music, and lyrics by Micki Grant. Award-winning musical which deals with the black (and universal) problem of coping with life, utilizing songs and dances based on blues, gospel, jazz, rock, calypso, and traditional ballad rhythms. Winner of the Outer Critics' Circle Award, two Obie awards, two Drama Desk awards, and an NAACP Image Award. Nominated for a Tony Award. First presented by UAC in small theatres around New York and elsewhere, during the 1970–71 season, prior to its world premiere at Ford's Theatre in Washington, DC, opening Sept. 15, 1971, for 32 perfs. With Micki Grant, Alex Bradford, HOPE CLARKE, Arnold Wilkerson, Carl Bean, Charles E. Campbell, Marie Thomas, Bobbie L. Hill, and Willie James McPhatter. Opened on Bway in a slightly revised version, at the Playhouse Theatre, April 19, 1972, transferring to the Edison Theatre, June 13, 1972, where it continued to run, closing Oct. 23, 1973, after 1,065 perfs., with substantially the same cast. Prod. by the Center Theatre Group, at the Mark Taper Forum, Los Angeles, opening Aug. 10, 1972, for 54 perfs. Transferred to the Huntington-Hartford Theatre, Los Angeles, where it had a long run, featuring Paula Kelly. Also prod. at the Happy Medium, Chicago, 1972, featuring Loleatta, a singer formerly with Alberta Walker's Caravans. Again prod. at Ford's Theatre, opening April 23, 1973, for more than 44 perfs. Prod. as a guest prodn. at the American Conservatory Theatre, San Francisco, opening July 21, 1973, for 55 perfs. Cast recording by Polydor. Pub. by Samuel French, New York, 1972.

Croesus and the Witch (musical, full length, 1971). Book by Carroll. Music and lyrics by Micki Grant. Based on a fable. Prod. by UAC, in repertory, opening Aug. 10, 1971, at Ft. Green Park, and was still being presented by the group in 1975; dir. by Carroll. Pub. by Broadway Music Publishing, New York, 1984; copy in the Hatch-Billops Collection.

The Ups and Downs of Theophilus Maitland (musical, full length, 1974). Conceived, adapt., and dir. by Carroll from a West Indian folk tale. Music and lyrics by Micki Grant. The story of an old man who scandalizes his family and the community by taking on a beautiful young bride, but discovers on his wedding night that he is impotent. After consulting several doctors without success, he finally goes to a witch woman who gives him an aphrodisiac potion. Prod. by UAC, opening Nov. 13, 1974. This prodn. was also presented at the Black Theatre Alliance annual festival, New York, 1974. Revived Nov. 1–Dec. 5, 1976.

Your Arms Too Short to Box with God [*sic*] (gospel musical, full length, 1975). Conceived by Carroll. Music and lyrics by Alex Bradford. Additional music by Micki Grant. The Gospel of Matthew told in the black idiom, with title taken from a poem in *God's Trombones* (1927) by †James Weldon Johnson. Received two Tony nominations, 1966–67, for the best book of a musical and the best director. Developed by UAC for presentation at the Spoleto, Italy, Festival of Two Worlds, where it was first performed in 1975. American premiere was held at Ford's Theatre, opening Nov. 4, 1975, for 168 perfs. With Dolores Hall, who won a Tony Award as best featured actress. Revived at the Ambassador Theatre, New York, June 2–Oct. 12, 1980, for 149 perfs. Restaged by dancer-choreographer Ralf Haze, who first took the show on a national tour before opening with it at the Alvin Theatre, New York, Sept. 9, 1982, for a limited engagement, featuring Patti LaBelle and Al Green, with Haze in the role of Judas. Cast recording of the orig. prodn. by ABC, on records, cassettes, and eight-track cartridges. Also recorded by MCA, 1981–82.

When Hell Freezes Over, I'll Skate (musical, full length, 1979). Conceived and dir. by Carroll. Reflects on the positive and negative aspects of the black experience in America, through poetry, song, and dance. First prod. by UAC, Jan. 1979. Also presented as the first event in the Black Theatre Festival, U.S.A., May 1, 1979. Televised on NET, 1980–81. Revived in a pre-Bway tryout at the Forrest Theatre, Philadelphia, April 1984.

OTHER PLAYS AND DRAMATIC WORKS:
The Great Gettin' Up Morning (full length, 1963). Adapt. by Carroll and Alfred E. Cain from *God's Trombones* (1927) by James Weldon Johnson. Prod. at the White Barn Theatre, Westport, CT, opening Aug. 11, 1963. [See also **Trumpets of the Lord** above.] **Jubilation** (musical, 1964). Prod. by UAC, New York, 1964. [See also **Beyond the Blues** above.] **Step Lively, Boy** (musical, full length, 1972). Adapt. by Carroll from *Bury the Dead,* an antiwar play by Irwin Shaw. Music and lyrics by Micki Grant. Prod. by UAC, opening Feb. 7 1972; dir. by Carroll. **All the King's Men** (musical, full length, 1974). Adapt. by Carroll from the play of the same title by Robert Penn Warren. Music and lyrics by Malcolm Dodds. Prod. by UAC, opening May 14, 1974; dir. by Carroll. **Love Power** ("theatre event" with music, full length, 1974). Conceived by Carroll and Micki Grant. Prod. by UAC, Dec. 1974. **I'm Laughin' but I Ain't Tickled** (musical, full length, 1976). Conceived and dir. by Carroll. Music by Micki Grant. Based on poetry anthologized in *A Rock Against the Wind* (Patterson, 1973). Prod. by UAC, May and Dec. 1976. **What You Gonna Name That Pretty Little Baby** (musical, full length, 1979). Conceived and dir. by Carroll. Prod. by UAC, Dec. 1978, for 12 perfs.

CARSON, GERALD, Screenwriter and poet. An alumnus of the Sonia Sanchez Writers Workshop, held at the Countee Cullen Lib. in Harlem, 1970–71. His work has been published in *Three Hundred and Sixty Degrees of Blackness Comin at You* (Sanchez, 1971).

DRAMATIC WORK:
The Unforgettable Experience of Billy Joe McAlester (screenplay, 1977). Adaptn. of "The Ballad of Billy Joe McAlester," about love affair between a black man and a white woman, in which the man is killed by a jealous white rival. Pub. by Vantage Press, New York, 1977.

CARTER, STEVE (1929–), Playwright, scene designer, and theatre administrator. Winner of the Outer Critics Circle Award as the season's most promising playwright for his play **Eden** (1976), which also won an AUDELCO Award as best play of the year. Born in New York City, of part-West Indian heritage; his father came from Richmond, VA, his mother from Trinidad. Graduated from the H.S. of Music and Art, New York City, 1948, where he majored in art and dreamed of becoming a scene designer. Served as a radio operator with flight status in the U.S. Air Force until 1953, with the rank of staff sgt. Gained experience with MAXWELL GLANVILLE's American Community Theatre (ACT), where he designed costumes and sets, operated lights and sound, taught body movement, and wrote plays. Member of the Negro Ensemble Company (NEC) from 1968 to 1981, as director *(Raisin' Hell in the Son,* 1962), costume designer *(The Sty of the Blind Pig,* 1971), production coordinator and director of the Playwrights' and Acting Workshops, artistic director and set designer for the Season-Within-a-Season series, and playwright-in-residence. Directed the London production of Mustafa Matura's *Bread* at the Young Vic Theatre, 1976. Currently playwright-in-residence with the Victory Gardens Theatre, Chicago. Member of New Dramatists since 1981. In addition to the awards cited above, he received an NEA Creative Writing Award, a Rockefeller Foundation and a Guggenheim Foundation Creative Writing Fellowship, and a New York State Council on the Arts Dramaturgy Grant. His drama **Nevis Mountain Dew** (1978) was a Burns Mantle Theatre Yearbook "Best Play" of 1978–79. *Address:* P.O. Box 7217, Corona, NY 11368.

COLLECTION:
PLAYS BY STEVE CARTER. Broadway Play Publishing Co., New York, 1968. Contains **House of Shadows** (1982), **Dame Lorraine** (1981), **One Last Look** (1987), **Mirage** (1985), and **Tea on Inauguration Day** (1985).

GROUP OF RELATED PLAYS:
"THE CARIBBEAN TRIOLOGY" (3 full length plays. 1976–c. 1980). Includes **Eden** (1976). **Nevis Mountain Dew** (1978), and **Dame Lorraine** (pre-1980).

REPRESENTATIVE PLAYS AND DRAMATIC WORKS:
One Last Look (comedy, 1 act, 1967). A look at a man's life through the eyes of those who loved or hated him. The setting is his funeral, and the characters are the dead man, his mistress, his wife, and his children. First prod. Off-Off-Bway, at the Old Reliable Theatre Tavern, opening Nov. 13, 1967; dir. by Arthur French. Prod. Off-Bway by NEC, at St. Marks Playhouse, 1968. Prod. by the Afro-American Total Theatre, at International House, New York, Aug. 1970. Televised on ABC-TV's "Like It Is," 1970; rerun 1971. Prod. at Black Expo, San Francisco, 1972. Excerpt (1 scene) pub. in *Black Scenes* (Childress, 1971). Pub. in *PLAYS BY STEVE CARTER.*

As You Can See (comedy, 1 act, 1968). Concerns blind man who is not above using his affliction to con and wheedle and make the sighted feel guilty. Prod. Off-Off-Bway by ACT in Harlem, 1968. Prod. Off-Off-Bway at the Old Reliable Theatre Tavern, opening June 17, 1968.

Terraced Apartment (comedy, 1 act, 1968). A black couple move into a middle-class apartment building, but find that they are out of their element. First prod. at ACT in Harlem, 1968. Prod. Off-Off-Bway, at the Old Reliable Theatre Tavern, 1968. Prod.

as a work-in-progress by NEC, at St. Marks Playhouse, opening Jan. 30, 1971, for 2 perfs., with Denise Nicholas in the cast. Later adapt. to a full length play [see **Terraces** below].

Terraces (4 sketches, full length, 1974). Adapt. from his one-act play **Terraced Apartment** above. Concerns four views of life in a terraced apartment building in Harlem. Three of the sketches are satiric, and one melodramatic, in their criticism of wealthy black lifestyles. Prod. by NEC, as a Season-Within-a-Season experimental prodn., at St. Marks Playhouse, New York, April 2–7, 1974, for 8 perfs.; dir. by Frances Foster. With Mary Alice, Joyce Hanley, Robert Christian, Leon Morenzie, Ronald Sanchez, and Michele Shay. Nominated for an AUDELCO Award.

Eden (domestic drama, 3 acts, 1976). Part of a series which the author calls **"THE CARIBBEAN TRILOGY"** [see GROUP OF RELATED PLAYS above]. Romeo-and-Juliet-type story, with setting in New York City, dramatizing the love of a West Indian girl for a southern black American youth, whose families are in open conflict. Prod. Off-Bway by NEC, at St. Marks Playhouse, New York, opening March 3, 1976. Transferred to the Theatre De Lys, May 14–Aug. 1, 1976, for 181 perfs. With Barbara Montgomery and Graham Brown in the leading roles. Won for the author an Outer Critics' Circle citation as the season's most promising playwright. Winner of an AUDELCO Award as Play of the Year. AUDELCO awards were also won by both performers and by Saundra Ross for Lighting. Also adapt. as a screenplay, entitled **A Time Called Eden,** soon to be made into a film. Pub. by Samuel French, New York, 1976.

Nevis Mountain Dew (drama, 3 acts, 1978). Part of a series which the author calls **"THE CARIBBEAN TRILOGY"** [see GROUP OF RELATED PLAYS above]. Described by *The Best Plays of 1978–1979* as "A candid but respectful family portrait of a Queens household of West Indian background, with the man of the family confined to an iron lung and his sisters and friends attempting doggedly to create a party mood for his 50th birthday celebration." As the family members become intoxicated on West Indian rum (Nevis Mountain Dew), they begin to reveal their unhappiness and anxiety. The head of the family, realizing the effect that his illness has had on those who love him, begs his family to unplug the iron lung and release him and themselves from the imprisonment that his illness has caused. A *Burns Mantle Yearbook* "Best Play" of 1978–79. Prod. Off-Bway by NEC, at St. Marks Playhouse, Dec. 7–17, 1978, for 14 perfs. Reopened Feb. 22–April 1, 1979. Also presented at the Arena Stage, Kreeger Theatre, Washington, DC, opening April 20, 1979, for 35 perfs.; dir. by Horacena J. Taylor. With Frances Foster, Ethel Ayler, Arthur French, Graham Brown, Barbara Montgomery, Charles Brown, and SAMM-ART WILLIAMS. Abridged in *The Best Plays of 1978–1979*. Pub. by Dramatists Play Service, New York, 1979.

Dame Lorraine (drama, full length, 1982–83). Part of a series which the author calls **"THE CARIBBEAN TRILOGY"** [see GROUP OF RELATED PLAYS above]. A West Indian family, living in Harlem, waits for the return of their only surviving son, who has spent more than 25 years in prison. As they wait, they reveal their feelings of love and hatred. First prod. at the Victory Gardens Theatre, Chicago, March 28, 1981, dir. by Chuck Smith. Prod. by the Los Angeles Actors Theatre, during the 1982–83 season. Pub. in *PLAYS BY STEVE CARTER*

House of Shadows // Orig. title: **Shadows** (drama, 1 long act, 1982). According to the publisher's description, "Two baby-faced, would-be criminals decide to rob the home of two women of advanced age who live in contention with their past, their present, their future and each other. The brats get more than they've bargained for . . . including possible great futures behind bars in Joliet."—Pub. text, back cover. The author states that the play "was written to display the talents of . . . as the French would say . . . 'deux femmes du certaine age,' " a phrase which he later paraphrases as two "mature and experienced character actresses."—Ibid. First prod. at the Victory Gardens Theatre, Chicago, opening April 1, 1982, under its orig. title, dir. by Chuck Smith. prod. Off-Bway by NEC, Opening Jan. 16, 1986; dir. by Clinton Turner Davis. With Frances Foster and Joan Grant as the two old women; and Teddy Abner and Raymond Rosario as the young criminals. Pub. in *PLAYS BY STEVE CARTER*.

Mirage and **Tea on Inauguration Day** (2 very short plays, 1985). The author describes the two plays as follows: "MIRAGE . . . so like 'marriage' in its spelling and some pronunciations, is about how much more interesting mundane situations could be . . . if people would only 'apply' themselves." "TEA ON INAUGURATION DAY (which I should have called 'The Inaugural Tea') is a tragi-comical look at the current state of our country. However, one of the reasons I wrote it is that Americans (even the learned ones) tend to mispronounce 'Nuclear,' 'Acapulco,' 'Realtor' and 'Inauguration.' " Pub. in *PLAYS BY STEVE CARTER*. Also in *Short Pieces from the New Dramatists* (Broadway Publishing Co., 1980s).

OTHER PLAYS AND DRAMATIC WORKS:
(Undated plays are all pre-1980s.) **Rampart Street** (musical). Based on jazz musician Buddy Bolden's life. **The Courage and the Grace** (TV "soap," first 3 episodes). Prod. on PBS, Hartford, CT. **Shoot Me While I'm Happy** (musical, full length, 1986). Book by Carter. **Primary Colors** (1986). Public reading at Sounds in Motion Studio, New York, April 11–12, 1986, dir. by Alma Becker.

CARTER, THOMAS G., JR., Former student playwright at UCLA.

PLAY:
Angel of the Mourning (drama, 1976). Concerns how a black married couple corresponds to the racism and lack of economic opportunities which they face in a small urban community. Prod. by UCLA, 1976. Also presented at the American Coll. Theatre Regional Festival, at Cypress Coll., Cypress, CA, 1978.

cha JUA, CHAKULA, Actor, director, playwright. Associated with the Free Southern Theatre (FST) in New Orleans. *Address:* 3936 Magazine St., New Orleans, LA 70115; or Act I, Alliance for Community Theatres, P.O. Box 50575, New Orleans, LA 70150.

PLAYS:
(All prod. by FST during the early 1970s.) **A Black Experience** (coauthor, with *Leppaigne Chiphe). **Langston and Company** (1974). **Langston Hughes: A Poet of the People.**

CHARLES, MARTI (or Martie). See EVANS-CHARLES, MARTI.

CHARLES, (Rev.) NORMAN, Playwright. Associated with the Theatre of Renewal, New York City, and the Regal Roots for the Performing Arts, Paterson, NJ.

PLAYS:

Infirmity Is Running (domestic drama, 2 acts, 1976). About the relationships within a black family. Prod. by the Theatre of Renewal, at the Stagelights Theatre, New York, Sept. 1976. **Friends** (1976). Prod. by the Regal Roots for the Performing Arts, at St. Joseph Hosp. Auditorium, Paterson, NJ, July 1976. **Jenny** (comedy-drama, 1 act, 1976). Prod. by the Theatre of Renewal, at the Stagelights Theatre, 1976.

CHILDRESS, ALICE (Mrs. Nathan Woodard) (1920–   ), Distinguished actress, playwright, director, author, and lecturer. Born in Charleston, SC. Educated at the Harlem Community of New York City, at P.S. 81, Julia Ward Howe Jr. H.S., and Wadleigh H.S. Recipient of a Harvard appointment to Radcliffe Inst. as a scholar-writer, 1966–68, where she graduated without a degree. Married to Nathan Woodard, a musician and film director. Gained early training (for ten years) as a member of the American Negro Theatre (ANT) in Harlem, where she acted, directed, and served on the Board of Directors. Made her professional debut in 1944 in ANT's Broadway production of *Anna Lucasta*. Has also performed in †Theodore Browne's *Natural Man*, †Abram Hill's *On Strivers' Row,* and other stage plays, as well as on television. In addition to her credits as an actress and director of several Off-Broadway productions, she has written more than a dozen stage plays, numerous essays, a regular column for the Baltimore *Afro-American* newspaper, and the following books: *Like One of the Family* (1956), about the experiences of a black domestic, and *A Hero Ain't Nothin' but a Sandwich* (1973), a novel which was also produced as a film [see below]. Member of the Dramatists Guild, AEA, New Dramatists, and the Harlem Writers Guild. Recipient of numerous awards and honors including an Obie Award for **Trouble in Mind** (1956); a grant from the John Golden Fund for Playwrights, 1957; the Sojourner Truth Award, presented by the National Negro Business and Professional Women's Clubs; and the Black Filmmakers First Paul Robeson Medal of Distinction, 1977; and AUDELCO Pioneer Award, 1985. *Agent:* Flora Roberts, 1958 W. 57th St., New York, NY 10019.

COLLECTIONS:

MOJO AND STRING: Two Plays. Dramatists Play Service, New York, 1971. Includes **Mojo** (1970) and **String** (1969).

BLACK SCENES: Collection of Scenes from Plays Written by Black People About Black Experience. Ed. Zenith Books/Doubleday, Garden City, NY, 1971. Includes **The African Garden** (excerpt) (1971).

PLAYS AND DRAMATIC WORKS:

Florence (drama, 1 act, 1949). A black mother in the South, who wishes to dissuade her daughter Florence from becoming an actress, changes her mind after meeting a southern white actress in the Jim Crow waiting room of a railway station. First prod. by ANT in Harlem, 1949. Prod. by the Committee for the Negro in the Arts, at Club Baron, Harlem, Sept. 1950. Prod. by the Negro Arts Players, Harlem, Aug. 25–30, 1952. Prod. by the Southside Center of the Performing Arts, Chicago, 1966. Pub. in *Masses and Mainstream,* Oct. 1950, pp. 34–37.

Just a Little Simple (musical revue, full length, 1950). Adaptn. of LANGSTON HUGHES's *Simple Speaks His Mind*. About a Harlem character named Jesse B. Semple. Prod. by the Committee for the Negro in the Arts, at Club Baron in Harlem, opening Sept. 1950, for a run of two months.

Gold Through the Trees (dramatic revue, 8 scenes, 1952). Historical play with music, surveying the black struggle against oppression from Africa to the United States and back to present-day South Africa. Prod. by the Committee for the Negro in the Arts, at Club Baron in Harlem, April 1952. (According to the author, it "opened on the day of Black South Africa's protest of civil disobedience with the Tricentennial of S.A. Boers.")

Trouble in Mind (comedy-drama, 2 acts, 1955). Concerns the racial and emotional tensions that arise among a group of black and white actors (and their white director) as they rehearse a play about lynching in the South. Received the Obie Award in 1956, as the best original Off-Bway play of the season. First prod. Off-Bway, at the Greenwich Mews Theatre, opening Nov. 4, 1955, for 91 perfs., featuring Clarice Taylor and Hilda Haynes. Sched. for a Bway prodn. in April 1957, under the title *So Early Monday Morning,* but was withdrawn by the author because of changes which the director wished to make. Twice telecast by BBC in Oct. and Nov. 1964. Pub. in *Black Theater* (Patterson, 1971).

A Man Bearing a Pitcher (drama, full length, c. 1955). Set in Biblical times, this play focuses on an imaginary family in whose home Christ's Last Supper was held, and their attempts to prevent him from being crucified.

Wedding Band (drama, 3 acts, 1966). Subtitled "A Love/Hate Story in Black and White." About an interracial relationship between a black woman and a white man in South Carolina during World War I. First prod. by the Univ. of Michigan as its Professional Theatre Production of 1966, with RUBY DEE (who played the leading role of Julia in this and all subsequent prodns.), ABBEY LINCOLN, and Jack Harkins. Prod. at the Ivanhoe Theatre in Chicago, 1971. Prod. Off-Bway by the New York Shakespeare Festival Public Theatre, Sept. 26, 1972–Feb. 25, 1973, for 175 perfs.; dir. by author and Joseph Papp. This prodn. was televised as a two-hour ABC-TV Theatre Special, April 24, 1975. Pub. by Samuel French, New York, 1973. In *The New Women's Theatre* (Moore, 1977).

The World on a Hill (drama, 1 act, 1968). In a West Indian setting, a white woman and her son begin to reevaluate their unsatisfactory lives after meeting a young black teenager at a picnic. Pub. in *Plays to Remember* (Macmillan, 1968).

The Freedom Drum // Orig. title: **Young Martin Luther King** (historical play, 1969). Subtitled "Martin Luther King at Montgomery, Alabama." With music by *Nathan Woodard (Ms. Childress's husband). A tribute to the slain civil rights leader and apostle of nonviolence. Prod. by the Performing Arts Repertory Theatre, first at Symphony Hall, Newark, NJ, May 6, 1969; then on bus and truck tour for two years, 1969/72.

String (drama, 1 act, 1969). Free adaptn., in the black idiom, of de Maupassant's short story "A Piece of String." A raggedy black character who, in the tradition of a true Rastafarian, honorably survives on the discards of others, is falsely accused by middle-class blacks of stealing a wallet. Prod. Off-Bway, by NEC, at St. Marks Playhouse, March 25– April 20, 1969, for 32 perfs., with Esther Rolle, Clarice Taylor, and Arthur French. Pub. in the author's collection, *MOJO AND STRING.*

Wine in the Wilderness (comedy-drama, 1 act, 1969). Multifaceted statement of black experience, centered around the relationship between a middle-class black artist and a "soul sister" from the streets of Harlem whom he selects as a model. First prod. in 1969 on NET in Boston as part of an experimental series of plays. Prod. by the Kuumba Workshop, Chicago, 1971. Prod. by the Howard Univ. Players, Washington, DC, 1972. Prod. by the National Black Theatre, New York, 1977. Pub. by Dramatists Play Service, New York, 1969. In *Plays by and About Women* (Sullivan & Hatch, 1973); and in *Black Theater, U.S.A.* (Hatch & Shine, 1974).

Mojo ("A Black Love Story" [subtitle], 1970). A meeting between a divorced, middle-aged Harlem couple reveals that they still love each other, in spite of the feuding and fussing that originally caused them to separate. First prod. by the New Heritage Theatre in Harlem, Spring 1970. Pub. in *Black World* (April 1971), pp. 54–82; in the author's collection *MOJO AND STRING;* and in *The Best Plays of World Theatre, 1968–73* (Richards, 1973).

The African Garden (drama with music: excerpt, 1971). Book and lyrics by Childress. Concerns the black man's search for closer identification with his African heritage. Written under a Harvard Univ. appointment to the Radcliffe Inst. for Independent Study. Excerpt (1 scene) pub. in the author's collection *BLACK SCENES*.

When the Rattlesnake Sounds (1 act, 1975). Harriet Tubman is depicted as a laundress in a New Jersey hotel, where she is working to help the cause of abolition. Pub. by Coward, McCann & Geoghegan, New York, 1975.

Let's Hear It for the Queen (drama, 1 act, 1976). A continuation of the Mother Goose story about "the Knave of Hearts who stole some tarts." Pub. by Coward, McCann & Geoghegan, 1976.

A Hero Ain't Nothin' but a Sandwich (film, full length: screenplay, 1977). Based on the author's novel by the same title. Tells the story of a teenage drug addict and the influences that have molded his life. Prod. by Radnitz & Mattel, 1977; released by New World, 1978; starring Paul Winfield and Cicely Tyson, with Larry B. Scott as the teenager. Pub. only as a novel by Coward, McCann & Geoghegan, 1973.

Sea Island Song (drama, full length, 1977). Commissioned by the South Carolina Arts Commission. About the Gullah-speaking people of the Georgia Sea Islands off the coast of South Carolina. Completed in 1977. Prod. in Charleston, SC, at Stage South, during Alice Childress Week, 1977.

Gullah (musical, full length, 1984). Apparently based on her drama **Sea Island Song** [see above]. Music composed by her husband, Nathan Woodard. Prod. at the Univ. of Massachusetts, Amherst, Spring 1984.

Moms (three-character show, full length, 1987). About the life and world of come-dienne Jackie "Moms" Mabley. Apparently commissioned by Clarice Taylor, who also collaborated on the script. "The play abounds with jokes, wry humor and terse obser-vations by Moms, dealing with all aspects of her life with sophistication and worldly wisdom."—*New York Amsterdam News,* March 21, 1987, p. 32. Prod. at the Hudson Guild Theatre, New York, Feb. 4–March 1, 1987; dir. by Walter Dallas, with Clarice Taylor as Moms; S. Epatha Merkerson as her secretary, housekeeper, and confidant; and Grenaldo Frazier as her pianist and lover. A second version of this script by BEN CALDWELL was produced at the Astor Place Theatre, New York, in Aug. 1987.

CLARK, CHINA (Debra) (Mrs. Jervey Pendarvis) (1952–   ), Playwright, TV scriptwriter, film writer, poet, and writing teacher. Born in Pennsylvania. Educated at Columbia Univ. and the American Academy of Arts. Taught writing for the Cell Block Theatre at Columbia Univ.; has also taught writing for films and TV. Staff writer for the "Bill Cosby Show," produced by ABC-TV, 1977. Member of the Writers Guild (presumably WGA), Arts and Letters, and Poets and Writers. Recipient of the Woolrich Foundation Award, 1973, the Hannah del Vecchio Award (Columbia Univ.), 1974, and a CAPS fellowship. *Address:* 145 E. 18th St., Brooklyn, NY 11226.

COLLECTION:
(Exact title not verified.) *NEFFIE AND IN SORROW'S ROOM.* Era Publishing Co., New York, 1976. Contains **Neffie** (1975) and **In Sorrow's Room** (1975).

PLAYS:
Perfection in Black (drama, 1 act, 1971). Deals with the conflicts between black women and men. Prod. Off-Bway by the Negro Ensemble Co., as a work-in-progress, at St. Marks Playhouse, Jan. 16, 1971. Pub. in *Scripts #7*, May 1972.
Neffie (fantasy, 2 acts, 1975). The mythical story of the undying love of a beautiful African woman for one man. Public reading by the Frank Silvera Writers' Workshop (FSWW), New York, 1975. Pub. in the author's collection *NEFFIE AND IN SORROW'S ROOM.* Tape recording (and unpub. script) in the FSWW Archives/Schomburg Collection.
In Sorrow's Room (domestic drama, 3 acts, 1975). Concerns a young black woman named Sorrow who tries to find her own identity in spite of a domineering mother and the men who see her only as a sex object. Prod. at the Henry St. Playhouse, New York, Jan. 1974. Pub. in the author's collection *NEFFIE AND IN SORROW'S ROOM.*

CLARKE, HOPE (1942–   ), Actress, dancer-choreographer, musical playwright, TV scriptwriter. Based in New York City. Received her early training as a member of the Katherine Dunham Dance Company. Appeared in *Hallelujah, Baby!* (1967), *House of Flowers* (1968), *Don't Bother Me, I Can't Cope* (1970), and the film *Book of Numbers* (1973). She has choreographed shows for the Urban Arts Corps and the Afro-American Total Theatre, of which she was a member of the Board of Directors.

DRAMATIC WORKS:
Mae's Amees (musical, 1 act, 1969). Written with HAZEL BRYANT and *Hank Johnson. Prod. by the Afro-American Total Theatre, at the Riverside Church Theatre, New York, opening Aug. 9, 1969. Apparently remained in repertory until Oct. 1969. NOTE: She has also written television scripts, but no titles have been located.

CLARKE, SEBASTIAN, Playwright, theatrical critic, short-story writer, and poet. Born in Trinidad. Currently resides in New York City. His work has been published in *Black World, Black Creation, Black Theatre, Journal of Black Poetry, Plays and Players, We Be Word Sorcerers* (Sanchez, 1973), and *Twenty-Five Stories by Black Americans* (1973). *Address:* c/o Hattie Gossett, 775 Riverside Dr., New York, NY 10032.

PLAYS:
Helliocentric World (morality play, 1 act, 1972). Depicts the disintegration of contemporary urban life through a series of short scenes and monologues. Apparently prod. by the New York Shakespeare Festival Public Theatre, prior to being pub. in *Scripts* 1,

May 1972, pp. 86–90. **Lower Earth** (early 1970s). May be the above play by an earlier title.

CLAY, BURIEL, II (1943–1978), Playwright, theatrical director, screenwriter, film producer, poet, editor, and teacher. Born in Abilene, TX. Educated at Old Dominion Univ., Norfolk, VA, 1963–65; the Univ. of Rome, Italy, 1967; California State Univ. (B.A. in creative writing, 1973); and San Francisco State Univ. (M.A. in English). Attended a number of writers' workshops in New York, Washington, DC, and California. Producer-writer-director of over 35 original plays and several independent films. Columnist, San Francisco *Sun-Reporter,* 1968–71; director/instructor, San Francisco Black Writers' Workshop, 1968–78; pres., Pioneer Productions (filmmakers), 1971–75; lecturer at several California colleges and universities, 1972–75; film and drama critic, "Black Renaissance," Channel 44, 1973. In addition to stage plays and films, he is the black editor of *Time to Greez! Incantations from the Third World* (1975), an anthology of prose and graphics by ethnic artists and writers, and *Broken Pieces of Clay* (1975), poetry. Until his untimely death, Clay was attempting to complete a history of blacks in California before 1900. His writings have appeared in *Black Creation, Entertainment News, Black Stage,* and *Entertainment Review,* as well as in *San Francisco Black Writers' Literary Magazine,* of which he was publisher/editor. Winner of California Writers Scholarship, 1970; Univ. of California Writers Fellowship, 1970; Eugene O'Neill National Playwrights Award, 1975; and American Conservatory Theatre Playwrights Fellowship, 1975.

REPRESENTATIVE PLAYS AND DRAMATIC WORKS:
Buy a Little Tenderness (domestic drama, 1 act, 1971). About the social and psychological pressures on people living in the ghetto, and the problems which result from these pressures. Prod. by the Negro Ensemble Co. (NEC), New York, Feb. 1975. Unpub. scripts in the Hatch-Billops Collection and the Billie Rose Collection/NYPL.

The Creation of the World (ballet musical, 1 act, 1972). An American folk tale of the creation of the world, the elements, and man, through dance, song, dialogue, and music. Unpub. script in the Hatch-Billops Collection.

Raw Head and Bloody Bones (hoodoo ritual drama, 1 act, 1972). A woman experiences the consequences, both good and evil, of her sexual involvement with a forbidden lover. Unpub. script in the Hatch-Billops Collection.

No Left Turn (black experience drama, 1 act, 1974). Focuses on the racial experiences and attitudes of seven boyhood friends who hold a reunion in a small country town. Public reading by the Frank Silvera Writers' Workshop (FSWW), at the Harlem Performance Center, New York, Nov. 1976. Unpub. script and tape recording in the FSWW Archives/Schomburg Collection.

Liberty Call (morality drama, 2 acts, 1974). Concerns the development and deterioration of a friendship between two sailors, one black and one white, in the U.S. Navy in Southeast Asia. The white sailor has a homosexual interest in his black companion. Public reading by FSWW, at the Martinique Theatre, Jan. 1975. Prod. by NEC, at St. Marks Playhouse, April 29–May 4, 1975, for 8 perfs.; dir by DOUGLAS TURNER WARD. With SAMM-ART WILLIAMS, Michael Jameson, Thelma Carter, Ramon Rafiur, George Campbell, Naola Adair, ELAINE JACKSON, Sam Finch, and Suavae Mitchell. Unpub. script and tape recording in the FSWW Archives/Schomburg Collection.

OTHER PLAYS AND DRAMATIC WORKS:
X's (domestic drama, 2 acts, 1972). Former subtitle: "Bridges over Troubled Waters". Focuses on the relationship among three people whose lives are intertwined. **A Dance for Demons** (1 act, 1973). A ritual to save one of three souls doomed to damnation. **Jesebelle** (satire, 1973). Examines and offers a solution to the political, sociological, economic, and psychological problems of black people. **The Gentle Rose Decays** (psycho-drama, 2 acts, 1975). About the psychological problems of women in prison. **Greasy Spoons** (morality drama, 2 acts, 1975). About four people waiting for a change, and what each does or fails to do to bring it about.

CLAY, CARL, Playwright, filmmaker, and theatrical director. Executive director of the Black Spectrum Theatre Co. (also known as the Black Spectrum Film & Theatre Co.), located in St. Albans, Queens, NY. *Address:* Black Spectrum [Film &] Theatre Co., 119th Ave. and Merrick Blvd., St. Albans, Queens, NY 11413.

PLAYS:
2000 Black (1975). Prod. by the Black Spectrum Theatre, 1975. **The Pit** (drama, full length, 1985). A dramatization of the Bernard Goetz subway shooting incident. Prod. by the Black Spectrum Film & Theatre Co., opening May 31, 1985. **Babies Making Babies** (film). **The Follower** (film).

CLEAGE, PEARL (formerly Pearl Cleage Lomax) (1948–   ), Poet, playwright, and writer of fiction and essays. Born in Springfield, MA., daughter of well-known author and clergyman Rev. Albert B. Cleage, Jr. Grew up in Detroit, MI. Attended Howard Univ. for three years, where she studied playwriting under OWEN DODSON, TED SHINE, and PAUL CARTER HARRISON. Graduated from Spelman Coll. (A.B. in drama and playwriting, 1971), where her first play was performed in 1972. Also pursued a master's degree in Afro-American Studies at Atlanta Univ. Worked at the Martin Luther King Memorial Center, as a member of the MLK Archival Library field collection staff, 1969–70. Director, Southern Education Program, Inc., 1970–71. Appointed director of communications by Atlanta's first black mayor, Maynard Jackson, 1973, and for the next few years was heavily involved in Atlanta politics. Columnist for the *Atlanta Constitution*. Interviewer/hostess, "Black Viewpoints," Channel 30, WETV, Atlanta, 1972; interviewer/writer/producer, "Ebony Beat Journal," Channel 11, WQXI-TV, Atlanta, 1972–. Since 1981 she has been playwright-in-residence with the Just Us Theatre Co., Atlanta. Her volumes of poetry include *We Don't Need the Music* (1976) and *Dear Dark Faces: Portraits of a People* (1980). Her fiction is included in *Christmas, 1967: Christmas, 1981* (1981) and *One for the Brothers* (1983). Other poems and essays are anthologized in *The Insistent Present* (1970), *We Speak as Liberators* (Coombs, 1972), and *A Rock Against the Wind* (Patterson, 1973), and published in such periodicals as *Ms., Black World, Journal of Black Poetry, Black Collegian, Contemporary Arts/Southwest,*

South and West, Essence, and *Poet Lore.* Recipient of first prize for poetry, *Promethean Literary Magazine,* 1968; Atlanta Mayor's Fellowship in the Arts, mid-1970s; NEA residency grants through Just Us Theatre Co., 1980s; Georgia Council for the Arts residence grant, from the city of Atlanta, 1980 and 1983. *Address*—Office (and location of scripts): Just Us Theatre Co., 710 Peachtree St., N.E., Suite 225, Atlanta, GA 30307. Home: 1543 Peachtree St., N.E. #31, Atlanta, GA 30309.

REPRESENTATIVE PLAYS AND DRAMATIC WORKS:

The Sale (farce, 1 act, 1972). Has as its setting "a store that sells 'token niggers'."— *Black World,* April 1973, p. 90. Prod. by the Morehouse/Spelman Players, Atlanta, 1972; dir. by CARLTON W. MOLETTE.

Puppetplay (piece for two actresses and a marionette, full length, 1981). "Bizarre love story that takes place in a time when puppets want the right to vote and smokey robinson *[sic]* is only a dim memory of another time and place."—Author. Prod. as a work-in-progress at the Atlanta New Play Project, 1981; broke all attendance records previously set during the five-year history of the project. Prod. by the Just Us Theatre Co., Atlanta, 1982–83 season. Prod. by the Negro Ensemble Co., New York, 1983.

Hospice (domestic drama, full length, 1983). The story of a mother and daughter struggling to communicate with each other after a 20–year absence. The mother, an expatriot poet who left her daughter behind when she went to Paris, is now dying of cancer just as her daughter is about to have her first child. Premiered Off-Bway at the New Federal Theatre, New York, 1983; prod. by WOODIE KING, JR. Winner of five AUDELCO awards, 1983, including Best Play, Best Playwright, Best Director, Best Actress, and one additional award. Sched. for prodn. by Just Us, Atlanta, during its 1985–86 season. Prod. by the National Black Touring Circuit, New York, c. 1986.

Good News (romantic comedy, full length, 1984). Romance for the eighties, complete with misunderstandings, feuding lovers, and a happy ending, which chronicles a weekend gathering of six friends with differing agendas. Premiered by Just Us, Atlanta, Feb. 1984. Also presented for 2 perfs. at the Springer Opera House in Columbia, GA, under the sponsorship of Delta Sigma Theta Sorority.

Essentials (1984/85). A play about people and politics, which focuses on the campaign of a black woman attorney who is forced to become her town's first black elected official. She must call on resources within herself and within her campaign workers that they did not even know existed. Prod. by Just Us, Atlanta, 1984–85 season. Prod. by the Passage Theatre Co., Trenton, NJ, April 1–11, 1987.

Banana Bread (two-character piece, 1985). Play about friendship and love, featuring two black women spending an evening trying to figure out how to deal with the men in or out of their lives. In the process, they also redefine the parameters of their friendship and discover a new level of their relationship. Videotaped and premiered as part of a local PBS series, "Playhouse 30," Atlanta; directed by Byron Saunders.

OTHER PLAYS AND DRAMATIC WORKS:

Hymn for the Rebels (1 act, 1968). First prod. by the Howard Univ. Players, Washington, DC, 1968. Prod. by Sons and Ancestors Players, San Francisco, 1974. **Duet for Three Voices** (1969). Prod. by Howard Univ. Players, 1969. **The Jean Harris Reading** (perf. piece, 1981). Solo perf. by author, Atlanta, 1981. **The Pearl and the Brood of Vipers** (perf. piece, 1981). Perfd. in collaboration with Avery Brooks, Indianapolis,

1981. **Nothin' but a Movie** (perf. piece, 1982). Solo perf. by author, Atlanta, 1982. **PR: A Political Romance** [working title] (1984/85). Developed in collaboration with Walter R. Huntley. Sched. for prodn. by Just Us, 1984–85 season. **Porch Songs** (1985). Presented by the Phoenix Theatre, Indianapolis, at a Festival of New American Theatre, Aug. 1985.

CLEMMONS, PHYLLIS, Playwright. Currently associated with the Dashiki Project Theatre in New Orleans, LA. *Address:* c/o Dashiki Project Theatre, P.O. Box 8223, New Orleans, LA 70182.

PLAY:
Siege on Dunncan Street (1982). Prod. by the Dashiki Project Theatre, New Orleans, where it won second place in the New Play Contest, 1982.

CLEVELAND, CARLES (Jonas) (1950–   ), Actor, playwright, screen-writer, and novelist. Born in Miami, FL. Educated at Bernard M. Baruch Coll. of CCNY, 1970–72. Actor in motion pictures, commercials, and on the stage. Films include *The Wiz* (1978) and *Slow Dancing in the Big City* (1978). Stage performances include *Anna Lucasta, A Raisin in the Sun, In Splendid Error,* and **Hail Hail the Gangs!** (1976). Stage manager of the Al Fann Theatrical Ensemble, 1972–74. Often collaborates with JAMES de JONGH, with whom he coauthored four plays (cited below) and two novels: *City Cool: A Ritual of Belonging* (1978), a first-person narrative by a black teenager who joins a Harlem street gang; and *Till Victory* (c. 1979), which, according to Cleveland, deals with "the rise and fall of black Harlem in the fictional character of Alexander Hamilton Shakespeare (1880–1942), lover, philanthropist, sportsman, and num-bers banker."—As quoted in *Contemporary Authors,* vols. 85–88, p. 109. Vice pres. and secy. of Cleveland/de Jongh Assocs., Inc. Member of AFTRA, SAG, and WGA/East. Recipient of a CAPS Fellowship in fiction, 1977, and an AU-DELCO Recognition Award, as musical creator, 1984. *Address and agent:* (c/o) Susan Schulman Lit. Agency, 454 W. 44th St., New York, NY 10036.

REPRESENTATIVE PLAY:
Hail Hail the Gangs! (experimental theatre piece, full length, 1976). Coauthor, with James de Jongh. About a black teenager who joins a Harlem street gang, with tragic results. Prod. Off-Off-Bway by the New York Theatre Ensemble, April 1976. Featured at the Black Theatre Alliance Festival and the Lincoln Center Outdoor Festival, New York, 1976. Pub. only as a novel, *City Cool: A Ritual of Belonging,* by Random House, 1978, also coauthored by Cleveland and de Jongh.

OTHER PLAYS AND DRAMATIC WORKS:
City Cool (first draft screenplay, 1977). Coauthor, with James de Jongh. Screen adaptn. of the novel *City Cool: A Ritual of Belonging,* cited above. Under prodn. consideration by Warner Bros. **"The Bet," Watch Your Mouth** (story idea for a TV series episode, 1977). Coauthor, with James de Jongh. Under prodn. consideration by NET-13. **Ladies First** (treatment and screenplay, 1981). About black WACs in World War II. Under prodn. consideration by Seymour Films. **Play to Win** (musical biography for children and young adults, full length, 1983). Coauthor, with James de Jongh. Commissioned by

Theatreworks/USA. The story of Jackie Robinson. Prod. by Theatreworks/USA, at the Martin Theatre, New York, 1983. With Marcus Olson and Christine Campbell. Then on national school tour, 1984–86.

CLIMONS, ARTIE, Neophyte playwright who in 1969 was a teenager associated with the Aldridge Players/West (AP/W) in Berkeley, CA.

DRAMATIC WORK:
My Troubled Soul (ethnic collage, full length, 1986). Play of black lifestyles, written out of the experience of the author, the cast, and crew (all teenagers), combining music, dance, Afro dress, light, and sound, to give a convincing picture of life in black neighborhoods. Prod. by AP/W in the San Francisco Bay area during the 1970–71 season.

CODLING, BESS. See BREWSTER, BESS E. CODLING.

COFFMAN, STEVEN, Playwright. Former graduate student at the Univ. of Michigan/Ann Arbor.

PLAY:
Black Sabbath (drama, 1 act, 1973). Explores the growing black awareness of a poet-playwright whose best friend—a young militant fighting to improve the slum conditions in his city—is killed in a race riot. Pub. in *Negro American Literature Forum,* Fall 1973, pp. 91–103.

COLES, ROBERT, Playwright. In 1975 he was associated (presumably in a writers' program) with Arizona State Univ., Tempe.

PLAY:
Woke Up This Mornin', Good Thing on My Mind (drama, full length, 1975). Conflict between a black couple and their activist son. Prod. and pub. at Arizona State Univ./Tempe, 1975. Copy of pub. script in the Hatch-Billops Collection.

COLES, ZAIDA (1933–   ), Actress, producer, and originator of a one-woman show. Born in Lynchburg, VA. Has performed in the film *Such Good Friends* (1971); on radio in "Sounds of the City" series; on TV in "The Doctors" series; and in numerous plays by black playwrights. Associate producer of *Inacent Black* (1981) on Broadway. *Address:* 90 Vaughan Ave., New Rochelle, NY 10801.

DRAMATIC WORK:
Scenes and Songs of Love and Freedom (one-woman show, full length, 1975). Conceived, compiled, adapt., and performed by Coles. Prod. by the Urban Arts Corps, New York, 1975.

COLLIE, BRENDA FAYE (1951–   ), Playwright and screenwriter. Winner of the Lorraine Hansberry Award in the American Coll. Theatre Fest. (ACTF) for her play **Silent Octaves** (c. 1978). A theatre graduate of three colleges— Hampshire Coll. (B.A., 1974), the Univ. of Connecticut (M.A. in playwriting and theatre history, 1975), and the Univ. of Iowa (M.F.A. in playwriting, 1979).

Playwright-in-residence at the Univ. of Michigan, in its Guest Artist Program, 1982. Winner of the Norman Felton Playwriting Award in 1976 and 1978. *Address:* 2660 8th Ave. #16 L, New York, NY 10030.

PLAYS AND DRAMATIC WORKS:
(The author has had readings of her plays at New Dramatists, La Mama E.T.C., the Frank Silvera Writers' Workshop [FSWW], and other theatres in the New York City area.) **Silent Octaves** (drama, c. 1978). About an ex-musician torn between his music and his family. Prod. in the ACTF, where it won first place in the Lorraine Hansberry Playwriting Competition. **Backsteps** (pub. screenplay, c. 1978). About a lonely woman who takes in a bum, changing both of their lives. **I Can't Hear the Birds Singing** (drama, 1982). About a black factory worker whose past catches up with him. Performed at the Univ. of Michigan, 1978. Prod. at the 18th St. Playhouse, New York, 1983. Unpub. script in the FSWW Archives/Schomburg Collection.

COLLIE, KELSIE E. (1935–   ), Educator, theatrical director, and playwright. Educated at Hampton Inst. (A.B. in English, speech, and drama, 1967), George Washington Univ. (M.F.A. in dramatic arts, 1970), and Howard Univ. (doctoral studies in communication arts, 1975–   ). Has taught English and drama at various colleges in Washington, DC, prior to joining the Dept. of Drama at Howard in 1975 as asst. prof. and director of the Children's Theatre. His theatrical experiences include TV appearances and presentations, as well as extensive acting, directing, and producing at Howard and in the DC area. In children's theatre, he has developed touring programs, conducted seminars and workshops, and served as resource person for numerous groups. Recipient of a number of awards for contributions to youth nurture. *Address*—Home: 7519 12th St., N.W., Washington, DC 20012. Office: Dept. of Drama, College of Fine Arts, Howard University, Washington, DC 20059.

REPRESENTATIVE PLAYS AND DRAMATIC WORKS:
Fiesta (children's musical, 1 act, 1969). A young man's search for truth and happiness leads him to a South American village where he saves the fiesta from becoming a fiasco when it is discovered that the ceremonial donkey has been stolen. Written and presumably prod. at George Washington Univ., Washington, DC, 1969. Unpub. script in the author's M.F.A. thesis, George Washington Univ., 1970.

Celebration (children's play with songs, 1973). A selfish, egotistical prime minister who has been voted out of office by the people of a West Indian nation almost gets away with stealing all of the money from the treasury and preventing the people from holding an Independence Day celebration. Prod. by the Howard Univ. Drama Dept., 1973.

Randy's Dandy Circus (children's musical, 1974). A young boy inherits a circus, and his envious aunt and uncle sabotage the opening by stealing all the animals; but the boy triumphs after all, with the help of his friends. Prod. by the Howard Univ. Children's Theatre, Washington, DC, Summer 1974, and presented on the "Young News" segment of WRC NBC-TV, Channel 4, Nov. 2, 1974.

Black Images/Black Reflections ("Children's Historical-Ritual Theatre Piece" [subtitle], 1975). A chronicle narrative of Afro-American experiences and contributions to the United States' development, depicted through song, movement, and dramatization.

Prod. by Howard Univ. Children's Theatre, 1975, and presented on "Howard University Presents . . . " over WRC NBC-TV, Channel 4, May 18, 1975.

OTHER PLAYS AND DRAMATIC WORKS:
Good Friday, or the End and the Beginning (morality drama, 1 act, 1962). Ten persons seek shelter in a cave from an atomic holocaust; they attempt to come to grips with themselves and each other. **It Happens Every Summer** (musical comedy, 2 acts, 1963). Deals with experiences shared by a group of young people who are working as summer camp counselors for a church youth program. **Where Is Love** (children's drama, 1 act, 1963). A little girl runs away from an orphanage in search of love. **The Gift** ("Sermon in Three Dramatic Sketches, Including a Litany" [subtitle], 1 act, 1964). Depicts how humans are often unmindful of the gift of love God has given each. **How to Succeed with a Little Bit of Luck** (musical comedy, 2 acts, 1964). A young woman visits her cousin in New York and gets a big theatrical break, but she has some minor problems in the romance department. **Hell's Belles** (musical comedy, 2 acts, 1965). An angel is sent from heaven as an emissary and promptly falls in love with an attractive hellion. **Kids!** (musical comedy, 1 act, 1966). The girls want to know what the boys are doing in their clubhouse, so they send in a spy. The parents want to know what both are up to. **Ash Wednesday** ("Morality Based on Ash Wednesday Scriptures" [subtitle], 1 act, 1967). Several persons at a cocktail party are revealed to be jealous, petty, and lustful, as they share the bread and wine served by the host, who is a priest. **It's a Mad, Mad, Mad, Mod World We Live In** (musical revue, 1 act, 1967). Topical issues including politics, religion, and minority problems are satirized in song and dance. **Maybe Some Day** ("Domestic/Black Experience Drama with Music" [subtitle], 1 act, 1968). A young woman's conflict with her mother's teachings and her desire to have a good time with her friend and neighbor, who is very hip and popular.

COLLIER, EUGENIA (1928–   ), Author, critic, editor, teacher, and playwright. Born in Baltimore, MD. Received Ph.D. from the Univ. of Maryland. Assoc. prof. of English in the Graduate School of Arts and Sciences at Howard Univ., Washington, DC. Coeditor, with RICHARD LONG, of *Afro-American Writing: An Anthology of Prose and Poetry* (1972). *Address:* 5401 Wilkins Ave., Baltimore, MD 21228.

PLAY:
Ricky (drama, 1 act, 1976). Based on her short story by the same title. Prod. by the Kuumba Workshop, at the Eugene Perkins Theatre, Chicago, Oct. 1976.

COLLINS, KATHLEEN, Playwright, writer, filmmaker, director, and producer. Assoc. prof. of film at CCNY. Received the B.A. in philosophy from Skidmore Coll., and the M.A. in French literature and cinema from the Middlebury Grad. School in France. Author of *The Mountain, The Stone* (1978) and *Teachers & Writers* (pre-1985). Coproducer of three films: *Gouldtown: A Mulatto Settlement,* **The Cruz Brothers and Miss Malloy,** and **Losing Ground** (a feature film, 1981), which won a prize as First Feature at the Portuguese International Film Festival. Nominated for both the Susan Blackburn Prize for Playwriting and an AUDELCO Award, 1983, for her play **Brothers.** Recipient of grants from the American Film Inst. (AFI), the New York State Council on the Arts, and NEA. Member of Professional Theatre Women, AAUP, and Professional Staff Congress. *Address:* 796 Piermont Ave., Piermont, NY 10968. *Agent:* The Prettyman Agency, 215 W. 98th St., Suite 12B, New York, NY 10025.

GROUP OF RELATED PLAYS:

"BEGIN THE BEGUINE" ("A Quartet of One-Act Plays" [subtitle], 1984). On the theme "Difficult Women." Commissioned by the American Place Theatre (APT) Women's Project, New York, 1984. Individual titles unknown.

REPRESENTATIVE PLAYS AND DRAMATIC WORKS:

Losing Ground (16 mm. color film, 90 min.: screenplay, 1981). A zany comedy about a young black couple in the midst of a marital crisis, precipitated by the wife's far-fetched search for "ecstasy." Prod. and dir. by author. Won for her an individual media grant from NEA, 1981, and an AFI Screenwriting Grant, 1981. Winner of a prize for "First Feature" at Portugal's Figueroa da Foz International Film Festival, c. 1981.

In the Midnight Hour (drama, full length, 1981). About an upper-class black family in turmoil at the beginning of the civil rights movement. Prod. at the Richard Allen Center for Culture and Art's International Black Theatre Festival, New York, 1982, under the direction of Duane Jones. Pub. in an anthology entitled *The Women's Project* (an American Place Theatre APT Performing Arts Journal, New York, 1981).

The Brothers (drama, 3 acts, 1982). A tale of the Edward family as told through the eyes of six women whose lives have all been rendered brittle, abstract things through the obsessive preoccupation of their men (six brothers) with race and ambition. According to LIONEL MITCHELL *(New York Amsterdam News,* April 17, 1982, p. 28), "This is about those Blacks—say of Tidewater Virginia, who have the blood of the Jeffersons, Randolphs, Henrys, and so forth, in their veins. . . . What kind of people have these descendents become? . . . Well, according to Kathleen Collins, they are a pretty shaky lot, almost decadent." Prod. at the Kuntu Repertory Theatre, Pittsburgh, 1982; dir. by Dr. Vernell Lillie. Prod. Off-Bway, at APT, 1982; dir. by Billie Allen. Finalist for the Susan Blackburn International Prize in Playwriting, 1983. Nominated as one of the Best Plays of 1982 by the AUDELCO Awards Committee. Pub. in *Plays-in-Process, 1982– 83* (anthology of the Theatre Communications Group, 1983); in the second *The Woman's Project Anthology* (1984); and in *Nine Plays by Black Women* (Wilkerson, 1986).

In the Midnight Hour (domestic drama, full length, 1982). "An intimate study of a black middle-class family's relationships."—*Nine Plays by Black Women* (Wilkerson, 1986), p. 298. Prod. by the Richard Allen Center for Culture and Arts, New York, 1982.

Only the Sky Is Free (fictional meditation, full length, 1986). About the life of the first black aviatrix, Bessie Coleman. Prod. Off-Bway at the Richard Allen Center for Culture and Arts, Spring 1986.

OTHER PLAYS AND DRAMATIC WORKS:

Where Is Love? (drama, 1 act, 1972). A black man of middle age reminisces on a youthful love affair that still haunts him. Has been prod. several times. (The author considers it an early/amateur work and does not encourage its circulation.) **Love Comes but Once** (poetic drama, 1 act, 1972). Two-character piece in which a woman loves a man who does not return her love. **Portrait of Kathleen** // Orig. title: **Portrait of Katherine** // Also known as **Almost Music** (musical fantasy, 5 acts, 1974). A middle-aged black couple reminisces about the wife's early life, their courtship, and marriage. (The author states that this play, which has been rewritten several times, has now been abandoned, and its salvageable elements—mainly its music—have been reassembled in the film **A Summer Diary** [next entry.] **A Summer Diary** (16 mm. color film, 120 min.: screenplay, 1983). Musical about love and separation, as seen through the eyes of two black women and the men who surround them. Prod. and dir. by author; shot in Summer 1983 for Spring 1984 release. **The Cruz Brothers and Miss Malloy** (16 mm. color film, 54 min., pre-1985). Adapt. by Collins and Henry H. Roth from Roth's novel, *The Cruz Chronicle*. Three Puerto Rican brothers are hired to renovate the mansion of a dying Irish dowager; adventures ensue. Prod. and dir. by Collins prior to 1985. **While Older Men Speak** (drama, full length, pre-1985). About two middle-aged black men. **Remembrance** (drama, 1 act, 1985). Sched. as part of the Women's Festival of One-Act Plays, to be prod. at APT, Dec. 1985.

COLLINS, RISË, Poet-playwright. Based in New York City, where her work has been produced by the New Federal Theatre (NFT).

PLAY:
Incandescent Tones (poem-play, full length, 1983). Described by Laurie Stone, writing in the *Village Voice* (Aug. 2, 1983, p. 75), as "a series of autobiographical monologues and fugues, openly derivative of, but a good deal less pungent and varied than, NTOZAKE SHANGE's For Colored Girls, in which Collins performed. Collins also writes about writing, men, sex, and parents" (capitalization added). Prod. by NFT, July 20–Aug. 7, 1983, for 11 perfs., as a part of "The Woman's Series: Four New Black Playwrights"; dir. by Marjorie Moon. With Collins, Terria Joseph, S. Epetha Merkerson, and Pamela Poitier.

COLSON-WALKER, CELESTE. See WALKER, CELESTE COLSON.

COMER, J. DOUGLAS (d. 1980), Playwright. Resided in Columbus, OH, where he was associated with East H.S. Author of an unpublished novel. Died as a result of a heart attack and automobile accident. *Literary Executor* (and widow): Mrs. Ruby Comer (Mrs. J. Douglas Comer), 660 Wilson Ave., Columbus, OH 43205.

PLAYS:
(All coauthored with *William E. Graham.) **Beyond the City** (musical comedy, 3 acts, 1970s). Injured baseball player gives up his profession to work in a remote community. **The Continuous Struggle, Part II** (1970s). Subtitled "Stand Up East High." Concerns the problems faced by several teenagers whose parents are both college graduates. Written for and presumably prod. by East H.S., Columbus, OH. **Mabel Jones and the Devil** (musical, 3 acts, 1970s). Domestic comedy about poverty. **Outta This World** (musical comedy, 1970). With the aid of an ex-astronaut, a black mother gets rid of her rebellious hippie son by sending him to another planet. Prod. at East H.S., March 1970. **Six Broken Wires** (drama, 1970s). Six rehabilitation counselors from an Ohio graduate school set out to rehabilitate the world, with disastrous results.

COMPTON, JIMMY DAVIS, JR., Playwright, Resides in Detroit, MI. *Address:* 18660 Waxford, Detroit, MI 48234.

PLAY:
Why Chickens, Turkeys, and Ostriches Don't Fly // Alternate title (or subtitle): **Why Chickens, Turkeys, and Ostriches Don't Be Around Other Birds** (children's fantasy, 1 act, pre-1975). Parable on the destructive effects of greed.

CONWAY, MEL, Playwright. Resides in Detroit, MI.

PLAY:
Best One of 'Em All (domestic drama, 3 acts, 1975). "Deals with a preacher, his daughter, his sons from a previous marriage, and how the preacher is pushed by his family to a higher level of consciousness."—*Black Playwrights, 1823–1977* (Hatch & Abdullah, 1977), p. 34. Prod. by Parkway Community House, Chicago, Feb. 1975.

COOPER, GRACE (Grace Cooper Ihunanya), Actress, playwright, and educator. Resides in Washington, DC, where she received her early education. Holds a doctor's degree in psycholinguistics from Howard Univ. Gained theatrical experience from the age of five performing with the Children's Theatre of Washington. Married to T. G. COOPER, former chairman of the Drama Dept. at Howard Univ. Currently assoc. prof. of English at the Univ. of the District of Columbia. *Address:* c/o Univ. of the District of Columbia, Washington, DC 20009. Alternate: c/o Prof. Theodore G. Cooper, Dept. of Drama, College of Fine Arts, Howard University, Washington, DC 20059.

PLAYS:
A Dress for Annalee (domestic drama, 1 act, 1972). Concerns a young unwed mother who comes home early to find her baby bitten by rats. **Finding Easter** (children's play, 1 act, 1972). The children find out that the real meaning of Easter is not in material possessions. **Behold! A Unicorn!** (morality play, 1 act, 1973). Concerns a conflict in the cultural identity of a nearly white black woman. **The Rain Is Cold in December** (morality play, 3 acts, 1973). A black woman's career is in conflict with the men she loves. **Kojo and the Leopard** (children's musical, 1 long act, 1973). Her best-known play. Concerns a young African boy who completes his tribal initiation into manhood by conquering a leopard. Has been produced at college, school, and community theatres throughout the United States.

COOPER, JOAN "CALIFORNIA," Playwright and short-story writer. Born in Berkeley, CA, in the 1930s. Currently resides in Oakland, CA. The mother of one daughter. Her writing style has been compared to that of Tennessee Williams (hence the name "California"), LANGSTON HUGHES, Zora Neals Hurston, and Alice Walker. A "closet writer" since childhood, her plays were discovered and first produced in the 1970s by Nora Vaughan of the Berkeley Black Repertory Theatre. Since then her dramas have been performed on stages throughout northern and central California, on public television, radio, and college campuses. Encouraged by Pulitzer Prize-winning author Alice Walker, Cooper completed 12 short stories which were subsequently published by Walker's publishing company, Wild Tree Press, as *A Piece of Mine* (1984) and nominated by the American Lib. Assn. for its List of Notable Books in 1985.

A second volume of short stories was scheduled for publication in 1985, and a third volume is being prepared for publication. Cooper was named Playwright of the Year in 1978, for her play **Strangers**. *Address:* P.O. Box 7431, Oakland, CA 94601. Alternate: P.O. Box 2061, Marshall, TX 75670.

REPRESENTATIVE PLAYS AND DRAMATIC WORKS:

How Now? (drama, 1973). A crippled girl wants an education, but her mother wants her to get pregnant so she can stay on welfare. Prod. by the Black Repertory Group, Berkeley, 1973.

Strangers // Also known as **Ahhh, Strangers** (drama, 1978). A couple married for 50 years discovers that they may never have loved each other, and wonder why, and whether or not it is too late to make a fresh start. Performed at the San Francisco Palace of Fine Arts, 1978, and earned for the author a citation as Playwright of the Year.

Loners (drama, 1 act, pre-1981). A young man who values everything except his family finds that he is absolutely nothing when he loses them. First prod. by the Black Repertory Group Theatre, late 1970s. Subsequently prod. at Mills Coll., Oakland; by Encore Theatre Group, Washington, DC; and at the Univ. of Massachusetts/Amherst. Pub. in *Center Stage* (Ostrow, 1981).

The Unintended (drama, c. 1983). Described in an unidentified newspaper clipping of a review by Thea Johnson (supplied by the author) as a "serious contemporary drama," involving a love story between "a 35–year-old virgin as the protagonist" and a gentle hunchback with whom she first becomes sexually involved in order to get money to pay her motel bill, after she has been ditched and bilked out of her cash by a "jiving Goman." The reviewer compares the protagonist to "the painfully introverted...Laura in Tennessee Williams' *The Glass Menagerie*." Prod. as a play-in-progress by the Black Repertory (Group) Theatre, June 1983.

OTHER PLAYS:

(1970s–80s.) **Everytime It Rains.** A lonely woman makes a rapist change his mind and eventually marries him. **System, Suckers and Success.** A young man seeking success and happiness finds it wasn't education, money or many things he was taught; he finds it on his own. **The Mother.** A woman with too much to offer leaves the country for the Big City, abandoning her three children; she returns 25 years later, sick and broke. **(The) Killing of Kindness.** A kind, kind woman is so taken advantage of by her family and the world that her kindness literally kills her. **Loved to Death.** A crippled woman tells of her young, pretty sister who was loved to death by the world in general, until she— like the preceding protagonist—fulfills the prophecy implied by the play's title. **Moments** (a light musical). Concerned with old people looking back to the past. **Monologues.** Solo dramas, with actors in the background. **Not One of a Kind.** A totally selfish woman tells about the world as she sees it. **One for the Money** (short 1 act). A female narcotic addict and her relationship to her man and her mother. **One Hour or Forever** (short 1 act). Experimental play, set in darkness, about a pair of clandestine lovers and what they pay for one hour. **Shed a Tear.** At a man's funeral, no one cries for him except a small, young illegitimate son. **Weight of Clay.** A young black woman, depending on the world for approval, discovers a much better way to be happy. **Say What You Willomay.** An older, humorous woman discusses the trials and tribulations of a younger one. **Too Hep to Be Happy.** An older woman (in her eighties) talks about a male friend, an old bachelor, who was "too hep to be happy."

COOPER, T. G. (Theodore G., or Ted G.), Playwright, actor, producer, and educator. Member and former chairman of the Drama Dept. of Howard Univ., Washington, DC, where he has produced and directed more than two dozen plays. Educated at Howard (B.F.A. in drama), the Univ. of Miami (M.A. in theatre management and directing), and Laurence Univ., Santa Barbara, CA (specialist in higher education, 1976). Has worked for numerous government agencies in Washington and other cities, including the Office of Economic Opportunity, Social Security Admin., the White House, U.S. Post Office, Dept. of Commerce, and Justice Dept. Teaching experiences include Booker T. Washington H.S. and Miami-Dade Jr. Coll., both in Miami, FL; Roosevelt H.S. in Washington, DC; Virginia State Coll. in Petersburg, 1974; and the Frank Silvera Writers' Workshop (FSWW) in New York City, 1974. Has also performed in a number of plays and served as technical director and stage manager for numerous others. In addition to the works cited below, he has written two unpublished novels ("Mack" and "Obeah") and has contributed articles to several periodicals. *Address:* Dept. of Drama, College of Fine Arts, Howard University, Washington, DC 20059.

REPRESENTATIVE PLAYS:

A Town Called Tobyville (protest drama, 3 acts, 1971). A brother investigates the unusual death of his sister while she is on a freedom ride in the South. Prod. by Howard Univ. Drama Dept., Washington, DC, 1971. Also prod. at the Univ. of Miami, Coral Gables, FL, 1972.

Goodnight, Mary Beck (morality melodrama, 3 acts, 1974). A young black woman finds it more convenient to have a male roommate, to the displeasure of her boyfriend. Prod. by the Howard Univ. Drama Dept. Also Prod. at Lincoln Univ. in Pennsylvania the same year.

OTHER PLAYS:

(All prod. at Howard Univ., Washington, DC.) **Chocolate Boy** (morality drama, 3 acts, 1968). The principles of a righteous white family are challenged when the son brings home a black friend for Christmas. **Have You Seen Mommy Lately** (morality drama, 1 act, 1970). A black man's attempt at finding reality in insanity. **Strawman** (3 acts, 1970). **Queen's Children** (domestic comedy, 1 act, 1970). Situation of a black woman with three children by three different men. Potential husband must accept the already formed family. **Chickenbone Special** (morality melodrama, 3 acts, 1972). Malcolm X returns to convince the Blackman of the need to love one another. **Shade of Black: Portrait of a Woman** (morality drama, 3 acts, 1973). (Also listed by subtitle alone.) A middle-class black woman's attempt to free herself from the social restrictions put on her by family ties. **Cutting Loose** (1970s). Unpub. script in the Schomburg Collection, presumably in the FSWW Archives.

COUSINS, LINDA, Poet, playwright, freelance writer, editor, and publisher. Received the B.S. in business administration from the Univ. of Tennessee at Knoxville. Founder/editor/publisher of the Universal Black Press, Brooklyn, which publishes *The Universal Black Writer (TUBW)*, a biannual magazine for black writers and readers. Has had ten years' experience in freelance writing, research, and editing. Her articles have appeared in *TUBW, Essence* (as contributing editor, 1981–83), *Black New York Illustrated, New York Amsterdam News,* and the *Black American.* Her poetry has been published in several anthologies, including *A Rock Against the Wind* (Patterson, 1973) and *Three Hundred and Sixty Degrees of Blackness Comin at You* (Sanchez, 1971). One of her poems was featured in the Broadway show *When Hell Freezes Over, I'll Skate.* Editor of two anthologies of black writers: *Black and in Brooklyn: Creators and Creations* (c. 1982), which earned for her a proclamation from the Brooklyn Borough President's Office, 1983, and *Ancient Black Youth and Elders Reborn* (1985), subtitled "The Poetry, Short Stories, Oral Histories, and Deeper Thoughts of African-American Children and Senior Citizens." Memberships include Poets and Writers, Committee of Small Magazine Editors and Publishers (COSMEP), Coordinating Council of Literary Magazines (CCLM), and Black Women in Publishing. Recipient of awards from Central Brooklyn Coordinating Council and *West Indian Tribune,* both 1982; Fannie Lou Hamer Award, from the Women's Center of Medgar Evers Coll., Brooklyn, 1984; and Editor's Award, from CCLM, 1984. Also recipient of publishing grants for *TUBW* from Brooklyn Arts and Culture Assn., 1982, 1983, and 1985; CCLM, 1982 and 1983; and Lucius Eastman Foundation (for historical publishing), 1985. *Address*—Office: The Universal Black Writer, P.O. Box 5, Radio Station, New York, NY 10101.

REPRESENTATIVE PLAYS AND DRAMATIC WORKS:

Karma (comedy, 2 acts, 1976). A huge and erudite "baby" is born to a woman who was his nagging wife in another lifetime. The former husband and wife, now mother and infant son, seek to resolve their karmic differences after the initial shock has worn off of their deja-vu hospital maternity ward reunion. Prod. at the Hudson Guild Theatre, New York, Aug. 1976.

The Divorcing (comedy, 1 act, 1976). An "un-bride" and "un-groom," decked out in full wedding regalia, go before a justice of the peace for a stormy "un-marriage" ceremony. Prod. at the Hudson Guild Theatre, Aug. 1976.

The Night Before // ** Aug. title: **The Night Before the Buryin' (drama [monologue and flashbacks], 2 acts, 1981). An elderly southern black woman sits up all night with her husband's body during a solitary wake/vigil after his death. Through dramatic flashbacks she relives both the intensely painful and joyful experiences of their 50–year union in the Jim Crow South. Prod. by the Alonzo Players, Brooklyn, Nov. 1981 and April 1982; revived Jan.-Summer 1986.

Capturing Dreams (drama, 2 acts, 1982). A young couple, who have long worked toward their dream of a husband-wife singing team, watch helplessly as their marriage is put to an exacting test by the skyrocketing of the wife's career while the husband is forced to become an unhappy backstage shadow. Prod. at the Paul Robeson Theatre, Sept. 1982.

A Three-Piece Suit (drama, 2 acts, 1982). A middle-aged, highly educated black janitor, whose racist environment has never afforded him the opportunity to advance in life, stages a last act of protest on his job of many years by insisting on sweeping offices and cleaning bathrooms in an expensive three-piece suit and derby. His quiet defiance, and his influence on a maid who subsequently joins with him in a two-person picket line, almost bring to a standstill the operation of the firm for which he works. Prod. at the Paul Robeson Theatre, Sept. 1982. Performed before the Shaw Univ. Alumni Assn., May 1983.

The 85-Year Old Swinger (comedy, 2 acts, 1982). An energetic and shockingly pregnant senior citizen stands up (with the help of her cane) for the rights of her twilight motherhood and a trembling marriage to her bedridden nursing home lover, as her doctor, family, and the world around her look on in amazement. Prod. at the Alonzo Players Theatre, April 1982. Sched. to open the OSSIE DAVIS/RUBY DEE series on PBS-TV entitled "In Other Words—Ossie & Ruby," in Oct. 1985.

The First Wife (drama, 2 acts, 1985). An escaped slave, resigned to the fact that he will never be reunited with his family again, remarries after several years and begins rearing a new family in the Reconstruction Era South. With steel-bent determination, his first wife, now freed, finds him after a desperate search. The play revolves around the dilemma faced by this ex-slave upon the appearance of "the first wife." Performed at the the ATA Theatre, Jan. 1985. Sched. to open the fall season of the Alonzo Players Theatre, Brooklyn, Oct. 1985. Prod. by the Alonzo Players, Jan.-Summer 1986.

OTHER PLAYS AND DRAMATIC WORKS:
Sheer Guts (1970s). Program of poetry on the black condition in America. **Free Groceries Thursday Morning** (domestic drama, 1 act, 1970s). Black woman of 35 attempts to sustain her family without going on welfare. **Return to Apt. 8K (or Back Home from Detroit)** (drama, 2 acts, 1980s). Concerns the unsuccessful efforts of a black woman to rescue her husband and children from grueling poverty by journeying to Detroit to pursue her dream of being a blues singer. Although she achieves her goal, her plan to reunite with her family is never realized. She falls into the life of a streetwalker and dies in poverty. Only after death does the family reunion occur.

COX, JOSEPH MASON ANDREW (1923–   ), Journalist, poet, novelist, and playwright. Based in New York City. *Pertinent address*—For possible location of author's published script: J. Brooks Dendy III, 1713 North 21st St., Philadelphia, PA 19121.

PLAY:
Ode to Dr. Martin Luther King, Jr. (3 acts, 1970). First prod. at a CreataDrama Theatre, Univ. of Pittsburgh, PA, 1970. Pub. by J. BROOKS DENDY, 1970.

COX, TONY, Playwright. Was residing in Los Angeles during the 1970s.

PLAYS:
(All scripts in the Hatch-Billops Collection.) **Man's Best Friend** (domestic comedy, one-act version, pre-1975). Concerns the sexual conflict of a shy boy who lives with his widowed mother. **Man's Best Friend** (domestic comedy, three-act version, pre-1975). A rewritten version of the above play, continuing the boy's sexual conflicts into young manhood. In this version, the boy lives with his widowed father, who has remarried. **Take a Long Look** // Also cited in some sources as **Take a Look** and **Take a Good Look** (ritual, 1 act, 1971). Designed to make blacks aware of freeing themselves from mental enslavement. Unpub. script in the Hatch-Billops Collection.

CRAWFORD, ROBERT. See AJAMU.

CRAWLEY, HAZEL L. (1921–c. 1978), Poet-playwright. Born in Newark, NJ. Educated at Washington Square Coll., New York. Served in the WAC Corps during World War II, receiving an honorable discharge in 1946. An alumna of the Frank Silvera Writers' Workshop (FSWW) and the Douglass Creative Arts Center, both in New York City. Author of *Erratica*, a volume of poetry. *Literary executor:* Ms. Bea Winde, 148 Stanton St., Apt. 3, New York, NY 10002. *Agent:* Esther Taylor-Evans, 26 Horatio St., New York, NY 10014.

   PLAYS:
   (Unpub. scripts of all plays are located in the FSWW Archives/Schomburg Collection.) **Ten Past (The Soft Underbelly)** (drama, 3 acts, 1975). Concerns a wealthy mental patient who is destroyed by his three private nurses, in retaliation against his unpleasant conduct during a critical period of his confinement in a mental hospital. Public reading by FSWW, at the Martinique Theatre, May 1975. **The Square Root of Two** (drama, 3 acts, 1976). A black girl of 19 tries to free herself from the domination of her foster parents and their two sons. Public reading by FSWW, at the Martinique Theatre, Jan. 1976. Prod. at Salem Methodist Church, New York. **The Sunset Gun** (1976). Public reading by FSWW, at the Harlem Cultural Council, June 1976. **Two Left Shoes** (drama, 3 acts, mid-1970s). A woman in her mid-forties leaves her husband and their two grown children in order to locate (through the aid of a psychic) a former lover of her youth. Her course of action ends in tragedy. Public reading by FSWW, at the Martinique Theatre, during the mid-1970s. **Nello** (1970s). Public reading by FSWW, 1970s.

CRUSE, HAROLD (Wright), Author, educator, film and drama critic, and playwright. Best known for his controversial book *The Crisis of the Negro Intellectual* (1967). Born in Petersburg, VA. Educated in the public schools of Petersburg and Norfolk, VA; the high schools of New York City; and the United States Armed Forces Institute (USAFI) in the field of journalism, 1941–42, while serving in the United States Army from 1941 to 1945. He was intensely involved in the Black Theatre movement in New York City from 1952 to 1962, during which time he wrote the plays listed below. He had an extensive career in freelance journalism, civil service, television communications, community and public affairs, and higher education. Since 1968 he has been writer-in-residence, visiting professor of history, and director of the Center for Afroamerican and African Studies at the Univ. of Michigan at Ann Arbor. Other major publications include *Rebellion or Revolution* (essay collection which includes his early film reviews, 1968), *Black Studies—Interpretations and Methodology and the Relationship to Social Studies* (monograph, 1971), *The Afro-American in the Creative and Performing Arts and the Struggle for Identity and Credibility* (1978), and the biographical profile of the actor Canada Lee (1907–1952) for the *Dictionary of American Biography, Supplement Five* (1951–1955). Recipient of recognition for "Outstanding Contribution to the Tri-Service Adult Education Conference" (U.S. Military), Berchtesgaden, Germany, April 8–11, 1974. *Ad-*

dress: Center for Afroamerican and African Studies, University of Michigan, 809 Monroe, Ann Arbor, MI 48109.

PLAYS AND DRAMATIC WORKS:
The Delta Rose (historical play set in the 1890s, full length, c. 1952). **Irma Tazewell** (drama, 2 acts [11 scenes], 1960). Subtitled "The Maid's Dilemma." Unpub. script in the Schomburg Collection. **A Lady of Consequence** (musical play, full length, 1961–62). Libretto and lyrics by Cruse. Musical score by *Frank Fields (deceased). Sched. for prodn. around 1962, with Pearl Bailey in the lead, but the planned prodn. did not materialize.

CUMMINS, CECIL, Playwright, critic, director. Cofounder of the Brownsville Laboratory Theatre, Brooklyn, NY, now inactive. Former member of the Writers' Workshop of the New Lafayette Theatre (NLT) in Harlem.

PLAY:
Young Blood, Young Breed (antidrug play, 1 act, 1970). Dramatizes the destructive effect of drugs, alcohol, and prostitution on the black community. Prod. by the Brownsville Laboratory Theatre, at Jr. H.S. 263, Brooklyn, Dec. 2–29, 1969, and March 6, 1970. Later presented in schools and auditoriums throughout the Brooklyn community, remaining in repertory through Summer 1970.

CUNNINGHAM, ARTHUR (1928–   ), Contemporary composer whose compositions include a number of scores for musical theatre works. Educated at Fisk Univ.; Teachers Coll., Columbia Univ. (M.A. in musical theory and conducting); and the Metropolitan Music School, studying with composer Wallingford Reigger. In addition to stage works, he has written a number of compositions for symphony orchestra, chamber ensemble, and solo voices.

MUSICAL THEATRE WORKS:
(Musical scores only.) **Ostrich Feathers** (children's rock musical, 1964). **Patsy Patch and Susan's Dream** (musical for very young children, 1963). **His Natural Grace** (mini rock-opera, 1969). **Shango** (stage work, 1969).

CUNNINGHAM, SCOTT, Playwright. Based in New York City.

PLAY:
Beautiful Dreamer (historical drama, 34 scenes, 1968). Pageant of the civil rights movement, from the Montgomery bus boycott to the murder of Martin Luther King, Jr. Prod. by Resurrection City, Washington, DC, 1968.

CURRELLEY, LORRAINE, Poet, writer, playwright, and producer. Author of *The Gospel in Rainie's Shout, An Autopoemography* (1985) and other books of poetry. Her work has been published in numerous anthologies, and she has appeared on radio and television, lectured, and performed her work for schools, colleges, and universities. Founder and director of Growing Theatre, Inc. Member of Gaptooth Girlfriends: The Third Act, a writer's collective founded by ALEXIS DeVEAUX. Other memberships include Harlem Arts Fund (former pres.); Feminist Writers Guild; Frank Silvera Writers' Workshop; Negro Ensemble Co. (NEC) Playwrights Workshop; Women's Sports Foundation; Poets & Writers; and Dance Theatre Workshop. *Address:* Growing Theatre, Inc., P.O. Box 562, College Station, New York, NY 10030.

PLAYS:

Breasts Oppressed (drama, 7 scenes, 1974). On the theme of lesbianism and its effect on a marriage. **The Unsuccessful Raping of James' Mother** (domestic drama, 6 acts, 1974). Deals with the problems that develop between a son and his mother after she marries again. **And the Gang Played On** (drama, 4 acts, pre-1974). Deals with conflicts that develop among members of a youth gang when faced with a choice between right and wrong. **The Red Flowered Basin** (1970s). Prod. and aired over the National Black Network, 1980s.

CURTIS, NORMAN, Composer and musician. Based in New York City.

DRAMATIC WORK:

Walk Down Mah Street! (musical, 2 acts: music only, 1967). Subtitled "A Topical Musical Revue." Script and lyrics by PATRICIA TAYLOR (then Patricia Taylor Curtis), who also dir. and choreographed. Special material by James Taylor, Gabriel Levenson, and members of the Next Stage Co. Songs and skits on racial subjects. Apparently first prod. as a TV adaptation on "Camera Three," CBS-TV, New York, 1967. Prod. Off-Bway at the Players Theatre, located on Macdougal St., New York, June 12–Oct. 6, 1968, for 123 perfs., with members of the Next Stage Co.

D

DAMU. See STOKES, HERBERT.

DANIELS, RON, Playwright. Formerly associated with the DC Black Repertory Co., Washington, DC

PLAY:
Swing Low Sweet Steamboat // Also known as **The Wake of Nan Walker** (drama, full length, 1973). Set on a New Orleans pier and in a middle-class living room, this drama revolves around a group of wine-drinking derelicts, among whom is a young Vietnam veteran whose death precipitates the action. The derelicts are brought together with the snobbish family of the veteran at his funeral. First prod. as a workshop production by the DC Black Repertory Co., 1973. World premiere by DC Black Repertory, opening Nov. 12, 1974, for 20 perfs.; dir. by Motojicho (VANTILE WHITFIELD).

DARRELLE, DHARVI (Arlene Morgenstern), Playwright. Associated with the Frank Silvera Writers' Workshop (FSWW) in New York City.

PLAYS:
Goodbye to Yesterday (musical, 3 acts, 1972). Domestic love story dealing with the conflicts between a black couple's married life and the wife's desire to be a successful dancer. **New Couple** (dance drama, 2 acts, 1975). Subtitled "Lovers." Triangular relationship involving a black woman, a white European man, and a black homosexual. Public reading by FSWW, at the Martinique Theatre, New York, June 1975. Unpub. script in the FSWW Archives/Schomburg Collection.

DAVID, JAMAL. See POLE, CHARLES.

DAVIDSON, N. R., JR. (Norbert R.) (1940–   ), Playwright and magazine editor. Born in New Orleans, LA. Received the A.B. from Dillard Univ. and the M.F.A. from Stanford Univ. During the 1960s, he was playwright-in-residence with the Dashiki Project Theatre in New Orleans. One of the editors of

The Black Collegian magazine. *Address:* c/o Contemporary Arts Center, 900 Camp St., New Orleans, LA 70150; or 2811 Audubon St., New Orleans, LA 70115.

PLAYS:

El Hajj Malik (ritual drama, 2 acts, 1967). Subtitled "The Dramatic Life and Death of Malcolm X." Based on Malcolm's biography, writings, and speeches, utilizing drama, prose, poetry, slides, and dance. Developed out of a group improvisation by students in the M.F.A. program at Stanford, Spring 1967. First prod. at Dillard Univ., New Orleans, 1968. Prod. Off-Bway by the Afro-American Studio, at the Martinique Theatre, Nov. 29, 1971–Jan. 9, 1972, for 40 perfs.; dir. by ERNIE McCLINTOCK. Prod. in Chicago during the 1973–74 season, both by the Ebony Talent Assocs. and by the LaMont Zeno Community Theatre, Cleveland, May 1974; dir. by Gale Hollie of Western Reserve Univ. Pub. in *New Plays from the Black Theatre* (Bullins, 1969). **The Further Emasculation Of . . .** (comedy, 1 act, 1970). During his rehabilitation, a mental patient continues to face the same hostile forces in his family and community that originally caused his mental breakdown. Prod. by Dashiki Project Theatre, New Orleans, July 11, 1970. Unpub. script in the Schomburg Collection. **Window** (psychological drama, 3 acts, 1970). "Explores the homosexual scene of two black college instructors and a young ex-student on the verge of a mental breakdown." —*Black Theatre* #6, 1972, p. 6. **Jammer** (comedy, 1 act, 1970). "Based on the stud metaphor of American racist origin."—Ibid. **Short Fun** (comedy, 1 act, 1970). Unpub. script in the Hatch-Billops and Schomburg collections. **Falling Scarlet** (musical, 2 acts, 1971). Satire of black life in the South during slavery times. Sched. for prodn. by Dashiki Project Theatre, 1971. **Jimy Cry** (musical, 2 acts, 1975). Subtitled "The Reason Why." Satire of black life in the South during the Depression. Prod. by Dashiki Project Theatre, April 1975.

DAVIDSON, WILLIAM F., Playwright. (Racial identity not verified.)

PLAY:

Learn, Baby, Learn (comedy, full length, 1969). According to the publisher, this play, which is "set in a large high school . . . concerns two couples with utterly different ambitions, who find unexpected help in each other." Pub. by the Dramatic Publishing Co., Chicago, 1969.

DAVIS, A. I., Playwright and short-story writer. Born in Harlem, New York City. His short stories have appeared in *Essence* magazine. Wrote a radio script for WHA/Earplay, Univ. of Wisconsin, in addition to the plays cited below. Recipient of a grant from the New York Council on the Arts, 1972. *Address:* c/o Gloria Davis, 439 Grand Ave., Leonia, NJ 07605.

PLAYS AND DRAMATIC WORKS:

Man, I Really Do (1 act, 1969). Prod. by the Touring Ensemble Workshop of the Free Southern Theatre (FST), New Orleans, Dec. 1969–Jan. 1970. **The Cock Crows** (drama, 1 act, 1971). Concerns the negative effects of welfare on a black family. Prod. by the Afro-American Total Theatre, at the Riverside Church Theatre, New York, Feb. 22–27, 1972. **Better Make Do** (domestic drama, 1 act, 1971). A rebellion against the attitude of some adults who expect others to be grateful for their hand-me-downs. **The Crab Barrel** (film scenario or treatment, 1971). Deals with the concept of blacks as "crabs in a barrel," trying to pull each other down. Other thematic elements include the loss of illusions of a black revolutionary, the corruption of both black and white policemen, the mother-son relationship within the black family, and the decline of the black community. **A Man Talking** (1 act, 1971). Prod. by the Afro-American Total Theatre, at the Riverside Church Theatre, Feb. 22–27, 1972, on double bill with **The Cock Crows** (1971). **Black Sunlight** (drama, 2 acts, 1974). The head of state of a mythical African nation and a government official who once worked with him in the cause of independence are now divided by their different political views concerning their nation's future goals. Prod. Off-Bway by the Negro Ensemble Co. (NEC), at St. Marks Playhouse, opening March 19, 1974, for 8 perfs.; dir. by Kris Keiser. Unpub. script in the Hatch-Billops Collection. **Cinema, the Beautiful** (symbolic drama, 3 acts, pre-1975). Five stereotyped black characters, presumably created by Hollywood films, meet and reveal their secret desires. **Episode** (drama, pre-1975). The destructive effect of drugs on the black family.

DAVIS, LAWRENCE E., Playwright. Associated with Oduduwa Production, Black Studies Dept., Univ. of Pittsburgh, PA.

PLAY:
Three Blind Mice (satire, 1 act, 1970). A black family, living in an integrated suburban neighborhood, are shot by their white friends and neighbors during a black uprising. Pub. in *Connection* (Porter, 1970).

DAVIS, MILBURN, Playwright, actor, freelance writer, newspaper reporter, public relations director. Educated at the U.S. Armed Forces Inst. (USAFI) (journalism, newswriting, and public relations, 1959), apparently while serving in the U.S. Air Force during the late 1950s. Studied English and sociology at Morgan State Coll. (now Univ.), 1967; public relations at Pace Coll., 1969; and acting at the Negro Ensemble Co. (NEC) with HAL DeWINDT, and at the New Lafayette Theatre (NLT) with ROBERT MACBETH. Freelance writer, 1969– present. Staff writer with *Time* magazine, 1962–65. Copy editor with the *Afro-American* newspapers, 1965–67. Reporter for the *New York Post* and the *Baltimore News American*, 1965–67. Performed as an actor with the Black Magicians of NLT, 1969–73, during which he also played roles in two of his own plays. Has also performed in *Macbeth* and in a pilot soap offered to a cable TV company, *The First and the Fifteenth*. Since 1959 has published more than 40 short stories in such popular magazines as *Tan, Bronze Thrills, Hep, Jive,* and *Soul Confessions*. His articles have been published in *Muhammad Speaks, Liberator, Black Dialogue, Black Troop,* and in the newspapers named above. Winner of second and third prizes in the USAF short story contest, 1958; fourth prize in the Freedoms Foundation writing contest, 1959; and honorable mention in *Boy's Life* writing contest, 1959.

REPRESENTATIVE PLAYS:
The $100,000 Nigger (black experience comedy, 1 act, 1969). Subtitled "You Can Take the Nigger Out of the Country, But—." A black hustler tries to defraud his country cousin out of his inheritance by engaging the services of a fake medium. Presented as

workshop readings by NLT, 1970, and by NEC, 1973. Prod. by the Spelman Coll. Drama Dept., Atlanta, 1979.

Sometimes a Switchblade Helps (drama, 1 act, 1969). Concerns the dilemma of a black man working for a large corporation, when he sees a white manager flirting with a black woman. Should he assert his black consciousness, or should he play the game? Prod. as a workshop production by NLT, 1970, with the author in the cast.

Gallivantin' Husband (drama, 2 acts, 1973). Concerns the domestic problems that develop when a Harlem husband abandons his wife and baby for another woman. Prod. Off-Bway by NEC, as a workshop production, Jan. 27–31, 1973, with the author in the cast. Also prod. in Greenwich Village by Players' Workshop, 1973. Unpub. script in Billy Rose Collection/NYPL.

Sporting Times (black experience comedy, 1 act, 1973). A black Harlem pimp goes around reciting street rhymes he has composed to drum up business for his prostitute. Staged reading by NEC, 1973.

OTHER PLAYS:

Nighmare (fantasy, 1 act, 1970). A messenger of Truth visits a black man in his dreams and teaches him a lesson in black awareness. Unpub. script in the Schomburg Collection. **Love Songs** (short skit for street theatre, 1972). A singer singing about love is interrupted by a female heckler, who insists that love is a lie and that only songs of hate represent truth; but the singer does not stop singing his love songs. **More Power to the Grape** (domestic comedy, 1 act, 1974). Concerns the conflict between a black New Yorker who has changed his "slave" name to an African one, and his wife, who prefers to cling to her Western identity as well as to her friends. As the title implies, the drinking of wine is an integral part of the play. **Black Rage in Suburbia** (drama, 3 acts, 1974). A group of Harlem blacks try to "rip off" some wealthy suburban whites but are impeded by the maid, who is also black. Unpub. script in the Schomburg Collection. **Precious** (drama, 3 acts, 1975). About the difficulties of a black father trying to raise two daughters and cope with the realities of a ghetto environment.

DAVIS, NOLAN (1942–   ), Freelance writer, TV scriptwriter, and producer. Born in Kansas City, MO. Educated at San Diego Evening Coll., 1964–65, and Stanford Univ., 1967–68. Resides in Los Angeles, CA, and Trinidad. Staff writer for the *San Diego Evening Tribune,* 1963–66. Director of public relations, Economic Opportunity Commission (EOC), San Diego, 1966–67. Staff correspondent, *Newsweek* magazine, 1967–70. Producer and senior writer, KABC-TV, Hollywood, 1970–71. Copartner and vice pres., SHARK TV Productions, 1971–76. Author of *Six Black Horses* (1971); *O'Grady* (with John O'Grady, 1974); and *Empire of Eternity* (novel, in progress, 1974).

DRAMATIC WORK:

Grave Undertaking (TV comedy, half hour, 1970). From the "Sanford and Son" TV series. Prod. by NBC-TV, 1970. **Further than the Pulpit** (TV doc., 1972). Prod. by NBC, 1972. **Six Black Horses** (screenplay, pre-1976). Based on the author's novel by the same title. **O'Grady** (pilot teleplay, pre-1971). Based on the author's book by the same title.

DAVIS, OSSIE (1917–   ), Veteran actor, playwright, and film director. Best known as the author of **Purlie Victorious** (1961), the original play which was adapted into the highly acclaimed musical **Purlie** (1970). Born in Cogsdell, GA.

Grew up in Waycross, GA. Studied for three years at Howard Univ., leaving in his junior year to pursue a theatrical career in New York. Gained experience with the Rose McClendon Players, 1941–42, before induction into the U.S. Army in 1942. Served first in the Medical Corps, then in Special Services. Stationed in Liberia, where he wrote a number of musical shows. After discharge in 1945, tried out for and won the leading role in *Jeb,* a new Broadway play which launched his professional career. Also in the production was his future wife and acting partner, RUBY DEE, whom he married in 1958. The Davises have three children. The couple has costarred in numerous productions, including plays, films, TV shows, spoken recordings, and performances on college and university campuses. Ossie Davis's numerous stage acting credits include *Stevedore* (1949), *The Green Pastures* (1951), *Jamaica* (1957), and *A Ballad for Bimshire* (1963). His films include *The Joe Louis Story* (1953) and *The Scalphunters* (1968). TV credits include "Kraft Theatre" (1965), "The Defenders" (several episodes, 1961/65), "The Fugitive" (1966), "N.Y.P.D." (1968), and "Night Gallery" (1969). Coproducer and cohost of "The Ruby Dee/Ossie Davis Story Hour" (1974) on the National Black Network; cohost of "With Ossie and Ruby" (1981) and "The American Revolution" (1984), a two-part segment of "A Walk Through the 20th Century with Bill Moyers," both produced on PBS. Among the films that Ossie Davis has directed are *Cotton Comes to Harlem* (1969), which he also coscripted, *Kongi's Harvest* (1970), *Black Girl* (1972), *Gordon's War* (1973), and *Countdown at Kusini* (1976), another of his coauthored screenplays. Memberships include the Masons, NAACP, Grace Baptist Church, AEA, DGA Advisory Board, CORE, Urban League, SNCC, SCLC, NAG, SAG, and AFTRA. Honors and awards include Emmy Award for his role in "Teacher, Teacher" (Hallmark Hall of Fame, 1969); Frederick Douglass Award by the Urban League of New York, 1970; AEA Paul Robeson citation, 1975; induction into the Black Filmmakers Hall of Fame, 1974; and honorary doctorates from Howard Univ., the Univ. of Massachusetts, Wilberforce Univ., and Virginia State Univ. *Address:* P.O. Box 1318, 44 Cortlandt Ave., New Rochelle, NY 10801. *Agent:* Clifford Stevens, 888 Seventh Ave., New York, NY 10019.

REPRESENTATIVE PLAYS AND DRAMATIC WORKS:

Alice in Wonder (drama, 1 act, 1952). Concerned with political harassment of militant blacks during the era of McCarthyism. A happily married black television performer faces either the loss of a large TV contract or the compromise of his principles when asked to testify before a congressional committee against the political activities of his brother-in-law. Coprod. and codir. by MAXWELL GLANVILLE. at the Elks Community Theatre, New York, Sept. 1952, starring Ruby Dee as the wife, Ed Cambridge as the brother-in-law, and Glanville as the husband. Later made into a three-act version entitled **The Big Deal** (1953).

Purlie Victorious (comedy, 3 acts, 1961). (Also prod. as a full length feature film, **Gone Are the Days:** screenplay, 1963.) Satire of traditional (white-created) black and white stereotypes, to demonstrate how effective laughter can be as a weapon against racial prejudice. A black preacher triumphs in the use of his wits to get a white plantation owner to contribute $500 toward the building of an integrated church in the black community. Prod. on Bway, at the Cort Theatre, Sept. 28, 1961–May 13, 1962, for 231 perfs.; dir. by Howard Da Silva. With Ossie Davis in the title role, Ruby Dee, Helen Martin, GODFREY CAMBRIDGE, Alan Alda, BEAH RICHARDS, and Sorrel Booke. Made into a film, under a new title, **Gone are the Days,** prod. by Nicholas Webster; released by Hammer Bros., 1963. With Ossie Davis, Ruby Dee, Godfrey Cambridge, and most of the orig. actors from the Bway cast. Again prod. as a stage play, Off-Bway, at the Equity Lib. Theatre, opening March 7, 1969, for 9 perfs. Also adapt. into a musical, **Purlie** (1970). Pub. by Samuel French, New York, 1961; in *Speaking for Ourselves* (Faderman & Bradshaw, 1969); *Afro-American Literature: Drama* (Adams, Conn, & Slepian, 1970); *Black Drama—An Anthology* (Brasmer, 1970); *Black Drama in America* (Turner, 1971); *Black Theater* (Patterson, 1971); *Contemporary Black Drama* (Oliver & Sills, 1971). Excerpts *in Black Scenes* (Childress, 1971); *Cavalcade* (Davis & Redding, 1971); and *Thirty-two Scenes for Acting Practice* (Elkind et al., 1972).

Teacher, Teacher (TV script, full length, 1963). Prod. on "East Side/West Side" series by CBS-TV, 1963.

Curtain Call, Mr. Aldridge, Sir (dramatic reading, 1 act, 1963). Highlights the life and career of Ira Aldridge, the eminent black Shakespearean actor of the early nineteenth century. Designed for reader's theatre prodn. Commissioned by the Ira Aldridge Soc., New York, which first prod. the play as a showcase production, at the Henry Hudson Hotel, May 26, 1963, with an interracial cast of six professional actors, including the author and Ruby Dee. Prod. by the Univ. of California/Santa Barbara, Summer 1968. Pub. in *The Black Teacher and the Dramatic Arts* (Reardon & Pawley, 1970).

Cotton Comes to Harlem (feature film, full length: screenplay, 1969). Coauthor, with Arnold Perl. Based on the novel of the same title by CHESTER HIMES. Described as a cops-and-robbers thriller offering "a picturesque glimpse of Harlem . . . depicted as [an] exotic playground."—*Toms, Coons, Mulattoes, Mammies, and Bucks* (Bogle, 1973), p. 231. Although criticized as mere entertainment, the film was highly successful with black audiences at the box office, and largely responsible for setting the pattern for black films of the 1970s. Prod. by Samuel Goldwyn, Jr., and Warner Bros., 1969; dir. by Ossie Davis; costarring Raymond St. Jacques and Godfrey Cambridge as two Harlem policemen, with Redd Foxx making his film debut as a junk man.

Purlie (musical, 2 acts [6 scenes], prologue and epilogue, 1970). Book by Davis, Philip Rose, and Peter Udell, who also wrote the lyrics. Music by Gary Geld. Based on Davis's play **Purlie Victorious** (1961). Opened on Bway at the Broadway Theatre, March 15, 1970; moved to the Winter Garden, Dec. 15, 1970, then to the ANTA, March 15, 1971, closing Nov. 7, 1971, for a total of 688 perfs.; dir. by Philip Rose. With Clevon Little in the title role, Melba Moore, Novella Nelson, Sherman Hemsley, C. David Colson, Helen Martin, and John Heffernan. For their perfs., Little and Moore won Drama Desk awards, Tony awards, and *Variety*'s annual New York Drama Critics' Poll. Little also won the New York Drama Critics Circle Award. Prod. by the Repertory Co. of the Virginia Museum Theatre, Richmond, opening Nov. 8, 1974; dir. by Albert B. Reyes, with choreography by Nat Horne. Orig. cast recording by AMPEX Records (A40101). Script and musical score pub. by Samuel French.

Countdown at Kusini (feature film, full length: screenplay, 1976). Coauthor, with AL FREEMAN, JR. About the liberation of a fictional African country (actually Lagos, Nigeria), with a romantic subplot. Financed by DST Telecommunications, a subsidiary of Delta Sigma Theta Sorority. Prod. by Nigerian (a film company), 1976; dir. by Ossie Davis. With Ruby Dee, Davis, Greg Morris, Tom Aldredge, Michael Ebert, and Thomas Baptiste.

Escape to Freedom (historical play for children, full length, 1978). Subtitled "The Story of Young Frederick Douglass." Adapted from Douglass's autobiography. About the boyhood of the famous abolitionist and orator, who was born a slave. Centers on Douglass's struggle to read, an important step in obtaining his freedom. Had its debut in Town Hall, New York City, March 8, 1976. Pub. by Viking Jr. Books/Viking Press, New York, 1978, and by Samuel French, New York.

Langston: A Play (biographical play, full length, 1982). About the poet-playwright LANGSTON HUGHES. Pub. by Delacorte, 1982.

Bingo (musical, full length, 1985). Book by Davis and Hi Gilbert. Music by George Fischoff. Lyrics by Gilbert. Musical director, NEAL TATE. Based on William Brashler's book, *Bingo Long's Traveling All Stars and Motor Kings* (which had been made into a film in 1976), about the black baseball team of the 1930s. Prod. by the AMAS Repertory Theatre, New York, Oct. 24–Nov. 17, 1985; dir. by Davis. Featuring Norman Matlock. Also presented at the AUDELCO Black Theatre Festival, Oct. 16–19, 1986.

OTHER PLAYS AND DRAMATIC WORKS:
Goldbrickers of 1944 (variety show, full length, 1944). One of several musical shows written and prod. by the author in Liberia while he was serving in the U.S. Army. **Alexis Is Fallen** (1947). **They Seek a City** (adaptn., 1974). Based on the book of the same title by †Arna Bontemps, about black migration from the South. **Point Blank** (1949). **The Mayor of Harlem** (1949). **The Last Dance for Sybil** (c. 1950). **Clay's Rebellion** (1951). **The Big Deal** (drama, 3 acts, 1953). Expanded from his one-act play **Alice in Wonder** (1952), about the political harassment of blacks during the McCarthy era. Prod. by the New Playwrights Co., at Yugoslav Hall, New York, opening March 6, 1952. **What Can You Say to Mississippi** (1 act, 1953). **Montgomery Footprints** (1 act, 1956). About the civil rights incidents in Montgomery, AL, that brought Martin Luther King and Mrs. Rosa Parks into the national spotlight.

DAVIS, WILLIAM ANGELO, Playwright.

PLAY:
Dalton's Dream (allegorical drama in poetic prose, 3 acts, 1973). Revolves around the theme of universal brotherhood. Pub. by Vantage Press, New York, 1973.

DEAN, PHILLIP HAYES, Actor and playwright. Recipient in 1971–72 of a Drama Desk Award as the year's most promising playwright, and the Dramatists Guild Award—both awards for **The Sty of the Blind Pig,** which was also selected by *Time* magazine as one of the year's ten best plays. Born in Chicago, IL. Educated in the public schools of Pontiac, MI. Moved to New York City in the late 1950s to pursue an acting career, appearing on Broadway in *Waiting for Godot* and *The Wisteria Trees*. His plays have been produced by the American Place Theatre (APT), the Chelsea Theatre Center, the Negro Ensemble Co. (NEC), and the Afro-American Studio in New York City. Clive Barnes, drama critic for the *New York Times,* has called him "a young black writer of major potential," with "a genuine command of dialogue and the ability to create dramatic tension and atmosphere." George Oppenheimer, critic for *Women's Wear Daily*, stated that "he has a gift of writing dialogue that has humor, veracity and power." Charles Ryweck, critic for the *Hollywood Reporter*, has described Dean as "an impassioned writer who creates with a touch of the poet." *Address:* 639 West End Ave., New York, NY 10023.

COLLECTIONS:
STY OF THE BLIND PIG AND AN AMERICAN NIGHT CRY: A Trilogy. Bobbs-Merrill, Indianapolis, 1972. Contains **The Sty of the Blind Pig** (1971), **Minstrel Boy** (1972), and **Thunder in the Index** (1969).

*AMERICAN NIGHT CRY.*Dramatists Play Service, New York, 1972. Contains **Thunder in the Index** (1969) and **Minstrel Boy** (1972).

THE STY OF THE BLIND PIG AND OTHER PLAYS. Bobbs-Merrill, Indianapolis, 1973. Contains **the Sty of the Blind Pig** (1971), **Thunder in the Index** (1969), and **This Bird of Dawning Singeth All Night Long** (1968).

GROUP OF RELATED PLAYS:
"AMERICAN NIGHT CRY" (3 one-act plays, 1968/72). (Not to be confused with the author's two pub. collections listed above, which do not include the first play in the trilogy.) Includes **This Bird of Dawning Singeth All Night Long** (1968), **Thunder in the Index** (1969), and **Minstrel Boy** (1972). Prod. as a trilogy by the Actors Studio, New York, opening March 7, 1974, for 12 perfs.; dir. by RICHARD WARD.

REPRESENTATIVE PLAYS AND DRAMATIC WORKS:
This Bird of Dawning Singeth All Night Long (drama, 1 act, 1968). Two-character play in which a white prostitute is confronted by a black woman claiming to be her twin sister. First prod. by APT, at St. Clement's Church, Dec. 12, 1968, on a program of three one-act plays, featuring Billie Allen and Nancy Ferrett. Prod. as a part of the trilogy "AMERICAN NIGHT CRY" [see GROUP OF RELATED PLAYS above] with Sylvia Miles and Josephine Premice. Pub. in the author's collections *AMERICAN NIGHT CRY* and *THE STY OF THE BLIND PIG AND OTHER PLAYS*.

Every Night When the Sun Goes Down (drama, 2 acts, 1968). Concerns a racketeer who has just come back from prison, and his relationships with his old friends, all inhabitants of an inner-city flophouse. First prod. by APT, 1969 (see also its revival below). Prod. by the Eugene O'Neill Theatre Center, National Playwrights Conf., Waterford, CT, at the Amphitheatre, opening Aug. 2, 1974, for 2 perfs.; dir. by Harold Scott. Revived by APT, Jan. 16–Feb. 22, 1976, for 46 perfs; dir. by GILBERT MOSES. With Frank Adu in the role of Blood, the former prisoner. Pub. by Dramatists Play Service, New York.

Thunder in the Index (drama, 1 act, 1969). Concerns a racial confrontation between a Jewish psychiatrist and his young, hip, black patient. Prod. at the Chelsea Theatre Center, Brooklyn, opening Jan. 23, 1969. Prod. as part of the trilogy "AMERICAN NIGHT CRY" [see GROUP OF RELATED PLAYS above], with Don Blakely as the mental patient. Prod. separately by the New Media Studio, Aug. 1975; dir. by Mary Hayden. Pub. in the author's collections *STY OF THE BLIND PIG AND AN AMERICAN NIGHT CRY, AMERICAN NIGHT CRY* and *THE STY OF THE BLIND PIG AND OTHER PLAYS*.

The Owl Killer (drama, 1 act, 1971). A black blue-collar worker, who has bowed and scraped to white folks all his life, takes out his frustrations and bitterness on his family, and particularly his son and daughter—both of whom have been evicted from the home after years of mistreatment and deprivation. Prod. by the Afro-American Total Theatre, New York, Dec. 1973. Pub. in *Black Drama Anthology* (King & Milner, 1972).

The Sty of the Blind Pig (drama, 3 acts, 1971). Play of black family life in Chicago, in which a blind street singer exercises a disturbing influence on the relationship between an aging unmarried woman and her old-fashioned, domineering mother, with whom she shares an apartment. Honored by *Time* Magazine as one of the year's best plays. Won for its author a Drama Desk Award, 1971–72, as the year's most promising playwright. First prod. by NEC, at St. Marks Playhouse, for 64 perfs., opening Nov. 16, 1971; dir. by SHAUNEILLE PERRY. Featured Frances Foster, Clarice Taylor, and Moses Gunn. Prod. by the Karamu Theatre, in the Proscenium Theatre, Cleveland, for one month, Jan. 11–Feb. 11, 1973. Prod. by the Howard Univ. Players, Washington, DC, during the 1972–73 season. Prod. by the Afro-American Studio Theatre in Harlem, during the 1973–74 season; dir. by ERNIE McCLINTOCK. Prod. on "Hollywood Television Theatre," May 29, 1954. Prod. by the Alley Theatre, Houston, opening Oct. 21, 1976, for 45 perfs.; dir. by Beth Sanford. Pub. by Dramatists Play Service, New York, 1972. In the author's collections *STY OF THE BLIND PIG AND AN AMERICAN NIGHT CRY* and *THE STY OF THE BLIND PIG AND OTHER PLAYS*; also in *Kuntu Drama* (Harrison, 1974).

Ministrel Boy (tragedy, 1 act, 1972). Depicts the frustrations, fears, and uncertainties of an aging black vaudeville performer and his wife following an unsuccessful out-of-town engagement. Prod. as part of the trilogy **"AMERICAN NIGHT CRY"** [see GROUP OF RELATED PLAYS above], with Don Blakely and Cleo Quitman. Pub. in the author's collections *STY OF THE BLIND PIG AND AN AMERICAN NIGHT CRY, AMERICAN NIGHT CRY,* and *THE STY OF THE BLIND PIG AND OTHER PLAYS*.

Freeman (drama, 2 parts, 1973). Concerns the unsuccessful rebellion of the free-spirited son of black bourgeoisie parents in a Michigan community. First prod. by APT, Jan. 25–Feb. 24, 1973, for 37 perfs.; dir. by Lloyd Richards. Featuring Bill Cobbs, who won a Drama Desk Award. Prod. on NET during the 1976–77 season, with Dick Anthony Williams in the title role, and featuring Richard Ward, Pauline Myers, and Chip Fields. Prod. by the Afro-American Studio, opening March 31, 1977; dir. by Ernie McClintock. Revived April 15, 1978. Pub. by Dramatists Play Service, New York, 1973.

Paul Robeson (one-man show, full length [1 long act], 1978). Portrayal of the conflicts in the life and career of singer-actor-political activist Paul Robeson. Prod. on Bway at the Lunt-Fontanne Theatre, Jan. 19–Feb. 26, 1978; then reopened in repertory with *For Colored Girls Who Have Considered Suicide/When the Rainbow Is Enuf* (by NTOZAKE SHANGE), March 9–April 30, 1978, for a total of 77 perfs.; dir. by Lloyd Richards. Starring James Earl Jones as Robeson and Burg Wallace as Lawrence Brown, his accompanist. The controversial prodn. was attacked by a group of prominent black leaders, in newspaper ads and other media, for allegedly misrepresenting the facts of Robeson's life and the principles for which he stood. The charge was answered by Carl Stokes of NBC News, who defended the play on its merits, and by over 30 leading playwrights, members of the Theatre Guild, who agreed that although a playwright should be prepared to accept criticism, no matter how harsh or unjust, group censorship of a play was in violation of the First Amendment principles of freedom of expression. Pub. as *Paul Robeson (The Play)* by Doubleday, 1978.

Mount Hope (drama, 2 acts, 1983). "A young minister, taking charge of a failing, urban church, confronts his religion and his past in a haunting, mysterious story of faith, justice and murder.''—Program Notes. Prod. by Rites and Reason, Brown Univ., Providence, RI, May 13–June 5, 1983; dir. by Akin Babatunde and Thelma Carter.

OTHER PLAYS AND DRAMATIC WORKS:
Johnny Ghost (TV play, 1969). **Noah** (1979). **The Flight of the Koo-Koo Bird** (1970). **The Dream Time** (historical satire, 2 acts, 1974). **The Collapse of the Great I Am** (pre-1975). **Relationships** (pre-1975). **If You Can't Sing, They'll Make You Dance** (1978). Prod. Off-Off-Bway by the WPA Theatre, opening Jan 27, 1978; dir. by author. With Margie Elliot, Patricia O'Toole, and Frank Adu.

DeANDA, PETER (1938–   ), Actor and playwright. Born in Pittsburgh, PA, one of nine children. Educated in the public schools there, and attended acting classes for teenagers at the Pittsburgh Playhouse. Dropped out of school and served in the U.S. Air Force, 1955–59, where he was assigned to Special Services and appeared in a number of theatrical productions. Completed high school while in the service. Married; the father of three children. Graduated from the Pittsburgh Playhouse School of Drama and performed with the Irene Kaufman Players. Studied with the Actors' Workshop in New York City. Appeared in the New York stage productions of *The Blacks* (1963), *Dutchman* (1964), *A Sound of Silence* (1965), *The Zulu and the Zayda* (1965), *Inherit the Wind* (1970), *The Guide* (1978), *Passing through Exotic Places: Sunstroke* (1969), and *The House of Leather* (1970). TV appearances include the role of Dr. Price Trainor on "One Life to Live" (1971), the title role of a black private eye on the NBC-TV special "Cutter" (1972), and appearances on "Cannon" (1975), "Joe Forrester" (1976), and "Police Woman" (1976). Films include *Lady Liberty* (1971), *The Blue Centurions* (1972), and *Come Back, Charleston Blue* (1972).

PLAYS:
Sweetbread (drama, 3 acts, 1964). A young black who faces opposition from his brother because of his Black Muslim religion is finally shot by a white policeman for refusing to obey an order. Performed by the author on Bway in 1964, as part of Talent 64, a showcase for new faces. This perf. was repeated on NBC-TV's premiere show of "Kaleidoscope" during the summer of 1964.
Ladies in Waiting (drama, 2 acts [8 scenes], 1968). A pretty, young, liberal-minded white girl, arrested for marching in a picket line to protest prison conditions for women, is incarcerated in the same cell with three black women—a lesbian, a prostitute, and a mentally unstable woman. Prod. Off-Bway in a workshop production by the Negro Ensemble Co. (NEC), at St. Marks Playhouse, June 17, 1968. Prod. by the Urban Arts Corps in Greenwich Village, 1970–71; dir. by VINNETTE CARROLL. Prod. by the New Federal Theatre (NFT), New York, 1973. Prod. by the Alonzo Players, at the Billie Holiday Theatre, Brooklyn, 1974; dir. by CECIL ALONZO. Pub. in *Black Drama Anthology* (King & Milner, 1971).

DEAS, (Dr.) GERALD W., Doctor-playwright. *Address:* 109–07 197 Ave., Hollis, NY 11432.

DRAMATIC WORKS:
Paper Bird // Orig. title: **A New Breed Is Now the Seed** (musical, 2 acts, 1974). Story, lyrics, and music by Deas. Book and direction by TAD TRUESDALE. Title taken from a poem by Deas, which deals with man's universal desire to fly like an eagle, only to discover that he is just a paper bird. A story of street gangs—black and Hispanic versus white ethnic groups—exploring some of the problems under its orig. title of survival in the big city ghettos. Prod. by William Hunter at Town Hall, New York, 1975. Prod. by Now the Seed Productions, Inc., at the Storefront Museum, Queens, NY, Nov. 17–Dec. 3, 1977, for 9 perfs. **Oh! Oh! Obesity** (musical comedy, 2 acts [13 scenes], 1984). Story, lyrics, and music by Deas. Script collaboration (book) and direction by Bette Howard. Concerned with the problem of obesity and how to control it. Characters include Fat Momma, Fat Daddy, Blimpie, and Fatsie; musical numbers include "I Can't Eat a Thing," "I'm Fat," and "I Fried All Night Long." Prod. by the New Federal Theatre (NFT), at the Louis Abrons Arts for Living Center, New York, June 7–24, 1984, for 15 perfs. Prod. by the Paul Robeson Theatre, Brooklyn, Nov. 1986.

DeCOY, ROBERT H. (1920–   ), Playwright, screenwriter, radio scriptwriter, author, actor, broadcaster, historian, and philosopher. Born in New Orleans, LA. Cofounder and director of the Inst. of Nigritian Studies; pres. of Nigritian, Inc., Publishers. (Nigritian is his preferred ethnic term for Americans of African descent.) Author of *Cold Black Preach* (1967) and *The Nigger Bible* (1971), both published by Nigritian. Radio broadcaster for more than a decade; writer and consultant for CBS and ABC radio networks.

PLAYS AND DRAMATIC WORKS:
This Is Progress (radio doc., 1969). Created, written, and narrated by DeCoy. History of the contributions of black Americans. Apparently broadcast over CBS or ABC radio, date unknown. **The Castration** (1970). **The Black Prodigal and the Priest** (screenplay, 1971).

DEDEAUX, RICHARD (Anthony) (1940–   ), Playwright, TV scriptwriter. Born in New Orleans, LA. Member, writer, and producer of the Watts Prophets, a group of Los Angeles poets who have performed in concerts throughout the United States. Cofounder of the Wattstax Summer Concert. Instructor and consultant for the Watts Writers Workshop, 1971–72. Consultant for Stax Records, 1974. Assoc. producer for KCET's weekly series "Doin' It at the Waterfront." Scriptwriter, teacher and consultant at Mafundi Inst., and editor of the *Mafundi Monthly* newspaper. His writings include four volumes of poetry, two novels, and an anthology of six short stories.

PLAYS AND DRAMATIC WORKS:
And Baby Makes Three (family comedy-drama, 1973). Prod. by Mafundi Inst., Los Angeles, Jan. 1973. **The Rising Sons—Wisdom and Knowledge** (staged poetry reading, 1973). Written with *Otis Smith and *Killu Hamilton. Performed by the Watts Prophets, 1973. **Victory Will Be My Moan** (TV doc., 1970s). Written with the Watts Prophets. Prod. in Los Angeles, and nominated for an Emmy. **The Decision** (1970s). **A Duel with Destiny** (TV script, 1970s). **The Big Rip Off** (screenplay, 1970s).

DEE, RUBY (Ruby Ann Wallace; Mrs. OSSIE DAVIS) (1924–   ), Veteran actress of stage, screen, and television; playwright, screenwriter. Born in Cleveland, OH. Educated at Hunter Coll. (A.B., 1945). Received theatrical experience with the American Negro Theatre (ANT) in Harlem, 1941–44. Also studied with Morris Carnovsky, 1958–60, and with the Actors Workshop. She has costarred with her husband Ossie Davis in numerous productions, including plays, films, TV shows, spoken recordings, and performances on college and university campuses. Appeared in both the stage and screen versions of *A Raisin in the Sun* (1959, 1961) and *Purlie Victorious* (1961, 1963). Other stage credits include *Walk Hard* (1944), *On Striver's Row* (1946), *Tell Pharaoh* (1972), and *Wedding Band* (1973). Films include *The Jackie Robinson Story* (1950), *St. Louis Blues* (1958), *Take a Giant Step* (1960), *Black Girl* (1973), and *Countdown at Kusini* (1976). Recipient of Frederick Douglass Award, New York Urban League, 1970; Obie Award for *Boesman and Lena,* 1971; and Actors Equity Assn. (AEA) Paul Robeson Citation, 1975. Elected to Black Filmmakers Hall of Fame, 1975. *Address:* 44 Cortlandt Ave., New Rochelle, NY 10801; or P.O. Box 1318, New Rochelle, NY 10802.

PLAYS AND DRAMATIC WORKS:

Uptight (feature film, full length: screenplay, 1968). Script coauthored with JULIAN MAYFIELD and Jules Dassin. Adapted from Liam O'Flaherty's novel *The Informer,* which had been previously made into a film by John Ford in 1935. According to the *Ebony Handbook* (1974, p. 457), it was the first film to depict the black revolution. Whereas *The Informer* deals with Irish rebels in Dublin, **Uptight** was set in the black ghetto of Cleveland, and its leading characters were black militants. Prod. by Paramount Pictures, 1968, starring joint authors Dee and Mayfield. Mayfield appeared as the leader of the black militant group, and Dee as a young welfare mother who supplemented her income by prostitution. The supporting cast included Raymond St. Jacques, Frank Silvera, ROSCOE LEE BROWNE, and Janet MacLachlan.

Twin Bit Gardens (comedy-drama, 1 act?, 1974). Disgusted by the way man has messed up the world, God gives him 30 days to get things straightened out. Public reading by the Frank Silvera Writers' Workshop (FSWW), at the Martinique Theatre, New York, March 1976. Unpub. script in FSWW Archives/Schomburg Collection.

Tomorrow Is Ours (children's TV script, 1970s). Prod. on CBS-TV, 1970s.

Take It from the Top (musical, full length, 1979). Words and lyrics by Dee. Prod. Off-Bway by the New Federal Theatre (NFT), opening Jan. 18, 1979; dir. by Ossie Davis, who also performed in the cast. Unpub. script and tape recording in the Hatch-Billops Collection.

de JONGH, JAMES (Laurence) (1942–   ), College professor, novelist, actor, and playwright. Born in St. Thomas, Virgin Islands. Educated at Williams Coll. (B.A., 1964). Currently assoc. prof. of English, City Coll. of New York. Initially attracted to the theatre by an interest in acting and still works occasionally as a performer (last featured in WOODIE KING, JR.'s *Death of a Prophet*). Often collaborates with CARLES CLEVELAND, with whom he coauthored four dramatic works (cited below) and two novels: *City Cool: A Ritual of Belonging*

(1978), a first-person narrative by a black teenager who joins a Harlem street gang with tragic results; and *Till Victory* (c. 1979), which (according to Cleveland, the coauthor) deals with "the rise and fall of Black Harlem in the fictional character of Alexander Hamilton Shakespeare (1880–1942), lover, philanthropist, sportsman, and numbers banker."—*Contemporary Authors,* vols. 85–88, p. 109. Recipient of Fulbright Fellowship, Univ. of Madrid, 1964; CAPS Fellowship in fiction, 1977; NEH Summer Fellowship, Yale Univ., 1980; appointment as Fellow of the Center for Black Studies, Univ. of California/Santa Barbara, 1981–82; AUDELCO Recognition Award, as musical creator, 1984. *Address:* English Dept., City College, New York NY 10031. *Agent:* Susan F. Schulman, Susan Schulman Literary Agency, 454 W. 44th St., New York, NY 10036.

PLAYS AND DRAMATIC WORKS:
Hail Hail the Gangs! ("an experimental theatre piece," full length, 1976). Coauthor, with Carles Cleveland. About a black teenager who joins a Harlem street gang. Prod. Off-Off-Bway by the New York Theatre Ensemble, April 1976. Featured at the Black Theatre Alliance Festival and the Lincoln Center Outdoor Festival Pub. only as a novel, *City Cool: A Ritual of Belonging,* by Random House, New York, 1978, also coauthored by Cleveland and de Jongh.

City Cool (screenplay [first draft], 1977). Coauthor, with Carles Cleveland. Adaptn. of the novel *City Cool: A Ritual of Belonging,* cited immediately above. Was under prodn. consideration by Warner Bros. in 1984.

"The Bet," Watch Your Mouth (story idea for a TV series episode, 1977). Coauthor, with Carles Cleveland. Under prodn. consideration by NET, Channel 13, New York City.

Do Lord Remember Me ("Memory play with music," full length, 1978). Exploration of the collective triumph of African-Americans over the institution of slavery through the recollections of former slaves recorded in the 1930s, under the WPA Federal Writers' Project. First prod. by the New Federal Theatre, New York, opening March 3, 1978; dir. by REGGE LIFE. Prod. Off-Bway at the American Place Theatre, opening Oct. 20, 1982; also dir. by Regge Life. With Glynn Turman (replaced by Carlos Esposito), Frances Foster, and Charles Patterson (as narrator).

Play to Win (musical biography for children and young adults, full length, 1983). Coauthor, with Carles Cleveland. The story of Jackie Robinson. Commissioned by Theatreworks/USA, New York, which prod. the play in 1983. With Marcus Olson and Christine Campbell. Went on national school tour, 1984–86.

DENDY, J. BROOKS, III, Playwright, artist, editor. Founder and director of CreataDrama Theatre Laboratory Co. in Philadelphia, which apparently established CreataDrama Centers at the Univ. of Pittsburgh and the Univ. of Arkansas at Pine Bluff. *Address:* 1713 N. 21st St., Philadelphia, PA 19119.

PLAYS:
Environmental Dramas (series of sketches, early 1970s). These sketches dramatize how a person's character determines his responses to another person or object. Prod. at CreataDrama Centers in Philadelphia and Pittsburgh, early 1970s. **Julius Caesar's Doomsday** (mid-1970s). CreataDrama, based on Julius Caesar's assassination, focusing

on the crowd's reaction to the event. Prod. by the Isaac Hathaway Fine Arts Center, Univ. of Arkansas, Pine Bluff, during the mid-1970s. Unpub. script in the Hatch-Billops Collection.

DENNIS, DOROTHY LORENE, Playwright. Former member of the Southern Assn. of Dramatic and Speech Arts (SADSA), renamed the National Assn. of Dramatic and Speech Arts (NADSA).

PLAY:
Outcast (1 act, 1951). Pub. in *SADSA Encore* (Nashville, TN), 1951.

DENT, TOM (Thomas Covington Dent; also known as Kush) (1932–   ), Poet, editor, playwright, essayist, and theatrical director. Born in New Orleans, LA, the son of Dr. Albert Dent, former pres. of Dillard Univ. Received the bachelor's degree in political science from Morehouse Coll., 1952, and the master's degree in poetry from Goddard Coll., 1974. Served in the U.S. Army, 1947–59. Gained experience in journalism as an editor of Morehouse's student newspaper, the *Maroon Tiger,* and as a reporter for the *Houston Informer* during his summers off from college. Following his army service, he went to New York to become a writer. First worked as a reporter for the *New York Age,* and assisted in the publication of *On Guard for Freedom,* a fledgling political newspaper. Was one of the organizers in 1952 of the Umbra Workshop, and cofounder of *Umbra,* a poetry magazine which became an important publication of the Black Arts movement. Left New York in 1965 to become assoc. director of the Free Southern Theatre (FST), then based in New Orleans. Cofounder of Blkartsouth, a community writing and acting workshop of FST, which published *Nkombo,* a quarterly journal of the black arts. Coeditor, with Richard Schechner and GIL-BERT MOSES, of *The Free Southern Theatre by the Free Southern Theatre* (Bobbs-Merrill, 1969). Author of two books of poetry: *Magnolia Street* (1976) and *Blue Lights & River Songs* (1982). His articles and poems have appeared in *Black World, Freedomways, Umbra, Black Creation, Black River Journal, New Negro Poets: USA* (Hughes, 1964), *New Black Voices* (Chapman, 1968), *The Black Poets* (Randall, 1971), *Black Culture* (Simons & Hutchinson, 1972), and *An Introduction to Black Literature in America* (Patterson, 1968). One of the founders of the Congo Square Writers Union in New Orleans, and of *Callaloo,* a literary magazine published at the Univ. of Kentucky in Lexington. Currently involved in the cowriting of Andrew Young's autobiography. *Address:* P.O. Box 50584, New Orleans, LA 70115.

REPRESENTATIVE PLAY:
Ritual Murder (drama, 1 long act, 1966). The theme is stated by one of the characters (a black psychiatrist): "When murder occurs for no apparent reason but happens all the time as in our race on Saturday nights, it is ritual murder.... When a people who have no method of letting off steam under the source of their oppression explode against each other, homocide, under these conditions, is a form of suicide."—Pub. script. First prod. at the Ethiopian Theatre, New Orleans, Summer 1977; dir. by CHAKULA cha JUA, who

dir. all New Orleans productions, and is credited by the author with "important contributions in staging which make the play effective."—Letter to Peterson, July 24, 1983. Prod. in New Orleans by the Congo Square Theatre, and by Act One Theatre (at Xavier Univ.); in Baton Rouge, LA, and in Opelousas, LA, for the Southern Development Cooperative; in Jackson, MS, at Tougaloo Coll.; and in Elizabeth City, NC, at Elizabeth City State Univ. Pub. by the author, New Orleans. Also pub. with director's notes in *Callaloo* (Dept. of English, Univ. of Kentucky, Lexington), Feb. 1978, pp. 67–81.

OTHER PLAYS AND DRAMATIC WORKS:
Negro Study #34A (drama, 1 act, 1969). White businessman is tricked by black couple into financing a phony scheme. Written in Fall 1969 as part of the FST Workshop, but not performed by FST. Unpub. script in the Hatch-Billops Collection. **Riot Duty** (drama, 1 act, 1969). Black policeman in plain clothes is mistaken by white policeman for a rioter and is subjected to brutality. Written in Winter 1969 as part of the FST Workshop, but not performed by FST. Unpub. script in the Hatch-Billops Collection. **Snapshot** (1 act, 1969). Prod. as an FST Workshop production, 1970. Pub. in *Nkombo*, Dec. 1969, pp. 85–90. **Feathers and Stuff** (1 act, 1960). Prod. by FST Touring Ensemble Drama Workshop, New Orleans, Dec. and Jan. 1969–70. **Song of Survival** (ritual, 1 act, 1969). Coauthor, with KALAMU YA SALAAM (Val Ferdinand). For the raising of black consciousness. Prod. by FST, 1969. **Inner Black Blues** (ritual, 4 parts, 1972). Subtitled "A Poem/Play for Black Bros. and Sisters." Ritual for the raising of the consciousness of black youth to resist the brainwashing of the white oppressor. Pub. in *Nkombo*, Aug. 1972, pp. 28–43.

dePALM, NORMAN, Playwright. Based in New York City.

PLAY:
Desiree ("A One Woman, One Act Drama" [subtitle], 1983). Based on a newspaper item, "Woman Burns Baby to Death." Prod. at the No-Smoking Playhouse, New York, Dec. 1–30, 1983, for 24 perfs.; dir. by Felix de Rooy. With Marian Rolle as Desiree.

DePASSE, SUZANNE, Corporation executive and screenwriter. Born and reared in Harlem, New York City. President of Motown Productions, the television and film division of Motown Industries. Recipient of an Academy Award nomination for the best story and screenplay for **Lady Sings the Blues,** 1973. *Address:* Motown Record Corp., 6225 Sunset Blvd., Los Angeles, CA 90028.

DRAMATIC WORK:
Lady Sings the Blues (feature film, full length: screenplay, 1972). Written jointly with Terrence McCloy and Chris Clark. Based on Billie Holiday's autobiography of the same title, written with William Duffy. Musical biography of the well-known blues singer. Prod. by Berry Gordy and others; released by Paramount Pictures, Oct. 1972; featuring Diana Ross in her screen debut, Billy Dee Williams, and RICHARD PRYOR. Earned for the authors a 1973 Academy Award nomination for best story and screenplay. Gil Askey was also nominated for his musical arrangements for this film. Available on VCR videotape.

DeRAMUS, BETTY, Freelance writer, reporter, journalist. Resides in Detroit, MI. Graduated from Wayne State Univ., 1963. Worked for four years as a reporter for the *Michigan Chronicle*, during which time she received three citations for her news and feature writings from the National Publishers Assn. Her short stories and articles appeared frequently in *Negro Digest/Black World*.

PLAY:
Just What I Said (1971). Prod. by the Concept East Workshop, Detroit, Nov. 26, 1971.

DeSHIELDS, ANDRE (1946–   ), Multitalented actor-playwright, director. Born in Baltimore, Md. Educated at the Univ. of Wisconsin. Played the title role in *The Wiz* (1975) on Broadway and was a principal star in *Ain't Misbehavin'* (1978) and *Jazzbo Brown* (1980). Other stage performances include *Warp* (Bway debut, 1973), *Rachel Lily Rosenbloom, 2008 1/2* (Off-Bway), *The Soldier's Tale, The Little Prince,* and **Haarlem Nocturne** (1983).

DRAMATIC WORKS:
Haarlem Nocturne (musical, 2 acts, 1983). Conceived by DeShields. Cowritten and directed by DeShields and Murray Horowitz. Vocal arrangements by Marc Shaiman. Self-publicized as a "blistering, passionate, and lusty vision of New York life." One of its production numbers, "New York Is a Party," is an accurate description of what the whole play is about. Prod. by La Mama E.T.C. (Experimental Theatre Club), New York, presumably in 1983, where it had a long and successful run. Expanded for Bway, opening at the Latin Quarter, Oct. 30–Dec. 30, 1984, for 64 perfs. Featuring DeShields, Debra Byrd, Ellia English, Marc Shaiman, and Freida Williams. **Blackberries** (minstrel-vaudeville spectacular, 2 acts [16 scenes], 1984). Book by Joseph George Caruso. Sketches by Billy K. Wells. Additional material/dialogue and direction by DeShields. Celebrates the contributions that blacks have made to American musical comedy. Prod. by AMAS Repertory Theatre, New York, April 19–May 13, 1984, for 16 perfs.

DeVEAUX, ALEXIS (1948–   ), Poet, playwright, fiction writer, teacher, self-taught artist, and political journalist/activist in black feminist causes. Born and grew up in New York City. Received the B.A. from Empire State Coll. of SUNY, 1976. Asst. instr. of English for the WIN Program of the New York Urban League, 1969. Creative writing instr. for the Frederick Douglass Creative Arts Center, New York City, 1971. Community worker for the Bronx Office of Probations, 1972. Reading and creative writing instr. for Project Create, New York City, 1973. Cultural coordinator of Black Expo for the Black Coalition of Greater New Haven, CT, 1975. Cofounder of Coeur de l'Unicorne Gallery, New Haven, 1975; own paintings were exhibited. Freelance writer, 1976–present. Currently a contributing editor of **Essence** magazine. Her poetry and drama have been performed in and around New York in such places as Greenhaven Prison, the Brooklyn Academy of Music, Cathedral of St. John the Divine, Empire State Coll., Riverside Church, F. Douglass Creative Arts Center's Experimental Theatre, and Westchester Community Coll. Her work has been broadcast in New York on Radio Stations WBAI, WRVR, WVLR, and WNYC, and televised on

WABC-TV's "Like It Is," WTTG-TV's "Panorama" in Washington, DC, and KCET-TV in California. Has been a guest lecturer at Livingston Coll. (Rutgers Univ.) in New Jersey, and in 1975 was invited to speak before a graduate seminar in writing taught by Paule Marshall at Columbia Univ. Her books include *Spirit in the Street* (1973), a novel; *na-ni* (1973), a children's book; *Li Chen/Second Daughter First Son* (1975), a novel; *Don't Explain: A Song of Billie Holiday* (1980), a biography of the famous blues singer; and *Adventures of the Dread Sisters* (1982). Her short stories, poems, and other writings have been published mainly in *Black Creation, Essence, Hoo-Doo Magazine, Encore,* and *Sunbury Magazine.* Recipient of first prize in *Black Creation's* national fiction contest, 1972; best production award, Westchester Community Coll. Drama Festival, 1973; and two Art Books for Children awards from Brooklyn Museum in 1974 and 1975. *Address:* 115 Easter Parkway, Suite 8K, Brooklyn, NY 11238; or c/o *Essence* Magazine, 1500 Broadway, New York, NY 10003.

REPRESENTATIVE PLAYS AND DRAMATIC WORKS:

Circles (drama, 1 act, 1973). A young black woman attempts to break away from the influence of her domineering grandmother in order to realize her dreams of becoming a dancer. Performed by the F. Douglass Players at the F. Douglass Creative Arts Center, Harlem, March 4–28, 1973, playing only on weekends, for 14 perfs.; dir. by Ernestine Johnson. Performed by the same group at the Westchester Community Coll. Drama Festival, New York, May 1973, winning a "Best Production" award. Televised by KCET-TV in California, Jan. 1976, and presented on PBS-TV on a dramatic series called "Visions"; dir. by MAYA ANGELOU. Cast included Ruth Beckford-Smith (well-known black dancer) and Raymond Allen (of "Sanford and Son").

The Tapestry (drama, 2 acts, 1976). A young black female law student who is about to take her bar exams attempts to come to grips with her own womanhood and her relationships with her boyfriend and her best girlfriend. A chorus of "spirits" helps her to resolve her inner conflicts. Televised by KCET-TV in California, Jan. 1976, and presented on PBS-TV on a dramatic series called "Visions"; dir. by Maya Angelou. Cast included Glynn Turman, Ebony Wright, Alvin Childress, Ruth Beckford-Smith, and JIMMY JUSTICE. Public reading by Frank Silvera Writers' Workshop (FSWW), at the Harlem Cultural Center, New York City, mid-1970s. Prod. by the West Coast Black Repertory Theatre, c. 1976. Prod. by the Quaigh Theatre, New York City, March 1977; dir. by Kimaki Baraka. Pub. in *Nine Plays by Black Women* (Wilkerson, 1986). Unpub. script and tape recording in the FSWW Archives/Schomburg Collection.

A Season to Unravel (psychological drama, 1 long act, 1979). A Freudian-type play which takes place in the mind of the leading character, a woman, who is also a psychologist. The other characters are various aspects of herself, some of whom are portrayed as animals. Prod. by the Negro Ensemble Co. (NEC), at St. Marks Playhouse, New York City, Jan 25–Feb. 4, 1979, for 15 perfs.; dir. by *Glenda Dickerson.* With Olivia Williams, Barbara Montgomery, Michele Shay, L. Scott Caldwell, Graham Brown, and ADOLPH CAESAR.

OTHER PLAYS AND DRAMATIC WORKS:

A Little Play ("dream fantasy," 1 act, 1972). Concerns a young girl's conversation with her lover. Performed by the Young People's Workshop of All Soul's Church in Harlem, Nov. 1973, for one weekend (3 perfs.); dir. by author. **Whip Cream** (drama,

1 act, 1973). Involves a young woman who is caught jumping the turnstile of a New York City subway. Performed by the Young People's Workshop of All Soul's Church, 1973. **The Fox Street War** (drama, full length, c. 1979). A group of black female tenants uses folk magic (voodoo) to get their landlord to improve the conditions of their dwelling house.

DeWINDT, HAL (Harold) (1934–   ), Theatrical director, actor, playwright, teacher; former model, semiprofessional basketball player. A featured model in *Ebony* Magazine and in the Ebony Fashion Fair for several years. Appeared in the New York productions of *Entertain a Ghost* (1962), *Day of Absence* and *Happy Ending* (1965), and *Volpone* (1967). Stage manager for the New York Shakespeare Festival Mobile Theatre during the summer of 1965. Director of the Summer Lab for the Working Actor at the Stanleigh School of Theatre in New York during the 1960s. Associated with the Inner City Repertory Co. (of the Inner City Cultural Center [ICCC]) of Los Angeles as producing director in the late 1960s. Workshop director of the Negro Ensemble Co. (NEC), New York, 1972. Founder-director of the Hal DeWindt Theatre, San Francisco, 1977.

PLAYS:
Raisin' Hell in the Son (satire, full length, 1962). Satirizes the black actor, the black politician, the white liberal, and LORRAINE HANSBERRY's play *A Raisin in the Sun*. Prod. Off-Bway, at the Provincetown Playhouse, opening July 2, 1962, for a run of three weeks; dir. by author, and featuring BARBARA ANN TEER. **Us Versus Nobody** (1 act, 1971). Prod. Off-Bway by NEC, as a work-in-progress, at St. Marks Playhouse, Feb. 2, 1971.

DICKERSON, GLENDA (J.) (1945–   ), Director, folklorist, adaptor, writer, choreographer, actress, black theatre organizer, and teacher. Recipient of an AUDELCO Award for her **Magic and Lions** (1978). Born in Houston, TX, the daughter of a career army officer. Traveled extensively with her family throughout the United States, Europe, and the Orient. Received the B.F.A. from Howard Univ., 1966, and the M.F.A. from Adelphi Univ., 1968. Also studied with British director Peter Brook. Married; one daughter. A former actress, she started directing in 1968 because of her dissatisfaction with the "cattle call" system of auditions in New York. Founder-director of TOBA (Tough on Black Actors) Players in New York City, 1967–68. With this group she explored a theatrical format that combined poetry, drama, and black heritage, which was to become one of the trademarks of her style as a playwright and director, in which special emphasis is placed on the adaptation of myths, legends, poetry, and black classic novels to drama. Artistic director, Black American Theatre, Washington, DC, 1969–72. Asst. prof. of speech and acting, Howard Univ., 1969–72. Director, Theatre Dept. of the School of Arts, Western H.S., Washington, DC, 1970s. Assoc. director of Starbecker Films, Inc. Teacher and conductor of workshops, 1970–74, for the Bureau of Indian Affairs, the African People's Repertory Theatre, San Francisco, and the Workshop for Careers in the Arts. Former staff member, Negro Ensemble Co. (NEC). Founding director of the Lyric Theatre (now the Owen Dodson Lyric Theatre), a New York–based traveling company, 1983–. Currently asst. prof. of speech and theatre at SUNY/ Stony Brook. Has directed over 50 dramatic productions for stage and television, including her own works, cited below. Her more recent directorial credits include *The Daughters of the Mock* (1978) and *A Season to Unravel* (1979) for NEC, and *Reggae* (1980), which was produced on Broadway at the Biltmore Theatre. One of her theatrical projects is the "Living Library Series," a videotaped series of adaptations of black classics, 1967–76, which includes her own play **Unfinished Song** (1969), and dramatizations of novels by JAMES BALDWIN (*If Beale Street Could Talk*), †Arna Bontemps *(Black Thunder)*, and Margaret Walker *(Jubilee)*—apparently housed in both the theatre depts. of the School of Arts of Western H.S. and Howard Univ. In addition to the AUDELCO Award, she is recipient of a Citation by the mayor of Washington for **Unfinished Song;** a Peabody Award for her production of *For My People* (on WTOP-TV); and an Emmy nomination for her production of *Wine in the Wilderness* (WRC-TV).

REPRESENTATIVE PLAYS AND DRAMATIC WORKS:
Unfinished Song (theatrical collage, full length, 1969). Subtitled "Reflections in Black Voices." A theatre piece which preserves African oral poetry and selected poetry by black Americans, from Jupiter Hammond to LARRY NEAL. Staged with drums, finger instruments, and choreography. First prod. at Howard Univ., 1969. Recipient of a Citation from the mayor of Washington. Subsequently prod. in New York and California. Videotaped for the author's "Living Library Series."

Jesus Christ—Lawd Today (Biblical musical, full length, 1971). Music by *Clyde Barrett. The Christ story set in an urban black American setting. Prod. by the Black American Theatre, Summer 1971; dir. by author, with choreography by Debbie Allen (of TV's "Fame" series). Also presented at Howard Univ., 1970s.

Trojan Women (adaptn., full length, 1971). From the play by Euripides, set in West Africa. Presents a new perspective on the ravages of war and oppression. Prod. in the Ira Aldridge Theatre, Howard Univ., 1971.

Jump at the Sum (adaptn., full length, 1972). From †Zora Neale Hurston's novel *Their Eyes Were Watching God* (1937). The happy, singing love story of a young woman in the rural South who meets a magic man named Tea Cake. According to Taquiena Boston and Vera J. Katz, Hurston's novel "shows the earthbound folk of the rural black experience. The production depicts a woman's journey to find love and deals with the hardships of holding onto love."—*Black American Literature Forum*, Spring 1983, p. 26. Prod. at the Theatre Lobby, Washington, DC, 1972.

The Torture of Mothers (adaptn., full length, 1973). From Truman Nelson's novel by the same title. "Tells the story of six Black mothers whose sons allegedly played key roles in igniting the Harlem riots in 1964."—*Black World*, April 1973, p. 84. The story is told through the eyes of the mothers. Prod. by the Back Alley Theatre, 1973.

Owen's Song (theatrical collage, 2 acts, 1974). Subtitled "A Tribute to Owen Dodson." Conceived, directed, and choreographed by Dickerson and MIKE MALONE. Music by Clyde Barrett and *Dennis Wiley. Adapt. from the dramatic and poetic works of OWEN DODSON. Described by the coauthors (Dickerson and Malone) as a "weaving together [of] lines from [Dodson's] works, including *Divine Comedy, Powerful Long*

Ladder, his many poems, and his full-length play *Bayou Legend.''* ''The story line . . . is inspired by the magnificent theme that runs through all of his works: climbing a powerful long ladder to catch the bird of freedom''—Program Notes. Boston and Katz *(Black Literature Forum,* Spring 1983) view the play as ''a prodigal son story in which the wanderer sacrifices his innocence, but returns home to his people with wisdom.'' Prod. by the DC Black Repertory Co., at the Last Colony Theatre, Washington, DC, opening Oct. 24, 1974, for six weeks. Also performed in New York City at the Harlem Cultural Center; then transferred back to Washington, to the Eisenhower Theatre in the John F. Kennedy Center for the Performing Arts, opening Dec. 31, 1974, for two weeks. Unpub. script in the Hatch-Billops Collection.

Magic and Lions (theatrical collage, full length, 1978). Conceived from the prose and poetry of *Ernestine Walker. A lyric, choreographic piece steeped in Egyptian mythology. First prod. by the Women's Interart Theatre, New York City, 1978. Recipient of an AUDELCO Award.

OTHER PLAYS AND DRAMATIC WORKS:

Rashomon (adaptn., full length, 1982). From the Japanese classic; set in Ethiopia in the thirteenth century. Includes elements of the story of the Queen of Sheba and African trickster tales. Prod. in Ethiopia, 1982. **No** (literary collage, 1983). Conceived from the works of ALEXIS DeVEAUX. Presented as a parlor reading in New York City, 1983. **Saffron Persephone Brown** (one-woman show, full length, 1983). The flower story of an archetypal brown woman. Conceived and enacted by the author, 1983. **Haitian Medea** (adaptn., full length, 1983). From the tragedy of Euripides. Set in Dahomey in the early nineteenth century. Medea is a Haitian woman loosely based on Marie Laveau, the ''Voodoo Queen of New Orleans,'' and Celestine Simon, a Haitian folk heroine. Jason is a Brazilian slave. Through Medea's powers they fly across the Atlantic Ocean and return to Dahomey.

DINWIDDIE, MICHAEL, Playwright. Educated at NYU, where he received the B.A. in liberal arts in the Gallatin Div., 1980, and the M.F.A. in dramatic writing at the Tisch School of the Arts, 1983, with a major in stage/screenplay writing and a minor in film and video production. Currently associated with the Wonderhorse Theatre in New York City. *Address:* 120 E. 4th St. #4D, New York, NY 10003.

PLAYS:

Script Chatter (1981). Prod. by the Satori Theatre Co., Detroit, 1971. **The First Day** (1973). Prod. by the Finneytown Players, Cincinnati, 1973. **Dale** (teleplay, 1974). Prod. by WXYZ-TV (ABC), Southfield, MI, 1974. **Montana Young** (musical, 1975). Book, music, and lyrics coauthored with Kenneth Kylton, Jr. Prod. on college tour of Michigan, 1975. **Martians Don't Speak English** (1976). Prod. by Satori Theatre Co., 1976. **Remake of a Chance Remark** (video play, 1978). Prod. by Caranci Studios, New York, 1978. **Liferoses** (1979). Prod. by Westbeth Theatre, New York City, 1979. **Death of a Canvas Gazer** (1980). Prod. by Tennessee State Univ., Nashville, 1980. **Jill Reed, Read!?** (children's musical, 1980). Book, music, and lyrics by Dinwiddie. Prod. by the Grand St. Settlement, New York, 1980. **Dacha** (1 act, 1981). Play of Harlem life, set in a brownstone building. Staged reading by the Wonderhorse Theatre, 1981; full prodn. by the same group, on double bill with **Masque,** April 18–May 18, 1982, for 15 perfs.; dir. by Leslie Hurley. **Masque** (1 act, 1982). Play of black life in Louisiana during the

1850s; the setting is the balcony of a ballroom. Prod. by the Wonderhorse Theatre, April 18–May 18, 1982, for 15 perfs. **The Beautiful LaSalles** (1984). Play of black upper-middle-class life, set in the LaSalles' Riverside Drive apartment. Prod. by the Wonderhorse Theatre, Feb. 9–26, 1984, for 20 perfs.

DIXON, MELVIN, Playwright, black theatre administrator, and essayist. Resides at Stamford, CT. Currently teaching at Queens Coll., Jamaica, NY. Director and coordinator of the Black Repertory Theatre, Wesleyan Univ., Middletown, CT, which in 1969 produced *Sails and Sinkers* by *Ronald Fair. Member of the National Black Theatre (NBT), where he came under the tutelage of actress-playwright BARBARA ANN TEER. Author of an essay on black theatre published in *Black World*, July 1969.

PLAYS AND DRAMATIC WORKS:

Confrontation (drama, 1 act, 1969). Two black men of different social classes and political views meet on a subway and discover that, in spite of their apparent differences, they have one goal in common. Prod. by Wesleyan Univ. Theatre, Middletown, March 1969. Unpub. script in the Hatch-Billops Collection. **In the Beginning: A Ceremony in the Evolution of Black Folks** (ritual/collective creation, 1969). Created and performed by the Black Repertory Theatre, Wesleyan Univ., Dec. 11, 1969, under the direction of Dixon. **Kingdom, or the Last Promise** // Orig. title: **Thy Kingdom Come** (ritual, 3 acts, 1969). Black characters after death attempt to gain the freedom they have been promised and avoid the threat of further mistreatment and damnation. Apparently first prod. by the Black Repertory Theatre, Wesleyan Univ., 1969. Prod. by Brown Univ., Providence, RI, 1972; dir. by Benny S. Ambush. Unpub. script in the Hatch-Billops Collection. **Black People** (collective creation, 1970). Created and performed by Black Repertory Theatre, Wesleyan Univ., May 6, 1970, under the dir. of Dixon. **Ritual: For Malcolm** (1970). Compiled and dir. by Dixon. Prod. by Black Repertory Theatre, Wesleyan Univ., at the Malcolm X House, Nov. 1, 1970.

DODSON, OWEN (Vincent) (1914–1983), Poet, novelist, playwright, teacher, and theatrical director; for many years prof. of drama and chairman of the Dept. of Drama at Howard Univ., Washington, DC. Recognized as one of the most influential directors in the black academic theatre from the 1940s to the 1970s. Recipient of an AUDELCO Outstanding Pioneer Award, 1975, "for his contribution to the growth and development of Black theatre." Born in Brooklyn, NY. Educated in the public schools of New York City; at Bates Coll. (B.A., 1936), where he was elected to Phi Beta Kappa, and from which he received an honorary Doctor of Letters in 1967; and at Yale Univ. (B.F.A. in playwriting and directing, 1939), under a General Education Board Fellowship. Taught and directed plays at Atlanta Univ., 1939–42; Hampton Inst., 1943–44; and Howard Univ., 1949–70. Served in the U.S. Navy, 1942–43, where he wrote, produced, and directed a number of short, morale-building plays while stationed at Camp Robert Smalls at the Great Lakes Naval Training Station in Illinois. Author of several books of poetry, including *Powerful Long Ladder* (1946), *The Confession Stone* (1970), and *The Harlem Book of the Dead* (with Camille Billops and James

Van Der Zee, c. 1981); two novels: *Boy at the Window* (1951; republished as *When Trees Were Green*, 1974) and *Come Home Early, Child* (1977; orig. titled *The Bent House*); short stories, articles, and poems in periodicals and anthologies; and over 30 plays, operas, and theatrical works. In 1935 he directed the premiere production of JAMES BALDWIN's *The Amen Corner*, nine years before it was presented on Broadway. One of the founders of the Negro Playwrights Co., 1940. Credited with having discovered, encouraged, or influenced a number of well-known, successful theatrical talents, including Gordon Heath, Earle Hyman, OSSIE DAVIS, CHARLES SEBREE, TED SHINE, Hilda Simms, RICHARD WESLEY, Frank Silvera, and many others. In addition to the AUDELCO Outstanding Pioneer Award, 1975, Dodson was winner of the Maxwell Anderson Verse Play Contest, 1940, for his **Garden of Time** (1939); and first prize of $100 in a playwriting contest sponsored by Tuskegee Inst., 1941, for his **Gargoyles in Florida** (1936). Recipient of a Rosenwald Fellowship, 1944–45; a Guggenheim Fellowship, 1953–54; and a Rockefeller Grant, 1969–70.

PLAYS AND DRAMATIC WORKS WRITTEN, PRODUCED, AND/OR PUBLISHED SINCE 1950:

Divine Comedy (verse drama with music, 2 acts, 1938). Based on the life and career of Father Divine, the famous black religious cult leader. First prod. at Yale Univ. Theatre, New Haven, Feb. 16–18, 1938. Prod. at the Atlanta Univ. Summer Theatre, July 1938. Prod. at the Hampton Inst. Summer School Theatre, Hampton, VA, July 23, 1942. Prod. at Jackson State Coll., Jackson, MS, Oct. 23, 1952. Prod. by the New Federal Theatre (NFT), New York, opening Jan. 14, 1977. Excerpt pub. in *The Negro Caravan* (Brown, Davis & Lee, 1941); reprinted in *La Caravella* (Italy). Complete script pub. in *Black Theatre, U.S.A.* (Hatch & Shine, 1974). Unpub. script in the J.W. Johnson Memorial Collection/YUL.

Bayou Legend (adaptn., 2 acts, 1948). Poetic black American version of Henrik Ibsen's *Peer Gynt*, set in Louisiana's bayou. First prod. at Howard Univ., Washington, DC, May 1948. Prod. by the theatre workshops of Hunter Coll. and CCNY, in the Hunter Coll. Playhouse, May 13–21, 1950. Prod. as a puppet play at the Southeastern Theatre Conf., Atlanta, March 1952. Prod. by the Howard Univ. Players, at Spaulding Hall, Washington, DC, May 1, 1957; dir. by SHAUNEILLE PERRY. Pub. in *Topic* No. 5, Special Issue, "The Negro in the American Arts" (Washington Press and Publications Service, U.S. Information Agency, 1965?); copy in the Schomburg Collection. Also in *Black Drama in America* (Turner, 1971).

Constellation of Women (pageant, 1950). Premiered at Bennett Coll., Greensboro, NC, Oct. 1950.

A Christmas Miracle // Orig. title: **A Southern Star** (opera, 1 act: libretto, 1958). Musical score by *Mark Fax. Begun in 1940; completed in 1958. Twice performed at Howard Univ., by Phi Kappa Lambda National Music Fraternity, March 1958. Libretto of **A Southern Star** in the J.W. Johnson Memorial Collection/YUL.

Medea in Africa (adaptn., full length, 1959). Afro-American version of Euripides's play, set in Africa. Presumably based on †Countee Cullen's play, *The Medea*, publ. by Harper, New York, 1935, and Dodson's **Garden of Time** (1939). Prod. by the Howard Players and the Howard Univ. Drama Dept., Sept. 1959; revived April 25–May 3, 1963, and taken on tour of a number of colleges in New England, including Dartmouth, the Univ. of New Hampshire, Bowdoin, Middlebury, and Williams; dir. by author.

Till Victory Is Won (opera: libretto, 1965). Musical score by Mark Fax. Traces the highlights of the black man's history from Africa to the present. Written for the centennial celebration of Howard Univ. and performed there in April 1965. An excerpt was presented to Bermuda audiences, under the auspices of the Howard Univ. Alumni Assn. Also sched. for prodn. in New York.

The Confession Stone (song cycle, full length, 1968). Music by *Noel Da Costa. Dramatizes the lives of Biblical figures, including Mary, the mother of Jesus. First prod. at Carnegie Hall, New York, Feb. 3, 1968, then at the Canadian Expo, and other places in the United States; sung by Canadian contralto Maureen Forrester. Prod. by Theatre Off Park, New York, opening Feb. 14, 1979, for 8 perfs.; dir. by Dodson. With Ruth Attaway.

The Dream Awake (radio drama and filmscript [also adaptable to the stage], 1969). Highlights in the history of the black man from Africa to the present. Prod. by Spoken Recordings, 1969.

Owen's Song (theatre work, 2 acts, 1974). Subtitled "A Tribute to Owen Dodson." Conceived, directed, and choreographed by GLENDA DICKERSON and MIKE MALONE. Based on the plays and poems of Dodson. Described by the presenters as "a collage, weaving together lines from [Dodson's] works, including *Divine Comedy, Powerful Long Ladder*, his many poems, and his full length play *Bayou Legend*." "The story line, conceived by the directors, is inspired by the magnificent theme that runs through all of his works: climbing a powerful long ladder to catch the bird of freedom."—Program Notes. Prod. by the DC Black Repertory Co., at the Last Colony Theatre, Washington, DC, opening Oct. 24, 1974, for six weeks. Also performed in New York at the Harlem Cultural Center; then transferred back to Washington to the Eisenhower Theatre in the John F. Kennedy Center for the Performing Arts for two weeks, opening Dec. 31, 1974. Unpub. script in the Hatch-Billops Collection.

The Morning Duke Ellington Praised the Lord and Seven Little Black Davids Tap-Danced Unto (ceremonial entertainment, with blues, jazz, and dance, full length, 1976). Music by Roscoe Gill. After death, several black entertainers are brought before Jesus for judgment. Staged reading by the Frank Silvera Writers' Workshop (FSWW), at the Martinique Theatre, New York, Jan. 1976. Unpub. script in the Hatch-Billops Collection.

The Story of Soul (musical, combining dance, music, and poetry, 1978). Coauthor, with Gary Keys. Premiered at Howard Univ., Dec. 1978. Apparently taken on European tour of Switzerland and other countries, Jan.-April 1979.

Justice Blindfolded (three plays, in progress late 1970s).

OTHER PLAYS AND DRAMATIC WORKS PRIOR TO 1950:
Garden of Time // Former title: **With This Darkness** (drama, 4 acts [6 scenes], 1939). **Jane** (incomplete script, 2 scenes, c. 1936). Coauthor, with *William Swallow. **Including Laughter** (poetic play, 3 acts, 1936). **Gargoyles in Florida** (drama, 1 act, 1936). **The Shining Town** (drama, 1 act, 1937). **The Amistad** (historical drama, 5 scenes, 1939). **Doomsday Tale** (drama, 1941–42). **Someday We're Gonna Tear the Pillars Down** (short poetic semi-drama for speech choir, 1942). **Heroes on Parade** (series of 16 short plays on military, naval, and civilian heroism, 1942/43). (Only eight titles in this series have been discovered: "Lord Nelson, Naval Hero," "Old Ironsides," "Robert Smalls," "Don't Give Up the Ship," "Everybody Join Hands," "Freedom, the Banner," "The Ballad of Dorrie Miller," and "Climbing to the Soil.") **The Midwest Mobilizes** (radio

doc., 1 act, 1943). **St. Louis Woman** (radio script, 1949). **New World A-Coming** (pageant, 7 scenes, 1944; also a historical radio drama, 1945). **They Seek a City** // Alternate titles: **Migration, Journey to Paradise,** and **Where You From?** (screenplay, 1945). **The Third Fourth of July** (symbolic drama, 1 act, 1945).

DOLAN, HARRY (E., Jr.) (1927–1981), TV scriptwriter, screenwriter, play-wright, author, editor, and teacher. Winner of the Golden Pen Award and an Emmy nomination for his NBC-TV special **Losers: Weepers** (1967). Writer for Warner Bros. studios, 1957, and credited with being the first black to work on a major film *(No Strings,* 1967) for a major studio. Born in Pittsburgh, PA. Educated at the Univ. of Pittsburgh, Carnegie Inst. of Technology, and Howard Univ. Extension (Certificate in Writing, 1959). Newspaper editor, *Boston Sun,* 1960. Moved to California, 1960s, where he was editor of *Los Angeles Next Week;* director of the Frederick Douglass Writers' Workshop, and associated with both the Douglass House Foundation and the Watts Theatre. Contributor of stories and articles to numerous periodicals, including the *New York Times* and *Esquire.*

PLAYS AND DRAMATIC WORKS:
Losers: Weepers // Orig. title: **Love Song for a Delinquent** (TV drama, 2 acts, 1966). Concerns a man who loses both his wife and children in an attempt to prove his manhood. Prod. under its orig. title by NBC-TV, Feb. 9, 1967. Pub. under its present title in *From the Ashes* (Schulburg, 1967).

The Iron Hand of Nat Turner (drama, 3 acts, 1970). Described by MARGARET WILKERSON as "a chronicle of Nat Turner's life. Told in a series of episodes, the play depicts the revolutionary preacher as a 'black Moses' who felt called upon to liberate his own people."—*The Drama Review,* Dec. 1972, p. 36. This prodn. "established a clear connection between the abortive Turner insurrection and the Watts revolt, bringing the play very close to the history and experience of the viewers."—Ibid., p. 26. First prod. by the Watts Writers' Workshop, at the Douglass House Foundation, Los Angeles 1970. Revived by Watts Theatre, 1972; dir. by actor/playwright TED LANGE (of "The Love Boat" TV series).

DOUGLAS, RODNEY K., Actor-playwright. Appeared in the New York pro-duction of *Scuba Duba* (1967).

PLAYS:
Voice of the Ghetto (morality drama, 1 act, 1968). "A ghetto politician appears unannounced at a Suspension Hearing to protest the suspending of his god-daughter from school. The conclave, with the exception of the Psychiatrist, takes umbrage to his intru-sion, but . . . accept[s] him with polite sarcasm. The panel claims the education system a saving grace for the community. [The politician], however, lays bare its evils and in a menacing narrative of ghetto life, warns Authority to produce solutions quickly or be faced with grave consequences (of a ghetto uprising)."—*Samuel French's Basic Catalog of Plays.* **The Marijuana Trip** (pre-1975).

DRAYTON, RONALD, Author and playwright whose work has been greatly influenced by AMIRI BARAKA (LeRoi Jones). He has written poetry and a novel, *Morning Before the Dawn.* His plays have been produced by the Back Alley Theater in Washington, DC.

PLAYS:
Nocturne on the Rhine (drama, 1 act, 1968). Two-character piece, in which a black priest attempts to seek salvation for a black man who stole money for a humanitarian cause. Pub. in *Black Fire* (Jones & Neal, 1968). **Notes from a Savage God** (monologue, 1 act, 1968). A lonely boy, locked in the prison of his sleazy roominghouse bedroom, where he is even afraid to use the filthy toilet in the hall, tries to cope with his depression, fears, and loneliness by appealing to a god whom he thinks is dead. Prod. by the Back Alley Theatre, 1975. Pub. in *Black Fire* (Jones & Neal, 1968).

DuBOIS, JA'NET (Jeanette), TV actress, songwriter, playwright, and former model. Based in Los Angeles, CA. Best known for her portrayal of Wilona on the "Good Times" TV series. Coauthor of the theme song, "Movin' on Up," of "The Jeffersons" TV series. Began her theatrical career as a model; then as an understudy in *The Long Dream, A Raisin in the Sun,* and *Nobody Loves an Albatross.* Appeared for two years in the serial "Love of Life" before being discovered by Norman Lear for her role in "Good Times." Performed in a number of films, including *The Pawnbroker* (1965) and *Five on the Black Hand Side* (1973).

PLAY:
Maybe It's All in My Mind (TV play, pre-1974). According to the author, this play "has to do with the street situation and [a] drunk is the medium [i.e., narrator]. He tells the story. . . . And we have situations on the corner, . . . situations which are really happening—we can't live together, we can't love each other (maybe it's all in my mind)."— *Black Stars*, Aug. 1974, p. 26. Prod. by an NBC-TV station in Los Angeles during the 1970s, and reportedly was nominated for an Emmy for writing, directing, and producing.

DUKE, BILL, Actor, poet, playwright, and film director. A graduate of the American Film Inst. in Los Angeles. Former director of the Weusi Kuumba Troupe in Brooklyn, NY. Stage acting credits include *Slave Ship* (1970) and *Ain't Supposed to Die a Natural Death* (1971). Appeared in such films as *Car Wash* (1976) and *American Gigolo* (1980), and directed a number of episodes of prime time television shows, including "Dallas," "Knots Landing," "Falcon Crest," "The Killing Floor" (PBS), and "McGruder & Loud" (ABC). His poetry has been published in *Black Creation.*

PLAYS:
An Adaptation: Dream (1 act, 1971). Prod. by the Negro Ensemble Co. (NEC), New York, Jan. 1971. **Sonata** (1975). Prod. by Theatre Genesis, at St. Marks-on-the-Bowery, New York, 1975.

DUMAS, CHARLES (frequently cited as C. dUmas), Actor, writer, playwright. Managing director of Loaves & Fish Theater Co., Jersey City, NJ. Toured Europe in 1986 with his one-man show about Booker T. Washington, entitled "Up from Slavery" (based on Washington's autobiography). Also played the role of Booker T. Washington in *Boogie Woogie and Booker T.* (1987), presented by the New Federal Theatre. *Address*—Home: c/o Farrell, 540 Main St., Roosevelt Island, NY 10044. Office: Loaves & Fish Theatre Co., 2 Liberty Ave., Jersey City, NJ 07306.

PLAYS:
Return to the River (drama, full length, 1985). Concerns a black attorney who is opposed to his company's policies in South Africa. Prod. by the O'LAC Repertory Ensemble, at the 18th St. Playhouse, New York, April 18–May 12, 1985; dir. by Randy Frazier. **Anna** (drama, full length, 1986). About a girl who is sexually abused by her stepfather. Prod. by the O'LAC Repertory Ensemble, at the 18th St. Playhouse, New York, June 12–July 13, 1986. **Surfacing** (drama, full length, 1986). A black love story set against the background of the student political activism of the 1970s. Prod. by the American Folk Theatre, New York, May 1986, dir. by Dick Gaffield. **Durante Vita** (1987). Public reading by the Frank Silvera Writers' Workshop, March 16, 1987.

DUMAS, DAISY IRENE. See DUMAS-FEATHERSTONE, DAISY I.

DUMAS, MILDRED, Playwright, producer, and director. Educated at Pikes Peak Community Coll., Colorado Springs, CO. (A.S. in broadcasting), and Hubbard's Business Coll., St. Louis, MO (secretarial course). Has also taken several writing courses. Writer, director, and producer for several dramatic societies, including the Dumas Dramatics Soc., East St. Louis, IL, 1969–72, and the Dumas Players, Colorado Springs, 1981–83. Director of drama and TV services at St. John's Baptist Church in Colorado Springs, 1978–83. *Address:* 742 E. 79th St. #2, Los Angeles, CA 90001.

REPRESENTATIVE PLAYS:
The Power of Will (dramatic comedy, 2 acts, 1966). Aunt Savannah, stricken with a fatal heart disease, has summoned her nieces and nephews to her side to await her death and their inheritances. One of her nephews decides to give Old Man Death a helping hand, but he underestimates Aunt Savannah. Prod. by the Dumas Players, 1983.

Uncle Rufus (mystery-comedy, 2 acts, 1978). Uncle Rufus, a millionaire, announces to his relatives that he is about to be married to his fourth wife, but he is murdered the same evening. A surprise discovery is that his bride-to-be is a transsexual. Prod. by the Dumas Players, at Colorado Springs, Ft. Carson, CO, and Los Angeles, 1978. See also **Connie** (1980), below

OTHER PLAYS AND DRAMATIC WORKS:
Terrace of Doom (mystery, 2 acts, 1965). A group of college students, returning from a homecoming, runs into a violent storm and must seek shelter in an old, apparently abandoned house—not knowing that it is, in fact, occupied by a maniacal old woman. **You Gotta Live it** (comedy, 2 acts, 1976). A white Vietnam veteran from an affluent background comes to live with his black ex-army buddy in the ghetto, in order to get the

first-hand experience that he needs to write a book about black life. **Checkerboard** (drama, 2 acts, 1978). Confrontation between two sets of brothers and sisters by the same black father—one by his black wife and the other by his white ex-wife. **No Room at the Inn** (Christmas musical drama, 1 act, 1979). Prod. annually at St. John's Baptist Church, Colorado Springs, 1979–82. **Out on Calvary** (Easter musical drama, 1 act, 1979). Prod. annually at St. John's Baptist Church, Colorado Springs, 1979–82. **Connie** (dramatic comedy, 2 acts, 1980). A sequel to **Uncle Rufus** (1978). Connie, one of Uncle Rufus's nieces, is about to bury her late husband; she is also having an affair with a younger man. Her children, who are opposed to this affair, threaten to have her committed. **The Confession** (comedy, 1 act, 1983). A husband's confession of infidelity turns his formerly loving wife into a mad, screaming, fighting tyrant. **Daddy's New Role** (domestic comedy, 1 act, 1983). Bruce Kennedy, 39, who has lost his job, is forced into the role of family housekeeper while his wife becomes the breadwinner. His new role touches upon family ties, cohesiveness, and responsibilities. **His Grace Is Leading Me** (musical, 2 acts, 1984). Subtitled "Society's People." Utilizes traditional spiritual, jazz, and blues songs and a play-within-a-play to tell a story of love, sorrow, ambition, joy, and hope. **My Brother's Blood** (drama, 2 acts, 1985). Coauthor, with Ernestine Harbour. A story of gang violence, in which four gang leaders are invited to meet with concerned citizens in order to discuss why they choose to engage in their devastating activities. **Victims of the System** (drama, 2 acts, 1985). About a destitute family, whose father/husband leaves them after losing his job, forcing them to live on the street. Deals with their efforts to carry on their lives while attempting to fight with their feelings of love/hate for the man who caused their misery.

DUMAS-FEATHERSTONE, DAISY I. (Daisy Irene Dumas), Playwright, teacher, and student. Received the B.A. in English from Long Island Univ., Brooklyn, NY, 1966. In pursuit of her career objective of an M.D. or Ph.D. in medicine, she has taken courses at San Francisco State Coll., the Univ. of Upsala, Sweden, the Univ. of California at Berkeley, Columbia Univ., Albert Einstein Coll. of Medicine (New York), City Coll. of New York, and St. Joseph's Coll. (Brooklyn). Has taught English and science, and has been a counselor and substitute teacher, at various high schools and alternative schools in New York City and San Francisco. Studied playwriting with the Frank Silvera Writers' Workshop (FSWW) and the Negro Ensemble Co.'s (NEC's) Playwrights Workshop, New York City. Recipient of numerous academic scholarships, grants, and awards, including the Charles Drew Fellowship, Columbia Univ., 1969–70; Martin Luther King/Robert Kennedy Fellowship, Albert Einstein Coll. of Medicine, 1970–71; National Congress of Neighborhood Women Award, 1982; and Woolrich Writing Award, Columbia Univ., 1982. *Address:* 214–B Carlton Ave., Elmira, NY 14901.

PLAYS:

Jumeau's Mama (domestic drama, 3 acts, 1977). Subtitled "La Maman de Jumeau." Public reading by FSWW, at the Teachers, Inc., New York, Jan. 1977. Unpub. script and tape recording in FSWW Archives/Schomburg Collection. **Wamba's Mother** (domestic drama, 3 acts, c. 1978). Presumably a revised and expanded version of the above play. Deals with the struggle of a professional black woman to be accepted as equal to or better than her white counterpart, and the conflicting values among the black middle class.

DUNCAN, JOHN, JR., Playwright.

PLAY:
A Crimson Fountain for Harlingcourt (1976). Pub. by Ashley Books, New York, 1976.

DUPREE, HERBERT H., Playwright.

PLAY:
How White Is the Moon ("A Light Comedy in a Serious Vein" [subtitle], 1 act, 1958). White passengers on a spaceship, who have fled to the moon to escape black people, are disappointed to discover the racial coloring of the moon's inhabitants. Pub. in *Black Expression,* Fall 1958, pp. 52–54.

DURHAM, ALICE MARIE, Former student playwright at Wilberforce Coll. (now Univ.), Wilberforce, OH.

PLAY:
Golden Gloves (1951). Won second place in the 1950–51 playwriting contest of the Southern Assn. of Speech and Dramatic Arts (SADSA), held at Alabama State Coll., Montgomery, AL, May 3, 1951.

DURHAM, RICHARD (1927–   ), TV scriptwriter, freelance writer, and editor. Resides and works in Chicago, IL. A graduate of Northwestern Univ. Member of the Nation of Islam (formerly the Black Muslims) and former editor of *Muhammad Speaks,* 1960s. Biographer of Muhammad Ali. Winner of a Peabody Award.

PLAYS:
Here Comes Tomorrow (radio drama series, 1960s). The first radio series about a black family. Broadcast in Chicago during the 1960s. Based on original concept by Durham, who also regularly contributed scripts (apparently coauthored with Bill Quinn). Title taken from an 1847 speech by Frederick Douglass on the sons and daughters of Africa in the United States: "They have been a bird of iron feathers, unable to fly to freedom."—*Jet,* Oct. 10, 1969, p. 72. Telecast on WTTV, Chicago, Channel 11, beginning in 1969. **Destination Freedom** (TV drama series, 1970–). "Underwritten by a $600,000 grant from the Ford Foundation."—Ibid. Sched. to begin telecasts in Jan. 1970.

DURRAH, JAMES W. (Jim), Playwright and theatrical director. Based in New York City. Drama critic Willie L. Hamilton said of him: "It is easy to see that in Durrah a new Black playwright of immense talent has come on the scene. For satirical and dramatic writing, he is better than most. . . . As a director, Durrah brings lively creativity to the stage."—*New York Amsterdam News,* Dec. 15, 1973, p. D–5.

GROUP OF RELATED PLAYS:
"THE DREAMKEEPERS" (program of 3 one-act plays, 1973). Includes **Available in Winter** (1 act), "About the memories of an old man"—ibid.; **Miss DoFunny Speaking** (1 act), "a takeoff on two homosexual mental intake workers"—ibid.; and **Saturday Militant** (1 act), "an eerie futuristic but now type of work which forecasts ahead to a time when the earth is ruled by the Perfect White and robots"—ibid. Prod. in New York, Dec. 1973.

OTHER PLAYS:
The Ho–Hum Revolution (1973). One scene was broadcast over Denmarks Radio in Copenhagen, 1972, as part of a program on black theatre in the United States. **How Do You Spell Watergait** (satirical musical, full length, 1977). Book and lyrics by Durrah. Music by Victor Willis and Donna Brown. Concerns the Watergate scandal and politics in general. Prod. by Sutton East Theater, New York, Jan. 1977.

DYSON, DIEDRA, Drama teacher, director, and playwright. During the mid-1970s she was a member of the Kuumba Workshop and secretary of the Black Theater Alliance (BTA) in Chicago.

PLAY:
Black Ritual (1974). Written "to show that the folklore of Black people is an integral part of Black drama, and that theatre must not be defined only through the stage and creativity of the playwright."—Author, *Black World,* April 1975. Prod. by Kuumba Workshop, Chicago, at the beginning of the 1974 season.

E

EARLY, ANN, Playwright. Based in New York State, where she was associated with Writers-in-Residence, at Great Neck, during the 1970s.

PLAYS AND DRAMATIC WORKS:

I Am (blues musical, 1973). Written partly with inmates of C-76, Riker's Island, NY, where it was prod. in 1973. **Do You Take This Woman** (domestic drama, 1 act, pre-1976). The trials of a devout black mother of two sons, one of whom is dying from drug addiction, and the other living in her home with his common-law wife. Prod. by Writers-in-Residence, Great Neck, NY, before 1976. **Is George Responsible** (courtroom comedy, pre-1976). George Washington is placed on trial for the failure of the American governmental system. Prod. by Writers-in-Residence, Great Neck, NY, before 1976. **Mishap** (drama, 2 acts, pre-1976). An unwed mother who has brought up her son to believe that he is her brother tries to prevent him from entering into an incestuous relationship with a neighbor's daughter who is really his sister. Prod. by Writers-in-Residence, Great Neck, NY, before 1976.

EARLY, JACQUELINE, Playwright. Associated with the Harlem Cultural Council in New York City. *Address:* c/o Harlem Cultural Council, Inc., 1 W. 125th St., New York, NY 10027.

DRAMATIC WORK:

Sheba (improvisational song play, 1971). Prod. at Tomkins Square Park, New York, Aug. 1971.

EATON, AL, Actor-playwright. Based in New York City. A graduate of Emerson Coll. in Boston. He has performed with the National Center for Afro-American Artists as well as with a Shakespearean company.

PLAY:

M.L.K. (one-man drama, full length, 1985). Based on the life of Martin Luther King, Jr. According to Joe Spencer, writing in the *New York Amsterdam News* (June 1, 1985), "What makes the drama . . . a standout is that [Eaton] takes us into the lives of several characters who were touched by the non-violent life style of King during the turbulent civil rights struggle of the 60s." Written, prod., dir., and perfd. by the author at the American Place Theatre, New York, May-June 1985.

EDMONDS, HENRIETTE, Drama director and playwright. Daughter of the prolific pioneer playwright and drama director †S. Randolph Edmonds. Received the M.A. in drama from Western Reserve University. Currently assoc. prof. of drama at Howard Univ., Washington, DC, where she has also been chairperson. *Address:* Dept. of Drama, College of Fine Arts, Howard University, Washington, DC 20059.

PLAY:
Mushy Mouth (children's musical, 1975). Prod. by Howard Univ.'s Children's Theatre, Washington, DC, 1975.

EDMONDS, IRENE COLBERT, Children's playwright. Pioneer in educational theatre at Dillard Univ. and Florida A. & M. Univ. (FAMU). Educated at Syracuse Univ. (A.B.) and Johns Hopkins Univ. (M.A. in writing, speech, and drama). Formerly married to playwright †S. Randolph Edmonds.

PLAYS:
(All children's plays, prod. at FAMU, Tallahassee, FL, prior to 1963.) **The Lost Gem. Their Time and Our Time. The Wedding of Peer Gynt.**

EDWARDS, GUS (1939–   ), Playwright, actor, and director. Born in Antigua. Grew up in St. Thomas, U.S. Virgin Islands. Encouraged by actor Sidney Poitier, he came to the United States in 1959 to pursue a career in the theatre. Studied acting and theatre in New York City, worked at a number of jobs, and appeared in minor roles in two films, *The Pawnbroker* (1965) and *Stilleto* (1969), while developing his skills as a playwright. In 1977 he became resident playwright with the Negro Ensemble Co. (NEC), which produced his first two scripts in a single season and has since produced three more of his plays. Since 1983 he has been resident playwright at Arizona State Univ./Tempe. Edwards has conducted theatre workshops for Lehman Coll., Bronx, NY, and the North Carolina School of the Arts (where he was also judge of a playwriting contest); has served on literary advisory committees for the Theatre Communications Group and the New Dramatists, among other organizations; was a judge for the Obie Awards, 1981–82; and was a script panelist for the Artists Foundation, 1982, and a member of the TV Panel on Playwriting for the American Theatre Wing. Member of the Dramatists Guild and the New Dramatists. Recipient of a Rockefeller Foundation Playwrights Award, 1979–80, and grants from the National Endowment for the Arts and the Drama League. *Address:* 1502 S. Price Rd., Apt. #106, Tempe, AZ 85281. *Agent:* Susan Schulman, 454 W. 44th St., New York, NY 10036.

REPRESENTATIVE PLAYS AND DRAMATIC WORKS:

The Offering (drama, 2 acts, 1977). Concerns a psychological struggle for dominance between a young black hired killer and his aging down-and-out mentor who is now living on welfare. The title refers to a large sum of money offered by the younger man to his older friend, ostensibly to help him out. The offering and its refusal by the mentor serves as the catalyst for a power struggle and a psychological battle of wits in which the older man becomes the victor. Prod. by NEC, at St. Marks Playhouse, Nov. 26, 1977–Jan. 1, 1978; reopened Feb. 7–28, 1978, for a total run of 59 perfs.; dir. by DOUGLAS TURNER WARD, who also starred as the older man. With Charles Weldon, Olivia Williams, and Katherine Knowles. Pub. by Dramatists Play Service, New York, 1978.

Black Body Blues (melodrama, 2 acts, 1977). The portrait of a black ex-boxer, now working as a servant to a kindly white man, and his clash with his brother, a dope pusher, whose lifestyle is vastly different. The pusher eventually shoots the employer to liberate his brother from the master-slave relationship. First prod. as a staged reading by the Eugene O'Neill Theatre Center's National Playwrights Conf., as part of its TV Project, June 1977. Prod. by NEC, at St. Marks Playhouse, Jan. 19–March 5, 1978, for 40 perfs.; dir. by Douglas Turner Ward. With SAMM-ART WILLIAMS in the role of the former boxer, Norman Bush, Catherine E. Slade, Frankie R. Faison, and Douglas Turner Ward.

Old Phantoms (drama, 2 acts [15 scenes], 1979). After the death and funeral of their father—a domineering black man who had set impossible standards for his family and had tried to instill in them his exaggerated sense of pride, determination, and desire to excel—his three children (two sons and a daughter) reminisce about the destructive effect that his domination has had on each of their lives and that of their mother, who died in childbirth. Prod. by NEC, at St. Marks Playhouse, Feb. 7–18, 1978; dir. by Horacena Taylor. With Douglas Turner Ward as the father, Samm-Art Williams and Chuck Patterson as the sons, and L. Scott Caldwell as the daughter.

Fallen Angels // Orig. title: **Scenes from the City** (drama, 1 act, 1979). Commissioned by the North Carolina School of the Arts. A young college-bred drifter becomes involved in a triangular relationship with a factory coworker and his attractive wife, whom the drifter falls in love with and seduces. He walks out of the couple's lives just as he walked in, leaving the wife pregnant and the unsuspecting husband happy that he is going to be a father. Apparently first prod. by the North Carolina School of the Arts, under its orig. title, Oct. 1979. Prod. by the American Premiere Stage, Boston, Nov. 1981. Pub. in *Center Stage* (Ostrow, 1981).

Weep Not for Me (domestic drama, 2 acts, 1981). Portrait of the life and psyche of a black family living in a decaying section of New York City, the South Bronx. Prod. by NEC, Jan. 28–March 8, 1981, for 48 perfs.; dir. by Douglas Turner Ward. Featuring Ethel Ayler and Bill Cobbs.

Manhattan Made Me (drama, 2 acts, 1983). Four-character play, set in a Manhattan apartment, depicting blacks and whites living together while trying to find employment as actors. Prod. by NEC, at Theatre Four, New York, for 32 perfs.; dir. by Douglas Turner Ward. With Eugene Lee, Katherine Forbes, Robert Gossett, and David Davies.

Go Tell It on the Mountain (TV adaptn., full length, 1985). Dramatization of JAMES BALDWIN's novel by the same title. About his growing up in Harlem under the oppressive domination of his preacher-father. Filmed for PBS, 1985, telecast on the "American Playhouse" series. With Paul Winfield, Rosalind Cash, Olivia Cole, Douglas Turner Ward, Ruby Dee, and Alfre Woodard. Available in 16 mm. and 12″ video from New Line Cinema Corp., 575 Eighth Ave. (16 Fl.), New York, NY 10018.

Ramona (drama, full length, 1986). "Set in the Caribbean in the '50s; about an uninhibited woman who lives all for love, or the illusion of it."—*New York Amsterdam News*, Sept. 27, 1986. Prod. by NEC, during the 1986–87 season.

OTHER PLAYS AND DRAMATIC WORKS:
Aftermath (TV script, 1979). Public reading by the Eugene O'Neill Memorial Center, New London, CT, July 1979, as part of the center's TV Project. Script not available. **Tenement** (1983). Prod. by New Dramatists, New York, opening March 30, 1983. **Ages of Douglass** (dramatic collage, full length, pre-1985). On the life of Frederick Douglass, focusing on the struggles of his adult life—his triumphs and the legacy of freedom he left behind. **Black Is Black** and **New Ice Age** (2 one-act plays, pre-1985). Pub. in *Short Pieces from the New Dramatists* (Broadway Play Publishing, New York, 1985).

EDWARDS, JUNIUS (1929–   ), Short-story writer, novelist, playwright, and advertising agency owner. Born in Alexandria, LA. His stories have been included in *Beyond the Angry Black* (Williams, 1966), *The Best Short Stories by Negro Writers* (Hughes, 1967), *Black Short Story Anthology* (King, 1972), and *A Native Sons Reader* (Margolies, 1970).

PLAY:
If We Must Die (drama, full length, 1963). Pub. by Doubleday, New York, 1963.

EL, LEATRICE. See EMERUWA, LEATRICE W.

ELDER, LONNE, III (1931–   ), Actor, playwright, screenwriter, and TV scriptwriter. Best known for his play **Ceremonies in Dark Old Men** (1965), which won both the Vernon Rice/Drama Desk Award and the Outer Critics' Circle Award and was nominated for a Pulitzer Prize; and his film **Sounder** (1972), which was nominated for an Academy Award. Born in Americus, GA. Grew up in Jersey City, NJ. Educated at Jersey City State Teachers Coll. (now Trenton State Teachers Coll.), c. 1959–60; the Jefferson School and the New School for Social Research, c. 1950–52; Yale Univ. School of Drama, 1965–67; and privately, under Mary Welch (acting). Moved to New York City's Harlem at age 19, prior to being drafted into the army in 1952; returned to Harlem after being discharged. Joined the Harlem Writers Guild, where he was encouraged by Dr. Robert Hayden and JOHN OLIVER KILLENS to write poetry and fiction. Turned his talents to playwriting after meeting, becoming friends with, and sharing an apartment with DOUGLAS TURNER WARD, 1953–56. Married to actress Judy Ann Elder; the father of one son. Played the bit part of Bobo in the Broadway and road productions of **A Raisin in the Sun** (1958), and later the role of Clem in the New York production of Ward's *Day of Absence* (1965). Scriptwriter for the "Camera Three" TV series, 1963; coordinator of the Directors and Playwrights Unit, Negro Ensemble Co. (NEC), New York, 1967–69; staff writer, Talent Assocs., New York, and scriptwriter, "N.Y.P.D." TV series, 1968; writer-producer, Cinema Center Films, Hollywood, 1969–70; staff writer, Universal Pictures, Hollywood, and scriptwriter, "McCloud" TV series,

1970–71; staff writer, Radnitz-Mattel Productions, 20th Century-Fox Studios, Hollywood, 1971; writer-producer, Talent Assocs., Hollywood, 1972; currently under contract with Columbia Pictures, Television Div. In addition to the awards listed above, he is the recipient of ABC Television Fellowship, 1965–66; John Hay Whitney Fellowship for Playwriting, 1965–66; John Golden Fellowship, 1966–67; and Joseph E. Levine Fellowship in Filmmaking, Yale School of Drama, 1966–67; for **Ceremonies in Dark Old Men** (1969), recipient of Stella Holt Memorial Playwrights Award and Christopher's TV Award; for **Sounder** (1972), recipient of Writers Guild of America Award, Atlanta Film Festival Silvera Award, Chistopher's Award, NAACP Image Award, Stanley Award, and Los Angeles Drama Critics Award; for **Part 2, Sounder** (1976), recipient of a second Christopher's Award. *Address:* 14400 Valley Vista Blvd., Sherman Oaks, CA 91423.

REPRESENTATIVE PLAYS AND DRAMATIC WORKS:

Ceremonies in Dark Old Men (drama, 2 acts [4 scenes], (1965). Set in a Harlem barbershop run by an old-time vaudevillian who operates a whiskey still in the back room, this realistic drama focuses on the disintegration of an oppressed black family through their inability to face responsibility and cope with their frustrations, and their frantic schemes to combat racism and to secure money by illegal means. His most successful play. Won the Outer Critics' Circle Award, the Vernon Rice Drama Desk Award, the Stella Holt Memorial Playwrights Award of $300, the Stanley Drama Award of $500, and the Los Angeles Drama Critics Award, and placed second in the voting for the Pulitzer Prize of 1969. First presented as a workshop reading by the New Dramatists Committee, 1965. Presented as a concert reading at Wagner Coll., Staten Island, NY, mid-1960s. Revised and prod. Off-Bway by NEC, at St. Marks Playhouse, Feb. 2–March 9, 1969, for 40 perfs.; dir. by Edmund Cambridge. With Douglas Turner Ward, Arthur French, William Jay, David Downing, Rosalind Cash, Samuel Blue, Jr., and Judyann Johnsson. Reopened Off-Bway in a second professional prodn. at the Pocket Theatre, April 28, 1969–Feb. 15, 1970, for 320 perfs.; also dir. by Cambridge. With Richard Ward, Arnold Johnson, Billy Dee Williams, Richard Mason, Bette Howard, Carl Lee, and Denise Nicholas. Prod. by the Guthrie Theatre Co., at the Guthrie Theatre in Minneapolis, June 19, 1970, for 33 perfs.; dir. by Israel Hicks. With MAXWELL GLAN-VILLE, Gerry Black, Ron Glass, Arnold Wilderson, Bette Howard, and Ed Bernard. Prod. by Benjamin Banneker Productions at the Ivar Theatre, Hollywood, CA, opening July 14; dir. by Cambridge. With Billy Dee Williams, Arthur French, Barbara Clarke, Pamela Jones, Jay Montgomery, Edmund Cambridge, and Robert Hooks. Prod. by the Center Stage in Baltimore, March 5, 1971, for 29 perfs. Prod. by the Players Workshop, located in the East Village, New York City, at the festival of black plays, Oct. 2, 1972. Prod. by the Washington Theatre Club, Washington, DC, opening Jan. 17, 1973, for 30 perfs. Telecast on ABC-TV, 1975, where it won the Christopher's Television Award. Revived by NEC, and presented at Theatre 4, New York, May 10–June 16, 1985. Pub. by Farrar, Straus, and Giroux, New York, 1969; by Noonday Press, New York, 1969; by Samuel French, New York, 1970; in *New Black Playwrights* (Couch, 1970); in *Black Theater: A Twentieth Century Collection of the Work of Its Best Playwrights* (Patterson, 1971); and in *Drama: Principles and Plays* (Hatlen, 1975).

Charades on East Fourth Street (drama, 1 act, 1967). Described by Darwin T. Turner as "a thesis drama," which "urged young blacks to combat the oppression of corrupt police by legal means rather than by violence."—*Contemporary Dramatists* (Vinson, 1977), p. 233. Commissioned by Mobilization for Youth, Inc., New York. Performed at Expo 67 in Montreal, 1967. Pub. in *Black Drama Anthology* (King & Milner, 1972).

Melinda (feature film, full length: screenplay, 1972). Based on a story by Raymond Cistheri. The drama of a black disc jockey and his efforts to extricate himself from entanglement with a white crime syndicate. Prod. by Pervis Atkins; released by MGM, Aug. 16, 1972; dir. by Hugh A. Robertson; starring Calvin Lockhart and Rosalind Cash.

Sounder (feature film, full length: screenplay, 1972). Based on the award-winning children's book of the same title by William H. Armstrong. Although the original story focuses on the travels of the dog Sounder, the film version told the story of a black sharecropping family and their constant efforts to survive during the Depression, with the dog as an incidental character. *Black Creation* (Winter 1973, p. 35) called it "one of the ten most important Black films between 1962 and 1973. (Based upon their combined existing or potential impact on the Black community and movie industry.)" Prod. by Radnitz/Mattel Productions; released by 20th Century-Fox, Sept. 24, 1972; dir. by Martin Ritt. Cast included Cicely Tyson and Paul Winfield as the wife and husband, both of whom received Academy Award nominations; Kevin Hooks as the oldest son; and Janet MacLachlan as a progressive young black teacher. The author also received an Academy Award nomination for the best screenplay and a CORE (Congress of Racial Equality) plaque.

A Woman Called Moses (TV script, full length [2 parts], 1978). The story of Harriet Tubman, the slave who escaped to freedom in the North, then returned numerous times to rescue other slaves through her famous Underground Railroad. Telecast on NBC-TV, Dec. 11 and 12, 1978; narrated by Orson Welles, and starring Cicely Tyson as Harriet Tubman.

Part 2, Sounder (TV film, full length: screenplay, 1976). Follow-up of **Sounder** (1972), continuing the story of black sharecropping family and their efforts to survive during the Depression. Winner of the Christopher's Award, 1976. Prod. by Robert Radnitz, dir. by William Graham, and telecast by ABC-TV, 1976; starring Harold Sylvester, Nathan Morgan, Ebony Wright, Darryl Young, and Annazette Chase.

Bustin' Loose (feature film, full length: screenplay, 1981). Based on a concept by RICHARD PRYOR. About an ex-convict who drives a teacher and a busload of her physically and mentally handicapped students through overwhelming obstacles, including the Ku Klux Klan, to a new location where the teacher will reestablish her school. Released by Universal Pictures, 1981; dir. by Oz Scott; starring Pryor and Cicely Tyson.

OTHER PLAYS AND DRAMATIC WORKS:

A Hysterical Turtle in a Rabbit Race (drama, 3 acts, 1961). Concerns the efforts of a social-climbing black matriarch to help her husband and children achieve the success that she thinks they rightfully deserve, while they attempt to extricate themselves from her social manipulation and tyranny. Unpub. script in the Hatch-Billops Collection. **"Camera Three"** Series (TV scripts, early 1960s). Prod. by ABC-TV, 1963. **Kissin' Rattlesnakes Can Be Fun** (tragicomedy, 1 act, 1966). "Deal[s] with the black-white relationships in Greenwich village."—*Jet*, Sept. 26, 1969, p. 49. Sched. for prodn. in New York, May 1970. **Seven Comes Up, Seven Comes Down** (comedy, 1 act, 1966). About a double congame. Prod. by the National Black Theatre, New York, 1977. **"N.Y.P.D."** series (TV scripts, 1967–68). **"McCloud"** series (TV scripts, 1970–71). **Deadly Circle of Violence** (TV script, 1970s). **A Splendid Mummer** (1970s).

el-SHAIR, JAMIL F. (1954–   ), Playwright, editor, and publisher. Born in Tallahassee, FL. Educated at Hempstead H.S., Hempstead, NY; Clark Univ., Worcester, MA; and Georgia State Univ., Atlanta. *Address:* 1128 Lawton Place, Atlanta, GA 30310.

PLAYS:
A View Through the Blinds (1 act, 1981). Presents the dynamics of blacks beginning to place their elders in nursing homes. Prod. by Mass Communications Dept., Clark Coll., Atlanta, GA, dir. by Joan Lewis. **BloodKnot** // Also known as **BloodTies** (1 act, 1982). Presents the bizarre turns and twists that a relationship can take when the people involved fail to talk and be honest. **Praying for Lynn** (3 acts, 1982). The story of an older man who has left his wife for a younger woman. It focuses on the awakening of the central character to the error and cost of his ways over the years. **Street Corner Symphony** (3 acts, 1984). A play about the trust and friendship presented in the context of the reunion of five men that used to sing together in a group while in high school. Songs from the sixties as well as orig. songs are used to move the plot along and conjure up memories. **The Sandman** (2 acts, pre-1985). A macabre play that deals with human obsession and demonic possession. **Crik Crak** (children's play, 1 act, pre-1985). Dramatization based on African folklore, explaining why adult frogs do not have tails. **Joshua and David** (children's play, 1 act, pre-1985). A story of trust and true friendship. One child gets in trouble because of a friend's reluctance to tell the truth.

EMERUWA, LEATRICE W. (Leatrice El), Author, poet, playwright, and educator. Born and currently residing in Cleveland, OH. Received the B.A. from Howard Univ., c. 1947, and was a graduate fellow in English and education, 1947–49; the M.Ed. from Kent State Univ., 1957; and the Ed.D. from the Univ. of Akron, 1981. Has taught in the public schools of Cleveland and been a participant in the Poets-in-Schools project since 1968. Currently assoc. prof. of English at Cuyahoga Community Coll., Cleveland, where she has been teaching since 1965. Her writings on the theatre have been published in *Black World,* and her poetry has appeared in a number of periodicals and in *Rising Tides,* an anthology. She has written professional articles on reading and has coauthored three reading manuals and textbooks for schools. Her books of poetry include *Ev'Ry Shut Eye Ain'T Sleep* (1977) and *Black Girl Black Girl* (1976). An outstanding contributor to black arts in Cleveland, Emeruwa was director of the One World Theatre Project, which sponsored workshops in music, dance, poetry, and play productions by local Cleveland playwrights, 1971–73. *Address*—Home: 3514 E. 153rd St., Cleveland, OH 44120. Office: Communications Learning Center, Cuyahoga Community College, 200 Community College Avenue, Cleveland, OH 44115.

DRAMATIC WORK:
Black Magic Anyone? (musical, full length [approximating 3 acts], 1971). Combines ritual, chants, music, slides, poetry, and song into the drama. According to the author, it is "a religious play, . . . and the theme involves the religiosity of the two principal characters—Sister Williams and Madame Zenobia. It is actually Sister's story, of her conflict with oldtime religious beliefs in the face of the conditions still confronting Black

people, her son's and his friend's propensity toward radicalism and Mohammedanism, and Madame's mysticism." Presented as a work-in-progress by the Negro Ensemble Co., at St. Marks Playhouse, New York, for 2 perfs., opening Jan. 19, 1971; dir. by Buddy Butler. First prod. at the First One World Theatre Project, Cleveland, 1971; also dir. by Butler. Prod. at the Second One World Theatre Project, Cleveland, 1973; dir. by author and Anna Boles-El.

ENSLEY, EVERETT (1931–1986), Actor-playwright. Lived in New York City, where he was associated with the American Community Theatre, Theatre in Progress, and the Frank Silvera Writers' Workshop (FSWW), Appeared in New York stage productions of *Automation* (Off-Bway, 1961), *My Sister, My Sister, One Last Look, A Yank in Beverly Hills,* and *Blues for Mr. Charlie.*

PLAYS:
(All scripts, pre-1985, are located in the FSWW Archives/Schomburg Collection.) **Go Start the Rainbow. Ruebella and the Castle Crowd. Weep the Living.**

EUBANKS, THELMA, Elementary school teacher and playwright. Resided in Detroit, MI, during the 1950s.

PLAY:
The Spirit of Negro History (black history play, 1 act [3 scenes], 1954). For elementary school children, grades 4–7. Concerns the achievements of Crispus Attucks, Harriet Tubman, and †Paul Laurence Dunbar, which were not included in the children's textbooks at that time. Pub. in *Negro History Bulletin,* May 1952, pp. 171–72.

EULO, KEN, Playwright. Based in New York City, where he was associated with the William Morris Agency.

PLAY:
Black Jesus (drama, 3 scenes, 1972). After helping to steal a Guatemalan statue of Black Jesus, a blind black American regains his eyesight prior to his death. Prod. by the Stage Directors and Choreographers Workshop Foundation at the Lib. and Museum of the Performing Arts at Lincoln Center, New York, Dec. 17, 1983.

EVANS, DON (Donald T.) (1938–   ), Author, playwright, teacher, and lecturer. Born in Philadelphia, PA. Educated at Cheyney State Coll., PA (B.S. in secondary school English, 1962); Temple Univ., Philadelphia (M.A. in communications and theatre, 1968; M.F.A. in theatre arts, 1974). Has also studied acting and directing at Berghof Studios in New York, 1969–70. Taught secondary English in the public schools of Bristol, PA, 1962–65. Consultant in theatre arts for Princeton Regional School, NJ, 1965–70, and for the Philadelphia Board of Education, 1968–69. Exec. director, Princeton Youth Center/Hansberry Arts Workshop, 1970–72. Currently chairman, African-American Studies, and director, Minority Executive Council, Trenton State Coll. Has taught courses in black theatre or African American Studies at Cheyney State Coll., 1969–70; Rutgers Univ., Douglass Coll., New Brunswick, NJ; and Princeton Univ., 1972–74. His articles and reviews have been published extensively in *Black World,*

English Journal, Essence, and other periodicals. In 1974 he was editing a collection of plays by black authors, to be entitled *Behind the Mask.* His awards and citations include Best Director and two Best Production awards in the Rider Coll. Drama Festival, 1966 and 1968, respectively; Arena Theatre award for Outstanding Contribution to Black Theatre, 1974; and numerous service awards from such organizations as the Princeton Regional Schools, the Minority Programming Committee, Kappa Alpha Psi Fraternity, and Omega Psi Phi Fraternity. *Address*—Home: 32 Oak Lane, Trenton, NJ 08618. Office: Chairman, African-American Studies, Trenton State College, Trenton, NJ 08625. *Agent:* Lucy Kroll, 390 West End Ave., New York, NY 10024.

COLLECTIONS:

THE PRODIGALS: Two One Act Plays. Dramatists Play Service, New York, 1977. Includes **Orrin** (1972) and **Sugar Mouth Sam Don't Dance No More** (1972).

REPRESENTATIVE PLAYS AND DRAMATIC WORKS:

Sugar Mouth Sam Don't Dance No More (drama, 1 act, 1972). Sammy, a sweet-talking but irresponsible drifter, returns to Verda Mae's life after a three-year absence, hoping that they can resume their former love affair. She tells him, however, that she can no longer share him with his wife, and he leaves her once again. First prod. Off-Bway by H.B. Playhouse, New York, Fall 1972. Prod. by the Concept East Theatre (CET), Detroit, 1973. Prod. by the Freedom Theatre, Philadelphia, Spring/Summer, 1974. Prod. Off-Bway by the Negro Ensemble Co. (NEC), May 6–11, 1975, for 8 perfs.; dir. by Helaine Head. With Lea Scott and Carl Gordon. Pub. in *Black World,* April 1973, pp. 54–77; in the author's collection *THE PRODIGALS*; and in *The Best Short Plays of 1978* (1978).

Orrin (domestic drama, 1 act, 1972). A young man with a history of dope and thievery comes home to "check things out." He hopes to be invited back without having to change his life. His father, solid as a rock, holds fast to his responsibility to the family and refuses his son's reentry on those terms. Prod. Off-Bway by the H.B. Playhouse, 1972. Prod. as part of the ANTA Matinee Series at Theatre De Lys, Jan. 1972. Presented by the Hansberry Arts Workshop, Princeton Youth Center, Princeton, New York, March 1972, under the direction of the author. Prod. by CET, Detroit, 1973–74 season. Prod. by NEC, New York, May 6–11, 1975, for 8 perfs.; dir. by Helaine Head. With Lea Scott, Taurean Blacque (as Orrin), Eric Coleman, and Carl Gordon. Pub. in the author's collection *THE PRODIGALS*.

Change of Mind (comedy, 2 acts, 1972). [May be an earlier version of the author's **It's Showdown Time** (pre-1976), cited below.] Concerns a black man from the South who initiates his own black revolution in the North by using the sexual myths about black men to his own advantage in his romantic conversation. Prod. by the Hansberry Arts Workshop, May 1972. Presented under option for Bway, presumably in New York, in April 1974. Prod. by the Morehouse-Spelman Players, Atlanta, 1974; dir. by CARLTON W. MOLETTE II.

Matters of Choice (serious comedy, 2 acts, 1974). The Washingtons, a middle-class black couple, return home from a night out to find that their home has been broken into. The police show no interest, and Oscar has to investigate on his own. He finds that he does not know the dynamics of his own people when he goes back to the black ghetto.

Prod. by the H.B. Playhouse, New York, Fall 1974. Prod. by the Karamu Playhouse, Cleveland, Feb. 1975. Prod. by the Players Co., Trenton, NJ, Spring 1975.

It's Showndown Time // Orig. title: **Showdown** (comedy, 2 acts [7 scenes], pre-1976). Adaptation of Shakespeare's *The Taming of the Shrew* for a black cast, in a Philadelphia setting. Apparently first prod. as **Change of Mind** (1972) (see above). Prod. as **Showdown** in Philadelphia, presumably by the Freedom Theatre, prior to 1976. Also prod. as **Showdown** by the New Federal Theatre, New York, Feb. 1976; dir. by SHAU-NEILLE PERRY, then taken on national tour. Pub. as **It's Showdown Time** by Dramatists Play Service, New York, 1976.

Mahalia (musical, 2 acts, 1978). Book and lyrics by Evans. Music by John Lewis. Based on the life of Mahalia Jackson, and may be an adaptation of *Just Mahalia Baby*, by Laurraine Goreau. First prod. by NFT, at the Henry St. Playhouse, New York, May 31–June 11, 1978, for 14 perfs.; dir. by Oz Scott. With Esther Marrow as Mahalia. Prod. by the Hartman Theatre, Stamford, CT, during the 1981–82 season; dir. by Gerald Freedman. Also with Esther Marrow.

Louis // Orig. title: **Satchmo** (musical, full length, pre-1980). Book and lyrics by Evans. Music by Michael Renzi. Prod. by NFT, at the Henry St. Playhouse, Sept. 18–Oct. 4, 1981, for 12 perfs.; dir. by GILBERT MOSES. With Norther J. Calloway as Louis.

A Lovesong for Miss Lydia (drama, full length, 1981). About a romantic relationship which develops between a respectable widow and her gentleman boarder, to the consternation of her friends. Prod. by the Crossroads Theatre, and televised by Arts Playhouse on the Arts and Entertainment Network, May 29, 1981. With Pauline Myers and Earle Hyman.

One Big Happy Family (comedy, full length, 1983). "Explores white and Black sexual attitudes, fantasies, and more through the tale of a successful white business woman's efforts to reunite with her college-aged daughter, who has been raised by a Black foster parent, the mother's best friend."—*New York Amsterdam News,* May 21, 1983, p. 7. Prod. by the American Folk Theatre's Emsemble Acting Co., at the Richard Allen Center for Culture and Art, New York; dir. by Dick Gaffield, May 18–June 5, 1983.   ◉

One Monkey Don't Stop No Show (domestic comedy, full length, 1984). About the life of a middle-class black family, the Harrisons, with all of their pretensions. Prod. by the National Black Theatre, New York, March 29–May 13, 1984; dir. by Shirley Clemons Faison.

Sweet Daddy of Love (farce, full length, 1985). "About the pursuits and passions of Philmore Reeves, a 250-lb. lover of poetry, pulchritude and pasta."—*Black Masks,* April 1985, p. 4. Prod. by the Crossroads Theatre Co., New Brunswick, New Jersey, April 12–May 12, 1985; dir. by Lee Richardson.

OTHER PLAYS AND DRAMATIC WORKS:
Nothing but the Blues (full length, 1972). Prod. by the H.B. Playwrights Foundation, New York, Sept. 1972. Prod. by CET, Detroit, May 1973. **The Trials and Tribulations of Stagerlee Booker T. Brown** (1985). Prod. by the National Black Theatre, New York, Nov.-Dec. 1985. Pub. by Dramatists Play Service, New York, 1985. **Call It What You Will** (2 acts, pre-1986). **Blues for a Gospel Queen** (musical, full length, 1986). Book and orig. lyrics by Evans. Orig. music by John Lewis. Prod. at the Billie Holiday Theatre, Brooklyn, Nov. 1986.

EVANS, MICHAEL ("Mike") (1950–   ), Television actor and scriptwriter. Best known as the original Lionel Jefferson on "All in the Family" (1971–75) and "The Jeffersons" (1975–76 and c. 1979–). Appeared in several films, including *The Love Ins* (1967) and *Now You See Him, Now You Don't* (1972).

DRAMATIC WORKS:

"Good Times" (TV comedy series, 1974–). Cocreator, with ERIC MONTE. A spinoff from the "Maud" TV series. According to *Jet* magazine (undated clipping): "Producer Norman Lear asked writer Mike Evans to create a Black pilot show and Good Times was the result. Evans named [Ralph Carter] the baby brother in the show Michael Evans 'as a sort of ego trip.' Now Ralph Carter is more widely known as Michael Evans than the real Michael Evans." Prod. by CBS-TV, Feb. 1974, continuing into the mid-1980s. With Esther Rolle, JOHN AMOS, Jimmie Walker, JA'NET DuBOIS, Ralph Carter, and BernNadette Stanis. **"Sanford and Son"** (TV scripts, 1970s).

EVANS-CHARLES, MARTIE (also known as Martha Evans Charles and Martie Charles), Actress-playwright, described by *Black World* (April 1972, p. 52) as "one of the more powerful new women playwrights on the scene." Daughter of actress Estelle Evans and niece of actress Esther Rolle. Educated at Fisk Univ. and Hunter Coll. (A.B., M.A.). An alumna of the Harlem Black Theatre Workshop and the New Lafayette Theatre (NLT), New York City Asst. prof. of speech and drama at Medgar Evers Coll., Brooklyn. Recipient of a Rockefeller grant.

PLAYS AND DRAMATIC WORKS:

Job Security (drama, 1 act, 1970). A sensitive, intelligent, but seemingly incalcitrant pupil gains revenge on a school system which has subjected her to the hostility, neglect, and indifference of techers more interested in job security than in their students. Prod. by the Black Magicians at Third World House, New York, June 25, 1970. Prod. by the Univ. Players, Elizabeth City State Univ., Elizabeth City, NC, Spring 1975; dir. by Bernard L. Peterson, Jr. Pub. in *Black Theater, U.S.A.* (Hatch & Shine, 1974).

Black Cycle (drama, invocation and 2 acts, 1971). Revolves around "a beauty shop and its particular life style, which has no parallels. Everyone is there, from the operators to the "operators," and in this setting [the author] manages to tell a poignant story."— *Black World*, April 1972, p. 52. Also described as "a black girl's rebellion against her mother and her older generation."—*Black Theater, U.S.A.* (Hatch & Shine, 1974), p. 875. First prod. by the Black Theatre Workshop, at NLT, 1971. Prod. by the Afro-American Studio, New York, 1973. Prod. by the Kuumba Workshop, Chicago, during the 1973–74 season. Pub. in *Black Drama Anthology* (King & Milner, 1972).

Jamimma (drama, 3 acts, 1971). Described by Kushauri Kupa as "the story of a Black woman in love with a man and her attempts to keep him despite hostilities of varying nature facing her from all sides."—*Black Theater* #6, 1972. First prod. as a workshop production by the Black Playwrights Workshop (presumably of NLT), New York, 1971. Prod. Off-Off-Bway by the New Federal Theatre (NFT), at the Henry St. Playhouse, March 16–26, 1972, for 8 perfs. Reopened May 15, 1972, at NFT, for 41 additional perfs., closing June 25, 1972; dir. by SHAUNEILLE PERRY. With Marcella Lowery in the title role. Unpub. script in the Hatch-Billops Collection.

Where We At? (1 act, 1971). Dramatizes "the humiliation and degradation of a black woman who refuses to help her unfortunate sister."—*Black Theater, U.S.A.* (Hatch & Shine, 1974), p. 876. First prod. Off-Bway as a work-in-progress by the Playwrights Workshop of NEC, at St. Marks Playhouse, 1972. Unpub. scripts in the Hatch-Billops Collection and the Schomburg Collection.

African Interlude (1978). Prod. by NFT, opening March 2, 1978, for 12 perfs.; dir. by Shauneille Perry.

F

FABIO, SARAH WEBSTER (Mrs. Cyril L. Fabio) (1928–1979), Playwright, poet, critic, and college teacher. Born in Nashville, TN. A prominent literary figure in the Black Arts movement in California during the 1960s. Her poetry and articles appeared frequently in *Negro Digest/Black World*. Her many volumes of poetry include *A Mirror, a Soul* (1969), *Black Talk: Soul, Shield and Sword* (1973), and *Soul Ain't, Soul Is* (1973).

DRAMATIC WORKS:
M. L. King Pageant (black history pageant, 1967). Prod. at Merritt Jr. Coll., Oakland, CA, and at the Students Theatre, Univ. of California/Berkeley, 1967. **The Saga of the Black Man** (1975). Pub. in the *Iowa Review*, Spring 1975. **No Crystal Stair: Steps to Emancipation for the Black Woman** (1975).

FAISON, GEORGE (1947–   ), Choreographer, director, and musical playwright. Best known for his choreography of "Earth, Wind and Fire" and *The Wiz* (1975). Also choreographed the Radio City Music Hall production of *Porgy and Bess* (1973).

DRAMATIC WORK:
Sing, Mahalia, Sing (gospel musical, 2 acts, 1985). Book by Faison. Music and lyrics by Faison, Richard Smallwood, and Wayne Davis. About the life and times of Mahalia Jackson. Prod. as a national touring production, opening March 18, 1985, at the Shubert Theatre in Philadelphia, then traveling to 11 other cities during its run. With Jennifer Holliday, alternating with Esther Marrow, in the title role, supported by a cast of more than 20.

FANN, AL (Albert Louis Fann) (1925–   ), Actor, director, producer, and playwright. Born in Cleveland, OH. Studied at the Cleveland Inst. of Music, 1956. Asst. director for 15 years of the Karamu Theatre in Cleveland. Founder, exec. director, and resident playwright, since 1967, of the Al Fann Theatrical

Ensemble, a Harlem group whose alumni have appeared on Broadway, on television (as featured actors and in commercials), and in films. Film credits include asst. director, *Cotton Comes to Harlem* (1970); actor and assoc. producer, *Come Back Charleston Blue* (1972); actor in *The French Connection* (1971), *Buck and the Preacher* (1972), and *Supercops* (1974). Television credits include "The Bob Hope Show" (1952), "Search for Tomorrow," "Love of Life," and "Edge of Night." Stage appearances include *Porgy and Bess* (City Center, 1964), *Tambourines to Glory*, *From This Time Forward* (Off-Bway, 1975), and *The Wiz* (1975). Recipient of an AUDELCO Black Theatre Recognition Award, 1973, and an Andy Award from the Advertising Club of New York, 1969.

REPRESENTATIVE PLAYS:

Masks in Black // Orig. title: **Masks in Brown** (series of annual dramatic shows, 1970/74). Blanket title for an annual series of shows prod. in repertory by the Al Fann Theatrical Co., New York, from 1970 to about 1974. The 1970 show was prod. under its orig. title. The 1974 show featured scenes from Bway shows and was presented at the Hofstra Univ. Playhouse, Hempstead, NY. The 1975 show, which emphasized the Bicentennial theme, presented the contribution of blacks from the American Revolution to the present, and was prod. at St. Phillips Church, New York, in June 1975.

King Heroin (drama, 1971). "Drama of drug addiction in Harlem written partly as a reaction to the death of Walter Vandermeer, a 12-year-old schoolboy."—*The Best Plays of 1970–1971*. Prod. by the Al Fann Theatrical Ensemble, under the auspices of the St. Phillip's Community Service Council, at the St. Phillip's Community in Harlem, opening March 17, 1971, for 30 perfs.; dir. by author, who also played the Voice of King Heroin. Also toured colleges, high schools, and community centers. Prod. by the Black Image Players, at Booker T. Washington H.S., Atlanta, opening in Nov. 1972; dir. by Andrea Frye.

OTHER PLAYS AND DRAMATIC WORKS:

Sweet Jesus (screenplay, early 1970s). Music by Danny Meehan. Described in advance of its prodn. as "the truest and most devoted movie treatment of Harlem yet."—*Jet* (undated clipping, early 1970s). No record of the actual prodn. **Strivin'** (theatrical collage, 1975). Written, dir., and choreographed by Fann for the Beaux Arts Ball, New York, 1975.

FANN, ERNIE, Community theatre director and playwright. Based in Cleveland, OH, where he has been associated with both the Humanist Theatre and the Karamu Theatre

PLAYS AND DRAMATIC WORKS:

Colors // Also known as **Blue, Green, Yellow, Orange, Red and Brown** (1974). "About racial confrontations."—*Black World,* April 1974. Prod. by the Humanist Theatre, Cleveland, Fall 1972. Also performed at various neighborhood centers in Cleveland, 1973.**The Hymie Finklestein Used Lumber Company** (musical comedy, 1973). Co-authored with MARGARET F. TAYLOR SNIPES. First prod. by the Karamu Theatre, Cleveland, in the Arena Theatre, during the summer of 1973. Revised and restaged by Karamu Theatre for a run of four weeks, opening Sept. 28, 1973. **The First Tuesday in November** (1975) and **A Fair and Impartial Verdict** (1975). Both sched. for prodn. by the Humanist Theatre, Cleveland, Fall 1975, to be performed at the Horseshoe Lodge

Country Club in Rome, OH, as part of a Labor Day Weekend Ball, but the perf. was canceled because of rain. No record of the actual prodn.

FARLEY, RICHARD, Playwright. *Address:* 332 E. 53rd St., New York, NY 10022.

PLAY:
The Great American Race War (drama, 3 acts, pre-1975). Concerns a white liberal who discovers that he is a racist when faced with a genuine test of his beliefs.

FENTY, PHIL (Phillip), Screenwriter, former advertising copywriter, and agency owner. Born in Cleveland, OH. Studied art, with an aim to becoming a painter and sculptor. Dropped out of school to work for an advertising agency specializing in radio commercials. There he won two prizes for his work after only six months, and was persuaded to become a copywriter. Went to New York, where he landed a job as copy trainee at Gray Advertising, and within a year became a full-fledged copywriter. Moved to Ted Bates & Co., where within two years he was made head of the television commercial copywriters, and by age 25 became vice pres. Resigned this position to form his own ad agency and design company (with another black man), which soon went broke because of the failure of the design company. At this point he decided to try his hand at writing a screenplay, and teamed up with producer Sig Shore and actor Ron O'Neal to produce his first film.

DRAMATIC WORK:
Superfly (screenplay, full length [98 min.]: 1972). Highly successful but controversial film that romanticized the life of a black drug pusher who tries to quit but is opposed by his white suppliers. Financed by blacks. Prod. by Sig Shore; dir. by Gordon Parks, Jr., with Ron O'Neal in the leading role; released by Warner Bros., 1972.

FERDINAND, VAL, III. See SALAAM, KALAMU YA.

FIELDS, JULIA (1938–   ), Poet, short-story writer, playwright, and teacher. Born in Bessemer, AL. Received the A.B. from Knoxville Coll., 1961, and the M.A. in English from the Bread Loaf School of English, Middlebury, VT, 1972. Also studied at the Univ. of Edinburgh in Scotland. Served as poet-in-residence at Miles Coll. (Birmingham), Hampton Inst., and East Carolina Univ. Contributed poetry to numerous magazines and anthologies, including *Negro Digest/Black World,* in which she was featured in the annual poetry issue, and in 1972 was awarded *Black World*'s Seventh Conrad Kent Rivers Memorial Award for Literature (which included a cash prize of $500). Among her books of poetry are *Poems* (1968), *East of Moonlight* (1976), and *A Summoning, A Shining* (1976). Other poems are anthologized in *Beyond the Blues* (Pool, 1962), *American Negro Poetry* (Bontemps, 1963), *New Negro Poets: USA* (Hughes, 1964), *For Malcolm* (Randall & Burroughs, 1967), *Kaleidoscope* (Hayden, 1967), *An Introduction to Black Literature in America* (Patterson, 1968), *City in*

All Directions (Adoff, 1969), *The New Black Poetry* (Major, 1969), *Black Out Loud* (Adoff, 1970), *The Poetry of the Negro: 1746–1970* (Hughes & Bontemps, 1970), *A Galaxy of Black Writing* (Shuman, 1970), *Blackamerican Literature* (Miller, 1971), *The Poetry of Black America* (Adoff, 1972), *Afro-American Poetry* (Bell, 1972), and *A Rock Against the Wind* (Patterson, 1973). Her short stories have been published in *Black World* and anthologized in *Black Fire* (Jones & Neal, 1968) and *Short Story Anthology* (King, 1972). Recipient of a $1,500 grant from NEA, 1968. *Address:* P.O. Box 209, Scotland Neck, NC 27874.

PLAYS:

All Day Tomorrow (drama, 3 acts, 1966). About the progressive deterioration of relationships between the races and generations in a small southern village. The main character is a young black woman who refuses to offer sympathy to an old white woman who had once been kind to her but is now dying of a malignant disease. First prod. at Knoxville Coll., TN, 1966; dir. by Earl Alston.

Up the Country (drama, 4 acts, 1975). Explores the relationships among diverse types of people in a small southern town: people who have been part of the urban North and South; young explorers—including drug addicts and prison inmates—and ordinary hardworking southern people who make their situation work for them; old people and children who live in a fantasy world of plastic and electronics. In 1975 it was being considered for New York prodn.

FIELDS, MAURICE C., Poet-playwright. Based in Philadelphia, PA. Author of two volumes of poetry: *The Collected Poems of Maurice C. Fields* (1940) and *Testament of Youth* (1940).

PLAYS:

The Dead Are Not Forgotten (domestic drama, 1 act, 1974). When a black man runs for public office, his son, whom he believed dead, returns to enjoy the benefits of his father's future position. **Nowhere to Go, Nowhere to Get Over** (domestic drama, 3 acts, 1974). Concerns the conflicts within a black home caused by the Muslim beliefs of a son who has just been released from jail.

FISHER, JOHN (1926–   ), Journalist, poet, and playwright. Born in Goose Creek, TX. Now living in San Francisco, where he has been managing editor of *The Grapevine,* a community newspaper in Watts, and involved in the activities of the Mission Neighborhood Playhouse. His poetry has been published in *Black Dialogue, Black Journal,* and the *Journal of Black Poetry.*

PLAY:

Beyond the Closet (pre-1976). Prod. by the Mission Neighborhood Playhouse, San Francisco, prior to 1976.

FITZ, ANDREE, Playwright. Former student member of the Virginia Union Univ. Players, Richmond.

PLAY:

Black . . . Out! (contemporary thesis revue, full length, late 1960s). Coauthor, with SYLVIA HAMPTON. Explores the problems and frustrations of the American Negro.

Resulted from a black drama competition sponsored by the Virginia Union Univ. Players, which prod. the play during the late 1960s. Also toured Concordia Coll., Moorehead State Coll., St. John's and St. Benedict's Coll. (all in Minnesota,) and North Dakota State Univ.

FLAGG, ANN (Kathryn), Playwright and children's theatrical director. Born in Charleston, WV, where she was educated in the public schools. Received the B.A. in theatre at West Virginia State Univ., where she studied under Dr. Fannin S. Belcher, the noted black theatre historian. Received a graduate fellowship at Northwestern Univ. during 1961–62 to pursue the M.A. in children's theatre under Winifred Ward. Taught in the public high schools of West Virginia until 1952, when she joined the staff of Karamu House in Cleveland as director of Children's Theatre, remaining until 1961, when she went on leave to study at Northwestern. Won first prize in the National Collegiate Playwriting Contest in 1963.

PLAY:
Great Gettin' Up Morning (drama, 1 act, 1963). Concerns the experiences of a southern black family on the morning that their daughter is to enter a previously all-white school. Won first prize in the National Collegiate Playwriting Contest, 1962. Televised by CBS, New York, 1963. Prod. at the American Place Theatre, New York, 1974. Pub. by Samuel French, New York, 1964.

FLETCHER, B. B. (Bernice B. Fletcher), Playwright. Associated with the Frank Silvera Writers' Workshop (FSWW) in New York City. *Address:* 160 W. 71st St., New York, NY 10023.

PLAYS AND DRAMATIC WORKS:
A Mysterious Light (comic fantasy for children, 1 act, 1965). Combines spectacular light, music, and dance to point up "good Samaritan" heroism involving a crying lightning bug. Prod. at the No Smoking Theatre, New York, Sept. 26–Oct. 19, 1983. **The Shelter** (1 act, 1972). About a temporarily destitute mother. **The Letter of White Law** (1 act, 1973). One man's attempt to stand up to "the system." Public reading by FSWW, New York, 1982. Unpub. script in the FSWW Archives/Schomburg Collection. **Haveanice-weekend** (3 acts, 1976). A slice-of-weekend-life in the lives of employees of a large company in New York City. Public reading at the Script Development Workshop, New York, 1979. **Collision** (comedy, 1 act, c. 1978). Concerns the colliding of lives in an elevator. Public reading at the Script Development Workshop, New York, 1979. Prod. as an Equity Showcase at ATA, 1984, on triple bill with **Game Cancelled Due to Rain** (c. 1979) and **The Reading** (c. 1981), under the blanket title **"CRACKED." Les Enfants Perdus** ("Lost Children") (1 act, c. 1978). A man and woman confront each other, after a lengthy separation and other partners, via telephone. Prod. at the Pretenders Theatre, New York, 1978. **Boogieee!** (3 acts, 1979). About a young adult coming of age in an era preoccupied with the "body beautiful." Public reading by FSWW, 1981. Unpub. script in the FSWW Archives/Schomburg Collection. **Game Cancelled Due to Rain** (comedy, very short 1 act, c. 1979). Spoof of television. Prod. as an Equity Showcase at ATA, 1984 [see **Collision** above]. **Three** (1 act?, c. 1980). Unmasks the lives of three modern women living in the same apartment building. The first of four related one-act plays, of which only two have been completed. [See also **Ramona** below.] Public reading

by FSWW, 1981. Unpub. script in the FSWW Archives/Schomburg Collection. **Flag Street Stop** (mystery, in progress since 1981). Involves a chance meeting between a black man and woman. **The Guest House** (1 act, c. 1981). An outrageous tale of urban life. Prod. at the 18th St. Playhouse, New York, 1982; dir. by Paul Davis. **The Reading** (comedy, 1 act, c. 1981). Prod. as an Equity Showcase at ATA, 1984 [see **Collision** above]. **Ramona** (1 act, c. 1982). The second of four related one-act plays, of which only two have been completed. [See also **Three** above.] Ramona and Walter, two characters introduced in **Three**, are embroiled in a love triangle. Pub. reading by FSWW. Unpub. script in the FSWW Archives/Schomburg Collection. **Daisy's Dilemma** (children's play, 1 act, c. 1984). Lighthearted tale about how a daisy finds a home of her own. **A Pair of Short Shorts Flappin' in the Breeze** (pre-1985). Unpub. script in the FSWW Archives/Schomburg Collection.

FOARD, SYLVIA-ELAINE, Playwright. Based in New York City.

PLAY:

A Fictional Account of the Lives of Richard and Sarah Allen (historical/biographical play, full length, 1976). About the founder and first bishop of the A.M.E. Church and his wife. Prod. by the Negro Ensemble Co., New York, as a Season-Within-a-Season production, April 20–25, 1976; dir. by Horacena J. Taylor.

FONTENOT, (Dr.) CHESTER J., Editor, teacher, and playwright. *Address:* Asst. Prof., Africana Studies and Research Center, Cornell University, 310 Triphammer Rd., Ithaca, NY 14853.

PLAYS:

Author of several plays, including **The Seventh Son** (c. 1977), which have been performed by local black drama groups.

FOREMAN, FARRELL J., Poet, writer, playwright, and drama teacher. A native of Philadelphia, PA. Educated at Antioch Univ., Philadelphia (B.A. in elementary education, 1977), and Univ. of California/San Diego (M.F.A. in theatre and playwriting, 1982). Currently on the faculty of the Drama Dept. of UC/San Diego, 1980–. Has taught English at Mesa Coll., San Diego. Playwright-in-residence at Northern Illinois Univ., Dekalb, 1982, and earlier, in 1978, was faculty asst. at the Center for Minority Studies. Author of *Null & Void* (poetry, 1970). Other poems and articles are published mainly in *Imprints* magazine (Antioch Univ.), *Encore* magazine, and *Towers* magazine (Northern Illinois Univ.). One of his poems, published in *Atlantic Monthly,* won a student writing award in 1971. Other awards include NADSA Award for Playwriting, 1978; Lorraine Hansberry Award for Playwriting, American Coll. Theatre Festival, 1978; Samuel Goldwyn Award for Creative Writing, 1980; NEA Award for Playwriting, 1980s; McDonald's Gold Award, 1983. *Address—* Office: c/o Drama Dept./Humanities Library Bldg., University of California at San Diego, La Jolla, CA 92037. Home: 3565 1/2 Strandway, San Diego, CA 92109.

REPRESENTATIVE PLAYS AND DRAMATIC WORKS:
The Ballad of Charley Sweetlegs Vine (1978). Winner of the Lorraine Hansberry Award for Playwriting, American Coll. Theatre Festival (ACTF). Prod. by Northern Illinois Univ., Dekalb, and entered in ACTF, 1978.

Daddy's Seashore Blues ("A Play in Three Tides" [subtitle], full length, 1979). According to the author: "This play is about folks trying to make it. Folks trying to run away. Folks trying to love when it would be a lot easier to hate. Black people fall in love . . . they also have to survive. Most ordinary folk are just trying to get by with a little happiness. Some are doomed to fail, but they aren't any less human for trying."—Introduction to pub. script. Prod. at Northern Illinois Univ., Dekalb, 1979; Berkeley Stage, 1981; Lawrenceville Community Center, NJ, 1982; Inner City Cultural Center, Los Angeles, 1982; Eden Theatrical Workshop, Denver, 1983; and Victory Gardens Theatre, Chicago, 1983. Pub. in *Center Stage* (Ostrow, 1981).

OTHER PLAYS AND DRAMATIC WORKS:
The Teachers' Lounge (1 act, 1977). Prod. at Texas Southern Univ., Houston, 1977, where it was the recipient of an award. **Lone Eagle** (1985). Deals with black flyers in World War II. Prod. at UC/San Diego, Summer 1985. **Black Gravy** (1982). Prod. at Northern Illinois Univ., Dekalb, 1982. **Gym Rats** (1982). Prod. at the Olde Globe Theatre, San Diego, 1982, and by New Dramatists, New York, 1983.

FOREMAN, KENT, Poet-playwright and director. Based in Chicago, where he has read his poetry in coffee houses and bars.

DRAMATIC WORK:
Summer in the City (musical, full length, 1965). Cowritten with OSCAR BROWN, JR. "Although the motif in the production had an integrated background, the gut and beauty of it came entirely from Black life." —*Black World,* April 1973, pp. 28–29. Prod. at the Harper Theatre in Hyde Park, Chicago, 1965.

FOSTER, ALEX, Playwright. Based in New York City.

PLAY:
Community Kitchen (comedy-drama, 3 acts, 1974). Deals with the problems faced by a group of hardworking black people who are fired from their jobs in order to make way for automation. Prod. by the Harlem YMCA, New York, 1974.

FRANKLIN, J. e. (Jenny E.), Playwright, author, and teacher. Born in Houston, TX. Received the B.A. degree from the Univ. of Texas. Has also taken graduate courses at Union Theological Seminary in New York. Formerly a lecturer in the Education Dept. of Herbert H. Lehman Coll., a branch of CUNY. She has developed her skills as an artist-therapist, and is director of the Theatre for Artcentric Living, Church of Crucifixion, New York City. Has written a number of short stories, one of which was published in *Black Short Story Anthology* (King, 1972). Her book *Black Girl from Genesis to Revelations* (1976) contains an introduction to her best-known play, **Black Girl** (1969). She has also completed a series of articles on education through art, and what she terms a "schizo-genesis," or "the theological roots of racism." Recipient of the New

York Drama Desk Award, as most promising playwright, 1971; Media Women Award, 1971; New York State Council on the Arts (NYSCA) Public Service Grant, 1972; CAPS Fellowship, 1972; Institute for the Arts and Humanities Dramatic Arts Award, Howard Univ., 1974; Better Boys Foundation Playwriting Award, 1978; NEA Creative Writing Fellowship, 1979; and Rockefeller Grant, 1980. *Agent:* Victoria Lucas Associates, 888 Seventh Ave., Suite 400, New York, NY 10019.

REPRESENTATIVE PLAYS AND DRAMATIC WORKS:

The In-Crowd (thesis play, 1 act, 1967; also a rock musical, full length, 1977). Members of a youth gang sentence their parents to death and kill them in effigy as punishment for what they perceive as parental cruelty. After the mock-murders, they come to realize that family ties are stronger than any other bonds. Prod. by Mobilization for Youth (New York) at Montreal Expo, Canada, 1967. Prod. as a rock musical for the young by New Federal Theatre, New York, 1977.

Black Girl (domestic drama, 2 acts, 1969; also a feature film, full length: screenplay, 1972). Autobiographical play in which a teenager with ambitions of becoming a dancer struggles to break away from her family without losing their love. Won for the author a Drama Desk Award, 1971–72, as most promising playwright. First prod. as a videotape production (presumably by NFT) on NET, WGBH/Boston, 1969. Prod. Off-Off-Bway by NFT, at St. Augustine's Chapel, New York; transferred to Bway at the Theatre De Lys, June 16, 1971–June 16, 1972, playing for one year (247 perfs.); dir. by SHAUNEILLE PERRY. With Kishasha, Arthur French, Lorraine Ryder, Gloria Edwards, Loretta Greene, Louise Stubbs, MINNIE GENTRY, Jimmy Hayeson, and SAUNDRA SHARP. Prod. by the Bennett Coll. Little Theatre, Oct. 18–20, 1973, for 3 perfs. Made into a film prod. by Lee Savin, released by Cinema Releasing, 1972, and dir. by OSSIE DAVIS. With Leslie Uggams, Brock Peters, Claudia McNeil, Peggy Petitt, and RUBY DEE. Pub. by Dramatists Play Service, New York, 1973.

Prodigal Daughter (1962). Explores the problems of a young unwed mother. The orig. play on which her musical **The Prodigal Sister** (1974) was based. Prod. in New York as a street-theatre project at Lincoln Center, and on street corners in the Bronx.

Cut Out the Lights and Call the Law (drama, full length, 1972). A group of black students attending a white college prepare themselves to fight if they are attacked by white students. Sched. for production by NFT, 1972, but apparently not prod. Prod. by NEC, 1970s. The author states that two scenes were read at the literary events of FESTAC in Lagos, Nigeria, 1977.

The Prodigal Sister (musical, 2 acts [8 scenes], 1974). Book by Franklin. Lyrics by Franklin and MICKI GRANT. Music by Grant. Apparently based on Franklin's play **Prodigal Daughter** (1962). Follows the basic plot and theme of the Prodigal Son. A young girl becomes pregnant, leaves her home and family for the big city, and sinks into a sordid life, finally returning home to the love and protection of her parents. Prod. Off-Bway at the Theatre De Lys, New York, Nov. 25–Dec. 29, 1974, for 40 perfs.; dir. by Shauneille Perry. With Paula Desmond and Saundra McClain. Pub. by Samuel French, New York, 1975.

Throw Thunder at This House (1970s). A group of undergraduate students desegregates a southern university and learns that freedom is a constant struggle. Prod. by the Theatre for Artcentric Living, 1970s. Presented at Skidmore Coll., Saratoga Springs, New York, 1970s.

Where Dewdrops of Mercy Shine Bright (1983). A sequel to **Christchild** (pre-1983) [see OTHER PLAYS AND DRAMATIC WORKS below]. An insensitive parent loses a second child to the world. Prod. by Rites and Reason, Brown Univ., Providence, RI, Feb. 4–7, 1983; dir. by Thelma Louise Carter.

Under Heaven's Eye til Cockcrow (1983). A young girl searches for her roots but is not sure she wants to embrace them once she has found them. Prod. at the Theatre of the Open Eye, New York 1984.

OTHER PLAYS AND DRAMATIC WORKS:
The First Step to Freedom (thesis play, 1964). Her first play. Written as part of the Mississippi CORE SNCC Summer Project to interest students in reading. Prod. at the Sharon Waite Community Center, Harmony, MS, 1964. **Mau Mau Room** (1969). Prod. as a workshop production by NEC, 1969. **Two Flowers** (1960s). Prod. at the New Feminists Theatre, New York, during the 1960s. **The Enemy** (1973), **Four Women** (1973), **MacPilate** (1974), and **The Creation** (1975). All prod. by Eureka Theatre Group, at Herman Lehman Coll., New York, during the years indicated. **Crusade for Justice** (film treatment, 1975). On the Life of Ida-Welles Barnett, antilynch crusader, apparently written for the Boston Committee, 1975. **Another Morning Rising** (1976). Prod. by the Company of Us, Greenwood, SC, 1976. **The Hand-Me-Downs** (1978). Prod. by the Theatre for Artcentric Living, New York, 1978, and presented at the LaMont-Zeno Theatre the same year. **Cristchild** (pre-1983). A boy born with six fingers on his left hand wrestles a bear to earn his father's love. **Guess What's Coming to Dinner** (mime show, 1980s). **Will the Real South Please Rise?** (musical, 1980s).

FRAZIER, HANK, Playwright. Associated with the Frank Silvera Writers' Workshop (FSWW) in New York City.

PLAYS:
The Businessman (1 act, 1972). A black man fails to find fulfillment in life, partly because he does not know what he wants, and partly because of his mistrust of knowledge. **A Black Market** (mystery-comedy, 2 acts, 1977). A young man searches for the murderer of his twin brothers. Public reading by FSWW, at the Studio Museum, New York, March 1977. Unpub. script and tape recording in the FSWW Archives/Schomburg Collection. **Nothing but the Truth** (drama, 1 act, pre-1977). Blacks on death row reveal their views about religion and morality. Unpub. script in the Schomburg Black Theatre Collection.

FRAZIER, LEVI, JR. (1951–), Playwright, author, and broadcast journalist. Based in Memphis, TN. Has written over 30 plays for radio, TV, and the stage. Educated at Southwestern Coll. at Memphis (B.A. in communications arts and psychology, 1973), Memphis State Univ. (M.A. in speech and drama, with emphasis on playwriting and directing, 1975), State Technical Inst. at Memphis (accounting, 1976), and Memphis State Univ. (advanced film, 1976–77). News reporter and talk show producer for Radio Station WREC, 1972–74; local coordinator/writer for Chicago Educational TV (WTTW-TV); scriptwriter for Audiovisual Dept., State Technical Inst./Memphis, 1975–76; audivisual coordinator, Memphis Correctional Center, 1976–79. His poetry and short fiction have been published in local and regional periodicals, and his poems are included in *Good Citizens of Gomorrah* (1979). Member, Tennessee Arts Commission,

Literary Advisory Panel, 1979–82, and American Federation of Radio and TV Artists. *Address:* 3090 Carnes, Memphis, TN 38111.

PLAYS AND DRAMATIC WORKS:

A Tribute to Richard Wright (script for readers' theatre, full length [1 hr., 45 min.], 1972). Compiled from various works by and about Wright, including letters, short stories, essays, and poetry, to tell the true story of his constant battles with racism and colonialism the world over. Prod. in Tennessee and Mississippi at Millington Naval Air Station, Memphis, 1980; Univ. of Mississippi/Oxford, 1980; Shelby State Community Coll., Memphis, 1981, 1982; Oxford Black Arts Coalition, Oxford, 1981; Rust Coll., Holly Springs, MS, 1981, 1982; Radio Station WLOK, Memphis, 1977; and Itawamba Jr. Coll., Fulton, MS, 1981.

Wrong Place/Right Time // Orig title: **The Way We Was; or The Wrong Place at the Right Time** (surrealistic play, 1 act, 1972). A play-within-a-play, about the sixties and a character named Sidney who tries to borrow money from a white friend to go to New York to become an actor. Unfortunately, the director of the play-within-a-play seems to think that it should end differently. Prod. in Memphis, at Southwestern Coll. Lab Theatre, 1973; Memphis State Univ. Ball Room, 1975; Circuit Playhouse Attic Theatre, 1975; and Radio Station WLOK, 1978.

Down on Beale St. (musical, full length, 1973). Deals with the life of W. C. Handy, Father of the Blues, and the legendary Beale Street of Memphis. There is also a shorter musical version that deals more with Beale Street. Prod. in Memphis at LeMoyne-Owen Coll., 1973; Memphis State Univ., Lab Theatre, 1974; WKNO-TV, 1974; Mid-America Mall, at May Festival, 1978; Memphis State Univ., Main Stage, 1979; Martin Luther King Performing Arts Center, 1982; and Radio Station WLOK, 1979. Prod. in New York at the Richard Allen Center for Culture and Art, 1980.

Paul Robeson—All American (drama, 1 act, 1973). Gives the essence of the greatness of Paul Robeson—scholar, world traveler, and superb athlete. Beginning with his boyhood, this play shows Robeson in the glory and splendor of his youth, as well as the low periods of later years when he was hounded by the U.S. government for his outspoken positions against racism and capitalism. Prod. in Memphis at Southwestern Coll., 1973, and Radio Station WLOK, 1977.

The Homecoming (domestic drama, 1 act, 1974). Shows a black family awaiting the arrival of a son who had been listed as missing in action in Vietnam, but who was recently found. Has he been hurt? Was he a traitor? Is he a junkie? All of these questions are running through everyone's mind as a clear picture of who their son is eludes them. Prod. by Radio Station WLOK, Memphis, 1977.

A Sad State of Affairs (series of satires, full length [1 hr.], 1975). Prod. in Raleigh, NC, at the Southern Black Cultural Alliance Conf., 1980. Prod. in Memphis at Radio Station WLOK, 1979; at the Memphis Correctional Center, 1980; Shelby County Penal Farm, 1980; Blues Alley Bar & Restaurant, 1980; Cook Convention Center 1981; Channel 7, cable TV, 1982; Melrose H.S., 1982; Shelby State Community Coll., 1980; and State Technical Inst., 1982. Prod. at Meharry Medical School, Nashville, 1977, and at Alcorn Coll., Alcorn, MS, 1982.

Sis' Moses (drama, 1 act, 1975). About Harriet Tubman, ex-slave and conductor of the Underground Railroad. Depicts her return to the South to get her parents and other slaves in the area, and their difficult journey up North to freedom. Prod. in Memphis at Memphis Public Lib., Levi Branch, 1975; NAACP Freedom Fund Dinner, 1976; Radio Station WLOK, 1977.

The Grapevine (comedy, 1 act, 1978). A parody of the Tarzan story. Two irate mothers, Ms. Chipanowitz and Ms. Gibbon, lambast the king of the jungle, in his absence, for his "human qualities," especially the advances he makes toward their daughters and all the other "little monkey girls" in the jungle. Prod. in Memphis by Beale St. Repertory Co., 1978, and at Radio Station WLOK, 1978.

Ratman & Bobbin I & II (radio script, full length [1 hr.], 1978). A take-off on Batman and Robin that satirizes local government, politicians, contemporary issues, and fads. Prod. in Memphis on Radio Station WLOK, 1978 and 1980, and by Arts in the Park, 1980.

Ain't No Way I & II (radio script, full length [1 hr.], 1980). A murder mystery, originally written for radio, in which the general manager of a theatre is killed and his estranged friend (a former theatre person-turned-cop) takes on the task of finding the murderer. Prod. by Radio Station WLOK, Memphis, 1980.

Big Ten (drama, 2 acts, 1980). Written jointly with Rommy Ray, Hosea Henderson, Quincy Mckay, Akeba Patton, and Mary Robinson. Deals with a young athlete's loss of self-esteem when he is injured and his glorious football career comes to an end. He finds that he must make a choice either to give up on life or go on and make a new life for himself. Prod. at the Cook Convention Center, Memphis, 1982.

Children of Production (children's play, 1 act, 1980). Machines have taken over the earth, and a family of children travels to the future via a time machine. In the future they learn the secrets of the past that they must use to keep the world from coming to such a horrible end. So they journey back to the past with a new resolve of "Clean air, clean earth, clean water, and clean minds!" Written for the Jacks & Jills of America, Inc. Prod. in Topeka, KS, 1980. Prod. in Memphis at Hickory Ridge Mall, 1981, and on Radio Station WLOK, 1980.

A Chance for Charley (comedy, 1 act, 1981). About a family and some friends who like drinking beer and watching TV more than anything else, until the wife has had enough and calls it quits. The friends also want to straighten up and live constructively, but the husband and ringleader is committed to his ways until a few ghostly visitors pay him a call. Originally written for the Kingsbury High–Sears Adopt-a-School Program of the Memphis City Schools. Prod. in Memphis by Sears Mid-town Store, 1981; Sears Poplar Store, 1981; and Holiday Inn Rivermont, 1982.

You're Different (drama, 1 act, 1981). Takes place at a small predominantly white university, where a young black coed is trying desperately to leave in favor of greener (or blacker) pastures; however, her leaving is not a simple matter because she is forced to confront herself and her future by two untimely visitors. Prod. on Radio Station WLOK, Memphis, 1981.

Alpha Kappa Alpha's Pledge Review (sorority revue, 1982). Prod. in Memphis, 1982.

FREEMAN, AL, JR. (Albert Cornelius Freeman, Jr.) (1934–   ), Veteran actor of stage, screen, and TV; screenwriter and director. Born in San Antonio, TX. Studied theatre at Los Angeles City Coll., where in 1957 he was named Outstanding Drama Student. Formerly associated with the Ebony Showcase in Los Angeles, 1954; and with the Negro Ensemble Co. and the New York Shakespeare Festival, New York City, during the 1960s and 1970s. Made his Broadway debut in *The Long Dream* (1960) and has performed in numerous Off-Broadway and Broadway plays, including *Kicks and Company* (1961), *Trumpets of the Lord* (1963), *The Slave* (1964), *Blues for Mister Charlie* (1964), *Dutchman* (1965), *Golden Boy* (1965), *Look to the Lilies* (1970), and *The Great MacDaddy* (1974). His many films include *Dutchman* (1967) and *Finian's Rainbow* (1968). TV appearances include the title role in *My Sweet Charlie* (1970), for which he received an Emmy nomination; Bingham in the "Hot l Baltimore" series, c. 1975; "Roots: The Next Generations," Episode Seven, for which he received an Emmy nomination, 1979; and Lt. Ed Hall in the daytime drama series "One Life to Live," for which he received an Emmy Award, 1979.

DRAMATIC WORK:

Countdown at Kusini (feature film, full length: screenplay, 1976). Coauthor, with OSSIE DAVIS and Ladi Ladebo. About the liberation of a fictional African country (actually Lagos, Nigeria), with a romatic subplot. Financed by DST Telecommunications, a subsidiary of Delta Sigma Theta Sorority. Prod. by Nigerian (film company), 1976; dir. by coauthor Davis. With RUBY DEE, Ossie Davis, Greg Morris, Tom Aldredge, Michael Ebert, and Thomas Baptiste.

FREEMAN, CAROL (1941–   ), Poet, playwright, and short-story writer who in 1968 characterized herself as a "revolutionary Black nationalist." Born in Rayville, LA; resides in Oakland, CA. Received the B.A. in English from Mills Coll.; also studied at Oakland City Coll. and the Univ. of California. Her poetry has been anthologized in *The Magic of Black Poetry* (Abdul, 1972), *The Poetry of Black America* (Adoff, 1972), *The Poetry of the Negro* (Hughes & Bontemps, 1970), *3000 Years of Black Poetry* (Lomax & Abdul, 1970), *Blackamerican Literature* (Miller, 1971), and *Black Culture* (Simmons & Hutchinson, 1972). Winner of the Mary Merrill Henry Prize in poetry and verse, 1971–72.

PLAY:

The Suicide (drama, 1 act, 1967). A quiet wake in a ghetto apartment turns into a cursing, screaming brawl because a neighbor refuses to turn her radio down in proper respect for the dead. Prod. by Black Folks Theatre, Northwestern Univ., Evanston, IL, 1971. Pub. in *Soulbook* (1967?). Reprinted in *Black Fire* (Jones & Neal, 1968).

FRENCH, ARTHUR, III, Son of veteran actor Arthur French II, and godson of actor–director–playwright MAXWELL GLANVILLE.

PLAY:

Teens Today (1982). Play of adolescent life, "about the problems of . . . sexuality in teenage values."—*New York Amsterdam News,* May 8, 1982, p. 31. Prod. at the Harlem YMCA, May 1982; dir. by Maxwell Glanville.

FRIEDMAN, STEVE, Playwright. Based in New York City. (Racial identity not verified.)

PLAY:

Freedom Days (1984). "Saga of the civil rights movement."—*New York Amsterdam News,* Feb. 25, 1984. Prod. at the Washington Square Church, Feb. 1984.

FUDGE, ANTHONY R., Poet-playwright. Based in Cleveland, OH. Has published two volumes of poetry: *Book of Arf: Migration* (1972) and *Hough: A World Flight* (1975). Cofounder of *Black Ascensions,* a literary magazine, at Cuyahoga Community Coll., 1971; and organizer of Bartuss Experience, a Cleveland poetry-performing group, 1972.

PLAY:
Migration: Up from This Earth (poetic drama, 1973). "A futuristic play depicting one man's spiritual development."—*Black World,* April 1974, p. 36. According to the author, its "setting is in the future, covering a period of twenty years that ends around the year 2001. it is a narrative tale spun from a manuscript left by the most influential character in the play, ab'rajl. the narrator is ab'rajl's brother, te'bral."—Letter to Peterson, 1976. Prod. by the Humanist Theatre, Cleveland, Oct. 1973; dir. by Annette Jefferson. Also performed at the One World Theatre Workshop, Cleveland, 1973.

FULLER, CHARLES H., JR. (1939–   ), Playwright, screenwriter, and TV scriptwriter; former journalist, theatre director, and teacher. Winner of the Pulitzer Prize for Drama, 1982, for **A Soldier's Play** (1981). Born in Philadelphia, PA, the son of a printer. Served in the U.S. Army, 1959–62. Educated at Villanova Univ. (1956–58) and LaSalle Coll. (B.A., 1967). Married; two sons. Began writing short stories, poetry, and essays at night while working in Philadelphia during the 1960s on a number of different jobs, including bank loan-collector, Temple Univ. counselor, and city housing inspector. Has edited several newspapers in Philadelphia. Was one of the founders of Kuntu, an organization of black writers and artists; cofounder and codirector of the Afro-American Arts Theatre in Philadelphia. 1967–71. Taught black American literature at LaSalle Coll., 1970; lectured on the same subject on a tour of seven universities, 1970–71. A number of his television scripts, cited below, have been produced on local Philadelphia TV channels. Recipient of the following honors and awards, in addition to the Pulitzer Prize cited above: Rockefeller Foundation Fellowship, 1975; CAPS Playwriting Fellowship, 1975; Obie Award for playwriting, 1980, for **Zooman and the Sign** (1980), which was also selected by the Burns Mantle Theatre Yearbook *Best Plays* series as a "Best Play" of 1980–81; and the following additional awards for **A Soldier's Play:** the New York Drama Critics' Circle Award, as the Best American Play; the Outer Critics' Circle Award, as the Best Off-Broadway Play; the Theatre Club Award as the Best Play; and selected by the Burns Mantle Theatre Yearbook *Best Plays* series as a "Best Play" of 1981–82. *Address*—Home: 15 Langford St., Philadelphia, PA 19136. *Agent:* William Morris Agency, Inc., 1350 Avenue of the Americas, New York, NY 10019.

GROUP OF RELATED PLAYS:
"THE SUNFLOWERS" (5 one-act plays, full length program, 1968/69). Includes **Ain't Nobody Sarah, But Me** (1969), **Cain** (1969), **Indian Giver** (1969), **J.J.'s Game** (1969), **The Layout** (1968), and **The Sunflower Majorette** (1969).

REPRESENTATIVE PLAYS AND DRAMATIC WORKS:

The Perfect Party // Orig. title: **The Village: A Party** (drama, 2 acts, 1968). Deals with the problems of interracial marriage. "The plot centers around five mixed couples . . . who have established a utopia-type community where the racial problems of the outside world can be forgotten or completely ignored."—*Jet,* April 17, 1969, p. 58. However, at a surprise birthday party thrown by one of the white wives for her black husband, "the harmonious facade is exposed as a fraud as all the couples are discovered to be having problems based on racial feelings."—Ibid. Prod. under its orig. title at the McCarter Theatre, Princeton, NJ, opening Oct. 18, 1968. Prod. Off-Bway, at Tambellini's Gate Theatre, New York, March 1969, with Moses Gunn and Virginia Kiser.

The Rise // Also known as **Brother Marcus** (historical drama, 4 acts, 1968). Based on the life of Marcus Garvey, the early black nationalist from Jamaica, who attempted to arouse black consciousness in America, and who advocated the return of blacks to their ancestral homeland in Africa. Prod. by the Afro-American Arts Theatre, Philadelphia, around 1968. Prod. by the Harlem School of the Arts, New York, 1974. Pub. in *New Plays from the Black Theatre* (Bullins, 1969).

The Layout // Orig. title: **The Layout Letter** (domestic drama, 1 act, 1968). Included in the author's series, **"THE SUNFLOWERS"** [see GROUP OF RELATED PLAYS above]. After the death of a mother, the family receives a letter which she has written to them. Prod. by the Afro-American Arts Theatre, 1969. Prod. by the Freedom Theatre, Philadelphia, 1974.

The Sunflower Majorette (monologue, 1 act, 1969). Included in the author's series, **"THE SUNFLOWERS"** [see GROUP OF RELATED PLAYS above]. Deals with the problems of a woman in love with a married man. Prod. by the Afro-American Arts Theatre, 1969.

Emma (domestic drama, 1 act, 1970). Concerns a black family in the South whose son has been killed in a railway strike. Prod. by the Afro-American Arts Theatre, 1970.

An Untitled Play (domestic drama, 1 act, 1970). A woman's lover comes back to claim her after many years have passed. Prod. by the Afro-American Arts Theatre, 1970.

First Love (drama, 1 act, 1971). Deals with the problem of adolescent love among boys and girls in the eighth grade during the 1950s. Prod. by the Afro-American Arts Theatre, 1971. Prod. at the Billie Holiday Theatre, Brooklyn, NY, June 1974.

In My Many Names and Days (composite of 6 of the author's one-act plays, 1972; individual titles unknown). About the life of a black family. Prod. Off-Bway by the New Fed. Theatre (NFT), 1972. Unpub. script in the Hatch-Billops Collection.

The Candidate (drama, 1974). A black candidate seeks to win an election as mayor. Prod. by NFT, 1974.

In the Deepest Part of Sleep (domestic drama, 2 parts, 1974). A sequel to **In My Many Names and Days** (1972). Continues the life of the black family begun in the earlier play, and focuses on the relationship between an emotionally disturbed mother and her adolescent son. Prod. Off-Bway by the Negro Ensemble Co. (NEC), at St. Marks Playhouse, June 4–30, 1974, for 32 perfs.; dir. by Israel Hicks. With Mary Alice, Todd Davis, Michele Shay, and Charles Weldon.

The Brownsville Raid (historical drama, 3 acts, 1975). "Dramatization of an actual incident in which an entire black army regiment received an honorable discharge, with the collusion of everyone up to and including the President, for an incident of racial violence in which they did not take part."—*The Best Plays of 1976–1977,* p. 335. First prod. by the Eugene O'Neill Theatre Center National Playwrights Conf., Waterford, CT, at the Amphitheatre (outdoors), opening Aug. 5, 1975, for 2 perfs.; dir. by Harold Scott. Prod. by NEC, at Theatre De Lys, Dec. 5, 1976–Jan. 30, 1977, for 112 perfs.; dir. by Israel Hicks. With DOUGLAS TURNER WARD, SAMM-ART WILLIAMS, and ADOLPH CAESAR. Unpub. script in the Hatch-Billops Collection.

Jerry Bland and the Blandelles Featuring Miss Marva James // Orig. title: **Charles Fuller Presents the Dynamic Jerry Bland and the Blandelles, with the Fabulous Miss Marva James** (musical, 3 acts, 1974). The story of an aging blues singer attempting to make a comeback. Prod. Off-Bway by NFT, Spring 1977.

Zooman and the Sign (melodrama, 2 acts, 1980). Examines the crime and punishment of a black teenage Philadelphia youth, Zooman, who has terrorized a whole neighborhood and accidentally killed a 12-year-old black girl in full view of witnesses who are afraid to identify him. In an effort to get someone to come forth and identity his daughter's killer, the girl's father puts up a sign accusing the neighborhood of cowardice. According to Ethel Githii, the play "shows the disintegration and decline of the killer, the dead girl's grieving family, the neighborhood, and society at large."—*Afro-American Writers After 1955: Dramatists and Prose Writers* (Davis & Harris, 1985), p. 108. Won for the author an Obie Award for playwriting. Selected by the Burns Mantle Yearbook *Best Plays* series as a "Best Play" of 1980–81. Prod. Off-Bway by NEC, at Theatre Four, Dec. 7, 1980–Jan. 4, 1981, for 33 perfs.; dir. by Douglas Turner Ward. Featuring Giancarlo Esposito as Zooman, who also won an Obie Award and a Theatre World Award for his perf. Abridged in *The Best Plays of 1980–1981*. Pub. by Samuel French, New York, 1982.

A Soldier's Play (drama, 2 acts, 1981). In the context of a murder mystery, this play examines the roles that black men are often forced to play in a racist society. A tyrannical, race-conscious black technical sergeant, whom both whites and blacks have reason to hate, is murdered just outside a segregated army camp in Louisiana during World War II. Was it the Klan, a white army officer, or one of the black men from his own company who did it? A black captain, who is also an attorney, is sent in to investigate the murder. In a climate of racial hostility and mistrust on the part of both blacks and whites, the captain conducts a thorough and probing investigation leading to a surprising discovery of the murderer and the motives for the crime. Winner of the Pulitzer Prize for Drama, 1982; the New York Drama Critics' Circle Award, 1982, as the Best American Play; the Outer Critics' Circle Award, 1982, as the Best Off-Bway Play; and the Theatre Club Award as Best Play. Also selected by the Burns Mantle Theatre Yearbook *Best Plays* series as a "Best Play" of 1980–81. First prod. Off-Bway by NEC, at Theatre Four, opening Nov. 28, 1981, for 13 months, closing after 481 perfs. in early 1983. Also presented at the Mark Taper Forum in Los Angeles for a long run. Then went on a 13-city tour beginning at the Goodman Theatre in Chicago, June 3, 1983, and ending at the Coconut Grove Playhouse in Miami, May 1984. Both prodns. starred Adolph Caesar as Tech. Sgt. Vernon Waters and Charles Brown as Capt. Richard Davenport, the investigating officer. Also prod. as a film entitled **A Soldier's Story** (1984). Pub. by Hill & Wang, New York, 1983, and by Samuel French, New York, 1983. Abridged in *The Best Plays of 1981–1982* (1982).

A Soldier's Story (feature film, full length: screenplay, 1984). Adapt. from the author's Pulitzer Prize-winning play, **A Soldier's Play** (1981), concerning the investigation by a black captain of the murder of a black sergeant during World War II. [See preceding entry for plot synopsis.] The film was praised by *Essence* magazine (Nov. 1984, pp. 83–84) for its dignified and realistic portrayal of black men, who are "usually portrayed as buffoons and dunces.'' The article goes on to state that ''because the film's characters exhibit a full range of humanity, *A Soldier's Story* represents a first for the Black movie actor and, by extension, a first for the mass-media image of the Black male.'' Prod. by Norman Jewison and Caldix Films Ltd.; dir. by Jewison; released and distributed by Columbia Pictures, 1984. Starring Howard E. Rollins as Capt. Davenport and Adolph Caesar as Tech. Sgt. Vernon Waters. With Patti LaBelle in the cameo role of Big Mary, the owner of a bar. Caesar was nominated for an Academy Award as best supporting actor in 1985.

OTHER PLAYS AND DRAMATIC WORKS:

Roots, Resistance and Renaissance (series of 12 weekly TV scripts, 1967). Telecast over WHY-TV, Channel 12, Philadelphia, 1967. **Love Song for Robert Lee** (1 act, 1968). Prod. by the Afro-American Thespians, at the Heritage House, Philadelphia, 1968. **Ain't Nobody, Sarah, But Me** (1 act, 1969), **Cain** (1 act, 1969), **Indian Giver** (1 act, 1969), and **J.J.'s Game** (1 act, 1969). All included in the author's **''THE SUNFLOW-ERS''** [see GROUP OF RELATED PLAYS above], and prod. by the Afro-American Arts Theatre, Philadelphia, 1969. **Black America** (TV script, half hr., 1970). Telecast on WKYM-TV, Channel 3, Philadelphia, 1970–71. **J.T.** (TV pilot, 1972). Story edited by Fuller. Prod. by WABC-TV, New York, 1972. **The Selling of the President** (TV doc.: additional dialogue only, 1972). Prod. by Franklin Rober Productions, 1972. **Sparrow in Flight** (musical, full length, 1974). Prod. Off-Bway by the AMAS Repertory Theatre, New York, Nov. 1978. **The Sky Is Gray** (TV script, 1980). Adapt. from a short story by Ernest J. Gaines. Prod. on ''The American Short Story Series,'' and telecast on PBS, 1980. **A Gathering of Old Men** (TV film feature, full length; screenplay, 1987). Based on a novel by *Ernest J. Gaines. The elderly black men of a southern community unite to share the blame for the murder of the town's most feared racist. The murder has been committed by only one of them. Telecast on CBS-TV, May 10, 1987, starring Louis Gossett, Jr., as the man who has actually committed the crime, and Richard Widmark as the local sheriff, who is also a racist.

FULLER, LORENZO, Musician, entertainer, and TV coach. Best known for his participation in the original productions of *Kiss Me, Kate* and *Finian's Rainbow*. Also appeared in *St. Louis Woman* (1946) and *The Time of Your Life* (1969).

DRAMATIC WORKS:

A Temporary Island (musical, full length, 1948). With songs by Fuller. Prod. in New York, 1948. **The World's My Oyster** (musical, full length, 1956). By Fuller and Carley Mills. South Sea Island fantasy, with music reminiscent of Cole Porter. Prod. at the Actors Playhouse in Greenwich Village, New York, Aug. 1956, with Fuller as the romantic lead and Butterfly McQueen also in the cast. **Look at Me** (musical, full length, 1962). Music and lyrics by Fuller. Prod. in New York, 1962.

FURMAN, ROGER (1924–1983), Playwright, theatrical designer, actor, and community theatre organizer/director. Studied theatre arts with the Drama Workshop of the New School for Social Research under Edwin Piscator. Apprenticed under Rafael Rijospray at the National Theatre of Puerto Rico. Was a student of the American Negro Theatre (ANT) under †Abram Hill. Designed scenery and costumes for ANT, 1947–48. Designed scenes for the motion picture *The Cool World* and was asst. director to OSSIE DAVIS in the filming of *Cotton Comes to Harlem* (1969). Founder of the Negro Arts Players, New York, 1950s, and the New Heritage Theatre (NHT), now called the New Heritage Repertory Theatre (NHRT). A founding director and member of the Board of Directors of the Black Theatre Alliance (BTA) in New York, 1960s. Performed in the films *Georgia, Georgia* (1972) and *The Long Night* (1976). Directed the Off-Broadway productions of *The Three-Penny Opera* (1972), *Madam Odum* (1973), *Striver's Row* (1974), and *Trucking* (1974), as well as the production tour of *Harlem Heyday* (with the Voices, Inc., 1973–74). Taught black theatre courses at NYU and Rutgers Univ. Field supervisor of HARYOU Act Cultural Program, 1963–71. Coauthor, *The Black Book* (1974). Winner of the AUDELCO Board of Directors Award, 1973. *Pertinent Address:* New Heritage Repertory Theatre, P.O. Box 146, Manhattanville, New York, NY 10027.

REPRESENTATIVE PLAYS AND DRAMATIC WORKS:

Three Shades of Harlem (comedy-drama, 3 acts, 1964). Coauthor, with DORIS BRUNSON. Depicts the problems (shade 1), joys (shade 2), and hopes (shade 3) of the Harlem community. Prod. by NHT, in repertory, 1964–66, and presented at the Harlem YWCA, opening June 18, 1965, where it played for a number of weekends; then moved to Walter Cooper's Sunset Ballroom in Harlem, where it continued to play throughout the summer of 1965; opened again at the Harlem YWCA, Feb. 18, 1966.

Hip, Black and Angry (variety program, full length, 1967). Conceived and dir. by Furman, using pieces written by *Jim Williams, *Nathaniel Juni, *Warren Cuney, *Tad Joans, *Carl Boissiere, and *Frances Ernest Kobina Parks from South Africa. Prod. by NHT, in repertory, and presented at the following locations: Intermediate School 201, Harlem, April 1967, June 23, 1967, July 20 and 21, 1967; Bancroft H.S., Wilmington, DE, March 1968; 318 Livonia Ave., Brooklyn, March 15–17, 1968; Boston Technical H.S., Roxbury, MA, April 27, 1968; River St. School, Red Bank, NJ, Oct. 19, 1968; Mt. Kisco School, Westchester, NY, Dec. 1, 1968; Westchester Women's Club, Mt. Vernon, NY, March 1, 1969; Intermediate School 201, Harlem, Feb. 20 and 27, 1971; and John Jay Coll. of Criminal Justice, New York, May 2, 1972.

The Gimmick (fantasy, 1 act, 1970). All the characters are social outcasts of a kind, and the events are made to unfold as in a dream or nightmare. Prod. at Columbia Univ. School of the Arts, Nave Theatre, New York, March 27 and May 28, 1970. Unpub. script in the Hatch-Billops Collection.

To Kill a Devil (drama, 1 act, 1970). "Takes a look at a black mother who loves her son but is trapped by her own need for love that the son simply cannot satisfy."—*Times-Picayune* (New Orleans), Jan. 16, 1972. Prod. by the New Heritage Players, and presented at the Columbia Univ. School of the Arts, Nave Theatre, New York, March 27–28, 1970; presented at NHT, Nov. 19, 1972. Prod. by the Free Southern Theatre's Student Workshop, Jan. 1972. Prod. by the East River Players, at the Black Theatre Alliance annual festival, New York, 1972. Excerpt (1 scene) pub. in *Black Scenes* (Childress, 1971). Unpub. script in the Hatch-Billops Collection.

The Long Black Block (drama with music, 2 acts, 1971). Music dir. by Jackie McLean. Concerns the occupants of a Harlem tenement building. According to the author, it "deals with the aspects of Black people's struggles against apathy, exploitation, dissension, and the destructive moral crises brought on by the drug plague. It is full of vignettes based on the 'long black blocks' in the Black communities all across this country.''—*Black Theatre* #6, 1972, p. 3. Prod. by the NHT in repertory, 1972–73, with its premiere perf. at its theatre on 125th St., Jan. 21, 1972. Presented at the Brooklyn Academy of Music, Sept. and Nov. 1972. Again presented at NHT's 125th St. theatre, Nov. 19, 1972 and July 20, 1973.

Fat Tuesday (musical comedy, full length, 1975). Subtitled "Drawers Down, Bottoms Up," and apparently based on a nonmusical comedy by that title, written by *Dee Robinson, who also wrote the music and lyrics of *Fat Tuesday*. Centers on the activities in a New Orleans brothel during the 1930s. The title is an English rendition of the term *Mardi Gras*. Prod. by the New Heritage Players, in repertory, opening Oct. 1975, dir. by Furman. Won AUDELCO Awards in 1976 for Louis Meyers (performer) and Joseph Gandy (scenic designer).

OTHER PLAYS AND DRAMATIC WORKS:

Fool's Paradise (1 act, 1952). Prod. by the Negro Art Players, at the Elks Theatre, New York, Aug. 25, 1952, on triple bill with ALICE CHILDRESS's *Florence* and LANGSTON HUGHES's *Soul Gone Home*. **The Quiet Laughter** (1 act, 1952). Prod. by the Negro Art Players, New York, 1952. **Live Soul Drama** (1967). Prod. by NHT at Purple Manor, 65 E. 136th St., New York, Sept. 3, 1967. **Renegade Theatre** (1968). Prod. by NHT, at Purple Manor, New York, March 3, 1968. **The Spring Thing** (readings of black poetry, 1969). Prod. by NHT, at Town Hall, New York City, May 16, 1969. **Another Shade of Harlem** (comedy-drama, 1970). Related to the author's **Three Shades of Harlem** (1964) [see above]. Furman's most recent plays include **4 O'Clock on a Rainy Afternoon** and **Monsieur Baptiste the Con Man** (comedy, adapt. from Molière's *Tartuffe*).

G

GAINES, J. E. ("Sonny Jim" Gaines) (1928–   ), Playwright, actor, and director. Former member of the New Lafayette Theatre (NLT) in New York City, where he used the stage name of "Sonny Jim" for his work as an actor. Described by ED BULLINS as "the best playwright I know."—*The Theme Is Blackness: The Corner and Other Plays* (1973). He performed in Bullins's *In the Wine Time* (1968); *The Fabulous Miss Marie* (1971), for which he won an Obie Award for acting; and *The Corner* (1972), which he also directed at the Public Theatre. Other acting credits include *What the Winesellers Buy* (Off-Bway, 1972); the film *The Long Night* (1976); and TV appearances on "Good Times" (1976) and "Sanford and Son" (1977). Won a Drama Desk Award as most promising playwright, and was a Variety Poll nominee, for his play **Don't Let It Go to Your Head** (1970). Won both the Obie Award and an AUDELCO Award for his play **What If It Had Turned Up Heads** (1972). *Address:* 2349 Seventh Ave., New York, NY 10030.

PLAYS AND DRAMATIC WORKS:
Don't Let It Go to Your Head (drama, 3 acts, 1970). An American prisoner of war returns home to find that his wife has been unfaithful. Prod. by the New Federal Theatre (NFT), at the Henry St. Theatre, New York, opening Jan. 17, 1972; dir. by GILBERT MOSES. Won for the author a Drama Desk Award for 1971–72, as most promising playwright. Unpub. script in the Hatch-Billops Collection and the Schomburg Collection.

What If It Had Turned Up Heads (drama, 2 acts, 1972). (Title has also been cited as *What If It Turns Up Heads.)* Music and lyrics coauthored with *James Macbeth. Dramatizes the seamier side of black life among a group of so-called drunks (including one woman) who frequent a basement flat where wine is sold. First prod. as a workshop production at the American Place Theatre, New York, March 1972; dir. by ROBERT MACBETH. Cast included Whitman Mayo, Betty Howard, George Miles, and the author ("Sonny Jim"). Prod. by NLT, Oct. 13, 1972; dir. by William E. Lathan, featuring Carole Cole and the author. Won an Obie Award for the play, and AUDELCO awards for both the author and the director. Pub. in *The New Lafayette Theatre Presents* (Bullins, 1974).

Sometimes a Hard Head Makes a Soft Behind (drama, 1 act, 1972). "A play about a Harlem family with a drug problem . . . who cannot stand to have their coats pulled by the Black people who love them."—*Jet,* Aug. 10, 1972, p. 52. Also described as being "about pushers, junkies, whores, and their hangups."—*Black World,* April 1973, p. 17. Prod. by NLT, opening July 28, 1978; dir. by Bill Lathan. Unpub. script in the Schomburg Collection.

Heaven and Hell's Agreement (drama, full length, 1974). Subtitled "A Myth." Related to the author's play **Don't Let It Go to Your Head** (1970). "A soldier presumed to be dead in Vietnam returns to find his place again with his wife and mother in the family environment."—*The Best Plays of 1973–1974.* Prod. as a workshop production by the Negro Ensemble Co. (NEC), at St. Marks Playhouse, New York, April 9–14, for 8 perfs.; dir. by Anderson Johnson. Cast included Nick Latour, Lea Scott, Michele Shay, Leon Morenzie, Gary Bolling, Ronald Sanchez, Mary Alice, and Red Davis. Unpub. script in the Hatch-Billops Collection.

Twenty Year Friends (drama with music, 3 acts [9 scenes], 1984). Described by Al Morris in the *New York Amsterdam News* (undated clipping, March 1984) as "a story about a middle-aged couple who learn about love and friendship when [they are] faced with a crisis." LIONEL MITCHELL, writing in the same paper, April 14, 1985, states that the play not only concerns the 20–year friendship of the couple, but also "is a story about a group of hustlers who know their businesses are dying but they are trying to come together before they do." Prod. by WOODIE KING, JR., and NFT, at the Colonnades Theatre, March 22–April 8, 1984, for 15 perfs.; dir. by Andre Mtumi. With Clebert Ford, Joyce Jospen, Jack Neal, Roscoe Orman, and Louise Stubbs.

GAINES, "SONNY JIM." See GAINES, J. E.

GARRETT, JIMMY (1944?–   ), Activist-playwright. Born in Dallas, TX. Reared in Los Angeles, CA. Educated at San Francisco State Coll., where he was chairman of the Black Student Union. Worked as an organizer with SNCC in Mississippi and Los Angeles. A discovery of AMIRI BARAKA. From 1969 to 1974 headed the Center for Black Education, a community school in Washington, DC. In 1975 he was director of the Black Studies Program at the Claremont Colls., Claremont, CA. He has written several articles on education, politics, and Pan-Africanism, including a historical sketch of the Sixth Pan African Congress in *Black World* (March 1975).

PLAY:

(And) We Own the Night ("agitprop" melodrama, 1 act, 1967). Subtitled "A Play of Blackness." Takes its title from a poem by Amiri Baraka, which also serves as an epigraph to the play. A romanticized view of the black revolution, in which a young black militant, dying from wounds that he has received in a race war, kills his own mother—portrayed as a symbol of the black matriarch and the "White man's nigger"— in order to assert his black manhood and his belief in a new value system for blacks which must be brought about by any means necessary, even the destruction of one's own family. First prod. by the Spirit House Movers and Players, Newark, NJ, 1977; dir. by

Amiri Baraka. Pub. in *Black Fire* (Jones & Neal, 1968), pp. 527–40. In *The Drama Review,* Summer 1968, pp. 62–69. In *Right On!* (Chambers & Moon, 1970).

GATEWOOD, L. A., Playwright. Formerly associated with the Karamu Theatre and the Humanist Theatre in Cleveland, OH.

PLAYS:
A Place // Orig. title: **Ghetto: A Place** (1 act, c. 1973). About the problems of ghetto life. Prod. by the Karamu Theatre and by the Humanist Theatre, Cleveland, c. 1973. **Jones** (1 act, c. 1973). About drug addiction. Prod. by the Karamu Theatre and the Humanist Theatre, Cleveland, c. 1973.

GEARY, BRUCE O., Playwright. An alumnus of the Sonia Sanchez Writers Workshop, held at the Countee Cullen Lib. in Harlem, 1970–71.

PLAY:
Cadillac Alley (drama, 1 act, 1971). Deals with the negative forces that plague ghetto blacks—mainly dope and prostitution. Pub. in **Three Hundred and Sixty Degrees of Blackness Comin at You** (Sanchez, 1971).

GENTRY, MINNIE (Minnie Lee Watson) (1915–   ), Playwright, actress (stage, screen, TV, and radio), singer, composer, and poet. Born in Norfolk, VA. Received a Tony Award for *Ain't Supposed to Die a Natural Death* (1971). Films include **Georgia, Georgia** (1972) and *Claudine* (1974). TV appearances include *Sojourner* (on ''General Electric Theatre,'' 1976). *Address:* 400 W. 42rd St., New York, NY 10036.

PLAY:
My House Is Falling Down (2 acts, 1975). Public reading by the Frank Silvera Writers' Workshop (FSWW), New York, at the Martinique Theatre, May 1975. Unpub. script in the FSWW Archives/Schomburg Collection.

GERIMA, HAILE, Ethiopian playwright, screenwriter, and director.

DRAMATIC WORKS:
Bush Mama (play, 1970s). **Bush Mama** (screenplay, c. 1977). Based on the author's play by the same title. Prod. or distributed by Transcontinental Film Center, Berkeley, CA., and listed in its 1977–78 catalog, p. 44.

GIBSON, P. J. (Patricia Joann Gibson, or Pat Gibson), Playwright and teacher. Winner of two AUDELCO Awards, one for playwright of the year, and the other for production of the year—both for her play **Long Time Since Yesterday** (1958), which also won awards for direction, costuming, and scenic design. Born in Pittsburgh, PA. Grew up in Trenton, NJ. Currently resides in New York City. Educated at Keuka Coll., Keuka Park, NY (B.A., 1973), and Brandeis Univ., Waltham, MA., under a Shubert Fellowship (M.F.A., 1975). Also studied under J. P. Miller (*Days of Wine and Roses*). Production stage manager, Voices, Inc., New York, 1971–73. Scriptwriter, public service announcements, Office of Youth Development/Human Development, U.S. Dept. of Health, Education and Welfare, 1973. Administrator, Summer Introductory Preparatory Program, Brandeis Univ., 1974. Creative arts dir., Roxbury Children's Theatre, Dorchester, MA., 1974–75. Instr. of drama, creative writing, and fundamental writing skills, Boston Coll., Chestnut Hill, MA., 1975–76. Asst. theatrical director, "Say Brother," WGBH-TV, Boston, 1976–77. Project administrator, Rites and Reason Theatre, Brown Univ., Providence, RI, 1976–77. Instr., creative writing/playwriting, Frederick Douglass Creative Arts Center, New York, 1978–83. Instr., creative writing, Project Reach Youth/Family Reception Center, Brooklyn, NY, sponsored by Poets and Writers, Inc., 1979–82. Playwright-in-residence, CETA Arts Program, Cultural Council Foundation/ Black Theatre Alliance, New York, 1979–80. Instr., creative writing, Teachers and Writers Collaborative, New York, 1980. Instr., creative writing, and mentor, independent study, Coll. of New Rochelle, NY, 1982–present. Guest lecturer at numerous colleges, schools, and organizations, including Boston Coll., 1975; Quinnipiac Coll., 1976; Music and Drama Inst., Khartoum, Sudan, 1978; Afro-American Cultural Center, Yale Univ., 1981. Consultant to Educational Testing Service, 1969–74; Massachusetts Desegregation Magnet Program, 1975; Third World Cinema Productions, New York, 1977–78. Author of publications for Media Assocs., Inc., Washington, DC, including *Basic Management* (4 vols.), *Building an Institution, Ideas into Practice,* and *Dealing with Space.* In addition to the AUDELCO Awards mentioned above, she was recipient of a commission from Rhode Island Committee for the Humanities to write her historical drama, **My Mark, My Name,** 1977–78; NEA playwriting grant; artist-in-residence, Music and Drama Inst., Khartoum, Key to the City, Mayor of Indianapolis, IN. *Address:* 400 W. 43rd St. #14L, New York, NY 10036.

GROUP OF RELATED PLAYS:

"PRIVATE HELLS, SKETCHES IN REALITY—A TRILOGY" (program of 3 one-act plays, 1981). Includes **You Must Die Before My Eyes as I Have Before Yours** (1981), **"But I Feed the Pigeons"/"Well, I Watch the Sun"** (1981), and **Can You Tell Me Who They Is?** (1981). Prod. by the Frederick Douglass Creative Arts Center, New York, May 1981. [AUTHOR'S NOTE: "These three plays are accompanied by satirical, dramatic commercials. The One Acts may be produced separately from the trilogy."]

REPRESENTATIVE PLAYS AND DRAMATIC WORKS:

Shameful in Your Eyes (drama, 3 acts, 1971). A young woman is forced to live with a fanatical religious aunt in a small southern New Jersey town. Her development into womanhood and love is suppressed by the aunt's cruelty. Prod. at Keuka Coll., Keuka Park, NY, Feb. 1971.

The Black Woman (poetic prose drama of monologues, 1–3 acts [length variable], 1971). Traces the black woman—her life, survival, and pain—chronologically through American history. Twenty characters, all women. First prod. in a one-act version, at Keuka Coll., Nov. 1971. Prod. in a three-act version at SUNY/Cortland, NY, March 1972.

Void Passage (realistic/surrealistic drama, 1 act, 1973). The setting is a vast pyramidal structure considered the "void passage." Addresses the conflict of two women who have had to live with the title "strong Black woman." The two women at first distrust one another and later find solace in each other. A companion piece to the author's **Konvergence** (below), with which it was prod. on double bill by Players Co., Trenton, NJ, March 1973; Rites and Reason, Providence, RI, April 1977 (as part of its "Image and Reality" project); and Kuumba Workshop, Chicago, 1978.

Konvergence (drama, 1 act, 1973). In the setting of a mountain lodge, a couple seeks reconciliation after a year's separation. A companion piece to **Void Passage** (above), with which it was prod. on a double bill by Players Co., Trenton, NJ, March 1973; Rites and Reason, Providence, April 1977 (as part of its "Image and Reality" project); and Kuumba Workshop, Chicago, 1978. Also prod. alone at the Oakland Ensemble Theatre, Dec. 1982.

The Ninth Story Window (drama, 1 act, 1974). A young woman, plagued by accusations of causing the tragic death of her baby sister, finally learns (after many years) the truth of the circumstances which led to the tragedy. Prod. at Brandeis Univ., Waltham, MA, Nov. 1974.

Spida Bug (children's play, 1 act, 1975). In the setting of an isolated construction site, some children learn the meaning of "trust." Prod. at Brandeis Univ., Waltham, MA, April 1975. Also presented in schools of the Boston School System, May 1975.

My Mark, My Name (research-to-performance play, 2 acts, 1978). Apparently commissioned by Rites and Reason, Providence, RI. Based on the historical data of the First Black Regiment of Rhode Island. Drama addresses the world facing the "freed" black men and women after the American Revolution. It is a time when "freedom" does not mean security, and a slave in the midst of freed men must choose which life he will lead. First prod. by Soul People's Repertory, Indianapolis, Feb. 1981. For this prod., the author was presented the key to the city of Indianapolis. Prod. at the International Black Arts Festival, Richard Allen Center for Culture and Art, New York, Aug. 1982.

The Androgyny (surrealistic/symbolic drama, 2 acts, 1979). Set in a deserted coliseum area of a park, this play concerns the androgynous nature of people and the purging of "life lies." Prod. at the Cardboard Clowns Theatre, Frankfurt, Germany, 1979. Unpub. script in the FSWW Archives/Schomburg Collection.

Ain't Love Grand? (poetic drama with music, 2 acts, 1980). A play of humor, reality, and the triangles of love, set in "Any Place USA." The four couples involved range in age from the teens to the late forties. Prod. on U.S. tour, 1980. Prod. by the Black Spectrum Theatre, St. Albans, Queens, NY, Feb. 1984.

Miss Ann Don't Cry No More (drama, 2 acts, 1980). A house in a northern urban city is divided into four separate apartments. The drama reflects the lives, conflicts, desires, passions, and "deferred dreams" of those who live in the house. Earned for the playwright an NEA Grant. Prod. by the Frederick Douglass Creative Arts Center, New York, March 1980.

Angel (realistic/stylized drama, 2 acts, 1981). In the setting of a small town, four women find themselves living the remainder of their lives without men. One resorts to booze, one to religion, one to bed partners, one to a man created by her mind—"Angel," a suspected incubus. She must choose between a living man who pursues her and "Angel." Prod. as a staged reading at the Family Theatre, New York, March 1981.

You Must Die Before My Eyes as I Have Before Yours (satire, 1 act, 1981). A wife who has given up her identity for her spouse rebels, taking both their lives. Prod. in

1981, as part of the trilogy **"PRIVATE HELLS, SKETCHES IN REALITY"** [see GROUP OF RELATED PLAYS above]. **"But I Feed the Pigeons"/"Well, I Watch the Sun"** (satire, 1 act, 1981). An obese submarine-eating woman and a homosexual male who watches from the rooftop are confronted by the religious aspects of their lifestyles. The two fight the conflict of philosophy, religion, and reality as presented to them by a born-again Christian. Prod. 1981, as part of the trilogy **"PRIVATE HELLS, SKETCHES IN REALITY."**

Can You Tell Me Who They Is? (satire, 1 act, 1981). Addresses the individual stories of the characters and the question "Are they really insane?" Prod. in 1981, as part of the trilogy **"PRIVATE HELLS, SKETCHES IN REALITY"**.

Unveilings // Orig. title: **The Unveiling of Abigail** (drama, 2 acts, 1981). An ex-college professor chooses to spend her last days on her parents' vast estate in Virginia. It is her birthday. Her gifts are the revelation of lies, deception, and cheated years with the man she loved. First presented, under its orig. title, at the Torino, Italy, Black Arts Festival, July 1981.

Brown Silk and Magenta Sunsets (stylized drama, 2 acts, 1981). In the setting of the luxurious apartment of Lena Larden Salvinoni, a wealthy recluse, three life-size paintings, representative of persons in her life, come alive and confront her with the effects of her passionate and obsessive love. The subjects of the paintings, portrayed by actors, remain frozen in time until brought to life in the mind and world of Lena Salvinoni. Staged reading of one act at the Frederick Douglass Creative Arts Center, New York, Nov. 1981. Pub. in *Nine Plays by Black Women* (Wilkerson, 1986).

Clean Sheets Can't Soil (drama with music, 2 acts, 1983). A woman fleeing from her emotions is brought back to the source of her fears only to find that she is not the only member of the family who is running. Described by the producers as "the tale of a professional singer, returning to Providence [RI] and her family and musical roots. . . . [It] is a moving portrait of black families, churches and, most of all, the soul of gospel music."—Program Notes. Prod. by Rites and Reason, Providence, RI, March 25–April 7, 1983; dir. by Akin Babatunde.

Long Time Since Yesterday (drama, 2 acts, 1985). A group of ex-college women is reunited after the suicide of one of their friends. Through an examination of their experiences, their strengths and weaknesses, and the discovery of lesbianism among the group, their lives are changed forever. Twice prod. by the New Federal Theatre, Feb. 1–24, and Oct. 1985; dir. by Bette Howard. These prodns. won five AUDELCO awards, including Best Dramatic Production and Playwright of the Year, 1985. Pub. by Samuel French, New York, 1985.

OTHER PLAYS AND DRAMATIC WORKS:

Doing It to Death (1977). Public reading by FSWW, Nov. 12, 1977. Unpub. script in the FSWW Archives/Schomburg Collection. **The Zappers and the Shopping Bag Lady** (1 act, 1979). Prod. on summer tour, New York, Aug. 1979. **"The Edge of Night"** (TV script, 1 episode, 1981). Televised Aug. 1981. **A Man, Masculine and Glass Fist** (realistic drama, 1 act, pre-1985). Concerns a married couple stuck in the routine of their relationship. The wife, in anger and frustration, demands that her husband "be a man." This results in her finding the true meaning of the man her husband is. **Marie** (realistic drama with song, 1 act, pre-1985). A conjure woman's preparation to do battle with the "man thief" is interrupted by the presence of an interviewer seeking information about the "woman in her." **In Search of Me** (drama of adolescence, 1 act, pre-1985). In a courtroom setting, four teenage girls and two teenage boys defend their actions, conditions, needs, and addictions.

GILLIAM, THEODORE E. (Ted), Black theatre director, college professor, and playwright. Executive and artistic director of Dashiki Project Theatre, New Orleans, and asst. prof. of drama at Loyola Univ. in New Orleans. Received the M.F.A. from Yale Univ. School of Drama and the Ph.D. from Tulane Univ. *Address:* 2559 Wisteria St., New Orleans, LA 70122; or c/o Dashiki Project Theatre, P.O. Box 8323, New Orleans, LA 70182. Theatre location: Contemporary Arts Center, 900 Camp St., New Orleans, LA 70130.

PLAYS AND DRAMATIC WORKS:
What You Say? (or How Christopher Columbus Discovered Ray Charles) (children's play, 1 act, 1970). Based on a story ("Columbus") by *Flip Wilson. Prod. by Dashiki Project Theatre, New Orleans, Summer 1970. **The Pride of Lions** (family drama, 3 acts, 1973). Based, in part, on two short stories from *Lover Man* by Alston Anderson. Prod. by Dashiki Project Theatre, 1973. **Mahalia** (doc. narrative with songs, 1 act, 1982). Subtitled "My Name Is Naomi." Prod. by Dashiki Project Theatre in collaboration with the Desire Community Housing Corp., at two churches in New Orleans. Expanded into present full length form, and presented at the New Orleans Jazz and Heritage Festival, 1983. **Praisesong!** (adaptn., first draft, 1983). From the novel *Praisesong for the Widow* by *Paule Marshall. Work in progress, planned in collaboration with the author of the novel.

GLADDEN, FRANK A., Poet, short-story writer, and playwright. Born in Winnsboro, SC. Co-head of the fiction section of the DC Black Writers Workshop, Washington, DC. Has published short stories and poems in *Black World* and other periodicals.

PLAY:
The Distant Brother (1972). Prod. in Washington, DC, 1972.

GLANVILLE, MAXWELL (1918–   ), Veteran actor, director, playwright, producer, journalist, editor, poet, writer, and teacher. Has appeared in numerous Off-Broadway, Broadway, community theatre, summer stock, and touring productions, as well as in films and on television. Credited with having trained numerous black actors and playwrights who have gone on to professional careers in the theatre and films. Born in Antigua, British West Indies. Educated in New York City, where he attended P.S. 89, Jr. H.S. 139, DeWitt Clinton H.S., and the New School for Social Research (on scholarship), 1942–43, studying acting and drama. Served three years in the U.S. Air Corps, 1943–46. Gained early theatrical experience as actor and member of the Board of Directors with the American Negro Theatre (ANT) in Harlem, c. 1942–43 and 1946–50. Appeared in ANT productions of *Natural Man* (1941), *Home Is the Hunter* (1942), *Walk Hard* (Bway debut, 1946), *Anna Lucasta* (Bway, 1946), and *Freight* (1950). Other theatrical affiliations include People's Drama (actor); Coordinating Council of Negro Performers (Board of Directors); Committee for the Negro in the Arts (actor, producer); Greenwich Mews Theatre (actor, producer, stage manager, member of Board of Directors); Bed-Stuy Theatre (director, drama instr.); CETA Program (Theatre for the Forgotten) (drama instructor, Rikers Island); St. Christopher School for Children (drama instr., producer, and director); Ward's Island, Drug Rehabilitation Program (theatre arts); Burlap Summer Theatre (Club Baron, New York); Skyline Theatre (Theresa Hotel, Harlem); Glanville-Jett Productions; Glanville-Mayfield Productions; Glanville-Greene Productions. Founder and artistic director, American Community Theatre (ACT), now known as the ACT/Pro/Workshop, Inc., 1958–present. Currently director, Drama Dept., Theatre International, Inc. Coproducer of *Alice in Wonder, The Other Foot,* and *A World Full of Men* (1952); also director of the first two plays. In addition to productions of ANT, his extensive stage acting credits include *How Long Till Summer* (1969), *The Autumn Garden* (1951), *Take a Giant Step* (1953), *In Splendid Error* (1954), *Cat on a Hot Tin Roof* (1955), *The Shrike* (1955), *Interlock* (1958), *Simply Heavenly* (1959), *Nat Turner* (1960), *The Cool World* (1960), *Golden Boy* (1964), *We Bombed in New Haven* (1969), *Zelda* (1969), *Lady Day* (1972), *Light in the Cellar* (1975), and *Branches from the Same Tree* (1980). Films include *Cotton Comes to Harlem* (1970), *The Out of Towners* (1970), and *Come Back Charleston Blue* (1972). Has appeared in more than 75 TV shows. Former newspaper columnist for several New York newspapers, including *Amsterdam News, Daily News, New York Age,* Chicago *Defender* (New York edition), and *Big Red* (Brooklyn); many of his articles on black theatre history have been published in the latter. Author of more than a thousand poems, many of them published in the *Amsterdam News* (1932–35) and other periodicals. Has published two books, *The Bitch,* an autobiographical account of his life in the theatre, and *The Bonus,* a novel, apparently based on his play by the same title. Other memberships include Frank Silvera Writers' Workshop, AEA, AFTRA, SAG, and American Federation of Teachers. Recipient of numerous awards, including three poetry awards, from the Junior Page of *Amsterdam News,* 1932–35; Rosenwald Scholarship, 1943 (declined because of induction into the U.S. Air Corps); YMCA Community Service Award for contributions in the theatre, 1954; Bedford-Stuyvesant Civic Club (Brooklyn) Award for community work in theatre, 1972; American Community Theatre Award from members of ACT for dedication and direction from 1958–80; and WLIB Community Civic Award for contribution to the arts. *Address:* 775 Concourse Village East, Bronx, NY 10451.

REPRESENTATIVE PLAYS AND DRAMATIC WORKS:
Swing Wedding (short skit, 1945). A wedding in swingtime! Chanted and spiced with slang. Performed at Champaign, IL, USO, 1945, and Harlem YMCA, 1947.

Subway Sadie (comedy, 1 act, 1955). With Charles Griffin. About a lady who makes a subway station her home. Performed at Greenwich Mews Theatre, New York, 1955.

Long Stretch—Short Haul (romantic drama, full length, 1960). Triangular love relationships among three unemployed actors, a woman and two men. She loves one who is indifferent, while another loves her to whom she is indifferent. Prod. by ACT, 1969, with presentations later in Brownsville, Brooklyn, and other locations in New York.

The Bonus (comedy, 1 act, 1961). Prod. under several titles. A newly married couple is visited by the wife's off-beat mother while the couple is on vacation. Whether to leave or stay and entertain Mother-in-law is the dilemma facing the newlyweds. Prod. by ACT; Clark Center YWCA; Westchester Community Theatre; Bed-Stuy Civic Theatre, Brooklyn; Yonkers Community Theatre; and other New York community groups.

Cindy (children's play, 1 act, 1970). Black adaptn. of the Cinderella story. Prod. by ACT, 1962, the Adam Clayton Powell, Jr., Theatre, New York, 1976, and the Drew Hamilton Community Center, 1976.

Dance to the Nosepicker's Drum (drama, 2 acts, 1970). Coauthor, with RUDY GRAY. Domestic drama involving interrelationships among three generations of a black family, focusing particularly on the relationships between a young boy and his estranged mother and father. The boy steals to draw attention to himself, while the parents are too busy with their problems to give him their proper attention. Prod. by ACT, 1970, and subsequently by Clarke Center YWCA and by Concourse Village Community Center, Bronx, New York.

The Wire (screenplay, 1973). Coauthor, with GERTRUDE GREENIDGE. Based on police files of an actual case involving a Harlem policeman who goes undercover to solve his father's murder, linked to dope-dealing.

Twit // Orig. titles: **Twit for Twa'** and **Twit for 'Wat** (musical farce, full length, 1974). Book coauthored with Gertrude Greenidge. Musical score by *Ben F. Carter. Additional lyrics by Bessye Scott. Loose adaptn. of Shakespeare's comedy *Measure for Measure*, set in the country of Blackolovia, "where Blacks rule and sex without marriage is a hanging offense." —*New York Amsterdam News*, June 28, 1986, p. 32 (Fuller). As in the orig. play, the Mayor hands over the government of his country to a hypocrite who promptly revives an old edict banning fornication, thus bringing near tragedy into the lives of several characters. The mayor, however, remains on the scene in disguise, and at the end "villains are unmasked and everything ends happily." Book and lyrics completed 1974; music completed 1979. Public reading at New Florida Theatre, New York, under one of the orig. titles. Full prodn. by Cynthia Belgrave Artist (CBA) Theatre Workshop, at Long Island Univ.'s Triangle Theatre, Brooklyn, June 19–29, 1986; dir. by Belgrave. With Randy Flood, Lawrence James, David Morris, and Lillias White in the leading roles.

OTHER PLAYS AND DRAMATIC WORKS:
For Any Evil (3 acts, 1960). **The Injectors** (playlet, c. 1960). Agents of the devil convene to discuss improving their lot. **The Cycle** (1 act, pre-1970). Coauthor, with Roberta Watson. Performed at the Harlem Branch YMCA, at Drew Hamilton Community Center; and at James Monroe School, Bronx. **A Walking Disorder** (screenplay, full length, 1970). An unmarried 16-year-old boy with five children in Minnesota's "Harlem" has no roots but finds his way with his (adopted) integrated family when faced with an unusual set of circumstances. **China Gold** (short playlet—an acting exercise, 1983). Two methadone clinic attendants in street dialogue spiced with their habit and habits. **The Commutables** (1 act, pre-1985). Emotional involvement of two couples linked by commuting between Harlem and Westchester. The setting is the 125th St. Park Ave. Station.

GLENN, ROBERT, Director and playwright. Resides in New York City. Directed the New York productions of *Soul Gone Home* (1959), *Victims of Duty* (1960), *Time to Go* (1960), and *The Coggerers* (1960), as well as his own adaptations cited below.

DRAMATIC WORKS:

Shakespeare in Harlem (poetic collage, full length, 1959). Adapt. from the poetry of LANGSTON HUGHES. Music by *Margaret Bonds. The title was taken from one of Hughes's earlier volumes, *Shakespeare in Harlem* (1942), but most of the poems came from Hughes's *Montage of a Dream Deferred* (1951). Prod. during the 1959–60 season at various locations in New York City—first Off-Bway at the Theatre De Lys (ANTA Matinee Series), then at the White Barn Theatre—all directed by Glenn. Prod. by the Karamu Theatre, Cleveland, April 1961. **God's Trombones** (poetic collage, full length, 1960). Adapt. from †James Weldon Johnson's book of poems by the same title. Prod. in New York, Feb. 1960; dir. by Glenn.

GOODWIN, ROBERT L., Television and film scriptwriter, film producer, and director. Started writing and producing stage plays in 1948. Prior to 1970 had written TV scripts for seven major TV series, as well as two screenplays which as yet have not been produced. In 1970 he founded Robert L. Goodwin Productions, his own independent motion picture company.

DRAMATIC WORKS:

(TV scripts for the following shows, all pre-1970s.) **"Bonanza," "Love American Style," "Julia," "And Then Came Bronson," "The Outcasts," "Uptight,"** and **"Dundee and the Culhane."** Two filmstrips, titles unknown, both pre-1970s, one for Dick Clark Productions, and the other for the Mirisch Brothers. **Black Chariot** (film: screenplay, 1970). Concerns the efforts of a young black man to become involved in the black civil rights struggle. Prod. by Robert L. Goodwin Productions, 1970; dir. by author, with financial backing from the Black Muslims, a few black professionals in the city of Los Angeles, and a number of black film and TV stars, including Diahann Carroll, Barbara McNair, William Marshall, Maidie Norman, and Bernie Casey, who starred in the prodn.

GORDONE, CHARLES (1925–   ), Actor, director, and playwright. The first black winner of the Pulitzer Prize for drama, for his **No Place to Be Somebody,** 1970. Born in Cleveland, OH; grew up in Elkhart, IN. Educated at Los Angeles State Coll. (B.A. in acting, 1952) and NYU, TV Workshop (Certificate, 1961). Served for a time in the U.S. Air Force, earning the rank of second lieutenant. Married; one daughter. Moved to New York, where he tried his hand at acting while working in a Greenwich Village bar. There he had experiences and met characters which he was later to use in **No Place.** Won an Obie Award in 1964 for his performance as George in an all-black production of *Of Mice and Men*. Other New York stage performances include *The Climate of Eden* (1952), *Mrs. Patterson* (1955), *Fortunato* (1956), *The Blacks* (1961/65), *Faust* (1959), *The Trials of Brother Jero* (1967), *Escurial* (Actors Studio), *Crazy Horse Have Jenny Now* (NLT), *Liliom* (AMDA Studio One), and his own theatrical tour de force, **Gordone Is a Mutha** (1970). In New York he directed *Faust* at Judson's Poet's Theatre, 1959; *Peer Gynt* at the Bowery Theatre, 1959; *Tobacco Road* and *Three Men on a Horse* at the Vantage Theatre, 1960; *Detective Story, Moon of the Caribbees* and *Hell Bent for Heaven* at the Equity Lib.

Theatre, 1960; and *Hallway* at Curt Dempster's Ensemble Studio Theatre, 1982. Cofounder, with Susan Kouyomjian, of American Stage in Berkeley, CA., where he has directed numerous productions. Film credits include production manager, U.S. Information Agency documentary for *The Negro in America* (1963), and assoc. producer and casting director for *Nothing but a Man* (1963) and *Black Like Me* (1963). In 1981 he was writing screenplays in Hollywood for Paramount Pictures. Instr., Cell Block Theatre, Yardville and Bordontown detention centers, NJ, 1977–78; instr. of Playmaking, New School for Social Research, Sept. 1978–Jan. 1979. Cofounder, with GODFREY CAMBRIDGE, and chairman of the Committee for the Employment of Negro Actors, 1962. Appointed by President Lyndon Johnson to the research team of the Commission on Civil Disorders, 1967. Member, Ensemble Studio Theatre and Actors Studio. Other awards, in addition to the Pulitzer Prize an Obie awards previously mentioned, include New York Drama Critics Circle Award, 1970; Drama Desk Award, 1970; and a grant from the American Academy of Arts and Letters, 1971—all for **No Place to Be Somebody**. *Address:* American Stage, 2320 Dana St., Berkeley, CA 94704.

REPRESENTATIVE PLAYS AND DRAMATIC WORKS:

No Place to Be Somebody ("A Black-Black Comedy" [subtitle], 3 acts, 1967; also adapt. as a screenplay and a musical [as yet unprod.]). According to cultural historian Margaret Just Butcher; "The play covers a fifteen year time span in the life of Johnny Williams, a Black hustler who is a victim of his awareness of Black Power. The owner of a bar, Johnny is seen in the company of black and white prostitutes, gangsters, politicians, ex-convicts. Gordone says his play's meaning has to do with the question of identity. 'We're all of us looking . . . to try to find out just who and what we are.' "— *The Negro in American Culture* (Butcher rev. and updated ed., 1971). A Burns Mantle Yearbook "Best Play of 1968–69," and winner of the Drama Desk Award for the playwright the same year. Winner of the Pulitzer Prize, 1969–70, the first play by a black playwright to win this award. Also won the New York Drama Critics Circle Award, 1970, and an American Academy of Arts and Letters Grant, 1971. Earned for the leading actor (Ron O'Neal) a *Theatre World* Award, 1968–69, and a Clarence Derwent Award. First presented at the Sheridan Square Playhouse, New York, Nov. 1967. Prod. at Richard Barr's Playwrights Unit, New York, Dec. 1967. Prod. Off-Bway by Joseph Papp at the Other Stage, April 1969. Presented by the New York Shakespeare Festival at the Public Theatre, May 2, 1969–Oct. 18, 1970, for a total run of 312 perfs. This run was interrupted for a special engagement presented on Bway by ANTA at the ANTA Theatre for 16 perfs., 1970. Orig. prodn. was dir. by Ted Tornell, starring Ron O'Neal and Nathan George; with Bonnie Thompson, Susan Pearson, Lynda Westcott, Marge Eliot, Henry Baker, PAUL BENJAMIN, Laurie Crews, Iris Comma, WALTER JONES, Nick Lewis, Ed Van Nuys, Richard Seals, Malcolm Hurd, and Martin Shaker. Again prod. on Bway at the Promenade Theatre, 1970–72; dir. by author. Prod. by the National Touring Co., 1970–74; dir. by author, with a cast headed by Philip Thomas and Terry Alexander. Following national tour, this prodn. returned to the Morosco Theatre on Bway in 1974, for a limited run. Has been translated into Spanish, Russian, French, and German, and continues to be prod. periodically throughout the world. Pub. by Bobbs-Merrill, Indianapolis, 1969; by Samuel French, New York, 1969; abridged in *The Best Plays of 1968–1969;* in *Black Theater: A Twentieth Century Collection of the Work of Its Best Playwrights*

(Patterson, 1971); in *Contemporary Black Drama* (Oliver & Sills, 1971); in *Drama of the Modern World* (Weiss, 1974); in *Masterpieces of the Theatre* (Ritter, 1976).

Gordone Is a Mutha ("Mother") (collection of monologues, full length program, 1970). In collaboration with *Marge Eliot and *Julius Harris. A series of monologues, similar in type to the ones introduced in the author's **No Place to Be Somebody;** of these, two-thirds (or about ten) were written by Gordone, and the rest by his two collaborators, who were also leading performers in **No Place.** Presented in a tryout perf. at Carnegie Recital Hall, New York, May 1970, featuring Gordone, with the expectation of being presented on Bway in the spring of 1971; however, this prodn. apparently never materialized. Pub. in *The Best Short Plays, 1973* (Richards, 1973).

The Last Chord (melodrama, full length, 1976). A black church official becomes involved with the Mafia. Prod. at the Billie Holiday Theatre, Brooklyn, Aug. 1976.

OTHER PLAYS AND DRAMATIC WORKS:
A Little More Light Around the Place (adaptn., 1964). From the novel by †Sidney Easton. Prod. at Sheridan Square Playhouse, 1964. **Worl's Champeen Lip Dansuh an' Watah Mellon Jooglah** ("World's Champion Lip Dancer and Water Melon Juggler"). Prod. by NYSF, at the Other Stage, May 26, 1969. **Baba Chops** (1975). Prod. at Wilshire Ebell Theatre, Los Angeles, 1975. **Under the Boardwalk** (screenplay; also adapt. for the stage, 1976). Public reading by Frank Silvera Writers' Workshop, at Teachers, Inc., New York, Dec. 1976. **The Block** (musical, pre-1983). **From These Ashes** (screenplay, pre-1983). **Liliom** (screenplay, adapt. for a mixed cast, pre-1983). **The W.A.S.P.** (screenplay, adapt. from the novel by Julius Horwitz, pre-1983). **[Untitled Stage Western]** (play in progress, 1983). **Ambiosis** (play in progress, 1983).

GOSS, CLAY (Clayton E. Goss) (1947–   ), Poet, playwright, and writer. Born in Philadelphia, PA. Educated at Howard Univ. (B.F.A. in drama, 1972). Married; the father of two children. Drama specialist with the Dept. of Recreation, Washington, DC, 1969. Playwright-in-residence at Howard Univ., first with the Drama Dept., 1970–73, then with the Inst. for the Arts and Humanities, 1973–75. Instr. of poetry, Antioch Coll., Washington, DC, and Baltimore, MD, campuses, 1970–72. Author of a novel, *Bill Pickett: Black Bulldogger* (1970). His poems, short stories, articles, and reviews have been published in *We Speak as Liberators* (Coombs, 1970), *The Drama of Nommo* (Harrison, 1972), and *The Sheet* (Kirkendall, 1974), and in such periodicals as *Black World, Blackstage,* and *Liberator. Agent:* Dorothea Oppenheimer, 866 United Nations Plaza, New York, NY 10017.

COLLECTION:
HOMECOOKIN': FIVE PLAYS. Howard Univ. Press, Washington, DC, 1974. Contains **Oursides** (1972), **Homecookin'** (1970), **Andrew** (1970), **On Being Hit** (1970), and **Mars** (1972).

GROUPS OF RELATED PLAYS:
"CHANGES: THREE PLAYS FOR ELGBA" (program of 3 one-act plays, 1970). Includes **Ornette** (1970), **On Being Hit** (1970), and **Homecookin'** (1970). Prod. by the Drama Dept., Howard Univ., Washington, DC, Winter 1970.

"HOMECOOKIN', ANDREW, AND OURSIDES" (program of 3 one-act plays, 1971). Includes **Homecookin'** (1970), **Andrew** (1970), and **Oursides** (1972). Prod. Off-Bway by the New Federal Theatre, New York, 1971–72.

"THREE DISHES: HOMECOOKIN', SPACES IN TIME, AND ON BEING HIT" (program of 3 one-act plays, 1972). Includes **Homecookin'** (1970), **Spaces in Time** (1972), and **On Being Hit** (1970). Prod. Off-Bway by the DC Black Repertory Co. at the Last Colony Theatre, for 20 perfs., opening Dec. 8, 1972.

REPRESENTATIVE PLAYS AND DRAMATIC WORKS:

Homecookin' (drama, 1 act, 1970). "Concerns itself with destinations, when two young men who knew each other as youngsters meet years later on a subway train headed toward their futures."—*The Best Plays of 1972–73*. First prod. at Howard Univ., Washington, DC, in the Ira Aldridge Theatre, 1970. Prod. Off-Bway, as a work-in-progress and showcase for New York Univ. students, by the Negro Ensemble Co. (NEC), at St. Marks Playhouse, New York, for 2 perfs., Jan. 30–31, 1971. Prod. Off-Bway by the New Fed. Theatre (NFT), New York, during the 1971–72 season, on a program of three one-act plays by the author, under the prodn. title "**THREE DISHES.**" [See GROUPS OF RELATED PLAYS above.] Pub. in the author's *HOMECOOKIN'*.

On Being Hit // Alternate title: **Of Being Hit** (tragedy, 1 act, 1970). "A portrayal based on Holly Mims, a real-life black boxer from Washington who fought for 19 years, getting his head punched, his kidneys battered, his dream smashed, until he died . . . [in 1969] working as a janitor, from his bad kidneys."—*Ledger Star* (Norfolk, VA), undated clipping, 1973 (Woodlief). Prod. by the Drama Dept. of Howard Univ., Winter 1970. Prod. by the DC Black Repertory Theatre, at the Last Colony Theatre, opening Dec. 8, 1972, for 20 perfs. on a program of three one-act plays by the author, under the prodn. title "**THREE DISHES.**" Prod. at the Billie Holiday Theatre, Brooklyn, NY, 1973. Prod. at Yale Univ., New Haven, CT, 1974. Pub. in *The New Lafayette Theatre Presents* (Bullins, 1974) and in the author's *HOMECOMIN'*.

Ornette (ritualistic drama, 3 acts, 1970). Concerns the avant-garde innovators of jazz music during the 1940s, including Charlie Parker. Prod. by the Drama Dept., Howard Univ., Winter 1970, on a program of one-act plays by the author entitled "**CHANGES: THREE PLAYS FOR ELGBA**" [See GROUPS OF RELATED PLAYS above.] Prod. by NYU, 1973. Prod. by the Univ. of Massachusetts, 1975.

Andrew (tragedy, 1 act, 1970). "A murder victim symbolically confronts his killers." —*The Best Plays of 1972–1973*, p. 368. First prod. at Johns Hopkins Univ., Baltimore, around 1970. Prod. Off-Bway, as a work-in-progress and showcase for NYU students, by NEC, at St. Marks Playhouse, for 2 perfs., opening Jan. 28, 1971. Prod. Off-Bway by the New York Shakespeare Festival, at the Public Theatre, June 22–July 30, 1972, for 46 perfs., on a program of three one-act plays by various authors, under the prodn. title *The Corner*. Prod. Off-Bway by NFT, 1972, on a program of three one-act plays by the author, under the prodn. title "**HOMECOOKIN', ANDREW, AND OUR-SIDES.**" [See GROUPS OF RELATED PLAYS above.] Prod. by the La Mont-Zeno Community Theatre, Chicago, 1975. Pub. in the author's *HOMECOMIN'*.

Mars (drama, with music, 1972). Subtitled "Monument to the Last Black Eunuch." An article concerning black life on the planet Mars, published in a Black Muslim newspaper, regenerates the spirit of a middle-aged black man who has become tired of his meaningless life. Prod. by Howard Univ., Washington, DC, 1972. Pub. in the author's *HOMECOMIN'* and in *Kuntu Drama* (Harrison, 1974).

Oursides (experimental drama, 1 act, 1972). A black experience drama, set in a subway in which a black man and woman, both strangers, discuss their lives and problems. Prod. by NFT, on a program of three one-act plays, under the prodn. title **"HOMECOOKIN',** **ANDREW, AND OURSIDES."** [See GROUPS OF RELATED PLAYS above.] Prod. at the Billie Holiday Theatre, Brooklyn, 1973. Pub. in the author's *HOMECOOKIN'*.

OTHER PLAYS AND DRAMATIC WORKS:

A Hip Rumplestiltskin (juvenile rock/soul musical, 1969). Hip, black version of the well-known fairy tale. Prod. by the Dept. of Recreation, Washington, DC, 1969. Prod. by Ebony Impromptu, Washington, DC, 1971. Prod. by Theatre Black, at the Third Annual Black Theatre Alliance Festival, held at Brooklyn Academy of Music, 1973. Prod. by Summer in the Parks of New York City, 1974. **Spaces in Time** (staged poetry reading, 1 act, 1972). Prod. by the DC Black Repertory Theatre, at the Last Colony Theatre, for 20 perfs., opening Dec. 8, 1972. Prod. at the Billie Holiday Theatre, Brooklyn, 1973. Prod. by the National Park Tour of Washington, DC. **Billy McGhee** ("comedy teleplay" [author], 1 act, 1974). Concerns the dilemma of a young boy who must choose between his normal life among his family and circle of school friends and the glamorous but hectic life of a professional actor. Prod. on "The Place," over WRC-TV, Channel 4, Washington, DC, Sept. 1974. **Keys to the Kingdom** (domestic drama, 3 acts, pre-1975). Concerns the family problems which arise when one young member receives a property inheritance on the death of the grandmother.

GRAHAM, ARTHUR J. (1939–   ), Playwright, educator, and accountant.
Born in Kingston, Jamaica. Became a U.S. citizen in 1963. Educated at San Diego State Univ. (B.A. in accounting, 1967) and the Univ. of California at San Diego (Ph.D. in English and American literature, 1980). His doctoral dissertation, entitled "The Manichean Leitmotif," "deals with the ideology and psychology of racism in American fiction." Also wrote **The Captain and His Crew** (children's story, 1972). In 1983 he was living in San Diego.

PLAYS AND DRAMATIC WORKS:

The Nationals ("A Black Happening in Three Acts" [subtitle], 1968). Black pimps, prostitutes, and winos take their part in the civil rights struggle of the 1960s. Pub. by Black Book Productions, San Diego, 1968.

The Last Shine (drama, 1 act, 1969). An old "shoe shine boy" comes to grips with his racial identity. Described by the publisher as "a modern allegory of the tragic impasse between black Americans locked into the acceptance-denial 'mental set' produced by three hundred years of oppression, and the oncoming generations who in the closing decades of the 20th century are perhaps passing through fires more searing than any of their predecessors knew." Prod. by the Inner City Reader's Theatre, Los Angeles, Feb. 1976; dir. by Roland McFarland. Prod. by the West Coast Black Repertory Theatre, Inc., June 1976, San Francisco; dir. by Fred Blanchard. Pub. by Black Book Productions, San Diego, 1969. Reprinted by McNally & Loftin, Santa Barbara, 1975.

Daddy Was a Welfare Check (drama, 3 acts, 1975). According to a review by Carlene Gayle, "A family once torn apart by welfare assistance, joined together to create a stable household without any type of government assistance. . . . The final act ended on a somewhat happier note."—*The Voice News & Viewpoint* (San Diego), Nov. 26, 1975. Developed at San Diego State Univ. Experimental Theatre. Performed at Stage 7, 1941

Seventh Ave., San Diego, in Aug. and Nov. 1975. Presented as a special showing by the Performing Arts Soc. of Los Angeles, Dec. 21, 1975.

GRAHAM, BILLY, Actor, writer, commercial artist/cartoonist, playwright, and set designer. His work has been showcased by the Frank Silvera Writers' Workshop (FSWW), the Negro Ensemble Co. (NEC), and the New Federal Theatre (NFT) in New York City. Born in New York City. A graduate of the H.S. of Music and Art and the School of Visual Arts (on the G.I. Bill, after serving a four-year enlistment in the U.S. Navy). Also studied acting with Jim Moody and playwriting with STEVE CARTER at NEC; acting under BILL DUKE, GILBERT MOSES, and Dick Anthony Williams at NFT (the Henry St. Settlement); and theatre with MAXWELL GLANVILLE at the ACT/Pro/Workshop. Began his career as a commercial artist, first becoming art director of Warren Publishing, the world-famous horror magazine company (publishers of *Creepy, Eerie, Vampirella,* and *Famous Monsters* magazines. Turned to free-lance art work, and was the first black cartoonist/illustrator hired by the Marvel Comics Group; became illustrator for many of their comic books (which include *Superman, Spiderman,* and *The Hulk.*) Among the strips which he illustrated for Marvel Comics were "Luke Cage (Powerman) Hero for Hire" and "The Black Panther." Copies of comic books containing his illustrations are preserved in the archives of the Schomburg Collection. He also created the syndicated cartoon character "Bertha Butt," known for her abundant figure and her too-tight clothes, which appeared in a number of black magazines, including *Players* magazine, where a few of Graham's short stories were also published. Since 1974 Graham has turned his talents to the theatre, as actor, playwright, set and poster designer, and publicist. He has also written "spec" scripts for television and films. Twice nominated for AUDELCO Recognition Awards for Set Design, and winner of this coveted award in 1982–83, for his designs for GARLAND LEE THOMPSON's play *Tut-Ankh-Amen* (1982). He was also nominated by AUDELCO as most outstanding playwright of 1983–84, for his play *The Trial of Adam Clayton Powell, Jr.* (1981). *Address:* 115 W. 143rd St. #2, New York, NY 10030.

REPRESENTATIVE PLAYS:
The Trial of Adam Clayton Powell, Jr. (drama, 2 acts, 1981). Described by DICK CAMPBELL as "the fall of Adam Clayton Powell, Jr. from his place in the House of Representatives," focusing on the "raw bigotry of the members of the House Committee in Congress to censor and oust the powerful Black chairman of the Education and Labor Committee, whose seven-term, 14-year tenure in Congress had given him top seniority and power in the House, which only veteran Southern politicians had ever achieved."— *New York Amsterdam News,* Oct. 22, 1983, p. 23. First prod. by FSWW for a long, successful run, c. 1982–83. Presented for three perfs. at the Second Annual AUDELCO Black Theatre Festival, prod. by Vivian Robinson at CCNY, 1983. Presented Off-Bway by NFT, Oct. 20–Nov. 20, 1983, for 24 perfs.; dir. by Dianne Kirksey. With Timothy Simonson in the title role, for which he won an AUDELCO Award as best actor of the year. Graham was also nominated for an AUDELCO Recognition Award as most outstanding playwright of 1983–84.

The Dreams of Dr. King and **The Memphis Mission** (2 one-act plays about Martin Luther King, Jr., 1985). Both plays deal with the next to the last day in King's life. According to a review by Mel Tapley, " 'Dreams of Dr. King' . . . utilizes speeches and sermons of the great civil rights leader and shows some of his fears, frustrations and his premonition of his death from an assassin's bullet; and 'The Memphis Mission' dramatically reveal[s] how King defied warnings and journeyed to Tennessee to give his support to the striking sanitation workers."—*New York Amsterdam News,* Jan. 12, 1985. Prod. by Theatre in Progress, New York, Dec. 27, 1984–Jan. 27, 1985; dir. by Wyatt Paul Davis. Cast included Randy Frazier as Dr. King, JERRY MAPLE, JR., as Ralph Abernathy, Chauncy de Leon Gilbert as Andrew Young, with three cameo roles by the playwright.

OTHER PLAYS AND DRAMATIC WORKS:
Death of a Young Boy's Father (1978). Public reading by FSWW, Jan. 30, 1978. Unpub. script in the FSWW Archives/Schomburg Collection. [NOTE: In addition to the following plays, all written between 1983 and 1986, the author has also written TV "spec" scripts for **"Poppi," "The Redd Foxx Comedy/Variety Show," "Sanford and Son," "What's Happenin'?," "Palmerstown, USA,"** and **"The White Shadow."**] The Young Mr. Bojangles // Orig. title: **Young Mr. Bo** (cabaret musical play, 1 act, c. 1985). Commissioned by the Harlem Cultural Council. About the early years of Bill "Bojangles" Robinson. **Papa Charlie's Place** (1 act). Prod. by One-West Dinner Theatre, a Harlem supper club. **William and Franklin** (1 act). Prod. by One-West Dinner Theatre. **The Wino's Wake** // Formerly **Don't Step on Mah Foots** (1 act). Performed as a public reading under its orig. title by NEC. Performed under its present title at One-West Dinner Theatre. **Waiting for Joyce Miller** (soap opera-type melodrama). **The Street Magician** (film script). Was being shot for a movie for independent producer Wayne Anthony of Red Anway Productions, 1984–85. **The Lottery Ticket** (film script). **The Ashante Princess** (screenplay). For a low-budget horror film. **The Albino** (screenplay). For PBS. **Careers for the Future** (two-part TV script) for the syndicated show "Fame." **Crack, the Ultimate High** (antidope drama, 30 min., 1986). About a family whose son is on crack. Presented by numerous churches, schools, and community groups in New York City since 1986. **Telebrain** (drama, 1 act, 1986). Futuristic love story, set in the mid-twentieth century. Public reading at the Fourth Friday Playwrights Reading, 249 E. 4th St., New York, April 18, 1986, dir. by Randy Frazier.

GRANT, MICKI (Minnie Perkins; Mrs. Ray McCutcheon) (1941–   ), Prize-winning actress, author, composer, and lyricist. Born in Chicago, IL. Educated at the Univ. of Illinois, Roosevelt and DePaul universities, and Geller School. Appeared in the New York productions of *Brecht on Brecht* (1961), *The Blacks* (1961), *Fly Blackbird* (1962), *The Cradle Will Rock* (1963), *Funnyhouse of a Negro* (1964), *Leonard Bernstein's Theatre Songs* (1965), *To Be Young, Gifted and Black* (1969), and her own production of *Don't Bother Me, I Can't Cope* (1970). Her TV credits include a regular role as Peggy Nolan, attorney-at-law, on NBC's "Another World"; a continuing role on "Edge of Night"; host for a period on the CBS children's show "Around the Corner"; featured appearances on "The Today Show," "Camera Three," and NET's "Vibrations." In 1983 she joined the cast of the Emmy Award-winning "Guiding

Light.'' Since 1970 she has been composer-lyricist and artist-in-residence of the Urban Arts Corps (UAC) in New York City, where many of her original dramatic works were written in collaboration with the UAC's artistic director, VINNETTE CARROLL. Recipient of numerous awards in 1972, mainly for **Don't Bother Me, I Can't Cope** (1970), including two Drama Desk awards (one as composer-lyricist and the other as performer), an Obie Award (as composer-lyricist), two Outer Critics' Circle awards (one as composer lyricist and the other as performer), a Grammy Award, a Mademoiselle Achievement Award, two Tony nominations, and an NAACP Image Award. *Address:* Migra Music Co., Inc., 250 W. 94th St. #6G, New York, NY 10025.

REPRESENTATIVE DRAMATIC WORKS:

Don't Bother Me, I Can't Cope (musical entertainment, 2 acts, 1970). Conceived by Vinnette Carroll, who directed all professional prodns. Book, music, and lyrics by Grant. Award-winning musical which deals with the black, (and universal) problem of coping with life, utilizing songs and dances based on blues, gospel, jazz, rock, calypso, and traditional ballad rhythms. Winner of an Outer Critics' Circle Award, two Obie awards, two Drama Desk awards, and an NAACP Image Award. Nominated for a Tony Award. First presented by UAC in small theatres around New York and elsewhere during the 1970–71 season, prior to its world premiere at Ford's Theatre in Washington, DC, opening Sept. 15, 1971, for 32 perfs. With Grant, Alex Bradford, HOPE CLARKE, Arnold Wilkerson, Carl Bean, Charles E. Campbell, Marie Thomas, Bobbie L. Hill, and Willie James McPhatter. Opened on Bway in a slightly revised version, at the Playhouse Theatre, April 19, 1972, transferring to the Edison Theatre, June 13, 1972, where it continued to run, closing Oct. 23, 1973, after 1,065 perfs., with substantially the same cast. Produced by the Center Theatre Group, at the Mark Taper Forum, Los Angeles, opening Aug. 10, 1972, for 54 perfs. Transferred to the Huntington-Hartford Theatre, Los Angeles, where it had a long run, featuring Paula Kelly. Also prod. at the Happy Medium, Chicago, 1972, featuring Loleatta, a singer formerly with Alberta Walker's Caravans. Again prod. at Ford's Theatre, Washington, DC, opening April 23, 1973, for more than 44 perfs. Prod. as a guest production at the American Conservatory Theatre, San Francisco, opening July 21, 1973, for 56 perfs. Cast recording by Polydor. Pub. by Samuel French, New York, 1972.

Croesus and the Witch (musical, full length, 1971). Book by Vinnette Carroll. Music and lyrics by Grant. Based on a fable. Prod. by UAC, in repertory, opening Aug. 10, 1971, at Ft. Green Park, and was still being presented in April 1975; dir. by Carroll. Pub. by Bway Music Publishing, New York, 1984; copy in the Hatch-Billops Collection.

Step Lively, Boy (musical, full length, 1972). Adapt. by Carroll from *Bury the Dead*, an antiwar play by Irwin Shaw. Music and lyrics by Grant. Prod. by UAC, opening Feb. 7, 1972; dir. by Carroll.

The Prodigal Sister (musical, full length [8 scenes, called ''beats''], 1974). Book and lyrics by J. e. FRANKLIN. Music by Grant. Apparently based on Franklin's play *Prodigal Daughter* (1962). Follows the basic plot and theme of the Prodigal Son. A young girl becomes pregnant, leaves her home and family for the big city, and sinks into a sordid life, finally returning home to the love and protection of her parents. Prod. Off-Bway by the New Federal Theatre (NFT), New York, Nov. 25–Dec. 29, 1974, for 40 perfs.; dir. by SHAUNEILLE PERRY. With Paula Desmond and Saundra McClain. Pub. by Samuel French, New York, 1975.

The Ups and Downs of Theophilus Maitland (musical, full length, 1974). Conceived, adapt., and dir. by Vinnette Carroll from a West Indian folk tale. Music and lyrics by Grant. The story of an old man who scandalizes his family and the community by taking on a beautiful young bride, but discovers on his wedding night that he is impotent. After consulting several doctors without success, he finally goes to a witch woman who gives him a potion. Prod. by UAC, opening Nov. 13, 1974. This prodn. was also presented at the Black Theatre Alliance (BTA) annual festival, New York, 1974. Revived Nov. 1–Dec. 5, 1976.

Your Arms Too Short to Box With God (gospel musical, full length, 1975). Conceived by Vinnette Carroll. Music and lyrics by Alex Bradford. Additional music by Grant. The gospel of Matthew told in the black idiom, with title taken from a poem in *God's Trombones* (1927) by †James Weldon Johnson. Received two Tony nominations, 1966–67, for the best book of a musical and the best director. Developed by the UAC for presentation at the Spoleto, Italy, Festival of Two Worlds, where it was first presented in 1975. American premiere was held at Ford's Theatre, Washington, DC, opening Nov. 4, 1975, for 168 perfs. This prodn. transferred to Bway, at the Lyceum Theatre, Dec. 22, 1976–Jan. 1, 1978, for 429 perfs. With Dolores Hall, who won a Tony Award as the best featured actress. Revived at the Ambassador Theatre, New York, June 2–Oct. 12, 1980, for 149 perfs. Restaged by dancer-choreographer Ralf Haze, who first took the show on a national tour before opening with it at the Alvin Theatre, New York, Sept. 9, 1982, for a limited engagement, featuring Patti LaBelle. Orig. prodn. by ABC, on records, cassettes, and eight-track cartridges. Also recorded by MCA, 1981–82.

I'm Laughin' but I Ain't Tickled (musical, full length, 1976). Conceived and dir. by Carroll. Music by Grant. Based on poetry anthologized in *A Rock Against the Wind* (1973), edited by LINDSAY PATTERSON. Prod. by UAC, May and Dec. 1976.

Working (musical, full length, 1977). Adapt. and dir. by Stephen Schwartz from the book by Studs Terkel. With music and lyrics by Grant and others. Prod. by the Goodman Theatre, Chicago, opening Dec. 30, 1977, for 44 perfs. Opened on Bway at the Forty-Sixth St. Theatre, May 14, 1978, for 30 perfs. Nominated for a Tony Award, 1977–78.

Alice (musical, full length, 1978). Conceived, written (book), and dir. by Vinnette Carroll. Music and lyrics by Grant. Based on *Alice in Wonderland* and *Through the Looking Glass* by Lewis Carroll. A reworking of *But Never Jam Today* by Vinnette Carroll. Presented in a pre-Bway tryout at the Forrest Theatre, Philadelphia, May 31–June 11, 1978; closed prior to Bway opening.

It's So Nice to Be Civilized (musical, full length, 1980). Focuses on the lives and romantic involvements of people in a city neighborhood. Prod. at the Martin Beck Theatre, New York, June 3–8, 1980, for 8 perfs.

Hansel and Gretel (in the 80's) (musical, full length, 1984). Book by *Marie Thomas. Music and lyrics by Grant. Pub. by Bway Play Publishing, New York, 1984.

Phillis (musical, full length, 1986). Book by LESLIE LEE. Music and lyrics by Grant. Based on the life and world of the eighteenth century black American poet Phillis Wheatley, a slave born in Senegal, who learned to read and write and gained international fame as America's first published woman poet, also earning the admiration of George Washington and Thomas Jefferson. Prod. by Ralph Madero Productions, in assoc. with the United Negro Coll. Fund. Previewed at the Apollo Theatre, New York, Oct. 30, 1986; dir. by Ronald G. Russo. Sched. to open at Ford's Theatre, Washington, DC, in late 1986.

OTHER PLAYS AND DRAMATICS WORKS:
An Evening of Black Folktales (full length, 1974). Apparently adapt. by Grant. Prod. by UAC, 1974.; dir. by Vinnette Carroll. **Love Power** ("theatre event" with music, full length, 1974). Conceived by Vinnette Carroll and Grant. Prod. by UAC, Dec. 1974.

GRAY, RUDY (Alfred Rudolph Gray, Jr.) (1933–   ), Playwright, director, teacher, and sports enthusiast. Born and currently living in New York City. Educated at CCNY (A.B., 1945), Hunter Coll. (M.A., 1974), and the Graduate Center of CUNY (Ph.D. in progress). Currently teaches English at the John Philip Sousa Jr. H.S., Bronx, New York, where he has also produced and directed full-scale student productions, including *The Student Prince, Finian's Rainbow*, and *Inherit the Wind*. Has also taught science, mathematics, and art. Has played semiprofessional baseball, basketball, and football, and had a tryout with the New York Yankees and was scouted by the Pittsburgh Pirates, the Boston Braves, and the Philadelphia Phillies. His plays have been produced in New York by the American Community Theatre (ACT), the Hunter Coll. Playwrights' Unit, the New Lafayette Theatre (NLT), and Company in Black, of which he is the director. Memberships include DG, WGA/East, CCNY Black Alumni Assn., New York City Teachers of English, United Federation of Teachers, Frederick Douglass Creative Arts Center (FDCAC), and Frank Silvera Writers' Workshop. Recipient of the following awards: three John Golden playwriting awards, 1972, 1973, and 1974; WGA Screenwriting Fellowship, 1980; CAPS Playwriting Fellowship, 1980; the American Award for Filmmaking; nominee for an AUDELCO Award for excellence in black theatre. *Address:* 615 Fort Washington Ave., Apt. 1–H, New York, NY 10040. *Agents:* Mr. Adam Berg, Paul Tush Management, 119 W. 57th St., New York, NY 10019. Mrs. Berthan Clausner, International Literary Agency, 71 Park Ave., New York, NY 10016.

PLAYS AND DRAMATIC WORKS:
Tryout (domestic drama, 1 act, 1959). Concerns the frustrations of a former star athlete who hopes to perpetuate the memory of his glorious career through his talented teenage son. Prod. by MAXWELL GLANVILLE and ACT, New York, 1959.

Lucy, My Rose Petal (bitter comedy, 1 act, 1964). A married couple who have been mugged, robbed, and tied together by burglars attempt to assess their marriage in the aftermath of their experience. Prod. by NLT, 1964.

Dance to a Nosepicker's Drum (drama, full length, 1970). Coauthor, with Maxwell Glanville. The marriage of a young black couple is strained by interference from family members, particularly the wife's minister-father. Their young son's concern and love bring about their reconciliation. Produced by Maxwell Glanville and ACT, 1970. Also presented at the Clark Center in New York City, and at Concourse Village in the Bronx, 1971.

Feeling to the Pain (domestic drama, 1 act, 1971). A black father rejects the inadequate public school system to educate his son at home. Prod. by Rudy Gray's Co. in Black at the Clark Center for the Performing Arts, New York, 1971; dir. by author.

Dreams from a Far Region of the Soul (drama, 1 act, 1972). A prostitute attempts to break away from her pimp. Prod. by the author's Company in Black, 1972.

Eye for an Eye (drama, 1 act, 1972). A white high school teacher is kidnapped and terrorized by a black street gang. Prod. by Harvey Vincent and Hunter Coll., New York, 1972. Unpub. script in the Hunter Coll. Lib. Later expanded into **Blood Brothers** (1976), described below.

The Visitor // Orig. title: **The Visit** (domestic drama, 1 act, 1972). Psychosexual fantasy of a middle-class black woman contrasted with the reality of her marital relationship. Prod. by the Hunter Coll. Playwrights Unit, 1972. Unpub. script in the Hunter Coll. Lib.

Open School Night (absurdist comedy, 1 act, 1973). A mother and her teenage son meet his teacher on an "open school night." Prod. by Prof. Edwin Wilson and Hunter Coll. Playwrights Unit, 1973. Unpub. script in the Hunter Coll. Lib.

The Dean (drama, 2 acts, 1974). Concerns the personal and professional conflicts leading to the suicide of the black dean of an inner-city high school. Inspired by an actual incident. Prod. by the Hunter Coll. Playwrights Unit and the West Side YMCA, New York, 1974. Unpub. script in the Hunter Coll. Lib., New York City.

A Package of Ball Point Pens (domestic drama, 3 acts, pre-1975). Concerns the conflict of values within a black family between husband and wife, and between the parents and their son.

Young Faustus (philosophical drama, 3 acts, pre-1975). Modern treatment of the Faust legend through the life of a contemporary black playwright.

Blood Brothers (comedy-drama, full length, 1976). An expanded version of the author's one-act play **Eye for an Eye** (1972). A "rat pack" of disaffected black youths kidnaps and terrorizes a white school teacher. This version has strong comic overtones. Prod. by Harvey Vincent and CUNY, 1976.

Trio (drama, full length, 1978). Two young black women and a young black man share an apartment and become entangled in each other's lives. Prod. by FRED HUDSON and Frederick Douglass Creative Arts Center, during the 1978–79 season.

Before the Flood (musical, full length, 1979). Book by Gray. Music by Paul Piteo. Lyrics by David Blake. A whimsical treatment of the story of Noah's Ark. All the characters except Noah are animals. Prod. by ROSETTA LeNOIRE and the AMAS Repertory Theatre New York, opening Nov. 29, 1979, for 12 perfs. Unpub. script and tape recording in FSWW Archives/Schomburg Collection.

Away from the Wolves (film script, full length, 1980). The story of a black family struggling to escape the terror of poverty and violence surrounding them in the inner-city neighborhood. For this play and the following one, the author received a WGA Screenwriting Fellowship, 1980.

The Revenge (film script, full length, 1980). About a man who takes wrongful revenge following the rape of his wife. For this play and the preceding one, the author received a WGA Screenwriting Fellowship, 1980.

Linty Lucy (drama, full length, 1981). The struggle of an upwardly mobile black family to come to terms with themselves and each other—played put against the intellectual and moral crisis of the husband/father/son. Public reading by FSWW, 1981. Prod. by FSWW, 1982. Prod. by the Lorraine Hansberry Theatre, San Francisco, 1983. Unpub. script in the FSWW Archieves/Schomburg Collection.

Solomon Northrup's Odyssey // Orig title: **Solomon Northrup** (teleplay, 90 min., 1983/85). Based on the life of Solomon Northrup, a free black man kidnapped into slavery from 1841 to 1853. Originally sched. to air on PBS-TV in Fall 1983. Rewritten and prod. by PBS-TV, 1985.

Medea and the Doll (psychological drama, full length, 1984). "Portrays a young Black psychiatrist's examination of a desperate young woman's struggle with the hellish effects of child abuse."—*New York Amsterdam News,* Jan. 28, 1984, p. 22. First showcased at FSWW, Jan. 26–Feb. 12, 1984; dir. by Randy Frazier. Starring Maria Ellis and Juney Smith. Prod. Off-Bway at the Samuel Beckett Theatre, New York, Oct. 9–Nov. 4, 1984; dir. by Randy Frazier. Starring Marie Ellis and Morgan Freeman. Prod. by the Theatre of Universal Images, New York, Oct.-Nov. 1985.

Scylla and the Faithful (1986). Public reading by FSWW, Oct. 1986, dir. by Richard Hughes. Unpub. script in the FSWW Archives/Schomburg Collection.

GREAVES, DONALD (1943–   ), Poet-playwright. Born in New York City's Harlem Community.

PLAY:

The Marriage (domestic drama, 2 acts, 1972). Written while the author was in high school. A contract between two generations of a black family. A young woman who really loves her husband has decided to leave him because of her strong ambition for a better life and her husband's apparent inability to grow up and face responsibilities. She changes her mind after her mother-in-law reveals that she had made a similar mistake in her youth which resulted in a loveless relationship with another man and a lifetime of regret. Prod. by the Players Workshop, New York, opening April 12, 1974; dir. by James Whitten. Pub. in *Black Drama Anthology* (King & Milner, 1972).

GREAVES, WILLIAM ("Bill") (1926–   ), Actor, producer, director, and filmmaker. Credited with having produced more than 200 documentary films, for which he has won more than 16 international film festival awards, 1970–73. Inducted into the Black Filmmakers Hall of Fame, 1980. Born in New York City, one of seven children. Educated at CCNY, 1949–51; also studied at the Actors Studio, 1948, of which he is a distinguished alumnus. Dropped out of CCNY to enter the theatre as a dancer with the Asadata Dafora Dance Co. and the Pearl Primus Dance Troupe. Became interested in acting and joined the American Negro Theatre (ANT), appearing in ANT's productions of *Three's a Family* (1943) and *Henri Christophe* (1945). Continued to act in plays and films until 1952, appearing in New York stage productions of *A Young American* (1946), *Finian's Rainbow* (1946), *John Loves Mary* (1948), and *Lost in the Stars* (1949); and in two films, *Miracle in Harlem* (1948) and *Lost Boundaries* (1949). Dissatisfied with the portrayal of blacks in American films, he decided on a career as a filmmaker. Unable to obtain a scholarship or apprenticeship in cinema in the United States because of the unacceptability of a black person working in certain capacities in this medium, Greaves applied to the National Film Board of Canada (NFBC), which was outstanding in the field of documentary films, and was accepted as an apprentice in 1952. He was soon made a regular member of its staff, in which position he remained for eight years as editor, writer, and director. While with NFBC, Greaves founded the Canadian Drama Studio (modeled after the Actors Studio), with branches in Montreal, Ottawa, and Toronto, and there directed theatrical productions from 1953 to

1963. Became information officer in charge of film and television for the International Aviation Org., an agency of the United Nations in Canada, which led to his return to the United States to take a position on the staff of U.N. TV, 1963–64. Left the U.N. to found his own company, William Greaves Productions, Inc., 1964–present, which produces an average of four or five films per year. Outstanding films include *In the Company of Men* (1969), for *Newsweek* magazine (which won 8 awards); *Voice of La Raza* (1971), with Anthony Quinn, for the Equal Opportunity Commission (which won 4 film festival awards and received 3 Emmy nominations); *From These Roots* (1974), narrated by Brock Peters (which won 22 national and international awards); and *Space for Women* (1982), narrated by Ricardo Montalban, for NASA (which won 8 awards). Cohost and exec. producer for NET's "Black Journal," 1968–70, which was twice nominated for an Emmy and which won one in 1970. Producer of "Black News," 1975. Executive producer of Universal Pictures' box office hit *Bustin' Loose* (1981), starring RICHARD PRYOR and Cicely Tyson. Memberships include New York Actors Studio since 1948; SAG; AEA; AFTRA; DGA; WGA; founder, National Assn. of Black Media Producers, 1970. Winner of the John Russworm Award, from the National Newspaper Publishers Assn. of America, for "Black Journal"; a Doctor of Humane Letters from King Memorial Coll.; an Actors Studio Award, 1980; and a Distinguished Alumnus Award from Stuyvesant H.S. *Address:* William Greaves Productions, Inc., 80 Eighth Ave., New York, NY 10011.

REPRESENTATIVE DRAMATIC WORKS:

The Sweet Flypaper of Life (feature length screenplay, pre-1971). Based on the book by LANGSTON HUGHES and Roy DeCarava. The story of a grandmother's faith in her street-gang grandson, set in Harlem during the 1940s. Prodn. pending, 1985.

Booker T. Washington: The Life and the Legacy (doc. film, 30 min., early 1980s). Written with Lou Potter. The life of the controversial black American leader and founder of Tuskegee Inst., whose "policies of Black economic self-reliance and political accommodation to the reactionary white power were debated nationwide [and] brought him into conflict with other leaders of the Black community as well as liberal and progressive whites."—Distributor's publicity. Winner of ten film festival awards. Prod. and dir. by Greaves for the National Park Service, early 1980s, with Maurice Woods as Booker T. Washington, AL FREEMAN, JR., as W.E.B. Du Bois, and narration by Gil Noble. Available on VHS video cassette, distributed by Your World Video, 80 8th Ave., Suite 1701, New York, NY 10011.

Frederick Douglass: An American Life (doc. film, 30 min., early 1980s). Written with Lou Potter. A portrait of the famous abolitionist and human rights advocate of the nineteenth century, who was a leader in the fight against slavery and racism in the United States. "Born a slave, and entirely self-educated, Douglass played a critical role as orator, writer, newspaper publisher and editor, and political leader in the struggle for the emancipation of the African-American and in the early Women's Rights movement."—Distributor's publicity. Prod. and dir. by Greaves for the National Park Service, early 1980s, with Hugh Morgan as Frederick Douglass. Available on VHS video cassette, distributed by Your World Video, 80 8th Ave., Suite 1701, New York, NY 10011.

Tribute to Paul Robeson (multi-media prodn, pre-1985). Cowritten with Paul Robeson, Jr. Prod. at Carnegie Hall for the Paul Robeson Archives, featuring Ellen Burstyn, Harry Belafonte, Simon Estes, Maureen Stapleton, Eli Wallach, Anne Jackson, Rip Torn, and many others.

OTHER PLAYS AND DRAMATIC WORKS:
(All doc. films, written, prod., and dir. by Greaves, 1975/85.) **The Marijuana Affair** (1975). Coauthor, with *Woodie Robinson. **Symbiopsychotaxiplasm: Take One.** Avant-garde prodn., awaiting release. **Ali the Fighter.** Starring Muhammad Ali and Joe Frazier in "the fight of the century," at Madison Square Garden.

GREEN, JOHNNY L., Playwright. Based in New York City, where he was a participant in the New York Black Writers Conf. in 1971.

PLAYS:
(All sched. for publication by Amuru Press, New York, 1974, but apparently never pub.) **Black on Black** (mystery-drama, 1 act). The action occurs in the interior of an old cabin in the woods, where a traitor is discovered among the group. **The Night of Judgment** (drama of ethics, 1 act). Four black men are brought to trial by a hooded figure, who determines whether they live or die by their actions in the community. **The Sign** (2 acts). **The Trials and Tribulations of Ma and Pa Williams** (domestic drama, 3 acts). A young wife puts status and image before the human interests of her husband's mother and father.

GREEN, MILTON, JR., Student playwright at Occidental Coll., Los Angeles, during the 1970s.

PLAY:
Mama (domestic drama, 1976). "A tightly knit family held together by love and respect for the widowed mother opens its doors to an attractive, illegitimate, half sister from California. Instead of responding to the warmth of the family, she seduces the youngest son and blackmails him into helping her sell drugs. Violence and tragedy bring the family closer together in dealing with the reality of the world around it." —*ACTF* [American Coll. Theatre Festival] *Newsletter,* Dec. 1976. Prod. at the American Coll. Theatre Festival, at Cypress Coll., Cypress, CA, 1975.

GREENIDGE, GERTRUDE, Playwright, librettist, screenwriter. A native New Yorker who has been writing plays since 1962. Employed by one of the agencies of the city of New York until her retirement in the spring of 1984. Oil painting was her hobby prior to her involvement in writing. Although she does not consider herself an actress, she has made two stage appearances: the first as Miss Hatch in a community theatre production of *Detective Story,* and later in three minor roles in *A Streetcar Named Desire.* She has been a member of the Negro Ensemble Co. (NEC) Playwrights Workshop, under the direction of STEVE CARTER, and has been associated with the Frank Silvera Writers' Workshop (FSWW), the Harlem YMCA Little Theatre, the Adam Clayton Powell II Repertory Co., the Afro-American Total Theatre, and the Franklin Thomas Little Theatre—all in New York City—as well as the TAPS Community Theatre and the Paul Robeson Players in Brooklyn, NY. Currently, she is playwright-in-residence at the ACT/Pro/Workshop (American Community Theatre Professional Workshop), New York City. In 1967 she was presented with an award for the Best Play by the Harlem YMCA Little Theatre for her play **Shadows.** In 1983 she received an Award for Literary Excellence from the Paul Robeson Players in Brooklyn. *Address:* 715 St. Mark's Avenue, #2F, Brooklyn, NY 11216.

REPRESENTATIVE PLAYS AND DRAMATIC WORKS:

Shadows // Orig. title: **Shadow of the Birth Tree** (domestic drama, 2 acts, 1963; revised 1977). On a midwestern farm, the oldest of three brothers is tormented by a family secret only he knows. The arrival of his youngest brother and his new bride proves the catalyst that erodes his facade and throws the family into violent and bitter conflict. Prod. under its orig. title (as a three-act play) by the TAPS Community Theatre, Brooklyn, 1973, for 4 perfs.; and by the Harlem YMCA Theatre Group, 1967, for 3 perfs., where it was also presented an award for Best Play. Under its present title, it was presented by the Franklin Thomas Theatre Group, New York City, July 1977. Unpub. script located in the Billy Rose Theatre Collection/NYPL.

The Interrogator (drama, 1 act, 1965). In a small Latin American country, a ruthless general takes hostages in his efforts to find the mysterious rebel leader who opposes the government. He succeeds, but finds it an empty victory. Prod. as a staged reading by the Brooklyn Public Lib. (Central Lib.) at the Grand Army Plaza, Jan. 6, 1979. This play was among the finalists under consideration for prodn. by the Repertory Workshop Series of WCAU-TV in Philadelphia

Shadowplay (fantasy, 1 act, 1966). A young couple enters a theatre that is due for demolition and finds two men seated on the bare stage. Their meeting changes the course of the young couple's lives. Prod. as a "Riverdale Showcase" at Christ Church Parish House, 252nd St. and Riverdale Ave., Bronx, NY, opening Jan. 19, 1968, for 6 perfs. Prod. by the Adam Clayton Powell II Repertory Co., New York, June 24–July 17, 1977. Unpub. script in the Billy Rose Theatre Collection/NYPL.

Makin' It (musical, full length, 1970). Book written in collaboration with HAZEL BRYANT and WALTER MILES. Music by JIMMY JUSTICE and HOLLY HAMILTON. Concerns the trials and tribulations of a young man from a small town as he tries to make it in show business. Performed exclusively by the Afro-American Total Theatre at the following locations in New York City: International House, opening Jan. 1972, for 3 perfs.; Finch Coll. Museum of Art (excerpts), June 18, 1972; Riverside Church Theatre, July 1972, for 20 perfs.; and Lincoln Center Plaza—Street Theatre Festival, Sept. 9, 1972. Also presented in Boston at the "Summer Thing" sponsored by Mayor Kevin White, week of Aug. 14, 1972.

Bricks (protest play, 1 act, 1971). A white couple and their teenage daughter are forced from their car at gunpoint and sealed up in an apartment in a black slum dwelling for no apparent reason. Was among the finalists at the Eugene O'Neill Playwrights Conf., Waterford, CT, 1972.

Something for Jamie (musical, full length, 1972). Book coauthored with Holly Hamilton, who also wrote the music and lyrics. About a black storefront preacher whose sexual activities cause him to land in jail when one of the church women falsely accuses him. The experience leads him to reevaluate his life. Prod. by the Franklin Thomas Little

Theatre, New York City, Oct. 23–Nov. 2, 1975; dir. by Franklin Thomas. Prod. at Robeson House, Brooklyn, Sept. 25–Oct. 18, 1982.

Laundry (drama, 1 act, 1972). A young woman faces a test of her own self-sufficiency during a terrifying experience in a laundry room. Prod. by NEC, Jan. 23–26, 1973. Produced by the Ebony Talent Creative Artists Foundation, Chicago, Aug. 1978. Unpub. script located in the Billy Rose Theatre Collection/NYPL.

Snowman (domestic drama, 1 act, 1972). A brother's love is placed on trial when he is forced to make a difficult decision. Public reading by the FSWW, at the Harlem Performance Center, New York, May 3, 1976.

Outside ("A Psychological Evaluation in 1 Act" [subtitle], 1983). A young woman, the victim of amnesia, tries desperately to convince the director of the mental institution where she is confined that she is not insane. Presented by the ACT/Pro/Workshop, New York, Jan. 1983, for 3 perfs. Prod. by the HADLEY Players, New York, Dec. 12–22, 1985, and Feb. 21–Mar. 16, 1986; dir. by MAXWELL GLANVILLE.

The Mask // Orig. title: **Lover Man** (drama, 1 act, 1973). In an empty bar, a cynical ladies' man drinks one too many and reveals his tortured past to the bartender. Prod. by the ACT/Pro/Workshop of the Harlem YMCA ("Showcase '80"), June 20–22, 1980.

Playgrounds (6 short plays for children, 1973). Includes the following individual one-act plays: **The Baby Sitter,** about a boy who realizes how important his responsibility is when he discovers that the baby left in his care is gone. **A Good Job,** about a boy who is ordered to scrub the subway station walls which he has marked up; he looks at vandalism in a different light when his friend decides to mark up the station he is cleaning. **Lemonade,** about a boy who learns how to beat his competitor in lemonade sales. **New Kid on the Block,** about a boy who has just moved onto the block, but is not accepted by those who live there. **The Outing,** about the things that go wrong as a group of children go on a picnic to the mountains. **Rosa Mae's Baby,** about an extremely liberated mother who comes to realize that her little girl should have a doll.

Twit // Orig. titles: **Twit for Twa'** and **Twit for 'Wat** (musical farce, full length, 1974). Book coauthored with Maxwell Glanville. Musical score by *Ben F. Carter. Additional lyrics by Bessye Scott. Loose adaptn. of Shakespeare's comedy *Measure for Measure,* set in the country of Blackolovia, "where Blacks rule and sex without marriage is a hanging offense."—*New York Amsterdam News,* June 28, 1986, p. 32 (Fuller). As in the orig. play, the Mayor hands over the government of his country to a hypocrite who promptly revives an old edict banning fornication, thus bringing near tragedy into the lives of several characters. The Mayor, however, remains on the scene in disguise, and at the end "villains are unmasked and everything ends happily." Book and lyrics completed in 1974; music completed in 1979. Public reading at New Florida Theatre, New York, under one of the orig. titles. Full prodn. by Cynthia Belgrave Artists (CBA) Theatre Workshop, at Long Island Univ.'s Triangle Theatre, Brooklyn, June 19–29, 1986; dir. by Belgrave. With Randy Flood, Lawrence James, David Morris, and Lillias White in the leading roles.

Ma Lou's Daughters // Orig. title: **Daughters** (domestic drama, 1 act, 1974). A woman raped by two white men as a teenager returns South for her mother's funeral. She finds that she must now deal with her mulatto daughter whom she has left behind since infancy. Pub. reading by FSWW, Oct. 28, 1974. Produced by the Afro-American Total Theatre, March 17–May 3, 1975. Prod. by ACT/Pro/Workshop, at the Harlem YMCA, Jan. 25–27, 1980. Presented as a staged reading on a series of Works by Women, at the Spectrum Theatre, New York, 1981; this play was selected from the reading series as one of two plays to have an Equity Showcase Production. Prod. as an Equity Mini-Showcase at the Redfield Theatre of the No Smoking Playhouse; dir. by GLENDA DICKERSON, Sept. 21–25, 1983. Prod. by the HADLEY Players, New York, Dec. 12–22, 1985, and Feb. 21–Mar. 16, 1986, dir. by Maxwell Glanville. Unpub. script in the Billy Rose Theatre Collection/NYPL.

The Game (protest play, 1 act, 1972). During a desert sandstorm, a prejudiced white couple who live in an isolated diner attempt to thwart a black couple in their efforts to seek shelter from the storm. Prod. by the Adam Clayton Powell II Repertory Theatre, June 24–July 17, 1977. Unpub. script in the Billy Rose Theatre Collection/NYPL.

OTHER PLAYS AND DRAMATIC WORKS:

Incident in a Southern Town (protest play, 1 act, 1962). An innocent black man is accused of rape by two white girls in a small southern town. When their father learns the truth, he finds it expedient to let the innocent man be lynched. **Red Rain** (protest play, 1 act, 1965). Racial conflict in a small southern town erupts into violence in which a prominent white racist is critically injured. His only hope for survival is a donor with his rare blood type who happens to be a young, militant black man. **Poison** (soap opera, 1 act, 1966). A loving husband, who used an unorthodox method to successfully reha-bilitate his alcoholic wife, now faces the prospect of losing her. **The Lifeguard** (short curtain raiser, 1967). A man is jealous of his wife's infatuation with the handsome lifeguard, until a near-drowning sets things right. **The Strippers** (filmscript for a short 10–15 min. film, 1971). A young woman's car breaks down in a deserted part of a large metropolitan city. She is forced into a deadly game of cat and mouse in the empty buildings and streets as three thugs pursue her. " . . . **And Now from the Sponsors of World War II . . .** " (multi-media black comedy, 1 act, 1972). A wife wants to see a comedy program on TV while her husband wants to see the news. The husband wins, but wishes he hadn't. **The Gift of Saturday** (domestic drama, 1 act, 1972; also a filmscript for a short 10–15 min. film, 1972). A woman who is divorced and remarried resents her ex-husband's once-a-month visitation rights to their daughter. On special Saturday, she is forced to realize how selfish she has been and what she has lost. **Red . . . As Blood Is Red** ("1 Act Anti-War Play" [subtitle], 1972). The witch doctor of a prehistoric tribe feels that his position is threatened by a couple he had previously cast out of the tribe. He learns that the couple plans to challenge his power, and he decides to kill them to prove that his magic is stronger. **The Wire** (screenplay, feature length, 1973). Coauthor, with Maxwell Glanville. A detective in a large metropolitan city goes undercover to find his father's murderer. **Overnight Sensation** (musical, pre-1983). Book coauthored with *Chez Smith. **A Present for Debby** (short Christmas play for children, pre-1983). Debby is not invited to sing with the Christmas carolers on the block because she has a terrible singing voice. A little baby left in her care for a few minutes helps to make her prayer for a beautiful voice come true. **Old Toys for Christmas** (short Christmas play for children, pre-1983). A group of girls are fixing up their old toys to donate as Christmas presents. One of the girls suddenly discovers the true meaning of giving.

GREENLEE, SAM (1930–   ), Novelist, short-story writer, poet, play-wright, and self-styled "professional propagandist" for black people. Born in Chicago, Il. Educated at the Univ. of Wisconsin (B.S. in political science, 1952); the Univ. of Chicago (graduate studies in political science and interna-tional relations, 1954–57); and the Univ. of Thessaloniki (Greek history and language). Served as an officer in the U.S. Army Infantry, 1952–54. Worked as a foreign service officer with the U.S. Information Agency (USIA), 1957–65; resigned to devote full time to writing. Author of three books: *The Spook Who Sat by the Door* (a novel, 1969; also adapted as a play and a film); *Blues for an African Princess* (poetry, 1971); and *Bagdad Blues* (a novel, 1973). His short stories have been published in *Black World/Negro Digest* and anthologized in *Ten Times Black* (Mayfield, 1970), *Black Short Story Anthology* (King, 1972), and *We Be Word Sorcerers* (Sanchez, 1973). Recipient of numerous awards, including a meritorious service award, USIA, and a Book of the Year Award by the British Press, 1969.

DRAMATIC WORK:
The Spook Who Sat by the Door (drama, full length, 1969; also prod. as a feature film, full length: screenplay, 1973). Adaptn. by Greenlee and Melvin Clay of Greenlee's novel by the same title. About a black revolution which begins on the South Side of Chicago. As described by the author, it is "a study of the revolutionary character in general; and the farcical nature of racial integration in the U.S. in particular."—*Blackstage,* Dec. 1973, p. 8. First prod. by the Southside Center for the Performing Arts, at the Louis Theatre, Chicago, 1969. Prod. as a film by Ivan Dixon and Greenlee, with screenplay by Greenlee and Clay; directed by Dixon and released by United Artists, Sept. 1973. With Lawrence Cook, Paula Kelly, and Janet League.

Blues for Little Prez (musical play, 3 acts, 1976). About the life and tragic drug-related death of a Chicago jazz musician, Little Prez. Public reading by the Frank Silvera Writers' Workshop (FSWW), at the Martinique Theatre, New York, Jan. 1976. Unpub. script possibly in the FSWW Archives/Schomburg Collection.

GREENWOOD, FRANK, Playwright. Has resided in Los Angeles and New York City. Currently resides in Los Angeles,

PLAYS:
Cotton Curtain (1 act, 1951). Received honorable mention in the playwriting contest of SADSA, held at Alabama State Coll., Montgomery, May 20, 1951. **Cry in the Night** (1 act, 1963). Explores the subject of black militancy. Pub. in *Liberator,* Sept. 1963, pp. 18–19. **Burn, Baby, Burn** (1966). **Brother Malcolm X** (biographical drama, full length, 1986). Subtitled "Reminiscences of a Black Revolutionary." About the life of one of the most influential leaders of the Civil Rights Movement. Prod. by the National Black Touring Circuit, and presented first at ROGER FURMAN's New Heritage Theatre, New York, May 15–June 1, 1986; then on national tour, where it was still running in April 1987; dir. by RON MILNER, and featuring Duane Sheppard as Malcolm.

GREER, BONNIE (1948–   ), Playwright. Born in Chicago, IL, where she attended parochial and public schools and graduated from DePaul Univ. with a degree in American history, 1974. Studied playwriting in Chicago with David Mamet and in New York with AISHAH RAHMAN and STEVE CARTER. Studied film and television with Corinne Jacker, award-winning playwright, screenwriter, and former headwriter of "Another World." Began her professional career in Chicago in 1977, when her plays were first produced by the

Chicago Black Ensemble and the Black Experimental Theatre. Moved to New York City in 1978, joining the Negro Ensemble Co.'s (NEC's) Playwrights Workshop, where she studied playwriting for three years off and on. Left NEC to become involved with the downtown New York experimental theatre scene. Joined Studio ReCherChez, under the direction of two experimental theatre directors, Ruth Maleczech and Lee Breuer, where she developed two of her plays, **Incidents** and **Diaspora: A Black Woman's Odyssey.** Works in both traditional and experimental forms; also interested in exploring African performance forms to find their roots in black American theatre. Member of the Playwrights/Directors Unit of Actors Studio; also member of the screening group which makes policy and recommends admissions. Vice chairperson of the Dramatists Guild's Committee for Women; and in 1982 cochaired the group's annual event entitled "Third World Women in American Theatre," which was the first time that an event of that organization had centered around the concerns and issues of women of color in the theatre. Member of Women in the Theatre/New York, an organization comprised of the top 100 women in the American theatre. Member of the preselection committee of the Young Playwrights Festival. *Agent:* Helen Merrill, 337 W. 22nd St., New York, NY 10010.

REPRESENTATIVE PLAYS AND DRAMATIC WORKS:

(NOTE: The author's plays have been read by the NEC, the New Federal Theatre [NFT], Actors Studio, Playwrights Forum, Phoenix Theatre, and the Hartford Stage Co.)

1919 (1977). The story of a black woman during the riots of 1919 in Chicago. Her first play. A one-night perf. was given by the Chicago Black Ensemble, Dec. 1977. It had a short run at the Black Experimental Theatre, also in Chicago, Summer 1978. Public reading by the NEC's Playwrights Workshop, April 17, 1980. In 1983 the author was preparing for a prodn. of this play in New York under the direction of John Stix, who directed *Take a Giant Step* in the 1950s. It has been nominated for the DuNouy Prize in Playwriting.

Incidents (late 1970s). Cowritten with playwright Ethan Taubes. Developed at Studio ReCherChez, New York, after 1978. An examination of the slave diary of Linda Brent, told as if she appeared on the "Johnny Carson Show."

Diaspora: A Black Woman's Odyssey (late 1970s). Developed since 1978, at Studio ReCherChez. An examination of a black woman's mental breakdown.

Vigil (late 1970s). An analysis of the murder of a white family by their black maid, as told through video and mime. Prod. since 1978 at Franklin Furnace and Inroads Multi-Media Arts Center, both located in Soho, New York City. Sched. for publication in Fall 1983 in *Acting Up,* a journal of women's writing in the theatre, pub. by *Heresies* magazine.

Pictures (1970s). A black photographer's attempt to escape reality during the Harlem Renaissance. Public reading by NEC, 1970s.

OTHER PLAYS AND DRAMATIC WORKS (written between 1978 and 1983):

Alive . . . in Winnetka. Black Sun. Fulani (screenplay, full length). **In Darkness There Is Light** (TV script). **Mask** (video piece). **Night. Triptych: Eleanora McKay. Tokyo Rose.**

GREGGS, HERBERT D. (1931–   ), Poet-playwright. A product of the Karamu Theatre, Cleveland, OH. His poetry was anthologized in *The Magic of Black Poetry* (Abdul, 1972).

DRAMATIC WORK:
The Ballad of a River Town (musical play, 1968). Sched. for Bway prodn., 1968. No record of the actual prodn.

GRIFFIN, ANTHONY E., Playwright. Associated with the Frank Silvera Writers' Workshop (FSWW) in New York City. *Address*: c/o Katherine Horton, 400 Riverside Dr. #10, New York, NY 10024.

PLAY:
A Reason to Live (pre-1985). Public reading by FSWW, prior to 1985. Unpub. script in the FSWW Archives/Schomburg Collection.

GRIMES, KEN, Playwright. Former director of the Black Arts Co., Denver, CO. Studied theatre at the Univ. of Denver and voice with Donald Todd, a noted Denver actor and director.

DRAMATIC WORK:
Barca! Men of Lightning (musical, full length, 1982). Book and lyrics by Grimes. Music by CARLTON BACON. Written by the author after two years of research, the story was based on Hannibal's historic attempt to conquer Rome. Hannibal was the black man who took the elephants over the Alps. In this prodn., the elephants were portrayed by dancers. Prod. by the Black Arts, Co., at the Community House Theatre, Denver, July 28–Aug. 7, 1982; dir. by JOHN McCALLUM.

GUILLAUME, ROBERT (Robert Williams) (1927–   ), Actor, playwright, and singer, best known for his television role as Benson, which was first performed on the "Soap" series, then on his own ABC-TV series, "Benson." Born in St. Louis, MO. Gained early theatrical experience with the Karamu Theatre in Cleveland, and later with the Afro-American Total Theatre in New York (as artistic director). Stage performances include *Kwamina* (Bway debut, 1961), *Tambourines to Glory* (1963), *Golden Boy* (1964), *The Life and Times of J. Walter Smintheus* (1970), the title role in *Purlie* (1970 and 1975), *Big Man* (1974), and *Guys and Dolls* (1976). TV appearances include "All in the Family," "Sanford and Son," and "The Jeffersons." Also appeared in the film *Super Fly T.N.T.* (1963).

DRAMATIC WORKS:
Montezuma's Revenge (and Everybody Else's) (1970). Prod. by the Afro-American Total Theatre, at International House, New York, Feb. 19 and 22, 1970. **Music! Music!** (musical comedy, 1974).

GUNN, BILL (William Harrison Gunn) (1934–   ), Playwright, actor, director, novelist, and screenwriter. Born in Philadelphia, PA, where he attended the public schools. Served for a short term in the U.S. Navy. Performed as a stage, television, and film actor during the 1950s and 1960s. Stage acting credits include *Member of the Wedding* (1950), *The Immoralist* (1954), *Take a Giant Step* (Off-Bway, 1954), *Sign of Winter* (1958), *Moon on a Rainbow Shawl* (1962), *Anthony and Cleopatra* and *A Winter's Tale* (both produced by the New

York Shakespeare Festival, 1963). TV appearances include "American Parade" (Sojourner episode), "Danger," "The Fugitive," "Dr. Kildare," "The Interns," "Outer Limits," "Route 66," "Stoney Burke," and "Tarzan." Films include *The Sound and the Fury* (1959), *The Interns* (1962), and *The Spy with My Face* (1966). Author of at least two novels, *All the Rest Have Died* (1964) and *Rhinestone Sharecropping* (1981), which was adapted into a musical play, 1982. Winner of an Emmy for the Best Television Play, **Johnnas** (1972). Recipient of an AUDELCO Black Theatre Recognition Award, 1975.

REPRESENTATIVE PLAYS AND DRAMATIC WORKS:

Marcus in the High Grass (1960). Produced Off-Bway by the Theatre Guild, at the Greenwich Mews Theatre, 1960, starring David Wayne and Elizabeth Ashley.

Johnnas (drama, 1 act, 1966). The tragic portrait of a sensitive, talented young black poet who destroys himself because he cannot cope with the realities of black survival in a hostile, racist, conformist society. His death shatters the hopes of his mother and father who, many years earlier, had given up their careers in show business to make a better life for their children, of whom all except Johnnas had died in infancy. First prod. at the Chelsea Theatre Center, Brooklyn, 1966. Prod. by the Dashiki Project Theatre, New Orleans, as a Premiere Production, Summer 1971; dir. by THEODORE GILLIAM. Telecast over WRC-TV (NBC), Washington, DC, 1972; according to the *New York Amsterdam News* (March 23, 1974, p. D-15), it "won an Emmy as Best Teleplay in 1972." Prod. as a workshop production by the Negro Ensemble Co. (NEC), Feb. 1–4, 1973; dir. by Michael Fleming. Prod. by the Afro-American Studio New York, 1973–74. Pub. in *The Drama Review*, Summer 1968, pp. 126–32.

Don't the Moon Look Lonesome (feature film, full length: screenplay, 1979). "An interracial love story adapted from Don Asher's novel by the same title."—*Jet*, April 3, 1969, p. 99. Prod. by Chuck Barris Productions, 1970.

Angel Levine (feature film, full length: screenplay, 1970). Based on "The Angel Levine," a story by Bernard Malamud. Co-adaptation by Gunn and Ronald Ribman. An angel in the form of a black street hustler, played by Harry Belafonte, is sent from heaven to help rescue an old Jewish tailor from his troubles. Prod. by Harry Belafonte Enterprises, and released by United Artists, 1970; dir. by Jan Kadar. Cast included Zero Mostel as the Jewish tailor and Gloria Foster as the hustler's girlfriend. This film, shot in East Harlem, was used by producer Belafonte as a vehicle to teach several young apprentices filmmaking techniques under the supervision of professionals.

The Landlord (feature film, full length: screenplay, 1970). Based on *Kristin Hunter's novel by the same title. A black ex-beauty queen seduces the young white landlord of the apartment building in which she lives while her black militant husband is in prison. When the husband returns, learns about the affair, and seeks revenge, he proves to be psychologically unable to harm the white man who has cuckolded him, suffering instead a mental breakdown which results in his hospitalization. Prod. by United Artists, 1979, featuring Diana Sands as the seductress, Louis Gossett as her husband, Beau Bridges as the white landlord, Pearl Bailey as one of the building's most colorful tenants, and Melvir Stewart as the operator of a black nationalist school.

Bessie (screenplay for a full length film, 1972). Based on Chris Albertson's novel by the same title. Screen biography of the well-known blues singer Bessie Smith.

Ganga and Hess; reedited as Blood Couple (feature film, full length: screenplay 1973). Orig. title: **The Vampires of Harlem.** About a doctor who is obsessed with blood but more symbolically about the black experience in America. Prod. independently; released by Kelly-Jordan, 1973; dir. by author, who also appeared in the film, which featured Duane Jones, Marlene Clark, SAM WAYMON, and Leonard Jackson. It has been shown with much success at the Cannes Film Festival, the Mexican Film Festival, the Philadelphia Art Museum, and the Museum of Modern Art. Rights sold by Kelly-Jordan to Heritage Enterprises, which reedited, retitled, and rereleased it as a vampire film, without its symbolic message.

Black Picture Show (musical play, full length, 1975). Book by Gunn. Music and lyrics by Sam Waymon, who also functioned as vocalist and musical director. According to *The Best Plays of 1974–75,* it depicts "the intellectual decay and death of a Black poet [-playwright] seduced by ambition and movie money." Its setting is a psychiatric unit in a Bronx hospital, and the poet-playwright "is looking back over his life from the vantage point of the last day," to see "how and why it all went wrong." Prod. by the New York Shakespeare Festival (NYSF) and Joseph Papp, at the Vivian Beaumont Theatre, Lincoln Center, New York, Jan. 6–Feb. 9, 1975, for 41 perfs.; dir. by author, featuring Dick Anthony Williams (who received a Tony nomination for his acting performance). Pub. by Reed, Cannon & Johnson, Berkeley, CA, c. 1975.

The Greatest, The Muhammad Ali Story (film: screenplay, 1977). Released by Columbia Pictures, 1977; dir. by Tom Gries. With Muhammad Ali, Ernest Borgnine, James Earl Jones, Roger E. Mosely, Paul Winfield, Lloyd Haynes, and Dina Merrill.

Rhinestone (drama with music and dance, 3 acts, 1982). Adapt. by Gunn from his novel *Rhinestone Sharecropping* (1982). Music and lyrics by Sam Waymon. Choreography by GEORGE FAISON. Explores the director-writer relationship between a racially insensitive European producer and a sensitive black screenwriter who has been assigned to do a screenplay of a film about a famous black football hero. Prod. in New York during the 1982–83 season; dir. by author. With Joe Morton as the black writer, Novella Nelson as his wife, and Michael Wager as the insensitive white producer.

Family Employment (domestic drama, full length, 1985). The story of an upwardly mobile black middle-class family whose wealth and power have come mainly from exploitation of the black community through gambling. Scheduled for prodn. by the NYSF Public Theatre, 1985, with the author in the leading role.

OTHER PLAYS AND DRAMATIC WORKS:
Fame Game (film: screenplay, 1968). For Columbia Pictures, 1968. **Friends** (film: screenplay, 1968). For Universal Studios, 1968. **Stop** (film: screenplay, 1969). Shot in Puerto Rico, under contract to Warner Bros., 1969, but never released.

GUY, ROSA (1928–   ), Short-story writer, novelist, essayist, and playwright. Born in Trinidad, West Indies. Member and past pres. of the Harlem Writers Guild. Author of *Bird at My Window* (novel, 1966) and *The Friends* (children's book, 1973). *Address:* c/o Harlem Writers Guild, 372 Central Park West, Suite 19J, New York, NY 10025.

PLAY:
Venetian Blinds (1 act, 1954).

H

HAIRSTON, WILLIAM (Russell, Jr.) (1923–   ), Actor, playwright, the-
atre manager, director, and writer. Born in Goldsboro, NC. Educated at NYU;
Columbia Univ.; Univ. of Northern Colorado/Greeley (B.A.); and through spe-
cial drama and theatre studies with such top professionals as Robert Lewis, Betty
Cashman, and Harry W. Gribble. Wrote films and TV shows for the U.S.
Information Agency (USIA) and the Social Security Admin., Washington, DC.
As a professional actor, performed in such plays as *The Hasty Heart, No Time
for Sergeants, Rain, The Petrified Forest, Louisiana Purchase,* and *The Respectful Prostitute,* in New York City, on tour, and in summer stock, 1950–57.
Acted in many live TV dramatic shows in New York City, 1950–55. Had the
leading role in "Harlem Detective," a TV series on WOR-TV, 1953. Had a
featured role in the MGM picture *Take the High Ground* (1953), with Richard
Widmark, Karl Malden, and Steve Forest. As a theatre administrator, held
positions as production coordinator, Greenwich Mews Theatre, New York, 1963,
and coproducer, 1963–64; theatre manager, Delacorte Amphitheatre in Central
Park, New York Shakespeare Festival (NYSF), May 1963–Sept. 1964, and
codirector of community relations for the Mobile Theatre Unit, NYSF, during
its tour of the five boroughs of New York City, season of 1965; asst. to the
exec. director of Arena Stage, Washington, DC, Sept. 1965–Sept. 1966, also
working as general manager, box office manager, public relations director, and
theatre manager. Directed *Jerico-Jim Crow,* a full length folk musical, written
by LANGSTON HUGHES, produced in New York, Jan. 1964, and recorded
on Folkways Label, FL-9571. Author of *The World of Carlos* (a novel, 1968).
Editor and publisher of *D.C. Pipeline,* a monthly newspaper of the District of
Columbia government employees. Wrote and broadcast radio news reports, feature stories, and specials, which were fed to major and minor radio networks
and stations throughout the United States. Public administrator, city government,
Washington, DC, 1970. Member, American Society of Public Administrators;

Authors League; Dramatists Guild; chairman, District of Columbia Police and Firefighters Retirement and Relief Board, 1979–; active in the National Capitol Area Council, Boy Scouts of America. Recipient of NEA Literary Study Grant, 1967, to assist NEA in its search for young, talented writers; Ford Foundation Theatre Administration Grant, to work with Arena Stage, Washington, DC, Sept. 1965–Sept. 1966. *Address:* 9909 Conestoga Way, Potomac, MD 20854

REPRESENTATIVE PLAYS AND DRAMATIC WORKS:

Swan Song of the 11th Dawn (domestic drama, 3 acts, 1962). Workshop reading, New York, June 1962.

Walk in Darkness (drama, 3 acts, 1963). Adapt. from the novel of the same title by Hans Habe. Set in a small Bavarian village near Munich after World War II, the play concerns a black soldier in occupied Germany whose plans to marry a German girl are thwarted by the army. Prod. Off-Bway at the Greenwich Mews Theatre, Oct. 28–Nov. 23, 1963, for 24 perfs.; dir. by Sidney Walters. With Clarence Williams III as the young soldier.

Black Antigone (adaptn., 1 act, 1966). Black version of the play by Sophocles. Prod. at the North Carolina Drama Festival (district and state), Feb. 1966.

The World of Willie (screenplay, 1965). The story of a young Puerto Rican boy with red hair and Irish features, set in New York City. Sched. for filming in New York during the summer of 1965.

OTHER PLAYS AND DRAMATIC WORKS:

Curtain Call, Mr. Aldridge, Sir! (adaptn., 1 act, 1963). One-act play based on the radio script of the same title by OSSIE DAVIS. Prod. in New York, May 1966. **The Honeymooners** (1 act, 1967). About newlyweds who reveal too much of their past loves. **Passion Flowers** (full length, pre-1983). Adolescent girls set up a mini-brothel in a high-class New England school for girls. **Ira Frederick Aldridge** (historical drama, full length, pre-1980s). The early struggles of the great black American tragedian, set in the early 1800s.

HALL, PHYLLIS, Playwright. Formerly associated with the Afro-American Studies Program at Brown Univ., Providence, RI.

PLAY:

Two Wings (6 episodes, 1975). Written with DELORES McKNIGHT and ELMO MORGAN. Performed as a series of episodes for one semester, as an adjunct to the course "Images and Myths of African People in New World Consciousness," for Brown Univ.'s Afro-American Studies Program, Providence, Feb.-May 1975.

HALSEY, WILLIAM, Playwright.

PLAY:

Judgment (satire, 1 act, 1969). A black artist leads a revolution to destroy the white court that is trying him for advocating violence. Pub. in *Black Dialogue,* Spring 1969, pp. 40–43.

HAMILTON, HOLLY (Asbury Verdelle Smith) (1939–   ), Actress, singer, composer-lyricist, and playwright. Born in Petersburg, FL., one of nine children; her family moved to Neptune, NJ, when she was one year old. Her musical talents were nurtured by her parents, who both sang with gospel groups earlier in their marriage. Her writing talents surfaced while in grammar school, at age 11 or 12, when she began to write poetry. Graduated from Asbury Park H.S., 1958, and decided to drop the Asbury from her name, calling herself Verdelle Smith. Later changed her name to Hamilton Holly at the suggestion of a friend. Moved to New York to try her luck as a singer, without much success at first. Took a job with the New York City Welfare Dept. as a transcribing typist and met playwright GERTRUDE GREENIDGE, with whom she later collaborated in the writing of songs and plays. Was persuaded to take the leading role in Greenidge's original drama *Shadow of the Birth Tree*, which was produced locally with much success in 1963. After many auditions and disappointments in trying to break into the theatre, she teamed with tap dancer Billy Byrd as a part of the duo "The Byrds," and together they performed in the Catskill Mountains for two or three summers, 1964–67—she as a singer, dancer, and cocktail drummer who also told jokes. Worked extensively with the Job Corps during the 1960s, touring through Virginia, Minnesota, Maryland, Wisconsin, and other states. During the late 1960s and early 1970s, performed in a number of productions at the 135th St. YMCA, under the direction of Franklin Thomas. Began receiving recording contracts in 1966 with Capitol Records; appeared in a Kurt Weill-Bertolt Brecht production in New York City—*Lost in the Stars* (1967), at the Equity Lib. Theatre. Performed in TAD TRUESDALE's *Safari 300,* a musical experience of 300 years of black culture, at the Mayfair Theatre, 1972, in which she sang a slave song, one of her own musical compositions which she translated into African dialect. In 1979 she coproduced "The Spiritual Radio Family," a weekly program on WBNX 130, consisting of Bible readings, singing, and discussion of spiritual experiences. The theme song, "God in Me Loves You," and the music to Psalm 91 were both composed by Hamilton and recorded with Gertrude Greenidge. She has twice appeared on "The Johnny Carson Show," once with Count Basie and his orchestra, and once with Muhammad Ali. Presently she is performing as an "Evangelist of Song" in nightclubs, churches, nursing homes, prisons, and hospitals. She has compiled a book of poetry which she expects to publish in the near future. A member of Rev. Ike's Church and Choir at United Palace in Washington Heights, NY, she is currently studying at the church's Science of Living Inst., while simultaneously working toward a degree in humanities at Touro Coll. in New York. *Address:* P.O. Box 646, New York, NY 10163.

REPRESENTATIVE PLAYS AND DRAMATIC WORKS:

Makin' It (musical, full length, 1970). Book by Gertrude Greenidge and WALTER MILES. Music and lyrics in collaboration with JIMMY JUSTICE. The trials and tribulations of a young man from a small town as he tries to make it in show business. Written in 1970. Prod. by the Afro-American Total Theatre, and performed at the following locations: at International House, Jan. 14–16, 1972; at Riverside Church, March 6–12, 1972; at Finch Coll., March 1972; as a street theatre prodn. in the five boroughs of New York City, July 31–Aug. 14, 1972; at Lincoln Center, Nov. 3, 1972. Remained in repertory until June 10, 1973.

Something for Jamie (musical, full length, 1972). Book coauthored with Gertrude Greenidge. Music and lyrics by Hamilton alone. Jamie, a storefront preacher with a proclivity toward women, winds up in prison after one testifies falsely against him. Completed in 1972. Presented by the Franklin Thomas Little Theatre, New York City, Oct. 23–Nov. 2, 1975; dir. by Franklin Thomas. Nominated by AUDELCO's third annual Recognition Awards in three categories of achievement: Best Producer, Best Playwright, and Best Play of the Year. Excerpts were performed for the John Greenidge Cable TV show on Channel "C," New York, 1975. More recently has been performed at the Paul Robeson House in Brooklyn, NY, prod. by Josephine English and Charles Hancock, Oct.-Nov. 1981.

OTHER PLAYS AND DRAMATIC WORKS:
Daniel (musical, full length, 1978). About the Biblical character of the Old Testament. Includes 15 songs. **Tree Free the Free Tree** (mini-musical, 1 act, 1979). About how a tree was freed from imprisonment by a rock, the rock symbolizing any obstacle or problem in our lives. NOTE: The following are all children's plays, pre-1983: **How David and Meatball Became Friends With God** (10 min.). Two friends become friends with God after having to call on Him for help and receiving it. **Extended Engagement** (drama, 2 acts with music [40 min]). Music by Elise Carnegie. Lyrics by Hamilton. A woman waits 32 years for her fiance to return. Theme song: "Tell Me You Remember." **Beulah Butterfly Meets Farmer Big Feet** (dramatic reading, 5 min.). About a butterfly who wanted to be everybody and everything but herself, until she became aware of her own beauty. **Faith Offering** (5 min.). About a girl who gives an offering on faith and receives her wish. **Frank Meatball** (3 min.). Subtitled "Be Your Own Parade." A funny, fat-woman parade comes to town. Her enthusiasm and self-confidence inspires Frank Meatball who, up to that time, had no enthusiasm. **Inter-Graded Xmas** (children's poem-play with 1 song, 20 min.). Gives an event-by-event account of the 12 months which came to be called our year. **The Treasure** (5 min.). A little boy sells all his valuables, including his pet frog, to purchase a treasure chest. He does not know what's inside, but he finds a real treasure. **The Road to "I Believe"** (musical). Coauthor, with Edythe Hepner. About children traveling to "I Believe Land," gathering a number of nonbelieving animals along the way. Surprise ending. **Lovers Are Winners and Winners Are Lovers.** Theme: to be a winner, one must believe in oneself.

HAMPTON, SYLVIA, Playwright. Former student member of the Virginia Union Univ. Players, Richmond, VA.

PLAY:
Black . . . Out! (contemporary thesis revue, late 1970s). Coauthor, with ANDREE FITZ. Explores the problems and frustrations of the American Negro. Resulted from a black drama competition sponsored by the VUU Players, Richmond, which prod. the play during the late 1960s. Also toured Concordia Coll., Moorehead State Coll., St. John's Coll., and St. Benedict's Coll. (all in Minnesota) and North Dakota State Univ.

HANSBERRY, LORRAINE (1930–1965), Playwright, journalist, and editor. Credited with being the first black woman to be produced on Broadway and the first black dramatist to win the New York Drama Critics Circle Award, in 1959, for **A Raisin in the Sun,** which is probably the best-known black American play. Born in Chicago, IL; died of cancer in New York City. Educated at the

Univ. of Wisconsin; the Art Inst. of Chicago; Roosevelt Coll.; and the New School for Social Research. Married to Robert Nemiroff, editor, composer, music publisher, and playwright, from whom she was divorced prior to her death. They remained friends, however, and he was named her literary executor and has devoted himself to keeping her literary legacy alive. Prior to her debut as a playwright, Hansberry worked variously as a department store clerk, waitress, hostess, restaurant cashier, journalist, and editor of a monthly magazine. Author of *The Movement: Documentary of a Struggle for Equality* (1964); contributor to *American Playwrights on Drama* (Frenz, 1965). Her writings are also represented in *Theatre Arts, Village Voice, Freedomways,* and *Negro Digest.* Member of DG, Inst. for Advanced Study in the Theatre Arts, and Ira Aldridge Soc. In addition to the New York Drama Critics Circle Award, 1959, she was recipient of a Cannes Film Festival Award, 1961, nominated by the Screen Writers Guild, 1960–61; and elected posthumously to the Black Filmmakers Hall of Fame, 1975.

COLLECTIONS:

A RAISIN IN THE SUN AND THE SIGN IN SIDNEY BRUSTEIN'S WINDOW. New American Lib., New York, 1969. Contains **A Raisin in the Sun** (1959) and **The Sign in Sidney Brustein's Window** (1964).

LES BLANCS: The Collected Last Plays of Lorraine Hansberry. Edited by Robert Nemiroff. Random House, New York, 1972; and Vintage, 1973. Contains **Les Blancs** (1960), **The Drinking Gourd** (1961), and **What Use Are Flowers?** (1961).

PLAYS AND DRAMATIC WORKS:

A Raisin in the Sun (drama, 3 acts, 1959; also a feature film, full length: screenplay, 1961). Domestic drama revolving around the clash of dreams among the members of a black family in Chicago who are eagerly awaiting the arrival of a $10,000 check, which represents Mama Lena Younger's deceased husband's insurance settlement. Mama dreams of moving her family into a suburban home; her son (a chauffeur) dreams of owning his own liquor store and becoming an independent businessman; her younger daughter dreams of becoming a doctor. The play also explores a multiplicity of themes, including black identity, power, and pride; assimilation versus separation of the races; the structure and strength of the black family; black male-female relationships; and black America's African heritage. The first play written by a black woman to be prod. on Bway; the first to be dir. by a black director in more than a half century; and the first black playwright to receive the New York Drama Critics Award. Prod. at the Blackstone Theatre, Chicago, for 4 weeks, 1958–59, prior to opening on Bway, at the Ethel Barrymore Theatre, March 11, 1959, for 530 perfs.; dir. by Lloyd Richards. Starring Claudia McNeil, RUBY DEE, Sidney Poitier, Diana Sands, and Ivan Dixon; with Louis Gossett, LONNE ELDER III, John Fiedler, and DOUGLAS TURNER (WARD). Prod. in London, 1959–60, with Juanita Moore, Kim Hamilton, and Earle Hyman. Other prodns. include the Blackstone Theatre, Chicago, 1960–61; the Gilpin Players, Cleveland, 1961; Playhouse in the Park, at the Robert S. Morse Theatre, 1973; the Hartford Stage Co., 1975; the Goodman Theatre, Chicago, 1983–84; the Studio Arena Theatre, Buffalo, NY, 1983; and the McCarter Theatre, Princeton, NJ, 1985. Cast recording (3 records) released by Caedman Records (355), 1972. Prod. as a film by David Susskind and Philip Rose; released by Columbia, 1961; dir. by Daniel Petrie. Starring Sidney Poitier, Claudia McNeil, Ruby

Dee, and Diana Sands; with Ivan Dixon, John Fiedler, and Louis Gossett. Winner of the Gary Cooper Award for "outstanding human values" at the Cannes Film Festival, 1961. Widely available for rental as a film or video cassette tape. Pub. by Random House, New York, 1969; by Signet/New American Lib., New York, 1961; orig. acting edition by Samuel French, New York, 1961; revised Twenty-Fifth Anniversary [Acting] Edition by Samuel French, New York, 1984. Pub. in *Broadway's Best, 1959* (Chapman, 1959); in *Theatre Arts,* Oct. 1960, pp. 27–58; in *Four Contemporary American Plays* (Cerf, 1961); in *Six American Plays for Today* (Cerf, 1961); in *Literary Cavalcade (Scholastic* Magazines), Nov. 1965; in *An Anthology for Introduction to the Theatre* (White, 1969); in *The Art of Drama* (Dietrich, Carpenter, & Kerrane, 1969); in *Plays of Our Time* (Cerf, 1967); in *Discovery and Recollections* (Heish, 1970); in *Afro-American Literature: Drama* (Adams, Conn & Slepian, 1970); in *Exploring Literature* (Altenbernd, 1970); in *Playreader's Repertory* (White & Whiting, 1970); in *Black Theatre* (Patterson, 1971); in *Generations: An Introduction to Drama* (Barringer & Dobson, 1971); in *Contemporary Black Drama* (Oliver & Sills, 1971); in *The Realities of Literature* (Dietrich, 1971); in *Quartet* (Simon, 1973); in *Eight American Ethnic Plays* (Griffith & Mersand, 1974); in *Introduction to Theatre and Drama* (Cassady & Cassady, 1975); in *Two Voices: Writing About Literature* (Symes, 1976); in *The Range of Literature: Drama,* 3rd ed. (Schneider, Walker, & Childs). Abridged in *The Best Plays of 1958–1959;* excerpt (Act III, Scene 1) in *Right On!* (Chambers & Moon, 1970); one scene in *Twenty-Eight Scenes for Acting and Practice* (Elkind et al., 1971). Pub. as *Un Raisin au Soleil,* adaptn. by Emanuel Robles of a French translation by Philippe Bonniere, by Editions Seghers, Paris, 1963; copy in the Schomburg Collection. [See also **Raisin** (1973) below.]

   Les Blancs ("The Whites") (historical drama, 2 acts [plus prologue and 12 scenes], written 1960–61). Adapt. by Robert Nemiroff. As described by the publisher of the acting script:

The young English-educated son of an African chieftain returns with his white wife to his village to bury his father. Soon, he's unwittingly caught up in the cross-fires of an impending revolution. He finds his younger brother's an alcoholic and his elder one's become a priest and a traitor to liberation. The play includes a fascinating tapestry of characters: a missionary's matriarchal wife; a dedicated, idealistic, homosexual doctor; a white military commander determined to preserve the colonial way of life; a "faithful" house servant who's actually a liberation leader and a well-intentioned, liberal, white American journalist. The play is a collision course between the races and electrifying in the drive and finality of its tragedy. [*Samuel French's Basic Catalog of Plays* (1985)]

Prod. at the Longacre Theatre, New York, opening Nov. 15, for 40 perfs.; dir. by John Berry. With James Earl Jones, who received a Drama Desk Award, Earle Hyman, and Cameron Mitchell. Pub. in *LES BLANCS: The Collected Last Plays of Lorraine Hansberry;* also pub. by Samuel French, New York, 1972.

   The Drinking Gourd (TV drama, 3 acts [90 min.], 1961). Commissioned by NBC-TV. Drama of American slavery in the 1850s, focusing on the plight of one black woman and her family. Emphasizes the brutality and dehumanizing aspects of the system, as well as the overt and underground resistance of blacks to their treatment. Prod. by the Harlem School of Arts at the Black Theatre Alliance (BTA) annual festival, New York, 1974. Pub. in *LES BLANCS: The Collected Last Plays of Lorraine Hansberry;* in *Black*

Theater, U.S.A. (Hatch & Shine, 1974); in *Upstage/Downstage: A Theatre Festival* (Farrell et al., 1976).

What Use Are Flowers? // Orig. title: **Who Knows Where?** (first written in 1961– 62 as a television fantasy; revised as "A Fable in One Act" [present subtitle], 1967). An old hermit who had once renounced civilization returns to find that it has been detroyed by an atomic holocaust, of which the sole survivors are a group of wild children. It becomes his task to teach them what he knew about civilization—music, love, literature, science, and the use of flowers. Pub. in *LES BLANCS: The Collected Last Plays of Lorraine Hansberry;* and in *The Best Short Plays, 1972* (Richards, 1972).

The Sign in Sidney Brustein's Window (comedy-drama, 3 acts [7 scenes], 1964; also adapt. as a musical, 1972). The story of a white, Jewish, liberal Greenwich Village intellectual, his aspiring-actress wife, and their circle of bohemian and colorful friends, set against the background of a heated political campaign. Often cited as the first play by a black playwright which does not focus on black characters and themes. The major focus of the play is on the necessity for the concerned individual to make a strong personal commitment toward political activism in times of moral corruption, conformity, and alienation. Although the play does deal with such subthemes as racism, integration, and assimilation, these are examined mainly from a Jewish point of view rather than a black one, and for this the play was highly criticized by black reviewers. First prod. on Bway by Robert Nemiroff and others at the Longacre Theatre, Oct. 15, 1964–Jan. 12, 1965, for 101 perfs.; dir. by Peter Kass, closing on the day of the author's death at age 34. With Gabriel Dell, Rita Moreno, Ben Aliza, Frank Schofield, John Alderman, Dolph Sweet, Alice Ghostley, Cynthia O'Neal, and Josip Elic. Pub. by Random House, New York, 1965; by Samuel French, 1965; in the author's *A RAISIN IN THE SUN AND THE SIGN IN SIDNEY BRUSTEIN'S WINDOW*; in *Three Negro Plays* (1969); and in *The Best American Plays, 6th Series* (Gassner & Barnes, 1971). Presented in a musical version, first prod. on Bway, at the Longacre Theatre, Jan. 26, 1972.

To Be Young, Gifted and Black ("A Portrait of Lorraine Hansberry in Her Own Words" [subtitle], 2 acts [plus prologue and epilogue], 1971). Adapt. by Robert Nemiroff. A kaleidoscope, weaving together appropriate materials from her pub. and then unpub. stage plays, screenplays, essays, fiction, poetry, speeches, memoirs, journals, letters, and transcripts of interviews, to present a unique self-portrait of the playwright as an artist, a black woman, and a spirited human being. The present work grew out of two broadcasts, "Lorraine Hansberry in Her Own Words," presented on Radio Station WBAI in New York City, 1967, narrated by OSSIE DAVIS and Harold Scott, and featuring a cast of 61 distinguished participating artists. In its present play form, it was first prod. by Nemiroff, in association with Harry Belafonte and others, at the Cherry Lane Theatre, New York City, opening Jan. 2, 1969, where it ran for 12 months, amassing a total of 380 perfs.; dir. by Gene Frankel; featuring Barbara Baxley, John Beal, Rita Gardner, GERTRUDE JEANNETTE, Janet League, Stephen Strimpell, Cicely Tyson, and Andre Womble. Others who starred in this production during the course of the play's run were PAUL BENJAMIN, Clifton Davis, MICKI GRANT, Moses Gunn, SAUNDRA SHARP, and CAMILLE YARBROUGH. A second production, starring Claudia McNeil, was prod. at Playhouse-in-the-Park, Philadelphia, Summer 1969; dir. jointly by Gigi Cascio (the orig. stage manager) and Nemiroff. Prod. as a touring production of New York State colleges in Fall 1969; dir. by Sidney Walters. Prod. as a national road tour production of 112 cities and colleges, 1970–71; dir. by Will Mott. Televised by NET Playhouse, 1972, starring Claudia McNeil and Ruby Dee. Prod. by Dallas Theatre Center, at the

Down Center Stage, opening Dec. 21, 1972, for 15 perfs. Presented by Stamford, CT, Street Theatre, at the Third Annual Community/Street Theatre Festival, held at Lincoln Center for the Performing Arts, at Lincoln Center Plaza, opening Aug. 21, 1973. The complete play recorded on three records by Caedmon Records, 1971; dir. by Gigi Cascio and Robert Nemiroff. With James Earl Jones, Barbara Baxley, Claudia McNeil, Tina Sattin, Camille Yarbrough, Garn Stevens, and John Towey. Pub. by Prentice-Hall, Englewood Cliffs, NJ. 1969; by Signet Books/New American Lib., 1970; and by Samuel French, New York, 1971.

Raisin (musical, full length, 1973). Book by Robert Nemiroff and Charlotte Zaltzberg. Music by Judd Woldin. Lyrics by Robert Brittan. Based on Hansberry's A Raisin in the Sun (1959). Prod. by Robert Nemiroff at the 46th St. Theatre, Oct. 18, 1973–Dec. 7, 1975, for 847 perfs.; dir. and choreographed by Donald McKayle. With Virginia Capers, Ralph Carter, Joe Morton, Ernestine Jackson, Deborah Allen, and Robert Jackson. Winner of a Tony Award as the Best Musical of 1973–74. Virginia Capers also won a Tony as Best Actress in a Musical, for her portrayal of Mama Lena Younger. Ralph Carter was nominated for a Tony Award as Best Supporting Actor in a Musical and for a Drama Desk Award as the most promising young actor. Ralph Carter, Ernestine Jackson, and Joe Morton won *Theatre World* Awards as the most promising newcomers in Off-Bway prodns. New York cast album issued by Columbia Records (KS 32754; also on cassettes and eight-track cartridges). Pub. by Samuel French, New York.

HARDY, WILLIAM, Actor, singer, and musical writer. Broadway star of *Your Arms Too Short to Box with God* (1976). *Address:* P.O. Box 2572, Paterson, NJ 07509.

DRAMATIC WORK:

God's Creation (gospel musical, full length, 1984). Apparently based on †James Weldon Johnson's poem "The Creation" and the King James Version of the Bible. Prod. by the Paul Robeson Theatre, New York, Jan.-Feb. 1984, with the author in the leading role.

HARDY-LEONARD, SHIRLEY M. (Shirley Hardy), Playwright. Based in Chicago, IL. Educated at Roosevelt Univ. (studies in speech and journalism, completed 1985). Founder-director, Catalyst Writers' Workshop, 1981. Wrote "The Unterview," a training film for Inland Steel Co. Illinois Arts Council Artist-in-Residence, 1983. Member, DG, Authors League of America, International Women's Writing Guild. Recipient of Joseph Jefferson Citation, 1975; NEA Playwrights Fellowship, 1981; and Artist's Grant, Illinois Arts Council, 1984. *Address:* P.O. Box 1828, Harvey, IL 60426.

PLAYS AND DRAMATIC WORKS:

Where Is the Pride; What is the Joy? (1974). Prod. by Experimental Black Actors' Guild (X-BAG), at Parkway Community Theatre, 1974. **Booj-Wah-Zee** ("Bourgeosie") (1975). Prod. by Parkway Community Theatre, 1975. **No Welcome for the New Day** (1975). Prod. by Olive-Harvey City Coll., Chicago, 1975. **Stairways Lead Up** (1979). Prod. by Education Through Theatre Assn., Chicago, 1979. **Window Boxes** (1980). Prod. as readers' theatre, at Victory Gardens, Chicago, 1980. **Ezzie and Doc** (1981). Public reading at Commons Theatre, Chicago, 1983. **Cabell Story** (1983). Prod. by Fleetwood-Jourdain Theatre, Evanston, IL, 1983. **Be Still Thunder** (1983). Prod. as an Equity Showcase production by Equity Lib. Theatre/Lincoln Center, New York, 1983.

That Jazz Life (1984). Prod. as an Arts Council Showcase by Harlen Productions, at Parkway Playhouse, Chicago, 1984.

HARRIS, BILL, Playwright and creative writing teacher. Based in Detroit, MI, and New York City. Received a master's degree in creative writing from Wayne State Univ. Began writing in the 1960s. Wrote his first play while in the army. Has worked as an arts administrator for the Detroit Council of the Arts, JazzMobile, Inc., and the New Federal Theatre (NFT). Taught creative writing, humanities, and adult education courses at Wayne State and the Center for Creative Studies. Writing awards include the Tompkins Writing Award for Drama at Wayne State, the Mary Roberts Rinehart Foundation Grant for the completion of a novel, the Greater Detroit Motion Picture Council Merit Award for drama, and the Paul Robeson Cultural Arts Award given by the state of Michigan for cultural contributions. *Address:* 466 Central Park West, #6D, New York, NY 10025; or 667 W. Bethune, Detroit, MI 48202.

GROUP OF RELATED PLAYS:
"TRIO" (program of 3 one-act plays, 1983). Includes **Smoke** (1st and 2nd movements) (1983), **Holy Smoke, Society of Men** (1983), and **Every Goodbye Ain't Gone** (1983). Prod. by NFT April 28, 1983; dir. by Nathan George.

REPRESENTATIVE PLAYS AND DRAMATIC WORKS:
No Use Cryin' (drama, 3 acts, 1973). A black family attempts to cope with a crisis which may destroy it as a unit. Written while the author was in the army. First prod. by the Southside Center of the Performing Arts, at the Louis Theatre, Chicago, Oct. 1969; dir. by THEODORE WARD. Also produced in Chicago by Malcolm X Coll., the Independent Professional Performing Artists, and Parkway Community Theatre; and in Detroit by Concept East Theatre and Mwongi Arts Players.

Warn the Wicked (drama, full length, 1974). Concerns the clash of political beliefs and ideologies within a black family and the effect of the murder of one of its militant members on the rest of the family. Prod. by the Experimental Black Actors Guild (X-BAG), Chicago, Nov. 29, 1974–Jan. 27, 1975. Also prod. by Indiana Univ. and by the Parkway Community Theatre, Chicago.

What Goes Around (drama, full length, 1975). A black couple attempts to cope with the psychological forces which threaten to separate them. Prod. by Wayne State Univ., Detroit. Staged readings by the Negro Ensemble Company, New York.

Smoke (1 act [2 movements], 1983). First movement: "A street scene with the hawkers pushing smoke, uppers, downers, coke and what have you."—*New York Amsterdam News,* May 1983, p. 19. Second movement: An exploration of man/woman relationships. Prod. on a program of three one-act plays, under the blanket title **"TRIO"** [see GROUP OF RELATED PLAYS above], by the New Federal Theatre (NFT), New York, April 28, 1983; dir. by Nathan George. With Otis Young-Smith as the man and Barbara Smith as the woman.

Holy Smoke, Society of Men (comedy, 1 act, 1983). About black preachers, male and female. Featured were MINNIE GENTRY "doing the sidewalk preacher thing and LeeRoy Giles [as] a smooth Reverend Sweet hawking an incense over the radio that will make one able to sin without suffering the consequences, funeey!"—Ibid. Prod. on a

program of three one-act plays, under the blanket title **"TRIO"** [see GROUP OF RE-
LATED PLAYS above], by NFT, April 28, 1983; dir. by Nathan George.

Every Goodbye Ain't Gone (drama, 1 act, 1983). A black woman who wishes to
make it as a singer tries to get rid of the man she loves because she considers him a
distraction and an obstacle to her goal. She wants and needs the psychic nourishment
that he provides, but is unwilling to meet the demands that loving a black man entails.
Winner of an AUDELCO Award, 1984. Prod. on a program of three one-act plays, under
the blanket title **"TRIO"**[see GROUP OF RELATED PLAYS above], by the NFT,
April 28, 1983; dir. by Nathan George. With S. Epatha Merkerson as the woman and
Obaka Adedunyo as the man. Also presented at the Colonnades Theatre Lab, New York,
as a project of the National Black Touring Circuit, May 1984.

Stories of the Old Days // Orig. title: **Stories About the Old Days** (drama, full length,
1986). Set in a Detroit church scheduled for demolition, this play concerns a confrontation
between a female gospel singer and a male, former blues singer. Prod. under its orig.
title by the Arts for Living Center, New York, opening May 18, 1986; dir. by LaTanya
Richardson. Featuring ABBEY LINCOLN and Clebert Ford. This production was nominated for an AUDELCO Award, 1986. Prod. under its present title by the National Black
Touring Circuit, 1987, featuring Lizan Mitchell and Clebert Ford.

OTHER PLAYS:
The Pimp's Pimp (comedy, 1 act, 1974). **He Who Endures** (pre-1985). **Journeys**
(pre-1985).

HARRIS, CLARENCE, Playwright.

PLAY:
The Trip (drama, 1 act, 1970). A black man gets the best of his Aunt Jemima landlady
and the white policeman that she calls to have him arrested. Pub. in *Black Voices from
Prison* (Knight, 1970).

HARRIS, NEIL (1934–   ), Playwright, black theatre director, and conductor
of theatrical workshops. Born in Valhalla, NY. Grew up in New Rochelle, NY,
where he graduated from New Rochelle H.S. Attended Shaw Univ. for two
years, 1958–60. A self-taught playwright, he established and directed a number
of drama/writers' workshops in New York during the 1970s, including a creative
writing workshop at the Mount Morris Drug Rehabilitation Center, in the Bronx,
under the New York State Narcotic Commission; the Dickie Austin Theatre
Workshop, at New Rochelle; the Black Osmosis Drama-Writers Workshop in
Pelham; and the "Shades" Drama Workshop at the Coll. of New Rochelle.
Founder-director of the Neil Harris Experimental Theatre, Mount Vernon, NY
(now quiescent). Has written scripts for the "Sanford and Son" TV series.
Recipient of grants from the Westchester Council of the Arts, 1972, and the
American Film Inst., 1973.

REPRESENTATIVE PLAYS AND DRAMATIC WORKS:
Cop and Blow (melodrama, 1 act, 1972). Barroom drama, set in Harlem. Reveals
"the corruption and stink that exist in the black ghetto community among both white and
black police (taking pay-offs and threatening to trump-up charges)."—*Plays and Players,*
Dec. 1972, p. 35. Prod. on a program of four one-act plays, under the production title

Black Visions, by the New York Shakespeare Festival Public Theatre (NYSF/PT) at the Annex, opening April 4, 1972, for 64 perfs.; directed by Kris Keiser. Pub. in *Scripts* 7, May 1972, pp. 72–80.

Players Inn (melodrama, 1 act, 1972). Harlem barroom play. Concerns "the ubiquitous presence of black dope-pushers and hustlers" in the black community —*Plays and Players,* Dec. 1972, p. 35. Prod. on a program of four one-act plays, under the production title *Black Visions,* by the NYSF/PT, at the Annex, opening April 4, 1972, for 64 perfs.; dir. by Kris Keiser.

So Nice They Named It Twice (drama, full length, 1976). "A giant slice of black life in the Big Apple. Middle-class romance crosses paths with the raw passions of the street world and marriage becomes the ultimate confidence game in a deceitful society."— *The National Playwrights Directory* (Kaye, 1977), pp. 132–33. Prod. by the NYSF/PT around 1974. Presented as a public reading by the Frank Silvera Writers' Workshop (FSWW), at the Martinique Theatre, New York, March 1975. Unpub. script in the FSWW Archives/Schomburg Collection.

Straight from the Ghetto (musical revue, full-length, 1976). Coauthor, with MIGUEL PIÑERO. Based on a book of poems and stories about Harlem street life written by members of the Black Osmosis Drama Workshop, under the direction of the author. Prod. by NYSF at Lincoln Center; as "street theatre" in New York; and on tour throughout the New York penal system, Summer 1976–Jan. 1977. Pub. under the imprint of Black Osmosis, Pelham, NY, c. 1977.

OTHER PLAYS AND DRAMATIC WORKS:

The Portrait (1 act, 1969). Prod. by the New Lafayette Theatre Workshop in Harlem, 1969. Again prod. in 1973 (presumably as a film), under a grant from the American Film Inst. **The Vampire** (melodrama, 3 acts, 1971). Concerns a junkie vampire who gets his victims hooked on drugs. **Passion Without Reason** (1977). Public reading by FSWW, Nov. 14, 1977. Unpub. script and tape recording in FSWW Archives/Schomburg Collection.

HARRIS, TED, Playwright. A product of the Playwrights' Workshop of the Negro Ensemble Co. (NEC), New York City.

PLAYS:

Playstreet (drama, 1 act, 1973). A married couple relives the experiences of their unfulfilled life together while staying in an abandoned building. Prod. as a workshop production of NEC, Feb. 1–4, 1973. **Sandcastles and Dreams** (drama, 1 act, pre-1976). Explores the fantasies, dreams, and unfulfilled sexual desires of two lonely, middle-aged women on vacation at a beach resort.

HARRIS, TOM (W.) (1930–   ), Prolific playwright, librarian, former dancer, and actor. Born in New York City, where as a child he began writing skits and playlets for local groups. Served in the U.S. Army, 1951–53. Educated at Howard Univ. (B.A., 1957), where he was also a star basketball player and captain of the team; UCLA (M.A. in playwriting, 1959); and the Univ. of Southern California (M.L.S., 1961). Began his professional career as a writer and actor for the Voice of America Radio Programs, Washington, DC, 1953–55. Has been a librarian with the Los Angeles Public Lib. since 1961. Writer-director for Channel 22 TV and for Studio West, both in Los Angeles. Teacher, Inner City Cultural Center, Los Angeles, 1967. His plays have been prod. by Pasadena Playhouse and Actors Studio, 1967. Author of two novels, *Always with Love* (1973), based on his play by the same title, 1966; and *No Time to Play* (1977), about two orphaned boys in the Los Angeles ghetto coming of age before their time. Member of the California Librarians Black Caucus and NAACP. Recipient of a citation from the Los Angeles City Council for outstanding contributions to the theatre in Los Angeles, 1967. *Address:* 1786 South Fairfax Ave., Los Angeles, CA 90019. *Pertinent address*—For location of author's unpub. scripts: Los Angeles Public Library, 630 W. 5th St., Los Angeles, CA 90041.

REPRESENTATIVE PLAYS:

Always with Love (diabolical comedy, 2 acts, 1966). A black maid murders the members of a rich white family in humorous ways. Prod. by the Pasadena Playhouse, Pasadena, CA, 1967. Pub. in *New American Plays,* vol. 3 (Hoffman, 1970).

Suds (drama, 2 acts, 1972). A young girl who works in an outdoor hand laundry, c. 1912, dreams of sailing on a fine ship. Prod. by the Actors Studio, Los Angeles, 1984.

OTHER PLAYS AND DRAMATIC WORKS:

(Most scripts are located in the Los Angeles Public Lib. [see address above].)] **The A Number One Family** (drama, 1 act, 1956). The struggles of a black immigrant family and the educational system. **Fall of an Iron Horse** (drama, 3 acts, 1957). Life beneath the 3rd Avenue El as the trains are stopped. **Pray for Daniel Adams** (drama, 1 act, 1958). Love triangle and mercy killing with a religious background. **City Beneath the Skin** (master's thesis play, 3 acts, 1959). College student torn between modern morality and his religion. **Daddy Hugs and Kisses** (drama, 2 acts, 1960). Spirit of executed youth returns to fight for his widow's mind. **All the Tigers Are Tame** (comedy, 3 acts, 1962). Prisoners on daily work furlough outside; they return at night. **Beverly Hills Olympics** (comedy, 2 acts, 1963). One of the many ways in which Olympic participants are chosen. **The Relic** (drama, 3 acts, 1964). An innocent goes to war and experiences its many mental and physical horrors. **Divorce Negro Style** (comedy, 2 acts, 1965). Battle between the sexes. **Who Killed Sweetie** (comedy, 1966). Rock star is assassinated and an investigation ensues. **Cleaning Day** (drama, 1 act, 1968). Human disposal at city morgue. **Shopping Day** (drama, 1 act, 1968). Are the organs of a dying man subject to eminent domain? **Moving Day** (drama, 1 act, 1968). Ghetto dwellers are herded to greener pastures. **The Golden Spear** (drama, 1 act, 1969). An African warrior reduced to life on America's skid row. **At Wits' End** (comedy, 2 acts, 1969). Murder mystery. **Mary, Queen of Crackers** (drama, 2 acts, 1970). Mary Lincoln spends five weeks in seclusion in the White House, with Elizabeth Keckley, her black dressmaker and confidante, following Lincoln's assassination. **The Brothers** (screenplay, 1971). **Then Came the Winter** (screenplay, 1974). **When I Grow Up** (screenplay, 1975). **The Solution** (drama, 2 acts, 1975): a combination of **Moving Day** (1968) and **Shopping Day** (1968). **Street Heat** (screenplay, 1976). **A Streetcar Salad** (comedy-drama, 2 acts, 1979). History of rapid transit in Los Angeles as background to a management-labor strike. **The Ally** (screenplay, 1981). **Desert Killing** (screenplay, 1981).

HARRIS, VALERIE (1952–   ), Playwright, film consultant, scriptwriter, and essayist. Born in Philadelphia, PA. Received the B.A. from Cheyney State Coll. in Philadelphia and the M.A. in performing arts and theatre from American Univ. in Washington, DC. Her essays have been published in several periodicals, including *Glamour* and *Artworker's News,* and anthologized in *Black Art and Fireweek: Women and Performance* (1970s). Story consultant and scriptwriter for Camera News, Inc., an independent film company. *Address:* c/o Camera News, Inc., 160 Fifth Ave., Suite 911, New York, NY 10019.

PLAYS:

Nights Alone in the Naked City // Orig. title: **Nights Alone** (drama, 1 act, 1970s). Concerns the interactions between an old white woman and a young black derelict who shares her bungalow and experiences from her past, which they reenact at night. Prod. under its orig. title in Washington, DC (presumably at American Univ.), and Cleveland, OH. Unpub. scripts (under both the orig. and present titles) in the Hatch-Billops Collection.

The Redesther Play (fable, 1970s). Unpub script in the Hatch-Billops Collection.

Ice Game (harlequinade, 1 act, 1970s). Pierrot, the premier performer of a troupe of hired entertainers, refuses to "go on" and wishes to leave the troupe, which is scheduled to perform at a masquerade ball. The others try unsuccessfully to persuade him to stay, then entice him into playing a deadly game that ultimately gives Pierrot the release from his contract that he is seeking. Unpub. script in the Hatch-Billops Collection. Unpub. script and a tape recording of a reading by the Frank Silvera Writers' Workshop (FSWW) in the FSWW Archives/Schomburg Collection.

HARRISON, PAUL CARTER (1936–   ), Playwright, director, critic, editor, and teacher. Born and reared in New York City. Educated at Indiana Univ. (B.A. in liberal arts, 1957); New School for Social Research (M.A. in psychology, 1962); and Ohio Univ. (graduate study as National Science Foundation Fellow, Summer 1959 and 1960). Also associated with the Playwrights Unit of the Actors Studio. Has traveled extensively; speaks Dutch and Spanish. Lived and worked in Amsterdam, 1962–68, where he developed and directed stage productions; published plays and essays on the contemporary theatre; wrote and produced films for television; was freelance journalist in art and politics; and was dramaturgical consultant for the Mickery Theatre, Loenesloat, the Netherlands. Has also traveled to the Caribbean, Brazil, and Africa, 1980s. Visiting artist-in-residence, SUNY/Buffalo, Summer 1965; assoc. prof. of Afro-American Literature, Kent State Univ., Summer 1969; asst prof. of theatre arts, Howard Univ., 1968–70; prof. of theatre arts and Afro-American studies, Univ. of Massachusetts/Amherst, 1972–76; adjunct prof. of theatre communications, Univ. of Illinois/Circle Campus, Chicago, 1978–82; chairman and artistic producer, Theatre/Music Dept., Columbia Coll., Chicago, 1976–80; visiting prof. in Afro-American studies, Smith Coll., Northampton, MA, and Wesleyan Univ., Middletown, CT, Spring 1984. Currently writer-in-residence, Columbia Coll., Chicago, 1980–present. Published books include *The Modern Drama Footnote* (edited collection of essays on modern theatre, Amsterdam, 1965); *Dialogue*

from the Opposition (essays based on his play **The Experimental Leader** [1965],
Amsterdam, 1966); *The Drama of Nommo* (essays on the African Continuum
as a formulation for the aesthetics of black theatre, 1972); *Kuntu Drama* (anthology of African diaspora plays, 1974); and *Chuck Stewart's Jazz Files* (a
photo documentary, 1965). His essays and reviews have been published in
numerous periodicals. His extensive directing credits include MELVIN VAN
PEEBLES's *Ain't Supposed to Die a Natural Death* (conceived and directed the
orig. version based on poems by the author, 1970; it was subsequently performed
on Bway under the direction of GILBERT MOSES, 1971); CLAY GOSS's
Homecookin' (Negro Ensemble Co. [NEC], New York, 1971); AISHAH RAH-
MAN's *Lady Day: A Musical Tragedy* (Chelsea Theatre Center, New York,
1972); LONNE ELDER III's *Ceremonies in Dark Old Men* (Univ. of Illinois,
Circle Campus, 1979); LARRY NEAL's *In an Upstate Motel* (NEC, New York,
1981); ADRIENNE KENNEDY's *The Owl Answers* (conceived and directed
modern operatic version at Columbia Coll. Performance Co., Chicago, 1980);
RAY ARANHA's *My Sister, My Sister* (NYU School of the Arts, 1981); and
CHARLES GORDONE's *No Place to Be Somebody* (Columbia Coll., Chicago,
1983). Literary advisor, Lincoln Center Repertory Co., New York, 1972–73;
consultant, Theatre Panel, Theatre Communications Group, New York, 1972–
74; consultant on New England Regional Committee for Pan African Cultural
Festival in Lagos, Nigeria, 1973–74; theatre panelist, Illinois Arts Council,
1976–79; theatre and contributing editor, *Elan* magazine, New York, 1981–83.
Member of ATA, Soc. for Directors and Choreographers, and DG. Recipient
of Obie Award for **The Great MacDaddy,** 1974; AUDELCO Award, as Best
Musical Creator, for **Tabernacle,** 1981; and Illinois Arts Council Grant for
playwriting, 1984. *Address:* P.O. Box 143, Leeds, MA 01053.

COLLECTION:
KUNTU DRAMA. Edited by Harrison. Grove Press, New York, 1974. Contains **The
Great MacDaddy** (1972).

REPRESENTATIVE PLAYS AND DRAMATIC WORKS:
The Postclerks (existential drama, 1 act, 1961). Three postal clerks (one young, one
middle-aged, and one old) vainly dream of freedom from the routine, rhythmical slavery
of their jobs. Written in Amsterdam, 1961. Prod. as a workshop production by Actors
Studio, New York, 1963.

Tophat // Also **Top Hat** (dramatic tone poem with music, 1 act, 1962). A sexual
fantasy is enacted a by black junkie with the woman of his dreams, while a black musician
plays in the background. Written in Amsterdam, 1962. Prod. by Buffalo Univ. Summer
Theatre, 1965. Prod. as a workshop production by the Negro Ensemble Co. at St. Marks
Playhouse, New York, Jan. 12, 1972, for 2 perfs.; dir. by author. Prod. by the Players'
Workshop in Greenwich Village, New York, opening Jan. 5, 1973. Prod. by LaMont
Zeno Theatre, Chicago, 1980. Prod. by Chicago Theatre Co., 1985.

Pavane for a Dead-Pan Minstrel (avant-garde drama with music, 1 act, 1963). A
pseudo-minstrel show with a tragic ending, involving the attempted seduction of a white
girl (as a contest) by two men—one white, one black—who have exchanged their racial
identities. The white man wears black makeup and the black man wears white makeup.

At intervals, they also joke and dance as in a minstrel show. Prod. as a workshop production by Actors Studio, New York, 1964. Prod. by Buffalo Univ. Summer Theatre, 1965. Pub. in *Podium Magazine* (Amsterdam), Nov. 1965.

The Experimental Leader // Also known as **The Leader** (avant-garde drama, 1 act, 1965). An integrated couple presents a failing black leader with an experiment to improve race relations. Prod. by the Dove Co., at St. Peter's Church, New York, opening April 19, 1968. Pub. in *Podium Magazine* (Amsterdam), 1965.

Pawns (expressionistic play, 1 act, 1966). The leading character is an old German Jew, awaiting the arrival of the Gestapo, who plays a game of chess to determine his fate. The pawns in the game are puppets of a black soldier and a white general. Prod. by 2nd Story Players, New York, 1966. Prod. by SARST Foundation, Rotterdam, the Netherlands, 1967.

Folly 4 Two ("Folly for Two") (expressionistic drama, 1 act, 1967). (Rewritten and title changed to **Interface,** 1980). Symbolic play in which a black African native liberates himself from white colonialism through playing a game of folly. Pub. in *Podium Magazine* (Amsterdam), 1967.

Tabernacle (staged ceremony, 2 acts, 1969). "Based on the Harlem riots of Summer, 1964," it attempts "to articulate Black experience through a synthesis of all elements of the stage—plasticity of set design, dance and improvisation. The commanding theme is justice, probed with classical range and austerity."—*New Black Playwrights,* paperback ed. (Couch, 1970). First prod. by Howard Univ., Washington, DC, 1969. Prod. by State Univ. of California/Sacramento, for a tour of California state universities, 1971. Prod. by the Afro-American Studio, New York, 1974, 1976, 1979, and 1981; dir. by ERNIE McCLINTOCK. Pub. in *New Black Playwrights* (Couch, 1970); and in *The Design of Drama* (Hubenka & Garcia, 1973).

The Great MacDaddy ("ritualized African/American event" [program notes], 2 acts, 1972). Based on the novel *The Palm Wine Drinkard* by Amos Tutuola. MacDaddy, the immature son of a wealthy bootlegger (now deceased) goes on an odyssey in search of the spirit of Wine, in order to learn the secret formula of a palm wine that was the basis of his father's successful business. His journey takes him to a number of different locales in the U.S. South, Midwest, and West, where he encounters a variety of characters, including an inimical character called Scag (whose real name is Heroin), whom he meets in several places and in various disguises. Steven R. Carter called the play a "spiritual odyssey through Afro-American life," in which the leading character "gains force by encountering manifestations of the oppression and spiritual resistance of blacks throughout American history."—*Afro-American Writers After 1955: Dramatists and Prose Writers* (Davis & Harris, 1985). Prod. by the State Univ. of California/Sacramento, May 1972. Prod. by Black Arts/West, Seattle, WA, 1973. Prod. Off-Bway by NEC, at St. Marks Playhouse, New York, Feb. 12–April 14, 1974, for 72 perfs.; dir. by DOUGLAS TURNER WARD. With David Downing in the title role, later raplaced by Robert Hooks and Clevon Little. AL FREEMAN, JR., played the part of Scag. Revived by NEC, April 5–May 22, 1977, for 56 perfs.; again dir. by Ward. This revival had previously been presented in St. Croix and St. Thomas, Virgin Islands. Recipient of an Obie Award, 1973–74, as a distinguished play. Pub. in the author's *KUNTU DRAMA.*

Ameri/cain Gothic (drama, full length, 1977). "Two lonely people caught in the violence in Memphis on the day of Martin Luther King's assassination."—*Black Masks,* April 1985, p. 2. First prod. by Columbia Coll. Performance Co., Chicago, 1977. Prod.

by the New Federal Theatre (NFT), New York, March 28–April 7, 1985; dir. by WOODIE KING, JR. With Moses Gunn and Sylvia Miles.

Youngblood (feature film, full length: screenplay, 1978). Antidrug film which also deals with the pressures that cause black teenagers to join gangs. Prod. by Aion Communications; distributed by American International Pictures, 1978; dir. by Noel Nosseck. With Lawrence-Hilton Jacobs. Available on VCR videotape.

Abercrombie Apocalypse (drama, 2 acts, 1981). Subtitled "An American Tragedy." Confrontation between a mentally disturbed young man and the black caretaker of his family estate. Prod. as a workshop production at Columbia Coll., Chicago, 1981. Prod. by NEC, June 22–July 18, 1982, for 32 perfs.; dir. by Clinton Turner Davis. With Graham Brown, Timothy B. Lynch, and Barbara Montgomery.

OTHER PLAYS AND DRAMATIC WORKS:

Impressions of American Negro Poetry (TV scripts, 1963). Apparently a TV series devoted to the reading and discussion of black American poetry for Dutch viewers. Prod. for VPRO-TV, Hilversum, the Netherlands, 1963. **The End of the Beginning** (1968). Prod. at St. Peter's Church, New York, March 19, 1968. **Strangers on a Square** (film for TV, 1964). Written for and prod. by VPRO-TV, Hilversum, 1964. **Intrusion** (American short feature film, 1965). Filmed in Belgium, 1965. **Brer Soul** (1970). **Lord Shango** (film, 1974). Prod. and distributed by Bryanston Pictures, New York, 1974. **Doctor Jazz** (1975). **The Death of Boogie Woogie** (1976). Prod. by Smith Coll., Northampton, MA, 1975; Harvard Univ., Cambridge, MA, 1977; and by Richard Allen Center, New York, 1979. Pub. by *Callaloo* #24 (Univ. of Kentucky Press), 1985. **Gettin' to Know Me** (TV scripts, 1980). Four segments written out of the nine-part dramatic folklore series. Prod. by Children's Television International, Washington, DC, 1980. **Anchorman** (drama, 1982). Workshop prodn. by Columbia Coll., Chicago, 1982. NOTE: A new blues operetta by Harrison, with music by *Julius Hemphill, was scheduled as the fourth production by NEC during its 1986–87 season.

HASSAN, UMAR BIN (or Umar Ben Hassen), Playwright. Based in New York City, where his plays have been produced by the New Federal Theatre (NFT).

PLAYS:

Aid to Dependent Children (1975). Prod. by NFT, at the Brooklyn Academy of Music, 1975; dir. by Helaine Head. **Suspenders** (1979). Prod. by NFT, Oct. 1979, for 12 perfs.; dir. by AL FREEMAN, JR. Unpub. script in the Hatch-Billops Collection.

HAWKINS, CHERYL, Playwright. Grew up in New Orleans, LA. In 1981–82 she was associated with the Frank Silvera Writers' Workshop (FSWW) in New York City.

PLAY:

Shattered Home (domestic drama, full length, 1981). Concerns "a Black family in New Orleans as its fiber and nerve are toned and tested by the tensions resulting from calamities and strivings of its individual members."—*New York Amsterdam News*, Dec. 11, 1982, p. 32. Public reading by FSWW, 1981. Prod. by the National Arts Club, New York, 1981; dir. by Randy Frazier; winner of the club's Joseph Kersserlring Award. Unpub. script in the FSWW Archives/Schomburg Collection.

HAY, SAMUEL A. (1937–   ), Playwright, critic, educator, and theatre historian. Born in Barnwell, SC. Educated at Bethune-Cookman Coll. (B.A. in speech and theatre, 1955), Johns Hopkins Univ. (M.A. in playwriting, 1967), and Cornell Univ. (Ph.D. in theatre history and criticism, 1971). Currently chairperson, Dept. of Communication and Theatre Arts, and prof. of theatre, Morgan State Univ., Baltimore, MD, 1979–84. Director of theatre, Roosevelt H.S., West Palm Beach, FL, and at Dunbar H.S. in Baltimore, 1959–66. Asst. prof. of English and African American Studies, Univ. of Maryland/Baltimore Co., 1974–78; director, Africana Studies and Research Center, and assoc. prof. of theatre, Purdue Univ., 1974–78; director, Black Studies Program, and prof. of theatre, Washington Univ., St. Louis, MO, 1978–79. Director of the annual National Conference on Black American Drama and Theatre, at Morgan State Univ., held in April, since 1984; funded by the Maryland Council for the Humanities. Coeditor of the six-volume series *Focus on Literature* (1978). Author of *Black Theatre of the Sixties* (in process, c. 1986) and *Teaching Theatre Production to Non-theatre Students* (forthcoming). His articles, reviews, and criticism have appeared in the *Baltimore Afro-American, Black World, Negro History Bulletin, Maryland English Journal,* and other periodicals. Has lectured, read papers, and participated on panels at numerous colleges and universities since 1975. His research includes a Television Station Feasibility Study, funded by the Corp. for Public Broadcasting, 1981. Other research grants include Ford Foundation Fellowship for doctoral studies, Cornell Univ., 1968–71; grant by the Univ. of Maryland, for study of West African theatre, 1972; grant by the American Bi-Centennial Commission, for the study of oral history of blacks in Indiana, 1976; and grant by the U.S. Dept. of Education, to improve reading via black studies, 1979. Currently seeking a grant from NEA and several private foundations for the writing of a comprehensive history of Black American theatre and criticism. *Address*—Office: Dept. of Theatre Arts, Morgan State University, Baltimore, MD 27239. Home: 2704 Woodsdale Ave., Baltimore, MD 21214.

PLAYS AND DRAMATIC WORKS:
Yes in a Pleasant Country (2 one-act fantasies, 1970). Includes **Parting Shocks,** which shows the pain experienced by a couple who decide to stop their extramarital affair; and **Getting Some,** which shows a 14-year-old seducing the 28-year-old friend of his mother. Prod. at Cornell Univ., 1970.

The Robeson Place Singers (drama, full length, 1976). Inspired by the life of Paul Robeson, the play charts the effects of the events on the lives of some drunks in an alley. Prod. at Purdue Univ., 1976.

An American Passport (drama, full length, 1981). The story of Paul Robeson's appearance before the House Un-American Activities Committee. Prod. at Morgan Theatre, 1981.

Sistah Rachel (music drama, full length, 1982). Adaptn. of OWEN DODSON's *Divine Comedy,* showing the rise and fall of Father Divine. Prod. at Morgan Theatre, 1982; dir. by author.

A Woman Against Apartheid (drama, full length, 1985). Winner of the National Playwriting Contest sponsored by the Detroit Center for the Performing Arts. The story of a South African woman who is tortured for her struggles against the system. Prod. by the Detroit Center for the Performing Arts, 1985.

HEMPHILL, A. MARCUS (d. 1986), Playwright, director, and musician. Born in Fort Worth, TX. Educated at Houston-Tillotson Coll., Austin, TX. (music major). A member of the Frank Silvera Writers' Workshop (FSWW) in New York City since 1973, where he moderated and conducted readings. Also a member of the New York Shakespeare Festival Workshops. Former member of the jazz duo The Pair Extraordinaire, which cut five albums for Liberty Records and toured extensively with Bill Cosby. In 1985 he became one of the writers for "The Cosby Show." Was artistic director of the Riverside Drama and Cultural Club at Riverside Church, New York City, where he directed a number of productions, including NTOZAKE SHANGE's *For Colored Girls . . .*, and JAMES BALDWIN's *The Amen Corner*. His play **Inacent Black** was the recipient of six AUDELCO awards—for best playwright, best lighting, best set, best costume design, best director, and best production of the year, 1984.

REPRESENTATIVE PLAY:
Inacent Black // Title varies: also prod. as **Inacent Black and the Five Brothers** and as **Inacent Black and the Brothers** (mystery-comedy, full length 1978). Inacent Black, a domestic servant working for a middle-class black family, is in reality an angel sent by God to help the family change their greedy ways and to gain faith in themselves. Public reading under the title *Inacent Black and the Five Brothers* by FSWW, April 22 and 24, 1978. First prod. under the same title as a Writer-Directors Staged Project of FSWW, at the New World Theatre of Columbia, New York, Nov. 29–Dec. 3, 1978; dir. by Billie Allen. Prod. at the Billie Holiday Theatre, Brooklyn, 1979, where it ran for almost a year; dir. by Mikell Pinkney. Prod. on Bway as *Inacent Black* by Spirit Will Producers, at the Biltmore Theatre, New York, opening May 6, 1981, for 15 perfs.; dir. by Mikell Pinkney. With Melba Moore as Inacent Black and featuring Barbara Montgomery, Rosanna Carter, Gregory Miller, REGINALD VEL JOHNSON, County Stovall, Bruce Strickland, Ronald "Smokey" Stevens, Joyce Sylvester, Lorey Haynes, and Ed Cambridge. Again prod. at the Billie Holiday Theatre, Brooklyn, Winter 1984; dir. by Mikell Pinkney, under the title *Inacent Black and the Brothers*. Featuring Louise Stubbs, Maurice Carlton, Gwendolyn Ricks-Spencer, Jay Aubrey Jones, and Karen Charles. Unpub. script, registered with WGA, in the Hatch-Billops Collection.

OTHER PLAYS AND DRAMATIC WORKS:
Breakin' Light: The Life and Times of John Henry. I.B. Murphy Down the Stretch. NOTE: Scripts and tape recordings of the following plays are deposited in the archives of the Frank Silvera Writers' Workshop, located in the Schomburg Collection: **Backstage: Do's Don'ts of Submitting a Short Skit. Seven Days Before the Flood. The Eternal Question** (first play in a trilogy). **And I Killed Him** (second play in a trilogy). **The Big Game** (third play in a trilogy). **Harlem Lives.**

HENDERSON, NANCY, Playwright.

COLLECTION:
WALK TOGETHER: Five Plays on Human Rights. Julian Messner, New York, 1972. Copy in the Hatch-Billops Collection. Contents not analyzed.

HERSHEY, VICTORIA, Playwright. Associated with Writers-in-Residence, Great Neck, NY, during the 1970s.

PLAY:
Heritage House (drama, pre-1976). A five-character piece about the celebration of Christmas in a welfare rooming house. Prod. by Writers-in-Residence, Great Neck, NY, prior to 1976.

HICKS, RALPH, Playwright. Resides in Kansas City, MO. In 1969–70 he was associated with the Black Workshop Theatre Group of the Univ. of Missouri/Columbia. *Address:* 3807 Bellefontaine, Kansas City, MO 66142.

PLAYS:
From Where Confusion Comes (domestic drama, 3 acts, 1969). A black militant tries to hide his beliefs and activities from his drunken father, who believes in the middle-class economic and social values of the white world. Prod. by the Black Workshop Theatre Group, Univ. of Missouri/Columbia, 1969. **When Am I Gonna Know My Name** (domestic drama, 3 acts, 1969). A tyrannical upper-middle-class black father tries to control the destinies of his three sons. **The Last Act of a Revolutionary** (drama, 1 act, 1970). Defeated leaders of a black revolution wrestle with the decisions that they must make regarding the future of their people and their cause. Prod. by the Black Workshop Theatre Group, 1970. **Whatever Happens to All Those Motherless Children?** (domestic drama, 3 acts, 1971). The brothers and sisters of an urban black family attempt to cope with their generational differences and the problem of dealing with an antagonistic white society. **The Revolution?—Is It Time?** (symbolic drama, 1972). Diverse members of a black family attempt to free themselves from their "cages," where they are confined like animals, tormented by black trainers who are in turn controlled by whites.

HIGGINSEN, VY, Author, journalist, radio and TV broadcaster, producer, director, actress, and playwright. Grew up in New York's Harlem community. Cocreator of the longest-running black Off-Broadway musical since *Shuffle Along* in 1933. Married to Ken Wydro, an author and professional speaker. First woman radio broadcaster in prime time daily radio in New York City, over WBLS-FM, 1971–75. Since 1975 she has hosted numerous shows in New York City, including WRVR-FM, 1977; National Black Network, 1979–80; WWRL-AM, 1980–81; WNBC-AM and WBLS-FM, 1982. Cohost of "Positively Black," on NBC-TV, early 1980s. Sales representative for *Ebony* magazine and publisher of *Unique New York,* a monthly guide to black entertainment in New York City, 1975–78. Regular monthly columnist for *Elan* and *Essence* magazines, 1982. *Address:* The Heckscher Theatre, 1230 Fifth Ave. at 104th St., New York, NY 10029.

DRAMATIC WORK:
Mama, I Want to Sing (musical, full length, 1982). Book by Higginsen. Lyrics and additional story consultatation with *Ken Wydro. Music composed, arranged, and dir. by *Grenoldo [Frazier]. Described by the producers as the longest-running black Off-Bway musical since the 1933 prodn. of *Shuffle Along*. Loosely based on the "story of

Higginsen's sister, Doris Troy, who left the church choir at Mount Calvary 130th St. and Lenox Ave. against her mother's wishes to sing rhythm-and-blues and popular music at 17.''—*Manhattan Daily News,* April 11, 1984. Presented in an early workshop version at the AMAS Repertory Theatre, New York, 1980, for 13 perfs.; dir. by Duane L. Jones, with music by Richard Tee. Rewritten with her husband and composer Grenoldo and first presented by the Molimo Players of Fordham Univ. as a benefit in Jan. 1983, for 4 perfs. Independently prod. by the coauthors at the Heckscher Theatre, New York, opening in March 1983, where it was well into its fifth year in May 1987. At least one touring prodn. is on the road, simultaneously carrying the show to audiences outside New York City. The leading role is played by Desiree Coleman, winner of Miss Teenage Universe in 1982. The cast includes several members of the Higginsen family: Vy Higginsen is the narrator; her sister Doris Troy plays her own mother (intermittently, between singing engagements); and her brother Randy Higginsen plays the role of Rev. Winter, the minister of the church. The entire prodn. has been called ''A Family Affair,'' because Vy's other sister Joyce Higginsen Davis is in charge of group sales and public relations, and Vy's nephew Kery D. Davis is the attorney for the company.

HILL, ALBERTA, Playwright. Attended the Playwrights' Workshop of the Negro Ensemble Co. (NEC) in New York City.

PLAY:

Sunshine, Moonbeam (fantasy, 1976). Adaptation of the fairy tale about the frog who turned into a prince. Prod. by NEC, as a Season-Within-a-Season production, New York, April 27–May 2, 1976, for 8 perfs. Unpub. script in the Hatch-Billops Collection.

HILL, ERROL (Gaston) (1921–   ), Playwright, author, editor, critic, director, and educator. Born in Trinidad. Educated at the Royal Academy of Dramatic Art, London (diploma, 1951); Yale Univ. (B.A., summa cum laude, 1962; M.F.A. in playwriting, 1962; D.F.A. in theatre history, 1966). Assoc. of the Drama Board, London, 1952. Announcer and actor, BBC, London, 1951–52. Stage director for the Arts Council tour of the provinces in Wales and North England, 1952. Author-director of Dimanche Gras carnival shows for the government of Trinidad and Tobago, 1963 and 1964. Has performed over 30 major roles in amateur and professional productions, and produced and directed over 120 plays and pageants in the United States, West Indies, England, Wales, and Nigeria. Tutor in drama and radio, Univ. of the West Indies 1953–58; tutor in creative arts, Univ. of the West Indies 1962–65; guest lecturer in creative writing, Univ. of British Columbia, Vancouver, Summer 1964; teaching fellow in theatre history, dramatic literature, and playwriting, Univ. of Ibadan, Nigeria, 1965–67; assoc. prof. of drama, Richmond Coll., CUNY, 1967–68; guest lecturer/director, Graduate Theatre Workshop, Leeds Univ., England, Fall 1978; prof. of drama, Dartmouth Coll., 1961–present; visiting prof., Univ. of California/San Diego, Winter, 1982; and Chancellor's Distinguished Professor, Univ. of California/Berkeley, Spring 1983. Author and editor of numerous books, including *The Artist in West Indian Society: A Symposium* (ed. and contr., 1964); *Caribbean Plays,* vols. 1 and 2 (ed., 1958, 1965); *Bulletin of Black Theatre,*

Nos. 1–6 (ed.; American Theatre Assn., 1971–75); *The Trinidad Carnival: Mandate for a National Theatre* (1972); *Why Pretend? A Conversation About the Performing Arts* (coauthor, 1973); *A Time and a Season: 8 Caribbean Plays* (ed., 1976); *Three Caribbean Plays for Secondary Schools* (ed. and contr., 1979); *The Theatre of Black Americans*, 2 vols. (ed. 1980); and *Shakespeare in Sable: A History of Black Shakespearean Actors* (1984). His articles have been published in *West Indian Review, Public Opinion, The Caribbean, Trinidad Guardian, Theatre Survey, Shakespeare Quarterly, Caribbean Quarterly, Ethnomusicology, Bulletin of Black Theatre, Cultures,* and *Black Scholar,* and included in the following publications: *Contemporary Dramatists* (Vinson, 1973), *Caribbean Rhythms* (Livingston, 1974), *Women in American Theatre* (Chinoy & Jenkins, 1981), *Showcasing American Drama* (Jiji, 1983), and *McGraw-Hill Encyclopedia of World Drama*, 2nd ed. (1984). Memberships include American Theatre Assn., American Society for Theatre Research, Univ. and Coll. Theatre Assn, New England Theatre Conf., National Assn. of Schools of Theatre (evaluator), Alpha Chapter of Phi Beta Kappa (pres., 1982). Recipient of British Council Scholarship, 1949–51; Rockefeller Foundation Fellowship, 1958–60 and 1965; Theatre Guild of America Fellowship, 1961–62; gold medal for drama, government of Trinidad and Tobago, 1973; Visiting Scholar, Bellagio Study and Conf. Center, Italy, Fall 1978; and regional citation for teaching and scholarship, New England Theatre Conf., Fall 1980. *Address:* 3 Haskins Rd., Hanover, NH 04755.

PLAYS AND DRAMATIC WORKS:

Square Peg (domestic drama, 1 act, 1949). About a young man who runs away from home. Prod. by the Univ. of the West Indies (UWI), Port of Spain, Trinidad, 1966. Pub. by the Extra-Mural Dept., UWI, 1966.

The Ping Pong ("A Backyard Comedy-Drama in One Act" [subtitle], 1950). About a West Indian steel band and the problems that they encounter while trying to win a band contest. Broadcast over BBC, London, 1950. Prod. by UWI, Trinidad, 1958. Pub. by the Extra-Mural Dept., UWI, 1958; repub. 1966; copy in the Schomburg Collection.

Dilemma (drama, 1 act, 1953). About industrial pollution of the environment. Prod. by UWI, 1966. Pub. by Extra-Mural Dept., UWI, 1966; repub. by the Chatham Bookseller, Chatham, NJ; copy in the Schomburg Collection.

Man Better Man ("Trinidad folk musical" [subtitle], 3 acts [7 scenes], 1954). A young Trinidadian suitor resorts to folk magic (voodoo) to try to win a stick-fighting contest in order to impress the girl he wishes to marry. Prod. by the Yale School of Drama, 1960 and 1962. Prod. in Trinidad and in England, 1965. Prod. by the Negro Ensemble Co., at St. Marks Playhouse, New York, July 2–20, 1969, for 23 perfs., with music by *Coleridge-Taylor Perkinson; dir. by DOUGLAS TURNER WARD. With David Downing. Pub. in *Three Plays from the Yale School of Drama* (Gassner, 1964) and in *Plays for Today* (Hill, 1985).

Wey-Wey (comedy, 1 act, 1957). Concerns the dreams, frustrations, and superstitions revolving around an illegal lottery in the West Indies. Prod. by UWI, 1957. Pub. by the Extra-Mural Dept., UWI, 1958; repub. by the Chatham Bookseller, Chatham, NJ, 1966; copy in the Schomburg Collection.

Strictly Matrimony (domestic comedy, 1 act, 1959). A West Indian couple who enjoy a happy common-law relationship are tricked into marriage; then everything begins to go wrong. Prod. by Yale Univ., New Haven, CT, 1959. Pub. by Extra-Mural Dept. UWI, 1959; repub. by the Chatham Bookseller, Chatham, NJ, 1966; copy in the Schomburg Collection. Pub. in *Black Drama Anthology* (King & Milner, 1972); also in *Whodunits, Farces & Fantasies* (Boynton & Mack, 1976).

Dance Bongo (fantasy, 1 act, 1965). About the dead-wake ritual dance. Prod. at UWI, 1965. Pub. in *Caribbean Literature: An Anthology* (Coulthard, 1966); also in *Three Caribbean Plays for Secondary Schools* (Hill, 1979).

OTHER PLAYS AND DRAMATIC WORKS:
The Silver Palace (drama, full length, 1948). **Oily Portraits** // Orig. title: **Brittle and the City Fathers** ("A Satiric Comedy in One Act" [subtitle], 1948). About political corruption in the West Indies. Prod. under its orig. title in Trinidad, 1948. Pub. by the Extra-Mural Dept., UWI, 1966. **Dimanche Gras Carnival Show** (1963). Prod. in Trinidad, 1963. **Whistling Charlie and the Monster** (carnival show, 1964). Prod. in Trinidad, 1964. **Broken Melody** (1954). Prod. in Jamaica, 1954. Pub. by the Extra-Mural Dept., UWI, 1954; repub. by the Chatham Bookseller, 1966; copy in the Schomburg Collection. **What Price a Slave, or, Freedom Brother Is . . .** (drama, full length, 1970).

HILL, MARS (Andrew) (1927–   ), Black theatre organizer, director, performer, and teacher; civil engineer, community organization worker, poet, lecturer, and playwright. Born in Pine Bluff, AR. Educated at the Univ. of Illinois (B.S. in architectural engineering, 1954); the Univ. of Washington (business law, 1971–72); Russell Sage Coll., Troy, NY (history of theatre, 1971–72); SUNY/Albany (M.A. in Afro-American studies with a minor in theatre, 1974); and the Afro-American Studio, New York (theatre). From 1954 to 1957, worked as a civil engineer for Kornacker Assn. in Chicago; Seattle (WA) Dept. of Public Works; and Boeing Aircraft in Seattle. From 1958 to present, employed as asst. civil engineer/bridges for the New York State Dept. of Transportation. Math instructor for Adult Education Program, Evening Div., Albany Public Schools, 1966–67. Organized a black theatre course at SUNY/Albany, 1970. Has had administrative and professional experience with the Arbor Hill Community Theatre, Kenwood Academy, Trinity Inst., CORE, and the Congress of African People—all in Albany. Founder in 1968 of the Black Experience Ensemble, a theatre group which has produced most of his plays, and with which he served as artistic director and playwright. Has conducted a series of drama workshops and community Black Arts festivals in Albany, and performed in and directed a number of plays in Seattle, Albany, and New York City. *Address:* 5 Homestead Ave., Albany, NY 12203. *Agent:* Richard Fulton, 850 Seventh Ave., New York, NY 10019.

REPRESENTATIVE PLAYS:
The Man in the Family (domestic comedy, 1 act, 1969). Domestic triangle involving a man, his new wife, and his "mother," who turns out to be the man in the family. Prod. by the Black Experience Family, at Siena Coll., Albany, NY, 1969; dir. by author, who played the role of Sticks.

House and Field (drama with chorus, 1 act, 1970). Ideological confrontation between the "house nigger" and the "field nigger." Prod. by Trinity Inst. in Albany, 1970 and

1971, with the author playing the role of House in the first prodn. and Field in the second. Also prod. at Uhuru Sasa School in Brooklyn.

The Huzzy (comedy, 1 act, 1970). Two gossiping old sisters, traveling on a bus from Chicago to the South, maliciously gossip first about a woman in their home town, then about a couple who are kissing in front of them on the bus. Prod. at the First Church, presumably in Albany, 1970 and 1973; dir. by author, who played the role of Sister Carry. Prod. by Black Arts, Inc., of Albany, at the Afro-American Studio, New York, April 7, 1973. Public reading by the Frank Silvera Writers' Workshop (FSWW), at the Harlem Performance Center New York, Jan. 1977. Unpub. script in the FSWW Archives/ Schomburg Collection.

The Street Walker (1 act, 1971). Subtitled "From the Black Experience." The tables are turned on a black hustler, who also has a bout with his "Conscience," a character in the play. Prod. by the Black Experience Ensemble at Trinity Inst. in Albany, 1971, with the author in the role of Conscience. Also prod. at SUNY/Albany, at Siena College in Albany, and at the House of Kuumba in New York, around 1973. Unpub. script in the Schomburg Collection.

Occupation (1 act, 1972). Prod. by the Black Experience Ensemble, in the open court of the Arbor Hill Community Center, Albany, 1972, with the author in the role of The Old Man. Unpub. script in the Schomburg Collection.

Eclipse (drama, 3 acts, 1974). An upper-middle-class black man and his son are saved from drowning by a fisherman who works as a trash man. When the father tries to show his gratitude by a small gift, he learns that the trashman and his wife want more than a simple reward, and their demands for money and favors eclipse the original deed of heroism. Prod. by the Black Experience Ensemble in Albany, Dec. 1974; dir. by Daniel Barton, with the author in the role of Grover Cleveland Bell. Televised on Channel 10 in Albany, 1974. Public reading by the Frank Silvera Writers' Workshop (FSWW), New York, during the mid-1970s. Unpub. script in the FSWW Archives/Schomburg Collection.

Malice in Wonderland (domestic drama, 2 acts, 1976). About a prosperous, middle-class black family whose secrets are maliciously revealed by an embittered, alcoholic sister, precipitating a family crisis by the disclosures. Produced by Black Arts, Inc., Albany, 1976; dir. by MAXWELL GLANVILLE.

First Movement (ritual drama, 16 movements [length], late 1970s). Didactic play offering Seven Principles (the *Nguso Saba)* as a possible solution to the problem of black liberation in America. Unpub. script in the Schomburg Collection.

OTHER PLAYS AND DRAMATIC WORKS:
Celebration (1 act, early 1960s). Prod. at Trinity Inst., Albany, during the early 1960s, with the author in the role of Crazy Legs. **First in War** (1 act, 1969). Prod. by Trinity Inst., Albany, 1969, and at Arbor Hill Community Center, 1973; dir. by author. **Monkey Motions** (1 act, 1969). Prod. in Albany, 1969; dir. by author, who played the role of The Man. **Cavorting with the Whartons** (1970s). Unpub. script and tape recording in the FSWW Archives/Schomburg Collection.

HIMES, CHESTER (1909–1986), Prolific expatriot short-story writer and novelist. Included in this directory because several of his works have been made into films. He has also written an original screenplay. Educated in the public schools of Augusta, GA, Pine Bluff, AR, and St. Louis, MO; graduated from high school in Cleveland, OH; and attended Ohio State Univ., 1925–29. After years of struggle to establish himself as a writer, he eventually found success in France writing detective stories. His novels include **If He Hollers Let Him Go** (1945—filmed 1968); *Lonely Crusade* (1947); *Cast the First Stone* (1952); *The Third Generation* (1954); *The Primitive* (1955); *For Love of Imabelle* (1959); *The Real Cool Killers* (1959); *The Crazy Kill* (1959); *All Shot Up* (1960); *The Big Gold Dream* (1969); **Cotton Comes to Harlem** (1965—filmed 1972); *Pinktoes* (1965); *Run Man, Run* (1966); *The Heat's On* (1966—filmed as **Come Back, Charleston Blue,** 1972); and *Blind Man with a Pistol* (1969). His short stories have been published in numerous anthologies and periodicals.

COLLECTION:

BLACK ON BLACK: BABY SISTER AND SELECTED WRITINGS. Doubleday, Garden City, NY, 1973. Contains **Baby Sister** (1973).

DRAMATIC WORKS (BASED ON HIS NOVELS):

If He Hollers, Let Him Go (feature film, full length, 1964). Adapt. from Himes's novel by the same title. Author of screenplay unknown. Concerns "a fugitive on the run from Georgia, where he had been wrongly convicted of assaulting a white girl."—*The Ebony Handbook* (1974). Prod. and dir. by Charles Martin. Released by Cinerama, 1968. Starring Raymond St. Jacques and Barbara McNair. Pub. only as a novel by Doubleday, 1945, and New American Lib., 1971.

Cotton Comes to Harlem (feature film, full length, 1970). Adapt. from Himes's novel by the same title. Screenplay by OSSIE DAVIS and Arnold Perl. Described by Donald Bogle as "a standard-thriller-cops-and robbers type" film, which "offered a picturesque glimpse of Harlem . . . depicted as [an] exotic playground."—*Toms, Coons, Mulattoes, Mammies, and Bucks* (Bogle, 1973), p. 231. Although criticized as mere entertainment, the film was eminently successful at the box office (with black audiences) and was largely responsible for setting the pattern for black films of the 1970s. Prod. by Samuel Goldwyn and Warner Bros., 1969; dir. by Ossie Davis; costarring Raymond St. Jacques and GODFREY CAMBRIDGE as two Harlem policemen, with Redd Foxx making his film debut as a junk man. Pub. only as a novel by Putnam, 1965, and Dell, 1966.

Come Back, Charleston Blue (feature film, full length, 1972). Based on Himes's novel *The Heat's On* (also pub. as *Come Back, Charleston Blue)*. Author of screenplay unknown. A sequel to **Cotton Comes to Harlem,** which "poked fun at everything and had blacks laughing at themselves."—*The Ebony Handbook* (1974), p. 455. Prod. by Warner Bros.; dir. by Mark Warren, a TV director, who piloted the project. Featured Raymond St. Jacques and Godfrey Cambridge. Pub. only as a novel by Putnam, 1966; Dell, 1967; and Berkley, 1972.

Baby Sister (screenplay, 1973). An orig. film script by Himes, set in Harlem. Pub. in the author's collection *BLACK ON BLACK: BABY SISTER AND SELECTED WRITINGS*.

HINES, JOHN, Playwright.

PLAYS:

(All pub. by New Dimensions, New York, and distributed by the Chatham Bookseller, Chatham, NJ.) **The Boyhood Adventures of Frederick Douglass** (88 pp., 1968). **The Celebration** (56 pp., 1968). **The Genius of Benjamin Banneker** (64 pp., 1968). **In Memory of Jerry** (64 pp., 1970). **The Outsider** (64 pp., 1970).

HOBBES, DWIGHT (1951–   ), Playwright, author, singer, songwriter, and actor. Born in Brooklyn, NY. In 1969 one of his lyrics, set to music by Thom Modeen, was made into a Chime Records single, and the same year one of his poems won Suffolk County's Prose and Poetry Contest. While in high school he wrote for the literary club's magazine. In 1970 he entered SUNY/Stony Brook, where he studied playwriting for one semester under LOUIS PETERSON, performed the role of Clay in a local production of *Dutchman,* and played guitar at the university and in local coffee houses before dropping out in 1973. Sang for a while on WSNL-TV, which landed him a scholarship at Long Island Univ./ C. W. Post Coll., from which he graduated with an A.B. in theatre in 1979. There he wrote several plays, two of which were produced, was nominated for the Irene Ryan Acting Award and the Lorraine Hansberry Playwriting Award, and received the Louis P. Bunce Award for creative writing. In 1980 one of his short stories was published in *Essence* magazine, and the following year one of his plays was anthologized. Most recently he established his own independent company, Beat Bad Productions, under whose label he recorded his ballad "Atlanta Children." In 1981 he had completed the manuscript of a novel, "Renegade: Journey of a Rock Messiah." *Address:* Beat Bad Productions, 1145 E. 35th St. #1–E, Brooklyn, NY 11210.

PLAYS AND DRAMATIC WORKS:
Pain in the Midst (drama with music, 1 act, 1976). A young couple find their relationship strained by the man's insistence on protecting his quite capable woman, who is willing to fight her fights, including sexual harassment on the job. Prod. by Long Island Univ., Greenvale, NY, 1976; dir. by Steven B. Nash. With Bway and TV actor Samuel E. Wright featured in the cast.

Flying on the Ground Is Wrong (vignette, mid-1970s). Written for and prod. by WSNL-TV while a student at C. W. Post Coll., Long Island Univ., mid-1970s.

You Can't Always Sometimes Never Tell (drama, 2 acts, 1978). A fair-skinned, flaxen-haired black woman and her brother both have identity problems. They take their troubles to bed in the hope of finding themselves, but they don't. First prod. by the Post Coll. Theatre Co., Long Island Univ.; dir. by Jack Poggi, with the author in the role of the brother. He was nominated for the Irene Ryan Acting Award and received the Louis P. Bunce Award for creative writing. Also presented as a staged reading at Pennsylvania State Univ., under the auspices of the John F. Kennedy Center (apparently in the regional contest of the American Coll. Theatre Festival [ACTF]), where the play was nominated for the Lorraine Hansberry Playwriting Award, but was not entered in the finals.

Renegade: Let the Black Boy Rock and Roll (play/screenplay, in progress, 1980s). Based on the author's novel (in manuscript) "Renegade: Journey of a Rock Messiah."

HODGES, JESSE J., Playwright, poet, short-story writer, and teacher. Educated at Los Angeles Community Coll. (A.A. in theatre arts and speech, 1973) and California State Univ. (B.A. in English and creative writing, 1975; M.A. in theatre arts, specializing in playwriting and history of the theatre, 1980). Teaches in the California Community Coll. system. The author of three unpublished novels, two for adults and one for children. He has also written over 30 poems and several short stories. Member of the Los Angeles Actors' Playwriting Lab, Frances Williams' Playwriting Workshop, and the California Council for Adult Education. Won three first place trophies in a modeling contest, 1970, and one in a tennis tournament, 1978. *Address:* 393 Adena St., Apt. 31, Pasadena, CA 91104.

PLAYS:

Away from Home (comedy, 2 acts, 1979). About a "down home" black man in his mid-fifties who has recently moved to the city. He is prejudiced against intellectuals and whites on all levels. Because of his biased behavior, he loses his wife and daughter. Presented in the 7/11 Theatre Unlimited at California State Univ., Los Angeles, 1980.

Heartshift (drama, 2 acts, 1982). Focuses primarily on a neurotic, incestuous father, whose objective is to keep his daughter Yolanda in bondage for his sexual pleasure. Yolanda fights desperately to overcome her father's outrageous demands. Prod. by the playwright at the TOBA West Theatre in Pasadena, 1983.

The Courtship (romantic comedy, 2 acts, 1983). About two young, interracial lovers. The black female is from a family of higher education and wealth; the white male is from a poverty-stricken home where he is being raised only by his mother. The parents of the black girl do not want their daughter to marry any man from such an environment and threaten to disinherit her.

Never Enough (serious comedy, 2 acts, 1984). About an egotistical male who has absolutely no respect for women, but gives an excellent impression that he does right up to the end of the play, when he is found out.

Equal Time (comedy, 1 act, 1964). Deals with two wives competing with the television for their husbands' attention.

HOLDER, LAURENCE, Playwright. Based in New York City. Associated with the New York Theatre Ensemble, La Mama E.T.C., and the Frank Silvera Writers' Workshop. Recipient of an AUDELCO nomination as best musical creator for **Juba** (1978), and winner of an AUDELCO Award as Best Playwright for **When the Chickens Came Home to Roost** (1981). *Address:* 625 Riverside Dr., New York, NY 10024.

REPRESENTATIVE PLAYS:

Open (drama, 2 acts, 1969). A minister, a playwright, and a teacher meet at the Agatha Johnson Memorial Sanitorium under unusual circumstances. Unpub. script in the Schomburg Collection.

Streetcorners (drama, 3 acts, 1972). A group of dead characters, including a black photographer, a black-and-white holdup team, and some transvestites, inhabits a street corner. Unpub. script in the Schomburg Collection.

The Journey (drama, 3 acts, 1972). Concerns a revolution planned and executed by black middle-class Americans. Unpub. script in the Schomburg Collection.

Juba (musical, 1978). Prod. by La Mama E.T.C., 1978; dir. by John Vaccaro. Nominated for an AUDELCO Award for best musical creator.

Zora // Orig. title: **Zora Neale Hurston's Their Eyes Were Watching God** (biographical sketch, 1 act, 1978). Subtitled "A Play About Zora Neale Hurston." A portrait of the well-known author and folklorist of the Harlem Renaissance. Public reading under its orig title by FSWW, Jan. 14, 1978. First prod. in 1979; dir. by Yvonne Cheyne.

Prod. by the New Federal Theatre (NFT), New York, opening June 18, 1981, for 12 perfs.; dir. by Elizabeth Van Dyke. With Phylicia Ayers-Allen, Kirk Kirksey, and Denzel Washington. Prod. by the National Black Touring Circuit, in association with ROGER FURMAN's New Heritage Repertory Theatre (NHRT), opening Oct. 25, 1984; dir. by Elizabeth Van Dyke. With Yvonne Sutherland.

When the Chickens Came Home to Roost (biographical sketch, 1 act, 1981). Subtitled "A Play About Malcolm X and Elijah Muhammad and Their Last Confrontation." Prod. by NFT, opening June 18, 1981, for 12 perfs.; dir. by Allie Woods. With Kirk Kirksey as Elijah Muhammad and Denzel Washington as Malcolm X. Prod. by the National Black Touring Circuit in association with NHRT, opening Oct. 25, 1985; dir. by Kirk Kirksey and WOODIE KING, JR. With Kirk Kirksey and Basil Wallace. Winner of an AUDELCO Award for Best Playwright.

Dreams Deferred (1981). Prod. by NFT, Jan. 7, 1982, for 12 perfs.; dir. by Allie Woods. With Erma Campbell, Kim Sullivan, Clebert Ford, Phyllis Stickney, Kathleen Morrison, and Michael Alsen. Unpub. script in the Hatch-Billops Collection.

Hot Fingers (1 act, 1984). The story of ragtime jazz pianist, bandleader, and blues singer "Jelly Roll" Morton. Prod. at the Vital Arts Center, New York, Dec. 1984; dir. by Glenn Weiss. Featuring Bruce Strickland.

What It Is What It Ain't (1 act, 1984). The story of a man who becomes the first black mayor of New York City. Prod. by the Vital Arts Center, New York, Dec. 1984; dir. by Elliott Ware. Featuring Emil Herrera.

Woman (drama, full length, 1984). "The story of a female migrant worker who has to confront the world alone."—*Black Masks,* May 1985, p. 3. Prod. by the Paul Robeson Cabaret Theatre, Brooklyn, NY, April 12–May 12, 1985; dir. by Yvonne Sutherland. Featuring Judy Thames.

OTHER PLAYS AND DRAMATIC WORKS:
The Prophylactic (1970). **The Shadows** (1970). **Closed** (1972). **The Jackass** (1972). **The Mob** (1972). **The Shores** (1972). **Grey Boy** (1973). **Bird of Paradise** (1974). Prod. 1974; dir. by Jacquie Berger. Prod. 1975; dir. by Ornette Coleman. **The Whore** (1974). Prod. by the New York Theatre Ensemble during the 1974–75 season; dir. by Kirk Kirksey. **They Were All Gardenias** (1979). Prod. 1979; dir. by REGGE LIFE. **Five Points** (1982). Prod. 1982; dir. by Bill Maher.

HOLIFIELD, HAROLD, Playwright. A member of the Harlem Theatre Movement of the early 1950s.

PLAYS:
(Both prod. by the Council on the Harlem Theatre during the 1950–51 season.) **Cow in the Apartment** (late 1940s). **J. Toth** (1950).

HOLLAND, ENDESHA IDA MAE (1944–   ), Playwright, actress, director, activist, lecturer, and teacher. Born in Greenwood, MS. Educated at the Univ. of Minnesota (B.A. in Afro-American studies, 1979; M.A. in American studies, 1984; Ph.D. in American studies, 1985). Grew up in pre–civil rights Mississippi, the daughter of a prostitute-turned-madam who became a midwife in order to achieve respectability. Because of her early childhood experiences, which also included sexual molestation by her white employers, Endesha also turned briefly to prostitution as a temporary means of survival. Her life was turned around when civil rights workers came to Greenwood in 1963. Seeing the women doing such responsible jobs as typing and helping with voter registration, she joined the group as a volunteer and never returned to her old life. Holland is currently prof. and coordinator of Third World Women's Studies in the Dept. of Afro-American Studies at the Univ. of Buffalo. Her professional activities, too numerous to list, include supervisor, resident planners, Model City, Minneapolis, 1970–71; founder and executive director, Women Helping Offenders, Minneapolis, 1971–75; founder and chairwoman, National Assn. of Women Helping Offenders, Inc., Bloomington, 1975–77; playwright-in-residence, the Playwrights' Center, Minneapolis, 1980–81 and 1981–83; founder and artistic director, Lorraine Hansberry Writers' Workshop, Minneapolis, 1982–. She performed in, directed, and served as stage manager and choreographer for several dramatic productions at the Univ. of Minnesota while a student. She has also been involved in productions of At the Foot of the Mountain Theatre and the Penumbra Theatre. Because of her unusual background, she is in great demand as a lecturer, dramatic reader, and guest on radio and television shows. Her community activities are extensive and include contributions in the fields of theatre, education, religion, criminal justice, feminist issues, and race relations. Member of BTA, DG, and the American Studies Assn. Recipient of the following theatre awards: ACTF Student Playwriting Award, Univ. of Minnesota, Region 5, 1981; ACTF, Second Place, Lorraine Hansberry Playwriting Award, 1981; First Annual Playwriting Award presented by the Theatre Arts Dept., Univ. of Minnesota, 1981. Address—Office: Department of American Studies, University of Buffalo, 1010 Coemens Hall, Buffalo, NY 14260.

REPRESENTATIVE PLAYS AND DRAMATIC WORKS:

Second Doctor Lady (drama, 1 act, 1980). "Based on her mother's mid-wifery. The black midwife assists a white woman with a difficult birth in a hospital, then delivers a baby in a poor black home."—*Minneapolis Tribune,* Nov. 30, 1980, p. 1A. Selected for reading at the Mid-Western Theatre Conf., Omaha, March 1980. Produced as a workshop production by the Univ. of Minnesota, Dec. 1980. Broadcast over radio station WFAI, 1981. Entered in the Regional Festival of ACTF, 1981, where it earned for the author a commendation for excellence in playwriting. Finalist, Women Playwrights Festival, the Woman's Theatre, Seattle, WA, 1981. Reading, the Playwrights' Center, Minneapolis, followed by a rewrite, March 1982.

The Reconstruction of Dossie Ree Hemphill (drama, 1 act, 1980). Based on the author's mother's experiences as "madam" and midwife. As described by one journalist:

In her dual occupations, Holland's mother was privy to information and gossip from women of the town. "My mother didn't want me listening in on those conversations, but I'd be there, pretending I was asleep," Holland said. Incest was a common topic. "The Reconstruction of Dossie Ree Hemphill" springs from those overheard conversations. In the play a young woman has sex with her father. So does her younger sister, creating rivalry between the sisters. The older sister leaves the South and tries to overcome her feeling of worthlessness. [*Minneapolis Tribune,* Nov. 30, 1980, p. 1A]

Prod. as a workshop production by the Univ. of Minnesota, Experimental Theatre Workshop, Dec. 1980. Entered Regional Festival of ACTF, 1981, where it earned a commendation for excellence in playwriting. Produced by the Univ. of Minnesota during its theatre season.

Requiem for a Snake (TV and stage versions, 1980). Reading at the Playwrights' Center, Minneapolis, 1980. Staged reading, the Playwrights' Center, 1981. Public reading by the Frank Silvera Writers' Workshop, New York, Nov. 1981. Reading, Los Angeles Theatre Workshop, Nov. 1981.

Mrs. Ida B. Wells (one-woman show, full length, 1982). Highlights the life of the renowned activist-journalist, whose contributions to the black press were extensive. She became well-known for her writings in the *New York Age,* and for lecturing with other activists. Public reading at the Playwrights' Center, Minneapolis, July 1982. Prod. on a Black Theatre program at the American Coll. Theatre Assn. National Convention, St. Paul, MN, Aug. 1983.

OTHER PLAYS:
(In progress, 1984.) **From the Mississippi Delta** (series of 7 plays). **Fanny Lou. Prairie Women. The Autobiography of a Parader Without a Permit** (doctoral dissertation, now completed).

HOLLAND, J. HOWARD (Joseph H. Holland), Playwright. Based in New York City. A graduate of Hampton Inst.

PLAY:
Cast Me Down (historical play, full length, 1984). Stage documentary of incidents in the controversial life of Booker T. Washington, founder and first pres. of Tuskegee Inst. The story is told through the eyes of one of his enemies, Thomas D. Fortune, the dynamic black editor of the *New York Age,* whose editorials were highly critical of Washington's leadership. Prod. at Aaron Davis Hall, CCNY, Oct. 1984. Prod. as a Black History Month Special at Theatre Four, New York, opening Feb. 6, 1987, for a limited engagement.

HOLMAN, M. CARL (1919–   ), Poet and civil rights leader. President of the National Urban Coalition. One of the 100 Most Influential Black Americans, listed by *Ebony* magazine in 1968. Born in Minter City, MS. Currently lives in Washington, DC. His poetry has been published in numerous periodicals and anthologies. Member of the District of Columbia Board of Higher Education. Recipient of a Rosenwald and a John Hay Whitney Fellowship. Winner of the John Fisk Poetry Prize, Univ. of Chicago, and the Blevins Davis Playwriting Prize, Yale Univ.

PLAY:
The Baptizin' (1971). Premiered by the Little Theatre, Tulsa, OK, Summer 1971. Won first prize in the National Community Theatre Festival of the American Community Theatre Assn., 1971.

HOPKINS, LINDA (1925–   ), Singer-actress. Discovered by Mahalia Jackson. Sang for more than ten years with the Southern Harp Spiritual Singers. First appeared on Broadway in a supporting role as church soloist in *Purlie* (1970). Won both a Tony Award and a Drama Desk Award for her performance in *Inner City* (1971).

DRAMATIC WORK:
Me and Bessie (musical, full length, 1974). About the life and legend of Bessie Smith, portrayed through reminiscences, anecdotes, and songs. First prod. at the Mark Taper Forum in Los Angeles, and at Ford's Theatre in Washington, DC, prior to opening in New York at the Ambassador Theatre, Oct. 22, 1975, eventually moving to the Edison Theatre, for a combined run (in New York) of 453 perfs.; dir. by Robert Greenwald, and starring Hopkins as Bessie Smith, with Lester Wilson, and Jerry Dean.

HORNE, J. W. ROBINSON (1927–   ), Playwright, theatre critic, and U.S. Postal Service employee; also an actor, designer, choreographer, and impressario. Born in Richmond, VA, the brother of Nat Horne, the professional New York dancer, choreographer, teacher, and founder of the Nat Horne Musical Theatre and School. Educated at Virginia Union Univ. (B.S.), the Fashion Academy of New York City; and Virginia Commonwealth Univ. (theatre production). Founder, playwright, and producing director, the Christian Arts Co., 1951–present, a resident performing arts company of the Second Baptist Church, Richmond, VA, where for the past 32 years Horne has written, produced, and codirected the church's annual Easter Sunrise Service production—for which he has received numerous awards from various church groups, including a plaque (1974), a trophy (1976), and a golden cross (1981). He has also written, directed, and choreographed numerous community productions in Richmond for such groups as Delta Sigma Theta and Alpha Kappa Alpha sororities; and designed costumes for dance revues of the Leigh St. YMCA, 1951 and 1952, and for a theatrical production of the Richmond Community Theatre Guild, 1962. He has acted in, designed for, and choreographed several of his own productions, and was the first to introduce movement to music (dance) in a church production in Richmond—a trend that has since been emulated by others. Formerly a freelance writer, and currently performing arts critic, for the *Richmond Afro-American* newspaper. As an impressario, he originated and presented, with Vera E. Taylor, a series of concert galas, featuring outstanding Richmond artists and choral groups, to augment the musical culture of the community and to benefit the production of the Easter Sunrise Service pageants at Second Baptist Church. *Address:* 11 W. Clay St., Richmond, VA 23220.

PLAYS AND DRAMATIC WORKS:
(NOTE: Except where indicated, the following plays were first prod. at the annual Easter Sunrise Service of the year indicated, on the Sacred Stage of the Sanctuary of the Second Baptist Church, Idlewood Ave. and Randolph St., Richmond, VA; dir. by Vera E. Taylor.)

The Garden [of Easter] (Easter pageant with music, 1 act, 1952). Drama in free verse style, with sacred music composed by *Anne Harris Williams, and liturgical dance, reliving those crucial moments of the last days of Christ, in six sequences, depicted in a magnificent garden setting. The six sequences include The Garden of the Palms; The Last Supper; The Garden of Gethsemane; The Garden of Golgotha; The Garden of a Revelation; The Garden of the Resurrection. Prod. 1952, 1963, and 1973.

The Acts of Four Men (drama with music, 4 scenes 1959). Concerns the actions of four men at climactic moments when their lives were shaken by Jesus of Nazareth on the day he died. Performed in a contemporary setting and with modern costumes, denoting the timeless relationship of God and man. The four men portrayed are Joseph Caiaphas, High Priest of the Hebrew Nation; Judas Iscariot, Disciple-Betrayer; Simon, Called Peter, Disciple-Denier; and Pontius Pilate, Roman Governor of Judea. Prod. 1959, 1969, and 1975.

That Man John (religious drama with music, 1 act [4 scenes], 1961). About the last days of John the Baptist, the zealous evangelist and forerunner of Christ. Commissioned by the Virginia State Baptist Church School & Virginia State Baptist Training Union associations for their 1961 annual convention. Presented at the Fourth Baptist Church, Sixth Mt. Zion Baptist Church, and Mt. Olivet Baptist Church, all in Richmond.

Great Day (narrative with music, 13 sequences, 1964). The birth, passion, death, resurrection, and ascension of Jesus Christ based on 14 Negro spirituals. Prod. 1964.

The People vs. the Nazarene (drama, 2 acts [2 scenes], 1965). A Messianic drama with music in a courtroom style (the Sanhedrin, the Supreme Court of the ancient Jewish nation), about the most controversial man ever born, Jesus of Nazareth. Prod. 1965, 1966, and 1977.

Exultations (Easter program, 1967). A narrative of great Biblical events, from Genesis to Revelation, with selected sacred music that elicits exultations from man, the created, to God the Creator. Prod. 1967.

Soul at Sunrise (pageant with music, 3 sequences, 1970). Subtitled "The African-American Christian Experience." A saga of the soul man, the American of African descent, from his glorious age in ancient Africa (Alkebu-lan) to his arrival in America. As a slave he gave birth to the sacred sound of soul—the spiritual; and as a free man, he created the syncopated sound of soul—the black gospel sound. Sequence I—Souls in the Sun; Sequence II—Souls in Slave Ships; Sequence III—Souls' Sacred Sounds. Prod. 1970, 1973, and 1982.

Joy to Jesus Christ (religious musical, 1972). Subtitled "A Contemporary Conception of the Christ Chronicle with Rock/Gospel/Folk Music." Two black brothers in Christ meet and rap about Jesus in this musical happening, which set a precedent in the Second Baptist Church, Richmond, where it was originally performed—the introduction of choreography by the Christian Arts Co. Performing Celebration Chorus. Prod. 1973 and 1979.

Miracle Morning (Easter program, 1974). Subtitled "A Celebration in Christ for Singers, Musicians and Liturgical Dancers with Spirituals, Gospel, Rock, Sacred Music and also Jazz." Prod. 1974.

Entrances & Exits (Easter pageant, 1976). A collage of the most memorable moments from past prodns. of the author, with music, drama, and dance, commemorating the Silver Anniversary of the Annual Easter Sunrise Pageants at Second Baptist Church, Richmond, 1951–76. Prod. 1976.

Maggie Lena Mitchell Walker: Vanguard Virginian (a semi-documentary play with music and projections, 2 acts, 1980). Based on a suggestion by *Dr. Frances M. Foster. About a little-known incident in the life of Mrs. Maggie L. Walker, Virginia's most famous black woman. The plot revolves around Mrs. Walker's Senior Class of 1883 at the Richmond Normal School. Ten black members of this class in a high school with an all-white faculty set a precedent in the fight for human rights by going on strike in protest because they were refused commencement exercises in the same theatre as whites. First prod. at the Second Baptist Church, Richmond, Nov. 2, 1980; dir. by Frances G. Gordon. Also presented by the Arts and Humanities Center of the Richmond Public School, 1980.

Sisters (drama with music, 1980). Subtitled "The African-American Experience of the Black Woman." A saga of the "Soul Sister" from the great black queens of Africa, through slavery and emancipation, to the American Christian experience and achievements. Premiered Easter 1980.

Easter: A Jesus Jubilee ("A Musical Jubilation in Jesus Christ" [subtitle], 1981). "A potpourri of rewritten scenes from the author's eight religious productions over the past 30 years."—*Richmond Times Dispatch,* May 16, 1981 (Briggs). Also described as "a musical journey from the birth of the Lord into modern religious rock, capitalizing on the talents of a superbly trained array of singers and actors."—*Richmond News Leader,* April 18, 1981 (Templeton). Prod. 1981.

Rejoice in the Redeemer ("A Pageant of Rejoicement in Jesus Christ with Music and Drama" [subtitle], 3 acts, 1983). Featured music includes hymns, spirituals, and gospel and sacred selections from oratorios woven into a tapestry with dramatic interludes from the life of Christ. Prod. 1983.

Morningstar ("A Musical of the Messiah" [subtitle], 12 sequences, 1985). "A narrative with spirituals, hymns, gospel and rock music, of the Messiah. . . . The text of the musical is found in the Book of Revelation 22:16, 'I, Jesus, I am the bright Morning Star.' "—*Richmond Afro-American,* March 30, 1985. Prod. 1985.

Praises (Easter pageant, 1986). Musical and dramatic "praises" (highlights) from the author's past productions. Prod. 1986.

HORNE, JAN, Playwright. Associated with the Freedom Theatre of Philadelphia, PA.

PLAY:
East of Jordan (1969). Deals with some of the age-old problems of black family life. Prod. by the Freedom Theatre, 1969.

HOUSTON, DIANNE (1954–   ), Actress, director, and playwright, with a special interest in children's theatre. Born in Washington, DC. Received training in the theatre at DC's Workshops for Careers in the Arts and at Howard University, where as a drama student she was named best director for two consecutive years for her productions of PETER DeANDA's *Ladies in Waiting,* KELSIE COLLIE's *Black Images/Black Reflections,* and SAUNDRA SHARP's *The Sistuhs.* At Howard she formed a professional association with composer Latteta Brown, with whom she has collaborated on a number of children's songs and a children's musical. Has worked with several theatre groups, including the Ebony Impromptu Theatre in Washington, DC, and the City Street Theatre in New

York City. Has taught theatre at Duke Ellington School of the Arts, and theatre and photography at community centers in the District of Columbia. Codirector of the Children's Theatre Funshop, which has performed at a number of locations, including public schools, in New York City. One of three finalists in the Kennedy Center/Karamu House division of the National Black Playwrights Competition, late 1970s. *Address*—Home: 545 W. 148th St., Apt. 5D, New York, NY 10031. Office: Artistic Director, Creative Arts Team, New York University, New York, NY 10003.

PLAYS AND DRAMATIC WORKS:
The Fisherman (drama, full length, 1979). Musical score and theme by *Latteta Brown. It was inspired by the death of one of Houston's associates and the imprisonment of one of her friends during what has been called the "Hanafi Takeover" in Washington, DC. According to the playwright, "It does not tell the story of the Takeover, nor does it parallel the lives of the people and events involved. It attempts . . . to show that passion and/or grief unanswered can, and does turn to violence, to exploded rage and grief." For this play, the author was a finalist in the National Black Playwrights Competition. First prod. by the New Back Alley Theatre, Washington, DC, April 1980. Pub. in *Center Stage* (Ostrow, 1981). **The Tale of Peter Rabbit: A Musical Re-telling** (musical, 3 acts, pre-1981). Musical score by Latteta Brown.

HOUSTON, VELINA HASU, Amerasian playwright who describes her racial heritage as half-Japanese, one-quarter black, and one-quarter American Indian. ("I suppose that makes me legally all 3 and biologically none of the above.") Began to write plays at the age of 15. Received the B.A. in mass communications with a minor in drama from Kansas State Univ. at Manhattan, 1979, and the M.F.A. in playwriting from UCLA, 1971. Also studied at Playwrights and Co., the Lee Strasberg Creative Center, Hollywood. Member of DG, Pacific Asian American Women Writers/West, Assn. of Asian/Pacific American Artists, Amerasian Tamshii, and Board of Advisors of Cold Tofu Asian American Comedy-Improvisation Company. Assoc. artistic editor, *Time Capsule*, a literary magazine. Honors and awards include Phi Beta Kappa; honorable mention, one-act category, American College Theatre Regional Festival, St. Louis, 1976; winner, Best New Plays Festival, for *Petals and Thorns,* one of five new plays selected by the Los Angeles–based Company of Angels from nationwide submissions; national first prize, the David Lib. Playwriting Award, for the "Best New Play about American Freedom," 1982; national first prize, Lorraine Hansberry Playwriting Award, for the "Best Play about the Black Experience," 1982; Author of the Year, Friends of Little Tokyo of Los Angeles, 1984; Rockefeller Foundation Playwriting Fellow, 1984. *Agent:* Ms. Bobbi Thompson, Bloom, Levy, Shorr & Associates, 800 South Robertson Boulevard, Los Angeles, CA 90035.

PLAYS OF THE BLACK EXPERIENCE:
(Only Houston's plays of the black experience are listed below. Her play *Petals and Thorns* has been mentioned above. She has also written *Shinseku* ("New World") produced by the Asian American Theatre Co., San Francisco, March-April 1985.)

AsaGa Kimashita ("Morning Has Broken") (drama, full length, 1982). Winner of two national first prize awards in the American Coll. Theatre Festival (ACTF), 1982: the Lorraine Hansberry Award, for the "Best Play about the Black Experience," and the David Lib. Playwriting Award, for the "Best New Play about American Freedom." First prod. at the Studio Theatre, Macgowan Hall, UCLA, Dec. 1981; dir. by David Hillbrand. Entered in the ACTF at the John F. Kennedy Center for the Performing Arts, Washington, DC, 1982. Prod. by East West Players, Inc., Los Angeles, Jan.-Feb. 1984; dir. by Shizuko Hoshi. Prod. by Pacific Rim Productions, Center-Space/Theatre Artaud, San Francisco, Feb.-March 1985; dir. by David Hillbrand.

American Dreams (drama, full length, 1984). Post–World War II story in which a black American G.I. returns home with his Japanese bride and must face the objections of his family and the realities of life in America. Prod. by the Negro Ensemble Co., New York, Jan.-Feb. 1984; dir. by Samuel Barton.

HOWARD, VILMA, Playwright. Associated with the Southern Assn. of Dramatic and Speech Arts (SADSA) during the 1950s.

PLAY:
The Tam (1951). Pub. in *SADSA Encore* (McQuiddy Co., Nashville, 1951).

HUDSON, FRED (Frederick Douglass Hudson) (1928–   ), Playwright, screenwriter, and business executive. Born in Miami, FL. Received the B.A. from the Univ. of California/Berkeley, where he also attended graduate school. Pres. and artistic director of the Frederick Douglass Creative Arts Center, New York City, 1971–present. Recipient of an AUDELCO Award, 1979, and a Eugene O'Neill Playwrights Grant. *Address:* Frederick Douglass Creative Arts Center, 276 W. 43rd St., New York, NY 10036.

DRAMATIC WORKS:
If We Must Die (1975). Prod. by the B & B Experimental Theatre, San Francisco, CA, 1975. **The Education of Sonny Carson** (feature film, full length, 1974). Coauthor, with Michael Campus. Based on Carson's autobiography by the same title. About the growing up of a rebellious black youth in the ghetto of the Bedford-Stuyvesant area of Brooklyn, NY, during the 1950s. Prod. by Paramount Pictures, 1974; dir. by Michael Campus. With Ronny Clanton (in the title role), Don Gordon, Joyce Walker, and PAUL BENJAMIN.

HUGHES, (James) LANGSTON (1902–1967), Author, poet, playwright and editor. One of America's most prolific black writers, who has been called "the poet laureate of the Black race" and "the dean of Black American professional writers." One of the best-known products of the Harlem Renaissance. The author or editor of more than 35 published volumes, including poetry, novels, short stories, plays, biography, history, and anthologies. Born in Joplin, MO. Grew up in Lawrence, KS, and Cleveland, OH. Graduated from Central H.S. in Cleveland, 1920, where he began writing poems and edited the senior yearbook. Spent one year, 1921–22, at Columbia Coll. (now Univ.), after which he decided to see the world, traveling to Africa, Italy, Paris, Spain, and Russia. Completed

his education at Lincoln Univ. in Pennsylvania (B.A. 1929). Resident play-
wright, Karamu Theatre, Cleveland, 1936 and 1939. Correspondent, *Afro-American* Newspapers, Baltimore, 1937. Founder, Harlem Suitcase Theatre, 1938;
founder, New Negro Theatre, Los Angeles, 1939; founder, Skyloft Players,
Chicago, 1941. Columnist, *Chicago Defender,* 1943–67. Poet-in-residence,
Univ. of Chicago Laboratory School, 1949. Volumes of poetry include *The
Weary Blues* (1926), *Fine Clothes to the Jew* (1927), *Dear Lovely Death* (1931),
The Dream Keeper (1932), *Shakespeare in Harlem* (1942), *Fields of Wonder*
(1947), *Montage of a Dream Deferred* (1951), *Ask Your Mama* (1961), and *The
Panther and the Lash* (1967). Novels include *Not Without Laughter* (1930) and
Tambourines to Glory (1959). Short stories include *The Ways of White Folks*
(1934), *Laughing to Keep from Crying* (1952), and *Something in Common and
Other Stories* (1963). Autobiographies include *The Big Sea* (1940) and *I Wonder
as I Wander* (1964). Books on black history include *A Pictorial History of the
Negro in America* (with Milton Meltzer, 1963) and *Black Magic: A Pictorial
History of the Negro in American Entertainment* (with Milton Meltzer, 1967).
His "Simple" books (about a character named Jesse B. Semple) include *Simple
Speaks His Mind* (1950), *Simple Takes a Wife* (1953), *Simple Stakes a Claim,*
and *Simple's Uncle Sam* (1965). His children's books include *The First Book
of Negroes* (1952), *Famous American Negroes* (1954), *The First Book of Jazz*
(1955), and *Famous Negro Heroes of America* (1958). His edited anthologies
include *The Poetry of the Negro 1946–1949* (with Arna Bontemps, 1949), *The
Langston Hughes Reader* (1958), *The Book of Negro Folklore* (with Arna Bontemps, 1958), *New Negro Poets: U.S.A.* (1964), *The Book of Negro Humor*
(1966), and *The Best Short Stories by Negro Writers* (1967). Memberships
included AFTRA, ASCAP, Authors Guild, DG, NAG, P.E.N., and WGA/East.
Recipient of *Opportunity* Poetry Prize, 1925; Harmon Gold Medal for Literature,
1931; Guggenheim Fellowship, 1935; Rosenwald Fellowship, 1942; American
Academy of Arts and Letters Grant, 1947; Anisfield-Wolf Award, 1953; Spingarn
Medal, 1960.

COLLECTIONS:
FOUR POEMS AND A PLAY IN VERSE. Golden Stair Press, New York, 1932.
Contains **Scottsboro Limited** (1931).

THE LANGSTON HUGHES READER. George Braziller, New York, 1958. Contains
Glory of Negro History (1958), **Soul Gone Home** (1937), and **Simply Heavenly** (1957).

FIVE PLAYS BY LANGSTON HUGHES. Edited by Walter Smalley. Indiana Univ.
Press, Bloomington, 1963. Contains **Mulatto** (1930), **Soul Gone Home** (1937), **Little
Ham** (1935), **Simply Heavenly** (1957), and **Tambourines to Glory** (1963).

**PLAYS AND DRAMATIC WORKS WRITTEN, PRODUCED, AND/OR
PUBLISHED SINCE 1950:**
Mulatto (tragedy, 2 acts, 1930). Based on his short story "Father and Son." Later
adapt. into an opera, **The Barrier** (1950). Concerns the tragic conflict between a white
plantation owner and his mulatto son in the Deep South. Written 1930. First prod. on
Bway in a version adapt. by producer Martin Jones at the Vanderbilt Theatre, Oct. 24,

1935, where it established a record of 373 perfs.—the longest run on Bway up to that time for a play by a black playwright. Toured for eight months in the United States, including a three-week stay in Chicago at the Studebaker Theatre, opening Dec. 25, 1936; dir. by Martin Jones. With Stuart Beebe as the white colonel, Morris McKenney as the son, featuring †Rose McClendon as the mother (and after her death, Mercedes Gilbert). First prod. in the author's orig. version by the Gilpin Players at the Karamu Theatre, Cleveland, March 8, 1938. Prod. in Italy, with Italian actors in blackface, as a part of the repertory of the Compagnia del Teatro Italiano in Rome and Milan, during the 1950s, where it ran for two years. Also prod. in Buenos Aires in the late 1950s. Text of the orig. version pub. in *FIVE PLAYS BY LANGSTON HUGHES*. Also in *Black Drama: An Anthology* (Brasmer & Consolo, 1970). Text of the Martin Jones adaptn. used for the Bway prodn. pub. in *Three Negro Plays* (Bigsby, 1964). Italian edition: *Mulatto, Drama in Due Atti e Tre Scene,* translated by A. Ghireli, pub. by A. Mondadori, Milan, 1949. Spanish edition: *Mulato, Drama en Dos Actos,* translated by J. Galer; pub. by Editorial Quetzal, Buenos Aires, 1954. Czechoslovakian edition: *Mulat,* translated by B. Becher; pub. by Dilia Publishers, Prague, date unknown. Copies of all texts, including foreign editions, are located in the Schomburg Collection.

Little Ham (comedy, 3 acts, 1935). Play of Harlem life during the 1920s, revolving around the escapades of Hamlet Jones, a carefree, antiheroic Harlem "sporting" type. First prod. by the Gilpin Players at the Karamu Theatre, Cleveland, June 9–14, 1936, for 6 perfs. Revived by the Karamu Theatre, May 25–June 6, 1938, for 9 perfs. Pub. in *FIVE PLAYS BY LANGSTON HUGHES*.

The Emperor of Haiti (tragedy, 3 acts, 1935). Concerns the heroic rise from slavery and the tragic downfall of the Haitian emperor Dessalines during the Napoleonic era. First prod. as *Troubled Island* by the Gilpin Players, at the Karamu Theatre, Nov. 18–23, 1936, for 6 perfs. Prod. as *Drums of Haiti* by the Roxanne Players, Detroit, c. 1937. (Revised under its present title, 1938.) Prod. in Harlem as *The Emperor of Haiti* by the Manhattan Art Theatre, at St. Martin's Episcopal Church Theatre, for 4 perfs; and at the Joseph P. Kennedy, Jr., Memorial Community Center Theatre, for 4 additional perfs., 1958. (Adapt. into the opera **Troubled Island,** 1949.) Again revised as a drama, 1963. Pub. under its present title in *Black Drama in America* (Turner, 1971). Manuscript of **Drums of Haiti** in the James Weldon Johnson Memorial Collection/YUL.

Mule Bone (folk play, 3 acts, 1930s). Coauthor, with †Zora Neale Hurston. Based on folk material collected by Hurston, some of which later appeared in her book, *Mules and Men*. Written during the 1930s. Sched. for prodn. by the Gilpin Players, but never prod. because of a literary quarrel between the coauthors, which Hughes reported in his autobiography, *The Big Sea*. Excerpt (Act III) pub. in *Drama Critique* (The Negro in the Theatre), Spring 1964.

The Barrier (opera; also called a musical drama, 2 acts, 1950). Libretto and lyrics by Hughes. Musical score by Jan Meyerowitz. Based on the author's play **Mulatto** (1930) and his earlier short story "Father and Son," both concerning the tragic conflict between a white plantation owner and his mulatto son in the Deep South. First prod. by the Columbia Univ. Opera Workshop at Brander Mathews Theatre, New York, Jan. 18, 1950. Prod. on Bway, at the Bradhurst Theatre, Nov. 2–4, 1950, for 4 perfs. Principals included Lawrence Tibbett, Muriel Rahn, Lorenza Herrera, and Wilson Clary, with Reri Grist in the supporting cast. Then went on tour, including a week at the Lydia Mendelssohn Theatre, Ann Arbor, MI. Prod. as a concert perf. in NYU's third annual summer concert series, July 24, 1961. Copies of libretto in the Schomburg Collection and the James

Weldon Johnson Memorial Collection/YUL. Full musical score pub. by Edward B. Marks Music Corp., New York.

Just Around the Corner (musical, 2 acts, 1951). Lyrics by Hughes. Book by Abby Mann and Bernard Drew. Music by Joe Sherman. First prod. as a summer theatre production at the Ogunquit Playhouse, ME, Aug. 1951. Copy in the Schomburg Collection.

The Wizard of Altoona (musical, 3 acts, 1951). Music by Elie Siegmeister. About carnival people, focusing mainly on their love affairs and business relationships. Apparently incomplete. Copy in the James Weldon Johnson Memorial Collection/YUL.

Soul Gone Home (opera, 1 act, 1954). Adaptn. with musical score by *Ulysses Kay of Hughes's play in one act by the same title (1937) [see OTHER PLAYS . . . below]. The "spirit" of a dead son accuses his prostitute mother of misconduct and neglect for his untimely death. Copy in the James Weldon Johnson Memorial Collection/YUL.

Simple Takes a Wife (folk comedy, full length, 1955). The orig. dramatic version of Hughes's novel *Simple Takes a Wife,* which in 1957 was expanded into the musical **Simply Heavenly** (1957) [see below]. Prod. in Prague, Czechoslovakia, 1959. Unpub. script in the Schomburg Collection.

Esther (opera, 3 acts, 1957; also in one act version, 1957). Musical score by Jan Meyerowitz. Biblical opera, based on the Book of Esther and other sources. Commissioned by the Fromm Music Foundation. First prod. by the Univ. of Illinois, at the Urbana Musical Festival, March 1957. Prod. by the New England Conservatory of Music, Boston, 1958. Libretto in German (without music), translated by Jean Geiringer; pub. by Associated Music Publishers, New York; copy in the Schomburg Collection.

Simply Heavenly (musical comedy, 2 acts [17 scenes], 1957). Book and lyrics by Hughes. Music by *David Martin. Based on Hughes's nonmusical play, **Simple Takes a Wife** (1955), which was in turn based on his novel by the same title, concerning the courtship and marriage of Jesse B. Semple, a colorful Harlemite. First prod. Off-Bway at the 85th St. Playhouse, May 21, 1957, for a highly successful run; dir. by Joshua Shelley. Featuring Melvin Stewart and Claudia McNeil. Opened on Bway, at the Playhouse Theatre, Aug. 20, 1957, for 62 perfs., with the same director and cast. Prod. Off-Bway, at the Renata Theatre, beginning Nov. 8, 1957, with the same director and cast. An English version opened in London at the Adelphi Theatre, May 20, 1957, following a successful tour of the British provinces. Prod. by the Gilpin Players at Karamu House, May 5, 1958. Prod. on national TV by the "Play of the Week" series during the week of Dec. 7, 1959. Also prod. by a number of colleges and universities, including Howard Univ., Talladega Coll., and Florida A. & M. Coll. (now Univ.) which presented it on a seven-week tour of Europe. Pub. by Dramatists Play Service, New York, 1959. In *THE LANGSTON HUGHES READER;* in *FIVE PLAYS BY LANGSTON HUGHES;* and in *Black Theater* (Patterson, 1971). Condensed version for a recording script in the Schomburg Collection. Cast recording by Columbia (OL5240).

Glory of Negro History (pageant, 1958). Pub in *THE LANGSTON HUGHES READER.* Recorded by Folkways (FP752).

Shakespeare in Harlem (theatre work, full length, 1959). Adaptn. by ROBERT GLENN of the poetry of Hughes, utilizing the music of †James Weldon Johnson. Although the title is based on a 1942 volume by Hughes, most of the poems were taken from his *Montage of a Dream Deferred* (1951). A staged reading with characterizations, movement, music, and dance, designed to give a dramatic portrait of the poet/playwright himself. Thrice prod. in New York, during the 1959–60 season—at the White Barn Theatre, at the Theatre De Lys (ANT Matinee Series), and at the 41st St. Theatre. Prod. by the Karamu Theatre, Cleveland, April 1961.

Port Town (opera, 1 act, 1960). Libretto by Hughes. Musical score by Jan Meyerowitz. First prod. with the Boston Symphony, at the Berkshire Music Festival, Tanglewood, MA, Aug. 4, 1960.

Ballad of the Brown King (Christmas cantata; also called a Christmas song play; 2 acts, 1960). Music by †Margaret Bonds. The story of the dark king among the three wise men; dedicated to Martin Luther King, Jr. (a modern king), prior to his death. (Much of this material was later reworked into Hughes's widely produced Christmas song play, **Black Nativity** [1961].) Prod. at the Clark Auditorioum of the New York YMCA, Dec. 11, 1960. Prod. by the East Side Development, New York, 1961.

Mr. Jazz (musical theatre work, 1960).

Black Nativity ("Christmas Song Play" [subtitle]; also called a gospel song play as well as a gospel pageant; 2 acts, 1961). Celebration of the birth of Christ and the spread of the gospel, in the black idiom, with gospel music, spirituals, dance, drama, and narration. (Included some material from his Christmas cantata, **The Ballad of the Brown King** [1960].) Winner of the Catholic Dove Award at Cannes, France. First prod. Off-Bway, at the 41st St. Theatre, opening Dec. 11, 1961. Moved to the New York Theatre, Jan. 9–28, 1962, for a total of 57 perfs.; dir. by VINNETTE CARROLL. Featuring Marion Williams and the Stars of Faith. Presented at the Festival of Two Worlds in Spoleto, Italy, June 1962. Opened in London at the Criterion Theatre, Aug. 14, 1962; toured elsewhere in England, as well as Oslo, Copenhagen, Hamburg, and Brussels. Returned to New York for 7 perfs., during the Christmas season at Philharmonic Hall, Lincoln Center, Dec. 23–30, 1962. Resumed European tour, opening in Paris at the Theatre Champs Elysees, Jan. 3, 1963, followed by a six-month tour through Italy, Germany, the Netherlands, Belgium, Switzerland, and Sweden. Began American tour, opening in Boston, Oct. 14, 1963, and closing in Chicago, Jan. 12, 1964. Prod. Off-Off-Bway by the Afro-American Studio, in repertory, during the 1968–69 season; dir. by ERNIE McCLINTOCK. Unpub. script in the Schomburg Collection. Cast recording by Vee Jay (VJS-8503).

Gospel Glow // Orig. title: **The Gospel Glory** ("A Passion Play" [subtitle]; also called a gospel song play; 1 long act [revised from its former two-act version], 1962). Title revised to distinguish it from **Tambourines to Glory** (1963), one of Hughes's more important plays. Described by the author as "the first Negro passion play, depicting the life of Christ from the cradle to the cross."—Program Notes. Utilizes spirituals, gospel hymns, and pantomime for the purpose of telling the story. First prod. under orig. title at Washington Temple, Church of God in Christ, Brooklyn, NY, opening Oct. 26, 1962, for 2 perfs.; and in Westport, CT, 1962, for 1 perf. Prod. by the Wheatley Players at the dedication of the Don Valles Theatre, Cleveland, 1973. Unpub. scripts of **The Gospel Glory** in the Schomburg Collection and in the Archives of the Manuscript Div., State Historical Soc. of Wisconsin, at Madison. Unpub. script of **Gospel Glow** in the James Weldon Johnson Memorial Collection/YUL.

Tambourines to Glory (gospel song play, 2 acts [12 scenes], 1963). Music by *Jobe Huntley. Envolved from some of Hughes's poems which had been previously turned into gospel songs by Huntley, an earlier play written around these songs, and Hughes's novel *Tambourines to Glory*. Comic melodrama in which two women are assisted by the Devil in disguise in their efforts to establish a storefront church in Harlem. First prod. at the Little Theatre, West 44th St., New York, Nov. 2–23, 1963, for 24 perfs.; dir. by Nikos

Psacharopoulos. Featuring Louis Gossett, Hilda Simms, Clara Ward, and ROSETTA LeNOIRE. Pub. in *FIVE PLAYS BY LANGSTON HUGHES*. Songs from the musical are pub. in *Tambourines to Glory Gospel Songs,* by Hughes and Jobe Huntley, New York, 1958. Recorded by Folkways Records (FG3538), 1958.

Jerico-Jim Crow (song play, full length, 1963). (Also spelled *Jericho* in some listings.) The story of the black man's long struggle for freedom and equality in America, utilizing freedom songs, gospel music, spirituals, poetry, and narrative. First prod. Off-Bway by the Greenwich Players, Inc., "in coordination" with CORE, NAACP, and SNCC, at the Sanctuary, 143 W. 13th St., New York City, opening Dec. 28, 1963, and running on Saturdays and Sundays until April 26, 1964, for about 40 perfs.; dir. by Alvin Ailey and WILLIAM HAIRSTON. Cast included Gilbert Price, Hilda Harris, Joseph Attles, Rosalie King, James Woodall, and Dorothy Drake. Also perfs. in other halls and churches. Revived Off-Bway during the 1967–68 season. Unpub. script in the James Weldon Johnson Memorial Collection/YUL, the Billy Rose Theatre Collection/NYPL, and the Schomburg Collection. Orig. cast recording by Folkways/Scholastic (FL9671).

Beyond the Blues (TV script with music, 1964). Utilized several of Hughes's poems, read to music, including "Mother to Son," "Negro Dancers," "The Negro Speaks of Rivers," and "When Sue Wears Red." Prod. 1964.

It's a Mighty Wind (TV script with music, 1965). Easter program, utilizing a few of Hughes's poems from *Fields of Wonder,* sung by Odetta strolling on the California coast. Prod. by CBS-TV, Spring 1965.

Mother and Child (theatre vignette, 1 act, 1965). Based on his short story by the same title, pub. in *The Ways of White Folks* (1934). The members of the black ladies' missionary society gossip about the white woman whose newborn child was fathered by a black man. Prod. Off-Bway by the American Place Theatre, 1965; dir. by WOODIE KING, JR. Pub. in *Black Drama Anthology* (King & Milner, 1972).

The Prodigal Son (gospel song play, 1 act, 1965). Rousing retelling of the well-known Biblical parable in song, dance, and drama. First prod. Off-Bway at the Greenwich Mews Theatre, opening May 20, 1965, for more than 14 perfs.; dir. by Vinnette Carroll, and featuring Philip A. Stamps and GLORY VAN SCOTT. Went on tour abroad in the fall of 1965, playing in England, Belgium, the Netherlands, and France. Pub. in *Players* Magazine, Dec. 1967–Jan. 1968.

The Weary Blues (theatre work with music, 1966). Authorized adaptn. by Woodie King, Jr., of Hughes's poetry and prose. Based mainly on Hughes's first book of poems, *The Weary Blues* (1926), using additional prose and poetry from his other works, with setting in Harlem, and W.C. Handy's blues added as an integral part of the concept. Prod. by Actors Equity Theatre, at Lincoln Center, New York, Oct. 31, 1966.

Strollin' Twenties (TV script, 1966). With music by *Duke Ellington. A TV spectacular, set in Harlem in the 1920s. Conceived and prod. by *Harry Belafonte, who starred in this prodn., which also featured such top black stars as Sidney Poitier, Sammy Davis, Jr., Diahann Carroll, Nipsey Russell, Joe Williams, Gloria Lynn, and George Kirby.

Soul Yesterday and Today (theatre work, 1966). By Hughes and *Bob Teague, arranged by Rosetta LeNoire. A historical treatment of "soul" as it relates to black lifestyles, using some of the works of Hughes and others. Prod. by AMAS Repertory Theatre, at Central Park Mall, New York, Aug. 28, 1969.

OTHER PLAYS AND DRAMATIC WORKS PRIOR TO 1950:
The Gold Piece (children's play, 1 act, 1920s). **Scottsboro Limited** (play in verse, 1 act, 1931). **Cock o de World** (musical comedy, 3 acts, 1931). Adapt. by Hughes from a play by †Kaj Gynt. With lyrics by †Duke Ellington. **Angelo Herndon Jones** (drama, 1 act, 1936). **No Left Turn** (comedy, 1 act, 1936). **St. Louis Woman** (adaptn., full length, 1936). Revision by Hughes of the orig. play by †Arna Bontemps and †Countee Cullen. **When the Jack Hollars, or Careless Love** (folk comedy, 3 acts, 1936). **Don't You Want to Be Free** (musical pageant, 1 long act, 1937; revised 1963). **Soul Gone Home** (fantasy, 1 act, 1937). **Joy to My Soul** (farce, 3 acts, 1937). **The Em-Fuehrer Jones** (satirical skit, 1 act, 1938). **Limitations of Life** (satirical skit, 1 act, 1939). **Little Eva's End** (satirical skit, 1 act, 1938). **Front Porch** (3 acts, 1938). **Like a Flame** (drama, 1 act, 1938). Dramatization by Alice Holdship Ware of Hughes's poem "Tomorrow." **De Organizer** (blues opera, 1 act, 1938). **Way Down South** (feature film, full length: screenplay, 1939). Coauthor, with †Clarence Muse. **Trouble with the Angels** (drama, 1 act, 1930s). Based on Hughes's short story by the same title. **Booker T. Washington in Atlanta** (radio script, 1940). **Cavalcade of the Negro Theatre** (theatre script, 1940). Coauthor, with Arna Bontemps. **Tropics After Dark** (musical theatre work, 2 acts, 1940). Coauthor, with Arna Bontemps. **Jubilee: A Cavalcade of the Negro Theatre** (radio script, 1941). Coauthor, with Arna Bontemps. **Sun Do Move** // Orig. title: **Sold Away** (musical drama, 3 acts and prologue, 1941). **Brothers** (radio script, 1942). **For This We Fight** (radio script with music, 1942/44). **That Eagle** (patriotic play with music, 1942). **Freedom's Plow** (radio script, 1943). **John Henry Hammers It Out** (radio script with music, 1943). **In the Service of My Country** (radio script, 1944). **The Man Who Went to War** (radio script with music, 1944). **Pvt. Jim Crow** (radio script, 1945). **Street Scene** (folk opera, 2 acts, 1947) Libretto by Elmer Rice. Lyrics by Hughes. Musical score by Kurt Weill. **Swing Time at the Savoy** (radio script, 1949). Coauthor, with †Noble Sissle. **Troubled Island** (opera, 4 acts, 1949). Musical score by †William Grant Still. Based on Hughes's play **The Emperor of Haiti** (1935). NOTE: The following additional scripts are all undated: **Adam and Eve and the Apple** (opera, 1 act: libretto). **At the Jazz Ball** (musical theatre works: lyrics, with others). **Five Foolish Virgins** (opera, 2 acts: libretto). Musical score by Jan Meyerowitz. **Outshines the Sun** (drama). **Tell It to Telstar** (musical play, 1 act). **Wide Wide River** (folk opera: libretto). Music by Granville English.

HUGHLEY, YOUNG, Playwright. One of the founding members of the Black Image Theatre, Atlanta, GA, consisting of many of the products of the Morehouse-Spelman Players.
PLAY:
Peace for the Manchild (1972). "About George Jackson (Soledad Brother) and his family."—*Black World,* April 1973, p. 89. Deals with many of the problems of the black male in general, as well as the problems of black family relationships. Prod. by the Black Image Theatre, at their Studio Theatre, "way out on Peachtree Street" in Atlanta, Dec. 1972.

HULETT, MICHAEL, Playwright. Based in New York City.
PLAY:
Basin Street // Orig. title: **Storyville** (musical, 2 acts, pre–1983). Book coauthored by Hulett and G. WILLIAM OAKLEY, who also directed. Lyrics by Hulett. Music by

Turk Thom Bridwell. Jazz-blues musical, set in the Storyville District of New Orleans in 1917. Prod. under its present title by the New Federal Theatre, New York, Sept. 8–25, 1983. Unpub. script entitled **Storyville** in the Hatch-Billops Collection.

HULT, RUBY, Playwright.

PLAY:

The Saga of George Bush (1962). Pub. in *Negro Digest,* Sept. 1962, pp. 88–96.

HUNKINS, LEE (Leecynth) (1930–   ), Playwright, television scriptwriter, retired federal employee. Born in New York City's Harlem community, where she graduated from George Washington H.S. Also attended NYU. Gained theatrical experience with MAXWELL GLANVILLE's American Community Theatre (ACT) in Harlem, where she learned her craft from the ground up, and where several of her early plays, now unavailable, were first produced. Has also been affiliated with the Writers Workshop of the New York Shakespeare Festival. Recently retired from the Social Security Admin., after 34 years with the federal government. During all these years, most of her writing was done in the evenings and on weekends. A believer in positive thinking and a practitioner of Religious Science and yoga. Also enjoys chess and dancing. Recipient of ABC Theatre Award in the "New Drama for Television" project of the Eugene O'Neill Theatre Center's National Playwrights Conf. *Address:* P.O. Box 408, New York, NY 10024. *AGENT:* Flora Roberts, 157 W. 57th Street, New York, NY 10019.

REPRESENTATIVE PLAYS AND DRAMATIC WORKS:

26501 (fantasy, 1 act, early 1960s). A guide for the souls of the newly dead tires of his job and is punished by being returned to earthly existence. Prod. by ACT in Harlem, early 1960s. Also prod. by the Old Reliable Theatre, in the East Village, New York, 1960s.

Maggie (drama, 1 act, late 1960s). Concerns a prostitute who tries to change her life by becoming a nun. Prod. by the Negro Ensemble Summer Festival, New York, late 1960s. Not available.

The Dolls (drama, 1 act, 1969). About three life-sized puppets who come alive. First prod. by the Afro-American Total Theatre, at International House, New York, Nov. 1–2, 1969. Prod. by the Old Reliable Theatre, New York, 1971, with music by Steve Chambers. Prod. by The Family, New York, 1970s.

Hollow Images (TV play, 2 hours, 1973). Explores the question, Can one go home again? Based on the author's experience of leaving Harlem and returning years later to find it drastically changed. Selected by the Eugene O'Neill Writers Conf., Waterford, CT, and prod. by the National Playwrights Conf., 1978; dir. by Marilyn Mossman. There it was winner of the ABC Theatre Award, which consisted of $10,000 and the right of ABC to option the script. Telecast by the ABC Theatre, as a Tutus Production, June 24, 1979; dir. by Marvin Chomsky.

Revival (sketch, 1 act, early 1970s). Slice-off-life vignette, involving the relationships among four vagrants, two black, two white, and their efforts to revitalize their lives. Their opportunity comes when they see an announcement of a religious revival meeting, and they elect one of their group to pose as a minister at the meeting. Pub. in *Center Stage* (Ostrow, 1981).

OTHER PLAYS:
(Prod. in the 1960s—not currently available.) **The Square Peg** (3 acts). **Fading Hours** (1 act). **Another Part of Tomorrow** (3 acts). **The Visitor** (monologue). **The Leper** (monologue).

HUNTLEY, ELIZABETH MADDOX, Playwright and drama teacher.

PLAYS:
Legion, the Demoniac (1950). Pub. in *American Literature by Negro Authors* (Dreer, 1950). **What Ye Sow** (drama, full length [97 pp.], 1955). "Concerned with the trials and triumphs of a dedicated and forward-looking pastor."—*Crisis*, Feb. 1955, p. 85. Pub. by Court Press (or possibly Comet Press), 1955.

HUNTLEY, MADELINE, Playwright. Resides in New York City. *Address:* 2181 Madison Ave., New York, NY 10037.

PLAYS:
The Sheltered (drama, 1 act, 1968). A middle–aged couple who have loved each other for many years but were never married finally unite, only to live out their lives separately. **A Piece of the Action** (drama, 1 act, 1969). Concerns the reformation of an ex-junkie. **Havoc in Harlem** (pre-1985). Unpub. script in the Hatch-Billops Collection.

I

IHUNANYA, GRACE COOPER. See COOPER, GRACE.

IMAN, YUSEF (1933–   ), Poet, singer, actor, playwright, and director. Born in Savannah, GA. Married; five children. Gained theatrical experience as a member of AMIRI BARAKA's Spirit House in Newark, NJ, and with ROGER FURMAN's New Heritage [Repertory] Theatre in New York City. For several years he has been director of the Weusi Kuumba Troupe in Brooklyn, NY. Performed in the New Federal Theatre prodn. of *What the Wine-Sellers Buy* (1973). Recorded his poetry on the Jihad Productions recording *Black and Beautiful.* His volumes of poetry include *Something Black* (1967) and *Poetry for Beautiful Black Women* (1969). Has contributed poetry to *The Journal of Black Poetry* and to numerous anthologies. Some of his poetry was used as a grand finale for the cultural exhibit "Harlem on My Mind." *Address*—Office: 10 Claver Place, Brooklyn, NY 11238.

REPRESENTATIVE PLAYS AND DRAMATIC WORKS:
Praise the Lord, but Pass the Ammunition (revolutionary drama, 1 act, 1967). Explores the effectiveness of violence versus nonviolence in the solution of racial problems. First prod. at Spirit House, Newark, NJ, 1967. Sched. for prodn. by the Hill Arts Theatre, New Haven, CT, 1970. Pub. by Jihad Productions, Newark, NJ, 1967.

Sociology 700 (Clean Up Time) (didactic play, 1 act, 1970). Urges black pimps, prostitutes, and homosexuals to transform their lives and become aware of their blackness. Prod. at Sethlow Community Center, New York, July 1970.

The Junkie (monologue, 1 act, 1974). A junkie complains that his case is no worse than anybody else's, because most people have some kind of hangup, such as alcohol, tobacco, or sex. Prod. at The East, New York, Aug. 1974.

Yesterday, Today, Tomorrow (historical pageant, full length, 1974). Coauthor, with BEN CALDWELL. A dramatization of the Seven Principles of the Black Value System, called the *Nguso Saba*. Produced by the Weusi Kuumba Troupe at the Black Theatre Alliance annual festival, New York, Summer 1974.

Book Worm (didactic play, 1 act, 1975). Exhortation to black men to change the lives of black women, including prostitutes. Prod. by the Weusi Kuumba Troupe, Brooklyn, 1975.

OTHER PLAYS AND DRAMATIC WORKS:
Nigger House (didactic domestic drama, 1 act, 1965). **Dope: The Cause, the Cure** (antidrug play with music, 1 act, 1967). **Santa's Last Ride** (anti-Christmas play, 1 act, 1967). **Jihad** (didactic play, 1 act, 1968). **Resurrection** (didactic play, 1 act, 1969). **The Joke's on You** (satire, 1970). **The Verdict Is Yours** (protest play, 1 act, 1970). **Libra** (morality drama, 2 acts, 1971). **The Pride of Revolution** (revolutionary drama, 1 act, 1971). **Blowing Temptation Away** (1972). **Mr. Bad** (1972). **Respect** (didactic drama, 1 act, 1973). **We Wear the Mask** (morality play, 1 act, 1973). **Dope Pusher** (antidrug play, 1 act, 1970s).

IRVINE, WELDON, JR., Playwright. Associated with the Frank Silvera Writers' Workshop (FSWW) in New York City. *Address:* 110–21 195th St., Hollis, NY 11412.

PLAYS:
Young, Gifted and Broke (musical, 1977). Prod. at the Billie Holiday Theatre, Brooklyn, NY; dir. by Marjorie Moon. NOTE: The following plays received a public reading by the FSWW, and their unpub. scripts are located in the FSWW Archives/ Schomburg Collection: **How Long Must I Wander. The Priest and the Prostitute. The Will.**

IYUAN, IFA, Playwright. Associated with the New Federal Theatre (NFT) in New York City.

DRAMATIC WORKS:
Drinkwater (musical, 1975). Book by Iyaun. Music by *Johnny Taylor. Presented by NFT, opening April 18, 1975; dir. by Denise Hamilton. **You Don't Get Off Here to Catch the Express** (musical comedy, 1 act, 1975). Lyrics coauthored with BARRY AMYER KALEEM. Music arranged by Andre Ingram and Palmer Lampkin. About the stratified society within the so-called melting pot of New York's Lower East Side. Prod. by NFT, July 1975.

J

JACKMON, MARVIN E. See MARVIN X (alphabetized under "M").

JACKSON, ANGELA, Poet, playwright, and fiction writer. Chairperson of the OBAC (Organization of Black American Culture) Workshop, Chicago. Contributor to *Black Scholar*. Her work has been produced in New York by the New Federal Theatre (NFT).

PLAY:
Shango Diaspora (musical, full length, 1982). Music by Eli Joenai. Prod. by NFT, opening July 9, 1982; dir. by Abena Joan Brown.

JACKSON, C. BERNARD (Clarence) (1927–   ), Composer, playwright, theatrical director, and theatre administrator. Born in Brooklyn, NY. Educated at the H.S. of Music and Arts (art major), Brooklyn Coll., and UCLA (B.A., M.A.). Musical director, Dance Center, Los Angeles, 1954–56. Choral director, Los Angeles Bureau of Music, 1956–57. Staff member, Dept. of Dance, UCLA, 1957–61; musical director of graduate concerts, 1963; lecturer, 1966–67. Musical director, Alvin Ailey Dance Co. (South American tour), 1963. Musician and resource consultant, Neuropsychiatric Inst., Mental Health Programs, UCLA, 1966–67. Exec. director, Inner City Cultural Center (ICCC), Los Angeles, 1966–. Senior lecturer, Dept. of Ethnic Studies, Univ. of Southern California, Los Angeles, 1967–. Founding director, Inner City Inst. for the Performing and Visual Arts, Los Angeles, 1967. Director, Leonard Davis Center, and chairman, Theatre Dept., CCNY, 1979–81. In addition to his own plays and dramatic works he has directed the following plays at the ICCC: *Street Scene* (the musical, by Hughes, Weill, & Rice, 1971), *One in a Crowd* (by BEAH RICHARDS, 1971), *Monkey's Paw* (by. W. W. Jacobs, 1971), and *A Black Woman Speaks* (by Beah Richards, 1974, revived 1975). Composer of numerous compositions for orchestra, chorus, and string quartet, including "Arena," "Blood of the Lamb," "Invisible Kingdom," "Schudorama," "Montage," "Chameleon and the Lady," and "Two of Me." Member of the following panels and boards: NEA, Dance Advisory Panel; California Arts Council, Performing Arts Panel; President's Commission on Mental Health, Arts Advisory Panel; California Arts Council, Arts Education Panel; American Bi-Centennial Commission, Arts Advisory Panel; American Theatre Assn., Los Angeles Convention, Advisory Board; UCLA Arts Advisory Panel; Radio Station KUSC, Advisory Board; California Theatre Council, Board; National Arts Awards, Advisory Board. Also member of AEA, DG, American Theatre Assn., Musicians' Union, Broadcast Music, Inc., AAUP, and National Theatre Conf. Recipient of the following awards: Obie Award for Best Musical, 1961–62; Unity Award, Los Angeles, 1960; John Hay Whitney Fellowship, 1963–64; Special Commendation from the Los Angeles City Council, 1969, 1978; three DramaLogue awards (one each for writing, production, and direction), for **Iago**, 1979; *Los Angeles Weekly* Award for Best Play, **Iago,** 1980; DramaLogue Award for directing **Piano Bar**, 1980; City of Los Angeles Certificate of Appreciation, 1982; Los Angeles Human Relations Commission Certificate of Merit, 1982. *Address:* Inner City Cultural Center, 1308 South New Hampshire Ave., Los Angeles, CA 90006.

REPRESENTATIVE PLAYS AND DRAMATIC WORKS:

Fly Blackbird (musical play, 2 acts, 1960). Book by Jackson. Music and lyrics coauthored with James V. Hatch. Born out of the sit-in movement of the 1960s, it satirizes the conflicts within the ranks of a group of blacks in the Deep South as to the most effective methods of securing civil rights. Expanded from a one-act play first prod. at the Shoebox Theatre, Los Angeles, Fall 1960. First prod. as a two-act musical at the Metro Theatre, Los Angeles, Feb. 10, 1961, with student performers (many of whom, including MICKI GRANT and Thelma Oliver, went on to professional stage and film careers). Prod. Off-Bway in a revised and expanded version, with additional material by the director, Jerome Eskow, at the Mayfair Theatre, for 127 perfs., opening Feb. 6, 1962, with Avon Long in the leading role. Earned for the authors an Obie Award, 1961–62. Prod. at the Inst. in Black Repertory Theatre, held at the Univ. of California at Santa Barbara, Summer 1968. Pub. in the Off-Bway version in *The Black Teacher and the Dramatic Arts* (Reardon & Pawley, 1970). Pub. in the orig. Los Angeles version in *Black Theater, U.S.A.* (Hatch & Shine, 1974). Cast recording by Mercury Records (OCS-6206).

Departure ("musico-drama," also called an oratorio; full length, 1965). Music and lyrics by Jackson. Completed under a grant from the John Hay Whitney Foundation. A staged mass for the dead; a musical work which deals with a young black man who refuses to die (presumably symbolizing the black man's struggle for survival). First prod. in 1965. Prod. by ICCC, in repertory, May 23–June 22, 1975; dir. by author.

Earthquake // Also called **Earthquake I** (musical revue, full length, 1973). Utilized a modified musical revue format to explore those aspects of life in Southern California that tourists seldom see; subjects dealt with include birth control, the construction of Watts Towers, the increase in Los Angeles's nonwhite population, the election of Los Angeles's first black mayor, the institution of marriage, aging, theatre criticism, and violence in the schools. Prod. by ICCC, in repertory, Dec. 20, 1973–July 14, 1974; dir. by author.

Looking Backward (adaptn., full length, 1974). Based on the Edward Bellamy classic novel, which deals with life in America in the year 2000. Prod. by ICCC, in repertory, April 20–May 12, 1974; dir. by Jackson.

The Second Earthquake // Also called **Earthquake II** (musical revue, full length, 1974). A sequel to **Earthquake** (1973). Subjects covered in this edition include the demise of a famous Southern California amusement park (Pacific Ocean Park), theatre reviews and reviewers, aspiring Hollywood actors, institutional religion, street construction, adult nursery rhymes, the "dozens," American violence, and art as entertainment. Prod. by ICCC, in repertory, Oct. 18, 1974–March 8, 1975; dir. by author.

Sweete Nutcracker (adaptn., full length, 1974). A Christmas musical adapt. for the stage from Alexander Dumas's version of "The Nutcracker of Nuremburg." (The famous Tchaikovsky ballet, *Nutcracker Suite*, is based on the Dumas story.) This version is a sort of Inner City *Nutcracker Suite* dealing with life in the ghettos of Los Angeles. Prod. by ICCC, in repertory, Dec. 13, 1974–Jan. 12, 1975; dir. by Jackson.

Sortilegio (translation/adaptn., full length, 1975). Based on the play by black Brazilian *Abdias do Nascimento, presented to educate the community concerning the similarities between the black struggle in Brazil and the black struggle in the United States. In the story a black Brazilian is faced with the choice of becoming "Europeanized" or accepting his African cultural heritage. Produced by ICCC, Feb. 12–23, 1975; dir. by Jackson.

Langston Hughes Said . . . (adaptn., full length, 1975). A musical evening dedicated to the life of LANGSTON HUGHES, which includes some of his best poetry, song lyrics, short stories, and a one-act play, *Soul Gone Home*. Prod. by ICCC, March 28–31, 1975.

Earthquake III (musical revue, full length, 1975). A sequel to **Earthquake** (1973) and **The Second Earthquake** (1974). This version covers such subjects as Los Angeles trying to cope with the U.S. Bicentennial, mating, piano bars, UFOs, and unemployment. Prod. Oct. 1975.

Maggie de Mouse Meets d'Dirdy Rat Fink // Orig. title: **Maggie de Mouse** (musical, 1976). Music and lyrics by Jackson. A sequel to **Sweete Nutcracker** (1974), in which a young girl dreams about Maggie, a socially aware mouse who organizes the other mice against their common enemy, the Exterminator. Prod. by ICCC, Dec. 5, 1975–Jan. 4, 1976; dir. by Reggie Montgomery. Subsequent prodns. were dir. by Jackson.

Piano Bar // Orig. title: **Piano Bar and Other California Stories** (musical, full length, 1976). Centers around the customers who frequent a California bar and the people who work there. Prod. by ICCC, March 5–June 6, 1976, dir. by author.

B/C // Orig. title: **B.C. (Before the Completion)** (historical doc., full length, 1976). Points out the relationships between African (Moorish) and Spanish music and women, to determine what relationship existed between black and Spanish peoples. Prod. by ICCC, June 11–20, 1976; dir. by author.

Iago (adaptn., full length, 1979). Based on the works of Giraldi Cinthio and William Shakespeare. Prod. at Lincoln Center, New York, 1979, and ICCC, the same year. Winner of three DramaLogue awards for writing, production, and direction, 1979; and the *Los Angeles Weekly* Award for Best Play, 1980.

OTHER PLAYS AND DRAMATIC WORKS:
Aftermath (theatrical collage, full length, 1977). Selections from **Earthquake** (1973) and **The Second Earthquake** (1974). Prod. by ICCC, 1977. **Wanted Experienced**

Operators (musical adaptn., 1978). Based on *La Factoria* by Estela Scarlata. Music and lyrics by Jackson. Prod. by ICCC, 1978. **A New Liliom** (adaptn., full length, 1980). Based on *Liliom*, by Ferenc Molnar. Prod. by ICCC and the Richard Allen Center, New York, 1980; dir. by Jackson.

JACKSON, CHERRY, Philosopher-playwright. Based in Oakland, CA.

PLAY:

In the Master's House There Are Many Mansions (fantasy, 1 act, 1978). A young black man, dressed in black, visits a funeral parlor to view the remains of his childhood friend, a Vietnam veteran, who has been shot while committing a robbery and is laid out on an embalming table in an expensive white silk suit. During the course of the play, the living and the dead exchange identities as well as clothes, and at the end the corpse leaves the funeral parlor in the guise of the visitor, and the visitor unwillingly assumes the place of the corpse on the embalming table. Pub. in *Center Stage* (Ostrow, 1981).

JACKSON, ELAINE, Actress-playwright. In 1971 she was living on the West Coast. Currently resides in New York City. A graduate of Wayne State Univ. Appeared in the Negro Ensemble Co.'s production of *Liberty Call* (1975), by BURIEL CLAY II. *Address:* 609 Columbus Ave. #16N, New York, NY 10024.

PLAYS:

Toe Jam (drama, 3 acts [7 scenes], 1971). (The title is taken from a black term for the offensive matter that collects between the toes of dirty feet.) Concerns a black girl in search of her own identity who tries to escape from the sordidness of ghetto life by dreaming of herself as a great actress-poet-playwright. Prod. by the New Federal Theatre. Pub. in *Black Drama Anthology* (King & Milner, 1972).

Cockfight (drama, 2 acts [4 scenes], 1976). "The play takes a heavy-handed look at the dissolution of a marriage and why the break-up is occurring."—*New York Theatre Review*, Dec. 1977, p. 44 (Frank). In a larger sense, it examines the relationships between black women and men in American society from the feminist point of view. Originated in the Frank Silvera Writers' Workshop (FSWW), New York, 1976. Prod. at the Greenwich Mews Theatre, Oct. 7–30, 1977, for 28 perfs.; dir. by WOODIE KING, JR. Cast included Mary Alice, Morgan Freeman, Charles Brown, GYLAN KAIN, and Cynthia McPherson. Unpub. script and tape recording in the FSWW Archives/Schomburg Collection.

Birth Rites (comedy-drama, full length, 1987). In the setting of a maternity ward in New York City, this play focuses on the hopes and aspirations of expectant mothers of diverse racial and ethnic backgrounds as they are about to give birth. Prod. by the American Folk Theatre, New York, Apr. 23–June 1, 1987, dir. by June Pyskacek.

JACKSON, JOSEPHINE (Jo), Musical playwright. Associated with The Voices, Inc., and Arts for Racial Identity, New York City.

DRAMATIC WORKS:

The Believers ("The Black Experience in Song" [subtitle], 3 acts). Coauthor, with JOSEPH A. WALKER. A chronicle of the black experience in America through song and dance. First prod. Off Bway, at the Garrick Theatre, New York, May 9, 1968; dir. by BARBARA ANN TEER. With the cast of The Voices, Inc. Cast recording by RCA

Victor (LSO-1151). **Martin and Malcolm** (early 1970s). About Martin Luther King and Malcolm X. **Harlem Heyday** (musical, full length, 1973). Recreation of the Harlem of the twenties in old songs, old dances, old humor. Songs, all written by blacks, included "Honeysuckle Rose," "In My Solitude," "Love Will Find a Way," "I'm Just Wild About Harry," "Do Nothing till You Hear from Me," "Darktown Strutter's Ball," "Ain't Misbehavin'," "A Good Man Is Hard to Find," "Memories of You," "Sweet Georgia Brown," "Nobody," "There'll Be Some Changes Made," and "Please Don't Talk About Me When I'm Gone." Prod. Off-Bway by The Voices, Inc.; dir. by ROGER FURMAN, and on tour of colleges and universities, c. 1973. **Journey into Blackness** (musical, full length, 1974). Traces highlights and achievements during the black man's sojourn from Africa during the seventeeth century to life in the urban centers of America in the 1970s. Scenes include African Sequence, Slavery Sequence, Emancipation, Blues and Jazz, Religious Experience, and "After Sunday Comes Monday" (to remind the audience "that life goes on seven days a week"). Prod. in New York and on tour by The Voices, Inc.; dir. by Rod Rogers.

JACKSON, (Rev.) SPENCER (1910–   ), Clergyman, choir director, singer, actor, playwright, theatrical director, and author. Born in Thomaston, AL. Currently resides in Chicago, IL. Educated at Gregg Business School, 1935; Midwestern Conservatory of Music, 1946–48; Chicago Conservatory of Music (certificate 1951). Married; the father of six children. Music teacher and choir director for various churches, 1938–55. Pastor, Good Shepherd Baptist Church, Chicago, 1955–63. Leader, Rev. Spencer Jackson Family, a family gospel singing group which performed regularly in the Chicago area. Director of the Black Heritage Theatrical Players; had an extensive list of theatrical credits in the early 1970s. In the 1960s he was associated with the Afro-Arts Theatre as singer, actor, choral director, and theatrical director. Author of a book, *Black Survival,* for which he received a recognition award from the Chicago Black Cultural Council in 1970. Recipient of awards from International Black Writers Conf. (IBWC), for outstanding achievement in drama, 1973; Chicago Black Theatre Alliance (4th Annual Paul Robeson Award), 1978; and the Olive Harvey Black Studies Commission, for outstanding contributions to black theatre, 1979.

PLAYS AND DRAMATIC WORKS:
A New Day (1969). Prod. by the Afro-Arts Theatre, 1969 and 1972. **Come Home** (1969). Prod. by the Afro-Arts Theatre, 1969. **Chi-Star** // Title also cited as **Shyster** and **Slyster** (comedy, 1973). Described by playwright EUGENE PERKINS as "an amusing story of a country boy who comes to the city, where he becomes exposed to the tribulations of urban living."—*Black World,* April 1974, p. 52. First prod. by the Black Heritage Theatrical Players, Chicago, 1973. Again prod. in a revised version by the same group, at the PUSH (Rev. Jesse Jackson's "People United to Save Humanity") organization's Dr. Martin Luther King Workshop, 1975. Apparently this was the play that earned for the author an award in 1973 from IBWC.

JAHANNES, JA A. (Arthur) (c. 1943–   ), Poet, dramatist, lecturer, and behavioral scientist. Educated at Lincoln Univ./Pennsylvania (B.A., cum laude, 1964); Hampton Univ. (M.A. in educational administration and supervision,

1966; M.A. in guidance and counseling, 1975); Coll. of William and Mary (postgraduate studies in educational administration, 1966–67); and the Univ. of Delaware (Ph.D. in behavioral science, 1972). Served in the U.S. Air Force, 1964–68. Married; four children. Currently dean of the School of Humanities and Social Sciences, Savannah State Coll., Savannah, GA, and prof. of psychology; former dean, School of Education, and chairman, Dept. of Secondary Education, 1973–81. Assoc. director of development, Lincoln Univ./Pennsylvania, 1968–69; director of education, Community Action of Greater Wilmington, and director of Head Start, Wilmington, DE, 1969–72. Visiting prof., Faculty of Education, Haile Selassie I Univ., Ethiopia, Summer 1972; senior lecturer and head, Dept. of Professional Studies, National Teacher Coll., Kampala, Uganda, 1972–73. Author of *The Poet's Song* (1981), and other poems published in *Black Scholar Encore, Journal of Ethnic Studies,* and *College Poetry Anthology.* Author of the essay on LOFTEN MITCHELL in the *Dictionary of Literary Biography, Vol. 38* (1985). Founding member of the Peshawar Players, an international theatre touring company, and has had extensive experience as an actor and director in the United States, Asia, and Africa. Columnist for the *Savannah Tribune,* 1984; weekly commentator on WSOK Radio, Savannah, 1983–85. Member of American Council on Education; National Black Child Development Inst.; NADSA; Langston Hughes Soc. (charter member); Coastal Jazz Assn. (Board of Directors); and Advisory Council, Chatham-Effington Area Mental Center. Recipient of numerous awards and citations for contributions to culture and education. *Address*—Office: School of Humanities and Social Sciences, P.O. Box 20059, Savannah State Coll., Savannah, GA 31404. *Pertinent address* (for obtaining author's scripts and tapes of premiere perfs.): New Foundations Institute Inc., 2304 Noble Oaks Dr., Savannah, GA 31406.

REPRESENTATIVE PLAYS AND DRAMATIC WORKS:

One More Sunday (gospel folk opera, 2 acts, 1985). "About a fictitious Black baptist church; and the machinations of a typical congregation, as they prepare for a special Sunday service, commemorating the life and death of Rev. Martin Luther King, Jr. . . . The play scenes covered a church committee meeting, a choir rehearsal, culminating with the memorial service to Rev. MLK."—*The Herald,* (Savannah), Jan. 23, 1985. Premiered at the Johnny Mercer Theatre, Savannah Civic Center, Savannah, Jan. 13, 1985; presented at Kennedy Fine Arts Theatre, Savannah State Coll., the following day. Script and video of premiere perf. are available through New Foundations Inst. [See address above.]

Ain't I Something (musical play, 2 acts, 1985). Music by Gary Swindell and Scope Harris. "Variations on the theme of growing up Black in America during the 1950s and 1960s."—*Savannah Tribune,* May 15, 1985, p. 4. Takes eight main characters through childhood, adolescence, and adulthood. Orig. music includes blues, jazz, and pop. Premiered at the Johnny Mercer Theatre, Savannah Civic Centre, May 5, 1985. Script and video are available through New Foundations Inst.

And Yet We Sing (musical play, 3 acts, 1986). Series of dramatic pieces that reflect episodes in black life, showing the continuity of strength, joy, and humor through the lives of a mythical black family from Africa of 1600 to America in the 1980s. Utilizes drama, dance, and orig. music. Premiered at the Johnny Mercer Theatre, Jan. 18, 1986. Script and video are available through New Foundations Inst.

La Dolorosa (oratorio, 3 parts, 1986). Libretto by Jahannes. Musical score by Marshall J. Fine. A fusion of classical music and African American music—jazz, blues, and gospel—to prod. a unique three-part musical version of the life, death, and resurrection of Jesus. Dance accompaniment is classical and jazz forms drawing upon African American expressions. Premiered at the Johnny Mercer Theatre, March 28, 1986.

OTHER DRAMATIC WORKS:
(According to the author, these have been produced at various places, prior to 1985).
Go Down Death (dramatic and musical adaptn. of †James Weldon Johnson's poem, 1 act). **Ding Dang It** (musical spoof, 2 acts). About knights and dragons and the like. **The Burning of the Dead** (melodrama, 1 act). First presented at NADSA's 48th National Conf., Miami, FL, 1985.

JAMES, (Minister) FRANK W. (Wellington), Artist, freelance photographer, playwright, minister, judo instructor, and hospital equipment technician. Born, raised, and educated in New York City's Harlem community, where he states that he also found God and subsequently discovered himself. Began studying art at age 12, and at age 15 was awarded honorable mention by Stern's Dept. Stores, New York City, for landscapes in oil and water color. Studied at the Art Student League in New York, 1971; traveled to Haiti to study art and the lifestyle of the Haitian people, 1972. Graduated from the New York Theological Seminary. His art has been exhibited at the U.N. Building and other locations in New York, Washington, DC, Philadelphia, and Bermuda. His photography has been published in such periodicals as *City Scene,* a Harlem-based community newspaper, *Bilalian News* (formerly *Muhammad Speaks), New York Amsterdam News*, and *Jet* magazine. Studied judo in 1967 and began teaching the art to underprivileged youth at We Care Community Center and Northside Center for Child Development, in New York. Recently became an ordained minister of the Church of God in Christ. In 1979 he was employed at the New York Hospital as a respiratory therapy equipment technician. *Address:* P.O. Box 455, Bronx, NY 10473.

PLAY:
Gods at War (musical/gospel drama, full length, 1977). Music by *Orvye Ray Gordon. The central theme is the struggle between the forces of good and evil in the black community. The plot revolves around a Muslim minister and his followers who are constantly at odds with the pimps and hustlers that are claiming his neighborhood as their territory. In addition to drama, the play makes use of gospel and jazz music, dancing, and the martial arts. First presented at the Harlem Performance Center, New York, 1978. Prod. by Theatre In Progress, New York, Oct. 11–Nov. 4, 1984; dir. by JERRY MAPLE, JR.

JAMES, IAN ELLIS. See BLACK, WILLIAM ELECTRIC.

JAMES, LUTHER (1928–   ), Actor, director, producer, playwright, and teacher. Born in New York City, where he attended the Dramatic Workshop of the New School for Social Research. Studied in England, France, Germany, and

the Soviet Union on a John Hay Whitney Fellowship, 1959–60. Studied Broadway theatre on a Ford Foundation Fellowship, 1962. Organized Comet Productions in the 1950s, which produced LOFTEN MITCHELL's adaptation of John
Steinbeck's *Of Mice and Men* for a black cast. Exec. producer, CBS-TV Network, Los Angeles, 1966–68. Affiliated with the Negro Ensemble Co., New
York, 1968–69. Producer, "On Being Black," Allston, MA, 1968–70. Taught
at Portland State Univ., Oregon, 1971; California State Univ./Los Angeles, 1971;
and California State Univ./Northridge, 1972–73. Currently prof. of drama at the
Univ. of California/San Diego. Member of DGA and WGA. *Address*: 1308 S.
New Hampshire, Los Angeles, CA 90006.

PLAY:
Liberty (TV play, 1 act, early 1970s). Concerns "an important confrontation between
a street-hardened Puerto Rican and a young Black law student in jail for the first time."—
Pub. script. Prod. on national television during the early 1970s, starring BOOKER T.
BRADSHAW, JR., as the law student. Pub. in *Interactions* (Altshuler, 1972).

JAMISON, BILL, Playwright. Based in Philadelphia, PA.

PLAY:
Soul Bus to Brotherhood (drama, 1 act, 1970s). A white passenger who is picked
up by a bus loaded with black passengers of diverse political and racial views is murdered
at the instigation of the only female aboard, who is also a middle-class black.

JEANNETTE, GERTRUDE (1948–   ), Playwright, actress, director, and
black theatre founder and executive. Born in Little Rock, AR, where she graduated from high school. Moved to New York in the 1940s, becoming affiliated
with the American Negro Theatre (ANT) in Harlem, where she studied acting
under the tutelage of the late Osceola Archer. Also studied at the New School
for Social Research. Has acted in a number of Broadway and Off-Broadway
plays, including *Lost in the Stars* (1948), *Deep Are the Roots* (1960), *The Long
Dream* (1960), *Moon on a Rainbow Shawl* (1962), *Nobody Loves an Albatross*
(1963), *The Amen Corner* (1965), and *To Be Young, Gifted and Black* (1969).
Also performed in the Prospect Park Theatre production of *A Raisin in the Sun*.
Films include *Cry of the City* (1948), *Nothing but a Man* (1964), *Cotton Comes
to Harlem* (1970), *Shaft* (1971), *The Legend of Nigger Charley* (1972), and
Black Girl (1972). Has made numerous TV appearances, beginning in 1950
when she costarred with Frederick O'Neal in Fred Waring's production of *God's
Trombones*. Founder and exec. director of the Elks Community Theatre in Har-
lem, around 1950. Founder and artistic director of the HADLEY Players, 1984–.
(HADLEY is an acronym for Harlem Artistic Development League Especially
for You.) Recipient of the AUDELCO Outstanding Pioneer Award in 1984 for
her talents and continued dedication and service of the theatrical world. *Address*:
HADLEY Players, Community Service Council of Greater Harlem, Inc., 207
W. 133rd St., New York, NY 10030.

PLAYS:

This Way Forward (dramatic comedy, 2 acts, 1948). Set in a small southwestern farm town in the mid-1920s, this play concerns how a black "city woman," considered an "outsider" by both unprogressive blacks and racist whites, pioneered against strong resistance from both groups to improve racial and educational conditions for blacks. This included advancing a one-room school that only went as high as the fifth grade to an up-to-date high school. First prod. by the ANT Workshop in Harlem, 1949. Prod. by the author at the Elks Community Theatre in Harlem, opening May 7, 1951. Prod. by the Harlem Renaissance Theatre, Aug. 1979. Prod. by the HADLEY Players, New York, Oct. 1984.

(A) Bolt from the Blue (drama, 2 acts, 1950). Concerns a middle-class black family whose happiness is threatened by ties to the past. Specifically, it deals with a woman who meets and becomes pregnant by a man at the height of the Great Depression, when she is young, destitute, and alone in New York City. He is sent to prison for a crime, and their paths do not cross until years later when she is happily married and the child is 17. First prod. by the Elks Community Theatre in Harlem, 1952. Has since been presented by a number of theatre groups and schools. Most recently produced by the HADLEY Players at the Community Service Council of Greater Harlem, March 1985.

Light in the Cellar (domestic comedy-drama, 2 acts, 1960). A sequel to **This Way Forward** (1948). The story of the son of the pioneering woman in the previous play and his family. Because of southern unrest and the closing of schools during the civil rights movement of the 1960s, a black man sells his farm and other properties in the Southwest and moves his family to New York City to seek better educational and cultural advantages for them. He buys an apartment building, in which he and his family also live in the basement, keeping it a secret that he is the real owner. The play turns on the resentment of the family that they are being treated by the other tenants as if they were servants, and the rebelliousness of the son, who believes that his father is a coward for running away from the racial struggle in the South. The family discovers during the course of the play the complacency, superficiality, and frailties of northern blacks, and learns that there is not much difference between southern and northern racism. Written and showcased in 1960. Rewritten and prod. by Our Theatre, New York, 1964. Prod. by Adam Clayton Powell, Jr. Theatre, New York, May 1975. Prod. by the HADLEY Players, at the Community Service Council of Greater Harlem, Dec. 1984, and Feb.-March 1985; dir. by author.

Who's Mama's Baby, Who's Daddy's Child? (dramatic comedy with songs and dance, 2 acts, 1985). Music and lyrics by Louise Mike. "The play, which centers on the trials and tribulations of foster-parents . . . and their talented brood, is a mixed bag of drama, comedy, and song."—*New York Amsterdam News*, June 15, 1985, p. 25 (Boyd). About a retired middle-class couple who, after raising three successful career children of their own, are now devoting their time to abused and unwanted children. Prod. by the HADLEY Players, at the Community Service Council of Greater Harlem, May 31–June 23, 1985.

JEFFERSON, ANNETTA LOUISE GOMEZ (1927–   ), Playwright, TV writer-producer, poet, director, and educator. Born in Detroit, MI. Graduate of the Dramatic Workshop, New York City, 1950. Received the M.A. in English from Western Reserve Univ., Cleveland, OH; further graduate work at John

Carroll Univ., Cleveland (where she also taught for one year in the M.A. Training Program), and Notre Dame Univ. Taught English and drama for seven years in the public schools of Cleveland, and served two years as chairman of English, Glenville H.S. Married; two sons. Was a writer for one year with the Educational Research Council of America. Writer-producer for seven years at WVIZ Educational Television Station, where she produced a number of TV series, comprising more than 60 individual programs, for one of which she received an Emmy Citation. Formerly asst. prof. of English at the Coll. of Wooster, where she taught black literature, creative writing, theatre, and oral interpretation, and directed college productions; currently chairman, Dept. of Theatre, Coll. of Wooster, a newly established dept., since Sept. 1981. Director of the Stage Right Repertory Co., Wooster, 1983–85. Has lectured and/or served as guest director at Karamu House, Humanist Theatre, Cuyahoga Community Coll., Cleveland State Univ., Kent State Univ., Findlay Coll., and Case Western Univ. Taught writing for television at Oberlin Univ., 1973. Member of the Governor's Commission for Educational TV in the State of Ohio. Recipient of grants for her TV series from the Ford Foundation (two grants); the Ohio Educational TV Assoc.; and the Martha Holdings Jenning Foundation. *Address:* Chairman, Dept. of Theatre, College of Wooster, Wooster, OH 44691.

PLAYS AND DRAMATIC WORKS:

In Both Hands (drama, 3 acts, 1974). Takes place in the late 1960s. Conflict between a militant son and father, a Baptist minister, who is opposed to direct action and protest. First prod. as a special on WVIZ, c. 1974. Prod. Winter 1974 at the Humanist Theatre, Cleveland Prod. Jan. 1975 at the Coll. of Wooster.

My Soul Looks Back in Wonder (gospel drama, full length, 1974–75). Prod. on WVIZ, Cleveland; and at the Coll. of Wooster, 1974–75.

Drown the Wind (musical, 3 acts, 1975). Book and lyrics by Jefferson. Music by Brian Dykstra. Story of a middle-class black mother who has adopted white middle-class values and abandoned those of her race. As a result, she almost completely alienates her husband and children. Prod. by the Freelander Theatre, Coll. of Wooster, May 1975.

Amandla (drama, 3 acts, pre-1985). Deals with the evils of apartheid in South Africa. Based partly on the story of Steve Biko, the black martyr. In this play the hero's name is Nkosi, and his experiences are somewhat different.

The Fishmonger (drama, 3 acts, pre-1985). Rudy decides to avenge his father's suicide by writing a play which supposedly exposes the weaknesses of the patrons who frequent the Fishbowl, his mother's restaurant. In the end, he is exposed to the weaknesses of his father and is self-exiled to the Fishbowl.

JEFFRIES, IRA L., Playwright, journalist, short-story writer, and theatre technician. Educated at CCNY (drama major, studies completed 1987), where she was feature editor of *The Campus,* the college newspaper. Has been published in *New Harlem Magazine,* a community oriented publication of CCNY. Currently a reporter for the *New York Amsterdam News.* Has been writing plays and short stories since 1970. Was property supervisor for Theatre in Progress; traveled regionally with the Negro Ensemble Co. (NEC) as property supervisor for STEVE

CARTER's *Nevis Mountain Dew;* was stage manager for Butterfly McQueen and Ebony Jo-Ann's "Blackgold" nightclub act. Member of the Golden Key National Honor Society. Recipient of an AUDELCO certificate of excellence for playwriting for her drama *Odessa,* which was nominated in six categories and won awards in three, at the AUDELCO Theatre Awards, 1985. *Address:* 1990 Lexington Ave. #26A, New York, NY 10035.

PLAYS:

The Cactus and the Rose (dramatic fantasy, 1 act [with or without music], pre-1985). Based on her short story by the same title. About a cactus plant that arouses awe, ambivalence, jealousies, and rejection among plant and human characters because of its unusual appearance. Rose, the oldest and wisest of all the flora, consoles and counsels Cactus in the ways of the real world of flora and humans. Unpub. script in the FSWW Archives/Schomburg Collection.

Odessa (drama, 2 acts, 1985). The story of twin sisters, one dark and one fair, born to a mulatto mother during the 1930s. The darker twin, Odessa, is rejected because of her strong resemblance to her father; the fairer twin achieves success in the world of show business, under the tutelage of her mother, by "passing" for white. A family reunion, after many years, results in conflict, tension, confrontation, and ambivalent feelings. Prod. by Theatre in Progress, 1985. Nominated for six AUDELCO awards, and winner of three awards in 1985.

JENNINGS, CORRINE, Playwright. Prof. of English at Queens Coll., CCNY.

DRAMATIC WORK:

Snakeshiiit (tragicomic pageant, 3 acts, 1975). Written with STEVE CANNON and JOE OVERSTREET. Public reading by the New Federal Theatre, New York, 1975. Unpub. script in the Hatch-Billops Collection.

JOHNSON, CHARLES F., Television producer and screenwriter. Educated at Howard Univ. (B.A.), Howard Univ. Law School (J.D.), and the Univ. of Delaware. Producer of the following television shows: "The Rockford Files" (associate producer, 1974–76; producer, 1976–80), for which he received an Emmy Award, 1978; "Baa Baa Black Sheep"; "The Black Filmakers Hall of Fame"; "Hellinger's Law"; "Simon and Simon"; "Voices of Our People"; and "Bret Maverick."

DRAMATIC WORKS:

Hammer (feature film, full length: screenplay, 1972). About a champion boxer who is trying to hold on to his title while fighting corruption in the boxing game. Prod. by Al Adamson. 1972; released by United Artists; dir. by Bruce Clark; starring Fred Williamson.

Slaughter's Big Rip-Off (feature film, full length: screenplay, 1973). Violent film about an ex-Green Beret who murders the leaders of the syndicate before they can murder him. Prod. by Monroe Sachison, 1973; released by American International, dir. by Gordon Douglas; starring Jim Brown.

JOHNSON, CHRISTINE C., Poet-playwright. Her poetry was anthologized in *For Malcolm: Poems on the Life and Death of Malcolm X* (Randall & Burroughs, 1967).

PLAY:
Zwadi Ya Africa Kwa Dunwa (Africa's Gift to the World) (historical play for young people, 2 parts, 1960s). Classroom play, emphasizing the contributions of Africa to world civilizations. Pub. by Free Black Press, Chicago, 1960s.

JOHNSON, DOUGLAS, Director of the Black Arts West Theatre in Seattle, WA. *Address:* Black Arts West Theatre, 1404 34th Ave., Seattle, WA 98122.

DRAMATIC WORK:
Black Is a Beautiful Woman (one-woman show, full length, 1973). Compiled by Johnson and MARGO BARNETT. A performed reading of the works of Mari Evans, Nikki Giovanni, LANGSTON HUGHES, Margaret Walker, and other black writers. Performed by Barnett at the Back Alley Theatre, Washington, DC, opening Jan. 18, 1973. Also telecast on NET, 1973.

JOHNSON, HANK, Musical playwright. Formerly associated with the Afro-American Total Theatre in New York City.

DRAMATIC WORK:
Mae's Amees (musical, 1 act, 1979). Written with HAZEL BRYANT and HOPE CLARKE. Prod. at the Riverside Church Theatre, Aug. 9–10, 1969. Apparently remained in repertory until Oct. 1969. **Origins** (musical, 1 act, 1969). Written with BEVERLY TODD and Hazel Bryant. Prod. at the Riverside Church Theatre, Oct. 1969.

JOHNSON, HERMAN, Playwright. Attended the Playwrights' Workshop of the Negro Ensemble Co. (NEC) in New York City.

PLAYS:
The Death of Little Marcus (domestic drama, 1 act, 1973). A long absent father returns home to cause a crisis for his family. Prod. as a workshop production by NEC, Jan. 27–31, 1973. **Nowhere to Run, Nowhere to Hide** (drama, 2 acts, 1974). A rebellious Harlem youth is framed for murder by two drug-dealing cops. Prod. as a Season-Within-a-Season production by NEC, at St. Marks Playhouse, March 26–31, 1974, for 8 perfs.; dir. by Dean Irby. Cast included Todd Davis as the youth and Leon Morenzie and Frankie Faison as the policemen. Also in the cast were SAMM-ART WILLIAMS and ADOLPH CAESAR. **17 Sycamore Court** (drama, 3 acts, pre-1975).

JOHNSON, HUGH M., Playwright. Inmate of the Norfolk (VA) Prison at the time he wrote the following play.

PLAY:
Justice or Just Us (Part I) (protest drama, 1 act [3 scenes], 1972). Explores the injustice of the judicial system for the black man. Pub. in *Who Took the Weight?* (Norfolk Prison Bros., 1972).

JOHNSON, REGINALD VEL, Playwright. Based in New York City, where his plays have been produced by the New Federal Theatre (NFT) and the Negro Ensemble Co. (NEC).

PLAYS:
Section D (drama, full length, 1975). "A close look at seven brothers in a juvenile home, and as [they] interact, we get a penetrating look into the whole misconception of so many young dudes on what is a man. To them manhood is a physical and verbal brutality, exaggerated coolness and irresponsible sexual conquest of their women."— *Black World,* April 1976, p. 55 (Bailey). Prod. by NFT, 1975; dir. by Anderson Johnson, Jr. With JACQUES WAKEFIELD, Herb Rice, Lawrence Fishburn III, J. Eric Bell, Eddie Perez, George "Smokey" Campbell, and Elliott Williams as the seven brothers. **The Trap Play** (1976). Prod. by NEC, as a Season-Within-a-Season production, opening April 6, 1976, for 8 perfs.; dir. by Edmund Cambridge. Unpub. script in the Hatch-Billops Collection.

JOHNSTON, PERCY EDWARD (1930–   ), Poet, playwright, essayist, editor, publisher, and teacher. Born in New York City. Received the A.B. degree in philosophy, history, and English from Howard Univ., 1960; and the M.A. in English from Montclair State Coll. Graduate School, 1968. Has taught at Howard Univ. and in the public schools of Washington, DC, and in New Jersey at Essex Coll., Caldwell Adult School, and St. Peter's Coll. Prof. of English and comparative literature at Montclair State Coll., Upper Montclair, NJ, 1968–82, and chairman and coordinator of Afro-American Studies, 1977–82. Instr. of acting (part-time) at Rinjohn Studio, artistic director and theatre instr. at Studio Tangerine, and artistic director of Percy Johnston & Friends Theatre Co., all in New York City. Former pres. of Dasein Literary Soc.; founding editor and first publisher of *Dasein,* a journal of aesthetics, literature, and philosophy, 1961–present. Author of a number of articles on aesthetics, philosophy, history, and biological/behavioral sciences. Volumes of poetry include *Continental Streamlets* (with Leroy O. Stone, 1959); *Concerto for Girl and Convertible* (1960); *Six Cylinder Olympus* (1964); *Sean Pendragon Requiem* (1964); *Brushed* (1977); and *Loft Jazz and Miriny Blues* (1982). His poems have also been widely published in anthologies of contemporary black poetry and in numerous journals and periodicals. Memberships and affiliations include Prose Committee, Literary Fellowship Grants, New Jersey State Council of the Arts, 1981–83; vice pres., R. C. Richardson Foundation, Washington, DC, 1983–present; pres., Falashfa International Honor Soc. in Philosophy, 1983–present. Honors include Phi Sigma Tau, National Honor Fraternity, 1957; Howard Univ. Teaching Fellowship in English, 1960–61; National Defense Education Act Fellowship in English and Linguistics, 1967–68; Pi Delta Epsilon National Honor Fraternity in Journalism; and Calliope Poetry Award, 1977. *Address:* JAF Box 7831, New York, NY 10016.

REPRESENTATIVE PLAY:
Antigone (adaptn., full length, 1977). Modern version of the tragedy by Sophocles. In Johnston's version of the classical myth, the deaths of Antigone's two brothers (which

are merely reported in Sophocles's version) are actually depicted on stage; Ismene (Antigone's sister) is given an expanded role; Tiresias is depicted as a woman (since the original blind seer is traditionally hermaphroditic); and the entire play is presented as a tragicomedy. Prod. by Studio Tangerine, New York, 1977–78.

OTHER PLAYS AND DRAMATIC WORKS:
John Adams, A Historical Drama, Parts I and II (full length, 1972). Prod. by Rinjohn Productions, 1972. **Dewitt II** (full length, 1973). Prod. by Rinjohn Productions, 1973. **Crispus Attucks, Part I and II** (historical drama, full length, 1974). Prod. by Rinjohn Productions, 1974. Also prod. on tape, 1975. **Boston Common: A Morality Play** (1 act, 1977). Prod. by Dasein Literary Soc., New York, 1977. Again prod. in Washington, DC, Feb. 1977. **Frankie & Johnnie**. ("A Blues/Jazz Opera" [subtitle], full length: in progress, 1985). Lyrics, book, and music by Johnston.

JONES, E. H. (1925–   ), Poet, playwright, and technical writer. Born in Lexington, MS. Currently lives in Washington, DC, where he is involved in speechwriting, preparing reports, and other special projects in his position as special assistant to the project director of a neighborhood health center. Author of *A Pleasant Encounter and Other Poems* (1964) and an unpublished novel, "Manifest Destiny."

PLAY:
Our Very Best Christmas (pre-1975).

JONES, GAYL (1949–   ), Poet, novelist, short-story writer, and playwright. Born in Lexington, KY. Received the B.A. degree in English from Connecticut Coll., 1971, and the M.A. in creative writing from Brown Univ., 1973. Author of two novels, *Corregidora* (1975) and *Eva's Man* (1976); a collection of short stories, *White Rat* (1977); and a book of poems, *Songs for Anninho* (1981). Her poetry and short stories have also appeared in numerous magazines and journals, including *Essence, Laureate, Ms., Silo, Callaloo, Ploughshares,* and *Obsidian;* and anthologized in *Soulscript* (Jordan, 1970), *Amistad 2* (Williams & Harris, 1971), and *Dues* (Welburn, 1974). She has also written a long poem entitled "Chile Woman," which has been produced as a dramatic work [see below]. Twice recipient of the Connecticut Coll. Award for the best original poem, 1969 and 1970; the Frances Steloff Award for Fiction; a Breadloaf Writers' Conf. Scholarship, 1971; and the New Play Award, New England Region, 1974. *Address:* English Department, 7607 Haven Hall, University of Michigan, Ann Arbor, MI 48109.

REPRESENTATIVE PLAYS AND DRAMATIC WORKS:
Chile Woman (a "show off" with music, 1 act, 1973). Dramatization of the author's poem by the same title. With music by *Brother Ahhh Folayemi. Utilizes the forms of the black folk tradition, blues, jazz, and the sermon motif to relate black history to contemporary listeners (represented as people in a bar). Prod. at Brown Univ., Providence, RI, 1973. Published in *Schubert Playbook Series,* no. 5, vol. 2 (Emigh, 1974).
    Beyond Yourself (The Midnight Confessions) for Brother Ahhh (ritual drama, 1 act, 1975). A young black man and woman, attempting to heal their lives through learning

to love themselves and each other, are observed by an elder grassroots couple who have gone through this experience at an earlier time. Published in *BOP (Blacks on Paper)*, Brown Univ., Providence, 1975.

OTHER PLAYS:
Mama Easter (1974). **The Ancestor—A Street Play** (late 1970s). Pub. in *Yardbird Reader*, vol. 5 (Reed, late 1970s).

JONES, GUIL, Playwright. Based in New York City. A participant in the New York Black Writers Conf. in 1971.

PLAY:
The Power of the African Eye (mystical drama, 3 acts, 1974). A pimp supplies a magical black powder, which he has stolen from an old African woman, to the community. Sched. for publication by Amuru Press, New York, 1974, but apparently never pub.

JONES, HERMAN LeVERNE (1954–   ), Actor, director, technical director, theatre administrator, and playwright. Based in North Carolina; currently resides in New York. Educated at North Carolina State Univ. (B.A. in theatre, 1980) and the Univ. of North Carolina/Chapel Hill (M.F.A. in acting, 1983). Also studied for one summer in Nigeria at the Univ. of Ile-Ife (tribal dance, drumming, and theatre, 1979). Prior to attending North Carolina State Univ., he had worked in theatre at Virginia Commonwealth Univ. and at Montclair State Univ. in New Jersey. Founder and artistic director of the LaVerne (*sic*) Players, Inc., Raleigh, NC, his own theatre company for which he wrote and received three North Carolina Arts Council grants and one $50,000 CETA grant for theatre administration. Has performed in and directed numerous college, university, and regional productions. His most recent theatrical affiliations as actor-director include the American Folk Theatre, New York, 1983; the New Federal Theatre, 1983, and his current position as asst. director to WOODIE KING, JR., National Black Touring Circuit, Inc. (NBTC), 1983–present, where he is the booking agent for NBTC, and performed in 1985 as an actor in the touring circuit's production of SAMM-ART WILLIAMS's *Home*, directed by King. Member of AEA and AFTRA. *Address*—Home: 89–35 193 St., Jamaica, NY 11432. Office: National Black Touring Circuit, Inc., 417 Convent Ave., New York, NY 10031.

PLAYS AND DRAMATIC WORKS:
Black Woman: Sime Simba Sim Luye Koon (dramatization of a narrative poem by Jones, 1 act, 1975). Described by Lynn Wogan of the Raleigh *Times* (undated clipping) as "written to express the pressures black women have experienced through the years and the plight of the black man in his relationship with them. . . . The title means, 'I have nothing' in Swahili." Presented by the LaVerne Players at Stewart Theatre, during the Pan African Festival at North Carolina State Univ, 1975. **The Silent Murder** // Also known as **Death of a Nationalist** (c. 1975–76). Prod. by the LaVerne Players, around 1975. **Let's Make a Slave** (drama, 1976). Prod. by the LaVerne Players, and presented at North Carolina State Univ., Feb. 1976. **Do You Really Know What Time It Is** (theatre of the absurd, in progress, late 1970s).

JONES, LeROI. See BARAKA, AMIRI.

JONES, LOLA E. (formerly Lola Jones Amis) (1930–   ), English teacher, short-story writer, and playwright. Born in Norfolk, VA. Educated at Hampton Inst. (B.S., 1950), the Univ. of Rhode Island (1958), the Univ. of Maryland (1965), and Johns Hopkins Univ. (M.L.A., 1967); currently enrolled in the M.F.A. Program in Fiction at the Vermont School of Norwich Univ., Montpelier, VT, 1985–. Other studies include courses with the Union Graduate School for Experimenting Colls. and Univs., as well as several writing seminars. Taught English in the public schools of Norfolk, VA, 1954–62; Charlottesville, VA, 1962–63; and Baltimore (Frederick Douglass H.S.), 1963–67. In addition to the two collections cited below, she is the author of two books of short stories, *Dear Aunt & Till Fen Comes Back!* (c. 1976) and *The Edge of Doom, or Honor Thy Father* (1985). Founding editor of *Outreach,* a creative writers' journal, 1982–, in which many of her writings have been published. Other writings have appeared in *Janus* magazine, *Black American Literature Forum,* and *Student.* Author of *Native Son Notes* for the *Cliff's Notes* series (1971). Recipient of an Arena Players Citation in Drama for her collection *THREE PLAYS* (1965), republished as *FATAL FEMALE FIGURES IN 3 PLAYS* (1982). *Address*—Home: 1727 Ingram Rd., Baltimore, MD 21230. Office: Morgan State University, Cold Spring Lane & Hillen Rd., Baltimore, MD 21239. *Pertinent Address*—for purchasing author's scripts: Morgan State University Bookstore, Cold Spring Lane & Hillen Rd., Baltimore, MD 21239.

COLLECTIONS:
THREE PLAYS. Exposition Press, New York, 1965. Repub. as *FATAL FEMALE FIGURES IN 3 PLAYS.* Morgan State Univ., Baltimore, 1983; available from Morgan State Univ. Bookstore. Contains **The Other Side of the Wall** (1965), **The Places of Wrath** (1965), and **Helen** (1965).

EXPLORING THE BLACK EXPERIENCE IN AMERICA. F. Peters, Franklin Square, New York, 1976; reprinted by Morgan State Univ., Baltimore; available from Morgan State Univ. Bookstore. Contains **The New Nigger, or Who's Afraid of William Faulkner?** (1976) and **The Deal** (1976).

PLAYS:
Helen (drama, 2 acts, 1965). A young mother refuses to grow up and allow her 16-year-old daughter to call her "Mother." Her refusal grows out of her own frustrated and unhappy childhood, stemming from her own mother's personal rejection of her in favor of her brother. Pub. in the author's *THREE PLAYS*; reprinted as *FATAL FEMALE FIGURES IN 3 PLAYS.*

The Other Side of the Wall (drama, 3 acts, 1965). Hinges on the conflict between a sensitive, compassionate wife and her cloddish husband, who prevents her from coming to the aid of another wife in the next apartment whose husband beats her nightly. Prod. by the Norfolk (VA) Public Lib. Culture Center, April 5, 1971. Pub. in the author's *THREE PLAYS*; reprinted in *FATAL FEMALE FIGURES IN 3 PLAYS.*

The Places of Wrath (drama, 3 acts, 1965). An unfaithful husband, who has also apparently caused his daughter's suicide, becomes repentant and begs his cold, bitter, and vindictive wife for forgiveness, to no avail. Pub. in the author's *THREE PLAYS*; reprinted as *FATAL FEMALE FIGURES IN 3 PLAYS*.

The Deal (drama, 2 acts, 1976). Greed leads to the misfortune of two men and two women when they make a deal in which each hopes to outsmart the other three. Prod. by the Morgan State Univ. Players, Baltimore, Feb. 24–March 6, 1983, running on weekends; dir. by Richard Pope. Pub. in the author's *EXPLORING THE BLACK EXPERIENCE IN AMERICA*.

The New Nigger, or Who's Afraid of William Faulkner? (drama, 2 acts, 1976). Satire on racism in America, utilizing black and white stereotypes and a play-within-a-play structure to answer the question, Who writes the black man's script? Pub. in the author's *EXPLORING THE BLACK EXPERIENCE IN AMERICA*.

JONES, SILAS (1942–   ), Short-story writer and playwright. Born in Cynthiana, near Paris, KY. Educated at Washington State Univ. (writing and literature), Los Angeles City Coll. (theatre and screenwriting), and the Open Door Program of WGA. Directed a writing workshop for the Performing Arts Soc. of Los Angeles (PASLA), 1974. A number of his short stories have been published in *Black World* and other publications. He is the author of two books: *The Price of Dirt* (a novel, 1974) and *Children of All* (featuring black superheroes, 1978). Member of WGA/West and DGA. Recipient of the Gwendolyn Brooks Literary Award (for best short story), 1972, and an ARTACT Playwriting Award, around 1976. *Address:* 7818 South Hobart Blvd., Los Angeles, CA 90047.

PLAYS AND DRAMATIC WORKS:

Waiting for Mongo (comedy-drama, full length, 1975). "Nightmare comedy," combining reality and fantasy, concerning a black teenage rapist who is hiding out in a dilapidated church basement, waiting to be rescued from a white lynch mob by a black revolutionary leader. Prod. Off-Bway by the Negro Ensemble Co., at St. Marks Playhouse, New York, May 18–June 15, 1975, for 33 perfs.; dir. by DOUGLAS TURNER WARD. Cast included Reyno, Bill Cobbs, Bebe Drake Hooks, Barbara Montgomery, Roland Sanchez, Ethel Ayler, ADOLPH CAESAR, Graham Brown, and SAMM-ART WILLIAMS. Won an AUDELCO Award for the lighting director, Saundra Ross.

The Afrindi Aspect (c. 1976). Prize-winning play in the ARTACT Playwrights' Competition.

Denise Douglass, D.D.S. (filmscript or screenplay, full length, 1970s). Situation comedy, which in the late 1970s was under option to Twentieth Century-Fox.

JONES, T. MARSHALL (1934–   ), Musician, composer, arranger, band director, and college professor. Currently resides in Albany, GA. Educated at Virginia State Coll. (B.S. in instrumental music education, 1956); Univ. of Oklahoma (M.Mus. in instrumental music education, 1960); Univ. of Oklahoma (D.Mus. Ed., 1961; music education, 1972); with further study at Eastern Michigan Univ., 1961, Northwestern Univ., 1968, and Westminster Choir Coll. at Princeton Univ., 1974. Served in the U.S. Army, Adj. Gen. Corps, 1957–59. Married; four children. Prof. and chairman, Dept. of Music, Albany State Coll., Albany, GA, 1977–present; previously director of bands, 1963–77. Director of instrumental music, Lapeer State Training School, Lapeer, MI, 1960–63. Has performed as a trombonist with numerous musical groups, including Virginia State Coll., Univ. of Michigan, Univ. of Oklahoma, and in the U.S. Army. Serves as musical director for the Albany State Coll. Players, and has conducted musicals at the Univ. of Oklahoma and at the Mummers Theatre of Oklahoma City. Member of numerous professional national and state music associations. Other memberships include Alpha Phi Alpha Fraternity, Alpha Phi Omega National Service Fraternity, Georgia Alliance for Arts Education (state secy., 1974–76), and National Soc. for Literature and the Arts. Recipient of numerous honors, awards, and appointments for outstanding service in music, education, and the arts. *Address:* 3332 Sweetbriar Rd., Albany, GA 31707.

PLAYS AND DRAMATIC WORKS:
Ghetto Vampire (comedy with music, 2 acts, 1973). Play by CURTIS L. WILLIAMS. Music (8 songs) by Jones. A black man seeks to escape the ghetto by becoming a vampire. First prod. at Albany State Coll., opening Feb. 20, 1973, for a three-day run. Extensively revised and rewritten, and prod. by the Afro-American Players of Austin, TX, at the Methodist Student Center, opening Oct. 24, 1975, for a five-week run of Fri. and Sat. night perfs. Unpub. script without music included in the coauthor Curtis L. Williams's Ph.D. dissertation, "Two Plays on the Black Experience: From Conception to Production" (Univ. of Texas at Austin, 1977).

Swap Face (children's play with music, 1 long act, 1974). Play by Curtis L. Williams. Music (6 songs) by Jones. Swap Face goes to the magic forest of San Ban Tisco to demand a new face of Mr. Meanie, to whom he has sent his old socially rejected face. Hocus is Swap Face's ally. Prod. at Albany State Coll., 1978. Script without music pub. in *Encore* magazine, 1975.

JONES, WALTER, Actor, director, and playwright. Founder and artistic director of the Cornbread Players, New York, now quiescent. In addition to his own plays, Jones directed the original production of CHERRILYN MILES's *X Has No Value* and performed in the New York productions of *The Toilet* (1964), *No Place to Be Somebody* (1969), and *The Life and Times of J. Walter Smintheus* (1971).

REPRESENTATIVE PLAYS:
Nigger Nightmare (ritual, full length, 1969). The story of 400 years of black oppression in the West. Coprod. by the Cornbread Players and the New York Shakespeare Festival Public Theatre (NYSF/PT), at the Other Stage, New York, June 24–27, 1972, for 4 perfs.; dir. by Novella Nelson. With HOPE CLARKE, Norma Darden, Judi Dearing, Tommy Jonsen, GARRETT MORRIS, Freda Vanterpool, Lennal Wainwright, and Dick Williams. Prod. by a performing group called Langston Hughes's House of Kuumba, New York, Feb. 1972.

Jazznite (drama, 1971). About a Yale-educated black intellectual who brings back to the ghetto what he has learned about "the games that the Whiteman plays." Prod. by NYSF/PT, at the Other Stage, opening April 13, 1971, for a run of more than 38 perfs., on double bill with *The Life and Times of J. Walter Smintheus* by EDGAR WHITE, both prod. under the production title *Underground;* dir. by Jones. With Robin Braxton, Demond

Wilson, Lennal Wainwright, Sam Singleton, Walter Cotton, MacArthur Flack, and Norma Darden. Pub. in *Scripts* 6 (NYSF/PT), May 1972.

OTHER PLAYS AND DRAMATIC WORKS:
The Boston Party at Annie Mae's House (1971). Written and dir. by Jones. Prod. by the Cornbread Players, at Cafe La Mama in the East Village, New York, 1971. **Fish and Chips** (comedy-drama, 1 act, 1972). Prod. by the Cornbread Players, New York, Fall 1972. **Rev. Brown's Daughter** (comedy-drama, 1 act, 1972). Prod. by the Cornbread Players, Fall 1972. Prod. by La Mama E.T.C., New York, opening Nov. 1, 1972. **Dudder Love** (1972). Prod. by the New Federal Theatre, during the 1972–73 season. Prod. at the Third Annual Black Theatre Alliance Festival held at Brooklyn Academy of Music, New York, 1973. **Sunnyboy's Poems** (1973). Prod. by the Cornbread Players, at the Billie Holiday Theatre, Brooklyn, the second week of Oct. 1973; dir. by MEL WINKLER.

JONES, WILLA SAUNDERS (Mrs. Charles E. Jones) (1901–1979), Playwright, producer, director, singer, pianist, organist, and composer. Born in Little Rock, AR. Resided for more than 50 years in Chicago, IL, where she was an important contributor to the cultural and religious life of the black community. A member of the National Baptist Convention, and director of its 1,000-voice chorus, which sang at conventions in Chicago, Arkansas, California, Cleveland, Detroit, and New York. Author and producer of an annual passion play, described below.

DRAMATIC WORK:
Black Passion Play (full length, 1926/1973). An "interpretation of the suffering and ultimate glory of Jesus as seen through the eyes of the Black man's experience in the U.S."—*Jet*, March 26, 1970, p. 43. Prod. annually in Chicago since 1926, where it was "reputed to be Chicago's oldest continuous cultural event."—Ibid. The 1970 prodn. was sponsored by SCLC. The 1973 prodn. was the forty-fourth annual prodn.

JONES-MEADOWS, KAREN, Playwright. Associated with the Negro Ensemble Co. (NEC) in New York City.

PLAY:
Henrietta (drama, 2 acts, 1985). In a Harlem setting, this play, according to *Black Masks* (Feb. 1985, p. 2), presents a portrait of "a mature, dishevelled woman . . . [who] sits outside her brownstone hurling insults at passers-by. However, closer attention to her words reveals her truly uncanny insight into human behavior." Prod. by NEC, Feb. 1985; dir. by Samuel P. Barton. With Frances Foster, Elain Graham, and William Jay.

JORDAN, NORMAN (1938–   ), Poet-playwright and filmmaker. Born in Ansted, WV. Grew up in Cleveland, OH, where he was educated in the Cleveland Public Schools and in "the University of life." Dropped out of high school after the ninth grade to serve a four-year hitch in the navy. Worked on a number of jobs before becoming associated with neighborhood youth centers in Cleveland, first as a youth leader, then as an outreach worker, and eventually as director of the Hough Youth Center, 1965–68. Participant in the U.N. International

Playwrights Workshop, 1967. The first writer-in-residence at Karamu House and Karamu Theatre in Cleveland, 1970–71. Taught writing at the Muntu Workshop. Was associated with Le Theatre Noir in Cleveland, and Theatre Black and the Bed-Stuy Theatre in New York City. The author of two volumes of poetry: *Destination Ashes* (1967; 1971); and *Above Maya (to a Higher Consciousness)* (1971). His poems have been published in numerous periodicals, including *Cricket, Black World, Journal of Black Poetry,* and *Umbra,* and anthologized in *Black Fire* (Jones & Neal, 1968), *New Black Poetry* (Major, 1969), *Right On!* (Chambers & Moon, 1970), and *Blackspirits* (King, 1972). More recently he has turned his talents to screenwriting and filmmaking. Technical advisor to the film *Uptight* (1968). Recipient of a United National Playwright's Award, 1967, and the Harriet Eels Performing Arts Fellowship at Karamu House, 1971.

REPRESENTATIVE PLAYS AND DRAMATIC WORKS:

We Free Kings (drama, 1 act, 1967). Two brothers become increasingly intoxicated as they drink while awaiting news of their father's death. Prod. by Le Theatre Noir, Cleveland, Aug. 1967.

Cadillac Dreams (comedy, 2 acts, 1967). A blue-collar worker devises a get-rich-quick scheme which involves tricking a professional basketball player into marrying his girlfriend's niece. Prod. by Theatre Black, in association with the Harlem Dramatic Arts Theatre, at Judson Hall in Harlem, opening Oct. 11, 1968. Prod. by the Bed-Stuy Theatre, Brooklyn, NY, 1970. Unpub. script in the Hatch-Billops Collection.

OTHER PLAYS AND DRAMATIC WORKS:

Corrupted American Dollar (1 act, 1967). Prod. by Le Theatre Noir, Cleveland, Aug. 1967. **Destination Ashes** (poetry "ensemble" piece, full length, 1971). Based on the author's poetry volume by the same title, 1967. Prod. by Theatre Black, New York, Summer 1971. Prod. by Karamu House, Cleveland, 1971. Pub. only as a volume of poetry, 1967 and 1971. **In the Last Days** (poetic ritual, 1971). Prod. by the Karamu House Arena Theatre, Cleveland, May 1971. Prod. by Theatre Black, at the Bed-Stuy Theatre, New York, May 1973.

JOSHUA, GEORGE E., Playwright. Associated with the Frank Silvera Writers' Workshop (FSWW) and the O'LAC Repertory Ensemble in New York City.

PLAYS:

The Plantation (1977). Public reading by FSWW, at the Teachers, Inc., New York, Jan. 1977. Unpub script in the FSWW Archives/Schomburg Collection. **Across the Pond** (drama, full length, 1984). "Deals with the plight of several G.I.'s stationed in the Philippines during the Vietnam War. Joshua, a New Yorker, served in the U.S. Air Force and has treated this play with careful realism and clarity."—*New York Amsterdam News,* Feb. 18, 1984. Prod. by the O'LAC Repertory Ensemble, New York, Feb. 1984; dir. by Randy Frazier. **The Flame** (pre-1985). Unpub. script in the FSWW Archives/Schomburg Collection.

JULIEN, MAX, Actor, screenwriter. Born in Washington, DC. Attended Howard Univ., where he was a premedical student, before dropping out to pursue a career in the theatre. Enrolled in the Carnegie Hall Dramatic Workshop in New

York City. Made his acting debut with the New York Shakespeare Festival, and appeared in a number of Off-Broadway productions, including *The Blacks* and *The Beggar's Opera,* before beginning his career in films. Film appearances include *Psyche-Out, The Savage Seven, Uptight* (1968), *Getting Straight* (1970), and *The Mack* (1973), his best-known film, in which he gave a memorable portrayal of a cold-hearted but very successful pimp and the lifestyle that he exhibited. TV appearances include "Mod Squad," "Deadlock" (1969), "Name of the Game" (1970), and "Tattletales" (1974). Member of SAG. *Address:* c/o Allen Susman, 9601 Wilshire Blvd., Beverly Hills, CA.

DRAMATIC WORKS:
Cleopatra Jones (feature film, full length: screenplay, 1973). Written with *William Tennant and *Sheldon Keller. Antidrug crime melodrama, featuring Tamara Dobson as a sexy narcotics agent who is also a sharpshooter, karate expert, and motorcyclist; and Shelly Winters as Cleopatra's archenemy, a white lesbian gang leader. Coprod. by Julien and William Tennant; dir. by Jack Starrett. Released by Warner Bros., 1973. Also featured Bernie Casey and Brenda Sykes.

Thomasine and Bushrod (feature film, full length: screenplay, 1974). Western love story, about the bank-robbing black couple Thomasine, (played by Vonetta McGee) and Bushrod (played by Julien). Prod. by Harvey Bernard and Julien; dir. by Gordon Parks, Jr., and released by Columbia Pictures, 1974.

JUSTICE, JIMMY (1941–   ), Musician and actor. For many years musical director of the Afro-American Total Theatre in New York City. Born in Erie, PA. A graduate of Juilliard. Made his Broadway debut in *The Cuban Thing,* followed by *Indians.* Recent New York appearances include *Timbuktu!* (1978) and *Dementos* (1983). Musical director of *Sancocho* (1979), produced Off-Broadway by the Public Theatre.

DRAMATIC WORKS:
(Music only.) **Makin' It** (musical, full length, 1970). Book by HAZEL BRYANT, GERTRUDE GREENIDGE, and WALTER MILES. The trials and tribulations of a young man from a small town as he tries to make it in show business. Prod. by the Afro-American Total Theatre, at various locations in New York, 1970–73. **Jimmy's Carousels** (1972). Prod. by the Afro-American Total Theatre, May 1972. **Soul Politiken** (musical, 1973). Prod. as a street theatre production, at Lincoln Center, New York, July 27, 1973.

K

KABABA, LAWRENCE, Former artistic director and resident playwright of the New Concept Theatre (NCT), Chicago.

PLAYS:
(All prod. by NCT.) **Darts Anyone?** (1967). **The Pride of Africa** (1968). **Home Grown War** (1974). Concerns the murder of a young black militant by the police.

KAIN, GYLAN, Poet, actor, playwright. Born and raised in Harlem, New York City. Former leader of the famed performing group The Last Poets, who performed at The East Wind, a black cultural center in Harlem of which Kain was also the director. The Last Poets appeared in the hit film *Right On!* (1971), and their poems were recorded by Juggernaut Records (JUG-ST/LP 8802). Kain appeared in the play *The Black Terror* (1972). His poetry has been published in *Essence* magazine and in his collection, *Black Spirits* (1970). *Address:* 1295 Fifth Ave. #8B, New York, NY 10029.

PLAYS AND DRAMATIC WORKS:
Epitaph to a Coagulated Trinity (1 act, 1968). A black wino points up the absurdities of white Christianity to a group of white priests, nuns, and churchgoers, until someone calls the police. Prod. by The Last Poets, at The East Wind, New York, 1968; dir. by ERNIE McCLINTOCK. **The Urination of Gylan Kain** (1973). Prod. by the Players' Workshop, Feb. 23, 1973.

KALEEM, BARRY AMYER (Amyer Kaleem), Playwright. Formerly associated with the New Federal Theatre (NFT) in New York City.

PLAYS AND DRAMATIC WORKS:
System of Green Lantern Solos (drama, 3 acts, 1973). About black survival in the twenty-first century. Prod. by NFT, Feb. 1973; dir. by SAMM-ART WILLIAMS. **You Don't Get Off Here to Catch the Express** (musical comedy, 1 act, 1975). Lyrics coauthored with IFA AYAUN. Music arranged by Andre Ingram and Palmer Lampkin.

About the stratified society within the so-called melting pot of New York's Lower East Side. Prod. by NFT, July 1975. **Birdland** (drama, 2 acts, pre-1975). Deals with the struggle to cope with corruption and the rackets. **One Mint Julep** (tragedy, 2 acts, pre-1975). The return of an absent relative precipitates a family dispute that leads to the rape of one of its members.

KAMBON, OBAYANI, Playwright.

PLAY:

The Pendulum (avant-garde play, 1 act, 1975). The title is a metaphor for the shifting identities of the characters in this play, which concerns two young junkies in a shoeshine parlor who rip off an old man in order to get a "fix." The two men may possibly be brothers, or even the same person; the old man may be their father or possibly facets of themselves. Pub. in *Obsidian*, Winter, 1975, pp. 73–80.

KAY, ULYSSES (Simpson) (1917–   ), Composer whose works include compositions for the stage; violinist, pianist, and conductor. Born in Tucson, AZ, the son of a musical family. Attended local schools and graduated from the Univ. of Arizona (B.S. in public school music, 1938); studied further at the Eastman School of Music/Univ. of Rochester (M.Mus., 1940), Yale Univ. (1941–42), Columbia Univ. (1946–48), and privately. Served in the U.S. Navy, 1942–45, where he played in a navy band and dance orchestra. Lived in Italy, and traveled in Europe, 1949–52, as a Prix de Rome and Fulbright Fellow. Worked as music consultant for Broadcast Music, Inc., New York, since 1953. Served as visiting prof. of music at Boston Univ., Summer 1965, and at UCLA, 1966–67. Became prof. of music at Herbert H. Lehman Coll. of CCNY, 1968; appointed distinguished prof. of music, 1972. Has composed extensively in various media, including works for orchestra, chamber music, and choral groups, as well as for films and television. Significant works include his *Concerto for Orchestra* (1948) and his music for the film *The Quiet One* (1948); orchestral scores *Portrait Suite* (1948), *Sinfonia in E* (1950), and *Southern Harmony* (1975); and cantatas *Song of Jeremiah* (1947) and *Inscriptions from Whitman* (1963). He was a member of the first group of American composers to visit the USSR, 1958, under the cultural exchange program. Served as the American judge on the Prix Italia competition in Trieste, 1960, and toured England in 1961 with the American Wind Symphony. Recipient of numerous awards including the Alice M. Ditson Fellowship, 1964; Rosenwald Fellowship, 1947; Fulbright Fellowship, 1950; Guggenheim Fellowship, 1964; and NEA Grant, 1978. Won the Prix de Rome, 1949 and 1951; an award from the American Academy of Arts and Letters, 1947; and an Alumni Award from the Univ. of Rochester, 1972. Received honorary doctorates from Lincoln Coll./Illinois, 1963; Bucknell Univ., 1966; the Univ. of Arizona, 1969; and Illinois Wesleyan Univ., 1969. *Address:* 1217 Alicia Ave., Teaneck, NJ 07666. *Sole selling agent:* Serious Music Dept., Carl Fischer, Inc., 62 Cooper Sq., New York, NY 10003.

DRAMATIC WORKS/STAGE WORKS—Mainly as composer:

The Boor (opera, 1 act, 1955). Libretto adapt. by the composer from the play by Anton Chekhov. Premiered in a concert prodn. at the Univ. of Kentucky/Lexington, April 2, 1968, Phillip Miller, conductor. Pub. by Pembroke Music Co.; available from Carl Fischer Music, Inc., New York.

The Juggler of Our Lady (opera, 1 act, 1956). Libretto by Alexander King. Premiere prodn. by the Xavier Univ. Opera Workshop, New Orleans, Feb. 23, 1962, Richard Harrison, conductor. Pub. by Pembroke Music Co.; available from Carl Fischer Music, Inc.

The Capitoline Venus (opera, 1 act, 1970). Libretto by Judith Dvorkin. Based on a story by Mark Twain. Commissioned by George Irwin and the Quincy Soc. of Fine Arts. Premiered by the Univ. of Illinois Opera Group, Urbana, March 12, 1971. Pub. by Pembroke Music Co.; available from Carl Fischer Music, Inc.

Jubilee (opera, 3 acts, 1976). Libretto by *Donald Dorr. Based on the novel *Jubilee* by *Margaret Walker. Commissioned by Opera/South, which also premiered the prodn. in Jackson, MS, Nov. 20, 1976. Pub. by Pembroke Music Co.; available from Carl Fischer Music, Inc.

Frederick Douglass (opera, 3 acts, 1985). Libretto by Donald Dorr. Created with the support of NEA and the Rockefeller Foundation. Pub. by Pembroke Music Co.; available from Carl Fischer Music, Inc.

KELLY, JO-ANN (1949–   ), Playwright, songwriter, and poet. Born and currently living in Philadelphia. Studied playwriting with T. DIANNE ANDERSON. Has been associated with the Freedom Theatre in Philadelphia, where she studied playwriting, acting, poetry, and creative writing. Her poetry has been published in *Black World*.

PLAYS:
A Gift for Aunt Sarah (1970). Prod. by the Freedom Theatre, Dec. 1970–Jan. 1971.
Where the Sun Don't Shine (pre-1976).

KEMP, ARNOLD, Playwright and author. Reared in Harlem, New York City. Attended Queens Coll., majoring in English. Author of a novel, *Eat of Me I Am the Savior* (1972). His poetry and a short story have been published in *We Speak as Liberators* (1970) and *What We Must See*.

PLAY:
White Wound, Black Scar (1970s).

KENNEDY, ADRIENNE (Adrienne Lita Hawkins) (1931–   ), Playwright and creative writing teacher. Born in Pittsburgh, PA. Grew up in Cleveland, OH, where she graduated from the Cleveland Public Schools. Educated at Ohio State Univ. (B.A. in education, 1952), with additional studies at Columbia Univ., 1954–56; the New School for Social Research, 1957; the American Theatre Wing, 1958; and Edward Albee's workshop at the Circle in the Square, 1962–64. It was under Albee's tutelage that her playwriting efforts received recognition, and she acknowledges him as the major influence on her career. Married to

Joseph C. Kennedy, 1953; the mother of two children. Lecturer in playwriting at Yale Univ., 1972–73, on a Yale Teaching Fellowship. Author of *People Who Led to My Plays* (a memoir, 1987). Member of the playwriting unit of Actors Studio, 1962–65; New Black Playwrights; P.E.N.; National Soc. of Literature and Arts, 1975–; National Register of Prominent Americans, 1975–. Recipient of a Stanley Drama Award of $500 from Wagner Coll., Staten Island, New York, for **Funnyhouse of a Negro** and **The Owl Answers,** 1963; an Obie Award for **Funnyhouse,** 1964; a Guggenheim Fellowship for creative writing, 1967; two Rockefeller grants, 1967–69, 1970; a National Endowment for the Arts Fellowship, 1972; and a New England Theatre Conf. Grant, 1970s. *Address:* 325 W. 89th St., New York, NY 10024. *Agent:* Bridget Aschenberg, 40 W. 57th St., New York, NY 10019.

COLLECTION:

CITIES IN BEZIQUE: Two One-Act Plays. Samuel French, New York, 1970. Contains **The Owl Answers** (1963) and **A Beast's Story** (1965).

GROUP OF RELATED PLAYS:

"**CITIES IN BEZIQUE**" (program of 2 one-act plays, 1969). Includes **The Owl Answers** (1963) and **A Beast's Story** (1965). Prod. Off-Bway by the New York Shakespeare Festival Public Theatre (NYSF/PT), Jan. 4–March 2, 1969, for 57 perfs. Pub. in the author's *CITIES IN BEZIQUE: Two One-Act Plays* (1970) and in *Kuntu Drama* (Harrison, 1974). **The Owl Answers** also in *New American Plays* (Hoffman, 1968).

REPRESENTATIVE PLAYS AND DRAMATIC WORKS:

Funnyhouse of a Negro (avant-garde play, 1 long act, 1963). About a mulatto girl's unsuccessful attempts to resolve the psychological conflicts of her black/white heritage. Set in a surrealistic rooming house, where she is visited by various historical figures who represent facets of her divided self. Won for the author a Stanley Award from Wagner Coll., Staten Island, NY, 1963; and an Obie Award, 1964. First prod. as a workshop production for one night, at the Circle in the Square, New York, 1963; dir. by Michael Kahn, and featuring Diana Sands, Yaphet Kotto, Lynn Hamilton, and Andre Gregory. Opened Off-Bway, prod. by Edward Albee and others, at the East End Theatre, Jan. 14– Feb. 9, 1964, for 46 perfs.; dir. by Michael Kahn. With Billie Allen as the young girl, Ruth Volner, Leonard Frey, Leslie Rivers, Cynthia Belgrave, Ellen Holly, Gus Williams, and Norman Bush. Prod. in London, 1968. Prod. as a student production by the Univ. of Houston, Oct. 19–21, 1984; dir. by NTOZAKE SHANGE. Prod. by the Undergraduate Dept. of Drama at NYU, Nov. 28–Dec. 2; dir. by Billie Allen, with music by Carman Moore. Pub. in *Anthology of the American Negro in the Theatre* (Patterson, 1967); by Samuel French, New York, 1969; in *The Best Short Plays, 1970* (Richards, 1970); in *Black Drama—An Anthology* (Brasmer & Consolo, 1970); in *Contemporary Black Drama* (Oliver & Sills, 1971).

A Rat's Mass (avant-garde play, 1 act, 1963). Described by JOHN S. SCOTT as "a vitriolic struggle of a Black brother and his sister [characterized as Brother and Sister Rat] to rid themselves of white-Christian oppression."—*Players,* Feb.-March 1972, p. 131. First prod. in Rome, Italy. Prod. by the Theatre Co. of Boston, April 1966. Prod. Off-Bway by La Mama E.T.C., opening Aug. 17, 1969, with music by LAMAR ALFORD. Prod. in London, 1970. Again produced by La Mama E.T.C., March 1976;

dir. by Cecil Taylor. Pub. in *More Plays from Off-Broadway* (Smith, 1976); in *New Black Playwrights* (Couch, 1968); in *The Off-Broadway Book* (Poland & Mailman, 1972).

The Owl Answers (avant-garde drama, 1 act, 1963). "Series of reveries of a Mulatto girl who can find no place for herself in either white or black society."—Program Notes. Recipient of a Stanley Award, 1963. First prod. at the White Barn Theatre in Westport, CT, 1965. Prod. Off-Bway by the NYSF/PT Jan. 4–March 2, 1969, for 67 perfs., on double bill with her **A Beast's Story** (1965), under the blanket title **"CITIES IN BEZIQUE"** [see GROUP OF RELATED PLAYS above]. Dir. by Gerald Freedman. With Joan Harris, Cynthia Belgrave, Moses Gunn, and Henry Baker. Pub. in *New American Plays* (Hoffman, 1968); in the author's *CITIES IN BEZIQUE: Two One-Act Plays*; in *Kuntu Drama* (Harrison, 1974).

A Lesson in Dead Language (avant-garde play, 1 act, 1964). A white dog teaches a class of adolescent girls, with understandable lack of communication. Prod. in London, 1968. Prod. by Theatre Genesis, at St. Marks Church, New York, opening April 22, 1971. Pub. in *Collision Course* (Parone, 1968).

A Beast's Story (avant-garde drama, 1 act, 1965). Symbolic play about the sexual fears of a black woman. First prod. in New York, 1965. Prod. Off-Bway by the NYSF/PT, Jan. 4–March 2, 1969, for 67 perfs., on double bill with her **The Owl Answers** (1963), under the blanket title **"CITIES IN BEZIQUE"** [see GROUP OF RELATED PLAYS above]. Dir. by Gerald Freedman. With Amanda Ambrose, Moses Gunn, Cynthia Belgrave, and Tony Thomas. In the author's *CITES IN BEZIQUE: Two One-Act Plays* and in *Kuntu Drama* (Harrison, 1974).

The Lennon Play: In His Own Write (adaptn., full length, 1967). (Sometimes listed by subtitle alone.) Adapt. by Kennedy and Victor Spinette from John Lennon's stories and poems. Deals with the problems of growing up and becoming aware. First prod. in London by the National Theatre Co., 1967. Prod. at the Summer Theatre Festival, Kingston, RI, opening Aug. 20, 1968. Prod. by the Arena Summer Theatre, State Univ. of New York/Albany, Aug. 1969. Pub. by Simon & Schuster, 1972. In *The Best Short Plays of the World Theatre, 1968–1973* (Richards, 1973).

Sun (avant-garde monologue, 1 act, 1969). Subtitled "A Poem for Malcolm X Inspired by His Murder." About the scattering of a man's atoms into the Cosmos, after his body has been shattered into fragments. Prod. in London's West End at the Royal Court Theatre, Aug. 1969. Pub. in *Scripts* #1, (NYSF/PT), Nov. 1971; and in *Spontaneous Combustion* (Owens, 1972).

An Evening with Dead Essex (doc., 1 act, 1973). Memorial to Mark Essex, a youth who was shot by police in New Orleans. Prod. Off-Bway at the American Place Theatre, opening Nov. 28, 1973. Prod. by the Yale Repertory Co., New Haven, March 15, 1974.

A Rat's Mass/Procession in Shout (improvisational jazz opera, full length [1 act, 2 hrs.], 1976). Adapt. and staged by Cecil Taylor from Kennedy's play **A Rat's Mass** (1963). Produced by La Mama E.T.C., New York, March 1976.

A Movie Star Has to Star in Black and White (full length, 1976). Prod. Off-Off-Bway as an experimental workshop production by the NYSF/PT, opening Nov. 1976; dir. by Joseph Chaikin. Prod. at the Univ. of Houston, opening Feb. 8, 1985; dir. by NTOZAKE SHANGE. Pub. in *Wordplay* 3 (Performing Arts Journal Publications, New York, 1984).

A Lancashire Lad (children's musical, 1980). A fictionalized version of the boyhood of Charlie Chaplin, commissioned by the Empire State Youth Theatre Inst. Prod. in

Albany, NY, at Gov. Nelson A. Rockefeller Empire State Plaza Performing Arts Center, May 1980.

Black Children's Day (children's play, 1980). Commissioned by Brown Univ. (while artist-in-residence there). Based on the black experience in Rhode Island. Prod. by Rites and Reason, Brown Univ., Providence, during the reopening of the Walker-Smith House, a historical site in Rhode Island, Nov. 1980; dir. by GEORGE HOUSTON BASS.

Diary of Lights ("A Musical Without Songs" [subtitle], full length, 1987). Concerned with "The youthful idealism of a young black [married] couple on the inter-racial Upper West Side" of New York City.—Advt., *Black Masks,* May/June 1987, p. 6. Prod. at Davis Hall, CCNY, June 5–14, for 8 perfs., dir. by David Willinger.

OTHER PLAYS AND DRAMATIC WORKS:
The Pale Blue Flower (1 act, 1955). Her first play, modeled on Tennessee Williams's *The Glass Menagerie.* Script not available. **Boats** (1969). Prod. in Los Angeles, at the Forum, 1969. **Orestes and Electra** (adaptn., full length, 1980). Commissioned by Juilliard Conservatory of Music, 1980.

KENNEDY, J. SCOTT, Writer, director, playwright, composer, actor, and company manager. Born in Knoxville, TN. Recipient of the B.A., M.A., and Ph.D. degrees from NYU. Has also studied in London, Paris, and Heidelberg, and has attended professional schools of theatre and acting. Currently professor of theatre arts, School of Performing Arts, Brooklyn Coll., CUNY. Married to Janie Sykes Kennedy, actress and educator; they have three children. A university teacher and prof. for more than 25 years, he has held positions at Prairie View A. & M. Coll., Texas Coll., Hampton Inst., Morgan State Coll., Long Island Univ., Hofstra Univ., and the New School. Senior Fulbright Scholar, the Flinders Univ. of Southern Australia, where he introduced African theatre and black theatres to the continent, 1973–74. Founder/director of a number of university, community, and professional theatre groups, including Off-Broadway Players, New York City, 1956; Scott Kennedy Players, New York City, 1959; the New School Players, New York City, 1959; Brooklyn Coll. Interpretative Readers Workshop, 1962; BSYIA Repertory Theatre, Brooklyn, 1964; New Studio Players Professional Theatre, Accra, Ghana, 1967; the South Australian Black Theatre Co., 1973; the Amistad Players of the Brooklyn Coll. Black Theatre's Workshop, 1974. As a performer, he has appeared in films and on stage, radio, and television in the United States and abroad. Participant as actor-director and Africanist at the following: First World Festival of Negro Arts, Dakar, Senegal, 1966; and First Pan-African Cultural Festival, Algiers, Algeria, 1969. Author of *In Search of African Theatre* (1973). Other nondramatic writings include *Speak the Speech* (1958), *African Theatre in Ghana* (1970), *Cries from the Ghetto* (1973), and *Africa Is a Woman* (1973). Member of the American Theatre Assn., the Broadway Soc. of Choreographers and Directors, and Broadcast Music Inc. Recipient of a Rockefeller Foundation Acting Grant. Holds several honorary degrees. Listed in numerous biographies, including *Who's Who in America* and the *International Who's Who of Intellectuals. Address:* 114–91 179th St., Albany, NY 11434; or Theatre Dept., Brooklyn College, Brooklyn, NY 11210.

PLAYS AND DRAMATIC WORKS:

Ham's Children (drama with music, 3 acts, 1962). A drama of the civil rights struggle. Settings include a church and a jail in the Deep South. Prod. by African Theatre and the Related Arts (ATRA), New York, 1962.

Dramatic Voices of Protest (theatrical collage, 2 acts, 1964). Utilizes music, poetry, narration, and drama to present various figures of history who represent the "Voices of Freedom." Prod. by ATRA, 1964.

Commitment to a Dream (historical drama with music and dance, full length, 1965). Historical black heroes who fought in the cause of freedom are resurrected by a High Priestess from Ghana in order to inspire a group of players who are rehearsing a play about freedom. Figures invoked include Cinque, Nat Turner, and Frederick Douglass. Prod. by ATRA, 1965.

Threshold of the Dawn (historical drama with music and dance, full length, 1965). A sequel to **Commitment to a Dream** (1965). Another group of historical black heroes who fought in the cause of freedom is resurrected by a High Priestess from Ghana in order to inspire a group of players rehearsing a play about freedom. Figures invoked include Harriet Tubman, Sojourner Truth, and W.E.B. Du Bois. Prod. by ATRA, 1965.

Negritude: A Speak Out on Color (morality play with music, 1 act, 1965). A criticism of color prejudice in America and the world. Prod. by ATRA, 1965.

Beyond the Veil (historical drama with music, 2 acts, 1965). An inarticulate, punch-drunk boxer becomes inspired to speak out for black pride and dignity. Prod. by ATRA, 1965.

Behind the Mask (historical drama with music, 2 acts, 1965). Thematically related to **Commitment to a Dream** and **Threshold of the Dawn.** Historical figures come alive to speak out against prejudice and to call for freedom. Prod. by ATRA, 1954.

Cries from the Ghetto (morality drama with music, 1 act, 1966). Similar in theme and content to **Negritude: A Speak Out on Color**. May be the same play by a different title. Prod. by ATRA, 1966.

The Poetic Life of Langston Hughes (theatrical collage, 2 acts, 1957). Coauthor, with his wife *Janie Kennedy. A portrait of the poet as seen through his poetry, with music and dance. Prod. by ATRA in Freetown, Sierra Leone, 1967.

They Sang of a Nation (theatrical collage, 2 acts, 1968). A portrait of America, through music, dance, and dramatic sketches using the works of Robert Frost, LANGSTON HUGHES, and Carl Sandburg. Prod. by ATRA, 1968.

The Rivers of the Black Man (historical drama with music, 3 acts, 1969). Coauthor, with his wife Janie Kennedy. Depicts through gospel, blues, and jazz music, African drums, and poetry, the black man's connection to his past, especially to Africa, and the experience that he has gone through in his search for freedom. Prod. by ATRA, in Accra and in West Africa, 1969.

The Spirit That Creates (drama with music, 1970). The spirit cannot create in a society where people are consumed by commercialism and material values. Prod. by ATRA in Washington, DC, 1970.

The King Is Dead (ritual drama with music, 2 acts, 1971). Subtitled "The Ballad of Dr. Martin Luther King." King is used as a symbol in the black man's fight for respect and dignity in America. Prod. by ATRA at Brooklyn College, 1971.

Cries! How African! (ritual, 1 act, 1973). Utilizes mime and drama to teach racial pride, black consciousness, and a need for more positive images. Prod. by ATRA in Adelaide, Australia, 1973.

KENNEDY, MATTIE, Playwright. Based in New York City. Studied play-writing at UCLA, where she received the M.F.A., 1974.

PLAY:

A Love Supreme (M.F.A. thesis play, 1974). Performed by the Black Vibrations, at the third annual Black Theatre Alliance Festival, held at the Brooklyn Academy of Music, 1973. Prod. by UCLA, Spring 1974.

KENYATTA, DAMON, Playwright and director. Based in New York City. Directed the New York Public Theatre production of *The Ambassadors* by MBA ACAZ in 1970.

PLAY:

The Black Experience (1971). Prod. by Black Arts/West, Seattle, WA, 1971.

KILLENS, JOHN OLIVER (1916–   ), Novelist, short-story writer, essay-ist, critic, editor, playwright, and screenwriter. Born in Macon, GA. Received his undergraduate education at Edward Waters Coll. and Morris Brown Coll.; studied law at Howard Univ. and Terrel Law School, with intent to pursue a legal career; did further graduate study in creative writing at Columbia Univ. and NYU. Married; the father of two children. Began writing while serving in the U.S. armed forces in the South Pacific during World War II, 1942–45. Books include *Youngblood* (1954), an autobiographical novel; *And Then We Heard the Thunder* (1963), a novel about racism against black soldiers during World War II, based on his army experiences; *Black Man's Burden* (1969), a collection of essays; *The Cotillion: Or One Good Bull Is Half the Herd* (1971), a satirical novel about the social strivings of the black middle class; *Great Gittin' Up Morning: A Biography of Denmark Vesey* (1972); and *A Man Ain't Nothin but a Man* (1975). Several of his novels have been adapted, either wholly or in part, for the stage or screen. His stories have been included in such anthologies as *American Negro Short Stories* (Clarke, 1966), *The Best Short Stories by Negro Writers* (Hughes, 1967), and *Black Short Story Anthology* (King, 1972). His essays and criticism have appeared in *Arts in Society, African Forum, Black World, The Black Aesthetic* (Gayle, 1971), *Holiday, Library Journal, New York Times, Pageant, Redbook,* and numerous other publications. Former staff mem-ber of the National Labor Relations Board, 1936–42, and 1946. Founder and first chairman of the Harlem Writers Guild Workshop, 1950. Teaching fellow in creative writing at Fisk Univ., c. 1954. Adjunct prof. and chairman of the Creative Writing Workshop and Black Culture Seminar at Columbia Univ., 1969. Writer-in-residence at Howard Univ., 1971–c. 1973. Has lectured and conducted writing seminars at the New School for Social Research, Southern Univ., Cornell Univ., Howard Univ., Rutgers Univ., Brandeis Univ., Springfield Coll., the Univ. of Western Michigan, and Savannah State Coll. Has traveled extensively through West Africa, and has chaired the Writers Committee of the American Soc. of African Culture. Member of the executive board of American P.E.N.; vice pres. of Black Academy of Arts and Letters. Recipient of the Afro-Arts

Theatre Cultural Award, 1955; Brooklyn Branch NAACP Literary Arts Award, 1957; and awards from Association for the Study of Negro Life and History, Empire State Federation of Women's Clubs, New York State Fraternal Order of Elks, and Waltann School of Creative Arts. Was one of the playwrights who benefited from a $225,000 Ford Foundation grant presented to the American Place Theatre (APT) in New York, 1965. Elected to the Black Filmmakers Hall of Fame in 1976, for his film **Odds Against Tomorrow** (1959). *Address:* 1392 Union St., Brooklyn, NY 11212. *Agent:* c/o Phyllis Jackson, International Creative Management, 40 W. 57th St., New York, NY 10019.

PLAYS AND DRAMATIC WORKS:

Odds Against Tomorrow (feature film, full length: screenplay, 1959). Musical score by John Lewis. Melodrama in which a nightclub musician, motivated by gambling debts and a failing marriage, turns to crime. Considered the first major modern black-authored film, and earned for the author election to the Black Filmmakers Hall of Fame, 1976. Prod. by Harry Belafonte (Harbel Productions), 1959; dir. by Robert Wise. Featured Harry Belafonte, Carmen de Lavellade, Robert Ryan, Shelley Winters, and Ed Begley.

Ballad of the Winter Soldier (dramatic doc, full length, 1965). Coauthor, with LOF-TEN MITCHELL. According to Mitchell, "It dealt with freedom fighters throughout history. The term 'winter soldiers' grew out of Thomas Paine's statement: 'these are the times that try men's souls. The summer soldier and the sunshine patriot will in this hour shrink from the service of his country.' The winter soldier, the authors felt, was one who did not, who continued to fight for freedom."—*Black Drama* (Mitchell, 1966). Prod. as a benefit show for the Congress of Racial Equality (CORE), at Philharmonic Hall, Lincoln Center, New York, Sept. 28, 1964; dir. by James E. Wall. Cast included Frank Silvera, Dick Gregory, RUBY DEE, Robert Ryan, Shelley Winters, and Madeline Sherwood.

Lower than the Angels (drama, 3 acts, 1965). Adapt. from a chapter of his autobiographical novel *Youngblood*. The conflicts between a black and a white family on a Georgia plantation during the late 1950s are complicated by the friendship between the sons of both families. Prod. by APT, Jan. 1965.

And Then We Heard the Thunder (drama, full length, 1968). Adapt. by MILTON McGRIFF from Killens's novel by the same title. About the mistreatment of black soldiers during World War II, based on Killens's military experiences. Prod. by Lee Cultural Center, Philadelphia, Nov. 1968. Pub. only as a novel by Knopf, New York, 1963.

Slaves (feature film, full length: screenplay, 1969). In collaboration with Herbert J. Biberman, who also dir. the film. Depicts the inhumanity and incongruities of the American slavery system, focusing on the breaking up of families, their sale at the auction block, their physical abuse, the squalor of their living conditions, and the sexual relationships between black women and their slave masters. A rebellion against the system is led by a courageous slave, played by OSSIE DAVIS. Prod. by the Theatre Guild, New York, 1969; filmed in Louisiana. Also featured BARBARA ANN TEER, Dionne Warwick, Robert Kya-Hill, Julius Harris, and Eva Jessye. Pub. by Pyramid, New York, 1969.

Cotillion (comedy-drama, full length, 1975). Adapt. from his novel *The Cotillion*. A satire of the social strivings of the black middle class and their attempts to imitate white upper-class society. Prod. by the New Federal Theatre (NFT), New York, July 1975. Also presented at the Harlem Performance Center, New York, Sept. 11–12, 1975. Pub. only as a novel by Trident, New York, 1971.

KILONFE, OBA. See PENNY, ROB.

KIMBALL, KATHLEEN, Playwright. Based in New York City, where she was associated with Theatre Genesis, the Afro-American Studio, and the New York Shakespeare Festival Public Theatre (NYSF/PT) during the 1970s.

PLAYS:

Meat Rack (comic fantasy, 1 act, 1972). About the mental wanderings or dreams of a black prostitute who wants to quit her profession ("the meat rack"). Her fantasies concern what she might otherwise have become. Prod. by the Afro-American Studio, New York, Jan. 1975. Pub. in *Scripts* #7 (NYSF/PT), May 1972. **Jimtown** (1972). Prod. by Theatre Genesis, New York, April 1972.

KING, CURTIS, Playwright. Associated with the Jr. Black Academy of Arts and Letters in Dallas, TX.

PLAYS:

(All pre-1976). **Development of the Black Man. Sharecroppers. A Tribute to the Oppressed.**

KING, RAMONA, Actress-playwright. Based in New York City, where she is associated with the Negro Ensemble Co. (NEC) and the New Federal Theatre (NFT).

PLAYS:

Steal Away (comedy, full length, 1981). Five matriarchs of a Chicago church turn to bank robbery in order to raise money for the church's scholarship after their previous money-raising efforts—selling pies—have failed. First prod. by NFT, July 16–Aug. 2, 1981, for 12 perfs.; dir. by Anderson Johnson. With Joyce Sylvester, MINNIE GENTRY, Beatrice Winde, Estelle Evans, Juanita Clark, and Dorothi Fox. Prod. by the Crossroads Theatre Co., New Brunswick, NJ, Sept. 19–Oct. 14, 1984; dir. by Lee Richardson. With Minnie Gentry, Rosanna Carter, and Leila Danette. Prod. by the New Workshop Theatre, Paterson, NJ, Feb. 14–March 14, 1985; dir. by Duane Coles. With Debra Smith, Ayesha M. Vasati, Mia Price, Charlotte Gaither, Felecia Wrights, and Darlene Crowell. **Daniel & Simara** (1984). Public reading by NEC's Playwrights Workshop, April 15, 1984. Prod. by the HADLEY Players, New York, Oct. 24–Nov. 10, 1985, dir. by GERTRUDE JEANNETTE. Prod. by the Black Spectrum Theatre, at Roy Wilkins Park, Jamaica, NY, May 6–27, 1987.

KING, WOODIE, JR. (1937–   ), Producer, director, playwright, screenwriter, TV scriptwriter, actor, essayist, short-story writer, and consultant. Described by Peter Bailey as the "Renaissance Man of Black Theatre." Born in Mobile, AL. Moved with his family to Detroit, MI, at five years of age. Educated at Cass Technical H.S., Detroit, mid-1960s; Will-O-Way School of Theatre, Bloomfield Hills, Michigan, 1958–62; Wayne State Univ. (two years of postgraduate study in theatre); and the Detroit School of Arts and Crafts. Later studied in New York City with Lloyd Richards on a John Hay Whitney Fellowship, 1965. Married; father of three sons. Began his theatrical career as a model in Detroit, 1955–68, when his picture was printed on church fans and insurance calendars. Joined an all-white drama group in Grosse Pointe, MI, c. 1957–58, where he performed in a number of "buddy-type roles" before realizing that there were few opportunities for black actors in white theatre schools and groups. Cofounded (with RONALD MILNER) the Concept East Theatre (CET) in Detroit, 1960–63, also functioning as manager and artistic director. There he directed a number of all-black and integrated plays, including *The Toilet* and *The Slave* by AMIRI BARAKA; *The Zoo Story* and *The Death of Bessie Smith* by Edward Albee; *A Study in Color* and two other plays by the Rev. Malcolm Boyd (a white Episcopalian minister); and *Life Agony* (an early version of *Who's Got His Own*) by Ron Milner. While associated with CET, he also wrote drama criticism for the Detroit *Tribune,* 1960–63. Came to New York City in a touring production of Malcolm Boyd's *A Study in Color,* 1964, which was presented at both the Union Theological Seminary and the American Place Theatre, then just forming. There he remained to direct five plays, including Ron Milner's *Who's Got His Own* (1965) as a work-in-progress. This led to his involvement with HARYOU-ACT (Harlem Youth Opportunities Unlimited, Inc. Associated Community Teams) and to his meeting with Congressman Adam Clayton Powell, Jr., who asked him to write a proposal showing how a cultural arts program could be developed and funded under the antipoverty program. As a result of his proposal, King was made cultural arts director of Mobilization for Youth, New York City, 1965–70, and given a budget of $225,000 to set up a theatre program. He then brought in a group of talented people to teach dance, arts, and theatre, and produced and directed a number of plays and award-winning short films. The films produced with Mobilization for Youth include *The Game* (based on the play *Games* by GEORGE HOUSTON BASS), *Ghetto, Where We Live, You Dig It?, Epitaph,* and *Right On!* (with The Last Poets, 1970). While with Mobilization for Youth, King was also involved in several other projects: he adapted several of LANGSTON HUGHES's writings, which were produced as *The Weary Blues* (1966) and *Simple Blues* (1967)—these were his first efforts at scriptwriting; he was consultant in arts and humanities to the Rockefeller Foundation, 1968–70, and was responsible for making a survey of black theatre in 1969 and for suggesting theatre groups and playwrights for possible funding; and he performed in a number of professional plays, including *The Displaced Person* (1966), *Benito Cereno* (c. 1966), *The Great White Hope* (1968), and *The Perfect Party* (1969). Several years later, in 1973, he also performed in two films, *Serpico* and *Together for Days.* After the termination of Mobilization for Youth, King cofounded the New Federal Theatre (NFT) at the Henry St. Settlement in New York City, 1970–present, where he also serves as artistic director. Since 1969 he has also been president of Woodie King Associates, which he also founded. In addition to his own plays and dramatic works cited below, King has coproduced plays by Amiri Baraka (LeRoi Jones), J. E. FRANKLIN, WILLIAM WELLINGTON MACKEY, ED BULLINS, J. E. GAINES, WALTER JONES, UMAR BIN HASSAN, Ron Milner, LESLIE LEE, NTOZAKE

SHANGE, and MELVIN VAN PEEBLES. In 1972 he also produced two record albums for Motown: *New Black Poets in America* and *Nation Time* (by Amiri Baraka [LeRoi Jones]). Wrote TV scripts for "Sanford and Son" (1974) and "Hot l Baltimore" (1975). Was script editor for TV's "Sanford Arms," 1970s. Author of *Black Theatre: Present Condition* (a collection of essays originally published in periodicals; National Black Touring Circuit [publishers], New York, 1981). Editor of the following books: *A Black Quartet* (four plays by Baraka, Bullins, Caldwell, and Milner, 1970); *Black Drama Anthology* (with Ron Milner, 1972); *Black Poets and Prophets: The Theory, Practice and Aesthetics of the Pan-Africanist Revolution* (with EARL ANTHONY, 1972); *Black Short Story Anthology* (1972); *Black Spirits: New Black Poets in America* (1972); and *The Forerunners: Black Poets in America* (1975). His essays and criticism have been published in *The Drama Review, Negro Digest/Black World, Rockefeller Foundation Quarterly, Variety, Liberator, Black Theatre Magazine, Black American Literature Forum,* and *Anthology of the American Negro in the Theatre* (Patterson, 1967). His short stories have been published in *Liberator, Negro Digest, Negro History Bulletin, Black Creation, Black Scholar, Best Short Stories by Negro Writers* (Hughes, 1967), *Rappin' and Stylin' Out: Communication in Urban Black America* (Kochman, 1972), and *We Be Word Sorcerers* (Sanchez, 1973). Recipient of a John Hay Whitney Fellowship, 1965–66, to study directing; a Venice Festival Award, 1968, and an Oberhausen Award, 1968, for his short film **The Game;** an A. Phillip Randolph Award from the New York Film Fest., 1971, for his short film *Epitaph;* an AUDELCO Black Theatre Recognition Award, 1973, an AUDELCO Board of Directors' Award, 1975, for his work as a producer, and a third AUDELCO Award as director of a dramatic production, *Appear and Show Cause* (by *Leon Gidden and *Stephen Taylor), 1985. *Addresses*—Office: New Federal Theatre, 466 Grand St., New York, NY 10002. Office: 417 Convent Ave., New York, NY 10031.

PLAYS AND DRAMATIC WORKS:

The Weary Blues (dramatization, 2 acts, 1966). Based mainly on LANGSTON HUGHES's first book of poems by the same title (1926), using additional prose and poetry from his other works, with *W. C. Handy's blues music added as an integral part of the concept. According to King, "The idea [is] to follow a young Black American from a storefront church through the Harlem streets and finally to [his experiences as a soldier on] the foreign soil of some distant land."—*Negro Digest,* April 1969, pp. 31–32. First prod. at the Lincoln Ctr. Lib. in New York City, sponsored by Equity Theatre, Oct. 31, 1966, for 3 perfs. Cast included Theresa Merritt, Eleo Pomare as a junkie dancer, Norman Bush as a preacher, and Cliff Frazier as a hustler. Apparently prod. again by the Adventure Corps, NY, Feb. 1968.

Simple Blues (dramatization, 1 act?, 1967). Adapt. from the stories of LANGSTON HUGHES which deal with Jesse B. Semple, a colorful Harlem character. Written at Hughes's request, after King had successfully adapted his **Weary Blues.** Prod. at the Clark Ctr. of Perfg. Arts, New York City, 1967.

Cotillion (musical, full length, 1975). Adapt. by King, RICHARD WESLEY, and others from the novel by JOHN O. KILLENS. Satirizes the imitation of white upper-class society by the black middle classes. Prod. by King at NFT, July 1975; dir. by Allie Woods.

Black Dreams (screenplay, pre-1976). "Based on the short story 'Beautiful Light and Black Our Dreams.' "—*Black Playwrights, 1823–1977* (Hatch & Abdullah, 1977), p. 141.

The Long Night (feature film, full length, 1976). Based on JULIAN MAYFIELD's novel by the same title (1968). According to Stephen M. Vallillo, it concerns "an adolescent boy in Harlem (played by King's son W[oodie] Geoffrey King), whose father has disappeared. Throughout one night, the boy tries to recover $27 which he owes to mother and which has been stolen from him. At the same time, in flashbacks, he recalls the events that led to his father's departure."—*Afro-American Writers After 1955: Dramatists and Prose Writers* (Davis & Harris, 1985), p. 174. Prod. by Woodie King Assocs., New York, 1976.

The Black Theatre Movement: "A Raisin in the Sun" to the Present (doc. film, full length: film script, 1978). According to Stephen M. Vallillo (ibid.), this film "traces the rise of black theatre through interviews with actors, directors, writers, and producers, and film footage of past and current black theatre productions." Prod. by the National Black Touring Circuit, 1978, and shown on public television in 1979.

The Torture of Mothers (doc. film, full length, 1980). According to Stephen M. Vallillo (ibid., p. 177), it "dramatizes a 1964 Harlem incident that ballooned from children's mischief to the imprisonment of six innocent youths. King based the film on tape recordings of the children's mothers."

OTHER PLAYS AND DRAMATIC WORKS:
"Sanford and Son" (TV script, 1974). Prod. by NBC-TV, 1974. **"Hot l Baltimore"** (TV script, 1975). Prod. by ABC-TV, 1975. **Jet** (screenplay, pre-1976). **Harlem Transfer** (filmscript, 1 act, 1970s). Adapt. from a short story by EVAN WALKER. **Death of a Prophet** (screenplay, 1982). Prod. by the National Black Touring Circuit, 1982.

KIRKSEY, VAN, Actor-playwright. Performed in *Big Time Buck White* (1973).

PLAY:
The Hassle (early 1970s).

KULJIAN, ROY R., Playwright. A member of the Negro Ensemble Co. (NEC) in New York City.

PLAY:
Big City Blues (A Trilogy) (3 monologues, 1 act, 1980). Three vignettes describing problems of life in Los Angeles: "Jackhammer Man," portrayed by SAMM-ART WILLIAMS; "Revival," portrayed by Chuck Patterson; and "Goodbye to Mrs. Potts," portrayed by Frances Foster. "Jackhammer Man" concerns a construction worker who felt that he was being controlled by his machine. Prod. by NEC, Feb. 7–24, 1980, for 22 perfs.; dir. by Horacena J. Taylor.

KURTZ, CLEVELAND, Playwright. Associated with Brown Univ. in Providence, RI.

PLAYS:

A Voice in the Wilderness (gospel song play, 1 act, 1973). Coauthor, with *Sandra Franklin. Prod. by Congdon St. Baptist Church, Providence, Nov. 1973. **Sarge** (1 act, 1974). A trip by two ex-Marine buddies to visit their sergeant after the Vietnam War leads to unexpected consequences. Prod. by Brown Univ., May 1974. Pub. in *Schubert Playbook Series,* vol. 2, no. 1 (Emigh, 1974).

KUSH. See DENT, TOM.

L

LANG, JAMES, Inmate of Norfolk (VA) Prison at the time he wrote the following play.

PLAY:
The Plague (drama, 1 act, 1972). Subtitled "Don't Let the Joneses Get You Down." Dramatizes the dilemma faced by a black man who is torn between his addiction to narcotics (called "the plague" or "the Joneses") and his wish to be rehabilitated for the sake of his wife and children. Pub. in *Who Took the Weight?* (Norfolk Prison Bros., 1972).

LANGE, TED (1947–   ), Actor and film director. Born in Oakland, CA. Currently resides in Beverly Hills. Attended San Francisco City Coll., 1967; graduated from the American Film Inst. (AFI) in Los Angeles. Best known for his TV roles as Junior in "That's My Mama" and Isaac Washington, the bartender, in "The Love Boat." Stage performances include *Golden Boy* (1964), *Big Time Buck White* (1969), *Hair* (1969), and *Ain't Supposed to Die a Natural Death* (1971). Film appearances include *Blade* (1973) and *Friday Foster* (1975). Has directed segments of "The Love Boat," "Fall Guy," and "Fantasy Island." Member of SAG, SDG, and AFI.

PLAYS AND DRAMATIC WORKS—All pre-1980:
Day Zsa Voo. A Foul Movement. Pig, Male and Young. Sounds from a Flute. Booker's Back (screenplay). **Boss Rain Bow** (screenplay). **Little Brother** (screenplay). **Passing Through** (1973). Prod. by UCLA, 1973.

LEA (one name), Playwright. Associated with Theatre Black, New York City, in 1971.

PLAY:
Old MacDonald Had a Camp (children's play, full length, 1971). Described by Sati Jamal, codirector of Theatre Black, as follows: "Old MacDonald had a different farm.

It consisted of Black people—just everyday people on the street. This (the street) was the farm and MacDonald was the Man, the devil . . . he had a white face and the members of the farm were simply the people on the street, the junkies, the pimps, and the average working man.''—Interview recorded in ''The Black Theatre Alliance: A History of Its Founding Members'' (Ph.D. dissertation, Robert Jerome Wilson, 1974), p. 85. Performed in repertory by Theatre Black, as part of its Children's Theatre Series, at the Langston Hughes House of Kuumba for African Peoples, Harlem, New York, 1971. Later presented in 12 school districts around New York.

LEAGUE, RAYMOND A. (1930–1975), Playwright, producer, communications and media executive, marketing and sales consultant. Cofounder and president of Zebra Assocs., a New York marketing-advertising firm. Producer of *A Sound of Silence* New York, 1965.

PLAY:
Mrs. Carrie B. Phillips (1971). Prod. by the Lambs' Club, New York, 1971.

LEAKS, SYLVESTER (1927–   ), Author, playwright, former dancer, public relations specialist. Born in Macon, GA. Educated at CCNY and Cambridge School of Radio Broadcasting. Currently resides in Brooklyn, New York. Former dancer with Asadata Dafora African Dancers and Singers. Director, Public Information, Bedford-Stuyvesant Restoration Corp., Brooklyn, 1969–73. Editor, *Muhammad Speaks,* Chicago, 1960–65. Former pres., Harlem Writers' Guild. Author of poetry, short stories, biography, and nonfiction.

DRAMATIC WORKS
Both pre-1976). **Trouble, Blues N' Trouble** (drama). **My God, My God Is Dead** (screenplay).

LeBLANC, WHITNEY J. (1931–   ), TV producer-director, theatre and lighting designer, and playwright. Educated at Southern Univ./Baton Rouge, LA (B.A., 1954), and State Univ. of Iowa (M.A., 1958). Stage manager and asst. technical director, Karamu House, Cleveland, 1959; asst. prof. and theatre designer, Antioch Coll., 1959–64; assoc. prof. of theatre, Howard Univ., 1964–65; assoc. prof. of theatre, Towson State Coll., 1955–69. Set designer for Center Stage, Baltimore, MD, 1965; cofounder, with his wife, dancer Elizabeth Walton, of Theatre Univ., Baltimore, 1968–; designer of the orig. prodn. of *Ceremonies in Dark Old Men* for the Negro Ensemble Co., New York, 1969; TV director of the Maryland Center for Public Broadcasting, and director of the ''Our Street'' TV series, 1969–; assoc. producer, ''Good Times'' TV series, c. 1974–. Presently TV/film director, Hollywood, CA. Member, National Assn. of Educational Broadcasters, ATA, Alpha Phi Alpha. Recipient of Arena Players Citation, Baltimore, for contributions as designer and educator, 1968; and Ohio State Award, 1970, for excellence of TV series ''Our Street.''

PLAYS AND DRAMATIC WORKS:
It's a Small World (TV drama, 1 act, 1972). Deals with the recurring aspects of friendship, needs and aspirations which do not know color lines. Set in a ghetto where

a black and a white discover that they knew each other many years ago. Prod. and dir. by the author at the Maryland Center for Public Broadcasting, Baltimore, May 1971; aired many times in repeats on PBS. Earned for the author an Ohio State Award, 1972, for the series "Our Street," of which this play is one episode.

Dreams Deferred ("A Real Fairy Tale" [subtitled], 2 acts, 1975). The story of a beginning relationship between a black man, a white woman, and a Cuban clown during the early 1960s. It is told by a storyteller as a fairy tale, but the times move from fantasy to reality and end with the assassination of Martin Luther King. Prod. as a workshop production by the Frank Silvera Writers' Workshop (FSWW), at the Martinique Theatre, New York, on Feb. 24, 1975. Unpub. script in the FSWW Archives/Schomburg Collection.

The Killing of an Eagle ("A Surrealistic Religious Epic" [subtitle], 3 acts, c. 1975). Deals with the burden placed on interracial friendships by our religious teachings. Takes place in an abandoned church which was Catholic, then Jewish, and finally a Church of God in Christ. Complete with dead bodies, rites remembered by the occupants, cantos spoken by the former deities, revolutionaries revolting, and dances which mystically transform time from real to surreal.

LEE, CARL (Carl Vincent Canegata), Actor and screenwriter. The son of noted actor Canada Lee. Performed in numerous films, including *The Connection* (1962), *A Man Called Adam* (1966), *The Landlord* (1970), *Superfly* (1972), and *Gordon's War* (1972). TV appearances include "The Nurses," "Mannix" (1975), and "Good Times" (1977).

DRAMATIC WORK:

The Cool World (feature film, full length, 1963). Based on Warren Miller's novel, which had been prod. as a play by the same title, 1960. Coauthored with Shirley Clarke, who also directed. As described by Donald Bogle:

The film showed the plight of a fifteen-year-old ghetto victim, and his gang, the Pythons. Duke searches for a gun, the great power symbol that will assure him of leadership and help him defeat the rival gang, the Wolves. In between the search for the gun, director Clarke presents a disciplined and realistic portrait of Harlem as Divine Hell. The Pythons trade comic books for marijuana, share their gangland whore, drink booze, snatch purses, storm the city streets in anger, in boredom, in utter hopelessness. *Toms, Coons, Mulattoes, Mammies, and Bucks* (Bogle, 1973).

In commenting on the contribution of Carl Lee to the script, Bogle also states: "Here again a perceptive black writer was able to bring new insights to a filmic exploration of the black experience."—Ibid. Prod. by Frederick Wiseman, 1963. Featured Gloria Foster, Clarence Williams, and author Carl Lee in the role of Priest.

LEE, JAMES, Playwright. Associated with the Frank Silvera Writers' Workshop (FSWW) in New York City.

PLAYS:
The Rag Pickers (1 act, 1975). Public reading by FSWW, at the Martinique Theatre, June 1975. Unpub. script and tape recording in the FSWW Archives/Schomburg Collection. **The Shoeshine Parlor** (melodrama, full length, 1975). About life in a black ghetto, involving dope, death, and revenge, set in a shoeshine parlor. Prod. by a group of ex-inmates called The Family, through the Mobile Theatre, at various locations in New York City, from Aug. 1975 to July 1976.

LEE, LESLIE (1935–   ), Playwright, TV scriptwriter, fiction writer. Born in Bryn Mawr, PA. Educated at the Univ. of Pennsylvania (B.A. in biology and English) and Villanova Univ. (M.A. in theatre). After receiving his undergraduate degree, he planned to enter the medical profession, and worked for several years as a research technician. He changed his mind and began writing plays while attending Villanova. Gained theatrical experience working for Ellen Stewart's La Mama E.T.C., 1969–70, where his first two plays were produced. Taught playwriting at the Coll. of Old Westbury, NY, 1975–76. Playwright-in-residence, Black Centenary, Univ. of Pennsylvania, 1980. Author of two novellas: *The Day After Tomorrow* (1974) and *Never the Time and Place* (1985). Theatre panelist, New York State Council on the Arts, 1982–84; playwriting coordinator, Playwriting Workshop, Negro Ensemble Co. (NEC), 1985; instr., Beginning Playwriting, Frederick Douglass Creative Arts Center New York; member, WGA and DG. Recipient of Rockefeller Foundation Playwriting Grant, 1966–68; Shubert Foundation Playwriting Grants, 1971 and 1972; Obie Award for **The First Breeze of Summer,** 1975, which also won a Tony nomination and a John Gassner Medallion for Playwriting, awarded by the Outer Circle Critics, as well as a Mississippi ETV Award, and Special Mention by Black Filmmakers, 1977; Isabelle Strickland Award for excellence in the fields of arts and human culture; Playwriting Grant, NEA, 1982; and Playwriting Fellowship, Eugene O'Neill Playwriting Conf., Waterford, CT, 1980. *Address:* 152 Bank St., Apt. 1B, New York, NY 10014.

REPRESENTATIVE PLAYS AND DRAMATIC WORKS:
Elegy to a Down Queen (tragicomedy, 2 acts, 1969). Deals with the disturbing effects of social change on the members of a black family. Believed to be the original play on which the author's Obie Award-winning play **The First Breeze of Summer** (1975) was based. Prod. at Cafe La Mama (La Mama E.T.C.), New York, Feb. 1969. Again prod. in a musical version at La Mama E.T.C., 1972.

Cops and Robbers (absurdist tragicomedy, 1 act, 1970). Deals with the problem of change versus holding on to tradition. Prod. by Cafe La Mama (La Mama E.T.C.), April 1970–71.

The First Breeze of Summer (semi-autobiographical drama, 2 acts, 1975). "A reflection on three generations of a black, now middle-class family, as the quarrels of the younger members set their much-admired grandmother to remembering some of the sacrifices and heartaches she had to suffer in order to bring them all this far." —*The Best Plays of 1974–1975*. Developed from a one-act play first written in the mid-1960s, presumably **Elegy to a Down Queen** (1969). The play was expanded to include the grandmother as a speaking character. In the original version, information about her past was reported by other members of the family. Winner of an Obie Award as the Best Play of 1974–75 in addition to the three distinguished acting awards cited below. Also earned a Tony nomination, and won for the author a John Gassner Medallion for Playwriting, awarded by the Outer Circle Critics. First prod. Off-Bway by NEC, in association with WOODIE KING, JR., at St. Marks Playhouse, March 2–April 27, 1975; dir. by DOUGLAS TURNER WARD. With Frances Foster as the grandmother, Reyno (who won both an Obie Award and a Clarence Derwent Award), and Moses Gunn (who won an Obie Award). Transferred to Bway, opening at the Palace Theatre, June 10–July 20, 1975, for 48 perfs. Prod. in a film adaptn. by PBS on WNET-TV's "Theatre in America" series, 1976, starring Moses Gunn. Winner of a Mississippi ETV Award, for best film adaptn., 1977. Prod. at the Center Stage, Baltimore, opening March 11, 1977, for 36 perfs.; dir. by Woodie King, Jr., with Claudia McNeil as the grandmother. Prod. by the Theatre of Universal Images, New York, Jan.-March, 1983. Pub. by Samuel French, New York, 1975.

Between Now and Then (drama, 2 acts, 1975). "Centers around the traumas of a white man who is afraid that the white race and culture will disappear as the colored peoples of the world mix with whites."—*Essence,* Oct. 1975, p. 9. Prod. by the New Dramatists, New York, Feb. 6, 1975; dir. by Dana Roberts. Prod. by the Billie Holiday Theatre, Brooklyn, 1983. Pub. by Samuel French, New York, 1984.

The War Party (political drama, 1975). About a young mulatto woman's search for her identity, set against the background of a power struggle within a civil rights organization. Deals with opposing views within a civil rights organization, based on the author's own experiences. Prod. by the New Dramatists, New York, 1975. Prod. by NEC, at Theatre Four, New York, Oct. 7–Nov. 16, 1986, dir. by Douglas Turner Ward.

Colored People's Time (historical play, full length, 1982). "Series of scenes depicting highlights of black American history."—*The Best Plays of 1981–1982,* p. 381. Deals with events from the Civil War to the Montgomery bus boycott. According to the publisher, "The play consists of 13 tiny vignettes, each with different fictional characters, each set at a moment when momentous social change is in the wind. The hero is not a character, but the Black spirit for survival." —*Samuel French's Basic Catalog of Plays* (1985) (quoting from a review in the *New York Post).* Prod. by NEC, March 30–April 24, 1982, for 32 perfs.; dir. by Horacena Taylor. With L. Scott Caldwell, Charles Weldon, Juanita Mahone, Chuck Cooper, Charles H. Patterson, Robert Gossett, Curt Williams, Debbie Morgan, and Jackee Harry. Nominated for an AUDELCO Award, as best play, 1983. Pub. by Samuel French, New York, 1983.

Phillis (musical, full length, 1986). Book by Lee. Music and lyrics by MICKI GRANT. Based on the life and world of the eighteenth-century black American poet Phillis Wheatley, a slave born in Senegal, who learned to read and write and gained the admiration of George Washington and Thomas Jefferson. Prod. by Ralph Madero Productions, in association with the United Negro Coll. Fund. Previewed at the Apollo Theatre in Harlem, Oct. 30, 1986, dir. by Ronald G. Russo. Sched. to open at Ford's Theatre, Washington, DC, in late 1986.

Hannah Davis (domestic drama, full length, 1987). "Focuses on the grown children of an upper-middle-class Black family coming to terms with their own lives as well as with the illness of their father."—*Black Masks,* Mar./Apr. 1987, p. 5. Prod. by the Crossroads Theatre, New Brunswick, NJ, Mar.-Apr. 1987, dir. by L. Kenneth Richardson.

OTHER PLAYS AND DRAMATIC WORKS:

As I Lay Dying, a Victim of Spring (1972). Prod. by the New Dramatists, New York, 1972; presented at the Walnut St. Theatre, Philadelphia. **The Night of the No-Moon** (1973). Prod. by the New Dramatists, New York, 1973. **The Book of Lambert** (1977). Prod. as a workshop production by the Theatre at St. Clements, opening May 26, 1977; dir. by Dick Gaffield. **Almos' a Man** (film script, 1977). Adapt. from the short story by Richard Wright. Prod. by PBS on "The American Short Story" TV series, 1977. Selected by the U.S. State Dept. and shown at the Ionesco Film Festival, Paris, 1978. **Nothin' Comes Easy** (1978). Prod. at the Village Gate, New York, 1978. **Summer Father** (TV mini-series, 1978). Prod. by PBS on the "Vegetable Soup TV series, 1978. **Killing Time** (play with music, pre-1980s). Prod. at the Village Gate, New York, late 1970s. **Life, Love and Other Minor Matters** (musical revue, 1980). Written in collaboration with June Carroll and Arthur Siegel. Prod. at the Village Gate, New York, 1980. **"Another World"** (TV scripts, 1982–83). Scripts for the TV soap series, prod. by NBC, 1982–83. **Willie** (1983). Prod. by the O'Neill Center's National Playwrights Conf., 1983. **Golden Boy** (revision of the 1964 musical, 1984). In collaboration with Charles Strouse and Lee Adams. Prod. at the Billie Holiday Theatre, Brooklyn, 1984. Sched. to open Off-Bway, Jan. 1986. **The Killing Floor** (film drama, 1984). Prod. in 1984. Presented at the New York Film Festival, the Locarno Film Festival, the Sundance Film Festival, and the Cannes Film Festival. First prize, the National Black Film Consortium, 1984. **The Wig Lady** (1984). Prod. at the Harold Clurman Theatre, New York, 1984. **Go Tell It on the Mountain** (film script, 1985). Adaptn. of JAMES BALDWIN's novel by the same title. In collaboration with GUS EDWARDS. Prod. in 1985, starring Douglas Turner Ward, Rosalind Cash, Alfre Woodard, Linda Hopkins, and Paul Winfield. **Langston Hughes** (film script, 1986). Semidoc. about the poetry of Hughes, for the Center for Visual History, to air on PBS as part of a new poetry series which includes Robert Frost, Ezra Pound, and others. **Martin Luther King, Jr.** (musical biography for children, 1986). Music and lyrics by Charles Strouse. Prod. by Theatreworks/USA, and opened in New York at the Brooklyn Center for the Performing Arts, Brooklyn Coll., Jan. 6–8, 1987.

LeNOIRE, ROSETTA (Rosetta Olive Burton) (1911–   ), Actress, black theatre founder/director, producer, and conceiver of dramatic works. Born in New York City. Educated at Betty Cashman Dramatic School, 1946; American Theatre Wing, 1950; ASFTA Dramatic School, 1955–58, where she studied acting with Morris Carnovsky. Also studied singing with Reginald Beane, Nat Jones, Kenneth Welch, and Robert Gorman, 1947–c. 1960. Formerly married to William LeNoire, from whom she took her stage name. Made her Broadway debut in the Federal Theatre production of *Macbeth* (1936), in which she appeared as the First Witch. Since then she has appeared in numerous plays, TV shows, and films. Stage appearances include *The Hot Mikado* (1939), *Head of the Family* (1941), *You Can't Take It with You* (USO touring prodn., 1943), *Anna Lucasta* (1947), *Kiss Me Kate* (1950), *Four Twelves Are 48* (1951), *Show Boat* (1951 and 1956), *Carmen Jones* (1952), *Finian's Rainbow* (1955), *The White Devil* (1955), *Mister Johnson* (1956), *Ceremonies of Innocence* (1956), *Take a Giant Step* (1956), *Lost in the Stars* (1958 and 1972), *The Bible Salesman* (1960), *The*

Oldest Trick in the World (1961), Bloody Mary in *South Pacific* (1961), *Tambourines to Glory* (1963), *Cabin in the Sky* (1964), *Blues for Mr. Charlie* (1964), Mrs. Holiday in *Lady Day* (1972), *Streetcar Named Desire* (1973), *God's Favorite* (1974), and *Northern Boulevard* (1985). TV appearances include "Love of Life" series, Emma in "Search for Tomorrow" series, "The Nurses," "The Doctors and the Nurses," Mrs. Noah in *The Green Pastures* ("Hallmark Hall of Fame," 1957), "Another World," and numerous commercials. Films include *Anna Lucasta* (1959) and *The Sunshine Boys* (1975). Founder and artistic director of AMAS Repertory Theatre, Inc., a multiracial performing arts organization in New York City, 1969–present. Member of AEA, AFTRA, AGVA, NAG, SAG, Catholic Actors Guild of America, Actors Fund of America. Recipient of the Dallas, TX, Blue Bonnet Musical Award (for *Show Boat)*, 1963; special citation, Tribute to Greatness Award Ceremony, 1975; Harold Jackman Memorial Award, 1976, in recognition of her contribution to the cultural life of the national community; Pierre Toussaint Medallion, 1985, by the (Catholic) Office of Black Ministry of the Archdiocese of New York, for outstanding service to the African American Community; St. Genesius Award, by the Catholic Actors Guild of America, for special service to the guild, the profession, and the Church; Richard Coe Award, 1986, for her contribution to the development of American theatre. *Address:* AMAS Repertory Theatre, 1 E. 104th St., New York, NY 10029.

REPRESENTATIVE DRAMATIC WORK:

Bubbling Brown Sugar (musical revue, 2 acts, 1976). By LOFTEN MITCHELL. Based on a concept by LeNoire. Encapsulates the history of black entertainment from 1910 to 1940, focusing on the all-black musical revues that flourished in Harlem during this period. Featured music by †Eubie Blake, Duke Ellington, Billie Holiday, †Andy Razaf, Cab Calloway, Earl Hines, and †J. C. Johnson. Described by Alex Bontemps *(Ebony,* Feb. 1976, p. 129), as "about a young man who has just graduated from college and is eager to leave Harlem, a place he believes has no history and no future. . . . A trio of veteran entertainers . . . try to change his mind by taking him on an imaginary tour of Harlem in its hey-day—1910 to 1940." The tour includes stops at such famous night spots as Small's Paradise and the Cotton Club, a visit to a house rent party, and a variety of street scenes. Nominated for a Tony Award, 1975–76, as best musical. Prod. successfully by the AMAS Repertory Theatre, playing Off-Bway and on tour for a year before opening on Bway at the ANTA Theatre, March 2, 1976–Dec. 31, 1977, for 766 perfs., dir. by Robert M. Cooper, with choreography by Billy Wilson (who was nominated for a Tony Award as best choreographer). With Avon Long, Josephine Premice, Joseph Attles, Vivian Reed (who won a *Theatre World* Award and a Drama Desk Award, and was nominated for a Tony Award as best actress in a musical), Chip Garnett (who also won a *Theatre World* Award), Ethel Beatty, and Barry Preston (who won a Clarence Derwent Award). Opened June 22, 1976, at the Shubert Theatre in Chicago, and closed at the National Theatre, Washington, DC, Oct. 9, 1977. Opened Aug. 23, 1977 in Uihlein Hall, Milwaukee, WI, and closed April 22, 1978, at National Arts Center, Ottawa, Canada. Prod. by the Papermill Playhouse, Milburn, NJ, during the 1977–78 season. According to the author, it was prod. in London, Paris, Central Europe, the Netherlands, Germany, on extensive U.S. tour, and by numerous independent groups throughout the

United States Pub. by Broadway Play Publishing Co., 1984. Cast recording released by H & L Records (HL-69011).

OTHER PLAYS AND DRAMATIC WORKS:
Soul Yesterday and Today (theatre work, 1966). By LANGSTON HUGHES and *Bob Teague, arranged by LeNoire. A historical treatment of "soul" as it relates to black lifestyles, using some of the works of Hughes and others. Prod. by AMAS Repertory Theatre, at Central Park Mall, New York, Aug. 28, 1969. **House Party—A Musical Memory** (1973). With music by Manny Cavaco and John Lenahan. Prod. by the AMAS Repertory Theatre, April 15, 1973. **Hound Dog Party** (variety show, 1974). Collective creation of the AMAS Repertory Theatre Workshop; dir. by LeNoire, June 9, 1974. **Rag Time Blues** (musical history of †Scott Joplin, 1975). Collective creation of the AMAS Repertory Theatre, dir. by LeNoire, c. 1975. **Come Laugh and Cry with Langston Hughes** (theatre work, 1977). Adapt. by LeNoire and *Clyde Williams from Hughes's *Shakespeare in Harlem*. Prod. Feb. 3, 1977; dir. by Bill Mason. **Mikado Amas** (operetta, full length, 1975). Adapt. from *The Mikado* by Gilbert and Sullivan. Prod. by the AMAS Repertory Theatre, Oct. 14, 1975; dir. by Irving Vincent. **Miss Waters, to You** // Also called **Miss Ethel Waters** (musical, full length). Book by Loften Mitchell. Based on a concept by LeNoire. Music from Waters's repertoire. Prod. by AMAS Repertory Theatre, opening Feb. 24, 1983; dir. by Billie Allen.

LESTER, JULIUS (1939–   ), Militant author and spokesman. Born in St. Louis, MO. Best known for his books *Look Out, Whitey! Black Power's Gon' Get Your Mama* (1968) and *To Be a Slave* (1968) for which he was a runner-up for the Newbery Award.

DRAMATIC WORK:
Black Folktales (full length, 1971). Based on his book by the same title. Dramatizes such popular stories from black folklore as "Stagolee" and "High John the Conqueror," which Lester has retold in his book. Prod. in Central Park, New York, opening Aug. 27, 1971. Pub. only in its orig. form by Richard W. Baron, 1969, and as a Grove paperback, 1971.

LEWIS, DAVID (1939–   ), Playwright. Born in Spanish Harlem, New York City. Currently resides in the Bronx, NY. Educated at the Murray Hill Vocational School (1957) and the New School for Social Research. Winner of the New American Playwriting Series Award, Brooklyn Coll., 1959.

PLAYS:
Gonna Make That Scene (morality, 1 act, 1967). An elevator is used as a metaphor to dramatize the aspirations of two black men to rise to the middle class (upper floors); but their encounter with the elevator operator greatly discourages them, and they go back down. **Do Your Thing** (comedy, 1 act, 1970). A black man visits a paranoid friend in Harlem, who refuses to let him in. **Georgia Man and Jamaican Woman** (comedy, 1 act, 1970). Satirizes the cultural differences between black Americans and West Indians. **My Cherie Amour** (comedy, 1 act, 1970). Concerns a lovers' quarrel in a discotheque. **Sonny Boy** (comedy, 1 act, 1970). A boy tries unsuccessfully to hustle a newspaper from various people passing by on a street corner. **A Knight in Shining Black Armour** (domestic drama, 1 act, 1971). Encounter between a middle-class black school principal

and his former sweetheart just before he is to be married to a younger woman. **Miss America of 1910** (morality, 1 act, 1971). An encounter between a barmaid and a drunk in a bar. **Mr. B.** (domestic drama, 1 act, 1971). A love story is told against the background of a poolroom setting, in the mid-1950s. **Heaven—I've Been There; Hell—I've Been There Too** (1972). Script apparently pub. by the author, Bronx, 1972. **One Hundred Is a Long Number** (children's comedy, 1 act, 1972). Two parents are faced with the problem of antagonism between their two boys, wherein the older son wishes to dominate the younger one. **Those Wonderful Folks (of the First Baptist Church of New Jerusalem in Harlem)** (children's comedy, 1 act, 1972). Black religious and cultural values are explored in this story of a teenage girl who attempts to get the best of her mother on a Sunday morning, just before leaving for church. **Bubba, Connie, and Hindy** (satire, 1 act, pre-1976). Through the metaphor of a job interview, this play explores a black view of life after death. **Sporty** (pre-1976). **Wally Dear** (pre-1976).

LEWIS, ED "BIM " Playwright. Of West Indian heritage, based in New York City.

PLAY:
The Gun Court Affair (comic melodrama with music, full length, 1975). According to TOWNSEND BREWSTER, "The protagonist, George Bucket, divides his time off from his illegal operations between a long suffering wife and a new mistress."—*Newsletter*, Harlem Cultural Council, vol. 2, no. 7, 1975. Prod. by Jamaica Progressive League and Carib Films, Inc., New York, Spring 1975.

LEWIS, ERMA D., Playwright. Formerly associated with the Sojourner Truth Players, Ft. Worth, TX.

PLAYS:
Our Heritage (black history collage, full length, 1970s). Drama, dance, poetry, and song are utilized to present the black man's history from Africa to the present day. Prod. by the Sojourner Truth Community Theatre, prior to 1975. **The Sharecroppers** (drama, 1 act, 1970s). A family of black sharecroppers struggles to attain its independence on a white plantation. Prod. at Jackson State Univ., Jackson, MS, prior to 1975.

LIFE, REGGE, Director and playwright. Associated with the AMAS Repertory Theatre and the Frank Silvera Writers' Workshop (FSWW), both in New York City. Directed the AMAS productions of *The Peanut Man, George Washington Carver* (1980) and *The Buck Stops Here* (1983).

PLAY:
The Natural (1975). Public reading by FSWW, at the Martinique Theatre, Dec. 1975. Unpub. script in the FSWW Archives/Schomburg Collection.

LIGHTS, FREDERICK L. (Fred) (1922–   ), Stage manager, director, and playwright. Born in Houston, TX. Grew up in Chicago. Lives in New York City. Brother of Ellen Stewart, the celebrated founder, director, and prime mover of La Mama E.T.C. Educated at Morehouse Coll. (B.A., 1974), Howard Univ. (School of Religion, 1946–48; Dept. of Drama, 1948); Yale Univ. (M.F.A.,

1951), and Columbia Univ. (1952). Served in the U.S. Army, 1943–46. Also studied in the Army Specialized Training Programs at North Carolina A. & T. Coll., 1944, and West Virginia State Coll., at Institute, 1944. At Morehouse Coll. he was actively involved as stage manager of all of the productions of the Atlanta-Morehouse-Spelman Players. Employed by NBC, 1951–present, first as a clerk-typist, from which he moved to film librarian, stage manager, and assoc. director. Member of DG, New Dramatists, 1951–54, and DGA, 1953–present. *Address:* 200 West 90th Street, New York, NY 10024.

REPRESENTATIVE PLAYS AND DRAMATIC WORKS:

All Over Nothin' (domestic play, 1 act, c. 1948). Adults become involved in a children's squabble. Written as a student workshop production at Yale School of Drama, New Haven, with an all-white cast. Produced by AMAS Repertory Theatre, New York, 1975.

The Underlings (adapt., 1 act, c. 1948). Based on LANGSTON HUGHES's poem "Father and Son," which deals with the theme of miscegenation. Prod. as a workshop production at Yale School of Drama, around 1948, with an all-white cast.

Samson and Lila Dee (Biblical adaptn., full length, 1952). Retelling of the Biblical story in terms of South Side Chicago in 1933. Optioned for production in 1952, but never prod.

OTHER PLAYS AND DRAMATIC WORKS:

(All pre-1976.) **Barbershop Boogie** (drama, 1 act). An incident of reverse racial prejudice in the South of 1946. **Boys Like Us** (drama, 1 act). Deals with prejudice in a white fraternity when it confronts its first black pledge. **Mood Indigo** (full length). A play based around the music of Duke Ellington. **Peripity** (drama, full length). A young black preacher is martyred by a sudden reversal of fortune. **Pigeons en Casserole** (adaptn., 1 act). Based on a short story by Bessie Bruer. A royal couple immigrates to America; the wife is unable to adjust.

LINCOLN, ABBEY (Aminata Moseka) (1930–   ), Vocalist, actress, writer, director, playwright. Best known for her film performances in *Nothing but a Man* (1965) and *For Love of Ivy* (1968). Born in Chicago, IL. Began career as a nightclub singer, 1950–; also performed with former husband Max Roach, the well-known drummer. Former asst. prof. of Afro-American Theatre and Pan-African Studies, California State Univ., mid-1970s. Recently appeared in a new music and dance presentation, "I Got Thunder," sponsored by the African Jazz-Art Society (AJASS) and Unity in Action, in conjunction with African International Perspective. She had previously starred in an AJASS production, "Naturally '62," before going to Hollywood to star in the two films mentioned above. Elected to the Black Filmmakers Hall of Fame, 1975.

PLAYS:

A Streak o' Lean (full length, 1967). A black man's morality is put to the test when he finds a large sum of money. Excerpt (1 scene) pub. in *Black Scenes* (Childress, 1971). **A Pig in a Poke** (1975). May be an alternate title for **A Streak o' Lean** above. Prod. by Mafundi Inst., Los Angeles, CA, 1975.

LLOYD, DARRYLE, Playwright. A resident of Jamaica, NY. Associated with the Univ. of Vermont/Burlington, where one of his plays was produced.

PLAYS:
P. J. Jones (drama, 2 acts, 1974). About the life and downfall of a Harlem dope dealer. Prod. by the Royal Tyler Theatre, at Univ. of Vermont/Burlington, April 1974. **You're Welcome, but You Can't Stay** (drama, 2 acts, 1975). About a middle-class family who are brutalized and held as prisoners in their own home by a gang of white terrorists.

LOFTIN, WAYNE (1949–   ), Playwright. Based in Omaha, NE. Served in the U.S. Air Force. Interested in freelance writing and photography. Member of the Frank Silvera Writers' Workshop (FSWW) in New York City.

PLAY:
Where? (political satire, 1 act, 1974). Prod. at Creighton Univ. in Omaha for 3 perfs., and on a number of local campuses, as well as at the State Prison in Nebraska, 1974/75. Unpub. script may be in the FSWW Archives/ Schomburg Collection.

LOMAX, LOUIS E. (1922–1970), Author and journalist. Born in Valdosta, GA. Journalist for the *Afro-American* Newspapers; later joined the staff of the *Chicago American*. Author of *The Negro Revolt* (1962), about black civil rights organizations, and *When the World Is Given* (1963), a study of the Black Muslim movement.

PLAY:
The Bitter Cup (TV drama, half hr., 1961). Prod. by NBC-TV on the "Frontiers of Faith" series, early 1961, starring Elwood Smith and RUBY DEE.

LOMAX, PEARL CLEAGE. See CLEAGE, PEARL.

LONG, BARBARA A., Playwright.

PLAY:
Midnight Brown (1 act, 1968). Seventeen black male and female characters symbolize the mythical "Black Subconscious." Unpub. script in the Schomburg Collection.

LONG, RICHARD A. (Alexander) (1927–   ), Author, editor, playwright, and educator. Born in Philadelphia, PA. Educated at Temple Univ., Philadelphia (B.A., MA) and the Univ. of Poitiers, France (doctorate in medieval studies). Prof. of English and Afro-American Studies at Atlanta Univ., and chairman of the Afro-American Studies Dept. Coeditor, with EUGENIA COLLIER, of *Afro-American Writing: An Anthology of Prose and Poetry* (1970). Author of *Black Americana* (1985), a pictorial history of black achievement in the United States; *Ascending and Other Poems;* and numerous critical articles in *Black World/ Negro Digest, CLA Journal, Modern Language Notes,* and *Phylon. Address:* Director, Center for African and Afro-American Studies, Atlanta University, Atlanta, GA 30314.

PLAYS:
Pilgrim's Price (sketches, 1963). Joan of Arc (folk opera, 1964). Stairway to Heaven (gospel opera, 1964). Reasons of State (1966). Black Is Many Hues (1969).

LOTT, KARMYN, Playwright, screenwriter, and producer. Born in Amarillo, TX. Currently resides in New York City. Graduated from West Texas State Univ. in Canyon (B.S. in theatre and journalism); completed one year of graduate work at NYU (toward an M.F.A. in dramatic writing); also studied playwriting at the Henry St. Settlement with RONALD MILNER, and with the Negro Ensemble Co. (NEC) New Playwrights Workshop, under the auspices of STEVE CARTER. Founder of AMTEX Productions, a theatrical company which produces plays in New York, and AMTEX Drama School, located in Amarillo, TX. Recipient of the Ragdale Foundation Writers Scholarship, 1985; Playwrights Center/McKnight Foundation Fellowship, second alternate, 1985; and CAPS Public Service Playwriting Grant, 1984. *Address:* 400 W. 43rd St., Suite 35A, New York, NY 10036; or AMTEX Drama School, 421 Third St., Amarillo, TX 79101.

REPRESENTATIVE PLAYS AND DRAMATIC WORKS:
Old Soldier (comedy, full length, 1978). Horace Mann, a hunchbacked transient con artist, is accused of robbing a bank in Oklahoma. A bounty hunter goes looking for Mann; however, he is set free when no evidence is found. Staged reading by the Henry St. Settlement (New Federal Theatre [NFT]), New York, June 1978. Public reading by the Frank Silvera Writers' Workshop (FSWW), New York, 1979. Unpub. script and tape recording in the FSWW Archives/Schomburg Collection.
Asphalt Gallery (drama, full length, 1979). A former student returns to his alma mater to coach basketball, and discovers that his team is encumbered with problems. Public reading by FSWW, Jan. 1979. Unpub. script and tape recording in the FSWW Archives/ Schomburg Collection.
Hot Sauce (drama, full length, 1980). Examines the subject of incest and the psychological problems that it causes. Public reading on the NEC New Playwrights Play Reading Series, May 1980. Presented by Distant Voices, Inc., New Haven, CT, June 1981. Presented by John Jay Coll. and SAG Conservatory, July 1982. Prod. by the American Theatre of Actors, at the Annex Theatre, New York, April 1983. Prod. by Vassar Coll., Poughkeepsie, New York, Feb. 1984. Prod. by Theatre Off Park, New York, June 1984.
Hush Sweet Baby (drama, 5 scenes, 1981). Sally is a corporate executive who wants to have a baby before she turns 30. After the baby is born, she cannot cope with the responsibilities of single parenthood. Public reading on NEC's New Playwrights Play Reading Series, March and April 1981.
From Africa to Amarillo (comedy with music, songs, and dances, approx. 25 min. without choir and preacher/approx. 55 min. with choir and preacher, 1984). A series of scenes, monologues, and dance interpretation of poems from the author's works, including Asphalt Gallery (1979) and Hot Sauce (1980) above.
Magic Is Ours (comedy, 1 act, 1985). A program consisting of magic acts, an oral interpretation of a story, poems, improvisations, and skits. Prod. at AMTEX Drama School, Amarillo, July 1985.

OTHER PLAYS AND DRAMATIC WORKS:
Nice Girls (drama, full length, 1982). Evolves around a group of women with various female problems. Set in the gynecology floor of the Dalworth Memorial Hosp. in Dalworth, TX. **My Hometown** (drama with music, full length, 1984). In a format similar to Thornton Wilder's *Our Town,* this play is a satire on the integration of the movie theatre in Amarillo, TX, during the 1960s. **Expo of a Black Writer** (series of scenes, 50 min., 1985). Scenes and monologues from the author's works, including **Hot Sauce** (1980), **Nice Girls** (1982), **My Hometown** (1984), and **Drugs** (not listed). **We Shall** (drama, full length, 1987). A tribute to Martin Luther King, the title based on the first words of the civil rights anthem, "We Shall Overcome." Prod. at the Guinevere Theatre, New York, sponsored by the New York State Committee for Dr. Martin Luther King, Feb. 1987, for 3 perfs. NOTE: The following plays are all pre-1986, or in progress: **Breakfast for My Friend** (drama, 1 act). About two alcoholics. **Empty Bottles** (screenplay for a 30–min. video). **Private Affair** (black soap opera). **Under the Mulberry Bush** (love story, full length). **Come See the Sun** (musical drama, full length, in progress). About a smart kid who wants to become a bug doctor. **Once upon a Time** (musical comedy, full length, in progress). Adaptn. of Shakespeare's *Twelfth Night.*

LOVETT, WINSTON C. (1947–   ), Actor, poet, and playwright. Born in Baton Rouge, LA. Graduated from McKinley Sr. H.S. and Dillard Univ., New Orleans (B.A. in business administration, 1969). Received training in scriptwriting for film and television; advanced literary writing; and acting, speech, and drama from the Frederick Douglass Creative Arts Center, New York. Studied playwriting with the Negro Ensemble Company (NEC) Playwriting Workshop, the New York Shakespeare Festival (NYSF) Playwrights' Workshop, and the Frank Silvera Writers' Workshop (FSWW), all in New York City. Has performed as an actor in the following Off-Broadway productions, 1973–76: *Waiting for Godot* (Afro-American Total Theatre); *Transcendental Blues* (Manhattan Theatre Club); *Requiem for George Jackson* (Harlem Renaissance Theatre); and *Homeboy* by ED BULLINS (Perry Street Theatre). Has appeared as an extra on TV's "Saturday Night Live" and in *Madigan, the Harlem Beat,* a made-for-TV movie. Author of three books, all unpublished: an untitled book of poetry and short stories (1978), "Creativity and the Arts" (1981), and "The World of Creativity" (1983). His poems have also been published in the *New York Amsterdam News* and *Grafica* magazine. In addition to the organizations named above, he has been associated with the Afro-American Total Theatre, the Henry St. Settlement Theatre (New Federal Theatre), and the Manhattan Playwrights Unit, and is a member of the New York Dramatists Club and Poets and Writers, Inc. The author states: "No books have been published, no plays produced, yet I continue to write feverishly." *Address:* P.O. Box 610, Rockefeller Center, New York, NY 10185.

PLAYS:
The Greatest Lion in the Circus ("A Children's Play with Music and Dance" [subtitle], pre-1979). **Mutt and Jeff** (1979). Public reading by NYSF, 1979. **The Hunchback of Harlem** (1980). Public reading by NEC, 1980. **The Comic** (1981). Public reading

by NYSF, 1981. **The Creation** (1982). Public reading by FSWW, 1982. Unpub. script in the FSWW Archives/Schomburg Collection. **A Modern Destructive Negro Tragedy** (1986). Public reading by FSWW, Oct. 13, 1986, dir. by Randy Frazier. Unpub. script in the FSWW Archives/Schomburg Collection.

LUCAS, W. F., Playwright, poet, screenwriter. Currently resides in Knoxville, TN, where his plays have been produced at the Univ. of Tennessee and the Carpetbag Theatre, where he was apparently playwright-in-residence from 1970 to 1973. Previously, his plays had been produced in Pennsylvania at Lincoln University, and at the Black Arts Spectrum Theatre and the Lee Cultural Center in Philadelphia. *Address:* 1936 Prospect Place, S.E., Knoxville, TN 37915.

REPRESENTATIVE PLAYS:

Patent Leather Sunday (domestic comedy, 1 act, 1967). Explores the relationship between two black women—one West Indian and the other southern American. First prod. at Lincoln Univ., Pennsylvania, 1967. Prod. at Lee Cultural Center, Philadelphia, Fall 1968; dir. by Tom Butler. Prod. at the Univ. of Tennessee, Knoxville, 1974.

Fandango's for Miss X (monologue with music and voices, 1 act, 1968). Comedy in which a black woman explores her identity. Prod. by the Black Arts Spectrum Theatre, Philadelphia, 1969.

Africa Foo Young (comedy, 1 act, 1970). The comedy revolves around four black customers trying to get what they want in a Chinese restaurant. Prod. by the Carpetbag Theatre, Knoxville, 1971.

Aunt Lottie's Wake (comedy, 1 act, 1970). Aunt Lottie's mourners discover at her wake that she was not as well-off as she pretended to be. Prod. by the Carpetbag Theatre, Knoxville, 1971. Prod. at the Univ. of Tennessee at Knoxville, 1974.

Elevator Stomp (comedy. 1 act, 1970). The setting is a stalled elevator in an apartment building in which four blacks and four whites are stranded. Prod. by the Carpetbag Theatre, 1971.

Bosun's Blues (monologue with voices, 1 act, 1971). A black seaman who has returned from a long journey at sea recalls his arduous experiences. Prod. by the Carpetbag Theatre, 1972.

The Mint (comedy, 1 act, 1971). Some black men and women try to get inside the U.S. Mint. Prod. as a workshop production by the Carpetbag Theatre, 1972.

OTHER PLAYS:

The Triflers, Red, Black, and Green (comedy, 2 acts, 1971). Satire of black scholars trying to find their own identity. **Rudyard's Confections** (comedy, 2 acts, 1972). Conflict between a rabbi who is on the verge of being converted to Christianity and a West Indian candy shop proprietor. **Wisemen in Stocking Caps or The First Supper** (parody, 2 acts, 1973). A contemporary version of the Last Supper.

LYLE, K. CURTIS (Kansas Curtis Lyle) (1944–   ), Poet, playwright, and critic. Born in Los Angeles, CA. Gained early writing experience as a member of the Watts Writers Workshop. Received the M.A. from California State Coll., 1968. Instr. at the Coll. of New Rochelle, NY, 1980s. Member of Black Arts/ West (BA/W), Seattle, WA. His poetry has been anthologized in *Watts Poets* (Troupe, 1968), *The Poetry of Black America* (Adoff, 1972), and *New Black*

Voices (Chapman, 1972), and published in the following periodicals: *Black World, Journal of Black Poetry,* and *Negro American Literature Forum.*

PLAYS:

Days of Thunder, Nights of Violence; Guerrilla Warfare; and **(Da) Minstrel Show** (3 one-act plays, 1969). All prod. by BA/W, 1969/70. **The Process of Allusion** (pre-1976). **Wichita** (pre-1976).

M

MACBETH, ROBERT (1934–   ), Actor, director, playwright, filmmaker, critic, and teacher. During the 1970s, he was considered one of the leading black directors in New York. Born in Charleston, SC. Educated at Morehouse Coll., 1950–52; Newark Coll. of Engineering, 1952–53; CCNY, 1957–60. Served in the U.S. Air Force, 1953–57. Married; the father of two children. Performed in a number of Broadway and Off-Broadway productions during the 1960s, including *The Merchant of Venice* (1962), *Tiger Tiger Burning Bright* (1962), *Who's Got His Own* (1967), which he also directed, and *The Blood Knot* (1964). Founder and artistic director of the New Lafayette Theatre (NLT) in Harlem, 1967–73. Has directed many of ED BULLINS's plays, at NLT, the American Place Theatre, and the New York Shakespeare Festival, including *A Son Come Home* (1968), *The Electronic Nigger* (1968), *In the Wine Time* (1968), *Clara's Ole Man* (1968), and *The Fabulous Miss Marie* (1971). Producer of the film *In the Streets of Harlem/The Ritual Masters* (1972). His critical writings and interviews have appeared in *Black Theatre* magazine (which he cofounded), *The Drama Review*, and *The Probe*. Visiting instr., NYU School of the Arts, since 1976; prof., CCNY, Leonard Davis Center for the Performing Arts, since 1977. *Address:* 1947 Seventh Avenue, Apt. #10, New York, NY 10026.

DRAMATIC WORKS:
A Black Ritual (short ritual, 1968). Designed to raise the consciousness of blacks for the conquest of the "White monster." Performed by the NLT Workshop, 1968. Pub. in *Black Theatre* #2, 1969, pp. 8–9; also in *The Drama Review,* Summer 1969, pp. 129–30.

The Box Office ("A Scenario for a Short Film" [subtitle], 1970). "By Ed Bullins As Related by Robert Macbeth."—Pub. script. Apparently planned as a short film commercial showing the curiosity and interest aroused in the black community when a theatre opens in the neighborhood. Pub. in *Black Theatre* #3, 1970, pp. 17–19.

McBROWN, GERTRUDE PARTHENIA, Actress, elocutionist, theatre director, high school English teacher, and author of plays and poetry for children. Based in Washington, DC. Educated at Emerson Coll. of Drama, the Conservatoire National de Musique et d'Art Dramatique, and the Institute Britannique of the Sorbonne. Founder of the District of Columbia Children's Theatre and Drama Workshop. Contributor to *Crisis, Negro History Bulletin* (and member of the Educational Board), and *Saturday Evening Quill.* Author of *The Picture-Poetry Book* (children's book, 1935).

PLAYS:
Bought with Cookies (children's radio play, 1 act, 1949). An early incident in the life of the abolitionist Frederick Douglass. Pub. in *Negro History Bulletin,* April 1949, pp. 155–56, 165–66. **The Birthday Surprise** (sketch, 1 act, 1953). Brief classroom play designed to introduce high school literature classes to the dialect poetry of Paul Laurence Dunbar and to encourage literary efforts on the part of students. Pub. in *Negro History Bulletin,* Feb. 1953, pp. 102–3. **Africa Sings** (ethnic collage, 1 act, 1954). Program of African folk tales, dance, and song. Pub. in *Negro History Bulletin,* Feb. 1954, pp. 133–34.

McCALLUM, JOHN, Musical theatre specialist, author, director, and musician. Based in New York City, and formerly in Denver, CO. Educated at the Univ. of Northern Colorado (music major); Antioch Univ. (B.A. in musical theatre); and Long Island Univ./C. W. Post Center (M.A. in theatre). Has served as a former director of the Denver Black Arts Co., and as musical director for several Bonfils Theatre/Denver Center for the Performing Arts productions. Has written a number of musical compositions for dramatic works which he has directed, including complete scores for *The Writing on the Wall, Thesmorporiazousae,* and *Gods Before Olympus;* as well as songs for already existing scores, including *The Wiz, Tambourines to Glory, For Colored Girls . . . , In the House of Blues,* and *Slow Dance on the Killing Ground.* Recipient of the Paul Robeson Award and the Barney Ford Award for his cultural contributions to the Denver community. *Address:* 555 Edgecombe Ave. #13J, New York, NY 10032.

REPRESENTATIVE DRAMATIC WORKS:
(The following musicals, all full length: book, lyrics, and score by McCallum, were prod. in Denver in the late 1970s, except where indicated:)
Daft. Takes place in a mental institution. The inmates like it there and have devised tricks to keep up their pretense of insanity. The head physician closes her eyes to reality because the inmates' play-acting gives her a role; but a tight-lipped state inspector appears and sees to it that the game is over.
Avatar // Also called **Waiting on Avatar** (1979). After the next world war, one man, a member of a survivalist clan, finds he cannot idly watch the remaining civilization melt away. After he is cast out from the survivalist camp for giving food to some persons outside of the clan, he leads a group of humans through territories claimed by self-appointed czars in order to reach the safety and warmth of the land to the south. Prod. by the Denver Black Arts Co., Summer 1979.

Are There Really Angels in the Sun? Set in a small midwestern town, this musical centers around SunAngel, a housewife and frustrated poet. Living in the limelight of her tennis star husband, she decides she must grow and discover herself and develops her poetic talents through Miranda, a famous published poet who flourished long ago. The play follows the challenge she has made to her husband and to herself—to become published within four months. It plots her earnest attempt to draw out her talent, even at the expense of her marriage; her violent conflict with Miranda; and the climactic challenge in the end—an international poetry contest.

The Banshee Boys (1983). Break-dancing young street men dominate the Bronx corner where we see the survival tactics used by these young men to embellish their environment. A young female lawyer opens a voter registration office near the corner and is deeply loved by one of the young men. She is socially above him and only dates rich doctors, but he still has plans for her. According to the author, "This show is a fast-paced, colorful, upbeat musical discovery of the mysterious, feared and dangerous young men who have come to be known as the Banshee Boys." (Apparently not among the musicals prod. in Denver.)

PLAYS AND OTHER DRAMATIC WORKS:
A Wish for Avatar. The Hobbit (adaptn.). **Rhapsody in Black. Happiness Together.** NOTE: The following are all one-act plays (prodn. data unknown): **Don't Lose. In Pursuit of Happiness. Footsteps. The Midnight Visit. To Be, or Not to Be.**

McCARTY, JOAN FOSTER (1949–   ), Playwright. Born and resides in Chicago, IL. In 1975 she was working on a master's degree in speech and theatre at the Univ. of Illinois, Chicago Circle Campus. She was also involved as a volunteer in the Illinois Prisoners Org.

PLAYS:
Prison Scenes (1975). Examines the experiences of prisoners through the eyes of their warden, the lawyer, and the inmates' families. All proceeds from the play went toward the free prisoner transportation which takes community people to visit friends or relatives in the various prisons in the State of Illinois. Performed in Chicago, 1975, at Northeastern Univ. during their Black Week, at the New World Resources Center, at Washington Park YMCA, and at the Midland Hotel as part of a benefit for the American Indian movement. **[Untitled Play].** In 1975 she was working on a second play, then untitled, about the life of George Jackson, which was sched. to be performed by the Theatrical Component of the Illinois Prisoners Org.

McCAULEY, ROBBIE, Actress-playwright. Studied playwriting with the Playwrights' Workshop of the Negro Ensemble Co. (NEC). Acted in *A Beast's Story* (1969), *So Nice They Named It Twice* (1975), and *The Taking of Miss Janie* (1975). Currently teaches acting in the Black Theatre Workshop of the New Federal Theatre. Winner of an Obie Award and an AUDELCO Award. *Address:* 233 East Fourth St., New York, NY 10009.

PLAY:
Wildflowers (1973). Prod. by NEC, New York, as a workshop production, on a program of plays by three black women. **My Father and the Wars** (one-woman, mixed-media show, full length, 1986). "Personal and historical images, songs, slides and video

combine to explore the contradictions within memory."—*Black Masks,* Oct./Nov. 1986, staged by Laurie Carlos, and perfd. by the author.

McCLINTOCK, ERNIE, Theatrical director. Based in New York City. Former director of the Academy Theatre Co.; former pres. of the Black Theatre Alliance; since 1968 executive director of the Afro-American Studio for Acting and Speech—all in New York City. Director, *Epitaph to a Coagulated Trinity* (1968), performed by The Last Poets. Director of *El Hajj Malik* (1971), produced by the Afro-American Studio. Recipient of an AUDELCO Black Theatre Recognition Award, 1973.

DRAMATIC WORKS:

(All collective theatre works, created under the direction of McClintock:) **African Collage** (1 act, 1965). Conceived, prod., and performed by the Academy Theatre Co., 1965. **Two Rooms** (1 act, 1965). Conceived, prod., and performed by the Academy Theatre Co., 1965. **Where It's At** (ethnic collage, full length, 1969). Described as a "Black theatrical event," which "combined drama, dancing, poetry, and music."— *Black Theatre* #4, 1962, p. 6 (Bailey). Created, prod., and performed by the Advanced Theatre Workshop of the Afro-American Studio, New York, opening Oct. 31, 1969.

McCRAY, NETTIE. See SALIMU.

McDOWELL, MELODIE M. (Maria), Playwright. Associated with the Experimental Black Actors Guild (X-Bag) in Chicago, IL.

PLAYS:

Nigger Nacks (satirical comedy, 17 scenes, 1974). Depicts the foibles of black folks in a series of short sketches. **March 22** (drama, 3 acts, 1975). The lives of three women of different backgrounds come together in a dramatic way on March 22. **The Conscience** (drama, 3 acts, 1975). The kidnapping of a black mayor's wife is depicted from three different viewpoints. Prod. by X-Bag, 1975. **The Car Pool** (morality play, pre-1976).

McFARLAND, H. S., Playwright.

PLAY:

Majority, Minority, Etcetera (poetic tract, 3 acts, 1975). Philosophical treatment of racism in America. Pub. in *Crest* (Vantage Press, New York, 1975).

McGLOWN, JERRY (c. 1948–   ), Playwright and teacher. Born in Oxford, MS. Received the B.A. degree in sociology and history from the Univ. of Mississippi, 1970, and the M.F.A. in speech and drama with a concentration in playwriting and directing from Memphis State Univ., 1976. Since 1970 has taught social studies, speech, and theatre in Tennessee/Mississippi area secondary schools and colleges, including one year at Tougaloo Coll., MS. Since 1980 has been director of theatre at LeMoyne-Owen Coll. in Memphis. Member of DG, the Black Cultural Alliance, and NADSA. *Addresses*—Home: 1377 Court Ave. #201, Memphis, TN 38104. Office: LeMoyne-Owen College, 807 Walker Ave., Memphis, TN 38126.

PLAYS:
King Uzziah (drama, 1 act, 1975). A white college teacher confronts a black, former student lover who is the mother of his only son. The teacher tries to take the son away from the mother; the mother tries to force the teacher to recognize that he has no legitimate claim to the child because of the absurdity of their relationship. Prod. at Memphis State Univ., March 1975. Has been prod. at least five other times, one of which was televised. Pub. in *Southeastern Theatre Conference Journal,* Spring 1976. Sched. for publication in *Mississippi Writers: Reflections of Childhood and Youth* ([Dorothy Renshaw] Abbott).

The Lonely Christmas Tree (comedy, 1 act, 1976). A group of children decide to make Christmas a joyous time for a lonely old widow. Three prodns. since 1976, one televised.

Mansions in the Sky // Orig. title: **To Mansions in the Sky** (comedy/drama, 3 acts, 1976; original length: 2 acts.) Concerns a successful black businessman who has won his fortune in California. He discovers his roots and truths in the rich, black earth of his native Mississippi, and his life in California is less tranquil on his return. First prod. at Memphis State Univ., 1976.

Lamentations and **The Great White Sea,** (2 related one-act plays, 1977). In **Lamentations,** a successful black nightclub singer has deserted his white wife and is living with a black woman. He is plagued by guilt over his wife's mock suicide attempts. In **The Great White Sea,** a black woman is struggling with her divided loyalty to a white gay confidant and her black lover who is hopelessly tied to his white wife. Both prod. in 1977.

The Lamps by the Golden Door (readers theatre piece, 1 act, 1978). Four gallant women from black history are interviewed shortly before they address an imaginary audience. They are Sojourner Truth, Mary McCleod Bethune, Bessie Smith, and Fannie Lou Hamer. First prod. in 1978.

The Quiet in the Land (drama, 2 acts, 1982). A marriage has taken place between a 36–year-old innocent man and a 12–year-old girl. Society, represented by the man's mother and the girl's aunt, conspires to separate the couple.

McGRIFF, MILTON (Milt), Playwright and TV program host. Former director of the Black Arts Spectrum Theatre in Philadelphia, PA. Also associated with the Lee Cultural Center in the city. During the late 1960s, he hosted a program entitled "New Mood, New Breed," which was telecast on Channel 12 at 7:30 P.M. every other Thursday.

PLAYS:
And Then We Heard the Thunder (drama, full length, 1968). Adapt. from JOHN O. KILLENS' novel by the same title, 1963, about the racial mistreatment of black soldiers during World War II, based on Killens's military experiences. Prod. by Lee Cultural Center, Philadelphia, in early Nov. 1968; dir. by Tom Butler. **Nigger Killers** (1971). Prod. by the Black Arts Spectrum Theatre, Philadelphia, 1971.

McIVER, RAY (1913–deceased), Teacher, actor, poet, playwright, and radio-TV personality. Born in Darien, GA. Educated at Morehouse Coll. (B.A., 1935). Served in the U.S. Army, 1942–45. Married; father of two children. Teacher of English, French, speech, and drama in the Atlanta, GA, public schools, 1942–.

For many years, also worked as an announcer and performer on various local radio and television stations, including Radio Station WERD.

PLAYS:

God Is a (Guess What?) ("Modern Musical Morality Play" [subtitle], full length, 1968). Music by *Coleridge-Taylor Perkinson. A satire on race relations in the Deep South—employing elements of the minstrel show and vaudeville routines—in which the lynching of a devout black man is prevented in the nick of time by the personal intervention of God, who turns out to be neither black nor white. Prod. Off-Bway by the Negro Ensemble Co., at St. Marks Playhouse, New York, opening Dec. 17, 1968, for 32 perfs.; dir. by Michael A. Schultz. Revived in May 1969, at the Aldwych Theatre in London. Prod. by the Burough of Manhattan Community Coll., of CCNY, in collaboration with OmiZelli Productions, Feb. 20–24, 1985, for 6 perfs. **The Fly in the Coffin** (comedy, 1 act, pre-1986). Based on a story by Erskin Caldwin, concerning a man, thought to be dead, who rises from the coffin during his funeral.

MACK, ETHEL, Playwright.

PLAY:

Phyllis (1961). Pub. in *Dasein* (Washington, DC), March 1961, pp. 15–28.

MACK, RON, Actor-playwright. Appeared in the New York productions of *Moon on a Rainbow Shawl* (1962) and *The Two Executioners* (1964). Member of the Negro Ensemble Co.'s (NEC's) Playwrights' Workshop.

PLAY:

Black Is—We Are (1970). Advocates black pride as a basis of black strength. Prod. by NEC's Playwrights' Workshop, at Riverside Church, New York, May 21, 1970s.

McKETNEY, EDWIN CHARLES, Playwright.

PLAYS:

Virgin Islands (3 acts, 1951). Pub. by Williams-Frederick Press, New York, 1951; copy in the Schomburg Collection. **Mr. Big** (3 acts, 1953). "Based on the numbers racket and illicit traffic of drugs." —*Crisis*, Feb. 1954, p. 87. Pub. by Pageant Press, New York, 1953; copies in the Schomburg Collection and the Moorland-Spingarn Collection.

MACKEY, WILLIAM WELLINGTON (c. 1938–   ), Playwright and actor. Born in Miami, FL. Received the bachelor's degree in 1958 from Southern Univ. in Baton Rouge, LA, where he was actively involved in the theatrical productions of the Riverbend Players, under the tutelage of Rhoda Carmichael. Taught for a year at a high school in Miami before entering graduate school at the Univ. of Minnesota in 1960. Began writing his first two plays while completing his master's degree at the Univ. of Minnesota, 1965. These scripts were completed after graduation, while Mackey worked as a recreational therapist at the Colorado State Hosp. in Pueblo, and were eventually premiered in Denver, under the direction of Donald Todd. From Denver, Mackey went to Chicago, and thence to New York City, where he currently resides, and where his plays have been produced Off-Broadway. In 1975 he was selected by the Bicentennial Committee of his home town to write the script for the Model City's cultural contribution to the celebration. Recipient of a Rockefeller Foundation playwriting grant. *Address:* 1590 Madison Ave., Apt. 17C, New York, NY 10029.

REPRESENTATIVE PLAYS AND DRAMATIC WORKS:

Behold! Cometh the Vanderkellans (drama, 3 acts, 1964). Dramatizes the effects of the black student rebellion during the late 1950s on an upper-middle-class black family which had produced generations of college presidents. Based on the author's experiences at Southern Univ., where he was an undergraduate student. Written while he was a graduate student at the Univ. of Minnesota. First prod. by the Eden Theatrical Workshop in Denver, 1965; dir. by Donald Todd. Prod. Off-Bway by WOODIE KING Associates, at Theatre De Lys, March 31–April 18, 1971, for 23 perfs.; dir. by Edmund Cambridge. With Graham Brown, Frances Foster, Roxie Roker, Carl Byrd, and Robert Christian. Pub. by Azazel Books, New York, 1957.

Requiem for Brother X (dramatic monologue, 1 act, 1965). Described by Hoyt Fuller *(Negro Digest,* April 1967, pp. 49–50) as "a drama of a black family living in the psychological shadow of Malcolm X's murder but it has nothing to do with Malcolm." Described by the author as "the angry defiance of a young slum-bred Muslim. It's a play about black people trapped in the ghetto, the trillion hallelujahs and amens of a dirge, a black mass, a requiem for the dead—the dead black people buried in the stone jungles of American Cities."—Quoted in *Denver Post,* May 20, 1966. Written while the author was a student at the Univ. of Minnesota. First prod. by the Points East Theatre Workshop, Denver, May 1966; dir. by Donald Todd. This prodn. was also televised in the Denver area. Prod. by the Parkway Theatre, Chicago, 1968; dir. by Dick Gaffield. Prod. Off-Bway by the Players Workshop, Greenwich Village, New York City, opening Jan. 5, 1973. Pub. in *Black Drama Anthology* (King & Milner, 1972).

Family Meeting (surrealistic drama, 1 act, 1968). Described by JOHN S. SCOTT *(Players,* Feb.-March 1972, p. 130), as

a satirical denouncement of fraudulent middle-class Blacks aspiring to white assimilation, [which] clearly reflects that some Black people are so inextricably confused about their Blackness that their actions shift with the unreasonableness of a hurricane. . . . Therefore, unless one understands and, further, accepts this shifting as being a truthful and powerful plotting of the "Black thang" [sic] one would likely attack the pendular structure of the play and its character movements as lacking in unity. Whereas, the unity—in this instance—springs from the "shaping principle" of Black people shifting with and on the nuances of Black identity.

First prod. by La Mama, E.T.C., New York, March 1972. Prod. by the Coll. of the Albemarle, Elizabeth City, NC, March 24, 1972; dir. by Lucy Vaughan. Pub. in *New Black Playwrights* (Couch, 1968) and by Dramatists Play Service, New York, c. 1972.

Billy Noname (musical, 2 acts [15 scenes], 1970). Book by Mackey. Music and lyrics by Johnny Brandon. Black history from 1930 to 1970 is paralleled in the life of a young black writer named Billy. Prod. Off-Bway by the Truck &

Warehouse Theatre, New York, March 2–April 12, 1970, for 48 perfs.; dir. by Lucia Victor. With Donny Burks (who won a *Theatre World* Award for his perf.) in the title role.

Love Me, Love Me, Daddy—or I Swear I'm Gonna Kill You! (drama, 3 acts, pre-1976). Just prior to the death of a powerful and wealthy black man, his seven sons fight for control of the family dynasty. Presented at the Holy Name House, New York, 1980.

Saga (Bicentennial musical, five acts, 1976). Commissioned by Third Century, the Bicentennial Committee of the author's home town, Miami, FL. Designed "to illustrate the impact of Africans on the development of the United States of America."—*Black World,* April 1975, p. 49. Based on a concept by Joan Bruner Timmons, a cultural planner for the Model Cities Program. Sched. to be the Model City's cultural contribution to the Bicentennial celebration, and to be prod. by the Miami Cultural Arts Center of the Model Cities Program, 1976. No record of the actual prodn.

OTHER PLAYS:
(Both pre-1976.) **Death of Charlie Blackman. Homeboys.**

McKIE, JOHN, Playwright. Associated with the Frank Silvera Writers' Workshop (FSWW) in New York City.

PLAY:
Living Is a Hard Way to Die (tragicomedy, 2 acts, 1974). Concerns the final days of a drunken father and the effect of his life and dying upon his son, who is preparing for the funeral. Public reading by FSSW, at the Harlem Cultural Center, March 1976. Unpub. script and tape recording in the FSWW Archives/Schomburg Collection.

McKNIGHT, DELORES, Playwright. Associated in 1975 with the Afro-American Studies Program at Brown Univ., Providence, RI.

PLAY:
Two Wings (6 episodes, 1975). Written with PHYLLIS HALL and ELMO MORGAN. Performed as a series of episodes for one semester, as an adjunct to the course "Images and Myths of African People in New World Consciousness," for Brown Univ.'s Afro-American Studies Program, Feb.-May 1975.

McNIGHT, JO-ANNE, Playwright. Based in Hollis, NY. Associated with the Frank Silvera Writers' Workshop (FSWW) in New York City.

PLAYS:
(Some of the author's unpub. scripts are in the FSWW Archives/Schomburg Collection [specific titles unknown]). **The Last Day** (monologue, 1 act, 1968). A black ex-soldier-turned-wino tells how he feels about life, death, love, and war. **Dialogue Between Strangers** (drama, 1 act, 1969). A white man attempts to rape a black woman, during which both reveal their different ethnic/cultural backgrounds, personal fantasies, hangups, and misunderstandings. **Train Through Hell** (drama, 1 act, 1970). Concerns the conflict between a white capitalist and his wife with regard to their images of self and attitudes concerning the racial problem. **Clara** (domestic drama, 2 acts, 1971). Futuristic play

concerning an interracial marriage during a time when America is involved in a race war; the husband and wife are condemned by their respective families for marrying each other. **Tones of the Lady** (drama, full length, 1974). A black girl struggles in New York to become a successful dancer. **Incense Burners** (historical ritual with music, full length, 1975). A pageant of black spiritual (i.e., religious) development, from African roots to America, through traditional Christianity, and back to Africa again.

McRAY, IVY, Playwright. Associated with the Frank Silvera Writers' Workshop (FSWW) in New York City.

PLAYS:
Unpub. scripts and tape recordings of readings or perfs. located in the FSWW Archives/ Schomburg Collection) **But There's Gonna Be Music** (1 act, 1974). Public reading by FSWW, at the Martinique Theater, New York, Nov. 1974. **Stepping Stones** (1975). Prod. by FSWW, at the Afro-American Total Theatre, New York, opening Nov. 24, 1975. **Run'ers** (drama, 1976). (Title also cited in some sources as *Run-Ners.)* Considered by Peter Bailey as a recent play of note, and described by him as "a thought-provoking look at the relationship between four female world-class track stars and their coaches."— *Black American Literature Forum,* Spring 1984. Public reading by FSWW, at Teachers, Inc., New York, Nov. 1976. Prod. Off-Bway in a full prodn. by FSWW, at the Theatre of the Open Eye, Nov. 13, 1977, as a project of the Writers/Directors Project Series. Prod. Off-Bway by the New Federal Theatre, April 27, 1978, for 12 perfs.; dir. by Novella Nelson.

MADDEN, WILL ANTHONY (1923–), Short-story writer, poet, and playwright. For many years an aide to Atty. Louis Nizer. Author of *Let's Read a Story About Princess Carolyn* (children's story, 1970), *Five More* (short stories, 1963), and *Sextette* (short stories, 1972).

COLLECTION AND PLAY:
TWO AND ONE: Two Short Stories and a Play. Exposition, New York, 1971. Contains **The Killer and the Girl** (melodrama, 1 act, 1961). Dramatization of Parris Flammond's poem, "Killer," about a young woman who delivers a letter and a package to a hired assassin, not realizing that she herself is to be the murder victim.

MAJOR, FRANCINE (1952–), Performing arts administrator, actress, and playwright. Born in New York. Studied acting with ERNIE McCLINTOCK at the Afro-American Studio Theatre Center in New York City. Was a participant in the FEDAPT Middle Management Training Program at the Eugene O'Neill Theatre Center, and was selected as a finalist for the National Fellowship in Performing Arts Management. Since 1970 has held a number of jobs in theatre administration in New York and Seattle, WA, and in 1976 was community coordinator for the Victory Gardens Theatre in Chicago. As an actress, she has performed as the Devil Lady in *Madheart* by AMIRI BARAKA, prod. by the Afro-American Studio in New York. Founder and pres. since 1984 of Major Concepts, her own New York–based firm specializing in public relations and artist management. Featured as an outstanding *Essence* Woman in *Essence* magazine, March 1978. *Address:* 1763 Bartow Ave., Bronx, NY 10469. (This is also the address of Major Concepts, her public relations and artist management firm.)

PLAY:
Evolution of a Sister (one-woman show, full length [1–1/2 hrs.], 1970). According to the author, it was written "out of necessity." "The really great Black actresses weren't working at the time, so I decided to put something together for myself."—*Essence,* March 1978. The play traces the lives of eight black women from Sojourner Truth to a sassy six-year-old girl, providing a positive portrait that brings to light their varied, yet universal, experiences, including the pride, self-determination, and sense of humor that helped them survive. Performed between 1970 and 1984 by the author at various locations in New York City; Seattle, Olympia, and Spokane, WA; and Chicago, IL.

MAJOR, TONY (Anthony Major) (1939–   ), Actor, director, and producer. Born in Sarasota, FL. Currently resides in New York City. Has been associated with the New York Shakespeare Festival. Founder and director of the Tony Major Grassroots Theatre, 1965. Acted in *For Love of Ivy* (1968); prodn. asst. and actor in *The Angel Levine* (1970); prodn. asst., asst. director, and actor in *The Landlord* (1970); asst. dir. for *Ganga & Hess* (also known as *Blood Couple,* 1973). Numerous other film, radio, TV, and theatrical credits.

DRAMATIC WORKS:
Off Duty (film short, 1972). Written, dir., and ed. by Major, 1972. **Super Spook** (film, 1975). Written, dir., and prod. by Major, 1975.

MALCOMB, BARBARA. See NAYO.

MALÍK (Hakim Sulaiman Malík II), Poet, actor, and playwright. Based in New York City. Educated at Queens College, Script Development Workshop (with Trent Gough), Frank Silvera Writers' Workshop (FSWW) (with CHARLES FULLER and RICHARD WESLEY), and the Negro Ensemble Co. (NEC) (with STEVE CARTER). Has performed his poetry at Fordham Univ. (Lincoln Center Campus), on an evening of poetry and drama entitled "Praying for a Miracle," 1978; at Riverside Church, New York City, 1979; and at the Countee Cullen Lib., Harlem, on a program entitled "When the Noise Downstairs Was Too Much," 1980. He has performed in such plays as *Ceremonies in Dark Old Men, The Sign in Sidney Brustein's Window,* and *Othello,* and has stage managed *A Raisin in the Sun, An Evening with Josephine Baker* (AUDELCO Award nominee, 1980), and a benefit performance of NTOZAKE SHANGE's *Boogie Woogie Landscapes.* Resident playwright at the Afro-American Repertory Theatre, 1975–76, and at the Riverside Theatre Workshop, 1977–78. Conducted a playwrights' seminar at Fordham Univ. (Lincoln Center campus), 1978. Member of AEA and SAG. *Address:* Malík c/o Browne, 104–20 189th St., Jamaica, NY 11412.

GROUP OF RELATED PLAYS:
sketches from the i (master title for a quartet of one-act plays, 1979–). Includes only one title at present: **the transients** (1983).

PLAYS AND DRAMATIC WORKS:
get the one with the star on the side (one-character drama, 1 act, 1973). Explores the relationship of a young black woman to her recently departed husband. Colloquially, she pokes jibes at her ex-husband's sexual insouciance, their high-falutin' friends, and the reasons he left her for a white woman. First prod. by the Afro-American Repertory Theatre, New York, 1975; dir. by Henry Miller. Subsequent prodns. at the Harlem Performance Center, 1976. Also presented by a black theatre group in Columbus, OH, 1978.

what it is (collection of satirical vignettes, full length, 1976). Asks the thematic question, What is it like to be black and be in the theatre? Follows the lives of the eight characters from the "spit and gum" amateurism of a community theatre, run by an egomaniacal artistic director, to their ultimate fame and subsequent decadence. Presented at the Harlem Performance Center, New York, 1976; dir. by author.

in the service of the chairman (drama, 3 acts, 1977). Explores the plight of an elderly gentleman who has been forced into retirement after winning the "Employee of the Month Award." Despite suggestions from his daughter and an elderly compatriot that he relax and enjoy his "autumn" years, he takes it upon himself to do something about a neighbor who, from the window above, shouts racial slurs and throws garbage. Presented as a staged reading at the Script Development Workshop, New York, 1977. Presented as a reading at the Riverside Theatre Workshop, New York, 1978. Presented as a reading at FSWW, New York, 1979. Unpub. script in the FSWW Archives/Schomburg Collection.

the murder of cyrene vignette (expressionistic drama, full length [7 titled scenes], 1977). Explores the perpetual identity crisis of a middle-aged black woman. The title character is taunted by a white husband and a blue-black warrior, both figments of her imagination, both vying for dominant positions within her identity. First presented as a reading by FSWW, 1978. Full prodn. by FSWW, 1979; dir. by Betty Howard. Unpub. script and tape recording in the FSWW Archives/Schomburg Collection.

the transients // Originally prod. under the title **sketches from the i** [see GROUP OF RELATED PLAYS above] (speculative drama, full length, 1983). Centers around the meeting of a man and woman in the afterworld. He has been perpetually incarnated as a soldier, while she has always been a whore. Both attempt to change their respective classifications, but only one is successful. Presented as a reading under the second title above by FSWW, 1980. Presented in a private reading under the first title, in New York City, 1983. Unpub. script in the FSWW Archives/Schomburg Collection.

MALONE, MIKE (1943–   ), Dancer, choreographer, director, playwright, and arts administrator. Born in Pittsburgh, PA. Educated at Georgetown Univ. (B.A. in French), spending his junior year abroad at the Sorbonne in Paris; Howard Univ. (M.A. in French literature, 1969); and Catholic Univ. (M.A. in theatre). Studied dance at the Howe Studio, the Barth Studio, and the Pittsburgh Playhouse; European training in modern jazz at the Studio Constant and the Scola Cantorium in Paris; with further study at the National School of Ballet and the Baltimore School of Ballet. Teaching experience includes elementary, secondary, collegiate, and professional levels in community, recreational, educational, and professional settings. Instr. of French and Spanish at Gonzaga (Jesuit Prep.) H.S., Washington, DC, 1967–70; asst. prof. of dance and dance history, Dept. of Dance, Federal City Coll. Washington, DC, 1970–71; asst. prof. of movement and theatre history, Dept. of Drama, Howard Univ., 1970–73; artistic director, Duke Ellington School of the Arts (Western H.S.), Washington, DC, 1974–75; founder and artistic director, DC Repertory Dance Co., 1970–71; director, Workshops for Careers in the Arts, George Washington Univ., 1968–77; director of performing arts, Karamu House, Cleveland, 1977–82; assoc. artistic director, Richard Allen Center for Culture and Art, New York, 1983–present; artistic director, Young Audiences of the District of Columbia, 1983–present; and opera-musical theatre program on-site evaluator, NEA, Washington, DC, 1984. Has performed as a dancer in such musicals as *Stairway to Heaven, West Side Story,* and *Bye, Bye, Birdie.* His experience as a choreographer includes *The Great White Hope* (Arena Stage, 1967; Bway, 1968); *Fly Blackbird* (George Washington Univ., 1969); **Genesis, Juba & Other Jewels** (WTOP-TV, Washington, DC, 1976); **Orpheus** (WETA-TV, Washington, DC, 1977); **Muntu Magic** (1977); *Daddy Goodness* (pre-Bway, Washington, DC, 1979); *Confession Stone* (Theatre Off-Park, New York, 1979, and Karamu House, 1980); *Take It from the Top* (Theatre in the Park, Philadelphia, 1979); *Reggae* (Bway, 1980); the following productions at Karamu House: *Don't Bother Me, I Can't Cope* (1978), *Bones* (1980), *On Toby Time* (1980), *Black Nativity* (also Hansberry-Sands Theatre, Milwaukee, 1981, on international tour, 1982, Cleveland Theatre Assn., 1983, and Theatre of Universal Images, Newark, 1984), *Breakfast in Harlem* (1981), *The Cotton Club Review* (1981), *The Wiz* (1981), *Shango De Ima/Shamgo Diaspora* (1982), *The Taming of the Shrew* (1982), *Black Gospel* (international tour, 1982–83), *Take Me Along* (Richard Allen Center, New York, 1983); *Greechies* (Dance Theatre Workshop, New York, 1983); seven episodes of the "Fame" TV show—1983–84 season (1) and 1984–85 season (6); *Mahalia's Song* (WHMM, Howard Univ., 1983, and Victory Theatre, Dayton, OH, 1984); and *Peace Child* (school touring version, Washington, DC, 1984). Public service in the arts includes dance program panelist, District of Columbia Commission on the Arts and Humanities, 1974; chairman, District of Columbia Bicentennial Dance Task Force, 1975–76; consultant, U.S. Dept. of HEW, Program for Gifted Children, 1975; theatre panelist, Ohio Arts Council, 1977–78; consultant, NEA, 1979; grants panelist, NEA, Opera-Musical Theatre Program, 1980–82; board member, Ohio Assn. of Dance Cos., 1981–82; board member, the Ellington Fund, 1982–present; and participant, Sixth Annual Colloquium of the National Opera Inst., "New Alliances for Music Theatre," 1983. Member, Soc. of Stage Directors and Choreographers. Honors and awards include Emmy nomination for Best Special, Washington, DC, 1977, for **Genesis, Juba & Other Jewels;** Emmy nomination for Best Special, Washington, DC, 1978, for **Orpheus;** Cine Golden Eagle Certificate of Excellence, 1978, 1979; the Duke Ellington Arts Award for contributions to the arts and education, Washington, DC, 1981; Cleveland Critics Circle

Award, 1978, 1979, 1982; and Certificate of Appreciation, City of Cleveland, George V. Voinovich, Mayor, 1983. *Address:* 147 W. 130th St., New York, NY 10027.

REPRESENTATIVE PLAYS AND STAGE WORKS:

Owen's Song (theatrical collage, 2 acts, 1974). Subtitled "A Tribute to Owen Dodson." Conceived, dir., and choreographed by Malone and GLENDA DICKERSON. Based on the plays and poems of OWEN DODSON. Described by the presenters as "a collage, weaving together lines from [Dodson's] works, including Divine Comedy, Powerful Long Ladder, his many poems, and his full length play *Bayou Legend.* . . . The story line, conceived by the directors, is inspired by the magnificent theme that runs through all of his work: climbing a powerful long ladder to catch the bird of freedom."—Program Notes. Prod. by the DC Black Repertory Co., at the Last Colony Theatre, Washington, DC, opening Oct. 24, 1974, for six weeks. Also performed in New York City, at the Harlem Cultural Center; then transferred back to Washington, to the Eisenhower Theatre in the John F. Kennedy Center for the Performing Arts for two weeks, opening Dec. 31, 1974. Unpub. script in the Hatch-Billops Collection. Also in the Billy Rose Theatre Collection/NYPL.

Genesis, Juba & Other Jewels (TV script, full length, 1976). Subtitled "A Songstep of Black America." A history of the role of dance in the lives of black Americans. Prod. by WTOP-TV, a CBS affiliate, Washington, DC, 1976, featuring the DC Repertory Dance Co.; dir. and choreographed by author. Recipient of an Emmy nomination as Best Special, 1977.

Orpheus (TV script, full length, 1977). Dance adaptn. of the Orpheus myth. Prod. by WETA-TV, Washington, DC, 1977, featuring the DC Repertory Dance Co., with special guest artist Debby Allen (of TV's "Fame"); dir. and choreographed by author. Recipient of an Emmy nomination as Best Special, 1978.

Spirits (dance drama, 1970s). "Asserts [that] Black people need to be raised up and connected with the higher positive forces within them by dispelling the evil spirits."— *Black American Literature Forum,* Spring 1983, pp. 23–24. Prod. by the DC Black Repertory Theatre, at the Last Colony Theatre, Washington, DC, 1970s.

Langston (play with music and dance, full length, 1978). With orig. music by *H. Q. Thompson. Compilation of LANGSTON HUGHES's poetry and prose which dramatizes a day in the life of eight factory workers in the 1930s. Recipient of Cleveland Critics Award, for the best new script, and an Emmy Award for best orig. music. Prod. by Karamu House, Cleveland, c. 1978. Prod. at the Lincoln Center Black Theatre Festival, New York, 1970s. Telecast on WETA-TV ("Ellington Live"), Washington, DC, 1970s. Script available only with permission of Langston Hughes estate, after contacting author.

Breakfast in Harlem (theatrical collage, full length, 1982). A celebration of the Harlem Renaissance, using poetry and music of the period. Prod. at Karamu House, Cleveland, 1982.

Ribbon in the Sky (theatrical collage, full length, 1982). Beginning on graduation day and through the music of Stevie Wonder, the adventures of three graduates of the Ellington School of the Arts are traced: a singer who goes to Los Angeles and ruins his career through drugs; an overly ambitious actress who loses friends seeking her career; and a dancer who through hard work finds success. They all meet again at the school reunion. Prod. by the Everyman St. Theatre Co., Washington, DC, 1982.

Spirit Songs (gospel parable, full length, 1983). An exploration of contemporary gospel music through individual songs. Based on black folklore and a visit to a rural country church. Prod. by Everyman St. Theatre Co., Washington, DC, 1983. Prod. by Black Theatre Troupe, Phoenix, AZ, 1984.

OTHER STAGE WORKS:
Muntu Magic (adaptn., full length, 1977). With orig. music by H. Q. Thompson. An adaptn. of William Shakespeare's *A Midsummer Night's Dream,* set in modern Nigeria. Prod. by the Maryland Centre for Public Broadcasting, 1977. NOTE: The following scripts were written or adapt. for street theatre, pre-1980s: **God Is in the Streets Today. The Life & Times of Stagolee** (adaptn). Prod. at Karamu Theatre, Cleveland, 1977– 78. **Singin' & Shoutin'** (adaptn.). Coauthor, with H. Q. Thompson. Prod. by Karamu Theatre.

MAMET, DAVIS, Playwright. Based in New York City.

PLAY:
American Buffalo (drama, full length, 1984). Described by *Black Masks* (Nov. 1984, p. 2) as "the story of one day in the existence of three low-class losers." Prod. by Crossroads Theatre Co., New Brunswick, NJ, Nov. 1984; dir. by Lee Richardson.

MANAN, LAILA. See SANCHEZ, SONIA.

MANDULO, RHEA MAKEDA ZAWADIE (Patricia Ann Wilkins Browne; Pat Wilkins) (1950–   ), Journalist, playwright, short-story writer, and poet. Born in New York City. Received the B.A. in communication arts from Mary-mount Manhattan Coll., 1973. Studied technical theatre with the Negro Ensemble Co., and playwriting with the Frank Silvera Writers' Workshop (FSWW), both in New York City Member of Theatre Black, 1968–71. Directed RICHARD WESLEY's *Gettin' It Together,* Brooklyn, 1971. Has performed poetry shows at various locations in New York City and New Jersey. Taught second grade in a public school in the Bronx, and reading at Boys Harbor. Currently editor-writer with UPI, where she is responsible for national wire copy for smaller newspapers and does feature writing and reporting assignments. Her articles have been published in *Black Enterprise, Virgin Islander, New York Amsterdam News, City Sun,* and other periodicals. Has also written short stories and poetry, as yet unpublished. *Address:* 82 Clinton Ave., Brooklyn, NY 11205. Alternate (family home): 92 Aberdeen St., Brooklyn, NY 11207.

PLAYS:
2 T's and G (1971). An early play, written in drama class at Marymount Manhattan Coll., 1971. Not available. **In Search of Unity** (drama, 2 acts, 1972). Explores the complex relationships between and among three black couples, all residing in the same inner-city apartment dwelling, presumably in New York City. Focuses on how each couple relates not only to his/her partner and to the other two couples, but also to the larger American and African ancestral societies of which they are an integral part. Written 1972. Prod. at Marymount Manhattan Coll.; dir. by author. Public reading by FSWW. Twice revised by the author since its first prodn., the most recent in 1985. Unpub. script and tape recording (under author's orig. name, Pat Wilkins) in the FSWW Archives/ Schomburg Collection.

MAPLE, JERRY, JR., Actor, director, choreographer, and playwright. Based in New York City. Admin. asst. in the Frank Silvera Writers' Workshop (FSWW). Former member of Voices, Inc. Appeared in the New York production of *I Can't Hear the Birds Singing*. Cofounder/director of Theatre In Progress, a Harlem group, 1983–. Directed and choreographed *Flat Street Sa'Day Night* (1985) by LENGA TOOKS, prod. by Theatre In Progress.

PLAYS:
Stop By for Christmas (pre-1983). Unpub. script and tape recording of a reading by FSWW in the FSWW Archives/Schomburg Collection. **That Little Baker Girl** (pre-1983). Unpub. script and tape recording of a reading by FSWW in the FSWW Archives/Schomburg Collection. **The Room** (absurdist play, 1 act, 1983). To test the limits of greed, four actors, placed in the audience, are invited to enter "the room" through a side door on stage, and are promised a million dollars if they can remain there for 24 hours. The stage then becomes the room, and the mismatched set of characters begins immediately to get on each others' nerves to the point of near-insanity, until the end and final payoff. Prod. by Theatre In Progress at a temporary "building owned by Mt. Nebo Church on 127th St. between 8th and St. Nicholas Avenues" in Harlem, Dec. 1983. **Life at the Limits of Existence** (melodrama, full length, 1985). Depicts the takeover of life as we know it by computer programming. Prod. by Theatre In Progress, Nov. 15–Dec. 16, 1984; dir. by Chuck Wise.

MARRS, STELLA (Stella Booker; "Miss Soft Soul") (1932–   ), Jazz singer. Born in New York City. A product of the New Heritage Repertory Theatre Workshop. Toured as a vocalist with Lionel Hampton's band during the late 1960s and early 1970s. Has performed in numerous clubs and concert halls; on radio, TV, and records; in theatrical productions; and in such films as *Cotton Comes to Harlem*, *Angel Levine*, *The Landlord*, and *Come Back Charleston Blue*.

DRAMATIC WORK:
I a Black Woman (one-woman show, pre-1976). Written, prod., and performed by the author.

MARSHALL, PAULE (1929–   ), Novelist and short-story writer. Born in Brooklyn, NY, of West Indian heritage. Phi Beta Kappa. Instructor at Columbia Univ. Former writer and researcher for *Our World* magazine. Author of three novels: *Brown Girl, Brownstones* (1959), *The Chosen Place, the Timeless People* (1969), and *Praisesong for the Widow* (1983). Other books include *Soul Clap Hands and Sing* (collection of novellas, 1961) and *Rena and Other Stories* (short stories, 1983). Member of the Harlem Writers Guild.

DRAMATIC WORK:
Brown Girl, Brownstones (TV script, full length, 1960). Adapt. from her novel by the same title; scriptwriter unknown. Presentation of a black woman's search for identity within a black community. Prod. as a CBS-TV Workshop Production, April 24, 1980. With OSSIE DAVIS and Cicely Tyson.

MARTENS, ANN COULTER, Playwright. (Racial identity not verified.)

PLAY:

These Are My People (assembly program for an all black or integrated cast, 1960s). "This unusual program introduces a large group of Negro leaders who in various ways have helped to make America great. The list ranges from . . . Phillis Wheatley through George Washington Carver to . . . Crispus Attucks. . . . The program has a slight plot that holds together lightly and effectively interesting elements."—Publisher. Pub. by Dramatic Publishing Co., New York, during the 1960s.

MARTIN, HERBERT WOODWARD (1933–   ), Poet, playwright, singer, actor, and drama director. Born in Birmingham, AL. Educated at the Univ. of Toledo (A.B., 1964), SUNY/Buffalo (M.A., 1967), and Middlebury Coll. (M.Litt. in drama, 1972). Has taught English at SUNY/Buffalo; Aquinas Coll., Grand Rapids, MI; the Univ. of Dayton (OH), where he was poet-in-residence, 1970–73; and Central Michigan Univ., where he was a Distinguished Prof. in 1973. Among his teaching specialities are sixteenth and seventeenth century literature and drama—including acting, directing, and technical theatre. Author of *New York: The Nine Million and Other Poems* (1969), *The Shit-Storm Poems* (1972), and *The Persistence of the Flesh* (1976). Recipient of scholarships and fellowships at Antioch Coll., the Univ. of Colorado, and the Bread Loaf Writers Project at Middlebury Coll. *Address*— Home: 715 Turner St., Toledo, Ohio 43607.

PLAY:

Dialogue (drama, 1 act, 1973). A black man is stopped on the street in a shower of rain by a policeman who appears to be human but isn't. Prod. at the Hardware Poets Playhouse, New York, 1963. Pub. in *The Urban Reader* (Cahill & Cooper, 1971).

MARTIN, SHARON STOCKARD (1948–   ), Poet, playwright, theatre critic, freelance writer, and editor. Born in Nashville, TN. Educated at Howard Univ., Bennington Coll. (A.B. in general studies, 1969), Yale School of Drama (M.F.A. in playwriting, 1976), and the Univ. of Southern California (Ph.D. studies, cinema/TV, 1982–present). Also studied with the Ed Bullins Black Theatre Workshop, New York, 1968–69; the Free Southern Theatre (FST) Writers' Workshop, New Orleans, 1970–73; the Frank Silvera Writers' Workshop (FSWW), New York, 1973–76; the Congo Square Writers Union, New Orleans, 1976–77; and the Los Angeles Actor's Theatre Playwrights Workshop, 1980. Gained theatrical experience during the 1960s with FST and the Dashiki Project Theatre in New Orleans. Assoc. editor of *Black Collegian* magazine, 1978–80, and communications director for the Urban League of Greater New Orleans during the same period. Has been a script reader for the Yale Repertory Theatre in New Haven, CT, and NEA, Washington, DC. Currently lives in California, where she has been associated with the NBC Story Dept. at Burbank, the Carson Film Co. at Studio City, and the UCLA Extension/KCET-TV in Los Angeles. Theatre critic for the Los Angeles *Reader,* 1982–present. Her poetry and critical articles have been published in *Black Creation, Encore, Black Sports,* and *Essence* magazines. Recipient of a Shubert Fellowship, Yale School of Drama, 1974–75, and also a Eugene O'Neill Award while a student at Yale; a CBS Foundation Prize in Playwriting, 1976; a John F. Kennedy Center Black Playwright Award, 1979; a Mary Roberts Rinehart Foundation Grant, 1980; and a Beaumont Fellowship, UCLA, c. 1982. *Address:* 1574 South Hayworth Avenue, Los Angeles, CA 90035.

REPRESENTATIVE PLAYS AND DRAMATIC WORKS:

Proper and Fine: Fanny Lou Hamer's Entourage (comedy, 1 act, 1968). About two black shoppers, loaded down with goods, who wait to be waited on by an indifferent salesman in a department store in the segregated South. Prod. by the Touring Ensemble of FST, 1969. Pub. in *The Search* (Scholastic Book Services, New York, 1972).

Further Elaborations on the Mentality of a Chore (domestic comedy, 1 act, 1972). (Orig. title: *Edifying Further Elaborations on the Mentality of a Chore.*) A middle-class couple who have recently evolved from Negro to black must now prepare themselves for the next change in the fashions and foibles of black pride. Prod. by FST, Spring 1972; then on tour with the same group.

Entertaining Innumerable Reflections on the Subject at Hand (domestic comedy, 1 act, 1973). Through word play, a woman tries to get her elderly husband to take out the garbage. Prod. by the Dashiki Project Theatre, New Orleans, Summer 1973.

Canned Soul (absurdist protest play, 1 act, 1974). Two white diners muse over the sudden absence of blacks as they gorge themselves on a tasty meal. Prod. by the Cabaret Workshop of Yale School of Drama, Fall 1974. Pub. in *Callaloo,* Spring 1978.

Deep Heat (absurdist comedy, 1 act, 1975). Described by the *American College Theatre Newsletter* (1976) as "a lust story . . . about the heightening of passions—misdirected, obsessive, finalistic—and the reuniting of desire with its long lost and sought after object." While looking for their lost pets, a man and a woman (both married and living in the same apartment building) fall in love with each other. They and their spouses must deal with the resulting effect that their lust has on their respective marriages. Prod. as a playwright's workshop production at the Yale School of Drama, April 1975. Prod. by Davenport Coll., at the Harlem Performance Center, New York, Oct. 10, 1976.

Moving Violation (absurdist drama, 2 acts, 1976). A family struggles to overcome the unfair restrictions of a mysterious ordinance that systematically takes away their various freedoms. As described by a press release from the Dashiki Theatre, "It does not resort to accustomed protest or propagandistic diatribes, but poetically reveals human survival techniques and responses under a rigid authoritarian system or police state." According to the author's introduction to the pub. script, "Everyone in the play is divided into two categories: those who are free to move and those who are not. One group has last names ending in 'man' and the other in 'son.' It's as irrational a division as Black and White." Public reading by the FSWW, at the Harlem Performance Center, New York, Nov. 1976. Produced by the Dashiki Project Theatre, 1979. Received the John F. Kennedy Center Black Playwright's Award for southeast region in 1979. Pub. in *Center Stage* (Ostrow, 1981).

S.O.S. (monologue, 1 act, 1976). A single parent does battle with apartment roaches, dirty dishes, and nagging memories in the early morning hours. Prod. by the author at the Yale Cabaret, New Haven, 1976; at FST, 1977; and at Brandeis Univ. and Texas Southern Univ., 1977.

Bird Seed (comedy, 1 act, 1976). Armageddon is here, but one harried couple struggles to go on living. Prod. by FST, 1977.

OTHER PLAYS AND DRAMATIC WORKS:
To My Eldest and Only Brother (realistic playlet, 1 act, 1969). A rural extended family reacts to the unorthodox marriage of one of its members. **The Old Ball Game: A Song Without Words or Music** (pantomime, 1 act, 1972). Symbolic characters act out the competitive notion of race through a struggle to control the ball in an atypical game. Characters are designated by their costumes, i.e., one man in white-on-white, one man in black-on-black. **The Undoing of the 3–Legged Man** (morality play, 1 act, 1972). A man with three legs searches for the meaning of his condition. **The Interim** (domestic comedy, 1 act, 1973). **Disintegration: A Television Play** (1 act, 1974). The devastating effects of integration on a middle-class family. **A Final Exultation Followed by the First Execution of the Obsession of an Imaginary Color from a Temporary Scene** (drama, 1 act, 1974). A man rids the world of the color white. **Make It Funky Now: The Syntactical Error** (comedy, 1 act, 1974). Four college students act to eliminate a foul odor, caused by the misinterpretation of a word. **Second Story** (domestic drama, 3 acts, 1985). Problem of a family of women; deals with the conflict between men and women, between races and classes, and with the expression and suppression of the realization of ambition. **Hair Products** (comedy, 2 acts, 1980). Patrons of an inner-city beauty salon clash over the intrusion of an unlikely customer. **State of the Art** (screenplay, full length, 1981). The white male conservative whose audit closes a mismanaged poverty organization tries to rehabilitate the militant black female who has come to share his space. **The Lagniappe** (screenplay, full length, 1983). A going away party turns from devilment to desperation as hunters become the hunted against the backdrop of the French Quarter in New Orleans. **The 20–Minute Workout** (comedy, 1 act, 1983). Two women seek refuge in a fitness center and try to dissolve their troubles in frenetic aerobic exercise.

MARVIN X (Marvin E. Jackmon) (1944–   ), Black nationalist playwright, poet, short-story writer, and essayist. Born in Fowler, CA. Educated at Edison H.S. in Fresno, Oakland City Coll. (now Merritt College) (A.A., 1964), and San Francisco State Coll. (now Univ.) (B.A. in English, 1974; M.A. in theatre, 1975). Cofounder and codirector (with ED BULLINS) of Black Arts/West (BA/ W), a theatre group in the San Francisco Bay area. Cofounder and secretary of Black House, the San Francisco headquarters of the Black Panther Party during the 1960s. After becoming a member of the Black Muslims (Nation of Islam), Jackmon adopted the name Marvin X, under which most of his writings have been published. (He has also used several other Arabic names.) Served as associate editor of *Black Theatre* magazine, 1969–72, and as contributing editor of the *Journal of Black Poetry*. Founder of Al Kitab Sudan Publishing Co., San Francisco and Fresno, 1967. Founder of Your Black Educational Theatre, San Francisco, 1972. His books include *Sudan Rajula Samia* (1967), *Black Dialectics* (1967), *Fly to Allah* (poems, 1969), *The Son of Man* (1969), *Black Man Listen* (poems and proverbs, 1969), *Confessions of a Wife Beater and Other Poems* (1981), and *Liberation Poems for North American Africans* (1982). His writings (poems, stories, essays, and interviews) have also been published in *Muhammad Speaks, Soulbook, Black Dialogue, Negro Digest/Black World,* and other periodicals. *Address:* Box 12583, Fresno, CA 93778; or 338 Fresno St., Fresno, CA 93706.

REPRESENTATIVE PLAYS AND DRAMATIC WORKS:
Flowers for the Trashman (also known as **Take Care of Business**) (drama, 1 act, 1965). (Orig. title: *Flowers for the Whiteman.*) Set in a jail cell, this play explores the lack of understanding and communication between a young college student who wants to be a writer, and his father, a florist whose business is on the decline and who is unkindly called "The Trashman" by some of his customers. First prod. by the Drama Dept. of San Francisco State Coll., 1965. Prod. as *Flowers for the Whiteman* by BA/W in the San Francisco Bay area, Spring 1966. Prod. by the Afro-American Studio, New York, opening Oct. 3, 1969. Prod. in a musical version, *Take Care of Business,* by Your Black Educational Theatre, in San Francisco and Fresno, 1971. Pub. in *Black Dialogue* (issue and date unknown). Pub. as *Flowers for the Trashman* in *Black Fire* (Jones & Neal, 1968). Pub. as *Take Care of Business* in *The Drama Review,* Summer 1968.

The Black Bird (Black Muslim allegory, 1 act, 1969). Arabic subtitle: "Al tair aswad." Utilizes drama, narrative, and dance to teach a lesson in black awareness to two little girls. The title is taken from a Muslim parable about a black bird who refuses to leave his cage to fly to freedom, even though the door is open and the house is on fire. Pub. in *New Plays from the Black Theatre* (Bullins, 1969). Illustrated edition pub. by Al Kitab Sudan Publishing Co., San Francisco, 1973.

Resurrection of the Dead (ritual, 1 act, 1969). Ceremony or rite for an all-black cast and any number of participants, modeled on pagan and voodoo rites, designed to rally blacks to the cause of liberation. Prod. by the New Lafayette Theatre, New York, 1969. Prod. by Your Black Educational Theatre, 1972. Pub. in *Black Theatre* #3, 1969.

Woman—Man's Best Friend (musical dance drama, full length, 1973). Prod., presumably by Your Black Educational Theatre, at Mills Coll., Oakland, CA, 1973. Pub. by Al Kitab Sudan Publishing Co., 1973.

OTHER PLAYS AND DRAMATIC WORKS:
Come Next Summer (drama, 1 act, 1968). Prod. by BA/W, 1966. **The Trial** (1970). First prod. in Harlem by the Afro-American Studio, 1970. **How I Met Isa** (1975). Master's thesis prodn., San Francisco State Univ., 1975. **In the Name of Love** (1981). Prod. by Laney Coll. Theatre, Oakland, 1981.

MASON, CLIFFORD (1932–   ), Playwright, actor, director, producer, administrator, author, critic, and teacher. Born in Brooklyn, NY. Educated at Queens Coll. (B.A., 1958). English teacher at Manhattanville Coll. of the Sacred Heart in Purchase, NY, 1969–75; asst. prof. in the Graduate School of Education, Rutgers Univ., New Brunswick campus, 1971–74; teacher, Medgar Evers Coll., CUNY/Brooklyn, 1981–83. As an actor, he has appeared in *The Cherry Orchard* at the Public Theatre, in his own play **Time Out of Time** (1980), and has had featured roles at La Mama E.T.C. and the Henry St. Settlement (New Federal Theatre), as well as bit parts on television and in films. He has produced three of his own plays in Equity Stock contracts in Baltimore and Washington, DC, Off-Broadway in New York, and in regional theatre productions at Brooklyn Coll. and the Univ. of Maryland. He has directed undergraduate and graduate theatre productions; at least six Equity approved workshop productions at the

New Dramatists; Off-Off-Broadway at the Richard Allen Center; and at Brooklyn Coll. Author of two books, which were scheduled to be published in 1980: *Macbeth in Harlem,* a selective history of black theatre; and *When Love Was Not Enough,* a murder mystery introducing Joe Cinquez, private detective. Has a weekly column in the *Long Island Weekly Voice,* 1966–67. His freelance writings on drama, literature, and the West Indies have been published in the *New York Times* (Sunday Drama Section and Magazine Section), *Life, New York, Black World,* the *New York Amsterdam News,* and the *Daily Gleaner* (Jamaica, West Indies). He had his own radio show on WBAI-FM, 1967–68, called "Clifford Mason on Theatre." Has also made TV appearances on Channels 5 and 13 in New York in connection with his articles. Memberships include DG, AEA, and New Dramatists. Recipient of $1,000 first prize for **Gabriel,** from the Elmwood Playhouse, Nyack, NY, 1968; NEH grant of $15,000, 1978, to research black theatre of the thirties through the sixties; NEA writer-in-residence grant of $5,000, 1979, to develop play material and hold workshops at the Gene Frankel Theatre in New York; and NEA grant of $10,000, 1980, for playwriting (with no specific project involved). *Address:* 201 W. 89th St., New York, NY 10024. *Agent:* Bertha Klausner, 71 Park Ave., New York, NY 10016.

REPRESENTATIVE PLAYS AND DRAMATIC WORKS:

Gabriel (historical drama, 3 acts, 1965). Subtitled "The Story of a Slave Rebellion." Dramatization of the unsuccessful slave rebellion led by Gabriel Prosser in Virginia in 1800. Prod. in workshop at the New Dramatists, Fall 1968. Entered in a nationwide contest by Elmwood Playhouse, Nyack, NY, where it won first prize of $1,000, and was also prod. in 1969. Has been prod. by several colleges. Pub. in *Black Drama Anthology* (King & Milner, 1972).

Sister Sadie // Orig. title: **Sister Sadie and the Son of Sam** (domestic drama, 3 acts, 1968). Deals with the problems of the black matriarchal family and its devastating effects on the father and son. First prod. in a workshop production at New Dramatists, June 1968. Prod. by the Eugene O'Neill Playwrights Conf., Waterford, CT., July 1968. Prod. at the Mark Taper Forum, Los Angeles, 1968. Prod. at La Mama E.T.C., 1973. Prod. at New Dramatists, 1975, with Virginia Capers in the title role.

Midnight Special (drama, 3 acts, 1971). Play of black experience, set in a bar and featuring a variety of character types. Prod. as a workshop production at New Dramatists, 1972. Prod. Off-Off-Bway at U.R.G.E.N.T. Theatre, 1975. Prod. in Baltimore, MD, and Washington, DC, 1976, with Raymond St. Jacques. Under Equity Stock contract with St. Jacques in 1985.

The Verandah (drama, 5 scenes, 1976). About upper-middle-class life in Jamaica in the late 1930s. Prod. as a staged reading at New Dramatists, March 1978. Prod. Off-Off-Bway at the Gene Frankel Theatre, May 1978. Pub. in *Center Stage* (Ostrow, 1981).

Time Out of Time (domestic drama, full length, 1980). Concerns the bittersweet reunion of the last generation of a well-to-do Jamaican family, set against a background of political unrest and the striving for Jamaican independence which is beginning to stir within the country. Prod. by the Black Theatre Alliance (BTA), New York, opening Oct. 17, 1980; dir. by Billie Allen. Prod. by the New Federal Theatre, New York, opening Nov. 15, 1986, for a two-week engagement.

Captain at Cricket (Caribbean play, full length, 1982). Comedy, set in Jamaica, about the bedroom activities of a cricket player. Prod. by Brooklyn Arts and Culture Assn., at Brooklyn Coll.'s Gershwin Theatre, Aug. 11–Sept. 4, 1983.

OTHER PLAYS AND DRAMATIC WORKS:
Jimmy X (domestic drama, 1 act, 1969). About a black youth trying to find his identity within the black revolution. Prod. in workshop at the New Dramatists, 1969. **Sammy Dead** (1 act, 1970). Prod. in workshop at the New Dramatists, 1970. **Half-Way Tree Brown** (drama, 3 acts, 1972). About the class struggle in the West Indies, focusing on the conflicts within a well-to-do black family that is part of the past colonial sociopolitical system. **The Trial of Denmark Vesey** (historical drama, 3 acts, 1974). The courtroom trial of the slave who led a rebellion in Charleston, SC, in 1823. Prod. in workshop at the New Dramatists, 1974. **The Black Brigade** (screenplay, 1979). **Royal Oak** (Caribbean play, 1981). Set in Jamaica. Prod. by CBA Theatre (a Caribbean theatre group in residence at Long Island Univ./Brooklyn Campus), at the University's Triangle Theatre, opening June 18, 1987, dir. by Charles Turner. **Return to Guy's Hill** (Caribbean play, 1981). Set in Jamaica. **The Boxing Day Parade** (Caribbean play, 1983). **Lady in Three Acts** (1983). **Return to Villa Borghese** (1984). **Bassington Comes Back** (1984). **The Black Brotherhood** (full treatment/screenplay, pre-1983). **Danny Boy** (outline/screenplay, pre-1985). **The Case of the Ashanti Stool** (full treatment/screenplay, pre-1985). **Savannah Sunday** (outline/screenplay, pre-1985).

MASON, JUDI ANN (1955–   ), Playwright and freelance journalist. Born in Shreveport, LA. Educated at Grambling State Univ. (B.A., 1977). Named by *Glamour* Magazine as one of the Top Ten College Women in 1976. One of the youngest women to have an Off-Broadway play produced in New York, at age 20. A vice pres. of the National Assn. of Dramatic and Speech Arts (NADSA). Member of the Southwest Theatre Conf.; Louisiana State Arts Council (the youngest and only black member appointed by the governor); Delta Sigma Theta Sorority; Theta Alpha Phi Fraternity; and WGA. Recipient of the Norman Lear Award, 1974, and the Lorraine Hansberry Award, 1976, both in the American College Theatre Festival (ACTF) of each year, and the first two-time winner of ACTF awards. Also won the S. Randolph Edmonds Award, given by NADSA, c. 1975. *Agent:* Susan Schulman, International Creative Management (ICM), 40 West 57th Street, New York, NY 10019.

PLAYS:
(Partial list only. Mason is credited with having written at least seven plays.)
Livin' Fat ("soul farce," 2 acts, 1974). The play deals with a bank janitor who finds $15,000 dropped in a bank robbery, and takes it home to his family, who are members of a strict religious sect. The comedy revolves around the dilemma of the family members trying to preserve their basic morality while also enjoying the benefits of their windfall. First prod. by Grambling Univ., Grambling, LA, 1974, where it won the Norman Lear Award in the ACTF. Produced by the Negro Ensemble Co. (NEC), New York, June 1–July 18, 1976, for 61 perfs. With MINNIE GENTRY, Frances Foster, Wayne Elbert, Joyce Sylvester, Dean Irby, and Frankie Faison. Prod. by the HADLEY Players, at St. Philip's Church, New York, c. 1984; dir. by GERTRUDE JEANNETTE. Pub. by Samuel French, New York, 1976.

A Star Ain't Nothin' but a Hole in the Heaven (tragicomedy, 1976). "A dramatic chronicling of the agonies of a young Black girl who is breaking the bonds of the old way of life in the country to take advantage of newly offered opportunities for education and personal development. It speaks for an entire generation of Black people faced with making a choice between the old and the new, between family ties and a life on the different and venturesome plane."—*ACTF Newsletter,* Dec. 1976. Prod. by Grambling State Univ.; entered in the ACTF, where it won the Lorraine Hansberry Award, 1976.

Daughters of the Mock (drama, full length, 1978). An old matriarch wishes to pass her voodoo power (called "the mock") on to her daughter, who wishes to get married instead of assuming this awesome family responsibility. Performed by the NEC, at St. Marks Playhouse, New York, opening Dec. 23, 1978, for 23 perfs. Prod. at the Billie Holiday Theatre, Brooklyn, March 1987, for an extended engagement, dir. by Mikell Pinkney. It was still playing in June 1987.

Jonah and the Wonder Dog (domestic drama, full length, 1986). "About a self-made Black politician and his ivy-league son, who are brought together by a family crisis that sparks a bittersweet confrontation between the two."—*Jet,* March 17, 1986, p. 55. Prod. by NEC, at Theatre Four, New York, opening Feb. 27, 1986, starring DOUGLAS TURNER WARD as the father and Kevin Hooks as the son.

Tea at Kat's Place (1 act, 1986). Prod. as a work-in-progress by Black Women in Theatre, Inc., New York, Dec. 11–12, 1986, dir. by Frances Foster.

MAUTI (one name). Inmate of Norfolk (VA) Prison at the time of writing the following play.

PLAY:
Cop 'n' Blow (drama, 1 act [3 scenes], 1972). Black prison parolee, who has given up all hope of finding a job, robs the very company which is about to give him employment. Pub. in *Who Took the Weight? Black Voices from Norfolk Prison* (Norfolk Prison Brothers, 1972).

MAYFIELD, JULIAN (Hudson) (1928–1984), Novelist, playwright, screenwriter, journalist, actor, director, producer, teacher, and political activist. Born in Greer, SC; grew up in Washington, DC. Enlisted in the peacetime army; served in the Pacific. Attended Lincoln Univ. (PA); also studied at the Paul Mann Actors Workshop, 1951–54. Actor-playwright, Group 20 Players, Unionville, CT, 1949. Acted in *Lost in the Stars,* 1949–50. Directed OSSIE DAVIS's *Alice in Wonder* (1952). Playwright, Camp Unity, NY, 1962–63. Acted in *City of Kings* (Blackfriars Guild, 1969). Author of three novels: *The Hit* (1957), *The Long Night* (1960), and *The Grand Parade* (1961). Aide to Pres. Kwame Nkrumah, Ghana, 1963–66; founding editor, *The African Review* (Accra, Ghana), 1964–66; editor, *The World Without the Bomb: The Papers of the Accra Assembly* (1963). Editor, *Ten Times Black: Stories from the Black Experience* (1972). Contributor of short stories to *Black World;* his nonfiction, criticism, reviews, and political articles published in *African Forum, African Review, American Negro Writer and His Roots, Black Literature in America* (Baker, 1971), *Black Expression and The Black Aesthetic* (Gayle, 1969 and 1971), *Black Scholar, Boston Univ. Journal, Commentary, Dark Symphony* (Emanuel & Gross, 1968),

Freedomways, The Nation,), Negro Digest, The New Republic, and *The Young Black American Abroad* (Klein, 1963). Lecturer, Afro-American Studies, Univ. of Maryland, c. 1966; fellow, Society for the Humanities, Cornell Univ., 1967–68; lecturer, Schweitzer Program in the Humanities, NYU, 1968–70; Distinguished Visiting Fellow, Africana Studies and Research Center, Cornell Univ., 1970–71; writer-in-residence, Howard Univ., 1978 to his death in 1984. Member, AEA, WAG/East, SGA, P.E.N., and Ghanaian Assn. of Journalists. Honored with a memorial tribute on Nov. 28, 1984, at the Henry St. Settlement Playhouse, Harry Dejur Theatre, by an organizing group of Friends of Julian Mayfield. The event featured tributes by a number of actors, writers, educators, and political activists who had worked with him through the years.

REPRESENTATIVE PLAYS AND DRAMATIC WORKS:
417 (domestic drama, 1 act, 1954). Deals with life in Harlem in the early 1950s. Prod. Off-Bway, 1961. Excerpt (1 scene) pub. in *Black Scenes* (Childress, 1971).

Uptight (feature film, full length: screenplay, 1968). Script by Mayfield, RUBY DEE, and Jules Dassin. Adapt. from Liam O'Flaherty's novel *The Informer*, which had been made into a film by John Ford in 1935. According to *Ebony Handbook* (p. 457), it was the first film to depict the black revolution. Whereas *The Informer* dealt with Irish rebels in Dublin, *Uptight* was set in the black ghettos of Cleveland, OH, and its leading characters were black militants. Mayfield appears as Tank, the leader of the black militant group, and Dee as a young welfare mother who supplements her income by prostitution. The supporting cast included Raymond St. Jacques, Frank Silvera, ROSCOE LEE BROWNE, and Janet MacLachlan.

OTHER PLAYS AND DRAMATIC WORKS:
The Other Foot (drama, 1 act, 1950). Prod. by the Elks Community Theatre, New York, opening Sept. 29, 1952, for a run of two weeks. Prod. by the Burlap Summer Theatre, at Club Baron, New York, July 9, 1953. **A World Full of Men** (drama, 1 act, 1952). Prod. by the Elks Community Theatre, New York, opening Sept. 29, 1952, on double bill with **The Other Foot** (above). **"Johnny Staccato"** (TV scripts, 1959–60). Prod. by NBC and ABC, 1959–60. **Fount of the Nation** (drama, 1963). Deals with the domestic problems of a West African nation (presumably Ghana) whose president wishes to build a $20 million harbor, which can only be done with American aid; his efforts are opposed by a faction within the country, led by his oldest friend, who must be sacrificed if the aid is to be forth-coming. **Fire** (drama, 1969). **Children of Anger** (doc. film, 1970). **The Long Night** (film, 1975). Dramatization of his novel by the same title. Prod. by ST. CLAIR BOURNE and Chamba Productions, New York, 1975. Has played in theatres in the United States and on television networks in Europe. **Christophe** (screenplay).

MAYFIELD, WILLIAM F. (Francis), Electrician, playwright and author, specializing in computerized playwriting and publication. Resides in Pittsburgh, PA. Graduated from Lindbloom Tech. H.S., Chicago, IL, 1968; also studied at the Kuntu Writers' Workshop, Black Studies Dept., Univ. of Pittsburgh. Employed as a journeyman electrician in Pittsburgh. Author of *Playwriting for the Black Theatre* (1985), available from the playwright. His articles have appeared in *Black Masks*. Member of the Frank Silvera Writers' Workshop (FSWW), New York. *Address:* 127 Mayflower St., Pittsburgh, PA 15206.

PLAYS:
(All pre-1985.) **Vintage Wine** (a woman's spoof). Received a staged reading in Memphis, TN. Unpub. script and tape recording in the FSWW Archives/Schomburg Collection. **Willi T** (black sci-fi). A future black hero tries to save the universe. Staged reading at FSWW. Unpub. script and tape recording in FSWW Archives/Schomburg Collection. **Queen Bee** (black sci-fi). Two bees are born. One is a potential queen, but no one knows which. Unpub. script and tape recording in the FSWW Archives/Schomburg Collection. **Catfish Murder** (black sci-fi). This costumed underseas story uses scavenger fish to explore a society. Staged reading at FSWW. **Morphis.** A black man and his wife try to change a welfare pattern. An excerpt was performed by a dormitory group at Howard Univ. **Little Black Boys** (musical, 2 acts, 1985). Script, lyrics, and melody by Mayfield. A celebration of the treasures and secrets that link black men. Staged reading at FSWW. One workshop reading in Pittsburgh. Workshop prodns. sched. at Kent State (OH), Shreveport, LA, and San Diego, CA. Pub. by the author, 1985.

WORKS IN PROGRESS:
Osiris. A modern look at the Egyptian gods as real people. Many of the early interpretations were tainted by racism and misinformation. Staged reading at a Computer Playwriting Workshop conducted by Mayfield at the Eden Theatrical Workshop, Denver, Colorado, Nov. 28, 1986. **Odella.** A look into the frustrations hitting modern women of the 1980s. The action takes place in a video arcade.

MEADOWS, LEROY, Playwright. From Miami, FL. Currently associated with the Inner City Cultural Center (ICCC), Los Angeles, CA. Educated at Florida A. & M. Univ., Tallahassee, where he was a technical theatre major, and Howard Univ., Washington, DC., where he majored in theatre on a William Morris Agency Scholarship. Also an alumnus of the WGA/West's Open Door Program, 1977–78. Currently a member of the Round Table Writers Workshop, Los Angeles, 1978–. Served in the U.S. Army, 1970–73. Technical asst. at St. Marks Playhouse, New York, 1969. Lighting designer, U.S. Army, winning the Best Lighting Designer Award, 1971. Floor director, MPLG-TV, Miami, 1973–74. News announcer, WMBM-Radio, Miami, 1974. Technical director, Ebony Showcase Theatre, Los Angeles, 1975–78. Has lectured on the techniques of writing at a number of schools in California. *Address:* 4715 South Arlington Ave., Los Angeles, CA 90043.

REPRESENTATIVE PLAYS:
Nothing Beats a Failure . . . (drama, 2 acts, 1978). A group of unemployed buddies discovers that starting a business requires more than enthusiasm. Prod. by the "M" Ensemble Company, Miami. Staged reading by the Crossroads Arts Academy, Los Angeles.

Blues Song ("continuing drama," also called "a soap opera for live theatre," 45 pp. each episode, 1983–). Serial of the manipulations of a narcissistic matriarch. Produced since 1983 by the Inner City Cultural Center, Los Angeles, where it was still being presented as of January 1984 on the downstairs stage, and had developed a loyal following.

According to the author, as quoted in an article by SHARON STOCKARD MARTIN in *Theatre L.A.* magazine (Dec. 1983/Jan. 1984), "This can go 249 episodes. . . . I plan to stay with the show. If it leaves the Center, there are other places it can go, like cable TV. I'm confident that it will succeed."

OTHER PLAYS:
Everything's Happening Here (musical, 2 acts, 1976). A young girl in a rural town has her high image of big cities shattered. **When It Rains** (drama, 1 act, 1980). According to the author, "Life throws a cunning lesbian, a crooked partner, and a dying mother against an up-and-coming professional woman." **Ellen** (drama, 2 acts, 1981). A play about the crisis of a black family, hard-pressed by proverty, and their efforts to come to grips with themselves and their problem. **The Avenue Kids** (children's show, 4 pp., 1984). Two neighboring youth gangs find a unifying purpose. **Julio** (multimedia theatrical work, 2 acts, pre-1985). An Olympic boxing hopeful's priorities are put to the test by pre-Olympic competition and offers to become a professional fighter.

MILES, CHERRILYN (Cherry), Playwright. Formerly associated with the Cornbread Players and the Frank Silvera Writers' Workshop (FSWW), both in New York City.

PLAYS:
X Has No Value (1970). Prod. by the Cornbread Players, New York, c. Feb. 17, 1971; dir. by WALTER JONES. **Eleanora** (1970s). **To Each His Own** (1970s). **Miss T** (pre-1985). Unpub. script in the FSWW Archives/Schomburg Collection.

MILES, ROLAND (Lloyd, Jr.) (1952–   ), Actor, singer, songwriter, percussionist, entertainment consultant. Based in Denver, CO. Educated at Los Angeles City Coll. (music) and the Univ. of Colorado/Denver (candidate for double master's degree in music merchandising and business administration); also enrolled in the Bailie School of Broadcasting. Has had 25 years' experience as a singer/showman. Performed as an atmosphere player (extra) in *Roots II* (1979) and *Skatetown, U.S.A.* (1980). Toured the Pacific with the USO, under the sponsorship of the U.S. Dept. of Defense, 1982. Winner of numerous talent competitions in Los Angeles, 1985. *Address:* 2830 Forest St., Denver, CO 80207.

DRAMATIC WORK:
Legends—Voices from the Past (cabaret, or musical entertainment, full length, 1985). Coauthor, with Marlene Vincent. Among the legends/voices presented are Nat King Cole, Otis Redding, Billie Holiday, Elvis Presley, Judy Garland, Mahalia Jackson, and Josephine Baker. Prod. by Bill-Mar Production, at Los Angeles Cabaret, Encino, CA; coprod., codir., and costarring the author.

MILES, WALTER, Musical playwright. Member of the Board of Directors and treasurer of the Afro-American Total Theatre, New York City, 1967–73.

DRAMATIC WORK:
Makin' It (musical, full length, 1972). Book written with GERTRUDE GREENIDGE and HAZEL BRYANT. Music by JIMMY JUSTICE and HOLLY HAMILTON. Prod.

by the Afro-American Total Theatre, at the following locations in New York: at International House, Jan. 14–16, 1972; at the Negro Ensemble Co., Feb. 7, 1972; at Riverside Church Theatre, March 6, 1972; at Finch Coll., March 1972; as a Street Theatre prodn. in the five boroughs of New York City, July 31–Aug. 14, 1972; as a Street Theatre prodn. in Boston, MA, Aug. 15, 1972; at Lincoln Center, Nov. 3, 1972. Remained in the company's repertory until June 10, 1973.

MILLER, AL (Alfred), Musical playwright and theatrical director. Based in New York City.

PLAY:
God Is Back, Black and Singing Gospel at the Fortune Theatre (musical entertainment, full length, 1969). Conceived from the black Christian heritage. "For scenery, the walls of the stage contained graffiti such as 'God Is Love' and 'Let No Man Deceive You With Words.' The audience participates in a camp meeting presided over by a red-gowned revivalist preacher who gives out sermonettes. There was joyful singing and dancing in the aisles to the musical renditions of Clara Walker, the Gospel Clefs, Tommy Brown and the Gospel Starlets."—*Black Images in the American Theatre* (Archer, 1973), pp. 286–87. Prod. Off-Bway at the Fortune Theatre, opening Nov. 18, 1969; dir. by author.

MILLER, ALAN E., Playwright. Based in New York City, where he was a participant in the New York Black Writers Conf. in 1971.

PLAYS:
All sched. to be pub by Amuru Press, New York, 1974, but never pub. **The Death of a Man** (drama, 1 act). **I Am My Brothers' Soul** (drama, 1 act). **Kiss Life for Me** (fantasy, 2 acts). Concerned with Nat Turner's son. **Mama! We Have Rats** (drama, 1 act). Young man is confronted by prison guard to sell dope.

MILLER, CLIFFORD L. (Leonard), Minister, poet, and playwright. Educated at Fisk Univ. and Andover-Newton Seminary. Served as chaplain in World War II. Author of two volumes of poetry: *Imperishable the Temple* (1963) and *Haunting Voice*.

PLAY:
Wings over Dark Waters (poetic drama, 5 parts [57 scenes], 1965). Called by *Crisis* magazine (Feb. 1966, p. 87) "a long ambitious 'closet' drama in prose and verse." Dramatizes the major events and contributions in black American history since slavery times. Pub. by Great Concord Publishers, New York, 1954; copies in the Schomburg Collection and the Hatch-Billops Collection.

MILLER, HENRY D., Playwright. Formerly associated with the Afro-American Repertory Theatre in New York City.

PLAYS:
A Little Langston Plus Three (1975). Based at least partly on the writings of LANGSTON HUGHES. Prod. by the Afro-American Repertory Theatre, New York, 1975; dir. by author. **Death of a Dunbar Girl** (1 act, 1975). Prod. by the Afro-American Repertory Theatre, at the Masque Theatre, New York, March 1975.

MILLER, LAURA ANN, Playwright. Associated with the UCLA Theatre, Los Angeles, 1967–68.

PLAYS:
The Cricket Cries (1 act, 1967). Prod. by UCLA Theatre, 1967. **The Echo of a Sound** (1 act, 1968). Prod. by UCLA Theatre, 1968. **Fannin Road, Straight Ahead** (3 acts, 1968). **Git Away from Here, Irvine, Now Git** (full length, 1969). **Freight Train** (drama, 3 acts, pre-1976). Provides a contrast between two girls living in a rooming house with their lovers: one becomes pregnant by her disreputable lover; the other falls for a handsome, well-to-do, and respectable young man. Unpub. script in the Hatch-Billops Collection.

MILNER, RONALD (Ron) (1938–   ), Playwright, author, editor, and director. Born in Detroit, MI, where he graduated from high school and attended Highland Park Jr. Coll. and the Detroit Inst. of Technology. Also attended Harvey Swados's writing workshop at Columbia Univ., 1965. One of the founders, with WOODIE KING, JR., and David Rambeau, and artistic director, of the Concept East Theatre (CET) in Detroit, 1962–; also a founding director of Spirit of Shango Theatre Co., early 1970s, which merged with CET, and founder of the Langston Hughes Theatre, Detroit, 1975–. Came to New York City with King in 1964, in a touring production of three plays by the Rev. Malcolm Boyd, and remained in New York with King when King joined the staff of the American Place Theatre (APT), which was then just being formed. At APT, King directed Milner's **Who's Got His Own,** as a work-in-progress in 1965, and Milner's **The Warning: A Theme for Linda** in 1969. They also continued their artistic collaboration by coediting *Black Drama Anthology* (1972), one of the earliest collections of plays by new black American playwrights. Milner was writer-in-residence at Lincoln Univ./Pennsylvania, 1966–67; and also taught and conducted a cultural workshop at Michigan State Univ./East Lansing, 1971–72, before returning to Detroit to try to develop a viable community theatre (through the Spirit of Shango Theatre Co. and the Langston Hughes Theatre). His prose writings (including short stories and articles on black theatre) have been published in *Negro Digest/ Black World* and other periodicals, and anthologized in *Best Short Stories by Negro Writers* (Hughes, 1967), *Five Black Writers* (Gibson, 1970), *The Black Aesthetic* (Gayle, 1971), and *Black Poets and Prophets* (King & Anthony, 1972). Recipient of a John Hay Whitney Award, 1962–63, and a Rockefeller Foundation grant, 1965–66. *Address:* 15865 Montevista, Detroit, MI 48238.

REPRESENTATIVE PLAYS AND DRAMATIC WORKS:
Life Agony (drama, 1 act, early 1960s). The orig. version of the author's three-act play **Who's Got His Own** (1965). Prod. by the Concept East Theatre in Detroit, during the early 1960s, with Woodie King, Jr., in the leading role. Later prod. in New York by Robert Hooks's Group Workshop, and on New York TV's Channel 47 Experimental Negro Theatre, again starring King.
Who's Got His Own (drama, 3 acts, 1965). Depicts a heated confrontation between a prodigal black youth and his mother and sister immediately following his father's funeral. Explores the problems of black manhood in a racist society and the conflicts between

generations and the sexes in a black family. An expanded version of the author's one-act play **Life Agony** (1960s). First presented as a work-in-progress at the American Place Theatre (APT), New York, Oct. 1965; dir. by Woodie King, Jr. First prod. in its completed form at APT, Oct. 12, 1966, for 19 perfs.; dir. by Lloyd Richards. With Glynn Turman, BARBARA ANN TEER, Estelle Evans, L. Errol Jaye, Sam Laws, and Roger Robinson. This prodn. also toured New York state colleges under the auspices of the New York State Council of the Arts. Prod. by the New Lafayette Theatre (NLT) in Harlem as its premiere prodn., Oct. 13–Nov. 12, 1967. Prod. by THEODORE WARD at the South Side Center of the Performing Arts in Chicago, during 1968, for a ten-week run. Revived by NLT, Feb. 28–March 30, 1969. Prod. at Cheyney State Coll. in Cheyney, PA, early 1970s. Pub. in *Black Drama Anthology* (King & Milner, 1971).

The Monster (drama, 1 act, 1968). According to a review by Leander Jones (*Black World,* Nov. 1969, p. 63), this play "depicts the dilemma of Black students on the nation's campuses. Here they must confront a professional negro and deal with him if they are to realize any self-fulfillment. They devise a stratagem to make the professional negro reveal his true self. He is the dean of the college." Prod. at the Louis Theatre, Chicago, Oct. 1969. Pub. in *The Drama Review,* Summer 1968, pp. 94–105; in *Black Arts* (Alhamisi & Wangara, 1969); in *Nommo* (Robinson, 1972).

The Warning: A Theme for Linda (drama, 1 act [4 scenes], 1969). The youngest in a household of three generations of black women hopes to find happiness in love, despite the fact that both her mother and grandmother have had unpleasant experiences with their husbands. First prod. by Woodie King Assocs., Inc., at Tambellini's Gate Theatre, New York, July 30, 1969, for 111 perfs., on a program of four one-act plays, under the blanket title *A Black Quartet;* dir. by Woodie King, Jr. With Vikki Summers, Louise Heath, Loretta Greene, Jo-Anne Robinson, L. Errol Jaye, Jimmy Hayeson, Paul Rodger-Reid, MINNIE GENTRY, and Joan Pryor. Prod. by the Studio Theatre of the Atlanta Memorial Art Center on Peachtree St., during the 1972–73 season; dir. by Young Hughly. Excerpt (scenes 3 and 4) in *Negro Digest,* April 1969, pp. 53–54 (includes synopses of scenes 1 and 2); in *A Black Quartet* (Caldwell, Milner, Bullins, & Jones, 1970).

M(ego) and the Green Ball of Freedom (symbolic play, 1 act, 1971). The green ball of freedom can only be obtained through cooperation and the giving up of one's ego. Prod. by the Theatre of Shango, Detroit, 1971. Pub. in *Black World,* April 1971, pp. 40–45.

What the Wine-Sellers Buy (drama, 3 acts, 1973). A professional black pimp tries to persuade a young high school student to follow the same profession and convert his girlfriend into a prostitute in order to get the money needed to care for the student's sick mother. First prod. at the Henry St. Settlement House, New York, May 1973. A second prodn. was staged at the Mark Taper Forum in Los Angeles, Oct. 1973. Prod. by the New York Shakespeare Festival at the Vivian Beaumont Theatre at Lincoln Center, Feb. 14–March 17, 1974, for 37 perfs.; dir. by Michael Schultz. With Glynn Turman, Loretta Greene, Marilyn Coleman, and Dick A. Williams, who won a Drama Desk Award in the role of Rico, the pimp. Pub. by Samuel French, New York, 1974.

Season's Reasons (*a cappella* operetta, full length, 1976). Subtitled "Just a Natural Change." Music by Charles Mason. "Conceived as a black musical, this work sets out to demonstrate to young people how conditions in the black community changed from the 1960s to the 1970s. Milner accomplishes this aim by dramatizing the state of 'future shock' suffered by a young revolutionary who escapes from jail after a long period of incarceration."—*Dictionary of Literary Biography,* vol. 38 (1986), p. 207. First prod. at the author's Langston Hughes Theatre, Detroit, 1976. Prod. by NFT, July 14, 1977, for 18 perfs.; dir. by author.

Roads on the Mountaintop (drama, full length, 1986). "About the internal struggles of Martin Luther King, Jr., and his family after he received the Nobel peace prize."— *Black Masks,* Feb./Mar. 1986, p. 5. Prod. by Crossroads Theatre, New Brunswick, NJ, Feb. 12–Mar. 9, 1986, dir. by Rick Khan.

OTHER PLAYS AND DRAMATIC WORKS:
These Three (early 1960s). Prod. by Concept East Theatre, Detroit, early 1960s. **Color Struck** (c. 1970). **The Greatest Gift** (children's play, 1973). Prod. by the Detroit Public Schools, 1973. **Crack Steppin'** (1981). Prod. at the Music Hall in Detroit, Nov. 1981. **Jazz Set** (1980). Story of the members of a jazz sextet. First prod. at the Mark Taper Forum, Los Angeles, 1980. Prod. at NFT, July 1982; dir. by Norman Riley, with musical score by *Max Roach.

MILTON, NERISSA LONG, School teacher and playwright.

PLAY:
The Challenge—A Fantasy (black history pageant for children, 4 parts, 1953). Black children in America are challenged by the Spirit of Truth to learn the true history of their people. Pub. in four installments in *Negro History Bulletin:* Part I, Oct. 1953, pp. 15–16; Part II, Nov. 1953, pp. 43–44; Part III, Dec. 1953, pp. 66–68; Part IV, Jan. 1954, pp. 87–88.

MITCHELL, LIONEL H. (1942–1984), Critic, novelist, and playwright. Born in New York City, son of Alexander John ("Razz") Mitchell, a drummer with Louis Jordan's Tympany Five and also with the Savoy Sultans. Attended LSU, 1961–63. Freelance writer prior to 1977. Drama critic, *New York Amsterdam News,* 1977–84. Author of a novel, *Travelling Light* (1980). Contributor to *Notes from the New Underground* (Kornbluth, 1968). Recipient of an American Book Award from Before Columbus Foundation, 1981, for literary excellence. *Agent:* Ned Leavitt, William Morris Agency, 1350 Ave. of the Americas, New York, NY 10019.

PLAYS:
L'Ouverture (ritual drama with choreography, full length, 1972). Focuses on three figures of the Haitian Revolution—Toussaint L'Ouverture, Dessalines, and Henri Christophe. Described by the author as "an original, starkly modern work in non-realistic style, utilizing masks . . . inspired by the Peter Brook production of *Marat/Sade.*" Public reading by the Frank Silvera Writers' Workshop (FSWW), New York City, 1975. Unpub. script and tape recording in the FSWW Archives/Schomburg Collection.

Uncle Tom's Cabin (updated adaptn., full length, 1974). Based on the orig. novel by Harriet Beecher Stowe and the George L. Aikin dramatization. With choral arrangements by Mitchell. Depicts Tom as a visionary figure, a martyr in the style of Martin Luther King, Jr. Story runs from Eliza's escape across the river to the North to Simon Legree's beating Tom to death, asking the latter when he is near death, "What do ya see, Tom?" Tom replies, "I see Jesus, Massa, I see Jesus!" According to the author,

"St. Clair's spouting of the Communist Manifesto in the orig. novel is also included." Produced by the WPA Theatre Group, New York, Feb.-March 1975.

MITCHELL, LOFTEN (1919–   ), Playwright, black drama historian, essayist, and teacher. Born in Columbia, NC.; reared in New York City (Harlem). Educated at DeWitt Clinton H.S. (graduating with honors, 1937); CCNY (playwriting, 1937–38); Talladega Coll. (A.B. 1943); Columbia Univ. Graduate School (playwriting, with John Gassner, 1947–51); with special studies at Union and General theological seminaries. Began his theatrical career/performing with the Salem Community Dramatizers, New York City, 1936–37, a church group for which he also wrote some sketches; the Pioneer Drama Group, 1936–37, which produced two of his early plays [see OTHER PLAYS AND DRAMATIC WORKS below]; and the Rose McClendon Players, 1937–38, performing in their workshop production of *Having a Wonderful Time* (1938). Also appeared in †Dennis Donoghue's *The Black Messiah* (1939). Since 1946 he has devoted his theatrical energies primarily to writing for and about the theatre. In addition to plays, films, and TV and radio scripts, he is the author of *Black Drama: The Story of the American Negro in the Theatre* (1967); *Voices of the Black Theatre* (1974); and *The Stubborn Old Lady Who Resisted Change* (novel, 1974). His articles have appeared in *Theatre Arts, The American Negro Writer and His Roots, The Talladegan, Freedomways, Anthology of the Negro in the American Theatre, Harlem, U.S.A., Crisis, In Their Own Words: A History of the American Theatre, Negro Digest, The Black American Writer, Black World, The Black Aesthetic,* the *Amsterdam News,* the *New York Times* and numerous other periodicals and anthologies. Author of special articles on blacks in the American theatre for the *Oxford Companion to the Theatre* and the *Enciclopedia Della Spettacolo.* Editor, *Freedom Journal,* NAACP, 1964. Prof., State Univ. of New York, Univ. Center at Binghamton, Depts. of Theatre and Afro-American Studies, 1971–present. Recipient of Guggenheim Award for creative writing in the drama, 1958; Harlem Cultural Award for writing, 1969; award for playwriting, Research Foundation, SUNY, 1974; Tony Award nomination for **Bubbling Brown Sugar,** 1976; award for Best Musical of the Year, London, for **Bubbling Brown Sugar,** 1977; AUDELCO Outstanding Theatrical Pioneer Award, 1979. *Address:* Dept. of Theatre, Division of Humanities, State University of New York at Binghamton, Binghamton, NY 13901.

REPRESENTATIVE PLAYS AND DRAMATIC WORKS:
Blood in the Night (drama, 3 acts, 1938). The author's first play, set in the Deep South during the 1940s. The title is taken from the lines of a poem by one of his fellow classmates at Talladega Coll., James Cliftone Morris: "Years will pass, another brown maid's heart will pain, / and I shall weep blood in the night for him again." Prod. by the People's Theatre Workshop, at the 115th St. Library in Harlem, March 22, 1946.
The Cellar (drama, 2 acts, 1947). A black blues singer in Harlem harbors a black fugitive from the South who is being pursued by her fiancé, a ruthless detective. Prod.

by the People's Theatre in Harlem, Oct. 24–Nov. 14, 1957. Prod. by the Harlem Show-case, Nov. 1952–late April 1953.

The Bancroft Dynasty // Orig. title: **The Depression Years** (domestic drama, 3 acts, 1947). Portrait of an upper-middle-class Harlem family during the Depression. Deals with the family's struggle to cope with changes brought on by the changing economic times, and with the problem of color consciousness among middle-class blacks. Prod. by the 115th St. People's Theatre, New York, 1948.

A Land Beyond the River (doc. drama, 3 acts, 1957). Dramatizes the story of Rev. Dr. Delaine, a minister and schoolteacher in Clarendon Co., SC, whose suit for equal school facilities and bus transportation for the rural black children in his area was one of the cases that resulted in the famous Supreme Court school desegregation decision of 1954. Prod. by the Greenwich Mews Theatre, New York, March 28–June 30, 1957, for 99 perfs.; dir. by Michael Howard. With Robert Graham Brown as Dr. DeLaine and the late Diana Sands as a member of the cast. Orig. prodn. taken on tour of Great Neck, Brooklyn, and Newark, 1958–59. Many independent prodns. by college and community groups. Pub. by Pioneer Drama Service, Cody, WY (now Denver, CO), 1963; in *Afro-American Literature: Drama* (Adams, Conn, Slepian, 1970); and in *The Black Teacher and the Dramatic Arts* (Reardon & Pawley, 1970).

The Phonograph (domestic drama, 2 acts, 1961). About a young boy growing up in the Harlem community during a period of struggle and adversity. (Believed to be an autobiographical play.) Prod. at the State Univ. of New York/Binghamton, 1974. Also prod. at the Maidman Theatre, New York, and by colleges throughout the United States, 1969–84, according to the author. Unpub. script in the Hatch-Billops Collection.

Ballad for Bimshire (musical, 2 acts [with prologue and 11 scenes], 1963). Book coauthored with IRVING BURGIE, who also wrote the music and lyrics. Love story with island atmosphere, involving a native girl and a New York playboy, set in Barbados (nicknamed "Bimshire"). First prod. Off-Bway at the Mayfair Theatre, Oct. 15–Dec. 15, 1953, for 74 perfs.; coprod. by OSSIE DAVIS, who also starred in the production; dir. by Ed Cambridge. Also in the cast were Frederick O'Neal, Robert Hooks, and Christine Spencer. Orig. cast recording (selections) released by London Records, in both monaural (48002) and stereo (78002).

Star of the Morning (musical play, 2 acts, 1963; revised 1984). Subtitled "Scenes in the Life of Bert Williams." Biographical drama, with song and dance, about the life and struggles of the well-known entertainer and comedian, who with his partner George Walker wrote and starred in many early black musicals. Orig. version prod. in Cleveland, OH, 1965. Revised version prod. by the American Folk Theatre, Inc., at the No Smoking Playhouse, New York; dir. by Dick Gaffield, with music and lyrics by Louis D. Mitchell, Romare Bearden, and Clyde Fox. Orig. version pub. in *Black Drama Anthology* (King & Milner, 1972).

Ballad of the Winter Soldiers (dramatic doc., described by the author as "more of a pageant than a play," 2 acts, 1964). Coauthor, with JOHN OLIVER KILLENS. According to the author, "It dealt with freedom fighters throughout history. The term 'winter soldiers' grew out of Thomas Paine's statement: 'These are the times that try men's souls. The summer soldier and the sunshine patriot will in this hour shrink from the service of his country.' The winter soldier . . . was one who did not, who continued to fight for freedom."—*Black Drama* (Mitchell, 1967), p. 202. Prod. as a benefit show for CORE, at Philharmonic Hall, Lincoln Center, Sept. 28, 1964; dir. by James E. Wall.

The cast included such well-known white and black professionals as Robert Ryan, Shelley Winters, Dick Gregory, Madeline Sherwood, †Frank Silvera, and RUBY DEE.

Tell Pharoah (a concert drama, 2 acts, 1967). A panoramic black doc—history in readers' theatre style, with traditional black music—of the black man from Africa to present-day America, with emphasis on his struggle for freedom. The title is based on a line from the well-known spiritual "Go Down Moses" ("Tell ole Pharoah / To let my people go!"). Prod. on the occasion of a black history-brotherhood program, at Golden Auditorium, Queens Coll., New York, Feb. 19, 1967, with an all-star cast of professional actors, including Ruby Dee, MICKI GRANT, Louis Gossett, Frederick O'Neal, Gloria Daniel, and Mary Alyce Glenn; assisted by singers Lucille Burney, Robert Alexander, and the St. Albans Children's Choir. Has been frequently performed, with other such notable actors as Hilda Simms and Ossie Davis. Prod. at the National Maritime Union Theatre, May 8, 1967, as a benefit for the Schomburg Collection, under the dir. of Albert Grant; at the Concord Baptist Church, with McKinley Johnson as the leading singer; and by the Kutana Players, a drama group from Southern Illinois Univ., at the Metropolitan Campus of Cuyahoga Community Coll., Cleveland, 1973. Recently prod. by the American Folk Theatre, at Symphony Space, New York, June 21, 1984; dir. by Henry Miller. Starring OSCAR BROWN, JR., Frances Foster, and Earle Hyman. Pub. in *The Black Teacher and the Dramatic Arts* (Reardon & Pawley, 1970).

Sojourn to the South of the Wall (historical drama, 1973; revised 1983). Subtitled "And the Walls Came Tumbling Down." About black people in seventeenth century New Amsterdam, NY, and their attempts to persuade the Dutch to fight against the British. Subsequently rewritten as the libretto of an opera entitled **The Walls Came Tumbling Down** (1976).

Bubbling Brown Sugar (musical revue, 2 acts, 1976). Based on a concept by RO-SETTA LeNOIRE. Encapsulates the history of black entertainment from 1910 to 1940, focusing on the all-black musical revues that flourished in Harlem during this period. Featured music by †Eubie Blake, Duke Ellington, Billie Holiday, †Andy Razaf, Cab Calloway, Earl Hines, and †J. C. Johnson. Described by Alex Bontemps (*Ebony*, Feb. 1976, p. 129), as "about a young man who has just graduated from college and is eager to leave Harlem, a place he believes has no history and no future. . . . A trio of veteran entertainers . . . try to change his mind by taking him on an imaginary tour of Harlem in its hey-day—1910 to 1940. The tour includes stops at such famous night spots as Small's Paradise and the Cotton Club, a visit to a house rent party, and a variety of street scenes." Nominated for a Tony Award, 1975–76, as best musical. Prod. successfully by the AMAS Repertory Theatre, playing Off-Bway and on tour for a year before opening on Bway at the ANTA Theatre, March 2, 1976–Dec. 31, 1977, for 766 perfs.; dir. by Robert M. Cooper and choreographed by Billy Wilson (who was nominated for a Tony Award as best choreographer). With Avon Long, Josephine Premice, Joseph Attles, Vivian Reed (who won a *Theatre World* Award and a Drama Desk Award and was nominated for a Tony Award as best actress in a musical), Chip Garnett (who also won a *Theatre World* Award), Ethel Beatty, and Barry Preston (who won a Clarence Derwent Award). Opened June 22, 1976 at the Shubert Theatre in Chicago, and closed at the National Theatre, Washington, DC, Oct. 9, 1977. Opened Aug. 23, 1977 in Uihlein Hall, Milwaukee, WI, and closed April 22, 1978, at National Arts Centre, Ottawa, Canada. Prod. by the Papermill Playhouse, Milburn, NJ, during the 1977 season. According to the author, it was prod. in London, Paris, Central Europe, the Netherlands, Germany, on extensive U.S. tour, and by numerous independent groups throughout the United States. Pub. by

Broadway Play Publishing Co., 1984. Cast recording released by H & L Records (HL-69011).

The Walls Came Tumbling Down (opera, 1 act, 1976). Libretto by Mitchell. Music by Willard Roosevelt. Based on Mitchell's play **Sojourn to the South of the Wall** (1973). Prod. by the Harlem School of the Arts, at Alice Tully Hall, Lincoln Center, New York, March 1976.

Miss Waters, to You // Also called **Miss Ethel Waters** (musical, full length, 1983). Book by Mitchell. Based on a concept by Rosetta LeNoire. Music from Waters's repertoire. Prod. by AMAS Repertory Theatre, New York, Feb. 24–March 20, 1983, for 17 perfs; dir. by Billie Allen.

OTHER PLAYS AND DRAMATIC WORKS:
Cocktails (satirical comedy, 1 act, 1938). Music by Catherine Richardson. What would happen if black cult leader Father Divine were elected president of the United States? Prod. by the Pioneer Drama Group of Harlem, New York, 1938. **Shattered Dreams** (1938). Prod. by the Pioneer Drama Group of Harlem, 1938. **Crossroads** (drama, 1 act, 1938). About the Harlem riot of 1935. **Of Mice and Men** (adaptn., full length, 1953). An all-black version of John Steinbeck's drama. Prod. by LUTHER JAMES and Comet Productions at the Cabaret Theatre, a Greenwich Village cafe, June 10–14, 1953; dir. by James. The cast featured Clayton Corbin, Howard Augusta, and two future black playwrights, CHARLES GORDONE and BILL GUNN. **Young Man of Williamsburg** (screenplay, 1954). Apparently prod. by the YM and YWHA of Brooklyn, 1954. **City Called Norfolk** (drama, 3 acts, 1950s). Prod. by the People's Showcase Theatre in Harlem, early 1950s. **Integration—Report One** (screenplay, 1959). Prod. by Andover Productions, 1960. **Ballad of a Blackbird** (musical play, full length, 1968). Book by Mitchell. Lyrics by W. F. Lucas. On the life and career of Florence Mills, a major black musical comedy star of the 1920s, who appeared in several editions of Lew Leslie's *Blackbirds,* and died at the age of 32 after an appendectomy. Projected for Bway showing in 1967, but apparently never prod. **The Afro-Philadelphian** (1970). Prod. in 1970, with Frederick O'Neal. **The Final Solution to the Black Problem in the United States: or the Fall of the American Empire** (drama, 1 act, 1970). About black genocide. Prod. in New York and on tour, 1973. **The Vampires of Harlem** (film, 1972). Prod. by Vanguard Productions, 1972. **Cartoons for a Lunch Hour** (musical, 1978). Prod. at the Perry St. Theatre, New York, 1978. **Harlem, USA** (1977). About the struggles of black Americans in Harlem, utilizing dialogue, music, and dance. Prod. at FESTAC, Lagos, Nigeria, Feb. 1977. **A Gypsy Girl** (musical, full length, 1982). Prod. in Pine Bluff, AR, 1982. Prod. as a benefit perf. for the Sickle Cell Anemia Foundation, at the Elks Home in Harlem, Oct. 14, 1984, under the supervision of Cameo Fashions and Gladys Blair Productions, under the auspices of †Dick Campbell, director of the foundation.

MOLETTE, BARBARA JEAN. See MOLETTE, CARLTON W., II, and BARBARA JEAN MOLETTE.

MOLETTE, BHUNNIE BERNIER (Bhunnie Bernier), Playwright and writer. Resides in Mount Vernon, NY. Educated at NYU (B.S.) and Columbia Univ. (M.A.). Wrote a weekly column, "Today's Child," for the *Westchester Observer,* 1970. Wrote two educational booklets for the Mount Vernon Board of Education which were distributed to children throughout the elementary schools.

Has also completed six children's stories (1984) and a novel, "Harlem Was My Hometown," all as yet unpublished. Her playwriting career began when she was introduced by WALTER JONES to the Frank Silvera Writers' Workshop (FSWW) in New York City, where she has been a member since 1975, and where most of her plays have been read or produced. *Address:* 620 South Seventh Avenue, Mount Vernon, NY 10550.

PLAYS AND DRAMATIC WORKS:

Ola & B (1975). Concerns a 65–year-old Cotton Club chorus girl trying to revive her youth through companionship with a 20–year-old divorcee neighbor; the past versus the present. Public reading by FSWW, at the Martinique Theatre, New York, 1975. Full prodn. mounted by FSWW at the Harlem Cultural Center, New York, 1976. Public reading for Joseph Papp, at the Public Theatre, New York, 1976. Unpub. script and tape recording in the FSWW Archives/Schomburg Collection.

An Almost Unmarried Female (comedy, 1976). About a nurse residing in Harlem with her husband, when her ex-husband comes to her for financial aid, having been refused by the welfare agency. Public reading by FSWW, at the Martinique Theatre, 1976. Unpub. script and tape recording in the FSWW Archives/Schomburg Collection.

Barbara Died and the Pumpkins Are Gone (1977). Concerns a slightly mad single mother whose children have to adjust to her new lifestyle. Public reading by FSWW, at the Martinique Theatre, 1977. Unpub. script and tape recording in the FSWW Archives/ Schomburg Collection.

Who Broke the Damn Bell? (1977). Five troubled girls and a social worker are locked in a dayroom by accident in a detention home in New York. Public reading by FSWW, at the Martinique Theatre, 1977. Unpub. script and tape recording in the FSWW Archives/ Schomburg Collection.

Partake of de Goat Meat (comedy, 2 acts, 1976). About a handsome West Indian man and a black American woman who begin a business in the back bedroom of his Caribbean grocery store. Public reading by FSWW, at the Harlem Performance Center, Dec. 1976. Prod. Off-Bway in a full production by FSWW, at the Theatre of the Open Eye, New York, Oct. 26–30, 1977; dir. by MANSOOR NAJEE-ULLAH. Unpub. script and tape recording in the FSWW Archives/Schomburg Collection.

Mama's Doing Her Thing! (script for a musical, 1980). Songs by Emma Kemp. A senior citizen who is recently widowed and decides to have a fling with a young minister meets with disapproval from her adult children and the spirit of her late husband. Public reading by FSWW, 1980. Unpub. script and tape recording in the FSWW Archives/ Schomburg Collections.

MOLETTE, CARLTON W., II (1939–   ), and **BARBARA JEAN MO-LETTE** (1940–   ), Husband and wife playwriting and theatrical team. Together they have written at least four plays: **Dr. B. S. Black** (1969), **Rosalee Pritchett** (1970), **Booji** (1971), and **Noah's Ark** (1974); a filmstrip: *Stage Makeup for Black Actors* (1975); a newspaper column about theatre, motion pictures, and television: "Upstage/Downstage," for the *Houston Informer,* 1976–79; and a recently published book: *Black Theatre: Premise and Presentation* (1986), describing the nature of Afro-American theatre as an expression of culture and a medium for communicating values.

Carlton Molette is a college and theatre administrator, producer, playwright, director, designer, stage manager, technician, actor, author, and editor. He was born in Pine Bluff, Arkansas. Educated at Morehouse Coll. (B.A., 1959), the Univ. of Iowa (M.A., 1962), and Florida State Univ. (Ph.D., 1968). Currently dean of arts and sciences, Lincoln Univ. of Missouri. From 1975 to 1984, he was prof. of communications and theatre at Texas Southern Univ. and dean of the School of Communications, during which period he established graduate and undergraduate programs in theatre/cinema, telecommunications, speech communication, and journalism; and developed a radio station and a dinner theatre. From 1969 to 1975, he was assoc. prof. of drama at Spelman Coll. in Atlanta, GA, and chairman of the Div. of Fine Arts, 1974–75. He has also held faculty positions at Tuskegee Inst., 1960–61; Howard Univ., 1963–65; and Florida A. & M. Univ., 1964–69. He has been visiting prof. at the Univ. of Iowa (Afro-American Drama Summer Inst., 1973) and the Univ. of Michigan (guest director, Professional Theatre Program, 1974). He has been involved in more than 100 productions at the above institutions and with the Negro Ensemble Co. (NEC), the Free Southern Theatre (FST), and the Des Moines Community Playhouse. Scenic designer for the film *Together for Days* (1971), written by WILLIAM BRANCH, directed by Michael Schultz, and starring Clifton Davis. Editor of *NADSA Encore*, 1965–71. Member, editorial advisory board, *Journal of Black Studies*, 1970–73. His articles and research have been published in NADSA Encore, Southern Speech Journal, Players, Negro Digest, Phylon, Bulletin of Black Theatre, Journal of Black Studies, and *Nommo*. Member of DG, ATA, NADSA, U.S. Inst. for Theatre Technology, International Council on Fine Arts Deans, Assn. for Communication Administration, Speech Communication Assn., Assn. for Education in Journalism and Mass Communication. Also member of Board of Directors, Arts Festival of Atlanta, 1971–74; Mayor's Advisory Committee for the Arts, Atlanta, 1974–75; founding chairman, Neighborhood Arts Center, Atlanta, 1975; and Miller Theatre Advisory Council, 1978–84. Recipient of Ford Foundation early admissions scholarship, Morehouse Coll., 1955–59; graduate fellowship, Univ. of Kansas City, 1959–60; doctoral fellowship, Carnegie Foundation Florida State Univ., 1955, and research grant, Atlanta Univ. Center, 1970–71.

Barbara Molette is a playwright, costume designer, makeup artist, director, actress, author, editor, and publicist. She was born in Los Angeles, CA. Educated at Florida A. & M. Univ. (B.A. with highest honors, 1966) and Florida State Univ. (B.F.A., 1969). Since 1975 she has been asst. prof. at Texas Southern Univ., teaching scriptwriting, theatre history, film criticism, and a survey of theatre, dance, visual arts, and music. From 1969 she was an instructor at Spelman Coll., Atlanta, teaching theatre history, scriptwriting, dramatic theory and criticism, and costume. She has been associated with more than 75 theatre productions at the above colleges and at the Negro Ensemble Co., Des Moines Community Playhouse, and Atlanta Univ. Summer Theatre, and has conducted drama workshops at Smith Coll., Dallas Independent School District, U.S. Inst.

for Theatre Technology, Atlanta School System, Atlanta Arts Council, Clark Coll., and Florida A. & M. Univ. Member of the editorial board of *Technical Theatre Course Guide, K-12,* U.S. Inst. for Theatre Technology, 1979. Her research, reviews, and criticism have been published in *Phylon, Black World, NADSA Encore,* and other publications. Member of DG, ATA, NADSA, National Coalition of 100 Black Women, and Soc. for Accelerative Learning and Teaching. Recipient of graduate fellowship in theatre, Florida State Univ., 1967–68, and Spelman Coll. faculty development grant for playwriting, 1972.

PLAYS AND DRAMATIC WORKS:

Dr. B. S. Black (comedy, full length, 1969; also prod. as a musical, 1972). Adaptn. of Moliere's *The Doctor in Spite of Himself.* By Carlton and Barbara Molette. According to the *National Playwrights Directory* (Kaye, 1977), a "Black con artist is recipient of [his] wife's revenge. He is beaten by two rural gentlemen into confessing that he is a doctor of black medicine and sets out to cure Magnolia, the daughter of Chauncy White, III. Sidetracked at the White estate by Tilly Mae and the 'sweet utensils of her trade,' B. S. eventually solves the dilemma by uniting Leroy and Magnolia and sets his sights on politics." First prod. as a play by the Morehouse-Spelman Players, at Spelman Coll., Atlanta, Nov. 10, 1969. Adapt. as a musical, with the collaboration of *Charles Mann. Prod. by the Atlanta Univ. Summer Theatre, July 20, 1972. Prod. as a musical by the Morehouse-Spelman Players, Atlanta, April 1983. Pub. as a play in *SADSA Encore,* 1970.

Rosalee Pritchett (drama, 1 act [4 scenes], 1970). By Carlton and Barbara Molette. According to *Black World* (April 1973, p. 33), "In *Rosalee Pritchett,* an ultra-grand bridge-playing colored lady constantly downs [Black] Movement people and feels secure that her professional husband's 'station-in-life' will protect her from the racists. She finds out differently." First prod. by the Spelman Coll. Dept. of Drama and the Morehouse-Spelman Players, Atlanta, March 23, 1970; dir. by Carlton Molette. With Glenda Stevens in the title role. Prod. by NEC, at St. Marks Playhouse, New York, opening Jan. 12, 1971, for 44 perfs.; dir. by SHAUNEILLE PERRY. With Frances Foster in the title role. Pub. by Dramatists Play Service, New York, 1972, and in *Black Writers of America* (Barksdale & Kinnamon, 1972).

Booji // Orig. title **Booji Wooji** (drama, full length, 1971; also prod. as a teleplay, 1982). By Carlton and Barbara Molette. The search for some significance to his life by a young, black middle-class lawyer is the main problem in this play, which also focuses on drug addiction in black communities. Prod. by the Atlanta Univ. Summer Theatre, July 8, 1971. Revised and prod. by the Morehouse-Spelman Players, Atlanta, Dec. 1972. Televised by KPRC-TV, Houston, May 23 and 30, 1982.

The Escape, or a Leap for Freedom (adaptn., full length, 1976). By Barbara Molette. Based on the 1853 play of the same title by †William Wells Brown, about the tragic plight of a recently married slave couple whose master wishes to separate them in order that he may enjoy the sexual favors of the beautiful wife. They make a desperate but successful attempt to escape to freedom in the North. Prod. as a bicentennial offering by Texas Southern Univ., Houston, opening Nov. 3, 1976.

Noah's Ark (drama, 2 acts, 1974). By Carlton and Barbara Molette. According to the *National Playwrights Directory* (Kaye, 1977), "Noah, [a] college professor; [his] wife, Gladys; [and their] son, Daniel, live in the year before 1984. War rages in Africa and Daniel [now also] a college professor, is slated for induction in the army. Noah, an ardent pacifist, conducts his own private, non-violent war with the powers that be." Prod. by the Morehouse-Spelman Players, opening Feb. 12, 1974. Pub. in *Center Stage* (Ostrow, 1981).

MONTE, ERIC, Screenwriter, TV scriptwriter. Best known as the cocreator and scriptwriter of the "Good Times" TV series.

DRAMATIC WORKS:
Cooley High (feature film, full length: screenplay, 1975). Comedy depicting life among black high school students in Chicago during the 1960s. Often called the black version of *American Graffiti*. Evolved into the TV series "What's Happening." Released by American International, 1965; dir. by Michael Schultz. Featured Glynn Turman, Lawrence Hilton-Jacobs, and GARRETT MORRIS. "Good Times" (TV comedy series, 1974–c. 1979). Cocreator, with MICHAEL EVANS. Prod. by CBS-TV between 1974 and 1979. Cast included Esther Rolle as Florida Evans, JOHN AMOS as James Evans, Jimmie Walker as J. J., JA'NET DuBOIS as Willona Woods, BerNadette Stanis as Thelma Evans, Johnny Brown as Nathan Bookman, and Janet Jackson as Willona's daughter Penny. **Michael Gets Suspended** (TV comedy, half hr., 1975). From the "Good Times" series. Michael gets suspended from school for calling George Washington a racist; his parents, who try to get him to apologize, learn a valuable lesson in black history. Prod. by CBS-TV, c. 1974. Pub. for amateur stage prodn. by Samuel French, New York, 1975. **Getting Up the Rent** (TV comedy, half hr., 1975). From the "Good Times" series. The Evans family faces eviction from their apartment, and each of them is desperately trying to find a solution to the problem. Prod. by CBS-TV, c. 1974. Pub. for amateur stage prodn. by Samuel French, 1975. **The Slave Brothers** Also known as **The Engineers** (screenplay/teleplay, full length, pre-1985). Written with GENE BO-LANDE. A panoramic adventure story of two brothers, one a house slave, the other a field slave, who escape bondage and follow the Underground Railroad to "freedom" in the North.

MOORE, BILL, Playwright. Based in New York City.

PLAY:
Butchman (drama, 1 act, 1970). A black man seeks vengeance for his son's death from a drug overdose. Unpub. script in the Schomburg Collection.

MOORE, ELVIE A. See WHITNEY, ELVIE.

MOORE, HOWARD, Musical playwright. Apparently based in New York City.

DRAMATIC WORK:
Don't Call Me Man! (musical comedy-drama, full length, 1975). Book, music, and lyrics by Moore. About the troubled relationship between a jazz singer and her man. First prod. at the Billie Holiday Theatre, Brooklyn, NY, July 1975, with jazz singer Betty Carter making her acting debut. Prod. by the Chicago Black Ensemble, around 1976, with M. Samantha Spencer as the jazz singer and Charles Edward Bell as her lover; dir. by George Barletta.

MORGAN, ELMO, Playwright. Associated in 1975 with the Afro-American Studies Program at Brown Univ., Providence, RI.

PLAY:
Two Wings (6 episodes, 1975). Written with PHYLLIS HALL and DELORES McKNIGHT. Performed as a series of episodes for one semester, as an adjunct to the course "Images and Myths of African People in New World Consciousness," for Brown Univ.'s Afro-American Studies Program, Feb.-May 1975.

MORGENSTERN, ARLENE. See DARRELLE, DHARVI.

MORRIS, GARRETT (1937–   ), Actor, singer-musician, playwright; the first black comedian on "Saturday Night Live." Born in New Orleans. Resides in New York City. Off-Bway appearances include *The Bible Salesman* (1961), *Porgy and Bess* (1964), *Hallelujah Baby* (1967), *Slave Ship* (1969), *Ain't Supposed to Die a Natural Death* (1971), and *What the Winesellers Buy* (1973).

PLAYS:
The Secret Place (1975). Prod. by the Frederick Douglass Creative Arts Center New York, in association with La Mama E.T.C., 1975, featuring the author in the cast. Unpub. script in the Hatch-Billops Collection. **Patchwork** (1970s).

MORRISON, CARL F., JR. See ABUDU, MUNGU KIMYA.

MORRISON, TONI (1931–   ), Critically acclaimed novelist, author, editor, and playwright. Currently living in New York City. Educated at Howard Univ. (B.A., 1953) and Cornell Univ. (M.A., 1955). Novels include *The Bluest Eye* (1970), *Sula* (1974), *Song of Solomon* (1977), and *Tar Baby* (1981). Editor at Random House, 1965–present. Former prof. at Texas Southern Univ. and Howard Univ. Member of NEA. *Address:* c/o Lynn Nesbitt, International Creative Management (ICM), 40 W. 57th St., New York, NY 10019.

DRAMATIC WORKS:
New Orleans (musical, full length, c. 1982). Coauthor, with *Donald McKale (internationally famous black director-choreographer). Book and orig. music by Morrison. About the fabled black red-light district in New Orleans; apparently focuses on the conflict between the prostitutes and the respectable elements of the community. Sched. for Bway prodn. in Fall 1982, with direction and choreography by McKale and costumes by Geoffrey Holder. No record of the actual prodn. **Dreaming Emmett** (drama, full length, 1986). Written in celebration of the first national observance of Martin Luther King, Jr.'s, birthday; loosely based on the Emmett Till murder in Mississippi in 1955. Premiered at the Marketplace Theatre, Albany, NY, Feb. 1986.

MOSEKA, AMINATA. See LINCOLN, ABBEY.

MOSES, GILBERT (1942–   ), Director, actor, guitarist, and songwriter. One of the most sought-after black directors in New York City. Born in Cleveland, OH, where he began acting at the Karamu Theatre at age nine. Studied

French and German at Oberlin Coll., 1960–63, followed by a short period in France at the Sorbonne; attended NYU, 1966; and studied acting and playwriting with Lloyd Richards, Kristin Linlater, and Paul Sills. Cofounder and artistic director of the Free Southern Theatre, which flourished in Mississippi and Louisiana, 1963–69, while pursuing an acting and directing career in New York City. Performed in *The Good Soldier Schweik* (1963). Directed a number of Off-Broadway and Broadway plays, including *Slave Ship* (1969), for which he also cowrote the music, *Ain't Supposed to Die a Natural Death* (1971), *Charlie Was Here and Now He's Gone* (1971), *The Duplex* (1972), and *The Taking of Miss Janie* (1975). Directed the film *Willie Dynamite* (1973), for which he also wrote music and lyrics and scored several songs. Has also directed for San Francisco Opera, Arena Stage in Washington, DC, American Conservatory Theatre in San Francisco, Boston Theatre Co., and Henry St. Playhouse/New Federal Theatre. Editor (with TOM DENT and Richard Schechner) of *The Free Southern Theater by the Free Southern Theater* (1969), "A Documentary of the South's Radical Black Theatre with Journals, Letters, Poetry and Essays Written by those Who Built It" [subtitle], which also includes the script of his play **Roots.** Member of the DGA. Winner of two Obie awards, one for *Slave Ship,* 1969, and the other for *The Taking of Miss Janie,* 1975; a Tony nomination and a Drama Desk Award, for *Ain't Supposed to Die a Natural Death,* 1972; and an AUDELCO Theatre Recognition Award, 1975.

PLAY:

Roots (absurdist drama, 1 long act, 1966). A parable of the black man in America. An old "Negro couple" (played by young actors), living in extreme poverty and dressed in rags from head to foot, quarrel about their present misery, their unfulfilled past hopes and dreams, and especially why they have nothing and have not produced anything (including children). It is revealed in symbolic terms that the roots of their present physical, mental, emotional, and economic condition lie deeply imbedded in racism, prejudice, and the psychological castration, impotence, and "brainwashing" resulting from the experience of being black in America. First prod. by FST, New Orleans, Sept. 1966. Prod. by the Afro-American Studio in New York, Oct. 1969. Pub. in *The Free Southern Theater by the Free Southern Theater* (Dent, Schechner, & Moses, 1969). **Slave Ship** ("Historical Pageant" [subtitle], full length [1 long act], 1967). By AMIRI BARAKA. Incidental music by Moses and Archie Shepp.

MOSS, CARLTON (1910–   ), Film writer, producer, consultant, and critic; former actor, radio scriptwriter, and director of the WPA Federal Theatre. Born in Newark, NJ. Received his early education in North Carolina. Later graduated from Morgan (State) Coll. in Baltimore during the late 1920s, where he participated in dramatics under the tutelage of early playwright †Randolph Edmonds. Went to New York to pursue a career as an actor and writer. In 1931 one of his scripts was prod. by the Harlem Players. For a two-year period, 1932–33, wrote "scores of radio plays" for NBC, under such titles as *Careless Love, Folks from Dixie,* and *Noah.* Wrote and acted in a radio series called "Community Forum," which was broadcast over Station WEVD. Acted in a number of plays and appeared in some of the early films of †Oscar Micheaux. In 1934 he was a Harlem YMCA drama director, under a federal rehabilitation program launched by Roosevelt's New Deal. When the WPA Federal Theatre was begun in New York in 1935, he was one of the principal black consultants, and was later appointed a director of the Harlem Unit when white directors Orson Welles and John Houseman were replaced by three blacks. "Moss was the 'community man' who went to black lodges and churches to try to win audiences for the unit. His goal was to create an environment where the community felt comfortable and would consider the theatre their own."—*Free, Adult and Uncensored* (O'Connor & Brown, 1978), p. 198. While with the Federal Theatre, 1935–39, Moss wrote and directed an original show for the Philadelphia Negro Unit, apparently based on his own popular booklet, *Negro Music Past and Present,* also written for the WPA. During World War II, he served with the Information and Education Div. of the War Dept., where he was a consultant, information specialist, and writer of stage shows and documentary films for the armed forces. In 1943 he was given a place on the Schomburg Collection's Honor Roll for Race Relations because of the success of his film *The Negro Soldier,* which was considered one of the best documentaries on the black soldier produced during the war. Since World War II, he has written and produced a number of short film biographies of famous black Americans, some produced by his own firm, Artesan Productions, and others by Fisk Univ. in Nashville. Since the 1960s, he has written a number of articles and film criticisms which have been published in *Freedomways* and several catalogs. For several years, Moss was resident writer, producer, and cinema instructor at Fisk Univ., where he helped to establish the first film program at a black school. He has also worked as a lecturer in comparative culture at the Univ. of California/Irvine.

REPRESENTATIVE DRAMATIC WORKS WRITTEN AND PRODUCED SINCE 1950:

Frederick Douglass: The House on Cedar Hill // Also called by subtitle alone (biographical film, 17 min., 1953). Biography of Frederick Douglass, one of America's black leaders in the struggle against slavery, presented through narration from Douglass's writings, historical documents, photographs, drawings, and mementos found in Douglass's house in Washington, DC.; also dir. by Moss. Musical score based on American Negro folk songs. Available on 16 mm. film or video cassette tapes from Contemporary/McGraw-Hill Films, New York, or from Pyramid Films, Santa Monica, CA.

George Washington Carver (biographical film, 12 min., 1959). Depicts events in the early life of Carver, including his struggle to achieve an education and his experiments at Tuskegee Inst. to develop products from the peanut. Apparently prod. by Artesan Productions; dir. by Moss. Available on 16 mm. film or video cassette tapes from Pyramid Films, Santa Monica, CA.

Paul Lawrence Dunbar (biographical film, 22 min., pre-1972). Short film biography of America's first black poet to achieve international recognition, presented through narration, dramatization, poetry, and story readings. Prod. and dir. by the author at Fisk Univ., Nashville, TN. Available on 16 mm. film or video cassette tapes from Pyramid Films, Santa Monica. CA.

[NOTE: In addition to the above films, the following documentary films by Moss are also available on 16 mm. film or video cassette tape from Pyramid Films, Santa Monica, CA: *Two Centuries of Black American Art, All the World's a Stage,* and *Gift of the Black Folks.*]

OTHER DRAMATIC WORKS WRITTEN AND PRODUCED PRIOR TO 1950:
Sacrifice (1 act, 1931). Coauthor, with *Richard Huey. Prod. by the Harlem Players, at the 135th St. Lib. Theatre, New York, Feb. 2–13, 1931. **Careless Love, Folks from Dixie, Noah,** and "scores" of radio plays for NBC, 1932–33. **Prelude in Swing** (theatrical collage, full length, 1939). Text by Moss. Choreography and direction by *Malvena Fried. **Salute to Negro Troops** (patriotic stage show, 1942). **The Negro Soldier** (doc. film, 1943). **Team Work** (short doc. film, 1944). A sequel to the author's **The Negro Soldier** (above).

MOSS, GRANT, JR., Author and playwright. Attended Tillotson Coll. in Austin, TX, where he first began writing. Taught English at Grambling Coll. in Louisiana during the 1950s; while there, one of his short stories was published by the *New Yorker* (c. 1959). More recently, an article on Bessie Smith was published in *Essence* magazine, where it was also reported that Moss now lives and writes in Winchester, TN.

PLAY:
Death Come Creeping in the Room (1 act, 1951). Won first place in the 1950–51 playwriting contest of the Southern Assn. of Dramatic and Speech Arts (SADSA), held at Alabama State Coll., Montgomery, May 3, 1951.

MOTOJICHO. See WHITFIELD, VANTILE.

MUTIMA, NIAMANI, Playwright. Associated with the Hansberry Arts Workshop in Princeton, NJ, 1972–73.

PLAYS:
That's All (drama, 1 act, 1972). Concerns the dilemma of a young black woman in choosing between her social life and her career. Prod. by the Hansberry Arts Workshop, 1972. **The Revolution Has Been Cancelled** (drama, 1 act, 1973). May be a revision of the above play. A young black female artist decides to devote herself to the pursuit of a career. Prod. by the Hansberry Arts Workshop, 1973.

N

NAJEE-ULLAH, MANSOOR, Playwright. Associated with the Frank Silvera Writers' Workshop in New York City. *Address:* 175 W. 90th St., New York, NY 10024.

PLAY:
Quiet Desperation (1977). Public reading by FSWW, Nov. 7, 1977. Unpub. script in FSWW Archives/Schomburg Collection.

NASH, JOHNNY (1940–   ), Singer, actor, composer, and screenwriter. Starred in the motion picture *Take a Giant Step* (1961). Recorded songs for Epic, Picwick, Repeat, ABC, and JAD. Composed "What Kind of Love Is This?," "Let Me Cry," and "Lonesome Romeo."

DRAMATIC WORK:
Love Is Not a Game (screenplay, pre-1976).

NAYO (Barbara Malcomb), Poet-playwright. Associated with the Free Southern Theatre (FST) in New Orleans, LA. The author of a volume of poetry, *I Want Me a Home* (1969). Other poems have been included in *New Black Voices* (Chapman, 1972) and *Black Culture* (Simmons & Hutchinson, 1972).

PLAY:
Fourth Generation (drama, 1969). Prod. by FST, Summer 1969.

NEAL, LARRY (Lawrence P. Neal) (1937–1981), Poet, critic, editor, and major literary spokesman of the Black Arts movement of the 1960s. Born in Atlanta, GA; reared in Philadelphia, PA. Died of a heart attack in Hamilton, New York. Educated at Lincoln Univ./Pennsylvania (B.A., 1961) and the Univ. of Pennsylvania (M.A., 1963). Teacher, Drexel Inst. of Technology, 1963–64. Arts editor of *Liberator* magazine, 1964–65. Founder, with AMIRI BARAKA, of the Black Arts Repertory Theatre in New York, 1965; also organized the First

Harlem Black Arts Festival the same year. Instr. of English, CCNY, 1968–69. Writer-in-residence, Wesleyan Univ., 1969–70; also program director, the Langston Hughes House of Kuumba, the same years. Writer-in-residence, Case Western Reserve Univ., 1971. Taught at Yale Univ., 1971–74, and Williams Coll., 1975–76. Exec. director, District of Columbia Commission on Arts and Humanities, 1980s. Has been an editor of *The Cricket,* the *Journal of Black Poetry,* and *Pride* magazine. His poetry and literary and social criticism have appeared in numerous anthologies of black writers, and in such periodicals as *Soulbook, Black Dialogue, Negro Digest, Black World, Ebony, Black Scholar, The Drama Review,* the *New York Times,* and *Freedomways.* Coeditor, with Baraka (then LeRoi Jones) of *Black Fire* (1968). Author of *Black Boogaloo* (poetry, 1968), *Hoodoo Hollerin' Beebop Ghosts* (poetry, 1974), and *New Space: Critical Essays on American Culture* (1976). Memberships include Coordinating Council of Literary Magazines, New York State Council on Arts, Academy of American Poets, Metropolitan Museum of Art, the Gordy Foundation, the Frank Silvera Writers' Workshop, Poets and Writers. Recipient of literary prizes from Lincoln Univ., 1960 and 1961; Guggenheim Fellowship, 1970; Yale Univ. Fellow, 1970–75; Faculty Grant, Williams Coll., 1975.

PLAYS:
The Glorious Monster in the Bell of the Horn (poetic drama, full length, 1976). Focuses on the dreams and aspirations of a group of black artists and writers on the day before the atomic bomb is dropped on Hiroshima. Public reading by FSWW, at the Harlem Cultural Council, New York, May 1976. Prod. by the New Federal Theatre, New York, July 6, 1979, for 12 perfs.; dir. by GLENDA DICKERSON. With music by *Max Roach. Unpub. script in the Hatch-Billops Collection.

In an Upstate Motel (crime drama, full length, 1981). Deals with two criminals on the run from a big city mob, who hide out "in an upstate motel." Presumably developed in the FSWW, and had not been fully revised prior to the author's death. Prod. post-humously by the Negro Ensemble Co., New York, April 4–May 3, 1981, for 45 perfs.; dir. by PAUL CARTER HARRISON. With Phylicia Ayers-Allen, Carl Gordon, Donna Bailey, and Charles Henry Patterson. Unpub. script and tape recording in the FSWW Archives/Schomburg Collection.

NELSON, MARCUS, Black theatre director and playwright. Executive director of the New Concept Theatre in Chicago, now quiescent.

PLAYS:
The Essence of Pathos (drama, 1975). About Richard Wright, the novelist, short-story writer, and playwright, who in his final years lived as an expatriot in France. Prod. by the New Concept Theatre, 1975. **Temperance** (1970s). Presumably prod. by the New Concept Theatre, 1970s.

NELSON, NATALIE, Playwright.

PLAYS:
Things That Happen to Us and **More Things That Happen to Us** (children's plays, each in 4 scenes, 1970). Companion volumes, providing instruction, in dramatic form,

for elementary school children on how to cope with drug pushers. Pub. by New Dimensions, New York, 1970.

NOBLE, GIL (Gilbert E. Noble) (1932–   ), Broadcaster, producer, and TV scriptwriter, associated with the American Broadcasting Corp. (ABC) since 1971. His broadcasting credits with ABC include "Weekend News," "Eyewitness News," and producer and host of "Like It Is."

DRAMATIC WORKS:
(All TV specials, prod. by ABC around 1976.) **El Hajj Malik: El Shabazz. Paul Robeson: The Tallest Tree. The Life and Times of Frederick Douglass.**

nSABE, NIA, Poet-playwright and alumna of the Sonia Sanchez Writers Workshop, held at the Countee Cullen Lib. in Harlem, 1970–71.

PLAY:
Moma Don't Know What Love Is (drama, 1 act, 1971). An unmarried, pregnant black girl is confronted by her mother, who has had the same experience and wishes to protect her daughter from what she went through. Pub. in *Three Hundred and Sixty Degrees of Blackness Comin at You* (Sanchez, 1971).

NWANGWA, SHIRLEY BACON (1944–   ), Health educator and filmmaker. Born in Christian Co., KY. Based in Roanoke Rapids and Halifax, NC. Received the B.A. in elementary education from Lane Coll., Jackson, TN, 1966, and the M.S. in public health and community organization from the Univ. of North Carolina/Chapel Hill, 1970. Served in the Peace Corps in Jamaica, 1966–68. Has also lived in Nigeria, as the former wife of a Nigerian educator. Employed since 1983 by the Halifax Co. Health Dept., Halifax, NC, where she is directly involved with problems of teenage pregnancy. *Address:* 1207 Hurley St., Roanoke Rapids, NC 27870.

DRAMATIC WORK:
The Eye Can Story (short doc. film, 30 min., 1986). Story line by Nwangwa, who also served as executive producer. Described by the *Daily Herald* (Roanoke Rapids, NC, April 17, 1987, p. 3) as "a film designed to promote self-esteem in teenagers and discourage early sexual involvement." Concerns "a disadvantaged teenage girl in rural North Carolina who overcomes pressure for sexual involvement as she strives to become an engineer. The . . . title is taken from a simple visual aid used by Nwangwa—a paper covered can to which a large paper eye is affixed."—Ibid. The "Eye Can" is used as a device throughout the film to remind the teenager of her goals, to help her resist peer pressure toward early sexual activity, and to encourage her to overcome her economic disadvantages. The film was financed through a $60,000 grant (the proposal written by Nwangwa) from the Carolina Dept. of Human Resources. Filmed by Take One Productions of Raleigh, NC, at various locations in Halifax Co. and on the campus of Elizabeth City State Univ., Spring 1986, featuring Shirley Askew of Ahoskie, NC, as the young girl. Premiered in April 1987 at Weldon H.S. in Weldon, NC, under the sponsorship of

Northeastern North Carolina Tomorrow, the North Carolina Dept. of Human Resources, the Halifax Co. Health Dept., and Take One Productions. Film is currently being shown in the public schools of North Carolina and other states. Available for purchase through Nwangwa at the above address.

O

OAKLEY, G. WILLIAM, Playwright and director. Based in New York City.

DRAMATIC WORK:
Basin Street Orig. title: **Storyville** (musical, 2 acts, pre-1983). Book coauthored with Michael Hulett, who also wrote the lyrics. Music by Turk Thom Bridwell. Jazz-blues musical, set in the Storyville district of New Orleans in 1917. Prod. under its present title by the New Federal Theatre, New York, Sept. 8–25, 1983; dir. by Oakley. Unpub. script entitled **Storyville** in the Hatch-Billops Collection.

O'NEAL, JOHN (1940–   ), Theatrical director, civil rights organizer, playwright, poet, and essayist. Born in Mount City, IL. Currently residing in New Orleans, LA. Educated at Southern Illinois Univ. (B.A., 1962). Married; father of two children. Former field secretary, SNCC, 1962–65. Field program director, Commission for Racial Justice, United Church of Christ, 1966–68. Founder and producing director, Free Southern Theatre (FST), based in New Orleans, 1963–c. 1965. Contributing author to *Black World Magazine* and coeditor of *The Free Southern Theatre by the Free Southern Theatre* (1969). *Address:* 1307 Barracks St., New Orleans, LA 70115.

PLAYS AND DRAMATIC WORKS:
Black Power, Green Power, Red in the Eye (melodrama, 1972). A close look at the sorry situation that exists in the games played on black folk by some of the current crop of black politicians.

Where Is the Blood of Your Fathers (stage doc., 1973). Written by the FST Workshop. Edited by O'Neal and *Ben Spillman. An examination of the role that black people played in the pre–Civil War South. The question is: Did black folk sit idly by waiting for Massa Lincoln to set them free? Prod. by FST, Summer 1973, for 18 perfs. Prod. at Memphis State Univ., Winter 1974; and at Florida A. & M. Univ., Spring 1975.

Hurricane Season (drama, 1973). Examination of the impact of the unprincipled use of computer technology on the life and family of a New Orleans black dock worker.

Prod. by the FST, 1973, for 19 perfs. Prod. by Buffalo Theatre, Buffalo, NY, Winter 1974.

Going Against the Tide (melodrama, 1974). The story of the conflict between a conservative housing project mother and her revolution-minded daughter. Suggested by but not adapt. from *Black Cycle* by MARTIE EVANS-CHARLES. Prod. by the Free Southern Theatre, New Orleans, Summer 1974, for 18 perfs.

When the Opportunity Scratches, Itch It! (satire, 1974–75). An indictment of opportunism among certain elements of the black bourgeoisie. Prod. by the FST, 1974–75, for approximately 40 perfs.

O'NEAL, REGINA (Regina Solomon O'Neal) (Reggie), Author, teacher, TV scriptwriter, producer, and broadcaster. Born in Detroit, MI. Educated at Wayne State Univ. (B.A.; M.A., 1965). Widow; mother of two children. Teacher and reading coordinator in the Detroit Public Schools; workshop director at the Edward MacDowell School, Milwaukee, WI. Coproducer-director, African Fables, Wil-Cas Records. Writer-producer, Wayne State Univ. Memberships include National Association of Educational Broadcasters (NAEB), American Women in Radio and Television, NAACP, and Alpha Kappa Alpha Sorority. Recipient of Emmy Award from the Detroit Chapter of NATAS, 1979, and NAEB Leadership Award in Minority Telecommunications, 1979. *Address*: Wayne State University, 70 West Palmer, Detroit, MI 48202.

COLLECTION:
AND THEN THE HARVEST: Three Television Plays. Broadside Press, Detroit, 1974. Contains **Walk a Tight Rope** (1974), **And Then the Harvest** (1974), **Night Watch** (1974).

PLAYS:
Walk a Tight Rope (drama, 1974). Deals with the conflicts and frustrations of a young teacher who is the first black assigned to teach in an all-white midwestern school during the early 1960s. Pub. in the author's collection *AND THEN THE HARVEST: Three Television Plays*.

And Then the Harvest (drama, 1 act [30 min.], 1974). Explores the causes of the race riots of the late 1960s by focusing on the experiences of one black family which has moved from the rural South to a northern ghetto. Pub. in the author's collection *AND THEN THE HARVEST: Three Television Plays*.

Night Watch (drama, 1974). Explores the shallow nature of white liberalism when put to an actual test involving a black. Pub. in the author's collection *AND THEN THE HARVEST: Three Television Plays*.

OSBORNE, PEGGY ADAMS, Playwright.

PLAY:
The Meeting (educational play, 1 act, 1968). Designed to instruct school children from the sixth grade up about America's black heritage, with the entire class involved in the prodn. Originally issued in a boxed package containing a hardcover teacher's edition with prodn. guide, stage settings, costume guide, and character portraits of such well-known black historical and contemporary personages as Sidney Poitier, Jean Baptiste

Point Du Sable, and Frederick Douglass. Pub. by Afro-American Publishing Co., Chicago, 1968.

OVERSTREET, JOE (Joseph) (1934–   ), Painter and playwright. Born in Conehatta, MS. Grew up and studied painting in the San Francisco Bay area. Moved to New York City's Lower East Side in 1958, where he remained to pursue his career as a painter and developed a growing concern for black American political and social struggles. Developed friendships with a number of black musicians and writers. Wrote several plays during the early 1960s, under the influence of AMIRI BARAKA, while working with Baraka's Black Arts Repertory Theatre/School in Harlem. His paintings have been exhibited at a number of galleries in New York City.

PLAY:
(Only one of several has been located.) **Snakeshiiiit** (tragicomic pageant, 3 acts, 1975). Written with CORRINE JENNINGS and STEVE CANNON. Public reading by the New Federal Theatre, New York, 1975. Unpub. script in the Hatch-Billops Collection.

OWA (1944–   ), Playwright and photojournalist. Born in New York City. Studied playwriting with the Negro Ensemble Co.'s (NEC's) Playwrights Workshop. The first Rockefeller writer-in-residence with the Frank Silvera Writers' Workshop (FSWW) in New York City. A disciple of OYAMO (Charles Gordon). Has worked in East Africa and Europe as a photojournalist. His plays have been produced by La Mama E.T.C., Urban Arts Corps, Brooklyn Coll., CUNY, Hudson Valley Freedom Theatre, Bijou Theatre, and Eugene O'Neill National Playwrights Conf. *Address:* 616 Lyons, Irvington, NJ 07111. *Agent:* Weldon Irvine, P.O. Box 36, St. Albans, NY 11412.

GROUP OF RELATED PLAYS:
"THE SOLEDAD TETRAD" (group of four plays, 1975). Includes Part I: ‡**A Short Piece for a Naked Tale;** Part II: ‡**Transitions for a Mime Poem;** Part III (title uncertain): ‡**That All Depends on How the Drop Falls,** or **Rejections;** Part IV (title uncertain): **The Bloodrite,** or ‡**In Between the Coming or Going.** Prod. by the NEC Playwrights Workshop, New York, Spring 1975. [Titles marked with a double obelisk (‡) were a part of the program.]

REPRESENTATIVE PLAYS:
Transitions for a Mime Poem (1975). Subtitled "A Study in Transcendence." Part II of the author's **"THE SOLEDAD TETRAD"** [see GROUP OF RELATED PLAYS above]. Written as a living memorial to George and Jonathan Jackson and the Soledad Brothers. Prod. by NEC Playwrights Workshop, New York, Spring 1975. Prod. as a staged reading, presumably by FSWW; dir. by Kalima; moderated by TOWNSEND BREWSTER, with GYLAN KAIN and Loretta Greene. Pub. in *Center Stage* (Ostrow, 1983).
The Bloodrite (morality drama, full length, 1977). Part IV of the author's **"THE SOLEDAD TETRAD"** [see GROUP OF RELATED PLAYS above]. Conversation and confrontation between a businessman and an ex-offender on a New York pier. Public

reading by FSWW, Nov. 28, 1977. Also prod. by Eugene O'Neill Theatre Center's National Playwrights Conf.

Heaven Must Be a Very Complicated Place (1982). Concerned with how blacks fared in the 1940s. Prod. at the Billie Holiday Theatre, 1982; dir. by Mikell Pinkney, and featuring Lee Roy Giles, Cheryl Lynn Bruce, Venessa Williams, Avan Littles, Jr., and Greg E. Miller.

OTHER PLAYS AND DRAMATIC WORKS:
Rejections (morality drama, 1 act, 1973). Subtitled "A Study in Development." Listed as Part III of the author's **"THE SOLEDAD TETRAD."** Concerns a confrontation between a black boy and a white man on a park bench that leads to tragedy. **Egwuwu** (2 acts, 1974). Public reading by FSWW, at the Martinique Theatre, New York, Dec. 1974. **A Short Piece for a Naked Tale** (1975). Subtitled "A Study in Chaos." Part I of the author's **"THE SOLEDAD TETRAD"** [see GROUP OF RELATED PLAYS above]. Prod. by NEC, Spring 1975. **That All Depends on How the Drop Falls** (1975). Subtitled "A Study in Direction." Also listed as Part III of the author's **"THE SOLEDAD TETRAD"** [see GROUP OF RELATED PLAYS above]. Prod. by NEC, Spring 1975. **Funnylingus** (1979). Public reading bt FSWW, Oct. 8, 1979. Unpub. script in the FSWW Archives/Schomburg Collection. NOTE: The following plays are all pre-1980: **Concert Grand. Cyklops I.** Prod. at Fordham Univ., New York City. Unpub. script in the FSWW Archives/Schomburg Collection. **The Garden of Eden. Gotta Get Off.** Unpub. script in the FSWW Archives/Schomburg Collection. **Hip Niggas** (tragedy, 1 act). Two young, hip blacks mug an old black woman for three dollars to buy a bottle of wine. **Rascallion.**

OWENS, DAN (Daniel W. Owens) (1948–   ), Poet-playwright, teacher, and theatrical director. Born in Malden, MA. Educated at Bryant and Straton Jr. Coll. (certificate in computer programming, 1968); Boston State Coll. (1968); the Univ. of Massachusetts at Boston (B.A. in English, 1971); Yale Univ. School of Drama (playwriting, 1971–72); and Harvard Univ. School of Education (Ed.M.). Has taught black theatre and playwriting at Boston Univ. and the Univ. of Massachusetts, early 1970s. Resident playwright, New African Co. of Boston, 1969–71; assistant educational director, Store Front Learning Center, Boston, 1969–71; director of playwrights' workshops, National Center of Afro-American Artists, Boston, 1969–73. Coordinator, Columbia Point, MA, Summerthing, 1969; assoc. director, Roxbury, MA, Summerthing, 1971. One of 12 playwrights selected for the Eugene O'Neill Theatre Program, National Playwrights Conf., Waterford, CT, 1973. Produced his own plays in Boston and New Haven, 1969–72. Since 1972 his plays have been produced by the People's Theatre in Cambridge, MA, the Eugene O'Neill Theatre Center, National Playwrights Conf., and by the following groups in New York City: the Afro-American Studio, the Black Theatre Alliance, the Frank Silvera Writers' Workshop (FSWW), the New Federal Theatre (NFT), the Negro Ensemble Company (NEC), the Frederick Douglass Creative Arts Center, and the Richard Allen Center for Culture and Art. In 1972 he was writer for "Brotherlove," Channel 7, Boston. While at the Univ. of Massachussetts, he was assoc. editor of *Viewpoint,* a student publication. His poetry has been published in *Journal of Black Poetry,* and anthologized in *Today's Negro Voices* (Murphy, 1970). Pres. of the Youth Council of the NAACP, Malden-Everett, MA, 1963–65; advisor to the Youth Fellowship of Emmanuel Baptist Church, Malden, 1967; member, Board of Directors, Roxbury Ecumenical Center, 1969. *Address:* c/o Frederick Douglass Creative Arts Center, Inc., 276 W. 43rd St., New York, NY 10036.

PLAYS AND DRAMATIC WORKS:

The Box (symbolic drama, 1 act, 1969). Three young black people are trapped in a box and must learn to understand attitudes that are different from their own. Prod. by the New African Company of Boston, MA, at the Univ. of Illinois, Urbana, 1969.

Nigger, Nigger, Who's the Bad Nigger (drama, 1 act, 1969). Story of two brothers, one dark and one fair, and the color prejudices among blacks. Prod. by the New African Co., at the National Center of Afro-American Artists, Boston, Summer 1969.

Clean (tragedy, 1 act, 1969). The admiration of a young man for a black pimp leads to the young man's death. Prod. by the New African Co., Boston, 1969.

Joined (melodrama, 1 act, 1970). The conflict of a black assassin whose job is to kill a white liberal. Prod. by the People's Theatre, Cambridge, MA, 1970.

Imitatin' Us, Imitatin' Us, Imitatin' Death (absurdist drama, 1 act, 1970). Deals with the conflicts and contradictions within the black revolutionary movement. Prod. by the New African Co., at the Boston Centre for the Arts, opening Sept. 30, 1971.

Bus Play (drama, 1 act, 1972). Five black women compete for one supervisory position in a hospital. Prod. at the Summerthing, Boston, 1972.

Misunderstanding (drama, 1 act, 1972). The conflict that arises between a black man and his girlfriend because she does not share his dreams. Prod. by the National Center of Afro-American Artists, Roxbury, MA, 1972.

Where Are They? (drama, 2 acts, 1972). Asks the question, What has happened to the young black revolutionists of the 1960s? Prod. by the black drama students at Yale Univ., New Haven, CT, 1972.

Refusal (drama, 1 act, 1973). Asks the question, Who is the black writer writing for— black people or white critics? Prod. by the National Center of Afro-American Artists, Roxbury, MA, 1973.

Emily T // Title also cited as **Emily Tillington** (drama, 1 act, 1973). A black woman examines her life and tries to come to grips with her identity. First prod. at Emerson Coll., Boston, 1973. Prod. by the Frederick Douglass Creative Arts Center, New York, 1980s; dir. by Kimaki Baraka.

What Reason Could I Give (musical drama, 3 acts, 1973). Concerns the problems of a black writer who is unable either to create or to experience love. Written for and presumably prod. by the Eugene O'Neill National Playwrights Conf., Waterford, CT, 1973.

Bargainin' Thing (drama, 3 acts, 1975). Written for and presumably first prod. by the Eugene O'Neill National Playwrights Conf., 1973. Public reading by FSWW, opening April 1976; dir. by Harold Scott. Unpub. script and tape recording in the FSWW Archives/ Schomburg Collection.

Acife and Pendabis // Also known as **Noirhommes** (which was its orig. subtitle) (drama, 3 acts, 1974). According to Peter Bailey, "The play dealt with a young West Indian dude whose rejections of his people's tradition brought about his downfall."— *Black World,* April 1975, pp. 21, 25. Prod. by the Afro-American Studio, New York, opening Nov. 21, 1974; dir. by ERNIE McCLINTOCK. Also presented at the Black Theatre Alliance annual festival, New York, 1974.

One Shadow Behind (poetic drama, 2 acts, 1974). A struggle among three sensitive and talented people (two men and a woman) for self-expression, until one of them dies. Prod. by the People's Theatre of Cambridge, MA, 1974.

Debts (drama, 1975). Deals with the problems and consequences of past due debts. Prod. by the Eugene O'Neill Theatre Center, National Playwrights Conf., at the Amphitheatre (Outdoors), Waterford, CT, opening July 29, 1975, for 2 perfs.; dir. by Harold Scott.

The Michigan (comedy, full length, 1979). The title is a gambling term that refers to a phony wad of money, consisting of blank paper on the inside and large bills on the outside. The play concerns a con man who is trying to find the one big scam that will make him rich. Prod. Off-Bway by NEC, Nov. 16–Dec. 9, 1979, for 22 perfs.; dir. by Dean Irby. With DOUGLAS TURNER WARD and Hattie Winston.

Lagrima Del Diablo ("The Devil's Tear" [subtitle] (sociopolitical fantasy, two parts, 1980). "Confrontation between a guerrilla leader and an archbishop who is his prisoner."—*The Best Plays of 1979–1980*, p. 438. Prod. Off-Bway by NEC, Jan 10–Feb. 3, 1980, for 30 perfs.; dir. by Richard Gant. With Leon Morenzie, Graham Brown, ADOLPH CAESAR, Barbara Montgomery, Chuck Patterson, Charles Brown, and Zackie Taylor.

Forever My Darlin' (play with music, 1984). Music by Chapman Roberts. According to *Black Masks,* Dec. 1984, p. 2, "This humour-laced play with music shows the effect of the suicide of Rhythm and Blues star, Johnny Ace, on an adolescent girl singer who is obsessed with fantasies of fame." Prod. by the Richard Allen Center for Culture and Art, New York, Dec. 13, 1984–Jan. 6, 1985; dir. by Duane Jones. Featuring Maria E. Ellis, Connie Fredericks, Carolyn Lynn Maillard, Rome Neal, and Pamela Tyson.

The Game (1986). Public reading at Roger Furman's New Heritage Theatre (NHT), New York, May 10, 1986. Full prodn. by NHT, beginning June 18, 1986.

OYAMO (Charles F. Gordon) (Name usually appears as Oyamo) (1943–   ), Playwright and author. Born in Lorain, OH. Educated at the Coll. of New Rochelle, School of New Resources (B.A., 1979) and Yale Univ. School of Drama (M.F.A. in playwriting, 1981). Also studied at Miami Univ., Oxford, OH (American studies, 1963–65); U.S. Naval Reserve (journalism, 1966); NYU, Washington Square Coll. (journalism, 1967–68); Harlem Youth Speaks/First Light Video Inst. (educational/industrial videotape technology and prodn., 1960s); the Univ. of the Streets, New York City, 1967); and Brooklyn Coll., Theatre Lighting Program (lighting and stage design, 1968). Gained theatrical experience with the New Lafayette Theatre (NLT) as a member of the Black Theatre Workshop, asst. technical director, playwright, and contributor to *Black Theatre* magazine, 1967–70. Founder, the Black Magicians, a theatre company, 1970. Asst. stage manager, American Place Theatre, 1970; master electrician, Negro Ensemble Co. (NEC), 1971; playwright-in-residence, Afro-American Cultural Center, Buffalo, NY (taught playwrights workshop), 1972; director, Black Theatre Workshop, CCNY, 1973; scriptreader, New York Shakespeare Festival Public Theatre, 1973; director, Street Theatre, Eastern Correctional Inst., Napanoch, NY, 1975–76; instr., creative writing workshop, Afro-American Cultural Centre, New Haven, CT, 1978; instr., dramatic literature and theatre studies, Coll. of New Rochelle, School of New Resources, 1979–83; writer-in-residence, Emory Univ., Atlanta (also taught playwriting classes), 1982–83; writer-in-residence, Playwrights' Centre, Minneapolis, MN (counseled young playwrights), 1984. His poetry has been published in *Journal of Black Poetry, New Black Poets* and other anthologies. His poetry, prose, and plays are published in *Hillbilly Liberation* (1976) [see COLLECTION below]. His black children's story, *The Star That Could Not Play* (1973), was published separately by the author. Invited to participate in Eugene O'Neill Playwrights Conf., Waterford, CT, 1972, 1973, 1974, and 1985. Recipient of Rockefeller Foundation Playwright-in-Residence Grant, 1972; Creative Artists Public Service Program (CAPS) grants, 1972, 1975, 1982, and 1985; Guggenheim Fellowship, 1973; Ohio Arts Council Award, 1979; Molly Kazan Award, Yale Univ. School of Drama, 1980; Rockefeller Playwright-in-Residence, Frank Silvera Writers' Workshop (FSWW), 1983–84; McKnight Fellow, Minneapolis, 1984; and NEA Fellowship, 1985. *Address:* 157 W. 120th St., New York, NY 10027. *Agents:* Flora Roberts, Penthouse Sta., 157 W. 57th St., New York, NY 10019. Helen Marie Jones, P.O. Box 251, Morningside Station, New York, NY 10027.

COLLECTION:

HILLBILLY LIBERATION. Collection of plays, essays, and poems. Pub. by OyamO Ujamma, New York, 1976. Contents not analyzed.

REPRESENTATIVE PLAYS AND DRAMATIC WORKS:

Out of Site (agitprop drama, 1 act, 1969). A militant, self-styled black coalition group occupies a land site in Harlem, where they are ostensibly working for the Harlem community to prevent a state office building from being constructed on the site. However, they refuse to let a member of the community enter the site without a pass, dismissing him as a counterrevolutionary and a "typical deaf, dumb and blind nigga." Prod. by Black Troupe, at the New Lafayette Theatre (NLT), New York, 1970. Pub. in *Black Theatre #4*, 1969, pp. 28–31.

His First Step (satire, 2 acts, 1969). Explores the contradictions and conflicts between the college-educated and the ghetto points of view with respect to black liberation. Written in 1969. First presented Jan. 28, 1971, as a work-in-progress by the Negro Ensemble Co. (NEC), at St. Marks Playhouse, New York, for 2 perfs.; dir. by Kris Keiser. Previewed by the New York Shakespeare Festival Public Theatre (NYSF/PT), on a program of four one-act plays under the blanket title *Four for One*, at the Other Stage, May 17, 1972. Prod. in a full production by NYSF/PT, on a program of three one-act plays under blanket title *The Corner*, June 22–July 30, 1972; dir. by Kris Keiser. With Michael Coleman, ILUNGA ADELL, Yoland Karr, and Cornelius Suares. Pub. in *The New Lafayette Theatre Presents* (Bullins, 1974).

Willie Bignigga // Also called **Bignigga** (ritual/comedy, 1 act, 1970). A satire showing that a "nigga," big or small, is still a "nigga." Prod. by the Henry St. Settlement's New Federal Theatre (NFT), New York, 1970, and by the Street Theatre, Inc., New York, 1975.

The Breakout (symbolic drama, 2 acts, 1971). Utilizes the metaphor of a prison without bars, and a variety of character types, to show that "jail is wherever white people run black people's lives."—Pub. script. Whether the jail is sparsely or lavishly furnished (ghetto vs. middle-class blacks) makes no difference; blacks must break out of the system that has become their prison. First prod. at the Eugene O'Neill Theatre Center National Playwrights Conf., Waterford CT, for 2 perfs., opening July 27, 1972. Again prod. by the Manhattan Theatre Club, New York, opening April 27, 1975; dir. by Harold Scott. With Bill Cobbs, Brent Jennings, Terry Alexander, Robert Stocking, and Joe LoGrippo. Pub. in *Black Drama Anthology* (King & Milner, 1972).

The Lovers (street theatre, 1 act, 1970). Described by Kushauri Kupa as "a look at the Black man/woman relationship in two perspectives. First we see it as we would like it to be: Noble Black man standing tall, his Black Queen beside him, regal, proud, the mother of mankind. The second segment reveals us as we seem to be in reality: fighting, cussing each other, disrespectful, . . . singing the blues as it were."—*Black Theatre* #6, 1972, p. 47. Prod. by the Black Troupe of NLT's Drama Workshop, 1970. Performed by the Black Magicians, at the Third World Discotek, Bronx, New York, 1970.

The Thieves (street theatre, 1 act, 1970). Points out the negative side of black capitalism. Prod. by Black Arts/West, Seattle, WA, 1970. Prod. by the Black Magicians Road Co., on tour, 1970–71.

Crazy Nigger (street theatre, 3 acts, 1971). Educates the audience as to who the "crazy niggas" really are. Prod. by the Eugene O'Neill Theatre Center, Aug. 10, 1973. Prod. by the Street Theatre, Inc., at the Eastern Correction Facility Drama Workshop, New York, May 1975.

The Barbarians (street theatre, 2 acts, 1972). Teaches who the barbarians of this society are. Public reading by the Frank Silvera Writers' Workshop (FSWW), at the Martinique Theatre, New York, Dec. 1975. Unpub. script in the FSWW Archives/Schomburg Collection.

The Juice Problem ("An Erotic Love Chartune" [subtitle], 3 acts, 1975). About "doing what one has to do" in order to survive/succeed/"get over." Prod. by the Eugene O'Neill Theatre Center, National Playwrights Conf., at the Barn El (indoors), opening July 26, 1974, for 2 perfs.; dir. by Ed Hastings. With Mary Alice, Bill Cobbs, Jay Van Leer (JUNE VANLEER WILLIAMS), Michele Shay, Caroline Godfrey, and Hannibal Penny. Public reading by FSWW, at the Martinique Theatre, Jan. 1975. Prod. by the Heritage Repertory Co. of Yale Univ., at the Afro-American Cultural Center, New Haven, CT, 1980. Unpub. script in the FSWW Archives/Schomburg Collection.

Blue Journey (1977). A journey into the future. Public reading by FSWW, Jan. 9, 1978, and at NYSF/PT the same year. Staged Reading by Playwrights' Center, Minneapolis, 1984.

Mary Goldstein and the Author (1979). Prod. by Yale Playwrights Project, 1979. Prod. by Frederick Douglass Creative Arts Center, New York, 1979. Prod. by the Alliance Theatre Co. of New Haven, at the Educational Center for the Arts, 1980. Prod. by the Heritage Repertory Co. of Yale Univ., 1980. Unpub. script in the Hatch-Billops Collection.

The Resurrection of Lady Lester (musical, full length, 1980). Poetic mood-song, based on the life of Lester Young. Prod. by the Yale Cabaret Theatre, New Haven, 1980, and by the Yale Repertory Theatre, 1981. Prod. by CBS Cable TV, 1982. Prod. by Manhattan Theatre Club, New York, at the Upstage, Oct. 20–Nov. 22, 1981, for 40 perfs.; dir. by Andre Mtumi. With Cleavon Little as Lester Young. Prod. by Shelby State Community Coll., Memphis, TN, 1983. Prod. by Penumbra Theatre Co., Minneapolis, 1985. Pub. in *New Plays, USA*, 1 (1982).

Distraughter and the Grand Panda Scanda (musical, 1983). Concerns the loss of spirituality and the attempt to regain it. Prod. by Theatre Emory, Emory State Univ., Atlanta, GA, 1983. Staged reading, New Dramatists, New York, 1984.

Fried Chicken and Invisibility (1983). Concerns the illusion of being a black artist in Western culture. Prod. by FSWW, as a workshop production, 1983. Public reading at New Dramatist Noontime Series, 1983; and at Bay Area Playwrights' Festival, San Francisco, 1984.

OTHER PLAYS AND DRAMATIC WORKS:

Fuck Money (street theatre, 1969). **The Last Party** (street theatre, 1969). Prod. by the Black Magicians, at the House of Kuumba, New York, 1971. **The Store** (street theatre, 1969). **The Surveyors** (street theatre, 1969). **Unemployment** (street theatre, 1969). **Upcrusted** (street theatre, 1969). **When Our Spirit Awakens, Then Black Theatre Opens** (street theatre, 4 acts, 1969). Utilizes dancing, drumming, singing and drama to educate the audience as to what black theatre really is. **The Negroes** (street theatre, 1969). Public reading, Black History Week, Univ. of Connecticut, Storrs, 1970. Prod. by the Black Magicians, New York, 1970. Pub. in *Black Troupe* magazine, No. 2, 1970. **Chumpanzee(s)** (street theatre, 1970). Prod. by the Henry St. Settlement's NFT, 1970. Also presented July 1973, presumably as a street theatre prodn. **Never Look a Word in the Face** (ritual, 1 act, 1970). Explores the relationship of the male psyche to the female. **The Revelation** (ritual, 1970). Ethnic collage featuring dancing, drumming, and singing, as well as drama. **Chump Changes** (comedy, 1971). **The Advantages of Dope** (street theatre, 2 acts, 1971; also a screenplay). Prod. at the Afro-American Cultural Center, Buffalo, 1971. Prod. by the U.S. Army Bamberg Players, Bamberg, West Germany, 1972. Adapt. as a screenplay for Teko Productions, New York. **Nine Is One** (drama, 3 acts, 1972; also a screenplay). Deals with the problem of oppression, how to recognize its various facets, and how to cope with it. **The Ravishing Moose** (1972). Written for the National Theatre of the Deaf. **Called Up Fear** (street theatre, 1 act, 1972). Satire of the black experience. Performed 1974. **Kindest of the Finest** (street theatre, 1 act, 1973). Routine pick-up of Harlem blacks by New York City cops in order to meet their nightly quota. **Screamers** (drama, 3 acts, 1973). Pub. reading by FSWW, 1977. Unpub. script in the FSWW Archives/Schomburg Collection. Thesis prodn., SUNY/Binghamton, 1980. **Three Red Falcons** (screenplay, full length, 1973). Commissioned by Sidney Poitier and Harry Belafonte for Verdon-Cedric Productions, 1973. **A Star Is Born Again** (children's play, 1975). Adapt. from the author's story, *The Star That Could Not Play* (1973). Utilizes dialogue, dancing, drumming, and singing. First prod. by the Afro-American Cultural Center, Buffalo, 1975. Again prod. at the Police Athletic League Community Center, New York, 1978. Pub. privately, 1974. **Dangling Popsicles** (TV script, 1976). Sitcom episode for "Watch Your Mouth," WNET-TV, New York, 1976. **The Place of the Spirit Dance** (1980). Prod. by the Afro-American Cultural Center, Yale Univ., 1980. **Freedom Is a Long, Long Sigh** (1983). About a man who is forever learning, but always the hard way, never outgrowing his naivete. **Old Black Joe** (1984). Prod. at Bay Area Playwrights Festival, San Francisco, 1984. **Josh White—An American Folktale** (teleplay, 1985). Staged reading/taping at Eugene O'Neill Playwrights Conf., 1985.

OYEDELE, OBAMOLA, Playwright. Based in New Haven, CT, where he was actively involved in the black theatre activities of his community during the 1970s.

PLAY:

The Struggle Must Advance to a Higher Level. . . . (mock-ceremonial play, 1 act, 1972). Satirizes the screaming of radical slogans and cliché-ridden phrases by the pseudo-revolutionary, and calls for the advancement of the black struggle to a higher level of action. Pub. in *Black Theatre* #6, 1972, pp. 12–13.

P

PALMER, JEREE (Mrs. Adam Wade), Actress-singer-playwright. Based in New York City and Philadelphia, PA.

DRAMATIC WORK:
Shades of Harlem (cabaret musical, full length, 1984). A recreation of the famous Cotton Club. Prod. at the Village Gate Theatre, New York, Aug. 21, 1984–April 20, 1985, for 229 perfs.; dir. by Mical Whitaker. With Jeree Palmer, Branice McKenzie, and Ty Stephens. Prod. by the National Black Touring Circuit, opening in Jan. 1987. **Club Fifty** (cabaret musical, full length, 1986). Coauthor, with her husband *Adam Wade. A celebration of life after age 50. Prod. at the Kopia Dinner Theatre, Philadelphia, Mar. 6–Apr. 27, 1986, dir. by Wade. *Miss Lizzie's Royal Cafe* (cabaret musical, full length, 1986). Coauthor, with Adam Wade. A love story. Prod. at the Kopia Dinner Theatre, Oct. 1986, dir. by Wade.

PANNELL, LYNN K., Playwright. Associated with Theatre Black in New York City.

PLAYS:
It's a Shame (1971). Describes how black men misuse black women "in order to get over." Prod. by Theatre Black at the Bed-Stuy Theatre, Brooklyn, New York, May 1971. **Conversation** (early 1970s).

PARKER, LEONARD R. (1932–   ), Actor, producer, and director. Born in Cleveland, OH. Educated at Cleveland Inst. of Music (B.A. in music and voice, 1951) and Western Reserve Univ. (M.A. in theatre arts, 1956). Gained early experience with Karamu House and the Karamu Theatre, Cleveland, 1946–48, and 1956–58. Currently exec. director of Arts and Culture, Inc., New York. *Address*—Home: 2311 Fifth Ave., New York, NY 10037. Office: Arts & Culture, 79 West 125th St., New York, NY 10027.

DRAMATIC WORKS:
Second Chance (drama, full length, 1979). Dramatizes the lyrics to the song "Love Is Lovelier the Second Time Around." Prod. by Arts & Culture, New York, Fall 1979; dir. by GERTRUDE JEANNETTE. With Lorraine Jordan, Yoland Karr, and Curtis Harry. **Oh, My Mother Passed Away** (drama, full length, 1982). Described by LIONEL MITCHELL as "An afternoon in a Harlem bar," during which "lives unfold and fates are decided. Although there are the usual assortment of drunks, whores, numbers runners, and bankers, this play [rises] above mere stereotypes because of the subtleties that are written as interplay between the characters."—*Amsterdam News* (undated clipping). Prod. by the author and Arts & Culture, Inc., at the Renny Theatre, New York, May 6–23, 1982; dir. by Kirk Kirksey, with additional music by Herbert Jones. With Lucretia Collins, Steve Laws, and Ken Porter. **Skillet** (drama, 1984). Prod. at Aaron Davis Hall, CCNY, 1984.

PARKER, WILLIAM, Playwright. Based in New York City, where he was a participant in the New York Black Writers Conf. in 1971.

COLLECTION/PLAYS:
WILLIAM PARKER'S MINI-PLAYS. Includes five one-act plays, described by the publisher as "drama[s] of Impressionism. . . . Author presents circumstances that deal with the logical and illogical behavior/result of humans caught up in a mad world."—Amuru Press Catalog. Sched. for pub. by Amuru Press, New York, 1974, but apparently never pub.

PATTERSON, CHARLES (1941–   ), Poet-playwright. Born in Fayetteville, NC. Moved to New York at an early age, where he was educated in the public schools. Was associated with AMIRI BARAKA (LeRoi Jones) and his Black Arts Repertory Theatre School (BARTS), which had a short life in Harlem in 1965. His poetry has been published in *Umbra*, a journal of Black poetry, and anthologized in *The New Black Poetry* (Major, 1969). He has also made a recording for the *Umbra* Poets, 1967.

PLAYS:
Black Ice (drama, 1 act, 1965). Concerns an attempt by a group of black nationalists to obtain the freedom of one of their cohorts from prison by using a kidnapped congressman as hostage. Prod. by BARTS in Harlem, 1965. Pub. in *Black Fire* (Jones & Neal, 1965). **Legacy** (drama, 2 acts, 1970). A young black woman, who falls in love with a black nationalist, must deal with the reactions of her middle-class family. Pub. in *Nineteen Necromancers from Now* (Reed, 1970). **The Super** (1 act, 1965). Prod. by BARTS, 1965. The following plays are all pre-1975: **Circle in the Square. The Clowns. The Liberal. Longhair.**

PATTERSON, LINDSAY W., Author, critic, radio/TV show host, screenwriter. Author of numerous books on theatre and films, including *Anthology of the American Negro in the Theatre* (1967), *Black Theatre: A Twentieth Century Collection of the Work of Its Best Playwrights* (1971), *Black Films and Filmmakers: A Comprehensive Anthology from Stereotype to Superhero* (1975), and

A Critical Study of Black Playwrights (1977). *Address:* WPIX-TV, 220 E. 42nd St., New York, NY 10017.

DRAMATIC WORK:
Roper (screenplay, c. 1978).

PAWLEY, THOMAS D., III (1917–   ), Educator, theatrical director, author, and playwright. Born in Jackson, MS. Educated at Virginia State Coll. (A.B. with distinction, 1937), Univ. of Iowa (A.M., 1939; Ph.D., 1949), and the Univ. of Missouri at Columbia (postdoctoral study). Married; the father of two sons. Has held teaching positions at Atlanta Univ. Summer Theatre, 1939, 1940, 1941, and 1943; and Prairie View State Coll., as director of drama, 1939–40. Since 1940 has been a member of the faculty at Lincoln Univ., Lincoln, PA, where he was head of the Dept. of English, Speech, and Theatre, 1958–77; chairman of the Div. of Humanities and Fine Arts, 1967–77; dean of the Coll. of Arts and Sciences, 1977–83; and is currently head of the Dept. of Communications, Distinguished Professor of Speech and Theatre, and writer in residence, 1983–. He has been guest lecturer at numerous colleges and universities throughout the South and Southwest. Coauthor, with William Reardon, of *The Black Teacher and the Dramatic Arts* (1970). His articles on the theatre have appeared in numerous periodicals, including *SADA Encore, Negro College Quarterly, Central States Speech Journal, Player's Magazine, Black World, Encore,* and *Black American Literature Forum;* one of his articles was anthologized in *The Theatre of Black Americans,* vol. 2 (Hill, 1980). His poetry has been published mainly in *Crisis* and *Phylon,* and his book reviews mainly in *Central States Speech Journal* and *Quarterly Journal of Speech.* Professional organizations and appointments include president, NADSA, 1953–55; Advisory Committee, American Educational Theatre Assn. (AETA), 1953–55; Central Committee, American Coll. Theatre Festival (ACTF), 1971–75; Board of Governors, Speech and Theatre Assn. of Missouri, 1975–79; Advisory Screening Committee in Theatre Arts of the Committee on the International Exchange of Persons, 1973–76; Exec. Committee, Black Theatre Program, American Theatre Assn. (ATA), 1972–75; Commission on Theatre Education, ATA, 1977–79; Committee on International Relations, ATA, 1978; vice pres., Mid-western Region, Alpha Phi Alpha Fraternity, 1975–79; president, Speech and Theatre Assn. of Missouri, 1977–78; Board of Directors, American Conf. of Academic Deans, 1979–82; consultant, NEA, 1979, 1980; Theatre Advisory Committee of the Missouri Arts Council, 1979–; participant, Mid-American Assembly on the Future of the Performing Arts, Kansas City, Sept. 13–16, 1979; participant in CEMREL Conf. on Curriculum Development in Aesthetic Education, Aspen, CO, June 10–15, 1979; Exec. Committee, Black Theatre Program, ATA, 1980–83; Board of Directors, Mid-America Arts Alliance, 1980; consultant, Guggenheim Foundation, 1981, 1982; DG, 1983–; Missouri Assn. of Theatre, 1984–; Regional Committee on Special Initiatives, NEA, 1985. Honors and awards include winner, Shields-Howard Creative Writing Award, Virginia State Coll., 1934; Iota Sigma Lambda, Virginia State Coll., 1937; Purple Masque, Univ. of Iowa, 1939; Omicron Delta Kappa, Univ. of Iowa, 1949; Graduate Scholarship, Univ. of Iowa, 1938; Alpha Phi Alpha Graduate Scholarship, 1947–48; National Theatre Conf. Fellowship, 1947–48; winner of First Prize, Jamestown (VA) Corp. Playwriting Contest, 1954, for *Messiah* (1948); elected to Outstanding Educators of America, 1970; Outstanding Teacher Award, Speech and Theatre Assn. of Missouri, 1977; elected to the Coll. of Fellows, ATA, Aug. 1978; NADSA Outstanding Service Award, 1984. *Address*— Home: 1014 Layafette St., Jefferson City, MO 65101. Office: Dept. of Communications, Lincoln University, Jefferson City, MO 65101.

GROUPS OF RELATED PLAYS—Both prior to 1950:

The author's master's thesis plays, all prod. by the Dept. of Theatre Arts at the Univ. of Iowa, Iowa City, April 21, 1939. Copies in the Univ. of Iowa Lib. These include **Jedgement Day** (1938), **Smokey** (1938), and **Freedom in My Soul** (1938).

"EXPERIMENTAL PRODUCTIONS OF A GROUP OF ORIGINAL PLAYS." The author's Ph.D. dissertation, Univ. of Iowa, Iowa City, 1949; copy in the Univ. of Iowa Lib.

PLAYS AND DRAMATIC WORKS WRITTEN, PRODUCED AND/OR PUBLISHED SINCE 1950:

Crispus Attucks // Alternate title (and subtitle): **Son of Liberty** (tragedy, 3 acts [5 scenes], 1947; revised 1976). Examines Attucks' motivation for fighting against the Tories in Boston. First prod. by the Dept. of Speech and Dramatic Arts, at the Univ. of Iowa, March 18–19, 1948. Unpub. manuscript included in the author's Ph.D. dissertation, "EXPERIMENTAL PRODUCTIONS OF A GROUP OF ORIGINAL PLAYS" [see GROUPS OF RELATED PLAYS above]. Revised for the Bicentennial, 1976. WHITNEY LeBLANC also did a film treatment of this play, 1976.

F.F.V. "First Family of Virginia") (drama, full length, 1963). Deals with the problems of mixed marriage, as it affected a black family during the 1920s. First prod. by the Stagecrafters at Lincoln Univ. of Missouri, in a production dir. by author, Nov. 7–9, 1963.

The Tumult and the Shouting (drama, 2 acts, 1969). Described by Hatch (cited below), p. 475, as "the tragedy of a [black] college teacher who dedicates his life to lifting the veil of ignorance" from the children and grandchildren of slaves, only to find himself rejected by the system to which he sacrificed his life. Dedicated to the author's father, himself a teacher. First prod. by the Inst. in Dramatic Arts, Lincoln Univ., Jefferson, MO, for 4 perfs., July 15–18, 1969. Pub. in *Black Theater, U.S.A.* (Hatch & Shine, 1974).

The Eunuchs (comedy, 2 parts, 1977). Satirizes sexual myths about blacks and whites.
The Long Lonesome Ride of Charley Young (1984).

OTHER PLAYS AND DRAMATIC WORKS PRIOR TO 1950:

Jedgement Day (folk comedy, 1 act, 1938). An errant, non-church-going husband, who has failed to heed his minister's dire warning that his bones "will sink into the depths of Hell on judgement day," falls asleep and dreams of that harrowing day. One of three plays written by Pawley for his master's thesis, and first prod. at the Univ. of Iowa, Iowa City, April 21, 1939 [see GROUPS OF RELATED PLAYS above]. Pub. in

The Negro Caravan (Brown, Davis, & Lee, 1941); in an Italian periodical, *Sipario,* during the 1950s, translated by Gerardo Guerrieri, and prod. over several radio stations in northern Italy; in *Humanities Through the Black Experience* (Kotman et al., date unknown). **Smokey** (melodrama, 1 act, 1938). Character study of a black farmhand, formerly an ideal, well-liked worker, who is jailed for murdering a southern white plantation owner, apparently without motivation or regret. His character is contrasted with that of his black cellmate, a more stereotyped happy-go-lucky drifter, who dies with him as they both are shot while trying to escape an angry lynch mob. One of three plays written by Pawley for his master's thesis, and first prod. by the Dept. of Theatre Arts at the Univ. of Iowa, Iowa City, April 21, 1939 [see GROUPS OF RELATED PLAYS above], with the author in the title role. Also prod. by the Atlanta Univ. Summer Theatre, July 1939. **Freedom in My Soul** (drama, 1 act, 1938). One of three plays written by Pawley for his master's thesis at the State Univ. of Iowa, 1939 [see GROUPS OF RELATED PLAYS above]. **Messiah** (historical drama, 8 scenes, 1948). Concerns Nat Turner, the famous leader of a slave insurrection. According to Fannie Ella Frazier Hicklin's Ph.D. dissertation, "The American Negro Playwright, 1920–1964," p. 319, "Mr. Pawley's play gives his conception of the underlying motives and the preparation for the insurrection, as well as the actual incidents of the insurrection and the outcome for Nat Turner." First prod. at the State Univ. of Iowa, July 27–29, 1948. Unpub. script included in the author's Ph.D. dissertation, "EXPERIMENTAL PRODUCTIONS OF A GROUP OF ORIGINAL PLAYS" [see GROUPS OF RELATED PLAYS above]. Won first prize of $1,000 in a play contest sponsored by the Jamestown Corp., Williamsburg, VA, Dec. 1954. **Zebedee** (comedy, full length, 1949). **Postlude to Guns** (drama, 1940s). A black hero of World War I returns home to find that he is still wanted for homicide.

PENDARVIS, CHINA CLARK. See CLARK, CHINA.

PENNY, ROB (formerly Oba Kilonfe), Poet, playwright, and educator. Born in Opelika, AL; raised in Pittsburgh's Hill District, where he completed high school. Currently assoc. prof. of Black Studies, Univ. of Pittsburgh, where he has been teaching since 1969, from 1978–84 was chairperson, and where he is also playwright-in-residence of the Kuntu Repertory Theatre, 1975–present. Married; three sons. The author of more than 40 plays. His poetry has also been published in a number of anthologies, including *The Poetry of Black America* (Adoff, 1973), *A Rock Against the Wind* (Patterson, 1973), and *Love from Black Men to Black Women* (Barnes, 1976). *Address*—Home: 1845 Bedford Ave., Pittsburgh, PA 15219. Office: Dept. of Black Community Education and Development, University of Pittsburgh, Forbes Quadrangle, 230 S. Bouquet St., Pittsburgh, PA 15260.

REPRESENTATIVE PLAYS AND DRAMATIC WORKS:
Deeds of Blackness and **Dance of the Blues Dead** (2 one-act plays, 1967). Prod. on double bill by the Black Horizon Theatre of Pittsburgh, at A. Leo Weil Auditorium, Aug. 7–8, 1968; dir. by AUGUST WILSON.
Dance of the Blues Dead was again presented Nov. 25–27, 1968, on double bill of three one-act plays, also dir. by August Wilson.

Sugar and Thomas (melodrama, 1 act, 1970). After Sugar begins wearing a natural (Afro) hairstyle, Thomas leaves her for a white woman, but Sugar gets her revenge. Prod. by Oduduwa Production, Black Studies Dept., Univ. of Pittsburgh, prior to its publication in *Connection* (Porter, 1970).

Little Willie Armstrong Jones (drama, full length, 1973). Drama of southern racial oppression. According to the author:

It is arranged in three movements and pulses. The play has its major movements, with the pulses being minor modes. The action is spontaneous and grows out of the modes. For instance, in the second movement when [one of the characters] is accidentally shot, the characters begin to recognize their responsibility. They can no longer permit unprincipled spontaneity to exist and disrupt the harmony and rhythm of the community's stability. Thus, the characters resolve [their] problems by politically banding together and breaking the oppressive mode. [Program Notes]

Prod. by the Kuntu Repertory Theatre, Univ. of Pittsburgh, 1973; dir. by Vernell A. Lillie.

Good Black Don't Crack (drama of black life, full length, 1977). According to the program notes, "*Good Black Don't Crack* confronts several customary concepts: an older woman and younger man's relationship, young people attempting to define their own value system, and the human and social values society should prize. [In this play,] the playwright contends that the only values a society should prize are those that speed an individual toward social freedom and a full enriched life." Prod. by the Kuntu Repertory Theatre, April 6–9, 1977; dir. by Vernell A. Lillie.

Dianne's Heart Dries Out Still More (1976). Prod. by the Kuntu Repertory Theatre, July 21–29, 1976; dir. by Vernell A. Lillie.

Who Loves the Dancer (full length, 1976; revised 1985). First prod. by the Kuntu Repertory Theatre, Univ. of Pittsburgh, 1976. Prod. by the New Federal Theatre (NFT), New York, 1982; revised and presented by NFT, Feb. 25–March 13, 1985, at the Harry DeJur Henry St. Settlement Playhouse; dir. by SHAUNEILLE PERRY.

OTHER PLAYS AND DRAMATIC WORKS:
Night of the Hawk (1966). **Centre Ave., A Trip** (full length, 1968). Prod. by the Black Horizon Theatre, 1968. **Up to Life** (1968). **Coon Can** (1969). **The Way** (1969). **Bad News** (1970). **Blue Yonder** (1970). **The Republic of New Africa** (unfinished, 1970). **Uhh Survival Energy** (1970). **A Good Quick Feel—and Then We Build upon a Plan** (full length, 1971). Prod. by the Black Horizon Theatre, 1971. **LifeRise** (1971). **The Depths of Her Star** (adaptn., 1976). From †Richard Wright's short story "Bright and Morning Star." Prod. by the Kuntu Repertory Theatre, 1976. **A Question Mark on Her Face** (1 act, 1976). Prod. by the Kuntu Repertory Theatre, 1976. **Take on a Life/ or Live in a Crowded Colored Cocoon** (full length, 1981). Prod. by the Kuntu Repertory Theatre, 1981.

PERKINS, EUGENE (1932–   ), Social worker, teacher, poet, playwright, theatrical and literary critic. Born in Chicago, IL, where he graduated from Wendell Phillips H.S. Attended colleges in Winston-Salem, NC, and Knoxville, TN. Received the B.S. degree in group work from George Williams Coll. in 1961, and the M.S. in group work-administration from the same institution in

1964. Has had extensive professional experience as a social group worker in Chicago, where he was employed at the Ada S. McKinley House, 1959–60; Chicago Boys Club, Youth Development Project, 1963; Henry Horner Chicago Boys Club, 1963–66. Since 1963 has been assoc. director of the Chicago Better Boys Foundation. Has taught at Malcolm X Coll., 1968–72; Central YMCA Coll., 1968–69; Roosevelt Univ., Summer 1969; Lewis Univ., 1970–73; and Triton Coll., 1974. Has also lectured at over 30 colleges and universities throughout the United States, as a member of the Contemporary Speakers Forum and Ebony Talent, Inc. Has also conducted numerous creative writing workshops, at such locations as the South Side Community Art Center, 1969–71; Helen Robinson Lib., 1968–70; Cook County Jail, 1970–71; Farragut H.S., 1969–70; and the DuSable Museum of African-American History, 1973–present. Author of *Home Is a Dirty Word: The Social Oppression of Black Children* (1974). His published books of poetry include *An Apology to My African Brother* (1964), *Black Is Beautiful* (1968), *Silhouette* (1970), *Black Expression* (editor, anthology of new black poets, 1967), and *Poetry of Prison* (editor, 1970). His articles relevant to the black theatre, black arts, and black literary movement in Chicago were published in *Black World, Black Books Bulletin, Freedomways, Liberator, Illinois English Bulletin, Chicago Sun-Times, Inner City Studies Journal, George Williams College Bulletin, Panorama Magazine/Chicago Daily News,* and *Black Seventies* (Barbour, 1970). Memberships include National Black Educators, National Black Social Workers, Catalysts, African Information Center, Inst. of Positive Education, South Side Community Art Center, and Union of Black United Artists. Winner of Malcolm X Black Manhood Award, May 1968; Concerned Parents of Lawndale Award, June 1970; and Council on Interracial Books for Children, Special Prize, June 1972. *Address*—Home: 6800 South Jeffrey, Chicago, IL. Office: Better Boys Foundation, 1512 South Pulaski Road, Chicago, IL 60623.

REPRESENTATIVE PLAYS AND DRAMATIC WORKS:

Turn a Black Cheek (historical protest drama, 3 acts, 1965). About the black students who began the sit-in demonstrations in Greensboro, NC, during the 1960s. Prod. in Chicago, 1965.

Assassination of a Dream (revolutionary morality drama, 2 acts, 1967). A black politician of questionable moral character receives a lesson in black justice. Produced in Chicago, 1967.

God Is Black, but He's Dead (revolutionary morality drama, 1 act, 1968). A group of black militants comes into conflict with the black church. Prod. by Kusema [Repertoire Theatre], Chicago, Oct. 1974; dir. by Seitu Ambee. The prodn. was videotaped by Chicago State Univ.

Nothing but a Nigger (nationalistic play, 1 act, 1969). In the setting of a pool hall, five street blacks join together to fight a common enemy. Prod. in Chicago, 1969.

Cry of the Black Ghetto (domestic/protest drama, 1 act, 1970). Concerns the problems facing a black policeman and the members of his family. Prod. in Chicago, 1970.

Black Is So Beautiful (nationalistic play for children, 1 act, 1970). Teaches the value and importance of black pride. Prod. in Chicago, 1970.

Fred Hampton (revolutionary-historical drama, 1 act, 1970). About the circumstances leading to the death of Fred Hampton, chairman of the Black Panther Party of Illinois, who was killed in a police raid. Prod. by the Kuumba Workshop Theatre, Chicago, 1972. Revived by the same group, Feb. 7–March 29, 1975, playing on weekends only.

The Image Makers (satire/morality drama, 2 acts, 1973). "A satirical view of the Black movie boom" *Black World,* April 1973, p. 83, in which "Miss America and Mr. Hollywood plan [a] Black exploration film."—*Black World,* April 1974, p. 46. Prod. by the Kuumba Workshop, Chicago, during the 1972–73 season. Also enjoyed a one-week engagement at the Apollo Theatre in Milwaukee, WI.

Professor J.B. (domestic-nationalistic drama, 3 acts, 1974). Described by the author as "a drama of a Black family torn between political values and the African Liberation Struggle."—Prodn. poster. Prod. by the Experimental Black Actors Guild (X-Bag), Chicago, Sept. 28–Nov. 18, 1973.

Black Fairy (musical drama for children, 2 acts, 1972). About a black fairy who lacks understanding of her culture and feels that she has nothing to offer black children. Winner of Special Book Award, Council on Interracial Books for Children, 1972. Prod. by the La Mont Zeno Community Theatre, Chicago, in repertory, 1974–76. Also performed at the Univ. of Kentucky, and sched. for perfs. in Cincinnati and other midwestern cities. Pub. by Third World Press, Chicago, 1972.

Our Street (children's play, 1 act, 1975). Makes an "analogy . . . between the Nigerian civil war and the teenage gang conflicts which plague so many urban Black communities."—*Black World,* April 1976. Prod. by the Lamont Zeno Community Theatre, 1975. Also sched. for prodn. by the Children's Theatre of the Kuumba Workshop, Chicago, 1975.

Quinn Chapel (historical play, 3 acts, 1974). The story of the origin and development of Quinn Chapel A.M.E. Church, the first black church in Chicago, established in 1844.

OTHER PLAYS AND DRAMATIC WORKS:

The Legacy of Leadbelly (historical drama, 1 act, 1966). Explores the events leading up to the death of the famous blues singer. **Thunder Is Not Yet Rain** (revolutionary drama, 3 acts, 1968). Some black revolutionaries try to fight the white establishment. **It Can Never Be in Vain** (revolutionary drama, 1 act, 1973). About a black revolutionary leader who becomes dissatisfied with the racial struggle in the United States and leaves the country. **Brothers** (domestic-nationalistic drama, 3 acts, 1974). The conflict among four brothers concerning their political ideologies. **Cinque** (historical-morality drama, 3 acts, 1975). The story of the Amistad Mutiny, and the lessons of black survival that can be learned from this historical event.

PERRY, FELTON, Actor, writer, singer, and dancer, assocaited with the Experimental Black Actors Guild (X-BAG) in Chicago. He was featured in the film *Walking Tall.* Apparently also associated with the Frank Silvera Writers' Workshop (FSWW) in New York City.

PLAYS:

(At least one of his scripts is in the FSWW Archives/Schomburg Collection.) **Buy the Bi and By** (drama, full length, 1975). The reactions of an integrated group of five actors and actresses who attend the first reading of a new play by a White playwright/director, which presents a stereotypical picture of lower-class black life. Prod. by X-Bag, Chicago, 1975. Also presented at Ralph Waite's Actor's Theatre in Los Angeles, Jan. 1976. **Or**

(1976). Prod. by X-Bag, Chicago, May 1976. Also presented by Evergreen Stage, Hollywood, CA.

PERRY, JULIA (1927–1979), Composer, conductor, and teacher, whose dramatic works include three operas. Born in Lexington, KY; moved with her family to Akron, OH, at age ten. Received both her bachelor's and master's degrees at the Westminister Choir School in Princeton, NJ. Also studied at Juilliard, at the Berkshire Music Center, and privately abroad in Florence and Paris. Taught music at NYU and Bronx Community Coll. In addition to the three operas cited below, her works include compositions for voice, chorus, and orchestra.

DRAMATIC WORKS:
The Cask of Amontillado (opera, 1 act, 1954). Apparently based on the short story by Edgar Allan Poe. Prod. at the McMillin Theatre, Columbia Univ., New York, Nov. 20, 1954. **The Bottle** (opera, pre-1970s). **The Selfish Giant** (opera, pre-1970s).

PERRY, LESLIE DAVID, Playwright and musical writer. Based in the San Francisco Bay area. His plays have been produced at California State Univ./ Hayward and by the Afro-American Studies Dept. of Univ. of California/Berkeley.

PLAYS:
Rats (musical drama, 2 acts, 1974). Adaptn. of "The Pied Piper of Hamlin," a poem by Robert Browning, with the rats representing human corruption. Prod. at California State Univ., Hayward, 1974. **Sis Goose an' de Fox** (fable, 1 act, 1975). Dramatization of a black folk tale on justice. Prod. by the Afro-American Studies Dept., UC/Berkeley, prior to publication in *The Yardbird Reader,* vol. 4 (Reed, 1975), pp. 112–22.

PERRY, SHAUNEILLE (Mrs. Donald Ryder) (1930–   ), Director, actress, playwright, and teacher. One of the most sought-after black women directors in New York. A cousin of LORRAINE HANSBERRY. Educated at Howard Univ. (B.A. in drama), the Goodman Theatre Art Inst., Chicago (M.A. in directing), and the Royal Academy of Dramatic Art, London. Member of the Howard Univ. Players. Former feature writer for the *Chicago Tribune.* Has taught speech and theatre at Manhattan Community Coll., Dillard Univ., and Queens Coll. As an actress, she appeared in New York stage productions of *The Goose* (1959), *Dark of the Moon* (1960), *Talent '60* (1960), *Ondine* (1961), *Clandestine on the Morning Line* (1961), and *The Octoroon* (1961). Other performances include "The Catholic Hour" (TV series), "The Kimball Hour" (radio), and *The Long Night* (film). She has directed original productions for AMAS Repertory Theatre, the Negro Ensemble Co., and the New Federal Theatre (NFT). Among her most important directing credits are the premiere productions of *Rosalie Pritchett* (1971), *Black Girl* (1971), *The Sty of the Blind Pig* (1971), *Jamimma* (1972), *Terraced Apartment* (1972), *Ladies in Waiting* (1973), *The Prodigal Sister* (1974), *Bayou Legend* (1975), and *Who Loves the*

Dancer (1982), and Williams & Walker (1985). She has also directed numerous other plays, films, and television shows, including many of her own works cited below. Recipient of a Fulbright scholarship, a New York State Council on the Arts Young Audiences Play Commission, an AUDELCO Black Theatre Recognition Award (as best director, 1974 and 1985), and a Broadcast Media Award, the Black Rose of Excellence from *Encore* magazine.

REPRESENTATIVE PLAYS AND DRAMATIC WORKS:

Last Night, Night Before (melodrama, 3 acts, 1971). Coauthor, with *Donald Jackson. A party is given by the good people of the neighborhood, while a 16-year-old boy is being hooked on dope, from which he dies. Prod. by Impact Productions at the Black Theatre Alliance annual festival, New York, 1974.

"Sounds of the City" (black radio soap opera, 15 min. daily, c. 1973/75). Concerns the struggles of the Taylors, a black urban family. Prod. by Mutual Black Network; sponsored by Quaker Oats Co. for two years, c. 1973–75. Regular cast included ROBERT GUILLAUME (TV's Benson) as Calvin Taylor, ZAIDA COLES as Winona Taylor, Adam Wade as Jimmy Gates, and Helen Martin as Eula Taylor. CECIL ALONZO also performed in the cast.

Presenting the Pettifords (children's play, 1976). A circus family decides to give up their exciting work to live like ordinary people. Prod. by the Arts for Living Center, New York, Dec. 1976.

Daddy Goodness (musical, full length, 1979). Coauthor of book. Music by Ken Hirsch. Adapt. from the play of the same title by †Richard Wright and Louis Sapin (1968), based on the life of Father Divine. Prod. by Ashton Springer and others in a pre-Bway tryout at the Forrest Theatre in Philadelphia and the National Theatre in Washington, D.C., Aug. 16–Sept. 30, 1979; dir. first by Israel Hicks and later by Phil Oesterman. Closed before reaching Bway.

Things of the Heart: Marian Anderson's Story (play for young people, full length, 1981). About the famous concert and opera singer. Prod. by the NFT, opening Jan. 10, 1981; dir. by Denise Hamilton. With Franz Jones, Victoria Howard, Lucy Hollander, and Hy Mencher. Unpub. script in the Hatch-Billops Collection.

A Celebration ("The African-American Tradition Through Words and Songs" [subtitle], full length, 1985). Conceived and dir. by Perry. Prod. by ROGER FURMAN's New Heritage Repertory Theatre (NHRT), New York, in association with Danva Productions, Feb. 18–24, 1985. Featuring Carolyn Byrd, Clebert Ford, Andre Robinson, Jr., and Fran Salisbury. Prod. at the American Place Theatre, New York, 1986.

OTHER PLAYS AND DRAMATIC WORKS:

A Holiday Celebration (TV special, full length, 1971). Prod. 1971, with OSSIE DAVIS and RUBY DEE. **Mio** (children's play, 1971). Prod. by NFT Workshop, New York, Fall 1971; dir. by author. **The Music Magic** (musical odyssey, full length, 1975). Conceived and dir. by Perry. Music and lyrics by NEAL TATE. Prod. by the Urban Arts Corps, New York, opening April 1976. Also presented at the Billie Holiday Theatre, Brooklyn, Nov. 1976. **Love** (poetic revue, full length, 1982). Conceived and dir. by Perry. Featuring poems of Carolyn M. Rogers. Prod. and dir. by NFT, opening June 3, 1982. **Clinton** ("An Urban Fairytale" [subtitle], full length, 1976). Prod. by NHRT, opening Jan. 1984; dir. by Sloane Robinson.

PETERSON, LOUIS (Stamford, Jr.) (1922–   ), Actor, playwright, screen-writer, television scriptwriter, and talented pianist. Born in Hartford, CT, the son of a bank employee. Educated at Morehouse Coll. (B.A. in English and sociology, 1944); Yale Univ. School of Drama (1944–45); and NYU (M.A. in drama, 1947). Also studied with Sanford Meisner at the Neighborhood Playhouse School of the Theatre, 1948–49, and Clifford Odets (playwriting, 1950–51) and Lee Strasberg (acting, 1950–52) at the Actors Studio. Performed as an actor in *A Young American* (1946), *Justice* (1947), *Our Lan'* (1947), and the national tour production of *Member of the Wedding* (1951–52) during which he began writing his first and most important play, **Take a Giant Step** (1953). Member of Omega Psi Phi Fraternity (president of Morehouse College Chapter, 1943–44), DG, WGA/East, and AEA. Recipient of Benjamin Brawley Award at More-house (for Excellence in English); Emmy nomination, 1956, for **Joey**; and Black Filmmakers Hall of Fame Award, as a pioneer in the film industry. *Address:* 440 W. 22nd St., New York, NY 10011.

REPRESENTATIVE PLAYS AND DRAMATIC WORKS:

Take a Giant Step (drama, 2 acts [6 scenes], 1953; also prod. as a feature film, full length: screenplay, 1960). Described by the author as a semi-autobiographical play, which

has to do with a young Negro boy, living in a white neighborhood, who confronts his first negation of the white boys he has played with, when the boys become interested in sex. The first part of the play is a personal odyssey he goes on after he is aware of the situation, to the Negro section of town, where he hopes to find sex, or friendship among his own people. He becomes embroiled with some very funny prostitutes, who . . . finally turn on him and completely negate his wish, and also destroy the hope that this is an avenue of escape. The rest of the play concerns itself with the death of his Grandmother, his only friend, his conflict with his parents and the boys and his final emergence into adult understanding. [Letter to Bernard Peterson, June 29, 1953]

Selected by the Burns Mantle Yearbook *Best Plays* series as a "Best Play of 1953–54." According to the author, the play went into rehearsal Aug. 15, 1953, in New York. It opened in Philadelphia at the Forrest Theatre, Sept. 9–19, where it ran for 16 perfs. Opened on Bway at the Lyceum Theatre, Sept. 24–Nov. 28, 1953, for 76 perfs.; dir. by John Stix. Starring Louis Gossett in his acting debut; featuring Frederick O'Neal, Estelle Hemsley, Estelle Evans, Jane White, Pauline Myers, Frank Wilson, MAXWELL GLAN-VILLE, and Dorothy Carver. Prod. by the Gilpin Players, Cleveland, April 2–8, 1954; and revived by the same group Jan. 19–Feb. 13, 1960. Prod. Off-Bway at the Jan Hus Auditorium, Sept. 25, 1956–June 9, 1957, for 264 perfs.; dir. by Ira Cirker. Starring BILL GUNN; featuring BEAH RICHARDS, GODFREY CAMBRIDGE, Frances Foster, Hilda Haynes, and ROSETTA LeNOIRE. Prod. by Boston Summer Playhouse, at the Charles Playhouse, opening Sept. 21, 1958, for a run of two weeks. Prod. as a full length feature film, with screenplay by the author, by Julius J. Epstein; released by United Artists, 1960. Starring Johnny Nash; featuring RUBY DEE, Frederick O'Neal, Beah Richards, and Estelle Hemsley. Pub. by Samuel French, New York, 1954; abridged in *The Best Plays of 1953–54;* in *Black Drama in America* (Turner, 1971); in *Black Insights* (Ford, 1971); in *Black Theatre: A Twentieth Century Collection of the Work of Its Best*

Playwrights (Patterson, 1971); abridged in *Black Literature: An Anthology of Outstanding Black Writers* (Washington & Beckoff, 1972).

Class of 1958 (TV drama, full length, 1954). About an adolescent youth who is experiencing college difficulties; considered a sequel to the author's **Take a Giant Step** (1953). Prod. with an all-white cast by the "Goodyear TV Playhouse," on NBC-TV, Dec. 1954.

Joey (TV drama, full length, 1956). Nominated for an Emmy Award, 1956. Produced by the "Goodyear TV Playhouse," on NBC-TV, March 1956, starring Anthony Perkins and Kim Stanley. Sold to Hollywood "for an enormous sum," but apparently was not filmed.

Entertain a Ghost (drama, 2 acts, 1962). Described by Fannie Hicklin as "a play within a play. A married actress is rehearsing a play by her husband. Meanwhile, their personal relationship provides an interior play in which the egocentric actress causes the deterioration of the marriage by her increasingly selfish demands of her husband to function as an auxiliary in boosting her as an actress. A subplot deals with an interracial romance."—"The American Negro Playwright, 1920–1964" (Ph.D. dissertation, Hicklin, 1965), p. 401. Produced at the Actors Playhouse, New York, opening April 9, 1962, for 9 perfs.; dir. by Ira Cirker (who also coproduced the play). Cast included HAL DeWINDT.

OTHER PLAYS AND DRAMATIC WORKS:

Padlocks (TV drama, full length, 1954). Prod. on the "Danger" series (a dramatic anthology of psychological and murder mystery dramas), and telecast on CBS, Nov. 1954. **The Tempest** (adaptn., full length: screenplay, 1957). From the play by William Shakespeare. Prod. in Italy by Cinecitta, 1957. **The Emily Rossiter Story** (TV script, full length, 1957). Prod. on the "Wagon Train" series by NBC-TV, Sept. 1957. **Hit and Run** (TV drama, full length, 1961). Prod. on the "Dr. Kildare" series by NBC–TV, Dec. 1961. **Crazy Horse Have Jenny Now** (drama, full length, c. 1970). Prod. by New Federal Theatre, New York, opening Nov. 8, 1979, for 12 perfs. With CHARLES GORDONE in the cast. **The Confessions of Nat Turner** (feature film, full length: screenplay, 1970s).

PETERSON, QUENTIN, Former student playwright at the Univ. of Wisconsin at Green Bay.

PLAY:

Another Nigger Dead (domestic drama, 1976). "An urban Black family held together by a strong-willed mother encounters explosive tensions in a world they never made. Despite one son's passiveness and another's unsuccessful attempt at theft, the family fights to hold together in the face of destructive pressures." —*ACTF* [American Coll. Theatre Festival] *Newsletter,* Dec. 1976. Prod. by the Univ. of Wisconsin/Green Bay, 1976, and presented at the ACTF Regional Festival, held at Beloit Coll., Beloit, WI, 1976.

PEYTON, BRUCE, Playwright.

PLAY:

Street King (historical pageant, 1 act, 1973). Coauthor, with RENEE ROASHE. Depicts black enslavement through the ages, from its beginnings in Africa to the present day. Prod. by the Theatre for the Forgotten, Riker's Island, NY, 1973, as a project of the Work Release Program.

PIÑERO, MIGUEL, Hispanic playwright of part-black heritage. Based in New York City. Winner of the New York Drama Critics Circle Award and the Obie Award, 1974, for his play **Short Eyes**.

PLAYS:
Short Eyes (drama, 2 acts, 1974; also a feature film, full length: screenplay, 1977). Drama of prison life in which a young white inmate, jailed for child molestation, is mistreated and eventually killed by the other prisoners. Prod. by the New York Public Theatre, March 1974, and perfd. by The Family, a group composed mainly of ex-inmates; dir. by Marvin Felix Camillo, who won an Obie Award. Also won for the playwright a New York Drama Critics Circle Award and an Obie Award, 1974. Made into a film, prod. by Lewis Harris as a Film League Presentation, with musical score by *Curtis Mayfield. Both Piñero and Mayfield appear in supporting roles in the film, which features Bruce Davidson and Jose Perez. Available on a rental basis from Corinth Films, New York **Sideshow** (drama, 1 act, 1975). Portrays ghetto life among teenagers on the Lower East Side of New York City. Prod. at the Space Theatre, New York, Jan. 1975. **Straight from the Ghetto** (musical revue, full length, 1976). Coauthor with NEIL HARRIS. Combines music, poetry, and drama to provide a picture of street life in New York City's Harlem. Prod. by The Family, and performed as street theatre, New York, Summer 1976. Again presented by the Theatre for the New City, New York, Jan. 1977. **The Sun Always Shines for the Cool** (drama, full length, 1976). Confrontation in a bar between two New York street gangs. Prod. at the Booth Theatre, New York, Feb. 1976.

PITCHER, OLIVER (1923–   ), Poet, actor, playwright, and drama teacher. Born in Massachusetts. Has resided in Pittsburgh, PA; New York City; Atlanta, GA; and Palo Alto, CA. Received some of his theatrical training at Bard College, at the Dramatic Workshop of the New School, and with the American Negro Theatre. Taught black drama at Vassar Coll., 1970s. Has acted professionally as well as with college and little theatre groups. Author of a volume of poetry, *Dust of Silence* (1960). His poems, which Robert Hayden has described as "offbeat and sardonic," have been published in numerous periodicals, including *Negro Digest/Black World, Presence Africaine,* and *Umbra;* and anthologized in *Beyond the Blues* (Pool, 1962), *American Negro Poetry* (Bontemps, 1963), *New Negro Poets: USA* (Hughes, 1964), *Kaleidoscope* (Hayden, 1965), *3000 Years of Black Poetry* (Lomax & Abdul, 1970), and *The Poetry of Black America* (Adoff, 1972). *Address:* c/o Eaton, 945 Old Trace Rd., Palo Alto, CA 94306.

REPRESENTATIVE PLAYS AND DRAMATIC WORKS:
The Bite (1 act, 1970). Deals with black college students and prostitution. Pub. in the *Atlanta University Sampler* (Atlanta Univ. Press, c. 1970).

The One (monologue, 1 act, 1970). In an isolated setting that appears to be a mental institution, a black man attempts to come to grips with his psychological, sexual, and racial identity. Prod. as a work-in-progress by the Negro Ensemble Co., New York, opening Jan. 14, 1971, for 2 perfs.; dir. by Norman Bush. Pub. in *Black Drama Anthology* (King & Milner, 1972).

OTHER PLAYS AND DRAMATIC WORKS:
Spring Beginning (poetic drama, full length, 1940s). Prod. at the 115th St. People's Theatre in Harlem during the 1940s; dir. by Leslie Jones. With MAXWELL GLANVILLE and RUBY DEE. Apparently opened on Bway without success. **Snake! Snake!** (c. 1961). Prod. at the Poet's Theatre, New York, around 1961. Unpub. script in the Schomburg Collection. **So How're You Wearing Your Straitjacket?** (1 act, 1963). Excerpt pub. in *Umbra,* Winter 1963, pp. 13–14. **Shampoo** (1972). Pub. in the *Atlanta University Center Sampler* #3 (Atlanta Univ. Press 1972). **The Daisy** (avant-garde drama, 2 acts, pre-1975). A symbolic probe into a black man's psyche to determine the meaning of his life. **The Meaning of Strings** (drama, 1 act, pre-1975). Symbolic drama which utilizes the metaphor of the puppeteer to probe the question, Who pulls the strings?

PLANT, PHILIP PAUL, Playwright. Associated with the Frank Silvera Writers' Workshop (FSWW) in New York City.

PLAYS:
Switcheroo (fantasy, 1 act, pre-1975). Conflict between a man and his alter ego over the problem of masculinity. Unpub. script in the Schomburg Collection. **Different Strokes from Different Folks** (domestic drama, 1 act, pre-1975). Conflict of sexual and political values within a black family. **The Past Ain't Nothing but the Future Turned Around** (1970s). Unpub. script and tape recording in the FSWW Archives/Schomburg Collection.

PLOMER, WILLIAM, Playwright. (Racial identity not verified.)

GROUP OF RELATED PLAYS:
"I SPEAK OF AFRICA: Two Plays for a Puppet Theatre" (2 short plays, 1964). Includes **The Man in the Corner** and **The Triumph of Justice.** Pub. in *Drama Critique* (issue on the Negro in the Theatre), Spring 1964, pp. 110–14.

POINDEXTER, GWENDOLYN, Playwright. Based in Cleveland, OH, where she was associated with the Karamu Theatre. Formerly resided in Shaker Heights, OH.

PLAY:
We'll Show Them (play for marionettes, 4 scenes, 1975). An old man tells his grandchildren a black folk tale, in which a loving father and his son are sold separately from the wife and mother. The family is reunited with the aid of a conjure woman who changes the man and his son into birds. Prod. by Karamu Theatre, Nov. 1975.

POLE, CHARLES (Jamal David), Playwright, lyricist, and producer. Founder and chief administrator of the Everlasting Life Co., Bronx, NY, whose purpose is to promote and produce unknown talented artists in the area of the theatre and other arts. *Address:* The Everlasting Life, G.P.O. Box 623, Bronx, NY 10451.

PLAYS AND DRAMATIC WORKS:
Super Nigger Right Around the Corner (1973). Produced at St. Theresa's Church, New York, Sept. 29, 1973, and at Taft United Methodist Church and Community Centre, New York, Dec. 16, 1973. **Forty Years—Later** (domestic drama, 3 acts, pre-1976). "This is a story about a black family that has constant arguments and disagreements

about one another's life-styles, but they nonetheless have coherence and unity."—*Black Playwrights, 1823—1977* (Hatch & Abdullah, 1977). Unpub. script in the Hatch-Billops Collection. **Reality** (domestic drama, full length, 1976). Described by the director, Timothy H. Taylor (also known as Noken), as "about a young Black man caught in a whirlpool of conflict regarding his life-style, his father, his woman, and his spiritual realization of self."—Publicity release. Prod. by Robert E. David Enterprises, and presented at Lincoln Square Neighborhood Center, New York, opening April 4, 1976. Also performed at various theatres and community centers in New York City. (May be a rewritten or retitled version of **Forty Years—Later.**) **Black Woman in a Sunday Morning** (domestic drama, 1 act, 1977). Takes a look at the black man's insecurities and how his wife and children are affected. Prod. by the Everlasting Life, under the direction of Gwen Hardwicke, and presented at the Lincoln Square Neighborhood Center, Feb. and March 1977. Also presented at the 13th St. Theatre, St. Luke Methodist Church, Harlem YMCA, and the Little Theatre, April-May 1977. **Life Is a Trip** (drama, 1 act, 1977). The story of how two college students, both heavy drug users, cope with each other. Offers a close view of human beings trying to relate to each other. Prod. by the Everlasting Life, under the direction of Scottie Davis, and presented at the Lincoln Square Neighborhood Center, New York, Feb. and March 1977. Also presented at the 13th St. Theatre, St. Luke Methodist Church, Harlem YMCA and the Little Theatre, April-May 1977. **Gettin Over** (drama, full length, 1983). A play about the life styles and conflicts of people trying to make it in a rat-race society. The theme is about a young black aspiring actor who wants to go to Hollywood to achieve fame and fortune, while his common-law wife wishes to raise a family and settle down. Prod. by the Everlasting Life, in association with LSNC Salt & Pepper Mime Co., at the Harlem YMCA, opening June 2, 1983, for 2 perfs.; dir. by Scottie Davis.

PORTERFIELD, GORDON, Playwright. Based in New York City.

PLAY:
The Universal Nigger (1970). According to Howard Thompson, *New York Times* (March 21, 1970); "The purpose of Gordon Porterfield's play was plain. He has used the Christ figure as a pinpoint scapegoat for man's inhumanity to man differentiated by color." Prod. by the Chelsea Theatre Center, at the Brooklyn Academy of Music's Third Stage Auditorium, March 1970.

POTTS, JIM, Playwright. During the mid-1970s, he was residing in San Francisco, CA, where he was apparently associated with Benjamin Franklin H.S.

PLAYS:
Unfinished Portrait (historical musical, 1 act, 1971). The odyssey of the black woman from slavery to the black revolution. Prod. at Benjamin Franklin H.S., San Francisco, July 1971. Unpub. script in the Hatch-Billops Collection. **Beautiful Black Cat** (musical satire, 1 act, 1970s). A beautiful black cat, who has given up her freedom in the fields for the ordeals of civilized life, longs to be free again. **Deadline for Michael** (domestic drama, 1 act, 1970s). After the death of a playwright who does not live to see his first play produced, the hypocrisy of his fellow playwrights comes to light. **A Play for Me** (morality, 1 act, 1970s). Three-character play involving the interaction of a black playwright, a black prostitute, and a white male. **Requiem for Bethany Baptist** (drama, 2 acts, 1970s). The ordeal of a black youth who is the first to integrate a white Louisiana

college during the 1960s. **Roots of Evil** (musical satire, 1 act, 1970s). The odyssey of a $20 bill from the mint to the bank, through the black community, and back to the mint again, where it is finally destroyed.

POWELL, RICHARD, Playwright.

PLAY:
Aaron Answorth (1970). Pub. by New Dimensions, New York, 1970s.

PRICE, ROBERT EARL, Author and playwright. Born in Atlanta, GA. Educated at Clark Coll. (English and journalism) and the American Film Inst. (AFI) (advanced film studies and screenwriting). Has professional credits in every genre except the novel. Author of *Bloodlines* (collection of poems and short stories, 1978). His articles have been published in *Essence, Dayton Daily News,* and *Fannon Center Journal.* His poetry has appeared in *Black World, Negro Digest,* and *Rufus Magazine.* He has extensive credits as theatre, film, and TV director and coach. Member of WGA. Recipient of a Broadside Press Award for poetry, 1976, and AFI's William Wyler Fellowship for screenwriting, 1977. *Address:* 344 Camfield Ct., S.W., Atlanta, GA 30310. Alternate: 3610 W. 6th St. #810, Los Angeles, CA 90020.

DRAMATIC WORKS:
Seven short film scripts written for advanced study directors and prod. on film or tape at AFI, 1974–77. **Polished Ebony** (video tape, 20 min., 1976). Prod. at AFI, 1976. **A Place for Beau** (teleplay, mid-1970s). Script for "Palmerstown U.S.A." TV series, prod. by Haley/T.A.T. for CBS-TV, mid-1970s. **Pride of Dumas** (screenplay, feature length, 1977). Written for Advanced Fellows Program at AFI, 1977. **Lazarus Syndrome** (1978). Story created for VSC Enterprises, Inc., for ABC-TV, 1978. **Freedom Road** (TV mini-series, 1979). Wrote additional scenes and dialogue while serving as special consultant to the director, Jan Kadar. Series prod. for NBC-TV by Zev Braun Productions, 1979. **Black Cat Bones for Seven Sons** (drama, full length, 1982). Selected for prodn. in Summer Festival of One Act Plays, by Los Angeles Actors Theatre, 1982. **Bird's Vamp** (drama, 1983). **Cane's Theme** (drama, 1984). Prod. by the Francis Williams theatre, 1984. **Replay** (drama, 1984).

PRIMUS, MARC, Director, playwright, editor, theatrical researcher, and Afro-American folklorist. Resides in New York City. Assoc. director of the Theatre Communications Group, New York City. Former affiliate member of the Black Theatre Alliance, and director of the Afro-American Folkloric Troupe. Editor, *Black Theatre: A Resource Directory* (1973). In 1973 Primus was planning to work on his doctorate in the United States and in Australia for one year with the Aboriginal Theatre Arts and Cultural Movement. *Address:* 790 Riverside Dr., New York, NY.

PLAY:
High John De Conquer (musical, full length, 1969). Music written and conducted by *Bobby Banks. Based on the folk legend of High John the Conqueror. Performed on

Bway by the Afro-American Folkloric Troupe, at the New York City Center, opening April 23, 1969; dir. by Primus.

PRINGLE, RONALD J. (1942–   ), Playwright.

PLAYS:
The Finger Meal (drama, 1 act, 1968). Explores the master-slave relationship in a small southern town. Pub. in *Nineteen Necromancers from Now* (Reed, 1970). NOTE: The following plays are all pre-1975: **Dead Flowers on a Great Man's Grave. Deep Roots of Rotted Wood. The Fall of the Chandelier. Feed the Lion. The Lesser Sleep. The Price.**

PROVIDENCE, WAYNE, Playwright. An alumnus of the Sonia Sanchez Writers Workshop, held at the Countee Cullen Library in Harlem, New York City, 1970–71.

PLAY:
Where Are You Black Dream (ritual, 1 act, 1970). To realize the black dream, black people must overcome ignorance and inactivity. Pub. in *Three Hundred and Sixty Degrees of Blackness Comin at You* (Sanchez, 1971).

PRYOR, RICHARD (Richard Franklin Lennox Thomas Pryor III)

(1940–   ), Actor, comedian, and scriptwriter. Born in Peoria, IL, where his family operated a local bar and brothel, and where he was educated in the parochial and public schools. Became interested in show business by watching impromptu performances by Duke Ellington, Count Basie, and Louis Armstrong at Peoria's famous Door Club. Began his career as a stand-up comedian, working in small clubs in Canada and New York, prior to gaining an appearance on the "Ed Sullivan Show," which led to his first film, *The Busy Body* (1967), followed by *Wild in the Streets* (1968). His best-known films include *Lady Sings the Blues* (1972), *Uptown Saturday Night* (1974), *Car Wash* (1976), *Silver Streak* (1976), *Greased Lightning* (1977), *Which Way Is Up* (1977), *Blue Collar* (1978), *The Wiz* (1978), *Stir Crazy* (1980), *Bustin' Loose* (1980), *Some Kind of Hero* (1982), *The Toy* (1982), *Superman III* (1983), and *Brewster's Millions* (1985). His live concert performances, also seen on video, include *Richard Pryor—Live in Concert* (1979), *Richard Pryor—Live on the Sunset Strip* (1983), and *Richard Pryor—Here and Now* (1983). His best-known comedy records include *Pryor Goes Foxx Hunting* (with Redd Foxx), *That Nigger's Crazy* (1974), and *Bicentennial Nigger* (1976). He has written scripts and/or comedy material for "Sanford and Son"; "The Flip Wilson Show"; "The Richard Pryor Show"; two Lily Tomlin specials, for which he received an Emmy Award in 1973; and **Blazing Saddles** (1974), for which he received awards from the American Writers Guild and the American Academy of Humor. For his numerous comedy recordings, he has received four Grammy awards (1974, 1975, 1976, and 1981).

REPRESENTATIVE DRAMATIC WORKS:
Blazing Saddles (feature film, full length, 1974). Screenplay by Mel Brooks, Norman Steinberg, Andrew Berman, Richard Pryor, and Allan Uger. Based on a story by Berman.

Slapstick western film which satirizes every western film ever made. About a black sheriff who saves a bigoted town from being taken over by criminal elements in order to make way for a railroad. Prod. by Warner Bros., 1974; dir. by Mel Brooks. With Cleavon Little as the sheriff. For his contribution to this film (which he was led to believe he would star in), Pryor earned an American Writers Guild Award and an American Academy of Humor Award.

Jo Jo Dancer, Your Life Is Calling (feature film, full length, 1986). Screenplay by Rocco Urbisci, Paul Mooney, and Richard Pryor. Semi-autobiographical play, based "around events in Pryor's life including his upbringing in a brothel in Peoria, Ill."— *Jet,* May 26, 1986, p. 59. According to Pryor, "his own story was simply an outline for the movie, fleshed out with the fictional characters that he and his collaborators created."—Ibid. Prod. and dir. by Pryor, who also starred in the title role, 1986. With Debbie Allen, Paula Kelly, Art Evans, Barbara Williams, Carmen McRae, Scoey Mitchell, and E'Lon Cox.

OTHER DRAMATIC WORKS:

See also Pryor's TV writings and live concert performances mentioned in the biographical sketch above.

R

RADISON, NELSON, Playwright. Based in New York City.

PLAY:

Exiles in the Kingdom (poetic drama, 1 act, 1972). A Puerto Rican poet–drug addict relives his past. Prod. by the Hatch-Billops Studio, New York, May 1972. Unpub. script in the Hatch-Billops Collection.

RAHMAN, AISHAH, Playwright and educator. A native of New York City's Harlem, where she attended P.S. 184 and began writing plays in the sixth grade. Currently assoc. prof. in the English Dept. of Nassau Community Coll. in New York, and director of the Playwrights Workshop at the New Federal Theatre (NFT). Formerly a CETA artist with the Black Theatre Alliance (BTA) in New York.

GROUP OF RELATED PLAYS:

"THE MAMA" (trilogy of one-act plays, 1974/76). Includes **The Mama, a Folk's Tale** (1974), **Portrait of a Blues Lady** (1974), and **Mother to Son** (1976).

REPRESENTATIVE PLAYS AND DRAMATIC WORKS:

Lady Day ("A Musical Tragedy" [subtitle], full length, 1972). Book by Rahman. Music mainly by ARCHIE SHEPP. Based on the life, times, and career of Billie Holiday. Prod. at the Chelsea Theatre, Brooklyn, Oct. 17–Nov. 5, 1972, for 34 perfs.; dir. by PAUL CARTER HARRISON. Featuring Cecelia Norfleet as Billie Holiday. Also in the cast were ROSETTA LeNOIRE and MAXWELL GLANVILLE. Unpub. script in the Hatch-Billops Collection.

The Transcendental Blues (drama, 1 act, 1976). A companion piece to the author's **The Lady and the Tramp** [see OTHER PLAYS AND DRAMATIC WORKS below]. About a middle-aged woman who is abandoned by her young lover. Prod. by the Frederick Douglass Creative Arts Centre, New York, Aug. 1976; dir. by Kimaki Baraka. Nominated for an AUDELCO Award, 1976.

Unfinished Women Cry in No Man's Land While a Bird Dies in a Gilded Cage ("Play in 12 Scenes" [subtitle], 1977). Deals with the longing and fantasies of unwed teenage mothers, focusing on the time when they must decide whether to keep their babies or give them up for adoption. The "Bird," which is the central metaphor of the play, as implied by its title, is Charlie Parker (known as the "Bird"), whose death in the boudoir of a European lady is juxtaposed with the occurrences taking place in a home for unwed mothers; Parker's music is heard in the background of the play. First prod. by the New York Shakespeare Festival (NYSF), June 1977, dir. by BILL DUKE. Toured with the NYSF Mobile Theatre, Aug. 1977. Also prod. by NYU School of the Arts, and by California State Univ./Sacramento. Pub. in *Nine Plays by Black Women* (Wilkerson, 1986).

Myth-Mouth (play [or possibly opera], in progress, 1980). According to the author, it was "inspired by two historical figures, Marie Laveau and High John the Conqueror. It has a contemporary setting and evolves around two characters, an American soul singer and an African singer. What I deal with is the danger we constantly face of losing our souls as we tirelessly strive to 'Americanize' ourselves. If your sole interest becomes how best to 'crossover' you stand to lose what it was that got you over in the first place."—*Black Collegian,* April/May 1980, p. 10.

Tales of Madame Zora (blues musical, full length, 1986). Based on the life of †Zora Neale Hurston, the black folklorist and novelist of the Harlem Renaissance. Prod. by the Ensemble Studio, New York, Feb.-March 1986; dir. by GLENDA DICKERSON. Featuring Stephanie Berry, Keith David, Willie Barnes, and Deborah Malone.

OTHER PLAYS AND DRAMATIC WORKS:
Linus' Song (1 act, 1968). Prod. by Howard Univ., Washington, DC, 1968. **The Knitte Shop** (1 act, 1968). **Voodoo America** (drama, 3 acts, 1968). Prod. at Howard Univ., 1968. **The Jukebox** (drama, 1 act, 1974). Concerns the problem of high school integration. **The Mama, a Folk's Tale** (drama, 1 act, 1974). Part of the trilogy **"THE MAMA."** Based on a story of the relationship of George Jackson, a political prisoner, and his mother. **Portrait of a Blues Lady** (a memory play, 1 act, 1974). Part of the trilogy **"THE MAMA."** A black woman reviews her life to see if she can make a fresh start. **Mother to Son** (1976). Part of the trilogy **"THE MAMA."** Public reading by FSWW, at the Harlem Cultural Council, New York, May 1976. Unpub. script in the FSWW Archives/Schomburg Collection. **The Lady and the Tramp** (drama, 1 act, 1976). Deals with the problem of male-female alienation in contemporary society. **In Men's Eyes** (TV drama, 90 min., 1976). About the suicide of a black high school principal during a school integration crisis.

RANDOLPH, JEREMY, Playwright, director, composer, and literary agent. Resides in New York City. Cofounder, with Georgia Nicholas, of the Theatre of the Incentive, the Nicholas Literary Agency, and Rannick-Amuru Press (also known as Rannick Press and Amuru Press). Rannick-Amuru, which advertised itself as a press specializing in the work of new black writers, apparently never completed its ambitious publication project.

PLAYS:
(All except the first two plays were scheduled for publication by Rannick-Amuru Press, New York, 1973, but apparently were never pub.) **Cartouche 1990** (semi-musical drama, 3 acts, 1970). Book by Randolph. Music and lyrics by Randolph, Jerry Stevenson, and Richard Bone. Prod. simply as *Cartouche* at Cami Hall (formerly Judson Hall), 165 W. 57th St., New York City, for 2 perfs., Nov. 14–15, 1970; dir. by author. **Blowup in A**

Major (satirical farce, 2 acts, 1971). Set in the interior of the White House, where four senators plan a scheme to set blacks back by over 100 years. Pub. by Rannick Press, New York, 1971. **Negro Mama, Black Son** (drama of absurdity, 1 act, c. 1973). Young man tries to explain his reactions to his mother concerning their lives in the South and what has divided the family. **Rock Baby Rock While De Darkies Sleep** (prophetic drama, 1 act, c. 1973). According to the author, a discovery is made by a young man when he returns to his home in the South, and a prophecy is told. **To the Slave Mountain Alone** (drama of reverse loyalty, 3 acts, with music, c. 1973). A young man, pressured by a racist draft board, tries to make the final decision of whether or not to refuse induction on the grounds of religious principles. **Whiteman's Seal of Approval** (psychological comedy-drama, 1 act, c. 1973). Set in the workroom of a printing house, where a young male chauvinist publisher is confronted by a female egotist author.

RAPHAEL, LENNOX (1940–   ), Journalist, poet, and playwright. Born in Trinidad. Has resided off and on in New York City. Worked as a reporter in Jamaica before first coming to the United States as a U.N. correspondent. In 1969 worked with the Teachers and Writers Collaborative at P.S. 26 in Brooklyn, New York. Has also been a staff writer for the *East Village Other,* and an editor of *Umbra,* a poetry journal based in New York. His writings have been published in *Negro Digest, American Dialog, New Black Poetry,* and *Natural Process.* *Address:* c/o Home Theatre, Ten Pelham St., Belmont, Port-of-Spain, Trinidad, West Indies.

PLAYS:
Che! (drama, 1 act, 1968). Described by *Jet* (May 15, 1969) as a " 'leave nothing-to-the-imagination' way-out play.'' An extremely controversial play, which was the subject of alleged nudity and sex on stage and against which an obscenity charge was upheld in court. Characters include Che Guevara, a nymphomaniac nun, and the president of the United States, all used symbolically and metaphorically by the author to make a sociopolitical statement concerning contemporary ideologies. Opened Off-Bway, apparently in late 1968 or early 1969, but was closed by police after only one night. Reopened Off-Off-Bway at the Free Store Theatre, New York, March 22, 1969. Pub. by Contact Books, North Hollywood, CA, 1969. **Blue Soap** (pre-1975). Music by ARCHIE SHEPP.

RAVELOMANANTSOA, GLEN ANTHONY. See BUTLER, GLEN ANTHONY.

REAGON, (Dr.) BERNIECE, Singer, composer, and teacher. Based in Washington, DC. Director of the Smithsonian's Program in Black American Culture. Formerly associated with the DC Black Repertory Co. and the SNCC (Student Nonviolent Coordinating Committee) Freedom Singers.

PLAYS:
A Day, A Life, A People (song talk, 1975). Conceived and dir. by Reagon. "This theatre piece, using a spectrum of Black music, focused on the daily lives of some Black people living in the nation's capitol."—*Black World,* April 1976, p. 84. Prod. by the DC Black Repertory Co., 1975. **Upon This Rock** (song poem [also called a song talk], 1 act, 1974). Based on the black American historical and musical experience. Prod. by

the DC Black Repertory Co., 1974. **Tribute to Sojourner Truth** (1979). Coauthor, with
*June Jordan. Prod. by the New York Shakespeare Festival Public Theatre, 1979; dir.
by NTOZAKE SHANGE.

REDMOND, EUGENE B. (1937–   ), Poet, publisher, critic, and teacher
who has written and adapted a number of poetic works for the stage. Born in St.
Louis, MO. Reared in East St. Louis, IL. Educated at Southern Illinois Univ.
(B.A. in English literature, 1964) and Washington Univ. (M.A., 1966). Founding president of Black River Writers Press (now quiescent), which has published
several books of his poetry, including *Sentry of the Four Golden Pillars* (1970),
River of Bones and Flesh and Blood (1971), and *Songs from an Afro-Phone*
(1972). Has held editorships of a number of newspapers in East St. Louis, 1962–
67. His writings have appeared in numerous publications, including *Black Orpheus, American Dialog, Journal of Black Poetry, The Sou'wester, Reflections,
Free Lance, Rumble, Black World, Black Lines,* and *The Black Scholar*. Edited
the works of the late Henry Dumas for Random House, 1974. Visiting lecturer in
Afro-American literature at Webster Coll., Summer 1968; poet-in-residence and
director of language arts workshops at Southern Illinois Univ., 1968–69; writer-
in-residence and lecturer in Afro-American studies at Oberlin Coll., 1969–70;
English professor and poet-in-residence, Ethnic Studies Dept., California State
Univ. at Sacramento, 1970–; writer-in-residence at Southern Univ., Baton
Rouge, LA, summers of 1971 and 1972. Consultant to numerous public, private,
and community institutions in the design of black studies, writing, performing
arts, and educational programs. Received first prize in the Festival of Arts and
Poetry Contest, Washington Univ., 1965; honorable mention, Norma Lowery
Memorial Poetry Contest, 1965–66; first prize, *Free Lance* Poetry Contest, 1966;
honorable mention, Wednesday Club Sr. Original Verse Contest, 1968; a reso-
lution from the California State Assembly, 1974, for literary and community service; a writing grant from California State Univ., Sacramento, 1973; and
numerous other academic, literary, community service, and performance awards.

PLAYS AND DRAMATIC WORKS:
Shadows Before the Wall (1966). Prod. at Southern Neighborhood Center, East St.
Louis, 1966; dir. by Lena Weathers.
   The Face of the Deep (poetic ritual, full length, 1971). Uses music, song, dance, and
the works of several black poets and singers to extol the black mystique of endurance,
strength, and power. Prod. at California State Univ., Sacramento, Winter 1971; and at
Southern Univ., Baton Rouge, Summer 1971; dir. by author.
   9 Poets with the Blues (poetic ritual, full length, 1971). (Also prod. as *Poets with
the Blues.*) Apparently utilizes the works of nine poets and appropriate musical settings
to illustrate and display the "blues" concept embodied in the title. Prod. at California
State Univ., Sacramento, May 1971. Also performed at several other Northern California
sites during spring and summer of same year; dir. by author.
   River of Bones (poetic ritual, full length, 1972). Poetry, music (mainly drums), and
dance are utilized to illustrate the roots of black tradition. Adapt. principally from the

author's volume of poetry, *River of Bones and Flesh and Blood* (1971). Prod. at California State Univ., Sacramento, late Fall 1972; dir. by author.

The Night John Henry Was Born (poetic ritual, full length, 1972). Utilizes the work of several black poets, interspersed with choral interludes, to celebrate the legend of John Henry, black folk hero, as a symbol of the struggles and endurance of black people. Prod. at Southern Univ., Baton Rouge, during the summer of 1972; and at Cliff Top, WV, during the Second Annual John Henry Memorial Blues and Gospel Jubilee, during the summer of 1974; dir. by author.

Will I Still Be Here Tomorrow? (ritualistic eulogy with music, 1 act, 1973). On the death of Raymond Brewer, a 15–year-old youth who was murdered in 1972 in Sacramento. The dead youth speaks about his unrealized possibilities and potentialities. Prod. at California State Univ., Sacramento, and on KVOR-TV, during the spring and summer of 1973; dir. by Michael Gates, with the Sons/Ancestors Players. Public reading by the Frank Silvera Writers' Workshop (FSWW), at the Martinique Theatre, New York, May 1975. Unpub. script in the FSWW Archives/Schomburg Collection.

Kwanza: A Ritual in 7 Movements (poetic ritual, full length, 1973). To be performed during Kwanza, "a first fruits festival," created for black Americans by Ron Karenga, which combines traditional East African principles and concepts with elements of the black experience. According to Omonike Weusi-Puryear, author of the *Kwanza Handbook* (writing in *Essence*, Dec. 1979, p. 115), the purpose of the festival is "to celebrate our African heritage, to give thanks to our ancestors, to reaffirm the belief that elders should be respected, to reinforce our value framework for our children and to celebrate the seven principles of the Black value system, the Nguzo Saba." The seven movements in Redmond's ritual correspond to the seven principles of the black value system: (1) unity; (2) self-determination; (3) collective work and responsibility; (4) cooperative economics; (5) purpose; (6) creativity; and (7) faith. Prod. during the Christmas–New Year period (Kwanza begins Dec. 26 and ends Jan. 1), at California State Univ., and in the residential community, 1973–74; dir. by Michael Gates.

Music and I Have Come at Last (theatrical collage, full length, 1974). A stage adaptn. of the prose and poetry of the late *Henry Dumas. Performed at California State Univ., Sacramento, 1974, with the Sons/Ancestors Players; dir. by Tommy Ellis.

There's a Wiretap in My Soup, or Quit Bugging Me (morality play with music, 1 act, 1974). Satire of the Watergate scandal, in the context of a mock Independence Day celebration, with allusions to a number of famous historical and contemporary persons, including George Washington, Abraham Lincoln, Richard Nixon, Sigmund Freud, and Franz Fanon. Prod. in Miller's Park, Sacramento, before 4,000 people during Juneteenth celebration in June 1974; commissioned by the Sacramento area Black Caucus.

REED, EDWINA, Playwright.

PLAY:
A Man Always Keeps His Word (black history play, 1 act [4 scenes], 1963). About President Lincoln's decision to write the Emancipation Proclamation. Pub. in *Negro History Bulletin*, Jan. 1963, pp. 138–40.

REILLY, J. TERRANCE (1945–   ), Playwright, actor, director, university professor. Born in the Bronx, NY. Received the B.A. from Harpur Coll., and the M.F.A. from Cornell Univ., where he also worked toward the Ph.D. In

1972 was teaching literature at the State University of New York at Oswego, where he was also involved in acting, directing, playwriting, and radio broadcasting. Member of the Board of Directors of the Foundation for Research in Afro-American Creative Arts. Playwright-in-residence of the Black Masquers Guild, presumably of the State University of New York, 1972.

COLLECTION:
BLACK! Myra House, Poughkeepsie, NY, 1972. Contains **Enter at Your Own Risk, Bogie, Montage, Jejune Ju Ju** and **Waiting on the Man** (all 1972).

PLAYS AND DRAMATIC WORKS:
Enter at Your Own Risk (revolutionary theatre game, 1 act, 1972). Several white actors, thought to be members of the audience, are apparently abused, raped, or murdered by black actors carrying guns and knives, while other white actors, not known to be participants, react with horror and protest to the mock mayhem and violence. After finally being told that they are only watching a theatre game, the entire audience is shot. Pub. in the author's collection *BLACK!*

Bogie (drama, 1 act, 1972). The story of a black taxi driver who is no longer needed, and who places all his hopes on the outcome of a horse race. Pub. in the author's collection *BLACK!*

Montage (monologue, 1 act, 1972). Subtitled "An All Black Play." A character called E. Z. Raper makes a speech on "Black Power." Pub. in the author's collection *BLACK!*

Jejune Ju Ju (monologue, 1 act, 1972). Subtitled "A Mad Poem in the Form of a Play." Uses several types of word-play on the "black is beautiful" theme. Pub. in the author's collection *BLACK!*

Waiting on the Man (morality play, 1 act, 1972). Three characters, Yellow, Black, and Brown, representing different facets of black ideology, debate among themselves while "waiting on the [white] Man." Pub. in the author's collection *BLACK!*

Confrontation ("anti-abortion tract," 1 act, 1975). Prod. by the Weusi Kuumba Troupe, New York, 1975.

RENÉ, YVES, Actress-playwright. Born in Port-au-Prince, Haiti, where she attended school. Came to the United States in 1965 and studied acting with ERNIE MCCLINTOCK at the Afro-American Studio of Acting and Speech and the Sonia Moore Studio in New York. She has appeared on stage; in most of the New York based soap operas—most recently in "All My Children"; and as a Haitian in the movie *A Brother from Another Planet*. *Address:* 89–11 153rd St., Jamaica, NY 11432.

PLAYS:
Toussaint L'Ouverture: First of the Blacks (biographical drama, 3 acts, 1979). First reading at the Frank Silvera Writers' Workshop (FSWW), New York, April 1979. **Corvée** (drama, 1 act, pre-1986). About Haitian migration (the boat people). Sched. for a reading by UBU Repertory Theatre, 1986.

RHEA, BETTY L. (1940–   ), Poet, playwright, theatrical director, and teacher. Born in Denver, CO, where he was educated at Colorado Univ., Denver Univ., and The Community Coll. of Denver. Has also studied at Metro State

Coll., working toward a degree in communications with a minor in theatre. Freelance copyist and colorist for Vogel and Rothman Fine Arts, New York, 1965–69. Activities in the Denver community include creative writing instr., Model Cities Cultural Center, 1969–72; coproducer and writer for Channel 6 series, "Blacks Then and Now," 1972; codirector of *Five on the Black Hand Side* at Bonfils Theatre, 1972 (was the first black woman to direct a play at that theatre); director for the Creathon Theatre Group, 1971–78. Freelance writer, 1978–present. Three of her poems have been included in *Come to Think of It* (1972), an anthology of poems by local poets. Recipient of a grant from NEA to develop black theatre in Denver, 1974. *Address:* 2807 Jasmine, Denver, CO 80207.

PLAYS AND DRAMATIC WORKS:
The Holiday (domestic drama, 1 act, 1970). Concerns the anger and frustration faced by a black family after the death of the husband/father. Prod. at the Model Cities Cultural Center, Denver, Nov. 16, 1970. **Fantasy and Lies** (1972). Prod. at Lowry Air Force Base, Denver, Nov. 15, 1972. **Count Dracula Takes a Bride** (children's play, 1973). Prod. at the Forum Center for Children, Denver, Aug. 11, 1973. **A Time for Fun** (children's play, 1975). Prod. at Smith Elementary School, Denver, April 22, 1975. **Laying on of Hands** (historical musical, in progress, 1983). History of blacks in America from slavery time to the present.

RHODES, CRYSTAL V., Playwright, TV scriptwriter. A native of Indianapolis, IN, now residing in New York City. Educated at Indiana Univ. (B.A. in sociology, 1970), Atlanta Univ. (M.A. in sociology, 1974), Laney Coll., Oakland (television production and film production courses, 1979–81). Has also attended a number of workshops, including Circle Film Production Co.—TV/Film Workshop, San Francisco; Black Repertory Group Theatre Playwrights Workshop, Oakland; Attic Theatre Playwrights Workshop, Oakland; Media Alliance Television Scriptwriting Workshop, San Francisco; Western Public Radio Writers Workshop, San Francisco. Her plays have been produced by the Black Repertory Group Theatre, Berkeley, CA; Encore Theatre, Washington, DC; California Museum of Afro-American History and Culture, Los Angeles, 1983; Inner City Cultural Center, Los Angeles; Oakland Community Theatre; WPA Productions, Oakland; and Go Productions, San Francisco. Coproducer/scriptwriter for "Getting By," a 13–week, half-hour series, Oakland, telecast on Teleprompter cable TV stations in Oakland/Piedmont, 1981. Producer/hostess/writer for "Bay Arts Beat," an hour-long radio show on the arts for radio station KBLX, Berkeley, 1982–N83. Has published reviews in such newspapers and magazines as *California Voice, Metro-Reporter, Oakland Post, San Francisco Post, City Arts,* and *Black Collegian.* Member of DG and Media Alliance. Nominated as one of the Outstanding Young Women in America, 1983. *Address;* 276 Adams Street, #14, Oakland, CA 94610. *Agents—*Teleplays and screenplays only: Frank Stewart, 1745 Neil Armstrong #201, Montecello, CA 90604. Play inquiries only: c/o CVR, 5344 Kenwood, Indianapolis, IN 94608.

REPRESENTATIVE PLAYS:

The Trip (comedy, 1 act, 1979). Concerns an automobile trip from Chicago to California taken by four women friends who have known each other since college days, and its disastrous effect on their friendship. Almost from the beginning, things start to go wrong, which causes them one by one to begin bickering and pointing out small flaws and annoying habits that they can't stand in each other. By the time they reach their destination, they are at each other's throats, cursing and bitching and revealing their true feelings to such an extent that they can barely stay in the same car together. They decide to return home immediately—by different planes! Prod. by the Black Repertory Group Theatre, Berkeley, 1979; by the Soul People Repertory Co., Indianapolis, 1980; by PCTV cable TV station, Oakland, 1980; and by Encore Theatre, Washington, DC, 1983. Pub. in *Center Stage* (Ostrow, 1981).

Please Don't Bury Me Before I Die (drama, full length, 1980). Prod. by the Black Repertory Group Theatre, Berkeley, 1980. Also prod. as an hour-long pilot for a TV series, **"Getting By"** (1981).

Mama's Man (comedy, 1 act, 1980). Prod. by the Black Repertory Group Theatre, 1980; Soul People Repertory Co., Indianapolis, 1980; Oakland Parks and Recreation Dept., 1981; California Museum of Afro-American History and Culture, Los Angeles, 1982; and Inner City Cultural Center (ICCC), Los Angeles, 1982.

The Loot (comedy, 1 act, 1980). Prod. by Black Repertory Group Theatre, 1981; broadcast on KPOO Radio, San Francisco, 1980; prod. at the California Museum of Afro-American History and Culture, Los Angeles, 1982; prod. by ICCC, 1982.

"Getting By" (TV series, half-hour, 13 weeks, 1981) Coproducer and scriptwriter. Prod. by "Getting By" Productions, Oakland; telecast on Teleprompter cable TV station, Oakland/Piedmont, 1981. Scripts include the author's **Please Don't Bury Me Before I Die** (1980), which was the pilot for the series. Titles of some of the other scripts are **Pot Luck** (drama), **The Honorable Mr. Peter Carson** (comedy), **The Encounter** (comedy), **Competition** (drama), **David** (drama), **The Dilemma** (drama), **The Date** (comedy), **Between a Rock and a Hard Place** (drama), and **Lillian Comes Home** (drama).

Stoops (comedy/drama, 2 acts, 1983). Prod. by Go Productions, San Francisco, 1983, at the On Broadway Theatre; dir. by BEAH RICHARDS. Presented at the Carver Community Theatre, San Antonio, TX, 1983, and on Children's Radio Theatre, San Francisco, 1983.

OTHER PLAYS AND DRAMATIC WORKS:

Trial of Ruth Lewis (TV drama, 2 hrs., 1978). **Mommy I'm Pregnant** (TV drama, 2 hrs., 1979). **Crystal Palaces** (drama, 3 acts, 1981). Prod. by Oakland Community Theatre, 1981). **Lady Day Don't Pass This Way No More** (comedy, 1 act, 1982). **Loving Amber** (TV drama, 2 hrs., 1982. Thirteen scripts written for WPA Productions, Oakland, 1982. **Queen of the River Niger** (drama, 1 act, 1983).

RHONE, TREVOR (1940–   ), Caribbean playwright, whose plays have been produced and published in the United States, England, and the West Indies. Born in Jamaica. Educated in England, where he studied traditional European classical drama during the 1960s. At age 25, returned to Jamaica, where he came to discover the wealth of his native heritage. Founded the Barn Theatre in Kingston, and served as its resident playwright for 12 years. ADDRESS: c/o Broadway Play Publishing, Inc., 357 W. 20th St., New York, NY 10011.

COLLECTION:
OLD STORY TIME AND OTHER PLAYS. Essex, England: Longman House, 1981; distributed by Broadway Play Publishing Co., New York. Contains **Old Story Time** (1979), **School's Out** (1975), and **Smile Orange** (1971).

PLAYS:
The Harder They Come [*sic*] (feature film, full length: coauthor of screenplay, 1970–71). This film, which launched the international stardom of Jamaican reggae singer-actor Jimmy Clif, concerns a Caribbean singer and his attempts to establish himself within the "system." It also presents a revealing picture of Jamaican life. Prod. in Jamaica, and released by New World, 1973, dir. by Perry Henzell.

Smile Orange (Caribbean drama, 2 acts, 1970–71; also adapt. as a screenplay, 1975). Set in a "tourist-trap hotel" in Jamaica, the play, as described by Mervyn Morris in his introduction to the pub. script, is a "funny," "serious," and "devastating comment on tourism and attitudes the industry harbours or can breed." First prod. at the Barn Theatre, Kingston, opening Nov. 1, 1971, for 245 perfs.; dir. by Dennis Scott. Pub. in the author's *OLD STORY TIME AND OTHER PLAYS* (1981).

School's Out (Caribbean drama, 2 acts, 1975). Set in the staff room of a church school, this play depicts the shortcomings and despiriting conditions of a Jamaican educational system as seen through the eyes of an idealistic but self-righteous new teacher. First prod. at the Barn Theatre, Kingston, opening April 3, 1975; dir. by Yvonne Jones-Brewster, with the author in the role of the new teacher. Pub. in the author's *OLD STORY TIME AND OTHER PLAYS* (1981).

Old Story Time (Caribbean drama, 3 acts, 1979). Described by the publisher as "a poignant commentary on the pride of motherhood," which (according to the *Daily Gleaner*) makes "a serious comment on Jamaican and on human values."—Pub. script. First prod. by the Bahamas Drama Circle at the Dundas Centre for the Performing Arts in Nassau, opening April 19, 1979; dir. by the author. Subsequently perfd. for more than 200 perfs. in the Virgin Islands, Trinidad, Miami, Toronto, and Jamaica. Pub. in the author's *OLD STORY TIME AND OTHER PLAYS* (1981).

Two Can Play (domestic comedy, full length, 1984). "A husband and wife from Jamaica, W.I. devise a scheme involving the wife's marriage to an American and then divorce as a way of both gaining entry in the U.S., only to find their own relationship is put to the acid test by the wife's independence."—*Black Masks*, April 1985, p. 4. Prod. Off-Bway by the Negro Ensemble Co., New York, for two successful runs; the first in the Spring of 1985, and the second in the Summer of 1985. Prod. as a TV special by KET Enterprise (Lexington, KY), starring Grace McGhie and Charles Hyatt. This perf. is available for broadcast on one-inch Type C video tape, or for home use on 1/2–inch VHS or Beta formats from KET Enterprise, 600 Cooper Dr., Lexington, KY 40502.

OTHER PLAYS:
(All presumably prod. by the Barn Theatre, Jamaica.) **The Gadget** (1969). **Music Boy** (1970). **Comic Strip** (1973). **Sleeper** (1974). **The Game** (1985).

RICHARDS, BEAH (Beulah Richardson), Stage, screen, and television actress; playwright. Born in Vicksburg, MS. Studied at Dillard Univ., New Orleans, and San Diego Community Theatre. Best known for her role as Sidney Poitier's mother in the film *Guess Who's Coming to Dinner* (1967), for which she received an Academy Award nomination as Best Supporting Actress. Performed as Sister Margaret in JAMES BALDWIN's *The Amen Corner* (1965), for which she won a *Theatre World* Award. Other stage acting credits include *Take a Giant Step* (1956), *A Raisin in the Sun* (1959), and *Purlie Victorious* (1961). Other films include *Take a Giant Step* (1961), *Gone Are the Days* (1963), *In the Heat of the Night* (1967), *Hurry Sundown* (1967), *The Great White Hope* (1970), and *Mahogany* (1975). TV appearances include "The Bill Cosby Show" (1970), "I Spy" (1967), "Hawaii Five O" (1969), *Just an Old Sweet Song* (1976), and *Roots II—The Second Generation.* Elected to the Black Filmmakers Hall of Fame in 1974. *Agent:* Jack Fields & Associates, 9255 Sunset Boulevard, Suite 1105, Los Angeles, CA 90069.

DRAMATIC WORKS:

A Black Woman Speaks (performance piece, 1 act, 1950). A long poetic monologue in which a black woman addresses white women, and confronts them with their role in the oppression of black people. Winner of an Emmy Award in 1975. First performed by Richards for the Women of Peace in Chicago, 1950. Prod. by ICCC, Los Angeles, May 24–July 21, 1974; dir. by C. BERNARD JACKSON and performed by Richards. Revived by ICCC, May-Sept. 1975. This piece, which is in Richards's permanent repertoire, has been performed on tour of colleges, libraries, churches, book fairs, and other locations in Los Angeles and elsewhere. Pub. in *Freedomways,* 1st Qtr. 1964, under the name Beulah Richardson; in the author's *A Black Woman Speaks and Other Poems* (1974); in *Nine Plays by Black Women* (Wilkerson, 1986). Has also been recorded by the author.

One in a Crowd ("showcase," full length, 1951). "Combining a Shakespearean style and 'social' humor, the play contains subplots of the emancipation of the Black woman from Whites and from male domination." "Set in a New York penthouse [it] deals with the quest of a nightclub singer, Elizabeth Dundee, for revenge against her illegitimate brother's white father whom she perceives as the destructive force of her family."— "The History of Theatre Productions at the Los Angeles Inner City Cultural Centre, 1965–1976" (Sheffey-Stinson, Ph.D. diss., 1979), p. 82. First prod. by ICCC, May 28–Oct. 31, 1971 (20 years after it was written); dir. by C. Bernard Jackson. With the author in the role of Elizabeth Dundee, and featuring Thalmus Rasulala, Glynn Turman, Gloria Calomee, Ellen Harris, and Michael Cameron. Revived by ICCC May 5–June 24, 1973, with "a gala twenty-five dollar per seat premiere and dance . . . given in honor of Beah Richards and the cast. This premiere was hosted by fellow minority artists Paul Winfield, Cicely Tyson . . . ABBEY LINCOLN . . . and others."—Ibid., p. 84 (capitalization added).

RICHARDSON, MEL, Playwright. Based in the San Francisco Bay area.

PLAY:

The Breach (1969). A play "about the barrenness of a negroboni marriage."—*Black World,* April 1974, p. 91. Prod. at Merritt Coll., Oakland, CA, March 1969, and in the San Francisco Bay area, 1970–71.

RICHARDSON, VIRGIL, Playwright. Formerly associated with the Performing Arts Society of Los Angeles (PASLA), CA. In 1977 he was residing in Mexico.

PLAY:
After Hours (morality play, 3 acts, 1972). About a bar owner who becomes involved in a crime that leads to murder and blackmail. Prod. by PASLA, 1975.

RICHE, ROBERT, Playwright. (Racial and national identity not verified.)

PLAY:
Message from the Grass Roots (black history doc., 3 acts, pre-1968). Loosely based on the life and career of Malcolm X. Depicts the life of a contemporary black political figure who rises from a life as a thief and drug pusher to become one of the most influential black leaders in America. As described by the publisher, "The play moves from a tragic mid-West boyhood, to the search for the easy life in Harlem, to jail and Muslim conversion, to life on the outside as a Muslim minister, through the painful break with his religion and with his idolized spiritual leader, then on to new insights in Africa, the triumphant return to America and, finally, the tragic assassination in New York."—*Samuel French's Basic Catalog of Plays* (1985). Premiered by the Old Vic Theatre, at Bristol, England, prior to its prodn. in the United States by the James Weldon Johnson Theatre Center in Harlem, New York, Oct. 1958. Pub. by Samuel French, New York, c. 1969.

RILEY, CLAYTON (1935–   ), Author, director, playwright, and drama critic. One of the leading interpreters of the Black Arts movement. Born in Brooklyn, New York. Entertainment editor of the *New York Amsterdam News;* drama critic of *Liberator;* and a contributor to *Ebony,* the *New York Times, Black World, Black Creation,* and numerous other periodicals. His work is anthologized in *Harlem* (Clarke, 1970) and *The Black Aesthetic* (Gaylor, 1971). Wrote the introduction to *Black Quartet* (1970). Has taught courses in black drama, literature, music, filmmaking, and other subjects at Fordham Univ., Howard Univ., Sarah Lawrence Coll., and the American Film Inst. Served as production asst. in the filming of *Nothing but a Man* (1964). Television appearances include "Black Journal" (1971) and "Black News" (1971). Directed *On the Goddam Lock-in* (Off-Bway, 1975). Member of the Harlem Writers Guild and the Drama Desk. *Address:* c/o Joy Jones, 175 W. 12th St. #12–B, New York, NY.

PLAYS:
Over (1975). Public reading by the Frank Silvera Writers' Workshop (FSWW), at the Martinique Theatre, New York, Dec. 1975. Unpub. script in the FSWW Archives/ Schomburg Collection. **Gilbeau** (drama, full length, 1975). Concerns the life of an aging pimp who becomes involved with drug pushers and black revolutionaries. Staged reading by the Urban Arts Corps, New York, April 1975. Prod. Off-Bway by the New Federal Theatre, New York, Jan. 1976; dir. by author.

RILEY, NORMAN, Playwright. Based in New York City.

PLAY:
Runaway People (drama, 1 act, 1972). Concerns the unsuccessful efforts of two young black idealists to break away from their ghetto environment. Prod. by the Harlem School of the Arts, New York, March 1972.

RISON, ALTON D., Author, songwriter, lyricist, producer, and New York City junior high school principal. Grew up in Brooklyn, NY; currently lives in Uniondale, NY. Self-taught club musician and composer. The first black to graduate from the Univ. of Texas (sociology, early 1950s). Served in the U.S. Army as a psychiatric social worker technician. Worked in the New York City Dept. of Welfare before entering the New York City school system, eventually becoming principal of Brooklyn's Intermediate School 117 in Feb. 1971, which he transformed from its reputation as "The Criminal School" to one of the model junior high schools in the city, thereby gaining national recognition as a consultant for his successful innovative scientific methods of educational reform. Because of his accomplishments, in 1975 he was selected chairperson of the Urban Task Force Education Subcommittee on Math, Reading, and the Curriculum for the Federal Office of Education's Chicago Conference. An early member of the Harlem Writers' Guild, he began writing short stories and novels, and shifted to playwriting in the early 1960s. Founder of his own production company, Alton D. Rison Productions, Inc. *Address*—Home: 656 Winthrop Dr., Uniondale, NY 11553. Alternate: Alton D. Rison Prodns., Inc., Box 157, Uniondale, NY 11553.

REPRESENTATIVE PLAYS AND DRAMATIC WORKS:

In the Teachers' Lounge (comedy, full length, 1976). A funny play with an interracial cast, about black and white teachers in conflict over school integration. First performed at the Henry St. Settlement Theatre, 1976. Performed at the Flagstone Theatre Center, Hempstead, Long Island, New York, April 1977; reopened Dec. 1977–Jan. 1978.

Rich Like an Alabama Sheriff (musical comedy, 2 acts, 1979). "The story evolves around a farm boy from the South who is told and even encouraged by the white landlord of his mother's farm land how he could make it big on public assistance in New York with a check every two weeks without working," thereby becoming "as rich as the white sheriff who owns a big car and fine clothes—all on Welfare."—*New York Amsterdam News,* Feb. 2, 1980. Prod. at the Masonic Temple, Brooklyn, Jan.-Feb. 1980, dir. by Matthew Bernard Johnson; then on tour of Long Island from Feb.-March., returning to the Masonic Temple for a final engagement. Also dir. in another prodn. by Richard Wyr.

Oh Brooklyn You're My Home (musical satire, 2 acts, 1982). Centers around Harry Bowen, a new principal in a problem school in Brooklyn's Bayridge area. He must deal with a cantankerous staff, including a reluctant custodian, a mischievous but potentially bright student from Brownsville, and his irate parents. The musical presents, additionally, a rivalrous school staff, proud of their Brooklyn locales. In song and prose, various street names, places, and events in Brooklyn are brought to life with good-natured fun and humor. Prod. in Brooklyn at the Ethical Humanist Soc. in Garden City, and at Roosevelt H.S., Sept. 1982.

On Sunday I Am Somebody (musical, 2 acts, 1984). "A one-hour revue, peppered with excitement to keep an outdoor audience alive."—*Big Red News,* July 7, 1984. Draws its materials from the motifs, characters, and situations of the black church. Public reading at the Frank Silvera Writers' Workshop, New York. Played the Quintessence Theatre Club in Manhattan, 1981. Prod. in an outdoor production, at the request of the Nassau County (New York) Office of Cultural Development, and presented at the Lakeside Theatre in Eisenhower Park in East Meadow, New York, July 8, 1984; dir. by Charles David Brooks. Unpub. script in the FSWW Archives/Schomburg Collection.

Mr. B Changed the Key (musical, full length, 1984). Traces a pop singer's legendary rise to superstardom, while describing his bittersweet years prior to and during reaching public acclaim as top male vocalist during the 1940s. His crowning achievement was being the first black love idol among both black and white audiences and the breaking of a six-year-old attendance record established by a legendary white singer at the Paramount Theatre in New York. Prod. by FSWW, Dec. 6–23, 1984; dir. by Rey D. Allen. Unpub. script in the FSWW Archives/Schomburg Collection.

The Operetta of Bedford Stuyvesant (musical epic, full length, 1985). Book, music, and lyrics by Rison. Focuses on the "upheavals of the 60's, over jobs, poverty, and "community control of schools,' pitting various forces: radicals and ethnics, the Mayor and union officials in deep power struggles, creating heroes and villains, romances and love life."—Author's publicity. Backer's audition presented at the Latin Quarter, New York, Dec. 16, 1985.

OTHER PLAYS AND DRAMATIC WORKS:
In the Principal's Office (pre-1985). Unpub. script in the FSWW Archives/Schomburg Collection. **Is This the PTA or Not** (pre-1985). Unpub. script in the FSWW Archives, Schomburg Collection.

RIVERS, CONRAD KENT (1933–1968), Promising poet and author in whose honor *Black World* magazine established an annual Conrad Kent Rivers Poetry Award following his untimely death. Born in Atlantic City, NJ. Lived in Chicago, IL. Died in Gary, IN. Educated at Wilberforce Univ. (A.B., 1955), Indiana Univ., Chicago Teachers Coll., and Temple Univ. His volumes of poetry include *Perchance to Dream, Othello* (1959), *These Black Bodies and This Sunburnt Face* (1962), *Dust at Selma* (1965), *The Still Voice of Harlem* (1968), and *The Wright Poems* (1973).

PLAYS:
To Make a Poet Black (poetic collage, 1950s). Prod. by the Penthouse Players, Chicago, late 1950s, for "many performances." **Who's Afraid of Malcolm X** (morality play, 1 act, 1967). Explores the contrast in attitudes between a white playboy and his black servant concerning class and race. Incomplete script in the Hatch-Billops Collection.

RIVERS, LOUIS (Lou) (1922–   ), Actor, director, author, playwright, and English teacher. Born in Savannah, GA. Educated at Savannah State Coll. (B.S. in English, 1946); NYU (M.A. in dramatic arts, on an Experimental Teacher Fellowship, 1949); Fordham Univ. (Ph.D. in administration and supervision, 1976); with studies in playwriting at Catholic Univ. (with Walter Kerr), Yale Univ. (with Elmer Rice), and the Gene Frankel Studio, New York; and acting at the Brette-Warren Studio (with Howard da Silva). Married; four children. Language arts teacher at Center H.S., Waycross, GA, 1946–49; instr. of language arts at West Virginia State Coll., Southern Univ., and Tougaloo Coll., 1951–58. Has taught at high schools and junior high schools in the Bronx, Brooklyn, and New York City, 1958–69. Drama coach and consultant for Voices, Inc., New York City, 1966. Teacher of philosophy of design, Parsons Coll. of Fashion and Design, 1969–. Currently assoc. prof. of writing and speech at New York

City Community Coll., Brooklyn, c. 1976–. Consultant and program designer for ASPIRA's tutorial program, New York City, 1966; for Youth in Action's tutorial program, Bedford-Stuyvesant, Brooklyn, 1967; and for Knickerbocker-Wyckoff Community Services, Bushwick, Brooklyn, 1969. Member, National Advisory Subcommittee of Urban-Rural School Development Program, Washington, DC, 1969–present; panelist, New York City Council of English Teachers, 1968; panelist, New York State English Council, Syracuse, 1970. Affiliated with the New Heritage Repertory Theatre, New York, 1973. Joint author of *Pattern Practices to Learn and Write By* (1972). Poems in *Driftwood, Discord, Community Review,* and *Perspectives.* Member, National Writers Club, DG, Authors League of America, Phi Delta Kappa, and Kappa Delta Pi. Recipient of Experimental Teacher Fellowship, Catholic Univ., 1949; John Hay Whitney Opportunity Fellowship for theatre, 1957–58; NEA Fellowship, NYU; EPDA Fellowship, CUNY/Kingsboro Community Coll.; Experienced Teacher Fellowship, CUNY/Hunter Coll.; and Andrew Mellon Fellowship, CUNY/Graduate School and Univ. Center. *Address:* 333 Lafayette Ave., Brooklyn, NY 11238.

REPRESENTATIVE PLAYS AND DRAMATIC WORKS:

The Scabs (drama with music, 1 act, 1962). During the Depression years, a group of out-of-work Harlem musicians decides to "scab" the jobs of some white waiters who are on strike. Pub. in *First Stage: A Quarterly of New Drama* (Purdue Univ., Lafayette, IN), Fall 1962.

Madam Odum (comedy, 2 acts, 1973). A black woman educator at a southern college becomes a formidable opponent when the school tries to force her into retirement, to be replaced by a young man. Prod. by the New Heritage Theatre, New York, May 18–June 30, 1973, July 20, and Sept. 7–Oct. 29, 1973.

This Piece of Land (domestic drama, 1 act, 1974). Music by *Ben Carter. A terminally ill woman finds a way to help her husband hold on to a piece of land which he would otherwise lose. Prod. by the American Theatre Co., New York, Dec. 1974. Pub. in *Best Short Plays, 1977* (Richards, 1977).

More Bread and the Circus (1981). Pub. in *Center Stage* (Ostrow, 1981).

OTHER PLAYS AND DRAMATIC WORKS:

(All pre-1976, except where indicated.) **Black English** (comedy, 2 acts, 1974). A black college student who is having trouble passing his English course, and who is also romantically involved with the chairman of the English Dept., begins to revaluate his life, with a view to making some changes. **Black Pictures** // Also listed as **Portraits in Blackness** (a series of short scenes of black life, c. 1974). Scenes of black existence which take place in such locations as a public bus, a barber shop, a beauty salon, a bar, a street corner, a church, a house, and a front porch. **Bouquet for Lorraine** // Also listed as **A Rose for Lorraine** (drama, 2 acts). Concerned with the conflicts between black social classes, with regard to their different attitudes, values, and sexual roles. **A Case of Peppermint Gum** (comedy, 2 acts). Conflict of wills between a black maid and a white store manager in a Georgia five-and-ten-cent store. **Crabs in the Bucket** (drama, 1 act). A black woman in a southern town during World War II tries to influence her son and her community to work for political change. **Ghosts on My Land** (fantasy, 1 act). The reliving of an episode in history after the Civil War, involving a conflict between former slaves and whites over the possession of some land. **Mr. Randolph Brown** (drama,

2 acts). A black man is almost destroyed in a struggle for power. **Night's Passage into Purple Passion** // Also listed as **Purple Passages** (drama, 1 act). Deals with the black student revolts of the late 1960s, and is set on the campus of a southern black college. **Pictures for Jimmy, Jr.** // Also listed as **Jimmy Jr.** (drama, 1 act). Concerns the struggles of a young Harlem couple, who recently moved up from the South to improve their lives, when their plans are upset by the arrival of a new baby, Jimmy, Jr. **The Promise.** Unpub. script in the Hatch-Billops Collection. **Seeking** (tragedy, 2 acts). A religious black woman seeks to bring her family back together after it has been divided by alcoholism, political differences, and war. **Soldiers of Freedom** (1976). Prod. by the American Theatre Co., New York, 1976. **Spiritual Book Incident** // Also listed as **Spiritual Book Incident at Christmas Time** (musical, 2 acts). Music by *Ben Carter. The Biblical Christmas story retold in the modern black musical and dramatic idiom. **The Witnesses** (drama, 1 act). A black college professor tries to gain faculty support for a white colleague whose loyalty to the United States is being investigated by a legislative committee during the pre-McCarthy era.

RIVERS, SAM (Samuel Carthorne Rivers) (1980–   ), Composer, musician, orchestra leader, and performer on the flute, saxophone, and piano, Associated with the Harlem Opera Soc., New York City. *Address:* c/o Emory Taylor, Harlem Opera, 536 111th St., Suite 76, New York, NY 10025.

PLAYS:
Black Cowboys (musical, 1970). "A horse opera in jazz form."—*Black World,* April 1976, p. 57. Music by Rivers. Libretto by Emory Taylor. First prod. by the Afro-American Singing Theatre, New York, 1970. Again prod. by Emory Taylor's Harlem Jazz Opera (now Harlem Opera Soc.), New York, 1975. **Solomon and Sheba** (musical theatre work—presumably an opera, 1974). Coauthor, with ED TAYLOR (who apparently wrote the libretto). Prod. by the Harlem Opera Soc., at the Black Theatre Alliance annual festival, New York, 1974.

ROASHE, RENEE, Playwright.

PLAY:
Street King (historical pageant, 1 act, 1973). Coauthor, with BRUCE PEYTON. Depicts black enslavement through the ages, from its beginnings in Africa to the present day. Prod. by the Theatre for the Forgotten, Riker's Island, NY, 1973, as a project of the Work Release Program.

ROBERSON, ARTHUR (Art), Playwright. Apparently from Stockton, CA. Associated with the Performing Arts Soc. of Los Angeles (PASLA) and the Aldridge Players/West (AP/W) of Berkeley, CA.

PLAYS:
Don't Leave Go My Hand (1965). According to MARGARET WILKERSON, this play focuses on the "pathology within a [black] family."—*The Drama Review,* Dec. 1972, p. 29. One source, for which the citation has not been located, states that "an air of desolation and withdrawal from human comforts hovers about this play." Prod. by AP/W in Berkeley, 1965. Prod. by PASLA, 1969. **In the Shadow of Ham** (1968). **Run Sweet Child in Silence** (1968). **Melanosis** (1969).

ROBERSON, WILLIAM. See ROBINSON, WILLIAM.

ROBINSON, GARRETT (S. Garrett Robinson) (1939–   ), Playwright, songwriter, teacher, and librarian. Born in Columbus, OH. Received the B.S. in microbiology and physiological chemistry from Ohio State Univ., and the M.L.S. in library science and information science from Rutgers Univ. Has also done graduate work in environmental health science at Hunter Coll., CCNY. Has taught black theatre and creative writing courses in the Dept. of Black Studies, Jersey City State Coll. Currently head librarian, Hunter Coll. School of Health Sciences. In addition to writing plays, he has also written and published songs. His theatrical affiliations include the New Heritage Repertory Theatre (NHRT) and the Afro-American Repertory Theatre, both in New York. Recipient of a Schuster Faculty Fellowship Award for an Afro-Hispanic bilingual theatre project in East Harlem. *Address:* 313 E. 10th St., New York, NY 10009. *Agent:* Lily A. Robinson, Robinson Enterprises, 313 E. 10th St., New York, NY 10009.

REPRESENTATIVE PLAYS:
Hamhocks (comedy, 1 act, 1968). A dramatized tall tale about a man who loves to eat, a love-starved wife, and a stranger who eats the man's food and makes love to his wife. Prod. by NHRT in Harlem, in repertory, opening Aug. 16, 1968, and continuing through Feb. 28, 1971.

Whiteshop (comedy, 1 act, 1968). A cultural spoof about a charlatan who can turn black folks white for a fee. Prod. by NHRT in Harlem, opening Aug. 13, 1968, and continuing through Feb. 28, 1971, on double bill with the author's **Hamhocks** (1968).

Land of Lem (experimental play, 5 acts, 1971). A fusion of African and classical-European dramatic forms, to symbolize the spiritualistic and materialistic forces that have had their impact on the black American consciousness. Prod. by the Afro-American Repertory Theatre, at the Afro-Arts Cultural Center, New York, April 1971.

The Magic Drum (children's play, 1973). Dramatization of an African fable about three teenagers living alone in a village in Ghana. Prod. at Intermediate School 201, and at Harlem Hosp., May 1973. Pub. by Wazum Publications, Box 600, New York, NY 10009.

OTHER PLAYS:
Golden Apple (1970s). About two senior citizens in love. **Karma II** (1970s). About Appalachian urban whites.

ROBINSON, MATT (1937–   ), Producer, playwright, screenwriter, television scriptwriter, and songwriter. Born in Philadelphia, PA. Educated at Pennsylvania State Univ. (B.A., 1958). Staff writer for Station WCAU, Philadelphia, 1963–68, where he hosted "Black Book," "The Discophonic Scene," and "Opportunity Line." Writer-producer of "Sesame Street," 1968–71, for which he received a gold record, 1970. Writer for "The Cosby Show," 1986.

SELECTED PLAYS AND DRAMATIC WORKS:
Simmons from Chicago (musical, full length, 1973). Book by Robinson. Concerns "a small-time hustler who eventually out-hustles the biggest hustlers in town, including the mayor of New York City, the governor of New York, and the President of the U.S.,"

and "winds up as the secretary general of the UN."—*Jet*, May 10, 1973. Sched. for prodn. in 1973, to be dir. by Michael Schultz, and to feature actor-comedian RICHARD PRYOR, but the planned prodn. never materialized. [See also **Amazing Grace** (1974).]

Save the Children (black rock doc. musical film, full length [123 min.], 1973). Narration written and spoken by Robinson, who also prod. the film. Based on musical acts that were performed during Summer 1972 at the Black Expo in Chicago, sponsored by Jesse Jackson's Operation PUSH. The music is interpolated with montages of black children and vignettes of contemporary black urban life. Prod. by Robinson; dir. by Stan Lathan; released by Paramount Pictures. Individuals and groups appearing in the film include Jesse Jackson, the Jackson Five, Nancy Wilson, Gladys Knight & The Pips, Quincy Jones, Roberta Flack, Sammy Davis, Jr., Curtis Mayfield, James Cleveland, the Operation PUSH Mass Choir, JULIAN "CANNONBALL" ADDERLEY, Isaac Hayes, the Temptations, and Marvin Gaye.

Amazing Grace (feature film, full length: screenplay, 1974). Situation comedy, apparently based on his **Simmons from Chicago** (1973). According to *Variety*, "Amazing Grace stars Moms Mabley as a lovable but cantankerous old woman who reforms Moses Gunn into a successful but honest candidate for mayor in a large eastern city." Prod. by author, dir. by Stan Lathan, and released by United Artists, 1974. Other featured players include Slappy White, Rosalind Cash, Stepin Fetchit, and Butterfly McQueen.

Keyboard (1982). Prod. at the Henry St. Playhouse, early 1982; dir. by SHAUNEILLE PERRY, and featuring Cleavon Little, ZAIDA COLES, Giancarlo Esposito, Andre Robinson, Jr., Lex Mumson, and Louise Stubbs.

OTHER DRAMATIC WORKS:
Possession of Joel Delaney (screenplay, 1972). **"Sanford and Son"** (TV scripts, 1975). **"The Jeffersons"** (TV scripts, 1970s).

ROBINSON, WILLIAM (name uncertain; also cited in some sources as William Roberson), Significant playwright of the 1950s, whose work is cited by Darwin Turner in his article "The Negro Dramatist's Image of the Universe," reprinted in *Anthology of the American Negro in the Theatre* (Patterson, 1967), pp. 68, 72.

PLAYS:
The Passing Grade (1958). "Views education as . . . the hope of the [black] race" and "castigates the unjust administration of the rural Negro schools in the South."— Ibid. **The Anger of One Young Man** (1959). Describes the "frustration of a writer whose idealism is blighted by the mercenary materialism of the publishing trade."— Ibid.

RODERICK, D. B., Playwright. A member of the Negro Ensemble Co. (NEC) in New York City.

PLAYS:
The Gilded Window Box (morality play, 3 acts, 1974). About a black man's struggle to find his identity on both the physical and spiritual planes. **Blues for Kingston Street** (domestic drama, 3 acts, 1975; also adapt. as a screenplay). Concerns the problems of a southern black family now living in a Jewish community in Brooklyn, New York. Prod. Off-Bway by NEC, 1975. **Man, Woman, Life, Death, Infinity** (multimedia play, 3

acts, 1975). Designed to raise consciousness and spirituality and to facilitate the finding of one's identity. **Secondhand Rose** (morality play, 3 acts, 1975). Deals with a black man's struggle to escape alcoholism.

ROGERS, IRA, Playwright, actor, director, and musician. Based in Chicago, IL, where he graduated from Wilson Jr. Coll. Stage performances in Chicago include *Othello* (as Iago) and *The Emperor Jones*. Films include *Three Tough Guys* and *The Naked Ape*. Has made a number of TV commercials. Performed as a member of a two-man singing act called Inman and Ira, which toured the United States and abroad during the 1960s.

PLAYS AND DRAMATIC WORKS:
The Cellar Boheme (revue, full length, pre-1973). Prod. at the 8th St. Theatre, Chicago, prior to 1963. **To Reach a Circle** (1963). Prod. on TV in 1963, and later staged at The Church in Chicago. **Tetragrammanon Is** (surrealistic drama, full length, 1974). Coauthor, with *Chuck Davis. Apparently based on a work by François Dimanche. Described by the *Chicago Defender/Accent* (June 18, 1977, p. 2) as "a play of incendiary brilliance" and "a work of ingenius symbolism," in which "humans representing the spirit of life rush by with dramatic urgency." First prod. by the Experimental Black Actors Guild (X-Bag), at Parkway Community House, Chicago, July 5–Aug. 25, 1974. Prod. at the 11th St. Theatre, Chicago, Summer 1977; dir. by Rogers. With Bartholomew Miro, Jr., who appeared in the Bway prodn. of *Hair,* Corrine Rogers, who plays Pooter in *Cooley High,* Helene Barrett, and Donald X. Williams.

ROLLINS, BRYANT (1937–   ), Journalist, novelist, poet, and playwright. Born in New York City, where he currently resides. Educated at Northeastern Univ. (B.A. in English, 1960). Has been associated with or written for the *Boston Globe,* as copy boy and reporter, 1955–56; *Time* and *Newsweek* magazines, as stringer, 1963–66; the *Bay State Banner,* as cofounder and editor, 1965–66; and the *New York Amsterdam News,* as executive editor, 1971–72. Author of two novels: *Danger Song* (1967) and *Go Down Slow*. In 1968 he was associated with the OM Theatre Workshop of the Boston Theatre Co. *Address—* Home: 138 Manhattan Ave., New York, NY 10025. Office: Graduate School of Journalism, Columbia University, 116th St. and Broadway, New York, NY 10025. *Agent:* Anita Diamant, 51 E. 42nd St., New York, NY 10017.

PLAY:
Riot (drama, 1 act, 1968). Coauthor, with Julie Portman. An interracial panel consisting of two whites and two blacks, representing four different ideological positions concerning the racial problem in America, convenes for a discussion, but the meeting is broken up by a riot. Prod. by the OM Theatre Workshop of the Boston Theatre Co., at Broadway United Church of Christ, New York, 1968. Earned for the OM Theatre Workshop an Obie Award, 1969.

ROY, JESSIE H., Elementary school teacher and playwright.
PLAY:
Bridging the Gap (TV doc., 1 act, 1957). Coauthor, with GENEVA C. TURNER. Pub. in *Negro History Bulletin,* March 1957, pp. 133–37.

RUSSELL, CHARLIE L. (1932–   ), Playwright, freelance writer, teacher, editor, actor, and theatrical director. Born in Monroe, LA. Graduated from Technical H.S. in Oakland, CA. Received the B.S. degree in English from the Univ. of San Francisco, 1959, and the M.S.W. (Master of Social Work) from NYU, 1966. Also attended Santa Rosa Jr. Coll. and Oakland Jr. Coll. Studied acting in New York with the Actors Studio, the National Black Theatre (NBT), and privately under Clarice Taylor. Studied directing with GILBERT MOSES and the New Dramatists Guild Workshop. Asst. prof. and counselor, SEEK Program, CCNY, Dept. of Special Programs, 1967–74; writer-in-residence and chairman of Playwrights Workshop NBT, 1969–74; adjunct asst. prof., Livingston Coll. of Rutgers Univ., New Jersey, where he taught basic English and creative writing, 1972–73; adjunct asst. prof., filmscript writing, Visual Arts Dept., NYU, 1974–75; writer-in-residence, American Place Theatre (APT), 1977, 1978; drama instr., Contra Costa Coll., San Pablo, CA, 1977–82; exec. and artistic director, East Bay Players, a community theatrical group based in Richmond, CA. Has directed numerous plays in New York and California, including *In the Wine Time, Ain't Supposed to Die a Natural Death,* **Five on the Black Hand Side** (1969), *In White America,* **The Incident at Terminal Ecstacy Acres** (pre-1983), *Ceremonies in Dark Old Men,* and *Ten Little Indians.* Columnist for the *Manhattan Tribune;* editor, *Onyx* magazine, New York City; fiction editor, *Liberator* magazine. His articles have appeared in *Essence, Liberator, Encore, Black World, Onyx,* the *Manhattan Tribune,* and the *New York Amsterdam News.* His short stories have been anthologized in *The Best Short Stories by Negro Writers* (Hughes, 1967), *Afro-American Literature: Fiction* (Adams, Conn, & Slepian, 1979); and *The Urban Reader* (Cahill & Cooper, 1971). Has also published a novella, *A Birthday Present for Kathryn Kenyatta* (late 1970s). Serves as a coach for Little League basketball. Member of the NAACP and the Sickle Cell Anemia Foundation. Recipient of a grant from the Inst. of International Education to study African rituals and ceremonies in Nigeria for three months, 1973; NAACP Image Award, 1975, for Best Filmscript, **Five on the Black Hand Side;** Rockefeller Playwright's Grant, 1977. *Address:* P.O. Box 87074, San Diego, CA 92138; or 3895 Midway Drive, #208, San Diego, CA 92110.

REPRESENTATIVE PLAYS AND DRAMATIC WORKS:
Five on the Black Hand Side // Orig. title: **Gladys** (comedy, 2 acts, 1969; also prod. as a feature film, full length: screenplay, 1973). Concerns a hopelessly divided black middle-class family in Harlem, in which an intimidated wife and mother rebels against the domination of her stuffy, male chauvinist husband and succeeds in bringing her family back together in unity and peace. Public reading under its original title, at the APT Writers' Program, June 10, 1969. First prod. Off-Bway by the APT, with members of NBT, at St. Clement's Church, New York City, Dec. 10, 1969–Jan. 31, 1970, for 62 perfs.; dir. by BARBARA ANN TEER. Starring L. Errol Jaye (succeeded by MAXWELL GLANVILLE), Clarice Taylor, and Theresa Merritt. William Adell Stevenson (ILUNGA ADELL) was also in the cast. Also prod. by the Black American Theatre Co. of the New

Theatre School, Washington, DC, during the 1972–73 season. Prod. by the Kuumba Workshop, Chicago, 1974. Also prod. as a film. Pub. by Samuel French, New York, 1970; and by the Third Press, New York, c. 1974. In *Black Perspectives* (Murray & Thomas, 1971). In *The American Place Theatre: Plays* (Schotter, 1973). Unpub. script of **Gladys** in the Hatch-Billops Collection. Prod. as a film by Brock Peters and others; released by United Artists, 1973; dir. by OSCAR WILLIAMS. Starring Clarice Taylor, Leonard Jackson, and Virginia Capers. Sonny Jim (J. E. GAINES) and JA'NET DuBOIS were also in the cast.

(The) Revival! // Also prod. as **A Revival: Change! Love! Organize!** (ritual, full length, 1972). A frequently revived and revised ritual, utilizing music, drama, dance, "rapping," and the rhythms, fervor, and style of the black church to teach black people to unite, love one another, and appreciate the values and traditions of their heritage. First prod. by NBT in 1969; dir. by Barbara Ann Teer; Remained in repertory until about 1974.

OTHER PLAYS AND DRAMATIC WORKS:

The Black Church (TV script, 1950s). Telecast on CBS-TV. **A Man Is Not Made of Steel** (TV script, 1960s). Telecast on WGBH-TV, Boston. **What You Gonna Do on Monday, Blackman?** (1971). Sched. for prodn. by NBT. No record of the actual prodn. **Four No Trump!** (pre-1983). **The Incident at Terminal Ecstasy Acres** (pre-1983). Dir. by author.

S

ST. JOHN, CHRISTOPHER, Filmwriter, producer, director, and actor. Residing in Los Angeles, CA. Educated at the Univ. of Bridgeport (CT) and Actors Studio. Former member of the Yale Repertory Co. Founder of the Troupe Theatre. Acted in the films *For Love of Ivy* (1968) and *Shaft* (1971). Appeared in the television series "That's My Mama" (1975) and in the Off-Broadway play *No Place to Be Somebody* (1969). Directed the Off-Broadway productions of *Tennis Anyone?* (1968), *End of Summer's Drought,* and *Antigone. Agent:* Lew Sherrell Agency, 7060 Hollywood Blvd., Los Angeles, CA 90028.

DRAMATIC WORK:

Top of the Heap (film: screenplay, 1972). Writer, producer, director, star. "Personal statement about a tormented and outwardly abrasive black cop who retreats into a fantasy world as a moon explorer and national hero. There are some racial cliches in reverse but moments of biting irony and penetrating sensitivity." —*Black Creation,* Fall 1972, p. 64 (Murray). Prod. by Fanfare, 1972.

SALAAM, KALAMU YA (Val[lery] Ferdinand III) (1947–   ), Described by Arthenia J. Bates Millican as "a speaker, dramatist, literary and music critic, interviewer, short story writer, photographer, editor, poet, . . . essayist, . . . journalist, activist, and emissary." —*Afro-American Writers After 1955: Dramatists and Prose Writers* (Davis & Harris, 1985), p. 322. Salaam's biographical statement in *Black Theatre, U.S.A.* (Hatch & Shine, 1974) p. 864, gives the following information concerning himself (prior to adopting Kalamu ya Salaam as his "free name"): "my name is vallery ferdinand iii, ain't got no free name yet, am married got a daughter named Asante Salaam (which means thank you peace). my education went like this: dropped out of carleton college in northfield, minn., served three years in the army, got kicked out of southern univ. in new o. as a result of participation in a student movement to create a black university." According to *Black World* (April 1972), he "has been a long-time force in

Louisiana in the building of Black cultural communication, political and educational institutions." Millican (ibid.) states that "he has facilitated communication between *Afro-American* and communities all over the world by his travels to such diverse places as Tanzania, the People's Republic of China, Cuba, Barbados and Surinam." He has been a writer since 1962 and has been associated with the Free Southern Theatre (FST) in New Orleans since its founding in 1968. Codirector and resident playwright of Blkartsouth, the community writing and acting workshop of FST. Codirector of *Nkombo,* a quarterly journal of poetry and black arts, and managing editor of *The Black Collegian.* His best-known volumes of poetry are *The Blues Merchant* (Blkartsouth, 1969) and *Revolutionary Love* (1978). He has written more than eight other books of poetry, short stories, and essays, published mainly in New Orleans by Ahidiana. His poetry has been published in numerous journals, including *Obsidian, The Black Collegian,* and *Black Scholar;* and anthologized in *New Black Voices* (Chapman, 1972) and *Black Culture* (Simmons & Hutchinson, 1972). His short stories have been included in *What We Must See* (Coombs, 1977) and *We Be Word Sorcerers* (Sanchez, 1973). His theatre reviews have been published in *Negro Digest* and *Black World.* Founding member of Ahidiana, a Pan-African nationalist organization based in New Orleans, which operated an independent school for preschool children, 1973–84. Recipient of *Black World*'s Richard Wright Award for literary criticism, 1971; the ASCAP Deems Taylor Award for excellence in music criticism, 1980; and numerous awards for his work as editor of *The Black Collegian. Address:* 1240 South Broad Street, New Orleans, LA 70125; or New Orleans Jazz and Festival Foundation, P.O. Box 2530, New Orleans, LA 70176.

PLAYS AND DRAMATIC WORKS:
Black Liberation Army (drama, 1 act, 1969). Didactic play on the need for an army to fight for black liberation. Prod. by FST, Spring 1969.

Blk Love Song #1 (ritual, 1 act, 1969). Designed to raise the consciousness of blacks by reinforcing positive images and destroying negative ones. Produced by FST, 1969. Pub. in *Black Theater, U.S.A.* (Hatch & Shine, 1974).

Homecoming (drama, 1 act, 1969). About the change in attitude of a returning black veteran after his experiences in the service. Prod. by the FST Touring Ensemble, Dec. 1969–Jan. 1970. Pub. in *Nkombo,* Aug. 1972, pp. 3–15.

Mama (domestic drama, 1 act, 1969). A black family attempts to examine itself in order to achieve greater unity. Prod. by FST, March 1969.

The Pickett (drama, 1 act, 1969). "A short character study which sharply raises the question of whether blacks have more respect for white women than they do for their own black women." *—Times Picayune,* New Orleans), Jan. 16, 1972. Prod. by the FST Touring Ensemble, Dec. 1969–Jan. 1970.

The Destruction of the American Stage (ritual, 1972). Subtitled "A Set for Non-Believers". Shows how the theatre has been used to corrupt black consciousness and to destroy black unity. Pub. in *Black World,* April 1972, pp. 54–69.

OTHER PLAYS AND DRAMATIC WORKS:
Cop Killer (drama, 1 act, 1968). Prod. by FST, 1968. **Happy Birthday, Jesus** (drama, 1 act, 1969). Prod. by FST, 1969. **Sons of Survival** (drama, 1 act, 1969). Coauthor, with TOM DENT. Prod. by FST, 1969.

SALIMU (Nettie McCray), Playwright. Associated with the New Lafayette Theatre in New York City.

PLAY:
Growin' into Blackness (drama, 1 act, 1969). Over their mother's objections, three black girls vow to continue to wear their natural (Afro) hairstyles and to dedicate their lives to the cause of black people. May have been presented by the New Lafayette Theatre, New York, prior to publication in *Black Theatre* #2 (1969), pp. 20–22, and in *New Plays from the Black Theatre* (Bullins, 1969).

SANCHEZ, SONIA (Laila Manan) (1934–   ), Revolutionary poet, playwright, author, editor, teacher, performer, and lecturer. Born in Birmingham, AL. Educated at NYU, Hunter Coll. (B.A., 1955), and Virginia Commonwealth Univ. (M.F.A., 1985). Married to author Etheridge Knight; the mother of three children. Formerly associated with the Black Arts movement in Harlem. Teacher and staff worker, Downtown Community School, 1965–67, and Mission Rebels in Action, 1968–69, both in San Francisco. Taught black literature and creative writing at San Francisco State Coll., 1966–69; the Univ. of Pittsburgh, 1969–70; Rutgers Univ., New Brunswick, NJ, 1970–71; Manhattan Community Coll., 1971–73; Amherst Coll., MA., 1972–73; and is currently teaching in the Dept. of English at Temple Univ. in Philadelphia, PA. During the 1970s, she headed the Office of Human Development of the Nation of Islam in Chicago. One of the most prolific contemporary black poets in America, whose work is compared with that of AMIRI BARAKA (LeRoi Jones) and Nikki Giovanni. Volumes of poetry include *Homecoming* (1969), *We a BaddDDD People* (1970), *It's a New Day* (1971), *A Blues Book for Blue Black Magical Women* (1973), *Love Poems* (1973), *A Sound Investment* (1983), *I've Been a Woman* (1978), and others. Anthologies edited by Sanchez include *Three Hundred and Sixty Degrees of Blackness Comin at You* (1971), an anthology of poetry from students in her writers' workshop in Harlem, and *We Be Word Sorcerers* (1973), 25 stories by young black writers. Has also been guest editor of the *Journal of Black Poetry*. Children's books include *The Adventures of Fathead and Squarehead* (1974). Her writings have appeared in almost every important journal and anthology of black authors. Has frequently given performed readings of her poetry and has lectured on such topics as "The Relevancy of the Liberation Movement to the Black Woman," "Revolutionary Black Poetry," and "Black Art and Culture in America." A two-cassette journal, consisting of 120 minutes of poetry reading, with musical accompaniment by Robert Bly, was issued under the title *Black Box 3* in 1976. Recipient of grants from P.E.N., of which she is a member, and an honorary doctor's degree in humanities from Wilberforce Univ. in Ohio. *Address*—Home: 407 W. Chelton Ave., Philadelphia, PA 19144. Office: Dept. of English, Temple University, Philadelphia, PA 19122.

PLAYS:
The Bronx Is Next (drama, 1 act, 1968). An attack on poor housing in Harlem and the Bronx. First prod. by Theatre Black at the Univ. of the Streets, Oct. 3, 1970. Pub. in *The Drama Review*, Summer 1968; and in *Cavalcade* (Davis & Redding, 1971).

Sister Son/ji (semiautobiographical monologue, 1 act, 1969). A black woman searches for and finds her true identity. The events of her life parallel those of the black struggle in America. First prod. by Concept East, Detroit, Dec. 1970. Prod. Off-Bway as a work-in-progress by the Negro Ensemble Co. (NEC), at St. Marks Playhouse, opening Jan. 16, 1971, for 2 perfs. Prod. Off-Bway by the New York Shakespeare Festival (NYSF) Public Theatre, at the Public Theatre Annex, opening April 4, 1972, for 64 perfs. on a program of four one-act plays, under the prodn. title *Black Visions*. Also prod. by Sudan Arts/Southwest, Houston, TX, 1972; Univ. of the District of Columbia, Washington, DC, 1978; and Jomandi Productions, Atlanta, GA, 1979.

Malcolm Man Don't Live Here No Mo! (children's play, 1 act, 1969). About the life and ideals of Malcolm X. Pub. in *Black Theatre* #6, 1972.

Uh, Uh: But How Do It Free Us? (ritual, 3 scenes, 1970). Deals with black male/female relationships in the struggle for freedom. Pub. in *The New Lafayette Theatre Presents* (Bullins, 1974).

Dirty Hearts (poetic allegory, 1 act, 1971). The game of Dirty Hearts is used as a metaphor for race relations in America; the game is conducted by white men, and the black man always gets the Queen of Spades, which causes him to lose the game. Pub. in *Scripts* #1 (NYSF/Public Theatre), Nov. 1971, pp. 46–50.

I'm Black When I'm Singing, I'm Blue When I Ain't (1982). Prod. by Jomandi Productions, Atlanta, April 1982. Performed for the author's M.F.A. thesis, at Virginia Commonwealth Univ., Jan. 1985.

SANDERS, JOE, JR., Actor, poet, playwright. Associated with the Experimental Black Actors Guild (X-Bag), Chicago, IL. Attended the Univ. of Illinois, where he majored in psychology and speech.

PLAY:
All Men Are Created (adaptn., full length, 1972). Dramatization of J. A. Rogers's book, *From "Superman" to Man*. Prod. by X-Bag, Chicago, during the 1972–73 season.

SAUNDERS, RUBY CONSTANCE X (1939–   ), Nation of Islam (Black Muslim) actress, poet, and dancer, who gave up a career as a research chemist for the theatre. Has been a member of the Howard Univ. Players in Washington, DC, and the Negro Ensemble Co. (NEC) in New York City.

PLAY:
(Only one of several has been located.) **Goddam, Judy** (1 act, 1969). Written in the NEC's Playwrights' Wkshop, New York, where it was presumably prod. as a wkshop production.

SAUTI, INSAN, Playwright. Based in Norfolk, MA.

PLAY:
The Installment Plan (drama, 1 act, 1972). Deals with one man's attempt to cope with black prisoner recidivism. Pub. in *Drama and Theatre Magazine*, vol. 2, no. 1, 1982.

SCOTT, JOHN (S.) (1931–   ), Playwright, teacher, and critic. Born in Bellaire, OH. Educated at South Carolina State Coll. (B.A.) and Bowling Green State Univ. (M.A., 1966; Ph.D., c. 1970). Currently playwright-in-residence and artistic director of the Ethnic Cultural Arts Program at Bowling Green State Univ., where he also teaches playwriting and drama theory. His work has been produced by the National Playwrights Conf. of the Eugene O'Neill Theatre Center in Waterford, CT, and in New York City by the Negro Ensemble Co., the Afro-American Total Theatre, the Richard Allen Center for Culture and Art, and showcased by the Frank Silvera Writers' Workshop (FSWW). He has given lectures and workshops and directed plays at numerous universities and regional theatres in the United States and abroad. His articles on dramatic theory have been published in *Players* magazine and *Black Lines*. *Address*—Home: 2228 Gleenwood Ave., Toledo, OH 43620. Office: University Theatre, Bowling Green State University, Bowling Green, OH 43403. *Agent:* Viki McLaughlin-Cowell, Buttonwood Rd., Peekskill, NY 10566.

COLLECTION:
"THE BLACK SPIRIT: A Trilogy of Original Plays and a Treatise on Dramatic Theory in Contemporary Black Theatre." Ph.D. dissertation, Bowling Green State Univ., Bowling Green, OH, c. 1970. Includes **Ride a Black Horse, Black Sermon Rock, and Time Turns Black** (all 1970).

REPRESENTATIVE PLAYS AND DRAMATIC WORKS:
The Alligator Man (musical, 1 act, 1967). A black jazz musician attempts to escape the academic queries of a white Ph.D. and a black girl singer by hiding in the sewer system beneath a nightclub. The plot is concerned with their attempt to pursue him and his efforts to escape. First prod. at Bowling Green State Univ., 1967.

Ride a Black Horse (drama, 2 acts, 1970). Black sociologist is confronted by the bizarre demands of ghetto militants when he attempts to join with them to force commitments from the civic and educational leaders of the city. Failing to implement the militants' version of their joint plan and successfully develop his ideals of black unity, he is driven to the brink of irrationality, then pushed toward self-destruction. Part of the author's trilogy **"THE BLACK SPIRIT."** First prod. by the National Playwrights Conf. at the Eugene O'Neill Theatre Center, Waterford, CT, 1970. Prod. by Playhouse-in-the-Park, Cincinnati, OH, 1970. Prod. at Bowling Green State Univ., 1971. Prod. by the Negro Ensemble Company (NEC) at St. Marks Playhouse, New York, May 25–June 13, 1971, for 30 perfs.; dir. by DOUGLAS TURNER WARD. Cast: Graham Brown, Madison Arnold, Marilyn Chris, ADOLPH CAESAR, William Countryman, Bill Cobbs, Esther Rolle, David Downing, Charles Grant, Charles Weldon, Delores Gaskins, Barbara Clarke, and Jay Montgomery. Included in the author's Ph.D. dissertation, "THE BLACK SPIRIT": [see COLLECTION above].

Black Sermon Rock (drama, with music, 1 act, c. 1970). A black woman preacher tries to conduct a funeral service for two black men, but her efforts are complicated by the return of the dead and their effect upon the service. Part of the author's trilogy **"THE BLACK SPIRIT."** Prod. at Bowling Green State Univ., 1972. Unpub. script included in the author's Ph.D. dissertation, "THE BLACK SPIRIT" [see COLLECTION above].

Time Turns Black (drama, 2 acts, c. 1970). A black West Indian taxi driver and a black lawyer kidnap the white mayor of a city in order to forcibly bring about national economic and social improvements, but their efforts are complicated by the unleashing of uncontrollable black revolutionary forces. Part of the author's trilogy **"THE BLACK SPIRIT."** Prod. at Bowling Green State Univ., 1972. Unpub. script included in the author's Ph.D. dissertation, "THE BLACK SPIRIT": [see COLLECTION above].

I Talk With the Spirits (comic drama, 1 act, early 1970s). A young man, angered by the absurdity of miscommunication, lures a young woman and an old man into a series of threatening games in his attempt to shift the blame for his own shortcomings, uncertainties, and confusion. Prod. at Bowling Green State Univ., early 1970s.

Karma's Kall (drama, 2 acts, 1973). Examines the problems of black women particularly, who must maintain their femininity while struggling to develop the toughness required to survive in a milieu that demands competitive strength. Concerns a black woman activist/writer who attempts to find love while also dealing with the conflicting forces in her life—the demands of her ex-husband, her protective mother, her best friend, and drug pushers who threaten to kill her. First prod. at Bowling Green State Univ., 1973. Public reading by FSWW, at the Martinique Theatre, New York, 1974. Showcased by the Black Theatre Alliance, at the Harlem Cultural Council, New York, 1974. Prod. by the Urban Arts Theatre, New York, 1974. Also prod. as a musical [see **Karma** (1977) below]. Unpub. script in the FSWW Archives/Schomburg Collection.

The Good Ship Credit (musical, 2 acts, 1974). A HooDoo captain leads the inhabitants (inmates) of an island/asylum to greater racial understanding by teaching them that the spirit of racial or personal identity cannot be borrowed on credit. Public reading by FSWW, at the Martinique Theatre, 1974. Prod. by the Univ. of Toledo, 1974. Prod. at Bowling Green State Univ., 1977. Unpub. script in the FSWW Archives/Schomburg Collection.

Shades (2 connected one-act plays, 1974). On the theme of interracial love. Two couples look at the economic, career, social, and family pressures that their respective romances cause. One couple involves a black male and a white blonde; the other a black female and a white Jewish intellectual. Public reading by FSWW, New York, at the Martinique Theatre, 1974. Prod. at Bowling Green State Univ., 1974. Unpub. script in the FSWW Archives/Schomburg Collection.

Karma (musical, full length, 1977). Book and lyrics by Scott. Music by Stan Cowell. Based on the author's play, **Karma's Kall** (1973), described above. Prod. by the Afro-American Total Theatre, New York, opening Dec. 8, 1977; dir. by Elaine Head. Prod. by Bowling Green State Univ., May 1–June 1, 1978.

After Work (drama, 1 act, early 1980s). A young man competes with an old man for a janitor's job, and they learn some intricate dimensions of the generation gap when they are forced to confront each other's dream for a better life in front of the uncaring employer. Prod. at Bowling Green State Univ., early 1980s.

The Zaire Mark (comedy, full length, early 1980s). A parody of the film *The Sting*. On their trip to Zaire to the Foreman-Ali boxing match, three big-time hustlers and their ladies of the night conspire to swindle some Africans in a real estate venture. Their unexpected detour in the African bush country provides them with hilarious and unusual lessons on survival and international brotherhood. First prod. at Bowling Green State Univ., early 1980s.

OTHER PLAYS AND DRAMATIC WORKS:

Play Division (early 1980s). Apparently prod. at Bowling Green State Univ., early 1980s. **Shadow and Act** (early 1980s). Prod. at Bowling Green State Univ., early 1980s.

Ovet and Tevo (TV script, early 1980s). Prod. by Spectrum Productions and telecast on Public TV during the early 1980s. **Pieces of a Man** (TV script, early 1980s). Telecast on Public TV during the early 1980s.

SCOTT, JOHNIE HAROLD (1946–   ), Author, filmmaker, screenwriter, playwright, producer, and director. Born in Cheyenne, WY. Educated at Harvard Univ., 1964–65; East Los Angeles Jr. Coll., 1965–66; Stanford Univ. (B.A., 1970; M.A., 1972); American Film Inst., 1973. Coordinator of project development, Frederick Douglass House Foundation, Los Angeles, 1966. Research asst. and instr. of Cinema Arts Workshop, Dept. of Afro-American Studies, Stanford Univ., 1967–72. Filmmaker for Midpeninsula Urban Coalition, Fair Housing Campaign, 1970–71. Playwright, Studio Watts Workshop, 1970–72. Film director and member of the board of directors, Human Perspectives, Inc., filmmakers, Woodside, CA, 1971–72. Intern director (on scholarship) of *Across 110th Street,* a film produced by the Academy of Motion Picture Arts and Sciences, 1971–72. Student intern, *Newsweek,* San Francisco, 1969–70; correspondent, *Time,* 1972–73. Director of affairs, Afro-West: Theatre of the Black Arts, 1974. His poetry and fiction have been widely published in anthologies of black writers. *Address:* 2000 Cooley Ave. #24, East Palo Alto, CA 94303.

DRAMATIC WORKS:
The Angry Voices of Watts (TV doc., 1966). Prod. by NBC-TV, 1966; nominated for an Emmy Award. **The New Voices of Watts** (TV doc., 1968). Prod. by NBC-TV, 1968. **David** (drama, 3 acts, 1969). Commissioned and presumably performed by the Los Angeles Festival of Performing Arts, 1969.

SCOTT, SERET (1947–   ), Actress-playwright. Born in Washington, DC. Resides in New York City. Educated at North Carolina Coll. and NYU. Has performed with the Negro Ensemble Co. (NEC) in New York, the Center Stage in Baltimore, the Hartford Stage Co. in Connecticut, and the Free Southern Theatre in Mississippi and Louisiana. Winner of a Drama Desk Award for her outstanding performance as Sue Belle in *My Sister, My Sister* (1973). Other stage appearances include *Slave Ship* (1969), *Hot L Baltimore* (1974), *For Colored Girls . . .* (1976), *Mother Courage and Her Children* (1979), and *Weep Not for Me* (1981). *Address:* 106 Walgrave Dr., Teaneck, NJ 07666.

PLAYS:
Funnytime (satirical comedy, 1 act, 1973). About a married man who consents to spend a full night with his girl friend. Prod. Off-Bway by NEC, Feb. 15–18, 1973. **No You Didn't** (1 act, 1973). Prod. Off-Bway by NEC, on double bill with the author's **Funnytime,** Feb. 15–18, 1973.

SEBREE, CHARLES (1914–1986), Playwright, artist, designer. Born in Madisonville, KY. Moved with his family to Chicago, IL, in 1924. Educated at the Art Inst. of Chicago (3 years); also took art classes at the Community Arts Center on Chicago's South Side. Became a dancer-designer with the Katherine Dunham

Dance Co. Dunham introduced Sebree to Dr. Alain Locke at Howard Univ., who arranged for the artist to come to New York to do the illustrations for †Countee Cullen's book of poetry, *The Lost Zoo*. During the 1940s, Sebree designed costumes and sets for *Garden of Time* (1945), *Henry Christophe* (1945), and *Our Land* (1947), mainly for the Howard Univ. Players in Washington, DC, and the American Negro Theatre (ANT) in New York. He began writing plays in 1949 but continued to pursue his first love, painting, until the mid-1980s. Recipient of a Rosenwald Fellowship, 1944.

PLAYS AND DRAMATIC WORKS:

My Mother Came Crying most Pitifully (fantasy, 3 acts, 1949). The orig. version on which both the author's **The Dry August** and **Mrs. Patterson** are based. About a poor, young black girl who dreams of being a rich, white lady. Unpub. script in the Hatch-Billops Collection.

Mrs. Patterson (musical fantasy, 3 acts, 1954). Coauthor, with Greer Johnson. Music by James Shelton. Adapt. from Sebree's **My Mother Came Crying Most Pitifully** (1949). About a poor, black country girl who dreams of becoming a rich, white lady like Mrs. Patterson. Prod. on Bway, at the National Theatre, Dec. 1, 1954–Feb. 26, 1955, for 101 perfs.; dir. by Guthrie McClintick. With Eartha Kitt, Ruth Attaway, Avon Long, Enid Markey, and Estelle Hemsley. Then went on a three month national tour. Prod. by the Gilpin Players, Cleveland, Jan. 15–Feb. 16, 1957. Bway cast recording by RCA Victor (LOC-1017).

The Dry August (fantasy, 1 act, 1972). Adaptn. of the author's orig. script, **My Mother Came Crying Most Pitifully** (1949), which had been the basis of the Bway success, **Mrs. Patterson** (1954). A young black country girl, who dreams of running away from home to achieve fame and fortune in Chicago, is offered assistance by Satan. Pub. in *Black Theatre, U.S.A.* (Hatch & Shine, 1974).

OTHER PLAYS AND DRAMATIC WORKS:

(Both pre-1976) **A Talent for Crumbs** (1 act). **Fisher Boy.**

SELF, CHARLES, Playwright and fiction writer. Based in New Orleans, LA, where he was associated with Dillard Univ. and the Free Southern Theatre (FST). Took graduate courses at Columbia Univ. and lived for a brief period in Africa. One of his short stories was published in *Black Review, No. 2* (Watkins, 1972). In 1972 he was reportedly working on a novel.

PLAY:

The Smokers (1 act, 1966). Prod. by FST, at the Afro-American Festival held at Dillard Univ., New Orleans, 1968.

SHA-BETHEA, MAHALIEL HAROOM (writes under the name **Mahaliel; also known as Mahaliel H. Bethea**), Playwright, author, and theatre director. Currently studying for his Ph.D. in theatre education at CCNY, where he is also teaching. Founder and pres. of Sun People Theatre, Inc. Member of DG, ATA, and numerous other writing and teaching organizations. *Address*—Office: Sun People, Inc., 138th St. and Convent Ave., New York, NY 10031. Home: 115–49 180th St., St. Albans, NY 11434.

PLAYS:
We Must Eat the Black Root (domestic drama, full length, 1984). About the struggle for survival of a poor black family. Prod. by Sun People Theatre, Inc., at the African Poetry Theatre, Jamaica, NY, Oct. 14, 1984; / dir. by Pat White. **Sun People Turn Ice** (ethnic collage, full length, pre-1986). The African experience in America, presented through history, dance, and drama. Prod. in repertory by Sun People Th., Inc., pre-1986; dir. by Dana. **Malcolm's Time** ("A Collaborative Play" [subtitle], full length, pre-1986). The story of Malcolm X. Prod. as a collective creation of Sun People, Inc., and Mahaliel, and directed by Randy Frazier.

SHANGE, NTOZAKE (Paulette Williams) (1948–   ), Feminist, poet, playwright, author, dancer, actress, musician, director, and college teacher. Best known as the creator and developer of the "choreopoem" as a dramatic form, with her most successful theatre piece, **For Colored Girls Who Have Considered Suicide/When the Rainbow Is Enuf** (1976). Born in Trenton, NJ the daughter of a surgeon and a psychiatric social worker. Grew up in upstate New York and in St. Louis, MO. Educated at Barnard Coll. (B.A. with honors in American Studies, 1970 and the Univ. of Southern California (M.A. in American Studies, 1973). Also studied music and dance. Twice married; currently to jazz musician David Murray, 1977. Assumed her Zulu name (pronounced En-to-ZAH-ki SHONG-gay) in 1971. Her first name means "She who comes with her own thing"; her last name means "One who walks like a lion." Has taught English, creative writing, drama, and related subjects at Trenton State Coll., 1972; California State Coll. at Sonoma, 1973–75; CCNY, 1975; Medgar Evers Community Coll., 1975; Douglass Coll., Rutgers Univ., 1978; and Rice Univ., 1983. Performed in several jazz/dance/poetry ensembles in California and New York. Television appearances include "Straight Talk" (1976), "Sunday" (1976), "Black Journal" (1977), and "An Evening with Diana Ross" (1977). Radio appearances include "Celebrity Hour" (WRVR, 1976). In 1979 she directed several plays for the New York Shakespeare Festival (NYSF), including *The Mighty Gents* (RICHARD WESLEY, 1979) and *Tribute to Sojourner Truth* (BERNIECE REAGON and JUNE JORDAN, 1979). Her books include *Nappy Edges* (a book of poems, 1978); *Sassafrass, Cypress & Indigo: A Novel* (1982— originally published as *Sassafrass: A Novella,* 1977); *Melissa & Smith: A Story* (1983); *A Daughter's Geography: Poetry* (1983); *Matrilineal Poems* (1983); *See No Evil: Prefaces, Essays, and Accounts, 1976–1983* (1984); and *Betsy Brown* (a novel, 1985). Her short fiction, articles, and poems have appeared in numerous periodicals, including *Ms. magazine, Black Scholar, Hoodoo, Sojourner, Essence, Callaloo,* the *New York Times, TV Guide,* and most recently have been anthologized in *The Pushcart Press II* (1977), *Califia: The California Poetry* (1979), and *Anthology of Third World Women Writers* (1980). Professional and civic affiliations include P.E.N., WGA, DG, AEA, Poets and Writers, National Assn. of Third World Writers, Feminist Art Institute (Board of Directors), Women Against Violence Against Women and Children, NATAS, AFTRA, and national member of American Film Inst. Recipient of Outer Critics' Circle Award, Obie Award, AUDELCO Award, *Mademoiselle* Award, 1977, for *For Colored Girls Who Have Considered Suicide/When the Rainbow Is Enuf* (which was also nominated for a Tony Award and a Grammy Award); Frank Silvera Writers' Workshop (FSWW) Award, 1978; another Obie Award, 1980, for outstanding adaptn. of **Mother Courage** by Brecht (1980); Guggenheim Fellowship for writing, 1981; *Los Angeles Times Book Review* Award for poetry, for *Three Pieces,* 1981; Medal of Excellence, Columbia Univ., 1981; New York State Council of the Arts Award, 1981; NEA Fellowship for creative writing, 1981. *Address:* 12002 Chimney Rock Road, Houston, TX 77035. Alternate: 1122 S. Pembridge Drive, Houston, TX 77071. *Agent:* David M. Franklin Associates, Suite 1290, Omni International, Atlanta, GA 30303.

COLLECTION:
THREE PIECES. St. Martin's Press, New York, 1981. Penguin Books, New York, 1982. Contains **Spell #7** (1979). **A Photograph: Lovers-in-Motion** (1977), **Boogie Woogie Landscapes** (1979).

REPRESENTATIVE PLAYS AND DRAMATIC WORKS:
For Colored Girls Who Have Considered Suicide/When the Rainbow Is Enuf (choreopoem, full length, 1976). A drama of self-celebration, utilizing poetry, dance, color symbolism, and intimate personal experiences to explore the many facets of a black woman's psyche. It is performed by seven black women, called the Lady in Brown, the Lady in Yellow, the Lady in Red, the Lady in Green, the Lady in Purple, the Lady in Blue, and the Lady in Orange. According to Elizabeth Brown [ELIZABETH BROWN-GUILLORY]: "Shange presents all-too-human black women who are preoccupied with the business of living and surviving; *For Colored Girls* is also filled with the outcries of women who have been hurt. On the one level, the work speaks of the physical and emotional abuse that black women experience at the hands of insensitive black men; on another level, however, it is about the black women's ability to survive even after they have been knocked down repeatedly."—*Afro-American Writers After 1955: Dramatists and Prose Writers* (Davis & Harris, 1985), p. 241. Recipient of the Outer Critics' Circle Award. Nominated for a Tony Award, a Grammy Award, and an Emmy Award. Winner of three Obie awards—one each for the playwright, the director, and the entire cast. Winner of four AUDELCO awards—for the playwright, the two producers (Joseph Papp and WOODIE KING, JR.), and actress Tranzana Beverly (who also won a Tony Award and a *Theatre World* Award). Developed from poetry readings given by the author in San Francisco bars and clubs prior to 1973. With the addition of a second actress in 1973, it was presented at small colleges, bars, and community facilities around San Francisco, before being brought to New York City, where it played a number of East Village clubs, acquired a director, and was expanded to include seven actresses. Discovered by Woodie King, Jr., who prod. it Off-Off-Bway at the Henry St. Settlement's New Federal Theatre (NFT), April-May 1976, from which it was transferred Off-Bway to the NYSF Public Theatre, June 1–Aug. 29, 1976, for a total of 120 perfs. Transferred to Bway, prod. jointly by Papp and King, as a NYSF prodn. in association with the Henry St. Settlement's NFT, opening at the Booth Theatre, Sept. 15, 1978, for 746 perfs., amassing a total run of 876 perfs. All preceding perfs. were dir. by Oz Scott, and featured Janet League, Aku Kadogo, Tranzana Beverly, Paula Moss, RISË COLLINS,

Laurie Carlos, and Shange. Toured the major cities of the United States, opening Aug. 10, 1977, at the Mark Taper Forum in Los Angeles, and closing Dec. 31, 1978, in Washington, DC., with perfs. also in Chicago, Philadelphia, Baltimore, Boston, and other large cities. Also toured Kingston, Jamaica, Dec. 1977–March 1978; Rio de Janeiro, July-Sept. 1978, and London, Sept.-Nov. 1979, with the National Touring Co., under the sponsorship of Samuel French. Prod. by ACT (A Contemporary Theatre), Seattle, WA, opening May 8, 1980, for 24 perfs.; dir. and choreographed by Tawnya Pettiford. Prod. by PBS, WNET-TV, for the "American Playhouse" series, June 1981, and aired on PBS in Feb. 1982. Cast recording by Buddah (BDS-950070C). First pub. in an early version by Shameless Hussy Press, San Lorenzo, CA, 1976. Formal version pub. by Macmillan, New York, 1977. Also pub. by Eyre Methuen, London, 1978; by Bantam Books, 1980; in *Plays from the New York Shakespeare Festival* (1986); and in a Japanese translation pub. in Tokyo, 1982.

A Photograph: Lovers-in-Motion // Orig. title: **A Photograph: A Still Life in Shadows** // Also prod. as **A Photograph: A Study of Cruelty** ("Poemplay," 2 acts, 1977). Considered more of a play than a choreopoem. About a young, ambitious, and misogynistic photographer and his relationship with the three women in his life, who love him, and whom he needs to satisfy his ego. Although he pretends to be a strong black male, his facade collapses when he is rejected for a fellowship and a gallery exhibition which he considered necessary to launch his career. Prod. as a workshop production under its original title by the NYSF/Public Theatre, Jan. 1977. Prod. as **A Photograph: A Study of Cruelty** in a full prodn. by NYSF/Public Theatre, at LuEsther Hall, Dec. 16, 1977–Jan. 22, 1978, for 60 perfs. Produced as **A Photograph: Lovers-in-Motion** by the Equinox Theatre, Houston, TX, Nov.-Dec. 1979. Pub. in the author's *THREE PIECES*. Pub. by Samuel French, New York.

Where the Mississippi Meets the Amazon (a cabaret, full length, 1977). Written with *Jessica Hagedorn and *Thulani Nkakinda (T. Davis). According to Allen Woll, this piece was "orchestrated in the fashion of a musical composition. . . . [The three collaborators,] called The Satin Sisters, performed their own poetry, danced and sang alone or in ensemble, while a band, Teddy and His Sizzling Romancers, played jazz."— *Dictionary of the Black Theatre* (Woll, 1983), p. 249. Prod. by NYSF/Public Theatre, Dec. 1977–March 1978.

Spell #7 (choreopoem, 2 acts, 1979). Series of poetic vignettes built around the theme of what it means to be black in America, and set in a St. Louis bar frequented by black musicians and artists. The various characters unburden their souls through soliloquies, often supported by appropriate dances which illustrate the emotional content of their speeches. As described by Allen Woll, *Spell #7,* "unlike *For Colored Girls,* . . . uses both male and female characters who interact with one another. In the beginning, the characters wear grotesque black minstrel show masks, which they shed when revealing the truths about their lives. A narrator, an interlocutor, is instrumental in binding the vignettes together."—*Dictionary of the Black Theatre* (Woll, 1983), p. 157. Prod. by the NYSF/Public Theatre, April-Nov. 1979; dir. by Oz Scott. Pub. by Samuel French, New York, 1981. Included in the author's *THREE PIECES*.

Boogie Woogie Landscapes (experimental theatre piece, full length, 1979). A woman's experiences, memories, and dreams are presented through song and dance, and in a stream of consciousness style, to explore what it means to be black and female in America. First presented in a one-woman perf. by NYSF, in the Poetry at the Public Series, 1979. Presented in play form by FSWW at Symphony Space, New York, June 1979. Prod. by the Black Touring Circuit at the Kennedy Center's Terrace Theater, Washington, DC, June-July 1980. Pub. in the author's *THREE PIECES*.

Mother Courage and Her Children (adaptn., full length, 1980). From the play of the same title by Bertolt Brecht. "In this version, the time and place were changed from seventeenth-century Sweden, Poland, and Germany to post-Civil War America, with Mother Courage as an emancipated slave." —*Dictionary of the Black Theatre* (Woll, 1983), p. 249. Recipient of an Obie Award for Outstanding Adaptation. Prod. by NYSF, April-June 1980.

A Daughter's Geography // Orig. title: **Mouths: A Daughter's Geography** // Also prod. as **Triptych & Bocas** // Also pub. as **Bocas: A Daughter's Geography** (choreopoem, full length, 1981). "An experience of the topology of a woman's life on the planet as we now know it. From the point of view of Conakry and Tulsa, the Cosmic Couple, we travel the realms of Black people in the New World from slavery times to the recent Atlanta murders."—*Samuel French's Basic Catalog of Plays* (1985). Explores a number of feminist and nationalist issues and presents several love relationships throughout the play. The episodes are connected by appropriate dances arising from the ethnic or emotional content of the scene. First prod. as **Mouths: A Daughter's Geography: A Performance Piece,** at the Kitchen, New York, April 1981. Prod. as **Triptych & Bocas: A Performance Piece,** at the Mark Taper Theatre Lab, Los Angeles, March-April 1982; dir. by Oz Scott, with choreography by Michelle Simmons. Revised as **A Daughter's Geography: A Choreopoem** and presented by the Mark Taper Forum, July 1983. Pub. as **A Daughter's Geography** by St. Martin's Press, New York, 1983. Also pub. as **Bocas: A Daughter's Geography** by Samuel French, New York.

Betsy Brown ("A Rhythm & Blues Play" [subtitle], full length, 1981). Commissioned by NYSF. Music by Bakida Carroll. Staged readings by NYSF, Aug. 1981. Closed workshop prodn. by NYSF, Oct. 1982; dir. by author. Presented in a full prodn. by NYSF for only 1 perf., with music, Feb. 14, 1983 (after which the prodn. closed). Pub. as a novel by St. Martin's Press, 1985.

The Dancin' Novel: Sassafrass, Cypress, & Indigo (theatre piece, full length, 1982). Conceived and written by Shange with Dianne McIntyre and Rod Rogers. Based on her novella *Sassafrass, Cypress & Indigo,* which centers around two sisters from Charleston, SC. According to Elizabeth Brown, the two sisters "have chosen different ways of perceiving and relating to the world. Sassafrass is a weaver and a would-be writer who chooses to live with her lover Mitch regardless of the fact that he is a junkie and a musician who works sporadically and who abuses her mentally and physically. . . . Cypress, on the other hand, chooses to be a feminist. She has many male friends, but she does not take any of them as lovers." —*Afro-American Writers After 1955: Dramatists and Prose Writers* (Davis & Harris, 1985). According to Elizabeth Brown (cited above), the novella lends itself easily to translation to the stage: "Cypress and her friends act/ perform women's dance pieces. . . . Sassafrass bears Shange's trademarks of scenes which merge music, poetry and dancing. Mitch's music, literally and figuratively, does not sooth Sassafrass. . . . Sassafrass and Cypress cope through dance with frustration, pain, and insecurity."—Ibid. Prod. by the NYSF, March 1982. Pub. only as a novel by St. Martin's Press, New York, 1982.

OTHER PLAYS AND DRAMATIC WORKS:

From Okra to Greens (theatre piece, full length, 1978). Prod. at Barnard Coll., New York, Nov. 1978. Pub. as *From Okra to Greens: A Different Love Story* by Coffee House

Press, St. Louis, 1984. **Black & White Two Dimensional Planes** (theatre piece, full length, 1979). Prod. by Sounds-In-Motion Studio Works, New York, Feb. 1979. Prod. at the Houston Jazz Festival, Nov. 1979. **It Has Not Always Been This Way** (choreo-poem, full length, 1981). In collab. with Sounds-In-Motion Dance Co. Prod. at Symphony Space, New York, June 1981.**Dreamed Dwellings** ("An Installation & Performance Piece" [subtitle], 1981). In collab. with Wopo Holup. Prod. by Women's Interact Centre, New York, June-Oct. 1981.

SHANNON, JAMES-EDWARD, Playwright and teacher. Born on the South Side of Chicago, IL. The son of actress Laura Finne. Educated at John Jay Coll. of Criminal Justice (B.A.) and Long Island Univ (graduate work). Presently a writing prof. at Empire State Coll. (SUNY), since 1980. Has been writing since 1967; his plays have been performed in London, South Africa, Heidelberg, West Germany, and on and Off-Broadway. He is currently completing a novel. Member of DG. Was a candidate for the George Devine Award (British), and a literature scholar under the funding of the New York State Council for the Humanities. *Address:* 309 E. 81st St., New York, NY 10028.

REPRESENTATIVE PLAYS AND DRAMATIC WORKS:

Mama, Is Terry Home for Good? (drama, full length, 1971; revised, 1985). In a setting in the Deep South, a black mother of a deceased veteran struggles to carry out her son's wishes to be buried in an all-white cemetery. Given three staged readings at the Cubiculo, New York, Feb. 1971; dir. by Anthony De Vito. With MINNIE GENTRY as the mother, Yvonne Warden as the aunt, and Floyd Ennis as a boarder. Prod. at the Circle Theatre, Johannesburg, South Africa, 1974. Revised and prod. as an Actors Equity Approved Showcase, at the Brecht Theatre, New York, opening June 29, 1985, and performed on weekends through mid-Sept. 1985; dir. by Charles H. Patterson. With Michael Jefferson as the son, Joy Moss as the mother, and Zelda Patterson as the aunt. Pub. by Breakthrough Press.

Mother Mary's Honor Student (comedy, 1 act, 1971). Described by George L. George *(Back Stage,* Nov. 12, 1971), as "a trenchantly humorous slice of Harlem life." According to *Show Business* (Oct. 21, 1971), the plot revolves around "a poor, world- and wine-weary Harlem couple . . . who prepare for their son's high school graduation. The piece is a poignant one that somewhat resembles [TV's] 'The Honeymooners,' set one or two sad steps down the social and economic ladder." Prod. by the New York Theatre Ensemble, on a program of three one-act plays, Oct.-Nov. 1971; dir. by Anthony De Vito.

Testimonies (2 one-act plays, full length program, 1971). Includes the author's *The Menials,* about two boisterous sisters, Thomasena and Beatrice, "who are menial workers and always will be. One is chaste and filled with the spirit of the Lord, the other is more tolerant, the forgiving wife of an alcoholic husband."—*The Westsider* (New York), Aug. 5–11, 1982. "Thomasena uses religion and the memory of a proud, God-fearing mother to force her sister to renounce Malcolm X" (ibid.), and refuses to allow her to include his picture on the wall along with those of Jesus Christ and Martin Luther King. The other play, whose title is not known, concerns Rev. Hall, a preacher with a fifth-grade education who "will not submit to his daughter's imprecations that he free his son from jail (the 21–year-old has been picked up for carrying guns as part of a revolutionary program)."—Ibid. First prod. at La Mama E.T.C., New York, 1971, starring the late

Estelle Evans in *The Menials,* and presumably the author as Rev. Hall. Presented at the Black Heritage Festival, 1973; at St. Clements Church, New York, 1976; and at the Bijou, 1976. Again prod. at Trinity Lutheran Church, New York, July-Aug. 1982. With Minnie Gentry and Beatrice Winde as the two sisters, Thomasena and Beatrice, and the author as Rev. Hall.

OTHER PLAYS AND DRAMATIC WORKS:
Bill & William (1971). Prod. at the Playbox Theatre, New York, 1971. **Black Graduates** (1972). Prod. by the New York Theatre Ensemble, 1972; at Colby Coll., Waterville, ME, 1973; at the Royal Court Theatre, London, 1976; and at John Jay Coll., New York, 1978. **Young Prince Hall** (1973). About the founder of the first black masonic lodge. Commissioned by the Performing Arts Repertory Theatre, New York, 1973. **Truth Tabernacle** (comedy, 1 act, 1976). About a bishop reminiscent of Rev. Ike. Prod. in New York, 1976. **Al and Big Mama** (pre-1985). **Ain't Cake Supposed to Be Sweet?** (pre-1985).

SHARP, SAUNDRA (1942–   ), Actress, singer, poet, playwright, TV scriptwriter, screenwriter, and publisher. Born in Cleveland, OH. Received the B.S. degree from Bowling Green State Univ., 1964. Attended film school at Los Angeles City Coll. Producer of children's radio programs in Cleveland, before moving to New York City. Has performed with the Al Fann Theatrical Ensemble, Poets and Performers, and in prisons with the Theatre of the Forgotten. New York stage appearances include *To Be Young, Gifted and Black* (1969), *Five on the Black Hand Side* (1970), *Black Girl* (1971), and *The Great MacDaddy* (1974). Made her film debut in *The Learning Tree* (1969). Starred in two television movies, *Minstrel Man* (1977) and *Hollow Image* (1979). Has performed in numerous TV commercials and in such shows as "As the World Turns," "The Guiding Light," "Our Street," "The Jeffersons," "Wonder Woman," "Benson," "St. Elsewhere," and "Knots Landing." Radio appearances include "Sounds of the City," "The Story Hour" (with OSSIE DAVIS and RUBY DEE), and as moderator of "Black Dialogue." Director of Togetherness Productions, which focuses on young black creative artists; founder-director of the Lorraine Hansberry Playwrights Workshop, 1976. Has performed as a popular singer with a number of musical groups and in nightclubs in the United States, Mexico, and Antigua. Editor-publisher of *Directory of Black Film/TV Technicians & Artists, West Coast* (Togetherness Productions, 1980); cowriter/editor of *History of Blacks in Film Exhibit Catalog* (William Grant Still Gallery & City of Los Angeles, c. 1983). Copywriter for *TV Guide* magazine. Author of three volumes of poetry, published by Togetherness Productions: *From the Windows of My Mind* (1980), *In the Midst of Change* (1972), and *Soft Song* (1978). Her poems have been published in *Black World, Black Creation,* and other periodicals, and anthologized in *We Speak as Liberators* (Coombs, 1971), *The Magic of Black Poetry* (Abdul, 1972), and *A Rock Against the Wind* (Patterson, 1973). Cofounder of the Anti-Defamation League, an organization that monitors the images of blacks in the media. Member of AEA, AFTRA, SAG. *Address:* Togetherness Productions, Box 75796, Sanford Station, Los Angeles, CA 90075.

REPRESENTATIVE PLAYS AND DRAMATIC WORKS:

The Sistuhs (drama with music, 2 acts, 1975). About contemporary black American women, described by *Black World* (April 1976) as "a striking collage of interconnecting scenes that provide the audience with a penetrating glimpse into female-male relationships." Public reading by the Frank Silvera Writers' Workshop, at the Martinique Theatre, New York, Jan. 1975. Prod. by the Shaw Players, Raleigh, NC, 1977. According to the author, it has been "produced throughout U.S., including SRO runs in Los Angeles and Oakland, CA."—Resume, Oct. 1985.

Back Inside Herself ("A Film Short" [subtitle] 4 1/2 min., 1984). According to Kevin Thomas *(Los Angeles Times,* Jan. 27, 1984), this film was "inspired by her poem urging that black women reject images placed on them by others and discover their own identities. Sharp, who has been studying film at Los Angeles City College, communicates this process with a power and economy that seem remarkable, considering that this is her first film." Won first place in the Black American Cinema Society Grants Competition, 1984. Prod. by the author, and available as a 16mm film or videotape.

Life Is a Saxophone (cultural doc., 1 hr., 1985). Featuring the work of Kamau Daaood, "an oral poet" known as "the word musician," who has been culturally involved in Watts, CA, for more than 15 years. Includes a guest appearance by the renowned musician Billy Higgins, and interpretations of Kamau's work through martial arts (Dadisi Sanyika), dance (Lula Washington), portraits (Gale Fulton-Ross), and musicians Roberto Miguel Miranda, Dadisi Wells Komolafe, and Nirankar Singh Khalsa. Prod. and dir. by the author and cinematographer Orlando Bagwell, 1985. Available in color as a 16mm film or videotape. Received the Black American Cinema Soc.'s 1985 Award of Special Merit.

OTHER PLAYS AND DRAMATIC WORKS:

The Way It's Done (TV script, half hr., 1973). Written for the "Our Street" series, and prod. by WMPB for the PBS network, Baltimore, MD, during the summer of 1973. NOTE: The following scripts were written and prod. prior to 1984: **"Palmerstown, U.S.A."** (TV script, 1 hr.). Prod. by Haley-T.A.T. Productions for CBS-TV. **"Watch Your Mouth"** (TV scripts, 13 ten-min. interviews). Prod. and hosted by the author, on Black Entertainment TV, USA Cable Network. **"Lazarus Syndrome"** (TV script, 1 hr.). Prod. by Viacom Productions for ABC-TV. **"Surinam"** (doc., 1 hr.: script consultant only). Prod. by WTVS, Detroit. **Your Move** (doc. film, half hr.: story and script). Prod. by Berkeley Productions for the U.S. Dept. of Education. **Twice as Nice** (feature film, full length). Commissioned by J&L Films, New York. **We Write the Songs** (1 hr. script). Written for Quincy Jones Music Workshop, Los Angeles.

SHAW, C. TITO, Playwright. Formerly associated with the Paperback Theatre and the Greenwich Mews Theatre, both in New York City. Currently resides in California.

PLAYS:

Guerra (drama, 1 act, 1967). The tragedy of a black musician who, having lost both his talent and his wife, now loses his only son in the war in Vietnam. Prod. by the Paperback Theatre, New York, June 1970. **An Orchard for Romy** (morality play, 1 act, 1968). Deals with the moral and emotional conflicts of a black homosexual soldier whose white friend decides to get married. Prod. by the Paperback Theatre, New York, Nov. 1970. **He's Got a Jones** (historical drama, 3 acts, 1969). Two black sharecroppers on a southern plantation during the Depression dream of a better life up North. Prod. by the Greenwich Mews Theatre, New York, Jan. 1973. Again prod. by the Folger Theatre Group, Washington, DC, opening Feb. 4, 1974, for 28 perfs.; dir. by Harold Scott. **Jingle in a Broken Tongue** (historical drama, 1 act, 1973). Depicts the struggles of a family of black sharecroppers in the South during the 1920s.

SHEARS, CARL L. (Saggitarus [sic]), Playwright. Based in Washington, DC.

PLAY:

I Am Ishmael, Son of the Blackamoor (drama, 4 acts, 1975). Concerns the first black U.S. president and the problems he encounters, due in part to his marriage to a white woman. Pub. by Nuclassics and Science Publishing Co., Washington, DC, 1975; copy in the Hatch-Billops Collection.

SHELTON, IRVING, Playwright. Based in Brooklyn, NY. *Address:* 391 Grand Ave., Brooklyn, NY 11238.

PLAY:

Soul Iconoclast (1 act, pre-1976). Subtitled "Union." Concerned with the problems of union contract negotiations within an atmosphere of racial discrimination in a small community. Unpub. script in the Schomburg Collection.

SHELTON, SHERMAN NORMAN, JR. (Omowale), Poet, folklorist, short-story writer, and playwright. Educated at Hampton Inst. (B.A.), Univ. of Ibadan, Nigeria (diploma, African Studies), Trinity Coll., and Univ. of North Carolina/ Chapel Hill. Married to Jacki Shelton; father of two children. His poetry has been published in *Hyperion Poetry Journal,* the *Chapel Hill Sun,* and the *Hartford Times. Address:* Rt. 5, Box 402, Mebane, NC 27302.

PLAYS

(All pre-1980.) **He's Got the Whole World in His Hand** (3 acts). Examines the plight of a black man confronted with various kinds of activist philosophies and organizations in Harlem. **A Love Supreme** (1 act). A group of Philadelphia janitors evolves to understand the significance of jazz. **The Man with the Plan** (1 act). The role of Islam in dissolving gang warfare in West Philadelphia. **Moses on the Mountain** (drama, 2 acts). On the life and times of George Moses Horton.

SHEPP, ARCHIE (Vernon) (1937–   ), Musician, composer, jazz saxophone player, playwright, and teacher. Born in Ft. Lauderdale, FL. Educated at Goddard Coll., Plainfield, VT (B.A., 1959). Married; two children. Taught English in the public schools of New York City, 1961–63; currently adjunct prof. of Afro-American Studies, Univ. of Massachussetts/Amherst. Has also taught at the Univ. of Buffalo, late 1960s. Appeared in one of his first concerts at Goddard Coll., 1960, and in *The Connection* by Jack Gelber, at Living Theatre, the same year. A recording artist for more than 25 years, mainly under contract to ABC-Impulse Records, c. 1961–present. Coleader of the Archie Shepp-Bill Dixson Quartet, which toured Europe in 1962 and Scandinavia in 1963. Artist in residence, Mobilization for Youth, New York, 1963. Performed in the Newport Jazz Festival and Chicago Jazz Festival, 1965; also participated in John

Coltrane's *Ascension* recording, 1965. Has performed in such clubs as Five Spot Cafe, 1961; Village Gate, 1975; and Village Vanguard, 1975. Member of the Jazz Composers Guild. Winner of *Downbeat* magazine's new star award, 1965. His album *Mama Too Tight* was voted No. 6 in the top 20 jazz albums in a jazz award poll, 1967; his *Trouble in Mind* was voted album of the year in *Downbeat*'s 1981 readers' poll. *Address:* 27 Cooper Sq., New York, NY 10003.

REPRESENTATIVE DRAMATIC WORKS:

Junebug Graduates Tonight ("A Jazz Allegory" [subtitle], prologue and 2 acts [4 scenes], 1967). According to *Black World* (April 1972, p. 52), *Junebug* is a "contemporary Black tale inextricably woven with the 'American' one. The characters are symbols: America, White Woman, Junebug, Blackman, The Muslim, Uncle Sam, The Birchite, The Panther... It is good to see this marriage of music and drama happening at last. It is Africa, our roots, Langston, our poetry, jazz, and in Black Theatre there should be no separation." According to Doris Abramson, "The June Bug of the title is a sensitive young Negro who is plagued by questions on the eve of his graduation from high school as valedictorian of his class. The audience is asked to consider what goes on in his mind at this transitional moment in his life."—*Negro Playwrights in the American Theatre* (Abramson, 1969), p. 282. These questions concern whether or not he should play the game of integration and moderation (as advocated by white liberals) or the game of separation, action, and blood (as advocated by the Black Muslims). Or does he defend himself with his fists, or his words? Or does he forget about defense and start attacking?—Adapt. from a review by Dan Sullivan, *New York Times,* Feb. 21, 1967. First prod. in the Church of the Holy Apostles, New York, Feb. 20–March 2, 1967. With Glynn Turman, Rosalind Cash, MINNIE GENTRY, and Cynthia Belgrave. Prod. at Howard Univ., Washington, DC; dir. by PAUL CARTER HARRISON, late 1970s. Pub. in *Black Drama Anthology* (King & Milner, 1972).

Lady Day ("A Musical Tragedy" [subtitle], 2 acts: music only, 1971). Book by AISHAH RAHMAN. Music by Shepp. Based on the life, times, and career of Billie Holiday. First prod. at the Brooklyn Academy of Music, 1971. Prod. at the Chelsea Theatre, Brooklyn, Oct. 17–Nov. 5, 1972, for 34 perfs., dir. by Paul Carter Harrison. Featuring Cecilia Norfleet as Billie Holiday. Also in the cast were ROSETTA LeNOIRE and MAXWELL GLANVILLE. Unpub. script in the Hatch-Billops Collection.

OTHER DRAMATIC WORKS:

Co-composed incidental music of AMIRI BARAKA's (LeRoi Jones's) **Slave Ship** (1967) and music for LENNOX RAPHAEL's **Blue Soap** (pre-1975).

SHINE, TED (1936–   ), Playwright, university professor, and editor. Born in Baton Rouge, LA. Grew up in Dallas, TX, where he attended the public schools. Educated at Howard Univ. (B.A., 1953), where his writing was encouraged by OWEN DODSON and Sterling Brown; the State Univ. of Iowa (M.A., 1958); and the Univ. of California at Santa Barbara (Ph.D., 1973). After graduating from college, spent two years at the Karamu Theatre in Cleveland, 1953–55, and served for a brief period in the army, 1955–57. Taught at Dillard Univ. in New Orleans, 1960–61, and at Howard Univ., 1961–67. Currently teaching at Prairie View A. & M. Univ. in Texas. Company playwright of the Inst. in Black Repertory Theatre at the Univ. of California at Santa Barbara,

Summer 1968. Scriptwriter for the "Our Street" television series, produced by the Maryland Center for Public Broadcasting, Baltimore, 1969–73. Adjudicator for the Lorraine Hansberry Playwriting Award, presented by the American Theatre Assn. as part of the American Coll. Theatre Festival, 1980–81. Coeditor of *Black Theatre, U.S.A.* (with James V. Hatch), an anthology of 45 plays by black American playwrights [see COLLECTIONS below]. Recipient of a Rockefeller Scholarship to study at Karamu House in Cleveland, 1953–55, and a Brooks-Hines Award for Play-writing from Howard Univ. for his play **Morning, Noon, and Night** (1962). *Address*—Home: 10717 Cox Lane, Dallas, TX 75229. Office: Prairie View A. & M. University, Prairie View, TX 77446. *Agent:* Flora Roberts, 157 W. 57th St., New York, NY 10019.

COLLECTIONS:
CONTRIBUTIONS: Three One Act Plays. Dramatists Play Service, New York, 1970. Contains **Plantation** (1970), **Contribution** (1969), and **Shoes** (1969). [See also GROUP OF RELATED PLAYS below.]

BLACK THEATER, U.S.A.: Forty-Five Plays by Black Americans, 1847–1974. Coeditor, with James V. Hatch. The Free Press, a div. of Macmillan, New York, 1974. Contains **Herbert III** (1974).

GROUP OF RELATED PLAYS:
"CONTRIBUTIONS" (program of 3 one-act plays, 1970). Includes **Plantation** (1970), **Contribution** (1969), and **Shoes** (1969). Prod. Off-Bway at Tambellini's Gate Theatre, March 9–22, 1970. Pub. in the author's *CONTRIBUTIONS: Three One Act Plays*.

REPRESENTATIVE PLAYS AND DRAMATIC WORKS:
Cold Day in August (domestic drama, 1 act, 1950). Deals with the conflicts that arise between a young couple and the wife's mother, with whom they are forced to live. Written and prod. at Howard Univ., Washington, DC, while the author was an undergraduate.

Sho' Is Hot in the Cotton Patch // Alternate title: **Miss Weaver** (comedy, 1 act, 1951). Deals with the conflicts between the older and younger generation of blacks working in a YMCA kitchen in the South. Written and prod. at Howard Univ. while the author was an undergraduate. Again prod. at Howard Univ., Oct. 21–31, 1964; dir. by Roxie Roker (supporting star of "The Jeffersons"). Prod. Off-Bway by the Negro Ensemble Co. (NEC), 1968, under its alternate title. Pub. in *Encore* 11 (NADSA; Florida A. & M. Univ., Tallahassee), 1967, pp. 18–50.

Dry August (comedy-drama, 3 acts, 1952). A black man is entangled in the web of southern racial injustice. Prod. at Howard Univ., 1952.

Epitaph for a Bluebird (comedy-fantasy, 3 acts, 1958). A lonely girl finds love with a soldier in a small military town, only to lose it when he deserts her. Master's thesis play, written and first prod. at the State Univ. of Iowa, Iowa City, Dec. 1958; dir. by Oscar Brockett. With WHITNEY LeBLANC as the soldier-lover.

Morning, Noon, and Night (drama, 1 act, 1962). A Texas family is dominated by a peg-legged religious matriarch who systematically poisons her enemies. First prod. at Howard Univ., Dec. 1962, where it won for the author the Brooks-Hines Award for playwriting. Produced by the Inst. in Black Repertory Theatre, at the Univ. of California, Santa Barbara, Summer 1968. Prod. at Lincoln Univ. of Missouri, for 4 perfs., Feb. 5–8, 1970. Considered for Off-Bway prodn., but the proposed prodn. never materialized.

Flora's Kisses (comedy, 1 act, 1965). The story of a welfare mother's desperate attempt to find love. Prod. by Theatre U, Baltimore, MD, April 1969.

Comeback After the Fire (drama, 2 acts, 1967). Sequel to **Morning, Noon, and Night** (1962). After a nervous breakdown, a black woman evangelist tries to make a comeback. Prod. at the Inst. of Dramatic Arts, at Lincoln Univ. of Missouri, July 8–11, 1969.

Contribution (comedy, 1 act, 1969). An elderly black woman, considered a "good darky who loves us" by her white employers, makes her contribution in the fight for freedom by poisoning their whole family. First prod. Off-Bway by NEC, March 25–April 20, 1969, for 32 perfs., on a program of three one-act plays under the blanket title "CONTRIBUTIONS" [see GROUP OF RELATED PLAYS above]. Produced at the Federal City Coll. Environmental Theatre, Washington DC, during the 1972–73 season. Pub. in the author's *CONTRIBUTIONS: Three One Act Plays.*

Shoes (drama, 1 act, 1969). Three black youths, one with a passion for a pair of alligator shoes, reveal their extravagant plans for spending the money they have earned during the summer while working at a Texas country club. First prod. Off-Bway at Tambellini's Gate Theatre, March 9–22, 1970, for 16 perfs., on a program of three one-act plays by the author, under the blanket title "CONTRIBUTIONS" [see GROUP OF RELATED PLAYS above]. Prod. by the Federal City Coll. Environmental Theatre, during the 1972–73 season. Pub. in *Encore* 12 (NADSA, Florida A. & M. Univ., Tallahassee), 1969.

Hamburgers at Hamburger Heaven Are Impersonal // Alternate title: **Hamburgers Are Impersonal** (comedy-drama, 1 act, 1969). About a lovestarved schoolteacher who gets involved with an unsavory character in a Texas tavern. Prod. under its alternate title at the Harlem School of the Arts Community Theatre, opening July 9, 1971.

Idabel's Fortune (satire, 1 act, 1969). A black domestic worker, whose mistress is on her deathbed, uses her wits to gain her rightful inheritance (for a lifetime of devoted service) prior to the arrival of the woman's greedy relatives. Prod. at the Harlem School of the Arts Community Theatre, opening July 9, 1971.

"Our Street" (TV series, more than 60 half-hour scripts, 1969–73). Popular dramatic series aired by 22 public television stations. Prod. by the Maryland Center for Public Broadcasting, 1969–73. One of Shine's scripts, **Audition,** coauthored with T. DIANNE ANDERSON, was pub. in Anderson's collection *The Unicorn Died at Dawn* (1981).

Plantation (comedy, 1 act, 1970). The nightmare experience of a wealthy, racist plantation owner who discovers that his newborn son is black, and later learns that he himself is a mulatto. Prod. Off-Bway at Tambellini's Gate Theatre, March 9–22, 1970, under the blanket title "CONTRIBUTIONS" [see GROUP OF RELATED PLAYS above]. Pub. in the author's *CONTRIBUTIONS:* Three One Act Plays.

Packard (comedy, 1 act, 1971). A Texas white woman, whose black chauffeur-lover dies in her bed, is faced with the task of removing the body. Prod. at Hampton Inst., Virginia, March 1972.

Herbert III (domestic drama, 1 act, 1974). A black couple, arguing about the whereabouts of their missing son Herbert the Third, reveals more about the crisis in their marriage than they do about their missing son, who is found to be O.K., having fun at a bowling alley. Pub. in the author's *BLACK THEATER, U.S.A.*

The Night of Baker's End (tragedy, 3 acts, 1974). Concerns the struggle of a black father to keep his family together. Prod. at Lincoln Univ. of Missouri Dec. 1974.

The Old Woman Who Was Tampered with in Youth (comedy, 1 act, 1979). An elderly woman who was molested as a young girl is visited by the man who molested her. Prod. at the Starlight Lounge, Indianapolis, IN, Oct. 1980. Pub. in *Center Stage* (Ostrow, 1981).

Baby Cakes (drama, 2 acts, 1981). A woman in her fifties, alienated from her children and dissatisfied with her life, comes into a small fortune and decides to start a new life for herself. Prod. at the Univ. of Texas, Austin, Sept. 1982.

Poor Ol' Soul (tragicomedy, 1 act, 1982). An immature young man desiring a career in show business as a singer must choose between caring for his ill grandmother or performing in an amateur show at a local nightclub. Produced at Fisk Univ., Nashville, Oct. 1983.

OTHER PLAYS AND DRAMATIC WORKS:

Bats out of Hell (3 acts, 1955). Some children create havoc in a peaceful neighborhood while trying to locate their real mother. **Entourage Royale** (musical, 2 acts, 1958). A family of gypsies learns a valuable lesson while trying to swindle the members of a black community. **Rat's Revolt** (character study, 3 acts, 1959). A 17–year-old high school football hero loses his girlfriend, drops out of school, and struggles to find a place for himself in the world. **Miss Victoria** (1 act, 1965). An elderly woman is terrorized by a vicious, drug-crazed teenager who breaks into her home to rob her. **Pontiac** (1 act, 1967). A middle-aged white couple drives down the streets of a college town picking up young black students for the wife to seduce. **Jeanne West** (musical, 2 acts, 1968). A lonely girl, obsessed with collecting celebrity autographs and dominated by an unkind mother, severs the maternal bond and finds love, success, and happiness in show business. **Revolution //** Alternate title: **Riot** (drama, 2 acts, 1968). A group of blacks from all walks of life find themselves together in a basement of a burned-out building as riots in their city and all over the country threaten to annihilate them all. **The Coca-Cola Boys** (1 act, 1969). A recently wed young woman, angry with her husband, joins some older women in her neighborhood at the local tavern, where the older women hustle drinks and money from the Coca-Cola employees. **Waiting Room** (1 act, 1969). A homely teenage wife, estranged from her husband, nevertheless accompanies him to the hospital for emergency treatment. There she is belittled by the nurses on duty, her husband's relatives, and later by her husband. **Trinity** (drama, 1 act, 1983). An alcoholic poet is visited by his friend and former student whom he suddenly does not recognize, accuses him of theft, and orders him out of the apartment. **Goin' Berserk** (comedy, 1 act, 1983). A young man is faced with the problem of putting a female friend, who asked if she could share his apartment for the weekend and has remained for six weeks, out of his apartment. **Vestibule** (drama, 1 act, 1983). A black woman confronts her white in-laws following the death of her husband, whom they had disowned because of his marriage.

SHIPMAN, WILLIE B., Playwright. Formerly associated with the Back Alley Theatre in Washington, DC.

PLAY:

Pepper (comedy, 1 act, 1972). "In this drama, set in Georgia, an aging woman who wants to adopt a child tries to convince a fastidious, sanctimonious woman from the adoption agency that the child will live in a home where Christianity and soberness will prevail. The behavior of the hedonistic husband and elderly father contradicts her carefully rehearsed statements. And when the representative from the adoption agency, unknowingly, drinks punch to which liquor has been added, the comic moments erupt."—*Black World*, April 1973, p. 84. Prod. by the Back Alley Theatre, 1972.

SHOCKLEY, ANN ELLEN (1927–), Librarian, writer of nonfiction and fiction, TV scriptwriter. Born in Louisville, KY. Educated at Fisk Univ. (B.A., 1948) and Case Western Reserve Univ. (M.S.L.S., 1959). Freelance writer for newspapers and periodicals, prior to 1969. Librarian, Fisk Univ., 1969–present. Coauthor, with Sue P. Chandler, of *Living Black American Authors: A Biographical Dictionary* (1973). Compiler and editor, with E. J. Josey, of *A Handbook for Black Librarianship* (1977). Author of three novels: *Loving Her* (1974), *The Black and White of It* (1980), and *Say Jesus and Come to Me* (1982). Her short stories have been published mainly in *Negro Digest/Black World, Umbra,* and *Freedomways;* her nonfiction has been published in numerous periodicals, including *Negro History Bulletin, Library Journal, CLA Journal,* and *Phylon.*

DRAMATIC WORK:
Script for a film adaptation of **"The World of Rosie Polk"** (projected untitled teleplay, 1978). Sched. to be coauthored with Stan Taylor. Based on Shockley's prize-winning short story "The World of Rosie Polk," "about a woman with a young son in the deep South struggling against impossible odds until she finally meets someone who can provide new hope."—*Jet,* Aug. 24, 1978. Sched. to be prod. by Rollaway Productions, a television company formed by actress Esther Rolle, star of the long-running CBS comedy series "Good Times," who would also star in this film. No information concerning the completion of this project is available.

SHOCKLEY, ED, Playwright. Associated with the Frank Silvera Writers' Workshop (FSWW) and the Black Spectrum Theatre, both in New York City. Apparently a resident of St. Albans (Queens), NY.

PLAYS:
(Unpub. script and tape recordings of all plays except the last **[Hopewell]** are located in the FSWW Archives/Schomburg Collection.) **There Are No Fools** (1978). **(That Lil Dreamer Girl)** (1970s). **The Stalking Horse** (1970s). **The Box** (1970s). **Bessie Smith, Empress of the Blues** (1980s). **Hopewell** (historical play, full length, 1984). "The story of St. Albans (Queens, N.Y.) . . . Where the Stars Once Lived."—Advertisement, *New York Amsterdam News,* June 16, 1984. Prod. by the Black Spectrum Theatre, St. Albans, New York, Summer 1968.

SIMAMA, JABARI O., English and drama teacher, playwright. Attended the Univ. of Bridgeport (CT); received a master's degree in Afro-American Studies from Atlanta Univ., where he also pursued additional studies in Afro-American poetry. Founder and one of the "spiritual leaders" of the People's Revolutionary Art Ensemble in Atlanta. Was teaching at Atlanta Jr. Coll. in 1975.

PLAY:
Gonna Make These Bones Shake-N–Finger Pop (theatrical college, full length, 1975). Multimedia prodn., encompassing poetry, dance, jazz, readers' theatre, dramatization, and visual prodn., reflecting the inner feelings of the black community toward

society as well as how blacks perceive themselves. Prod. by the Drama Club of Atlanta Jr. Coll., at the Pittman Community Center, Atlanta, April 4, 1975.

SIMMONS, HERBERT A. (1930–   ), Novelist, poet, and playwright. Born in St. Louis, MO. Educated at Lincoln Univ. (MO), 1949–52, Washington Univ. (MO) (B.A., 1958), and the State Univ. of Iowa on a Writers Workshop Fellowship. Author of two novels: *Corner Boy* (1957), which won a Houghton Mifflin Literary Award, and *Walking on Eggshells* (1962), both published by Houghton Mifflin. His poetry has been published in *The New Black Poetry* (Major, 1969). Coordinator of the Watts Writers Workshop, and was one of the organizers of Watts 13, an all-black communications media industry in Los Angeles.

PLAYS:
The Stranger (1956). Won for the author a Sara B. Glasgo Award in 1956. **Corner Boy** (1960s). Based on the author's novel by the same title. Prod. by the Douglas House Foundation, Los Angeles during the 1960s; dir. by HARRY DOLAN. Pub. only as a novel by Houghton Mifflin, Boston, 1957.

SINGLETON, JACQUI, Playwright. Studied playwriting with the Frank Silvera Writers' Workshop (FSWW) in New York City.

PLAY:
The Breaking Point (drama, 1 act, 1983). Explores the relationship between an older woman and her young lover. Prod. by FSWW, as the premier prodn. of its Writers/ Directors Series for the 1982–83 season, opening Jan. 20, 1983, and continuing for three weekends, closing Feb. 6, 1983. Prod. at the Beckman Theatre, New York, Jan. 3–19, 1985; dir. by Juney Smith. Featuring Lavelle Zeigler and Betty Vaughan.

SMITH, CHARLES ROBERT, Playwright, director, and instructor. Based in Chicago, IL. Educated at the Univ. of Iowa (B.A. in English, with honors, 1981; M.F.A. in playwriting, 1984; postgraduate, 30 hours). Director of Black Action Theatre, Univ. of Iowa, 1981–83. Basic playwriting instructor, Univ. of Iowa, 1983–85; advanced playwriting instructor, 1983–85. Directing intern, ABC Circle Films, Los Angeles, CA, April-June 1983. Literary asst., Mark Taper Forum, Los Angeles, June-Aug. 1983. Asst. director, Iowa Playwrights Workshop, 1984–85. Directing intern, the Guthrie Theatre, Minneapolis, MN, April-June 1985. Literary asst., Victory Gardens, Chicago, 1985–present. Recipient of Lorraine Hansberry Playwriting Award, for **The Silent Warrior** (1982); Best New Play of 1983/Univ. of Iowa Theatres, for his play **Jelly Belly Don't Mess with Nobody** (1983); Univ. of Iowa Graduate and Professional Fellowship, 1983–85; Norman Felton Playwriting Award, Aug. 1984; and an award from the Cornerstone National Playwriting Competition, 1985, for his play **Jelly Belly**. . . . *Address:* 743 W. Cornelia, Chicago, IL 60657.

PLAYS AND DRAMATIC WORKS:
Bluff (1981). Prod. by the Pegasus Players, Chicago, March-April 1981; dir. by Ed Homewood.

Music in Paradise (drama, full length, 1981). Incorporates the use of music via an actor playing a single phrase on the saxophone. The story of Adrian Stone, a U.S. Army veteran, and his younger brother Billy, an aspiring jazz musician. The brothers are at odds once Adrian returns to his home in the inner city and attempts to uproot his family, moving them into what he believes to be a better life in suburbia. Sensing that such a move would not only destroy his musical creativity, but also the family's happiness, Billy struggles to stay close to all he knows—his music, his environment, and himself. Prod. by the Univ. of Iowa, at MacLean 301, May 1981. Staged reading at the Goodman Theatre, Chicago, Aug. 1982.

The Silent Warrior (black comedy, 2 acts, 1982). Set in modern-day suburbia, this is the story of Lonnie, the head of the Weatherspoon family, who intends to expose a crooked politician defaming the memory of his dead father, and of Lonnie's wife, Constance, an unfaithful wife and an unfit mother, who thinks Lonnie should "rub up against" the politician for a "cushy" job. Into this household comes a gun-toting revolutionary who by his own misdirection gives Lonnie a new perspective on morality. Prod. by the Univ. of Iowa, at Studio One, May 1983. Winner of the Lorraine Hansberry Playwriting Award in the American Coll. Theatre Festival (ACTF), c. 1983.

Jelly Belly Don't Mess with Nobody (drama, 1 act, 1982). A construction worker has taken under his wing an aggressive but slightly misguided young man who lives down the street from him. Into this setting comes Jelly Belly, a drug dealer recently released from jail, where he served six months for murder. Jelly Belly goes on a subtle but dangerous campaign to win the younger man over to a life of crime, drugs, death, and destruction. Prod. by the Univ. of Iowa, at MacLean 301, Dec. 1983. Prod. by the American Theatre of Actors, New York City, Aug. 1984. Prod. by Penumbra/Hallie Q. Brown Theatre, April 1986. Named the Best New Play of 1983 by the Univ. of Iowa Theatres. Winner of the Cornerstone National Playwriting Competition, 1985. Sched. to be included in a collection of plays pub. by the Univ. of Iowa Theatre Press, Oct. 1986.

Thief in a Basket (black comedy, 2 acts, 1984). The story of J. D. Brown, a slave who is in partnership with his owner, Col. Burnmaster. The relationship between the Colonel and J. D. changes from assurance and trust to doubt and suspicion as J. D. steals supplies from the Colonel and sells them for healthy profits to the Underground Railroad, aiding and abetting the escape of his fellow slaves. Eventually J. D. amasses enough money to buy his freedom and to purchase the Colonel's now financially strapped plantation, which he does. Once the change of power is complete, J. D. finds that living in postwar America with prewar attitudes is not as easy as he thought. Prod. by the Univ. of Iowa, at MacLean 301, April 1984. Again prod. by the Univ. of Iowa, at the Mainstage, Oct.-Nov. 1984; dir. by Paul Winfield.

Redemption (drama, full length, 1985). About the changing relationships between the members of a menage a trois, consisting of an older guru-type philosopher and lover of poetry, a young aspiring poetess, and a young, black ex-car thief, who is the subject of the poetess's poems. The play is a battle for supremacy among the three characters; it is finally won by the young black man, who finally dominates the poetess and the teacher. Prod. by the Univ. of Iowa, at Studio Two, May 1985. Staged reading at Victory Gardens, April 1986.

Pequito (drama, 1 act; adapt. as a teleplay, 1986). While on duty in the operating room of the Trauma Center, Dr. Paul Fallert finds himself holding the threads of the life of Pequito, a critically wounded leader of a local street gang, who was recently acquitted of the murder of the doctor's only son. Prod. by WMAQ/NEB, Chicago, Dec. 4 and 18, 1986. Also available for prodn. as a play.

SMITH, DEMON. See ABAKARI, DEMANI.

SMITH, DONALD, Playwright.

PLAY:
Harriet Tubman (biographical drama, 61 pp., 1970). About the fugitive slave and abolitionist, who was one of the most successful leaders of the Underground Railroad. Pub. by New Dimensions and distributed by the Chatham Bookseller, Chatham, NJ, 1970.

SMITH, EDWARD G. (Ed), Playwright, director, and actor. Assoc. prof. of theatre and African-American studies at SUNY/Buffalo; also director of the Black Drama Workshop in Buffalo. Cofounder of Black Theatre Canada in Toronto. Has performed as an actor Off-Broadway, in films, and on television. Has directed numerous plays and conducted acting workshops in the United States, Canada, and the West Indies. Recipient of a New York State Council on the Arts grant for playwriting, 1979–80. *Address*—Office: African-American Studies Dept., State University of New York at Buffalo, 206 Harriman Hall, Buffalo, NY 14216. Home: 182 N. Pearl St., Buffalo, NY 14202.

PLAYS AND DRAMATIC WORKS:
Now Time (radio drama, 30 min., 1970). Concerns one man's obligation to the black revolution. Prod. by the Black Drama Workshop, Buffalo, 1970.

It's Easier to Get Dope Than It Is to Get a Job (thesis play, 1 act, 1971). About the problems of drug traffic in the black community. Prod. by the Black Drama Workshop, Buffalo, 1971.

Games (ritual, 1 act, 1972). Moves from children's games to the assassination and murder of black people. Prod. by the Black Drama Workshop, Buffalo, 1972.

Mr. Stag'lee (drama with music, 1 act, 1974). The life and times of a black folk hero, done with music and ensemble. Prod. by Black Theatre Canada, Toronto, Aug. 1974, for 12 perfs. Prod. by Paul Robeson Theatre, Buffalo, July 1977, for 10 perfs. Prod by Kent State Univ., Kent, OH, Sept. 1980, for 8 perfs.

I Love You Madly (musical, full length, 1975). Book by Smith. Music by *Duke Ellington. About a musician who is looking to play in a band located in another city, but is having a hard time leaving his family. (Frank Foster from Count Basie's Band did the musical arrangements with an 11–piece orchestra.) Performed by the Dept. of Theatre, SUNY/Buffalo, April 1975, for 4 perfs.

What's Goin' On (comedy, short 1 act, 1975). About the judicial system. Cowritten with members of Attica Correctional Facility. Performed by members of Attica Correctional Facility, Attica, NY, May 1975, for 2 perfs.

Light Travelin' (drama, short 1 act, 1976). As described by the author: "Two people meet for the first time on a train. One is an out-of-work, hard-on-the-luck musician who has been in this life before but fears it now from taking off on drugs. The lady is someone who is already dead . . . Billie Holiday.''—Letter to Peterson Oct. 8, 1984.

Let the Sun Shine on Me (drama, 1 act, 1983). Concerns two bag people, both looking for something: one for the son he lost in a shoot-out with the police in the 1964 riots; the other, for the sun, which he lost while losing his mind in the Vietnam War. Performed by the New Freedom Theatre, Philadelphia, PA, Sept. 1983, for 16 perfs.

SMITH, JEAN WHEELER, Short-story writer and playwright. Born in Detroit, MI. "Left her studies at Howard University and went off to the Southern Wars with that valiant band of young SNCC workers in 1963. . . . Finally returned to Howard for her degree, married Frank Smith, a fellow-SNCC worker, and settled in Mississippi to carry on the fight and to try to make a life."—*Negro Digest,* Nov. 1967. In 1968 she was pursuing graduate studies and was an associate of the Center for Black Education in Washington, DC. Her writings have been published in *Negro Digest/Black World.*

PLAY:
O.C.'s Heart (drama, 3 acts, 1970). A young black man gets back his dead brother's heart after it has been transplanted into a white man's body. Excerpts (Act II, Scenes 2 and 3; Act III, Scenes 1 and 2) pub. in *Negro Digest,* April 1970, pp. 56–76.

SMITH, LOIS A., Playwright. Based in Chattanooga, TN.

PLAYS:
A Reversible Oreo (comedy of race relations in the United States, 3 acts, 1974). Depicts the contrasts in the lives of a black and a white family in the South, and how they are differently affected by the pressures of life. Prod. in Chattanooga, April 1974. **What's Wrong** (comedy, 1 act, 1974). Depicts the hustle, bustle, and selfish thinking that describes the pace, condition, and attitude of the average person during the Christmas holidays. Prod. in Chattanooga, Dec. 1974.

SMITH, VANCE, Playwright. Formerly associated with the Mwongi Arts Players, Detroit, MI.

PLAY:
S.T.R.E.S.S. (1973). "This play proved most beneficial in describing for the Black communities the Detroit Police Department's stratagem in using police decoys to apprehend street robbers. S.T.R.E.S.S., an acronym for 'Stop the Robberies—Enjoy Safe Streets,' shows how all the units' victims, 19 Black, fell to their fatal shooting."—*Black World,* April 1974. Prod. by the Mwongi Arts Players during the 1973 season.

SMITH, WELTON (1940–   ), Poet-playwright. Born in Houston, TX. Author of *Penetration* (poems, 1972). His poems have been published in numerous anthologies.

PLAY:
The Roach Riders (1970s).

SMYRL, DAVID LANGSTON, Actor, singer, comedian, and expert fencer. Former prisoner of Sing-Sing who was producing shows for prisoners during the mid-1970s.

PLAYS:

On the Goddam Lock-in or Lights Out (drama, 1 act, 1972). Focuses on the personal relationships that develop among fellow prison inmates. Public reading by the Frank Silvera Writers' Workshop (FSWW), at the Martinique Theatre, New York, March 1975. Prod. at the Hotel Alden Theatre, New York, July 1975. Unpub. script in the FSWW Archives/Schomburg Collection. **On the Lock-in** (musical, full length, 1977). Based on his one-act play, described above. A picture of prison life through scenes, soliloquies, and songs. Prod. Off-Bway, at the New York Shakespeare Festival Public Theatre, April 1977.

SNIPES, MARGARET FORD TAYLOR (Margaret Ford Taylor; Mrs. Kenneth E. Snipes) (1940–   ), Actress, director, playwright, public relations director. Born in Detroit, MI. Former director of public relations at Karamu House in Cleveland, where she was involved in the Karamu Theatre, and was described by LEATRICE EMERUWA in *Black World* (April 1974) as "a leading lady, playwright, director, TV-script writer, arts festival coordinator and newspaper editor." Cofounder of Ebony Tours, described as "the first Black professional performing arts organization in Ohio." At Karamu, she appeared as Idella Landy in *Purlie Victorious,* Sister Margaret in *The Amen Corner,* Grace Love in *Contribution,* Mama Rosa in *Black Girl,* and Lena in *Boesman and Lena.* In addition to directing her own plays at Karamu, she directed *Black Girl* at the African Cultural Center in Buffalo, NY, and ANNETTA GOMEZ JEFFERSON's *In Both Hands* at the Humanist Theatre in Cleveland.

PLAYS AND DRAMATIC WORKS:

Hotel Happiness (comedy, 1 act, 1971). Prod. at Karamu Theatre, March 1971, for 4 perfs. Revived by Karamu Theatre, 1972, for a four-week run. Prod. by Ebony Tours, Cleveland, 1974–75. **I Want to Fly** (comedy, 1 act, 1971). prod. at Karamu House, March 1971, for 4 perfs.; dir. by author. Revived by Karamu Theatre, 1972, for a four-week run. **Will Somebody Please Die?** (comedy, full length, 1973). Prod. by the One World Theatre Workshop, Cleveland, Summer 1973; dir. by author. **The Hymie Finklestein Used Lumber Company** (musical comedy, 1973). Coauthor, with ERNIE FANN. First prod. by Karamu Theatre, Cleveland, in the Arena Theatre, Summer 1973. Revised and restaged by Karamu Theatre for a run of four weeks, opening Sept. 28, 1983. **Folklore Black American Style** (1973). Prod. by Ebony Tours, Cleveland, 1974–75. **Sing a Song of Watergate** (musical comedy, 2 acts, 1975). A satire of the Watergate scandal. Prod. by the Humanist Theatre, Cleveland, Feb. 1975. **The Second Reconstruction** (TV doc. 1973). Narrated by OSSIE DAVIS, and prod. by NBC, 1973.

SOLOMON, FRANK, Novelist and playwright. Born in Allendale, SC, one of seven children, where he grew up working in the cotton fields. Spent two years in the army, 1955–c. 1957. Graduated from the South Carolina Area Trade School (now Denmark Technical Coll.) with a degree in radio and TV repair, 1960. Author of *A Hell of a Life,* a novel set in Allendale at the beginning of the civil rights movement.

DRAMATIC WORK:
Flat Street Sa'Day Night (musical drama, 2 acts, 1985). Book by Solomon. Music and lyrics by LENGA TOOKS. Based on Solomon's novel, *A Hell of a Life*. "Set in the late 1940s and early 1950s, the play depicts the lively happenings in the jukebox joints on Flat Street, a real street that croses U.S. 301 in Allendale. [It] spans a Saturday night from 6 p.m. to midnight, and depicts dancing, fighting, courting, joke-telling and singing."—*The State* (Columbia, SC), July 6, 1985. The joints were the only places for blacks to release their frustrations and unwind after working hard all week in the fields. Prod. by Theatre In Progress, and presented Off-Bway, at the Arts for Living Centre, Henry St. Settlement, in the facilities of the New Federal Theatre, May 16–June 30, 1985, and July 11–Aug. 4, 1985. At the invitation of the mayor, it was also presented in Allendale at the Allendale Primary School, July 5 and 6, 1985. Winner of five AU-DELCO awards for choreography (Sheryle R. Jones), outstanding performance in a musical/female (Patricia A. Clement), outstanding performance in a musical/male (Steve Beckman), outstanding musical creator (Lenga Tooks), and musical production of the year (Frank Solomon and Lenga Tooks).

SOUL, LAWRENCE. See WILLIAMS, X. LAWRENCE VIRGIL.

STANBACK, THURMAN W., Playwright, director, and teacher. Educated at Columbia Univ. (M.A.) and Cornell Univ. (Ph.D.). For many years, drama director at Bethune-Cookman Coll. and Florida Atlantic Coll. *Address*: Iona Enterprises, Inc., 520 N. Ridgewood Ave., Daytona Beach, FL 32014.

PLAYS:
(All pre-1970, except where noted) **Tomorrow Has Been Here and Gone** (domestic drama, 3 acts, 1969). Subtitled "A Change Has Got to Come." **Who Will Pay The Piper?** (drama, 3 acts). **The Delicate Thread** (full length).

STEED, RUTH (Dawkins) (1949–   ), Poet-playwright. Born in Marianna, FL. Resides in Pontiac, MI. Her work has been published in *Black World, Miami Times, and Liberty City News;* by Broadside Press; and was scheduled to be published by Amuru Press. She states that her writing objective is "to aid in pointing out some of the major contradictions in the *society of inhumanity* and to offer alternatives for the eradication of those contradictions."—Letter to Peterson, March 5, 1975.

PLAYS:
A Raindrop of Thunder (social drama, 2 acts, 1973–74). Examines the social attitudes of a revolutionary young mother; who is caught up in a conflict between white and black values. Prod. 1973–74. Sched. for publication by Amuru Press, New York, 1974, but apparently never pub. **Hyenas Can't Shoot** (satire, 1 act, 1984). Stresses the seriousness of careful in-depth planning of revolutionary activities. Prod. 1974. **Never Write Letters to the Dead** (protest play, 1975). Points out various contradictions in American society. Sched. for prodn. in New York City, 1975.

STEVENSON, WILLIAM ADELL, III. See ADELL, ILUNGA.

STEWARD, RON, Librettist, lyricist, and composer. Associated with La Mama E.T.C. and the New York Shakespeare Festival (NYSF). He has written music and lyrics for a number of New York shows, in addition to those listed below.

DRAMATIC WORKS:
The Believers ("The Black Experience in Song" [subtitle], 3 acts, 1968). Book by JOSEPH WALKER and JOSEPHINE JACKSON. Music and lyrics by Stewart. A chronicle of the black experience in America through song and dance. First prod. Off-Bway at the Garrick Theatre, May 9, 1968; dir. by BARBARA ANN TEER. With the cast of The Voices, Inc. Cast recording by RCA Victor (LSO-1151). **Sambo** (jazz musical, 2 acts, 1969). Subtitled "A Black Opera with White Spots." Previously subtitled "A Nigger Opera." Words by Steward and *Louis Johnson. Music by Steward and NEAL TATE. Described by *The Best Plays of 1969–1970* as a "protest musical," "with symbolic episodes depicting the black man's sense of alienation." First prod. by La Mama E.T.C., New York, June 14, 1969. Prod. as an indoor production by NYSF/Public Theatre, beginning Dec. 12, 1969; revived as an indoor production by NYSF Mobile Theatre, and presented at the parks and playgrounds of the five boroughs of New York City, beginning July 14, 1970.

STEWART, JAMES T., Poet, playwright, essayist, artist, and musician. Born in Philadelphia, PA. His poetry has been published in *Nommo* and the *Journal of Black Poetry,* and anthologized in *Black Arts* (Alhamisi & Wangara, 1969) and *Black Fire* (Jones & Neal, 1968). His essays on the revolutionary black artist have also been published in *Black Fire* and in *Black Dialogue* magazine. His paintings have been exhibited frequently in Philadelphia, and he has performed as an "altoist-baritonist" with a number of bands.

GROUP OF RELATED PLAYS:
"FIVE PLAYS FOR CHILDREN" (adaptns. of 5 African folk tales, 1971). Includes **Agbanli and the Hunter, The Messenger of God, How Men Came into the World, The Gourd Cup,** and **Jojo: The Storytellers** (all 1971). Pub. in *Black Lines,* Fall 1971, pp. 42–54.

PLAYS:
Agbanli and the Hunter (children's play: dramatization of an African folk tale, 1 act, 1971). Subtitled "Why One Never Tells the Truth to Women." A hunter tells a secret to his wife, with tragic consequences. Pub. in *Black Lines,* Fall 1971, pp. 43–45.
The Messenger of God (children's play: dramatization of an African folk tale, 1 act, 1971). Subtitled "Mamu's [God's] Ways Are Just." The Ways of Mamu are just, even though they do not always seem to be. Pub. in *Black Lines,* Fall 1971, pp. 45–48.
How Men Came into the World (children's play: dramatization of an African folk tale, 1 act, 1971). Subtitled "How the Lesser Gods Came into the World." Men came into the world by outsmarting Death. Pub. in *Black Lines,* Fall 1971, pp. 48–51.
The Gourd Cup (children's play: dramatization of an African folk tale, 1 act, 1971). Subtitled "A Play Spoken with Song and Dancing for Little Children." The gourd cup is the single source of both beauty and ugliness in women. Pub. in *Black Lines,* Fall 1971, pp. 51–52.

Jojo: The Storytellers (children's play: dramatization of an African folk tale, 1 act, 1971). Two morality tales are told: In the first, a father and his smart son are justly punished for not sharing food with the dumb son. In the second tale, a father receives his just punishment for not providing food for his starving wife and child. Pub. in *Black Lines,* Fall 1971, pp. 52–53.

STEWART, SALLY, Actress, director, poet, and playwright. Lives in Los Angeles, CA. Has attended Chicago Community Coll., West Los Angeles Coll., UCLA, and California State Univ./Dominguez. Received an Associate Arts degree in humanities. Studied acting with the Chicago Community Playhouse, the Dorsey Adult School, and the Inner City Cultural Center of Los Angeles. Studied writing through the Writers Guild West Open Door Program and the Frederick Douglass Writers' Workshop. Then formed a Roundtable Workshop at her home. Has worked as a secretary, administrative assistant, and in every aspect of the clerical field. Worked as an extra in a number of films, including *Let's Do It Again, Lady Sings the Blues, New York New York,* and *The One and Only.* Played a principal character in an educational film, *Uptight: Black and White,* and a bit part in a television special, *Kennedy.* Her poems have been published in *The Poetic Village* and *Of Thee I Sing.* She is the author of a book of poems, *The Dismal Blues. Address:* 5762 Clemson St., Los Angeles, CA 90016.

PLAYS:

Cadence (musical drama, 3 acts, 1976). Music and lyrics by *Harold Stewart and other song writers. Portrait of an aspiring entertainer whose dreams of stardom and travel are suddenly destroyed and turned to disaster as two boyfriends compete for her love and attention. Utilizes high-tech video effects and choreography. First prod. in Philadelphia, and presented in various high schools and community centers. Prod. in Los Angeles, May 1985, and shown in a number of recreational centers and community theaters.

Small Scope (historical satire, 2 acts, 1976). Dramatic account of political affairs during President Nixon's "reign." Prod. by the Performing Arts Soc. of Los Angeles (PASLA) and RON DANIELS, 1976, financed through a California State of Arts grant. A film version of this play is now being written by the author.

Corp Cry (drama, 3 acts, 1983). Based on the Patty Hearst story, this play depicts the attempt by revolutionaries to overthrow the government. Unpub. script in the Langston Hughes Lib., Inner City Cultural Centre, Los Angeles.

Sty Gose (detective drama, 2 acts, 1984). A Los Angeles police detective and a private eye team up to track down drug dealers in the United States and Mexico.

In My Father's House (political drama, 2 acts, 1985). A presidential contender addresses politically explosive issues, thus creating problems for his family and causing him to lose the election. A film version is being considered for prodn., according to the author.

STILES, THELMA JACKSON (1939–   ), Author, playwright, and editor. Born in Monroe, LA. Educated at the Univ. of California/Berkeley (B.A., 1961). Married; two children. Has worked for several years as a writer and editor for various industrial organizations, including Sage-Allen & Co., a department store chain in Hartford, CT, Litton Industries, Wells Fargo Bank in San Francisco, and Physics International Co. in San Leandro, CA. She has been a high school teacher and a faculty member at California State Univ./Hayward. Began writing fiction as a member of the San Francisco Black Writers Workshop, 1969–. Her articles and short stories have appeared in *Players, Essence, The California Monthly,* and other magazines and area newspapers. *Address:* P.O. Box 1805, Oakland, CA 94604

PLAY:

No One Man Show (domestic comedy, 1 act, 1971). The story of a single black woman in her late thirties who assumes the responsibility, after her parents' deaths, for caring for and running the lives of her 18–year-old sister and 20–year-old brother, while at the same time wishing that they would be more independent and responsible adults. She comes to realize that she has made them dependent on her, and takes action to remedy the situation. First prod. by the San Francisco Black Writers Workshop, 1971. Prod. by the B & B Experimental Theatre, at the On Broadway Theatre in San Francisco, 1972. According to the pub. script, "B & B has [also] launched several productions of *No One Man Show* in Oakland and San Francisco and at local colleges." Pub. in *Center Stage* (Ostrow, 1981).

STOKES, HERBERT (Damu), Agitprop playwright. A disciple of AMIRI BARAKA (LeRoi Jones) and a former member of Spirit House in Newark, NJ.

PLAYS:

The Uncle Toms (agitprop play, 1 act, 1968). About the conversion of two misguided "Negro boys" to militant young "Black men" through the rhetoric of a black "brother." Prod. by Spirit House, Newark, 1966; dir. by author. Pub. by Jihad Press, Newark, 1967. Pub. in *The Drama Review,* Summer 1968, pp. 58–60. **The Man Who Trusted the Devil Twice** (agitprop melodrama, 1 act, 1969). An "Uncle Tom" school principal twice betrays his own son by reporting him to white authorities, and learns too late the error of his ways. Pub. in *New Plays from the Black Theatre* (Bullins, 1969), pp. 119–28.

STRONG, ROMANER JACK, Playwright. Based in Los Angeles, CA, where during the 1960s he was associated with the Theatre of UCLA.

PLAYS:

(All prod. by the Theatre. of UCLA.) **Metamorphisms** (drama, 1 act, 1966). **Mesmerism of a Maniac** (tragedy, full length, 1967). **A Psychedelic Play or a Happening** (tragedy, 1 act, 1967). **A Date with the Intermediary** (drama, full length, 1968). **A Direct Confrontation in Black** (drama, 1 act, 1968).

STUART, DELANO H., Actor-singer, black theatre founder-director, and playwright. Born in the Panama Canal Zone, where he began his study of theatre arts. Moved with his family to New York City, where he pursued a career in the theatre and became dissatisfied with the opportunities available to blacks. Studied theatre administration at Brooklyn Coll. and Columbia Univ. During the mid-1960s, took singing engagements in Los Angeles and Hawaii. Cofounder in June 1968, with his wife Anne Marie Andrews Stuart, of the Bed-Stuy Theatre in Brooklyn, NY, a store-front theatre which was an integral part of the Brooklyn community until its demise in 1973. One of the founders of the New York Black Theatre Alliance (BTA). Brother of New York State Senator Waldaba Stewart.

PLAYS:
Rerun (1 act, 1973). First prod. by the Bed-Stuy Theatre, May 25, 1973, continuing in repertory through Oct. 25, 1973. **Uncle Tom** (1 act, 1973). A retrospective review of black history. First prod. by the Bed-Stuy Theatre, May 25, 1973, continuing in repertory through Nov. 1973. **Welcome Home, Joe** (1 act, 1973). First prod. by the Bed-Stuy Theatre, Sept. 13, 1973, continuing in repertory through Nov. 1973.

STUART, HAROLD, Playwright. Based in Boston, MA. Attended the Frank Silvera Writers' Workshop in New York City.

PLAYS: Calais and the Last Poets (2 acts, 1972). The technique of drama-therapy is used to rehabilitate a group of teenage drug addicts, as they enact the poetry of "The Last Poets." **There's a Struggle Going On** (musical, 2 acts, 1973). A black Vietnam veteran finds new meaning in life through involvement in the black American struggle. **Hunter** (comedy, 1 act, 1974). A man appears to be willing to provide for a woman and her son, until he discovers that the son is deaf, dumb, and blind. **The Truth About the Truth** (monologue, 1 act, 1974). A wise man (or woman) speaks on economics and its effects on black and minority people. Public reading by FSWW, Jan. 16, 1978. Prod. by Theatre Genesis, New York, April 6–16, 1978. Unpub. script in the FSWW Archives/Schomburg Collection.

SWANN, DARIUS LEANDER, Playwright.

PLAYS:
(All prod. by Friendship Press, New York) **The Crier Calls** (drama for verse choir, 1956). **A House for Marvin** (1 act, 1957). **I Have Spoken to My Children** (play for verse choir, 1 act, 1957). **The Circle Beyond Fear** (choral drama, 1960). **A Desert, a Highway** (1 act, 1963).

T

TANSEY, JUNE, Actress and musical librettist. Based in New York City.

DRAMATIC WORK:

Adam ("A . . . Musical About Adam Clayton Powell, Jr." [subtitle], full length, 1983). Book by Tansey. Music and lyrics by her husband, RICHARD AHLERT. Deals with the fall from power of the flamboyant black congressman, the forces that contributed to it, and its effect on the black community. Prod. Off-Bway by WOODIE KING, JR., and the New Federal Theatre, at the Henry St. Playhouse, New York, Jan. 20–Feb. 6, 1983; dir. by DON EVANS. With Reuben Green in the starring role.

TAPIA, JOSE (1942–   ), Playwright, specializing in musical theatre. Born in Santurce, Puerto Rico. Educated at Fordham Univ. (B.A., 1964, with one year at Fordham Law School). Was living in Amsterdam, the Netherlands, during the 1970s.

DRAMATIC WORKS:

Kenya (musical pageant, full length, 1969). Prod. at P.S. 29, New York, 1969. **EGO** (musical mystery play, full length, 1970). Prod. in Amsterdam, 1970. **Welcome Aboard the Space Ship O.R.G.Y.** (musical comedy, full length, 1971). Previewed in Dordrecht, 1971. **Thoughts** (collection of musical sketches, full length: additional lyrics only, 1972). Book, music, and lyrics by LAMAR ALFORD. First prod. Off-Off-Bway at La Mama E.T.C., Dec. 6, 1972; dir. by Jan Mickens. Presented Off-Bway, at Theatre De Lys, March 19–April 6, 1973, for 24 perfs.; dir. by Michael Schultz. Presented by the New Theatre Club of Washington, DC, at the Washington Theatre Club, Jan. 23, 1974, for 23 perfs. NOTE: The Following plays are all pre-1976: **Outrage** (musical). **Satin Man** (musical). **Sunny Explode** (opera, full length).

TATE, NEAL, Composer, musical director, arranger, conductor, and teacher. Born in Yonkers, NY. Educated at New York Univ. (B.S., 1955), with additional study at Manhattan School of Music and Juilliard School of Music. A specialist in theatre music, the training of singers and musicians, and the training of children in the theatre arts. Has been musical conductor, arranger, and director for a number of New York shows.

DRAMATIC WORK:
Sambo (musical, full length, 1969). Subtitled "A Black Opera with White Spots"; previously subtitled "A Nigger Opera." Book and lyrics by RON STEWARD and *Louis Johnson. Music by Steward and Tate. Described by *The Best Plays of 1969–1970* as a "protest musical," "with symbolic episodes depicting the black man's sense of alienation." First prod. Off-Bway by La Mama E.T.C. (Experimental Theatre Club), June 14, 1969. Prod. Off-Bway as an indoor production by the New York Shakespeare Festival Public Theatre, beginning Dec. 12, 1969; revived as an indoor production by the New York Shakespeare Festival Mobile Theatre, and presented at the parks and playgrounds of the five boroughs of New York City, beginning July 14, 1970. **Music Magic** ("Musical Odyssey" [subtitle], 1976). Book by SHAUNEILLE PERRY. Music and lyrics by Tate. Prod. at the Billie Holiday Theatre, Brooklyn, Nov. 1976.

TAYLOR, ED, Playwright. Affiliated with the Harlem Opera Society of New York City. *Address:* c/o Emory Taylor, Harlem Opera, 536 W. 111th St., Suite 76, New York, NY 10025.

DRAMATIC WORK:
Solomon and Sheba (opera, 1974). Coauthored with SAM RIVERS. Prod. by the Harlem Opera Soc., at the Black Theatre Alliance Festival New York. 1974.

TAYLOR, JACKIE, Playwright. One of the founders of the Chicago Black Ensemble, Chicago, IL.

PLAY:
The Other Cinderella (fantasy, 1975). Prod. by the Chicago Black Ensemble, 1975, apparently remaining in repertory until Dec. 1977.

TAYLOR, JEANNE, Author and playwright. Formerly associated with the Douglass House Foundation, Los Angeles, CA. Her nonfiction and short stories have appeared in the *Antioch Review, Negro American Literature Forum, Black Culture* (Simmons & Hutchinson, 1972), *From the Ashes* (Schulberg, 1967), and *New Black Voices* (Chapman, 1972).

PLAY:
House Divided (1968). Prod. by the Douglass House Foundation, Los Angeles, 1968.

TAYLOR, MARGARET FORD. See SNIPES, MARGARET FORD TAYLOR.

TAYLOR, PATRICIA (formerly Patricia Taylor Curtis), Playwright. Based in New York City, where her plays have been produced Off-Broadway and on television.

PLAYS AND DRAMATIC WORKS:
If We Grow Up (TV script/play, 1963). Prod. by WCBS-TV, New York, and Off-Bway by Audience Assn., 1963. **Unfinished Business** (TV script/play, 1964). Prod. by

the "Repertoire Workshop," WCAV-TV, New York (?), and Off-Bway by Audience Assn., 1964. **The People Watchers** (TV series for children, 1965). Prod. by "Camera Three," CBS-TV, Philadelphia, 1965. **Walk Down Mah Street!** ("A Topical Musical Revue" [subtitle], 2 acts, 1967). Script and lyrics by Patricia Taylor [Curtis], who also dir. and choreographed. Music by NORMAN CURTIS, who also performed as a musician. Special material by James Taylor, Gabriel Levenson, and members of the Next Stage Theatre Co. Songs and skits on racial subjects. Apparently first prod. in a TV adaptn. by "Camera Three," CBS-TV, New York, 1967. Prod. Off-Bway at the Players Theatre, June 12–Oct. 6, 1968, for 135 perfs., with members of the Next Stage Theatre Co. **A Whole Lotta World** (adventure series for children, 1971). Prod. by "The Electric Company," NET-TV, 1971. **The Play People** (children's theatrical work, 1971). Includes traditional black American children's rhymes, chants, songs, and games. Prod. by Voices, Inc., at Town Hall, New York, Dec. 1971.

TAYLOR, ROB (Robert Taylor), Playwright. In the early 1970s, he was an inmate at Riker's Island in New York. His plays, written in collaboration with CECIL ALONZO, were coauthored through correspondence. *Pertinent Address:* Cecil Alonzo, Alonzo Players, 317 Clermont Ave., Brooklyn, NY 11205.

PLAYS:
Somewhere Between Us Two (poetic love story, 1 act, 1972). Coauthor, with Cecil Alonzo. Story of two pen pals who finally meet and are disappointed that the words on paper do not match all the images that they have conjured up through their loving correspondence. Concerns their attempt to bridge the gap that lies "somewhere between the two" of them. Presented by the Alonzo Players, Brooklyn, NY, at the Billie Holiday Theatre; 1973, dir. by Alonzo. Performed at the Black Theatre Alliance annual festival, New York, 1974. Performed at the Seafood Playhouse, New York, June 1975. **Strike One Blow** (drama, 1 act, 1973). Coauthor, with Cecil Alonzo. A true story of the feelings and thoughts of an inmate on Riker's Island whose personal beliefs run afoul of the law and keep him in hot water with the authorities. Focuses on the joys and sadness of his past and his determination not to give in to the physical and emotional pressures of prison life. Based on the author's experiences, and written through correspondence with Alonzo. Prod. by the Tompkins Square Park Players, New York, and presented at the Billie Holiday Theatre, Brooklyn, 1973.

TEER, BARBARA ANN (1937–   ), Director, actress, author, educator, playwright, choreographer, black theatre founder and executive producer. Born in East St. Louis, IL. Educated at the Univ. of Illinois (B.A. in dance, 1957). Studied drama with Sanford Meisner, Paul Mann, Phillip Burton, and Lloyd Richards; studied dance in Berlin and Paris, and with the Vigmont School of Dance. Divorced from late comedian GODFREY CAMBRIDGE; two children. Danced with Alvin Ailey and Louis Johnson dance companies; dance captain on Broadway for Agnes DeMille in musical *Kwamina*. Taught dance and drama in New York City public schools. Founder, with Robert Hooks, of the Group Theatre Workshop, 1964, which later became the Negro Ensemble Co.; cultural director, teenage workshop, Harlem School of the Arts, 1967. Founder, producer, director, and resident playwright of the National Black Theatre (NBT),

1968–present. As the spiritual force and prime mover behind NBT, she developed
and taught a black art standard which has become the trademark of NBT. According to this standard, all theatrical presentations by NBT, including plays,
musicals, rituals, and "revivals" must (a) raise the level of consciousness, (b)
address political issues, (c) educate, (d) illuminate, and (e) entertain. With NBT,
she has also developed new art forms (including "ritualistic revivals" and
"blackenings") and has created what has been called the "Teer Technology of
Soul" as a technique of teaching "God Conscious Art" at NBT. She has toured
with NBT in theatres, colleges, and universities throughout the eastern United
States, the Caribbean, and Nigeria. Since early 1960s, she has performed frequently as an actress, appearing in New York productions of *Kwamina* (1961),
Raisin' Hell in the Sun (1962), *Living Premise* (1963), *Home Movies* (1965),
for which she won the Vernon Rice Award as best actress, *Prodigal Son* (1965),
Who's Got His Own (1966), *Does a Tiger Wear a Necktie?* (1967), *Where's
Daddy?* (1967), *The Experiment* (1967), and *Day of Absence* (1970). Film ap-
pearances include *Slaves* (1969) and *Angel Levine* (1970). In addition to directing
productions of NBT (including her own dramatic works cited below), she has
directed *The Believers* (Off-Bway, 1967), *The Spook Who Sat by the Door*
(Chicago, 1969), *The Beauty of Blackness* (with The Voices, 1970s), *Five on
the Black Hand Side* (Off-Bway, 1970), and "Black Heritage Series" (CBS-
TV, 1973). Guest lecturer on comtemporary black art, and guest director on the
"Black Heritage Series" (CBS-TV, 1973). Contributing writer to *Black Power
Revolt* (Barbour, 1968); contributing editor to *Black Theatre* magazine, 1969;
and contributor of numerous articles to *Negro Digest/Black World* and the drama
section of the Sunday *New York Times*. Memberships include Black Theatre
Alliance; Board of Directors, Theatre Communications Group; Harlem Philharmonic Soc.; and Theatre Committee for the Second International Black and
African Festival of Arts and Culture (FESTAC), 1975. Recipient of numerous
awards and citations for her contributions to the theatre and the community, only
a few of which include Vernon Rice/Drama Desk Award as Best Actress, 1965;
first annual AUDELCO Recognition Award in theatre, 1973; International Benin
Award, 1974; National Assn. of Media Women's Black Film Festival Award,
1975, for Best Film, **Rise: A Love Song for a Love People;** Cultural Arts
Service Award, Black Spectrum Theatre Co., 1978; Monarch Merit Award,
Special Council for Culture and Art, for outstanding contributions to the performing and visual arts, 1983; and the National Black Treasure Award, presented
by the Hamilton Arts Center, Schenectady, NY, for outstanding contribution to
black American theatre. *Address*—Home: 213 W. 137th St., New York, NY
10030. Office: National Black Theatre, Inc., 2033 Fifth Ave., New York, NY
10035.

PLAYS AND DRAMATIC WORKS:
Tribute to Brother Malcolm (historical doc., late 1960s). Dramatization of the tragic
assassination of Malcolm X. Performed by members of the NBT Workshop, late 1960s;
dir. by author.

(The) Revival // Also known as **A Revival: Change! Love! Organize!** (ritual, full length, 1969/72). Coauthor, with CHARLIE L. RUSSELL. An evolving theatrical work, completed in 1972 after almost three years of work, putting in dramatic form the author's black art standard, which has become the unifying philosophy and trademark of NBT. Utilizes a combination of music, drama, dance, "rapping," and the rhythms and fervor of the black church tradition to teach black people to unite, love one another, and work together for meaningful change. Prod. in repertory, with frequent revisions, by NBT since 1972.

Rise: A Love Song for a Love People (film: screenplay, 1975). Written, coproduced, and directed by the author. Based on the life of Malcolm X. May also be based on the author's **Tribute to Malcolm X,** previously produced as a play by NBT, late 1960s. Recipient of the National Assn. of Media Women's Black Film Festival Award, as Best Film, 1975.

Sojourney into Truth // Also known as **Soul Journey into Truth** (theatrical collage, full length, 1975). Written, directed, and choreographed by Teer. "Used music, chants, dance and audience participation to create a warm spiritual experience," described as similar to "those old Baptist revivals."—*Black World,* April 1976, p. 56 (Bailey). Prod. by the NBT, 1975. Also toured three West Indian/Caribbean countries. Won for costumer Larry Le Gaspi an AUDELCO Award, 1976.

We Sing a New Song (adaptn., full length, 1970s). Prod. by the NBT, 1970s.

TERRELL, VINCENT, Playwright. Former artistic director of the Society of Creative Concern, Boston, MA, 1969–75.

PLAYS:

(All prod. by the Society of Creative Concern, and pub. by Solar Press, Boston.) **The Caskets** (drama, 1 act, 1969). Concerns the murders of three civil rights activists— Medgar Evers, Malcolm X, and Martin Luther King, Jr. **Genuine Minstrel Show** (musical comedy, 3 acts, 1969). **Apollo #19** (1 act, 1970). Deals with the interactions of two astronauts during a space flight. **God's a Faggot (A Biblical Confession)** (morality drama, 1 act, 1970). Points out the contradictions in the Christian Bible and man's dilemma in attempting to choose between conflicting spiritual values. **Sarge** (drama, 1 act, 1970). About the trials of a black soldier who is recaptured after defecting to the enemy side in the Vietnam War. **Several Barrels of Trash** (morality drama, 1 act, 1970). Concerns the dilemma faced by trash and garbage collectors after finding a large amount of money. **Shuttle U.S.A.** (drama, 1 act, 1970). Offers revolutionary solutions to America's racial and political problems. **Us** (drama, 1 act, 1971). Similar to **Shuttle U.S.A.** (1970) above, in its proposal of radical solutions to America's racial problems. **Trotter** (historical drama, 1 act, 1972). Concerns the final tragic days in the life of William Monroe Trotter, Boston's militant black leader and editor of the turn of the century. **Will It Be Like This Tomorrow** (drama, 1 act, 1972). Concerns how a physical change in the president of the United States affects his presidency. **Trotter Debates** (historical drama, 1 act, 1973). Dramatizes the famous debate between President Woodrow Wilson and Boston's militant leader William Monroe Trotter on racial issues. **An Evening with William Wells Brown** (one-man show, 1 act, 1974). Deals with Brown's escape from slavery and his life as a free man and spokesman for the cause of abolition. **From These Shores, or Good Olde Crispus** (historical drama, 1 act, 1974). About Crispus Attucks, the first black American to be killed in the Boston Massacre. **Miss Phillis** (historical drama, 1974). About the literary development of black American poet Phillis Wheatley during colonial times in Boston. **Right, Reverend Nat Turner** (historical drama, 1 act, 1974). The life of Nat Turner, freedom fighter and leader of the Virginia Slave Rebellion. **Shoot-Out at St. Rafael County Courthouse** (political protest play, 1 act, 1974). About a younger brother's commitment to help his older brother escape from jail. **Trotter Woman** (1 act, 1974). About the love and dedication of Mrs. Gerald Louise Trotter, wife of William Monroe Trotter, Boston journalist, civil rights activist, and editor of the turn of the century. **Another Man Called William** (1 act, 1975). Concerns the opposition of William Monroe Trotter and members of the Boston Equal Rights League to the leadership and philosophy of Booker T. Washington, when Trotter spoke at a Roxbury, MA, church meeting which subsequently led to his arrest. (The title makes an obvious allusion to the much publicized dispute between W[illiam]. E.B. Du Bois and Booker T. Washington concerning Washington's approach to race relations.) **The Sunday the Preacher Did Not Show** (morality play, 1 act, 1975). Concerned with what happens when the black preachers throughout the United States mysteriously fail to show up at their churches one Sunday. **We Fought Too!** (historical drama, 1 act, 1975). About Peter and Salem Poor, two early black revolutionary heroes who fought in the Battle of Bunker and Creed's Hill. **13th Day After Christmas** (protest drama, 1 act, 1970s). About the mission and daily routine of an urban sniper. **Yours for the Cause** (historical drama, 1 act, 1970s). Praises the accomplishments of William Monroe Trotter, Boston's celebrated civil rights activist, journalist, and editor.

THOMAS, FATISHA, Short-story writer and playwright. One of her stories appeared in *Black Creation*. Associated with the Frank Silvera Writers' Workshop in New York City.

   PLAYS:
   (All pre-1975, except the last.) **Choice of Worlds Unfilled. It's Been a Long Time. Twenty Year Nigger. Attitudes** (1977). Public reading by FSWW, 1977. Unpub. script may be in the FSWW Archives/Schomburg Collection.

THOMAS, JOYCE CAROL (1938–   ), Poet, playwright, and novelist. Born in Ponca City, OK. Resides in the San Francisco Bay area of California. Educated at San Jose Univ. (B.A. in Spanish), the Univ. of California/Berkeley, and Stanford Univ. (master's in education). Author of five volumes of poetry; *Bittersweet* (1973), *Crystal Breezes* (1974), *Blessing* (1975), *Black Child* (1981), and *Inside the Rainbow* (1982), the last of which includes many of the poems from her first three volumes. Her latest works include two novels, *Marked by Fire* (1982), which won the Before Columbus American Book Award, and *Bright Shadow* (1983). Recipient of a Danforth Graduate Fellowship (to UC/Berkeley) and a Djerassi Fellowship for Creative Artists (at Stanford).

   PLAYS:
   Black Mystique (1974). Prod. by the Berkeley Community Little Theatre, Berkeley, CA, 1974. **How I Got Over** (1976). Prod. by Los Medanos Coll., California, 1976. **A Song in the Sky** (musical, 1976). Prod. by Montgomery Theatre, San Francisco, Summer 1976. **Look! What a Wonder** (musical, full length, 1976). Bicentennial play, presenting the contributions of black Americans. Prod. by California Community Theatre, Oct.

1976. **Magnolia** (1977). Prod. by the Old San Francisco Opera House, Summer 1977. **Ambrosia** (1978). Prod. by the Little Fox Theatre, Summer 1978.

THOMAS, VEONA, Author, playwright, writing teacher, and editor. Born in New York City. Raised and educated in New Jersey. Studied at the Frederick Douglass Cultural Arts Center, New York. Self-employed owner of a boutique shop for 15 years. Publisher and editor of *Write-On Newsletter.* Founder and editor of Rejoti Publishing Co., which is planning a book of ten female playwrights, scheduled for 1988. Contributing writer to *Black Masks,* a theatrical publication, *The Torchbearer,* and *New Directions for Women.* Author of a collection of poetry, commentary, and prose, *Laughter, Lyrics & Tears* (1985). Co-originator of The Power in You Workshop, National Black Theatre, New York. Originator of the Annual Black Writers Conf., held in late May of each year. Member of the National Writers Club, DG, AUDELCO, and TEAM Writers. *Address:* P.O. Box 852, Saddlebrook, NJ 07662.

PLAYS AND DRAMATIC WORKS:

Nzinga's Children (drama, 2 acts, 1983). Deals with the dilemma of a young black woman named Nzinga in choosing between a young black man whom she loves, but who "just can't seem to get his act together," and a successful young white attorney who loves her and wishes to marry her. Five generations of her deceased maternal grandmother, distressed by her consideration of making a break with her black heritage, visit her in a dream and resolve to help her strengthen her relationship with her black boyfriend. Throughout the rest of the play, he gradually matures into the responsible and considerate man that Nzinga wishes for her husband. Public readings at the Frank Silvera Writers' Workshop, New York, Oct. 1984; and at Theatre In Progress, Nov. 1984. Prod. by the National Black Theatre, New York, Feb.-June 1985, for an extended run. Sched. for prodn. by McCree Theatre, Flint, MI, Feb. 1986.

A Matter of Conscience (comedy-drama, 2 acts, 1985). A black woman becomes involved in a conspiracy to conceal the alleged theft of some undocumented money left outside of the vault of the bank where she works as a teller. According to the author, her Good and Bad Consciences, who are two characters in the play, "do a tug-of-war job on her head about everything from her religion or lack of it to her job and her sex life." The conclusion promises to be moral without being preachy. Showcased at the National Black Theatre, New York, c. 1986.

Martin Luther King—A Personal Look (one-person show, 10/15 min., 1985). Dr. King's life from a different perspective. The speaker is the gold watch on his wrist. Details of his life before, during, and after the civil rights movement are dramatically delivered, punctuated by ticking sounds of the watch. Specifically written for King's birthday, Black History Month, and other formats to show race pride. Performed Jan. 1985 for a group of black professionals, at Temple Emanuel, Saddlebrook, NJ.

Straight Street (musical drama, work-in-progress, 1985). The scene is a street in an inner city—a collage of all the streets we know—where a mixture of characters from teenagers to senior citizens all live, trying to survive among modern-day perils of crime. The plot revolves around two young men who grew up together—Slim, a devious character, and Hawk, his sidekick. Other interesting characters include a Jamaican fortune teller or obi woman, a young couple who try to find some place to make love, Danny the drunk, a senior citizen couple, and two brothers in jail. Sched. for completion Oct. 1985.

THOMPSON, CHEZIA B. (Brenda) (1951–   ), Freelance writer, playwright, actress, singer, director, editor, and teacher. Based in St. Louis, MO. Currently asst. prof. of African-American Studies, Univ. of Maryland/Baltimore County, 1982–83. Received the B.A. in English/Black Studies from the Univ. of Washington, 1972; the M.A. in Education/English from Washington Univ., St. Louis, 1975; and has completed studies for the D.A. in English/Communication from Carnegie-Mellon Univ. (all but dissertation). She has also had training in voice and dance. Has had teaching experiences at Wash. Univ, St. Louis, 1971–74; Forest Park Community Coll., St. Louis, 1975–79; Clarion State Coll., Pennsylvania, 1980–82; and Carnegie-Mellon, Pittsburgh, PA, 1981. Freelance researcher writer, *Proud* magazine, St. Louis, 1972–75; freelance fine arts reviewer, *St. Louis American,* 1973–79. Guest director, Mildred E. Bastian Performing Arts Center, St. Louis, 1978–79; writer, Publicity Dept., Mississippi Authority for Education, Jackson, 1982; cookbook editor, Bob McCall Enterprises, Pittsburgh; freelance fine arts reviewer, *New Pittsburgh Courier,* 1981–82. Her poetry, short stories, and articles have been published in *Afro-American St. Louis Poets: An Anthology, Proud Magazine, Blacks on Paper, Roots and Branches, Obsidian: Journal of Black Literature, The Griffith, New Writers,* and other publications. She has performed as an actress/singer in multiple productions of Maxwell Anderson's *Lost in the Stars,* and as a vocalist with the Kenneth B. Billups Legend Singers and the Alvin Major Jr. Messenger Singers, 1966–74. Awards and citations include Poetry Award, *Proud* magazine, 1971; Paul Robeson Black Artist Award, Washington Univ., 1972; W.E.B. DuBois Service Award, Washington Univ., 1973; citation, Outstanding Young Woman of America, 1973; citation, *Who's Who in American Colleges and Universities,* 1973; citation, *Dictionary of International Biography,* Cambridge, England, 1980; citation, *Who's Who in the East,* 1983. *Address*—Office: c/o African American Studies Dept., University of Maryland and Baltimore County, 5401 Wilkens Ave., Baltimore, MD 21228. All scripts through: Roots & Branches Workshop Publications, 2528 Rigsby, St. Louis, MO 63136.

PLAYS AND DRAMATIC WORKS:

Once upon a Time in a Garden // Also called **The Garden** ("A Morality Play for Children" [subtitle], 45 min., 1972). A ritual drama to be performed by young adults and children. Mother Oba, father Tala, and the children of the Garden (Africa) are celebrating the birth of twins to a young couple in love, when they are attacked by the stranded moon-ball people (white ex-terrestials *[sic]*), and must figure out how to reorder the world so that everyone can learn to live together. First performed at Graham Chapel, Washington Univ., and at the Black Awareness Workshop at the Learning Centre, St. Louis, 1972.

The Concubines ("A Carnival Mystery" [subtitle], 90 min., 1973). Ritual drama utilizing mythic Yoruba Orishas (religious figures). The entity Time thinks that he should visit the Earth to rest from his work of ordering things, but decides that it has so many problems that he needs to request aid for it. He asks his ultimate friends and lovers—Yemanja, Orisha of the sea and motherhood; Oshun, Orisha of inland rivers and love; and Oja, Orisha of the storm winds and health—to come live on Earth and help mankind through this difficult historical period. How they come to Earth and the lives that they affect is the subject of this play. First performed by the Experimental Theatre at Mallincrodt Performing Arts Centre, Washington Univ., St. Louis, 1975. Sched. for prodn. for the International African Literature Assn. Conf., at the Dunbar Performing Arts Center in Baltimore, April 1984.

Deathwalk (ritual drama utilizing Haitian folklore, 60 min., 1974). Subtitled "The Legend of Madame Ste Ile." In earlier times the great-grandmother of Mona Lisa had been seen carried beneath the water of Lake Erzulie in Port-au-Prince, Haiti, by a young loa in the house of Gene'. Mona Lisa makes a wish to be a better person (on a magical night, with a magical stone, on Lake Erzulie) and is abducted by a similar diety; she is transformed and is seen walking out of Lake Erzulie seven days (or seven years, or seven cycles) from when she disappeared. First performed at the Mildred E. Bastian Performing Arts Center, St. Louis Community College, 1979.

Jean Toomer's Cane (adaptn. for stage and TV, full length, 1978). Based on Jean Toomer's 1923 Harlem Renaissance classic, utilizing the "Vertical Technique" and "Blues Motif" as organizing vehicles. For a mixed cast of blacks and Euro-Americans. Orig. music written for Toomer's poems, which are labeled "songs." First performed at the Mildred E. Bastian Performing Arts Centre, St. Louis Community Coll., 1978. Prod. as one woman's vision, consisting of an hour-long, narrated instructional tape, featuring staged scenes from Toomer's work.

The Eyes of Black Folk ("A Dramatic Look at the Black Experience in America" [subtitle], full length, 1982). A primarily one-person show with musical accompanist, singer, two dancers, and slide photography to enhance the review of history as black people have seen it and recorded it in their literature and drama. First performed at Clarion State University Chapel and television studio, 1982. Prod. as an hour-long videotape (in collaboration with Mississippi Arts Commissioner John Horhn).

THOMPSON, GARLAND LEE (1938–   ), Actor, playwright, director, producer, stage manager, black theatre organization founder, black playwrights' workshop founder/director. Born in Muskegee, OK; grew up in Oregon. Took several writing courses, and spent a year at the Univ. of Oregon, which completed his formal education. Lived in Los Angeles during the 1960s, where he was associated with Actors Studio/West. Appeared in the film *South Pacific* and in a stage production of LANGSTON HUGHES'S *Simply Heavenly*. Wrote several plays for adults and children; produced a short film; and saw the production of his first play, **Sisyphus and the Blue-Eyed Cyclops** (1970). Came to New York City in 1971 as associate director of the national tour and production stage manager for the Broadway production of CHARLES GORDONE's *No Place to Be Somebody*. Coordinator of a new play reading at the Urban Arts Corps (UAC), 1972, from which one of his plays, **Papa Bee on the D Train** (1972), was selected for presentation at the Third Annual Black Theatre Alliance Festival at the Billie Holiday Theatre. Production stage manager of the Broadway production of JOSEPH WALKER's *The River Niger*, 1973. Founding director of the Frank

Silvera Writers' Workshop (FSWW), 1973–present. Founding board member and treasurer of the Black Theatre Alliance (BTA), New York. Member, Directors and Playwrights Unit, Actors Studio, New York. Founding director and president of the Board of Directors of the FSWW Foundation, Inc., 1980. Winner of the AUDELCO Board of Directors Award for superior and sustained contribution to community theatre, 1976. Winner of the AUDELCO Award, as producer of *Bessie Smith, Empress of the Blues*, 1981. *Address*—Home: 252 W. 76th St., Apt. 1A, New York, NY 10023. Office: Frank Silvera Writers' Workshop, 317 W. 125th St., New York, NY 10027.

PLAYS AND DRAMATIC WORKS:

Sisyphus and the Blue-Eyed Cyclops ("Black astrial play," 1 act [2 scenes], 1970). Explores the levels of consciousness between madness and sanity. Prod. by the Actors Studio/West, Los Angeles, Summer 1970, with Paul Winfield and D'Urville Martin in the cast. Prod. by the Negro Ensemble Co. (NEC) as a work-in-progress, at St. Marks Playhouse, New York, opening Jan. 14, 1971, with AL FREEMAN, JR., ADOLPH CAESAR, and William May. Prod. by the UAC, New York, opening Oct. 30, 1972, on double bill with the author's **Papa Bee on the D Train** (1972). Prod. by FSWW, at the Afro-American Total Theatre, New York, July 1975, and at the Harlem Performance Center, the same year. Winner of the 42nd Annual One Act Tournament, Washington, DC. Unpub. script and the tape recording in the FSWW Archives/Schomburg Collection.

Papa Bee on the D Train // Also called **Papa B on the D Train** and **Papa Bee on the Dee Train** ("Black astral play," full length, 1972). "A play-within-a-play look at the New York, late 1960s, Black rhetoric play. The writer stops the play. Is it the death of the play or the playwright?"—*Black Playwrights, 1823–1977* (Hatch & Abdullah, 1977), p. 225. Prod. by Howard Univ., Washington, DC, 1974. Prod. as a workshop production by FSWW, at the Harlem Performance Center, New York, opening June 15, 1976. Prod. as a Director's Project of FSWW, and presented by the Harlem Opera Soc. in association with the Harlem Performance Center, at the American Place Theatre, New York, July 15, 1976, with Charles Pegues, Kim Sullivan, Bob Molock, Joan Hart, Norman Jacobs, A. MARCUS HEMPHILL, Christine Campbell, Stephannie Howard, Chequita Jackson, and Jey Mon Treal. Apparently also prod. by the Actors Studio, New York. Unpub. script and tape recording in the FSWW Archives/Schomburg Collection.

The Incarnation of Reverend Goode Blackque Dress // Original title: **Incarnations or the Incarnation of Reverend Goode Black Dresse** ("A blacque astral mystic farce," full length, 1978). Described by UAC as "a delightful mysterious play about a man exorcising his demons and roaches during a surprise visit by his 'ex old lady.' "—Press release, Spring 1978. A study of human progress, from ancient Egypt to the future as seen through the eyes of an Egyptian tombmaker. Prod. by FSWW, at the Open Eye Theatre, New York, Feb. 1–5, 1978; dir. by Dean Irby, with Charles Brown, Dianne Kirksey, and Dave Connell. Prod. by the UAC, New York, April 20–May 7, 1978. Unpub. script and tape recording in the FSWW Archives/Schomburg Collection.

Tut-Ankh-Amen, the Boy King (historical drama, full length, 1982). About King Tut, the adolescent pharoah who ruled Thebes, the ancient capital of upper Egypt, during the 18th Dynasty. Focuses on the King's investigation of the death of his father, who had disappeared after denouncing polytheism and expressing his belief in one God. The Chief Priest, fearful that King Tut has inherited his father's religious convictions and that his own role in his father's death will be uncovered, orders the young king to be assassinated at the hands of one of his generals. Prod. by FSWW, Summer 1982. With Emil Herrera as King Tut and Helmar Augustus Cooper as the Chief Priest.

Jesse and the Games (drama, full length, 1984). A dramatization of the events leading up to Jesse Owens's victory in the Olympic games of 1936, held in Berlin. Explores the friendship between Owens and Lutz Long, the champion broad jumper on whom Hitler and the Third Reich had pinned their hopes for a German victory. According to Abiola Sinclair, writing in the *New York Amsterdam News* (June 30, 1984, p. 27), Owens and Lutz became avowed friends during the Olympics and continued to write each other monthly after the games and during the war. Prod. by FSWW, at the Amphi Theatre in Harlem, June 1983; dir. by Chuck Wise. With Zachary Minor as Jesse Owens and John McGinley as Lutz Long. The event was hosted by the Schomburg Center for Research in Black Culture, and was written and presented for the Schomburg Center's "Salute to the 20th Century Stage and Tribute to Black Theatre in America."

THOMPSON, LARRY (1950–   ), Poet-playwright. Born in Seneca, SC. His poetry has been published *Black Out Loud* (Adoff, 1968) and *It Is the Poem Singing into Your Eyes* (Adoff, 1970), as well as in *Negro Digest*.

PLAY:
A Time to Die (skit, pre-1975).

THORNE, ANNA V., Playwright. Associated with Black Arts/West (BA/W), Seattle, WA.

PLAY:
Black Power Every Hour (1969). "A collage of Black revolutionary poetry, music, dance, and drumming."—*Black Theatre* #5, 1971, p. 8. Prod. by BA/W, 1969.

TODD, BEVERLY, Actress and musical writer. For many years associated with the Afro-American Total Theatre in New York City. Stage performances include *Deep Are the Roots* (1960), *No Strings* (1964), *Carry Me Back to Morningside Heights* (1968), and most recently *Gettin' It Together* (1972).

PLAY:
Origins (musical, 1 act, 1969). Written with HAZEL BRYANT and HANK JOHNSON. Prod. by the Afro-American Total Theatre, at the Riverside Church Theatre, New York, Oct. 1969.

TOOKS, GEORGE ARNOLD. See TOOKS, LENGA.

TOOKS, LAWRENCE EDWARD. See TOOKS, LENGA.

TOOKS, LENGA (joint pseud. for Lawrence Edward aNd George Arnold Tooks), Team of musical playwrights, writers, and composers. Lawrence E. (Ed) and George A. Tooks are brothers who have been collaborating since early childhood. Born in Altoona, PA, where they graduated from high school. They formed their own gospel group, The Velvets, in their early teens, and traveled throughout Pennsylvania, singing in churches. Unable to make money singing gospel, they switched to rhythm and blues—called "the Devil's music" in Altoona. After high school, Ed attended Trenton Jr. Coll. in New Jersey, majoring in art; George studied speech and drama at the Altoona Undergraduate Center, a division of Pennsylvania State Univ. Going to New York in the early 1960s, they joined The Genies, a vocal group whose record "Who's That Knocking" sold over 1.75 million copies. They toured the country and appeared on American Bandstand and at the famed Apollo Theatre, Howard Theatre, and all the major uptown theatres and nightclubs. Their voices can be heard on the records of Ruth Brown, Roy "C," and others as back-up singers. As Lenga Tooks, composers, they are recipient of the 1985–86 AUDELCO awards for Outstanding Musical Creators, and for Musical Production of the Year, for their **Flat Street Sa'Day Night** (1985). In 1982–83 they received their first AUDELCO Award nomination for RICHARD WESLEY's *The Sirens*. Ed and George also composed music for and were musical directors for the following plays: *Cockfight* and *Toe Jam* by ELAINE JACKSON; *Buelah Johnson* by CECIL ALONZO; *Hi Steppin' in Harlem* by JERRY MAPLE, JR., and for the AUDELCO Awards program, "Winners All," June 21, 1986.

As an actor, George has appeared in 93 major motion pictures, including *Cotton Club, Ghost Busters, Death Wish III* (as an assassin), *Rag Time, In the Still of the Night* (elevator operator), *Fort Apache, the Bronx* (stuntman), *Grace Quigley,* and *We're Fighting Back.* He has appeared in every New York–based soap opera, including "All My Children," "Another World," and "Ryan's Hope," and had the continuing role of Tony the Maitre D' on "Texas" for two years. His stage credits include about 50 plays, including **Beulah Johnson,** the world's first live soap opera, written, produced, and directed by Cecil Alonzo. Has also appeared in numerous TV commercials and newspaper and magazine ads.

Ed's motion picture, TV, and theatre credits as a technician are as long and varied as George's. He served as production asst. and still photographer on "To Be a Man" (two-time Emmy Award-winning film), "The Ossie Davis-Ruby Dee Show" (PBS), and "A Walk Through the Twentieth Century" with Bill Moyers" (Emmy Award-winner). TV credits include "Video Wave" (32 episodes), "Jewish Life" (13 episodes), "The Sonny Taylor Show," "A Chat with Glendora" (CBS pilot), "Small World" (ABC-TV), and "Don, Jose and the Country Brothers." Has also worked on several films and TV commercials and has been in-house video producer for a number of agencies, firms, sports functions, and private weddings. Both George and Ed are graduates of Third World Cinema Productions, whose name was changed to Inst. of New Cinema Artists. This school was founded by OSSIE DAVIS, RUBY DEE, the late Diana Sands, and Cliff Frazier to pump "new technical blood" into a very anemic TV, radio, and recording industry. *Address:* 120 W. 44th St., Rm. #1207, New York, NY 10036.

REPRESENTATIVE DRAMATIC WORK:
Flat Street Sa'Day Night (musical drama, 2 acts, 1985). Book by FRANK SOLOMON. Music and lyrics by Lenga Tooks. Based on Solomon's novel, *A Hell of a Life.*

"Set in the late 1940s and early 1950s, the play depicts the lively happenings in the jukebox joints on Flat Street, a real street that crosses U.S. 301 in Allendale. [It] spans a Saturday night from 6 p.m. to midnight, and depicts dancing, fighting, courting, joke-telling and singing." —*The State* (Columbia, SC), July 6, 1985. The joints were the only places for blacks to release their frustrations and unwind after working hard all week in the fields. Prod. by Theatre-in-Progress, New York, and presented Off-Bway, at the Arts for Living Center, Henry St. Settlement, in the facilities of the New Federal Theatre, May 16–June 30, 1985, and July 11–Aug. 4, 1985. At the invitation of the mayor, it was also presented in Allendale, SC, at the Allendale Primary School, July 5 and 6, 1985. Winner of five AUDELCO awards for choreography (Sheryle R. Jones), outstanding perf. in a musical/female (Patricia A. Clement), outstanding perf. in a musical/male (Steve Beckman), outstanding musical creator (Lenga Tooks), and musical production of the year (Frank Solomon and Lenga Tooks).

OTHER PLAYS AND DRAMATIC WORKS:
(All pre-1986.) **Small World, Huh?** (WNYC-TV doc.). **The Black West** (TV script). With author William Loren Katzh and filmmaker Bill Miles. Prod. by PBS. **The Great Ocalla Foot Race** (mini-series for TV). Black love, action, and adventure. **Who's That Laughing. Jamaica Marie. The Life and Death Game. Uncle Harry. Revenge, Inc.** (screenplay). **Beat the Killer** (screenplay). **Lamby** (screenplay). **Spencer's Dream** (audio/video presentation). For the black insurance market. **E-Man** (musical comedy-drama, full length, 1987). Free adaptn. by Michael Dagley, from the anonymous medieval morality play *Everyman*. With additional material, special effects, and music by Lenga Tooks. Prod. by Theatre-in-Progress and the Lenga Tooks Musical Workshop, opening April 30, 1987, at the ACAR Theater, 317 W. 125th St., New York City; staged and dir. by Randy Frazier.

TOUSSAINT, RICHARD P. (1948–   ), Playwright, producer, director, and counselor. Based in New York City. Educated at (Borough of) Manhattan Community Coll. (A.A., 1971), and City Coll. of CUNY (B.A. in theatre, 1971; graduate courses in theatre arts, 1973–74; and M.S. in guidance and counseling, 1978). During the 1960s, he was associated with HARYOU-ACT, the Black Mask Players (of Manhattan Community Coll.), and Damani Productions, Inc., all in New York City. For Damani Productions, he directed *Plumes* by †Georgia Douglas Johnson and *Take Care of Business* by MARVIN X at the annual Staten Island Community Coll. One Act Play Festival, held in Nov. 1972. Worked for WCBS-TV, as a journalism apprentice, then asst. administrator of special projects, 1969–71; financial aid officer at Staten Island Community Coll./CUNY, 1971–74; and counselor for the Higher Education Development Fund, 1974–77. Employed by Consolidated Edison Co., New York, as employee representative/counselor, 1978–present. *Address:* 2160 Madison Ave., New York, NY 10037.

PLAYS:
If You Get Stepped On ... Tough! // Orig. title: **These Black Ghettoes** (domestic drama, 3 acts, 1964). A portrait of life in the black northern urban community, depicting the problems which created the pathology of the ghetto. Concerns the fight of one black youth to get out of this environment, in spite of the opposition of family and friends. First prod. as a one-act play, under its orig. title, at the 135th St. Harlem YMCA, 1964.

First prod. as a three-act drama, under its orig. title, by the Black Mask Players of Manhattan Community Coll./CUNY, at the Kennedy Community Center, New York, opening May 2, 1969, for about 3 perfs., and again on Dec. 5, 6, and 13, 1969. Public reading, under the title **If You Get Stepped On . . . ,** by the Frank Silvera Writers' Workshop (FSWW), Jan. 21, 1978. Unpub. script of **These Black Ghettoes** in the Billy Rose Theatre Collection/NYPL. Unpub. script of **If You Get Stepped On . . .** in the FSWW Archives/Schomburg Collection.

A Visitor with a Mission (fantasy, 1 act, 1970). A black prostitute discovers that the strange character who has propositioned her is the Angel of Death. Prod. by Damani Productions, New York, 1970.

TRASS, VEL, Playwright. Formerly associated with the Paul Robeson Players, Los Angeles, CA.

PLAY:
From Kings and Queens to Who Knows What (Bicentennial play, full length, 1975). On the theme of black heritage. "Many of the young actors were members of rival gangs, who, in working together . . . created a theatrical family . . . a family in which gang warfare had no place."—*Black World,* April 1976, p. 80. Prod. by the Paul Robeson Players, during the summer of 1975, with 40 youths from the Los Angeles community, dir. by Robert Browning.

TREADWELL, ANTHONY B., Actor, vocalist, author, and playwright. Born in Memphis, TN, where he graduated from Carver H.S. Attended Lane Coll. in Jackson, TN (with studies in music, elementary education, and creative writing; graduated 1979). Moved to Brooklyn, NY, 1979, where he studied creative writing and performed with the Staten Island Preparatory, as an actor and vocalist, 1980. Also studied music in New York City. Returned to Memphis, 1981, where he toured with Denise LaSalle as a background vocalist for one year; in 1982 left LaSalle's band to record with an all-male vocal group entitled Speed Limit. Wrote a book of poetry, *Family Tree* (1981), and a children's story book, **Dr. Smoke vs. Kick the Habit** (about cigarette smokers, 1983), which was also adapted as a play. *Address:* 236 Majuba Ave., Memphis, TN 38109.

DRAMATIC WORKS:
The Waste Basket (musical drama, 1 act, 1982). Prod. and dir. by author, Memphis, 1982. **Dr. Smoke vs. Kick the Habit** (children's musical play, 1 act, 1983). **Once over the Rainbow** (musical, in progress, 1986).

TRUESDALE, TAD (1926–   ), Actor, singer, and playwright. Born in Farrell, PA, where his father worked in the steel mills until the Depression closed them down. After the death of his parents, he was raised by his maternal grandparents in South Carolina; later moved to Leonia, NJ, during World War II, to live with an aunt and finish school. There he became hooked on the theatre after seeing a production of *Deep Are the Roots* and meeting the star, Gordon Heath, who got him an audition with the American Negro Theatre (ANT) in Harlem. Appeared in several ANT productions during the 1940s, including *Freight,*

Family Portrait, Juno and the Paycock, and the Broadway production of *Anna Lucasta.* Also worked for a while with Claude Marchant, and obtained a booking with one of Katherine Dunham's dancers at the Savannah Club doing erotic dancing. In 1954 he got involved in the drug scene, was arrested, and served 27 months at Rahway State Prison, where he started writing song lyrics. After his release, he joined a singing trio with one of his friends and Richie Havens, and the group played uptown at the African Club for seven years. This experience led to the writing of his first show, **Safari 300,** an extension of their musical act, which was produced at the Mayfair Theatre in 1972. A meeting with Ellen Stewart of La Mama E.T.C. led to his joining La Mama as resident playwright, director, and asst. box office manager, where he has remained since 1975. Has appeared as an actor-singer in many other Broadway and Off-Broadway productions. TV appearances include "The Edge of Night," "One Life to Live," and the "Leon Bibb Show." He has also made recordings on Columbia Records, appeared in TV commercials and documentary films, and worked as a professional model. Currently artistic consultant to Stargate Productions, a Nigerian company based in New York. Member of AFTRA, AEA, and AGVA. *Address:* 55 Second Ave., New York, NY 10003.

PLAYS AND DRAMATIC WORKS:

Safari 300 (musical revue, 2 acts, 1971). Book by Truesdale. Three hundred years of the black experience in song and dance, exploring black culture in the Western Hemisphere through music and dance from Africa to today. Prod. by Richie Havens, at the Mayfair Theatre, New York, opening July 12, 1972, for 17 perfs.; dir. by Hugh Gittens. With Truesdale, Lari Becham, Ernest Andrews, Joyce Griffin, HOLLY HAMILTON, Onike Lee, Fredi Orange, Andre Robinson, Grenna Whitaker, and Dorian Williams.

Paper Bird // Orig. title: **A New Breed Is Now the Seed** (musical, 2 acts, 1974). Story, lyrics, and music by GERALD W. DEAS. Book and direction by Truesdale. Title taken from a poem by Deas, which deals with man's universal desire to fly like an eagle, only to discover that he is just a paper bird. A story of street gangs—black and Hispanic versus white ethnic groups—exploring some of the problems of survival in the big city ghettos. Prod. by William Hunter at Town Hall, New York, 1975. Prod. by Now The Seed Productions, Inc., at the Storefront Museum, Queens, NY, Nov. 17–Dec. 3, 1977, for 9 perfs.

The Ilo Experience (musical, 2 acts, 1974). Revised and retitled **The Journeychain Show** (1980s). A series of reincarnational experiences—from Africa to slavery in America to the civil rights explosion of the 1960s. Prod. as a workshop production by La Mama E.T.C., 1976.

(The) Godsong (gospel rock musical, 2 acts, 1975). An adaptn. of †James Weldon Johnson's *God's Trombones.* A spectacular theatrical event, integrating original contemporary songs and dances with traditional spirituals to dramatize the retelling of several Biblical stories. Prod. by AMAS Repertory Theatre, March 4, 1976; dir. by author. Prod. by La Mama E.T.C., Dec. 30, 1976. With Marcia McBroom, Barbara Montgomery, and Isaiah Smalls. Prod. by the Macedonia A.M.E. Church at Queens Coll., New York, 1978. Prod. by the Hospital Workers Union—Local 1199, at Hunter Coll., New York, 1979. Listed in the *Metropolitan Opera's Central Opera Service Bulletin* (vol. 22, no. 2) as a new American opera. Excerpts of the score were selected to be presented in a

Composers' Workshop sponsored by the Met in Lake George, New York, on Aug. 17, 1983. A prodn. of *The Godsong* was being planned by WOODIE KING, JR., at the New Federal Theatre, Fall 1984, to be dir. by Tom O'Horgan, with the author playing the leading role of Narrator/Minister; the prodn. would tour nationally beginning in the spring of 1984.

Daddy! Daddy! ("A Blues Drama with Music" [subtitle], 2 acts, 1980). A black father tries to retain his family and his farm during the Depression years in the South. Nominated for an AUDELCO Award in 1981 for choreography by Danna Manno. Prod. by La Mama E.T.C., 1981; dir. by author.

An Evening, an Afternoon . . . with Tad Truesdale (one-man musical, approx. 1 hr., 1982). A cabaret-theatre collection of songs, monologues, and commentary taken from the author's career of performing and writings. Prod. by La Mama E.T.C., 1983, and by Hospital Audiences, Inc., New York City, 1983; prodn. coordinated by Rick Richardson.

Choir Practice (musical, 2 acts, 1983). A story of two young ladies, both with exceptional voices, vying for the attention of the new young choir master and the solo spot in a small southern community church choir, and determined to win first place in the next State Choir Competition.

TURNER, BETH, Playwright, actress, publisher, editor, and teacher. Educated at Colby Coll., Maine (B.A., Phi Beta Kappa, magna cum laude in French literature and language, 1963), including her junior year at the Univ. of Paris, France; and NYU (M.A. in human relations and community studies, 1966). Currently publisher and editor of *Black Masks,* a periodical "featuring information about Black performing and visual arts in the Greater New York, neighboring New Jersey and Connecticut area and beyond," formerly published monthly, now bimonthly. Also currently teaching the Black Women's Playwriting Workshop at the New Federal Theatre (NFT) in New York City. Former researcher for CBS-TV's "Lamp unto My Feet" and "Look Up and Live." Instr. of sociology at the Univ. of New Haven, 1971; director of education, Urban League of Greater New Haven, CT. Recipient of the John Hay Whitney Opportunity Fellowship, 1965; and New York State Council on the Arts Grant, 1975, for development of quality plays for young audiences. *Address—Home*: 3048 Kingsbridge Terrace, Bronx, NY 10463. Other: *Black Masks,* P.O. Box #2, Riverdale Station, Bronx, NY 10471.

REPRESENTATIVE PLAYS AND DRAMATIC WORKS:

Ode to Mariah (historical drama, 2 acts, 1975; also adapt. as a screenplay). Subtitled "A Miracle of Sunshine." Concerns the conflict between personal aspirations and the demands of family life, complicated by racial and sexual stereotyping, which has long been the gristmill of the African-American woman. In the setting of Waterville, NY, a fictitious town near Albany, in 1898, the plot revolves around a black mother's desire to fulfill her own thwarted dreams through her daughter, Mariah, but finds that her daughter has aspirations of her own. A family crisis forces both mother and daughter to reevaluate their dreams and thereby strengthens the bond between them. Staged reading by the Frank Silvera Writers' Workshop (FSWW), at the Martinique Theatre, New York, April 1976.

Prod. by the Henry Street Settlement Family Theatre, March 1979. Unpub. script in the FSWW Archives/Schomburg Collection.

Sing on Ms. Griot (children's play, 1 act [1 hr.], 1976). An African griot (storyteller) appears on stage and joyfully announces a growing brotherhood between Africans and African-Americans. She is interrupted by Ananse, the Spider, a West African folklore character, who challenges her to a contest of dance, song, music, storytelling, and tradition in order to decide if African-Americans are still influenced by African heritage and traditions. Earned for the author a New York State Council on the Arts Grant to develop plays for younger audiences. Prod. by the Afro-American Total Theatre, at the Richard Allen Center for Culture and Art, New York, July 1976; performed at Lincoln Center, American Place Theatre (Black Theatre Alliance Festival) and on tour of New York City Parks and museums. Prod. by the Henry St. Settlement and the Smithsonian Institution, at the Smithsonian's Discovery Theatre, Feb. 1982.

The Hungering Lion (historical play, 1 act, 1976). About Sundiata Keita, Mali's first emperor. Pub. in *Scholastic* magazine's *Search,* Sept. 23, 1976.

Crisis at Little Rock (drama, 1 act, 1977). About the desegregation of Little Rock, AR's Central H.S. Pub. in *Scholastic* magazine's *Search,* April 7, 1977.

Gursky and the Fabulous Four (comedy for younger audiences, 1 act, 1980). Four junior high school students turn into bumbling but successful crime-fighters when they try to save a hapless friend and their school from the plans of two would-be crooks. Performed at the Henry St. Settlement's Family Theatre, Feb. and March 1980.

La Morena ("The Dark One") (drama, 2 acts, 1981). Depicts the struggles of an interracial Puerto Rican family in 1945. Focuses on the conflict between the desire to become Americanized and repulsion at the concomitant racial stratification that threatens to destroy the multiethnic Puerto Rican family. Prod. by the New Federal Theatre, New York, Feb.-March 1981.

OTHER PLAYS AND DRAMATIC WORKS:
A New Father for Father's Day (TV script, 1970). Accepted by MGM for "The Courtship of Eddie's Father," 1970, but apparently not prod. **Come, Liberty** (play for young people, 1978). Public reading by FSWW, at Teachers, Inc., Dec. 1976. Performed at Lincoln Center Library for the Performing Arts, and at the Loft, Tuckahoe, NY, 1978. **Visions: A Dream for the Bronx** (musical, 1 act, 1980). Performed by the Henry St. Settlement's Black Theatre Workshop, 1980. **Sweet Mama Stringbean** (play with music, pre-1985). Based on the life of Ethel Waters.

TURNER, GENEVA C., Elementary school teacher and playwright. Taught at the George Bell Elementary School of Washington, DC. Member of the editorial board of *Negro History Bulletin*.

PLAY:
Bridging the Gap (TV doc., 1 act, 1957). Coauthor, with JESSIE H. ROY. Pub. in *Negro History Bulletin,* March 1957, pp. 133–37.

TURNER, JOSEPH (1936–1987), Playwright, newspaper journalist, and television producer. Born in Phenix City, AL, where he received his elementary and high school education. Moved to Chicago during the mid-1950s, where he received the B.S. in business administration from Loyola Univ.; attended graduate school at Northwestern Univ.; received the M.A. in communication and theatre (including playwriting) from the Univ. of Illinois at Chicago. Worked as a reporter for the Negro Press International News Service, the Urban Research Corp., and the *Chicago Defender,* during the 1960s. During the 1970s he worked first as an editorial writer for WLS-AM Radio and later as a program producer of several shows for Channel 5, including "Today in Chicago" and Tilmon Tempo." During the past 20 years Turner wrote more than a dozen plays. He was a resident of the Chatham neighborhood on Chicago's West Side. For the past several years he suffered as a kidney patient, and died from a heart attack in the dialysis unit at Michael Reese Hospital in Chicago.

REPRESENTATIVE PLAYS:

A Change Gon' Come (drama, mid-1980s). An exploration of the shocking and mysterious death of singer Sam Cook in Los Angeles in 1964. Prod. for a lengthy engagement at Excellence Through the Arts (ETA), Chicago, mid-1980s.

The Family Gathering (drama, full length, 1987). "A highly charged drama dealing with the passionate interactions within a southern African-American family, and their conflicts when the matriarch becomes seriously ill." —*Chicago Defender,* June 3, 1987, p. 3. Prod. at the South Side Community Arts Center, Chicago, June 1987, dir. by Claudia McCormick. (Turner attended a perf. on the evening before his death.)

OTHER PLAYS:

The Scheme (drama, 1 act, 1968). During the civil rights riots of the 1960s, Black National Guard officers are faced with the dilemma of moral choice and corruption. **A Summer Rain** (pre-1980s). **The Prize Fighter** (pre-1980s).

TURNER, THOM W., Director of the Weeksville United Actors Co., a drama group of the Bed-Stuy Street Academy of Brooklyn, NY.

PLAY:

An Experience in Reality (series of skits, full length program, 1970). Collective creation of the Bed-Stuy Street Academy and Thom Turner. A montage of scenes drawn from the lifestyles and experiences of the students in the academy, written over a period of eight to ten months. Prod. by the Bed-Stuy Street Academy, and performed by the Weeksville United Actors Co. at local junior and senior high schools in New York, at Long Island Univ., at Spelman Coll. (Atlanta), at CCNY, and at Lincoln Center for the Performing Arts, 1970, under the direction of Thom Turner.

U-V

UWEN, NATHAN, Playwright.

PLAY:

Martin Luther King, Jr. (biographical drama, 62 pp., 1970). Pub. by New Dimensions, New York, 1970; distributed by the Chatham Bookseller, Chatham, NJ.

VAN PEEBLES, MELVIN (1932–   ), Actor, director, novelist, short-story writer, screenwriter, filmmaker, composer, singer, producer, promoter, and one-man conglomerate. Elected to the Black Filmmakers Hall of Fame, 1976. Born in Chicago, IL, where he studied in the public schools. Attended West Virginia State Coll. (at Institute), 1949–50. Received the A.B. degree in English literature from Ohio Wesleyan Univ. at Delaware, OH, 1953. Also studied at the Univ. of Amsterdam, 1959 [see below]. Served in the U.S. Air Force as a navigator for three and a half years following college graduation. After being discharged, he lived for a short while in San Francisco, working as a gripman on the famous San Francisco cable cars; tried his hand at making short films (of which only two titles have been located [see OTHER PLAYS AND DRAMATIC WORKS below], which he hoped unsuccessfully would be of interest to Hollywood; and wrote a book (with photographs) about his cable car observations called *The Big Heart* (1957). Failing to interest Hollywood in his short films, he went to the Netherlands in 1959 to study for a Ph.D. in astrology at the Univ. of Amsterdam, on the G.I. bill. There he added the ''Van'' to his name, joined the Dutch National Theatre, and toured the country in a production of Brendan Behan's play *The Hostage*. Hitchhiked to Paris, at the invitation of an executive of Cinematheque Française, who had seen some of his work. There he was encouraged to study the craft of filmmaking and directing; wrote several novels, short stories, and a screenplay; and independently produced his first film (subsidized by the French government and a wealthy Frenchwoman), **The Story of a Three Day Pass** (1967), which was entered by the French in the San Francisco

Film Festival the same year and won the highest award. Following this triumph, he was besieged with offers from Hollywood and accepted an assignment by Columbia Pictures to direct the satirical film *The Watermelon Man* (1970), starring GODFREY CAMBRIDGE and Mantan Moreland about a white man who turns black overnight, and the change in his life which accompanies his transformation when it becomes known to his family, friends and co-workers. His novels, originally published in Paris, include *Un Ours pour le FBI* (1964), translated as *A Bear for the FBI* (1968), about his experiences as a victim of the brutality of a Chicago neighborhood youth gang; *Un Americain en Enfer* ("An American in Hell") (1965), later republished in English as *The True American;* and *La Fete à Harlem* ("The Party in Harlem") (1967), which became the basis of his musical **Don't Play Us Cheap** (1970). Also wrote *La Permission* (a screenplay, 1967), which became the film **Story of a Three Day Pass** (1967), and *Le Chinois du XIV*ᵉ (short stories, 1966). Author of *Bold Money* (1986), a book based on his personal success in the American Stock Exchange for more than ten years, which provides guidelines for the small investor to earn money in the stock market, without the usual risks, by investing in stock options. Member of the French Directors Guild and recipient of numerous theatrical awards, including (in addition to those previously mentioned), the Belgian Festival First Prize, the NAACP Image Award (as best film director), and the Drama Desk Award, 1971–72 (for **Ain't Supposed to Die a Natural Death,** 1971). In addition, his dramatic works have been nominated for nine Tony Awards and one Grammy Award. *Address:* Suite 1203, 850 Seventh Avenue, New York, NY 10019.

REPRESENTATIVE PLAYS AND DRAMATIC WORKS:

Story of a Three Day Pass (feature film: screenplay and songs, 1967). Based on the author's filmscript *La Permission* (1967). Interracial story of a young soldier on leave in Paris, where he becomes romantically involved with a white French girl and comes in conflict with some white American buddies from his camp. Prod. and dir. by the author in Paris, around 1967; underwritten by a grant from the French government and some financial backing from a Frenchwoman. Released by Sigma III, July 8, 1968, after having been entered as the French offering in the San Francisco Film Festival, 1967, where it won the highest award. Screenplay pub. as *La Permission* by Jerome Martineau, Paris, 1967.

Don't Play Us Cheap ("comedy musical," 2 acts, 1970). Book, music, and lyrics by Van Peebles. Based on the author's novel *La Fete à Harlem* ("The Party in Harlem", 1967). A pair of inept demons are unsuccessful in their attempt to break up a Saturday night party in Harlem. Recipient of a Tony nomination for best book for a musical. Premiered at San Francisco State College, Nov. 1970. Presented on Bway at the Ethel Barrymore Theatre, May 16–Oct. 1, 1972, for 164 perfs.; prod. and dir. by the author. With THOMAS ANDERSON, Joe Armstead, Esther Rolle, and Avon Long. Orig. cast album released by Stax Records (STS-2–3006). Made into a film in New Mexico; also prod. by the author, and premiered in Atlanta, GA. First pub. in French as a novel, *La Fete à Harlem,* by Jerome Martineau, Paris, 1967. Pub. in English as a novel with lyrics, under the title *Don't Play Us Cheap: A Harlem Party,* by Bantam Books, New York, 1973.

Sweet Sweetback's Baadasssss Song (feature film, full length, 1970). Controversial X-rated film which began the vogue of the black superstud in the movies. Sweetback, a sexual athlete who performs exhibitions at a club for the amusement of whites, is picked up by the police for questioning in connection with a murder. While on the way to the police station, his two arresting officers also arrest and beat unmercifully a black militant, while Sweetback looks on. Enraged by this brutality, Sweetback uses his handcuffs to knock the two policemen unconscious and escapes. From then on, he is on the run. One of the most lucrative independently produced films ever made, it grossed over $20 million. Written, scored, dir., starred in, and prod. by the author in 1970, on funds borrowed from comedian Bill Cosby and other backers. Distributed under a seven-year lease by Cinemation, 1971. Cast album released on A & M records and tapes. Scenario included in the author's *The Making of Sweet Sweetback's Baadaasss Song,* pub. by Lancer Books, New York, 1971.

Ain't Supposed to Die a Natural Death (musical, 2 acts, 1971). Book, music, and lyrics by Van Peebles. Subtitled "Tunes from Blackness." Title taken from a line attributed to Ralph Famous Seidman: "A slave ain't supposed to die a natural death." A lusty, sensational portrait of impoverished black street life that deals with the negative side of the American dream. A contemporary urban black version of "The Threepenny Opera." Among the well-known ghetto types portrayed are pimps, prostitutes, punks, drunks, cops, hustlers, and militants. As described by the publisher, "It is a world of tragedy, injustice and hatred—but it is a dynamic and real world brought alive with its jazz-soul-rock music."—*Samuel French's Basic Catalog of Plays* (1985). The fifth longest running show on Bway. A Burns Mantle Yearbook "Best Play" of 1971–72. Earned for the author a Drama Desk Award, 1971–72, as the most promising book writer of a musical. Recipient of two Tony nominations, for best book and best score for a musical. Recipient of a Grammy Award for best score from the original cast show album (cited below). First prod. by PAUL CARTER HARRISON at Sacramento State Coll., 1971. Prod. on Broadway by CHARLES BLACKWELL and others at the Ethel Barrymore Theatre, New York, Oct. 21, 1971–July 30, 1972, for 325 perfs., dir. by GILBERT MOSES, who received a Tony nomination and a Drama Desk Award. With Beatrice Winde, who won a *Theatre World* Award, and MINNIE GENTRY, who received a Tony Award. Cast recording by A & M Records. Prod. by the Theatre of Universal Images (TUI) in Newark, NJ, May 1983; dir. by Chuck Patterson. With Antonio Fargas. Excerpts from the lyrics of 9 of the show's 19 numbers pub. in *The Best Plays of 1971–1972,* consisting of eight unnumbered pages following p. 180. Book, words, and music pub. by Samuel French, New York, 1971. Pub. as a novel with lyrics by Bantam Books, New York, 1973. Grammy Award-winning cast recording by A & M Records (SP-3510).

Out There by My Lonesome (one-man show, full length, 1973). (Apparently also presented as *Out There by Your Lonesome.)* Performed by the author on tour of several cities, 1973. Performed at the New York City Correctional Facility for Women, Riker's Island, NY, Feb. 14, 1973.

Just an Old Sweet Song (TV film special, full length, 1976). Concerns a young couple, Priscilla and Nate Simmons, and their three children, who take a two-week vacation from Detroit to Georgia to visit their Grandma. While on vacation, they discover their roots and gain experiences which change their lives forever. First telecast on CBS as a General Electric Theatre Special, Sept. 14, 1976; dir. by Robert Ellis Miller. With Robert Hooks and Cicely Tyson as the couple; Kevin Hooks, Eric Hooks, and Tia Ranch as their 3 children; and BEAH RICHARDS as Grandma. Pub. as a novel by Ballantine Books, New York, 1976.

Greased Lightning (feature film, full length: screenplay [joint author], 1967). Drama based on the life of Wendell Scott, the first black racing car driver. Prod. by Warner Bros., 1977; dir. by Michael Schultz. With RICHARD PRYOR and Pam Grier.

Bessie (screenplay, full length, 1970s). Adapt. from the book of the same title by Chris Alberton. Sched. to be made into a film on the life of blues singer Bessie Smith, to be prod. in Philadelphia by Portable Productions, and to star Roberta Flack in the title role. No information concerning the actual prodn.

Reggae (musical, full length, 1970). Concept and prodn. by Michael Butler. Story by *Kendrew Lascelles. Book by Van Peebles, Lascelles, and *Stafford Harrison. Music and lyrics by various composers (seven in all). Combines reggae music (a popular style of Jamaican rock and roll) with Rastafarian philosophy (which advocates a return to Ethiopia, the original Garden of Eden). The story concerns "the return of a Jamaican singer to her home after her career begins to soar in the United States. She meets her ex-lover who is now a marijuana farmer, and they get in trouble with local mobsters. They are saved by local Rastafarians who also bring them spiritual enlightenment."— *Dictionary of the Black Theatre* (Woll, 1983), p. 136. Prod. on Bway at the Biltmore Theatre, WOODIE KING, JR., executive producer, March 27–April 13, 1980, for 21 perfs.; dir. by GLENDA DICKERSON, with choreography by MIKE MALONE. Calvin Lockhart was featured as a Rastafarian leader; also in the cast was Philip Michael Thomas (who plays Tubbs on the "Miami Vice" TV show).

Sophisticated Gents (TV miniseries, 4 hrs., 1981). Adapt. from the book *The Junior Bachelor Society* by JOHN A. WILLIAMS. Concerns the events that occur during a 25–year reunion of nine members of a black athletic-social club for a testimonial banquet in honor of their football coach—the man who was responsible for molding their lives. One of the returning members is a pimp who is wanted for murder. Prod. for three nights as a four-hour mini-series on NBC, opening Sept. 29, 1981; dir. by Harry Falk. With Bernie Casey (as the coach), Rosie Grier, Robert Hooks, Ron O'Neal, Thalmus Rasulala, Raymond St. Jacques, Van Peebles (as the pimp), Dick Anthony Williams, Paul Winfield, and Albert Hall.

The Waltz of the Stork "comedy musical," full length, 1982). Book, music, and lyrics by Van Peebles. Prod. at the Century Theatre on 45th St., West of Bway, 1982, where it was billed as the "Longest Running Comedy Musical of '82." Prod. by the New Federal Theatre (NFT), New York, 1984; dir. by author. With Harold Nicholas and the Brewery Puppets.

OTHER PLAYS AND DRAMATIC WORKS:
Made a number of early short films, the titles of which only two are known: **Sunlight** (1957) and **Three Pickup Men for Herrick** (1957). **Champeen** (musical, full length, 1983). Book, music, and lyrics by Van Peebles. Winner of an AUDELCO Award, 1983. Prod. by NFT, opening March 18, 1983. **Star** (1980s). Coauthor, with Kendrew Lascelles. Unpub. script in the Hatch-Billops Collection.

VAN SCOTT, (Dr.) GLORY, Dancer, singer, playwright, actress. Born in Chicago. Attended Goddard Coll.; studied dance with Nat Horne; recipient of a Ph.D. degree. Appeared in *Fly Blackbird, Prodigal Son, Billy Noname, Don't Bother Me, I Can't Cope, The Great White Hope,* and numerous other Broadway and Off-Broadway shows. Founder and artistic director of Dr. Glory's Children's Theatre in New York City. *Address:* Dr. Glory's Children's Theatre, 2 West 64th Street, New York, NY 10023.

PLAYS AND DRAMATIC WORKS:

Poetic Suite on Arabs and Israelis (poetic musical, 1 act, 1969). A lyrical and dramatic portrait of the Arab-Israeli conflict. First presented at Lincoln Center Auditorium, New York, May 1969. Also presented by the New York Ethical Cultural Soc., at 2 W. 64th St., New York, June 12, 1969. **Miss Truth** (poetic suite, 1 act, 1971). Script and music by Scott. About the life of Sojourner Truth. First prod. by the Afro-American Studio for Acting and Speech, New York, 1971, with the author in the leading role. Prod. by the Negro Ensemble Co., New York, Jan. 1972. Unpub. script in the Billy Rose Theatre Collection/NYPL, and in the Hatch-Billops Collection. **Sylvilla Fort** // Alternate title: **The Sylvilla Suite** (poetic doc., 1 act, 1976). A dance-poem in tribute to Sylvilla Fort, dancer and teacher. Prod. at Lincoln Center Auditorium, New York, May 1977. Unpub. script (entitled *The Sylvilla Suite)* in the Hatch-Billops Collection.

VROMAN, MARY ELIZABETH (Mrs. Oliver M. Harper) (1923–1967),

School teacher, short-story writer, and author. Born in Buffalo, NY; raised in the West Indies. Received the B.A. degree from Alabama State Coll. Taught at Camden Academy in Camden, AL. Achieved national acclaim for her short story "See How They Run," first published in *Ladies Home Journal,* June 1951, anthologized in *Best Short Stories by Negro Writers* (Hughes, 1967), and made into a film, *Bright Road* (1953), for which she served as technical advisor and was the first black woman accepted into the Screen Writers' Guild. Author of two novels: *Esther* (1963) and *Harlem Summer* (1967). Wrote the history of the Delta Sigma Theta Sorority, *Shaped to Its Purpose* (1963). Her fiction, poetry, and essays have been published in *Ladies Home Journal, National Education Association Journal,* and *Freedomways.* Winner of a Christopher Award for Inspirational Magazine Writing.

DRAMATIC WORK:

Bright Road (feature film, full length, 1953). Screenplay by Emmet Lavery. From the short story "See How They Run" by Vroman. Focuses on the troubles of a bright, sensitive elementary school pupil and the attempts by his principal and teacher (who fall in love with each other) to help him cope with his problems. Prod. by MGM and Sol Baer Fielding; dir. by Gerald Mayer; starring Philip Hepburn as the young boy, Harry Belafonte as the principal, and Dorothy Dandridge as the teacher.

W

WADUD, ALI (Walter Mitchell), Author, critic, musician, and playwright. Associated with the Negro Ensemble Co. (NEC) in New York City, which has produced all of his plays. Recently spent three years traveling, working, and living in Africa, a year of which was spent teaching at the School of Music and Drama in Khartoum, Sudan. His experiences were reported by him in several episodes in the *New York Amsterdam News*.

PLAYS AND DRAMATIC WORKS:

Kingdom (drama, full length, 1976). As described by TOWNSEND BREWSTER (Harlem Cultural Council *Newsletter,* vol. 2, no. 10), "A young black man who has killed a policeman for brutalizing a black woman during a St. Louis race riot in 1968, and who has been shot himself, seeks help at the house of two sisters." Prod. by NEC, as a Season-Within-a-Season production, April 27–May 2, 1976, for 8 perfs. Unpub. script in the Hatch-Billops Collection.

Companions of the Fire (drama, 1 act, 1980). A liaison between an overweight, love-starved Harlem matron and a self-styled black orator and revolutionary whom she has picked up for the night. The encounter proves to be more than she had bargained for and becomes very intense and revealing. Prod. by NEC, Feb. 7–24, 1980, for 22 perfs.; dir. by Horacena J. Taylor. With Barbara Montgomery and Charles Brown. Pub. by Dramatists Play Service, New York, c. 1980.

Tigus (monologue, 1 act, 1983). A man talks about his women and his drinking buddies. Prod. by NEC, April 12–May 3, 1983, for 24 perfs.; dir. and performed by DOUGLAS TURNER WARD.

WAKEFIELD, JACQUES (Abayome Oji), Poet-playwright and actor. Born in Newport News, VA. Grew up in New York City (his family first moved to Queens, NY, when he was an infant, and finally to Harlem when he was 14). Educated at Brooklyn Coll. under the Brooklyn Coll. Scholars Program in English (B.A. in theatre and film). Has appeared in a number of network shows concerned with the cultural and political mores of the black community, including "Black

Heritage," "Positively Black," "Soul," the "CBS Repertory Theatre," and in two CBS productions under the direction of BARBARA ANN TEER: *Lennox Ave. Sunday* and *Black Spirit and Power of LeRoi Jones.* Also starred in a coproduced film, *Moja: The Last American,* which won first prize in the Brooklyn Coll. Film Festival and was runner-up in the Black American Film Festival. Author of a volume of poetry entitled *Luv* (1971). Other poems have been published in such periodicals and anthologies as *Black Creation, Journal of Black Poetry, We Speak as Liberators,* and *Black Fire. Address:* c/o Salt and Pepper Studio, Lincoln Square Neighborhood Center, 218 W. 64th St., New York, NY.

PLAYS AND DRAMATIC WORKS:

Brotherly Love (drama, 1 act, 1972). Antidrug play concerning a buddy who cares enough about a friend who is a dope addict to do something about it. Pub. by the author in mimeographed form, New York, 1972; copy in the Hatch-Billops Collection.

Perceptual Movement (short 1 act, 1979). Avant-garde drama, utilizing minstrel show techniques and poetic rhetorical devices to explore the progress of the black man, or lack of it, in the 1980s. Pub. in *Centre Stage* (Ostrow, 1981).

A Cocktail Moon (drama, full length, 1985). "A Black history tribute to the unknown Black playwright. An unconventional approach to the story of a Black Harlemite woman who discovers herself after a failed integrated marriage."—*Black Masks,* Feb. 1985, p. 2. Prod. by Salt and Pepper Studio, at Lincoln Square Neighborhood Center, New York; dir. by Scottie Davis. Featuring Rene Mason, Jeff Della Penna, Calvin Lawson, Richard Mooney, and Gerrie Beckham.

WALCOTT, BRENDA (1938–   ), Playwright, novelist, and educational media specialist. Born in Brooklyn, NY. Educated at Harvard Univ. (M.Ed. in educational media). One of her video shows on children and poetry, "A Child's World," was produced at the Harvard Educational Media Center. In 1975 she was working on a novel, tentatively entitled "My Man—Jones." Currently lives in Cambridge, MA.

PLAYS:

(All 1970s.) **The Black Puppet Show. Fantastical Fanny. Look Not upon Me. Temporary Lives.**

WALKER, CELESTE COLSON, Playwright. Associated with the Black Spectrum Theatre, formerly located in St. Albans, Queens, NY, now located in Jamaica, NY.

PLAYS:

Once Upon a Wife Time (comedy, full length, 1985). Explores the conflicts of a young married couple when the husband decides to make his monogamous marriage a polygamous one by taking on a second wife. Prod. by the Black Spectrum Film & Theatre Co., St. Albans, Queens, opening Jan. 10, 1985, with perfs. running on weekends, through April 1985. **Reunion in Bartersville** (tragicomedy, full length, 1985). About a class reunion of four 1933 graduates of a Bartersville, TX, high school, who presume that they are the only surviving members of that 53–year-old class. Their reunion is tragically interrupted by the unexpected arrival of a fifth surviving graduate. First prod. during the 1985 season in Los Angeles, CA, where it was seen by GERTRUDE JEAN- NETTE, who brought the play to New York City. Prod. and dir. by Jeannette, with members of the HADLEY Players, opening Nov. 7, 1986, for 4 weekends, at 207 W. 133rd St. **The Wrecking Ball** (drama, full length, 1987). A satire on those city-sponsored neighborhood improvement schemes which are designed to "fix up a neighborhood and price the current residents right out."—*N.Y. Amsterdam News,* March 7, 1987, p. 31. The play concerns a son's unsuccessful efforts to persuade his parents and other residents to stop the improvement plans in time to save their homes. Prod. by the Black Spectrum Theatre, Jamaica, NY, Feb. 14–March 8, 1987.

WALKER, DRAKE (1936–   ), Screenwriter, novelist, producer, and di- rector. Born in Birmingham, AL. Currently lives in Brooklyn, NY. Educated at the H. S. of Music and Art (New York) and at NYU where he majored in art. Author of the novel *Buck and the Preacher* (1971), which was made into a film.

DRAMATIC WORKS:
Buck and the Preacher (feature film, full length: coauthor of screenplay, 1972). Writ- ten with Ernest Kinoy. Based on Walker's novel by the same title. "It centers on an ob- scure part of history, the period following the Civil War, when freed slaves were tracked down by sadistic bounty hunters and forced to return to unofficial slavery in the South."— *Toms, Coons, Mulattoes, Mammies, and Bucks* (Bogle, 1973). Prod. by Joel Glickman; dir. by Sidney Poitier; released by Columbia Pictures, 1972. Starring Sidney Poitier and Harry Belafonte. Pub. only as a novel by Popular Lib., New York, 1971. NOTE: The fol- lowing films were all prod. by Drapat Productions, New York, and dir. by the author: **The Prodigals** (1974). **Henry O. and Jimmy D.** (1975). **The Joust** (1976).

WALKER, ETHEL PITTS (also Ethel Pitts-Walker), Educator, director, and critic. Exec. director of the African American Drama Co. of California. A native of Tulsa, OK. Received her B.S. in education and speech/drama from Lincoln Univ. of Missouri; her M.A. from the Univ. of Colorado; and her Ph.D. in theatre history and criticism from the Univ of Missouri/Columbia. Has taught at Southern Univ., Baton Rouge, LA; Lincoln Univ., Jefferson City, MO; the Univ. of Illinois/Urbana; and Laney Coll., Oakland, CA. Has had extensive experience as producer-director in the Summer Repertory Theatre at the Univ. of California/Santa Barbara, Lincoln Univ., and the African American Drama Co. Acted in *Bloodlines to Oblivion,* produced by the Julian Theatre of San Francisco. Her writings on the theatre have appeared in *The Theatre of Black Americans* vol. 2 (Hill, 1980), *Encore,* and *Black American Literature Forum.* *Address*: African American Drama Co., 494 Fifth Ave., San Francisco, CA 94118.

DRAMATIC WORK:
Yarnin' on a Friday Night ("Tales of Old Black Folk" [subtitle] full length, 1984). Compiled by Walker. "A colorful drama with music about legendary Black folk tales drawn from the works of noted authors such as Langston Hughes, Arna Bontemps, James

Weldon Johnson, Julius Lester and Norma R. Yates.''—*Black Masks,* Nov. 1984, p. 3. Prod. by Black Spectrum Theatre Co., St. Albans, NY, Nov. 2–16, 1984; dir. by Ajene Washington.

WALKER, EVAN K. (1937–1982), Playwright and fiction writer. A native of Georgia. Resided in New York City. His short stories were published in *Black World, What We Must See* (Coombs, 1971), *Black Short Story Anthology* (King, 1972), *Ten Times Black* (Mayfield, 1972), and *We Be Word Sorcers* (Sanchez, 1973). He has reportedly also completed a novel and a screenplay. His plays were produced by the DC Black Repertory Theatre (DCBRT) in Washington, DC, the Free Southern Theatre (FST) in New Orleans, the Freedom Theatre in Philadelphia, and the Performing Arts Society of Los Angles (PASLA). Winner of the 1970 Conrad Kent Rivers Award for a short story in *Black World.*

REPRESENTATIVE PLAYS:
The Message (comedy, 1 act, 1960). Satire on the black middle-class desire to be integrated into American society. Prod. by PASLA, 1960. Prod by DCBRT Washington, DC, 1973.

East of Jordan (drama, 2 acts, 1969). Explores some of the problems of a Harlem family and the efforts of the mother to keep a shocking episode in her past from coming to light. Prod. by the Freedom Theatre, Philadelphia, 1969. Also prod. by FST New Orleans the same year.

Coda (drama, 3 acts, late 1960s). (Also known as **Coda for the Blues.**) Concerns the conflicts within a black family, whose members include a recently returned war veteran, as to the best methods of combatting white oppression during the black unrest of the late 1960s. Prod. by DCBRT, at the Last Colony Theatre Washington, DC, opening Dec. 8, 1972, for 20 perfs.

OTHER PLAYS AND DRAMATIC WORKS:
A War for Brutus (drama, 3 acts, 1950). Concerns the initiation of a young black paratrooper into the realities of life in a segregated airborne infantry regiment just before the Korean War. **Harlem Transfer** (film script, 1970s). Adapt. by WOODIE KING, JR., from a short story by Walker.

WALKER, FAI DAVIS, Playwright. Associated with the Frank Silvera Writers' Workshop (FSWW) in New York City.

PLAYS:
The Everlasting Arm (domestic drama, 1975). About the problem of what to do with an aging, widowed mother. Public reading by FSWW, Dec. 1975. Unpub. script in the FSWW Archives/Schomburg Collection. **This Way Out** (1970s). Unpub. script and tape recording in the FSWW Archives/Schomburg Collection.

WALKER, JOSEPH A. (1935–   ), Playwright, actor, director, and educator. Winner of a Drama Desk Award as the most promising playwright of 1972–73, for **The River Niger** (1972), which also won several awards, cited below. Born in Washington, DC. Educated at Howard Univ. (B.A. in philosophy and drama, 1956), where he also worked with dramatic productions of the

Howard Players, and completed all requirements but thesis for a master's degree in philosophy; Catholic Univ. (M.F.A., 1970); and NYU (Ph.D. studies, Dept. of Cinema). Served in the U.S. Air Force, receiving his discharge as first lieutenant in 1960. Married to Dorothy Dinroe, his second wife. Taught in the public schools of Washington, DC.; taught drama at City College of New York; currently is full prof. of drama at Howard Univ. Was playwright-in-residence at Yale Univ., 1970–71. Has acted on stage, TV, and films. He had appeared in the premiere production of JAMES BALDWIN's *The Amen Corner,* at Howard Univ., in the role of Luke, the returned husband; performed in Jason Miller's first play while at Catholic Univ.; played the lead in his own production of *The Believers* Off-Broadway in 1967; appeared in an episode of "N.Y.P.D." on television; was Moses Gunn's replacement in the New York Shakespeare Festival Public Theatre's production of *Cities in Bezique;* and played the role of the black militant in Woody Allen's film *Bananas,* in 1971. Cofounder, with Dorothy Dinroe, of the Demi-Gods, a professional music-dance repertory company, for which he served as artistic director and his wife as musical director. Became associated with the Negro Ensemble Co. (NEC) in 1969, where several of his plays have been produced. In addition to the Drama Desk Award cited above, **The River Niger** earned for the playwright the following awards: a Tony Award for the best play of 1973–74; an Obie Award, 1973; selection by the Burns Mantle Theatre Yearbook as a Best Play of 1972–73; an AUDELCO Black Theatre Recognition Award, 1973; an Elizabeth Hull/Kate Warringer Award, 1973, "to the playwright whose work produced within each year dealt with controversial subjects involving the fields of political, religious or social mores of the time, selected by the Dramatists Guild Council"; and a Guggenheim Fellowship of $12,000 to study creative writing for the theatre, c. 1974–75. *Address:* Dept. of Drama, College of Fine Arts, Howard University, Washington, DC 20059.

GROUP OF RELATED PLAYS:
"THE HARANGUES" (program of 4 one-act plays, 1969). Includes **Tribal Harangue One, Tribal Harangue Two, Tribal Harangue Three, and Harangue** (all 1969). Prod. Off-Bway by NEC, at St. Marks Playhouse, Dec. 30, 1969–Feb. 15, 1970, for 56 perfs.; dir. by Israel Hicks, with music by *Dorothy A. Dinroe (Walker).

PLAYS AND DRAMATIC WORKS:
The Believers ("The Black Experience in Song" [subtitle], 3 acts, 1968). Coauthor, with JOSEPHINE JACKSON. Music and lyrics by RON STEWARD. A chronicle of the black experience in America through song and dance. First prod. Off-Bway at the Garrick Theatre, New York, May 9, 1968; dir. by BARBARA ANN TEER. With the cast of The Voices, Inc. Cast recording by RCA Victor (LSO-1151).

Ododo (Yoruba word for "Truth") ("Musical Epic" [subtitle], 2 acts [9 scenes], 1968). Music by Dorothy A. Dinroe (Walker). "A musical review of the black man's history in North America viewed as repeated episodes of hate and injustice leading to a present status as an inevitable revolutionary—a kind of release of pent-up fury on the stage."—*The Best Plays of 1970–1971,* pp. 28–29. Prod. by the Afro-American Studio,

New York, Sept. 13, 1968. Prod. by NEC, at St. Marks Playhouse, Nov. 17, 1970, for 48 perfs.; dir. and partly choreographed by the author. With RAY ARANHA, Ethel Ayler, Marilyn B. Coleman, Delores Gaskins, Tonice Gwathney, Robert Jackson, Jack Landron, GARRETT MORRIS, Roxie Roker, Garrett Sanders, Charles Weldon, and Anita Wilson. Prod. by LaMont Zeno Community Theatre, Chicago, 1973–74 season. Prod. by the Demi-Gods at Howard Univ., Spring 1973. Pub. in *Black Drama Anthology* (King & Milner, 1972). Available in manuscript from Samuel French, New York.

Tribal Harangue One (vignette, or interlude, 1 act, 1969). The action takes place in a slave dungeon off the coast of West Africa in the fourteenth or fifteenth century. Two African prisoners, a husband and wife, kill their infant son to prevent him from growing up in slavery. Prod. Off-Bway by NEC, Dec. 30, 1969–Feb. 15, 1970, on a program of one-act plays under the blanket title **"THE HARANGUES"** [see GROUP OF RELATED PLAYS above]. With Rosalind Cash and Damon W. Braswell, Jr. Unpub. script in the Hatch-Billops Collection.

Tribal Harangue Two (drama, 1 act, 1969). A young black man and his white girlfriend plan to murder her wealthy Texas stepfather and use the money in the cause of the black revolution; however, their plans backfire. Prod. Off-Bway by NEC, Dec. 30, 1969–Feb. 15, 1970, on a program of one-act plays under the blanket title **"THE HARANGUES"** [see GROUP OF RELATED PLAYS above]. With Irene Bunde, Robert Hooks, David Downing, Robert G. Murch, William Jay, Julius W. Harris, and DOUGLAS TURNER WARD. Pub. in *The Best Short Plays, 1971* (Richards, 1971).

Tribal Harangue Three (vignette, or interlude, 1 act, 1969). Set in the future, following the black revolution, the characters in **Tribal Harangue One** decide to let their child grow up in freedom, though his father will possibly be executed for leading a rebellion. Prod. Off-Bway by NEC, Dec. 30, 1969–Feb. 15, 1970, on a program of one-act plays, under the blanket title **"THE HARANGUES"** [see GROUP OF RELATED PLAYS above]. Unpub. script in the Hatch-Billops Collection.

Harangue (drama, 1 act, 1969). In the setting of a bar on New York's Lower East Side, a black man with a gun (who goes berserk after years of trying unsuccessfully to find a job as a television director) forces the customers to prove that they are of good character (i.e., virtuous) or else they will die. (The man thinks that he is putting on a television show.) Unfortunately, his plans backfire, and only the virtuous are unable to prove their goodness and are killed. Prod. Off-Bway by NEC, Dec. 30, 1969–Feb. 15, 1970, on a program of one-act plays under the blanket title **"THE HARANGUES"** [see GROUP OF RELATED PLAYS above]. With Julius W. Harris, William Jay, Elliot Cuker, Linda Carlson, and Douglas Turner Ward.

Yin-Yang (theatrical collage, 1972). Music by Dorothy Dinroe Walker. A ritualistic projection of black consciousness through drama, dance, poetry, and music. Presented by the Demi-Gods and dir. by the author, at the Afro-American Studio, New York, June 1972; at the Space for Innovative Development in downtown New York, Aug. 1972; at the Third Annual Black Theatre Alliance Festival, held at the Brooklyn Academy of Music, 1973; at Howard Univ., Washington, DC, Spring 1973; Off-Bway, Oct. 4, 1973; and again in New York City, Oct. 1974.

The River Niger (drama of black experience, 3 acts, 1972; also prod. as a feature film, full length screenplay, 1976). Explores relationships among three generations of a Harlem family—the father and his wife, their son, and the wife's mother—their friends, and the members of a black militant group who invade their home. Focuses on the frustrations of the father—a painter by vocation and a poet by avocation—whose problem springs from his inability to be a real man in a racist society. So he writes poetry, drinks too much, and puts his hopes in his son, who has problems of his own with which he must cope. As described by Peter Bailey, "The play delves deeply into black love, duty, loyalty, sacrifice and responsibility in the context of the black family and the political and social movement for black revolution."—*Ebony*, June 23, 1973, p. 88. This play won numerous awards, including the Drama Desk Award for the most promising play-wright, a Tony Award as the Best Play of 1973–74, an Obie Award, selection as a Burns Mantle Theatre Yearbook Best Play of 1972–73, and an AUDELCO Black Theatre Recognition Award. In addition, it earned for the principal performers two Obie Awards, cited below. First prod. Off-Bway by NEC, at St. Marks Playhouse, Dec. 5, 1972–March 3, 1973, for 120 perfs. Transferred to Bway, at the Brooks Atkinson Theatre, March 27–Nov. 25, 1973, for 280 additional perfs., amassing a total of 400 perfs. With DOUG-LAS TURNER [WARD] and Roxie Roker, who both won Obie Awards for their per-formances, Frances Foster, Graham Brown, Grenna Whitaker, Lennal Wainwright, Neville Richen, Saundra McClain, Charles Weldon, Dean Irby, and Les Roberts. Went on tour of 44 cities, Jan. 14–March 23, 1975. Prod. as a film by Sidney Beckerman, dir. by Krishna Shah, released by Cine Arts, 1976. With Cicely Tyson, James Earl Jones, and Louis Gossett. Pub. by Hill & Wang as a Mermaid Dramabook, 1973; by Samuel French, 1974; in *The Tony Winners* (Richards, 1977); and abridged in *The Best Plays of 1972–1973* (1973).

Out of the Ashes ("A Minstrel Show" [subtitle], 2 parts, 1974). Part I is called "The Legacy," and Part II "The Vow." Satire of the metamorphosis of the Old Negro into the new black man, in which minstrel elements are mixed with modern scenes, and characters are transformed from one role to another. Presented by the Demi-Gods, New York, 1973.

Antigone Africanus (African adaptn. of the tragedy by Sophocles, 1975). Prod. by the Demi-Gods, New York, March 1975; dir. by author.

The Lion Is a Soul Brother (jazz-rock musical, full length, 1976). Music by Dorothy Dinroe Walker. An African tribal doctor relates the story of a friendly, talking lion. Prod. by the Demi-Gods, New York, May 1976.

District Line (comedy-drama, full length, 1984). A day in the life of a group of DC cab drivers, during which both passengers and drivers (a diverse group of characters) are brought together at a taxi stand set on the border of Washington and Maryland, creating a series of humorous and dramatic situations. Prod. by NEC, at Theatre Four, Dec. 1984; dir. by Douglas Turner Ward. Featuring Graham Brown, Frankie Faison, Saundra McClain, Richard Gant, and C. dUMAS.

WALKER, LUCY M. (Margaret) (1927–   ), Playwright, theatrical direc-tor, and freelance journalist. Born in Memphis, TN, where she attended ele-mentary school. Attended secondary and high school in Denver. Received the B.S. in secondary education from Central State Coll., Wilberforce, OH; and has taken graduate courses in theatre from the Univ. of Denver. Founder, pres., and exec. director of the Eden Theatrical Workshop, Inc., since 1963. Cofounder and former editor of the *Montbello Bell;* former columnist for the *Denver Drum, Denver Weekly News,* and *Aurora Sentinel.* Feature writer for the *Senior Edition;* book reviewer for the *Denver Post;* newsletter editor for the First Unitarian Church of Denver, Opportunities Industrialization Center. Affirmative action officer of the Univ. of Colorado Medical Center, Greater Denver Council for the Arts and Humanities, and the Eden Theatrical Workshop. Secretary-treasurer of CTAR (Community Theatre Assn. of the Rockies); board member of the Denver League of Women Voters, 1964–65; board member of Camp Fire Girls, 1964–65; precinct committee-woman, 1963; and pres. of the Montbello Citizens' Committee, 1974–75. Second place winner in an essay contest sponsored by the Denver City Federation of Colored Women's Clubs; first place winner in essay writing contest sponsored by Colorado Bi-Centennial Commission. Recipient of numerous honors in the Denver community, including Rocky Mountain Writers Guild's Humanitarian Award (renamed the Lucy M. Walker Humanitarian Award), 1976; Woman of the Year, presented by the alumni chapter of Delta Sigma Theta Sorority, 1977; Founder's Award from the Eden Theatrical Workshop, 1979; Citizen of the Week by KOA Radio and Capital Federal Savings and Loan Assn., 1980; and Community Development, Services and Education Award, from the Regional Office of the U.S. Office of Human Development Services, 1982. *Address:* Eden Theatrical Workshop, 1570 Gilpin St., Denver, CO 80218.

COLLECTION/GROUP OF RELATED PLAYS:

SOCIAL ACTION IN ONE-ACT PLAYS. Pub. by the author, Denver, 1970. Contains **It's Only Money, A Dollar a Day Keeps the Doctor Away, We All Play, My Own Man, The Real Estate Man, To Cuss or Bus,** and **Grades—Plus or Minus.** Written and prod. for the Curtis Park Cultural Heritage Program, Denver, and prod. by the Eden Theatrical Workshop under the program title **"PLAYS FOR LIVING."**

PLAYS AND DRAMATIC WORKS:

It's Only Money (social action play, 1 act, 1970). A married couple whose furniture is repossessed learns the hard way to read the fine print of a sales contract before signing on the dotted line. For prodn. and publishing information, see COLLECTION/GROUP OF RELATED PLAYS above.

A Dollar a Day Keeps the Doctor Away (social action play, 1 act, 1970). Explores the inadequacy and inefficiency of neighborhood community health services, through the experiences of two patients in a doctor's office who are being treated very casually by a routine-oriented nurse. For prodn. and publishing information, see COLLECTION/GROUP OF RELATED PLAYS above.

We All Pay (social action play, 1 act, 1970). A housewife admits that she heard the screaming of a woman who was raped and stabbed as she got off the bus, but was reluctant to report the incident because she didn't want to get involved. She learns too late that the victim is her own daughter. For prodn. and publishing. information, see COLLECTION/GROUP OR RELATED PLAYS above.

My Own Man (social action play, 1 act, 1970). A young man has just reached voting age. After listening to politicians from the two major parties, he is still somewhat undecided as to which party he wants to join. For prodn. and publishing information, see COLLECTION/GROUP OF RELATED PLAYS above.

The Real Estate Man (social action play, 1 act, 1970). A realtor is more interested in making a sale or deal than in how it affects his clients. A young couple who sign their first housing contract learn too late about leases. For prodn. and publishing information, see COLLECTION/GROUP OF RELATED PLAYS above.

To Cuss or Bus (social action play, 1 act, 1970). Explores the pros and cons of busing, with the conclusion expressed that "no one really likes busing, but it's the best thing we've come up with so far to begin to solve a problem that existed long before busing." For prodn. and publishing information, see COLLECTION/GROUP OF RELATED PLAYS above.

Grades—Plus or Minus (social action play, 1 act, 1970). A son who is refused the use of the family car until his school grades improve debates the subject of grades with his family. For prodn. and publishing information, see COLLECTION/GROUP OF RELATED PLAYS above.

Blood, Booze and Booty (Bicentennial play, full length, 1975). Based on the life of Aunt Clara Brown a black pioneer who arrived in Aurara—an area later to be known as Denver—in 1859. Aunt Clara died Oct. 23, 1885. She was somewhere around 80 years old. First prod. by the Eden Theatrical Workshop, Denver, at the Changing Scene Theatre, 1975; dir. by author. One of Colorado's official offerings for the Bicentennial year, 1975–76.

WALKER, MARK, Playwright.

PLAY:
A Near Fatality ("A Two-Scene Statement for Niggers Only" [subtitle], 1968). About a black nationalist college professor whose militant efforts prove to be counterproductive to his intended purpose, thus aiding the system which he is trying to fight. Pub. in *Black Expression*, Fall 1968, pp. 48–51.

WALKER, PHILLIP E., Producer, director, actor. Artistic director of the African American Drama Co. of San Francisco, CA. Born in Chicago, IL. Received the B.A. degree in theatre from Loyola Univ.; the M.A. in theatre history/criticism from the Univ. of Illinois/Urbana; and the M.F.A. in acting from the Univ. of California/Davis. Has taught theatre at Lincoln Univ. of Missouri, the Univ. of Illinois, Yuba Coll. (CA), the Univ. of California/Davis, and the People's School of Dramatic Arts in San Francisco. His theatrical credits span almost 100 productions, including TV commercials and industrial films; the CBS-TV film *Flesh and Blood;* the NBC-TV series "The Duke"; and productions of the African American Drama Co., the San Francisco Mime Troupe, the Missouri Summer Repertory Theatre, the Earth Theatre (Chicago), Kuumba Workshop (Chicago), and other groups. Member of the exec. council of the American Theatre Assn.'s Black Theatre Program, and the California Arts Council. *Address:* African American Drama Co., 394 Fifth Ave., San Francisco, CA 94118.

PLAYS AND DRAMATIC WORKS:
Can I Speak for You Brother? (one-man show, full length, 1978). Inspired by VINIE BURROWS's one-woman show, *Walk Together Children*. Combines dance, poetry, drama, letters, storytelling, speeches, music, and puppetry, with a single actor using selective costuming and props to recreate the words and thoughts of nine extraordinary black leaders. The chronology opens during the "Middle Passage" and closes in "tomorrow." Developed as a class production project, while the author was teaching in the professional theatre training program of the Univ. of Illinois, 1978. Prod. by several

campus organizations of the Univ. of Illinois, as part of their Black History Month Celebrations, prior to being prod. by the African American Drama Co. of California on a national tour of colleges, churches, schools, community centers, libraries, etc., during Black History Month, Feb. 1982. **Get Down** (drama, 1 act, pre-1985).

WALKER, SULLIVAN, Actor and playwright. Born in the West Indies. Artistic director of the Caribbean Experience Theatre, Brooklyn, NY. Performed in the Negro Ensemble Co.'s production of TREVOR RHONE's comedy, *Two Can Play* (1984).

PLAYS:
Black Macbeth (adaptn., 1973). A Third World concept of Shakespeare's play. Prod. by the Caribbean Experience Theatre, 1973. **A Tribute to the Black Woman** // Also called **Black Woman** (1974). Prod. at the Church of St. Matthew and St. Thomas, New York. Revived by the Caribbean Experience Theatre, 1983. **8 O'Clock Time** (theatrical collage, 1977). Program of sketches, poetry, and dance. Presents aspects of Caribbean life in Trinidad and the United States. Prod. by the New World Theatre, at Lincoln Square Community Center, New York, July 1977. **Two Soldiers at a Crossroad** (1970s). "An account of the Black power uprising on a Caribbean island during the seventies."— *New York Amsterdam News,* Jan. 29, 1983, p. 12. Prod. by the Caribbean Experience Theatre, 1970s. Revived Jan.-Feb. 1983. **The Journey** (comedy-drama, early 1980s). Prod. by the Caribbean Experience Theatre, early 1980s. **Mother & Daughter** (early 1980s). Prod. by the Caribbean Experience Theatre, early 1980s. **Boy Days** (series of sketches with a prologue, full length, 1985). Monologues, dialogues, and narratives about growing up in the West Indies, written and performed by Walker. In the prologue, the author/actor states the theme of the play: "I want to tak' 'em back to de days when sugar was three cents a pound . . . back to the days in the Caribbean . . . the good old days . . . back to 'Boy Days.' "—*New York Amsterdam News,* June 29, 1985, p. 26 (Richardson). Prod. by the Caribbean Experience Theatre, at the Ozone Layer, a disco space in Brooklyn, June 1985. Sched. to be published "later in the year" (1985), according to the author.

WALKER, TITUS, School teacher, actor, artist, composer, and playwright. Founder and artistic director of the Ujamaa Black Theatre in New York City. A graduate of CCNY, he teaches theatre and drama at the Coll. of New Rochelle in New York. Recipient of the *National Newport News and Commentator* Achievement Award, 1987. *Address:* 1133 Ogden Ave. #22, Bronx, NY 10452. Alternate: Ujamaa Black Theatre, c/o Carter Theatre, 250 W. 43rd St., New York, NY.

PLAYS AND DRAMATIC WORKS:
Harlem Renaissance (historical jazz musical, full length, 1980s). Subtitled "To the Gospel of the Church to the Jazz Clubs of Harlem." Presented by the Ujamaa Black Theatre Co., at Bway's Carter Theatre, New York, 1980s. **Sun People** (children's musical, full length, 1982). Subtitled "An African Tale for Children and Adults." Prod. at the Carter Theatre, New York, April 18, 1982. **Please Don't Take My Rhythm & Blues** (rhythm and blues gospel musical, full length, 1983). Prod. at the Carter Theatre, New York, 1982.

WALKER, WILLIAM, Playwright. Based in Cleveland, OH. Former drama major at Baldwin Wallace Coll. in Berea, OH. Taught at the J.F. Kennedy H.S. in Cleveland during the early 1970s.

PLAY:
O-Ree-O (play with music, 1973). Music by *Otis Dancey, then a senior from Youngstown, OH. "A search for lost identity through Black consciousness."—Program Notes. Prod. by black students at Baldwin Coll., March 5, 1973.

WALLACE, G. L., Playwright. Associated with the Frank Silvera Writers' Workshop (FSWW) in New York City.

PLAYS:
Them Next Door (comedy-drama, 1 act, 1974). "The Jacksons, a Black Family[,] have moved into a formerly all-White neighborhood where live the lily-white Gibbs family. The drama revolves around the fact [that] the two families have never spoken to each other. It is this lack of communication and thus lack of understanding about each other's family problems that is the crux of the play."—*Samuel French's Basic Catalog of Plays* (1984). Pub. by Samuel French, New York, 1974. **Lyrics for a Sad Song** (pre-1980s). Public reading by FSWW, presumably in the late 1970s. Unpub. script and tape recording in the FSWW Archives/Schomburg Collection.

WALLACE, RUDY, Playwright. Apparently originally based in Philadelphia, PA, where he was associated with Theatre Advocate and the Annenburg Center. His plays have also been prod. in New York City by the Negro Ensemble Co. (NEC). According to the *Dictionary of the Black Theatre* (Woll, 1983), "While the New York Times considered Wallace 'a playwright of promise,' it criticized the dramatist's use of obvious stereotypes for his characters."

PLAYS:
Brothers of Blood and Thunder (tragicomedy, 2 acts, 1974). Deals with ideological conflicts within a black fraternity between the pledgees and the big brothers. Prod. by the Annenburg Center, Philadelphia, 1974. **The Friends of LeLand Stone** (tragedy, 1 act, 1974). Concerns the emotional trauma within a black family after the father shoots a man whom the youngest daughter has accused of rape. Prod. by Theatre Advocate, Philadelphia, Dec. 1974. **The Philosopher Limer** (comedy, 1 act, 1974). Caribbean man deserts his wife and children to live on the beach, where he meets a young island girl. **The Moonlight Arms** (tragedy, 1 act, 1974). A violent argument between a scholar and his low-brow wife which brings about the dissolution of their two-month marriage. First prod. by Theatre Advocate, Philadelphia, Dec. 1974. Prod. by NEC, at St. Marks Playhouse, New York (as a curtain raiser to the following play), opening May 13, 1975, for 8 perfs. **The Dark Tower** (psychological drama, 1 act, 1975). Two-character drama involving an artistic, intellectual, and emotional confrontation between a young poet and a seedy old artist, described as a "street fighter" and a "reprobate." Prod. by NEC, at St. Marks Playhouse, New York, opening May 13, 1975, for 8 perfs., on double bill with **The Moonlight Arms. The People Play** (symbolic drama, 2 acts, 1975). Four black intellectuals argue about the possibilities of human perfection. **The Phillis Wheatley Story** (biographical drama, 2 acts, 1975). About the first black woman poet in America,

from her childhood in Africa to the moment that she is about to give birth to her own child.

WALMSLEY, DEWDROP, Playwright. Based in New York City, where she was a participant in the New York Black Writers Conf. in 1971.

PLAY:

Genius in Africa (historical drama, 1 act, 1974). Concerns Thomas Fuller, a gifted mathematician and slave from Africa who plots a way to educate the field slaves in math. Sched. for publication by Amuru Press, New York, 1974, but apparently never published.

WALTOWER, EARL, Playwright. Formerly associated with the Tompkins Square Park Players in New York City.

PLAY:

The Landlord (domestic drama, 1 act, 1975). Concerns the disastrous effect of dispossession on a hard-working southern black family. Prod. by the Tompkins Square Park Players, New York, June 1975.

WARD, DOUGLAS TURNER (also known as Douglas Turner) (1930–   ), Actor, playwright, black theatre organizer, director. Born near Burnside, LA; grew up in New Orleans. Attended Wilberforce Coll. (now. Univ.), 1946–47; and the Univ. of Michigan, 1947–48. In 1948, came to New York City, where he worked as a journalist, 1948–51. Attended Paul Mann's Actors Workshop for over two years before making his acting debut Off-Broadway in the Circle-in-the-Square prod. of *The Iceman Cometh*. Under the name of Douglas Turner, he launched a successful career as an actor, appearing successively in the New York City Center production of *Lost in the Stars;* as Sidney Poitier's understudy in *A Raisin in the Sun,* afterwards taking over the lead during its ten-month national tour; opposite Diana Sands in *A Land Beyond the River;* on Broadway in *One Flew over the Cuckoo's Nest;* in the pre-Bway tour of *Rich Little Rich Girl;* Off-Bway in *The Blacks* and *Blood Knot;* in the New York Shakespeare Festival production of *Coriolanus;* on TV in "East Side, West Side," "The Edge of Night," the "DuPont Show of the Month," and as costar of a CBS special on "Look Up and Live." In 1960 he tried unsuccessfully to get his first two plays, **Happy Ending** and **Day of Absence** produced, but it was not until 1964 that actor Robert Hooks decided to produce them himself, with the help of Juanita Poitier and GODFREY CAMBRIDGE. The opening of these two plays Off-Bway at St. Marks Playhouse in 1965 was the beginning of a successful playwriting career for Ward, who decided to write plays under his family name while continuing to act under the name Douglas Turner. The two plays mentioned above established an Off-Bway record of 504 performances, winning for him a Vernon Rice/Drama Desk Award for playwriting and the first of his two Obie awards for acting. In 1968 he joined with Robert Hooks in founding the Negro Ensemble Co. (NEC), which has produced all of his plays. In addition to his writing and administrative functions, he has directed many of NEC's productions

and acted in most of them, including his own works. He won his second Obie Award in 1973 for his performance in *The River Niger,* also produced by NEC. Other awards include a Tony nomination as Best Supporting Actor, for his performance in *The River Niger,* 1973; an AUDELCO Board of Directors Award, 1974; and the first Adolph Caesar Performing Arts Award, presented by NEC, 1987. *Address:* c/o Negro Ensemble Co., 165 W. 46th St., Suite 1015, New York, NY 10036.

COLLECTION:
HAPPY ENDING AND DAY OF ABSENCE: Two Plays. Dramatists Play Service, New York, 1966. Contains **Happy Ending** (1960) and **Day of Absence** (1960).

PLAYS AND DRAMATIC WORKS:
Happy Ending (satirical comedy, 1 act, 1960). Two black domestics, a maid and a laundress, who have been enjoying a comfortable living at the expense of their unsuspecting affluent white employers, are now faced with a possible cut-off of their source of money, clothing, food, and other "purloined perquisites, because their employers are getting a divorce. One of the longest-running Off-Bway plays. Won for its author a Drama Desk/Vernon Rice Award and an Obie Award, 1965–66. First prod. on double bill with **Day of Absence,** by Robert Hooks, Inc., at St. Marks Playhouse, Nov. 15, 1965–Jan. 29, 1967, for 504 perfs.; dir. by Philip Meister. Starring Esther Rolle, Robert Hooks, Douglas Turner (Ward), and Frances Foster. Prod. on double bill with **Day of Absence** at the Seattle Repertory Theatre, Seattle, WA, for 21 perfs., opening Feb. 10, 1971. Pub. in *HAPPY ENDING AND DAY OF ABSENCE;* in *New Black Playwrights* (Couch, 1968, 1970); in *Black Drama–An Anthology* (Consolo & Brasmer, 1970); in *Keys to Understanding: Receiving and Sending–Drama* (Holmes & Lehman, 1970); in *Contemporary Black Drama* (Oliver & Sills, 1971).

Day of Absence (satirical comedy, 1 act, 1960). According to the author, "The play is conceived for performance by a Black cast, a reverse minstrel show in white face."—Published script. White citizens of a southern town discover that blacks have mysteriously disappeared from the community, thus bringing about economic and domestic chaos by their absence. One of the longest-running Off-Bway plays. Won for its author a Drama Desk/Vernon Rice Award and an Obie Award, 1965–66. First prod. Off-Bway (on double bill with **Happy Ending**) by Robert Hooks, Inc., at St. Marks Playhouse, Nov. 15, 1965–Jan. 29, 1967, for 504 perfs.; dir. by Philip Meister. Starring Douglas Turner (Ward) and Robert Hooks. Prod. (with the orig. cast) on NET in 1967; telecast frequently repeated. Prod. Off-Bway (on double bill with **Brotherhood**) by NEC, at St. Marks Playhouse, for 64 perfs., March 10–May 3, 1970. Prod. (on double bill with **Happy Ending** at the Seattle Rep. Theatre, Seattle, opening Feb. 10, 1971, for 21 perfs. Widely prod. by black theatre groups throughout the country. Pub. in *HAPPY ENDING AND DAY OF ABSENCE;* in *Black Drama—An Anthology* (Brasmer, 1970); in *New Black Playwrights* (Couch, 1968, 1970); in *Afro-American Literature, 1760–Present* (Miller, 1971); in *Contemporary Black Drama* (Oliver & Sills, 1971); in *Black Theater, U.S.A.* (Hatch & Shine, 1974); excerpt in *Black Culture: Reading and Writing Black* (Simmons & Hutchinson, 1972).

The Reckoning "A Surreal Southern Fable" [subtitle], full length drama in 1 long act, 1969). Concerns a bigoted southern governor who is being blackmailed by his black mistress (a prostitute) and a cunning black pimp. The play is primarily a test of wits between the governor and the pimp. First prod. Off-Bway by (Robert) Hooks Productions, Inc., in cooperation with NEC, at St. Marks Playhouse, Sept. 4–Nov. 23, 1969, for 94 perfs.; dir. by Michael Schultz. Starring Douglas Turner (Ward) as the pimp, Jeanette DuBois (JA'NET DuBOIS) as the prostitute, and Lester Rawlins as the governor. Pub. by Dramatists Play Service, New York, 1970.

Brotherhood (satirical comedy, 1 act, 1970). A white couple, pretending to be liberals, entertains a sophisticated black couple in their living room, trying frantically to avoid revealing the artifacts of racism with which their home is crowded—"nigger," "mammy," and "pickaninny" statuettes, ashtrays, lamps, cushions, footrests, and records—all covered with sheets or otherwise concealed while the black couple visits. First prod. Off-Bway by NEC (on double bill with **Day of Absence)** at St. Marks Playhouse, March 30–May 3, 1970; dir. by author. With William Jay and Frances Foster as the black couple, Tom Rosqui and Tiffany Henry as the white couple.

The Redeemer (comedy, 1 act, 1979). A strange assortment of characters waits for the Second Coming on Judgement Day. First prod. by the Actors Theatre of Louisville, KY, Jan. 26, 1979. Prod. by NEC, April 12–May 1, 1983, for 24 perfs.; dir. by author. With L. Scott Caldwell, David Davies, Kathleen Forbes, Eugene Lee, and Naomi Riseman.

WARD, RICHARD (Richard Waugh) (1915–   ), Distinguished actor of stage, screen, and television; director, producer, playwright, and short-story writer. Born in Glenside, PA. Educated at Tuskegee Inst. Performed in vaudeville, 1928–32. Was a member of the American Negro Theatre in Harlem. Founder and director of the International School of Performing Arts, 1960. His many stage performances include *Anna Lucasta* (1954), *A Land Beyond the River* (1957), *Blues for Mister Charlie* (1964), *The Amen Corner* (1965), and *Ceremonies in Dark Old Men* (1969). Produced *Giovanni's Room* (International School of Performing Arts, 1960). Directed *American Night Cry* (1974). Appeared in *Tarzan* films (M.G.M., 1937–39) and in *Black Like Me, The Cool World, Nothing but a Man* (1964), and *The Learning Tree* (1969). Television appearances include *Sty of the Blind Pig,* "Sanford and Son," "The Jeffersons," and "Good Times." Recipient of an award for best short story in *Saturday Evening Post,* 1947.

PLAYS AND DRAMATIC WORKS:
(All pre-1976.) **When the World Has Found a Man** (TV script). Prod. by Camera Three. **Penitence //** or possibly **Penance** (drama, 3 acts, 1975). Prod. at the Open Space, New York, May 1975. **Rock & Rolls Has Gotta Go** (musical, 2 acts). **The Long Chase** (TV script).

WARD, THEODORE (1902–1983), Pioneer playwright of the 1930s and 1940s, best known for his two early plays, **Big White Fog** (1938), written and first produced by the Negro Unit of the Chicago Federal Theatre, and **Our Lan'** (1941), winner of the Theatre Guild Award, 1947. Author of 31 plays, many of them written since the 1950s. Born in Thibodeaux, LA. His father was a schoolteacher and traveling salesman of books and patent medicines. Grew up and received his early schooling in New Orleans and St. Louis. Ran away from home at 13, after the death of his mother, and worked his way to Chicago by doing odd jobs. There he remained off and on for most of his life. Lived for a while in Seattle, WA., and in Salt Lake City, UT, while he studied at the Univ. of Utah. There his talents as a writer were discovered, and he won the Zona Gale Fellowship for Creative Writing, which enabled him to continue his education at the Univ. of Wisconsin, where he developed both his writing and acting skills, and worked as a staff artist at Station WIDA in Madison, WI. Returned to Chicago during the 1930s, as drama instructor for the Negro Unit of the WPA Federal Theatre there. Moved to New York City during the 1940s and was one of the founders of the Negro Playwrights Company. Moved back to Chicago in the 1950s, making it his permanent home. Director of the Southside Center of the Performing Arts, Inc. (also called Ted Ward's Southside Center, etc.), 1967–c. 1974, where many of his plays were revived. In addition to the Theatre Guild Award, 1947, he was recipient of a National Theatre Conf. Fellowship, 1947; a Guggenheim Fellowship for creative writing, 1948; and most recently an AUDELCO Outstanding Pioneer Award for contribution to the growth and development of black theatre, 1975. *Agent:* James V. Hatch, Hatch-Billops Collection, 491 Broadway, New York, NY 10012.

PLAYS AND DRAMATIC WORKS WRITTEN, PRODUCED, AND/OR PUBLISHED SINCE 1950:

Throwback (drama, 1 act, 1951). A black man kills a white man for molesting his wife. Prod. by the Skyloft Players, Chicago, 1951.

Whole Hog or Nothing (drama, 1 act, 1952). Black American servicemen fighting in the South Pacific during World War II must also combat white racism. Prod. in Chicago (?), 1952.

The Daubers (drama, 3 acts, 1953). Deals with the problem of drug addiction within an upper-middle-class black family. Prod. by the Experimental Black Actors Guild (X-Bag), Chicago, 1973. Excerpt (1 scene) in *Black Scenes* (Childress, 1971).

John de Conqueror (folk opera, 2 acts, 1953). Concerns a colony of former Jamaican slaves living in Biloxi, MS, on the coast of the Gulf of Mexico. Rather than submit to white slavery, they are led to their deaths into the sea by their leader, John de Conqueror.

Madison // Orig. title and present subtitle: **Creole** (musical, 2 acts, 1956). Adapt. from a short story, "The Heroic Slave," written by *Frederick Douglass in 1853. Concerns the heroism of Madison, a slave leader who leads an insurrection on the S.S. *Creole,* in which the slaves gain control of the ship and sail to their freedom in Nassau.

Charity (musical, 3 acts, 1960). The story of Blind Tom, an early black musician who was exploited by whites.

Big Money (musical comedy, 2 acts, 1961). A man who suddenly comes into possession of a small fortune finds that his life is no longer the same. He is exploited by his friends and interfered with by the police.

The Bell and the Light (musical, 2 acts, 1962). A group of slaves discover that they cannot continue to depend upon the good treatment of a benevolent master, and that their only salvation is through freedom.

Candle in the Wind (historical drama, 4 acts, 1967). Concerns the events leading up to the murder of a black senator from Mississippi during the Reconstruction period in 1875. Prod. by the South Side Center of the Performing Arts, Chicago, 1969.

OTHER PLAYS AND DRAMATIC WORKS PRIOR TO 1950:
Sick and Tiahd ("Sick and Tired") (drama, 1 act, 1937). **Big White Fog** (tragedy, 3 acts, 1938). **Falcon of Adowa** (drama, 1938). **Even the Dead Arise** (fantasy, 1 act, 1938). **Skin Deep** (drama, 1 act, 1939). **Our Lan'** (historical drama, 2 acts, 1941). **Deliver the Goods** (defense propaganda play, 3 acts, 1941). **Shout Hallelujah** (tragedy, 3 acts, 1941).

WARD, VAL GRAY (1932–   ), Actress, poet, playwright, producer, and theatre director. Cofounder, with husband Francis Ward, of the Kuumba Theatre (originally known as the Kuumba Workshop), of the South Side Community Arts Centre), the oldest black theatre in Chicago, which in 1986 celebrated its eighteenth year of operation. Former director of the Afro-American Culture Program of the Univ. of Illinois/Urbana. As an actress, she has performed her one-woman show, "Voice of the Black Writer," and other programs on a number of college and university campuses. She was recently honored by the Board of Directors of Kuumba for " 'her tireless' efforts to bring Black theater to Chicago," —*Jet,* May 5, 1986, p. 56. Her writings (many coauthored with Francis Ward) have appeared in *Black Scholar, Black World,* and other periodicals.

PLAYS AND DRAMATIC WORKS:
Gwendolyn Brooks Tribute (poetic collage, full length, 1969). Staged readings of works by and about the noted black poet. Prod. at the Afro-Arts Centre, Chicago, Dec. 1969. **The Life of Harriet Tubman** (biographical drama, full length, 1971). A dramatic portrait of the famous leader of the Underground Railroad. Prod. by the Kuumba Workshop, Chicago, 1971. **The Heart of the Blues** (musical collage, full length, c. 1984). Described by *Jet* magazine (ibid.) as "a nightlong celebration of the contributions of such important blues singers as Bessie Smith, Ma Rainey and Billie Holiday." Prod. by the Kuumba Theatre, in repertory, 1984–86; dir. by author. With Katherine Davis as the blues great Ma Rainey, and Ward's daughter, Rhonda Ward, as blues singer Alberta Hunter.

WARNER, MARION, Playwright. Associated with the Frank Silvera Writers' Workshop (FSWW) in New York City.

PLAYS:
Catch as Catch Can (pre-1979). Unpub. script and tape recording of a reading by FSWW in the FSWW Archives/Schomburg Collection. **The Bag** (drama, 1979). The successful struggle of a Harlem family against poverty, drugs, and internal conflicts. Public reading by FSWW, Oct. 15, 1979. Unpub. script in the FSWW Archives/Schomburg Collection.

WASHINGTON, ERWIN, Former student playwright at UCLA. His play was a second place winner in the Lorraine Hansberry Awards of the American College Theatre Festival (ACTF). *Address:* 609 Venice Way, Inglewood, CA 90302.

PLAY:
Oh Oh Freedom (drama, 1976). A black man lords it over his family as king and boss, because that is the only domain that he is able to rule in a white racist society.

Prod. at UCLA, 1976. Winner of second place in the Lorraine Hansberry Awards, ACTF, 1976.

WATI, JASO, Playwright. Studied playwriting with the Frank Silvera Writers' Workshop (FSWW) in New York City, 1977.

PLAYS:
Trouble Don't Last Always (1977). Public reading by FSWW, at the Teachers, Inc., New York, Jan. 1977. Unpub. script in the FSWW Archives/Schomburg Collection. **Lazarus** (1977). Public reading by FSWW, at CCNY, March 1977. Unpub. script in the FSWW Archives/Schomburg Collection. **All About Karma** (late 1970s). Unpub. script and tape recording of a reading by FSWW in the FSWW Archives/Schomburg Collection.

WATKINS, GORDON (Ronald) (1930–   ), TV and stage actor, producer, director, writer, composer, nightclub entertainer, and concert artist. Born in Baltimore, MD. Educated at Juilliard School of Music (B.S., 1958; M.S., 1960), Katherine Dunham School of Dance, Hunter Coll (M.A.), and the New School for Social Research (film directing). Served in the U.S. Air Force, 1947–51. Taught theatre and directed plays at Rutgers Univ.'s Newark, NJ, campus, 1968–70. Was staff producer and writer for WCBS-TV, New York City, 1969–70. Since 1970 has served as president of the Toussaint Group, Inc., independent producers of black-oriented films and TV shows. Has appeared in such Off-Broadway and Broadway shows as *Kwamina, Porgy and Bess, The Prodigal Singer,* and *South Pacific.* His TV appearances include "East Side/West Side," "The Nurses," and "The Defenders." Recipient of the Anne M. Gannett Scholarship, from the American Federation of Music Clubs, 1956; Juilliard School of Music Scholarship, 1954–60; John Golden Fellowship, for graduate study of directing and playwriting, 1968–69; National Assn. of Television Program Executives' Award, for excellence in the performing arts, 1971; Ohio State Award, for excellence in television production, 1972. *Address*—Home: 675 Water St. #19D, New York, NY 10002. Office: The Toussaint Group, Inc., 420 E. 51st St., New York, NY 10022.

REPRESENTATIVE PLAYS AND DRAMATIC WORKS:
A Lion Roams the Streets (1968). First prod. at the champlain Shakespeare Festival, Burlington, VT, Sept. 1968. Prod. by the New Hudson Guild, New York, Nov. 15, 1968. Pub. by Breakthrough Press, New York, 1969.

Caught in the Middle (play and screenplay, 1969). An ex-streetgang member returns to his old neighborhood as an investigator for the welfare department. He is spurned, rejected, and attacked by the very people that he is trying to help, until he is finally forced to resort to violence. First prod. by the Hunter Coll. Playwrights Workshop, New York, 1969. Also prod. by the Little Theatre, West Side YMCA, New York.

Cages (drama, full length, 1970s). Concerns the barriers, both internal and external, that separate people and cause them such loneliness and despair; these barriers also prevent us from bringing about positive change in our society. Prod. in New York and Wilmington, DE, 1970s.

OTHER PLAYS AND DRAMATIC WORKS:
College Time (1 act, 1960). First prod. at Glacier Park Lodge, MT, Summer 1960.
Tinkerman to the Promised Land (1 act, 1967). Prod. in New York, April 1967. Also
prod. in Washington, DC, and Newark, NJ. **Sojourner Truth** (historical drama, full
length, 1970s). About the famous black abolitionist, told in dialogue, song, and speeches.

WATSON, HARMON C. (1943–   ), Playwright and university professor.
Born in Baltimore, MD. Educated at Morgan State Coll. (B.A., 1964), where
he also studied playwriting under the tutelage of Profs. Waters Turpin and †Arthur
Clifton Lamb; and at the Univ. of Colorado (M.A., 1968), under a Shubert
Foundation Fellowship in Playwriting, which was renewed for a second year.
After graduation, he joined the faculty of Morgan State Coll. as an instructor
and asst. director of drama.

PLAYS:
Toy of the Gods (1964). Prod. at Morgan State Coll., 1964, and later at Columbia
Univ. **Clown in Three Rings** (c. 1966). Written on a Shubert Foundation Fellowship in
Playwriting at the Univ. of Colorado, and was so well received that his fellowship was
renewed for another year. **The Golden Gates Fall Down** (comedy, 1 act, 1966). About
prejudice in Heaven. St. Peter refuses to let in a black man because he is not wearing a
white robe. He is finally admitted, after much debate, because the Klan choir needs a
bass voice. First prod. 1966. Pub. in *Black Insights* (Ford, 1971). **The Middle Man**
(drama, 3 acts, 1972). A black man married to a white woman finds himself in the middle
of a situation that seems to defy a satisfactory solution.

WATT, BILLIE LOU, Playwright.
PLAY:
Phillis "A Play with Music" [subtitle], 1969). About the life of Phillis Wheatley, the
early black American poet. Pub. by Friendship Press, New York, 1969.

WAYMON, SAM (Samuel), Musical performer, composer, lyricist, vocalist,
and conductor. Contributed the music and lyrics to two plays by BILL GUNN,
and appeared as a performer in Gunn's film *Ganja and Hess* (1973). Brother of
singer/pianist Nina Simone, with whom he recorded "It's Finished." Has appeared in the major clubs in Los Angeles, San Francisco, and New York; and
has performed in Carnegie Hall, Philharmonic Hall, the Apollo, and numerous
other theatres. His television appearances include the "David Frost Show" and
the "Tonight Show."

PLAYS:
Black Picture Show (musical play, full length, 1975). Music and lyrics by Waymon,
who also functioned as vocalist and music director. Book by Bill Gunn. According to
The Best Plays of 1974–75, it depicts "the intellectual decay and death of a Black poet
[-playwright] seduced by ambition and movie money." Its setting is a psychiatric unit
in a Bronx, New York, hospital, and the poet "is looking back over his life from the
vantage point of the last day, to see where it all went wrong." Prod. by the New York
Shakespeare Festival and Joseph Papp, at the Vivian Beaumont Theatre, Lincoln Center,

New York City, Jan. 6–Feb. 9, 1975, for 41 perfs., dir. by the author, and featuring Dick Anthony Williams (who received a Tony nomination for his perf.). Pub. by Reed, Cannon & Johnson, Berkeley, CA, c. 1975.

Rhinestone (drama with music and dance, 3 acts, 1982–83). Adapt. by Bill Gunn from his novel *Rhinestone Sharecropping* (1981). Music and lyrics by Waymon and Gunn. Choreography by GEORGE FAISON. Explores the writer-director relationship between a racially insensitive European producer and a sensitive black screenwriter who has been assigned to do the screenplay of a film about a famous black football hero. Prod. in New York, during the 1982–83 season; dir. by the author, with Joe Morton as the black writer and Novella Nelson as his wife. Michael Wager played the white producer.

WEBSTER, PAUL, Playwright. Of Barbadian descent. Former director of the Barbados Theatre Workshop in New York City, 1970s. Currently associated with the Caribbean Theatre of the Performing Arts. *Address:* 230 Mill St., Westwood, NJ 07675.

DRAMATIC WORKS:
Under the Duppy Parasol (folk comedy, full length, 1975). A satire on Americanized Barbadians who return from the United States to the West Indies with their newly acquired accents and superior attitudes. Prod. by the Barbados Theatre Workshop, at Emory Taylor's Harlem Cultural Center, New York, and at the Billie Holiday Theatre, Brooklyn, 1975. **Sea Rock Children Is Strong Children** (comedy with music, full length, 1985). Written and dir. by Webster. Music and lyrics by Ricardo Cadogan. A comedy of the seamier side of life in Barbados, set in the red-light district. Prod. by the Caribbean Theatre of the Performing Arts, at the Billie Holiday Theatre, Brooklyn, May 1985.

WELCH, LEONA NICHOLAS (1942–   ), Poet, playwright, teacher. Born in Mobile, AL. Received the B.A. in English from Mills Coll., Oakland, CA, 1976, with credential for teaching in 1979; and an M.A. in English from Holy Names Coll., Oakland, 1983. Married; six children. Has taught high school English (6 years); currently instr. of English at Contra Costa Coll., San Pablo, CA. Since 1971 has worked as a creative writing specialist in schools and colleges and with community groups. She specializes in seminars directed toward creative women, although her work has been with all sexes and ethnic groups. Has published one book of poetry entitled *Black Gibraltar* (1971). Other poems have been published in such periodicals as *Berkeley Monthly, Journal of Black Poetry, Black Times, Voices International, Encore, College Poetry Review,* and *Callaloo;* and anthologized in *To Build a Fire* (a commemorative anthology celebrating Oakland writers, 1977) and *Shelly's #8* (1978). Recipient of award of achievement for "body of literary work published" from California Assn. of Teachers of English, 1973, and certificate of achievement for excellence in lyric writing, American Song Festival, 1977. *Address:* P.O. Box 5073, Richmond, CA 94804.

PLAYS:
Black Through the Looking Glass (full length, 1980). A woman takes a look at her mind, heart, soul, and body through her own mirror. She has come from a point of not

knowing who she is, through not liking who she is, to now embracing and loving who she is. The story is told through dialogue, some humor, poetry, dance, and song. Performed by Berkeley (CA) Black Repertory Theatre, March 27–May 3, 1980.

Hands in the Mirror "A Dramatic Dance/Poem" [subtitle], 7 segments, with prologue and conclusion, 1981). A solemn tribute to old black women. A highly dramatic dance-poem which focuses on the hands of the dancer. In the words of the author: "The motion, the sturdy and steady motion of the hands of old Black women in our lives, and in the lives of millions of Americans has been a forever flowing song, a dance, and a poem. It is high time we applaud the performance of old black women in our lives. It is high time we stood up and cheered. This play makes an effort, in a small way, to say 'THANKS!' "—Description received from author, Sept. 16, 1983. Sched. to be performed in Amhurst, MD, Sept. 1983. Pub. in *Center Stage* (Ostrow, 1981).

The Old Lady and the Ballet Boy (drama with dance, 1 act, 1983). Explores the universal theme of love and the crossing of the generation gap. A cantankerous old woman has withdrawn from society, shutting herself up in her room, full of mistrust of children. An eight-year-old boy who is a ballet student knocks on her door, selling tickets to a performance. Through his persistence, and via his ballet, he gets her to buy a ticket, and she admits him into her heart and her house. Performed by the 11th St. Players, at the East Bay Centre for the Performing Arts, California, Sept. 1–25, 1983.

WESLEY, RICHARD (Errol) (1945–   ), Playwright and screenwriter. Born in Newark, NJ. Educated at Howard Univ. (B.F.A., 1967). Married; the father of one child. Worked as a passenger service agent for United Airlines in Newark, 1967–69. Member of the New Lafayette Theatre (NLT) in Harlem, 1968–73, where he worked closely with playwright-in-residence ED BULLINS, also serving as managing editor of *Black Theatre* magazine, 1969–72, and as playwright-in-residence himself in 1973. Member of the WGA/East. Received Honorable Mention in the National Collegiate Playwriting Contest, and a Special Playwriting Award from the Samuel French Publishing Co., 1965, for **Put My Dignity on 307.** Winner of a Drama Desk Award for Outstanding Playwriting, 1972, for **The Black Terror** which also earned another Drama Desk Award for the leading actor, GYLAN KAIN. Recipient of an Rockefeller Grant, 1973; an NAACP Image Award, 1974, for his film **Uptown Saturday Night** (1974); and an AUDELCO Black Theatre Recognition Award, 1974. His play **The Sirens** earned an Obie Award for actress Loretta Green's outstanding performance in 1973. *Address:* 221 Montclair Avenue, Upper Montclair, NJ 07043. *Agent:* Jay D. Kramer, Esq., 36 East 61st St., New York, NY 10021.

REPRESENTATIVE PLAYS AND DRAMATIC WORKS:

Put My Dignity on 307 (satirical drama, 1 act, 1965). A black blue-collar worker tries to achieve middle-class status by playing the numbers. Received Honorable Mention and a special playwriting award from Samuel French Publishing Co., in the National Collegiate Playwriting Contest, 1965. Prod. by Howard Univ., Washington, DC; broadcast on WRC-TV's "Operation Awareness," Washington, DC, May 1967.

Knock, Knock—Who Dat? (comedy, 1 act, 1970). "Deals with the No-Knock Law . . . which gives police the right to enter a private home at any time without prior warning and/or without a warrant, if they have any reason to suspect the inhabitants of engaging in criminal activity."—*Black Theatre* #6, 1972, p. 42. The members of a black family open gunfire on police when their door is broken down. Prod. by Theatre Black, at the Univ. of the Streets' Auditorium, New York, Oct. 1970. Unpub. script in the Schomburg Collection.

Gettin' It Together // Alternate title: **Steady Rapp** (drama, 1 act, 1971). An exploration of the black male-female love relationship in its historical perspective. Earned for the author a Drama Desk Award for Outstanding Playwriting. First prod. at the Elma Lewis School of Fine Arts, New York, May 13, 1971. Prod. by Theatre Black, at the Bed-Stuy Theatre, Brooklyn, NY, 1971. Prod. Off-Bway by the New York Shakespeare Festival (NYSF) Public Theatre, at the Public Theatre Annex, opening April 4, 1972, for 62 perfs., on a program of four one-act plays, presented under the blanket title *Black Visions*. Prod. by Stage 73, New York, July 1977; dir. by George Lee Liles. Pub. by Dramatists Play Service, 1979, in a volume with the author's **The Past Is the Past** (1973). Pub. in *The Best Short Plays, 1980* (Richards, 1980).

The Black Terror (political drama, 2 acts [8 scenes], 1971). An executioner for a black terrorist group, reminiscent of the Black Panthers, begins to doubt the justification of killing other blacks to bring about improvement of the black condition, and is suspended from the organization. The author received the Drama Desk Award as the most promising playwright of 1971–72 for this play, which also won a Drama Desk Award for the leading actor, GYLAN KAIN, in the Off-Bway production. First prod. by the W.A.S.T.S.A. Players at Howard Univ., Washington, DC, Feb. 1971. Prod. Off-Bway by the NYSF Public Theatre, at the Other Stage, Nov. 19, 1971–March 26, 1972, for 180 perfs.; dir. by Nathan George. Pub. in *Scripts* 2 (NYSF/PT), 1972. In *The New Lafayette Theatre Presents* (Bullins, 1972). Unpub. script in the Schomburg Collection.

Ace Boon Coon (drama, 1 act, 1972). Dramatizes the conflicts between a person's moral beliefs and his social and political obligations. Produced by Black Arts/West, San Francisco, Feb. 1972. Unpub. script in the Hatch-Billops Collection.

Strike Heaven in the Face (political drama, full length, 1973). According to the author, "A black GI, Medal of Honor winner, returns to civilian life and really can't adjust."—*Sepia,* Jan. 1977. Prod. by the New Phoenix Theatre as a showcase production, at the Lyceum Theatre, New York, opening Jan. 15, 1973.

Goin' thru Changes (drama, 1 act, 1973). Depicts the outside presures that destroy marital relationships between black men and women. World premiere at the Eugene O'Neill Theatre Center National Playwrights Conf., Waterford, CT., Aug. 1, 1973, for 2 perfs.; dir. by Harold Scott. Prod. at the Billie Holiday Theatre, Dec. 1973–Feb. 1974; dir. by Lloyd Richards.

The Past Is the Past (drama, 1 act, 1973). Concerns a confrontation between a son and his father, who deserted his mother before he was born. Earned for the author an AUDELCO Award as playwright of the year, 1974. First prod. at the Eugene O'Neill Theatre Center National Playwrights Conf., Waterford, CT, opening Aug. 1, 1973. Prod. by the Billie Holiday Theatre, Brooklyn, Dec. 1973–Feb. 1974; dir. by Lloyd Richards. Prod. by the Manhattan Theatre Club, New York, April 27, 1975; dir. by Harold Scott. Pub. in *The Best Short Plays, 1975* (Richards, 1975). Pub. by Dramatists Play Service, New York, 1979, in a volume with the author's **Gettin' It Together.**

The Sirens (drama, 1 act, 1973). Described by the publisher as "a penetrating study of character, and the destructive cycle which so often characterizes life in a big city black ghetto. Employing a series of interlocking vignettes, made up of street encounters, dialogues and monologues, the author counterpoints the lives of two young·prostitutes; the man who earlier deserted one of them; and a high school age couple whose future is surely shadowed in the present existence of the others.'' Prod. by the author and Ed Bullins at the Manhattan Theatre Club, New York, in late May 1974; dir. by William E. Lathan. With Loretta Green, who won an Obie Award for her perf. Prod. by the Afro-American Studio, New York, opening March 17, 1978; dir. by ERNIE MCCLINTOCK. Pub. by Dramatists Play Service, New York, 1975.

The Mighty Gents // Orig. title: **The Last Street Play** (drama, full length, 1974). Former members of a Newark black street gang, now grown older, try to find their identities and to make a place for themselves in the adult world. First prod. as a play-in-progress by the Eugene O'Neill Theatre Centre National Playwrights Conf., at the Barn Theatre (outdoors), opening July 18, 1974, for 2 perfs.; dir. by James Hammerstein. Public reading, under its original title, by the Frank Silvera Writers' Workshop (FSWW), at the Urban Arts Corps (UAC), New York, Jan. 1977. Revised and produced under its original title by UAC, New York, Feb. 1977; this version also presented by the Manhattan Theatre Club on the Upstage, opening May 12, 1977. Prod. on Bway under its present title at the Ambassador Theatre, New York, April 6–23, 1978, for 9 perfs.; dir. by Harold Scott. With Morgan Freeman, Howard Rollins, and Dorian Harewood. Prod. as an outdoor production by the Mobile Theatre of NYSF, on tour of the New York City boroughs, Aug. 17–Sept. 9, 1979; dir. by NTOZAKE SHANGE. Pub. by Dramatists Play Service, New York, 1979.

Uptown Saturday Night (feature film, full length: screenplay, 1974). Based on a concept by *Sidney Poitier. A satirical comedy, set in Harlem, about two buddies who get robbed of their cash and a $50,000 winning lottery ticket. In trying to recover their losses, they become involved with the underworld and are caught in the middle of a gang war. Prod. as a First Artists Production by Melvin Tucker; dir. by Sidney Poitier; released by Warner Bros., 1974. Featuring Sidney Poitier, Bill Cosby, Harry Belafonte, RICHARD PRYOR, Flip Wilson, ROSCOE LEE BROWNE, Rosalind Cash, and Paula Kelly. Won for the author an NAACP Image Award.

Let's Do It Again (feature film, full length: screenplay, 1975). Conceived by Sidney Poitier. Musical Score by *Curtis Mayfield. A sequel to **Uptown Saturday Night** (1974). Comedy-satire, in which two members of a black lodge try to raise $50,000 for their financially defunct organization by fixing a boxing match that they are betting on and bilking some professional gamblers. Their scheme is to hypnotize a scrawny boxer (played by Jimmie Walker) into thinking that he is a superfighter. Needless to say, they run into serious trouble with the underworld. Prod. by First Artists Corp.; dir. by Sidney Poitier; released by Warner Bros., 1975. Featuring Poitier, Bill Cosby, Jimmie Walker, Calvin Lockhart, JOHN AMOS, Denise Nicholas, Lee Chamberlain, and OSSIE DAVIS, with Jayne Kennedy in a cameo role.

Cotillion (musical, full length, 1975). Adapted by Wesley, WOODIE KING, JR., and others from the novel by JOHN O. KILLENS. Satirizes the imitation of white upper-class society by the black middle classes. Prod. by Woodie King, Jr., at the New Federal Theatre, New York, July 1975.

On the Road to Babylon: A Musical Journey (musical, full length, 1979). Music and lyrics by Peter Link. Book by Wesley. Conceived and developed by Brent Nicholson. World premiere by the Milwaukee Repertory Theatre, at the Todd Wehr Theatre, Milwaukee, Dec. 14, 1979, for 46 perfs.

The Dream Team (musical, full length, 1985). Book by Wesley. Music by Tom Tierney. Lyrics by John Foster. ''About two basketball-playing brothers, one of whom is tapped for the newly integrated major leagues, while the other is not."—*Black Masks,* April 1975, p. 4. Premiered in Goodspeed-at-Chester, CT, April 23–May 19, 1985; dir. and choreographed by Dan Siretta.

Fast Forward (feature film, full length: screenplay, 1985). Based on a story by Timothy March. Described by *Jet* magazine (March 4, 1985, p. 60) as "the moving, upbeat story of eight teenagers from Sandusky, Ohio, who take off for New York City, hoping to get that one-in-a-million shot at stardom." Prod. and dir. by Sidney Poitier, with Quincy Jones as executive music producer; released by Warner Bros., 1985. With screen newcomers John Scott, Don Franklin, Tamara Mark, Gretchen Palmer, Tracy Silver, Debra Varnado, Cindy McGee, and Monique Cintron.

OTHER PLAYS AND DRAMATIC WORKS:
The Street Corner (1970). Prod. by Black Arts/West, Seattle, WA, 1970. Prod. at Lincoln Center Plaza, Summer 1972. Unpub. script in the Schomburg Collection. **Headline News** (1 act, 1970). Prod. by the Black Theatre Workshop of the New Lafayette Theatre, New York, 1970. **Steady Rapp** (1972). Believed to be an alternate title of his play **Gettin' It Together** (1971) above. Prod. by the Public Theatre, New York, 1972. **Springtime High** (1 act, 1972).

WESSON, KENNETH ALAN, Playwright, poet, psychologist, and educational consultant. Born in the San Francisco Bay area. Educated at the Univ of California/Berkeley, with undergraduate and graduate work in psychology. Has taught at San Jose State Univ, Foothill Coll., San Jose City Coll., and Santa Clara Valley Medical Centre. Has worked at Stanford Research Inst. as an educational consultant, and in 1981 was working with Laidlaw Bros. Publishing Co., the educational division of Doubleday. *Address:* 1028 Kitchener Circle, San Jose, CA 95121.

PLAY:
Miss Cegenation (drama, 3 acts, 1979). Based on the author's poem by the same title (which is also pub. along with the play). Concerns a story of miscegenation that occurred on a slave plantation in Virginia between both the master and mistress and their slaves. Pub. in *Center Stage* (Ostrow, 1981), along with the poem on which the play was based.

WEST, ALLISON, Playwright. Associated with ROGER FURMAN's New Heritage Repertory Theatre (NHRT) and the National Black Theatre (NBT) in New York City. *Address:* 193–33 85 Rd., Holliswood, NY 11423.

GROUP OF RELATED PLAYS:
"AN AFTERTASTE OF SHERRY" (2 one-act plays concerning women, 1984). Includes **Casualties** and **Lesson Plans,** described below. First prod. at P.S.W. Studios, New York, throughout the month of Oct. 1983; dir. by Sidney Best, and starring Ifeoma *(sic)* in both plays. Prod. by NBT, in association with NHRT, at NBT, June 30–Aug. 5, 1984; dir. by Andre Robinson.

PLAYS:
Casualties (1 act, 1984). "Two mothers examine their loves, sorrows, hopes, and scattered joys through the lives of their professional children." —*New York Amsterdam News,* March 4, 1984. Prod. as indicated above, 1984. **Lesson Plans** (1 act, 1984). "About two middle-aged teachers whose marriages have recently ended."—Ibid. Prod.

as indicated above, 1984. **The Catwalk** (1980s). Unpub. script and tape recording in the archives of the Frank Silvera Writers' Workshop, located in the Schomburg Collection.

WESTBROOK, EMANUEL, Playwright. Studied playwriting with the Frank Silvera Writers' Workshop (FSWW) in New York City, 1975–76.

PLAY:

In a Safe Place (comedy, 7 scenes, 1975). A miserly father is swindled out of his money by his own children. Public reading by FSWW, at Teachers, Inc., New York, Nov. 1976. Unpub. script in the FSWW Archives/Schomburg Collection.

WHITAKER, FRANCIS SCOTT KEY, Playwright.

PLAY:

Thirty Pieces of Silver (Biblical play, 47 pp., 1951). Subtitled "The Betrayal of Christ." Pub. by Exposition Press, New York, 1951.

WHITE, EDGAR B. (1947–   ), Playwright, fiction writer, musician, and composer. Born in the West Indies. Has lived in New York City; currently resides in London. Educated at CCNY (1964–65); NYU (B.A., 1968); and Yale University School of Drama (1971–73), where he was also playwright-in-residence (1971–72). The author of more than a dozen plays, several of which have been produced Off-Broadway. Has worked with the New York Shakespeare Festival (NYSF) Public Theatre and the Cincinnati Playhouse in Ohio. Has also been artistic director of the Yardbird Players Acting Co. Author of three books of fiction: *Omar at Christmas* (1973), *Sati, the Rastafarian* (1973), and *Children of Night* (1974). Also wrote *Nine Night and Ritual by Water* (1984). His short stories and a novel sketch were anthologized in *What We Must See* (Coombs, 1971), *Black Short Story Anthology* (King, 1972), and *Yardbird Reader I* (Reed, 1972). One of his radio scripts, "Survey of the Arts," was broadcast by WNYC-Radio, New York, 1973. Member of the Authors Guild of New York. Recipient of a Rockefeller Grant for Playwrights, a New York State Council Grant, and a CAPS playwriting grant. *Address:* 6 Baalbec Road, London N5. *Agent:* Marcia Abson, 22 Tavistock Street, London WC1.

COLLECTION:

UNDERGROUND: Four Plays. William Morrow, New York, 1970. Contains **The Burghers of Calais** (1970), **Fun in Lethe** (or *The Feast of Misrule),* (1970), **The Mummer's Play** (1965), **The Wonderful Year** (1969).

THE CRUCIFICADO: Two Plays. William Morrow, 1973. Contains **The Crucificado** (1971) and **The Life and Times of J. Walter Smintheus** (1971).

LAMENT FOR RASTAFARI AND OTHER PLAYS. Boyars, London, 1983. Contains **Lament for Rastafari** (1981), **Like Them That Dream** (1983), and **Trinity—The Long and Cheerful Road to Slavery** (1983).

REPRESENTATIVE PLAYS AND DRAMATIC WORKS:

The Mummer's Play (fantasy, 15 scenes, 1965). Involves two symbolic Harlem characters, Demosthenes Bellysong Jones, a retired sculptor, and his young poet friend Pariah Anon. A mythical drama with religious and historical overtones, dealing with the development and concerns of the black artist. Written when the author was only 16. First prod. in 1965. Prod. by NYSF, at the Public Theatre, 1971. Pub. in the author's *UN-DERGROUND: Four Plays*.

The Cathedral at Chartres; also known as **The Figures at Chartres** (1 act, 1968). "About a five-year old boy who is taken away from his island by an aunt who wishes to give him an American education."—*Afro-American Writers After 1955: Dramatists and Prose Writers* (Davis & Harris, 1985), p. 280. Prod. by NYSF, at the Other Stage, opening Jan. 24, 1969. Pub. in *Liberator*, July 1968.

The Wonderful Yeare (tragicomedy, 23 scenes, 1969). Symbolic play about a Puerto Rican family living in New York. According to Richard Harrier's foreword to the text, "This deeply ironic play is about the gift of life in the midst of death." "The allusion in [the title] is to London's deliverance from the plague, among other impending disasters." Prod. by NYSF, at the Other Stage, opening Oct. 24, 1969. Pub. in the author's *UNDERGROUND: Four Plays*.

The Life and Times of J. Walter Smintheus (allegorical play, 1 act, 1971). According to a review by Kushauri Kupa, this play depicts "in a humorous manner, the pitfalls and tragedies of a Black man who adopts the values and traditions of a culture that enslaves him to the degree that he can no longer identify either with his own people or with his oppressor or with himself!"—*Black Theatre* #6, 1972, p. 45. First prod. by the ANTA Matinee Theatre, at the Theatre De Lys, New York, Feb. 1971. Prod. Off-Bway by the NYSF/Public Theatre, at the Other Stage, opening April 17, 1971, for 38 perfs. Pub. in *Scripts* #6 (NYSF/PT), April 1972, pp. 4–28. In the author's *THE CRUCIFICADO: Two Plays*.

Seigismundo's Tricycle ("A Dialogue of Self and Soul" [subtitle], 1 act, 1971). Conversation between an old white man riding a silver tricycle and a crippled, old black man walking on crutches, concerning their respective lives. Prod. by NYSF, at the Public Theatre, New York, April 1971. Pub. in *Black Review No. 1* (Watkins, 1971).

The Crucificado (modern allegory, 25 scenes, 1971). To free himself from the pain of his existence in an insane, racist world, a character named Morose resorts to drugs, sex, and finally the murder of his white father. Prod. by the Urban Arts Corps (UAC), New York, June 1972. Prod. by the Frederick Douglass Creative Arts Center, New York, March 23, 1978; dir. by Basil Wallace. Pub. in the author's *THE CRUCIFICADO: Two Plays*.

Lament for Rastafari (West Indian ritual, 1971). Deals with a West Indian family which moves from the West Indies to London. Prod. by the Billie Holiday Theatre, Brooklyn, 1971. Prod. by La Mama E.T.C., New York, opening March 30, 1977; dir. by Basil Wallace. Performed by the Yardbird Players; dir. by author. Pub. in the author's *LAMENT FOR RASTAFARI AND OTHER PLAYS*.

Dija (children's fantasy, 1 act, 1972). In her dreams, a black girl is trying to find her birthday. Pub. in *Scripts* #10 (NYSF/PT), Oct. 1972, pp. 15–17

The Rastafarian (children's fantasy, 1 act, 1972). A black boy learns the meaning of death. Apparently based on his novel, *Sati: The Rastafarian* (1973). Published as a play in *Scripts* #10 (NYSF/PT), Oct. 1972, pp. 13–14.

Les Femmes Noires ("The Black Ladies") (theatrical collage, full length, 1974). Vignettes from the lives of several black women. Prod. by the NYSF, at the Public Theatre, Feb. 19–April 7, 1974; dir. by Novella Nelson.

The Pygmies and the Pyramid (allegory, 2 acts, 1976). Presents the Biblical creation story and the story of the Crucifixion in an African version. Prod. by the Yardbird Theatre Co., New York, Aug. 1976.

The Defense (fantasy, 23 scenes, 1976). With music composed by White. In a dream concerning his death, a guard in a New York housing project conducts an imaginary defense of his life. First prod. by the National Playwrights Conf. of the Eugene O'Neill Theatre Center, in the Amphitheatre, Waterford, CT, opening July 30, 1976, for 2 perfs.; dir. by Dennis Scott. Prod. by the New Federal Theatre, at the Henry Street Settlement, New York, opening Nov. 11, 1976; also dir. by Dennis Scott.

Trinity—The Long and Cheerful Road to Slavery (trilogy of short plays, 1982). "Explores the cultural consequences of the forcible abduction of so many Africans, of neo-colonialism in Africa, and of the sociopolitical restrictions thrust upon West Indians by the British."—*Afro-American Writers After 1955: Dramatists and Prose Writers* (Davis & Harris, 1985), p. 283. Prod. at the Riverside Studio, London, Feb. 25, 1982.

OTHER PLAYS AND DRAMATIC WORKS:

La Gente ("The People") (drama, 1973). Prod. by NYSF, at Astoria Park, Queens, NY, July 18, 1973. **Ode to Charlie Parker** (1973). Subtitled "Study for Sunlight in Park." Prod. by Studio Rivbea, New York, opening Sept. 28, 1973. **Offering for Nightworld** (morality, 1973). Prod. by the BTA Festival, at the Brooklyn Acad. of Music, New York, 1973. **Masada** (South African ritual, 1979). Prod. at the Royal Court Theatre, London, 1979. **Like Them That Dream** (1983). Subtitled "Children of Ogun." About the racial strife in South Africa. Prod. by the Roger Furman Theatre, New York, Nov. 13–Dec. 7, 1986; dir. by Andre Robinson, Jr. Pub. in the author's *LAMENT FOR RASTAFARI AND OTHER PLAYS*.

WHITE, JAMES E., III, Playwright. Based in Washington, DC.

PLAYS:

The Candy Store Is Still Closed (domestic drama, 2 acts, 1973). Explores the conflicts within a black family in the South, between a subservient older brother who must get along with "the white folks" in order to support the family, and a militant younger brother who wishes to rebel. **Don't Go to Strangers** (2 acts, 1974). About the mistreatment of a widowed mother by her son and his family, who send her to a nursing home when she comes to live with them, and her rebellion against this mistreatment. **African Adventure** (historical ritual, 1 act, 1975). About the conflicts within an African tribe, concerning the relative merits of the white man's materialism and its own cultural values and traditions.

WHITE, JOSEPH (1933–   ), Playwright, poet, short-story writer, radio announcer, newspaper columnist, and public information specialist. Born in Philadelphia, PA, where he graduated from Southside H.S. in 1952. Resides in Newark, NJ, where he has worked since 1967 as a newspaper columnist for the *Newark News,* and since 1969 as a radio announcer for Newark's Radio Station WNJR. Has also served as public information director in community antipoverty, employment, and manpower programs in New York and New Jersey during the 1960s. A discovery of AMIRI BARAKA, his plays have been produced by Baraka's Black Arts Repertory Theatre in Harlem during its short life between 1964 and 1966, and by Baraka's Spirit House Movers and Players in Newark. His short stories have been published in *Liberator;* his poetry has been published in *Dasein* and anthologized in the *Afro-Arts Anthology* (1960s), *Poets of Today*

(Lowenfels, 1964), and *The Poetry of Black America* (Adoff, 1972). Recipient of a John Hay Whitney Fellowship, 1963–64, and a New York Council on the Arts grant, 1969. *Address:* 74 Barclay Street, Newark, NJ 07103.

PLAYS:

The Leader (satire, 1 act [7 scenes], 1968). A flamboyant black leader is allowed to burn to death in a fire which he has staged for publicity purposes, because his idealistic young aide (who was supposed to put out the fire) believes that the leader has become more interested in prestige, publicity, power, and white women than in helping black people. Presumed to have been produced by the Black Arts Theatre in Harlem, prior to its Off-Bway premiere at the Old Reliable Theatre Tavern, New York, opening Feb. 5, 1968. Prod. (presumably by the Spirit House Movers and Players) at the Freedom Community Workshop, Newark, Oct. 18, 1968. Prod. by Kuumba House, Newark, 1970. Pub. in *Black Fire* (Jones & Neal, 1968).

Old Judge Mose Is Dead // Also known as **Old Judge Mose** (satire, 1 act, 1968). Two black laborers in a southern funeral establishment take out their vengeance on white folks by insulting two corpses that they hated when alive—Old Judge Mose and Miss Ann, a former post office worker. But when the white undertaker brings the Judge's grieving daughter in to view her father's body, the blacks return to their accustomed pretence of docility, subservience, and respect in the presence of whites. First prod. by Freedom Community Workshop, Newark, opening Oct. 18, 1968. Prod. by the Hudson Guild Theatre, New York City, opening Aug. 27, 1969. Pub. in *The Drama Review,* Summer 1968, pp. 151–57.

The Hustle (drama, 1 act, 1970). A companion play to **The Leader** (1968), with which it was prod. on a double bill. According to one reviewer, "Both *[The Leader* and *The Hustle]* are ideal for street theatre productions, and as one-act plays, they are just what the doctor ordered for those small Black theatres that are in search of scripts that do not require elaborate sets or large casts. They are humorous and enlightening. Brother White's insights into the decadence of Western life are the meat of both plays.''—Kushauri Kupa, *Black Theatre* #5, 1971, p. 53. Prod. by Kuumba House, Newark, Spring 1970.

WHITEHEAD, JAMES X., Playwright. Inmate of Norfolk (VA) Prison at the time he wrote the following play.

PLAY:

Justice or Just Us (Part II) (1 act, 1972). Gives reasons, from a prisoner's point of view, as to why a parole board should not be allowed to determine whether or not a prisoner is ready for release. Pub. in *Who Took the Weight?* (Norfolk Prison Bros., 1972).

WHITFIELD, GRADY D., Poet-playwright and TV technician. A native of Valdosta, GA, where he attended the public schools. Attended the School of New Resources at the Coll. of New Rochelle, NY, 1975–79; Long Island Univ./ Brooklyn Centre, 1979–81; Third World Cinema's TV News Workshop, 1971; and Channel 13 (New York) PBS's advanced TV program classes, 1975. Worked as the first black TV news cameraman at WCTV, Channel 6 in North Carolina. Served in the U.S. Army, 7th Infantry, stationed in Aschaffenburg, Germany, early 1980s. Member of DG, Harlem Writers Guild, Atlanta Black Press Assn., Negro Ensemble Co. (NEC) Writers Workshop, New York Shakespeare Festival/

Public Theatre (NYSF/PT) Playwrights Workshop, and a contributor to the Frank Silvera Writers' Workshop (FSWW). *Address:* c/o The Emma Hall Memorial Projects, 716 Third Ave., Valdosta, GA 31601.

REPRESENTATIVE PLAYS AND DRAMATIC WORKS:

Trapped in Cobweb // Orig. title: **Spiritually Trapped** (drama, 3 acts, 1974). Subtitled "A Woman's World." A young minister's daughter seeks revenge on a white politician for causing the death of her father and baby sister. Public reading by FSWW, at the Harlem Performance Center, New York, Nov. 1976.

The Legend of Ira Imhotep // Orig. title: **Beyond Fear** (drama, 1 act, 1975). A ghost story, involving the return of the dead, cutting off of a head, and moving objects. Deals with the tragic life of a half black Iroquois Indian from the Seneca tribe. Developed at NEC's Playwrights Unit, under the direction of STEVE CARTER, 1975. Tested in ED BULLINS's Workshop at the NYSF/PT, 1975. First presented during the summer of 1979 at Brooklyn's Prospect Park, at the historic Grecian Shelter, where it was again presented during the summers of 1979 and 1980. Prod. in Aschaffenburg, Germany, at Graves Recreation Center, Feb. 27, 1983, while the author was in the U.S. Infantry.

All About Money (morality play, 1 act, 1976). A young ex-con, now working for the Social Security Administration, believing that his mother is dead, and having no money to go home, raises the money by letting a prostitute and her unsavory friends operate from his sleazy mid-Manhattan hotel room. Among the characters are a cosmetic saleslady, a gambler, a lesbian, a revolutionary, and a homosexual. Public reading by FSWW, at the Teachers, Inc., New York, Jan. 1976.

David, Sara, and Hannibal (drama, 2 acts, 1979). The story of two circus-performer brothers, born with their backs joined, who were separated while they were babies. Because both of their parents (one white, one black) had been injured in a circus accident, resulting in the death of the father and the permanent disabling of the mother, one of the brothers wishes to give up the circus life, while the other desires to continue working in the dangerous duo act. First presented by the Student Activities of the Borough of Manhattan's Community Coll., Spring 1979. Performed at the Triangle Theatre at Long Island Univ./Brooklyn Center, 1980, during Martin Luther King's birthday celebration.

Chasing Dreams Is the Message (drama, 1980). Public reading by NEC's Developmental Stages (a series of evening readings), April 18, 1980; dir. by Steve Carter. With SAMM-ART WILLIAMS, Frances Foster, and REGINALD VEL JOHNSON.

OTHER PLAYS AND DRAMATIC WORKS:

The Missions of Eugene Bullard (1984). About one of the first black Americans to become a fighter pilot. **The Boys' Night Out** (comedy, pre-1985). About a blind man named Eddie who lost his sight in Hawaii during the Japanese raid on an American air base. Deals with Eddie's need to be accepted by everyone as a whole man. **Kamellia Dear Heart** (2 acts, pre-1985). Deals with the social and judicia system of a small southern town (Valdosta, GA). An "I-Know-Who-Done-It," based on a triangular adultery plot. After Kamellia murders her husband and his lover, the local detective falls in love with her and tries to save her by pinning the killings on a drunk. **Moses** (musical, 1985). Under consideration for prodn. by AMAS Repertory Theatre, according to the playwright.

WHITFIELD, VANTILE (Motojicho) (1930–   ), Director, scenic designer, playwright, arts consultant, and editor. Born in Washington, DC. Educated at Howard Univ. (B.A., 1957) and the Univ. of California (M.A., 1960). Served in the U.S. Air Force, 1950–51. Married; two children. Instr., Howard Univ., 1957–58; production manager and arts director, Ad Graphics of Hollywood, 1960–61; cofounder and general manager, American Theatre of Being, 1963–64; instr., Los Angeles School District, 1965–66; set designer, Universal City Studios, 1966–67; founder-director, Performing Arts Soc. of Los Angeles (PASLA), 1966–71; guest artistic director, DC Black Repertory Co. (DC/BRC), Washington, DC, 1970s; director, Expansion Arts, NEA, Washington, and currently associated with Arts Media Services, Washington, which publishes *GAP*, a periodical also edited by Whitfield. Scenic designer for the New York production of *The Amen Corner* (1965); director of *Give Me Back My Drum, The Lonely Crowd,* and *Tear Them Pillars Down* (all 1969) for PASLA; director and lighting manager of *Day of Absence* (1975) for DC/BRC. Member of DGA, SAG, AFTRA. Recipient of awards from the city of Los Angeles, 1968; Hollywood/Beverly Hills NAACP (Image Award), 1969; National Assn. of Media Women, 1970; and Los Angeles Critics' Circle, 1970. *Address:* Arts Media Services, 1940 Fifteenth St., N.W., Washington, DC 20009.

PLAYS AND DRAMATIC WORKS:
The Creeps (1 act, 1960). **In Sickness and in Health** (1 act, 1966). **Changes** (musical, full length, 1973). Book by Motojicho. Music and lyrics by Valerian Smith. According to a description by Jeanne-Marie A. Miller *(Black World,* April 1974, pp. 59–60), "Here were heard the language styles familiar to Blacks—the 'dozens,' tall tales, street rhymes. In some places *Changes* faintly recalled Melvin Van Peebles' *Ain't Supposed to Die a Natural Death.* In the Motojicho-Smith production, contemporary problems were colored by race. The generation gap, for example, pitted the young Blacks' concept of the proper life-style against their middle-class parents' desire to assimilate and to accept, without question, the values of the dominant race." Prod. by DC/BRC, opening Dec. 6, 1973, for 47 perfs.; dir. by Motojicho. **Daybreak Dreams** (musical, full length, 1975). Described by the *Washington Star News,* Sept. 30, 1975, as "a Tribute to Two Poets." **Wanted** (1973). Prod. by DC/BRC, 1973.

WHITNEY, ELVIE (Elvie A. Moore), Playwright. Based in the Watts area of Los Angeles, CA, where she was associated with the Douglass House Foundation.

PLAYS AND DRAMATIC WORKS:
(All apparently prod. by the Douglass House Foundation.) **Center of Darkness** (1 act, 1968). **Up a Little Higher** (1 act, 1968). **Pornoff** (1 act, 1969). **Angela Is Happening** (pageant/ritual, 1 act, 1971). Angela Davis's trial is observed and commented on by various historical characters who have participated in the black struggle, including Frederick Douglass, John Brown, and Harriet Tubman. Prod. March 1971. Pub. in *The Disinherited* (Ravitz, 1971); copy in the Hatch-Billops Collection, where the author's unpub. manuscript is also located. **Bring the House Down** (drama, pre-1976).

WHITTEN, JAMES, Playwright. Formerly associated with the Players Workshop in New York City.

PLAY:

Traps (drama, 1 act, 1974). Explores the difficulty of prison inmates and their families who come to visit them to reach out to each other. Performed by a group of mainly ex-inmates called The Family. Presented at the Players Workshop, New York, 1974; dir. by Clay Stevenson. Also presented by the Afro-American Studio, New York, 1974.

WILKERSON, MARGARET B. (Buford) (1938–   ), Playwright, author, and educator. Born in Los Angeles, CA. Educated at Univ. of Redlands (B.A., 1959), UCLA (1961), Univ. of California/Berkeley (M.A., 1967; Ph.D., 1972). Married; three children. Former director, Centre for the Study, Education and Advancement of Women, UC/Berkeley; currently assoc. prof. in the Afro-American Studies Dept. Founder-director, Kumoja Players, Richmond, CA. Has published and lectured on equal education, blacks in higher education, and black theatre and playwrights. Author of articles in *The Drama Review, Black American Literature Forum, Essays on Contemporary American Drama* (Hueber, 1981), and other publications. Wrote the introduction to *Lorraine Hansberry: The Collected Last Plays* (New American Lib., 1983) and is currently writing a literary biography of Hansberry. Editor of *Nine Plays by Black Women* (1986). Former vice pres., American Theatre Assn., having served for four years as chair of ATA's Black Theatre Program Member, Black World Foundation; American Soc. for Theatre Research; American Assn. for Higher Education; National Council of Negro Women. Recipient of a Ford Foundation fellowship, 1970. *Address*—Home: 8 Highgate Rd., Kensington, CA 94707. Office: Dept. of Afro-American Studies, University of California/Berkeley, 3335 Dwinelle Hall, Berkeley, CA 94720.

PLAY:

The Funeral (drama, 2 acts, 1975). Dramatizes the perspectives and reactions of a black family to the death of an elder. The concluding scene replicates a traditional southern black funeral with songs and sermon in celebration of life. Performed by the Kumoja Players, Richmond, CA, at the Sojourner Truth Presbyterian Church, on weekends, Sept. 26–Oct. 18, 1975; dir. by author.

WILKINS, PAT (Patricia). See MANDULO, RHEA MAKEDA ZAWADIE.

WILKS, PETER YOUNG, III (Jiwe Alamaji), Playwright. Associated with the Frank Silvera Writers' Workshop (FSWW) in New York City.

PLAYS:

Space Brother (fantasy, 2 acts, 1974). Futuristic play concerning an encounter between a black man from another planet and a black American family, in which the "Space Brother" finds it difficult to understand the strict moral code of the father. Unpub. script in the FSWW Archives/Schomburg Collection. **The Long-Game Merfy** (pre-1976). **The Soul of Willy** (pre-1976).

WILLIAMS, ANITA JANE, Playwright and music enthusiast. Born in Houston, TX, where she wrote her first play at age 16. Studied playwriting at San Francisco State Univ., from which she graduated with a B.A. in sociology and anthropology and an M.A. in elementary education. Studied voice at the San Francisco Conservatory of Music. She is interested in the origins of black music and has done extensive research tracing modern-day rhythm and blues back to its roots among the African slaves. She was a contestant on the "Name That Tune" program and has done radio broadcasting and appeared on local television. Her plays have been produced by the Black Repertory Group in Berkeley, CA. *Address:* 419 Arch St., San Francisco, CA 94132.

PLAYS:

A Christmas Story // Orig. title: **A Turkey Tale** (comedy, 1 act, 1979). Based on a true family incident. Written while a student in Ernest White's course at San Francisco State Univ. Extension. Deals with the problem of senility among the elderly. Grandma Freeman, hopelessly senile, steals the Christmas turkey and the family silverware from the kitchen and hides them in her room. The plot revolves around the family's attempt to secure the turkey and silver in time to have Christmas dinner prepared for the guests and relatives who will soon arrive. Prod. by the Black Repertory Group in Berkeley, 1979–80. Pub. in *Center Stage* (Ostrow, 1981).

The First Militant Protest of 42nd Street (drama, 1 act, 1980). Because of racial indignities suffered by a black basketball player while traveling North from his college in Virginia in 1959, the player decides to withdraw from his position as center on the team, which has been selected to play in the 1960 summer Olympic Games in Rome. The plot revolves around the player's attempt, with the aid of his family, to persuade his father to accept and support his decision to relinquish his place as center on the team in order to protest racial conditions in the South. The father is a conservative patriarch who still believes that the battle for racial equality lies in excellence and submissiveness. An important character is the young man's sister, who conducts a protest of her own. Prod. by the Black Repertory Group, Spring 1982.

WILLIAMS, CURTIS L. (Leroy) (1939–   ), Playwright, actor, director, and university professor. Born in KauKeenah, FL. Educated at Friendship Jr. Coll. (A.A. in liberal arts, 1959); Morehouse Coll. (B.A. in English, 1961); Atlanta Univ. (M.A. in English, 1962); and the Univ. of Texas at Austin (Ph.D. in drama, with playwriting emphasis, 1977). Married; father of two children. English instr., South Carolina State Coll., Orangeburg, 1963–64; teaching asst., Drama Dept., Univ. of Texas/Austin, 1973–74; currently assoc. prof. and chairman, Speech and Theatre, Albany State Coll., 1965–present (on study leave, 1973–76). Organizational memberships include AAUP, ATA, Georgia Theatre Conf., Modern Language Association, NADSA, and Phi Kappa Phi. Recipient of basketball scholarship, Friendship Jr. Coll., 1959–60; tuition scholarship, Morehouse Coll., 1959; regional fellowship, Atlanta Univ., 1961–62; Merrill Foreign Study-Travel Fellowship, Atlanta Univ., 1973–74; and university fellowship, Univ. of Texas/Austin, 1974–76. *Address:* 5726 Periwinkle Way, Albany, GA 31707.

COLLECTION:
"TWO PLAYS ON THE BLACK EXPERIENCE: FROM CONCEPTION TO PRO-
DUCTION." Ph.D. dissertation, Univ. of Texas/Austin, 1977. Available from University
Microfilms International, Ann Arbor, MI. Contains **Ghetto Vampire** (1973) and **Crispus
Attucks** (1973).

REPRESENTATIVE PLAYS AND DRAMATIC WORKS:
The Auction (domestic drama, 1 act, 1970). A mother's dilemma—shall she bury her
dead son or sell his body to a foundation in order to get the money desperately needed
to support the rest of her children? Prod. at Albany State Coll., Albany, GA; Georgia
Theatre Conf.; Bowling Green State Univ., Ohio; Bed-Stuy Theatre New York; and the
Univ. of Texas/Austin, since 1970.
Single Indemnity (drama, 2 acts, 1972). A terminally ill young man makes a desperate
attempt to leave some insurance to his wife and brother. Prod. at Albany State Coll. and
Savannah State Coll., Savannah, GA, since 1972.
Ghetto Vampire (comedy with music, 2 acts, 1973). Music (8 songs) by T. MAR-
SHALL JONES. "About Blacks trying to join a vampire union and thus improve their
status in American society. . . . A chronicle of discrimination on various levels."—Au-
thor's Ph.D. dissertation, cited below. First prod. at Albany State Coll., opening Feb.
20, 1973, for a three-day run. Extensively rewritten and prod. by the Afro-American
Players of Austin, TX, at the Methodist Student Center, opening Oct. 24, 1975, for a
five-week run of Fri. and Sat. night perfs. Unpub. script included in the author's Ph.D.
dissertation, "TWO PLAYS ON THE BLACK EXPERIENCE: FROM CONCEPTION
TO PRODUCTION" [see COLLECTION above].
M-ssing in Act-on (drama, 2 acts, 1974). A Vietnam veteran tries to adjust to having
lost his phallus during the war. Public reading in Conkle Workshop at the Univ. of Texas/
Austin, 1974.
Swap Face (children's play with music, 1 long act, 1974). Music (6 songs) by T.
Marshall Jones. Swap Face goes to the magic forest of San Ban Tisco to demand a new
face of Mr. Meanie, to whom he has sent his old socially rejected face. Hocus Pocus is
Swap Face's ally. Prod. at Albany State Coll., 1978. Pub. in *Encore* magazine, 1975.
Maiden Voyage (drama, 2 acts, 1976). Lorenzo Stamper comes back to his home
town as a preacher and must face those who remember him as an agnostic and criminal.
To further threaten his newfound career, he becomes involved in a murder. Prod. at
Albany State Coll., Nov. 1976.
Boy Child (ritual, 1 long act, 1981). While playing a prank, a man, unaware of his
kinship with an ancient tribe of African mystics, grants a father a long desired son. The
child can survive birth only if the father decides to give up his own life, which he cherishes
above all else. Prod. at Albany State Coll. as part of Pres. Billie C. Black's Inaugural
Week, 1981.
The Day the Devil Went Out of Business (comedy-satire, 1 act, 1982). Tired of
people scandalizing his name and generally making life miserable for him, H.O.T. Devil
decides to sell out. His decision is complicated by special interest groups (including Rev.
Rev) who encourage him to stay in business. Prod. at Albany State Coll., for Summer
Children's Play, 1982.

OTHER PLAYS AND DRAMATIC WORKS:
Synthesis (1963). Prod. at a drama festival in Greensboro, NC, and at Savannah State
Coll., since 1963. **Frozen Tears** (1967). Prod. at Albany State Coll., 1967. (Title song

written by T. Marshall Jones.) **Say Grace** (1970). Prod. at Albany State Coll.; Georgia Theatre Conf.; Hampton Inst., Hampton, VA; and Washington, DC, since 1970. Pub. in *The Art of Organizational Management from the Director's Approach* (H. D. Flowers, 1982). **Fairy Tales** (1973). Prod. at Albany State Coll., 1973. **Brick by Brick** (historical doc., full length, 1978). An adaptn. of autobiographical materials of Joseph W. Holly, founder of Albany State Coll. **The Foreshadowing** (historical doc., full length, 1982). Based on autobiographical materials of Pres. J. W. Holley, founder of Albany State Coll. Written and prod. by the college for Founder's Day, 1983.

WILLIAMS, EDWARD G. (1929–   ), Novelist, short-story writer, and playwright. Born in Fayetteville, NC. Educated at Virginia State Coll., Norfolk, VA Branch (now Norfolk State Univ.), 1950; CCNY; and NYU, Coll. of Continuing Education. Currently resides in Brooklyn, NY. Supervised a staff of typists at the U.N., 1959–63. Writer of promotional material and traffic manager in Promotion Dept., New York *Herald Tribune*, 1963–67. Manager of Traffic Dept., S. R. Leon Advertising Agency, 1967. Freelance writer, 1967–present. Under the auspices of the New York Chapter of P.E.N., he conducted a writers' workshop at Daytop Village, a drug rehabilitation program in New York City. Author of a novel, *Not Like Niggers* (1969). His nonfiction has appeared in the *Christian Science Monitor*. *Address:* 20 St. James Place, Brooklyn, NY 11205.

PLAYS:
Great Day for a Funeral (domestic drama, 2 acts, 1974). Dramatization of his short story by the same title, which deals with conflicts that arise among family members after the death of a husband. Public reading by the Frank Silvera Writers' Workshop (FSWW), New York, Oct. 1975. Unpub. script and tape recording in the FSWW Archives/Schomburg Collection. **Remembrance of a Lost Dream** (1976). Public reading by FSWW at the Harlem Cultural Council, New York, May 1976. Unpub. script and tape recording in the FSWW Archives/Schomburg Collection.

WILLIAMS, ELWOODSON, Actor-playwright. Born in Jacksonville, NC. Now living in New York City. Graduated from Tennessee A. & T. State Univ., Nashville. Since 1968 has appeared in the following Off-Broadway productions: *Cadillac Dreams, A Land Beyond the River, Voice Machine, A Man's a Man, Cry the Beloved Country, Mercury Island, Middle-Class Black, Ceremonies in Dark Old Men, Murderous Angels,* and *The Adding Machine.* Made his Broadway debut in *Two Gentlemen of Verona* (1971). Member of the Frank Silvera Writers' Workshop (FSWW) in New York City. *Address:* 176 W. 87th St., New York, NY 10024.

PLAYS:
Voice of the Gene (drama, 3 acts, 1969). Concerns the problems of color-consciousness among middle-class blacks. A fair-skinned black father rejects his darker son in favor of the lighter. Prod. by the Bed-Study Theatre, Brooklyn, Aug. 1969. Public reading by FSWW, April 17, 1978. Prod. at Theatre 22, New York, Nov. 12–25, 1984; dir. by Enie Ativie. Unpub. script in the FSWW Archives/Schomburg Collection. **Mine Eyes Have Seen the Glory** (biographical drama, 3 acts, 1970). Dramatizes the life of Booker

T. Washington. **Only Her Barber Knows for Sure** (1977). Public reading by FSWW, at the Studio Museum of Harlem, New York, March 1977. Unpub. script in the FSWW Archives/Schomburg Collection. **Tale of an Instant Junkie** (1978). Public reading by FSWW, Jan. 30, 1978. Unpub. script in the FSWW Archives/Schomburg Collection. **The Peanut Man** (1970s). About George Washington Carter. Unpub. script and tape recording in the FSWW Archives/Schomburg Collection. **What Would Happen if the World Turned Red** (1970s). Unpub. script and tape recording in the FSWW Archives/ Schomburg Collection.

WILLIAMS, JOHN A. (Alfred) (1925–   ), Author, editor, and playwright. Born in Jackson, MS. Currently resides in Newark, NJ. His novels include *The Angry Ones* (1960; repub. as *One for New York,* 1975), *Night Song* (1962), *Sissie* (1963; repub. as *Journey Out of Anger,* 1965), *The Man Who Cried I Am* (1968), *Sons of Darkness, Sons of Light* (1969), *Captain Blackman* (1972), *Mothersill and the Foxes* (1975), *The Junior Bachelor Society* (1976), and *!Click Song* (1982). Editor of *The Angry Black* (1962), *Beyond the Angry Black* (1971), *Amistad 1* (1970), and *Amistad 2* (1971). His nonfiction, poetry, short stories, and criticism have been widely published in periodicals and anthologies.

DRAMATIC WORKS:
Sweet Love, Bitter (Screenplay, 1967). Apparently prod. by Film 2 Assocs., 1967. **Reprieve for All God's Children** (drama, pre-1975). **(The) Sophisticated Gents** (TV mini-series, 4 hrs., 1981). Adapt. from his novel *The Junior Bachelor Society.* Screenplay by MELVIN VAN PEEBLES. Concerns the events that occur during a 25–year reunion of nine members of a black athletic-social club for a testimonial banquet in honor of their football coach—the man who was responsible for molding their lives. One of the returning members is a pimp who is wanted for murder. Prod. for three nights as a four-hour mini-series on NBC, opening Sept. 29, 1981; dir. by Harry Falk. With Bernie Casey (as the coach), Rosie Grier, Robert Hooks, Ron O'Neal, Thalmus Rasulala, Raymond St. Jacques, Melvin Van Peebles (as the pimp), Dick Anthony Williams, Paul Winfield, and Albert Hall.

WILLIAMS, JUNE VANLEER (Jay Vanleer; also Van Leer), Actress, jour-nalist, poet, casting director, and playwright. Received the B.A. from Case Western Reserve Univ., and has done further study at Stanford Univ. on a Professional Journalism Fellowship, 1970. Served as public information spe-cialist in the air force during the Korean War. Has written two volumes of poetry: *Will the Real You Stand Up* and *Moments in Repose.* Has earned both stage and film credits under the name of Jay Vanleer (also spelled Van Leer). Performed on Broadway in *Don't Play Us Cheap!* (1972). Participated in the National Playwrights Conf. of the Eugene O'Neill Theatre Centre, Waterford, CT, during the mid-1970s, and performed in several showcase productions at the conference, including *You're Too Tall, But Come Back in Two Weeks, The Juice Problem,* and *Every Night When the Sun Goes Down.* In 1965 she coordinated Karamu House's Golden Anniversary celebration. Has lectured at Cuyahoga Community Coll., Cleveland State Univ., and the Univ. of Mexico. Member of the Overseas

Press Club, the Authors League of America, DG, AEA, and SAG. Recipient of a journalism award from the Ohio Bar Assn. for the year's (1969) best story in the cause of jurisprudence. *Address:* 1588 Ansel Rd. #508, Cleveland, OH 44106. *Agent:* Bertha Klausner, International Literary Agency, 71 Park Ave., New York, NY 10016.

PLAYS AND DRAMATIC WORKS:

The Eyes of the Lofty (drama, 1 act, c. 1965). Concerns the conflicts and problems that arise between a retired vaudeville performer and his son and daughter-in-law, with whom he is forced to live. Prod. by Karamu House, Cleveland, around 1965.

The Face of Job (drama, 3 acts, 1975). Concerns the conflicts, greed, and malice that erupt within an important black family following the death and reading of the will of a strong black matriarch. Staged reading by the Frank Silvera Writers' Workshop (FSWW), at the Martinique Theatre, New York, Oct. 1975. Unpub. script in the FSWW Archives/Schomburg Collection.

The Wandering Sons of Ham (musical, full length, pre-1977). The story of the triumphs and tribulations in the careers of the two most famous musical comedy stars of the turn of the century, †Bert Williams and †George Walker, who appeared in such musicals as *Sons of Ham, In Dahomey, Abyssinia,* and *Bandanna Land.* Includes musical numbers from their most successful shows.

A Bit of Almsgiving (drama, 2 acts, pre-1985). Concerns the psychological, interpersonal relationships among two sisters, a mother, and a husband, and the effect of the dominant sister on her family and associates.

Hollow Daze (one-woman show, full length, pre-1985). A dramatic portrayal of the life of Billie Holliday, interspersed with her music. Approximately 18 songs.

WILLIAMS, MANCE, Playwright.

PLAY:

What's the Use of Hanging On? (dialogue, 1 act, 1970s). Two "soul brothers" debate the goals and possibilities of the black rebellion, and whether or not there is any use in "hanging on" Pub. in *Roots* (Texas Southern Univ., Houston), 1970.

WILLIAMS, MARSHALL, Lighting designer and playwright, associated with the Negro Ensemble Co. (NEC) in New York City. His lighting credits include *The Song of the Lusitanian Bogey* (1968), *God Is a (Guess What?)* (1968), *Open 24 Hours* (1969), *High John De Conquer* (1969), *But Never Jam Today* (1969), and *A Black Quartet* (1969). *Address:* 319 Convent Ave., New York, NY 10031.

PLAYS:

The Diary of a Black Revolutionary (monologue, 1 act, 1974). Satirical tour de force on the black militant plays of the 1960s, delivered from the prison cell of the revolutionary. Prod. by the Weusi Kuumba Troupe, at the New Lafayette Theatre in Harlem, as one of a series of one-act plays presented under the collective title *Yesterday, Today, Tomorrow Plus 7 Principles.* **A Tear for Judas** (1975). A reworking of the Orpheus legend, suggested by "The Coming of John" from †W.E.B. Du Bois's *The Souls of Black Folk.* Presented at the Freedom Theatre, Philadelphia, PA, Nov. 1975. One scene was presented on local television. **The Tenant** (comedy, 2 acts, 1982). Based on the Biblical story of Joseph and Mary, the two-character play centers around a young middle-class black couple. Presented as a workshop production by the Theatre for the New City, New York, Feb. 25, 1982; dir. by Anthony Major. **Go Start the Rainbow** (pre-1985). Unpub. script in the Archives of the Frank Silvera Writers' Workshop (FSWW)/Schomburg Collection.

WILLIAMS, OSCAR (1939–   ), Filmmaker, producer, director, and screenwriter. Born in the Virgin Islands. Educated at Lagos Egri School of Writing; New York Community Coll.; CCNY; San Francisco State Coll. (B.A., M.A. in radio, TV, and film); U.S. Army Signal Corps (cinematography, 1963), and American Film Inst. (AFI), 1972. He was an AFI intern on the production of *The Great White Hope* (1970) and directed *Five on the Black Hand Side* (1973), which premiered at the Kennedy Center, Washington, DC.

DRAMATIC WORKS:

Sudden Death (film, full length: screenplay, 1970?).

The Final Comedown (feature film, full length: screenplay, 1970). According to James Murray, writing in *Black Creation* (Fall 1972, p. 64), "This independent film attempts . . . to say something relevant about Black revolution" and "presents a grim, bloody gun battle between Black militants and police in ghetto alleys." Prod. and dir. by author, 1970; released by New World Pictures, 1972. With Billy Dee Williams, D'Urville Martin, Cecilia Kaye, and Raymond St. Jacques.

Black Belt Jones (feature film, full length: screenplay, 1974). Based on a story by Alex Rose and Fred Weintraub. Black martial arts film for the Kung-Fu market, designed as a sequel to *Enter the Dragon*. Some black students of martial arts are pitted against a group of white gangsters who pursue them throughout the film. Prod. by Fred Weintraub and Paul Heller; dir. by Robert Clouse. Released by Warner Bros., 1974. With Jim Kelly in the title role.

Truck Turner (feature film, full length: screenplay, 1974). Written with Leigh Chapman and Michael Allin. Black exploitation melodrama on the bounty-hunting theme, with the usual mixture of pimps, prostitutes, gun battles, car chases, and blood. Prod. by Paul Heller and Fred Weintraub; dir. by Jonathan Kaplan. Released by American International, 1974. With Isaac Hayes in the title role.

Hot Potato (feature film, full length: screenplay, 1976). Martial arts film, set in Thailand, starring Jim Kelly as a karate expert whose mission is to rescue a senator's daughter who has been kidnapped by an oriental villain. Prod. 1976; dir. by Williams.

WILLIAMS, ROBYN CLAIRE, Playwright and screenwriter. Winner of the Lorraine Hansberry Playwriting Award in the American Coll. Theatre Festival, 1983. Based in California Educated at Northwestern Univ. (B.S. in theatre, 1983), and the American Conservatory Theatre (ACT) in San Francisco. Currently a member of Theatre of N.O.T.E. and a major participant in their playwrights' workshops. *Address*—Current: 1645 N. Vista, Apt. 3, Hollywood, CA 90046. Permanent: 458 Michigan Ave., Berkeley, CA 94707.

PLAYS AND DRAMATIC WORKS:

Operation: Second Chance (drama, full length, 1982). A shuttle crew of seven, in the midst of a three-month cabin fever, rediscovers a form of home that humanity has lost sight of. Prod. as a workshop production at Northwestern Univ., 1982. **The Confidant** (drama, 1 act, 1983). In the course of an evening, a young girl learns the simple sad reality—that her idolized father isn't perfect. **Snooks McAllister Lives at My House** (drama, full length, 1983). A white foster family brings a black juvenile delinquent girl into their home and the conflicts arise as the street gang with which the girl affiliates refuses to release their hold on her. Prod. as a workshop production at Northwestern Univ., 1983. Prod. at Loyola Univ., 1983, and entered in the American Coll. Theatre Festival (ACTF), where it won the Lorraine Hansberry Award. Also prod. at Eden Theatre in Denver, CO. Currently being adapt. to a screenplay. **Snowbird and Thumper** (screenplay, 1984). An unusual friendship of mutual need develops between three teenagers: a heroin addict, a car thief, and the high school BMOC (Big Man on Campus). Script available through Scott Schwartz, ICM (International Creative Management), 8899 Beverly Blvd., Los Angeles, CA 90048. **The Company We Keep** (screenplay, 1985). Coauthor, with *Maiya Williams. A coterie of the New York jet set, headed by a famed gossip columnist/commentator, find themselves engulfed within wit, murder, and mayhem. **The World of Finn** (drama, full length, 1986). A young man who has finally maintained a balanced security between his estranged Texan family and his homosexual lifestyle sees his cherished homestead go awry as his lover threatens to leave him for a woman and the arrival of his bitter sister tips the scales.

WILLIAMS, SAMM-ART (1946–   ), Actor-playwright. Born in Burgaw, NC, a small town near Jacksonville and Wilmington. Decided at an early age to become a writer, and was encouraged by his mother, who was a high school English teacher and drama director, and who provided him with his first opportunities to perform in the plays which she directed. Attended Morgan State Coll. in Baltimore, graduating in 1968. There he participated in athletics and continued to write, but was unable to find an outlet in drama. At Morgan, he majored in political science, with the intent of becoming a civil rights lawyer. Moved to Philadelphia in 1968, where he joined the Freedom Theatre, wrote poetry, and gained the acting experience which would give him entry in the New York theatre. In 1974 he joined the Playwrights Workshop of the Negro Ensemble Co. (NEC), where two of his earliest plays were produced as Season-Within-a-Season productions, and two other plays were given full productions. At NEC, Williams also performed as an actor in numerous productions, including *Nowhere to Run, Nowhere to Hide, The First Breeze of Summer, Eden, The Brownsville Raid,* and *Nevis Mountain Dew.* Recipient of a Tony nomination for his **Home** (1979), which also won a John Gassner Playwriting Medallion, and was selected as a Burns Mantle Yearbook "Best Play of 1979–1980." Also recipient of a North Carolina Governor's Award for his contributions to the theatre. *Address:* 400 West 43rd St. #22N, New York, NY 10036. Alternate: 309 N. Wright St., Burgaw, NC 28425.

REPRESENTATIVE PLAYS AND DRAMATIC WORKS:
Welcome to Black River (drama, 2 acts, 1974). The portrait of a black sharecropper family in North Carolina during the 1950s, focusing on their experiences of poverty, exploitation, and racism. Prod. by NEC, New York, as a Season-Within-a-Season production, May 20–25, 1975, for 8 perfs.; dir. by Dean Irby. With Juanita Bethea, Marcella Lowery, Lea Scott, Taurean Blacque, Clayton Corbin, Peter DeMaio, and Carl Gordon. Prod. by the New Federal Theatre (NFT), New York, opening Nov. 15, 1984; dir. by

Walter Dallas. With Frances Foster, J. C. Quinn, Ejaye Tracey, Carl Fordon, and Joy Aaron.

The Coming (morality play, 1 act, 1974). God appears and talks with a skid-row bum, first as a prostitute, then as a slave, and finally as a dope addict. Prod. at the Billie Holiday Theatre, Brooklyn, NY, 1975; dir. by author.

Do unto Others (domestic drama, 1 act, 1974). Concerns the revenge of a Chicago housewife whose husband (a numbers racketeer) thought that he had killed her in a fire. Prod. at the Billie Holiday Theatre, Brooklyn, 1975, on double bill with the author's **The Coming.**

A Love Play (drama, full length, 1976). As described by TOWNSEND BREWSTER in the *Newsletter* of the Harlem Cultural Council (vol. 2, no. 10), the play is about "four female characters [who] size up their situation and decide that lesbianism is their best bet . . . given the men in their lives." Prod. by NEC, as a Season-Within-a-Season production, April 13–18, 1976, for 8 perfs.; dir. by Frances Foster.

Home (drama, full length, 1979). About a young black North Carolina farmer who loses his land to a tax collector and is forced to try to seek his fortune in the North. For a while, he lives the good life in the city, gets a new job, and has a sexy new girlfriend, but things soon change. Like the Prodigal Son, he finds himself on a downward path, becoming involved with dope and prostitution, and finally losing both his job and his self-respect. Just at the point of hopelessness, he decides to return to his home in North Carolina, where he begins to rebuild his life as a farmer and to find the fulfillment that he has been seeking. First prod. Off-Bway by NEC at St. Marks Playhouse, Dec. 14, 1979–Feb. 16, 1980, for 82 perfs.; transferred to Bway, at the Cort Theatre, May 7, 1980, for an additional 279 perfs.; dir. by Dean Irby. With Charles Brown (who was nominated for a Tony Award), L. Scott Caldwell, and Michele Shay. Return engagement at Theatre Four, opening May 8, 1981, for 29+ perfs.; dir. by DOUGLAS TURNER WARD. Prod. by the Nina Vance Alley Theatre, at the Large Stage, Houston, TX, opening Aug. 31, 1982, for 6 perfs.; dir. by Horacena Taylor. With members of NEC. Prod. by the Virginia Museum Theatre, Richmond, VA, at the Studio Theatre, opening Nov. 5, 1982, for 12 perfs.; dir. by WOODIE KING, JR., who also played the leading role. A Burns Mantle theatre yearbook "Best Play of 1979–1980"; nominated for a Tony Award; and winner of the John Gassner Playwriting Medallion for the most provocative new play by an American; and winner of an AUDELCO Award for best play of 1980. Synopsis (prepared by Jeffrey Sweet) pub. in *The Best Plays of 1979–1980*, pp. 219–31. Pub. by Dramatists Play Service, New York, 1981.

The Sixteenth Round // Orig. title: **The Pathetique** (drama, full length, 1980). A dishonest, down-and-out prize fighter tries to hide from an executioner who is trying to kill him for throwing a fight. Prod. by NEC, Oct. 7–Nov. 9, 1980, for 40 perfs.; dir. by Horacena J. Taylor. With PAUL BENJAMIN, Rosalind Cash, and Roscoe Ormand.

Friends (comedy, full length, 1980). "About a woman whose husband and boyfriend are both blind and both living with her." —*New York Daily News*, Sept. 22, 1983. Prod. at the Billie Holiday Theatre, Brooklyn, 1983; dir. by Marjorie Moon.

OTHER PLAYS AND DRAMATIC WORKS:
Sometime from Now (1974). **Kamilia** (morality play, 2 acts, 1975). A well-to-do married woman discovers, through the interpretation of a persistent dream, that she is a lesbian. (Possibly an earlier version of **A Love Play.**) **Mackron** (TV script, 1975). **The Last Caravan** (musical, full length, mid-1970s). A 65-year-old man, who discovers that

he is impotent, decides to seek a remedy from a hoo-doo woman, which restores his potency despite the fact that it is only a placebo. **Break of Day Arising** (1976). **Brass Birds Don't Sing** (1977). Prod. by author, 1978. **Kneeslappers** (TV script, 1980). Prod. on PBS, with OSSIE DAVIS and RUBY DEE, 1980.

WILLIAMS, SANDA BETH (Auransia) (1948–   ), Actress, poet, playwright. Born in New Haven, CT, where she studied at Yale Univ. and acted with the Long Wharf Theatre. Has performed with the Afro-American Arts Theatre in Philadelphia, where she also directed a drama workshop and a radio program at Temple Univ. Recipient of a grant from the New York State Council on the Arts for two of her plays. Her poetry has been included in *Night Come Softly* (Giovanni, 1969) and in the *Journal of Black Poetry*. *Address:* 243 E. 17th St., New York, NY 10003.

> **PLAYS:**
> (All 1970s:) **The Family. Hey Nigger Can You Dig Her. Jest One Mo** (New York State Council on the Arts Grant). **Zodiac Zenith. Sunshine Loving** (New York State Council on the Arts Grant).

WILLIAMS, X. LAWRENCE VIRGIL (Lawrence Soul), Actor, screenwriter, playwright. Originally from Houston, TX. Received a B.A. in radio-TV from Texas Technical Univ. and took a special filmmaking course at Rice Univ. He is described by *Reel Soul* magazine (Feb. 1976, p. 45) as "a young black Orson Welles," "a six-foot 145 pound vegetarian," and "a meditating Aries." In 1976 he was residing in Hollywood, where he had recently acted in *Leadbelly,* a Paramount film directed by Gordon Parks.

> **DRAMATIC WORKS:**
> **Richard Nixon: Bad Joke on America** (short feature film, pre-1976). Written, prod., dir., photographed, and edited by Williams. Winner of the Will Rogers/Charlie Chaplin Award, and was entered in the Atlanta Film Festival. **Happy Birthday, America** (screenplay, 1976). Described by the author as "a seriocomic political satire for Bicentennial '76 tailored for comedian-activist Dick Gregory.... It's a critically patriotic comedy-fantasy. It puts the constitution and bill of rights ahead of capitalism. It says 'Everything you always wanted to say about Uncle Sam but could never find the words.' "—*Reel Soul*, Feb. 1976, p. 45. No information about the actual prodn.

WILLIAMS-LAWRENCE, VALERIE J., Playwright. Born and reared in Gulfport, MS. Educated at Dillard Univ., New Orleans. Mother of three boys. Currently employed (since c. 1968) as human resources manager for Mellon Bank in Pittsburgh, PA. *Address:* 36 Foster Sq., Pittsburgh, PA 15211.

> **PLAYS:**
> **Royal Relations** (satire, full length, 1983). A satirical look at upper-middle-class black families. Two staged readings by Kuntu Repertory Theatre, Univ. of Pittsburgh, 1983. Sched. as the season opener at Kuntu Repertory Theatre, Nov.-Dec. 1985. **Magnolia Aid Society** (drama, full length, 1984). A drama of struggle, love, and hope in the African-American tradition. **Circle of Friends** (comedy, pre-1985). The black man's

search for whiteness. **Financial Planning** (satire, full length: in progress, 1985). Subtitled "Yo Mama Is on Welfare." A family's struggle to return to the source of their help, which is their African-American heritage, and the conflicts that make the return almost impossible.

WILLIAMSON, FRED ("The Hammer") (1938–   ), Actor, producer, director, screenwriter, former professional football player. Born in Gary, IN. Educated at Northwestern Univ. (B.A., 1959). Pro football player with the San Francisco Forty-Niners, Pittsburgh Steelers, Oakland Raiders, and Kansas City Chiefs, 1959–68. Launched his acting career with an ongoing role on the "Julia" TV series, 1969–70, as Diahann Carroll's boyfriend. Since that time, he has become one of the top black stars. His best-known films (mainly as actor) include *M*A*S*H* and *Tell Me That You Love Me, Junie Moon* (both 1970); title roles in *Hammer* and *The Legend of Nigger Charley* (both 1972); *Black Caesar, The Soul of Nigger Charley, That Man Bolt,* and *Hell Up in Harlem* (all 1973); *Black Eye, Three Tough Guys, Crazy Joe,* and *Three the Hard Way* (all 1974); *Bucktown* and *Take a Hard Ride* (both 1975); *Death Journey* (also director and producer, 1976); and *Joshua* (1977).

DRAMATIC WORKS:
(All full length feature films, written, prod., dir., and starred in by Williamson.) **Boss Nigger** (1970s). **No Way Back** (1970s). **Adios Amigos** (1975). The escapades of a con man and his fall guy in the Old West. Also starring RICHARD PRYOR and Jim Brown. **Mean Johnny Barrows** (1976).

WILLIAMSON, FREDA, Playwright. Based in North Carolina, where she was educated in the public schools of Yanceville, and received the B.A. in drama and speech from Bennett College in Greensboro, 1972.

PLAY:
Reflections (drama, full length, 1971). A glimpse into the turbulent relationship of a young black actress and a college recruiter with whom she is now living. Set in a predominantly white university in Chicago. Prod. at Bennett Coll., Nov. 17–20, 1981; dir. by Malachi Greene.

WILSON, ALICE T. (1908–   ), Poet, songwriter, and screenwriter. Born in Virginia. Currently living in Washington, DC. Attended the Margaret M. Nursing School and the National Academy of Radio and Television Broadcasting. Has written a number of country and western songs. Member of the National Platform Assn.

COLLECTION AND PLAY:
HOW AN AMERICAN POET MADE MONEY AND FORGET ME NOT (screenplay and poems, 1968). Pub. by Pageant Press, New York, 1969. Contains **How an American Poet Made Money** (screenplay, 1958).

WILSON, ANDI A. B., Playwright of Bahamian descent. Associated with the Horace Mann Theatre in New York City.

PLAYS:
Blacksheep (drama, 1976). About a young man who faces an important decision in his life, concerning what will be his new role following his country's independence. Prod. by the Horace Mann Theatre, May 1976.

WILSON, AUGUST, Self-educated poet-playwright and director. Winner of the Pulitzer Prize for drama in 1987 for **Fences** (1984). Born and grew up in Pittsburgh, PA, one of six children. Although an avid reader and a proficient writer, he dropped out of school after the ninth grade, continuing his education on his own. Began writing poetry while earning a living doing odd jobs; and his work has appeared in several magazines and periodicals. Became a part of the Black Arts movement in Pittsburgh during the 1960s. Founded the Black Horizon Theatre of Pittsburgh in 1968, where he produced and directed plays by ROB PENNY, JOSEPH WHITE, and other playwrights. Moved to St. Paul, MN, in 1978, where he now resides, and where some of his early plays were first performed. As a result of his play **Ma Rainey's Black Bottom** (which later won the Drama Critics Circle best play award in 1986), he was invited to become a participant in the Eugene O'Neill National Playwrights' Conf., which brought him in contact with Lloyd Richards, director of the conference, dean of the Yale School of Drama, and artistic director of the Yale Repertory Theatre, where his two most important plays have been produced. Member of New Dramatists since 1983; associate playwright-in-residence at the Playwrights Center in Minneapolis, where he was awarded a McKnight Fellowship in Playwriting. Also recipient of fellowships in playwriting from the Bush and Rockefeller Foundations. In addition to the Pulitzer Prize, *Fences* won four Tony Awards: for best play, best director, best performance by a leading actor, and best performance by a featured actress. *Address*: c/o Lloyd Richards, Yale Repertory Theatre, New Haven, CT 06520.

REPRESENTATIVE PLAYS:
Ma Rainey's Black Bottom (drama, full length, 1982). About the life of the legendary blues singer of the 1920s. "Set in a Chicago recording studio in 1927, the play uses a recording session of Ma's as a backdrop to explore the dynamics of the white/black relationship with her white manager and her backup musician Levee, who wants to jazz up her arrangements."—*Right On! Class*, March 1985, p. 32. The title comes from the name of one of Ma Rainey's classic recordings. First prod. by the Eugene O'Neill Theatre Center's National Playwrights Conference, 1982. Premiered at the Yale Repertory Theatre, New Haven, CT, 1982; dir. by Lloyd Richards. Opened on Bway at the Cort Theatre, Oct. 1984–May 1985; dir. by Lloyd Richards. With Theresa Merritt in the title role, and featuring Charles S. Dutton, Leonard Jackson, Robert Judd, and Joe Seneca. Winner of the Drama Critics Circle Award, as best play of 1986. Pub. by Plumes/New American Lib., Bergenfield, NJ. Also pub. in an "exclusive hardcover edition" by the Fireside Theatre, Garden City, NY.

The Janitor (short monologue, 1985). A janitor, sweeping a hotel ballroom where an important conference is to be held, imagines that he is the speaker for the meeting. Pub. in *Short Pieces from the New Dramatists*. (Broadway Play Publishing, New York, 1985).

Fences (drama, full length, 1984). Drama of conflict between a father and son. Described by the producers as "an intimate look at a family caught by changing times and conflicting values. *Fences* speaks in a voice both poignant and majestic; to all people who have ever remained silent, or misunderstood, or challenged their loved ones."— Advertisement in *Black Masks,* April 1985, p. 3. First presented at the National Playwrights Conference, 1983. Prod. by the Yale Repertory Theatre, New Haven, April 30–May 25, 1985, dir. by Lloyd Richards. Featuring James Earl Jones, Mary Alice, Charles Brown, Courtney Vance, RAY ARANHA, Russell Costen, Crystal Coleman, and LaJara Henderson. Opened on Broadway to laudatory reviews, at the 46th St. Theatre, beginning March 17, 1987; dir. by Lloyd Richards; starring James Earl Jones. Winner of the Pulitzer Prize for drama in April 1987. Winner of four Tony Awards: for best play, best director (Lloyd Richards), best performance by a leading actor (James Earl Jones), and best performance by a featured actress (Mary Alice).

OTHER PLAYS:

Joe Turner's Come and Gone // Orig. title: **Mill Hand's Lunch Bucket** (1984). Selected as a workshop play at the National Playwrights Conference, 1984. The following plays are all pre-1985: **Jitney. Fullerton Street. The Coldest Day of the Year.**

WINKLER, MEL, Actor-playwright. Based in New York City, where he has been associated with the Cornbread Players, the New Genesis Theatre Co., and the New Federal Theatre (NFT). Appeared in *The Great White Hope* (1968) amd NFT productions of *In New England Winter* (1971) and *Don't Let It Go to Your Head* (1972).

PLAYS:

The Reachers (astrological drama, 1 act, 1976). According to *Black Playwrights, 1823–1977* (Hatch & Abdullah, 1977, p. 249), "The jet stream has shifted, the polar caps are melting, the ionosphere is thinning out, new vibrations are getting through, and the earth's axis is beginning to tilt the other way." Prod. by the New Genesis Theatre, New York, Jan. 1976.

WISDOM, ANTHONY, Playwright. Studied playwriting with the Frank Silvera Writers' Workshop (FSWW) in New York City. Founding member of Theatre in Progress, also in New York City.

COLLECTION/PLAYS:

A LITTLE BIT OF WISDOM. Publisher unknown, c. 1982. Contains the following plays: **Something Lost.** Prod. at the Henry St. Theatre, c. 1982. **Till the Very End.** "The story is about a middle-aged pornography writer, Ralph Dumas, who had been a radical activist of the turbulent Sixties and is trying to [reestablish friendship with] his former radical cronies."—*New York Amsterdam News,* Nov. 6. 1982. Written in FSWW. Prod. at Theatre 22, New York, Nov. 4–7 and 11–14, 1982; dir. by Morgan Freeman. Unpub. script and tape recording in the FSWW Archives/Schomburg Collection. **A Song for You** (1 act). Prod. by Theatre in Progress, Aug. 1984.

WISE, ROBERT, Playwright. Associated in 1975 with the Weusi Kuumba Troupe in New York City.

PLAYS:
The Game (melodrama, 1 act, 1975). A devout black mother kills the white detective who has slain her son. Prod. by the Weusi Kuumba Troupe, 1975. **Portsmouth** (drama, 1 act, 1975). A charming and handsome young writer is supported by his hard-working sister, until she discovers that she is being exploited. Prod. by the Weusi Kuumba Troupe, 1975.

WOLFE, ELTON (Clyde), Playwright. Formerly associated with Aldridge Players/West (AP/W) in San Francisco. Received the Ph.D. in theatre from Stanford Univ., 1977. His doctoral dissertation, "An Analysis of the Language in Five Plays by Bullins," is available from University Microfilms International, Ann Arbor, MI. *Address:* 390 Page St., San Francisco, CA 94102.

PLAYS:
Men Wear Mustaches (domestic drama, 1 act, 1968). A woman tries to reunite with the husband whom she has deserted, but finds that it is now too late. Prod. by AP/W, Aug. 1968. **The Big Shot** (comedy, 1 act, 1969). A young man, who is really employed as a chauffeur, visits his mother in his rich employer's Rolls Royce, only to discover that his mother has informed everybody that he is wealthy. **The After Party** (comedy, 1 act, 1970). Physical and verbal battle between two men, with audience participation invited, concerning the superiority of "black" versus "Negro" attitudes.

WOLFE, GEORGE C. (1934–   ), Playwright and musical librettist. Born in Frankfort, KY. Received the B.A. in directing from Pomona Coll., Clairmont, CA, where he was twice winner of the regional festival of the American Coll. Theatre Festival (ACTF); and the M.F.A. in dramatic writing/musical theatre from NYU. Was associated with the Inner City Cultural Center (ICCC) in Los Angeles during the 1970s. Currently resides in New York City. His work has been produced by the Crossroads Theatre and the New York Shakespeare Festival Public Theatre (NYSF/PT). Recipient of a CBS/Foundation of the Dramatists Guild Playwriting Award for **The Colored Museum** (1986); and grants from the Rockefeller Foundation, the National Endowment for the Arts, and the National Institute for Musical Theatre.

PLAYS AND DRAMATIC WORKS:
Up for Grabs (comedy-satire, 4 one-act episodes [full length], 1975). "As Joe Thomas discovers the secret to being Black and the reasons for his existence, he receives a lesson in American exploitation and power, all the while being an unknown contestant on the ultimate TV game show."—*Black Playwrights, 1823–1977* (Hatch & Abdullah, 1977). Prod. by Pomona Coll. Theatre, Claremont, 1975, and was the Pacific South Regional winner in the ACTF at Las Vegas, NV, the same year.
Block Party (play of black life with music, 1976). According to Sylvia Drake of the *Los Angeles Times,* it "deals with two themes: What it's like to grow up black and male in America and how tough, or impossible, it is to move out of that predetermined condition—out of that block and on to new horizons."—*ACTF Awards Newsletter,* Dec.

1976. Prod. by Pomona Coll., Dec. 1976, and was the Pacific South Region winner in the ACTF held at Cypress Coll., Cypress, CA, Feb. 10–13, 1977, where Wolfe was "the first author to repeat as a regional winner."—Ibid.

Back Alley Tales (1978–79). Written and dir. by Wolfe. Music by Paul Belfour. Prod. by ICCC, during the 1978–79 season.

Paradise (musical, full length, 1985). Book and lyrics by Wolfe. Music by Robert Forest. Prod. at Playhouse in the Park, Cincinnati, OH, Feb. 20, 1985; dir. by Worth Gardner. Also prod. on Bway.

Queenie Pie (musical, full length, 1986). Subtitled "An Evening of Vintage Ellington." Libretto by Wolfe. Music by Duke Ellington. "A story about an aging beauty queen, who, weary of her career and competition, dreams of escape to a tropical island." —*Black Masks,* Oct./Nov. 1986, p. 8. Prod. at the Kennedy Center, Washington, DC, Fall 1986.

The Colored Museum (a lampoon of the black experience, full length, 1986). "A series of twelve museum exhibits come to life revealing the myths and madness of stereotypes of Black culture." —*Black Masks,* Oct./Nov. 1986, p. 5. Among the subjects hilariously and mercilessly satirized are Afro wigs, Josephine Baker, *A Raisin in the Sun,* black song-and-dance musicals, *Ebony* magazine, and many other aspects of the black heritage. According to reviewer John Simon *(New York,* Nov. 17, 1986, as quoted in the published text), "This is a sophisticated, satirical, seriously funny show that spoofs white and black America alike. It is remarkably unafraid of lampooning black foibles, which is a sign of artistic maturity." World premiere at the Crossroads Theatre, New Brunswick, NJ, opening March 26, 1986; dir. by Lee Richardson. Prod. by NYSF/PT, at the Susan Stein Shiva Theatre, opening Oct. 7, 1986; dir. by Lee Richardson. Featuring Loretta Devine, Tommy Hollis, Reggie Montgomery, Vickilyn Reynolds, and Danitra Vance. Winner of the 1986 Dramatists Guild Award. Published by Broadway Play Publishing, New York, 1987.

WOOD, DEBBIE (Deborah J. Wood) (1951–   ), Reporter-editor, poet, and playwright. Born in Chicago, IL, where she graduated from Harvard/St. George H.S., 1968. Studied playwriting and drama at Howard Univ. (B.F.A., 1972), where she also served as coproducer and director of the Experimental Theatre there, and earned hours toward the master's degree in counseling in the Graduate School of Education. Worked for Commercial Clearing House Publishing Co. in the District of Columbia as researcher, editor, and reporter of information pertaining to the federal tax system. Her poetry has been published in *Afro-American Review, Transition,* and *Black History Museum um um Newsletter.* Under an NEA grant given by the DC Art Commission, she served as poet-in-residence at Dunbar HS., 1972, and has also given poetry readings throughout the DC area as well as on radio. Member of Poets and Writers. *Address:* 5445 W. Iowa St., Chicago, IL 60651.

PLAYS:
Four Niggers (skit, 1 act, 1971). Four dope addicts—three men and one woman—literally scratch themselves to death. Prod. by the Ira Aldridge Theatre, Washington, DC, 1971. **Indiana Avenue** (experimental play, 1 act, 1972). Revolves around a Chicago disaster in 1967 in which "an L car jumped the track killing almost all of the passengers

and pedestrians on Indiana Avenue below . . . and no one stopped/not even for a minute/ not even for a minute.''—Pub. script. First prod. by the Drama Dept. of Howard Univ.'s Experimental Theatre, April 15, 1972; dir. by Denise Hamilton. Prod. Off-Bway as a workshop production by NEC, in the Studio of the St. Marks Playhouse Building, New York, Jan. 23–26, 1973, for 4 perfs.; dir. by HAZEL BRYANT.

WRIGHT, CHARLES STEVENSON (1932–   ), Author, journalist, and playwright. Born in New Franklin, MO. Wrote regular columns for the *Kansas City Call* and the *Village Voice*. His writings have also appeared in *Negro Digest*. Author of short stories. In 1975 was working on a screenplay, a play, and a novel or travel book about Vera Cruz.

PLAY:
Something Black (early 1970s).

WRIGHT, JAY (1935–   ), Poet, playwright, and essayist. Born in Albuquerque, NM. Lived in California during his early youth. Played professional baseball in the Arizona/Texas and California State Leagues. Attended the Univ. of New Mexico for two months, studying chemistry, before entering the U.S. Army Medical Corps for three years. Graduated from the Univ. of California/ Berkeley (B.A., 1961); attended Union Theological Seminary for one semester on a Rockefeller Bros. Theological Fellowship (1961–62); and completed his graduate work at Rutgers Univ. (M.A. in comparative literature, 1966). Toured the South on a Woodrow Wilson/NEA Poets-in-Concert fellowship. Was poet-in-residence at Tougaloo Coll. (Mississippi), 1968, and at Talladega Coll. (Alabama), 1969–70. Author of five books of poetry: *The Homecoming Singer* (1971), *Soothsayers and Omens* (1976), *Explications/Interpretations* (1984), *Dimensions of History* (1976), and *The Double Invention of Komo* (1980). His poetry has also been published in numerous periodicals and anthologies, including *Black World, Black American Literature Forum, Evergreen Review, Hiram Poetry Review, New American Review, New American Poets, New Negro Poets, New Black Voices, Negro Digest, The Nation,* and *Yale Review*. In addition to the fellowship and grant mentioned above, he was recipient of a Hodder Fellow in Playwriting at Princetown Univ., 1970–71, ''with no other obligations than to read, think, and write.''—Author. *Address:* Indian Pond Rd., Piermont, NH 03779.

   Balloons (comedy, 1 act, 1968). According to the publisher, this play ''concerns the contemporary Christian understanding of righteousness. Benjamin, non-Christian in religious practice but living in what is supposedly a Christian society, is the center in that his values are those understood by contemporary Christians as righteous. His confrontations with himself and with others are not in the church but in the world he lives in, of which the church is only a part.'' Commissioned by the Christian Soc. for Drama, New York. Pub. by Baker's Plays, Boston, 1968.

Love's Equations (mythical drama, 1 act, 1983). Based on a Ghanaian myth) of the Akan tribe. According to the author's description:

Three men (one Black, one brown, one White) and a woman (White, and sometimes Black) set out, walking from Santa Fe, to attend a wedding in Albuquerque. The men are thaumaturges and prophets; the woman is partially an incarnation of Asaase Ya [not explained by the playwright, but presumed to be a goddess of special significance, possibly Love]. Along the way, each man in his manner tries to possess the woman. In order to free her from her ordeal with them, one man causes her to disappear. The others persuade him to return her, but they find that she has died while away from them. Each then works to restore her to life. She is revivified and vows to love them all.

Pub. in *Callaloo,* Fall 1983.

The Adoration of Fire (mythical drama, 1 act, pre-1984). A synthesis of Yoruba, Egyptian, and Mexican myths. According to the author's description:

In a country spot, near a marsh, a woman looks for her cow. A young man, who has been following her, approaches. He apparently tries to seduce her, but she repels him. The young man offers to retrieve the cow and leaves. An older man now enters, looking for the young man. He speaks to the woman as though they were familiar, and asks her to return to him. The young man returns. He and the older man seem to be familiar to each other, and they come into conflict, which results in the older man shooting the younger one. The woman now vows to acknowledge her son and to return to the older man.

Sched. for pub. in *The Southern Review,* Summer 1985.

The Death and Return of Paul Batuata (mythical/historical drama, long 1 act, 1984). The play takes its impulse from an incident related in William Weber Johnson's *Heroic Mexico,* concerning Rodolfo Fierro, one of Pancho Villa's associates. According to the author's description:

New Mexico is undergoing a revolution. A [black] lawyer, living in Santa Rosa, challenges the new regime by refusing to honor its laws or to offer his services. Two of his friends are active participants in the counterrevolution. The three men meet each day in a local cafe. On this day, a revolutionary committee head comes to eat at the cafe. A young counterrevolutionary has been killed on the road to Gallup and the committee head has received a note denouncing him for the murder. The committee head confronts the lawyer over the accusation and, in turn, accuses the lawyer of having committed the murder. The committee head forces the two friends and a waiter to convict the lawyer on the spot and to execute him. The waiter does; the lawyer dies. The three who have been forced to convict him invoke [i.e., pray for] the lawyer's return. He returns. The five suffer another passion [i.e., angry dispute]. The lawyer is convicted again and the waiter shoots him a second time.

Pub. in *Hambone,* Fall 1984.

NOTE: The following plays are all pre-1985, and are described in the words of the author:

The Unfinished Saint, Part One (full length). "The story of David Watkins' conversion from hustler to militant leader of a black spiritual and political group, his battles within and without the group, his disabling doubts and finally his killing of an old man who has stalked him." The setting is the urban environments of New York and Philadelphia.

The Unfinished Saint, Part Two (full length). "The second part of a four-part movement. The story of David Watkins' struggle to maintain power and to overcome the tensions arising in his group because of his act and the group's necessary physical move to a suburban spot, the falling apart of relations within the group and the killing of . . . a white reporter . . . and David." The setting is New York City's urban environment and a country place.

Death as History, Part One (full length).

The third in a series [continuing] the movement begun in **The Unfinished Saint.** Though it can be played alone, to which the author would not object, it lies most comfortably within its four-play context. It takes place in an isolated community in the Hills of New Mexico, where a team composed of two anthropologists, a folklorist and a mathematician are studying a self-sufficient black community under the spiritual and political leadership of one man. . . . A tension develops when the younger members of the team question their own work and the community's direction, and begin to try to impose a different set of radical values upon it. The community leader has to withstand the group's fragmentation and the erosion of his own power. Underlying these battles for control are the question of the autonomy of culture, the reading and value of history and myth within the sociopolitical world.

The setting is a functioning hill community of scholars and workers.

Death as History, Part Two (full length).

The fourth and final play in the series begun with *The Unfinished Saint*. It, too, can be played alone, but fits best as the play which opens and explores the final cosmological, historical and political dimensions that motivate the three previous plays. It takes place in the same isolated New Mexico community [as Part One, directly above]. The play now explores the problems of theological, historical and cultural returns. The last movement brings the people out of the hills, headed for the challenges of the larger world they left behind.

A Sacred Impurity: The Dead's First Invention (ritual, long 1 act). Draws upon Dogak, Akan, Mexican, and Greek myths.

A [black] ritual musician, dedicated to keeping his village's walls intact, determines to achieve his "knowledge of death" and his own redemption. This day, a [brown] man enters, dragging a [brown] woman by a rope. They wear, or carry, [certain ethnic] emblems. . . . The musician tries to free the woman. A [black] man [carrying certain Afroethnic emblems] enters. He wants to buy the woman. The four now try to determine the roots of their freedom and the knowledge of death, and to effect, through historical and spiritual events, their own salvation.

The Hunt and Double Night of the Wood (full length).

In the Sandia Mountains near Albuquerque, three white men go hunting, taking their black cook with them. The youngest, a new businessman, needs the support and influence of the oldest. During the course of the trip, he realizes the tenuousness of his situation and, exaggerating its difficulties, arranges . . . to have the cook kill the two older men. The double hunt now reveals itself and the play, calling upon the resources of myth, moves to connect five lives to each other and to the historical dimensions of their existence in this new world context. The play becomes one in which the men's mutual redemption motivates it.

Homage to Anthony Braxton (long 1 act play). The play takes its impulse from the compositional methods and goals of Anthony Braxton, a black musician.

A man and woman, who do what they can to hustle money from strangers and associates, determine to disrupt the kick-off to the community preacher's city council election campaign. They enlist the aid of a friend and another man, who is trying to hustle them. A young singer, who has enlisted in the preacher's campaign, gets involved with the four when he tries to solicit contributions. He is taken for a ride, thinks of revenge, but, believing he can get the better of them, promises to help them. On the day of the action in the park, the four enter ready for disruption. The singer, coming to fulfill his part of the bargain, shoots the gang's leader on the platform set aside for the celebration.

The Crossing (mythical drama, 1 act). The play is based on one of the Dinka spear-master myths. "In an isolated spot near a river at the foot of a mountain, three men, on an errand for their boss, encounter a husband and wife, keepers of the river, whom the men must circumvent in order to reach the mountain top and complete their job. One man is killed, one runs away. The third, with the woman's help, finds a way to escape her husband's dangers and start toward his task's fulfillment."

OTHER PLAYS AND DRAMATIC WORKS:
The following plays are all 1960s.) **The Death of Mr. Parker** (radio play, 1 act), **Welcome Back, Black Boy** (radio play, 1 act), and **Woman with Charm** (radio play, 1 act). All prod. by Radio Station WPFA, Berkeley, CA. **The Doors** (1 act). Prod. at Exodus Coffee House, San Pedro, CA. **The Final Celebration** (full length). Described by the author as "the story of Franklin Lawrence's ordeal, as a Black NCO in the U.S. Army [stationed in Germany], with his subordinates and superiors, because of his detachment from the racial linkages that all others establish, and of how he attempts to resolve his professional and personal problems in the secure arms of the group he chooses."

Y

YARBROUGH, CAMILLE, Versatile theatrical artist and performer whose talents include acting, singing, dancing, songwriting, poetry, and plays. Born in Chicago. Currently resides in New York City. Spent many years in association with Katherine Dunham, both as performer and teacher. Acting credits include the New York and national tour productions of *To Be Young, Gifted and Black;* the Urban Arts Corps production of *Trumpets of the Lord;* the film *Shaft;* the New York Public Theatre's production of *Cities in Bezique* and *Sambo;* the TV special *Caught in the Middle;* and the NET program "Soul." Her song album, *The Iron Pot Cooker,* "deals with the moral and social struggle of African-Americans." —*New York Amsterdam News,* Sept. 1, 1984. Her award-winning children's book, *Cornrows,* presents a positive self-image for black children.

PLAY:
And Then There's Negroland (black ritual, full length, 1970s). Subtitled "Ain't No One Monkey." Deals with the theme of black survival in the past, present, and future.

YOUNG, BEATRICE, Director of Educational Services, Illinois Commission on Human Relations, during the 1960s.

DRAMATIC WORK:
I, Too, Sing America (pageant, full length [1 long act], 1960s). Subtitled "A Skit Depicting the Role of the Negro in America." Combines narration, dialogue, and poetry to dramatize the contributions of black Americans from Crispus Attucks to Martin Luther King. Title taken from a poem by LANGSTON HUGHES. Distributed in mimeographed form by the author, through the Illinois Commission on Human Relations.

YOUNG, BILLIE JEAN, Organizer, attorney, poet, and veteran worker in the civil rights movement, rural development, and the arts. A native of rural Alabama. Currently residing in Jackson, MS. Chairman of the Board of Directors of the Rural Development Leadership Network. Executive director of the Southern Rural Women's Network and assoc. director of Rural America, both organizations located in Jackson. *Address:* Rural America, 4795 McWillie Dr., Jackson, MS 39206.

DRAMATIC WORK:

Fannie Lou Hamer: This Little Light . . . (one-woman show, full length, pre-1984). Developed and performed by Young. A re-creation of the life of Fannie Lou Hamer, a voting rights pioneer of the 1960s, who rose to national prominence as a result of the mistreatment which she received—being beaten, arrested, jailed, and fired from her job—because of her efforts to register to vote in Mississippi. The play is considered a work-in-progress "which will evolve as new insights, anecdotes and documentation emerge."—New York *Amsterdam News,* Feb. 18, 1984. First presented at Tougaloo Coll. in Mississippi, in Ruleville, MS (Hamer's hometown), and in Washington, DC. Presented in St. Peter's Church at Citicorp Center in New York, on Feb. 23, 1984, in support of the Rural Development Leadership Network, and sponsored jointly by the National Coalition of 100 Black Women and the National Council of Negro Women.

YOUNG, CLARENCE, III (1942–   ), Actor, playwright, and producer. Born in Dayton, OH. Educated at Capital Univ. (B.A., 1979). Served in the U.S. Air Force, 1961–65. Director and resident playwright of Theatre West, Dayton, since 1969. His work as a playwright and performer has been twice televised on the Univ. of Michigan TV series on black theatre—"Black Theatre USA" and "Black Theatre and Its Audience," prod. in 1970. Appointed by the governor to the Ohio Council for the Arts, 1970–74; drama and dance coach, Dayton Urban Youth Behavioral Program, 1979; consultant to youth, Resurrection Church, 1980; consultant to the Dayton Board of Education, 1980. *Address:* 2043 W. 3rd St., Dayton, Ohio 45417.

PLAYS AND DRAMATIC WORKS:

Perry's Mission (drama, 1 act, 1969). According to Peter Bailey, writing in *Black World* (April 1972), it "showed the destructive influence whites can have on the Movement, especially in dividing Black folks. Perry, a white man, had an assignment to go into the Black Community and cause chaos, and he succeeded in chilling fashion." First prod. by the African Cultural Center, Buffalo, NY, 1969; dir. by Jonathan Wilson. Prod. Off-Bway by the Negro Ensemble Co., at St. Marks Playhouse, Jan. 12, 1971, for 44 perfs.; dir. by DOUGLAS TURNER WARD. Prod. at Spelman Coll., Atlanta, 1972.

The System (revolutionary black musical, full length, 1973). Described by *Black World* (April 1973) as "a highly entertaining musical psycho-drama about America." Prod. by Theatre West, Spring 1972, and presented on a number of college and university campuses, including Spellman Coll., Atlanta, Sept. 1972, and Cleveland State Univ., 1973.

Black Love (musical, 1975). Described by *Black World* (April 1976) as "a musical with some social commentary. . . . The theme of the piece is love, which is achievable once the barriers to it are removed." Prod. by Theatre West (of Dayton) in Washington, DC, 1975.

YOUNG, OTIS, Actor-playwright. Based in New York City. In 1964 he played in the Broadway production of *Blues for Mister Charlie,* in the role of Counselor for the Bereaved.

   PLAY:
   Right On, Brother (1969).

Z

ZUBER, RON (E'Ron Zuba), Playwright. Based in Detroit, MI, where he was introduced to the theatre by RONALD MILNER. Formerly associated with the Spirit of Shango Theatre Co., which merged with the Concept East Theatre, forming the Concept East/Spirit of Shango Repertory Co.

PLAY:

Three X Love (poetic ritual with music, 1 act, 1969). Written in praise of black women—as mothers, sisters, and lovers. Prod. by the Spirit of Shango Theatre Co., Detroit, 1969. Also prod. by the Mwongi Arts Players, at D-Sace Playhouse, Detroit, 1973. Pub. in *Black Drama Anthology* (King & Milner, 1972).

APPENDIX A

ADDITIONAL PLAYWRIGHTS WHOSE SCRIPTS ARE LOCATED IN SPECIAL REPOSITORIES

Unpublished playscripts and/or possibly tape recordings of public readings or performances are deposited (as indicated) either in the Archives of the Frank Silvera Writers' Workshop (FSWW), located in the Schomburg Collection (SC), New York City, or in the Hatch-Billops Collection (HBC), New York City. Use of scripts is subject to the regulations of the particular repository, the copyright laws, and the permission of the individual playwright.

PLAYWRIGHT	PLAY	REPOSITORY
Adams, George	*An Evening with Josephine Baker*	FSWW/SC
Ahmad, Sayeed	*The Thing*	HBC
Alfaro, Rosanna Yamagiwa (racial identity?)	*Behind Enemy Lines*	FSWW/SC
Alston, Nelson C.	*Sam's Magic House of Shine*	FSWW/SC
Anderson, Lionel	*The Forever Clause*	FSWW/SC
Apollon, Gerald	*Toussaint L'Ouverture and San Domingo*	FSWW/SC
	Oh, Jesus	FSWW/SC
Arrington, Gerald Ray	*Maximum Security*	FSWW/SC
Aybar, Trudy	*Morning Train* (1974)	FSWW/SC
Baker, Eloise	*The Jitney Vehicle*	FSWW/SC
Barton, Peter	*Dawn Song*	HBC
Bates, Benjamin	*Off Campus*	FSWW/SC
Benjamin, Shafik	*His Majesty, Queen Hatchepsut*	FSWW/SC
Berry, Steven Ronald	*You Win Some—You Lose Some*	FSWW/SC
Beverly, Tranzana	*Git on Board* (1980)	HBC
Birhan, Iawta Farika	*On the Third Day He Shall Arise*	FSWW/SC
	Boysie and Girlsie	FSWW/SC
Bishop, Michael E.O.	*Surviving Poetically*	FSWW/SC

Blackwell, Thomas William	*Three Sets*	FSWW/SC
Bogxy, Ady	*Festival of the Gods*	FSWW/SC
Bowman, Bolaji	*The Day Way (Siku)*	FSWW/SC
Bowne, Alan	*Forty Deuce*	FSWW/SC
Bradford, Roy	*The Blind Spot*	HBC
Bronson, James Graham	*Invasion of Addis Ababa*	FSWW/SC
Brown, Donramel	*Casket Full of Corpse Bones*	FSWW/SC
Buck, William J.	*Cold Spell*	FSWW/SC
Bunche, Peter	*The Player Not the Game*	FSWW/SC
Burkhalter, Mary	*Emperor of Kings*	FSWW/SC
Carlton, Patrick Wayne	*Mother's Mad Alice*	FSWW/SC
Carpenter, Sandy	*The Replacement*	FSWW/SC
Cascio, Anna	*Gabe*	FSWW/SC
	The Wake	FSWW/SC
Coleman, Eleanor	*I Ain't Got No Rainbow*	FSWW/SC
Cook, Ernestine	*Checkers* (1976)	FSWW/SC
	Peanut Butter and Jelly (1977)	FSWW/SC
Davis, Luther	*Across 110th* (filmscript)	HBC
Davis, Martin K.	*Head Returned*	FSWW/SC
	Is He Crazy	FSWW/SC
	The Ghetto Poet	FSWW/SC
Derouin, Raymond E.	*Silver Bordman Is Dead*	FSWW/SC
Duncan, Danny	*Generations* (musical drama, 1891)	HBC
Dundee, Calua (exact spelling uncertain)	*Running Fast Through Paradise* (1975)	FSWW/SC
	Rainlight (1977)	FSWW/SC
Fennessey, Alice	*Greenberg*	FSWW/SC
Frazier, Kermit	*Kernel of Sanity*	FSWW/SC
	Shadoes & Echoes	FSWW/SC
Gabb, Elaine	*Transition*	FSWW/SC
Gaertner, Ken	*The Old Man's Death*	FSWW/SC
Garnes, Jule	*The Cuts*	FSWW/SC
Gordon, Ken	*Black Fog Poem*	FSWW/SC
Griffin, Michael	*Bricks Without Straw*	FSWW/SC
Harris, Leonard	*Blues Trilogy*	FSWW/SC
Harris, Willie Thomas	*Harlem Nocturne*	FSWW/SC
	The Roar of a Distant Cannon	FSWW/SC
Harrison, Stafford	*Masqueraders* (1977)	FSWW/SC
Hauer [one name]	*A Matter of Opinion*	FSWW/SC
Hebald, Carol	*The Fat Lady* ("A Symphonic Fantasy in Three Movements")	FSWW/SC
Henderson-Holmes, Safiya	*Screams from a Keyhole //* Orig. title: *I'll Be Home Soon* (1984)	FSWW/SC
Hennings, C. J.	*Whose Woods Are These*	FSWW/SC
Herrick, O. D.	*WRTI-FM—Philadelphia*	FSWW/SC

Horton, Robert	*June Bug*	FSWW/SC
Hudson, Wade	*Sam Carter Belongs Here*	FSWW/SC
Jackson, Henry L.	*For Brother Malcom [sic]*	FSWW/SC
	We Shall Overcome	FSWW/SC
James, Mike E.	*The Bakers*	FSWW/SC
	We Ain't Poor, Just Broke	FSWW/SC
James, Shirley	*Salvation's Webb*	FSWW/SC
Jennings, Regina Belvy	*Second Hand Dreams*	FSWW/SC
Johnson, Anderson	*Utopia (Once Removed)*	FSWW/SC
Johnson, Jocelyn	*Forbidden Fruit*	FSWW/SC
Jones, Ruth C.E.	*A Coupla Hookers*	FSWW/SC
	A Short Short Story	FSWW/SC
	Four Generations in Conversation	FSWW/SC
	Hamilton, Jr.	FSWW/SC
	Investments	FSWW/SC
	Judgment	FSWW/SC
	Me and Mr. Tree	FSWW/SC
	The Intruder	FSWW/SC
Kilburn, Aileen	*Adult Games*	FSWW/SC
	The Friendship	FSWW/SC
Kirksey, Dianne	*Dreams*	FSWW/SC
Konie, Gwendolyn	*Not of a Kind* (1978)	FSWW/SC
Kunda, Chaka	*Garvey*	FSWW/SC
Landsman, Sandy	*Night Vision*	FSWW/SC
Langa, Bkeki	*Bird of My Luck*	FSWW/SC
(racial/national	*Tsotsis Is Volaak*	FSWW/SC
identity?)	*Vusumuzi*	FSWW/SC
	Kroc	FSWW/SC
Lataro, Ed	*Every Worker's Dream*	FSWW/SC
	The Man Who Saw Through Magic	FSWW/SC
Latty, Garth	*After All Is Said and Done*	FSWW/SC
	Catharsis	FSWW/SC
Lee, Billy J.	*A Bench in Central Park*	FSWW/SC
Lesko, Ruth Garland	*Surviving Spouse*	FSWW/SC
Littleway, Lorna C.	*Phyllis [sic] Wheatley: The Celestial Muse* (3 acts of a first draft)	FSWW/SC
Lizardi, Joseph	*Save the Children*	FSWW/SC
Lukeman, Brenda	*The Haiku Boys*	FSWW/SC
Mac Intyre, Tom	*Find the Lady*	FSWW/SC
McPherson, Andrew	*End of the Line*	FSWW/SC
McQueen, Bill	*The Left Hand Mirror*	FSWW/SC
Manatu, Norma	*Diane*	FSWW/SC
	Family Feeling	FSWW/SC
Mann, Johnny	*For the Night Has Eyes*	FSWW/SC
Marisco, Gio	*The Other Place*	FSWW/SC

Maronkeji [one name]	*Osiris Rises*	FSWW/SC
Marsh, Theresa	*The Dinner Guest*	FSWW/SC
Martin, David F., and Gayther L. Myers	*Hot Gilly Mo* (musical, 1978)	FSWW/SC
Mulligan, Carmel	*It's Our Time to Speak*	FSWW/SC
Myers, Bernard	*Bridges*	FSWW/SC
Obiesie, Adichie	*Festival of the Gods*	FSWW/SC
Oyewole, Abiodun	*Comments* (Subtitled "A Black Man's Response to the Broadway Hit, 'For Colored Girls Who . . . ' ")	FSWW/SC
Parris, Jack	*Into Thy Narrow Bed*	FSWW/SC
Parrish, Milton	*The Mountain*	FSWW/SC
Patrick, Bobbie Jean	*Old Friends*	FSWW/SC
Patterson, Palestrine	*Frenzy, in Flight and Search*	FSWW/SC
Pfeiffer, Pat	*The Feeding*	FSWW/SC
Poole, Larry Spencer	*An Autobiography to Be Somebody*	FSWW/SC
Qualles, Paris H.	*A Song for My People* (1977)	HBC
Rashid, Imani	*A Family Secret*	FSWW/SC
	Stopover in Barbados	FSWW/SC
Roberts, M. Younger	*Cousins*	FSWW/SC
Rodriquez, Ivan	*Fortune*	FSWW/SC
	Lem, One Tramp, an' Ol Dad	FSWW/SC
Rogers, Michael	*The Woman Expert*	FSWW/SC
Ruffin, Glyde	*Like a Tree Planted* (1977)	HBC
	Speak to Me of Love	
Shakoor, Salahu-Din	*Kosokola*	FSWW/SC
	Nappy	FSWW/SC
Shirakawa, Samuel	*The Royal Court*	FSWW/SC
Shiras, Frank	*Swap*	FSWW/SC
Smallwood, Lawrence	*Throwdown*	FSWW/SC
Smith, C. C.	*Dead Ends* (1978)	FSWW/SC
Smith, Michael	*The Book of Malcom [sic]*	FSWW/SC
Stambler, Sookie	*Serpent's Tooth*	FSWW/SC
Steel, John	*Vigil of Candles* (1 act, 1974)	FSWW/SC
Stenbar, Harold	*Child*	FSWW/SC
Stevenson, Albert D.	*To the Bone*	FSWW/SC
Sturdevant, Kathleen	*Scramble for Flight 407*	FSWW/SC
Styles, Teresa	*We Are All the Same*	FSWW/SC
Taylor, Arthur	*The Messiah*	FSWW/SC
Thomas, Ronald Tan	*Mrs. Rutherford Is Dead in That Old Fashioned Garden*	FSWW/SC
Traynham, W. R.	*Zeulu*	FSWW/SC
Uno, Roberta	*In the Rock Garden*	FSWW/SC
Vessells, R. T.	*A Course in Life* (1978)	FSWW/SC
Vundla, Mfundi	*Kalahart: A Folk Drama in One Act*	FSWW/SC

Waller, C. Hobson	*The Ladies* (1976)	FSWW/SC
Wardlaw, Xavier X.	*The Lone Ranger Overture*	FSWW/SC
Weaver, Abiola Roselle (Abiola Sinclair)	*The Matriarchs* (1976)	FSWW/SC
Whitehead, Brenda L.	*High on People*	FSWW/SC
Williams, Sidney Gordon	*Echoes of a Saturday Afternoon*	FSWW/SC

APPENDIX B

OTHER CONTEMPORARY BLACK AMERICAN PLAYWRIGHTS

All undated plays are pre-1980.

PLAYWRIGHT	PLAY
Achilles, Marcel	*Askia, the Great* (historical play, 1 act)
	The Black Mexican (historical play, 1 act)
Adams, Ray	*Ritual of the Blacks* (3 acts, 1974)
Bailey, Roberta	*New Life*
Barnes, Harold C.	*Quite at Random* (fantasy, 1 act)
Batchelor, Ronald	*At Home in the Sun* (historical musical, full length, 1975)
Bennett, Harriet V.	*Grandma's Hands* (1976)
Berry, David	*The Freedom Bird*
	G. R. Point
Best, Germaine	*To the Future* (1 act)
Bey, Salome	*And a Little Child Shall Lead Them* (musical play, 1 act)
	The Sweet Bitter Life (2 acts)
Birchfield, Raymond	*The Diamond Youth* (3 acts, 1973)
Black-Bragg, Norma	*Herman Jones* (domestic drama, 2 acts, 1975)
Blackwell, Don	*The Has Been* (1976)
Blount, Robert (Bob)	*Experience Blackness* (ethnic collage, 1971)
Bond, Horace J.	*Mother April's* (satire, 1977)
Bowen, John	*After the Rain* (1975)
Brandon, Johnny	*Sing Me Sunshine* (musical, 1974)
Brome, George	*Before Black Was Beautiful* (tragicomedy, 1 act)
Brown, Chris, Jr.	*Chocolate* ("A Black Musical," 1971)
Bugg, Arthur	*Where We Are . . .* (1975)
Burgess, Ivan	*Horseshoe House* (drama, 2 acts, 1970)
Butler, E.	*The Smile and Wonder Cycle* (1976)

Carter, James   *The Masks Behind the Clown's Face*
                                  (expressionistic drama, 2 acts, 1968)
Carter, John D.   *The Assassin* (1 act, 1971)
Causley, Ed   *The Paisley Convertible*
Chamber, Charlotte   *Education X* (1973)
Chambers, E. Morris   *July Jones* (domestic drama, 2 acts)
Chambers, Kennedy   *Miller High Life* (play, 1974)
Chatman, Xavier   *And It's Time for a Big Christmas* (musical, 1973)
Chimbamul (Jeri Fowler)   *How the Spider Became the Hero of Folk Tales*
                                  (children's play, 1971)
Chiphe, Leppaigne (with   *A Black Experience*
   Chakula cha Jua)
Chisholm, Earl   *Black Manhood* (1970)
                                  Two in the Back Room (1971)
Coleman, Annie R.   *Gaslight Square* (drama, 2 acts)
Collier, Simone   *In a City*
                                  Straw/Baby with Hay Feet
Connor, Michael Donnel   *Make Mad the Guilty* (drama, 1 act, 1973)
Cornish, Roger   *Open Twenty Four Hours* (1 act, 1972)
Cotton, Walter   *Candyman's Dance* (1974)
                                  Monday Morning of Homing Brown
Curry, Randie   *Zelda and Lucas Plotz* (1 act, 1975)
Cutter, Ron   *Willie Dynamite* (screenplay, 1973)
Dalzon, Wilfrid (coauthor)   *The Second Visitation* (fantasy, 3 acts, 1972)
Dallas, Walter   *Manchild*
                                  Willie Lobo
Daniel, Gloria   *The Male Bag*
Daniel, Helen   *The Hidden Knowledge* (1975)
Davis, Buster   *Doctor Jazz* (1975)
Davis, Geri Turner   *A Cat Called Jesus*
Dumas, Aaron   *Encounter: Three Acts in a Restaurant*
                                  Poor Willie
Dunster, Mark   *Sojourner* (1969)
Ekulona, Ademola (Ronald   *Last Hot Summer*
   Floyd)   *Mother of the House*
                                  Three Black Comedies
Elliott, Marjorie (Marge)   *You Can't Go Home Again* (filmscript, 1975)
                                  Branches from the Same Tree (1983)
Evans, Zitshaw   *Zetta* (1975)
Ezilie [one name]   *Have You Seen Sunshine?*
Ferguson, Lou   *Elton* (1973)
Folani, Femi   *A Play for Zubena* (1972)
Forbes, John (with Ilunga   *Stone and Steel* (TV script)
   Adell)
Forde, John   *The Passing Cloud*
Foster, Gregory (Greg)   *The Life in Lady Day* (1972)
                                  Freeze (1976)
                                  Mainline Blues
Fox, William Price   *Southern Fried* (musical, 1977)

Freeman, Nathan Ross	*The Contract* (1982)
French, David	*One Crack Out* (1978)
Gay, Cedric	*Survival* (musical, full length, 1977)
Gaye, Irwin	*The Spirit of Christmas*
Gelber, Jack	*Rehearsal* (1978)
Gioffre, Marissa	*Bread and Roses* (1976)
Good, Jack	*Santa Fe Satan* (musical)
Gouchis, R. A.	*The Tenement*
Gray, C.	*Family Name*
Greane, David	*Martin Luther King—Man of God*
Greene, Otis	*A Different Part of the World* (1967)
Griffin, Oscar	*Miss Ann Is Still Alive (M.A.I.S.A.)*
Hacket, Harley	*On Toby Time* (1977)
Hightower, Charlie	*Children's Games* (1969)
Hightower, Robert	*The Train Ride*
	The Wall
Hill, Armenter	*Forever My Earth* (1976)
Hill, F.	*Betrayal*
Holliman, O. C.	*Yacob* (c. 1972)
Holt, Steven	*Where the Onus Falls*
Iman, Kasisi Yusef	*Yesterday, Today and Tomorrow*
Jackson, Eugenia Lutcher	*Everything Is Everything*
Jackson, James Thomas	*Bye, Bye Black Sheep* (police drama, full length, pre-1977)
Jeremy, John	*Jazz Is Our Religion* (screenplay)
Johnson, Eugene	*Spaces in Between*
Jones, Arnold	*Cinderella Everafter* (musical, full length, 1977)
Jones, Gene-Olivar	*Based on Cinderella* (antidrug play, 1 act)
	No Church Next Sunday (comedy-drama, 2 acts)
Kenley, Calvin (coauthor)	*The Second Visitation* (fantasy, 3 acts, 1972)
Kinoy, Ernest	*Leadbelly* (1976)
Knudson, K.	*There Were Two Tramps, Now There Are None*
Koenig, Laird	*The Dozens* (1969)
Kyser, Erma	*The Day That Was* (comedy, 1 act)
	Pseudo/Drama of the Life and Times of Mammy Pleasant (biographical drama, 3 acts)
	She Was a Woman (domestic drama, 3 acts)
Lamb, Myrna	*Crab Quadrille* (social satire, 1976)
Lasdun, Gary	*As Long as You're Happy, Barbara* (1974)
Lea, Patricia	*Night Song* (1977)
Leake, Damien	*Child of the Sun* (musical, full length, 1981)
Lerner, Irwin	*Tea* (1975)
LeRoy, Leslie (Hurley)	*Festivities for a New World*
Luther, Katie	*He Will Hallow Thee* (protest drama, 3 acts, 1969)
Lynch, Kim Dejah	*Black Odyssey: 200 Years in America* (Bicentennial play with music and dance, 1976)
Lyons, Shedrick	*A Bird of Passage Out of Night* (domestic drama, full length, 1970)
McGriff, Thereda C.	*Able to Leap from Tall Buildings in a Single Bound* (1980)

McGuire, Lois	*The Lion Writes* (1970)
Merriam, Eve	*Inner City* (musical, 1973)
Miller, Jeffrey	*The Last Ditch Junkie*
	Who Dreamed of Attica?
Neals, Betty Harris	*The Miracle of Sister Love* (drama, 3 acts)
Neely, Bennie E.	*Sue*
Nichol, James W.	*Home, Sweet Home* (1969)
Nodell, Albert Charles	*A River Divided* (1964)
Ormes, Gwendolyn	*Untitled*
	Ome-Nka
Owomoyela, Oyekan	*The Slave* (master's thesis play, UCLA, 1976)
Palmer, Jon Phillips	*The Starting Five* (sports drama, 1975)
Patterson, Lindsay	*Roper* (screenplay, c. 1978)
Pefkins, John	*The Yellow Pillow* (1 act, 1973)
Perry, Manokay	*The House That Was a Country*
Peters	*Fine Print*
Pickett, (Rev.) Leon Ray	*Black-Eyed Peas for Dinner* (comedy, 1982)
Pontiflet, Sudan	*The Preacher's Son*
	Five Black Men
Preston, Tony	*On the Road* (1 act, 1972)
	Rags and Old Iron (1 act, 1972)
Redwood, John	*But I Can't Go Alone*
Reid, Hazel	*H.E.W. Down the People*
	Midnight Maze
Reyes, Albert B.	*P.O.W.*
Roach, E.	*Belle Fanto*
	Letter from Lenora
Roach, Freddie	*Soul Pieces* (1969)
Robinson, Betsy Julia	*The Shanglers*
Robinson, Woodie	*The Marijuana Affair* (screenplay)
Sahkoor, Salahudin	*Armageddon* (1977)
St. Clair, Wesley	*The Station* (1 act, 1969)
Salim (Harrell Cordell	*It's Mary's Boy*
Chauncey)	*We Heard from Martin*
Saunders, Bryon C.	*The Promised Land* (black soap opera)
Saunders, Frank G.	*Balloons in Her Hair*
Scott, Jimmy	*Money* (1968)
Scott, Joseph	*Hocus-Pocus* (domestic comedy, 2 acts)
Seals, Howard E.	*After 'Yuh, Mama* (1972)
Sharkey, Tom	*Togetherness Again*
	Cinderella Brown (musical)
Shelton, Jaki	*Blue Opal*
Sherman, Jimmie	*A Ballad for Watts* (1967)
Smith, Djeniba	*Please Reply Soon* (1971)
Smith, Earl D. A.	*Imani-Umoja* (1975)
Smith, Milburn	*Bloodsport* (1973)

Snave, Eiman	*Little Dodo*
	The Park on 14th Street
	Skin Deep
Spenceley, Philip	*The Nitty Gritty of Mr. Charlie* (1969)
Spillman, Ben	*Where Is the Blood of Your Fathers* (1971)
Starkes, Jaison	*J. D.'s Revenge* (screenplay)
Staten, Pat	*Heartland*
Steele, Richard	*The Matter of Yo Mind*
Stewart, Artie (or possibly Arlie Stewart)	*Trec* // Orig. title: *Voyages* (1969)
Stokes, Jack	*The Incredible Jungle Journey of Panda Maria* (1976)
Storey, Ralph	*Doww* (1971)
Teague, Tony	*Tuff T*
Thomas, Piri	*Saturday Night*
Thomas, Valerie M.	*The Blacklist* (morality, 1 act, 1971)
Thompson, Ron S.	*Cotton Club Revue* (musical, full length, 1976)
Tree, E. Wayne	*Yesterday Continued*
Trenier, Diane	*Rich Black Heritage* (satire, 1 act, 1970)
Ullman, Marvin	*And I Am Black* (1969)
Unger, Robert	*Bohikee Creek* (1965)
Verona, Stephen	*Pipe Dream*
Wanshel, Jeff	*The Disintegration of James Cherry* (1970)
Washington, Charles L.B.	*To Hell with It* (screenplay, 1974)
Washington, Sam	*A Member of the Fateful Gray* (1969)
Way, Bryant	*Magical Faces*
Weaver, Carl	*Wednesday Afternoon Is Sabbath Day*
Webb, Lorraine	*Why Do You Think They Call It Dope* (1974)
Weber, Adam	*Spirit of the Living Dead* (1969)
	To Kill or Die (1969)
White, Iverson	*The Ritual* (1970)
White, Jane (Mrs. Alfredo Viazzi)	*Jane White, Who?* (1980)
White, Kathleen Yvonne	*The Greatest Show on Earth* (1972)
White, Nat	*The Black Tramp* (1964)
	Damn That Miss Ann (1964)
	No One Was Ever Born for Bread (1964)
	Nigger
Wiggins, Ernest	*Song Way Mom Way* (comedy-drama, 1 act, 1973)
Williams, Dick Anthony	*One*
	Black and Beautiful
	A Bit o' Black
Williams, Gerald	*Myth Meat* (1970)
Williams, Harold	*With the Right Seed My Plant Will Grow*
Wilson, Lester	*$600 and a Mule* (musical, 1973)

Wise, Edward	*Zelda and Lucas Plotz* (1 act, 1975)
Wright, Art	*One Thursday Last May*
Wyatte, Farcita	*You Gotta Pay Your Dues* (1973)
Younger, Martin	*A String of Periods*
	Courting
Zellers, Ron	*A Tribute to Otis Redding* (1971)

INFORMATION SOURCES

A. Libraries and Repositories

The following libraries and repositories have strong collections in black theatre and drama. Those which also have play manuscript collections are marked with a double obelisk(‡).

ATLANTA UNIVERSITY CENTER
Robert W. Woodruff Library
111 James P. Brawley Dr., S.W.
Atlanta, GA 30314
    (Countee Cullen/Harold Jackman Collection and Hoyt Fuller Collection)

BOSTON PUBLIC LIBRARY
666 Boylston St.
Boston, MA 02117
    (Drama and Theatre Collections)

DETROIT PUBLIC LIBRARY
Music and Performing Arts Department
5201 Woodward Ave.
Detroit, MI 48202
    (E. Azalia Hackley Collection)

FISK UNIVERSITY
Library and Media Center
17th Ave. N.
Nashville, TN 37203
    (Black Literature Collections)

‡HATCH-BILLOPS COLLECTION
691 Broadway, 7th Floor
New York, NY 10012
    (Published Play Collection, Oral History Tapes, Owen and Edith Dodson Memorial Collection)

‡HOWARD UNIVERSITY LIBRARIES
Moorland-Spingarn Research Center Library
2400 Sixth St., N.W.
Washington, DC 20059
  (Moorland Collection and Spingarn Collection)

‡LOS ANGELES PUBLIC LIBRARY
630 W. 5th St.
Los Angeles, CA 90041
  (Tom W. Harris Play Manuscript Collection and Dobinson Collection of Drama and
Theatre)

‡NEW YORK PUBLIC LIBRARY
Performing Arts Research Center
111 Amsterdam Ave.
New York, NY 10023
  (Billy Rose Theatre Collection)

‡NEW YORK PUBLIC LIBRARY
Schomburg Center for Research in Black Culture
515 Lenox Ave.
New York, NY 10037
  (Schomburg Collection, Black Theatre Collection, and Archives of the Frank Silvera
Writers' Workshop)

NORFOLK PUBLIC LIBRARY
301 E. City Hall Ave.
Norfolk, VA 23510
  (Black Literature Collection)

NORFOLK STATE UNIVERSITY
Lyman Beecher Brooks Library
2401 Corprew Ave.
Norfolk, VA 23504
  (Ethnic Collection)

RICHMOND PUBLIC LIBRARY
101 E. Franklin St.
Richmond, VA 23219
  (Reference Collection)

UNIVERSITY OF NORTH CAROLINA LIBRARIES
Chapel Hill, NC 27514
  (Interlibrary Loan)

‡YALE UNIVERSITY
Sterling Memorial Library
120 High St.
New Haven, CT 06520
  (James Weldon Johnson Memorial Collection)

B. Title List of Play Anthologies Which Include One or More Plays by Black American Playwrights

For individually published plays and collections of plays by a single playwright, consult the playwright's entry in this directory.

Afro-American Literature, ed. by Robert Hayden, David Burrows, and Frederick Lapides. New York: Harcourt Brace Jovanovich, 1971.

Afro-American Literature: Drama, ed. by William Adams, Peter Conn, and Barry Slepian. Boston: Houghton Mifflin, 1970.

Afro-Arts Anthology. Newark: Jihad Press, 1968.

The American Place Theatre: Plays, ed. by Richard Scotter. New York: Delta/Dell, 1973.

Amistad 1: Writings Based on Black History and Culture, ed. by John A. Williams and Charles F. Harris. New York: Vintage/Random House, 1970.

An Anthology for Introduction to the Theatre, ed. by Melvin R. White and Frank Whiting. Glenview, IL: Scott, Foresman, 1969.

Anthology of the American Negro in the Theatre, ed. by Lindsay Patterson. New York: Publishers Co., under the auspices of the Association for the Study of Negro Life and History, 1967.

The Art of Drama, ed. by R. F. Dietrich, William E. Carpenter, and Kevin Kerrane. New York: Holt, Rinehart and Winston, 1969.

The Best American Plays, 6th Series, 1963–1967, ed. by John Gassner and Clive Barnes. New York: Crown, 1971.

The Best Short Plays, 1969, ed. by Stanley Richards. Philadelphia: Chilton, 1969.

The Best Short Plays, 1970, ed. by Stanley Richards. Philadelphia: Chilton, 1970; New York: Avon, 1970

The Best Short Plays, 1971, ed. by Stanley Richards. Philadelphia: Chilton, 1971; New York: Avon, 1971.

The Best Short Plays, 1972, ed. by Stanley Richards. Philadelphia: Chilton, 1972; New York: Avon, 1972.

The Best Short Plays, 1973, ed. by Stanley Richards. Philadelphia: Chilton, 1973.

The Best Short Plays, 1974, ed. by Stanley Richards. New York: Chilton, 1974.

The Best Short Plays, 1975, ed. by Stanley Richards. New York: Chilton, 1975.

The Best Short Plays, 1977, ed. by Stanley Richards. New York: Crown, 1977.

Best Short Plays of the World Theatre, 1958–1967, ed. by Stanley Richards. New York: Crown, 1968.

Best Short Plays of the World Theatre, 1968–1973, ed. by Stanley Richards. New York: Crown, 1973.

Blackamerican Literature, 1970–Present, ed. by Ruth Miller. Beverly Hills, CA: Glencoe Press, a div. of Macmillan, New York, 1971.

Black Arts: An Anthology of Black Creations, ed. by Ahmed Alhamisi and Harun Kofi Wangara. Detroit: Broadside Press, 1969.

Black Culture: Reading and Writing Black, ed. by Gloria M. Simmons and Helene D. Hutchinson. New York: Holt, Rinehart and Winston, 1972.

Black Drama—An Anthology, ed. by William Brasmer and Dominick Consolo, Columbus, OH: Charles E. Merrill, 1970.

Black Drama Anthology, ed. by Woodie King, Jr., and Ron Milner. New York: Columbia Univ. Press, 1972.

Black Drama in America: An Anthology, ed. by Darwin T. Turner. New York: Fawcett, 1971.

Black Fire: An Anthology of Afro-American Writings, ed. by LeRoi Jones and Larry Neal. New York: William Morrow, 1968.

Black Identity: A Thematic Reader, ed. by Francis E. Kearns. New York: Holt, Rinehart and Winston, 1970.

Black Literature: An Anthology of Outstanding Black Writers, ed. by William D. Washington and Samuel Beckoff. New York: Simon and Schuster, 1972.

Black Perspectives. The Scholastic Black Literature Series. Ed. by Alma Murray and Robert Thomas. New York: Scholastic Book Services, a div. of *Scholastic* magazines, 1971.

A Black Quartet. A collection of plays by Ben Caldwell, Ronald Milner, Ed Bullins, and LeRoi Jones (Amiri Baraka). New York: Signet/New American Library, 1970.

Black Scenes. Selections from plays by black playwrights. Ed. by Alice Childress. Garden City, NY: Doubleday/Zenith, 1971.

The Black Teacher and the Dramatic Arts: A Dialogue, Bibliography, and Anthology, ed. by William R. Reardon and Thomas D. Pawley. Westport, CT: Greenwood Press [Negro Universities Press], 1970.

Black Theater: A Twentieth Century Collection of the Work of Its Best Playwrights, ed. by Lindsay Patterson. New York: Dodd, Mead, 1971.

Black Theater, U.S.A.: Forty-Five Plays by Black Americans, 1847–1974, ed. by James V. Hatch and Ted Shine. New York: The Free Press, a div. of Macmillan, 1974.

Black Voices from Prison, ed. by Etheridge Knight. New York: Pathfinder Press, 1970.

Black Writers of America, ed. by Richard Barksdale and Kenneth Kinnamon. New York: Macmillan, 1972.

Broadway's Best, by John Chapman. Theatrical yearbook. New York: Doubleday, 1959.

Caribbean Literature: An Anthology, ed. by Gabriel R. Coulthard. London: Univ. of London Press, 1966.

Caribbean Plays, Vols. 1 and 2, ed. by Errol Hill. Extramural Dept., Univ. of the West Indies, 1964.

Cavalcade: Negro American Writing from 1760 to the Present, ed. by Arthur P. Davis and J. Saunders Redding. Boston: Houghton Mifflin, 1971.

Center Stage: An Anthology of 21 Contemporary Black-American Plays, ed. by Eileen Joyce Ostrow. Oakland, CA: Sea Urchin Press, 1981.

Classic Through Modern Drama: An Introductory Anthology, ed. by Otto Reinert. Boston: Little, Brown, 1970.

Collision Course: An Omnibus of Seventeen Brief Plays, ed. by Edward Parone. New York: Random House, 1968.

Connection, ed. by Curtiss Porter. Pittsburgh: Oduduwa Production, 1970.

Contemporary Black Drama: From "A Raisin in the Sun" to "No Place to Be Somebody," ed. by Clinton F. Oliver and Stephanie Sills. New York: Charles Scribner's Sons, 1971.

Contemporary Drama: Thirteen Plays, 2nd ed., ed. by Stanley Clayes and David Spencer. New York: Charles Scribner's Sons, 1970.

Cry at Birth, ed. by Merrel Daniel Booker, Sr., et al. New York: McGraw-Hill, 1971.

The Design of Drama: An Introduction, ed. by Lloyd J. Hubenka and LeRoy Garcia. New York: David McKay, 1973.

Discovery and Recollection: An Anthology of Literary Types, ed. by Elizabeth Heisch. New York: Holt, Rinehart and Winston, 1970.

The Disinherited: Plays, ed. by Abe C. Ravitz. Encino, CA: Dickenson, 1974.

Drama and Discussion, 2nd ed., ed. by Stanley A. Clayes. Chicago: Loyola Univ., 1978.

Drama and Revolution, ed. by Bernard Dukore. New York: Holt, Rinehart and Winston, 1971.

Drama for Composition, ed. by Bert C. Back and Gordon Browning. Glenview, IL: Scott, Foresman, 1973.

The Drama of Nommo, ed. by Paul Carter Harrison. New York: Grove Press, 1972.

Eight American Ethnic Plays, ed. by Francis Griffith and Joseph Mersand. New York: Scribner's, 1974.

Exploring Literature: Fiction, Poetry, Drama, Criticism, ed. by Lynn Altenbernd. New York: Macmillan, 1970.

Famous American Plays of the 1970s, ed. by Ted Hoffman. New York: Dell, 1981.

Foundations of American Drama, ed. by C. J. Gianakaris. Boston: Houghton Mifflin, 1975.

Four Contemporary American Plays, ed. by Bennett Cerf. New York: Vintage/Random House, 1961.

The Free Southern Theatre by the Free Southern Theatre, ed. by Thomas C. Dent, Richard Schechner, and Gilbert Moses. Indianapolis: Bobbs-Merrill, 1969.

From the Ashes: Voices of Watts, ed. by Budd Schulberg. New York: New American Library, 1967.

A Galaxy of Black Writing, ed. by R. Baird Shuman. Durham, NC: Moore, 1970.

Generations: An Introduction to Drama, ed. by M. S. Barranger and Daniel B. Dodson. New York: Harcourt Brace Jovanovich, 1971.

The Great American Life Show: Nine Plays from the Avant Garde Theatre, ed. by John Lahr and Jonathan Price. New York: Bantam, 1974.

Grove Press Modern Drama, ed. by John Lahr. New York: Grove Press/Evergreen, distributed by Random House, 1975.

Guerrilla Theatre: Scenarios for Revolution, ed. by John Weisman. New York: Anchor/Doubleday, 1973.

Humanities Through the Black Experience, ed. by Phyllis Roach Kotman et al. Dubuke, OH: Kendall/Hunt, date unknown.

Icarus: An Anthology of Literature, ed. by John H. Bens and Douglas R. Baugh. New York: Macmillan, 1970.

Interactions: Themes for Thoughtful Living, ed. by Thelma Altschuler. Beverly Hills, CA: Glencoe Press, a div. of Macmillan, 1972.

An Introduction to Black Literature in America: From 1746 to the Present, ed. by Lindsay Patterson. New York: Publishers Co., under the auspices of the Association for the Study of Negro Life and History, 1968.

An Introduction to Theatre and Drama, ed. by Marshall Cassady and Pat Cassady. Skokie, IL: National Textbook, 1975.

Introduction to the Play: In the Theatre of the Mind, ed. by Robert W. Boynton and Maynard Mack. Rochelle Park, NJ: Hayden, 1976.

Keys to Understanding: Receiving and Sending—Drama, ed. by Paul C. Holmes and Anita J. Lehman. New York: Harper and Row, 1970.

Kuntu Drama: Plays of the African Continuum, ed. by Paul Carter Harrison. New York: Grove Press, distributed by Random House, 1974.

The Literature of America: Twentieth Century, ed. by Mark Schorer. New York: McGraw-Hill, 1970.

Major Black Writers. The Scholastic Black Literature Series. Ed. by Alma Murray and Robert Thomas. New York: Scholastic Book Services, a div. of *Scholastic* magazines, 1971.

The Man in the Dramatic Mode, vol. 5, ed. by Lilla Heston. Evanston, IL: McDougal, Littel, 1970.

Masterpieces of the Drama, 3rd ed., ed. by Alexander W. Allison et al. New York: Macmillan, 1974.

Masterpieces of the Drama, ed. Charles C. Ritter. Columbus, OH: Collegiate Publishing, 1976.

Meeting Challenges, ed. by J. Nelson. New York: American Book Co., 1980.

Mirrors for Man: 25 Plays of the World Drama, ed. by Leonard R.N. Ashley. Cambridge, MA: Winthrop, 1974.

Modern Drama and Social Change, ed. by Robert A. Raines. Englewood Cliffs, NJ: Prentice-Hall, 1972.

More Plays from Off-Off-Broadway, ed. by Michael Smith. Indianapolis: Bobbs-Merrill, 1966.

The Negro Caravan, ed. by Sterling A. Brown, Arthur P. Davis, and Ulysses Lee. New York: Dryden Press, 1941; reprinted by Arno Press and the New York Times, 1969.

New American Plays, vol. 2, ed. by William M. Hoffman. New York: Hill and Wang, 1968.

New Black Playwrights, ed. by William T. Couch, Jr. Baton Rouge: Louisiana State Univ. Press, 1968; and New York: Avon, 1970.

The New Lafayette Theatre Presents, ed. by Ed Bullins. New York: Anchor Press/Doubleday, 1974.

The New Negro Renaissance, ed. Arthur P. Davis and Michael W. Peplow. New York: Holt, Rinehart and Winston, 1975.

New Plays from the Black Theatre, ed. by Ed Bullins. New York: Bantam, 1969.

New Theatre in America, ed. by Edward Parone. New York: Delta/Dell, 1965.

The New Women's Theatre: Ten Plays by Contemporary American Women, ed. by Honor Moore. New York: Vintage, 1977.

The New Writing in the USA, ed. by Donald Allen and Robert Creeley. New York: Penguin, 1967.

Nine Plays by Black Women, ed. by Margaret B. Wilkerson. NY: Mentor/New American Library, 1986.

Nineteen Necromancers from Now, ed. by Ishmael Reed. Garden City, NY: Doubleday, 1970.

Nommo: An Anthology of Modern Black African and Black American Literature, ed. by William H. Robinson. New York: Macmillan, 1972.

The Norton Introduction to Literature: Drama, ed. by Carl E. Bain. New York: W. W. Norton, 1973.

The Off-Broadway Book: The Plays, People, and Theatre, ed. Albert Poland and Bruce Mailman. Indianapolis: Bobbs-Merrill, 1972.

The Off-Off Broadway Book, ed. by Albert Poland and Bruce Mailman. Indianapolis: Bobbs-Merrill, 1972.

Plays by and About Women, ed. by Victoria Sullivan and James V. Hatch. New York: Random House, 1973.

Plays for Our Time, ed. by Bennett Cerf. New York: Random House, 1967.

Plays for the Theatre: An Anthology of World Drama, 3rd ed., ed. by Oscar G. Brockett and Lenyth Brockett. New York: Holt, Rinehart & Winston, 1979.

Plays from the New York Shakespeare Festival. New York: Broadway Play Publishing, 1986.

Playreader's Repertory: Drama on Stage, ed. by Melvin White and Frank M. Whiting. Glenview, IL: Scott, Foresman, 1970.

Plays of Our Time, ed. by Bennett Cerf. New York: Random House, 1967.

Plays on a Human Theme, ed. by Cy Groves. Toronto: McGraw-Hill Ryerson, 1967.

Points of Departure, ed. by Bernece B. Kelly. New York: John Wiley and Sons, 1972.

The Practical Imagination: Stories, Poems, Plays, ed. by Northrop Frye, Sheridan Baker, and George Perkins. New York: Harper and Row, 1980.

The Range of Literature: Drama, 3rd ed., ed. by Elizabeth W. Schneider, Albert L. Walker, and Herbert E. Childs. New York: Van Nostrand, 1973.

The Realities of Literature, ed. by Richard F. Dietrich. Xerox Coll., 1971.

Right On! An Anthology of Black Literature, ed. by Bradford Chambers and Rebecca Moon. New York: Mentor/New American Library, 1970.

Ritual, Realism, and Revolt: Major Traditions in the Drama, ed. by J. Chesley Taylor and G. R. Thompson. New York: Scribner's, 1972.

The Scene. The Scholastic Black Literature Series. Ed. by Alma Murray and Robert Thomas. New York: Scholastic Book Services, a div. of *Scholastic* magazines, 1971.

The Search. The Scholastic Black Literature Series. Ed. by Alma Murray and Robert Thomas. New York: Scholastic Book Services, a div. of *Scholastic* magazines, 1971.

Seventeen Plays: Sophocles to Baraka, ed. by Bernard F. Dukore. New York: Thomas Y. Crowell, 1976.

Six American Plays for Today, ed. by Bennett Cerf. New York: Modern Library, 1961.

Skits and Sketches. New York: New Theatre League, 1939.

Standing Room Only, ed. Dalgon and Bernier. Englewood Cliffs, NJ: Prentice-Hall, 1977.

A Theatre in Your Head, by Kenneth Thorpe Rowe. New York: Funk and Wagnalls, 1960.

Thirty-two Scenes for Acting Practice, ed. by Samuel Elkind et al. Glenview, IL: Scott, Foresman, 1972.

Three Hundred and Sixty Degrees of Blackness Comin at You, ed. by Sonia Sanchez. New York: 5 X Publishing distributed by Broadside Press, 1971.

Three Negro Plays, ed. by C.W.E. Bigsby. Harmondsworth: Penguin, 1964.

Three Plays from the Yale School of Drama, ed. by John Gassner. New York: Dutton, 1964.

Time to Greez! Incantations from the Third World, ed. by Buriel Clay (black editor) et al. San Francisco: Glide Publications, 1975.

The Tony Winners: A Collection of Ten Exceptional Plays, Winners of the Tony Awards for the Most Distinguished Play of the Year, ed. by Stanley Richards. New York: Dodd, Mead, 1977.

A Treasury of the Theatre, 4th ed., vol. 2: *From Henrik Ibsen to Robert Lowell*, ed. by John Gassner and Bernard F. Dukore. New York: Simon and Schuster, 1970; distributed by Dryden.

Twenty-Eight Scenes for Acting and Practice, ed. by Samuel Elkind et al. Glenview, IL: Scott, Foresman, 1971.

Two Voices: Writing About Literature, by Ken M. Symes. Boston: Houghton Mifflin, 1976.

Types of Drama: Plays and Essays, ed. by Silvan Barnet, Morton Berman, and William Burto. Boston: Little, Brown, 1972.

Upstage/Downstage: A Theatre Festival, ed. by Edmund J. Farrell et al. Glenview, IL.: Scott, Foresman, 1976.

The Urban Reader, ed. by Susan Cahill and Michele Cooper. Englewood Cliffs, NJ: Prentice-Hall, 1971.

We Are Black. Chicago: Science Research Assocs., 1969.

West Coast Plays, 11/12. Berkeley, CA: Theatre Council, 1982.

Whodunits, Farces, and Fantasies: Ten Short Plays, ed. by Robert W. Boynton and Maynard Mack. Rochelle Park, NY: Hayden, 1976.

Who Took the Weight? Black Voices from Norfolk Prison, by the Norfolk Prison Brothers. Boston: Little, Brown, 1972.

The Yardbird Reader, vol. 4, ed. by Ishmael Reed. Berkeley, CA: Yardbird, 1975.

C. REFERENCE BOOKS AND CRITICAL STUDIES

Includes specific studies of black American playwrights and their plays as well as more general resource materials pertinent to the subject.

Abramson, Doris E. *Negro Playwrights in the American Theatre, 1925–1959*. New York: Columbia Univ. Press, 1969.

Afro-American Encyclopedia. 10 vols. North Miami, FL: Educational Book Publishers, 1974.

Arata, Esther Spring. *More Black American Playwrights: A Bibliography*. Metuchen, NJ: Scarecrow Press, 1978.

———, and Nicholas John Rotoli. *Black American Playwrights, 1800 to the Present: A Bibliography*. Metuchen, NJ: Scarecrow Press, 1976.

Archer, Leonard C. *Black Images in the American Theatre*. Brooklyn: Pageant-Poseidon, 1973.

ArtSourceBook: A Directory of Minority Artists in Pennsylvania and Resource Guide for Pennsylvania's Arts Constituency. 1983 ed. Harrisburg: Pennsylvania Council on the Arts, 1983.

The Association of Theatrical Artists and Craftspeople, comps. and eds. *The New York Theatrical Sourcebook, 1985–1986 Edition*. New York: Broadway Press, 1985.

Barbour, Floyd B. *The Black Seventies*. Boston: Sargent, 1970.

Bardolph, Richard. *The Negro Vanguard*. New York: Rinehart, 1959; Vintage/Random House, 1961; now distributed by Greenwood Press.

Baskin, Wade, and Richard N. Runes. *Dictionary of Black Culture*. New York: Philosophical Library, 1973.

Beckerman, Bernard, and Howard Siegman. *On Stage: Selected Theatre Reviews from the New York Times, 1920–1970.* New York: Arno Press, 1973.

Bergman, Peter N., and Mort N. Bergman. *The Chronological History of the Negro in America.* New York: Bergman Publishers, 1969; distributed by Harper and Row; and by Mentor/New American Library, 1969.

The Best Plays of 1950–1951/1983–1984. (The Burns Mantle Theatre Yearbook.) Various editors, as follows: John Chapman, 1950/52; Louis Kronenberger, 1952/61; Henry Hewes, 1961/64; Otis Guernsey, 1965/85. New York: Dodd, Mead, 1951/1984.

Bigsby, C.W.E., ed. *The Black American Writer.* Vol. 2: *Poetry and Drama.* Deland, FL: Everett/Edwards; distributed by Penguin, 1969.

Biographical and Genealogy Master Index. 2nd ed. [8 vols.]. Also: *1981–85 Cumulation* [5 vols.]. Detroit: Gale Research, c. 1985.

The Black Resource Guide: The 1985 Edition. Washington, DC: Black Resource Guide, 1985.

Black Studies: A Dissertation Bibliography. Also: *Black Studies II: A Dissertation Bibliography.* Ann Arbor, MI: University Microfilms International, c. 1977, c. 1980.

Black Theatre Directory. A project of the National Committee on Cultural Diversity in the Performing Arts., with the technical assistance of the American Theatre Assn. Washington, DC: John F. Kennedy Center for the Performing Arts, 1981.

Bogle, Donald. *Toms, Coons, Mulattoes, Mammies, and Bucks: An Interpretive History of Blacks in American Films.* New York: Viking, 1973.

Bonin, Jane F. *Major Themes in Prize-Winning American Drama.* Metuchen, NJ: Scarecrow Press, 1975.

———. *Prize-Winning American Drama: A Bibliographical and Descriptive Guide.* Metuchen, NJ: Scarecrow Press, 1973.

Bordman, Gerald. *The Oxford Companion to American Theatre.* New York: Oxford Univ. Press, 1984.

Brooks, Tim, and Earle Marsh. *The Complete Directory to Prime Time Network TV Shows, 1946–Present.* New York: Ballantine, 1979.

Brustein, Robert. *Seasons of Discontent: Dramatic Opinions, 1959–1965.* New York: Simon and Schuster, 1965.

Butcher, Margaret Just. *The Negro in American Culture.* Based on materials left by Alain Locke. Revised and updated ed. New York: Mentor/New American Library, 1971.

Campbell, Dorothy W. *Index to Black American Writers in Collective Biographies.* Littleton, CO: Libraries Unlimited, 1983.

Celebrity Service International Contact Book, 1985. New York: Celebrity Service Inc., 1984.

Clarke, John Henrik. *Harlem: A Community in Transition.* Syracuse, NY: Citadel Press, 1964, 1969.

———. *Harlem, U.S.A.* Berlin: Seven Seas, 1964; revised ed., New York: Collier/Macmillan, 1971.

Clurman, Harold. *The Naked Image: Observations on the Modern Theatre.* New York: Macmillan, 1966.

Cohn, Ruby. *New American Dramatists: 1960–1980.* New York: Grove, 1982.

Contemporary Authors, vol. 1–4/vol. 115. (Orig. series and various revisions.) Detroit: Gale Research, 1962/86.

Cruse, Harold. *The Crisis of the Negro Intellectual.* New York: William Morrow, 1967.

Davis, Thadious M., and Trudier Harris. *Afro-American Writers After 1955: Dramatists and Prose Writers. (Dictionary of Literary Biography, Vol. 38.)* Detroit: Gale Research, 1985.

A Directory of American Poets and Fiction Writers, 1985–86 Edition. New York: Poets & Writers, 1985.

Directory of Minority Arts Organizations. Washington, DC: Civil Rights Div., National Endowment for the Arts, Dec. 1982; new ed. in prep. for Spring 1985.

Dramatists Play Service. *Complete Catalog of Plays, 1984–1985.* New York: Dramatists Play Service, 1984. Also earlier eds.

Dramatists Sourcebook: Complete Opportunities for Playwrights, Translators, Composers, Lyricists and Librettists, 1985–86 Edition. New York: Theatre Communications Group, 1985.

Ebert, Roger. *Roger Ebert's Movie Home Companion, 1987 Edition.* Kansas City, MO: Andrews, McMeel & Parker, A Universal Press Syndicate Affiliate, 1985.

The Ebony Handbook. Chicago: Johnson Publishing, 1974.

Eddleman, Floyd Eugene, comp. *American Drama Criticism: Supplement 1 to the Second Edition.* Hamden, CT: Shoe String Press, 1984.

Eisner, Joe, and David Krinsky. *Television Comedy Series: An Episodic Guide to 153 TV Sitcoms in Syndication.* Jefferson, NC: McFarland, 1984.

Ethridge, James M., and Cecilia Ann Marlow, eds. *The Directory of Directories, 1983.* Detroit: Gale Research, 1983.

Fabre, Geneviève. *Drumbeats, Masks and Metaphor: Contemporary Afro-American Theatre.* Trans. by Melvin Dixon of Fabre's *Le Theatre noir aux Etats Unis* (Black Theatre in the United States), originally pub. in Paris by Editions du Centre National de la research scientifique, 1982. Washington, DC: Howard Univ. Press, 1983.

————et al. *Afro-American Poetry and Drama, 1760–1975: A Guide to Information Sources.* Detroit: Gale Research, 1979.

Gayle, Addison, Jr., ed. *The Black Aesthetic.* New York: Doubleday, 1971.

————. *Black Expression: Essays by and About Black Americans in the Creative Arts.* New York: Weybright and Talley, 1969.

Gibson, Donald B., ed. *Five Black Writers: Essays on Wright, Ellison, Baldwin, Hughes and Jones.* New York: New York Univ. Press, 1970.

Gottfried, Martin. *Opening Nights: Theatre Criticisms of the Sixties.* New York: Putnam 1969.

Guernsey, Otis L., Jr. *Directory of the American Theatre, 1894–1971.* (An index to *The Best Plays* series, also called the *Burns Mantle Theatre Yearbook.*) New York: Dodd, Mead, 1971.

Hartnoll, Phyllis, ed. *The Oxford Companion to the Theatre.* 3rd. ed. London: Oxford Univ. Press, 1972.

Hatch, James V. *Black Image on the American Stage: A Bibliography of Plays and Musicals, 1770–1970.* New York: DBS Publications, 1970.

————, and Omanii Abdullah. *Black Playwrights, 1823–1977: An Annotated Bibliography of Plays.* New York: R. R. Bowker, 1977.

Hill, Errol, ed. *The Theatre of Black Americans: A Collection of Critical Essays.* 2 vols. Vol. 1: *Roots and Rituals/The Image Makers.* Vol. 2: *The Presenters/The Participators.* Englewood Cliffs, NJ: Prentice-Hall, 1980.

Hill, George H., and Sylvia Saverson Hill. *Blacks on Television: A Selectively Annotated Bibliography.* Metuchen, NJ: Scarecrow Press, 1985.

Hill, Herbert. *Anger and Beyond: The Negro Writer in the United States*. New York: Harper and Row, 1966.

Howard University Library, Washington, DC. *Dictionary Catalog of the Arthur B. Spingarn Collection of Negro Authors*. 2 vols. Boston: G. K. Hall, 1970.

————*Dictionary Catalog of the Jesse E. Moorland Collection of Negro Life and History*. 9 vols. Boston: G. K. Hall, 1970.

Hudson, Theodore R. *From LeRoi Jones to Amiri Baraka: The Literary Works*. Durham, NC: Duke Univ. Press, 1973.

Hughes, Catharine R., ed. *New York Theatre Annual, 1976–77/1977–78*, vols. 1 and 2. Also: *American Theatre Annual, 1978–79/1979–80*. (Continuing series. Title changed to cover regional theatre companies and national touring companies, in addition to New York prodns.) Detroit: Gale Research, 1978/1981.

Hughes, Langston, and Milton Meltzer. *Black Magic: A Pictorial History of the Negro in American Entertainment*. Englewood Cliffs, NJ: Prentice-Hall, 1967.

Index to Periodical Articles by and About Negroes. (Formerly *Index to Selected Periodicals*.) *Cumulated, 1960–1970*. Also:/Annual vols., 1970–1980s. Boston: G. K. Hall, 1970/1980s.

Index to Selected Periodicals Received in the Hallie Q. Brown Library. (Superceded by *Index to Periodical Articles by and About Negroes*.) *Decennial Cumulation, 1950–1959*. Boston: G. K. Hall, 1961.

Kallenbach, Jessamine S., comp. *Index to Black American Literary Anthologies*. Sponsored by the Center of Educational Resources, Eastern Michigan Univ., Ypsilanti. Boston: G. K. Hall, 1979.

Kaplan, Mike, ed. *Variety Presents the Complete Book of Major U.S. Show Business Awards*. (Rev. ed. of *Variety Major U.S. Showbusiness Awards, 1982*.) New York: Garland 1985.

————*Variety Who's Who in Show Business*. New York: Garland, 1983.

Kaye, Phyllis Johnson, ed. *(The) National Playwrights Directory*. 2nd ed. Waterford, CT: Eugene O'Neill Theatre Center, 1981. Also 1st ed., 1977.

Keller, Dean H. *Index to Plays in Periodicals—Revised and Expanded Edition*. Metuchen, NJ: Scarecrow Press, 1979. Also earlier vols.: *Index to Plays in Periodicals* (1971) and its *Supplement* (1973).

Kennedy, Scott. *In Search of an African Theatre*. New York: Scribner's Sons, 1973.

King, Woodie, Jr. *Black Theatre: Present Condition*. New York: Publishing Center for Cultural Resources, 1981.

Leab, Daniel J. *From Sambo to Superspade: The Black Experience in Motion Pictures*. Boston: Houghton Mifflin, 1976.

Little, Stuart W. *Off-Broadway: The Prophetic Theatre*. New York: Coward, McCann and Geoghegan, 1972.

MacNicholas, John. *Twentieth-Century American Dramatists*. *(Dictionary of Literary Biography, Vol. 7.)* 2 vols. Detroit: Gale Research, 1981.

McNeil, Barbara, and Miranda Herbert. *Performing Arts Biographies Master Index*. Detroit: Gale Research, Dec. 1981. Also earlier ed., 1979.

Maltin, Leonard, ed. *Leonard Maltin's TV Movies, 1985–86 Edition*. New York: Signet/ New American Library, 1984. Also earlier eds., 1969/82.

Mapp, Edward. *Directory of Blacks in the Performing Arts*. Metuchen, NJ: Scarecrow Press, 1978.

Marquis Who's Who, Inc. *Marquis Who's Who Publications/Index to All Books. Who's Who in America. Who's Who in the East. Who's Who in the Midwest. Who's Who in the South and Southwest. Who's Who in the West. Who's Who in the World. Who's Who of American Women.* Chicago, various eds., 1960/1986.

Martin, Mick, and Marsha Porter. *Video Movie Guide, 1986.* New York: Ballantine, 1986.

Matney, William C. *Who's Who Among Black Americans, 3rd ed., 1980–81.* Northbook, II: Who's Who Among Black Americans, Inc., 1981. Also 1st ed., 1975–1976, and 2nd ed., c. 1977–1978.

Miller, Elizabeth W. *The Negro in America: A Bibliography.* 2nd ed. Cambridge, MA: Harvard Univ. Press, 1970. Also 1st ed., 1966.

Mitchell, Loften. *Black Drama: The Story of the American Negro in the Theatre.* New York: Hawthorn, 1967.

————*Voices of the Black Theatre.* Clinton, NJ: James White, 1975.

Monaco, James. *American Film Now.* New York: Oxford Univ. Press, 1979.

Murray, James P. *To Find an Image: Black Films from Uncle Tom to Superfly.* Indianapolis: Bobbs-Merrill, 1974.

The Negro Handbook. (Superceded by *The Ebony Handbook.*) Chicago: Johnson Publishing, 1966.

Newman, Richard, comp. *Black Access: A Bibliography of Afro-American Bibliographies.* Westport, CT: Greenwood Press, 1984.

New York Public Library. *Dictionary Catalog of the Schomburg Collection of Negro Literature and History,* 9 vols., 1962. *1st Supplement,* 2 vols., 1967. *2nd Supplement,* 4 vols., 1972. *Supplement 1974,* 1976. Boston: G. K. Hall, dates as indicated.

The New York Times (On-Going Reference Services). *The New York Times Book Review. The New York Times Book Review Index. The New York Times Film Reviews. The New York Times Theatre Reviews.* New York: New York Times/Arno Press, 1970–.

The New York Writer's Source Book, 1983. New York: Dept. of Cultural Affairs, City of New York, 1983.

Notable Names in the American Theatre. (A revision of *The Biographical Encyclopedia & Who's Who of the American Theatre,* ed. Walter Rigdon, 1966.)

Nykoruk, Barbara, ed. *Authors in the News.* Vols. 1 and 2. Detroit: Gale Research, 1976.

Parish, James R. *Actors' Television Credits, 1950–1972.* Metuchen, NJ: Scarecrow Press, 1973.

Patterson, Lindsay. *Black Films and Film-Makers: A Comprehensive Anthology from Stereotype to Superhero.* New York: Dodd, Mead, 1975.

————*Anthology of the American Negro in the Theatre: A Critical Approach.* New York: Publications Co., Inc., under the auspices of the Association for the Study of Negro Life and History, 1967.

Play Index, 1949–1952/1978–1982. 5 vols. Various editors, as follows: *1949–1952,* ed. Dorothy Herbert West and Dorothy Margaret Peake; *1953–1960,* ed. Estelle A. Fidell and Dorothy Margaret Peake; *1961–1967* and *1973–1977,* ed. Estelle A. Fidell; *1978–1982,* ed. Juliette Yaakov. New York: H. W. Wilson, 1953/1983.

Ploski, Harry A., and Roscoe C. Brown. *The Negro Almanac.* New York: Bellwether Publishing, 1966. (Superseded by *Afro USA.*)

Ploski, Harry A., and Ernest Kaiser. *Afro USA: A Reference Work on the Black Expe-*

rience. (An expanded and enlarged version of the *Negro Almanac,* first pub. in 1967.) New York: Belwether Publishing, 1971; distributed by Afro-American Press. (See also next entry.)

Ploski, Harry A., et al. *Reference Library of Black Americans.* Book. III. New York: Bellwether Publishing, 1971. Contains identical material to that included in *Afro USA.*

Primus, Marc. *Black Theatre: A Resource Directory.* New York: Black Theatre Alliance, 1973.

Ralph, George. *The American Theatre, the Negro, and the Freedom Movement.* (Bibliography, 33 pp.) Chicago: Chicago City Missionary Soc., 1966.

Reardon, William R., and Thomas D. Pawley, eds. *The Black Teacher and the Dramatic Arts: A Dialogue, Bibliography, and Anthology.* Westport, CT: Greenwood Press [Negro Universities Press], 1970.

Regional Black Arts Directory, 1983. Atlanta: Southern Arts Federation, 1983.

Rigdon, Walter, ed. *The Biographical Encyclopedia & Who's Who of the American Theatre.* (Revised as *Notable Names in the American Theatre.*) New York: James H. Heineman, 1966.

Rush, Theressa Gunnels, Carol Fairbanks Myers, and Esther Spring Arata. *Black American Writers Past and Present: A Biographical and Bibliographical Dictionary.* 2 vols. Metuchen, NJ: Scarecrow Press, 1976.

Ryan, Desmond. *Video Capsule Reviews.* New York: Fireside/Simon and Schuster, 1985.

Salem, James. *A Guide to Critical Reviews.* Parts I, II, IV, and Supplement One to Part IV. *Part I: American Drama, 1909–1982,* 3rd ed., 1984. *Part II: The Musical, 1909–1974,* 2nd ed., 1976. *Part IV: The Screenplay From "The Jazz Singer" to "Dr. Strangelove,"* 2 vols., 1971. *Part IV: The Screenplay, Supplement One, 1963–1980,* 1982. Metuchen, NJ: Scarecrow Press, dates as indicated.

Samples, Gordon. *The Drama Scholars' Index to Plays and Filmscripts: A Guide to Plays and Filmscripts in Selected Anthologies, Serials and Periodicals.* 2 vols. Metuchen, NJ: Scarecrow Press; orig. vol., 1974; vol. 2, 1980.

Samuel, French, Inc. *Basic Catalog of Plays, 1985.* New York: Samuel French, Inc., 1985. Also earlier eds.

Schatz, Walter, ed. *Directory of Afro-American Resources.* (A project of the Race Relations Information Center, Nashville, TN.) New York: R. R. Bowker, 1970.

Scheuer, Steven H., ed. *TV: The Television Annual, 1978–79.* New York: Collier/Macmillan, 1979.

Seller, Maxine Schwartz, ed. *Ethnic Theatre in the United States.* Westport, CT: Greenwood Press, 1983.

Sharp, Saundra, ed. *Directory of Black Film/TV Technicians and Artists, West Coast.* Los Angeles: Togetherness Productions, Nov. 1980.

Shockley, Ann Allen, and Sue P. Chandler. *Living Black American Authors: A Biographical Directory.* New York: R. R. Bowker, 1973.

Southern, Eileen. *Biographical Dictionary of Afro-American and African Musicians.* Westport, CT: Greenwood Press, 1982.

Southgate, Robert L. *Black Plots and Black Characters.* Syracuse, NY: Gaylord Professional Publications, 1979.

Spradling, Mary Mace, ed. *In Black and White: A Guide to Magazine Articles, Newspaper Articles, and Books Concerning More than 15,000 Black Individuals and Groups.* 3rd ed., 2 vols. and Supplement. Detroit: Gale Research, 1980, 1985.

Taylor, J. Chesley, and G. R. Thompson. *Ritual, Realism, and Revolt: Major Traditions in the Drama*. New York: Scribner's, 1972.

Taylor, Karen M. *People's Theatre in Amerika*. New York: Drama Book Specialists, 1972.

Theatre 1: The American Theatre, 1967–1968. Theatre 2: The American Theatre, 1968–1969. Theatre 3: The American Theatre, 1969–1970. Theatre 4: The American Theatre, 1970–1971. Theatre 5: The American Theatre, 1971–1972. New York: International Theatre Inst. of the United States, 1969, 1970; Scribner's, 1971, 1972, 1973.

Theatre World, 1950–1951/1983–1984. (Annual "Complete Pictorial and Statistical Record of the . . . Broadway and Off-Broadway Theatrical Season." Title varies: Originally called *Theatre World;* later called *Blum's Theatre World;* now mainly listed as *John Willis' Theatre World*. Ed. by Daniel Blum, 1950/55; currently ed. by John Willis, 1965–. New York: Crown, 1951/1984.

Turner, Darwin T., comp. *Afro-American Writers*. Goldentree Bibliographies in Language and Literature (series). New York: Appleton-Century-Crofts/Meredith Corp., 1970.

University Microfilms International, Ann Arbor, MI. *The Arts: A Catalog of Current Doctoral Dissertation Research*, 1983. *The Arts: A Catalog of Selected Doctoral Dissertation Research*, 1985. *Theatre: A Catalog of Doctoral Dissertations*, 1981. (See also *Black Studies: A Dissertation Bibliography* and *Black Studies II: A Dissertation Bibliography*, listed above.)

Video Times: Movie Rating Guide. Skokie, IL: A *Video Times* Special, Sept. 1985.

Vinson, James. *Contemporary Dramatists*. 3rd ed. New York: St. Martin's Press, 1983. Also 1st ed., 1973, and 2nd ed., 1977.

Weales, Gerald. *The Jumping Off Place: American Drama in the 1960's*. New York: Macmillan, 1969.

Whitlow, Roger. *Black American Literature: A Critical History, with a 1,520–Title Bibliography of Works Written by and About Black Americans*. Chicago: Nelson-Hall, 1973.

Who's Who in Colored America: A Biographical Dictionary of Notable Living Persons of Negro Descent in America. 7th ed. Yonkers, NY: Christian E. Burckel and Assocs., 1950.

Williams, Mance. *Black Theatre in the 1960s and 1970s: A Historical-Critical Analysis of the Movement*. Westport, CT: Greenwood Press, 1985.

Woll, Allen. *Dictionary of the Black Theatre: Broadway, Off-Broadway, and Selected Harlem Theatres*. Westport, CT: Greenwood Press, 1983.

D. DISSERTATIONS AND THESES

Where order numbers are given in parentheses, dissertations and theses are available in paper or microform copies from University Microfilms International, P.O. Box 1764, Ann Arbor, MI 48106. For current pricing information, call the Dissertations Hot Line 1–800–521–3042, toll free.

Abramson, Doris Elizabeth. "A Study of Plays by Negro Playwrights, from 'Appearances' to 'A Raisin in the Sun' (1925–1959)." Ph.D. diss., Columbia Univ., 1967. (BEJ67–14016)

Alkire, Stephen Robert. "The Development and Treatment of the Negro Character as Presented in American Musical Theatre, 1927–1968." Ph.D. diss., Michigan State Univ., 1972.

Allen, Arthur Lee. "Five Contemporary Black Plays for the Contemporary Black Theatre." [Original plays.] Ph.D. diss., Univ. of Texas/Austin, 1980. (KWN81–00865)

Archer, Leonard Courtney. "The National Association for the Advancement of Colored People and the American Theatre: A Study of Relationships and Influences (Vols. I and II)." Ph.D. diss., Ohio State Univ., 1959. (BEJ59–02728)

Bekka, Abu. "The Black Theatre Movement in the United States: 1950–1975." M.A. thesis, California State Univ./Long Beach, 1984. (MAA13–23320)

Blitzgen, Sister John Carol. "Voices of Protest: An Analysis of the Negro Protest Plays, the 1963–1964 Broadway and Off-Broadway Season." Master's thesis, Univ. of Kansas, 1966.

Brady, Owen Edward, III. "This Consciousness Epic: LeRoi Jones's Use of American Myth and Ritual in 'The Baptism,' 'The Toilet,' 'Dutchman,' 'The Slave,' and 'A Recent Killing.' " Ph.D. diss., Univ. of Notre Dame, 1973. (BWK74–00044)

Brown, Elizabeth. [Now Elizabeth Brown-Guillory.] "Six Female Black Playwrights: Images of Blacks in Plays by Lorraine Hansberry, Alice Childress, Sonia Sanchez, Barbara Molette, Martie Charles, and Ntozake Shange." Ph.D. diss., Florida State Univ., 1980. (KWN81–00634)

Burke, Lee Williams. "The Presentation of the American Negro in Hollywood Films, 1946–1961. Analysis of a Selected Sample of Feature Films." Ph.D. diss., Speech and Drama, Northwestern Univ., 1965.

Coleman, Edwin Leon, Jr. "Langston Hughes: An American Dramatist." Ph.D. diss., Univ. of Oregon, 1971. (BWK72–08518)

Colle, Royal. "Negro Image and the Mass Media." Ph.D. diss., Cornell Univ., 1967.

Collins, Leslie M. "A Song, a Dance, and a Play—An Interpretive Study of Three American Artists." Ph.D. diss., Fine Arts, Western Reserve Univ., 1945.

Curb, Rosemary Keefe. "The Idea of the American Dream in Afro-American Plays of the Nineteen-Sixties." Ph.D. diss., Univ. of Arkansas, 1977. (BWK77–23372)

Davis, (Brother) Joseph Morgan. "A Compilation and Analysis Concerning the Contributions of the Negro to the American Theatre in 1950–1960." Master's thesis, Catholic Univ., 1962.

Dickenson, Donald Charles. "A Bio-Bibliography of Langston Hughes, 1920–1950." Ph.D. diss., Univ. of Michigan, 1964. (BWK65–05891)

Dippold, Mary Diane. "LeRoi Jones: Tramp with Connections." Ph.D. diss., Univ. of Maryland, 1971. (BWK72–01663)

Eaton, Gregory S. "Black Theatre and Drama in America to Baldwin." Ph.D. diss., Washington Univ., 1977.

Edwards, Flora Mancuso. "The Theatre of the Black Diaspora: A Comparative Study of Black Drama in Brazil, Cuba, and the United States." Ph.D. diss., New York Univ., 1975.

Eikleberry, Burton. "The Negro Actor's Participation and the Negro Image on the New York Stage, 1954–1964." M.A. thesis, Univ. of Kansas, 1965.

Feeney, Joan V. "Black Drama Echoes Black Desires Evoking Blackness." M.A. thesis, California State Univ./Fullerton, 1973. (BWK13–05846)

Goodman, Gerald Thomas. "The Black Theatre Movement." Ph.D. diss., Univ. of Pennsylvania 1974. (BEJ75–14566)

Grossman, Samuel L. "Trends in the Avant-Garde Theatre of the United States During the 1960's." Ph.D. diss., Univ. of Minnesota, 1974.

Haley, Elizabeth Galbreath. "The Black Revolutionary Theatre: LeRoi Jones, Ed Bullins, and Minor Playwrights." Ph.D. diss., Univ. of Denver, 1971. (BEJ72–06485)

Hall, Frederick Douglass, Jr. "The Black Theatre in New York from 1960–1969." Ph.D. diss., Columbia Univ., 1973. (BEJ73–24070)

Halliburton, Warren. "The Social Implication of Humor as Portrayed in the Contemporary Black Theatre." Ph.D. diss., Teacher's Coll., Columbia Univ., 1975.

Hardwick, Mary R. "The Nature of the Negro Hero in Serious American Drama, 1910–1964." Ph.D. diss., Michigan State Univ., 1968.

Harris, Frances Jeanette Gregory. "The Tragic Dimensions of Modern Black Drama." Ph.D. diss., East Texas State Univ., 1977. (BWK77–27550)

Hayes, Donald. "An Analysis of Dramatic Themes Used by Selected Black American Playwrights from 1950–1976 with a Backgrounder: The State of the Art of Contemporary Black Theatre and Black Playwriting (Vols. 1 and 2)." Ph.D. diss., Wayne State Univ., 1984. (MAA85–04881)

Hicklin, Fannie Ella Frazier. "The American Negro Playwright, 1920–1964." Ph.D. diss., Univ. of Wisconsin, 1965. (BWK65–6217)

Hill, Edward Steven. "A Thematic Study of Selected Plays Produced by the Negro Ensemble Company." Ph.D. diss., Bowling Green State Univ., 1975. (BEJ76–02756)

Hudson, Theodore R. "From LeRoi Jones to Amiri Baraka: The Literary Works." Ph.D. diss., Howard Univ., 1971. (BWK72–14024)

Jeyifous, Abiodun. "Theatre and Drama and the Black Physical and Cultural Presence in America: Essays in Interpretation." Ph.D. diss., New York Univ., 1975.

Johnson, Helen. "Stereotypes of the Black Man in American Drama." Master's thesis, Jackson State Coll., 1971.

Keyssar-Franke, Helene. "Strategies in Black Drama." Ph.D. diss., Univ. of Iowa, 1974. (BEJ75–13749)

Latimer, Louise Cunningham. "The Critical Reception of Major Black American Dramatists, 1959–1969." Ed.D. diss., Ohio State Univ., 1977. (BWK78–01281)

Mapp, Edward Charles. "The Portrayal of the Negro in American Motion Pictures, 1962–1968." Ph.D. diss., New York Univ., 1970. (BEJ70–21137)

Miller, Jeanne-Marie Anderson. "Dramas by Black American Playwrights Produced on the New York Professional Stage (from 'The Chip Woman's Fortune' to 'Five on the Black Hand Side')." Ph.D. diss., Howard Univ., 1976. (BWK78–05440)

Nash, Rosa Lee. "Characterization of Blacks in the Theatre of the Sixties." Ph.D. diss., Yeshiva Univ., 1971. (BEJ62–11162)

Ogunbiyi, Yemi. "New Black Playwrights in America (1960–1975): Essays in Theatrical Criticism." Ph.D. diss., New York Univ., 1975. (BEJ76–19529)

Sandle, Floyd Leslie. "A History of the Development of the Educational Theatre in Negro Colleges and Universities from 1911 to 1959." Ph.D. diss., Louisiana State Univ. and A. & M. Coll., 1959. (BEJ59–05527)

Scott, John Sherman. "The Black Spirit: A Trilogy of Original Plays and a Treatise on Dramatic Theory in Contemporary Black Drama." Ph.D. diss., Bowling Green State Univ., 1972. (BEJ72–19778)

Shakong, Samuel. "A Study of the Black Theatre from the 1930s Through the 1960s." M.A. thesis, Adelphi Univ., 1975. (BWK13–07610)

Sheffey-Stinson, Sandi. "The History of Theatre Productions at the Los Angeles Inner City Cultural Center, 1965–1976." Ph.D. diss., Kent State Univ., 1979. (BWK80–03484)

Silver, Reuben. "A History of the Karamu Theatre of Karamu House, 1915–1960." Ph.D. diss., Ohio State Univ., 1961. (BEJ62–0081)

Singleton, Carole Waters. "Black Theatre as Cultural Communication: An Educative Process." Ph.D. diss., Univ. of Maryland, 1975. (BEJ75–29133)

Stevenson, Robert Louis. "The Image of the White Man as Projected in the Published Plays of Black Americans, 1847–1973." Ph.D. diss., Indiana Univ., 1976. (BEJ76–21607)

Sumpter, Clyde Gene. "Militating for Change: The Black Revolutionary Theatre Movement in the United States." Ph.D. diss., Univ. of Kans., 1970. (BEJ71–13367)

Tedesco, John L. "The White Image as Second 'Persona' in Black Drama, 1955–1970." Ph.D. diss., Univ. of Iowa, 1974.

Turner, S.H. Regina. "Images of Black Women in the Plays of Black Female Playwrights, 1950–1975." Ph.D. diss., Bowling Green State Univ., 1982. (MAA82–14438)

Washington, Rhonnie Lynn. "The Relationship Between the White Critic and the Black Theatre from 1959–1969." Ph.D. diss., Univ. of Michigan, 1983. (MAA83–14379)

Williams, Curtis Leroy. "Two Plays on the Black Experience: From Conception to Production." Ph.D. diss., Univ. of Texas/Austin, 1977. (BWK77–23044)

Williams, Mance Raymond. "The Color of Black Theatre: A Critical Analysis of the Black Theatre Movement of the 1960s and 1970s." Ph.D. diss., Univ. of Missouri/Columbia, 1980. (KWN81–08856)

Williams, Roosevelt John. "Modes of Alienation of the Black Writer: Problem and Solution in the Evolution of Black Drama and Contemporary Black Theatre." Ph.D. diss., McGill Univ., 1974.

Wilson, Robert Jerome. "The Black Theatre Alliance: A History of Its Founding Members." Ph.D. diss., New York Univ., 1974. (BEJ74–30055)

Wolfe, Elton Clyde. "An Analysis of the Language in Five Plays by Ed Bullins." Ph.D. diss., Stanford Univ., 1977. (BWK77–25746)

Yancey, Gloria Pauline White. "The Evolution of Black Drama." M.A. thesis, Univ. of Louisville, 1974. (BWK13–05830)

Zastrow, Sylvia Virginia Horning. "Structure of Selected Plays by American Women Playwrights: 1920–1970." Ph.D. diss., Northwestern Univ., 1975.

Zietlon, Edward R. "Wright to Hansberry: The Evolution of Outlook in Four Negro Writers." Ph.D. diss., Univ. of Washington, 1967.

E. PERIODICALS

The following list includes both active periodicals and periodicals no longer published which regularly featured articles, reviews, and/or bibliographical materials on black plays and playwrights from 1950 to the present. No attempt has been made to list individual articles in these or other periodicals. For bibliographies of articles in periodicals, consult the following reference books and critical studies (cited above): *Black American Playwrights, 1800 to the Present: A Bibliography* (Arata & Rotoli, 1976); *More Black Amer-*

ican Playwrights: A Bibliography (Arata, 1978); *Afro-American Writers After 1955: Dramatists and Prose Writers (Dictionary of Literary Biography. Vol. 38)* (Davis & Harris, 1985); *Afro-American Poetry and Drama, 1760–1975: A Guide to Information Sources* (Fabre et al., 1979); *Black Playwrights, 1823–1977: An Annotated Bibliography of Plays* (Hatch & Abdullah, 1977); *Black Theatre in the 1960s and 1970s: A Historical-Critical Analysis of the Movement* (Williams, 1985); and *Dictionary of the Black Theatre: Broadway, Off-Broadway, and Selected Harlem Theatre* (Woll, 1983).

Periodicals no longer published are marked with a double obelisk (‡).

Accent (Chicago Defender's TV and Entertainment Guide)
ACTF Playwriting Awards Newsletter (American College Theatre Festival)
Afro-American (Richmond, VA, and Baltimore, MD)
‡*Afro-Asian Theatre Bulletin* (superceded by *Bulletin of the Black Theatre* (newsletter of
      the American Theatre Association Black Theatre Project)
Alpha Psi Omega Playbill (college theatre productions)
Atlanta Daily World
‡*Bibliographic Survey: The Negro in Print*
The Black American (newspaper)
Black American Literature Forum (formerly *Negro American Literature Forum)*
‡*The Black Arts (Magazine)*
Blackartsouth
‡*Black Books Bulletin*
The Black Collegian
‡*Black Creation*
‡*Black Dialogue*
‡*Black Information Index*
‡*Black Lines*
Black Masks (Black Theatre in New York, New Jersey, and Connecticut)
Black Perspectives in Music
Black Scholar
‡*Blackstage*
‡*Black Stars*
‡*Black Theatre* (Nos. 1–6, ed. by Ed Bullins; New Lafayette Theatre, 1968–72)
‡*Black Theatre Alliance Newsletter*
‡*Black Theatre Arts*
Black Theatre Bulletin (formerly *Afro-Asian Theatre Bulletin)*
‡*Black World* (formerly *Negro Digest)* (especially annual Black Theatre issues, April
      1971–April 1976)
‡*Bulletin of Black Theatre* (formerly *Afro-Asian Theatre Bulletin*) (newsletter of the
      American Theatre Association Black Theatre Project)
Chicago Defender (see also *Accent)*
Chicago Theatre Guide
CLA Journal (College Language Association)
Crisis (journal of the NAACP)
Daily Variety (also *Variety)*
Dawn Magazine (The Afro-American)
Drama and Theatre (formerly *First Stage)*
Drama Critique (especially special Negro theatre issue, Spring 1964)

The Drama Review (also cited as *TDR/The Drama Review)* (especially Black Theatre
    issues, Summer 1968 and Dec. 1972)
Drama Survey
Dramatics Magazine
Ebony
‡*Educational Theatre Journal* (superceded by *Theatre Journal)*
Encore (black theatre periodical—not related to *SADSA Encore* and *NADSA Encore)*
Essence
Facts on File
‡*First World*
‡*Free Lance*
Freedomways
Harlem Cultural Council Newsletter
Harlem Cultural Council Review
IAHnews (Institute for the Arts and Humanities Newsletter, Howard University)
Jet
Journal and Guide (Norfolk, VA)
Journal of Negro Education
Journal of Negro History
The Langston Hughes Review
Ledger Star (Norfolk, VA)
‡*Liberator*
Los Angeles Sentinel
MBM (Modern Black Man)
Michigan Chronicle
‡*NADSA Encore* (National Association of Dramatic and Speech Arts) (superceded by
    SADSA Encore)
‡*Negro American Literature Forum* (superceded by *Black American Literature Forum)*
‡*Negro Digest* (superceded by *Black World)* (especially annual Black Theatre issues,
    April 1966, March 1967, April 1968, April 1969, and April 1970)
Negro Educational Review
‡*Negro in Print: Bibliographic Survey*
Newsbank—Performing Arts
New York
New York Amsterdam News (also called *Amsterdam News)*
New Yorker
New York Theatre Critics' Reviews
New York Times
Obsidian
‡*Opportunity*
Other Stages: OOB Theatre & Dance
‡*Our World*
Partisan Review
People
Playbill
Playboy
Players (Magazine)
Plays and Players

PM
Right On! Class
‡*SADSA Encore* (Southern Association of Dramatic and Speech Arts) (superceded by
        NADSA Encore)
‡*Scripts* (New York Shakespeare Festival/Public Theatre)
Sepia
Showbill
Showbiz (newsletter by Maxwell Glanville)
‡*Soulbook*
South Atlantic Quarterly
Stagebill
TDR/The Drama Review (also cited as *The Drama Review)*
‡*Theatre Arts (Magazine)*
Theatre Crafts
Theatre Journal (formerly *Educational Theatre Journal)*
‡*Theatre of Afro-Arts*
Tuesday (Magazine)
TV Guide
Variety (also *Daily Variety)*
Washington Post
Write On Newsletter
Yale/Theatre

TITLE INDEX

This is an alphabetical index of all plays and dramatic works written or coauthored by the contemporary black American playwrights included in the main Directory and the two Appendixes of this volume. Italicized pages indicate main author entries. The following abbreviations are occasionally used in this index: (C) for published collection; (G) for group of related plays.

General Index

This is a selective, general index of significant theatrical persons, organizations, and awards mentioned throughout this Directory. Because of space limitations, many names—especially of individual actors, actresses, and other performers appearing in only one play—had to be excluded. Among the main criteria for selection of entries have been (a) the importance of the individual, organization, or award, and/or (b) the frequency of their mention in this book. A special effort has been made to include all black-oriented theatre groups, as well as all coauthors, librettists, composers, and directors. A name printed in all-capitals (e.g., BALDWIN, JAMES) indicates that the person is a black playwright whose entry is also included in the main Directory. A playwright in the main Directory is indexed only if he or she is also referred to in other entries or in other sections of the book.

About the Author

BERNARD L. PETERSON, JR., Assistant Professor of English and Drama at Elizabeth City State University, North Carolina, has had a long career in theatre and theatre education. His articles on black American theatre and dramatists have appeared in scholarly journals and other periodicals.